Electoral College Votes in the 2020 Presidential Election

Biden
Electoral Votes **306**

232 Electoral Votes
Trump

0 ────────────── 269 ────────────── 0
270 Needed to win

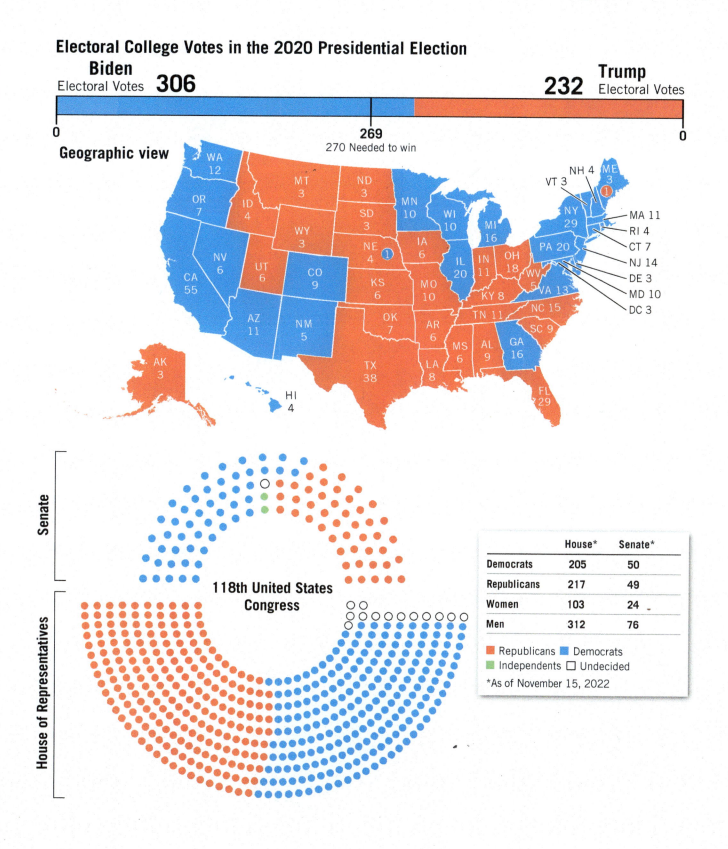

Geographic view

	House*	Senate*
Democrats	205	50
Republicans	217	49
Women	103	24
Men	312	76

■ Republicans ■ Democrats
■ Independents □ Undecided
*As of November 15, 2022

118th United States Congress

Senate

House of Representatives

BY THE PEOPLE

DEBATING AMERICAN GOVERNMENT

JAMES A. MORONE | ROGAN KERSH

BY THE PEOPLE

DEBATING AMERICAN GOVERNMENT | SIXTH EDITION

OXFORD
UNIVERSITY PRESS

Oxford University Press is a department of the University of Oxford.
It furthers the University's objective of excellence in research, scholarship,
and education by publishing worldwide. Oxford is a registered trade mark
of Oxford University Press in the UK and in certain other countries.

Published in the United States of America by Oxford University Press
198 Madison Avenue, New York, NY 10016, United States of America.

978-0-19-767069-9

Cataloging-in-Publication Data is on file with the Library of Congress.

Print number: 9 8 7 6 5 4 3 2 1
Printed by Lakeside Book Company, United States of America

Many teachers and colleagues inspired us. We dedicate this book to five who changed our lives. Their passion for learning and teaching set the standard we aim for every day— and on every page that follows.

Richard O'Donnell

Murray Dry

Maya Angelou

Jim Barefield

Rogers Smith

By the People comes from the Gettysburg Address. Standing on the battlefield at Gettysburg, President Abraham Lincoln delivered what may be the most memorable presidential address in American history—defining American government as a government "of the people, by the people, for the people." Here is the full address.

Four score and seven years ago our fathers brought forth on this continent, a new nation, conceived in liberty, and dedicated to the proposition that all men are created equal.

Now we are engaged in a great civil war, testing whether that nation, or any nation so conceived and so dedicated, can long endure. We are met on a great battle-field of that war. We have come to dedicate a portion of that field, as a final resting place for those who here gave their lives that that nation might live. It is altogether fitting and proper that we should do this.

But, in a larger sense, we can not dedicate—we can not consecrate—we can not hallow—this ground. The brave men, living and dead, who struggled here, have consecrated it, far above our poor power to add or detract. The world will little note, nor long remember what we say here, but it can never forget what they did here. It is for us the living, rather, to be dedicated here to the unfinished work which they who fought here have thus far so nobly advanced. It is rather for us to be here dedicated to the great task remaining before us, that from these honored dead we take increased devotion to that cause for which they gave the last full measure of devotion—that we here highly resolve that these dead shall not have died in vain—that this nation, under God, shall have a new birth of freedom—and that government of the people, by the people, for the people, shall not perish from the earth.

Contents

About the Authors xxiv

Preface xxv

Acknowledgments xxxiii

PART I IDEAS AND RIGHTS

1 THE SPIRIT OF AMERICAN POLITICS 2

Who Governs? 5

■ What Do You Think? Who Governs? 7

How Does American Politics Work? 8
   Ideas 8
   Institutions 9
   Interests 10
   Individuals 10
   History 11

What Does Government Do? 11
   Context: Government in Society 12
   No Big Government! 13
   What Government Does 14
   Taxed Too Much? 15
   COMPARING NATIONS 1.1 U.S. Taxpayers Less Burdened Than Other Advanced Countries 16
   The Hidden Government 16
   The Best of Government 17

Who Are We? 18
   COMPARING NATIONS 1.2 Aging Populations 19
   INFO DATA Demographics in America: How Are Race and Ethnicity Changing Over Time? 20

■ What Do You Think? Getting Engaged in Politics—Or Not 21

Conclusion: Your Turn 22

Chapter Summary 22

Key Terms 23

Study Questions 23

2 THE IDEAS THAT SHAPE AMERICA 24

BY THE NUMBERS American Ideas 26

A Nation of Ideas 26

Liberty 28
   "The Land of the Free" 28
   The Two Sides of Liberty 29

■ What Do You Think? Negative Versus Positive Liberty 29
   The Idea of Freedom Is Always Changing 30

Self-Rule: Democracy or Representation? 31
   One Side of Self-Rule: Democracy 31
   Another Side of Self-Rule: A Republic 32
   A Mixed System 33

Limited Government 34
   The Origins of Limited Government 34
   COMPARING NATIONS 2.1 Satisfaction with How Governments Are Working 35
   And Yet . . . Americans Keep Demanding More Government 36
   Limits on Government Action 37
   When Ideas Clash: Democracy and Limited Government 38

■ What Do You Think? Democracy Versus Limited Government 39

Individualism 40
   Community Versus Individualism 40
   COMPARING NATIONS 2.2 Should Government Take Care of the Poor? 41
   The Roots of American Individualism: Opportunity and Discord 42
      Golden Opportunity 42
      Social Conflict 43
   Who We Are? Individualism and Solidarity 43

■ What Do You Think? Individualism Versus Solidarity 44

The American Dream 45
   Spreading the Dream 45

Challenging the Dream 45
  Is the System Tilted Toward the Wealthy? 45
  COMPARING NATIONS 2.3 Social Mobility Around the
    World 47
  Does the American Dream Promote the Wrong Values? 47

Equality 48
Three Types of Equality 48
How Much Economic Inequality Is Too Much? 49
Opportunity or Outcome? 50

Religion 51
Still a Religious Country 52
So Many Religions 52
The Politics of Religion 53

Diversity 54
Two Powerful Statements 54
  **INFO DATA Diversity: How Different Nations Think
    About Themselves 55**
The Long Debate 56
Who Are We? 56

How Do Ideas Affect Politics? 57
Ideas in American Culture 57
Ideas in Political Institutions 57
Culture or Institutions? 58

Conclusion: Culture and Institutions, Together 59

Chapter Summary 59

Key Terms 60

Study Questions 61

3 THE CONSTITUTION   62

BY THE NUMBERS The Constitution 64

The Colonial Roots of the Constitution 65
  COMPARING NATIONS 3.1 The U.S. Constitution in
    Comparative Context 66

Why the Colonists Revolted 67
The Colonial Complaint: Representation 67
The Conflict Begins with Blood on the Frontier 68
The Stamp Tax and the First Hints of
  Independence 69
The Townshend Acts Worsen the Conflict 69
The Boston Tea Party 70
Revolution! 70
A Long Legacy 71

The Declaration of Independence 71
The Principle: "We Hold These Truths ..." 71
Grievances 73

The First American Government: The Articles of Confederation 73
Independent States 74
The National Government 74
Some Success ... 74

...And Some Problems 75
Secrecy 76
  ▪ **What Do You Think? Your Advice Is Needed 77**

The Constitutional Convention 78
1. How Much Power to the People? 78
2. National Government Versus State
   Government 79
3. Big States Versus Small States 79
   The Virginia Plan 79
   The New Jersey Plan 80
   The Connecticut Compromise 81
4. The President 82
   Committee or Individual? 82
   The Electoral College 82
   The President: Too Strong or Too Weak? 83
5. Separation of Powers 83
6. "A Principle of Which We Were Ashamed" 85
   The Three-Fifths Compromise 85
   The Slave Trade 86
   Fugitive Slaves 86
   "The National Calamity" 87

An Overview of the Constitution 88
Preamble 88
Article 1: Congress 88
  ▪ **What Do You Think? Have We Achieved These National
    Goals Today? 88**
Article 2: The President 89
  COMPARING NATIONS 3.2 The U.S. Government Is
    Different from Most Democracies 90
Article 3: The Courts 90
Article 4: Relations Between the States 91
Article 5: Amendments 91
Article 6: The Law of the Land 91
Article 7: Ratification 91
The Missing Articles 92

Ratification 92
The Anti-Federalists 92
The Federalists 93
Two Strong Arguments 94
A Very Close Vote 94
A Popular Surge Propels People into Politics 95

Changing the Constitution 97
The Bill of Rights 97
The Seventeen Amendments 98
The Constitution Today 99
  ▪ **What Do You Think? How Strictly Should We Interpret the
    Constitution? 100**
  **INFO DATA Amend the Constitution Today? On What
    Issue? 101**

Conclusion: Does the Constitution Still Work? 102

Chapter Summary 102

Key Terms 103

Study Questions 103

4 FEDERALISM 104

BY THE NUMBERS Federalism 107

Where Did Federalism Come From? 107

Who Should Wield Government Authority? 109

Advantages of State-Level Policy 109

INFO DATA Education Policies: Teaching About Race 111

Advantages of National Policy 112

What Do You Think? Preserving Local Values or Promoting Consistent National Policy? 112

How Federalism Works 114

The Constitution Sets the Ground Rules 114

The Constitution Grants National Authority 114

The Constitution Protects State Authority 115

The Constitution Authorizes Shared Power 116

The Layer Cake: Dual Federalism (1789–1933) 117

The Marble Cake: Cooperative Federalism (1933–81) 118

The Super-Swirl Cake: Contested Federalism (1981–2024) 119

Issues in Federalism 121

Climate Change 121

Health Care 123

Reducing the National Government's Size 123

On Both Sides of the Issue 124

In a Nutshell: Our Three-Dimensional Political Chess 125

Federalism in the Courts 125

Nationalism, American Style 127

The Rise of Nationalism 127

The Two Faces of Nationalism 127

Engagement 128

COMPARING NATIONS 4.1 Unitary Versus Federal Governments 129

Conclusion: Who Are We? 130

Chapter Summary 130

Key Terms 131

Study Questions 131

5 CIVIL LIBERTIES 132

The Rise of Civil Liberties 134

Civil Rights and Civil Liberties 134

BY THE NUMBERS Civil Liberties 135

The Purpose of Civil Liberties 136

The Slow Rise of Civil Liberties 137

Privacy 139

"Penumbras" and "Emanations" 139

What Do You Think? Is There a Right to Privacy? 140

Roe v. Wade 140

Dobbs v. Jackson Women's Health 141

Sex Between Consenting Adults 142

Clashing Principles 142

Freedom of Religion 143

The Establishment Clause 143

What Do You Think? May the Christian Youth Club Meet in School? 145

Free Exercise of Religion 145

Freedom of Speech 147

A Preferred Position 147

Political Speech 148

Symbolic Speech 149

COMPARING NATIONS 5.1 Civil Liberties Around the World 151

Limits to Free Speech: Fighting Words 151

Limited Protections: Student Speech 152

What Do You Think? Free Speech on Campus 152

Freedom of the Press 153

Prior Restraint 154

Obscenity 155

Libel 156

The Right to Bear Arms 157

A Relic of the Revolution? 157

The Palladium of All Liberties? 157

INFO DATA Guns on Campus: Should Colleges Allow Concealed Carry? 158

The Rights of the Accused 159

The Fourth Amendment: Search and Seizure 160

The Fifth Amendment: Rights at Trials 161

The Sixth Amendment: The Right to Counsel 162

The Eighth Amendment: Fines and Death Penalty 163

What Do You Think? End the Death Penalty? 165

Terrorism, Noncitizens, and Civil Liberties 166

Contacts with Forbidden Groups 166

Domestic Terrorism 166

The Rights of Noncitizens 167

Conclusion: The Dilemma of Civil Liberties 168

Chapter Summary 169

Key Terms 170

Study Questions 170

6 THE STRUGGLE FOR CIVIL RIGHTS 172

Winning Rights: The Political Process 174

Seven Steps to Political Equality 174

BY THE NUMBERS Civil Rights 175
The March to Civil Rights 177
How the Courts Review Cases 177
  Suspect Categories 177
  Quasi-Suspect Categories 178
  Nonsuspect Categories 178

Race and Civil Rights: Revolt Against Slavery 179
The Clash over Slavery 180
  Abolition 180
  Economics 180
  Politics 180
  Dred Scott v. Sandford 180
The Second American Founding: A New Birth of Freedom? 181
Freedom Fails 182

The Next Fight for Racial Equality 185
Types of Discrimination 185
The Modern Civil Rights Campaign Begins 185
The Courts 185
The Civil Rights Movement 187
Congress and the Civil Rights Act 189
The Rise of Black Nationalism 190

After the Southern Civil Rights Movement 191
Affirmative Action in the Workplace 191
Affirmative Action in Education 192
What Do You Think? Higher Education and Affirmative Action 193
The Black Lives Matter Movement 194

Women's Rights 195
Suffrage 195
COMPARING NATIONS 6.1 Percentage of Women in National Legislatures: Selected Countries 197
The Civil Rights Act of 1964: Unexpected Breakthrough 197
Equal Rights Amendment 198
The Courts 199
Progress for Women—Into High Offices 199
Abortion 200
#MeToo 200

Immigrants Help Build America 201
Latinos—A Rising Force in American Politics 201
  Barriers to Civil Rights 202
  Challenging Discrimination 202
The Politics of Immigration 203
  Ancient Fears 203
  Immigration by the Numbers 203
  Three Categories 203
  Undocumented Individuals 204
Immigration Policy 205
  Too Many Immigrants? Or Too Few? 205
  Language Controversy: "Speak English!" 205
Latino Political Mobilization 206
Asian Americans—The Fastest-Growing American Population 207

  Facing Discrimination 208
  Political and Cultural Influence 208

Native Americans 209
The Lost Way of Life 209
Native Americans and the Federal Government 210
The Struggle for Native American Civil Rights 210
Native Americans and the Courts 211

Groups Without Traditional Court Protections 212
People with Disabilities 212
Sexual Orientation and Gender Identity 213
  Same-Sex Civil Rights 213
  The Conflicts Continue 214
INFO DATA Who Faces Discrimination? The People Disagree 215

The Fight for Civil Rights Goes On 216
Voting Rights Today 216
Economic and Social Rights Today 217
  Health 217
  Income 217
  Incarceration 218

Conclusion: Civil Rights . . . By the People 218
Chapter Summary 219
Key Terms 220
Study Questions 221

PART II POLITICAL BEHAVIOR

7 PUBLIC OPINION 222
BY THE NUMBERS Public Opinion 226
Sources of Public Opinion 226
Political Socialization 227
  Parents and Friends 227
  Education 227
  Gender 228
  Race 228
  Religion 228
  Life Events 228
INFO DATA Democrats and Republicans on Climate Change: Far Apart or Coming Together? 229
Party 229
Self-Interest: Voting Our Pocketbooks 230
Elite Influence 230
Media 231
Wars and Other Focusing Events 231

Measuring Public Opinion 232
Polling Bloopers 233
Polling 101 233
  The Random Sample 233
  Sampling Frame 233

Refining the Sample 233

Timing 234

Wording 234

Lies, Damn Lies, and Polls 234

COMPARING NATIONS 7.1 Top Global Threats: Polling Around the World 235

Technology 235

Sampling Error and Response Bias 235

How Did They Do? 236

What Do You Think? **Is Polling Bad for Democracy? 237**

Do Opinion Surveys Influence Us? 237

What Do You Think? **Too Much Polling? 238**

Public Opinion in a Democracy 239

Ignorant Masses 239

The Rational Public 240

Public Opinion and Governing 241

Do the People Know What They Want? 242

How Do the People Communicate Their Desires? 242

Do Leaders Respond to Public Opinion? 242

Conclusion: Government by the People 244

Chapter Summary 244

Key Terms 245

Study Questions 245

8 POLITICAL PARTICIPATION 246

How We Participate 248

Traditional Participation 248

Voting 248

BY THE NUMBERS Political Participation 249

Electoral Activities 251

Political Voice 251

Direct Action 252

INFO DATA **Public Rallies: What Issues Draw People to Protest? 253**

What Do You Think? **Would You Have Protested? 254**

Civic Voluntarism 255

The Participation Puzzle 255

Why Do People Get Involved? 256

Background 256

Age 256

Wealth 257

Education 257

Race/Ethnicity 257

Friends and Family 258

Community 258

Political Mobilization 259

Government Beneficiaries 260

Historical Context 260

What Discourages Political Participation? 261

Alienation 261

COMPARING NATIONS 8.1 Voter Turnout in Selected Countries 262

Institutional Barriers 263

Complacency 264

Shifting Mobilization Pattern 264

Social Media, Big Data, and Gen Z 265

How Social Media Improves Democracy 265

How Social Media Challenges Democracy 266

Centralized Control 266

Din 267

Misinformation, Malice, and Trolls 267

Does Social Media Increase Political Participation? 267

How Millennials and Gen Z Participate 268

Conclusion: Revitalizing Political Participation 269

What Do You Think? **Should Voting Be Required by Law? 270**

Chapter Summary 270

Key Terms 271

Study Questions 271

9 MEDIA, TECHNOLOGY, AND GOVERNMENT 272

BY THE NUMBERS The Media 275

Media and American Democracy 276

Providing Information 276

Watching Political Leaders 276

Shaping the Political Agenda 277

U.S. Media Today: Traditional Formats Are Declining 278

Where People Go for News 279

Newspapers and Magazines: Rise and Decline 280

Radio Holds Steady 280

Conservative Talk 281

Public Radio 281

Podcasts 281

Television: From News to Infotainment 281

Cable 282

Infotainment 282

The Rise of Social Media 283

Worries About the News Media Today 283

Things to Cheer About the News Media Today 284

Is the Media Biased? 285

Are Reporters Politically Biased? 285

Profits Drive the News Industry 286

Drama Delivers Audiences 287

Investigative "Bias" 288

The Fairness Bias 289

What Do You Think? Is the Media Objective?
Should it Be? 289

How Governments Shape the Media 290
The First Amendment Protects Print Media from
Regulation 290
Regulating Broadcasters 291
Regulating Social Media 291
Local News: Most Trusted . . . and Fading Away? 292

INFO DATA **Disappearing Local Outlets: The Collapse of
Local Reporting** 293

Media Around the World 294
Government-Owned Stations 294
Censorship 295
COMPARING NATIONS 9.1 Censorship
Under Pressure? 295
American Media in the World 296

The Media in Context: War, Terrorism, and U.S. Elections 296
Covering Wars and Conflict 296
The Campaign as Drama 298
Candidate Profiles 299

Conclusion: At the Crossroads of the Media World 300

Chapter Summary 301

Key Terms 302

Study Questions 302

10 CAMPAIGNS AND ELECTIONS 304

BY THE NUMBERS Campaigns and Elections 308

How Democratic Are American Elections? 308
Frequent and Fixed Elections 308
Over 520,000 Elected Officials 309
COMPARING NATIONS 10.1 Election Timetables for
National Government 309
Barriers to Voting 310

What Do You Think? Are There Too Many Elective
Positions? 311

Financing Campaigns: The New Inequality? 312
Too Much Money? 312
Democracy for the Rich? 313
Major Donors: Easier to Give 313

INFO DATA **Money in Elections: The New Rules** 315

Presidential Campaigns and Elections 316
Who Runs for President? 316
The Three Phases of Presidential Elections 316
Winning the Nomination 316

What Do You Think? Why Iowa And New
Hampshire? 318

Organizing the Convention 320
The General Election 320
Winning Presidential Elections 320
The Economy 320
Demographics 321
War and Foreign Policy 321
Domestic Issues 321
The Campaign Organization 322
Parties Matter 322
The Electoral College and Swing States 322
That Elusive Winning Recipe 323
Predicting Presidential Elections 324

Congressional Elections 325
Candidates: Who Runs for Congress? 325
The Power of Incumbency 327
Patterns in Congressional Elections 328
Redrawing the Lines: The Art of the Gerrymander 329
Nonpartisan Districting and Minority
Representation 332
COMPARING NATIONS 10.2 American Parties in Context:
How Would They Look in Europe? 333

Congressional Campaigns 334
Candidate-Centered Elections 334
How to Run for Congress 335
Key 1: Money 335
Key 2: Organization 335
Key 3: Strategy 335
Key 4: Message 337

Conclusion: Reforming American Elections 338

Chapter Summary 340

Key Terms 341

Study Questions 341

11 POLITICAL PARTIES 342

BY THE NUMBERS Political Parties 345

Political Parties and the U.S. Government 345
What the Parties Do 346
Parties Champion Ideas 346
Parties Select Candidates 347
Parties Mobilize Voters 347
Parties Organize Governing Activity After the Election 347
Parties Help Integrate New Groups into the Political
Process 347
Two-Party America 347
Third Parties in American Politics 349
COMPARING NATIONS 11.1 Organizing Electoral/
Governing Systems 350

America's Party Systems: Origins and Change 351
Beginnings: First Party System (1789–1828) 352
Rise: Second Party System (1828–1860) 353

War and Reconstruction: Third Party System
(1860–1896) 354

Business and Reform: Fourth Party System
(1896–1932) 355

Depression and the New Deal: Fifth Party System
(1933–1968) 356

The Sixth Party System: Parties at Parity
(1969–Present) 357

Why the Party Period Matters 357

What Do You Think? **Does the 2020 Election Suggest a New Party System? 358**

Party Identification . . . and Ideas 358

Building Party Identification 359

What Do You Think? **Does Personality Predict Party Affiliation? 360**

The Power of Party Attachment 360
Voting/Participation 360
Filtering 360
Ideology 361
Negative Partisanship 361

INFO DATA **Growing Partisanship—On Core Issues: How Do Republicans and Democrats Divide? 362**

Republican Factions 363
American Nationalists or Trumpists 363
Religious Traditionalists 363
Fiscal Conservatives 363
Libertarians 363
Neoconservatives 363
Moderates 364

Democratic Factions 364
Progressives 364
The Civil Rights Caucus 364
Organized Labor 364
Centrists 365

Organizing the Parties 365
The Party Bureaucracy 366
Party in Government 366
Party in the Electorate 367
The Big Tent 367

Party Competition . . . and Partisanship 368

Parties Rise Again 368
Partisanship Intensifies 369

What Do You Think? **Should We Be Trying to Diminish Partisanship? 371**

Conclusion: A Party System Ripe for Reform? 372

1. Proportional Representation 372
2. Reduce the Barriers to Third-Party Competition in Elections 372
3. Reduce Partisanship in Government 373

Chapter Summary 373

Key Terms 374

Study Questions 375

12 INTEREST GROUPS 376

Interest-Group Roles in American Politics 378

BY THE NUMBERS Interest Groups 379
Informing Members 380
Communicating Members' Views 380
Mobilizing the Public 381
What Do Interest Groups Do for Democracy? 382

Types of Interest Groups 384

Economic Groups 384
Citizen or Public Interest Groups 385
Intergovernmental and Reverse Lobbying 386

Interest Groups Past and Present 387

1960s Advocacy Explosion 388
Not Your Grandparents' Lobbyists 388
COMPARING NATIONS 12.1 The Spread of American-Style Lobbying 389

Interest-Group Lobbyists in Action 391

Lobbyists' Multiple Roles 391
Researchers 391
Witnesses 391
Position Takers 392
Coalition Builders 392
Grassroots Campaign Builders 392
Nonprofits Lobby? 392

Interest Groups and the Federal Branches of Government 393

Rise of the Issue Network 394
Interest Groups and the Courts 395
Lobbying on Judicial Confirmations 395
Filing Amicus Curiae (Friend of Court) Briefs 396
Sponsoring Litigation 396

Interest Groups and Power 397

Interest Group Spending 397
Regulating Interest Groups 399

INFO DATA **Tech Lobbying Interests: How Do Interests Expand as Companies Grow? 400**

Are Interest Groups Bad or Good for America? 401

Four Concerns About Interest Groups 401
1. Corruption 401
2. Division and Hyperpluralism 402
3. Accountability 402
4. Unequal Representation 402
Four Defenses of Interest Groups 403
1. More Democratic Representation 403
2. Communication and Information 403

What Do You Think? **How Much Influence Should Interest Groups Have in American Government? 404**

3. Mobilizing and Organizing the Public 404
4. Stability 404

Conclusion: Interest-Group Influence
Revisited 405

Chapter Summary 405

Key Terms 406

Study Questions 406

PART III POLITICAL INSTITUTIONS

13 CONGRESS 408

BY THE NUMBERS Congress 411

Introducing Congress 412
Two Chambers, Different Styles 413

What Do You Think? **Senate Filibusters and Legislative Holds 415**
House and Senate: Unique Roles for Each 415

Congressional Representation 416
Does Congress Reflect America? 416
   Race 416
   Gender 417
   Religion 418
   Profession and Education 418
   Descriptive Versus Substantive Representation 418
Trustees and Delegates 418

What Do You Think? **Who Really Represents You? 419**
   Do the Right Thing 419
   Do What the People Want 419
   What Should Members Do? 419
   What Do Members Actually Do? 420

Getting to Congress—and Staying There 420
The Permanent Campaign 420
Home Style: Back in the District 421
A Government of Strangers 422

Congress at Work 422
The City on the Hill 423
Citizens of the City: Members and Staffers 423
Buzzing with Action: Life on Capitol Hill 425
Minnows and Whales: Congressional Leadership 425
House Leadership 425
Senate Leadership 427
Committees: Workhorses of Congress 427
The Enduring Power of Committees 428
Committee Assignments 430
COMPARING NATIONS 13.1 A Unique U.S. Committee
   System 430

How a Bill Becomes a Law 431
Drafting a Bill 432
Submitting the Bill 433
Committee Action 433
   1. Hold Hearings on Policy Topics 433
   2. Prepare Legislation for Floor Consideration 434

   3. Kill Legislation 435
   4. Exercise Oversight 435
Floor Action 435
   Getting to the Floor 436
   On the Floor 436
The Vote 438
Conference Committee 438
Presidential Action: Separated Powers
   Revisited 439

Why Is Congress So Unpopular? 441
Partisan Polarization in Congress 441

INFO DATA **Partisan Polarization: How Has It Changed
over Time? 442**

What Do You Think? **Is a Partisan Congress a
Good Thing? 443**
Divided Government 443

Some Popular Reforms—and Their
Limits 444
Limit Lobbyists 444
Educate the Public 445
The Real World of Democracy 445

Conclusion: Congress and the Challenge of
Governing 446

Chapter Summary 446

Key Terms 447

Study Questions 447

14 THE PRESIDENCY 448

BY THE NUMBERS The Presidency 451

Defining the Presidency 451
Defined by Controversy 452
The President's Powers 453
COMPARING NATIONS 14.1 Chief Executives' Power 454

Is the Presidency Too Powerful? 455
An Imperial Presidency? 455
A Weak Office? 456

What Presidents Do 458
Commander-in-Chief 458
Top Diplomat 459

What Do You Think? **Who Should Deploy American
Troops? 460**
The First Legislator 461
   Recommending Measures 461
   State of the Union 462
   Presidential "Batting Average" 462
   Veto 462
   Signing Statements 464
Chief Bureaucrat 465
   Appointments 465
   Executive Orders 465

Economist-in-Chief 466

INFO DATA Executive Orders Issued, Total and Per Year: Which Presidents Relied Most on This Power? 467

The Head of State 468
Party Leader 468
The Bully Pulpit: Introducing Ideas 468
The Impossible Job 469

Presidential Leadership: Success and Failure in the Oval Office 470

Managing the Public 470

What Do You Think? **Go Public or Play the Inside Game 471**

Approval Ratings 472
Presidential Greatness 473
Greatness in Context: The Rise and Fall of Political Orders 475
Step 1: A New Order Rises 475
Step 2: The Order Refreshed 475
Step 3: The Old Order Crumbles 475

The Personal Presidency 476

Presidential Style 476
The Burden of the Office 477

The President's Team: A Tour of the White House 479

The Political Solar System: Presidential Appointments 479
The Vice President 479
The Cabinet 480
The Executive Office of the President 481
The Office of Management and Budget (OMB) 482
The Council of Economic Advisers (CEA) and National Economic Council (NEC) 482
The National Security Council (NSC) 483
The Heart of Power: The White House Office 483
The First Spouse 484

What Do You Think? **Do Presidents Need Such a Large Staff? 485**

Conclusion: The Most Powerful Office on Earth? 486

Chapter Summary 487

Key Terms 488

Study Questions 488

15 BUREAUCRACY 490

BY THE NUMBERS The Bureaucracy 493

How the Bureaucracy Grew 494

Birth of the Bureaucracy 494
War 494
Morality 495
Economics 495

Geography 495
Race and Ethnicity 495
Toward Efficiency 495
The Bureaucratic Model 495
Hierarchy 496
Division of Labor 496
Fixed Routines 497
Equal Rules for All 497
Technical Qualifications 497
Bureaucratic Pathologies 497
The Democratic Dilemma 499

How Bureaucracies Work 500

Rule Making 500
Implementation 502

INFO DATA Regulating Health Systems: Do We Have Too Many Regulations? 503

How the Bureaucracy Is Organized 504

The Cabinet Departments 505
The Challenge of Governing 506
Cabinet Meetings 507
The Rotating Bureaucracy 507
COMPARING NATIONS 15.1 Parliamentary Systems 508
The Cabinet and Diversity 510
Other Agencies 510
Executive Agencies 510
Independent Regulatory Commissions 511
An Army of Their Own 513
Private Contractors 513

Who Controls the Federal Bureaucracy? 515

The People 515
The President 515
Congress 516
Interest Groups 517
Bureaucratic Autonomy 517
Challenging the Experts 517
The Courts Step In 518
Democracy Revisited 518

What Do You Think? **Change Versus Stability: Should We Have More Politically Appointed Bureaucrats? 519**

Reforming the Bureaucracy 520

Critiques 520
Cost 520
Inertia 520
Public Mistrust 520
Proposed Reforms 521
Open Up the System 521
More Efficiency! 521
Restore the Original Constitutional Logic 522
Privatization 522

Conclusion: The Real Solution Lies with You 523

Chapter Summary 523

Key Terms 524

Study Questions 524

16 THE JUDICIAL BRANCH 526

BY THE NUMBERS The U.S. Judiciary 530

Who Are We? A Nation of Laws . . . and Lawyers 530

Embracing the Law—and Lawsuits 530
Trust in Courts 531
COMPARING NATIONS 16.1 The United States Has a Lawyer for Every 248 People—a Lot More Than Other Countries 531
Courts in American Culture 532

Organizing the Judicial Branch 533

Divided We Rule 533
State and Local Courts 534
Judicial Selection 534
Judicial Selection in the States 534

What Do You Think? **How Should States Select Their Judges?** 535

Judicial Selection to the Federal Bench 535
The Federal Courts in Action 536
Specialized Courts 537
Diversity in the Federal Judiciary 538

What Do You Think? **Identity on the Bench 539**

The Court's Role 540

Judicial Review 540
Activism Versus Restraint 541
The Judicial Process 543
Too Much Power? 544
COMPARING NATIONS 16.2 Power of the Judiciary 544
. . . Or Still the "Least Dangerous" Branch? 545

The Supreme Court and How It Operates 546

Hearing Cases 546
Selecting Cases: Formal Requirements 547
Selecting Cases: Informal Factors 548
Conference Sessions and Written Decisions 549
Supreme Court Clerks 550
Confirmation Battles 550

Judicial Decision Making and Reform 553

The Role of Law 553
Ideology and Partisanship 554
Collegiality and Peer Pressure 555

INFO DATA **How Americans View the Supreme Court: Party Members See It Differently Today 556**

Institutional Concerns 556

Nineteen Cases You Should Know 557

1. *Marbury v. Madison* (1803) 557
2. *McCulloch v. Maryland* (1819) 557
3. *Dred Scott v. Sandford* (1857) 557
4. *Santa Clara Co. v. Southern Pacific Railroad* (1886) 558
5. *Plessy v. Ferguson* (1896) 558
6. *Lochner v. New York* (1905) 559
7. *Muller v. Oregon* (1908) 559
8. *Schenck v. United States* (1919) 560
9. *National Labor Relations Board v. Jones and Laughlin Steel Corporation* (1937) 560
10. *Korematsu v. United States* (1944) 560
11. *Brown v. Board of Education* (1954) 561
12. *Gideon v. Wainwright* (1963) 561
13. *Roe v. Wade* (1973) 561
14. *United States v. Nixon* (1974) 561
15. *Bush v. Gore* (2000) 562
16. *Citizens United v. Federal Elections Commission* (2010) 562
17. *National Federation of Independent Business v. Sebelius* (2012) 562
18. *Obergefell v. Hodges* (2015) 563
19. *Dobbs v. Jackson Women's Health Organization* (2022) 563
The Nineteen Cases—and the Power of the Court 563

What Do You Think? **Name Another Landmark Case 563**

Improving the Judiciary 564

Criticisms 564
Ideas for Reform 564
Policing Reforms 564
More Resources 565
Term Limits 565
Shift Authority to Congress 565

Conclusion: Democracy and the Courts 566

Chapter Summary 566

Key Terms 567

Study Questions 567

PART IV   POLICYMAKING

17 PUBLIC POLICYMAKING AND BUDGETING 568

Public Policymaking in Five (Not-So-Easy) Stages 570

BY THE NUMBERS U.S. Public Policy 571
1. Agenda Setting 571
2. Framing 574
3. Policy Formation 574
Analyzing Policy, Ex Ante 575
From Cost-Benefit Analysis to Politics 576
4. Policy Implementation 577
Rule Making Revisited 577
Top-Down Delivery 579
Bottom-Up Delivery 579
5. Policy Evaluation and Feedback 581
Ex Post Policy Evaluations 581
A Case in Point: Gang Violence 582
Policy Feedback 582

U.S. Social Policy 583

Wars and Social Policy 584

Old-Age Insurance: Social Security 585
Unemployment Benefits 586
Health and Disability: Medicare/Medicaid 587

What Do You Think? **Should We Expand or Contract Social Security and Medicare? 589**

Economic Policymaking: Fiscal and Monetary Policy 589

Fiscal Policy 590
Monetary Policy 591

Economic Policymaking: The Federal Budget Process 592

President's Budget Proposal 593
Congressional Budget Resolution 594
COMPARING NATIONS 17.1 Budget Policymaking 594
Reign of the Cardinals: Appropriations Committee Action 595

Making Good Policy 597

Moral Policies: Justice or Democracy? 598
Economically Efficient Policies 598
Capitalism Goes to the Movies 599

INFO DATA Views on Policymaking: Do Americans Feel That U.S. Policies Are Beneficial? 600

Reforming U.S. Policymaking 601

Systemic Reform 601
Policy Entrepreneurs 602
Eight Steps to Successful Policy Reform 603
Bring Passion 603
Act Fast 603
Bring a Plan 603
Mind the Symbols 604
Have a Philosophy 604
Go Public 604
Know the Rules 604
Learn How to Lose 604

Conclusion: Policy Matters 605

Chapter Summary 605

Key Terms 606

Study Questions 607

18 FOREIGN POLICY 608

Foreign Policy Goal No. 1: Security 610

Military Primacy 610
Basis for Primacy: Realism 610
BY THE NUMBERS Foreign Policy 611
COMPARING NATIONS 18.1 Military Spending Worldwide 612

A Different View: Liberalism 612
Soft Power 613
Foreign Aid and National Security 613
COMPARING NATIONS 18.2 Spending on Foreign Aid 614

Foreign Policy Goal No. 2: Prosperity 615

Economic Superpower or Nation in Decline? 615
Free Trade 617
Challenges to Free Trade 617
Cost 617
Social Displacement 617
Volatile Markets 618
Protectionist Pushback 618
Energy 619
Economic Weapons 619

Foreign Policy Goal No. 3: Spreading American Ideals 620

American Exceptionalism 620
The View from Abroad 621

What Do You Think? **Is America Exceptional? 621**

Foreign Policy Perspectives 623

Engage the World? Isolationism Versus Intervention 623
Go It Alone or Act with Others? 623
Four Approaches 625

What Do You Think? **Foreign Policy Perspectives 626**

Who Makes Foreign Policy? 626

Congress 627
The President 627
The State Department 629
The Department of Defense 629
Intelligence 630
The National Security Council 630
Other Executive Agencies 630
Interest Groups and the Public 630
Fragmentation or Success? 631

INFO DATA Global Corruption and U.S. Foreign Policy 632

Adding All of It Up: Grand Strategies in U.S. History 633

Standing Alone (1918–1939) 633
The Cold War (1945–1991) 634
The New World Order (1989–2001) 635
The War on Terror (2001–2009) 636

Conclusion: The Next Grand Strategy 637

What Do You Think? **Building a New Grand Strategy 638**

Chapter Summary 638

Key Terms 639

Study Questions 639

APPENDIX I
THE DECLARATION OF
INDEPENDENCE A-1

APPENDIX II
THE CONSTITUTION OF THE
UNITED STATES OF AMERICA A-3

APPENDIX III
THE FEDERALIST PAPERS A-21

APPENDIX IV
PRESIDENTIAL ELECTIONS,
CONGRESSIONAL CONTROL,
1789–2020 A-30

Glossary G-1

Notes N-1

Credits C-1

Index I-1

BY THE PEOPLE

DEBATING AMERICAN GOVERNMENT

MOST RECENT CHANGES

Version #2
1. Includes form for placing a disciplinary hold on the student's record with the Office of the Registrar
2. Removes the ability to appeal severity of an academic sanction
3. Establishes School Academic Integrity Committees
4. Clarifies policy and procedure

I. POLICY PURPOSE

A. This policy:
1. supports faculty and students through a fair, objective, and neutral process governing instances of alleged violations of academic dishonesty;
2. provides a procedure for CSN to record student violations of academic integrity;
3. enhances the existing CSN Student Code of Conduct with respect to violations of academic integrity; and
4. provides a procedure for:
   i. **instructors** to use when they suspect a student of academic dishonesty and intend to impose academic sanctions; and
   ii. **students** to use to appeal allegations of academic dishonesty.
5. Outlines the **Student Conduct Officer's** (SCO) role regarding conduct sanctions, as appropriate.

II. POLICY STATEMENT

A. CSN is first and foremost an academic community with its fundamental purpose being the pursuit of learning and student development. By joining the CSN community, students accept the expectation to always take the ethical path, uphold the standards for integrity and honesty in their individual academic studies, and encourage others to do the same.
B. CSN believes that instances of academic dishonesty harm the entire college community. The values of honesty, trust, respect, fairness, responsibility, and professionalism are paramount to maintaining the academic integrity of CSN's programs and courses. Students who violate these standards for academic honesty and integrity will be subject to CSN's disciplinary process as outlined in this Policy and the Student Conduct Code, as appropriate.
C. Academic dishonesty includes, but is not limited to, behaviors defined in the Glossary and generally classified under the categories of plagiarism; self-plagiarism; cheating; buying, selling, and possessing unauthorized materials; falsifying or altering information connected to academic evaluation; unauthorized use or possession of devices or content; substituting a person in a course for one who is not; and facilitating, permitting, or tolerating any of these behaviors.
D. This policy applies to behavior that may occur in or outside of class; during in-person, hybrid, or online courses; and at off-site locations, such as clinical settings.
E. Instructors shall reference the Academic Integrity Policy in their syllabi, as required by the Course Syllabus Policy, section III.J. Examples of syllabus statements can be found in Appendix C. It is recommended that instructors include:
   i. a brief definition of academic dishonesty as it pertains to the course;
   ii. the academic sanctions to be used for violations of the Academic Integrity Policy.
F. This policy is not intended to address disagreements over grades, which are addressed in the Student Grade Appeal Policy.
G. No student with a transcript notation shall be permitted to represent the college in any extracurricular activity, or run for or hold an executive office in any college student organization.
H. A student alleged to have committed a violation of the Academic Integrity Policy is not permitted to drop the course In question before the matter is resolved.

III. PROCEDURE

A. Instructor's responsibilities:

1. The instructor makes an initial determination that a student may have committed an act of academic dishonesty based on the instructor's own observations or grading and/or plagiarism detection software and/or a referral from a person with a legitimate factual basis to believe that an act of academic dishonesty may have occurred.

2. The instructor notifies the Office of the Registrar to place a disciplinary hold on the student's account (see Appendix D) to prevent the student from withdrawing from or dropping the course until the matter is resolved.

3. The instructor notifies the student of the allegation within seven CSN working days of discovering the alleged act of academic dishonesty and invites the student to meet, discuss, and respond.

   i. In setting up the meeting with the student, it is preferable to send the student an email. The email will explain what the meeting concerns, references this policy (for a sample email, see Appendix B), and provides documentation of the instructor's attempt to meet with the student.

   ii. The email should explain to the student that they:
      o will not be able to drop or withdraw from the class while the allegation is being investigated; and
      o may bring one person for support to the meeting, provided that the person is not a witness or legal representative; the support person will not be able to speak for the student, and they will be asked to leave if these guidelines are not followed.

   iii. The meeting should be in-person if possible, but can also occur via email, video chat, or on the phone if circumstances require.

4. At the meeting with the student, the instructor presents their reasons for the allegation and provides the student with an opportunity to respond.

5. Based on the meeting, one of the following shall occur:

   i. the instructor determines that no act of academic dishonesty occurred, notifies the student that the matter is concluded, and requests that the disciplinary hold be removed; or

   ii. the student denies that the act of academic dishonesty occurred; however, the instructor determines based on their observations and considering the student's response that a violation of academic integrity has occurred; or

   iii. the student acknowledges and/or takes responsibility for the act of academic dishonesty.

6. In the second and third scenarios (III.A.5.ii and III.A.5.iii), the instructor then:
   i. refers the student to the appeal process (III.C.6), if necessary;
   ii. continues with the remaining steps of the process, starting with step III.A.8.

7. If the student fails to meet with the instructor and respond to the allegation, the instructor will note this on the Academic Integrity Report form, attach a copy of the email that was sent to the student, then continue with the remaining steps of the process below.

8. The instructor decides on an academic sanction appropriate for the alleged offense committed. Academic sanctions may include but are not limited to:
   • Resubmitting an assignment
   • Reduction of points/letter grade for the assignment or other activity
   • Reduction of points/letter grade for the course
   • Failing grade for assignment or other activity
   • Failing grade for course

9. The instructor fills out the Academic Integrity Report form (see Appendix A). This will be completed during the meeting with the student so that the student may review and sign it. If the student declines to meet with the instructor, no student signature is necessary.

10. The instructor sends the Academic Integrity Report Form, with attached associated documentation, to the relevant School Academic Integrity Committee.

11. In cases when the student appeals the academic integrity violation, the procedure described in III.C.6 will be followed.

B. Student's responsibilities:
1. Students must pursue their coursework with integrity. Students must understand the instructor's standards and expectations for assignments, test taking and individual/joint work.
2. If an instructor alleges that the student committed an act of academic dishonesty, the student shall have an opportunity to meet with the instructor and discuss and respond to the allegation. The meeting should occur in person if possible, but if circumstances require, it can occur via email, video chat, or on the phone.
3. At the meeting with the instructor, the student should openly discuss the allegation. The student may bring one person for support to the meeting (see III.A.3.ii).
4. If the student denies the allegation but the instructor determines it occurred, the student may appeal the instructor's determination as outlined in section III.C.6.

C. Student Appeal to the School Academic Integrity Committees:
1. There shall be a School Academic Integrity Committee (SAIC) in each CSN School consisting of the following membership:
   i. One school faculty member appointed by the Dean for a two-year term
   ii. One representative from Student Affairs appointed by the Vice President of Student Affairs for a two-year term
   iii. The president of ASCSN Student Government shall select, in consultation with the President of CSN or designee, one member of the student body to serve a one-year term.
2. Before serving on an Academic Integrity Appeal hearing, any member who has not had FERPA training must complete it.
3. The Dean will seek replacement of any member of the Committee who is directly involved in a particular case. If a member of the Committee is unavailable, the Dean will replace the member for that individual appeal.
4. The Committee members will designate the chair of the Committee, who is responsible for ensuring that the procedure is correctly followed.
5. General procedure:
   i. The Committee will receive all relevant Academic Integrity Report Forms and associated documentation from instructors.
   ii. The Committee will check all paperwork for completion and send back incomplete forms and documentation to the instructor, if necessary.
   iii. The Committee will hold Academic Integrity Report Forms and associated documentation for seven CSN working days to allow students the opportunity to appeal the alleged violation.
   iv. If the Committee does not receive an appeal, it will forward all Academic Integrity Report Forms and associated documentation to the relevant SCO, who will begin the procedure in III.D.
   v. If the Committee receives a student appeal, it will commence the appeal process.
6. Appeal Process:
   i. A student may appeal an allegation of an Academic Integrity Policy violation for either of these two reasons:
      a. The student claims that they did not commit the alleged act of academic dishonesty.
      b. The student claims the instructor determined that the student committed an act of academic dishonesty on the basis of different factors than were used to evaluate other comparable instances in the same course section.
   ii. The student begins an appeal process by writing a statement of explanation of their reasons in support of the appeal. The student should attach any supportive documentation (at least the course syllabus, any relevant assignment instructions/criteria and copies of any disputed work). The statement of appeal is directed to the relevant School Academic Integrity Committee within seven CSN business days after the instructor notifies the student of their decision.
   iii. When an Academic Integrity Appeal is received by a School Academic Integrity Committee, the Committee will schedule a hearing at which the student and the instructor may each make a statement of the case. Additional material may be submitted to the Committee chair at least one week in advance, to be distributed to all parties at the chair's discretion. The Committee may hear other witnesses and examine all submitted materials from the student and faculty as they choose. The petitioning student must be present for the hearing. Absent extraordinary circumstances, the student's absence will result in forfeiting the appeal. The burden of proof is on the student. The Committee may not meet without all members present; a majority of members must agree to any Committee decision.

      iv.   The Committee may decide:
1. to deny the appeal, and uphold the determination that a violation of the Academic Integrity Policy occurred;
2. to accept the appeal, declare that the violation of the Academic Integrity Policy did not occur and void any sanctions based on the alleged offense.

      v.   if the appeal is denied, all documentation related to the Academic Integrity violation will be forwarded to the relevant campus SCO.

      vi.   the Committee will decide within one week and the Committee chair will prepare a summary of the appeal and the reasons for their decision, and each Committee member will sign indicating concurrence or dissent from the Committee's decision. The summary will be sent to the student and the faculty member.

      vii.   the Academic Integrity Appeal Committee's decision will be final and binding on all parties and unable to be appealed.

      viii.   when the matter is resolved, the SAIC will request that the disciplinary hold on the student's record be removed.

D. Student Conduct Officer's responsibilities:

After all decisions have been made regarding academic sanctions, SCOs will determine if conduct sanctions, as described in section III.D.3 should be pursued.

1. The relevant campus SCO receives and reviews the Academic Integrity Form and associated documentation from the School Academic Integrity Committee.

2. Once all paperwork is complete, the SCO will decide whether the circumstances warrant any actions by the Conduct Office. Instructors and/or members of the SAIC are invited to recommend whether any further action by the Conduct Office is appropriate.

3. Any actions by the SCO must be taken pursuant to the Student Conduct Code. By way of example only, conduct sanctions for academic dishonesty may include, but are not limited to, any one of the sanctions listed below singularly or in combination:

- Academic Integrity Seminar
- Reflection letter of understanding written by the student
- Transcript notation
- Disciplinary warning or probation
- Removal from course and/or program
- Suspension or expulsion
- Recommendation for revocation of a degree or certificate

4. Transcript notations for violations of the Academic Integrity Policy are reserved for cases in which the violation is both intentional and egregious, or there is a pattern of repeated infractions. Transcript notations, recorded on the student's official and unofficial transcript, are marked "Disciplinary Notation-due to violations of the Student Academic Integrity Policy in (course) during (semester)." The conduct sanction notation shall not affect the grade point average, course repeatability, or determination of academic standing.

5. If a conduct sanction notation is made on the student's transcript, the student may file a written petition to the Vice President of Student Affairs to have the notation removed providing that:

      i.   at the time the petition is received, at least 180 calendar days shall have elapsed since the conduct sanction notation was recorded; and,

      ii.   at the time the petition is received, the student shall have successfully completed the designated non-credit Academic Integrity Seminar, as administered by the Office of Student Conduct, or, for the person no longer enrolled at the college, an equivalent activity as determined by the Office of Student Conduct; and,

      iii.   the Office of Student Conduct certifies that to the best of its knowledge the student has not been found responsible for any other act of academic dishonesty or similar disciplinary offense at the College of Southern Nevada or another institution.

6. The SCO shall remove or reinstate a disciplinary hold on a student at the SCO's discretion.

IV. CONFIDENTIALITY OF RECORDS

All members of a School Academic Integrity Committee must sign a statement that they understand the materials they will review as a committee member are confidential academic records not to be disclosed outside the committee work.

V. GENERAL POINTS

All time limits specified in this policy may be extended for good cause.

VI. AUTHORITY AND CROSS REFERENCES

CSN Student Conduct Code; Chapter 10 of the NSHE Code

VII. DISCLAIMER

The President has the discretion to suspend or rescind all or any part of this policy or related procedure(s). The President shall notify appropriate CSN personnel, including the Administrative Code Officer and Faculty Senate Chair, of the suspension or rescission.

Questions about this policy should be referred to the CSN Administrative Code Officer (general.counsel@csn.edu, 702.651.7488) and/or the Recommending Authority.

VIII. SIGNATURES

Recommended by:

/s/ Alok Pandey   5/23/2017
Signature   Date

Faculty Senate Chair
Recommending Authority Title

Reviewed for Legal Sufficiency:

/s/ Richard Hinckley   5/23/2017
General Counsel   Date

Approved by:

/s/Michael D. Richards   5/24/2017
CSN President   Date

IX. ATTACHMENTS

> A. History
> B. Glossary
> C. Appendix A: Academic Integrity Report Form
> D. Appendix B: Initial Meeting Request Email
> E. Appendix C: Syllabus Statement samples
> F. Appendix D: Placing a Disciplinary Hold on a Student Account

About the Authors

JAMES MORONE (BA, Middlebury College; MA and PhD, University of Chicago) is the John Hazen White Professor of Political Science and Public Policy at Brown University and five-time winner of the Hazeltine Citation for outstanding teacher of the year. Jim, an award-winning author, has published eleven books. His most recent is *Republic of Wrath: How American Politics Turned Tribal from George Washington to Donald Trump* (2020). He is also author of *The Heart of Power* (2009, a "New York Times Notable Book"), *Hellfire Nation* (2003, nominated for a Pulitzer Prize), and *The Democratic Wish* (1990, winner of the American Political Science Association's Kammerer Award for the best book on American politics). He has written over two hundred articles and essays on subjects ranging from health care policy to Harry Potter. Jim has commented on politics in the *New York Times,* the *London Review of Books,* and the *American Prospect* and has testified before Congress multiple times. He has been elected to the National Academy of Medicine and the National Academy of Social Insurance. He has served as president of the politics and history section of the American Political Science Association and the New England Political Science Association. He also has served on the board of editors for eleven scholarly journals.

ROGAN KERSH (BA, Wake Forest University; MA and PhD, Yale University) just concluded ten years as provost at Wake Forest University, where he is Distinguished University Professor of Politics and International Affairs. A leading scholar in American political science, Dr. Kersh is best known for his work on generational politics and culture, the politics of obesity and public health, and interest-group lobbying. As a political science faculty member over the past quarter-century, he won five teaching awards and (at NYU) the Martin Luther King Jr. Award for scholarship, teaching, and university service. Dr. Kersh has published two books and more than sixty academic articles and has provided commentary on U.S. politics for dozens of different media outlets including CNN, *Newsweek,* and the *New York Times.* He has served as president of the American Political Science Association's organized section on health politics and policy, is an elected fellow of the National Academy of Public Administration, and has worked in political systems in the U.S., Japan, and Italy.

Preface

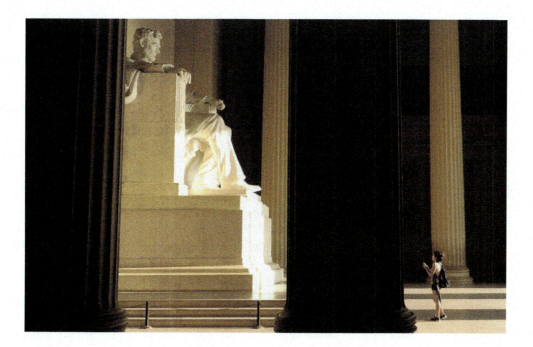

Americans are on edge. COVID lingers on (now joined by monkeypox). Prices are rising. Temperatures keep breaking records. And politics seem, well, crazy.

As we write this, Republicans are split over Donald Trump. Some admit that he lost the election of 2020; others join him in denying the results. The Trump debates go on and on. Did he incite the insurrection at the U.S. Capitol on January 6, 2021? Did he illegally remove highly classified material from the White House? Did he share it with anyone? And an increasingly urgent question: Who to support in the next presidential election in 2024?

Meanwhile, Democrats are divided as well. President Biden, after scoring a decisive victory (despite the "Stop the Steal" claims), sagged in opinion polls. Progressives charged that Biden had failed to live up to his campaign promises: to address global warming, advance anti-racism, and win support for working-class families. Moderates pushed the other way, accusing Biden of failing to work with Republicans and of veering too far to the left.

Even as pundits fretted that America was falling apart, however, the government marked significant achievements. Under President Biden's leadership, the U.S. was at the center of a coalition supporting Ukraine's brave fight against Russian invasion. Congress, amid charges of permanent dysfunction, passed significant legislation on climate change, healthcare protections, inflation reduction, and infrastructure expansion—much-needed funds for everything from repairing bridges and highways to expanding high-speed Internet access. Moreover, a lot of those achievements came with some Republican support—little hints of bipartisanship. Crime rates fell in 2022. And with all the nation's problems, the country opened its doors again, and more than a million new immigrants arrived on American shores, filled with hope for a better life.

Yes, U.S. government and politics is messy—at times bordering on chaos. And for the first time since we started writing about politics, the future of government by the people seems uncertain. Is the American republic in danger? Or is the whole system muddling along—pretty much as it was designed to do? Or maybe the truth lies somewhere in between? That was the overwhelming question on our minds as we wrote this edition.

And what about equality, social justice, and freedom? Are they rising or falling? Within reach or out of sight? We thought a lot about that too. In the end, we're cautiously optimistic on all these counts. Why? Because of our students. What do we mean? Read on!

By the People?

We picked the book's title—*By the People*—because Lincoln's phrase raises the deepest issue in American government: Who has the power? Or, to put it more pointedly, do the people rule in this day and age? Democracy is a constant struggle; it is an aspiration, a wish, a quest. In every chapter we'll ask how well Americans are living up to Lincoln's ideal. Does social media (Chapter 9) or the contemporary Congress (Chapter 13) or the bureaucracy (Chapter 15) or state governors, legislatures, and courts (Chapter 4) support or subvert government by the people? We'll present the details—and let you decide whether we should press for reform or leave things alone.

We'll be straight with you: We won't pretend there was a golden age in some imaginary past. After all, the United States has been home to political machines that enthusiastically stole votes, maintains an Electoral College designed to distort the people's vote for president, and governs through an elaborate system of checks and balances that blunts the popular will. (Again, you'll soon see two sides to each of these features of American government.) At the same time, you'll read about bold popular movements and unexpected electoral surges that changed the face of the nation. In many ways, these are the most exciting moments in American history. They spring up at unexpected times, inspiring ordinary people to achieve great things. Does Donald Trump's possible bid for a second term signify such a surge? Or are the protest movements that have sprung up around climate change and Black Lives Matter and #MeToo the larger agent of change?

Who Are We?

Here's Jim's very first political memory: My parents were watching TV, and as soon as I walked into the room I could see that my mother was trying hard not to cry. "What's going on?" I asked my parents nervously. My dad—a proud Republican who had fought in World War II—said, "Well, the U.S. had a racial problem, but that man there, he's going to get us past it." "That man there" was Martin Luther King Jr., giving one of the most famous speeches in American history: "I have a dream," said King, that "my four little children will one day live in a country where they will not be judged by the color of their skin but by the content of their character." My mother had been born in Poland and her near tears reflected pride in her new nation—and the uplifting aspirations of that August day.

Both of us grew up thinking about the dream—and about the nation that dreams it. America is constantly changing, constantly new. In every chapter we'll ask the same question: *Who are we*? We'll explore a lot of different answers.

Four themes are especially important in this book. **Race** touches everything in the United States, from the Constitution (Chapter 3) to our political parties (Chapter 11). The nation arose out of both freedom and slavery; race quickly became one of the great crucibles of American liberty. Likewise, **immigration** includes some of history's saddest passages involving the mistreatment of recent arrivals. And yet we are a nation of immigrants that continues to welcome the world's "huddled masses yearning to breathe free"—the famous words long associated with the Statue of Liberty. More than a fifth of all the emigrants around the globe come to the United States every year. Race and immigration are tied up in another powerful topic: **gender and sexuality**. From women in Congress to same-sex marriage, from teen pregnancy to abortion, we'll show how negotiating an answer to "Who are we?" always puts an emphasis on questions of gender and sexuality. Finally, we're especially interested in **American generations**, and more specifically the attitudes and contributions of today's young people, the millennial generation and so-called Generation Z. If you're among this group of teens/twenty- and thirty-somethings, the future belongs to you. This book is an owner's manual for the government that you're going to inherit. We'll have much to say about you as we go along—shaped by Rogan's decade of research on the rising generation's politics and culture.

The most important thing about all these categories is not their history, or the ways they've influenced voting behavior, or how the courts treat them—although we'll cover all those topics. Rather, what matters most about American politics are the opportunities to get involved. As you'll see, groups and individuals can and do make a difference in a nation that is always evolving. We hope our book inspires you to actively participate in making the American future.

 # How Government Works

We won't oversell the role of individuals. People's ability to advance political change is always shaped by the way the government is organized and operates. From the very start, this book emphasizes the unusual structure of American government.

Begin with a Constitution full of checks and balances, add a multilayered federalism, develop a chaotic public administration (President Franklin Roosevelt cheerfully called the uproar a three-ring circus), spin off functions to the private sector (especially during wars), complexify Congress (thirty-one different committees and subcommittees tried to claim jurisdiction over just one national health insurance proposal), and inject state and federal courts into every cranny of the system. Then throw the entire apparatus open to any interest group that shows up. The twenty-first century adds a 24/7 news cycle with social media commentary all the time and from every angle.

Turn to foreign policy, where high principles contend with tough-minded realism in a fractious world. When the most formidable military in human history is mustered into action, watch presidential power expand so rapidly that it sets off international debates about whether the great republic is morphing into an empire.

That Optimism We Mentioned

Finally, we come back to our optimism. It comes from our students. They display admirable values and ask tough questions. They're weary of partisanship, eager to build good communities, not so sure about American democracy, and even less sure about capitalism. That's pretty much been the recipe for big change in America: a rising generation eager to improve the way things work.

If that sounds like you, we've written this book to help guide you. And if not, we've written with an eye to converting you—to get you interested in American government and, just maybe, to induce you to leap in and participate in the great pageant of local, state, and national politics.

In Short

As you read this book, you'll repeatedly encounter four questions:

- *Who governs?* This is the question of democracy and power—or, as we phrased it earlier: Is this government by the people? And if and where it falls short, how might we refresh our democracy?

- *How does American politics work?* Our job is to help you think like a political scientist. What does that involve? You'll learn in the next chapter—and throughout the book.

- *What does government do?* You can't answer the first two questions if you don't know what the courts or the White House or Congress or interest groups actually do—and how they do it.

- *Who are we?* Americans endlessly debate America's identity. We are students, businesspeople, Hispanics, seniors, Texans, environmentalists, gays, Republicans, Democrats, Portlanders, Christians, Muslims, military families—and the list goes on. Sometimes it adds up to one united people; at other times we're left to wonder how to get along. Either way, American politics arises from—and shapes—a cacophony of identities and interests.

Changes to the Sixth Edition

In this new edition, we have:

- Embedded new videos and media tutorials in the enhanced e-book.

- Ensured that new examples are systematically balanced from left and right, to take into account political sensitivities in our highly partisan age.

- Provided updated coverage and analysis of the 2022 midterm elections and associated campaigns, including debates over voting rights and state election laws.

- Analyzed recent seismic events, from the Supreme Court's extraordinary set of 2022 summer decisions to landmark congressional legislation (on climate change, gun control, infrastructure, and American advanced-technology support) to the U.S. support of Ukraine—and growing tensions with China. We also continue to track inflation, with price increases at their sharpest in thirty years; the COVID pandemic; and ongoing protests against systemic racism, all of which have shaken up U.S. institutions, ideas, and interests.

- Included updates and rewrites throughout the book that speak to the influence of younger millennials and the rising generation/Gen Z in terms of participation in politics and the policy issues they find most salient.

- Introduced dozens of new topics, including potential speech restrictions on social media companies, government engagement with cryptocurrencies, and controversies over topics including critical race theory, "big data," the 2022 baby formula shortage, President Biden's executive order forgiving billions of dollars in student loans, and Florida's "Don't Say Gay" school legislation.

- Supplied new and updated statistics and figures in each chapter, tracking both long- and short-run political trends. Also expanded international comparisons, recognizing that trends in U.S. government both shape and are influenced by events and policy decisions around the globe.

- Emphasized the intensity of debates over ideas in our polarized age, and those debates' policy consequences, in our chapter on the Ideas That Shape America.

- Revised and updated discussions in the Federalism chapter to showcase new examples of how federalism is relevant today—given varying national, state, and local responses to the pandemic, the *Dobbs* Supreme Court decision on abortion, concerns about climate change, and immigration.

- Rewrote and updated multiple sections in the chapter on Media, Technology, and Government to reflect seismic changes in how people obtain their news, in particular through social media, and the widespread ramifications for political partisanship.

- Reworked the Campaigns and Elections (and Congress, and Parties) chapters to affirm the effects of continued very close national election outcomes (most recently, 2022's midterm contests) on party polarization, the hallmark of the U.S. party system over the past quarter-century.

- Added updates throughout the Presidency chapter to reflect Joe Biden's governing style—so different from both his predecessors, given Biden's five decades in Washington. Also included analysis of the ongoing influence of Donald Trump's presidency and postpresidential actions, most notably the January 6, 2021, insurrection.

- Affirmed in the Bureaucracy and Domestic and Foreign Policy chapters the immense value of trained, seasoned public officials in key government roles—and the impact on well-formed, enduring policies when that expertise is missing.

- Chronicled changes in American culture and their interplay with politics—including everything from BTS/K-pop to blockbuster movies with surprisingly anti-capitalist messages.

Getting Involved

By the People, when its first edition came out a decade ago, marked a new approach to courses in American government. The book displays U.S. politics and government in all its glory, messiness, and power. Like every textbook, this one informs our readers. But, as we hope you can already see, we don't describe government (or ideas about government) as inert and fixed. What's exciting about American politics, like the nation itself, is how fast it changes. And the constant, endless arguments about what it is and what it should be next. Our aim is to get you engaged—whether you already love politics, are a complete newcomer to government, or whether you are a newcomer to the United States itself. In the pages that follow, we'll bring American government to life. Get ready to start a great debate . . . about your future.

One final word: We've been working out the story line for this book throughout our teaching careers. We've taught everything from very large lectures to small seminars. Like all teachers, we've learned through trial and error. We've worked hard to pack this book with the stories, questions, and features that our students have found effective. That spirit—the lessons we've learned in the classroom—animates everything that follows.

Teaching and Learning Support for Instructors and Students

Oxford Learning Link

Oxford Learning Link delivers a wealth of engaging digital learning tools and resources to help both instructors and students get the most of their Oxford University Press title. Students can access self-study resources and instructors can view instructor resources at **oup.com/he/morone6e**. Instructors can integrate the digital learning content listed below directly into learning management systems. LMS integration enables instructors to easily assign these materials for a grade and track student success in the course. To find out more about integration, or if you have any questions about the course content, please contact your OUP representative at (800) 280–0280 or **http://learninglink .oup.com/support**.

Enhanced e-books

Included in *Oxford Learning Link*, Oxford's enhanced e-books combine high-quality text content with a rich assortment of integrated multimedia and practice questions to deliver a more engaging and interactive learning experience. The enhanced e-book version of *By the People* is also available via RedShelf, VitalSource, through inclusive access programs, and other leading higher education e-book vendors.

Oxford Learning Link for *By The People* includes the following text specific resources.

Instructor Resources

- **Test Bank**—Over 1,500 test questions in multiple-choice, short answer, and essay formats.
- **Instructor's Manual**—Includes learning objectives, chapter outlines, lecture suggestions, class activity and assignment suggestions, discussion questions, video resources, and internet resources.
- **Lecture PowerPoints**—These presentations review text content, integrating key art from the text.
- **Figure PowerPoints**—These presentations offer high-resolution images from the text for instructors to insert into their own presentation slide decks.

Student Resources

- **Enhanced E-book**—Contains section-level practice quizzes, topical videos, and flashcards in addition to search functionality, highlighting, note taking and printing capabilities.
- **Author Videos**—James Morone and Rogan Kersh provide 2–3-minute video introductions to each chapter's topic.
- **Learning Objectives**—Guide study and reinforce reading comprehension.
- **Key Terms Quizzes and Chapter Exams**—Assignable multiple-choice, matching, and drag-and-drop type questions to evaluate chapter comprehension. When assigned in an LMS environment, the results report to a gradebook.
- *In The News* **weekly news features**—Written by the authors, high-interest hot topics are discussed, providing additional links to news articles for a full understanding of the topic under discussion. Each feature includes a quiz and when used in an LMS environment, the results report to a gradebook.
- **Video Quizzes**—Extensive video clips show concepts in the real world and offer short assessments to capture students' understanding and application of key concepts. When used in an LMS environment, the results of these quizzes report to a gradebook.
- *Media Tutorials*—Twenty-six animated concept tutorials, 2–4 minutes in length, teach key concepts and address important contemporary issues, each with quizzes at the end. When used in an LMS environment, the results report to a gradebook.
- *Government in Action* **activities**—Ten simulations provide students with experiential learning activities in which students role play as political actors and decision makers responding to current political challenges. When used in an LMS environment, the results of these activities report to a gradebook.
- *Issue Navigators*—Eleven interactive data explorations explore major issues in American Politics and allow students to reflect on the sources of their opinions and views. When used in an LMS environment, the results of these activities report to a gradebook.
- **Web Activities and Links**—Provided for every chapter, these links and activities offer resources for research and civic engagement.

 ## Packaging Options

Adopters of *By the People* can package any Oxford University Press book with the text for a 20 percent savings off the total package price. See our many trade and scholarly offerings at www.oup.com, then contact your OUP sales representative to request a package ISBN. Below are additional suggestions to package with the text:

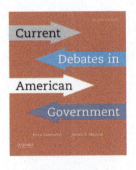

STAY CURRENT

For an additional $10, package *Current Debates in American Government, 3e.*

GET SPECIALIZED

Package with a *What Everyone Needs to Know* paperback **for only $5.** Written by leading experts, each volume in this acclaimed series offers a balanced and authoritative primer on complex issues and countries. To see a full list of these titles, visit http://bit.ly/OUPNtK.

WRITE AND RESEARCH BETTER

Package *Writing in Political Science* **for only $5** or *Research and Writing Guide for Political Science* for free!

KNOW YOUR RIGHTS

Package with *The United States Constitution: What It Says, What It Means* **for free!**

BECOME AN EXPERT IN NO TIME

Package one of Oxford's Very Short Introductions **for free!**

Acknowledgments

When he signed us up to write this book, publisher John Challice looked us each in the eye and said, "You know, this is going to be so much work—you're going to be married to us." He was right. Yes, it was a lot of work. And yes, the Oxford team has been like a family that carried us through the process.

There would be no book without Jennifer Carpenter, our extraordinary editor. She continues to guide us through the process of writing and rewriting with enormous skill. Along the way, Jen earned the highest praise authors can give their editor: She cared about the book as much as we did. Our development editor, Lisa Sussman, was also amazing. She has that rarest and most prized of gifts: knowing exactly when to make changes. We came to trust her wisdom more than any development editor we've worked with in four decades of writing.

Assistant editor Jane Handa guided the art program and tracked down every picture in the following pages. Senior production editor Keith Faivre coordinated a remarkable production process; we broke the publishing record for the number of times two authors wrote, "Good point!" in the margins of an edited manuscript. Danielle Michaely did a sterling copy edit on an impossible schedule (any errors you notice are the authors' fault, not Danielle's!). Art director Michele Laseau did the beautiful design. We are especially grateful to our marketing manager, Laura Ewen, for getting this book into your hands. To all of you in our immediate Oxford family: Thank you! Thank you!

We had an even more important team at our side—our families and our friends. Over the course of this book's initial conception and subsequent writing, Rogan moved from Syracuse University's Maxwell School to New York University's Wagner School, with a sabbatical leave at Yale along the way—and then, just as we were finishing the first edition, to Wake Forest University. Colleagues in all four places remain unfailingly generous with ideas and comments; thanks especially to Suzanne Mettler, Jeff Stonecash, David Mayhew, Ellen Schall, Shanna Rose, Shankar Prasad, Jonathan Lee Walton, and Katy Harriger. Because we strive throughout to get both the political science and the practical politics right, a group of experienced and reflective inside-the-Beltway friends cheerfully and patiently provided insight into their world: Bill Antholis, Matt Bennett, Laura Schiller, Erik Fatemi, Tom Dobbins, Dan Maffei, Bob Shrum, Marylouise Oates, Don Jodrey, and Darrel Cox. Grateful thanks to them as well as a wonderful set of current and former students, many now working in government and politics.

By the People's long journey to completion grew infinitely more enjoyable once Sara Pesek joined Rogan for the trip—through this book and everywhere else, from Australia to Ze Café in midtown New York City. Sara's insights into public policy made for the liveliest newlyweds' conversations (if you're a politics junkie) imaginable; my biggest bouquet of thanks to her for that rarest of gifts: a loving, fully joined partnership. Graylyn's arrival only days after the first edition marked a joyous confluence of timing; her intellectual curiosity and fearless verve have only grown across the decade since, and give both of us authors assurance that the American future is in good hands.

Jim offers warm thanks to my colleagues at Brown who form a wonderful community of scholars and teachers—always ready for coffee, lunch, or wine and a conversation about political science. Extra thanks to Peter Andreas, Mark Blyth, Corey Brettschneider, Ross Cheit, Elisabeth Fauquert, Alex Gourevitch, Bonnie Honig, Sharon Krause, Rick Locke, Susan Moffitt, Melvin Rogers, Wendy Schiller, Prerna Singh, Rich Snyder, and Ashu Varshney. And my wonderful students sampled every idea in this book. They are my constant teachers. Grateful thanks to Ryan Emenaker and Rachel Meade as well as Megean Bourgeois, Dan Carrigg, Ferris Lupino, Kevin McGravey, Rachel Meade, Aaron Weinstein, and Meghan Wilson.

My brothers, Joe and Peter Morone—and their families—are lifelong companions always ready with a cheerful take on the state of politics and the world. Special thanks to Lindsay, Ann, Joe, James (a newly minted Penn political scientist now in the same Wake Forest department as Rogan), Noreen, and Maegan Morone. My mother, Stasia, kept reminding me to enjoy the journey—and that there might be more to life than *By the People*. And the memory of my dad was a constant visitor as I read, and thought, and wrote. The revisions for the last edition were joyfully interrupted by Jim's wedding. If you detect a smile between the lines, it's because we're still celebrating my new family. Rebecca Henderson leapt into my life filling it with talk and ideas and dreams (and much more). And Harry, my wonderful son, takes me hiking and talks me through high ridges that I couldn't imagine trying without him. If this edition reads happier than the last— it's the spirit of Harry and Rebecca on the pages.

Reviewers

We have greatly benefited from the perceptive comments and suggestions of the many talented scholars and instructors who reviewed the manuscript of *By the People*. They went far beyond the call of duty in sharing thoughts and making corrections. Their insight and suggestions contributed immensely to the work. Over the many editions of this text, we've also benefited from the contribution of additional scholars and instructors who have class tested and provided their assessment of the completed manuscript, using this work with thousands of students in classrooms across the nation.

Gayle Alberda
Owens Community College

Ted Anagnoson
University of California, Santa Barbara

Herrick Arnold
Orange Coast College

Alex L. Avila
Mesa Community College

John Barnes
University of Southern California

Charles Barrilleaux
Florida State University

Steven Bayne
Century College

Brian A. Bearry
University of Texas at Dallas

Ronald Bee
Cuyamaca College

Paul Benson
Tarrant County College

Emily Bentley
Savannah State University

Joshua Berkenpas
Western Michigan University

Michael Berkman
Pennsylvania State University

R. M. Bittick
Sam Houston State University

Nathan Blank
Casper College, University of Wyoming, Kentucky Community & Technical College System

Jeff Bloodworth
Gannon University

Nichole Boutte-Heiniluoma
Jarvis Christian College

Wendell S. Broadwell Jr.
Georgia Perimeter College

Theodore C. Brown
Virginia State University

Allison Bunnell
Fitchburg State University

Aubrey Calvin
Tarrant County College

Bryan T. Calvin
Tarrant County College, Northwest

Frank P. Cannatelli
Southern Connecticut State University

John Carnes
Lone Star College–Kingwood

Jason P. Casellas
University of Texas at Austin

Kim Casey
Northwest Missouri State University

Angelina M. Cavallo
San Jacinto College

Jay Cerrato
Bronx Community College

Adam Chamberlain
Coastal Carolina University

Stefanie Chambers
Trinity College, Hartford, Connecticut

Matt Childers
University of Georgia

Suzanne Chod
Pennsylvania State University

Benjamin Christ
Harrisburg Area Community College

Ericka Christensen
Washington State University North

Michael Cobb
Carolina State University

Diana Cohen
Central Connecticut State University

Paul M. Collins
University of North Texas

Rosalind Blanco Cook
Tulane University

William Corbett
New Mexico State University

McKinzie Craig
Texas A&M University

Michael Crespin
University of Georgia

Kevin Davis
North Central Texas College–Corinth

Paul B. Davis
Truckee Meadows Community College

Michael Dichio
Fort Lewis College

Joseph Dietrich
California State Polytechnic
University, Pomona

Amanda DiPaolo
Middle Tennessee State University

Stewart Dippel
University of the Ozarks

Dennis Driggers
California State University, Fresno

Dawn Eaton
San Jacinto College South

Mark Ellickson
Missouri State University

Matthew Eshbaugh-Soha
University of North Texas

Blake Farrar
Texas State University

Jasmine Farrier
University of Louisville

Michaela Fazecas
University of Central Florida

Jennifer Felmley
Santa Fe Community College

Kathleen Ferraiolo
James Madison University

Deborah Ferrell-Lynn
University of Central Oklahoma

Paul Foote
Eastern Kentucky University

Joseph J. Foy
University of Wisconsin–Parkside

Peter L. Francia
East Carolina University

Megan Francis
Pepperdine University

Jim Fraser
Valencia College

Rodd Freitag
University of Wisconsin–Eau Claire

Margaret Garcia
Metropolitan State University of Denver

Joseph Gardner
Northern Arizona University

Andra Gillespie
Emory University

Lawrence L. Giventer
California State University Stanislaus

David Goldberg
College of DuPage

Frederick Gordon
Columbus State University

Paul Gottemoller
Del Mar College

Sara Gubala
Lamar University

Dan Guerrant
Middle Georgia College

Ingrid Haas
University of Nebraska–Lincoln

John I. Hanley
Syracuse University

Jeff Harmon
University of Texas at San Antonio

Jeff Hilmer
Northern Arizona University

James Hite
Portland State University

Jeneen Hobby
Cleveland State University

Michael Hoover
Seminole State College

Dirk Michael Horn
California State University, Bakersfield

Ronald J. Hrebenar
University of Utah
Pennsylvania State University

Daniel Hummel
Idaho State University

Mark S. Jendrysik
University of North Dakota

Aubrey Jewett
University of Central Florida

Gary Johnson
Weber State University

Jeremy Johnson
Carroll College

Nina Kasniunas
Goucher College

Michelle Keck
The University of Texas at Brownsville

William Kelly
Auburn University

Timothy Kersey
Kennesaw State University

Brian Kessel
Columbia College

Nicholas Kiersey
University of Texas Rio Grande Valley

John Klemanski
Oakland University

Richard Krupa
Harper College

Christopher L. Kukk
Western Connecticut State University

Sujith Kumar
University of Central Arkansas

Lisa Langenbach
Middle Tennessee State University

Michael Latner
California Polytechnic State
University

Nicholas LaRowe
University of Southern Indiana

William W. Laverty
University of Michigan–Flint

Jeffrey Lazarus
Georgia State University

Angela K. Lewis
University of Alabama at Birmingham

Gregg Lindskog
Temple University

Christine Lipsmeyer
Texas A&M University

Brad Lockerbie
East Carolina University

Brent A. Lucas
North Carolina State University

Margaret MacKenzie
San Jacinto College

Hamed Madani
Tarrant County College

Maruice Mangum
Texas Southern University

Thomas R. Marshall
University of Texas at Arlington

A. Lanethea Mathews
Muhlenberg College

Lanethea Mathews-Schultz
Muhlenberg College

Vaughn May
Belmont University

Jason McDaniel
San Francisco State University

Robert McGrath
George Mason University

Lauri McNown
University of Colorado at Boulder

John Mercurio
San Diego State University

Melissa Merry
University of Louisville

Patrick R. Miller
University of Cincinnati

Christina A. Medina
New Mexico State University

Donna Merrell
Kennesaw State University

Don Mirjanian
College of Southern Nevada

Michael K. Moore
University of Texas at Arlington

Patrick Moore
Richland College

Roger Morton
California State University, Long Beach

Gary Mucciaroni
Temple University

Yamini Munipalli
Florida State College at Jacksonville

Martha Musgrove
Tarrant County College–Southeast Campus

Jason Mycoff
University of Delaware

Carolyn Myers
Southwestern Illinois College

Marjorie K. Nanian
Schoolcraft College

Steven Nawara
Valdosta State University

Anthony Neal
Buffalo State College

Adam J. Newmark
Appalachian State University

Randall Newnham
Syracuse University

Roger Nichols
Northern Arizona University

Mark Nicol
Saginaw Valley State University

Anthony J. Nownes
University of Tennessee, Knoxville

Stephen A. Nuno
Northern Arizona University

Sunday P. Obazuaye
Cerritos College

Amanda M. Olejarski
Shippensburg University

Anthony O'Regan
Los Angeles Valley College

Kenneth O'Reilly
Milwaukee Area Technical College

Paul Parker
Truman State University

Michael Parkin
Oberlin College

Kevin Parsneau
Minnesota State University

Michelle Pautz
University of Dayton

Michael Petersen
Utah State University

Geoffrey Peterson
University of Wisconsin–Eau Claire

Richard Pious
Barnard College

Martin J. Plax
Cleveland State University

Robert Porter
Ventura College

Elizabeth A. Prough
Eastern Michigan University

Jane Rainey
Eastern Kentucky University

Wesley B. Renfro
St. John Fisher College

Sherri Replogle
Illinois State University

Kim Rice
Western Illinois University

John F. Roche, III
Palomar College

Joseph Romance
Fort Hays State University

Michael Romano
Georgia Southern University

Mikhail Rybalko
Texas Tech University

Joanna Sabo
Monroe County Community College

Jennifer Sacco
Quinnipiac University

Ray Sandoval
Dallas County Community College District

Laura Schneider
Grand Valley State University

Scot Schraufnagel
Northern Illinois University

Ronnee Schreiber
San Diego State University

Ronald C. Schurin
University of Connecticut

Eric Schwartz
Hagerstown Community College

John Shively
Longview Community College

Hayden Smith
Washington State University

Mitchel A. Sollenberger
University of Michigan–Dearborn

Chris Soper
Pepperdine University

Daniel Lavon Spinks
Stephen F. Austin State University

Jeffrey M. Stonecash
Syracuse University

Barry L. Tadlock
Ohio University

Edwin A. Taylor, III
Missouri Western State University

Kathleen Tipler
University of Oklahoma

John P. Todsen
Drake University

Delaina Toothman
Texas State University

Donald Travis
Gettysburg College

Toni-Michelle C. Travis
George Mason University

Andrew Trees
Roosevelt University

Dan Urman
Northeastern University

Ronald W. Vardy
University of Houston

Jan P. Vermeer
Nebraska Wesleyan University

Jennifer E. Walsh
Azusa Pacific University

Adam L. Warber
Clemson University

Gerald Watkins
Kentucky Community & Technical College System

Carl Wege
Social Sciences College of Coastal Georgia

Geoffrey Willbanks
Tyler Junior College

Patrick Wohlfarth
University of Maryland, College Park

Wayne L. Wolf
South Suburban College

Donn Worgs
Towson University

Jeff Worsham
West Virginia University

Larry L. Wright
Florida A&M University

Shoua Yang
St. Cloud State University

Mike Yawn
Sam Houston State University

Melanie C. Young
University of Nevada, Las Vegas

Khodr M. Zaarour
Shaw University

Finally, thanks to you for picking up this book. We hope you enjoy reading it as much as we did writing—and discussing, debating, sometimes deploring, and often marveling at the great kaleidoscope that is American politics and government.

Jim Morone and Rogan Kersh

BY THE PEOPLE

DEBATING AMERICAN GOVERNMENT

1

THE SPIRIT OF AMERICAN POLITICS

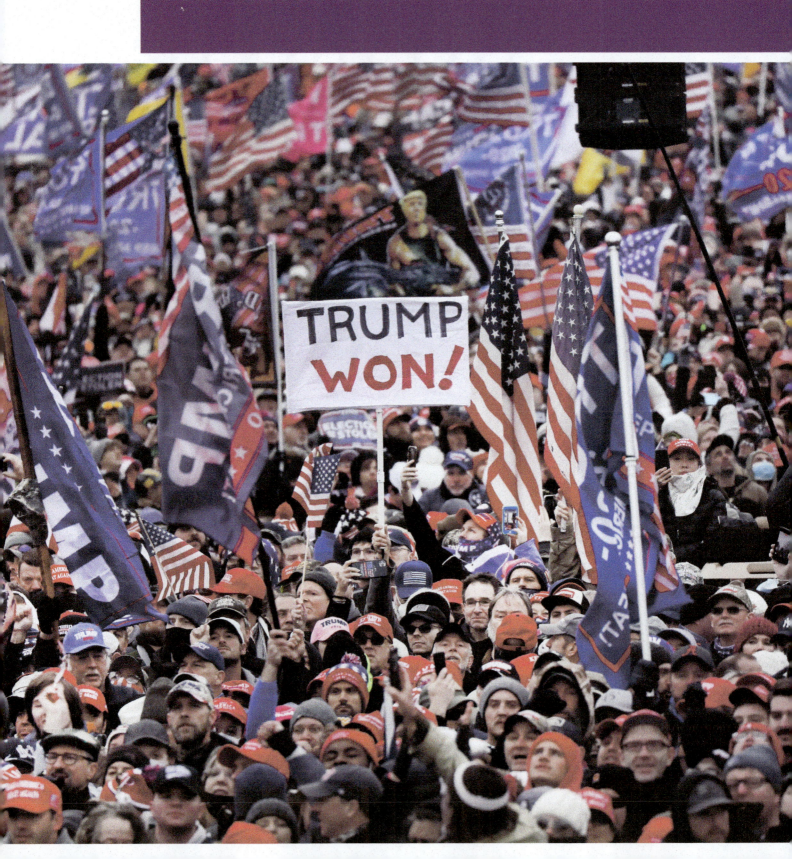

THOUSANDS OF AMERICANS STORMED INTO WASHINGTON, DC. "You have to fight like hell or you won't have a country," shouted President Trump to the cheering crowd. There was just one problem. Joe Biden had defeated Donald Trump by seven million popular votes and seventy-four Electoral College votes (we'll explain all about the Electoral College in Chapter 2). For the first time in American history, the loser and his followers refused to concede. Trump's team denied the results, pressed state officials to find extra votes, filed over fifty lawsuits, browbeat supporters in Congress to reject the results, criticized anyone who denied the false claims, and rallied in Washington to "stop the steal." His supporters mobbed the Capitol Building to try and stop Congress from officially declaring (or certifying) Biden the winner—five people died in the melee. Here's the biggest question in political science today: What does all this mean for government by the people in America?

There are two very different answers. One cheers the American system for holding firm. Yes, the losers challenged the results. But they did not get anywhere. Officials in every state faithfully counted the votes and certified the results—regardless of whether their party had won or lost. Courts across the nation weighed the evidence and rejected every major challenge. Vice President Mike Pence and Congress dutifully certified the results and declared Joe Biden the winner. Yes, it was messy, but American democracy has always been messy. The system worked—as it usually does.

Not so fast, say the pessimists. The assault damaged the electoral process, and it may not recover for a long time. The individuals who count the votes and certify elections across the country used to do their jobs in quiet anonymity. Not anymore. People who believe the false story of a stolen election now aim to take over those offices. They will be in a position to support false election claims in the future. Angry partisans, continue the pessimists, are trying to tilt the electoral rules in their own favor. Worst of all, Americans no longer agree on the most basic facts—like who won and by how many votes.

How should you think about all this? That's where this book comes in. After all, government by the people is about a lot more than choosing presidents.

In this chapter, you will explore four key questions:

 Who governs?

 How does American politics work?

 What does government do?

 Who are we?

● *Tens of thousands arrive in Washington, DC, for a "Stop the Steal" rally. For the first time in American history, the loser in a presidential election refused to concede. Is this a threat to government by the people? Read on!*

Americans elect more than five hundred thousand public officials—from the governors of their states to the mayors of their cities, from soil and water commissioners in Iowa City, Iowa, to cemetery trustees in Lempster, New Hampshire. Few other countries come close to voting on so many offices. All those officials preside over a powerful nation with the world's largest economy and long lists of immigrants eager to become Americans.

Yet, this democracy faced a lot of questions even before the 2020 election. Americans inaugurated presidential candidates who lost the popular vote five times. Think about that: More than one in every ten presidents (and two of the last four) was not the people's choice. Congress adds another peculiar twist to popular rule. Over the past ten years, its approval rating has averaged a dismal 19.3 percent. And in election after election, close to 95 percent of the House of Representatives win reelection—most by landslides.[1] The public expresses sharp disapproval of Congress—then votes to return nearly all its members to Washington for another term.

The Supreme Court's nine members represent still another limit on American democracy. Justices are not elected but are appointed for life. At times, the Court has looked more like a bastion of privilege than a protector of rights. Back in 1857, the Court ruled that, according to the Constitution, Black people "were so far inferior" that they had "no rights which the white man was bound to respect."[2] More recently, the Court struck down popular laws that started the school day with a prayer, regulated pornography, limited money in elections, and restricted public use of firearms. The Court protected a woman's right to end a pregnancy with an abortion (in 1973), then decided no such right had ever existed (in 2022).

There is still another tough question about American government. Is it up to the challenges of our time—like addressing climate change, a global pandemic, or systemic racial inequities? After all, the founders designed the government to move slowly most of the time. Is this a great strength? Or a terrible weakness?

To understand how American democracy is doing, you have to look at the big picture of politics and government. Over the course of this book, you'll be able to form your own judgment about whether the United States stands up as a formidable, popular government that on balance negotiates its many challenges pretty well. Or whether the nation faces deep trouble. Or perhaps a bit of both.

We address four questions throughout this book to help make sense of American politics and government. By the time you finish reading, you will understand the debates sparked by each question—and you will be ready (and, we hope, eager) to join the discussion.

1. **Who governs?** Do the people rule? Some answer, "Yes, and today more than ever." Others respond that the people have lost control—if they ever even had it. What if the people are *not* in charge—then who is?

2. **How does American politics work?** This may be the most confusing, messy, and fascinating government on earth. We will guide you through the political maze and help you understand what makes American politics and government tick.

3. **What does government do?** Many people view politics as dirty and see government as a problem, or irrelevant to their lives. We will show you how politics can be honorable, and why government is often important, even essential. By the time you finish this book, you will have the tools to judge whether government is a problem, a solution … or perhaps a mixture of both.

4. **Who are we?** In a rapidly changing, diverse, immigrant nation, this may be the deepest question of all. American politics helps define who we are—as a community, a people, and a nation.

Before we examine these four questions, we want to share a bias: We have always loved politics and government. We think there is nothing more interesting—not the new Drake album, not the Oscars, not the Super Bowl. (Actually, all those involve politics too.)

Yes, in recent years politics has gotten especially nasty and personal. Political leaders disagree about basic reality. Some sneer at science and expertise. We will not duck these issues. But, for all the tumult, we also aim to project the excitement that we see in politics and power and democracy. Or the way individuals and communities have made a difference—in big and little ways—throughout American history. We brief you on basic facts, then ask you to ponder the key questions and join in the debates. And we will suggest many ways that you can get involved in American politics.

There's one crucial thing we always ask our students to do: Respect one another. Try to find people you disagree with and see if you can understand what they care about and why. If you listen carefully to them, we bet you'll find that they share a lot of the same dreams (and worries). To help start the conversation, we will pose a lot of questions throughout the book and ask, simply—what do *you* think?

Now, let's turn to our four big questions.

 # Who Governs?

As Benjamin Franklin left the Constitutional Convention in 1787, a woman stopped him. "What kind of government have you given us?" she asked. According to legend, the wise old Franklin responded, "A republic, madam—if you can keep it." The Declaration of Independence began with a ringing proclamation of popular rule: Governments derive "their just powers from the consent of the governed." There are two different ways to put the people in charge—a **democracy** and a **republic** (we'll explore the differences further in the next chapter). Either way, Franklin knew that popular governments were extremely difficult to "keep." Previous efforts—such as Athens, Rome, and Florence—had collapsed. His point was that the people must be vigilant and active if they are to maintain control. Every American generation faces new challenges in keeping the republic. Many Americans fear we are now struggling to "keep" our republic. Are they exaggerating the dangers? Read on!

Democracy: A form of government in which the people hold power, either by acting directly or through elected representatives.

Republic: A government in which citizens rule indirectly and make government decisions through their elected representatives.

Popular rule in the United States was a bold breakthrough by eighteenth-century standards, but it did not empower everyone. The Constitution protected slavery and gave enslavers an extra three-fifths of a vote for every person they kept in chains. Women could not vote, nor could most poor men, white or Black. American Indians were considered foreigners in their native land. At the heart of American history lies the long, hard struggle to uphold the republic's founding ideals, to genuinely empower the people.

Today, most adults have the right to vote (although, as we will see, some states make voting more difficult than others), but does the public really rule? Or do the rich and powerful make most of the decisions? Americans have always worried that ordinary people will lose control. Back in 1961, for example, President Dwight Eisenhower, a Republican who was concerned about the size of government, warned that insiders wielded too much power. A juggernaut of big government, big business, and big contracts was creating a "military–industrial complex." Eisenhower's background gave him special credibility: He was a five-star general who had commanded U.S. forces during World War II.

Today, critics still charge that the very wealthy—the top 1 percent—have stripped the people of money and influence. How can we say the people rule in a land with 735 billionaires, they ask? Very rich people can pour money into their favorite causes (and fund their favorite politicians). Do the rich dominate our common lives by the sheer force of their wealth?[3] Or, as many conservative Americans worry, have government bureaucrats and mainstream media elites grabbed control?[4] Different voices across the political spectrum seem to agree on one thing: The people's voice is not being properly heard.

Alongside these fears, we will see many examples where ordinary Americans organized and made a big difference. People gathered in the streets and marched into voting booths to win civil rights, fight for lower taxes, come forward through #MeToo, insist that Black lives matter, press for a woman's right to choose, or demand an end to all abortions. Perhaps American government, past and present, does reflect the ideas and the passions of the people.

● Protests erupt after a police officer suffocated George Floyd. Civic protests sometimes get results. In this case, both parties called for reform, although they deeply disagreed about what reforms to pursue.

TABLE 1.1	Theories of Power	
THEORY	**LOCATION OF POLITICAL POWER**	**SOURCE OF INFLUENCE**
Pluralist theory	Interest groups represent most Americans—including those less well-off	A group's resources, political awareness, and connections
Elite theory	"Power elite"—billionaires and the heads of large corporations	Status based on money and leadership positions
Bureaucratic theory	Government organizations and top government officials	Organizational rules and day-to-day official decisions
Social movement theory	Protest movements	The ability to persuade the rest of the country to support their cause

Over the years, political scientists have developed different theories to answer the question of where power really lies in American politics. The following four theories (summarized in Table 1.1) are especially important:

- *Pluralist theory* suggests that people can influence government through the many interest groups that spring up to champion everything from fighting global warming to banning abortions. Pluralists suggest that interest groups give most people a voice.

- *Elite theory* maintains that power rests in the hands of a small number of wealthy and powerful individuals—particularly the richest Americans. Some political scientists argue that extreme income inequality erodes political equality; the very wealthy simply gain too much influence and dominate politics, economics, and culture.[5]

- *Bureaucratic theory* argues that real control lies with the millions of men and women who carry out the day-to-day operations of modern government. Bureaucratic experts establish policy and sideline the influence of most Americans.

WHAT DO YOU THINK?   Who Governs?

| Political scientists' two most popular theories of power are pluralism and elite theory. If you had to choose between them, which would you pick? | **Pluralism!** Power is spread out in America. Any group can have its say. | **Elitism!** A small circle of wealthy and powerful people hold most of the control in America. | Perhaps you would like to speak up for one of the other theories. Do you prefer social movement theory, which places power in the hands of an active, engaged group of citizens? If you are not sure, don't worry: We're just getting started. |

- *Social movement theory* emphasizes the power citizens can wield when they organize and march in protest—regardless of who is in control of day-to-day politics.

Notice that more than one of these theories can be true at the same time. Social movements, for example, can rise up, disrupt the status quo, and lead to change, even if the normal setting is pluralism or elite rule.

These theories represent very different answers to the vital question: Who rules in America? Are we a republic, governed by the people? Or does power rest with the rich and the well-connected? We will often return to this question—and ask you to consider which of these theories best describes power in the United States today. (And, yes, you'll be able to mix, match, and create your own theories.)

THE BOTTOM LINE

» In a republic, power rests with the people. However, this is a difficult form of government to maintain. The first question of American politics—raised in every generation—is whether the people hold power. Is the United States a government by the people?

» Scholars have developed four approaches to political power in America: pluralism, elite theory, bureaucratic theory, and social movement theory.

» We return to this issue of who holds power in every chapter of this book.

How Does American Politics Work?

Consider a classic definition of politics: *who gets what, when, and how.*[6] Every society has limited amounts of money, prestige, power, and other desirables. Politics helps determine how we distribute them—to which people, in what amounts, under which rules. A second definition is even simpler: *Politics is how a society makes its collective decisions.* Every nation has its own way of deciding. In this book we explain how collective decisions are made in the United States by focusing on four "I's": ideas, institutions, interests, and individuals.

Ideas

Powerful ideas shape American politics. The nation began with what was, at the time, a stunning idea: "All men are created equal." Yet, five of the nation's first seven presidents enslaved people. In Chapter 2, we explore eight essential ideas: liberty, democracy (or self-rule), individualism, limited government, the American dream, equality, faith in God, and diversity. At first glance, these ideas may look simple, but as you will quickly learn, each has at least two very different sides. Each idea provokes long, loud controversies.

Take democracy, for example. It sounds straightforward—government by the people—but defining and achieving democracy in America has been a constant struggle. The United States has seen a Constitution that limited the people's influence, an elaborate system of **checks and balances** that blunts the popular will, political machines in northern cities that enthusiastically stole votes in the

Checks and balances: The principle that each branch of government has the authority to block the other branches, limiting the power of any one branch or individual. This system makes passing legislation far more difficult in the United States than in most other democracies.

nineteenth century, a Jim Crow system in the South that drove Black people out of politics until the 1960s, and many other limits to popular rule. In fact, most people are shocked to learn that on the very first day of the Constitutional Convention in 1787, one delegate rose and said, to general approval, "The people should have as little to do as may be about the government. They lack information and are constantly liable to be misled."[7] Can checking the people's influence actually elevate popular rule? Most of the men at the Constitutional Convention thought so. Americans still debate this question.

● Bold popular movements can change the nation. Here, a call for action on climate change in March 2022 in New York City.

Instead of embracing popular sovereignty, many American leaders preferred the rule of a few—the elite founders of the nation, expert bureaucrats trying to solve technical problems, big banks regulating themselves, or judges appointed for life. All have aimed to protect government from the tumult of the masses—like you!

At the same time, bold popular movements and unforeseen electoral surges have changed the nation. In many ways, these are the most exciting moments in American history. They attract widespread attention, inspiring ordinary citizens to achieve great things. The chapters that follow highlight moments when the United States has reflected populist democracy, as well as periods when it has turned away from the people. We also explore the great contested zone between democracy and elitism. Ultimately, the struggle for power between the elite few and the democratic many goes back to our first question: *Who governs?*

The United States bursts with entrepreneurial energy. New ideas bubble up all the time. Ideas alone do not drive government decisions, but it is impossible to make sense of American politics without understanding ideas, big and small.

Institutions

When most people talk about politics, they think about individuals: President Biden, former President Trump, Senator Joe Manchin, Representative Alexandria Ocasio-Cortez, Governor Ron DeSantis, or commentator Tucker Carlson. Political scientists, on the other hand, stress **institutions**—*the organizations, norms, and rules that structure political action.*

Institutions: The organizations, norms, and rules that structure government and public action.

Congress, the Texas legislature, the Missoula (Montana) City Council, the Supreme Court, the Department of Homeland Security, and the news media are all institutions. If you want to understand why they do some things and not others, study the rules that govern their behavior.

Think about how institutions influence your own behavior, even without your noticing. You may compete in a classroom by making arguments. If the debate gets heated and you shove someone, however, you are in trouble. But if you play basketball after class, things are quite the opposite. There, a little shoving is fine, but no one wants to play hoops with someone who is always arguing. Different institutions—the classroom, the gym—have different rules, and most people adopt them without a second thought. Notice how shifting institutional rules give some people advantages over others. Smart, articulate students who think quickly have an advantage in one institution (the classroom), while fast, athletic students

● The U.S. Capitol, Washington, DC. Tourists see an impressive monument to democracy. Political scientists see an institution with complicated rules that give advantage to some individuals and groups.

with good post moves have an advantage in another (the gym). Political institutions work in the same way. The Department of Agriculture, the Chicago City Council, the Nevada legislature, Florida's state courts, the governor's office in Wisconsin, the Marine Corps, and thousands of other institutions all have their own rules and procedures. Each institution organizes behavior. Each gives an advantage to some interests over others.

By the time you finish this book, you will know to ask the essential question every time you look at a political issue: Which institutions are involved?

Interests

For many social scientists, interests lie at the center of the story. Political action flows from individuals, groups, and nations pursuing their own self-interest.

The traditional view of interests focuses on groups. If you want to influence environmental politics, join a group such as Greenpeace, ConservAmerica, or the Audubon Society. Their lawyers, lobbyists, and members all play an active role in American politics and society. Remember that pluralists believe interest groups are the central actors in American government—in contrast to France, for example, where the law forbids most interest groups from trying to influence the members of the national legislature.

Rational choice theory: An approach to political behavior that views individuals as rational, decisive actors who know their political interests and seek to act on them.

Other analyses focus on individual interests as the essential particles of politics. **Rational choice theory** suggests that people calculate the costs and benefits of any action to determine what will maximize their own self-interest. At an extreme, rational choice models suggest that all political outcomes—elections, the passage of a law, even mass rallies—are an aggregate of the public's individual interests.[8]

Don't overlook another interest—the public interest. Many people reject pandering to the interests of individuals or groups. Instead, they suggest that government ought to pursue the greatest good for the greatest number. Well, who decides what is the "greatest good"? This returns us to our first question: *Who governs?* The real answer lies in who can most effectively get his or her voice heard.

In the chapters that follow, we explore all three types of interests: group interest, self-interest, and public interest. Behavioral scientists add one more twist. Although we may think of our own interests, including our political views, as perfectly rational, most people sometimes deceive themselves and act nonrationally. Experiments repeatedly show, for example, that people do not change their views when confronted with evidence that they are mistaken—on the contrary, it only strengthens their attitudes. Experts are often no wiser than anyone else, for they may overlook data that does not fit their expectations. For a dramatic example, look no further than President Trump's 2016 election or the Democrats holding off a "red wave" in 2022—both of which surprised almost all public opinion experts.[9]

Individuals

Finally, individuals influence political outcomes. This book places special emphasis on how ordinary people change the world. Our hope is simple: We want to inspire you to get involved. Here we share one example.

Marla Ruzicka was a self-described "civics junkie" who visited Afghanistan and Iraq while U.S. forces were on the ground there. She was shaken when she saw the terrible toll that the wars took on civilians. With no foreign policy experience, the twenty-five-year-old established a public service organization in Iraq that she called the Campaign for Innocent Victims in Conflict, or CIVIC. Along with providing first aid, food, clothing, and comfort to ordinary Iraqis injured during the war, Marla formed survey teams of volunteers that kept a count of Iraqi civilians killed, regardless of who was responsible.

Marla's efforts attracted attention back in Washington, where Pentagon officials initially sought to dissuade her from publicizing her count. Eventually she received substantial support from Congress for her CIVIC efforts to aid civilian victims in both Iraq and Afghanistan.

● *Individuals can make a difference. Marla Ruzicka in Kabul, Afghanistan.*

There is a tragic note to Marla's story: As she traveled to an injured Iraqi's home, her car detonated a mine and she was killed. We highlight Marla's example both to honor her memory (she was our friend) and to emphasize the importance of individuals in every corner of American government. Today, the organization Marla founded has expanded its programs from Iraq and Afghanistan to Niger, Ukraine, Yemen, and other countries. She is an example of how individuals with a passion for political change can make a difference in politics—and in people's lives.

History

As the four "I's" reappear throughout this book, you will see that we pay special attention to the history of each. Why is an idea like freedom powerful? Why does an institution such as the U.S. military or the Supreme Court behave as it does? To understand you have to know how they developed over time. You cannot understand where the nation is, or where it might be going, without knowing where it has been.

THE BOTTOM LINE

» American political decisions are shaped by four "I" factors: ideas, institutions, interests, and individuals.

» Mastering how the four "I's" shaped politics also requires an understanding of history.

 ## What Does Government Do?

When Patrick Henry, one of the greatest orators in Virginia, read the newly written Constitution of the United States, he declared, "I smell a rat." This new government was too strong. President Ronald Reagan said the same thing, more politely, when he took the oath of office almost two hundred years later: "Government is not the solution to the problem. Government is the problem."[10] More recently, Donald Trump and his supporters railed against the "deep state" bureaucrats they believed were thwarting his administration's goals. Americans have always been critical of their own government. And yet there are more than 2.8 million people working as federal employees—roughly the same count as during the Reagan administration forty years ago. Is government still the problem? Before you can answer that, you need to know what government actually does.

Context: Government in Society

Let's start with the context. There are three sectors of society. *Private life* involves individuals, families, and friends connecting with one another. *Civil society* refers to people joining with others to do something—you might run for student government, form a Bible study circle, or volunteer at a recycling center. Finally, *government* is the set of institutions that make decisions for society.

The lines separating these different sectors are blurry. Successful democracy requires a vibrant civic spirit. When people join groups—even if it's just a soccer club or knitting group—they get used to interacting with others and solving problems together. They develop what Alexis de Tocqueville, a French visitor to America in 1831–32, called "habits of the heart"—the relationships they develop and the shared goals they pursue lay the foundation for robust democracy. Private groups foster the skills and attitudes that make people effective citizens.[11]

● *The three sectors of society. Individuals engage in all three sectors: personal life when they work or raise a family (a); civil society when they volunteer at a soup kitchen (b); and government when they get a driver's license or engage with a police officer (c). Here's the key point: All three are intertwined with one another; when one gets more robust, so do the others.*

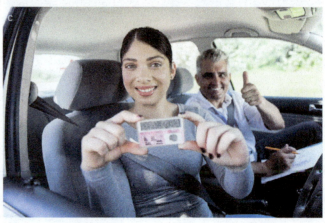

In addition, the different sectors come together to undertake public projects. **Public–private partnerships** bring private actors such as businesses together with government officials to renovate parks, construct sports arenas, or launch innovative schools.

No Big Government!

Americans have a very active civil society. In the abstract, at least, they prefer voluntary groups to government action. Today, only 20 percent of Americans trust the national government "to do the right thing most of the time"[12] (see Figure 1.1).

If Americans dislike "big government," then how did we get such a thicket of over thirteen hundred federal agencies and fifteen cabinet departments, populated by some 2.8 million civilian employees? Include another nearly 2.5 million members of the active and reserve armed forces, and you get a sprawling national government. Add 19.4 million state and local government workers alongside the five hundred thousand elected officials, and you get an idea of the sheer size of the U.S. government—more than 25 million men and women who touch every aspect of our lives.

Americans have long told admiring stories about individual heroes who won greatness on their own, free of government meddling. But often the public and private—the government and the people—were both involved. The brave settlers who populated the west? Before they settled in, the army forced the Native Americans off the land; Congress created land grants distributing western lands; and the national government carefully managed the process, regulating the settlements.[13] Or take those famous inventors, the Wright brothers. Working out of their bicycle shop, Orville and Wilbur created the first viable airplanes. What you may not have heard is that the Wrights were able to develop their invention because of timely investments from their first client: the U.S. military.[14]

Yes, government support was essential for settling the west and for launching the aviation industry—just as it was for exploring space; creating the Internet; and building the infrastructure we drive, walk, fly, run, and otherwise move around on every day. And despite the low trust in government generally, ask about specific agencies and people generally respond with thumbs up. Americans give high marks to the Post Office (91 percent approval), the Census Bureau (77 percent),

Public–private partnership: A government program or service provided through the joint efforts of private sector actors (usually businesses) and public officials.

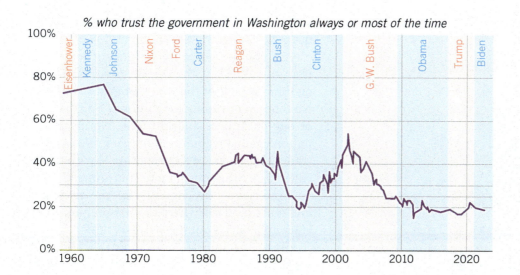

% who trust the government in Washington always or most of the time

FIGURE 1.1 *Americans' trust in government remains very low—stuck at about 20 percent.* (Pew Research Center)

the Department of Veterans Affairs (65 percent), and even the Internal Revenue Service, which has the unloved job of collecting taxes (65 percent).[15]

Still, the public's trust in government remains very low. That leads many people to ask: Could we—and should we—shift some of the national government's functions to the private economy and to civil society? Could private businesses and volunteers do some of that work more smoothly or efficiently? To answer these questions, you first have to know what government does.

What Government Does

The Constitution begins with the basic functions of government, circa 1787: "Establish justice, ensure domestic tranquility, provide for the common defense, promote the general welfare, and secure the blessings of liberty." Their list—we'll get to the details in Chapter 3—still describes the functions of the government, even as its size has grown. We can get a more focused look at the federal government's priorities by looking at what it spends its money on. Figure 1.2 shows the major categories in the national budget; normally, the total comes to about $4.5 trillion—although emergency spending for COVID relief pumped the 2022 budget up to $6.8 trillion.

Many people are surprised when they see the federal budget for the first time. More than 75 percent of all federal spending (in normal years) goes to just four categories: the military, Social Security (which provides a steady income for people over sixty-five, as well as payments for those with disabilities), Medicare (which provides healthcare for people over sixty-five), and Medicaid (which provides healthcare for children and lower-income Americans; about half of Medicaid spending also goes to those over sixty-five). These four programs add up to more than $3 trillion. They are all very popular, so most politicians are not going to meddle with them. Tune in to the budget debates and you will hear a lot of noise about budgets being out of control. But seriously reducing the size of government would require taking on the Big Four.

Notice how America's national government devotes the lion's share of its resources to the military and to seniors. Only one out of every six Americans is over sixty-five. What about the rest of us? We are mainly squeezed into the slice listed as "non-defense discretionary." That includes federal spending on education, housing, veterans, agriculture, infrastructure, the Supplemental Nutritional Assistance Program (SNAP), and a long list of other programs, which all stack up to less than 12 percent of the budget or, roughly, $600 billion.[16]

Of course, government does a lot more than spend. It sets the rules for society: Drive on the right side of the street. Stop at red lights. No tobacco or vaping for children. No rat hairs or bug parts in restaurant food. No discrimination against women when hiring. No insider trading in stocks. Most people agree with these rules. Others are much more controversial.

American government—on the national and state level—is where the nation makes its rules and hashes out its controversies.

Take the long debate about abortion as an example. In 2021 alone, twenty-one states

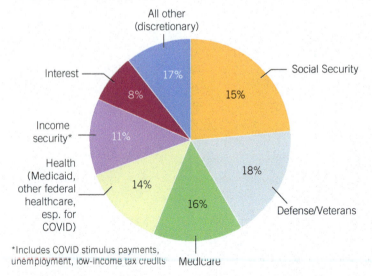

FY 2022 program spending

- All other (discretionary): 17%
- Social Security: 15%
- Interest: 8%
- Income security*: 11%
- Health (Medicaid, other federal healthcare, esp. for COVID): 14%
- Defense/Veterans: 18%
- Medicare: 16%

*Includes COVID stimulus payments, unemployment, low-income tax credits

● **FIGURE 1.2** *U.S. federal spending. Notice the Big Four: Social Security, Medicare, Medicaid, and national defense. (Treasury Department)*

passed abortion restrictions and twelve aimed to ban all abortions. On the other side, six states legislated protections for abortion. These debates all operate in the context of rules set by the Supreme Court. For almost fifty years, the Court protected a constitutional right to privacy that limited state restrictions on abortion; in 2022, the Court reversed itself and declared, "The Constitution does not confer a right to abortion."[17] The debates within each state now had a dramatically different legal context (see Chapter 5 for details).

Or take the great national debate over marijuana. In 2012, over 800,000 people were arrested on marijuana charges and the drug was banned for recreational use in all fifty states. A decade later, only twelve states ban all use. Even so, federal law prohibits marijuana and, in 2021, 318,000 people were arrested for simple possession. The trend toward decriminalization and full legalization, however, is very strong. Here's a case where strong opinions among young people—followed by the rise of a powerful economic interest—led to sweeping changes in a short time. (We'll return to this issue in Chapter 7.)

Firearms offer still another example of state debates in a federal context. If you want to buy a handgun in California, you'll need a safety certificate and proof of state residency. You'll also have to wait for ten days and to register with the state. In Texas or Ohio, you won't face any of those hurdles. And the state overrules (or preempts) any city that tries to impose its own restrictions. While the Supreme Court forcefully protects the right to bear arms, some states make it far easier to acquire guns than others.

Abortions are much easier to obtain in New York than in North Dakota. Guns are simpler to get in Texas than in California.

Government—national, state, and local—constantly sets the rules for society. Sometimes the rules make sense to most people; other times, they trigger fierce debates. Sometimes, federal, state, and local rules are all the same; in other cases, they clash. Government is the place where we debate and set (and change) the rules.

Governments affect what we do almost every minute of every day—from the moment you wake up and turn on the light (government is responsible for electricity), jump in the shower (local government provides water and makes sure it's clean), and eat breakfast (federal, state, and local governments all regulate food safety). As we go through this book, we keep coming back to a vital question: Should government do fewer things? Or more?

Taxed Too Much?

Although Americans dislike government in the abstract, by and large they support many of the things that government does. This paradox creates a chronic problem: How should we pay for government spending? Americans pay lower taxes compared to citizens of most other advanced industrial nations. Yes, you read that right. The U.S. tax burden (including federal, state, and local taxes) ranks thirty-second—right near the bottom—among the thirty-five wealthiest nations (see Comparing Nations 1.1).[18]

● *Americans often vote for budget cuts—but don't want their own favorite programs cut.*

COMPARING NATIONS 1.1

U.S. Taxpayers Less Burdened Than Other Advanced Countries

Citizens in the United States pay less in taxes than citizens in many other countries. In the countries near the top of the chart, nearly half of all economic activity goes into the government's coffers. In the United States, that figure is below one-quarter—and falling. Is this too little? Or still too much? These questions get back to the proper size of the government and what the government should do.

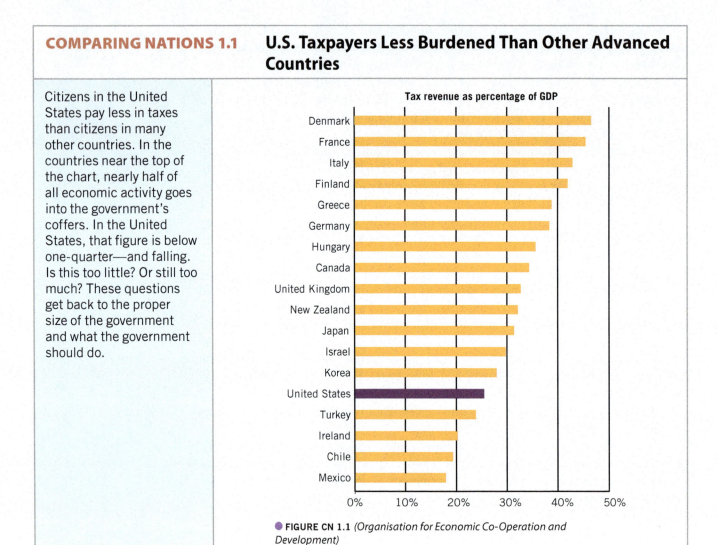

Tax revenue as percentage of GDP

● **FIGURE CN 1.1** *(Organisation for Economic Co-Operation and Development)*

Even so, many Americans think they are taxed too much. Americans like their federal programs, but many oppose paying taxes to support them. Each Republican administration in the last fifty years has made tax cuts central to its election campaigns and, with just one exception (George H. W. Bush), to its legislative agenda.

The Hidden Government

Another peculiar aspect of modern American government is that it can be hard to see. Scholars identify a "hidden" or "submerged" central government, with many functions deliberately tucked out of sight. Why is it people do not see their government at work?[19]

Because of Americans' antipathy to "big government," many federal programs work *indirectly*: They operate through the private sector. Take healthcare as an example. Rather than administering a national health insurance program as in Canada or France, the American government provides employers a major tax deduction if they offer employees health insurance. Today, the tax deduction for employers amounts to $275 billion a year.[20] That makes it one of the largest government-funded healthcare programs in the world. The national government offers similar tax deductions that help people buy homes, save for retirement, pay for schooling, or receive support if their income is low. However, the people who benefit do not see the government's hand at work.[21]

Political scientist Suzanne Mettler asked American citizens whether they receive federal benefits; more than half of the respondents incorrectly answered "no." They did not stop to think that the government had helped set up their retirement savings or their student loans by organizing the tax code to encourage their behavior. About a quarter of the people getting healthcare coverage through Medicaid or groceries through SNAP did not realize they were involved in government programs (see Figure 1.3).[22]

Liberal scholars conclude that the government does not get enough credit for helping people and creating a stronger nation. Conservatives, on the other hand, are more likely to worry that a hidden government is more difficult to control and cut back. Our job is to make sure you see all the ways that government operates—then you can decide whether it should grow, shrink, or stay about the same size.

The Best of Government

Despite powerful antigovernment sentiment—or perhaps inspired by it to promote change—millions of Americans cheer what is best in our national government and seek to improve it. In this book, you will meet dozens of people who act to improve government. They include policy entrepreneurs from across the political spectrum who promote innovative new solutions to pressing problems; organizers who engage their neighbors and larger communities in collective action for change; inventive bureaucrats who conceive ways to deliver public services more effectively; and civic-spirited tech wizards who devise faster, better connections between national policymakers and the public.

We will return repeatedly to ways you can get involved, have a say, and enhance the workings of American government. You can engage within our political system: volunteer on a Senate campaign, attend a town meeting, intern at a federal agency, join the school board, or run for the state legislature. You also can get involved from outside: call media attention to a problem, serve in (or start) an advocacy group, join a protest, or launch an online idea that might spotlight fresh solutions in crime prevention. In addition, you can get involved in the life of your

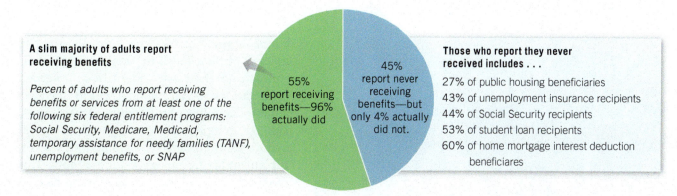

A slim majority of adults report receiving benefits

Percent of adults who report receiving benefits or services from at least one of the following six federal entitlement programs: Social Security, Medicare, Medicaid, temporary assistance for needy families (TANF), unemployment benefits, or SNAP

55% report receiving benefits—96% actually did

45% report never receiving benefits—but only 4% actually did not.

Those who report they never received includes . . .

27% of public housing beneficiaries
43% of unemployment insurance recipients
44% of Social Security recipients
53% of student loan recipients
60% of home mortgage interest deduction beneficiares

● **FIGURE 1.3** *One poll found that 55 percent of Americans report receiving government benefits, but Suzanne Mettler calculated that the number is closer to 96 percent. Even beneficiaries of the biggest programs do not realize they are getting benefits from the government. (Pew Research Center and Washington Post)* community. You are already enough of a social scientist to know that when you join a group or activity, you are participating in "civil society"—the basic building block of strong democracy.

THE BOTTOM LINE

» Every nation is made up of three primary sectors: private life; civil society, where people interact voluntarily; and government. Those sectors are increasingly blurred in the United States.

» Americans tend to dislike their national government—but like the benefits that government programs provide.

» Democratic government at its best involves popular involvement, either through direct engagement with public officials or through civil society activities that help develop "habits of the heart."

 # Who Are We?

The United States is a nation of immigrants, a country where individuals come to reinvent themselves. The nation is always changing. American politics constantly addresses the most fundamental question about a people: *Who are we?*

This question goes back to the earliest European settlers. When the Puritans landed in Massachusetts in 1630, they suddenly had to define their community for themselves. The colonists came up with a remarkable response: We are a collection of saints, a "city on a hill," a model for the whole world to follow. That city on a hill immediately discovered threats: The Puritans defined or imagined enemies that included Indians, witches, and heretics. These settlers learned to answer the question "Who are we?" both by affirming who they were ("us!") and by sharply declaring who they were *not* ("them!"). They defined themselves by celebrating their values, but also by demonizing their foes—promoting their cohesion by opposing dangerous "others."[23]

At the same time, different settlers were arriving in chains on ships with terrible conditions. Oppressors and traders tried to strip Africans of their families, their heritage, their names, and their very identities. Together, American enslaved people would have to remake their lives and redefine themselves. Through religion, close communities, great myths, secret gatherings, personal narratives, and an enduring struggle for freedom, this community too would help the nation face up to the great question: *Who are we?*

Every generation brings new Americans. They arrive from all corners of the world:

● *The United States grew as a nation of immigrants. Here a group from Ireland arrives during the 1870s.*

Ireland and Germany in the 1840s; Poland and Italy in the 1900s; Mexico, China, India, the Philippines, and El Salvador (among many other places) today. The new-comers, each in their own turn, wrestle with their identity in a new land. Many face discrimination when they arrive. But each generation helps remake American society, culture, and politics. Each tells us who we are. In 2022, more than forty-six million foreign-born people were living in the United States, making up about 14.1 percent of the population.[24]

New views also emerge from young people; each generation draws on different experiences and holds different attitudes. In one national poll, 59 percent of eighteen- to thirty-four-year-olds believed forms should offer gender options beyond male and female, and 62 percent believed racial diversity is good for society. In contrast, for the oldest Americans (seventy and older) who weighed in on these questions, 32 percent supported gender options on forms, and 42 percent believed racial diversity was good for society.[25]

Each generation of Americans embraces different values, engages in civic life to greater/lesser degrees, and accesses some but not other institutions.

Every feature of American government—the ideas, the Constitution, the president, Congress, the media, the political parties, the bureaucrats, and more—is

---

COMPARING NATIONS 1.2   **Aging Populations**

The U.S. population is getting older—2021 saw the slowest population growth in American history. Other countries, however, are experiencing even slower growth, which makes for aging societies. By the year 2050, 40 percent of the Japanese population will be over sixty-five. In Germany, senior citizens will make up 30 percent of the population, and in Canada, 27 percent. By 2050, only one in five Americans will be over sixty-five.

Why the different rates of aging in different countries? Partly because as nations get wealthier, families generally get smaller. And in most wealthy nations, people are living longer—though the United States lags behind the other nations listed here in life expectancy. In the United States, the large number of immigrants has kept the population younger than the population of other wealthy nations. *(U.S. Census Bureau)*

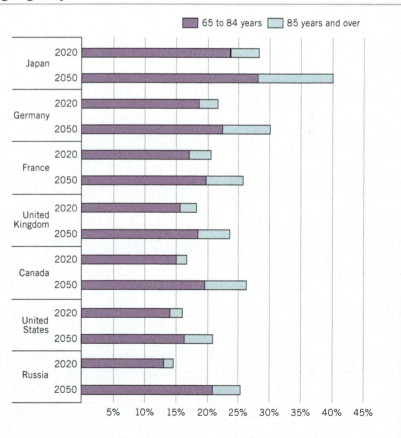

Demographics in America

How Are Race and Ethnicity Changing Over Time?

The mix of people in what is now the United States has been changing as long as there have been settlers on our shores, dating back to Native American inhabitants. White people dominated the country in 1960, but looking forward a half-century, we may see dramatic changes in our population: Some demographic models used by the Census Bureau project that the nation's fastest growth will occur among Americans of Hispanic, Asian, and African descent.

Changing Face of America

Percentage of total U.S. population by race and ethnicity, 1960–2060

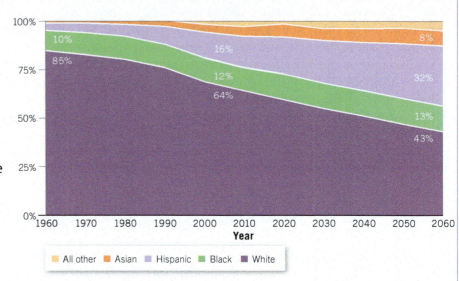

THINK ABOUT IT

First, what are the changes to the white population projected to be by 2060?

....

How does the projected growth of the Hispanic, Asian, and Black populations compare to that of the white population?

....

How do you think these demographic changes might change America and American politics?

....

Should the proportion of members of Congress or Supreme Court justices who are Hispanic also grow? Why or why not?

Source: Pew Research Center

part of the struggle to define and redefine the United States. We begin every chapter by showing you how the topic helps answer the same question: *Who are we?*

Who are we? The most important answer to that question is *you*. If you are part of Gen Z, individuals born after 1996, you are the future of American politics. To us, that is a comforting thought. This generation is, on average, more responsible, harder working, justice-minded, and more law-abiding than the generations that came before (including those of your authors). They tend to volunteer more, donate a higher share of their incomes to charity, and start more entrepreneurial

WHAT DO YOU THINK?

Getting Engaged in Politics—Or Not

Past public opinion data suggested that the younger generation has been less involved and interested in politics than were previous generations. Do you think this remains true today? What is your experience? Do you agree or disagree with this assertion?	**Disagree.** Millennials and Gen Z engage as civic volunteers like never before. From travel involving service learning to social media–fueled street protests to start-ups that disrupt traditional political forms, they are promoting new styles that more traditional observers have failed to appreciate. Moreover, young voters broke the turnout record in the 2020 election. Describe the types of activities you have seen or engaged in.	**Agree.** I do see a lack of political engagement around me. This may well be a problem for American democracy, but I shun electoral politics that seems to be dominated by two sides screaming at one another without engaging in civil discourse. I see more value in volunteering for a private organization or giving my time and money directly to causes that interest me.	**Unsure.** You may be new to the study of politics—or to the United States itself. If so, no worries. By the end of the book, we think you will have well-founded opinions on this and many other matters.

organizations with social impact. They are also a generation at home in a rapidly changing and diverse world.[26]

As we will see throughout the book, American politics has become especially rough—full of raised voices and bitter name-calling. Yet democracy thrives on tolerance. Our hope is that a new generation will take up the challenge of "keeping the republic" by expressing their own voices loudly and clearly while respecting and listening carefully to those of all others.

THE BOTTOM LINE

» American politics constantly addresses the most fundamental question about a people: Who are we?

» Because the nation is so diverse—and so rapidly changing—the answer to this question is constantly being rewritten.

» Each generation of Americans, including newly arriving immigrants, answers this question in its own way. Today we see millennials and Gen Z constructing their own version of a response.

🏛 Conclusion: Your Turn

The United States has solved many problems in the last two generations. It also has failed in some dramatic ways. The torch is now passing to you. We do not encourage you to get involved naively. This book details the many problems and frustrations of running for office, advocating on issues, or working in government. But we also hope our book will inspire you—whatever your age, whatever your background—to join the great debate about how to forge a better society. We invite you to use what you learn about American politics and government to help build a good community around you.

CHAPTER SUMMARY

⭐ To understand America's—or any other nation's—government and politics, keep four central questions in mind.

⭐ Who governs? This remains a deeply disputed topic, organized around four main theories. Pluralist thinkers claim that a wide array of interest groups, both private firms and public interest advocates, shapes government decisions and policy outcomes. Elite theorists view a handful of powerful and wealthy people as the most important source of political influence. Bureaucratic theorists look to millions of public officials in government organizations as the primary decision makers. Adherents of social movement theory argue that members of the public, when they join a protest movement, can have the ultimate say. Note that more than one of these theories can be true at the same time.

⭐ How does American politics work? Politics involves collective decisions about American society. To understand the decision-making process, we focus on four "I" factors. The first is *ideas*: Every day, people rally, debate, and even die on behalf of ideas such as freedom and democracy. Second, *institutions*: Congress, the Tennessee legislature, Immigration and Customs Enforcement (ICE), or regular elections provide the rules and procedures that shape political outcomes. Third, *interests* motivate people to act politically and come in different forms: individual self-interest, the goals of interest groups, and the overarching public interest we all share. Finally, *individuals* can have surprising amounts of political influence, even in a nation as large as the United States.

⭐ What does government do? Many Americans oppose a big, active national government, yet the United States has a very large one. The majority of the public embraces programs such as Social Security, Medicare, and a strong military. We also depend on vigorous civic engagement by the American public. In addition, government regulates the rules of everyday life, from who can get married to where to place a stoplight.

⭐ Who are we? American politics constantly addresses this most fundamental question about a people. Because the nation is so diverse—and so rapidly changing—the answer to this question is constantly being rewritten. Every feature of American politics—the foundational ideas, the Constitution, the media, Congress, the courts, and now Gen Z—engages in this vital debate over defining the nation and its people.

KEY TERMS

Checks and balances, p. 8   Institutions, p. 9   Rational choice theory, p. 10
Democracy, p. 5   Public–private partnership, p. 13   Republic, p. 5

STUDY QUESTIONS

1. Why do we describe American democracy as "paradoxical" at the opening of this chapter?

2. Why did Franklin add "if you can keep it" to his description of the new American nation as a republic?

3. What are some of the ways that ideas are influential in national government and politics?

4. Think of a political issue you care about—cutting taxes, global warming, immigration, healthcare, and so forth. Which government institutions are involved in determining how that issue is addressed and resolved?

5. What are the three types of "interests" that political scientists pay attention to in assessing whether political outcomes are interest based? Which seems most important? Why?

6. How might an individual make an impact on the vast U.S. system of government and politics? How might *you* be meaningfully involved?

7. Think of the various groups that you belong to. How would you describe each group? Social scientists call joining a group *social capital* and consider it the building block of democracy. Can you think of some ways that the things you do in your group might foster your role as a citizen?

2

THE IDEAS THAT SHAPE AMERICA

BACK IN 1955, developers focused mainly on moving traffic efficiently through cities and paid almost no attention to the consequences for urban life. So no one was surprised when city planners designed an expressway right through lower New York City—just as they were doing in cities from San Francisco to Atlanta. The proposed highway would run right over Washington Square Park and wreck the nearby neighborhoods—Greenwich Village and Little Italy.

A writer named Jane Jacobs loved the area and organized the neighbors to resist. In the fight, she came up with a fresh idea and a new way to see the city itself. Jacobs described what she saw happening on her own block: kids playing, neighbors gossiping, people shopping, and elderly people watching the pageant from their front porches. The highway, she said, would destroy a thriving community.

The professionals mocked her. They called her "a housewife" and a "militant dame" who didn't know what she was talking about. But Jacobs had come up with a powerful idea: The city should be seen as a series of rich, dense, living neighborhoods. Her idea spread, inspired residents, stopped the highway, and introduced a new era in urban design. Today, many urban planners celebrate Jane Jacobs's perspective; some cities have begun to move their highways. If you ever go to Manhattan, be sure to visit Washington Square Park and recall how one person's idea preserved the beautiful space you're standing in.[1]

Ideas are always changing, and over time people came to see cities in new ways. Today, some suggest that Jacobs had not paid enough attention to race, ethnicity, and class. A more diverse neighborhood, they argued, would be a better, richer, more satisfying place to live. Arguments about community, diversity, and what makes a good neighborhood—urban or rural—are still going strong.

Who are we? Our ideas tell us—and they tell the world. The United States is a nation built on ideas. You will see ideas at work in each chapter of this book, for they touch every feature of government and politics. This chapter introduces the most important American ideas and arguments. As you read about them—and as you continue through this book—think about other important ideas that you think we ought to add alongside the eight we discuss in this chapter. If you come up with a compelling idea, let us know and we may quote you in the next edition.

● *In 1955, city planners designed an expressway through lower New York City. There was just one problem. The proposed highway would pave over Washington Square Park. Then one writer had an idea that changed our image of the city itself.*

25

BY THE NUMBERS   American Ideas

86 Percentage of Americans who say a representative democracy is a good way to govern the country[2]

10 Number of times the word *rights* appears in the Declaration of Independence

15 Number of times the word *rights* appears in amendments to the Constitution

zero Number of times the word *rights* appears in the original Constitution

zero Number of times the word *democracy* appears in the Constitution

zero Number of times the word *equality* appears in the original U.S. Constitution

41 Number of the Declaration's signers who enslaved people

17 Percentage of Americans who say rule by military is a good way to govern the country[3]

70 Percentage of total wealth in the United States owned by the top 10 percent of the population[4]

30 Percentage of total wealth in the United States owned by the bottom 90 percent of the population[5]

78 Percentage of Americans who say that government should act to reduce economic inequality[6]

86 Percentage of Americans who say society is better off with people from many different backgrounds

What ideas are most important for making the United States a better place?

What ideas guide your own actions?

A Nation of Ideas

On July 4, 1776, American leaders issued a Declaration of Independence explaining their decision to break away from England. Its second paragraph describes the idea that animated them:

> *We hold these truths to be self-evident, that all men are created equal, that they are endowed by their Creator with certain unalienable rights, that among these are life, liberty and the pursuit of happiness.*

Most people have heard that line so often that it has lost its force, but it is one of the most powerful ideas in history. It explains the role of government—securing each

JOHN HANCOCK'S DEFIANCE.
JULY 4th 1776.

The Declaration of Independence being fully adopted, John Hancock, President of the Continental Congress, took up the pen and signed his name to it in a large bold hand: then rising he said, "There! John Bull can read my name without spectacles, and may double his reward for my head. That is my defiance!"

● *Ideas have consequences. John Hancock of Massachusetts defiantly signs the Declaration. According to legend, he signed it in big, bold letters so that King George III could read Hancock's name without his spectacles—and "double the reward for my head."*

individual's rights to life, liberty, and the pursuit of happiness. The Declaration states that people form governments for one purpose—*"to secure those rights."* And although the men and women who fought the Revolution fell far short of this ideal, they left the nation an inspiring goal. Every American generation argues about how it can best achieve the Declaration's shimmering promise to "secure" the rights of every citizen.

Many people believe that the United States is a unique nation, different from every other. That view is known as **American exceptionalism.** Others critique the idea of exceptionalism and note that every nation is distinctive in some ways. The United States is distinctive partially because of eight ideas that guide our politics. Most of them can be traced back to the Declaration of Independence.

What are the eight big ideas? Liberty, self-rule (which is often called democracy), individualism, limited government, the American dream, equality, faith in God, and diversity. These ideas touch almost everything we do as a nation. They are the foundation of American politics and lie at the core of what makes America distinctive.

But all these ideas come with an unusual twist: Americans rarely agree on what they mean. Instead, we constantly debate them. The Declaration of Independence declares that all men are created equal, but most of the men who signed it enslaved people. Our stamps and coins say "In God We Trust," but Americans passionately disagree about whether the Constitution permits prayer in schools or menorahs in public parks. All our foundational ideas have (at least) two sides and spark ardent disputes. To reveal the real truth about American politics, we should post signs at all the airports that say: *"Welcome to the great argument that is the USA."*

Now let's look at the first idea.

American exceptionalism:
The view that the United States is uniquely characterized by a distinct set of ideas such as equality, self-rule, and limited government.

> **THE BOTTOM LINE**
>
> » Eight ideas guide our politics: liberty, self-rule, individualism, limited government, the American dream, equality, faith in God, and diversity.

🏛 Liberty

As the Revolutionary War broke out, the royal governor of Virginia promised freedom to any enslaved person who joined the British. Eighty thousand enslaved people ran for the British lines. Some of them fought in Black units, with their motto—"liberty for the slaves"—sewn onto their uniforms.[7]

The enslaved men and women who fought for the British saw their hopes dashed when their side surrendered at the Battle of Yorktown in 1781—effectively ending the Revolutionary War. After the battle, the Redcoats, as the English soldiers were known, began to withdraw, rowing out to the warships bobbing in the harbor for their long retreat. One desperate group of Black men raced past the sentries on the wharf, dove into the sea, and swam toward the long rowboats that were ferrying the defeated British troops out to their naval vessels.

As the Black men tried to clamber aboard the small boats, British troops pushed them away. Fearful that the swimmers would swamp the craft, the troops pulled out axes and hacked off the Black men's hands and fingers. And *still* they kept coming, trying to surge aboard, thrashing after their fading dream of liberty. The image is unforgettable: These men were so desperate for freedom that even as the Redcoats swung their bloody hatchets, they kept clutching for the boats that might carry them away from bondage.

"The Land of the Free"

No idea comes up more often in American history than *freedom* or *liberty* (we use the words interchangeably in this book). The national anthem declares America "the land of the free." During the civil rights movement of the 1950s and 1960s, high school students spilled out of Baptist churches and marched toward dogs and high-pressure fire hoses, singing, "Everyone shout freedom, freedom, freedom!" In 2022, a truckers' convoy bore down on Washington, DC calling for "freedom, freedom, freedom" from masking and vaccination requirements.[8]

● *During the Revolutionary War, radicals met under trees they called "liberty trees" and erected poles they called "liberty poles." In this painting, Bostonians have dragged the British tax collector to the liberty tree and tarred and feathered him. The painting was British propaganda that mocked the liberty tree and the revolutionaries.*

What is **freedom?** It means that the government will protect your life, your liberty, and your property from the coercion of others (including public officials) to permit you to pursue the goals you define for yourself.

Freedom: The ability to pursue one's own desires without interference from others.

The Two Sides of Liberty

Everyone agrees that freedom is a basic American value. But what does it mean? Americans see it two very different ways: negative liberty and positive liberty.[9]

The more familiar view is **negative liberty**: *Freedom is the absence of constraints*. Society's responsibility, from this perspective, is to make sure that others (especially government officials) do not interfere with individuals. The government protects your right to believe what you wish, to say what you like, to declare any faith (or none), and to go into whatever profession you want—all without constraints or fear of punishment. Negative liberty firmly limits government action. Public officials violate your freedom when they stop you from protesting or punish you for smoking marijuana. Negative freedom is the right to act as you want.

Negative liberty: Freedom from constraints or the interference of others.

The alternative is **positive liberty**: *the freedom to pursue one's goals*. From this perspective, individuals cannot really be free—they cannot pursue their desires—if they lack life's basic necessities. Protecting liberty starts with ensuring that every citizen has food, shelter, healthcare, and educational opportunities. After all, how can people truly be free if they are hungry or homeless? This view requires government to give all people a legitimate shot at achieving their desires.

Positive liberty: The ability to pursue one's goals, which requires basic resources and power.

President Franklin D. Roosevelt forcefully expressed this view in 1941. As the United States prepared for World War II, he proclaimed that the nation was fighting for "four freedoms": freedom of speech, freedom of worship, freedom from want, and freedom from fear. The first two—freedom of speech and religion—were traditional negative liberties: No one could infringe on these individual rights. However,

WHAT DO YOU THINK?

Negative Versus Positive Liberty

Americans disagree about the meaning of "freedom." Is freedom the absence of constraints (negative liberty) or the freedom to pursue one's goals with equal opportunity (positive liberty)?	**Do you believe in negative liberty?** Government should not interfere with individuals. Freedom means leaving every person alone to do what he or she wishes—without interference. As President Reagan famously said, "As government expands, liberty contracts."	**Or do you believe in positive liberty?** Freedom simply is not a meaningful concept if you or your family are chronically hungry. A decent society has to lift everyone to a basic minimum. That is what living in a democracy should be about, said President Franklin D. Roosevelt: "True individual freedom cannot exist without economic security and independence."	**Or do your beliefs fall somewhere in between?** Think about how you might combine these two concepts. You may find it easier to answer this question after reading about the other major ideas. If you are not ready to choose, read on—and then return to this question.

"freedom from want" was something new, a positive liberty that entails helping needy people who have fallen on hard times. Roosevelt was suggesting that social welfare policies such as unemployment insurance and Social Security were part of the all-American idea of freedom. Contemporary ideas of positive freedom include efforts to ensure that all people are well educated, get healthcare when they need it, and do not ruin their health by smoking. The guiding notion is that a lack of education, or illness or addiction, makes it difficult for individuals to pursue their goals.

Which idea of freedom is right? That depends on your values. Beneath these two visions of liberty lie different ideas about a good society. The negative view emphasizes personal autonomy: Leave me alone. Taxing me violates my freedom of property. The positive view follows Roosevelt: Membership in a free society means sharing enough wealth so that everyone enjoys freedom from want. The two perspectives reflect different values, different visions of society, and different definitions of liberty.

The Idea of Freedom Is Always Changing

Once upon a time, Americans permitted slavery and passed laws requiring racial segregation. Women lost all their legal rights the day they were married; their possessions—even their very bodies—passed into the custody of their husbands. Immigrants from China, and later from India, were denied any hope of becoming Americans no matter how long they lived in the country. The ideal of freedom moved Americans to outgrow each of these prejudices.

Scholars disagree about how to interpret the results. Some see American history as a slow but steady march toward greater liberty. Yes, they admit, American history is full of oppression. However, our faith in freedom leads oppressed groups to fight for their rights. The American promise, wrote Samuel Huntington, is the "promise of disharmony," as a constant parade of groups—Black people, women, Irish, Latinos, and many others—successfully challenge the nation to live up to its ideals.[10]

Other political thinkers, such as Mary Frances Berry and Rogers Smith, warn against viewing American history as a steady rise of freedom. The outcome in the fight for freedom is never inevitable, they argue. Instead, freedom is won and lost . . . and won and lost again. Americans fought their bloody civil war to end slavery, only to watch terrorists rise up and impose new forms of racial segregation and oppression that lasted for another century. Native Americans have never had their place on the land or in society fully restored. Struggles to secure rights are still part of the long battle for freedom. No one can say how those conflicts will end. We should never take liberty for granted.[11]

THE BOTTOM LINE

» Liberty—or the freedom to pursue your goals—is the most often invoked American value.

» There are two different views of what liberty means. *Negative liberty* emphasizes a lack of constraints on individuals, even if those constraints are intended to help others. *Positive liberty* calls on the community to help everyone satisfy their basic needs.

» Freedom has expanded to new groups over time. Some scholars see the rise of freedom as inevitable, reflecting American ideals; others see it as a constant battle that can always go either way.

Self-Rule: Democracy or Representation?

As the American Revolution began, crowds gathered in the towns and cities. The people, they declared, would seize authority from their royal governors (appointed by the tyrannical king) and exercise power themselves. "The mob has begun to think for itself," complained one wealthy New Yorker. "Poor reptiles, before noon they will bite" (meaning *revolt*).[12]

Patriotic crowds ignored the skeptics. At mass meetings, the people voted for laws, enforced decrees, and even issued wedding licenses. Here is a powerful image of democracy: American people bypassing government officials and running the country themselves from the town commons. The people ruled.

That principle sounds simple. But from the beginning, a great debate arose about how to achieve **self-rule**. The Constitution was meant to settle the issue—but we are still arguing about its meaning more than 230 years later.

How do we achieve self-rule? Americans have long vacillated between two very different paths—a *democracy* and a *republic*.

Self-rule: The idea that legitimate government flows from the people.

One Side of Self-Rule: Democracy

Democracy involves citizen participation in making government decisions. (*Demos* is the Greek word for "the people," and *kratia* is the Greek word for "rule/power.") In early New England, citizens governed in town meetings—without relying on elected officials. To this day, some towns are still run this way. How high should taxes be? How much should the town pay its schoolteachers? Eligible voters have their say and then they vote to decide the matter.

Thomas Jefferson, who drafted the Declaration of Independence and served as the third U.S. president (1801–9), was the most vocal proponent of maximizing democracy. "The will of the majority," wrote Jefferson, is a "sacred principle" and "the only sure guardian of the rights of man." If the people cannot govern themselves, asked Jefferson, how can they possibly be trusted with the government of others?[13]

You might think that **direct democracy** like this wouldn't work in a country as big as the United States, but over the years reformers have looked for ways to take decisions away from the government and let the people make them directly. (Mark Twain captured the spirit of the efforts when he allegedly quipped, "No man's life, liberty or property are safe when the legislature is in session.")

Direct democracy: A form of government in which all laws and rules are made directly by the citizens, rather than through elected representatives.

One result is a rich American legacy of taking to the streets to demonstrate, rally, and protest. Millions of people rallied after a Minneapolis police officer killed a Black man named George Floyd. Immigrants and their supporters marched in cities across the country to protest deportation. Gun owners gathered to support the Second Amendment right to bear arms. Giant Earth Day demonstrations launched the modern environmental movement. Marches for and against abortion often draw hundreds of thousands. And—perhaps the most famous of all—Martin Luther King Jr.'s "I Have a Dream" speech electrified the people who participated in the March on Washington for Jobs and Freedom in 1963.

Every state tries to institutionalize the democratic ideal by letting the public vote directly on policy issues. In 2022, voters in thirty-eight states weighed in on 140 ballot questions: raising the minimum wage (in Nevada), expanding Medicaid to provide healthcare for more people (South Dakota), reducing the use of plastic (California), raising state university tuition fees for out-of-state students (Arizona), restricting or affirming a right to abortions (multiple states on each side), changing election laws (multiple states), and other issues.

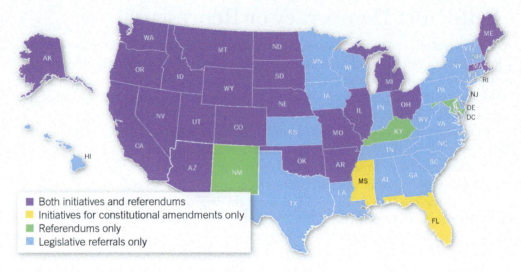

● **FIGURE 2.1** *Every state puts measures before the public. In the Midwest and Pacific Northwest referendums and initiatives bypass state legislatures. In the Northeast and South, people vote on issues that legislators put before them. (NY Constitution.org)*

Legend:
- Both initiatives and referendums
- Initiatives for constitutional amendments only
- Referendums only
- Legislative referrals only

Referendum: An election in which citizens vote directly on an issue.

Initiative: A process in which citizens propose new laws or amendments to the state constitution.

Legislative referral: The state legislature puts a proposal up for a popular vote.

Sunshine laws: Laws that permit the public to watch policymakers in action and to access the records of the proceedings.

Republic: A government in which citizens rule indirectly and make government decisions through their elected representatives.

People bypass the state legislatures and vote on an issue through a **referendum**, allowed by twenty-seven states and the District of Columbia (see Figure 2.1). Some states, like New York, permit referendums on the local level. **Initiatives** permit the public in twenty-four states to circulate a petition that would propose a new law or amendment to its Constitution. In forty-nine states, the legislatures sometimes ask voters to weigh in on controversial topics—known as **legislative referral**. And most city and state governments have **sunshine laws**, which require meetings to be open so the public can keep an eye on what the public officials are up to.

Thomas Jefferson's dream of direct democracy lives on in multiple ways. Idealists throughout American history have returned to his first principle: The people should exercise power as much as possible.

Another Side of Self-Rule: A Republic

Most of the men who drafted the Constitution disagreed with Jefferson about democracy. The states had tried to create direct democracy right after the American Revolution. George Washington thought the result was chaos. "We have probably had too good an opinion of human nature," he grumbled. James Madison put it most famously: "Democracies have [always] been spectacles of turbulence and contention . . . as short in their lives as violent in their deaths." The problem, said Madison, was that in direct democracy, the majority often gets carried away. They push their self-interest without paying attention to the rights of the minority. Direct democracy, he concluded, offers no barrier to lynch mobs.[14] Think of white nationalists chanting "Jews will not replace us" in Charlottesville, Virginia, or the individuals who tried to change the outcome of the presidential election by mobbing the Capitol Building on January 6, 2021.

The alternative to direct action by the people is a **republic**: The people rule indirectly through their elected representatives. When they designed this form of government, the Constitution's framers made an important contribution to the theory of self-rule. Classical democratic theory, which relied on direct popular participation, would only work if the people were virtuous—since there was nothing to check the public. The founders realized that people were often not very virtuous at all. "If men were angels," wrote Madison in *Federalist* No. 51, "no government

● *Another form of democracy in action: Americans take to the Michigan capitol to protest the lockdown during the COVID-19 pandemic.*

would be necessary." The great challenge, he concluded, was to devise government institutions that would protect individual rights even if a majority of the people and its leaders were selfish and corrupt. His solution: Let the people elect representatives who operated in an institutional framework full of checks and balances.

A Mixed System

Which view of self-rule holds in the United States? Both do. We can say that the United States is a democratic republic because it includes elements of a democracy *and* of a republic.

There are plenty of opportunities for direct participation. At the same time, American government is organized to check the majority. The House, the Senate, the president, and the Supreme Court all put the brakes on one another. And all of them face fifty different state governments, each with its own politics, powers, and programs. The American government operates through elected and unelected officials who answer (sometimes indirectly) to the public.

The sheer number of U.S. elected officials—more than five hundred thousand—reveals our hybrid form of government. There is one elected government official for every six hundred people in the country. Few other nations come close to this ratio. We elect representatives, reflecting our origins as a republic, but the enormous number of opportunities to serve in elective office moves us closer to a democracy.

Although our government combines elements of both democracies and republics, the debate continues about which way we should tilt. Which stance do you prefer? Jefferson's faith in direct democracy? Or Madison's warning that people are not angels and that government is best pursued indirectly, with the people electing representatives to make decisions for them?

You may have noticed that these two principles—the democratic and the republican—are also the names of America's two major political parties. However, to complicate matters, the party labels do not really correspond to the party principles. Many Republican Party members are committed democrats and vice versa. We always capitalize the names of the parties—Democrats and Republicans—to avoid confusing them with the two pathways to self-rule.

THE BOTTOM LINE

» Self-rule is a powerful and enduring idea guiding American government. Lincoln put it best: "Government of the people, by the people, for the people."

» There are two chief pathways to government by the people: a *direct democracy* and a *republic*. Americans have always sought to balance these two ideals.

Limited Government

Back in 1691, while America was still part of Great Britain, King William III appointed Benjamin Fletcher to be governor of New York and gave him control over the New England colonies (which had been independent until then). The Connecticut legislature did not want to cede its power to Governor Fletcher and immediately selected a new commander for the local militia—a direct challenge to the new governor's authority. Fletcher could not ignore this intransigence, so on a beautiful October day he sailed to Hartford, the capital of Connecticut, with a small detachment of troops. He assembled the Connecticut militia and had an officer read aloud the royal proclamation declaring his authority over the state—and its militia.

As the officer spoke, the Connecticut militiamen began to beat their drums in defiance. Fletcher tried to restore order by commanding his soldiers to fire their muskets in the air; in the ensuing silence, he threatened to punish the militia members for their insolence. In response, the commander of the Connecticut militia stepped forward, put his hand on the hilt of his sword, and issued his own warning: "If my drummers are again interrupted, I'll make sunlight shine through you. We deny and defy your authority." Outnumbered and in no mood for bloodshed, Fletcher beat a quick retreat to his vessel and sailed ignominiously back to New York City. Because the king and his ministers were more than three thousand miles away, they never heard about this little rebellion against their authority.[15]

The Origins of Limited Government

The tale of Governor Fletcher illustrates an enduring idea: Americans distrust centralized leadership and have consistently sought to limit its power. Eighty years before the Revolutionary War, Connecticut had grown used to electing its own leaders and going its own way. The people saw the king as a distant figure with no right to interfere in their affairs. The image of central government as a remote, unfeeling, untrustworthy authority that threatens our freedoms runs through American history.

Why did Americans develop this distrust? The answer lies in how the people secured their rights in the first place. In most nations, the central government—made up of kings or aristocrats, or both—grudgingly granted their people rights such as the vote or jury trials. Sometimes the people rebelled (as in France), sometimes they negotiated with kings (England), and sometimes monarchs expanded rights to modernize their nations (Thailand). All these countries share a common experience: Kings or the central governments that replaced them were the source of rights and liberties. No wonder citizens in these nations sometimes look to the government for help in solving their problems.

The United States was dramatically different. White male Americans enjoyed political rights such as voting long before they even had a central government. As Governor Fletcher's humiliation illustrates, for most of colonial history the king was too far away to meddle in colonial affairs. Experience taught Americans to see the central government not as a potential source of rights, but as a threat to their life, liberty, and happiness.

This is one reason why Americans are slow to trust their national government. Proposals such as national health insurance, a cap on carbon emissions to slow global warming, regulating the Internet, or a nationwide registry of gun sales all run up against a deep suspicion of government. The French aristocrat Alexis de Tocqueville was struck by this lack of trust. Any visitor from Europe, he wrote back in 1831, would be amazed that the American government is so "feeble and restricted." Fifty years later, the English ambassador to the United States summarized the American spirit: "The less of government the better."[16] Even today, Americans are less satisfied with how their government is working than citizens of many other nations (Comparing Nations 2.1).

There's one more reason for the rising distrust of government. Stoking anti-bureaucratic fervor is a good way to get voters to the polls. Attacking "those fools" in Washington gets people excited, but it also erodes the respect for our political institutions and makes governing a lot harder.[17]

COMPARING NATIONS 2.1   Satisfaction with How Governments Are Working

How do citizens in different nations view their government? In this survey, citizens were asked whether their country needed major reform in three areas: politics, economics, and healthcare.

Notice how Americans and Southern Europeans—Greece, Italy, and Spain—are dissatisfied in all three areas. But other nations—like the United Kingdom, the Netherlands, Sweden, Australia, and Singapore—are not looking for fundamental change. And perhaps the most striking difference lies in the contrast between North American neighbors—Canada and the United States.

Another way to look at it: Out of these seventeen nations, American satisfaction ranks eleventh (tied with France) for the economic system, thirteenth for the political system, and next to last on healthcare.

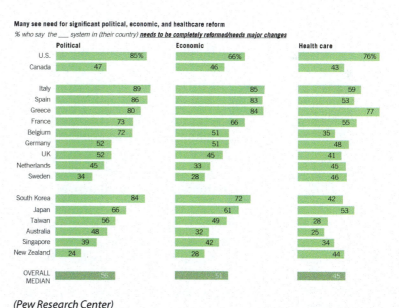

Many see need for significant political, economic, and healthcare reform

% who say the ___ system in (their country) **needs to be completely reformed/needs major changes**

	Political	Economic	Health care
U.S.	85%	66%	76%
Canada	47	46	43
Italy	89	85	59
Spain	86	83	53
Greece	80	84	77
France	73	66	55
Belgium	72	51	35
Germany	52	51	48
UK	52	45	41
Netherlands	45	33	45
Sweden	34	28	46
South Korea	84	72	42
Japan	66	61	53
Taiwan	56	49	28
Australia	48	32	25
Singapore	39	42	34
New Zealand	24	28	44
OVERALL MEDIAN	55	51	45

(Pew Research Center)

And Yet ... Americans Keep Demanding More Government

Here's the paradox lying at the heart of the limited-government idea. People across the political spectrum demand government action.

Many **conservatives** want government authority to crack down on illegal drugs, forbid abortions, harden the border against undocumented immigration, enhance homeland security, or ensure that teachers are not disparaging America in their classrooms. They also dream of restoring traditional morality by restricting obscenity, regulating video games, and bringing religion back into schools. Using government to restore moral values is not a new idea. Back in the 1920s, conservatives in both parties banded together with feminists and public health reformers to outlaw all sales of alcohol from coast to coast—a remarkably ambitious government effort to change people's everyday behavior. And many people still demand regulations of liquor and drugs; the United States is alone among advanced democracies in setting the drinking age at twenty-one, compared to Denmark and Costa Rica (where it is sixteen), Israel (eighteen), Japan (twenty), or Germany (fourteen for beer and wine if accompanied by an adult).

Most **liberals** reject the idea that public officials should meddle in people's private lives. You should be able to smoke marijuana, express your gender identity, and have an abortion, they say. But they are all for active government when it comes to fighting inequality, regulating business, addressing climate change, paying for college tuition, or offering school lunch programs (there's the positive freedom from want, again; Figure 2.2). From this perspective, everyone should have good access to healthcare. People over sixty-five appreciate Medicare, which provides them with health insurance; why not extend it to all Americans? And the same for good education.

Table 2.1 presents conservative and liberal positions on major issues.

While the main division in American politics lies between liberals and conservatives, there are two more perspectives that sometimes burst onto the scene.

Libertarians break with both liberals and conservatives; they are strong proponents of negative liberty and aim to reduce all government to a minimum. Government, libertarians insist, should protect public safety, private property, and national borders—and do little else. No giant army or navy; no public schools; no regulating banks; no telling people which drugs they cannot use; no helping people who are hungry, or homeless, or need healthcare; no laws against discrimination. The popularity of this perspective rises and falls over time because every national crisis—from tainted food to bank failures to terrorist attacks to the deaths of unarmed Black civilians at the hands of police—inspires widespread demands for government action.

Finally, **populists** believe the rich and powerful have captured the government. They distrust the media, the banks, the corporations, the political parties, and the experts who serve them. Their goal is to win back the government and use it to help the common people. Populists can be on the left (like Senator Bernie Sanders of Vermont) and call for massive economic assistance to those who have been left behind; or they can be on the right (like former President Donald Trump) and emphasize restoring a lost national culture. Right-wing populists sometimes slip into racism and immigrant bashing. But on both sides, populists aim for an active government that helps "real" Americans, restores economic mobility, or makes America great again.[18]

Conservatives: Americans who believe in reduced government spending, personal responsibility, traditional moral values, secure borders, and a strong national defense. Also known as *right* or *right-wing*.

Liberals: Americans who value cultural diversity, government programs for the needy, public intervention in the economy, and individuals' right to a lifestyle based on their own social and moral positions. Also known as *left* or *left-wing*.

Libertarians: Americans who are strong proponents of negative liberty and aim to reduce all government to a minimum.

Populists: Americans who believe the rich and powerful have captured the government and seek to win back government to help the common people.

Large partisan differences on the issues

% who say _____ should be a top priority for the president and Congress to address this year

	Dem/ Lean Dem	Rep/ Lean Rep	Rep-Dem diff.
Strengthening economy	63	82	+19
Reducing healthcare costs	53	69	−16
Dealing with coronavirus outbreak	35	80	−45
Improving education	48	66	−18
Securing Social Security	56	58	+2
Defending against terrorism	48	65	+17
Improving political system	40	61	−21
Reducing crime	45	60	+15
Improving job situation	49	55	+6
Dealing with immigration	35	67	+32
Reducing the budget deficit	31	63	+32
Addressing criminal justice system	40	48	−8
Dealing with problems of poor people	25	58	−33
Dealing with global climate change	11	65	−54
Addressing issues around race	14	53	−39
Strengthening military	22	55	+33
Dealing with global trade	30	40	+10
Dealing with drug addiction	27	32	−5

FIGURE 2.2 *Look at the stark differences between the parties. Democrats calls for action on global climate change, racial issues, poverty, and the coronavirus. Republicans focus on immigration, budget deficits, the military, and terrorism. Notice that only three issues attract a majority from both parties. (Pew Research Center)*

Here's an important point: Liberals, conservatives, and populists all look to government to win the things they care about. They simply disagree on what exactly government ought to do.

Most people do not agree with their party on every issue—although the more closely they follow politics, the more they tend to agree. How about you? What issues do you care about most? Do you fit into the blue or red columns? Or are you more comfortable mixing and matching? If so, you are a true independent.

Limits on Government Action

In short, Americans often say they do not like government and then demand that government address the problems they are concerned about. But, as rising political scientists, you already know that our institutions shape the way arguments play out.

When the framers designed our political system, they built suspicion of government right into the core. The federal Constitution includes an intricate system of checks and balances on power, which we explore in Chapter 3. The Constitution limits what Congress may do—and for two centuries, Americans have vigorously debated where those boundaries lie.

TABLE 2.1 Liberal and Conservative Positions on Strong and Weak Government

DEMOCRATS/LIBERAL	REPUBLICAN/CONSERVATIVE
MORE/STRONG GOVERNMENT	
Provide healthcare for all	Secure border
Reduce income inequality	Deport undocumented immigrants
Address climate change	Strengthen military
Raise minimum wage	Strengthen police/crack down on crime
Address racial injustice	Forbid abortions
Protect LGBTQ+ rights	Maintain binary gender categorizations
Protect the right to vote	Prevent voter fraud
Protect consumers	Limit pornography
Impose restrictions on guns	
Provide college tuition	
LESS/WEAK GOVERNMENT	
Prevent undocumented immigrants from being deported	Lower taxes
Reduce police authority	Reduce regulations on business
Reduce drug regulations	Let economic markets operate freely
Remove abortion restrictions	Reduce interference with gun rights
Remove binary gender categorizations	Enable religious freedom
	Resist government mandates (masks, vaccination requirements)

The policy positions of the conservatives (the right) and the liberals (the left). Notice how each party wants government to get involved in some things—and stay out of others.

Another institutional limit on government activity involves multiple levels of government—local, state, and national—constantly checking and balancing (and suing) one another. This federalist system is the subject of Chapter 4.

When Ideas Clash: Democracy and Limited Government

President Trump promised to repeal and replace "Obamacare," the health insurance plan that covers twenty million people. He pledged to build a wall on the border with Mexico paid for by Mexicans. Neither happened. President Biden promised to stimulate the economy, address climate change, and end the COVID epidemic with vaccines and mandates. So far, they've all proven elusive goals. Election winners get their followers fired up with their promises—and then face major hurdles in achieving them—thanks to the many limits that Americans have placed on their government.

What we face is a clash between two American ideas: popular rule and limited government. Popular rule (or democracy as it's usually called) says that the winning party should be able to put their policies into place. In a democracy, the majority should rule.

But another value, limited government, responds: not so fast. We do not like government meddling in our private lives, so we make it very difficult for elected officials to follow through on their promises and get things done. Even a president who wins a national election by a large margin must still convince a majority in the House of Representatives and 60 percent of the Senate to vote his way. (Why sixty of the one hundred senators? You'll see in Chapter 13.) And when Congress does pass a law—which is no easy task—the programs created by the law often face challenges in the courts for violating constitutional limits on government power.

Ironically, the limits on change make it difficult to repeal programs once they make it past all the hurdles and are up and running. For example, Social Security was passed in 1935 during the economic crisis of the Great Depression; Medicare passed in part because of a great electoral landslide in 1964. Both are now extremely popular; in fact, they are so widely embraced that they are known in Washington as "the third rails" of American politics—touch them and die (politically, of course). More recently, Republicans eagerly promised to repeal the Affordable Care Act, passed by the Obama administration, but despite controlling the White House and Congress, they failed. The program had grown too popular, and the same institutional process that makes it hard to win programs also makes it difficult to repeal them.

● *When people are suffering, even critics of the government set aside their views and ask for help. Here, tornado damage in Kentucky.*

Yes, Americans resist "big government," and it is difficult to pass new programs. But that is only half the story. Americans also demand government action and fiercely defend the programs they like.

How should we balance democracy and limited government? Erecting too many boundaries means that we undermine government by the majority. But remove the barriers and the winning party can pass all its preferred programs—until it loses in elections and the other party eliminates all those programs and pushes through the agenda that it promised.

WHAT DO YOU THINK?

Democracy Versus Limited Government

	I'm with Thomas Jefferson.	I'm with James Madison.	Not sure?
Some observers think we do not have a true government by the people because it is too difficult for elected officials to get things done, even with a large popular majority. These reformers seek an easier path to government action. However, that prospect raises fears of a more active government. Which should we emphasize, democratic self-rule or limited government? It's time to make your choice.	It should be easier for elected officials to enact the programs they promised. If they cannot do so, elections become less meaningful. When the people vote for change and their representatives fail to deliver, it fosters cynicism about the entire political process. Democracy requires us to follow the people's mandate. If the majority does not like the results, it can express its displeasure in the next election.	The checks and balances that make large-scale reforms difficult protect the United States from overbearing government and from sudden changes—whether rapidly expanding or cutting programs. The barriers to government action *should* be high. If the public really wants something, it will probably happen over time. Limited government is more important. Don't change the process.	This is a formidable question. You may very well change your mind—maybe more than once—as you continue to read this book.

THE BOTTOM LINE

» Americans distrust their government more than people in most wealthy democracies—though new pressures are making many other nations more like the United States. The Constitution builds that distrust into our governing rules by providing for limited government. The result is a very durable status quo.

» In many countries, politicians can usually deliver the programs they promised on the campaign trail. In the United States, winners confront multiple barriers to fulfilling their pledges—the antigovernment idea is expressed as checks and balances.

» However, once programs do go into effect, they often prove popular and difficult to change.

Individualism

Political scientist John Kingdon was visiting his niece in Norway. She was expecting a baby, and Professor Kingdon asked what she planned to do about her job. Casually, she replied that she would receive a full year's leave at 80 percent of her normal pay, and that her company was required to give her job back after the leave. "Who pays for all this?" asked Kingdon. "The government, of course," his niece replied. She was surprised the question had even come up. "Is it any different in the United States?" she asked innocently.[19]

It is completely different in the United States. Advocates fought for years to win the Family and Medical Leave Act (1993), which requires employers with more than fifty workers to allow up to twelve weeks of *unpaid* leave for pregnancy, birth, adoption, illness, or military service. On family leave, like many other issues, other countries share the responsibility—and often pay higher taxes to do so.

Individualism: The idea that individuals, not the society, are responsible for their own well-being.

Many Americans value **individualism**: *the idea that individuals, not the society or the community or the government, are responsible for their own well-being.* Government does not pay for maternity leave. Instead, we expect private individuals and families to handle birth, adoption, and caregiving. But that is only one part of the American story.

Community Versus Individualism

The idea of individualism is a source of controversy in every nation (see Comparing Nations 2.2). There are two ways to see any society: as a single *community* or as a collection of *individuals*. Every nation includes both, but government policies can be designed to emphasize the community or to focus on individuals. Let us take a closer look at these two principles.

Social democracy: The idea that government policy should ensure that all are comfortably cared for within the context of a capitalist economy.

Countries that emphasize the community are called **social democracies**. Social democrats believe that members of a society are responsible for one another. They view government as a source of mutual assistance. The government provides citizens with the basics: good health insurance, retirement benefits,

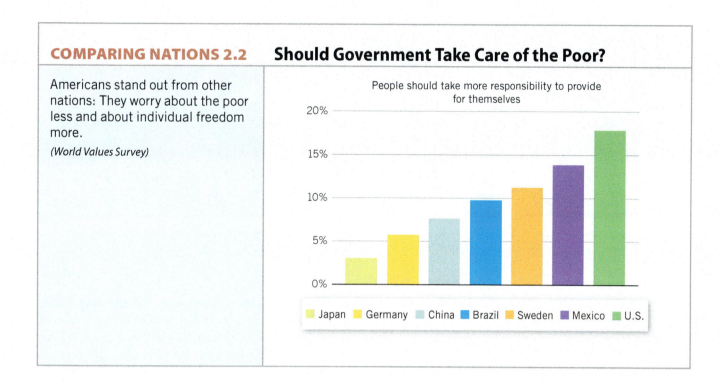

COMPARING NATIONS 2.2 **Should Government Take Care of the Poor?**

Americans stand out from other nations: They worry about the poor less and about individual freedom more.

(World Values Survey)

People should take more responsibility to provide for themselves

Japan ■ Germany ■ China ■ Brazil ■ Sweden ■ Mexico ■ U.S.

generous unemployment packages, and—as we saw in the Norwegian case—maternity benefits.

In exchange, people pay high taxes. Almost half of a Norwegian's income goes to taxes. One effect of high taxation is to make it difficult for most citizens to get very rich. At the same time, the extensive welfare state makes it far less likely that people will live in poverty. Communal societies are far more equal—not just in opportunity, but in outcome. Most Western European nations are social democracies.

Social democracies are based on *solidarity*, the idea that people have a tight bond and are responsible for one another. Some societies exhibit a very strong sense of solidarity. In general, solidarity increases during wars, economic depressions, or other crises that get everyone to pull together. Scholars have found that more homogeneous societies—those in which people look alike, share the same values, and practice the same religion—exhibit higher rates of solidarity than very diverse societies. They point out that even long-established social democracies in Europe (historically populated primarily by Christians) have seen their sense of solidarity falter with the arrival of Muslim immigrants. Growing diversity has challenged national solidarity.[20]

American politics includes a strong streak of solidarity, often expressed as empathy for those less fortunate, that balances its individualism. Martin Luther King Jr. put it eloquently: "I am inevitably my brother's keeper because I am my brother's brother."[21] However, the commitment to solidarity rises and falls in the United States. Public opinion surveys suggest it is rising again among people under forty—they express far more support for solidarity than older generations.[22]

Now let us turn to individualism. In this view, people and their families are responsible for their own welfare. The economist Milton Friedman famously

● *Images of individualism and solidarity. (a) This Republican National Convention backdrop emphasized self-reliance and individual achievement; (b) Democrat Bernie Sanders, in 2020, emphasized community and solidarity.*

argued that the world runs on individuals pursuing their separate interests. Leave people free to choose their interests, Friedman continued, and the public interest of the whole society will emerge.[23] Rather than taxing people and using funds to aid the less well-off, proponents of this perspective opt for low taxes and a green light for private entrepreneurs. People who work hard will succeed, they believe, and society will grow and prosper.

Individualists value the chance to get ahead more than they value a society in which everyone is equal. In social democracies, government regulations aim to protect workers. In contrast, individualists oppose government controls and believe that private companies should be able to expand or contract their workforce as they see fit (as long as they hire and fire without discriminating). People should take care of one another through churches, charities, or other private means. Individualism points toward limited government, faith in economic markets, and a strong emphasis on *negative liberty*.

The Roots of American Individualism: Opportunity and Discord

In the past, Americans generally leaned toward individualism and away from social democracy. Why? Two famous explanations look to American history. One finds the answer in golden opportunities. A second emphasizes social and racial discord.

Golden Opportunity. For centuries, most Europeans and Asians lived as serfs or peasants working small plots of land. Powerful rulers kept them firmly in their place—there was little chance for individuals to get ahead by working hard. In early America, by contrast, there appeared to be endless land and opportunity. With hard work and a little luck, anyone (at least any white male) could earn a decent living and perhaps even a fortune. Stories about early settlers clearing their own land were later reinforced by images of rugged individuals on the western frontier. Hard workers relied on themselves—not the government.

There is a lot of myth in these stories. Frontier life was less about brave individualism and more about communities. Settlers could not build a barn, a church, or a meetinghouse without their neighbors' help. But the image of hardy individuals on the frontier remains a powerful ideal in American culture and politics. And there was an important truth at its core: Few societies have ever offered so many individuals as much opportunity to rise and prosper as early America did.[24]

Social Conflict. Another explanation for American individualism emphasizes the enormous differences within our society. The country is too big and the population too diverse to develop a sense of solidarity. What, after all, did Calvinist Yankees in New England have in common with Roman Catholics in Baltimore or Anglican planters in Virginia—much less Spanish speakers in Florida or Texas?

● *Individualism in historical memory: At high noon on April 22, 1889, bugles sounded and a great mob surged across the Oklahoma border and snatched up as much land as they could stake out. Although the government sponsored the land giveaway, the image that has stuck is of people grabbing the land for themselves. Oklahoma still honors the scalawags that snuck in early ("sooner") and staked the best land—which is where the motto "The Sooner State" is said to come from.*

Moreover, a nation that enslaved four million Black people by 1860 had a terrible divide running through its heart. How do you build social solidarity in a land where four million people live in chains?

By the 1830s still another source of division had arisen. Irish immigrants speaking different languages and practicing what seemed like strange customs were arriving by the tens (and later hundreds) of thousands. Fifty years later, Italians, Poles, and Chinese seemed just as threatening to the Irish who, by then, had settled into their country. Each generation of immigrants unsettles those who came before.[25] All of these divisions made solidarity far more difficult to feel than in the more stable, homogeneous populations.

Which explanation is correct? Both are on target. Unprecedented economic opportunity and vast social divisions reinforced individualism in the American past. But that may be changing today.

Who Are We? Individualism and Solidarity

Americans are not individualists pure and simple. Rather, the two themes—individualism and solidarity—always compete in American politics. Individualism has been more robust and more often in evidence, but a sense of solidarity also unites the population. Americans often pull together as a nation. They take care of their neighbors and pass government programs to improve the lives of people they do not know. The United States may have deep divisions, but it is remarkable how quickly they can disappear. A substantial majority of Americans today are children, grandchildren, or great-grandchildren of immigrants—many of whom were once regarded as strange and different.

All this raises another question to ponder: Where would you draw the line between solidarity and individualism? The answer directly relates to one of this book's central questions: *Who are we?* Take the test in "What Do You Think?" to learn where you stand on the continuum between rugged individualism and strong solidarity.

WHAT DO YOU THINK?

Individualism Versus Solidarity

Please score yourself on the following ten statements:
0 = Disagree strongly
1 = Disagree
2 = Agree
3 = Agree strongly

Statement	Score
1. It is the responsibility of the government to take care of the least well-off in society.	0 1 2 3
2. Everyone should have health insurance.	0 1 2 3
3. In fact, everyone should have the same health insurance. It doesn't make sense for some people to get better care than others just because they can afford it.	0 1 2 3
4. I'd be willing to pay a little more in taxes so that no person in America goes hungry or homeless.	0 1 2 3
5. I'd be willing to pay a lot more in taxes so that everyone in America has a pretty decent life.	0 1 2 3
6. I agree with Dr. Martin Luther King Jr.: "I am inevitably my brother's keeper because I am my brother's brother [and my sister's sister]. . . . The betterment of the poor enriches the rich."	0 1 2 3
7. I don't believe big companies should be permitted to fire people without providing two months' salary and some retraining.	0 1 2 3
8. Most Americans want the same things out of life.	0 1 2 3
9. We should think about others as much as we think about ourselves.	0 1 2 3
10. It is wrong to step over others to get ahead in life.	0 1 2 3

Scoring
0–5 You are truly a rugged individualist!
6–14 You are largely an individualist.
15–20 You are a moderate who sees both sides of the issue.
21–24 You are a social democrat.
25–30 You are a true-blue believer in solidarity!

Now, speak to others who scored very differently from you. Try to explain how and why you came to hold your views.

THE BOTTOM LINE

» American politics includes both individualism and solidarity.

» Different leaders, parties, groups, and individuals weigh the two values in different ways. Compared to other nations, the United States is at the individualist end of the spectrum.

The American Dream

Benjamin Franklin perfected a classic American literary form—tips for getting rich. Anyone, he assured his readers, could be successful by following a formula: be frugal ("A penny saved is a penny earned"), hardworking ("No gains without pains"), steady ("Little strokes fell great oaks"), bold ("God helps those who help themselves"), and—most important—morally upright ("Leave your vices, though ever so dear").[26]

Franklin summarized what later became known as the American dream: *If you are talented and work hard, you can achieve personal (and especially financial) success.* A popular historian, James Truslow Adams, first defined the term. The United States, he wrote, is "a land in which life should be better and richer and fuller for everyone, with opportunity for each according to ability or achievement."[27] The idea scarcely changes across generations. "The American dream that we were all raised on is a simple but powerful one," averred President Bill Clinton more than two centuries after Ben Franklin. "If you work hard and play by the rules, you should be given a chance to go as far as your God-given abilities will take you." Affirmed Vice President Kamala Harris in summer 2022: "we are fueled by a common purpose: to help all people . . . achieve their own version of the American Dream."[28]

Spreading the Dream

The legacy of the Revolutionary War, according to historian Gordon Wood, was the spread of the American dream to all classes. National leaders originally imagined that they were establishing a classical republic, such as Athens, in which a few outstanding men would govern the people. Instead, the Revolution established the common people (at the time, that meant white men) as the basis of government and gave them an unprecedented chance to make their fortunes. What did the mass of people care about? "Making money and getting ahead," wrote Wood. Yes, it was vulgar, material, and crass. But such opportunity had never existed on such a broad scale before.[29]

Enabling the dream of success remains an important part of any policy debate. Will a proposal help small business? Will it create jobs? Will it stifle entrepreneurs? Immigrants still come to the United States in large numbers—far more than to any other country—partly to pursue the dream of success.

Challenging the Dream

As with every important idea, the American dream generates conflict. Critics raise two questions: Has the system become rigged to favor the wealthy at the expense of giving everyone a fair shot at success? And is the pursuit of wealth an undesirable value because it crowds out other important values?

Is the System Tilted Toward the Wealthy?   Some critics question whether the American dream is still open to everyone or whether it has grown biased toward the rich and powerful. When Tocqueville wrote *Democracy in America* in the 1830s, the United States offered more opportunities to get ahead than perhaps any nation in history. Vast open lands (open, that is, once Native Americans had been driven away—see Chapter 6) offered a fresh start for the ambitious and the resourceful.

For much of U.S. history, including the boom years after World War II, middle-class incomes rose faster than incomes at the top. Then, starting around 1979, this trend changed. Money began to flow to the wealthiest more than to the other classes. Figures 2.3a and 2.3b compare the two periods.

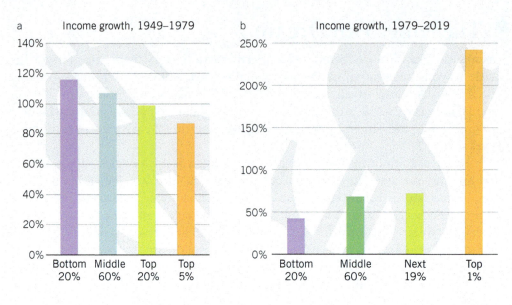

● **FIGURE 2.3** *Between 1949 and 1979, those on the bottom saw their earnings grow faster than those on the top (a). It was an era of growing equality. (Robert Frank,* Falling Behind) *... but look how that changed after 1979 (b). Now those on the bottom have very little income growth while the wealthy have very rapid growth. (Congressional Budget Office)*

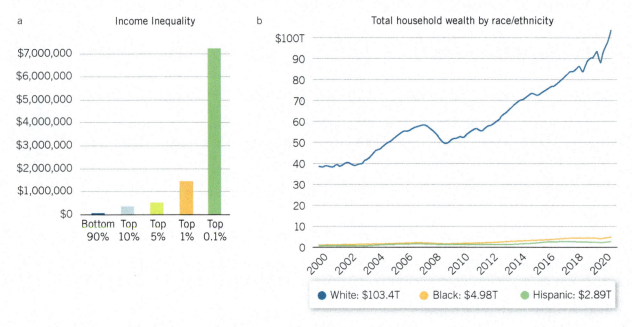

● **FIGURE 2.4** *Inequality in America: (a) The richest 200,000 American adults make more than the 188 million people in the bottom 90%; (b) White families have substantially more wealth than Black or Hispanic families.*

Today, the wealthiest 200,000 Americans, or the top one-tenth of the top 1 percent, earn more than the 188 million people who make up 90 percent of American adults (Figure 2.4a). The 60 million Americans at the bottom of the charts own almost nothing—one-tenth of 1 percent of the national wealth. The median white family is ten times wealthier than the median Black family (Figure 2.4b). Inequality continues to rise, as the gap between richest and poorest widens—and American popular uprisings targeting economic elites have arisen on both the left and right.[30]

Many social scientists conclude that the chance of moving up from poverty to wealth is fading in the United States. Studies suggest that someone in the bottom fifth of the income distribution is twice as likely to move up at least one category

COMPARING NATIONS 2.3 **Social Mobility Around the World**

Many nations—including Japan, New Zealand, and even Pakistan— have developed more social mobility than the United States. In 2015, China's president Xi Jinping began calling the aspirations of upward mobility the "Chinese dream," nudging the American dream aside—though China still has lower mobility rates than most Western democracies, including the United States. The chart displays how much more wealth is concentrated at the top in the United States than in other nations. *(Organization for Economic Cooperation and Development)*

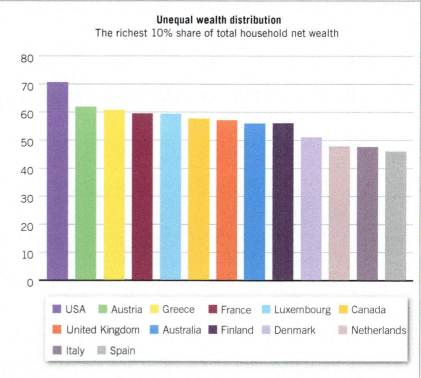

Unequal wealth distribution
The richest 10% share of total household net wealth

Legend: USA, Austria, Greece, France, Luxembourg, Canada, United Kingdom, Australia, Finland, Denmark, Netherlands, Italy, Spain

(or quintile) in Canada, Denmark, or France as they are in the United States (see Comparing Nations 2.3). Critics worry that the system is tilted toward insiders with good connections (known as crony capitalism) or the children of the wealthy. Both conservatives and liberals challenge the United States to live up to its promise of equality of opportunity.[31]

Does the American Dream Promote the Wrong Values? A second critique of the American dream questions the chase for wealth as a human value. Environmentalists criticize the damage caused by big houses, sprawling suburbs, gas-guzzling cars, and opulent lifestyles. Others cite the harm to old-fashioned communal ideals. "These dark days will be worth all they cost us," said President Franklin Roosevelt during the depths of the Great Depression, "if they teach us that our true destiny is . . . to minister . . . to our fellow man."[32] Today, young American evangelicals are offering an even sharper challenge to greed and the race for success as a threat to the biblical call to service.[33]

Voices like these have questioned the pursuit of economic success to the exclusion of community and social justice. Fifteen million children lived below the poverty line in the United States—and that was before the "COVID-19 recession." Critics charge that something is amiss with the American dream if we let one in five kids live in poverty.[34]

The capitalists who celebrate wealth often have to wrestle with economic populists who would rather share it. In a 2019 poll, just 16 percent agreed that "becoming wealthy" is a key feature of the American dream; far more (85 percent) emphasized "freedom of choice in how to live one's life" (the idea of liberty, highlighted previously), and 35 percent "making valuable contributions to my community" (the idea of solidarity).[35] In a 2022 poll, just 43 percent of American adults (and just 29 percent of those under 30 years old) agreed that the American dream still exists.[36]

Despite critics and challenges, many Americans continue to celebrate the gospel of success. The nation's politics, economics, and culture accommodate dreams of wealth. In comparison with other wealthy nations, our taxes are relatively low, we regulate business less, we take fewer vacations, and we place more emphasis on getting ahead. But given the skepticism toward the American dream among millennials and Gen Z, this idea is worth watching carefully in the coming years.

THE BOTTOM LINE

» The American dream is the belief that anyone who works hard can get ahead and grow wealthy.

» Critics argue that hard work is no longer enough. They offer two criticisms: First, the poor and the middle class are falling further behind the wealthy because of bias in the political economy; and second, other values are more important than wealth. These criticisms especially resonate among millennials and Gen Z.

» For many, the dream remains a powerful American idea.

Equality

When Tocqueville arrived in the United States in 1831, he was amazed by the widespread equality. In one of his first letters home, he reported watching servers in a tavern sit down at the next table to eat and drink alongside the guests. Here was a society in which people from all ranks shook hands, discussed politics, and chased money. Everyone seemed to be equals.

Tocqueville distilled this thought into the first sentence of his great book *Democracy in America*: "No novelty in the United States struck me more vividly . . . than the equality of condition." In a world that was still full of aristocrats and inherited privilege, American society embodied the great idea at the heart of the Declaration of Independence: "All men [and women] are created equal."[37]

Equality: All citizens enjoy the same privileges, status, and rights before the law.

Equality means that *every citizen enjoys the same privileges, status, and rights before the law*. There are three different types of equality to consider: *social*, *political*, and *economic*.

Three Types of Equality

Social equality: All individuals enjoy the same status in society.

Social equality means that all individuals enjoy the same status in society. There are no American barons or archdukes who inherit special benefits when they are born. This aspect of American society has not changed since the nation's founding. Except for slavery, there have never been fixed social classes. Few American politicians boast of noble origins or good family lineage. On the contrary, for the past 150 years candidates have flaunted (or invented) their working-class roots. Even very wealthy politicians often claim to have humble origins. If they are wealthy, they boast about their rise to riches. An old cliché in American politics is the saying that any little boy or girl could grow up to be the president—or a billionaire.

Political equality means that every citizen has the same political rights and opportunities. Americans enjoyed universal white, male *suffrage*—or the right to vote—much earlier than did citizens of most nations. Over time the opportunity to vote spread. Today there are lively debates about whether we still ensure everyone an equal opportunity to affect the political process.

Some reformers suggest, for example, that if everyone is to have the same chance to influence the political process, we should remove money from elections. Otherwise, the wealthy will have outsized influence over the outcome. Others counter that individuals who are excited by candidates should be allowed to contribute to them (we discuss the issue in Chapter 10).

The quest for political equality raises many other issues: Does everyone enjoy an equal right to a fair trial—or have the costs of going to court elevated this basic value beyond the reach of many people? Does the voting system make it too difficult for some people to register and cast their ballots? Does every citizen have an *equal opportunity* to influence the political process, and are they all treated the same way before the law?

Economic equality focuses on differences in wealth. When President Washington toured the country in 1790, he commented that in some regions there were few very wealthy people and little poverty. For more than a century and a half, the nation truly was exceptional in its relative economic equality.[38]

Today, the United States has changed dramatically—toward inequality. In 1970, the level of economic inequality in the United States was similar to that in most other wealthy democracies. On one measure of economic inequality, known as the Gini coefficient, the United States ranked between France and Japan on the equality tables. Today, in contrast, America has become far less equal than nations such as Japan, Sweden, and Germany. The United States is now closer to traditionally inegalitarian societies like Mexico, Bolivia, and Lesotho.[39] Should we adopt public policies that aim to limit economic inequality? Let us look more closely at this much-contested issue.

How Much Economic Inequality Is Too Much?

Inequality in America has reached levels not seen in almost a century. One illustration of national differences in economic inequality is the "salary gap." In 1965, the **median** (or typical) American chief executive officer (CEO) made twenty-six times more than a typical worker in his or her company. In Japan today the figure is roughly the same. But in the contemporary United States, the average CEO makes (depending on the study) three hundred to five hundred times the salary of the average employee. Is this a problem for the idea that all people are "created equal"?

People in many countries would answer "yes." Too much inequality, they say, divides society. In Japan, cultural norms encourage individuals to avoid attracting attention through great wealth or ostentation. In fact, Tocqueville warned Americans that they might be vulnerable to economic inequality: "The friends of democracy should keep their eyes anxiously fixed in [the] direction [of] . . . the manufacturing aristocracy we see rising up."[40]

Our public policies (and public opinions) often endorse the race to wealth. People who have won great success—hedge fund managers, basketball stars, successful musicians, CEOs, breakout entrepreneurs, and rock star professors— should enjoy the wealth they accumulate. On the other side, critics charge that

Political equality: All citizens have the same political rights and opportunities.

Economic equality: A situation in which there are only small differences in wealth between citizens.

Median: A statistical term for the number in the middle or the case that has an equal number of examples above and below it.

● *Alice Walton, daughter of Wal-Mart founder Sam Walton, inherited over $30 billion (a). Should we worry about economic inequality? Should we change the rules so that the wealthy get less and poor people more (b)?*

the richest 1 percent take advantage of everyone else. Tax laws and other rules are tilted in their favor. This debate stretches back over American history: Should our laws encourage or discourage the accumulation of terrific fortunes?

Opportunity or Outcome?

Many Americans accept high levels of economic inequality, contending that these are not fatal to our hopes for an egalitarian society. That is because of an important distinction between *equal opportunity* and *equal outcome.*

Equal opportunity is the idea that every American has a similar chance in life. In politics, this means that each person gets one vote and that the process is transparent and open to all. In economics, it means that every individual gets a fair shot at achieving the American dream. Whether you are white or Black, Anglo or Latino, male or female, rich or poor, you have a similar opportunity to influence the political process and to win economic success.

Equal outcome, in contrast, is the idea that a society guarantees not just opportunity but also results. Some nations reserve a minimum number of seats in the national legislature for women or members of specific ethnic groups. And, as we have already seen, others keep their taxes high and offer extensive social benefits, knowing that this arrangement will keep successful people from getting too far ahead of everyone else.

Today, the United States aims for equal opportunity. The winners fly in private jets; the losers may end up living on the streets. Questions—and hard political choices—about equal opportunity remain. How do we give people a real chance to affect the governing process? How much education is enough to help ensure that a graduate can make it in the marketplace? Do we need to provide early childhood reading programs? Offer English-language programs for everyone not fluent? And what should we do about past injustices? Does the long legacy of slavery, segregation, white privilege, and repressive policies toward Native Americans require our society to offer compensation to these groups? What about inheritance laws that permit some people to start life with billions and others with nothing?

These questions return us to the same policy debates we introduced during the discussion of positive and negative liberty. Should we guarantee the basics—or simply protect individual rights and let every person run the great race alone?

Concern has grown in recent years that the gap between rich and poor will grow so large that it destroys equality of opportunity. Americans have long pointed

Equal opportunity: The idea that every American has the same chance to influence politics and achieve economic success.

Equal outcome: The idea that citizens should have roughly equal economic circumstances.

proudly to our prosperous middle class—and indeed, for most of the nation's history middle-class Americans had the highest average incomes in the world. As the gap continues to widen, liberals warn that growing disparities are creating a land of a few billionaires and many hungry children. Conservatives respond that the effort to redistribute wealth from rich to poor discourages entrepreneurs from innovating and generating new wealth. Expanded wealth at the top, in their view, will help the many through job creation.

Over time, the United States has gone from the most equal society in the world to one that is considerably less equal than other wealthy nations. The past thirty-five years, in particular, have seen a very sharp spike in inequality. American politics has come to emphasize other ideas—negative liberty, individualism, the American dream of getting ahead—over equality. Still, we live in a dynamic and fluid society. Today, many Americans, both conservatives and liberals, call for renewed efforts to increase equality of opportunity. Populists, on both the left and right, increasingly emphasize this theme. Economic inequality may be one of the hottest political issues facing Americans today.

THE BOTTOM LINE

» Equality means that every citizen enjoys the same privileges, status, and rights before the law.

» Equality applies to social status, political rights, and economic conditions.

» Today, America generally aims for *equal opportunity* rather than *equal outcome*, though heated discussions rage over what society must provide to ensure equal opportunity.

Religion

In the 1630s, many Puritans escaped European persecution and sailed to New England with an ambitious aim: to establish a biblical commonwealth that would serve as a Christian model for the rest of the world. Governor John Winthrop called their settlement "a city upon a hill" and expected "the eyes of all people on us."[41] How did they fare? If people really were watching, they soon saw unexpected complications.

For example, Quakers from Pennsylvania—whom the Puritans despised for lacking discipline—began sailing north to convert the New Englanders. If the Quakers succeeded, they would subvert the whole idea of the model Puritan society. New England's women, the ministers worried, might be especially vulnerable to Quaker heresies—which emphasized the "inner light" shining in each person. The authorities banned Quakers from Massachusetts under threat of having an ear cut off (one each for the first and second offense), having their tongues pierced by hot pokers (third offense), and finally death. Quaker martyrs piously and joyfully challenged the Puritan authorities. Four were hanged before English authorities ordered an end to the punishment.

This story illustrates the importance of religion, the intense competition between sects, and a missionary fervor to save the world. Even today, politicians of every stripe repeat the idea of a "city on a hill" (although few realize that Winthrop was quoting the Sermon on the Mount from the New Testament). When Donald Trump wished to project an image of strength during the 2020 election, he stood in front of a church near the White House and waved a bible. His rival, Joe Biden, a devout Roman Catholic, responded that he wished the president "opened it once in a while instead of brandishing it."[42] Both seized on religion to win political points. Each thought religious morality was on their side.

Still a Religious Country

Religion plays an enduring role in American politics and society. The centrality of religion in U.S. national life may not surprise you. But it is a powerful example of American exceptionalism. As most nations grow wealthier, their religious fervor wanes. Citizens in developed countries, from Britain and France to Japan and South Korea, tell pollsters that God is not very important in their lives. In contrast, Americans maintain high levels of religiosity. More than 90 percent believe in a God (although over a third are referring to "a higher power" rather than the biblical God). And three out of four report that religion is "very important" or "somewhat important" to them.[43] To find higher levels you have to go to poorer nations such as India, Egypt, and Indonesia.

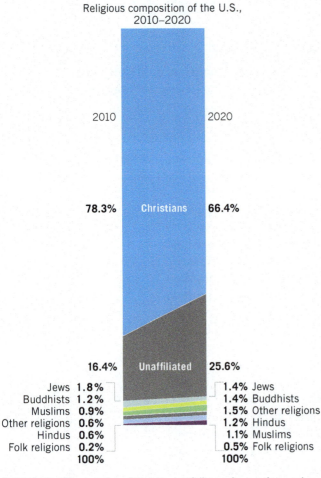

Religious composition of the U.S., 2010–2020

2010	2020
78.3% Christians	66.4%
16.4% Unaffiliated	25.6%
Jews 1.8%	1.4% Jews
Buddhists 1.2%	1.4% Buddhists
Muslims 0.9%	1.5% Other religions
Other religions 0.6%	1.2% Hindus
Hindus 0.6%	1.1% Muslims
Folk religions 0.2%	0.5% Folk religions
100%	100%

● **FIGURE 2.5** *The number of Christians is falling, whereas the number of unaffiliated is rapidly rising. Muslims, Hindus, and folk religions are also rising. Even with these changes the U.S. population remains more churched than most wealthy nations. (Pew Forum)*

However, the percentage of Americans who are religiously unaffiliated is growing. Church membership plummeted from 70 percent (in 2000) to 47 percent (in 2021), and the number of people who attended church, synagogue, or temple in the last week went down from 44 percent to 29 percent. The fall in faith is especially dramatic among young Americans. Why? Perhaps it's the perception that religions have gotten entangled in cultural and political wars.[44]

In short, the United States still stands out for its religiosity. But American faith is changing—and has, in the past decade, begun to decline. What about you? Is religion important to you? Would you describe yourself as spiritual but not religious? Or perhaps neither? Whatever your beliefs, you stand in a long, always changing, American tradition.

So Many Religions

Americans have a lot of religions to choose from (see Figure 2.5). One survey found sixteen different Christian denominations with more than a million members each.[45] That is just the beginning. Jews number over 7 million, Muslims some 3.5 million, and seven other non-Christian groups over 100,000 adherents each (two of the fastest growing are Wiccans and Pagans).[46] In contrast, many other nations have a single major faith, often supported by the government through tax dollars.

Why does the United States have so many religions? From the start, different colonies began with distinct religious affiliations. By forbidding the federal government from boosting any official faith, the

Constitution has kept the field open for any new preacher with a religious idea that might attract a following. Because none can win official recognition, each religious institution is only as strong as the congregation it can muster.

This open market explains why new religions spring up all the time. It does not explain why Americans respond. Religious leaders and scholars continue to explore why Americans continue to worship, while citizens in other wealthy nations show a sharply declining interest in religion.

Religious observance is not the same throughout the United States. Texas and Georgia (proud members of the "Bible Belt") have very high religiosity, Florida and Missouri are in the middle, Colorado and Wisconsin are not especially religious, and Maine is the least religious of all.

The Politics of Religion

How is religion relevant to politics? As we will see in Chapter 5, the Constitution appears to erect a "wall of separation between church and state," as Thomas Jefferson described it. Yet America's energetic religious life—marked by great evangelical revivals—injects three different types of political issues into American politics.[47]

First, there is the question of what exactly the Constitution forbids. Even the founders disagreed. Presidents George Washington and John Adams held national days of prayer; President Jefferson thought that this practice violated the First Amendment.

The argument about what is permissible continues to this day. May teachers lead prayers in public schools? May public school students in the bleachers organize prayers before football games? May judges post the Ten Commandments in a courthouse? Questions such as these spark intense debates about where to draw the line between church and state (see Chapter 5 for the details).

Second, religious faith often inspires people to throw themselves into politics. The civil rights movement spilled out from Baptist and Methodist churches across the South, with religious rhetoric, religious symbols, and religious zeal. Historically, even proponents of white supremacy—arguing for slavery and segregation—framed their response in religious terms. In American politics, both sides often invoke God. The controversies swirling around the politics of racial justice, abortion, the environment, same-sex marriage, and many other issues have all, to varying extents, made the same leap from pulpit to politics. Today, conservatives are more likely to take their faith into the political arena, but this has not always been true.

Third, religious fervor sometimes fosters a missionary sense in American politics. As the nation expanded westward, some Americans declared their "manifest destiny"—God had given an entire continent to his chosen people. At the time, conservative politicians warned against the arrogance and violence (against both Native Americans and Mexico) of claiming divine sanction for gobbling up land. During the Cold War, American leaders constantly invoked God as a way of contrasting the United States with communist nations. Congress added "under God" to the Pledge of Allegiance in 1954 and "In God We Trust" to paper money in 1955. A half-century later, President George W. Bush invoked "God's gift of freedom" to explain America's mission in Iraq. John Winthrop's idea—America as a model for the world—echoes from one generation to the next.

● *The Blackhawk Christian High School Braves pray at center court after winning the Indiana state championship. The scene would be strange in Japan and violate the rules in France, but it's not unusual in the United States.*

Political scientists often write about liberty, democracy, and equality. Religion usually flies below researchers' radar, but it is a constant element in American politics. Ignoring religion means regularly being surprised as intense religious feelings sweep past the separation between church and state.

THE BOTTOM LINE

» Religion plays an enduring role in American politics and society. This is unusual—almost unique—among wealthy countries.

» Americans have an unusually large number of faiths to choose from, although younger people are less likely than their elders to affiliate with an organized religion.

» Religious politics raise questions about the role and extent of religion in our national public life. They inspire political participation on a host of issues—from civil rights to abortion. And they foster a missionary sense in American foreign policy.

 # Diversity

The United States has always been extremely diverse, with many different types of people from many different places. The results were, for a long time, described as the American "melting pot"—a society that boils away differences and, in every generation, becomes homogeneous. More recently, diversity has been described in terms of a national mosaic—every different group retains its identity while adding to the American whole. Whatever the metaphor, both versions signal an unusually open nation: Come to America and help shape a diverse but unified people (remember the national motto: "out of many, one").

But as usual, Americans disagree. The celebration of diversity—the embrace of both unity and difference—has always run up against fears of cultural change. Each generation of newcomers runs into the same challenge: These new people do not understand the values that made America great. They will wreck the city on a hill.[48]

The debate goes on, but even so, the United States stands out. Almost nine out of ten Americans believe that society is better off with people from many backgrounds, a far higher percentage than countries like Germany, Italy, or Japan.

Two Powerful Statements

Two recent presidents burst onto the political scene, each promoting one side of the diversity debate. Future president Barack Obama first became a national star at the 2004 Democratic National Convention by offering himself as an example of a diverse America. "My father was a foreign student, born and raised in a small village in Kenya," said Obama. "He grew up herding goats, went to school in a tin-roof shack. . . . I stand here grateful for the diversity of my heritage[,] knowing that in no other country on earth, is my story even possible." Obama presented himself as the embodiment of a multiracial, immigrant, cosmopolitan, diverse nation unified around a common set of dreams and values.

Diversity

How Different Nations Think About Themselves

People in most nations celebrate a national mix of religions, ethnicities, and backgrounds. In contrast, some nations value a more homogeneous society where people are more alike. Americans support diversity in their country more than most nations, while the Japanese value diversity the least. Note that the median (the score right in the middle of these seventeen nations) cheers diversity by a three-to-one margin. (*Pew Research Center*)

Many believe their society to be better off with people of many backgrounds

% who say having people of many different backgrounds and races makes their country a worse/better place to live

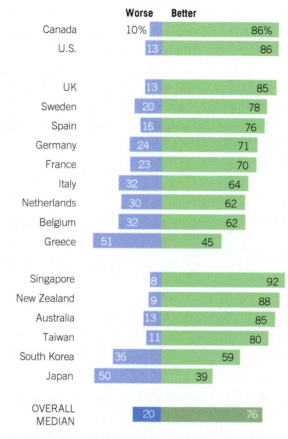

	Worse	Better
Canada	10%	86%
U.S.	13	86
UK	13	85
Sweden	20	78
Spain	16	76
Germany	24	71
France	23	70
Italy	32	64
Netherlands	30	62
Belgium	32	62
Greece	51	45
Singapore	8	92
New Zealand	9	88
Australia	13	85
Taiwan	11	80
South Korea	36	59
Japan	50	39
OVERALL MEDIAN	20	76

THINK ABOUT IT

In the United States, 86 percent say they welcome the nation's diversity. Why do you think that number is so high?

....

In the United States, 13 percent disagree with the majority. Why do you think that is?

....

How would you answer these questions: Does diversity make the United States a better or worse place to live? What kinds of diversity would you most support?

In contrast, Donald Trump stood before cheering supporters in New York City's Trump Tower and launched his long-shot campaign for the presidency with a very different message. "When Mexico sends its people, they're not sending their best. They're not sending you. . . . They're sending people that have lots of problems, and they're bringing those problems with them. They're bringing drugs.

They're bringing crime. They're rapists." Later in the same speech, Trump said, "It's coming from more than Mexico. It's coming from all over South and Latin America, and it's coming probably—probably—from the Middle East." Obama's interracial, international parents reaching for the stars had morphed into dangerous people overrunning the homeland.

The two men reflect a long and ferocious dispute about diversity. A very diverse nation has a culture war built in. Throughout American history, some people embrace the latest newcomers, while others fear them.

The Long Debate

The United States is a nation of immigrants—and, in most years, it's the largest immigrant destination in the world. The Fourteenth Amendment to the Constitution (passed after the civil war to integrate formerly enslaved Americans into the political community) offers an institutional framework for a diverse people with a wide-open definition of citizenship: Anyone born in the United States becomes a citizen. Almost no nation in Europe, Asia, or Africa offers similar **birthright citizenship** to every person born on the country's soil.

Birthright citizenship: Every child born in the United States is a citizen.

In addition, most American immigrants are eligible to apply for citizenship after five years in the country. A poem by Emma Lazarus, carved onto the Statue of Liberty in New York Harbor, celebrates the diversity and calls people from around the world to join the American mosaic: "Give me your tired, your poor, your huddled masses yearning to breathe free."

At the same time, every generation of newcomers also provokes fears. Some citizens have pointed to the newcomers (or people on the margins of power, like Black Americans, or Native Americans) and claimed: They do not understand America's values. They will take our jobs. They will make life harder for us. They will ruin the nation as we have known it.

Irish Catholics were reviled for decades, starting in the 1830s; "No Irish Need Apply" was still marked in job advertisements in the early twentieth century. Congress passed a "Chinese Exclusion Act" in 1882, responding to popular fears. Politicians whipped up bigotry, and people in the street harassed and spat at Chinese workers. More than a million Mexican Americans were deported during the Great Depression, amid widespread claims they were "stealing" jobs from white Americans. And the struggle by Black Americans to achieve full rights and inclusion stretches right across American history—from the first person killed during the Revolution (as you'll see when we describe the Boston Massacre in the next chapter) to a formidable Black Lives Matter movement in the 2020s.[49]

Opposition to a diverse people arises in part because each new group in the national mosaic really does change America. Each brings different customs, fresh ideas, distinct religions, and even new kinds of food.

In sum, another American divide: Should the nation celebrate the latest generation of immigrants, as Barack Obama encouraged? Or limit their numbers, as Donald Trump argued we should?

Who Are We?

The debate over diversity extends far and wide. It runs from immigration to race to generational change. After all, each generation rises up with new attitudes and ideas. Each generation challenges older people about the meaning of America. Today, the difference among generations is especially pronounced, with young people challenging older generations in their views of capitalism, socialism, gender identity, and many other issues (see Chapter 7).

These debates about diversity all go right back to a question running through this book: *Who are we?* The answer to that question is always changing.

THE BOTTOM LINE

» The United States is a nation of people from many different places.

» A great debate runs through American history. Some celebrate the national mosaic—the many people who make up a richly diverse, more or less unified whole. Others would like to limit the differences.

How Do Ideas Affect Politics?

Most political scientists agree that the eight ideas of this chapter are central to American society. But how do these ideas influence our politics? There are two familiar answers. Either ideas influence our culture, or they operate through our institutions. There is still another possibility to bear in mind: Perhaps ideas have a life all their own.

Ideas in American Culture

Each nation has a unique **political culture**, constructed over the years by a people and its leaders. Anthropologist Clifford Geertz described culture as the stories a group tells about itself. Ideas such as liberty, the fear of government, individualism, and the American dream together are the foundation of American political culture. They are the stories Americans tell about themselves.[50]

A culture shapes the way people think about politics and government. Culture develops over time, shaped by history and experience. Colonial Americans' shared beliefs, stories, and mental habits—their culture—inspired the founding generation to develop a Constitution that limits the power of government. Why did the framers add a bill of rights to the Constitution? Their faith in individualism. Why are there so many checks and balances in our national government? A fear of too much government, dating back to colonial times. Why do we regulate and tax less than other nations? The American dream's gospel of success. This shared culture leads men and women to fight for policies that reflect freedom or democracy; policies that reflect social-democratic solidarity are more difficult to win because they resonate more faintly in American culture. Americans' hopes and fears often seem peculiar to people in other nations—just as their hopes and fears may not make sense to us.

In short, the United States, like every other nation, has a rich national culture that should be read as a perpetual work in progress. Every era and each generation experience their own exuberant debate about what the nation has been, and what it should be.[51]

Ideas in Political Institutions

A different perspective suggests that ideas operate through political institutions. James Madison explained the *institutional perspective*. Past political theory expected republican citizens to virtuously seek the public interest. But,

Political culture: The orientation of citizens of a state toward politics.

● *Ideas move politics. A member of Americans for Prosperity, a conservative group, goes door to door to persuade voters about the benefits of tax cuts.*

Madison wrote sardonically in the *Federalist Papers*, "enlightened statesmen will not always be at the helm."[52] The Constitution did not ask people to be virtuous; instead, it envisioned a government that could operate smoothly even if its citizens were greedy and their leaders corrupt. The institution—the rules and organizations built into the government—would shape political behavior.

Many political scientists follow in Madison's footsteps. It is our governing institutions, starting with the Constitution, that shape American politics.

From an institutional perspective, the barriers to enacting new programs emerge not from a dislike of government but from the way the government is organized. The U.S. government is slow to act, according to this view, because we have *designed* it to be slow by building in multiple checks and balances on every level of government. When Americans criticize their policymakers for inaction, perhaps they miss the point: Gridlock is a consequence of the institutions we have inherited.

Culture or Institutions?

Although historians and sociologists tend to emphasize political culture, many political scientists are skeptical about its explanatory power. How, they ask, can something as static as national culture explain the fluid, fast-changing American political scene?

For example, the cultural perspective suggests that the United States has never had national health insurance, supplied and paid for by the federal government, because Americans do not trust government. (There's the "limited government" idea in action.) The institutional perspective counters that this lack of legislation is less a matter of popular belief and more the way we have designed the government. After all, they say, Harry Truman won the presidential election of 1948 in part by promising national health insurance. No deep-seated fear of government reared its head while Americans were voting. If we had been operating with a Canadian or an English legislature, Truman would have created the program right after he won the election. But the proposal was blocked by the checks and balances built into our system and died in Congress.

Proponents of culture as the primary driver of politics respond that cultural values are not meant to explain every possible political action. Events, leaders, movements, and government agencies all introduce change. But culture forms the boundary of those changes. It limits the possibilities, shapes our perceptions, and influences our reactions. It accepts a Congress that defeats the national health insurance program that a presidential candidate promised. Or, to take another example, when terrorists launch an attack, the American response is driven by the types of institutions we have built to provide for the common defense—but the debate about that response is deeply influenced by the values and ideas we share. Ideas, culture, and institutions all reinforce one another. Truly understanding a nation means understanding all three.

» Political scientists point to three different ways in which foundational ideas influence politics.

» First, ideas shape American culture, which in turn affects our politics.

» Second—and the most popular argument among political scientists—ideas operate through political institutions. We have to study those institutions to appreciate how ideas shape politics and policies.

» Third, ideas may have their own independent power.

 ## Conclusion: Culture and Institutions, Together

Do the ideas described in this chapter add up to a political culture that shapes the attitudes of American men and women? That cultural argument seems intuitive to many people. On balance, however, most political scientists underscore the importance of institutions.

As a political science student, you can decide for yourself on the relative power of ideas and institutions as you read this book. But you do not have to choose one or the other. We believe that culture and institutions together play a role in American politics. They reinforce each other. Yes, national institutions make it difficult to pass big national programs such as health insurance; and, yes again, opponents invoke powerful cultural norms—such as individualism and liberty—to persuade Americans that such legislation threatens their values. For us, the most interesting question is how ideas, culture, and institutions (along with interests and individuals—the four "I's" in the introductory chapter) all interact to shape American politics.

Finally, ideas have a power of their own—above and beyond the culture and institutions they have helped to shape. Ideas of liberty, democracy, and the American dream can move people to act.

As you read this book, you will constantly encounter the eight ideas we described in this chapter. Think about which seem most important and powerful to you. And pay attention to how they appear to operate—through the culture, through institutions, with a life of their own, or (as we believe) in all these ways at different times and in different circumstances.

CHAPTER SUMMARY

★ Eight important ideas influence American politics. Each idea has at least two different interpretations—differences that spur intense political debates. The eight key American ideas are freedom, self-rule, limited government, individualism, the American dream, equality, religion, and diversity.

★ *Freedom* means that the government will protect your life, liberty, and property from the coercion of others (including government) so that you can pursue the goals you define for yourself. In one view, freedom requires *positive government action* to make sure that everyone has the basics to permit them to pursue their goals. In another view, the government guarantees only *negative freedom*—the freedom to pursue your goals. You are free to succeed or to fail on your own, but there are no government guarantees about food, or homes, or healthcare.

★ *Self-rule* means that people govern themselves through clearly defined procedures such as elections. In a democracy, citizens participate directly in making government decisions. In a republic, the people rule indirectly through their elected representatives. The American system is a combination of the two, a democratic republic.

★ Americans value *limited government*: They distrust government and place limits on the authority it can exercise. And yet, at the same time, Americans value many government programs. Here's an all-American paradox: Value limited government; support an extensive government.

★ *Individualism* means that individuals—not society or the government—are responsible for their own well-being. For those who favor community or social democracy, the public interest is best served when members of a society use government to take care of one another. Americans take both an individual and a communal view, but in contrast to many other nations, the individualistic view is more powerful.

★ The *American dream* holds that if you are talented and work hard, you will succeed and grow wealthy. Critics argue that the system is rigged and that the dream promotes the wrong values. However, the dream remains a powerful force in American politics.

★ *Equality* allows each citizen to enjoy the same privileges, status, and rights before the law. Some define equality as a matter of *opportunity*—the idea that every American has an equal chance. Others promote equal *outcome*—a guarantee of results. There are three types of equality to consider: Social equality means that all individuals enjoy the same status in society. Political equality guarantees every citizen the same rights and opportunities to participate in politics. Economic equality minimizes the gap between citizens' wealth and earnings.

★ *Religion* plays an enduring role in American politics and society. The great question is how we limit government interference without limiting religion itself.

★ The United States is a *diverse* nation. That raises debates (and culture wars). Some Americans embrace the many different ethnic, racial, and national-origin groups that make up the whole. Others seek to limit differences and try to promote a more homogeneous whole.

★ These eight ideas mark Americans' beliefs as a people. They shape politics through national culture, through political institutions, and through their direct public influence.

KEY TERMS

American exceptionalism, p. 27
Birthright citizenship, p. 56
Conservatives, p. 36
Direct democracy, p. 31
Economic equality, p. 49
Equality, p. 48
Equal opportunity, p. 50
Equal outcome, p. 50
Freedom, p. 29
Individualism, p. 40
Initiative, p. 32
Legislative referral, p. 32
Liberals, p. 36
Libertarians, p. 36
Median, p. 49
Negative liberty, p. 29
Political culture, p. 57
Political equality, p. 49
Populists, p. 36
Positive liberty, p. 29
Referendum, p. 32
Republic, p. 32
Self-rule, p. 31
Social democracy, p. 40
Social equality, p. 48
Sunshine laws, p. 32

STUDY QUESTIONS

1. The second paragraph of the Declaration of Independence boldly explains why "governments are instituted among men." Why are governments formed? Do you agree with that assertion about government's most basic function?

2. *Liberty* is often described as the most important American idea. Describe the two different views of liberty known as positive and negative freedom. Which do you think is more accurate?

3. Review the eight key "American ideas" we have identified in this chapter. Are *new* foundational ideas bubbling up in American politics today? What examples can you imagine?

4. The Declaration of Independence asserts that all men are endowed by their creator with the inalienable rights to life, liberty, and the pursuit of happiness. Over time, Americans have extended that idea to more and more people, such as formerly enslaved people and women. Are there groups in our society today who are *not* getting the full benefits of this ideal? How might that change?

5. What is the difference between a democracy and a republic? Which principle does contemporary American government reflect, or does it reflect both?

If you were a founder, which of these principles would you emphasize?

6. George Washington declared national days of prayer during his presidency. Thomas Jefferson rejected this practice, saying that it violated the First Amendment. Who was right, in your view—and what does the First Amendment say about this? (See Appendix II for the exact wording.)

7. There are three forms of equality—social, political, and economic. Define each.

8. Describe the two approaches to economic equality: opportunity and outcome.

9. When it comes to religion, the United States is different from most wealthy societies. How? How do young people differ from previous generations in their approach to religion?

10. Many young Americans embrace the idea of a multicultural, diverse mosaic making up one people. Others resist diversity and seek to marginalize newcomers and minority groups. How, in your view, is the diversity of America best upheld in practice?

11. Ideas shape both culture and institutions. Explain.

3 THE CONSTITUTION

THE R. R. MOTON HIGH SCHOOL, in Farmville, Virginia, was a mess. The roof leaked, the heat barely worked, classrooms were over-crowded, and the school bus kept breaking down. When it rained, students sat under umbrellas and shivered in their coats. Moton was a majority-Black school; across town, the white students were warm and dry. On April 23, 1951, a Moton junior named Barbara Johns decided to take action. She fooled the principal into leaving the school and forged notes to the teachers calling an as-sembly. When the students had all filed into the auditorium, the sixteen-year-old stood on stage, called for a strike, and led a student march to the Prince Edward County Courthouse to protest the school's shabby state.

Barbara Johns and her fellow student protesters landed in trouble. The students and their families called a leading civil rights group, the National Association for the Advancement of Colored People (NAACP), which dispatched a team of lawyers. The lawyers explained that local governments run American schools, and there was not much the NAACP could do about the conditions at Moton High. However, continued the lawyers, they could challenge the entire policy of racial segregation. The NAACP sued the school district, arguing that forcing African Americans into a separate school violated the United States Constitution. The Supreme Court took the case, *Davis v. School Board of Prince Edward County*, bundled it together with four similar cases, and, three years after the student strike, delivered one of the most famous judicial decisions in American history, a ruling known as *Brown v. Board of Education*.

A sixteen-year-old took a bold risk, the Supreme Court unanimously ruled that she was right, and hundreds of laws across many states were struck down for violating the Constitution. The Court ruled that segregated education facilities are inherently unequal and violated the Fourteenth Amendment, which declares, "No state shall . . . deny to any person . . . the equal protection of the laws."

Stop and think about the power Americans invest in this document written more than 230 years ago. The **Constitution** is the owner's manual and rulebook for American government. It specifies how the government operates. It tells us what the government may do and how it should do it. If you want to learn about any feature of American politics, check the Constitution first.

Who are we? The answer to that question is always changing, but the Constitution provides the ground rules for those changes. It organizes

In this chapter, you will

 Discover the roots of the Constitution.

 See why Americans declared independence from England and learn about their first constitution, the Articles of Confederation.

 Follow the arguments that shaped the Constitution and the debate over its adoption.

 Learn how Americans have changed the Constitution—and how the Constitution has changed America.

Constitution: A statement of fundamental principles that governs a nation or an organization.

● *Student strikers at Moton High School (Farmville, Virginia), led by Barbara Johns. The protesters had an enormous impact because civil rights lawyers found a way to place their grievance in the context of the U.S. Constitution.*

our political life. The Declaration of Independence sets out the ideas shaping our nation. The Constitution takes those ideas and turns them into laws. It *institutionalizes* American ideas.

This sounds simple: The Constitution guides the government. But there is a wrinkle. It is often unclear how the Constitution applies to modern questions. After all, it is just 4,400 words written on four pages of parchment a long time ago. Many provisions can be read in two (or more) different ways, and the document is silent on topics Americans worry about—from abortion to global climate change. As a result, we have to *interpret* how the Constitution applies to a case today.

Segregation is a prime example. The Constitution says nothing about racial segregation. Back in 1896, the Supreme Court ruled that segregation did not violate the "equal protection" clause of the Fourteenth Amendment. In 1954, the Court ruled that it did (in the case that the Moton High students initiated). Different justices in different eras read the same words in changing ways. Likewise, in 1973 the Court ruled that the Constitution protected the right to an abortion but changed its mind in 2022 and ruled that it did not. We constantly debate how to read the Constitution's words—and how to apply them to the questions we face.

BY THE NUMBERS   The Constitution

17
Number of *successful* amendments since 1791

11,600
Number of *proposed* amendments to the U.S. Constitution introduced in Congress since 1791

6
Number of the 13 states that voted for the Constitution within 6 months

18 Number of delegates in New York, Virginia, and Massachusetts who could have defeated the entire Constitution by switching their votes

24 Number of states (of the 34 required) with at least one legislative chamber agreeing to a new constitutional convention, as of 2022

3 Percentage of the U.S. population that can block a constitutional amendment

202 Years after it was originally introduced that the most recent (27th) amendment was passed, in 1992

3 Number of states that initially voted against the Constitution

How easy is it to change the Constitution?
How easy should it be?

The Colonial Roots of the Constitution

No nation in the eighteenth century had anything like the American Constitution. Most nations wrote their governing documents much later; some countries, such as England and Israel, never wrote one at all (see Comparing Nations 3.1). However, the Constitution did not appear out of nowhere. Many features of colonial politics propelled the new nation toward its constitution.

- First, the colonies were three thousand miles away from the king and his armies. Authorities back in England debated policies and issued orders; the American colonists frequently ignored them and did what they wished. No one in London paid much attention. The English policy of ignoring colonies was known as *salutary neglect*; it permitted the colonies to develop their own political institutions. When England started interfering in colonial affairs, the Americans revolted.

- Second, beginning with the Virginia House of Burgesses in 1620, every colony elected its own legislature. As a result, the colonists had a great deal of experience with representation. New settlements demanded seats in the assemblies. New immigrants wanted the right to vote (Polish workers went on strike in Virginia over the issue). In some places, such as New Jersey, women with property could vote. America grew up arguing about representation—and that prepared them for the debate over the Constitution.

- Third, plentiful land created opportunities for ordinary people. Early America was not an equal society by any means: There were aristocratic families and enslaved people, prosperous merchants and **indentured servants**. However, by the standards of the time, the New World was a land of extraordinary social mobility. When North Carolina tried to establish a system of titles and social classes, the effort collapsed, as ordinary people made their fortunes and soon were wealthier than the would-be lords and dukes. Economic conditions helped foster a republic.

- Fourth, some colonies began with mutual agreements between the settlers, known as **compacts** or **covenants**. The Pilgrims, who landed in Massachusetts in 1620, introduced the idea; before they went ashore all forty-one adult males signed a mutual agreement known as the Mayflower Compact (named after their vessel, the *Mayflower*). In most nations, the right to rule stretched back through history and was based on tradition and force. In contrast, the individuals on the *Mayflower* formed a new society based on their mutual agreement. Many New England communities began with such compacts or covenants—often religiously inspired forerunners of a constitution.

- Fifth, many colonists came to the New World to practice their religion in peace. Across the colonies, different religions flourished: Calvinists in Boston, Quakers in Philadelphia, Catholics in Baltimore, Anglicans in Virginia, and a diverse mix of religions in Savannah, Georgia, which was home to Anglicans, Lutherans, and Jews, among others. All these different faiths did not always live in harmony; the Massachusetts Puritans hanged Quaker missionaries (discussed in Chapter 2). But beginning in Rhode Island in 1636, a revolutionary idea began to emerge: the individual's freedom to practice religion without government interference. In some colonies, this idea was followed by other rights, such as freedom of speech and freedom of the press. The rights of citizens would become the single greatest issue in the debate over whether to accept (ratify) the new constitution.

Indentured servant: A colonial American settler contracted to work for a fixed period (usually three to seven years) in exchange for food, shelter, and transportation to the New World.

Compact: A mutual agreement that provides for joint action to achieve defined goals.

Covenant: A compact invoking religious or moral authority.

● The Mayflower Compact. The settlers, who had begun to argue about who was in charge, agreed among themselves to enter into a "civic body politic"—a government. The authority of their government rose from their own agreement, which was signed only by white men, including two indentured servants.

- Sixth, border areas in early America were violent and insecure, often erupting in brutal wars between Native Americans and more recent settlers. The French claimed land to the north and west, the Spanish to the south and west. Colonists also constantly fought one another over their own boundaries, with most resisting attempts by any central authority—the Crown or, later, initial American government—to intervene. After the break with England, insecure borders helped inspire the colonists to adopt a strong central government.

Each colony governed itself in its own way. However, the six features described here—distance from English authority, representation, social mobility, covenants, individual rights, and insecure borders—all propelled Americans toward the Constitution of 1787. (Notice how many of these features helped shape the governing American ideas, like self-rule and limited government, discussed in Chapter 2.)

COMPARING NATIONS 3.1 — The U.S. Constitution in Comparative Context

The United States has the oldest constitution still in use. Of the eighteen democratic countries listed here, only Canada and the Netherlands wrote a still-operating constitution within a century of the United States. Many political scientists believe the American document has lasted so long because it works well. Others, however, charge that it has grown out of date and that our form of government is not effective or fair enough for the twenty-first century: One recent book calls the Constitution a "relic" and is subtitled "How Our Constitution Undermines Effective Government."[1] Keep this debate in mind as you read about how the U.S. Constitution came into existence and how it operates today.

NATION	YEAR THE CURRENT CONSTITUTION WAS WRITTEN
United States	1789
Argentina	1853 (revised text, 1994)
Austria	1920
Brazil	1988
Canada	1867 (revised text, 1982)
Costa Rica	1949
Denmark	1953
France	1958
Germany	1949
Great Britain	No written constitution
India	1950
Ireland	1937
Israel	No written constitution
Italy	1948
Japan	1947
Netherlands	1814
New Zealand	No written constitution
Thailand	2017

THE BOTTOM LINE

» Colonists developed their own political institutions that became forerunners of the Constitution.

» Six features of colonial life propelled Americans toward the Constitution of 1789: distance from English authority, long debates over representation, social mobility, covenants, individual rights, and insecure borders.

 # Why the Colonists Revolted

The roots of the American Revolution lie in a great English victory. Centuries of rivalry between England and France burst into war in 1754. Known in North America as the French and Indian War, the conflict spread through the colonies from Virginia all the way to Canada. Colonial American militias fought side by side with the British army and defeated the French in 1763. Thirteen years later the colonists declared independence and turned their muskets on the English—with crucial financial and strategic support from their former French foes.

Why did the Americans suddenly revolt? Because the victory over France introduced two fateful changes. First, ten thousand English troops remained in the colonies to protect the newly won land. The existence of those "Redcoats" meant that England could now enforce its policies: The days of salutary neglect were over. Second, the English had run up a crushing debt during the ten years of war and thought that the colonists should help pay it. The Americans' reaction was explosive.

The Colonial Complaint: Representation

It was not just Britain's demand for money that provoked the colonists. Americans had grown used to making their own decisions through their elected assemblies. When the English imposed new taxes, without the approval of the thirteen co-

lonial assemblies, they violated the idea of self-rule. The result was an unusual revolution. Most revolutionaries rise up against regimes that have long repressed them. In contrast, the Americans fought to *preserve* rights that they had been exercising during the many years of happy neglect.

Beneath the conflict lay a deep philosophical difference about representative democracy. The colonists considered their assemblies the legitimate voice of the people; if taxes had to be raised, they were the ones to do it. Colonial assemblies were very responsive to the voters and their daily concerns—they managed matters like building roads and surveying new lands. Political theorists call the colonial view **delegate representation**: Do what the voters want.

The British never understood this view of representation because they operated under an entirely different one. Unlike the colonists, the

Delegate representation: Representatives follow the expressed wishes of voters.

● *The colonial borders were the site of considerable fighting, with both the French and the Native Americans.*

English did not change their electoral districts every time the population shifted. English elected officials were expected to pursue the good of the whole nation. Your representative is not an "agent" or an "advocate," argued English statesman Edmund Burke, but must be guided by "the general good." This view is known as **trustee representation**—do what is best for the voters, regardless of what they wish.[2] The debate would spur an innovative provision in the U.S. Constitution: The United States would conduct a census every ten years to ensure that congressional districts matched up to the changing population—a direct reaction to Britain's trustee theory of representation.

Trustee representation: Representatives do what they regard as being in the best interest of their constituents—even if many constituents do not agree.

The Conflict Begins with Blood on the Frontier

After the French and Indian War, settlers poured westward (Figure 3.1). Native Americans fought back; they rallied around Chief Pontiac and overran colonial settlements and English forts in Virginia, Maryland, and Pennsylvania. To end the fighting, England closed the border and prohibited settlers from moving westward past the crests of the lengthy Appalachian Mountain chain. The colonists were stunned. The arbitrary boundary, announced in the Proclamation of 1763, had been drawn amid lobbying by land speculators. The proclamation threatened the westward thrust that spelled opportunity to the restless colonists. American settlers did not recognize Native American rights to the land. As they saw it, a corrupt English monarchy was blocking American pioneers from settling the wide-open spaces that they had helped win from France.[3]

● **FIGURE 3.1** *The colonies before (left) and after (right) the French and Indian War. Spain lost Florida but gained the land west of the Mississippi in compensation for backing France. Napoleon would later seize this land back from Spain; in 1803, the enslaved people in Haiti rebelled and, after a bloody war, defeated the French army. That ended Napoleon's plans for conquest in the New World, and he sold the vast lands, known as Louisiana, to the United States. The indomitable formerly enslaved people of Haiti made the Louisiana Purchase possible. Note the line formed by the Proclamation of 1763 on the map on the right. England tried to forbid settlers from crossing that line.*

The colonists responded in their traditional way—they ignored regulations that did not suit them. But now there was a British army in America to enforce the English policies. The Proclamation of 1763 was followed by the Quartering Act (1765), which required colonial assemblies to billet British troops in empty barns and warehouses. Suddenly, the Redcoats seemed like an occupying army.

Britain also began to enforce its **mercantilist** trade policies, which meant American ships had to bypass their traditional (and lucrative) partners and do business only with English colonies at higher prices. Colonists who ignored the decree were charged with smuggling—wealthy merchants now faced imprisonment or fines for trading with French colonies. To make matters worse, the English introduced taxes to help support their army of Redcoats. These widely reviled duties culminated in the Stamp Act of 1765.

Mercantilism: An economic theory according to which government controls foreign trade to maintain prosperity and security.

The Stamp Tax and the First Hints of Independence

Stamp taxes were a common way to raise money in England, but the effort to impose one on the colonies set off a firestorm. Parliament ignored the colonial assemblies (violating colonial ideas of representation) and simply announced the new tax. Colonists responded by convening a Stamp Act Congress that met in October 1765. Delegates from nine colonies sent a protest to the king and to Parliament. The English policies were pushing the colonists into working together.

Protests against the stamp tax spread throughout the colonies. Mobs hung, burned, and beheaded tax collectors in effigy. They attacked tax collectors' offices and homes. Across the sea, English authorities were incredulous. All they could see were ungrateful colonists who refused to pay for their own protection.[4]

The Townshend Acts Worsen the Conflict

After Parliament reluctantly lifted the stamp taxes, colonists celebrated the repeal and tensions eased—until Parliament followed up with the Townshend Acts in 1767. These acts instituted a fresh round of taxes; revenues were earmarked to pay a new colonial authority, the American Board of Customs, which would collect taxes independently of the colonial assemblies. Now an imperial bureaucracy was explicitly denying the colonists self-governance. The Townshend Acts also suspended the New York State Assembly for refusing to house and supply British troops.

Once again, American colonists responded with meetings, petitions, and mobs. New Yorkers and, later, Bostonians seethed with anger over having their legislatures dissolved. Mobs harassed the customs officials, who found it impossible to carry out their duties and called for help. A British warship arrived in Boston, discharging officials who seized a vessel owned by John Hancock, one of the resistance leaders, and charged him with smuggling (because he continued to trade with French colonies). That move set off riots, bringing British troops into the city to restore order. Before long, there were almost four thousand Redcoats in a city of fifteen thousand people. The Boston mobs harassed the soldiers with taunts, rocks, and snowballs until, on March 5, 1770, one detachment of Redcoats panicked and fired point-blank on the crowd.

The Boston Massacre, as the event quickly became known, left five civilians dead. The first to fall was a sailor named Crispus Attucks, the son of an African enslaved person and a Natick Indian who had escaped slavery some twenty years earlier. Ironically, the son of two groups who would not be liberated by the Revolution—African enslaved people and Native Americans—was the first to bleed for the cause. Paul Revere memorialized the massacre in an engraving

● An engraving of the Boston Massacre done by Paul Revere. This version of the event makes the British look like cold-blooded killers—not historically accurate, but powerful propaganda for independence.

First Continental Congress: A convention of delegates from twelve of the thirteen colonies that met in 1774.

that transformed the panicky soldiers threatened by a mob into a line of killers firing into a heroic cluster of civilians. Historian Gordon Wood described the engraving as "perhaps the most famous piece of antimilitary propaganda in American history."[5]

At the start of the crisis, six years earlier, colonial leaders had respectfully petitioned the king to rescind his policies. Now, blood had been shed and the colonists began to talk about rebellion.

The Boston Tea Party

The British repealed all the Townshend duties except a tariff on tea. Tea was a global industry in 1773; think of it as the must-have product of the eighteenth century. But the East India Tea Company, which had a monopoly in England, was on the verge of bankruptcy. In 1773, Parliament tried to rescue the company by granting it a monopoly over the tea trade in the New World. The colonial shippers who had long been trading tea would be shut out by this rival trading network.

When ships with East India tea arrived, mobs in Philadelphia and New York forced them to sail away without unloading their cargo. In Boston, however, Governor Thomas Hutchinson would not permit such nonsense. He insisted that the three ships in Boston Harbor not leave until their tea was safely delivered. On a dark December night, about fifty men, some "dressed in the Indian manner," boarded one of the ships. They hefted 342 chests of tea onto the deck, bashed them open with hatchets, and dumped the contents—worth about £9,600 (around $1.8 million today)—into Boston Harbor.[6]

Revolution!

British leaders were furious. Past insubordination paled next to this direct economic hit on a struggling British company. The English introduced what colonists dubbed the Intolerable Acts. The laws closed Boston Harbor until the tea was paid for, abolished town meetings, authorized the quartering of troops in any home in Massachusetts, and essentially put the state under military control. King George III himself put it bluntly: "The colonists must either triumph or submit."

Americans refused to submit. Instead, twelve colonies sent representatives to the **First Continental Congress** in September 1774. The Congress petitioned for an end to the Intolerable Acts, called for a boycott on British goods, and asserted colonial rights to "life, liberty, and property." They agreed to meet again in May 1775.

Before the Continental Congress reconvened, fighting had begun. In April 1775, the British commander in Boston, General Thomas Gage, sent one thousand troops from Boston to seize guns and ammunition stored at Concord, Massachusetts. Armed colonists who called themselves "minutemen" blocked the way and came under British fire at Lexington and Concord. Eight were shot dead. The British found and destroyed the weapons, but their march back to Boston was horrific. Minutemen hid behind rocks and trees and sniped at them all along the way.

By the time the English army limped back into the city, they had lost three hundred men.[7]

A Long Legacy

Revolutionary images and slogans still resonate in American politics today. Insurrectionists at the Capitol on January 6, 2021, brandished "Don't Tread on Me" flags, and right-wing Republican Congresswoman Lauren Boebert tweeted, "It's 1776." Tea Party Patriots continue to hold rallies and claim millions of members, while Democrats discuss a "tea party of the left."[8] Civilians anxious about immigration call themselves minutemen and patrol the border with Mexico. Self-proclaimed militias organize and train to defend their personal rights. And Americans from across the political spectrum aspire to live up to the Revolution's dreams of equality. The Revolution left the new United States with symbols, memes, and an enduring political concern: arbitrary government that threatens the people's liberties. But it also raises a provocative question: Are Americans too quick to exaggerate routine disagreements by making analogies to the revolutionaries?

THE BOTTOM LINE

» For over a century, England largely ignored its American colonies and elected assemblies governed the colonists. After the French and Indian War, the English bypassed the colonial legislatures and imposed new rules and taxes.

» These actions violated traditional colonial rights and exposed two different ideas of representation—the American concept of delegate representation (representatives respond to their constituents' desires) and the English concept of trustee representation (representatives do what they consider best for all, regardless of constituent demands).

» English action also harmed colonial economic interests.

» Americans fought an unusual revolution: Rather than demanding new rights, they were trying to preserve existing rights and economic interests.

The Declaration of Independence

The **Second Continental Congress**, which met in May 1775, faced the job of declaring independence, mobilizing an army, organizing a government, and rallying thirteen very different colonies around a single cause. A year later, on July 4, 1776, the Congress voted to adopt a Declaration of Independence as a statement to the world of America's purpose. The document has two parts: a statement of principles and a list of grievances. (The full Declaration is reprinted in Appendix I to this book.)

Second Continental Congress: A convention of delegates from the thirteen colonies that became the acting national government for the duration of the Revolutionary War.

The Principle: "We Hold These Truths . . ."

In one elegant paragraph, the Declaration of Independence distills America's political philosophy (see Table 3.1 for how the Declaration reflects the ideas discussed in Chapter 2):

- All people are equal.
- Their creator endowed them with rights that cannot be taken away.
- These rights include life, liberty, and the pursuit of happiness.

TABLE 3.1 The Declaration of Independence and America's Enduring Ideas

HOW DOES THE DECLARATION REFLECT THE KEY AMERICAN IDEAS DISCUSSED IN CHAPTER 2?
Liberty. The Declaration asserts that liberty is an "unalienable right" (meaning that no one can take it away), endowed to all people by their creator.
Self-rule. The right of representation is one of the Declaration's central themes: It contends that governments derive "their just powers from the consent of the governed." Ten of the twenty-seven grievances charged against the king directly address the issue of self-rule.
Limited government. The idea of limited government had more space than any other in both the Declaration and the Constitution. Most of the Declaration recites the ways King George III overstepped his "just powers." Eleven years later, the Constitution would carefully limit the powers given to the federal government.
Individualism. The Declaration states that "governments are instituted among men . . . to secure [the] rights" with which the creator has endowed each individual. These include "life, liberty, and the pursuit of happiness." Here is the cornerstone of American individualism. At the same time, the Declaration also talks about "one people" and "the people"—collective ideas that must be balanced with individualism. Recall the great American debate: How do we balance individualism and communalism? The Declaration emphasizes both.
The American dream. The Declaration of Independence promises the pursuit of happiness. What does this mean? The phrase is borrowed from John Locke, who wrote that governments are instituted to protect "life, liberty, and *property.*" Jefferson, in his first draft of the Declaration, changed "property" to "happiness." But right from the start, "the pursuit of happiness"—what we now call the American dream—was entangled with the pursuit of wealth.
Equality. This idea seems clear enough: Because "all men are created equal," they all have the same rights to life, liberty, and the pursuit of happiness. But do we as a society need to feed the hungry and clothe the poor (and provide a free education, arguably including college) to ensure that everyone has an equal shot at the pursuit of happiness? This remains a much-debated matter.
Faith in God. The words "the Creator" appear right at the start of the Declaration. But religion soon became controversial. Thomas Jefferson, who drafted the Declaration, was not a religious man. (As a deist, he thought that God did not interfere in human affairs.) Jefferson later ignited a controversy during his presidency when he refused to call national days of prayer as George Washington had done. Instead, Jefferson argued that there must be "a wall of separation between church and state." But Jefferson's wall raises as many questions as it resolves, as debates and court cases have attested for generations.
Diversity. The Declaration is clear: "all" are created equal, and the "thirteen united States of America" represented "one people." These stirring words ostensibly molded together the already diverse collection of Native Americans, Anglo-Saxon and Irish from the United Kingdom, immigrants—many "indentured" for years of servitude to pay for their passage—from across Europe, and enslaved African and Caribbean men and women brought by force. Settlers in the "New World" were already drawing lines around who was included and excluded, from the earliest colonial arrivals.

- People form governments to protect those rights.
- Governments derive their just powers from the consent of the governed.

These ideas were not new. Political philosophers, especially the English thinker John Locke, had used very similar "social contract" language. In his *Two Treatises on Government*, published more than a century earlier, Locke argued that in nature, there are no rules. Life is ruled by force and violence. To secure safety and freedom, people contract with one another, enter into civil society, and form governments to protect one another's life, liberty, and property. Locke was enormously influential in revolutionary America. One curious indicator: The elegant furniture of this era, which often featured carved busts of writers and religious figures, includes more carvings of John Locke than anyone else.[9]

As a statement of governing ideals, the Declaration of Independence was—and still is—breathtaking. In 1776, it was also a far cry from reality.

Thomas Jefferson, who drafted much of the document, was a slave owner. The Declaration essentially invites future cruelty when it refers to "merciless Indian savages." Its authors failed to live up to their noble sentiments. We do not fully live up to them today. Even so, the document stands as the great statement of American idealism—something every generation can fight for. It is the fountain-head of American government.[10]

Grievances

The second part of the Declaration lists twenty-seven grievances against King George III. These tell us what the American colonists cared about as they began the Revolution. Three complaints dominate the list:

- *Violations of the right of representation.* This complaint comes up in ten of the twenty-seven charges against England. It is by far the most intensely felt grievance described in the Declaration.

- *Maintenance of a standing army not under civilian control.* In particular, British soldiers acted in peacetime without the consent of American legislatures. Five complaints are about the British military.

- *Loss of an independent court.* This violation of traditional justice comes up six times.

Today the Revolution is often boiled down to the colonists' slogan "No taxation without representation." The Declaration emphasized *representation* much more than taxation; taxes did not show up until way down the list, as grievance number seventeen ("Imposing taxes on us without our consent"). Economics did matter, of course. Many of the British steps that preceded rebellion, from new taxes to tighter trade rules, were essentially economic challenges. However, those which reverberate most forcefully in the Declaration of Independence are the *right of representation* and the *consent of the governed.*

THE BOTTOM LINE

» The Declaration of Independence asserted philosophical ideals as the basis of the new American government.

» The first part of the Declaration features five ideals that sum up the nation's political principles.

» The second part of the Declaration lists twenty-seven grievances that led to the break. They emphasized the right of representation and consent of the governed.

 # The First American Government: The Articles of Confederation

When the United States declared its independence, it linked the thirteen former colonies—now states—into a **confederation**, or an *alliance of independent states.* Although this first American government lasted little more than a decade, it taught the new nation valuable lessons about effective government.

Confederation: A group of independent states or nations that yield some of their powers to a national government, although each state retains a degree of sovereign authority.

● *A series of legends have grown up around Molly Pitcher, whose real name was Mary Ludwig Hays McCauley. The most famous has her stepping in to take the place of her fallen husband at the cannon during the Battle of Monmouth. The stories are most likely a composite of descriptions of many women who fought with the American army.*

Independent States

The states organized their governments to reflect popular desires. They introduced annual elections, extended the right to vote, and opened their legislative deliberations to public view. Some states built benches in the assembly halls so that the public could watch their representatives in action. States also enlarged their legislatures so that members would be more responsive to citizens.

The new rules still left many people out. Women had participated in the Revolutionary War. Some dressed as men and fought; others cooked, worked as nurses, and buried the dead. The English estimated that "women and waggoners make up nearly half of their [American] army."[11] Nevertheless, women could not vote in most states. And, despite the Declaration of Independence's ringing statement of "unalienable rights," slavery persisted in every state.

Still, the revolutionary spirit unleashed a powerful egalitarian urge. States from Massachusetts to Virginia pondered the abolition of slavery. In some states, such as New Jersey, women with property were allowed to vote. And across the nation, state legislatures were, as historian Gordon Wood stated, "probably as equally and fairly representative of the people as any legislatures in history."[12]

The National Government

The Continental Congress approved its first constitution, called the Articles of Confederation, in November 1777. The document, which reflected Americans' recent experience with England, kept the national government weak and dependent on the states. The Articles named the new nation the United States of America and described the central government as "a league of friendship" among states: "Each . . . retains its sovereignty, freedom and independence, and every power, jurisdiction and right." In a sign of what was to come, Congress had to wait more than three years to get approval from all thirteen states for the Articles of Confederation.

There was no chief executive (the states would implement the laws), no central authority to tax (all revenues would come from state governments), and no central power to muster an army (the states supplied the troops). Each state had a single vote in Congress. Important matters required the vote of nine states. Any changes to the Articles of Confederation required the agreement of all thirteen states. Today, we call such extra-large majorities **supermajorities**—obviously, they are much harder to achieve than a simple majority. The Articles created a very weak central government.[13]

Supermajority: An amount higher than a simple majority (50 percent plus one)—typically, three-fifths or two-thirds of the voters.

Some Success . . .

Americans had good reason to be proud of their new government. Power remained close to the people. The new government overcame incredible odds and, by April 1783, had defeated the most powerful military force in the world. The population grew rapidly in the 1780s—the fastest rise of any decade in American history.

After a brief postwar recession, the economy also expanded. Americans considered themselves both democratic and prosperous.[14]

The Continental Congress also won a major policy success when it stopped the squabbling among states over claims to western land. The Northwest Ordinance of 1787 outlawed slavery in the territory and established a process by which individuals could buy western lands. When an area attracted a minimum number of settlers, it could apply to be a state with all the same powers and privileges as the existing states. With this act, the United States established its mechanism for western expansion.

... And Some Problems

But four major problems plagued the new American government.

First, the Continental Congress had limited powers, and the Articles provided for no executive official or judiciary. Congress had trouble supplying (much less paying) the army throughout the Revolutionary War. As the war ended, a growing population required everything from adjudicating border disputes to building roads and other infrastructure. But the requirement of unanimity made it impossible to amend the Articles to expand the weak central authority. George Washington drew a lesson that would always guide his politics: *The new republic needed a vigorous national government if it was to survive.*[15]

Second, the Articles government could not raise taxes and had no money of its own. The states were reluctant to provide funds. When Congress tried to fix its financial problems by levying a 5 percent tax on imported goods, Rhode Island's legislature blocked the proposal, calling it "the yoke of tyranny fixed on all the states."[16] When loans from France and Holland came due, there was no way to pay them. Again, many leaders shared a realization: *A vigorous national government needed a stable source of revenue.*

Third, state governments were dominated by their legislatures, which operated without any checks or balances. The result was often bias and even chaos. Legislatures wrote (and repealed) laws to benefit individuals. They forgave debts. They seized private property. Leaders eventually reached yet another important conclusion: *Different sources of government power should balance one another, governors should balance legislatures, and the central government should balance the states.*

Fourth, the weak national government had a difficult time standing up to foreign powers. Spain closed the Mississippi to American vessels. Britain's trade policy played the states against one another. Pirates brazenly seized American ships in North Africa. National-minded Americans drew an obvious conclusion: *A weak central government left the nation vulnerable.*

One event, Shays's Rebellion, dramatized the problems of government under the Articles. Captain Daniel Shays, a veteran of the Revolutionary War, led a protest that broke out in western Massachusetts in August 1786 and spread across the state. Thousands of farmers, facing rising interest rates, took up their muskets and shut down courthouses to stop foreclosures on their farms. When Governor James Bowdoin summoned the local militia to defend the Worcester courthouse, members refused;

● *Captain Daniel Shays led a rebellion in protest of farm foreclosures in 1786.*

● James Madison was the most diligent delegate. Small, shy, and unimpressive looking, no one would notice Madison next to the tall and muscular Washington or the charismatic Franklin. However, Madison was a brilliant thinker and one of the chief architects of the Constitution and Bill of Rights. He had more influence over the shape of the final text than any other individual.

some joined the rebellion. The same thing happened in Concord, just forty miles from Boston. By December, the rebels had seized six courthouses and an armory. Governor Bowdoin appealed to the national government for help, but Congress had no army and no money. Finally, Bowdoin hired a private militia and broke the rebellion. Shays's sympathizers shifted strategy: They won seats in the legislature the following year and legislated the debt relief the farmers had been fighting for—to the chagrin of the financiers who had lent them the money.[17]

For many national leaders, Shays's Rebellion was the last straw. Under the Articles of Confederation, neither the national government nor an individual state was strong enough to protect public property (e.g., courthouses) or private property (the repayment of loans). Shays's Rebellion pushed the most influential men in the colonies to write a new constitution. Not everyone agreed. Many Americans thought that problems such as Shays's Rebellion were the growing pains of a more democratic government that reflected the people's desires.

Secrecy

Spring 1787 arrived cold and blustery, delaying many of the delegates on their way to Philadelphia. James Madison from Virginia got there first, with a plan for a new constitution. Madison was short, shy, and balding; today, we recognize him as one of America's greatest political thinkers. The next delegate from Virginia arrived with more fanfare. As George Washington approached, church bells pealed, cannons thundered, army officers donned their old uniforms to ride escort, and local citizens lined the streets and cheered. The presence of the great American hero made the convention's success more likely.

On the first day, the delegates unanimously elected George Washington to chair the convention. Then they agreed on a controversial rule: The deliberations would be completely secret. Guards were placed at the doors. Windows were shut and remained closed, even after the Philadelphia summer turned stifling. George Washington made only three comments during the convention—and one was to rebuke a delegate who had carelessly dropped a copy of proposed resolutions. Most of what we know about the convention comes from James Madison himself, who sat at the front of the room and kept meticulous notes—though they were not made public until 1837, a year after Madison's death.

● Alarmed by spreading chaos, the Continental Congress called a national meeting. Only twelve delegates from five states arrived at Mann's Tavern in Annapolis (pictured above)—not enough to do official business. With Shays's Rebellion raging, the delegates requested each state to appoint representatives to meet in Philadelphia the following May, in 1787, and so quietly authorized a convention that would write an entirely new constitution—and permanently transform the United States.

WHAT DO YOU THINK?

Your Advice Is Needed

	Yes, stick with the Articles of Confederation.	No, build a new central government.	I am divided about this.
If you could go back and offer advice to American leaders in 1787, what would you tell them? Should they stick with the Articles of Confederation or write a new constitution? This debate is still alive today. Is the national government trampling on state and local authority, or does Washington provide a vital source of national leadership and funding? Keep current disputes in mind as you offer your advice to the founding generation.	A strong central government can become tyrannical—forcing the people to pay taxes or house soldiers without their consent and depriving them of their rights to express their beliefs, practice religion, or own guns. More power should reside with local government, which is closer to the people. Citizen militias can defend communities without a national army to tempt leaders to intervene in foreign conflicts.	The national government under the Articles is weak and chaotic. The national government must be powerful enough to repel foreign threats, to oversee national development, and to facilitate trade and good relations between the states.	The Constitution will enable the United States to eventually become a wealthy and powerful nation—but it will be less democratic than the local and state governments that dominated under the Articles.

Was it a good idea to impose secrecy? The young republic had only recently opened up its political process to the people. Thomas Jefferson called the decision to close the convention "an abominable precedent." In a republic, he argued, the people should always know what their leaders are doing.[18]

However, the delegates wanted to speak their minds freely without worrying about how their words would appear in the newspapers. Many also feared that powerful politicians in their home states would withdraw their delegation as soon as they heard that the convention was debating an entirely new constitution. Without secrecy, they might have to abandon their bold plan and simply amend the Articles of Confederation—which was all they had been authorized to do.

THE BOTTOM LINE

» Under the Articles of Confederation, thirteen independent states bound themselves into a confederation with a weak central government that had to rely on the states to implement its decisions.

» Though feeble, this first U.S. government was, by the standards of the time, a very democratic one.

» Delegates to the Constitutional Convention convened to fix the Articles of Confederation—but chose to go much further and propose a new American government.

The Constitutional Convention

As they thought about reorganizing their new government, American leaders balanced the two political dangers they had recently encountered.

- British officials' behavior warned them that a powerful central government could strip the people of their rights.

- Experience with the Articles of Confederation taught that a weak national government could fail to protect their rights.

The delegates debated from May into September 1787. They touched on almost every aspect of government, ranging from how to elect the legislature to what to do about slavery. Throughout the discussions, six major themes dominated their attention.

1. How Much Power to the People?

Most Constitutional Convention delegates believed the states had gone too far in empowering the voters. Too much democracy, they thought, had led to chaotic government. Several put their views bluntly right at the start of the convention. "The evils we are experiencing flow from an excess of democracy," argued Elbridge Gerry of Massachusetts. "The people . . . are the dupes of pretended patriots." Roger Sherman, a shrewd Yankee from Connecticut, summed up this perspective: "The people . . . should have . . . little to do . . . [with] government. They want [*lack*] information and are constantly liable to be misled."[19]

The delegates faced a dilemma. They wanted their government to answer to the public; that was why they had fought the Revolution. Recent experience, however, also made them fear a system that responded too readily to the people. The delegates wished to represent the public through better educated, wealthier, and more experienced leaders—men like themselves.

Over the course of the convention, the delegates developed a view of representation that Madison called *filtration*, or *indirect elections*: The public would vote for men (and later women) who would in turn vote for public officials. Examples of filtration appear throughout the Constitution. The speeches during the convention's first days can seem shocking today. The delegates wanted to make the public *less* involved in government than they had been in the eleven years since the United States declared its independence. The new Constitution would permit the public to vote for only one federal office—members of the House of Representatives.

The debate about public involvement did not end with the Constitution. Over time, Americans would play a more active role in their governance. Citizens would win more control over presidential

● Over time, common men began voting in American elections. This painting, by George Caleb Bingham, shows the raucous results. Note the heavy drinking—and how this, like most early American elections, was a completely male event.

elections beginning in the 1820s, when voting reforms were passed on the state level; they started voting directly for senators after passage of the Seventeenth Amendment in 1913. The "public" also would expand over time. Women became voters with passage of the Nineteenth Amendment in 1920; four years later, Congress ensured Native American voting rights. African Americans, who won the right to vote in 1870 (with the Fifteenth Amendment), were later violently denied suffrage, and finally won the right all over again with the Voting Rights Act of 1965. Younger Americans (eighteen- to twenty-year-olds) became eligible to vote in 1971.

The debate that began at the Constitutional Convention continues to this day. It animates one of the key ideas we discussed in Chapter 2: self-rule, balanced between direct democracy and indirect representation. At a still more fundamental level, the debate speaks to one of the greatest political questions: *Who governs?*

Public involvement in governance has grown dramatically over the centuries, but Madison's principle of filtration still keeps the people at arm's length from their government in many areas.

2. National Government Versus State Government

The Articles of Confederation left most power with the states. Madison's plan for the new government shifted that power to a strong national government. The very first motion that the delegates debated called for "a national government . . . consisting of a *supreme* legislature, executive, and judiciary." In fact, Madison's original plan would have shifted most governing authority to the national level.[20]

Many delegates disagreed with this dramatic change. They believed that state and local governments, closer to the people, could more accurately reflect public sentiments—precisely what Madison was trying to avoid. Some pro–states' rights delegates charged Madison and his allies with trying to "abolish the State Governments altogether." Ultimately, delegates from New York walked out of the convention; Rhode Island refused to send any delegates in the first place. The convention was soon down to eleven of the thirteen states.[21]

In the end, the delegates compromised on a system that included both national and state power. The federal government took over many functions—but far fewer than Madison had originally proposed. The states kept many duties—but far fewer than the states' rights advocates wanted. This mixed system, with a stronger national government that leaves considerable power with the state governments, is called **federalism** (we'll discuss it in Chapter 4). The debate about how to balance national government power and state power continues to the present day.

Federalism: Power divided between national and state government. Each has its own sovereignty (independent authority) and its own duties.

3. Big States Versus Small States

Another intense dispute at the Constitutional Convention revolved around a division we rarely notice today: the large, more populous states (led by Virginia and Pennsylvania) versus the smaller states (led by New Jersey and Delaware). Large states argued that representation should be based on population; small states wanted each state to have an equal voice. That debate led to two different plans, one put forward by Virginia (a big state) and the other by New Jersey (on behalf of the small states).

The Virginia Plan.   Governor Edmund Randolph of Virginia presented Madison's original plan for the Constitution. A powerful speaker, Randolph addressed the

Virginia Plan: Madison's plan, embraced by delegates from larger states; this plan strengthened the national government relative to state governments.

Bicameral: Having two legislative houses or chambers—such as the U.S. House and Senate.

delegates for four hours. The plan, which became known as the **Virginia Plan**, had five key points.

1. Congress would have two chambers, a form known as a **bicameral** legislature, with representation in both chambers based on state population.
2. Citizens would vote for members of the House of Representatives; the number of representatives reflected the size of the state. The House of Representatives would, in turn, vote for senators from a list of candidates provided by the state legislatures. These indirect elections limited the states' role and are a classic example of filtration.
3. Congress would elect the president. Here the Virginia Plan turned vague and did not specify whether the president would be one man or a committee; nor did it say how long the executive would serve. Madison told George Washington that he had not made up his mind.
4. A national judiciary with one or more supreme courts would be established, and the judges would have life tenure.
5. Congress would have broad powers to legislate in all cases where the states were "incompetent." A "council of revision" made up of the president and the Supreme Court would have the authority to review and nullify any state law.

Delegates who had not already been briefed by Madison were stunned. Randolph was urging them to embrace a robust national government. The Virginia Plan empowered Congress to "call forth the force of the union" against any state "failing to fulfill its duties" under the new constitution. The federal government could strike down state laws. Early votes indicated that the Virginia Plan enjoyed a small majority at the convention.

Delegates from small states were especially critical of Madison's blueprint and feared they would soon "be swallowed up." Each state had "its peculiar habits, usages, and manners," small-state advocates insisted, and these must be protected. Under Madison's plan, three states (Virginia, Pennsylvania, and Massachusetts) would have enough members in Congress to form a majority by themselves. Representatives from the smaller states repeatedly threatened to walk out of the convention.[22]

New Jersey Plan: Put forward at the Constitutional Convention by the small states, this plan left most government authority with the states.

Unicameral: Having a single legislative house or chamber.

The New Jersey Plan. The small states pushed back with their own plan, introduced by William Paterson of New Jersey and known as the **New Jersey Plan**. Rather than construct a new national government, this approach focused on strengthening the Articles of Confederation. It had four key points:

1. Congress would have only one chamber, a form known as a **unicameral** legislature. Each state would have one vote in Congress, regardless of its size—as in the Articles. But congressional acts would be the supreme law of the land, making the new constitution stronger than the Articles of Confederation.
2. Congress would elect a committee to serve as the federal executive for one term only.
3. The executive committee would select a supreme court, which would be responsible for foreign policy, economic policy, and the impeachment of federal officials.
4. The national government could tax the states and would have the exclusive right to tax imports.

The New Jersey Plan left the states at the center of American government but took a step toward union by building a stronger national government, one that could raise its own taxes and exercise more authority over interstate commerce. When the vote was called, only three states supported the New Jersey Plan.

The Connecticut Compromise. Convention delegates decisively approved the Virginia Plan's bicameral Congress with a House and a Senate. They voted for a House of Representatives based on population. Then debate turned to the Senate. If the delegates voted with the Virginia Plan—in which the House of Representatives would vote for senators—the big states would essentially win the debate. Tempers grew short. "I do not, Gentlemen, trust you," declared Gunning Bedford of Delaware. He hinted darkly that the small states would look for foreign allies if they lost this vote. William Paterson announced that he would rather "submit to a monarch, a despot," than accept the Virginia Plan. Luther Martin, a garrulous delegate from Maryland, wrote home that the convention was on the verge of breaking up over this issue.[23] Big states pushed back: "Will it require 150 voters from my state [Pennsylvania]," asked James Wilson, "to balance 50 from yours [New Jersey]?"[24]

Big states seemed to have the votes to carry seven states and win the Virginia Plan's version of Senate elections. But when the roll was called on July 2, one big-state supporter from Maryland and two from Georgia slipped out of the convention hall. With their exits, both states shifted, and the vote came out a tie: five states for the Virginia Plan, five against, and one evenly split.

To break the deadlock, the delegates formed a committee, which was tilted toward the small states. The committee came up with a compromise, brokered by Roger Sherman of Connecticut and therefore known as the Connecticut Compromise. The House would be based on population; the Senate would have two representatives for each state, chosen by the state legislature. (Americans did not vote directly for their senators in all states until 1914.) Because legislation had to pass through both houses, the public and the states would each have a say. Because the delegates wanted power over taxes and spending in the people's hands, they required that all finance-related bills be introduced first in the House.

The compromise squeaked through—five states voted "yes," four "no," and one split. The big states won the House of Representatives; the small states got their

● *Louis Glanzman's recent painting of the Constitutional Convention. Washington towers over everyone at the center in a black frock coat. To the right stands James Madison. Alexander Hamilton is the red-haired man standing sixth from the left. Benjamin Franklin, age eighty-one, sits at the center of the room chatting with Hugh Williamson, a delegate from North Carolina.*

way in the Senate. The compromise continues to give less populous states great clout in the Senate, engendering a debate as to whether small, mostly rural states like Vermont or Wyoming have too much power over vital national issues.[25]

4. The President

Even the master planner James Madison arrived at the convention without a clear design for the presidency—also known as the *executive authority* because it *executes* (or puts into effect) the laws. The delegates wavered at length about whether executive authority should be placed in one individual or a committee.

Committee or Individual?　Many delegates worried that a single executive would grow powerful and become, as Governor Randolph put it, "the fetus of monarchy." Madison and his allies, however, feared that the Connecticut Compromise opened the Senate door to the same petty state politics that had wrecked the Articles of Confederation. They decided that the president should be one individual, independent of Congress, who could represent the public. After much back and forth, they settled on a four-year term and permitted reelections. (In 1951, the Twenty-Second Amendment limited the president to two terms.)

The Electoral College.　How would the president be chosen? The Constitution's framers saw a problem with every option. They did not think the people had enough information or wisdom. They did not trust state legislators to put aside their own narrow concerns and think about the national interest. Delegates from the big states no longer wanted to give Congress the job, now that state legislators were picking the senators. What could they do? In response, they came up with the most complicated rigmarole in the Constitution: the **Electoral College**. Each state would select individuals known as *electors*—the delegates hoped that they would be well-known individuals with sound judgment—and the electors would then choose the president.

How many electors would each state have? Another compromise: Each state would have the same number of electors as it had members of Congress. That meant a state's population would matter (given proportional representation in the House) but also that every state was assured of two more votes (reflecting their Senate representation). If no individual received a majority of electoral votes—which last happened in 1824—the House of Representatives would choose from among the five candidates with the most votes. They would vote by state, and each state would get just one vote—again, a concession to small states.

Who would elect the electors? The convention left this question to the states. At first, the state legislatures got the job of voting for electors. But in the late 1820s, the states ceded this right to the people (again, white men, although by then they did not need to own any property). The people voted state by state for their electors—as we still do (see Figure 3.2). However, there is nothing in the Constitution to stop the state legislatures from taking back their original role of choosing electors.

Today, all electors in a state generally cast their votes for the candidate who won the state (except for Nebraska and Maine, which allocate one vote for the winner in each of the states' congressional districts). As we saw in Chapter 1, the system has elected five men who lost the popular vote—but won in the Electoral College. After President Trump lost the election of 2020, he pushed Republican state legislatures to select alternative electors—though most legal scholars and state legislators thought they could not properly do so after the people had voted. Now, partisans on both the left and the right are questioning the way the Electoral College works. Should the legislatures take this function back from the people?

Electoral College: The system established by the Constitution to elect the president; each state has a group of electors (equal in size to that of its congressional delegation in the House and the Senate). Today, the public in each state votes for electors, who then vote for the president.

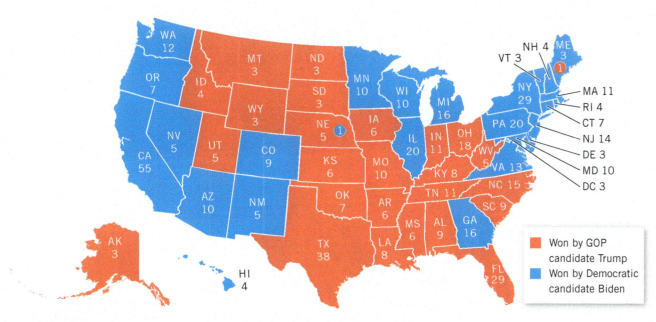

● **FIGURE 3.2** *Electoral College map for the 2020 presidential election.*

Should electors be allocated by the percentage of the vote each candidate gets in a state—rather than winner take all? Should the Electoral College be abolished altogether? What do you think?

The President: Too Strong or Too Weak?   All these details can obscure a crucial fact about the Constitution and the presidency. The delegates arrived at the Constitutional Convention less certain about this office than any other. Some feared putting too much power in one person's hands. Others recognized the need for a leader who could energetically pursue the nation's interests. Despite all that was at stake, arguments about the presidency never got very heated. Why? Because every delegate in the room knew exactly who the first president was going to be. There sat George Washington, calmly presiding over the convention. Knowing that Washington would almost certainly be thrust into the role of president cooled tempers. In the end, the delegates built a general framework and left many details to be defined by the presidents themselves.

Sometimes—when presidents push major legislation through Congress, or issue sweeping executive orders, or launch the U.S. military into action—the presidency is a very powerful office. At other times, it has seemed perilously weak. We explore this paradox when we examine the presidency in Chapter 14.

5. Separation of Powers

One idea that evolved during the convention was the separation of powers. Each branch of government—the president, Congress, and the judiciary—has its job to do: The delegates vested "all legislative powers" in Congress, the executive power in the president, and the judicial power (to try cases) in the courts. The Articles of Confederation had created only a national legislature; in Britain, power was also concentrated in Parliament, their national legislature. Now, the United States would have three independent branches.

The framers added a signature twist: checks and balances. Each power the Constitution grants to Congress or the presidency or the judiciary is balanced by a "countervailing" power assigned to another branch. Each branch is involved in the others' business. As Madison later put it, one branch's ambition for power would always check the other branches' ambitions (see Figure 3.3).

● **FIGURE 3.3** *Separation of powers—checks on the national branches. Multiply these checks across state and local levels and a vital question of American politics arises: Is this chaotic and fragmented state governable? Americans have wrestled with this dilemma since 1787.*

For example, Congress passes legislation but the president signs bills into law. The president can veto (reject) the bill (checking Congress); Congress can override the veto by a two-thirds vote of both chambers (balancing the president).

The president is commander-in-chief, but the Constitution gives Congress the power to declare war and set the military's budget. The president negotiates treaties, but the Senate must ratify them by a two-thirds vote. The president appoints cabinet officials and Supreme Court justices, but the Senate must approve (or confirm) them. Congress holds the ultimate power over all federal officers. The House can impeach (or formally accuse) the president or any other officer in the executive or judicial branch of "Treason, Bribery or other high Crimes and Misdemeanors"; the Senate looks into the accusation and decides whether to remove the person from office. What are "high crimes and misdemeanors"? Well, as the nation discovered during two separate impeachments of President Trump, they have never been fully defined and Congress must use its judgment.

These checks and balances are among the most distinctive features of the American Constitution. The French political philosopher Montesquieu wrote an influential treatise, *The Spirit of the Laws* (published in 1748), which argued that to avoid tyranny, the executive, legislative, and judicial functions of government must be separated—and never placed in a single individual or body. Very few governments have ever developed this principle as fully as the U.S. Constitution.

Checks and balances continue to spark disagreement in the present. Many scholars argue that American-style separated systems are too prone to gridlock—a paralysis of governing institutions—than other democracies. The danger of gridlock is that major issues such as mounting government debt or a national health crisis become harder to address. An even greater danger: Are people growing so tired of stalemate they vote for leaders who are willing to ignore the constitutional limits? [26] Or does power flow to the Supreme Court—unelected justices breaking the policy logjams, case by case? We explore these questions in Chapters 14 and 16.

Has the U.S. government developed too many checks and balances to meet today's immense challenges? Or do the Constitution's checks and balances remain in good working order, controlling power and preserving self-rule—just as James Madison planned?

6. "A Principle of Which We Were Ashamed"

The convention rethought almost every aspect of government—except slavery. Why? For some delegates, the answer involved self-interest. Of the fifty-five delegates, twenty-five were slave owners. George Washington brought three enslaved people with him to Philadelphia during the convention. In Georgia, South Carolina, and Virginia, enslaved people made up more than one-third of the population. And the men and women in bondage were a source of wealth and power. Each time the subject of slavery came up, delegates from South Carolina and Georgia offered the convention a stark choice—protect slavery or form a union without us.

In the end, the delegates wanted a strong union more than they hated slavery. The Constitution includes three major references to slavery—without ever mentioning the word itself. Each time, the slave-holding states got what they wanted.

The Three-Fifths Compromise. Slavery was first thrust on the convention's agenda with the question of how to count enslaved people when allocating seats in the House of Representatives. As Table 3.2 shows, nearly four in ten of Virginia's residents were enslaved persons. If enslaved people were counted as part of the population, southern states would have as many members in the House of Representatives as the northern states.

As soon as the issue came up, James Wilson of Pennsylvania offered yet another compromise. For the purpose of apportioning representation, Wilson proposed, let the total number of enslaved people count as three-fifths of the free

TABLE 3.2 Enslaved Proportion of the U.S. Population in 1790

STATE	TOTAL POPULATION	ENSLAVED PEOPLE	PERCENTAGE OF POPULATION ENSLAVED
Connecticut	237,655	2,648	1.1
Delaware	59,096	8,887	15.0
Georgia	82,548	29,264	35.5
Maryland	319,728	103,036	32.2
Massachusetts	378,556	0	0.0
New Hampshire	141,899	157	0.1
New Jersey	184,139	11,423	6.2
New York	340,241	21,193	6.2
North Carolina	395,005	100,783	25.5
Pennsylvania	433,611	3,707	0.9
Rhode Island	69,112	958	1.4
South Carolina	249,073	107,094	43.0
Virginia	747,550	292,627	39.1

Source: U.S. Census

people of a state. The strange fraction came from the Continental Congress. When it was trying to raise revenue from the states, Congress calculated each state's wealth on the basis of population. It then arbitrarily estimated that enslaved people would generate three-fifths as much wealth as free people.

This crude calculation now came back to haunt the Constitution. The delegates accepted the Three-Fifths Compromise. Its actual wording is as peculiar as the rule itself.

> *Representatives . . . shall be apportioned among the several states according to their respective numbers, which shall be determined by adding the whole number of free persons, including those bound to service for a term of years [indentured servants] and excluding Indians not taxed, three fifths of all other persons.*

The Constitution never says "slave," but simply "three fifths of all other persons." In fact, a reader who did not know that the passage refers to slavery would have a hard time understanding it. Why did the Constitution's framers—who were usually so precise—write such a convoluted sentence? They did not want the word *slavery* to appear in the Constitution. John Dickinson, a thoughtful delegate from Delaware, put it best: The awkward wording was, he said, "an endeavor to conceal a principle of which we were ashamed."[27]

The Slave Trade.   A second question involved the slave trade. Could the federal government regulate or abolish it? Many delegates were repulsed by the idea of stealing human beings from Africa, chaining them aboard ships bound for America, and selling the survivors to the highest bidder. George Mason from Virginia rose and gave the most prophetic speech of the convention: "Every master of slaves is born a petty tyrant. They bring the judgment of heaven on a country. As nations cannot be rewarded or punished in the next world they must be in this. Providence punishes national sins, by national calamities." It was a powerful speech. However,

● *A vivid example of slavery's brutality. Fifty years after the Constitutional Convention, abolitionists denounced the Constitution as a "covenant with death and an agreement with hell" because of its slavery compromises. Advertisements for runaway enslaved people reported identifying marks—such as horrific scars from whipping and even branding.*

Mason himself owned more than three hundred people. Their worth would rise if the slave trade were abolished.

No one at the convention was willing to follow Mason's attack. In the end, backers of a strong Constitution struck a bargain and permitted the slave trade for another twenty years, in exchange for more national power over interstate commerce and the authority to tax imports. Historian William Beeman calculated that by permitting the slave trade for another twenty years they condemned 200,000 Africans to slavery—close to the total (250,000) from the preceding 170 years.[28]

Fugitive Slaves.   In August, as the convention was winding down, delegates from the slave states proposed a fugitive slave clause—requiring the rest of the nation to assist in returning runaway enslaved people. This time there were no deals and barely any debate. The Northern delegates simply accepted the proposal. Northern merchants, after all, benefited from the slave trade right alongside Southern planters. Every region was complicit in the tragic decision.

"The National Calamity."   Many Americans revere the document that has guided the nation for more than two centuries. However, George Mason was right when he predicted a "national calamity." Seventy-two years later, Abraham Lincoln would echo Mason as he reflected on the carnage of the Civil War in his second inaugural address: "God . . . gives to both North and South this terrible war as the woe due to those by whom the offense [of slavery] came."

Embedding slavery in the Constitution had two consequences that would haunt the United States. First, of course, it entrenched slavery itself. Second and more subtly, it created a racial hierarchy that privileged whiteness, in both the North and the South. The Civil War led to the abolition of slavery. But racial hierarchy and privilege would be much harder to eradicate; the battle to do so extends to the present day, with widespread anti-racist efforts in some cases met by complaints about overzealous "woke" and "cancel" cultures.[29]

The Constitution's slavery passages remind us that the Convention was the beginning of an American journey. Each generation faces the same challenges that confronted the founders. *Who are we?* Can we make the United States more just, more democratic, and more inclusive? The Declaration of Independence states America's ideals: All people are created equal. The Constitution, in turn, provides the rules. Americans have wrestled with the meaning of the ideals and the implementation of the rules since these documents were written.

THE BOTTOM LINE

» The constitutional framers balanced two dangers: government that was too strong (the king of England) versus government that was too weak (the Articles of Confederation).

» Debates focused on five central issues:

1. Popular involvement in government. Most delegates believed in filtration, or indirect elections.

2. National versus state power, which came down to a standoff between larger and smaller states. Big states backed Madison's Virginia Plan. Small states countered with the New Jersey Plan. The Connecticut Compromise offered a solution: House members were elected on the basis of population, but every state had two Senate seats.

3. The nature of the presidency: A council? A single executive? Possessing what powers? Debate was limited, given the general expectation that George Washington would be the first president.

4. How best to separate governing powers, answered through a system of checks and balances. For the most part, these limits on concentrated authority would continue to develop long after ratification.

5. Slavery: Compromise in the name of union overcame morality. Delegates avoided the word *slavery* in the Constitution, but several clauses enabling the institution to expand would lead to the greatest conflict in the nation's future—and enshrine injustice that haunts the country still.

An Overview of the Constitution

By September 17, after four months of deliberation, the Constitutional Convention had done its work. Thirty-nine of the original fifty-five delegates lined up to sign the document. Benjamin Franklin, pointing to a sunburst painted on the back of the president's chair, remarked that he had gazed at that sun throughout the convention "without being able to tell if it was rising or setting. But now . . . I have the happiness to know that it is a rising and not a setting sun."[30] A pessimistic observer might have pointed out that sixteen delegates—almost a third—had either left the convention or refused to sign: a portent of the battles ahead.

There are seven articles in the Constitution, each comprising multiple sections. (The full text appears in Appendix II.) These passages remain the institutional foundation of American government.

Preamble

The Constitution begins with a preamble, the document's most elegant sentence:

> *We the people of the United States, in order to form a more perfect union, establish justice, insure domestic tranquility, provide for the common defense, promote the general welfare, and secure the blessings of liberty to ourselves and our posterity, do ordain and establish this Constitution for the United States of America.*

The Constitution's authority rests not on the states, but on "we the people." As we have seen, the Constitutional Convention produced a weak version of the people—one that affirmed slavery, excluded women, and permitted "we the people" to vote for exactly one branch of Congress. The next phrase—"in order to form a more perfect union"—addresses these limitations. Americans still struggle toward that improved union.

The preamble also offers six goals for a successful government. Ask yourself how you would rate today's U.S. government on each (see What Do You Think?).

Article 1: Congress

Article 1, the longest in the Constitution, describes the new Congress. Section 2 of the article establishes a House of Representatives elected every two years. In 1789, the average size of a House district was around 33,000 people—today the

---

Have We Achieved These National Goals Today?

Consider the goals listed in the preamble to the Constitution. Then give a grade to each: an "A" if you think the United States has lived up to its goals, and a . . . well, we're sure you know all about grades!

Goal:	Grade Today:
Form a strong union	_____
Establish equal justice for all	_____
Insure domestic tranquility (that is, peace at home)	_____
Provide for the common defense (today, we might say homeland security)	_____
Promote the general welfare	_____
Secure liberty for ourselves and posterity	_____

size of an average district has grown to over 760,000. Representatives must be twenty-five years old and have been a citizen for seven years. Section 3 establishes a Senate with two members from every state, elected every six years; they must be at least thirty years old and have been a citizen for nine years.

Section 8 is the most important passage in Article 1—and perhaps the entire Constitution. Its seventeen short paragraphs detail what Congress may do, including the "power to lay and collect taxes," declare war, regulate interstate commerce, coin money, and raise an army.

Think about the reach of congressional authority. The largest and most expensive program that Congress oversees is Social Security, which pays monthly pensions to older people. If you read all of Section 8, you may be puzzled—nothing in it remotely justifies paying for retirement pensions. How, then, could Congress create the Social Security program? Two different clauses stretch the government's reach. First, Congress has the authority to regulate commerce among the states—a power that can be stretched to touch everything that moves across state lines. And, more important, the very last paragraph of Section 8 empowers Congress "to make all laws which shall be necessary and proper for carrying into execution the foregoing powers, and all other powers vested by this Constitution in the government of the United States." That phrase, known as the *necessary and proper clause*, gives Congress—and the government—a great deal of creative leeway.

What are the limits of the power granted to Congress by this clause? Here again the delegates in Philadelphia disagreed, and scholars still argue about the necessary and proper clause. The states of the Confederacy broke away from the Union in 1861 and wrote their own constitution; although it largely mirrored the original, it ruled out an expansive reading of the interstate commerce clause to ensure that no future Confederate government would interfere with slavery.[31]

Section 9 of Article 1 lists the acts *forbidden* to Congress. Its second prohibition is especially important: "The privilege of the writ of habeas corpus shall not be suspended unless when in cases of rebellion or invasion the public safety may require it." *Habeas corpus* means that government cannot hold prisoners without formally charging them with a crime. The U.S. government may not simply throw someone in jail without a charge.

Article 2: The President

The Constitution's second article shifts focus from the legislature to the executive branch. The president, Article 2 specifies, must be a natural-born American at least thirty-five years old and is chosen by electors for a four-year term. Today every state has turned the power to choose electors over to the public. Very few other nations use the American process for selecting the head of state (see Comparing Nations 3.2).

Whereas Article 1 lists congressional do's and don'ts in detail, Article 2 spells out presidential powers and duties much less specifically. The president is commander-in-chief of the army and the navy.[32] Presidents can make treaties if two-thirds of the Senate approve; they appoint ambassadors, Supreme Court justices, and other officials—again with the advice and consent of the Senate.

Although these seem like a limited set of powers, the Constitution includes another clause that has permitted an enormous expansion of presidential powers: "The executive power shall be vested in a President of the United States." What that "executive power" is, and how far it can stretch, has been debated throughout American history.

President Biden, for example, in 2022 issued an executive order directing his Treasury Department to explore establishing a U.S. Central Bank Digital

COMPARING NATIONS 3.2   The U.S. Government Is Different from Most Democracies

Of these eleven advanced democracies, only two—Argentina and Brazil—mirror the American Constitution on all three dimensions. Most democracies are parliamentary systems, in which the lower house selects a chief executive (a prime minister). Ironically, that was the idea in both the Virginia and New Jersey Plans, the original drafts of the Constitution. No other democracy has as extensive checks and balances as the United States.

NATION	HEAD OF GOVERNMENT ELECTED BY	FEDERALISM	CHECKS/ BALANCES
United States	Public/electors	Yes	Yes
Argentina	Public	Yes	Yes
Australia	Parliament (lower house)	Yes	Some
Brazil	Public	Yes	Yes
Canada	Parliament (lower house)	Yes	No
France	Public	No	Sometimes
Germany	Parliament (lower house)	Yes	Some
Great Britain	Parliament (lower house)	No	No
India	Parliament (lower house)	Yes	No
Israel	Parliament	No	No
Japan	Parliament (lower house)	No	No

Currency—similar to a cryptocurrency. The big difference: A U.S. government "digital dollar" would be regulated by the Federal Reserve, effectively undermining many of the cryptocurrencies springing up almost daily. Critics complained that a government-run digital central bank would compete with (and snoop on) private currencies.[33] The Constitution, of course, makes no reference to "cryptocurrency"—or any form of money at all. Does the president have the authority to create a central-bank cryptocurrency? Courts would have to settle disputes over that question, and in recent years the federal judiciary has often deferred to presidents' claims of executive power.

Section 4 allows for removing a president "on impeachment for, and conviction of, treason, bribery, or other high crimes and misdemeanors." Four presidents, most recently Donald Trump, have faced formal impeachment proceedings; only one, Richard Nixon, resigned his office. The grounds for impeachment remain highly contested. Back in 1970, future president and U.S. House minority leader Gerald Ford remarked, "An impeachable offense is whatever a majority of the House of Representatives considers it to be at a given moment in history."[34]

Article 3: The Courts

Article 3 creates the Supreme Court and authorizes Congress to organize additional courts. Alexander Hamilton called the Supreme Court "the least dangerous" branch of government, and the Constitution describes it only briefly. The justices are selected by the president, are approved by the Senate, and have tenure for life—still another buffer against democratic politics. Article 3 grants the Supreme Court power over all cases "arising under this Constitution, the laws of the United States and treaties made."

The Constitution is silent on the Court's most formidable power: May it overrule an act of Congress? Or an executive declaration by the White House? Sixteen years after the Constitutional Convention, Chief Justice John Marshall, in deciding a case called *Marbury v. Madison*, ruled that the Court could strike down an act of Congress. (We review this case in detail in Chapter 16.) Because the Court has authority over all cases "arising under this Constitution," Marshall claimed it also had a responsibility to review the constitutionality of legislation. The delegates debated this power but, in the end, left the language vague. Ever since Marshall's decision, however, the courts have ruled whether Congress and the president are abiding by the Constitution's rules.

Notice how the powers of each branch have evolved over time. Americans are constantly challenged to interpret precisely what the Constitution requires.

Article 4: Relations Between the States

Article 4 defines the relationship between the states that had so plagued the Articles of Confederation. A state may not discriminate against citizens of other states, and each must give "full faith and credit" to official acts of other states and guarantee every state a republican form of government.

The "full faith and credit" clause can be explosive. When some states passed same-sex marriage legislation, others refused to recognize these unions. Congress passed the Defense of Marriage Act that permitted states to refuse "full faith and credit" for same-sex marriages conducted in other states. After more than a decade, the Supreme Court took the issue off the table by striking down the federal law and all state laws that limited marriage to a man and a woman. Now you know where they got the authority to do so: The Supreme Court's power to judge which laws and regulations violate the Constitution.[35]

Article 5: Amendments

Article 5 authorizes amendments to the Constitution. The process is extremely difficult, marked by multiple supermajorities. Two-thirds of both the House and Senate must approve the amendment. Then three-fourths of the states must ratify it—either through their state legislatures or through state conventions. The only amendment to be ratified through conventions is the Twenty-First Amendment, which in 1933 repealed the prohibition on alcohol.

Over one hundred thousand amendments have been suggested since 1791 (when the first ten amendments, or Bill of Rights, were ratified). Nearly twelve thousand have been proposed in Congress; only seventeen have passed into the Constitution. When Americans disagree with a Supreme Court ruling, they sometimes try to push through a constitutional amendment. Few ever succeed.

The Constitution forbids amendments on two matters: No amendment could stop the slave trade before 1808, and no state could be denied equal suffrage in the Senate (two seats) without its approval. In this way, the two fiercest debates at the convention were placed beyond the reach of future generations.

Article 6: The Law of the Land

Article 6 makes the Constitution the supreme law of the land. It also specifies that there must be no religious test for holding any federal office. Some states, however, had religious tests (requiring adherence to a specific religion, usually Protestant Christianity) for holding state and local office and even for voting, up until the 1830s.

Article 7: Ratification

Article 7 announced that the Constitution would go into effect after nine states had ratified—a controversial move, because the United States was still operating under the Articles of Confederation, which could be amended only by all thirteen states.

The Missing Articles

Many Americans thought that the original Constitution was missing something important. Only a handful of individual rights were mentioned in the document. It said nothing about free speech, a free press, freedom of religion, jury trials, or the right to bear arms. The debate over ratifying the Constitution would quickly expose this weakness. Ratification helped introduce an important addition: the ten amendments known as the Bill of Rights.

THE BOTTOM LINE

» The Constitution is a brief, elegant document with a preamble and seven articles (or major sections).

» The articles of the Constitution address (1) Congress, (2) the presidency, (3) the judiciary, (4) relations between the states, (5) instruction for amending the Constitution, (6) an assertion that the Constitution is the supreme law of the land, and (7) a process for ratifying the Constitution.

 # Ratification

The new Constitution next went to the states, where ratifying conventions would vote it up or down. Although most states were closely divided, the Constitution had two big advantages. First, it offered a clear plan in a time of trouble; opponents could only say "no" and force the nation to start all over again. Second, the convention had attracted many of the most prestigious men in America, beginning with Washington and Franklin. Supporters of the Constitution were known as *Federalists*—making their opponents the *Anti-Federalists*.

The Anti-Federalists

Classical republicanism: A democratic ideal, based in ancient Greece and Rome, that calls on citizens to participate in public affairs, seek the public interest, shun private gain, and defer to leaders.

The Anti-Federalists based their argument against ratification in **classical republicanism**. Popular government, in this view, should model itself on ancient republics such as Athens and Rome. Republics were small and local, permitting maximum popular participation in public affairs. When we discussed the idea of self-rule in Chapter 2, we introduced the idea of direct democracy (celebrated by Thomas Jefferson); classical republicanism is the original version of that idea.

The Anti-Federalists were not interested in a centralized nation-state such as the European empires (or the British monarchy Americans had just overthrown). They had four major criticisms of the new Constitution:

- First, it stripped political control from citizens and placed it in a powerful national government over which the people would have scant influence.

- Second, the president—a sole executive, with potentially vast authority—looked too much like a king.

- Third, standing armies and navies were a threat to peace and liberty. Republics relied on citizen militias—which could be mustered during wartime—to protect the people.

- Fourth and most important, the Anti-Federalists hammered away at the Constitution's missing piece, a bill of rights.[36]

Politics also played a role in the Anti-Federalist argument. Many of the men who opposed the Constitution were powerful political figures in their own states. A national government would diminish their influence.

Many of the Anti-Federalist (and civic-republican) arguments remain alive today. Americans often criticize the federal government and advocate restoring power to state and local officials, who are closer to the people. The Anti-Federalists may have lost the debate in 1788, but their fear of federal power and their yearning to return authority to the people endure—and shape one answer to our great question, *Who are we?*

The Federalists

The arguments in favor of the new Constitution were summarized by an editorial dream team. James Madison and Alexander Hamilton (with a little help from John Jay, who would become the first Supreme Court chief justice) wrote eighty-five short essays that appeared in several New York State newspapers to explain and defend the Constitution. Known as the *Federalist Papers*, these essays achieved three very different purposes. First, they are pro-Constitution editorials, even propaganda; the authors were fighting to get New York to approve the new Constitution, and they did not pretend to be neutral. Second, they are the single best guide to the thinking that guided the Constitution. However, we have to read them carefully, always weighing the *Papers* as persuasive rhetoric as well as explanations of constitutional logic. Finally, the *Federalist Papers* are outstanding theoretical essays about politics and government.

The two most famous *Federalist Papers*, no. 10 and no. 51, appear in Appendix III to this book. Their eighteenth-century language sounds strange to our ears, but the argument is brilliant. *Federalist* no. 10 argues, surprisingly, that a large national government can protect liberty more effectively than small local governments. Madison begins the essay by introducing the "mortal disease" that always destroys popular government. You might think that he was referring to tyrants like George III. Instead, he points to *factions*—groups that pursue their self-interest at the expense of others. And in the United States, said Madison, factions usually reflect economic interests. This insight is sometimes forgotten by American foreign policymakers today: Removing tyrants will not achieve stable popular government until the factions that divide a country are controlled.

How to diminish the effects of factions? Not through local governments, argued Madison. In each area, one economic interest is likely to predominate— farmers, merchants, big manufacturers, or even poor people eager to tax the rich. Because the same local group will always be in the majority, it is difficult to stop that group from taking advantage of the minority.

Madison's realistic assessment was a breakthrough in political theory. The classical view assumed that for popular government to survive, the people—that is, the voters—had to be virtuous and respect one another. Madison introduced a modern take: Expect people to pursue their own self-interest. As he wrote in *Federalist* no. 51, "If men were angels, no government would be necessary." If popular government is to survive, it must be organized to protect minorities from majorities who are going to pursue their own self-interest.

How can we do this? Move the debate to the national level, said Madison. A larger political sphere—a bigger government—will always have a great many diverse interests, arising from all the states. With so many different factions, no one interest will be able to dominate. Each faction forms a small minority of the whole, and will therefore need to form alliances. As the issues change, so will the groups that are in the majority and the minority. As a result, no one faction will have an incentive to impose its will on the minority for very long: They might need that minority as allies for the next political battle.

Madison's idea would run into trouble, however, if the same two sides face off against one another on every national issue. When that occurs, there is no need to form shifting alliances. That's what happened in the slavery debate in the 1850s. Some political scientists worry that intense party conflict today might again be creating fixed divisions—factions—on issue after issue and wrecking Madison's elegant solution. (We discuss that concern in Chapter 11.)[37]

Two Strong Arguments

To this day, both sides—Anti-Federalist and Federalist—sound persuasive. The Anti-Federalists tapped into a deep American preference for local governments that respond directly to popular concerns. The Federalists argued that only a national government could protect the people's rights and turn the new nation into a great power.

A Very Close Vote

The smaller states won considerable ground at the Constitutional Convention thanks to the Connecticut Compromise. Not surprisingly, they ratified quickly and unanimously—Delaware, New Jersey, and Georgia all signed by January 2, 1788. In Pennsylvania, some members of the assembly hid to slow down the process. Enthusiastic mobs found the reluctant members and marched them to the deliberations. The public crammed into the hall and swarmed outside the building. After a month, Pennsylvania ratified the Constitution by a large margin, and Benjamin Franklin led a cheering throng through the streets to Epple's Tavern for celebratory toasts (see Table 3.3 for a summary of the voting).

TABLE 3.3 Final Vote for the Constitution

STATE	DATE OF RATIFICATION	VOTE IN STATE CONVENTION
1. Delaware*	December 7, 1787	Unanimous (30–0)
2. Pennsylvania**	December 12, 1787	46–23
3. New Jersey*	December 18, 1787	Unanimous (38–0)
4. Georgia*	January 2, 1788	Unanimous (26–0)
5. Connecticut*	January 9, 1788	128–40
6. Massachusetts**	February 7, 1788	187–168
7. Maryland*	April 28, 1788	63–11
8. South Carolina*	May 23, 1788	149–73
9. New Hampshire***	June 21, 1788	57–47; required two meetings
10. Virginia**	June 25, 1788	89–79
11. New York**	July 25, 1788	30–27
12. North Carolina***	July 21, 1789 (after election of Washington)	194–77
13. Rhode Island***	May 29, 1790 (first Congress in session)	34–32

Key: *Easy Ratification   **Tough Fight   ***Originally Refused

In Massachusetts, Governor John Hancock, who was the first delegate to sign the Declaration of Independence, dramatically switched to the Federalist side—on one crucial condition. He asked that amendments protecting individual rights be introduced to the new Constitution. Even with his switch, the Constitution won ratification in Massachusetts only narrowly, 187 to 168. Once the votes were counted, the Anti-Federalists announced that they would "support the Constitution as cheerfully and as heartily as though [they] had voted on the other side." Other states followed the two Massachusetts precedents: Request a bill of rights and unite after the vote.

After Maryland and South Carolina approved the Constitution, the action moved to Virginia—the largest state and the most intense contest to date. Anti-Federalist opposition was led by Patrick Henry, known as "the son of thunder" for his rhetorical power; at one point he spoke without notes for seven straight hours. Governor William Randolph, who had presented the Virginia Plan at the convention, and George Mason, who had scorched the slave trade, both refused to sign the Constitution and joined Henry on the Anti-Federalist side. Despite the strong opposition, Virginia voted for the Constitution eighty-nine to seventy-nine.

New York was even more contentious than Virginia. New York City supported the Constitution, but the rest of the state opposed it. In the end, the new Constitution squeaked through by three votes.

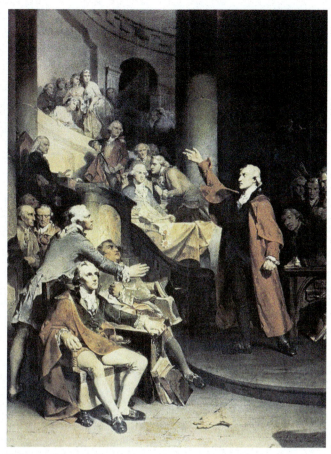

● *The ratification of the Constitution was a close call. Patrick Henry, a powerful orator, led the opponents (known as Anti-Federalists) in Virginia. Virginia was one of seven states where the vote was close.*

Not every state voted in favor. Rhode Island town meetings voted against holding a convention to debate the Constitution. Rhode Island would reluctantly join the Union after George Washington had been president for two months. North Carolina initially rejected the Constitution by a lopsided vote of 184 to 83. In New Hampshire a convention met, refused to ratify, and adjourned; four months later the delegates reconvened and voted yes, and on June 21, 1788, New Hampshire became the ninth state to ratify. The Constitution would now be the law of the land.

Ratification was a very close contest. If a total of just 3 percent of the delegates across Virginia, Massachusetts, and New York had changed their vote, the Constitution would have gone down to defeat. Americans came within a whisker of rejecting the Constitution that now defines the nation and its government. Figure 3.4 shows the number of men who signed several founding documents, by region, as well as the respective populations.

A Popular Surge Propels People into Politics

The Federalists ultimately won the constitutional debate and created a strong central government far removed from the people. At first it seemed as if Roger Sherman's "the people should have little to do with government" comment at the convention had won the day. But something unexpected happened. The Revolution

Signers by Document and Region, plus Population by Region

● **FIGURE 3.4** *This graph displays how many men from each region signed the founding documents: The Articles of Association called for a trade boycott against Britain in 1774; the Declaration of Independence, in 1776; the Articles of Confederation, signed between 1777 and 1781; and the Constitution, in 1787. Note the 1780 population count in each region. The middle states—New York, New Jersey, Pennsylvania, and Delaware—had a lot more participants than the other regions.*

set off a democratic surge that liberated popular energies. Not everyone was included in the Constitution's guarantees—not women, not Black people, not Native Americans. But the idea that ordinary citizens should be kept at arm's length from government was soon swamped by a great tide of participation that most founders neither imagined nor desired.[38] People raced to participate in both economic and political life. However, American history is not a simple story of ever-expanding participation. Rather, the battle for a more perfect union has been long and unpredictable. Over more than two centuries, rights, liberties, and democracy have been gained, lost, and gained again.

● *New York celebrated ratification by cheering Alexander Hamilton—still remembered as the major intellectual pressing for a strong central government. Here, global hit musical* Hamilton *recalls the most forceful Federalist. Original cast members, from left, Daveed Diggs, Okieriete Onaodowan, Anthony Ramos, and Lin-Manuel Miranda.*

THE BOTTOM LINE

» The debate over ratifying the Constitution featured two visions of American government.

» The Federalists argued that only an energetic national government could protect the nation and secure liberty. The Anti-Federalists called instead for a modest government that left power in state and local hands.

» The state-by-state voting on ratification was very close; it was well over a year before the Constitution was approved.

» Some 235 years later, Americans are still debating the same question: How strong should the federal government be?

Changing the Constitution

Although most Anti-Federalist leaders eventually rallied to the new Constitution, they insisted on a crucial addition to the Constitution: a bill of rights. The state ratification conventions proposed over two hundred amendments. When the first Congress met, in 1789, most members did not want to bother with amendments. The Constitution was ratified, Congress elected, and President George Washington's administration organized. However, one representative insisted on adding liberties to the Constitution. James Madison, during his tough House election campaign, pledged to support a bill of rights. With his word of honor at stake, Madison took the two hundred proposed amendments, boiled them down, and pushed his reluctant colleagues, who passed seventeen. The Senate reduced the list to twelve; the states ratified ten.

The Bill of Rights

Today, the first ten amendments to the Constitution, known as the **Bill of Rights**, form a crucial feature of American government. *These set out the rights and liberties—the protections from government—that every citizen is guaranteed.* Freedom of speech, freedom of the press, freedom of religion, the right to bear arms, and the long list of additional rights are an essential part of America's identity. Table 3.4 summarizes the amendments that make up the Bill of Rights.

Originally, the Bill of Rights applied only to the federal government. The First Amendment reads, "Congress shall make no law . . . abridging the freedom of speech." At the time, states that wanted to limit speech or set up an official religion were free to do so.

The Fourteenth Amendment, ratified after the Civil War in 1868 to protect the formerly enslaved people, commands that no *state* may deny "any person . . . the equal protection of the laws." In theory, this amendment extended the Bill of Rights to the states—meaning state governments must honor each right just as the national government must. However, the Fourteenth Amendment only kicked off a long process, known as **incorporation**: The Supreme Court applied (or "incorporated") each right to state government, one right at a time. That process continues still: The Supreme Court "incorporated" the right to bear arms in 2010 and protection against excessive fines in 2020. As a result, no state or city may

Bill of Rights: The first ten amendments to the Constitution, listing the rights guaranteed to every citizen.

Incorporation: The process by which the Supreme Court declares that a right in the Bill of Rights also applies to state governments.

TABLE 3.4 Summarizing the Bill of Rights

1. Congress may not establish a religion or prohibit the free exercise of religion; it may not abridge freedom of speech or of the press or of the people's right to assemble and to petition government.
2. Citizens have the right to bear arms.
3. No soldier may be quartered in any house without the consent of the owner.
4. There must be no unreasonable searches or seizures. Government authorities may not break into your house without a search warrant.
5. No one may be forced to testify against him- or herself (declining to do so is now known as "taking the Fifth"), and no one may be deprived of life, liberty, or property without due process of law. The government may not take private property (if, for example, it wants to build a highway) without just compensation.
6. Certain rights are guaranteed in criminal trials.
7. Accused persons are guaranteed the right to trial by jury.
8. The government may not force citizens to pay excessive bails, impose excessive fines, or impose cruel and unusual punishments.
9. The enumeration of certain rights does not diminish the other rights retained by the people.
10. Any powers not given to the federal government are reserved for the states and the people.

violate the Second Amendment right to bear arms or fund its police department by confiscating expensive possessions for minor drug offenses. The Third and Seventh Amendments have yet to be incorporated, and parts of others (the Fifth Amendment right to indictment by a grand jury) remain only applicable at the national level.[39]

Ratifying the Constitution and Bill of Rights was just the start of a long debate. We return to the story of the Constitution and individual rights in Chapter 5 and explore how they guide government today.

The Seventeen Amendments

After the Bill of Rights was passed, constitutional amendments became rare events—only seventeen have passed since 1791. Successful amendments all do at least one of four things: They *extend rights*—for example, guaranteeing the right to vote to eighteen-year-olds (seven amendments extend rights). They *adjust election rules*—for example, limiting the president to two terms (eleven amendments focus on elections). They *change government operations*—for example, switching Inauguration Day from March to January (four amendments focus on government rules). Or they *affect governmental powers over individuals*—for example, prohibiting alcohol and then (fourteen years later) permitting alcohol again. Table 3.5 summarizes the seventeen amendments that have been ratified since 1791: on average, one every 13.7 years.

Apart from formal amendments, American government—and how we interpret the Constitution—is always changing. We constantly debate how to apply the Constitution and its amendments to current issues. Should Congress limit the money corporations give political candidates? May a woman have an abortion? Does the First Amendment protect those advocating violent overthrow of the government? May universities consider an applicant's race in admissions decisions? Are governments free to require all citizens be vaccinated against a deadly

TABLE 3.5 **Amendments to the U.S. Constitution**

AMENDMENT	DESCRIPTION	YEAR RATIFIED	RESULT
11	Required state consent for individuals suing a state in federal court	1795	Modified government operations
12	Separated votes within the Electoral College for president and vice president	1804	Shifted election rules
13	Prohibited slavery	1865	Expanded individual rights
14	Provided citizenship to formerly enslaved people and declared that states could not deny civil rights, civil liberties, or the equal protection of the laws	1868	Expanded individual rights
15	Granted voting rights to members of all races	1870	Expanded individual rights
16	Permitted national income tax	1913	Expanded government powers over individuals
17	Provided direct election of senators	1913	Shifted election rules
18	Prohibited alcohol	1919	Expanded government powers over individuals
19	Extended the vote to women	1920	Expanded individual rights
20	Changed Inauguration Day from March to January	1933	Modified government operations
21	Repealed Prohibition	1933	Adjusted government powers over individuals
22	Limited president to two terms	1951	Shifted election rules
23	Extended the vote for president to citizens in Washington, DC	1961	Expanded individual rights
24	Prohibited a poll tax (one way to keep Black people from voting)	1964	Expanded individual rights
25	Established a succession plan in case of president's death or disability	1967	Modified government operations
26	Extended the vote to eighteen- to twenty-year-olds	1971	Expanded individual rights
27	Established that congressional pay raises could not go into effect until the next election	1992	Modified government operations

pandemic? The wording of the Constitution permits different interpretations. These questions—and many more—require Americans to reflect on what the Constitution tells us, more than two centuries after it was ratified.

The Constitution Today

The Constitution's ratification prepared the way for something no nation had done before: The United States organized a new government around a Constitution, written in the people's name and voted on by the people's representatives in every state. Celebrations broke out afterward, and the document has remained

A group of children pray together in their elementary school class. Does the Constitution permit prayer in public schools? Or would that mean the government was endorsing (or "establishing") a religion—violating the First Amendment? The issue is complex. For example, the Texas Attorney General sued to permit Bible quotes on one schoolhouse door but raised concerns about Muslim students reading the Koran. Recently, the Supreme Court has been far more accommodating to prayer in public places like schools.

Originalism: A principle of legal interpretation that relies on the original meaning of those who wrote the Constitution.

widely venerated ever since. "To live under the American Constitution," declared President Calvin Coolidge in the 1920s, "is the greatest political privilege that was ever accorded to the human race."[40] The document still guides American politics today. *Who are we?* Reading the U.S. Constitution is one important way to find out.

But Americans disagree, often heatedly, about how to read the Constitution. One view, called **originalism**, or strict construction, insists that Americans are bound to the literal meaning of the Constitution and its amendments, as their original authors understood them. From this perspective, the Constitution's meaning does not change with the times.

Another view was first articulated by Thomas Jefferson, who warned Americans not to view the Constitution with "sanctimonious reverence," as if it were "too sacred to be touched." The nation's founders should not be worshiped, he said, noting wryly that as one of the founders he was all too aware of their limitations. "I know also," concluded Jefferson, "that laws and institutions must go hand in hand with the progress of the human mind."[41] Many scholars and politicians have followed

WHAT DO YOU THINK?

How Strictly Should We Interpret the Constitution?

	I'm an originalist.	**I'm a pragmatist.**	**I'm in the middle.**
After considering the originalist and pragmatist approaches to interpreting the Constitution, choose a position.	Contemporary justices should not substitute their judgment for that of the Constitution's framers. We risk the arbitrary use of power if we permit everyone to read the Constitution as they like. Before long, the Constitution will mean nothing at all. When the Second Amendment protects the right to bear arms, for example, we must interpret that literally and allow individuals to purchase and carry guns.	Times change and conditions evolve. The modern world imposes challenges (and features new technologies) that the framers could not have imagined. The document cannot be an eighteenth-century straitjacket. The founders' idea of the right to bear arms protected state militias, not individual gun owners. We should consider the historical context when we interpret the Constitution.	I believe the difference between these positions is less stark than it appears. Even if we strive to get back to the document's original meaning, we always read the Constitution in light of the present. Every interpretation will be guided by our own ideas and our times. (We will come back to the Second Amendment debate in Chapter 5.)

Amend the Constitution Today?

On What Issue?

In the more than 230 years since the Bill of Rights was ratified, just seventeen more amendments to the U.S. Constitution have been adopted—the most recent in 1992. Yet proposals keep coming, with more than 850 introduced in the U.S. House or Senate over the past dozen years. Here are the most frequently proposed amendments over this period.

THINK ABOUT IT

What issues do most proposed amendments address? Which of these would you support? Why or why not?

....

If you could propose a constitutional amendment not on this list, what would the subject be? Protecting data privacy? Abolishing the income tax? Dismantling structural racism? Send your best idea to your senators or representative, and just maybe they will introduce it in the next session of Congress!

Source: Pew Research Center

Balanced budget is the most frequently proposed constitutional amendment since 1999

Most common subjects of proposed amendments, 1999–2018

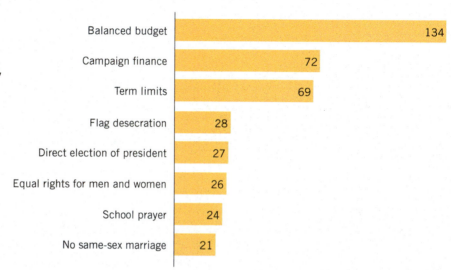

Subject	Count
Balanced budget	134
Campaign finance	72
Term limits	69
Flag desecration	28
Direct election of president	27
Equal rights for men and women	26
School prayer	24
No same-sex marriage	21

Jefferson's advice. They see a living, breathing, changing Constitution—one that speaks differently to each generation. This view of an evolving Constitution is known as **pragmatism**. *We cannot help bringing our own background, ideas, and judgments to bear as we think about the meaning of the document.*

As we will see throughout this book, it is often hard to tell exactly how the Constitution applies to our times. Different readers come to very different conclusions—even if they are searching for the original meaning. In the end, the difference between originalism and pragmatism may not be as large as proponents think.

Pragmatism: A principle of legal interpretation based on an evolving Constitution; interpreting the document must acknowledge contemporary realities.

THE BOTTOM LINE

» The Bill of Rights comprises the first ten amendments to the Constitution, which define the rights of American citizens.

» Seventeen more amendments (out of more than one hundred thousand proposals) followed over the next 230-plus years.

» Even amid vast changes, the Constitution still stands as the American political rulebook. However, the Constitution must be interpreted: It is often unclear what the document means and how it applies to contemporary cases.

Conclusion: Does the Constitution Still Work?

Every chapter that follows will focus on a different feature of the Constitution as it operates today—federalism, civil rights, Congress, the presidency, and so on. As you explore these institutions, keep asking: Does the world's oldest constitution still work? Most Americans believe that it does. That is why it has lasted so long. But some disagree. Robert Dahl, a much-revered political scientist, argued that the Constitution is not democratic enough.[42] It ignores many modern rights. Checks and balances are sometimes too cumbersome, making it difficult to pass needed laws. Congress no longer checks the president when it comes to war. The general effect, explained Dahl, is to diminish American democracy.

The debate takes us back to the very first question we asked in Chapter 1. Who governs? Do the people rule? Or do the rich and powerful wield the real power? These are questions that every chapter will address.

Regardless of whether you are an *originalist*, a *pragmatist*, or in between, check what the Constitution says every time you study another feature of U.S. government. Start with the Constitution to grasp the basic rules of American politics—and if you're looking to achieve significant political change, you'll find both the possible pathways and roadblocks there.

CHAPTER SUMMARY

★ The Constitution provides the ground rules for American politics. However, it is often unclear how the Constitution applies to contemporary issues. We must interpret its meaning.

★ The colonial experience prepared America for a constitution. The English practice of salutary neglect permitted the colonies to develop their own political institutions, centered on their legislatures. Americans became used to delegated, or actual, representation (reflecting voter sentiment), which contrasted with the British view of trustee, or virtual, representation (representing the whole nation regardless of public opinion).

★ The Declaration of Independence has two parts. First, it states the American ideal: All people "are created equal" and "endowed by their Creator with certain unalienable rights" including "life, liberty, and the pursuit of happiness." Second, it lists colonial grievances, emphasizing the rights of free people to elect their legislatures.

★ The first American government, under the Articles of Confederation, was an alliance of independent states that maximized popular participation. This government had some great successes, but many felt that it was too weak and left the United States vulnerable to foreign powers.

⭐ The Constitutional Convention, convened to fix the problems with the first American government, focused on six broad issues: popular involvement, national versus state power, big versus small states, checks and balances, the presidency, and slavery.

⭐ Ratification of the Constitution involved an extremely close battle between Anti-Federalists, who opposed the Constitution, and Federalists, who supported it. The first ten amendments, known as the Bill of Rights, came out of the ratification debates and were approved by the First Congress. Seventeen more amendments have followed since. American politics has changed enormously, but the Constitution remains the basic blueprint for American political life.

KEY TERMS

Bicameral, p. 80
Bill of Rights, p. 97
Classical republicanism, p. 92
Compact, p. 65
Confederation, p. 73
Constitution p. 63
Covenant, p. 65
Delegate representation, p. 67

Electoral College, p. 82
Federalism, p. 79
First Continental Congress, p. 70
Incorporation, p. 97
Indentured servant, p. 65
Mercantilism, p. 69
New Jersey Plan, p. 80
Originalism, p. 100

Pragmatism, p. 101
Second Continental Congress, p. 71
Supermajority, p. 74
Trustee representation, p. 68
Unicameral, p. 80
Virginia Plan, p. 80

STUDY QUESTIONS

1. Describe five ways that the colonial experience prepared the United States for a constitution.
2. Winning the French and Indian War drove two wedges between England and the colonies. What were they?
3. What is the difference between delegate (actual) representation and trustee (virtual) representation? How did the difference lead to the American Revolution?

Optional assignment: A Virginia colonist and a member of the English Parliament furiously debate the true nature of representation. You overhear them. Describe what each says during the debate. Try to make both sides sound reasonable.

4. What are the five overarching ideas introduced by the Declaration of Independence? In your opinion, how well are we achieving those aspirations today?
5. Describe the first government that Americans organized after declaring independence. Where was most of the power located? What problems arose under this government? What was successful?
6. When it came to writing the Constitution, the delegates had to balance two fears. One emerged from the battle with England, the other from American experience under the Articles of Confederation. Describe each fear.
7. What did Madison mean by "filtration of representatives"? List two examples of filtration in the original Constitution.

What do you think? Would you support filtration or the direct election of representatives?

8. Describe the differences between the Virginia Plan and the New Jersey Plan. If you had to vote for one or the other in 1787, which would you choose, and why?
9. Describe what the Constitution says about the following:

How the House of Representatives is elected.
How the president is elected.
How the Supreme Court is chosen.
How amendments can be added to the Constitution.

10. Describe the differences between the Federalists and the Anti-Federalists. Which side would you be on? Why?

Optional assignment: Choose one of the thirteen original states. Write a speech to be presented before its ratifying convention arguing for or against the new constitution.

4 FEDERALISM

THE REPORTER SPED ALONG A RURAL ROAD,

moving fast because it was election night in Texas, and he was facing a deadline. Then he heard the police siren. The sheriff pulled him over and walked slowly up to his car. "Young man," he said, leaning down and removing his sunglasses, "did you know that you were driving thirty miles over the speed limit?" Jose Antonio Vargas—who would win a Pulitzer Prize for outstanding reporting the following month—peed in his pants. As an undocumented immigrant, he was terrified. This traffic stop could result in his deportation back to the Philippines—a country he had left when he was twelve years old. This time, Jose lucked out. The sheriff's phone rang, and he said, "I gotta head back to the station. I'm gonna let you go. Slow down, young man."[1]

There are roughly eleven million undocumented people in the United States, about one out of every thirty Americans. Like Jose Vargas, most live in constant worry—any moment could mean detention and possible deportation. In response, more than five hundred cities and seven states (with a combined population of seventy-two million) have declared themselves "sanctuary" or "safe" havens: The police do not ask about legal status during routine encounters. That way, undocumented individuals can rely on vital services and protections—police, hospitals, schools, and so on. Many Americans argue that offering sanctuary protects the basic human rights that everyone deserves.

Others fiercely oppose the idea of sanctuary cities. They argue that undocumented immigrants take jobs away from American citizens and that by condoning unauthorized immigration, sanctuary cities compromise the rule of law. They further insist that the existence of undocumented immigrants divides society and makes it more difficult to win higher wages and expand social welfare policies—a fear expressed in many other countries worldwide, as well as in the United States.[2]

The Constitution gives the federal government—not the cities or states—authority over immigration. President Donald Trump vested expanded powers in the Immigration and Customs Enforcement (ICE) agency and made opposition to illegal immigration a signature issue of his administration.[3]

However, states and cities have primary responsibility over law enforcement. Proponents of the sanctuary movement insist that local officials have

● *Agents from U.S. Immigration and Customs Enforcement conduct raids on people without documents. They are officers of the national government who sometimes cooperate and sometimes clash with state and local government authorities. American federalism: creativity, cooperation, conflict, and a touch of chaos.*

In this chapter, you will

 Learn what federalism is.

 Discover how important federalism is for American government.

 Explore the strengths and weaknesses of federal and state governments.

 Examine how federalism works—and how it has evolved.

 Review the contemporary challenges of federalism.

 Explore American nationalism.

the authority to guide police practices. But this raises a further wrinkle: The state and city governments sometimes disagree. In Texas, for example, cities like Houston, Dallas, and San Antonio moved to protect undocumented people. In 2017, the state legislature pushed back and passed a law requiring local officials to cooperate with federal immigration law. A year later the Texas attorney general sued the city of San Antonio for violating the Texas statute. Stop and think about that: A state sued one of its own cities for opposing a *federal* policy.

When the Joe Biden administration came into office, it put a freeze on deporting undocumented people. Now, Texas turned around and sued the national government for not enforcing the law. Texas won its case against the freeze, but deportations still plummeted from 234,000 a year (under President Trump) to just 59,000 in President Biden's first year.

Welcome to American federalism. Federalism is simply *the division of power between national, state, and local government.* As you can already see from the immigration debate, the lines of authority between federal, state, and local government are all tangled up. This is unusual among countries. Some give most power to the national government (like France), others to the states or provinces (like Canada). But almost none mix it up quite like the United States.

Who governs? Every level of American government, from the largest (national) to the smallest (town and county), governs. The different levels of government share power, work together to solve problems, squabble over what to do, wrestle over funds, and vie for control. In the United States, most problems and programs fall under multiple jurisdictions. Responsibility across levels of government is often blurred and constantly renegotiated.

Chapter 3 highlighted the constitutional checks and balances between Congress, the executive, and the courts. Federalism involves an even more intricate balancing act. The interplay between national and state governments stretches all the way back to the founding era. The debate over adopting the Constitution pitted Federalists (who wanted a strong national government) against Anti-Federalists (who sought more power for the states). More than two centuries later, the debate continues.

Who are we? A nation of divided loyalties and governments. We are from the United States *and* Florida *and* Miami, or Michigan *and* Detroit. The results are innovation, liberty, and confusion. Fast-spreading coronavirus cases in American cities, wildfires in California, an outbreak of food poisoning in the Midwest, or a mass shooting in Uvalde, Texas, bring out local authorities, state officials, and national agencies, all scrambling to get on the same wavelength. The same goes for addressing the opioid epidemic, setting the minimum wage, protecting clean water, deciding what to teach in public schools, and legalizing pot. Federalism is ingrained in our Constitution, our institutions, and our national culture.

This chapter explains how federalism works. The story in a nutshell: Federalism is a source of creativity and innovation, but it makes effective and efficient governance far more difficult.

BY THE NUMBERS Federalism

1 Number of national governments

50 Number of state governments

3,031 Number of county or parish governments

87,044 Number of town or city governments or districts

2.8 Number, in millions, of nonmilitary personnel who work for the federal government[4]

5.1 Number, in millions, who work for state governments[5]

13.9 Number, in millions, who work for local governments[6]

53 Percentage of Americans who say they trust their national government to do what is right most of the time[7]

62 Percentage of Americans who say they trust their state government to do what is right most of the time[8]

72 Percentage of Americans who say they trust their local government to do what is right most of the time[9]

Why do you think Americans trust local government the most? Which level do you trust the most? The least?

Where Did Federalism Come From?

Early American government began on the state level—although at the time the states were called colonies. For 150 years, the people were primarily citizens of Virginia or Pennsylvania or New York. When Americans revolted against England, they had to unite thirteen very different places—now called states—under a single national government. History gave them two choices about how to organize their political system: a unitary government or a confederation. After trying each, the Americans invented a third approach.

Most nations in the 1780s had **unitary governments**. The national government—the king and Parliament in England, for example—made decisions for the whole nation. Local governments simply carried out their decrees. To this day, most nations are organized this way. Local government is an administrative extension of national government. Because Americans rebelled against Britain's unitary government, most did not want to reintroduce the same system all over again.

Unitary government: A national polity governed as a single unit, with the central government exercising most political authority.

Confederation: A group of independent states or nations that yield some of their powers to a national government, with each state retaining a degree of sovereign authority.

A second traditional form, **confederation**, leaves most power in the states or provinces, while a weak central authority provides common defense, economic policy, and general direction. Today, Switzerland leaves most decisions to its cantons and Canada governs primarily through its provinces. The European Union is struggling to turn very different nations from Portugal to Poland into a confederation. When the United States first broke from England, they tried this format under the Articles of Confederation. As we saw in Chapter 3, after a very heated debate, the nation decided that their confederation was too weak.

At the Constitutional Convention, the delegates devised a hybrid: a *federal system* in which power is shared between national and state governments. The Constitution gives some decisions to the national government (e.g., declaring war, coining money); it leaves others with the states (building schools, enforcing the laws); and many decisions are made at both levels (raising taxes, running courts, regulating business, allocating rights). Over time, the shared tasks mushroomed. Because each level is independent and their powers overlap, conflict is built into the system.

To complicate matters further, the United States also has independent local governments at the town, city, and county levels. These add still more layers of government—more elected officials, more experts, more taxes, more services, and more decision makers around the table. However, local governments are *not* sovereign units. Local jurisdictions derive their authority from the states.

Dillon's rule: Local governments may only exercise powers expressly granted to it by the state.

Back in 1868, Iowa Supreme Court Justice John Dillon ruled that local governments are an extension of state governments and may only exercise powers that the state expressly gives them. This is known as **Dillon's rule**—the Supreme Court affirmed it forty years later.[10] Some states (like New Hampshire and North Carolina) grant their local governments broad powers—known as **home rule**. Others (like New York and Virginia) jealously hold onto authority and approve or reject every local government action. As one famous description sums it up: "A city cannot operate a peanut stand at the city zoo without first getting the state legislature to [approve]."[11]

Home rule: States delegate authority to their cities, towns, and counties permitting them to govern themselves.

Here's an example of Dillon's rule in action: In 2007, New York City determined it would charge tolls on vehicles during busy hours to cut down on congestion and pollution in the city. The stakeholders negotiated an agreement, the city council adopted a plan, and the public approved of the plan, 67 percent to 27 percent. Then, the state assembly shot it down. The debate raged on for more than a decade before the state finally approved the proposal in 2018.[12] Another twist on American federalism: Cities lobby the state government for permission to enact policies in the cities. And the federal government also gets involved—in the case of the New York City tolls, it delayed the implementation of congestion pricing, at least until 2023.

Over time, states have slowly extended home rule—granting more authority to their cities. All the overlap and conflict between federal and state governments gets replicated—sometimes with even more intensity—between state and local governments.

On the surface, the state and local governments might seem to have a built-in advantage in any conflict with the national government. As Figure 4.1 shows, the more local the government, the more the people trust it. But the federal government has more resources, more expertise, and more capacity to address big problems that cross state and even national borders—like pollution, terrorism, economic slowdowns, and airline safety.

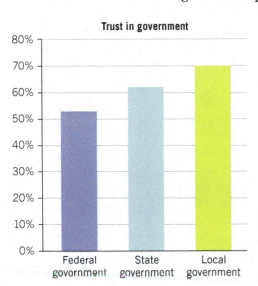

FIGURE 4.1 *Trust in government gets stronger as government gets closer to the public. (Gallup Poll, 2021)*

THE BOTTOM LINE

» The United States rebelled against a *unitary* system and rejected a *federation* after trying one for a decade.

» The Constitutional Convention created a new hybrid form of government: a federal system of shared and overlapping power. Power is divided and shared between national and state governments.

» American federalism is further complicated by local governments. Their authority to act comes from the state governments.

» American federalism in a nutshell: Governments on the national, state, and local level sharing authority and sometimes cooperating, sometimes competing.

Who Should Wield Government Authority?

A federal system constantly poses the same question: Who should wield authority? Political scientists see some advantages to leaving things up to the states. And others for making decisions on the national level.[13]

Advantages of State-Level Policy

First, proponents of state-level policy argue that states are *more responsive* to residents' needs and desires. The United States is a vast nation spanning states with very different problems and attitudes. Maine and Minnesota do not need to regulate water in the same way as desert states such as Arizona and Nevada. Large cities may try to curb gang violence with gun buy-back programs that rural areas would likely reject. Citizens of Delaware expect more government services (and pay higher taxes) than people in Florida. In short, state and local government can match policies to local conditions and values without a "one-size-fits-all" national policy.

Second, states sometimes offer more *protection for individual rights*. Same-sex couples found success on the state level long before federal officials were willing to support their right to marry. In the nineteenth century, national officials ridiculed the idea of women voting while feminists were busy winning suffrage across the western states. On the other hand, states violently denied Black people the right to vote, forcing reformers to take the fight to the national level (we explore all these topics in Chapters 5 and 6).

Third, federalism fosters *political innovation*. Different states can experiment with new programs, trying them out on the local and state levels before they get debated on the national level. Supreme Court Justice Louis Brandeis put it famously: "A single courageous State may . . . serve as a laboratory; and try novel social and economic experiments without risk to the rest of the country."[14] Ever since, states in a federal system have been called "laboratories of democracy"— allowing testing of policy options. Throughout American history, innovations have bubbled up locally, often diffusing from state to state, before going national. The list includes Social Security pensions for retirees, environmental protection laws, direct election of senators, welfare reform, child nutrition programs, alcohol prohibition, bankruptcy laws, and regulations for self-driving cars. This process of testing and spreading ideas is known as **diffusion**.

Diffusion: The spreading of policy ideas from one city or state to others, a process typical of U.S. federalism.

● Congress debates whether and how to regulate self-driving cars. States were first to pass such regulations, which vary from strong (in California and Pennsylvania, for example) to weaker (Arizona). Eventually, national officials may learn from the state experience and adopt national standards.

Unfortunately, diffusion can also spread dangerous ideas. Voting restrictions on Black voters spread from Mississippi to the entire South after 1890. Some conservatives worry that legalized gambling and decriminalized drug use spread moral danger. Meanwhile, some liberals charge that voting restrictions on people of color are rising again, leading two political scientists to spin Brandeis's phrase by tagging the states "laboratories of authoritarianism."[15] In short, all kinds of ideas—good, bad, and ugly—spread from innovative states.

Finally, a more controversial point: Some argue that federalism gives people more *choices*. Each state offers a different bundle of costs and services (see Figure 4.2). People who want or need many government services can

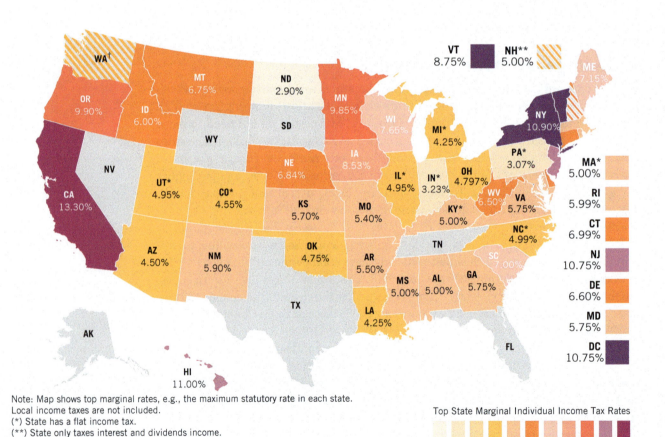

Note: Map shows top marginal rates, e.g., the maximum statutory rate in each state. Local income taxes are not included.
(*) State has a flat income tax.
(**) State only taxes interest and dividends income.
(†) State only taxes capital gains income.

Top State Marginal Individual Income Tax Rates

Lower   Higher

● **FIGURE 4.2** *Individual income tax rates in each state. Note the vast differences: Earn $100 in North Dakota, and state taxes peel off less than $3; in California, more than $13 goes to the state treasury. Seven states, colored gray on the map, levy no income taxes; two others tax only dividends and interest income. Here's the tough question: Can Americans really pick up and move to a state that reflects their own values? (Tax Foundation)*

Education Policies

Teaching About Race

The responsibility for education falls largely on state and local governments, and school policies often ignite conflicts over values and cultures. After the *New York Times* sponsored the 1619 Project tracing the legacy of slavery in American history, the issue exploded into the education curriculum.

Thirty-five states passed or proposed restrictions on what local schools could teach about race and American history, in some cases withholding funds from school districts where teachers emphasize "institutional racism, white privilege, and critical race theory." On the other side, seventeen states have passed or proposed laws and rules that expand the teaching about the history of race, ethnicity, sexual identity, or Indigenous people.

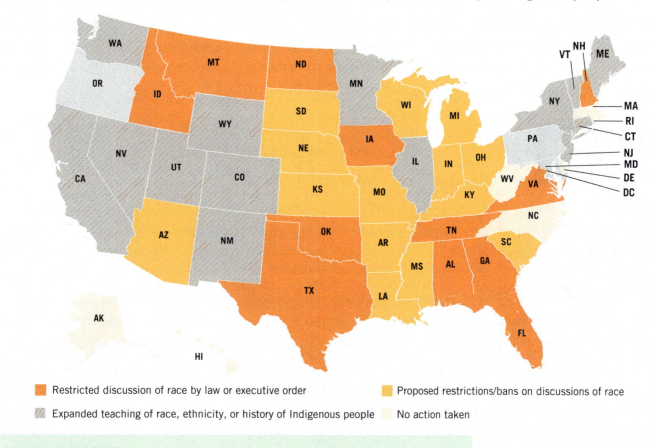

■ Restricted discussion of race by law or executive order   ■ Proposed restrictions/bans on discussions of race

▨ Expanded teaching of race, ethnicity, or history of Indigenous people   ☐ No action taken

THINK ABOUT IT

What has your state done to date? Is it expanding or restricting education about race?

....

How do you think states should approach the teaching of race in public schools?

....

And what about the essential federalism question: Who should be responsible for what is taught in public schools?

....

Should the federal government establish guidelines? Or the states? Local school districts? Parents? Or teachers and historians?

move to Connecticut or Alaska. Those who want a more limited government can choose the South or the red states of the Rocky Mountain West. Likewise, people who care about tough environmental standards can choose places with stringent rules such as California or Oregon.

This last point is disputed. Opponents point out that many Americans are not free to simply move—they have children in school, aging parents to take care of, or important ties to their community. If a policy is a good one, they argue, all Americans deserve to enjoy it—which brings us to the advantages of national policies.

Advantages of National Policy

First, national policy is often fairer than state or local policies. A single mother working full time for minimum wage can be treated for breast cancer under New York's Medicaid program but is not eligible for any treatment in Texas. Health advocates charge that this discrepancy is unjust and call for uniform national policies. Likewise, environmentalists argue that every citizen should have clean air and clean water, regardless of their state's history of supporting regulation; they also note that air and water pollution don't stop at state boundaries. Gun rights advocates point to the inconsistencies between Ohio, which permits residents to openly carry firearms; New Jersey, which requires a license for

WHAT DO YOU THINK?

Preserving Local Values or Promoting Consistent National Policy?

In 2014, Colorado permitted adults to buy up to an ounce of marijuana in licensed stores. Nine years later, seventeen states and the District of Columbia had followed Colorado's lead and legalized recreational marijuana. But federal laws outlaw the possession, manufacture, and sale of marijuana. In Colorado you can legally grow ninety-nine plants, in California you're limited to six, and in Idaho possession of an ounce is a felony. Should we leave marijuana use to the states, or insist on a national standard?

I'm a federalist; leave to each state to decide.
Because cultures differ by state, marijuana regulation should be handled state by state. Socially progressive states should have the right to legalize marijuana. Other states can learn from their experiments, assess the advantages and the disadvantages, and decide what policies to adopt. In fact, this is the laboratory of democracy at work: Legalization and decriminalization are spreading rapidly, even to traditionally conservative states.

I'm a nationalist; we should have one consistent standard.
The patchwork of changing laws—sometimes within a single state—is both confusing and counterproductive. Furthermore, the legalization of pot might negatively affect nearby states as stoned drivers and tainted merchandise cross borders. The national government should establish a policy that is best for all Americans.

Not sure.
On this, like other policies raised in this chapter, it can be hard to choose one side. Perhaps you would have stronger feelings about other illegal drugs like heroin—should they be controlled by national, state, or local laws?

handguns and forbids "open carry" of rifles and shotguns; and Massachusetts, which requires a license for any firearm. Finally, America's racial experience suggests that, at least sometimes, national decisions are required to overcome local prejudices.

This desire for fairness leads critics to worry that competition between states and localities leads to a *race to the bottom*. Leave social welfare policy to the states, argue defenders of national standards, and the result is a bidding war in which each state tries to cut programs (and taxes) more than neighboring states to attract middle-class people and new business. Although the race to the bottom hypothesis is hard to measure, social scientists have found some evidence that states do follow one another as programs are cut and benefits are reduced.[16]

Second, national policies can *equalize resources across the nation*. Every time there is a crisis—a hurricane, a terrorist attack, a wildfire, or a healthcare pandemic—all eyes turn to the U.S. government, which can bring more resources and expertise than individual states can. Support from Washington also can make day-to-day policies work across all fifty states. That way, even poorer states can obtain the resources they need.

Third, national policies can *standardize best practices* across the nation. After new policies are tested in the state "laboratories of democracy," a national policy can spread the lessons to everyone. Minimum standards ensure that no state chooses inadequate health or education policies for its children.

Finally, leaving authority in state hands introduces *problems of coordination* among federal, state, and local agencies. All respond to crises. All address chronic problems such as poverty, pollution, and crime. Simply getting every first responder onto the same communication frequency has taken many years and millions of dollars. With many different agencies responding to multiple layers of authorities, using different procedures, and trying to achieve slightly different goals, the result can be chaos. A patchwork of rules and regulations across the states can leave citizens and national companies bewildered about which rules apply where.

In sum, the ambiguity in federalism sets up a constant dispute about where to place authority. Do we leave decisions with the states because they are closer to the people? Or do we place them on the national level to try to promote equality and high standards across the country, even if local people resent them? For many Americans, the answer shifts with the issue.

Should federal laws outlawing marijuana possession override state efforts to decriminalize it? Liberals generally say no and support local choice. Should government programs provide health insurance for people with low incomes? Now most liberals switch sides and say yes, while conservatives want to leave it to the states.

Here's another twist: When a conservative administration governs, liberals discover the value of state governments, while conservatives learn to love national regulations.

Finally, the crucial point: These debates are all built into our federal institutions and are an integral part of our federalist system. *Federalism gives advocates many different political venues in which to address problems, challenge policies, and assert rights.* When people lose at one level, they can switch to another.

THE BOTTOM LINE

» The most important debate in federalism concerns where to place responsibility—on the state or national level.

» State-level policy has at least four advantages: It responds to local needs, enables innovation in the laboratories of democracy, protects individual rights, and enhances individual choice.

» National-level policy also has four main advantages: It enhances fairness (avoiding a race to the bottom), equalizes resources, promotes national standards and best practices, and facilitates coordination.

» Understanding the pros and cons of federalism is important as we decide whether to create national standards and programs or whether to leave judgment to local populations. This question is generally decided issue by issue and program by program.

 # How Federalism Works

So far this chapter's message is clear: Federalism offers endless opportunities for discord, confusion, and creativity, as different layers of government tussle over who has responsibility for what. However, there are well-defined patterns to this contest. Americans have hammered out rules that enable our federalist system to function pretty well most of the time. These rules evolve with time and are not always clear or straightforward. Even the terminology can be elusive: Americans routinely call the national government the "federal government," a practice we sometimes follow in this book, even though that term formally refers to the whole system of shared powers stretching across national, state, and local units.

The Constitution Sets the Ground Rules

Whenever you're trying to figure out something about American politics, the first step is to look at the Constitution. What does it say about federalism? Well, whether you want to empower an active national government or restrict the national government in favor of the states, you will find support in the Constitution. Let's look at the magic clauses—first those that empower and then those that limit the national government.

Delegated powers:
National government authority listed explicitly in the Constitution.

Commerce clause: The Constitutional declaration (in Article 1, Section 8) empowering Congress to regulate commerce with foreign nations, between states, and with Indian tribes.

The Constitution Grants National Authority. Article 1, Section 8, lists nineteen powers vested in the national government: Congress has the authority to pay debts, raise an army, punish pirates, establish a post office, handle U.S. foreign policy, and so forth. Because they are set out in black and white, we call these **delegated powers**—also known as *expressed* or *enumerated powers* (you can read them in the Constitution in Appendix II). This section of the Constitution lists the national government powers.

An especially important enumerated power grants the national government authority over international and interstate commerce. How far does that authority extend? A permissive reading gives Congress power over everything touched by goods shipped between states. For example, Congress used the **commerce clause** to forbid racial discrimination in restaurants—after all, their salt and sugar come from out of state. In this view, commerce can mean any profitable activity or even social interactions. Read this way, the clause permits the federal government to do a lot of different things, from desegregating restaurants to requiring that you have health insurance. "Wait a minute," respond people who favor a tighter reading. The commerce clause applies only to trade between states, they say; it's limited to passengers and cargo.

The final clause of Section 8 adds another ambiguity by authorizing Congress to make all laws *necessary and proper* for carrying out the delegated powers—*or any other power the Constitution vests in the national government*. The **necessary and proper clause** is also known as the *elastic clause* because it stretches national government authority. Over two centuries, the elastic clause—especially when combined with the interstate commerce clause—has expanded national authority to include everything from creating banks to regulating airlines to overseeing zoos. These new areas of jurisdiction are known as **implied powers**—powers that are implied by, but not specifically named in, the Constitution's text.

The **supremacy clause**, found near the end of the Constitution in Article 6, buttresses these granted (or explicit) and implied powers. The clause declares that the national government's laws and treaties are the "supreme law of the land," superior to state laws whenever the two clash. But there's a catch. The supremacy clause only holds for powers actually granted to the national government. As you can see, fierce debates (and many court cases) turn on when national officials indeed hold the authority to overturn state decisions.

Federal officials also wield a third set of powers known as **inherent powers.** They are not explicitly named or even implied in the Constitution. Instead, they are logical extensions of powers granted to the president or Congress, powers that national officials need to do their jobs. For example, the federal government tracks communicable diseases such as COVID-19, decides whether to acquire new territory, issues storm warnings, and sometimes intervenes in labor strikes. All rely on inherent powers rather than a clear or implied constitutional statement. Again, there is intense debate about how far these powers extend.

The Constitution Protects State Authority.   At the same time, the states have their own authority guaranteed by the Tenth Amendment—the final amendment in the Bill of Rights that "reserves" to the states all powers not specifically granted to the national branches in Washington. Small government conservatives emphasize this amendment and, in 2018, proposed a Tenth Amendment Restoration Act: Review every national executive agency (the Environmental Protection Agency, the National Weather Service, the National Aeronautics and Space Administration [NASA], and so on right down the bureaucratic roster) to determine whether its existence violates the Tenth Amendment. If so, the agency would be eliminated. The bill failed, but it illustrates the political importance of the Tenth Amendment.

What powers does the Tenth Amendment reserve for the states? Traditionally, the states' **reserved powers** include public education, public health, public morality, commerce within the state, and organizing elections.

Necessary and proper clause: The constitutional declaration (in Article 1, Section 8) of Congress's authority to exercise the "necessary and proper" powers to carry out its designated functions.

Implied powers: National government powers implied by, but not specifically named in, the Constitution.

Supremacy clause: The constitutional declaration (in Article 6, Section 2) that the national government's authority prevails over any conflicting state or local government's claims, provided the power is granted to the federal government.

Inherent powers: Powers neither specified nor implied by the Constitution, but judged necessary for the president or Congress to fulfill their duties.

Reserved powers: The constitutional guarantee (in the Tenth Amendment) that the states retain governmental authority not explicitly granted to the national government.

● *Federalism and speed limits. Permitting each state to set its own rules can reflect local culture and attitudes—from the meticulous Minnesotans (65.5) to aggressive New Yorkers (Limit this!) to no-rules Nevada (bat-out-of-hell). It's all in fun, of course, but the cartoon does make the point that federalism gives us more choices—and a bit of chaos.*

Police, prisons, and local courts are also in the state's hands. State and local officials carry out most investigations, arrests, trials, and incarcerations—unless a federal law has been violated. Most court cases are adjudicated in state courts, and state prisons and local jails hold nearly 90 percent of the inmates in the United States. Still, in actual practice, all these areas—education, health, police, morality—see some overlap between federal, state, and local action.

The Constitution Authorizes Shared Power. Federalism is not just about tension between government levels. State and national authorities properly share many responsibilities, termed **concurrent powers**. Both national and state governments have the power to raise taxes, build roads, construct bridges, build railways, update telecommunications networks, borrow money, and regulate business. The next time you are stuck in traffic inching past a sign announcing new transportation construction, look closely: You will usually see a combination of national, state, and local funds listed in support.

Federalism also involves relations among the states. The Constitution directs each state to give **full faith and credit** to the actions of other states. For example, your driver's license, issued in your home state, is honored everywhere else in the United States.

The Constitution also sets up some definite barriers for the states. A state may not launch its own navy, sign treaties with another country, or coin its own money. The Bill of Rights—though it originally applied only to the federal government—imposes a long list of limits on government in the name of individual rights and freedoms. In short, the Constitution empowers and limits both the national and the state governments. Figure 4.3 illustrates powers shared by and reserved to the different levels of government.

Emphasizing some parts of the Constitution—inherent powers, the interstate commerce clause, the necessary and proper clause, the supremacy clause—justifies a robust national government. This reading of the Constitution enables a national

Concurrent powers: Governmental authority shared by national and state governments, such as the power to tax residents.

Full faith and credit clause: The constitutional requirement (in Article 4, Section 1) that each state recognizes and upholds laws passed by any other state.

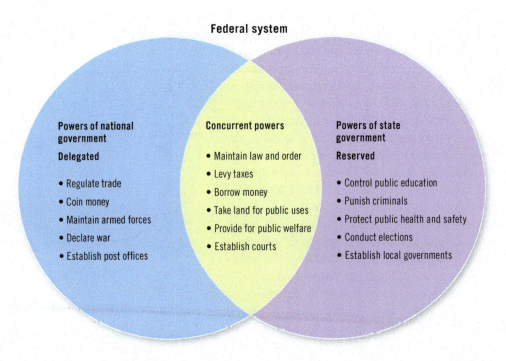

● **FIGURE 4.3** *The Constitution delegates some powers to the federal government, reserves some to the states, and allocates some to both. Those joint (or concurrent) powers have stretched dramatically over the years.*

American federalism
Layer cake, marble cake, or super-swirl cake?

Layer cake federalism
has a clear division of
governing authority between
national and state governments.

Marble cake federalism
mingles governing authority with
functions overlapping across
national and state governments.

Super-swirl cake federalism
extensively mingles government
authority as partisans try to influence
policies by shifting functions between
national and state governments.

● **FIGURE 4.4** *Different federalist styles throughout U.S. history.*

government that regulates toxic spills, forbids racial discrimination, enforces airport security, authorizes strong action against pandemics, signs people up for health insurance, and prosecutes the war on drugs. Emphasize other clauses (like the Tenth Amendment) or interpret the commerce clause narrowly (it only applies to trade between states) and you end up with a more modest national government that defers to the people of each state. That reading leaves states alone to decide environmental rules or regulate state universities.

Again, we return to a vital point: American government is a perpetual argument, a constant work in progress. The Constitution's ground rules for federalism are open to interpretation and reinterpretation. They have guided a long, often creative debate about which level of government should be doing what.

Over time, Americans have organized federalism in very different ways. The next section describes the three major eras.

The Layer Cake: Dual Federalism (1789–1933)

For its first 150 years or so, the United States practiced a form of **dual federalism,** in which state and national governments had relatively clear responsibilities. The state governments wielded at least as much authority as the federal government. American historians with an eye for metaphor describe this arrangement as "layer cake" federalism: The different levels of government—national, state, and local—exercised powers that fell, more or less, into separate layers. Each level of government was supreme within its own band of influence (Figure 4.4).

This division of labor left the national government in charge of three major areas. First, international relations—trade, war, diplomacy, and immigration. This was a big role, as the United States deployed troops overseas 165 times in its first 150 years—and that count does not include the long, bloody series of conflicts with Native American tribes.

Second, the national government was responsible for "internal improvements" such as transportation, a single currency, and overseeing westward expansion. In early America, it was cheaper to ship iron from London to Philadelphia than it was to move it fifty miles inland from Philadelphia. Developing transportation networks—roads, canals, and railroads—solved the problem of moving freight (and people). The U.S. post office united an increasingly far-flung people and placed at least one federal official—the postmaster—in every village across the nation.

Dual federalism: Also called layer cake federalism, the clear division of governing authority between national and state governments.

● *Constructing canals, bridges, roads—and later, railroads—was a major national government responsibility in the nineteenth century. So was delivering the mail, a task that briefly included the famous Pony Express.*

Finally, the federal government regulated relations and commerce between the states. This became an explosive issue when slave states demanded assistance in capturing men and women running for their freedom.

During this era, states retained control over almost everything having to do with individual citizens. The states oversaw education, marriage, divorce, professional regulation, business contracts, driving, drinking, and burials. To this day, state governments wield the primary responsibility over individual behavior, although the federal government now touches most of these matters directly or indirectly.

The layer cake was never quite as clear-cut as the metaphor suggests. The national government distributed land in the west. It wrestled endlessly over slavery before the Civil War and the rights of free people after the war. In the 1870s, it used control of interstate commerce to crack down on pornography, restrict contraception, and fight abortion. In 1920, the Eighteenth Amendment forbade the transportation and sale of intoxicating liquors. State and national authorities had overlapping jurisdiction in enforcing this act[17]—and when states like New York decided to ignore the ban on selling liquor, federal officials stepped in to enforce it (a 1920s version of today's drug wars). Still, despite many exceptions, government activity remained, very roughly, separated into layers.

"In Two Words, Yes And No"

● *Cooperative federalism means a trade-off—captured in 1949 and still an issue, some seventy-five years later.*

The Marble Cake: Cooperative Federalism (1933–81)

Dual federalism collapsed in the 1930s. President Franklin D. Roosevelt (FDR) and large Democratic majorities in Congress

TABLE 4.1	Comparing Dual and Cooperative Federalism	
DUAL FEDERALISM		**COOPERATIVE FEDERALISM**
NATIONAL POWERS		
Enumerated: The national government wields powers specifically listed in the Constitution.		**Elastic:** The national government wields powers "necessary and proper" to support its function.
LOCATION OF SUPREME AUTHORITY		
Separate sovereignty: National and state governments each have authority within their own spheres.		**National supremacy:** States retain important powers but are subordinate to the national government except where the Constitution strictly forbids it.
KEY PRINCIPLE		
States' rights: The federal government takes responsibility for some tasks (defense, infrastructure, interstate commerce) but leaves each state to govern its own affairs on all others.		**Power sharing:** National, state, and local officials work together in many areas—usually with federal funds, federal rules, and federal oversight.

responded to the Great Depression by passing policies that strengthened the national government's role. Their agenda, known as the New Deal, introduced **cooperative federalism**: Program after program involved both federal and state governments working together, with the federal government providing most of the funds—and writing the rules. The lines of authority blurred (Table 4.1). A new bakery metaphor emerged: a *marble cake*, in which the various ingredients—the different government functions—were all swirled together.

Officials in Washington provided federal funds through **grants-in-aid**—national funds accompanied by specific instructions to state and local officials about how the money could be spent. Governors and other state leaders, desperate for resources during the Depression, accepted these national grants for roads, bridges, hospitals, healthcare clinics, Social Security payments for seniors, welfare payments for poor people with children, and the list goes on.

After World War II, many state and local officials expressed resentment at the national meddling in their affairs. Federal funds continued to flow, however, and, during this era, supported items ranging from school lunches to multilane highways to student loans. Few politicians were going to deny their constituents this national bounty. Cooperative federalism, and Washington's domination of many policy areas, lasted from the New Deal (starting in 1933) through the 1970s. Senator Everett Dirksen (R-IL) quipped in 1964 that if the trend toward increasing national power continued, only mapmakers would care about the state boundaries.[18]

The Super-Swirl Cake: Contested Federalism (1981–2024)

Ronald Reagan's presidency (1981–89) ushered in a new era in which federalism became a major area of conflict, or what we call **contested federalism**. Republican administrations generally try to tip power away from national officials and toward the state and local government. Democrats try to swing it back toward the federal government. But neither side is consistent—each presses authority up to the federal government or down to the state and local level, depending on the issue and who holds power where. The lines of authority are more swirled together than ever. Now, federal, state, and local authorities all compete for influence over programs.

Cooperative federalism: Also called marble cake federalism, a system of mingled governing authority, with functions overlapping across national and state governments.

Grants-in-aid: National government funding provided to state and local governments, along with specific instructions about how the funds may be used.

Contested federalism: A system of mingled governing authority marked by high partisan conflict in which both parties try to influence policy by shifting functions among national, state, and local governments; also known as super-swirl-cake federalism.

New federalism: An approach to federalism that shifts authority from federal officials to state and local governments.

Block grants: National government funding provided to state and local governments with relatively few restrictions or requirements on spending. Block grant programs marked a trade-off for state officials: more authority, fewer funds.

Progressive federalism: Approach that gives state officials considerable leeway in achieving national programs and goals.

The Reagan administration replaced cooperative federalism with a fresh approach known as **new federalism**. Instead of programs in which national officials provided funding, rules, regulations, and oversight, the Reagan administration relied more heavily on **block grants**: Federal dollars flow to specific policy areas, such as education or transportation or health, but leave the program's details to state and local officials. The new flexibility comes with a catch—less money.

From the New Deal through the 1970s, cooperative federalism established large federal programs that provided unlimited funding for a specific purpose—for example, everyone who qualifies for Medicaid receives hospital coverage; every eligible person gets food assistance. In contrast, block grants provide a fixed amount of funds for healthcare or nutrition. The federal government limits its contribution and state officials make tough choices about who qualifies for the program and who does not.

The Obama administration, building on the George W. Bush administration, introduced yet another variant in 2009: **progressive federalism**. Here the national government sets program goals and relies on state innovations to achieve them. Note that Democrats now mix their traditional goals (set on the national level) with Republican means (foster state innovation).[19] The Obama administration deployed this progressive federalism across a host of policy areas—education, healthcare, the environment, and more.

For example, the biggest and most controversial Obama administration program, the Affordable Care Act (or ACA), aimed to deliver private health insurance to about twenty-eight million uninsured Americans. Congress mandated that all uninsured people buy coverage. The federal government issued rules and regulations defining the insurance products; the states were incentivized to build insurance exchanges where individuals could shop among competing health insurance plans. If the states were not up to the job—or simply opposed to the policy—the federal government came in and built the website that sold the insurance plans. Eventually, Republicans in Congress stripped away the mandate to buy health insurance, but the law remains in force.

The Trump administration tried to restore the Reagan-era tradition: fewer federal dollars, fewer federal regulations. It also aimed to weaken some federal regulations by giving states authority over regulatory programs, such as those protecting endangered species.

On the other hand, the Trump administration flexed federal muscle when it tried to strip California of its authority to set stricter auto emissions standards, a power that the state has exercised since 1968 (thirteen other states follow California's stricter rules). The Biden administration promptly restored California's authority.

Again, the Obama administration vastly expanded the Medicaid program (which pays for the healthcare of people with low incomes), the Trump administration tried (unsuccessfully) to turn it into a block grant and send it to the states, and the Biden administration pushed to expand the program.

More power to the states? It depends on the issue, for both Republicans and Democrats.[20]

In sum, federalism has become a major playing field for America's heightened partisan battles (Figure 4.5). Today, under contested federalism, each party tries to win policy battles by shifting the locus of programs—federal, state, and local. How long will the current era of hyperpolarized federalism continue? Stay tuned!

Partisan multistate lawsuits filed against the federal government, by administration

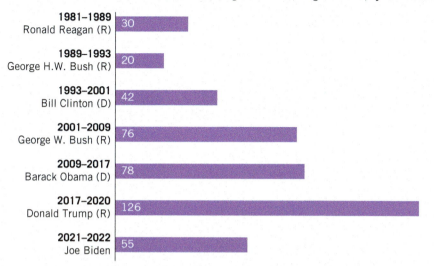

Administration	Lawsuits
1981–1989 Ronald Reagan (R)	30
1989–1993 George H.W. Bush (R)	20
1993–2001 Bill Clinton (D)	42
2001–2009 George W. Bush (R)	76
2009–2017 Barack Obama (D)	78
2017–2020 Donald Trump (R)	126
2021–2022 Joe Biden	55

● **FIGURE 4.5** *Contested federalism in action: when multiple states team up to sue the federal government. Notice the big rise in such lawsuits after the 2000 election, the outcome of which was disputed for weeks after Election Day and helped fuel the partisan fires that characterize American politics in the twenty-first century.*

THE BOTTOM LINE

» The Constitution grants the national government both delegated (or enumerated) powers and implied powers.

» You can read the Constitution as a broad grant of national powers, using the elastic clause, the interstate commerce clause, and the supremacy clause. Or you can see it as protecting state dominance, with a stricter interpretation of the commerce clause and an emphasis on the Tenth Amendment.

» Successive eras of federalism since the early twentieth century include dual federalism, with clearly demarcated authority (the layer cake); cooperative federalism, arising with FDR's New Deal, which introduced federal dominance and blurred the lines of authority (marble cake); and a modern era of contested federalism, alternating between new federalism, with less federal funding and more state discretion, and progressive federalism, in which states aim to shape national goals (super-swirl cake).

» Federalism reflects the hyperpolarization of American politics, as each party pushes authority and funding back and forth from the federal government to the states depending on the issue.

 # Issues in Federalism

Dual, cooperative, contested—these successive versions of federalism point to the perpetually shifting nature of government power and accountability. Today, a set of long-standing debates around federalism have become even more important. Let us review some current issues in this debate.

Climate Change

Every level of government oversees some aspect of climate change policy. The federal government regulates air quality and pollution, sets national goals for carbon emission, and negotiates international climate treaties. States establish

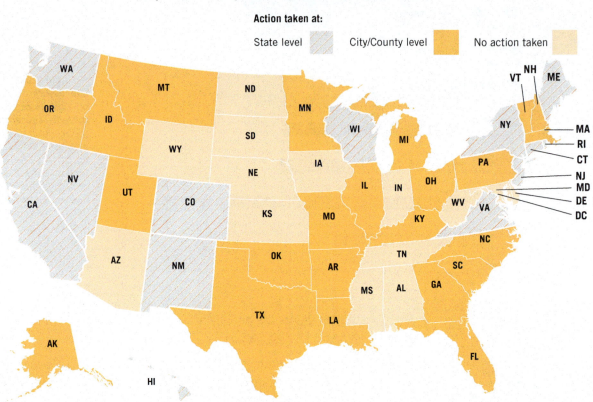

100 percent clean policies by state as of April 2020

Action taken at:

State level | City/County level | No action taken

● **FIGURE 4.6** *During the Trump years, fifteen states and territories committed to a 100% clean energy future. In situations where states were unwilling to commit to clean energy, city and county governments across twenty-two states made the pledge.*

transportation networks, oversee power generation, and manage the electric grid; they use federal funds and work within national regulations. Local governments are responsible for things like urban growth, land use, and waste disposal.

You can probably predict how the real world of federalism complicates this picture. The different levels push and pull in different directions. Start with the national government. In 2015, the Obama administration signed onto the Paris Climate Agreement, which aimed to limit rising temperatures. Five years later, the Trump administration officially withdrew from the accord. On his first day in office, in January 2021, President Biden rejoined the Paris Agreement.

Federalism gives reformers who lose out on one level the ability to move to another. When the United States withdrew from the Paris Climate Agreement, a coalition of mayors representing 468 cities—from Alameda, California, to Ypsilanti, Michigan—announced that they would continue to abide by the agreement. They proudly claimed to represent 74 million people and framed a new motto: "We're still in."[21]

Or take clean energy. When the national government turned away from this goal, some states moved right in: During the Trump years, fifteen states and territories committed to a 100 percent clean energy future. In situations where states were unwilling to commit to clean energy, city and county governments across twenty-two states made the pledge (see Figure 4.6). When the Biden administration began to commit to clean energy, other states began to push back, often via the courts.

What is America doing about climate change? We must look both at the national government—which passed a landmark climate-change bill in 2022—*and* the multilayered cake of states, counties, and cities, which both cooperate with and battle one another over fossil fuels or alternative energy or carbon taxes.

Healthcare

If you want to see a really fantastic marble cake, just look at American healthcare. Take Medicaid, which provides roughly eighty million Americans with health insurance (that's more than any other insurer, public or private). The national government established the program and offers funding (it pays 50 percent of Medicaid costs for wealthy states, 78 percent for the lowest-income states). The states provide the rest of the budget and decide who is eligible. In Connecticut, a single male making $40,000 a year qualifies; in Texas, no one without kids is eligible unless they are visually impaired, have a disability, or are pregnant. The Affordable Care Act aimed to expand Medicaid to all low-income people (with the federal budget paying for 90 percent of the new costs); thirty-eight states and the District of Columbia adopted the new national standards, while twelve have not.

Here's another example. The Affordable Care Act called for marketplaces where individuals can go online and shop for health insurance. Some states set up their own websites under national regulations; in other states, the national and state governments worked together to set up the insurance markets—sometimes they hid their cooperation to avoid political blowback; and in still other places, the national government built the website, while the state government sued to stop them.[22]

The COVID-19 pandemic further demonstrated the federalism tangle. The national government oversaw vaccine development, provided funds, issued guidelines, and announced mandates: for example, that you must wear masks on airplanes and cruise ships. States oversaw the healthcare response: allocating equipment to different hospitals, for example. Some states cooperated with the national mandates, while others refused. Florida banned mask mandates on cruise ships, insisting that individuals should be able to decide for themselves. Meanwhile, local governments ran the public health departments that were on the front lines of the response. The results? Typical American federalism: chaos, complexity, creativity, and many different choices.

Reducing the National Government's Size

The debate over federalism often reflects a particular American passion, which is especially strong among traditional conservatives: the desire to reduce the size and scope of national government. Their ideal is **devolution**, or the transfer of responsibility for government programs from national to state, from state to local, and from local government to the private sector.

Another conservative complaint about national action focuses on federal rules that require state and local government spending. For example, when federal regulations impose new safety requirements on commuter trains, state and local governments are left to buy and install the new technology, regardless of their own priorities. Critics call this an **unfunded mandate.**

In theory, Republicans prefer state and local control, while Democrats are more likely to seek Washington-based solutions. The reality is far more complicated: Both parties sometimes press for increased national authority and at other times defer to the states. It depends on the issue and who is in power—in Washington and in the state capital.

Devolution: The transfer of authority from the national to the state or local government level.

Unfunded mandate: An obligation imposed on state or local government officials by federal legislation without sufficient federal funding support to cover the costs.

On Both Sides of the Issue

Both Democratic and Republican administrations regularly stray from their parties' position on federalism. Why? Partly because both Democrats and Republicans are committed to different policies—state discretion is fine unless it challenges the party's priorities.

There is also another dimension. Republicans are often criticized for being hard-hearted budget cutters. In response, Republican administrations tend to introduce new social policies designed to show compassion and energetic management. For the last seventy-five years, every Republican president sponsored new, often very innovative, healthcare programs. The two largest expansions of the Medicare program, the health insurance program for people over sixty-five, came under Republicans Ronald Reagan (who covered high or catastrophic health costs—later repealed) and George W. Bush (who expanded the program to cover prescription drugs).[23]

The Democrats face the opposite criticism: too much federal government spending. As a result, Democratic administrations also regularly go against type and rely on state innovation and initiatives. As we just saw, the largest Democratic social program in the last half century, the Affordable Care Act, relies heavily on the states.

Notice how the old rule of thumb is often reversed: Republicans push authority to the states—unless the states use that authority to give benefits to undocumented immigrants or tighten environmental standards—which Republicans often **preempt** with new national laws. Likewise, Democrats support national authority—unless the states are raising minimum wages, decriminalizing drug use, expanding healthcare, or fighting climate change during a Republican administration.

Preemption: The invalidation of a U.S. state law that conflicts with federal law.

● As this cartoon humorously shows, which level of our federalist government a politician supports generally depends on the issue in question. (Nick Anderson)

In a Nutshell: Our Three-Dimensional Political Chess

These examples tell us to put aside the simple idea that conservatives want less federal government and liberals more. A more sophisticated view of federalism is to see it as a kind of three-dimensional political chess. Policy debates take place in Washington and in fifty state capitals, with thousands of municipalities as well as Native American tribal governments, independent school districts, and other local governing units also weighing in. Each decision about where to locate authority over a program advances some perspectives and limits others. At times, the raucous debates look more like wrestling than chess. Chess or wrestling, it is all part of the institutional framework that shapes American politics and policy.

Today, relations between national, state, and local levels take a dizzying array of forms—sometimes they work in partnership, and sometimes they are locked in combat. The one contemporary constant is *connection:* There are almost no issues in which the different levels of government exert separate functions, as in the old dual federalist system.

THE BOTTOM LINE

» Climate change and healthcare illustrate the contemporary politics of federalism: Decisions are spread out and often shift depending on who is in power.

» Devolution transfers responsibility back to state and local governments.

» Conventional wisdom suggests that liberals support national policies and conservatives seek to place power in state and local governments. In reality, both parties constantly shift, depending on the issue and who is in office on the different levels.

 # Federalism in the Courts

Most federalism disputes involve drawing a line where national power ends and states' authority begins—and, along with presidents and Congress, U.S. courts early on became a key player in allocating powers between the states and the nation. Judges have typically played a balancing role when it comes to federalism. Supreme Court decisions favored national prerogatives during the early republic, when many individual states had more power and prestige than the federal government in Washington. In a series of landmark decisions, the Supreme Court—led by Chief Justice John Marshall—protected national government powers from state incursions.

The first such case was *McCulloch v. Maryland,* decided in 1819.[24] Maryland's legislature had sought to impose a tax on the Baltimore branch of the first U.S. national bank. The bank refused to pay and was sued by the state. The Maryland Supreme Court ruled that the Constitution is silent about the federal power to establish a bank—and that the bank was therefore unconstitutional; Maryland was perfectly free to tax it. Writing for the Supreme Court, Marshall overruled the Maryland court and struck down the state tax. Invoking the necessary and proper (or elastic) clause, he ruled that Congress could draw on "implied powers" required to operate a national government and that states impairing the bank—in this case, by levying a tax on it—violated the Constitution. In these and later decisions,

Marshall and many other officials in the early republic were anxious to keep dual federalism in balance. At the time, doing so meant expanding national power.

As we will see in Chapter 16, in some eras—such as the period between the 1880s and the 1930s—the Court tilted away from federal authority to states and private corporations. On the other hand, the rise of activist government during the 1930s probably would not have been possible if the Supreme Court had not, quite dramatically, reversed its course and accepted New Deal legislation beginning in 1937. This transition to federal power led later courts to uphold congressional actions such as the Civil Rights Act (1964) and the Voting Rights Act (1965), which limited the ways that state and private actors could discriminate. It also led the Court to strike down state actions, as when they denied Texas's right to ban abortion (*Roe v. Wade,* 1973) or, in 2015, struck down several states' "three strikes" laws that jailed people for life, often for minor offenses.

In recent years—beginning under Chief Justice Rehnquist in the mid-1990s and gaining strength with a consistently conservative majority under Chief Justice Roberts since 2005—the Supreme Court has emphasized local and state power. In fact, the Rehnquist Court (1994–2005) struck down more acts of Congress than any previous Court in U.S. history; many of these decisions defended state authority. A series of prominent cases over the last three decades has shifted power away from the national government toward the states (see Table 4.2).

TABLE 4.2 Recent Supreme Court Decisions on Federalism

FAVORING NATIONAL GOVERNMENT
• *King v. Burwell* (2015). Ruled that premium tax credits provided under the Affordable Care Act (ACA) applied in every state.
• *Obergefell v. Hodges* (2015). Requires all states to issue marriage licenses to same-sex couples and to recognize same-sex marriages validly performed in other jurisdictions.
• *Cooper v. Harris* (2017). Ruled that North Carolina violated federal voting-rights laws by moving thousands of African American voters into congressional districts that had already elected African American Democrats.
• *Gamble v. United States* (2019). Affirmed federal government can prosecute defendants for the same crime they were tried for in a state court; these "separate sovereignties" (federal and state) do not violate the rule against "double jeopardy," or being tried twice for one crime.
• *New York State Rifle & Pistol Association v. Bruen* (2022). Invalidated a New York State law limiting residents' rights to carry arms outside their homes.

FAVORING STATE GOVERNMENTS
• *National Federation of Independent Business v. Sebelius* (2012). Struck down the national government's power to set standards for expanded Medicaid eligibility across the states, as mandated by the Affordable Care Act.
• *Shelby County v. Holder* (2013). Reversed a long-standing provision in the Voting Rights Act that required states with a history of voting discrimination to obtain federal permission before making changes to their election laws.
• *United States v. Windsor* (2013). Struck down a section of the federal Defense of Marriage Act (DOMA) and declared that same-sex couples who are legally married deserve equal rights to all federal benefits that other married couples enjoy.
• *United States v. Texas* (2016). Invalidated the Obama administration's executive act protecting from deportation certain unauthorized immigrants (parents of U.S. citizens, or legal permanent residents), and granting them work permits. Twenty-six states, led by Texas, challenged the White House policy.
• *Murphy v. NCAA* (2018). Invalidated a federal law prohibiting states from authorizing sports gambling. The Court ruled that states may legalize sports gambling—and that Congress does not have the power to stop them.
• *Kansas v. Garcia* (2020). Affirmed that states can set certain immigration policies, involving undocumented workers, instead of federal authorities.
• *Dobbs v. Jackson Women's Health Organization* (2022). Struck down *Roe v. Wade* and gave the authority over abortion policy to states, which can now prohibit or protect the practice. (See chapters 5 and 16.)

Nationalism, American Style

We have trained our focus, in the last two chapters, on the many ways Americans divide power. The Constitution scatters checks and balances across the national government. Federalism further fragments government authority across American space. However, something deeper has held the entire complicated apparatus in place. It is the elusive cultural sentiment known as *nationalism:* the American public's sense of identity as Americans. Nationalism helps maintain the federal balance by instilling loyalty to nation, state, and locality.

There were high barriers to the rise of American nationalism. After all, the thirteen colonies had proudly gone their own independent ways for 150 years. They practiced different religions, held different beliefs, lived in different kinds of societies, and represented different races, ethnicities, and nationalities. What would make these people (free, indentured, and enslaved), living up to a thousand miles apart, imagine themselves members of the same community?[25]

The Rise of Nationalism

What brought the people together was a piece of parchment. The Constitution became a touchstone for Americans' shared sense of belonging. Following ratification in 1789, celebrations broke out across the new nation. In Boston, a three-day festival featured a feast for twelve thousand people. Town leaders in Raleigh, North Carolina, fired so many twenty-one-gun salutes that elderly residents feared the Revolutionary War had started again. The Marquis de Lafayette, the French general who had fought alongside George Washington, wrote home to Paris that he was astonished to be "in the midst of perpetual fêtes [celebratory parties]."[26] It was the start of the nationalism that lives on to this day. In most ways, the United States was going through a familiar ritual: Nationalism usually springs up as nations are founded. The American difference was the Constitution's role in forging the national self.[27]

The Two Faces of Nationalism

But nationalism is always a double-edged sword. On the one hand, a strong sense of national identity fosters mutual support and loyalty. It is the bond that keeps a nation together despite all its inevitable differences. On the other hand, ardent nationalists in every nation are more likely to draw strict boundaries, and to restrict rights and aid only to people on one side of a border. Once those lines between us and them are cast, they tend to multiply.

People divide by race, by identity, by ideology—by who counts as a "true American." Groups push others to the periphery of wealth and power. In these ways, nationalism fragments even while it unifies.[28]

There are certainly signs of trouble today: In 2019, the Department of Homeland Security identified white nationalism as a primary terrorist threat. And in 2022, more than one in four Asian Americans reported fearing that members of their household would be attacked; African Americans reported their concern in roughly the same numbers. The dark side of nationalism is rising in the United States.[29]

Still, the search for common values, lying beneath all the American differences, remains a crucial part of our politics. Abraham Lincoln put it beautifully when he imagined that the "chorus of the union" would eventually be touched "by the better angels of our nature." How would that work today? We find those better angels by engaging with others in the community and, believe it or not, by the everyday work of politics.

Engagement

Civic voluntarism: Citizen participation in public life without government incentives or coercion (speaking at a town meeting vs. paying taxes, for example).

The sense of engagement with other people and of getting directly involved and cooperating with others is known as **civic voluntarism**. Early visitors to the United States were surprised to see how often Americans pitched in and did things for themselves—from adults building a road to children inventing the rules of a game. The American spirit of voluntary participation lives on, inspiring people's involvement in everything from town-meeting government to book clubs to civil rights organizations.[30]

Surprisingly, the effort to advance public policies in the fragmented American government also kindles widespread involvement. Federalism offers so many places to plunge into the debate—from the suburban school council to congressional town meetings to the Supreme Court—that it's difficult to get things done. That, in turn, forces public officials and private voices to build support for their policies in creative ways: They call on individuals to demonstrate support for an idea. They seek help from lobbyists. They mobilize powerful allies. They find new ways to publicize their ideas. They raise enormous amounts of money to fund future campaigns. We explore all these modes of action in future chapters.

● *Nationalism: A double-edged sword. Here one woman pledges allegiance (a) while another protests Asian hate (b).*

COMPARING NATIONS 4.1   Unitary Versus Federal Governments

As the clock strikes 11 in Paris, Pap Ndiaye, the Minister of National Education, knows exactly what every school child in France is studying because his ministry is responsible for the curriculum. France has a unitary government: Authority lies with the central government, which sets the policy for schools, hospitals, and farms in every corner of the country. The regional governments simply carry out directives from the national government. Roughly four out of five nations have unitary governments, including Great Britain, Peru, Iceland, and China—in fact, most countries in Europe, Africa, and Asia.

Other countries are federations. These nations are partially governed by local authorities under the umbrella of a central government. In Canada, for example, most policies are designed and funded on the regional (or state) level. The United States, Canada, Brazil, Russia, and India are all federal nations. Exactly how much power goes to the local government? The answer varies from country to country, with the United States in the middle of the federalist range.

Notice that there is not necessarily a link between unitary governments and authoritarian nations. Japan, Sweden, Britain, New Zealand, and Spain are all unitary countries—and highly democratic. On the other side, Russia is a federation—and authoritarian.

This chapter on American federalism has told a story of constant struggle for control between national, state, and local government. To some extent, this is true in every nation. Even in China, with its very powerful unitary government, regional authorities are constantly trying to expand their own influence.

Think of it this way: Every nation constantly balances national and local government authority. The rules in a unitary nation tilt heavily to the center; federalist nations push the balance of power closer to local governments.

Unitary states
Federal states

THE BOTTOM LINE

» The fragmenting institutions of federalism are balanced, sometimes too powerfully, by the bonding culture of nationalism.

» Nationalism helps bind together a large and diverse nation with a fragmented government.

» Nationalism is a double-edged sword: It both unites and splits a people. "Nationalists" claiming America stands only for Anglo-Saxons or Christians or English speakers sow division.

» Political engagement can help people overcome their divisions.

🏛 Conclusion: Who Are We?

Who finally decides whether Jose Antonio Vargas, whom we met in the introduction, will be arrested and deported? Or whether a person making $20,000 a year qualifies for Medicaid's health insurance? Or whether you must wear a face mask at your school's basketball games? Or whether you can carry a gun on campus? Or what children should learn about slavery in school? Or exactly what we should do about climate change? All these questions and many more raise the issue of federalism: the furious and perpetual American debate about where to put government power—on the nation, the state, or the local level. Think of it as a shifting philosophical debate etched into America's governing institutions.

Conflicting views about power and democracy, fairness, and liberty have always marked American politics. Successive eras allocated power differently. Dual federalism (the layer cake) largely kept the state and national spheres separate. The era of cooperative federalism saw the national government expand its role and mix with state and local functions (the marble cake). More recently, federalism has come to reflect the intense disagreements of twenty-first-century politics. Contested federalism (the super-swirl cake) reflects the hyper-partisan era we live in; where to vest authority depends on the issue, the power relations of the moment, and the national administration's ideological bent.

Federalism is the mark of a weaker national government. However, a paradox of American politics is that weak government is balanced by a powerful nation with a robust, patriotic sense of national identity. That force helps bind together all the centrifugal institutions of a federal system shot through with checks and balances on every level of government. Again, this sentiment can go too far—as the dangers of xenophobia and white nationalism illustrate.

Many critics suggest that limiting central government power diminishes America's capacity to face contemporary challenges. Others fear the opposite: An inexorably growing state marks the decline of American liberty. We will revisit these fears throughout this book. For now, recognize that this debate echoes those between Federalists and Anti-Federalists in the 1780s. The conflict involves balancing the most important American values, never an easy task . . . and forever an essential one.

CHAPTER SUMMARY

★ Americans are a people of multiple loyalties—to their nation, state, and home city or town. These divides are mirrored in our federalist politics.

★ Most other nations have more centralized (and therefore more powerful) unitary governments.

★ The American founders adopted a federalist system, in part to protect against concentrating too much power in one person or branch, but also to expand protections for individual rights, increase

government's flexibility, and enable more political innovations to flourish.

★ Different versions of federalism are evident in U.S. history, from dual federalism (in which the states and the national government perform largely separate functions) to cooperative federalism and, now, contested federalism.

★ Federalism is a key dimension to many policy issues ranging from healthcare to climate change.

⭐ Given this divided authority, we might wonder what has held the United States together, especially given regional differences that culminated in civil war. An uncommonly strong sense of national identity is a large part of the answer. Americans' devotion to national unity was instrumental in building a robust nation—although nationalism has its ugly sides as well.

⭐ Nationalism is a double-edged sword: It both unites and splits people. "Nationalists" claiming America stands only for Anglo-Saxons or Christians or English speakers sow division.

⭐ Political engagement can help people overcome their divisions.

KEY TERMS

Block grants, p. 120
Civic voluntarism, p. 128
Commerce clause, p. 114
Concurrent powers, p. 116
Confederation, p. 108
Contested federalism, p. 119
Cooperative federalism, p. 119
Delegated powers, p. 114
Devolution, p. 123

Diffusion, p. 109
Dillon's rule, p. 108
Dual federalism, p. 117
Full faith and credit
clause, p. 116
Grants-in-aid, p. 119
Home rule, p. 108
Implied powers, p. 115
Inherent powers, p. 115

Necessary and proper clause, p. 115
New federalism, p. 120
Preemption, p. 124
Progressive federalism, p. 120
Reserved powers, p. 115
Supremacy clause, p. 115
Unfunded mandate, p. 123
Unitary government, p. 107

STUDY QUESTIONS

1. Can you imagine the United States without federalism? Suppose that a central national authority ran the country, and governors and mayors—and other subnational officials—were entirely subordinate to the national government. Describe some of the changes that would likely result. Would this shift toward a unitary state be an improvement, in your view? Why or why not?

2. Define the following: dual federalism, cooperative federalism, and contested federalism (or, if you prefer: the layer cake, the marble cake, and the super-swirl cake). Can you see any themes that run across all three eras? Is the current era more like dual federalism or cooperative federalism? Why?

3. You're asked to advise senior members of Congress on a policy issue of great passion for you—environmental protection, gun rights, or whatever you choose. How would you advise them to approach the issue? Should they give more or less discretion to the states? To local communities? Why?

4. Think about your own political loyalties. Are they most strongly felt for your hometown or home city, the state where you grew up (or where you live now), or the nation as a whole? What do you think accounts for your outlook? If you are not from the United States, reflect on your own sense of political identity: Is it primarily to a nation, a region, or a local place?

5. If you feel a strong sense of national pride, do you think it comes with any undesirable aspects? If you are not an especially avid American nationalist, why not? What would happen if most citizens exhibited a skeptical outlook toward the country?

6. A wide range of reforms have been suggested for improving the American system of separated powers. Are there any other changes you would make to the federalist division of power across branches and between national, state, and local governments?

5 CIVIL LIBERTIES

SIMON TAM AND HIS DANCE ROCK BAND named themselves "The Slants" as a way to push back against a politically correct culture that tip-toed around racism. The band members, who are Asian Americans, told interviewers that they wanted to reclaim the slur. But when they applied for a trademark, the U.S. Patent and Trademark Office rejected their application because the name was "disparaging to people of Asian descent." Tam sued.

Many people agree with the copyright office: Hate speech has no place in our society. We should protect groups that have faced discrimination—for their race, ethnicity, religion, sexual orientation, gender identity, or anything else. Harsh language does more than demean people—it reinforces all the ways that our society privileges some and represses others. The issue has roiled many colleges. Some students and faculty members say that if a speaker has expressed hostility or hatred, they should be stopped from speaking on campus.

Wait a minute, say others. The First Amendment guarantees Americans the right to free speech—to say what they wish, including if it is unpopular and even hateful. You may denounce those peddling hate, this side argues, but you may not take away their rights.

Two important values collided when The Slants tried to copyright their name. On the one hand, a community should treat its members with respect. On the other, the ability to speak your mind is the basis of a free society. Both views are important—but when they collide, we must choose.

The Supreme Court made a clear choice and unanimously ruled in favor of The Slants. Even if they had been using the slur against Asians in a hateful way, the Court argued, the government was wrong to limit free speech by denying a trademark. "The proudest boast of our free speech jurisprudence," wrote the Court, is that we protect the freedom to express "the thought that we hate."[1] The Court has backed this view by emphasizing free speech over every other right in the Bill of Rights.

The First Amendment to the Constitution *does* guarantee people's right to free speech. This is the bedrock of American liberty: protecting individuals when they wish to state their views, practice their religion, or assemble to protest—even if what they say, or believe, or rally for is deeply unpopular.

In this chapter, you will

 Learn about the rise of civil liberties.

 Examine the right to privacy—a controversial liberty that is not mentioned in the Constitution and involves contraception, abortion, and same-sex marriage.

 Study the freedom of religion.

 Explore the right to free speech—and its special status.

 Weigh the right to bear arms.

 Consider the rights of the accused.

 Reflect on the difficult balance between fighting terrorism and protecting civil liberties.

● *Simon Tam and The Slants. The Supreme Court ruled unanimously that the First Amendment protected the band's name—even if it is a hateful slur.*

Over time the Court has struck down a series of popular efforts to limit free speech: The Court protected flag burning, unlimited campaign contributions, pornography, and hateful slurs shouted during the funeral services of Americans killed in combat—all decisions that we will explore. In 2019, the Court followed up the Tam decision by striking down a law barring "immoral" or "scandalous" trademarks. This time it was a clothing brand named "fuct." The justices rejected a government lawyer's argument that the word was the "past participle form of the paradigmatic profane word in our culture." Once again, they protected free speech.[2]

However, every right has limits. Individual protections always have to be balanced by community needs or by other people's rights. And the context matters. As Supreme Court Justice Oliver Wendell Holmes put it back in 1919, every action "depends upon the circumstances in which it is done. . . . The most stringent protection of free speech would not protect a man from falsely shouting fire in a crowded theater and causing a panic."[3]

Who are we? We are a nation always wrestling with a great trade-off—majority rule versus individual liberties. On the one hand, the United States is a democratic republic, which means the majority should get its way. On the other hand, every individual has rights that should be protected. In our democracy, a majority—even a very large majority—cannot violate the civil liberties of even a small minority.

The tension is exacerbated because we are (and always have been) a diverse nation of minority groups—Irish, lesbian, Muslim, Seventh-Day Adventist, gun owner, Hmong, Black, and the list goes on. When the majority feels threatened or offended, it sometimes moves to limit the minority's rights, making civil liberties all the more important.

Civil liberties: The limits on government that allow people to freely exercise their rights.

What are **civil liberties**? They are the limits we put on governments (and the majorities that elect them) so that individuals can exercise their personal freedoms. Americans have long embraced the figure of the brave individual, standing up for their rights. In practice, complexity abounds.

The Rise of Civil Liberties

May an anti-abortion protester shout at women entering family planning clinics? May states ban violent video games? May a skinhead stand on a street corner and urge people to attack Latinos, Sikhs, or Jews? May someone refuse to wear a mask during a health pandemic? The answer to all four questions is "sometimes." We always weigh the rights of individuals against the concerns and safety of the community. Who decides? Usually, the courts do. And there is often more than one reasonable answer when the courts take up a question.[4]

Civil Rights and Civil Liberties

Civil rights and civil liberties demand opposite things from government. Civil rights require government action to help secure individual rights; civil liberties restrict government action to protect individual rights. Until people have won their rights, the idea of protecting them is meaningless. When governments enforce

BY THE NUMBERS Civil Liberties

31 Number of rights listed in the Bill of Rights

134 Number of years after the Bill of Rights was ratified before the Supreme Court ruled that state governments could not interfere with freedom of speech

84 Percentage of adults who see it as a "very serious" or "somewhat serious" problem that some Americans do not speak freely in everyday situations because of worries about retaliation[5]

72.7 U.S. score on "World Press Freedom Index," 2022 (out of possible one hundred)[8]

2 Number of rights protecting freedom of religion

219 Number of years after the Bill of Rights was ratified before the Supreme Court ruled that states could not interfere with the right to bear arms

994 Total number of convicted felons executed in five states (Texas, Virginia, Oklahoma, Missouri, and Florida), 1976–2022[6]

38.8 Russian score on "World Press Freedom Index," 2022 (out of possible one hundred)[9]

19 Number of rights protecting people accused of crimes

1 Number of new rights secured by constitutional amendment in the past fifty years (the Twenty-Sixth Amendment extended the right to vote to eighteen- to twenty-year-olds)

64 Percentage represented by five states (Texas, Virginia, Oklahoma, Missouri, and Florida) of all U.S. executions, 1976–2022[7]

92.6 Norway score (highest) on "World Press Freedom Index," 2022 (out of possible one hundred)[10]

How has our interpretation of civil liberties and the government's responsibility to protect them changed over time?

civil rights for some people, they often limit the liberty of others. For example, as we will see in Chapter 6, the Civil Rights Act of 1964 outlawed segregated restaurants. That legal action freed Blacks and Latinos to eat wherever they wished but limited the liberty of racist restaurant owners to serve only those customers they wanted to serve.

In practice, the two concepts are not opposites. The battle for civil rights led to more robust civil liberties for everyone. The fight against slavery eventually led to the Fourteenth Amendment, which—as we will soon see—is the cornerstone

● *Legal? Sometimes! When? Read on . . .*

of modern civil liberties. Without the long American struggle for civil rights, Americans would have fewer civil liberties.

Both civil liberties and civil rights became increasingly important to American politics during the twentieth century. In this section, we look first at why civil liberties matter. We then explain how they grew and spread.

The Purpose of Civil Liberties

Lillian Gobitas was the seventh-grade class president in a Minersville, Pennsylvania, school in 1935. She refused to pledge allegiance to the flag because, as a Jehovah's Witness, she was taught that the pledge placed the nation ahead of God. Lillian was taunted, attacked, and expelled from school. Her father, Walter, sued the school district, and in 1940 the Supreme Court upheld the expulsion (8–1), declaring that "national unity is the basis of national security." (To add insult to injury, a clerk misspelled her name and the case is known as *Minersville School District v. Gobitis*.)

The American entry into World War II in December 1941 inflamed the prejudice against the sect. Mobs beat up five Jehovah's Witnesses in Wyoming, burned a Kingdom Hall in Maine, and allegedly castrated a Jehovah's Witness in Nebraska. The Court's ruling seemed to have made matters worse. "They're traitors," declared a sheriff in Maine, "the Supreme Court says so. Ain't you heard?"[11] This is the nightmare for civil liberties advocates: the powerful machinery of government invoked against a minority group.

Three years later, in 1943, the Court reversed itself and ruled that it was unconstitutional to require children to pledge allegiance if it violated their faith. In announcing its new position, the Court made a classic statement of civil liberties: "The very purpose of a Bill of Rights was to withdraw certain subjects from the vicissitudes of political controversy, to place them beyond the reach of majorities and officials."[12]

It has taken a long time for the United States to institute those principles. Civil liberties were barely visible in the nineteenth century. "What I find most dangerous in America," wrote Tocqueville in 1835, "is not the extreme freedom reigning there but the shortage of guarantees against the tyranny of the majority."[13] Because elected officials naturally tend to follow the will of the majorities that elected them (and, politicians hope, will re-elect them), it often falls to the judicial branch to protect the minority rights at the core of civil liberties.

● *Walter Gobitas with his children, William and Lillian. The Jehovah's Witnesses were expelled from school for refusing to salute the flag.*

The Slow Rise of Civil Liberties

The Bill of Rights barely touched American life because it only applied to the national government. The First Amendment states that "*Congress* shall make no law" prohibiting the exercise of religion or restricting speech. Well, what about the states? Were they also bound by the individual protections in the Bill of Rights?

In 1833, John Barron found out. Barron owned a thriving wharf in Baltimore Harbor until the city diverted the water and left his dock high and dry. Barron sued, arguing that the city had violated the Fifth Amendment by taking his property for public use "without just compensation." The Supreme Court ruled (in *Barron v. Baltimore*) that the Fifth Amendment applied only to the federal government. The Anti-Federalists, reasoned the justices, had demanded the Bill of Rights to protect them from the federal government. Washington could not strip Barron of his property rights—but Maryland or Baltimore could.[14]

The Bill of Rights eventually reached the states thanks to the quest for civil rights. After the Civil War, Congress passed the Fourteenth Amendment (ratified in 1868) to protect the newly freed slaves. Almost every discussion of civil liberties turns the spotlight on one passage in the Fourteenth Amendment:

> **No state** shall . . . *deprive any person of life, liberty, or property, without due process of law; nor deny any person within its jurisdiction the equal protection of the laws.* [emphasis added]

Look again at the first two words. The amendment directly addresses the states. None may deprive any person of life, liberty, or property, which is exactly what the Bill of Rights protects. The Fourteenth Amendment *seems* to apply the Bill of Rights to the states. In 1873, the Supreme Court disagreed, ruling that the Fourteenth Amendment did not mean that the states had to abide by the Bill of Rights.[15]

Slowly, the Court changed its mind—but it did so one right at a time. Over more than a century, the courts ruled that the states must honor the different rights listed in the Bill of Rights. This process began in 1897, when the Court returned to the issue raised in *Barron v. Baltimore* and ruled that state governments could not seize property without compensation. One phrase of the Fifth Amendment now applied to state and local government as well as to the federal government. We call the process **selective incorporation** because the Supreme Court selected a right and "incorporated" it into the Fourteenth Amendment. No state could violate the right once it was incorporated.

Selective incorporation: The extension of protections from the Bill of Rights to the state governments, one liberty at a time.

Over time, the Court incorporated almost every phrase of the Bill of Rights, protecting freedom of speech in 1925 (*Gitlow v. New York*), continuing with the free exercise of religion in 1940 (*Cantwell v. Connecticut*), the right to remain silent in 1966 (*Miranda v. Kerr*), and moving, most recently, to the right to keep and bear arms in 2010 and protection against excessive fines in 2019 (see Table 5.1). How did the Supreme Court decide which rights to incorporate? In 1937, it explained: States must respect rights that are essential to our idea of liberty.[16]

In the rest of the chapter, we examine the most important civil liberties and the issues they raise.[17]

TABLE 5.1 Incorporation of the Bill of Rights into the Fourteenth Amendment

THE BILL OF RIGHTS	YEAR	KEY CASE
I. Free exercise of religion*	1940	Cantwell v. Connecticut
No establishment of religion	1947	Everson v. Board of Education
Free press	1931	**Near v. Minnesota****
Free speech	1925	**Gitlow v. New York**
Right to peaceful assembly	1937	De Jonge v. Oregon
Right to petition government	1963	NAACP v. Button
II. Right to keep and bear arms	2010	**McDonald v. Chicago**
III. No quartering of soldiers		Not incorporated
IV. No unreasonable search and seizure	1949	Wolf v. Colorado
No search and seizure without a warrant	1961	**Mapp v. Ohio**
V. Right to grand jury indictment		Not incorporated
No double jeopardy	1969	Benton v. Maryland
No forced confession	1964	Escobedo v. Illinois
Right to remain silent	1966	**Miranda v. Arizona**
No seizure of property without compensation	1897	Chicago, Burlington, and Quincy Railroad Co. v. City of Chicago
VI. Right to public trial	1948	In re Oliver
Right to speedy trial	1967	Klopfer v. North Carolina
Right to trial by impartial jury	1966	Parker v. Gladden
Right to confront witnesses	1965	Pointer v. Texas
Right to compel supportive witnesses to appear	1967	Washington v. Texas
Right to counsel in capital punishment cases	1932	**Powell v. Alabama**
Right to counsel in any criminal trial	1963	**Gideon v. Wainwright**
VII. Right to jury trial in civil cases		Not incorporated
VIII. No excessive bail		Not incorporated
No excessive fines imposed	2019	**Timbs v. Indiana**
No cruel and unusual punishment	1962	Robinson v. California
IX. Rights not limited to rights listed in the first eight amendments		Not relevant to incorporation
X. Powers not delegated to the national government reserved to the states and the people		Not relevant to incorporation

* Notice that First Amendment rights were incorporated early in the process. Most protections for those accused of crimes were applied between 1962 and 1968.

** Boldfaced cases are discussed in this chapter.

THE BOTTOM LINE

» The Supreme Court neatly defined civil liberties in 1943: The Bill of Rights withdraws certain subjects from political controversy and places them beyond the reach of majorities and officials.

» The Bill of Rights did not apply to the states until the Fourteenth Amendment declared that no state could deprive any citizen of life, liberty, or property.

» The Court has applied the Bill of Rights to the states one right at a time between 1897 (no taking of property without compensation) and 2019 (forbidding excessive fines).

 # Privacy

We begin with an especially controversial civil liberty that, unlike all the others we will examine, is never directly mentioned in the Constitution. Instead, the Supreme Court found that it was implied by the First, Third, Fourth, Fifth, and Ninth Amendments. Fifty years after discovering this right, the Court appeared to deny it—leaving a series of explosive questions in its wake.

"Penumbras" and "Emanations"

In the mid-nineteenth century, contraceptives were widely available. Then, encouraged by the federal government in the 1870s, every state banned them—partly because of fears that immigrants would have more children than native-born Americans. Almost a century later, the director of Planned Parenthood of Connecticut defied that state's ban and dispensed condoms at a birth control clinic in New Haven. The Supreme Court heard the case, *Griswold v. Connecticut,* in 1965; struck down the law; and declared a dramatic new personal liberty: the right to privacy.[18]

How could the Court protect privacy if the Constitution does not even mention it? Justice William O. Douglas explained: Rights that are specifically mentioned in the Bill of Rights "have penumbras . . . that give them life and substance." The penumbras—literally, the shadows—of the First Amendment create "zones of privacy" in which people have a right to make their own choices free from government interference. As those "zones" overlap, individual Americans' privacy is strengthened. Douglas also affirms the *emanations* of the Bill of Rights. Those emanations are guarantees that flow out of other amendments such as the Third Amendment's ban on quartering soldiers in private homes. Douglas pointed out that such guarantees were designed to protect privacy. In addition, the Ninth Amendment declares that other rights exist besides the ones mentioned in the Constitution and that these rights are also "retained by the people." Privacy is one of those rights.

In 1787, when the Constitution was written, no one was thinking about condoms. But if you apply the logic of the Constitution to modern times, the right to privacy, and to contraceptives, emerges. These civil liberties reflect the spirit of the Constitution. After all, concluded Douglas, "would we allow the police to search the sacred precincts of marital bedrooms for telltale signs of the use

WHAT DO YOU THINK?

Is There a Right to Privacy?

	Yes.	No.	What it means.
Are you ready to try your first civil-liberties case? How would you rule in *Griswold v. Connecticut*? Do you agree that there is "a right to privacy" in the Constitution that permitted the Court to strike down the Connecticut ban on contraceptives?	Although the Constitution does not specifically mention privacy, a modern reading of the document would conclude that privacy is a basic liberty that the courts ought to protect. In addition, the consequence—a woman's right to control her own pregnancy—is an essential part of gender equality as we understand it today.	We have to stick to the simple language of the Constitution itself. We disrespect and even damage the document by reading things into it. Those who opposed Connecticut's ban on contraceptives should have gone to the legislature and lobbied them to change it.	Yes or no, you're part of a long intellectual tradition. If you said yes, you agree with the pragmatist school of thought, which says the courts must be guided by the *general ideas* that underpin the Constitution to determine the best outcome in a particular case. If you voted no, you're voting with *originalism* or *textualism*, the school of thought that limits judges to considering only what's explicitly stated in the Constitution's text.

of contraceptives? The very idea is repulsive." Is it acceptable to interpret the Constitution in this way—reading in rights that are implied but not stated? That question presents one of the great controversies in contemporary legal analysis.

The *Griswold* case itself did not stir much controversy. After all, most people thought married couples had every right to use condoms. In 1973, however, the right to privacy led to one of the most controversial Court decisions ever.

Roe v. Wade. In *Roe v. Wade* (1973), the Supreme Court drew on the right to privacy and struck down a Texas law banning abortion. The Court ruled that the right to privacy is "broad enough to encompass a woman's decision whether or not to terminate her pregnancy"—within the first three months of pregnancy (before the fetus can live outside the womb). During that first trimester, the state governments cannot *regulate* or *infringe on* a woman's right to abortion.

Roe v. Wade was not immediately controversial. Within a decade, however, two strong opposing perspectives had emerged. People who supported the decision—known as "pro-choice"—viewed the decision as essential to gender equality, for it enabled women to control when (and whether) they have children. From this perspective, *Roe* makes many more vocations and careers possible for women. It protects women's health by doing away with the dangerous back-alley abortions that desperate women sought out before *Roe* made abortions safe and legal. Democrats, for the most part, are pro-choice.

Those who oppose the decision—known as "pro-life"—believe that life begins at conception and that abortion is murder. Many religious activists took *Roe v. Wade* as a call to enter politics—although religious conservatives were originally deeply divided over the issue. The grassroots campaign to overturn the decision became a powerful force in modern conservatism. Within a decade, the Republican Party had committed itself to overturning *Roe*.

The debate added new intensity to American politics. Activists on each side felt they were fighting for the soul of the nation: On one side, equality for women rests on the ability to choose if and when to have children; on the other, the simple right of the unborn to life. The intensity has helped politicize Supreme Court appointments. Each new nomination, like Amy Coney Barrett's in 2020, raises key questions. What is their attitude toward abortion? Will it swing the Court? In 2022, we found out.

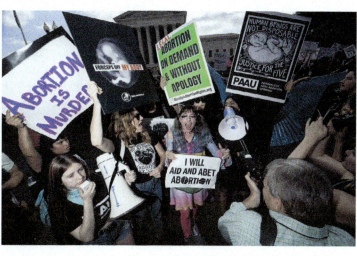

● *Abortion opponents (to left in picture) and supporters (to the right) clash after the Supreme Court's historic decision, in 2022, to reject the 1973 Roe affirmation of women's right to terminate their pregnancies. Subsequently the battle moved to the states, while Congress also debated whether to step in and create a national legislative solution to this burning issue.*

Dobbs v. Jackson Women's Health.   Challenges to *Roe v. Wade* led to a string of Supreme Court decisions. In 1980, the Court accepted a congressional ban on federal funding for abortions. In 1989, it upheld a Missouri prohibition on abortions in public hospitals. In 1992, in *Planned Parenthood v. Casey* (1992), the Court voted (5–4) to take a middle ground. The Court upheld a woman's right to terminate her pregnancy as a "component of liberty." However, it rejected *Roe v. Wade*'s trimester framework, which forbade any state limitations in the first trimester. Now the Court majority allowed states to legislate "measures aimed at ensuring that a woman's choice contemplates the consequences for the fetus." In short, the right to choose an abortion could be balanced—but not overruled—by the state's desire to protect potential life so long as state regulations did not impose "an undue burden" on the woman's choice.

The original *Roe* decision propounded a **judicial rule**. Rules set clear boundaries between what is lawful and what is not: In this case, the states may not interfere in the first trimester. Now, *Casey* replaced the rule with a **judicial standard**. A standard establishes a more general guiding principle in place of a hard-and-fast rule. What is an "undue burden" on a woman's choice? That's a judgment call.

Abortions continue to be fiercely debated—on and off the Court. *Roe* remained in place, however, until a historic 2022 decision. *Dobbs v. Jackson Women's Health* involves a 2018 Mississippi law banning abortions after fifteen weeks—a direct contradiction to *Casey*'s "fetal viability" standard, set at twenty-four weeks. Lower courts struck down the Mississippi statute, citing *Roe* and *Casey* as precedents. However, when the case got to the Supreme Court it made a bold pronouncement: "The Constitution does not confer a right to abortion." A right, protected by the Court for fifty years, was no longer a right at all. What about the *Roe* and *Casey* decisions? Both overruled—with a swipe at their "weak reasoning." What next? The Court was clear: It's now completely up to the states.[19]

State legislative battles that had been percolating for decades erupted in the decision's wake. Twenty-seven states passed abortion bans (many were already on the books); sixteen others protected the right to an abortion.[20]

But here's the curious thing about the *Dobbs* decision. It did not strike down the right to privacy on which the right to abortion had been constructed. It went out of its way to say *Griswold* (the right to buy contraceptives), *Lawrence v. Texas* (forbidding anti-sodomy laws, discussed next), and *Obergefell v. Hodges*

Judicial rules: Hard-and-fast boundaries between what is lawful and what is not.

Judicial standards: Guiding principles that help governments make judgment calls.

(protecting same-sex marriage) were not affected—*Dobbs* was only about abortion because abortion is "unique."

One justice, Clarence Thomas, did not buy that limit. If the right to privacy does not protect abortion, then it does not protect contraceptives or same-sex marriage either. Both the left and the right charged the Court with letting politics define rights. And remember the fundamental fact about civil liberties: Rights are meant to be protected regardless of what the majority wants; decisions about rights are meant to be lifted entirely out of politics.

Sex Between Consenting Adults

Does the right to privacy extend to same-sex couples? In 1986, the Supreme Court ruled it did not, upholding Georgia's anti-sodomy law. However, judicial mores were changing along with American culture. In 2003, the Supreme Court reversed itself in *Lawrence v. Texas* and extended the right of privacy to same-sex couples. In striking down a Texas anti-sodomy law, the majority echoed the original *Griswold* decision: "Liberty protects the person from unwarranted government intrusion into . . . private places." Three members of the Court disagreed and signed on to Justice Scalia's blistering dissent. In 2022, however, every justice but Clarence Thomas appeared to stand by this precedent.

Clashing Principles

The privacy cases generally reflect public opinion. By 1965, most Americans believed that couples should be permitted to use birth control. *Roe v. Wade* appeared to reflect the popular pro-choice view in the early 1970s but precipitated an enormous surge defending a right to life. Later decisions balanced the right to an abortion with state restrictions—roughly in line with popular preferences.

Commentary around the *Dobbs* case also suggests that the Court—by returning abortion regulation to state government—is deferring to public opinion.[21] It may seem a good idea for the courts to reflect majority opinion. But civil liberties are a bulwark *against* the will of the majority: The Constitution and the Court are designed to protect individual liberties in the face of popular opposition. They are supposed to protect the rights of unpopular minorities, such as Jehovah's Witnesses in the 1940s, same-sex couples in the 1980s, and women seeking safe abortions in the 2020s.

As we will see throughout this chapter, applying the Constitution is never simple. The United States is founded on two clashing values: We believe in government by the people. But at the same time, we believe that all individuals are endowed with inalienable rights. The story of civil liberties is the story of managing the collisions between the two core principles—the needs and desires of the community versus the rights of the individual.

● *John Geddes Lawrence (left) and Tyron Garner (right). The police, investigating a gun disturbance complaint, broke into Lawrence's apartment—which had gay posters prominently displayed on the walls. When Lawrence began to argue, the police arrested both men for "deviant sexual intercourse." In* Lawrence v. Texas *the Supreme Court struck down the Texas anti-sodomy law for violating the Constitution's privacy protections. After striking down* Roe v. Wade, *might the court reconsider* Lawrence? *Stay tuned!*

» The Court discovered a right to privacy implicit in the shadows of the First, Third, Fourth, Fifth, and Ninth Amendments.

» In *Roe v. Wade,* the Court issued a rule prohibiting states from interfering during the first trimester.

» Later cases permitted states to balance abortion rights with protections for the unborn; then, in the 2022 *Dobbs* decision, the Court rejected the right to abortion and returned decisions about it to the states.

» The Court extended privacy rights to same-sex couples by striking down anti-sodomy laws.

Freedom of Religion

As the Bill of Rights opens, the First Amendment lays down two succinct commands regulating religion:

> *Congress shall make no law respecting an establishment of religion, or prohibiting the free exercise thereof.*

The federal government may not establish an official religion—that's known as the **establishment clause**. And it may not interfere in religious practice—the **free exercise clause**.

But here's a complication buried within that constitutional sentence. What if the effort to avoid establishing a religion (for example, no Christian prayers to start the school day) clashes with the free exercise of religion (Christians want to pray at the start of the school day)? That tension has haunted jurisprudence for decades. And, once again, the Supreme Court recently made a blockbuster move to resolve the tension.

Establishment clause: The First Amendment principle that government may not establish an official religion.

Free exercise clause: The First Amendment principle that government may not interfere in religious practice.

The Establishment Clause

By the time the Constitution was written, Americans were practicing many faiths: Puritans (or Congregationalists) in Massachusetts, Quakers in Philadelphia, Baptists in Rhode Island, Anglicans in Virginia, Catholics in Maryland, and Jews in Newport, Rhode Island. The Constitution posed a threat. What if the federal government imposed a national religion? The First Amendment's establishment clause is designed to prohibit that. But what exactly did it forbid the government from doing? The debate began immediately.

President George Washington (1789–97) called for a national day of prayer each year. Was that encouraging religion? President Thomas Jefferson (1801–9) thought so and rejected the practice. The First Amendment, wrote Jefferson, builds "a wall of separation between church and state."[22] When the Supreme Court extended the establishment clause to the state governments in 1947, Justice Hugo Black quoted Jefferson's "wall of separation."[23] Until recently, Jefferson's metaphor guided the Court's efforts.

The difficulty with Jefferson's principle is that there has never been a true wall of separation. Congress starts every session with a prayer, a tradition that goes all the way back to its first meeting in 1789. The cash in Americans' pockets is inscribed "In God We Trust" and children pledge allegiance to "one nation under God"—Congress added "under God" in 1954 to distinguish America from the Soviet Union, which was officially atheistic. Visit the Supreme Court building and you'll find a carving of Moses holding the Ten Commandments. Presidents routinely end their speeches with "God bless America"—a spirit no leader would invoke in South Africa, France, or Japan. Despite these and many other interconnections, the courts have tried to separate church and state.

The establishment clause is clearly designed to keep government officials from favoring one religion—or religion over nonreligion. In a pathbreaking case, *Engel v. Vitale* (1962), the Supreme Court ruled that New York's practice of starting the school day with a nondenominational prayer violated the establishment clause.[24]

A long string of controversial decisions followed. Each decision returns to the vexing question of exactly where to construct Jefferson's wall.

In 1971, the Court established a test to guide decisions about separating church and state. In *Lemon v. Kurtzman*, the Court struck down a Pennsylvania law that paid teachers who taught nonreligious subjects in church-affiliated (mainly Catholic) schools. The Court promulgated what became known as the *Lemon test* for judging what government actions are permissible. A law does not violate the establishment clause if it meets a three-part test: First, the law must have a *secular* purpose. Second, its principal effect must *neither advance nor inhibit religion*. Finally, it must not *excessively entangle* government in religion. Paying the teachers in religious schools was, the Court ruled, an "excessive entanglement," and Pennsylvania could not do it.

As the Court grew more conservative, the Lemon test came under fire. Justice Scalia complained: "Like some ghoul in a late-night horror movie that repeatedly sits up in its grave and shuffles abroad . . . *Lemon* stalks our Establishment Clause jurisprudence."[25]

Strict separation: The strict principles articulated in the Lemon test for judging whether a law establishes a religion. (See "accommodation.")

Accommodation: The principle that government does not violate the establishment clause as long as it does not confer an advantage on some religions over others. (See "strict separation.")

Eventually, two different perspectives emerged. **Strict separation** tried to separate church and state using the Lemon test and remains the courts' guiding principle. An alternative view became known as **accommodation**: Government does not violate the establishment clause so long as it does not confer an advantage on some religions or discriminate against others.

In 2022, the Court finally put a stake through the Lemon test. The key case involved a high school football coach who prayed (with some of his students) on the field after three games. Well, that looked like "excessive entanglement" to the school district—after all, he was a role model teaching in a public school—and they fired him. The coach sued and, in *Kennedy v. Bremerton School District*, the Supreme Court sided with the coach. "In place of *Lemon*," ruled the court majority, "the Establishment Clause must be interpreted by 'reference to historical practices and understanding.'"[26]

● *Boston Pride Day, 2022: An LGBTQ+ Pride flag flies alongside the U.S. and Massachusetts standards. The U.S. Supreme Court ruled that a Christian-themed flag may also be flown outside Boston City Hall, using an accommodationist view and further burying the Lemon test.*

WHAT DO YOU THINK? ## May the Christian Youth Club Meet in School?

	Justice Stevens:	Justice Scalia:	Testing These Views:
The Good News Club is a Christian evangelical group that establishes youth clubs in schools across the United States. In Milford, New York, the school district refused to let the club meet in the school after classes, saying that such "religious worship" would amount to a public school's endorsement of Christianity. The case went to the Supreme Court. Justices Stevens (who argued against Good News) and Scalia (who supported Good News) each wrote opinions. Which opinion would you sign on to?	"Evangelical meetings designed to convert children to a particular faith . . . may introduce divisiveness and tend to separate young children into cliques that undermine the school's educational mission." The school district is right to stop the practice.	"Religious expression cannot violate the establishment clause when such exercise is (1) purely private and (2) open to all on equal terms." Milford [the school district] was discriminating against a religious group because it allowed other groups to meet.	As you ponder which side to take, consider how one would decide this case using the Lemon test (with Stevens) or the accommodation view (with Scalia). How did the court actually rule? The answer is in the endnote.[29]

What exactly is a "historical practice"? Future court decisions will have to spell that out, but one thing stands out: Since 2005, the Supreme Court has sided with religious organizations 83 percent of the time (compared to just 46 percent in the 1950s and 1960s).[27] In 2022 alone it ruled that the state of Maine could not exclude Christian schools from a tuition voucher program; the state of Texas could not execute an inmate without his pastor present; and a group in Boston could fly a "Christian flag" outside City Hall. Jefferson's wall of separation between church and state is lower than it has been for at least seventy years.[28]

Free Exercise of Religion

The First Amendment also prohibits government from interfering with the "free exercise" of religion. Once again, the Court's view has evolved.

The first landmark free exercise case was decided in 1963. Adell Sherbert, a Seventh-Day Adventist, refused to work on Saturday because it violated her faith. She was fired. South Carolina rejected her claim for unemployment benefits because she refused other jobs that also required work on Saturday. Claiming that the state was infringing on her "free exercise" of religion, Sherbert sued the state for her unemployment benefits. In deciding the case, Justice Brennan introduced a two-part test, known as the *Sherbert* or *balancing test*. First, was the government imposing a "significant burden" on an individual's ability to exercise his or her faith? Second, did the government have a "compelling interest" for imposing the burden? In this case, the Court ruled that there was a real burden on Adell Sherbert and no compelling state interest for denying her unemployment benefits.

The Sherbert test lasted until 1990, when the Court took a completely different approach. Two Oregon men participated in a Native American ritual that included taking peyote, a hallucinogen. The men were fired from their jobs at a private drug rehabilitation center and then were denied unemployment

● May a government end its contract with a foster-care provider because they refuse to place children with same-sex couples? No, ruled the Court in 2021—returning to an old "Sherbert balancing test" principle. Is Sherbert back for good? Keep an eye on the Court!

benefits for violating Oregon drug laws. The men sued, arguing that they should be exempted from the peyote ban because it was essential to their religious practice. Under the Sherbert test, they might have won. However, in *Employment Division v. Smith*, the Supreme Court ruled 6–3 against the two men and, in the process, made it much more difficult to sue the government for interfering with religious expression. In this case, the Court asked simply if the Oregon drug law was a neutral law applied in a neutral way. Yes, the law was neutral. It was not aimed at Native American religious practice—because it forbids *everyone* from smoking peyote.

The *Smith* case replaced the *Sherbert* balancing test with a *neutrality test*. The new test asks only whether the same law applies to everyone. So long as the law does not target a religious group, the Court will permit it. The result: It became more difficult to sue on the basis of "free exercise" of religion.[30]

Religious groups—from the Catholic Church to the *Witches' Voice*—mobilized against the Court's decision. Congress passed the Religious Freedom Restoration Act of 1993 (RFRA), which required federal and state governments to use the old Sherbert balancing test.

In 2014, the Supreme Court permitted the Hobby Lobby Corporation to deny its employees contraceptive coverage mandated by federal law, based on religious objections of the company's owners. The court relied on the Religious Freedom Restoration Act and, with this ruling, appeared to bring back the Sherbert balancing test—and to expand it beyond individuals to private employers like Hobby Lobby.[31]

In recent years, the Court appears to have quietly restored the Sherbert balancing test—without directly overruling *Smith* (the peyote case). In 2021, for example, in *Fulton v. City of Philadelphia*, the Court unanimously found that the city of Philadelphia had violated the free exercise clause when it ended a contract with Catholic Social Services (CSS). CSS certified foster care families but rejected same-sex couples (in accordance with church teachings)—violating Philadelphia's non-discrimination policy. The CSS had hoped that this case would lead the Court to overrule *Smith* once and for all, but the justices sidestepped the issue and simply said the non-discrimination policy did not apply in this case.[32]

Notice the trend: The Supreme Court leans toward defending religious practice—and, in many cases (like *Fulton*), permits individuals, companies, and agencies to ignore anti-discrimination laws (especially those designed to protect LGBTQ+ individuals and couples) if those laws violate a religious faith. The Court once again asks whether the government has a compelling reason to impose a burden (work on Saturday, work with same-sex couples) on religious practices.[33]

THE BOTTOM LINE

» The First Amendment has two clauses protecting religious rights: The government may not establish a religion (the establishment clause), and it may not interfere with the free exercise of religion (free exercise clause).

» Since 1971, the courts had ruled on establishment cases by trying to approximate Jefferson's wall separating church and state. Government action is permissible if it meets the three criteria known as the Lemon test: It must have a secular purpose, neither advance nor inhibit religion, and not excessively entangle government in religion. A more recent view known as accommodation simply requires that government not promote one religious view over another.

» In 2022, the Supreme Court replaced the Lemon test with a vaguer standard much friendlier to religion: "historical practices and understanding."

» In protecting the free exercise of religion, the courts traditionally asked if the government had a compelling interest for imposing a burden.

» A major fault line is emerging between two different liberties: Religious practice versus anti-discrimination laws (especially those that protect LGBTQ+ individuals). So far, the court has tilted toward religious claims.

 # Freedom of Speech

Next, we turn to the civil liberty that the courts now rank as the most important, freedom of speech. After its religious clauses, the First Amendment states:

> *Congress shall make no law . . . abridging the freedom of speech or of the press.*

A Preferred Position

The Supreme Court gives the First Amendment primacy among all the amendments to the Constitution. And among the rights listed in the First Amendment (freedom of speech, religion, press, assembly, and the right to petition government), free speech holds a "preferred position." When freedom of speech conflicts with any other right, the Court generally will "prefer," or protect, speech.[34]

Why do contemporary courts put so much emphasis on the right to express opinions? Because democracy requires vigorous debate. John Stuart Mill, a nineteenth-century English political theorist, put it this way: "However true a doctrine may be, if it is not fully, frequently and fearlessly discussed, it will be held as a dead dogma, not a living truth." Over time, the courts have followed Mill, placing their faith in the free marketplace of ideas.[35]

When the right to speak out clashes with other rights, free speech usually wins. How about **hate speech**—which demeans people on the basis of race,

Hate speech: Hostile statements based on someone's personal characteristics, such as race, ethnicity, religion, or sexual orientation.

ethnicity, gender, or other characteristics? In 2017, the Court unanimously protected hateful speech, in the case involving The Slants described at the start of this chapter.

When it comes to free speech, public opinion has been shifting against the court. More Americans (60 percent) support government prohibitions against racist or bigoted speech than at any time in modern history; in fact, a third even support prohibitions on "something rude or impolite to someone else."[36] Will public opinion make a difference? In *Dobbs* (the abortion case), the Court majority answered with a crisp "no": The courts do not "derive their legitimacy . . . from following . . . the vagaries of public opinion."[37] (In Chapter 16 we'll tell you how justices really decide.) Again, the whole point of civil liberties is to protect rights from the majority.

Political Speech

In every generation, political leaders are tempted to stop subversive talk—or harsh criticism. Under the John Adams administration, just ten years after the Constitution was ratified, Congress drafted the Alien and Sedition Acts. Tensions with France were running high, and the acts made it illegal to "print, utter, or publish . . . any false, scandalous, and malicious writing" against the government. The meaning of the acts was brutally simple: Criticize the government and face prosecution. Some of the nation's leading newspaper editors were prosecuted and jailed. The acts were repealed four years later—but stand as an eternal warning about the risks to free speech.[38]

The first modern free speech cases arose during World War I. Charles Schenck, general secretary of the Socialist Party of Philadelphia, was found guilty of violating the recently passed Espionage Act because his pamphlets urged men not to enlist for a war designed to pour profits into greedy Wall Street. Was his freedom of speech curtailed? Under normal circumstances it might be, wrote Justice Oliver Wendell Holmes for a unanimous Court in *Schenck v. United States* (1919), but this was wartime. Distributing these documents, Holmes wrote, was like falsely shouting "Fire!" in a crowded theater. Holmes then formulated the most famous test for free speech: Speech is not protected if it poses "a **clear and present danger** that it will lead to 'substantive evils.'"

In the early 1920s, many Americans, fueled by lurid media coverage, were anxious about foreigners, immigrants, socialists, communists, and anarchists. The Supreme Court hardened the "clear and present danger" test by ruling that judges did not have to "weigh each and every utterance." They could simply determine whether the "natural tendency and probable effect" of the speech was to "bring about something bad or evil"—even if that danger lay in the distant future.[39]

The clear and present danger test stood for decades. Then in *Brandenburg v. Ohio* (1969), the Court complained that "puny" threats, which no one took seriously except "nervous judges," were being declared a "clear and present danger." The issue arose when a Ku Klux Klan leader, Clarence Brandenburg, organized a rally at which Klan members burned crosses, waved guns, and called for "revengeance" against Jews and Black Americans. The Supreme Court struck down Brandenburg's conviction and rewrote the clear and present danger test. The state may not interfere with speech, it said, unless the speech "incites **imminent lawless action**" *and* is likely to actually "produce such action."[40]

The result makes it very difficult to curtail political speech—even when it is highly offensive. Members of the Westboro Baptist Church picket military funerals to protest homosexuality with signs that read "Fag sin = 9/11" and "You're

Clear and present danger: Court doctrine that permits restrictions on free speech if officials believe that the speech will lead to prohibited action such as violence or terrorism.

Imminent lawless action: Updated Court doctrine; restrictions on free speech only permitted if officials affirm a credible threat that dangerous illegal actions—such as acts of terror or assault—are an immediate and probable danger.

going to hell." Albert Snyder, the father of a Marine killed in Iraq, sued the church. Forty-eight states and numerous veterans' groups supported the suit. The Supreme Court acknowledged that the protests were hurtful but protected them as an exercise of free speech. The government may limit the speech only if the bad effects—a lynching, the overthrow of the government, or a terrorist attack—are likely to happen immediately.[41]

● *The expansive reach of free-speech protections: Members of the Westboro Church cheer for "more dead soldiers" in their fight against tolerance. Here they draw counterprotests at Brown University.*

The issue of free speech burst back into the headlines with the rise and spread of social media platforms. The First Amendment guarantees that the government cannot infringe on the right of free speech, but it does not apply to a private company like Facebook or Twitter. Even so, companies often use free speech as a guiding principle. Facebook founder and CEO Mark Zuckerberg has publicly rejected widespread criticism of the platform's refusal to remove disinformation and violent extremists—including charges that the January 6 Capitol insurrection was planned largely on the company's platform. "Facebook," Zuckerberg insisted, "follows the American free speech tradition."[42]

But as the "techlash" grew, social media platforms designed filters to objectionable speech, and flagged comments with warning labels about incitement to violence or falsehoods. In the wake of the January 6 Capitol insurrection, Facebook and Twitter banned former President Trump from their platforms; Twitter (until Elon Musk's 2022 takeover of the company) declared a permanent removal of "dangerous individuals and organizations."

Do these limits violate free speech? Most Americans say yes. In one poll, 61 percent said that the First Amendment requires Facebook "to allow all Americans to express themselves freely on the platform." But if you recall the actual language of the First Amendment, you'll know this is wrong. The First Amendment begins, "*Congress shall make no law*"—it applies only to government, not to private companies.[43]

Symbolic Speech

When Clarence Brandenburg burned his cross, he engaged in **symbolic expression**. He expressed a point of view with an act rather than through speech. The First Amendment protects symbolic speech—within limits.

In 2003, the Supreme Court identified those limits when it took two cross-burning cases on the same day. One involved a Ku Klux Klan (KKK) ceremony. The original cross burnings, after the Civil War, signaled the murder of a former slave—an emblem designed to frighten people during what amounted to a campaign of domestic terrorism. The Court drew a careful distinction. Individuals may burn crosses to express their views, but not to intimidate others. Sometimes, wrote Justice Sandra Day O'Connor, "the cross burning is a statement of ideology, a symbol of group solidarity. It is a ritual used at Klan gatherings, and it is used to represent the Klan itself." The Constitution protects these symbolic speeches.[44] The KKK burned the cross as part of a ritual without directly threatening or intimidating anyone. On the same day, however, the Court upheld the conviction of another cross burner. In this second case, two men had come home after a night of drinking and burned a cross on a Black neighbor's lawn. Their act directly

Symbolic expression: An act, rather than actual speech, used to demonstrate a point of view.

● *Social media or the First Amendment: Which do you know better? Five rights are listed in the First Amendment and five social media company logos are shown above. Only 1 percent of Americans can name all five First Amendment rights. Forty-five percent of Americans (and over 70 percent of eighteen- to twenty-nine-year-olds) can name all five social media company logos shown here. How about you? How many First Amendment rights can you name? How many logos? Answers: The logos, from left to right, are TikTok, YouTube, Twitter, Instagram, and Facebook. First Amendment rights: freedom of religion, speech, press, assembly, and the right to petition government. Source: Constitution Day Polls*

intimidated the neighbors. Even if there is no immediate (or clear and present) danger, intimidating people is not protected by the First Amendment.

Burning the American flag is another unpopular symbolic expression. Forty-eight states and the federal government banned flag burning. The Supreme Court narrowly struck down the laws. "If there is a bedrock principle underlying the First Amendment," argued Justice Brennan for a 5–4 majority, "it is that government may not prohibit the expression of an idea simply because society finds the idea offensive or disagreeable."[45] Congress responded by passing legislation defending the flag. The Court overturned that too.

In 2015, however, the Supreme Court narrowly upheld (5–4) Texas's refusal to issue a license plate with a Confederate flag. License plates are a form of government speech, and Texas can choose what to regulate. Notice the distinction: The government may not restrict Simon Tam's (fronting The Slants) hate speech, or any group's flag flying over City Hall, but it can choose what it "says." Today, that issue has boiled over across the South as the region confronts its Confederate legacy. On one side, many argue that Confederate flags and monuments (sometimes erected in response to the civil rights movement) commemorate those who fought for the enslavement of people of color and are symbols of racial oppression and white supremacy. On the other side, some people still contend that the monuments celebrate Southern heritage. The key question: When the state speaks, what should it say?[46]

● *Symbolic speech. Unpopular? Often. Protected? Yes. Burning an American flag (a) and players on the Houston Texans kneeling during the national anthem (b).*

COMPARING NATIONS 5.1   Civil Liberties Around the World

Every democracy protects civil liberties differently. Each makes choices based on its culture, its history, and who wields power. Consider some international differences.

The right to free speech is stronger in the United States. In Germany and France, it is against the law to deny that the Nazis murdered six million Jews between 1941 and 1945. In Turkey, the government will punish you for discussing the Ottoman Turks' genocide of Armenians in 1915. In Thailand, it is a serious crime to criticize the king. In Canada, there are strict limits on pornography because it demeans women. Most Americans despise Nazis, Holocaust deniers, and pornographers. However, the Constitution protects them all—at least in most cases. When it comes to speech, Germany, France, Thailand, Turkey, and Canada all tilt more toward community needs, whereas the United States distinctly emphasizes individual rights.

The United States is unique in protecting gun rights. No other nation explicitly mentions the right to bear arms in its constitution. And no other nation has so many guns per capita.

The United States puts special emphasis on property rights. For example, the Fifth Amendment forbids the government from taking private property "without just compensation." By contrast, the Canadian constitution does not even mention private property.

Most nations forbid the death penalty. One hundred and eight countries have abolished the death penalty for all crimes. Almost all industrialized democracies have done so (Japan, Taiwan, and the United States are the only exceptions). Abolishing the death penalty is a precondition for joining the European Union (the federation of European nations). In 2019, authorities in the United States executed twenty-two people in seven states; in 2021, five states and the federal government executed eleven people—the smallest number in more than fifty years. Even with these declining numbers, over 2,400 people have been sentenced to execution and remain on death row.[47] Only a handful of nations—China, Iran, Saudi Arabia, Iraq, and North Korea—have executed more people in recent years, although tyrannical governments often murder people outside the criminal justice system. Americans debate whether a clause in the Bill of Rights, the prohibition on "cruel and unusual punishment," should push the United States away from the death penalty.

American liberties are mostly negative: They tell the government what it may NOT do. Other constitutions include positive rights—things that the government must do—such as educate all citizens, provide universal healthcare, or ensure that women are well represented in the national legislature. As we saw in Chapter 2, President Franklin Roosevelt offered a new interpretation of liberty that included positive rights—but this is not something explicitly mentioned in the Constitution or its amendments.

Limits to Free Speech: Fighting Words

Is there any way to rein in cross burning, gay bashing, slurs against African Americans and other historically marginalized groups, and other forms of hateful speech? As you can see from Comparing Nations 5.1, other democracies are much tougher on hurtful speech; so are many colleges and universities. The logic is simple: How can you build a vibrant community if some members feel singled out, threatened, or diminished?

One legal doctrine offers a limit to hate speech by restricting **fighting words**. The Supreme Court defined these in 1942 as "personally abusive epithets which, when addressed to the ordinary citizen, are, as a matter of common knowledge, inherently likely to provoke violent reaction."[48] The Court stated the principle but has been very reluctant to apply it. Some legal scholars argue that it should simply be overruled.[49] However, reformers trying to create codes of decent language often rely on the logic of "fighting words." While the Supreme Court has been skeptical (unless the speech is accompanied by violence or other criminal acts), state courts continue to convict people for "fighting words"—most commonly when people confront police, harass women, or utter racial slurs.[50]

Fighting words:
Expressions inherently likely to provoke violent reactions and not necessarily protected by the First Amendment.

Limited Protections: Student Speech

How about students speaking out? In the 1969 landmark *Tinker* decision, the Court announced that students "do not shed their constitutional right to freedom of speech or expression at the schoolhouse gate." That decision, however, has been qualified in a series of cases that balanced student rights with the schools' educational mission.

In 1965, John (fifteen years old) and Mary Beth Tinker (thirteen) violated school rules by wearing black armbands to protest the Vietnam War. They were suspended and told that they could return only when they were ready to abide by the school's rules. The Supreme Court overturned the suspension and established what became known as the Tinker rule: The students' right to free speech could be curtailed only if it "materially and substantially interferes with the requirements of appropriate discipline in the operation of the school."[51]

In subsequent cases, the Court found that teachers and school officials had an obligation to teach students proper conduct and could regulate speech that was vulgar, indecent, offensive (1986), or inconsistent with the educational mission of the school (1988).[52] This perspective may have loosened recently, especially given a landmark 2021 case, *Mahanoy Area School District v. B.L.*, in which a Pennsylvania high school student, Brandi Levy, recorded a profane rant against her school while at a fast-food restaurant. The Court ruled in Ms. Levy's favor, holding that the school had no jurisdiction over her off-campus speech.[53] This marked the first free speech Supreme Court ruling in favor of students in decades.

Debates over student speech have intensified dramatically in recent years, as students from historically marginalized groups and their allies denounce speakers or viewpoints; they believe they are fighting for equity and inclusion.

WHAT DO YOU THINK?

Free Speech on Campus

Around the country, many universities forbid hate speech on campus. They forbid harassment (oral, written, graphic, or physical) against any group that might face discrimination—African Americans, Latinos, LGBTQ+ people, military veterans, religious denominations, age groups, and others. These codes, in turn, provoke fierce opposition. Critics argue that restrictions on speech create taboo subjects, and students with unpopular opinions could end up being expelled—and their teachers or professors fired. What should campus leaders do? Before your final answer, consider that public high schools and universities face stronger pressures on these themes (often with state legislatures taking action) than do private schools.

Yes. Forbid certain hurtful types of expression.
We must protect LGBTQ+ students, students of color, military veterans, and any other group that faces hatred and violence. Hate speech fractures communities and hurts people. It is frightening and painful to the targeted groups. It poses a threat to teaching and destroys the community spirit necessary for learning.

No. Forbid restrictions on speech regardless of how hurtful.
Everyone has the right to an opinion, even if it is a horrible opinion. We can punish criminal behavior, but we should never punish people for simply expressing their views—especially on a college campus, where exploration of ideas is a core value.

Others decry the "cancel culture" that—in their view—tramples on the right to free speech.[54] Some universities and private high schools, in attempts to balance between two strongly held views, have created "free speech zones" where community members or visiting speakers may speak as they wish. Critics respond that entire campuses *are* "zones" of free speech, and to set aside a small zone for free expression violates the spirit of civil liberties.[55]

School speech debates now face the digital frontier. Social media and other digital communications allow widespread, lightning-fast broadcast of information—as well as malicious gossip, cyberbullying, and cruel rumors. As of 2020 all fifty states and the District of Columbia had passed laws forbidding online cyberbullying, though some civil-liberties advocates critique them as restrictions on protected speech. Across the country, schools have suspended or expelled students for posts deemed inappropriate or illegal.

The First Amendment offers students—in high schools or colleges—less protection than it offers adults. School officials may regulate speech as long as they do not do so arbitrarily.

● Joseph Frederick was suspended from Juneau-Douglas High School (Juneau, Alaska) for ten days because of this banner. The Supreme Court upheld the suspension for advocating drugs in violation of the school's antidrug policy. [Morse v. Frederick, 551 U.S. 393 (2007)]

THE BOTTOM LINE

» Free speech is crucial to democracy, and the Court gives it a privileged position—even against angry public opposition to flag-burning, cross-burning, or homophobic displays at military funerals.

» Free speech can be curtailed if it poses a "clear and present danger." Today, the Court requires the danger to be both imminent and likely to occur.

» There are (much-debated) limits to free speech, including fighting words and student speech.

 # Freedom of the Press

Freedom of the press follows most of the same rules as freedom of speech. The written word has always been essential to politics. The form changes—pamphlets during the revolutionary period, newspapers in the mid-twentieth century, and digital media today. Written words share the "preferred position" enjoyed by speech. Broadcast media are slightly different and subject to federal regulation (as we explore in Chapter 9).

Prior Restraint

The effort to stop speech before it occurs is known as **prior restraint**. Although the Supreme Court has permitted government officials to punish people for what they have said or printed, it has never allowed federal government agents to gag citizens before they have had their say.

In 1931, public officials in Minneapolis shut down a newspaper, the *Saturday Press,* which was published by an avowed racist who claimed that Jewish gangs were running the city. In *Near v. Minnesota* (1931), the Court ruled that the state could not suppress the paper, no matter how obnoxious, but it left the door open to prior restraint for national security reasons. The government would be justified for stopping someone from publishing information about "the number and location of troops in the field," it said, but not for publishing anti-Semitic harangues.

In one famous case of prior restraint, a State Department official leaked a rich archive of classified material, the Pentagon Papers, that exposed the mistakes and deceptions that led the United States into the Vietnam War. The Richard Nixon administration, claiming a threat to national security, went to court to block the *New York Times* from publishing the papers. Within days, the Supreme Court heard the arguments and, by a 6–3 vote, lifted the ban and permitted publication. The majority opinion emphasized the "heavy presumption" against prior restraint.[56]

The shift from print media to the Internet has profoundly changed the logic of prior restraint. In 2008, WikiLeaks, a web-based venue for anonymous whistle-blowers, published internal documents from a Swiss bank that appeared to show tax evasion and money laundering at the bank's Cayman Islands branch. The bank went to court and won a restraining order against publication of the leaked documents. Stopping a newspaper from publishing is straightforward: The court enjoins the publisher. However, because WikiLeaks operates anonymously and globally, it is almost impossible for a court to suppress the information it publishes. In the WikiLeaks case, the court tried to seal the site's American address—but the documents simply appeared on mirror sites. After two weeks, Judge Jerry White dissolved the injunction and acknowledged that the court's effort had only publicized the documents. There is "a definite disconnect," he commented, "between the evolution of our constitutional jurisprudence and modern technology."[57]

Then in 2013, Edward Snowden, a contractor working for the National Security Agency (NSA), leaked a huge cache of documents detailing the NSA's extensive data collection. The reports, published in the *Washington Post*, revealed the NSA was collecting metadata on millions of cell phone calls and tapping data from tech companies.

Both the WikiLeaks and Snowden stories illustrate how digital media renders the government helpless against the spread of embarrassing and potentially harmful electronic information. By flowing anonymously across national borders and court jurisdictions, digital media—whether appearing on established media organizations' sites, social media platforms like Instagram and Twitter, or individual blogs—pose dilemmas for every nation trying to regulate the written word. The old question was "should prior restraint be permitted?" The new question is whether it is possible at all.

In some cases, it might be. In fall 2021, the *New York Times* published (online and in print) details that a secretive right-wing group, Project Veritas, had obtained, through possibly criminal means, a diary kept by President Biden's daughter, Ashley, as she recovered from addiction the previous year. Project Veritas, the *Times* reported, had planned to publish excerpts in an effort to embarrass candidate Biden shortly before the election.

The *Times* had also planned to publish further details of how Project Veritas had obtained the diary, but lawyers for Project Veritas brought a suit to prevent the *Times* from doing so. A senior New York judge agreed, and in late 2021/early 2022 forbade publication. Eventually a federal appeals court overturned the ruling, and the *Times* went public with details including the fact that Ashley Biden's diary had been passed around among donors at a Trump fundraising event.[58] Prior restraint still has some teeth even in the digital age.

Obscenity

The First Amendment does not protect obscenity. However, the courts always face the same problem: What is obscene? Justice Potter Stewart put it famously when he said simply, "I know it when I see it." Of course, different people see "it" in different things. The Court's emphasis on free speech leads it to reject most regulation of obscenity.

In *Miller v. California* (1973), the Supreme Court created a three-part test for judging a work to be obscene. The **Miller test** holds that speech is not protected by the First Amendment if it has all three of these characteristics:

1. "The average person, applying contemporary community standards, would find that the work, taken as a whole, appeals to the prurient interest" (meaning that it is meant to be sexually stimulating).

2. It depicts sexual conduct in a "patently offensive way."

3. The work lacks "serious literary, artistic, political or scientific value."

The Miller test only created new questions. What does it mean to be patently offensive? Offensive to whom? How do we rely on community standards of decency when digital media flow across borders?

In recent years, the Court has been hostile to most efforts at banning material. It struck down a congressional effort to ban online material that showed "sexual, excretory activities or organs." In an especially grisly case, it even rejected legislation prohibiting the portrayal of animal cruelty. The ban had tried to forbid "crush videos" in which women wearing high heels crush dogs, cats, and hamsters while engaging in "a kind of dominatrix patter."[59] Congress subsequently rewrote the law to get around this Court ruling and outlawed the animal cruelty.

Feminist scholars have tried to change the framework of this debate. Pornography, they have argued, subordinates women in the same way that hate speech demeans minorities. Nations such as Canada have accepted this perspective. Although U.S. courts have not taken this view—and continue to protect hate speech—the feminist position remains an important part of the debate.[60]

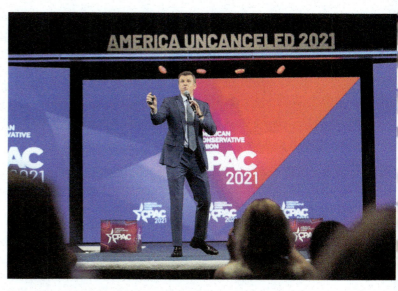

● Can the government restrain news organizations from publishing material, known as "prior restraint"? Here, James O'Keefe, the head of Project Veritas, speaks during the Conservative Political Action Conference in Dallas. O'Keefe successfully invoked prior restraint against the New York Times, *until a federal appeals judge removed the prohibition.*

Miller test: Three-part test for judging whether a work is obscene (if it has all three, the work loses First Amendment protection).

Social media has given rise to a new phenomenon, "revenge porn," in which explicit photos or videos are posted online without the subject's consent. All but two states now outlaw revenge porn and Congress has expressed rare bipartisan support for making it a federal crime. Judicial decisions on revenge porn have been mixed, with state supreme courts striking down laws in Arizona, Vermont, and Minnesota, while upholding state restrictions in Texas (2021) and Indiana (2022). The Supreme Court has yet to weigh in.

The Court flatly forbids child pornography—a sharp limit to free speech. Even here, the Court struck down one ban, the Child Pornography Act of 1996, because it criminalized too broadly—people might be prosecuted for possession of sexual images that were digitally altered or that involved people who were not minors. Led by evangelical conservatives, Congress rewrote the law to forbid presenting material that led someone to believe it included "minors engaging in sexually explicit conduct." In 2008, the Supreme Court upheld the revised law, and this exception to free speech protections has remained settled since.[61]

The issue was back in the headlines in 2022 during Senate Judiciary Committee hearings on Ketanji Brown Jackson's Supreme Court nomination. Some Republican senators opposing the nomination charged (wrongly, as it turned out) that Jackson, as a federal judge, had been lenient in sentencing defendants convicted of child pornography crimes.[62]

Libel

There are also limits to the false things one can write or say about someone. Written falsehoods are known as *libel*; spoken falsehoods are known as *slander*. The courts have made it very difficult for public officials or celebrities to win a libel (or slander) judgment. To do so, they must prove not just that a statement was false and that it caused them harm but that it was made with malice or "a reckless disregard for the truth."

Today, the Court allows even outrageous claims, cartoons, spoofs, and criticism directed at public officials and celebrities. By contrast, English law is just the opposite: It puts the burden of proof on the writers to prove the truth of what they have written. As president, Donald Trump brought multiple libel claims against

● *Almost anything goes. It is very difficult to win a libel judgment under American law. Former spouses and celebrated actors Johnny Depp (a) and Amber Heard (b) each brought libel suits against the other for defamation; after years of legal wrangling, Depp won a partial judgment—an exception to the usual U.S. judicial outcome.*

U.S. media outlets—in 2020, he sued the *New York Times, Washington Post,* and CNN for reporting widespread allegations about Russian interference in the 2016 presidential election. In England he might have had a case, but judges ruled against the president in American courts.[63]

THE BOTTOM LINE

» The rules for freedom of the press reflect those of free speech and strongly protect free expression.

» The courts are especially skeptical of any effort to impose prior restraint. Digital media make it almost impossible to even try.

» Obscenity is not protected by the First Amendment. The Court has spent years wrestling with what counts as obscenity and now uses the three-part Miller test. Child pornography is a clear exception.

 # The Right to Bear Arms

The Second Amendment asserts a uniquely American right. No other national constitution includes the right to bear arms. The text in the Constitution is ambiguous:

> *A well-regulated militia, being necessary to the security of a free state, the right of the people to keep and bear arms shall not be infringed.*

On one reading, this amendment simply protects colonial-era militias. On another, it guarantees the right to own weapons. Let's consider each side of the argument before we look at recent Supreme Court decisions that powerfully defended the right to carry firearms.

A Relic of the Revolution?

Skeptics question whether Americans have any right to bear arms at all. The Second Amendment, they say, protected state militias. Early Americans believed that only kings and tyrants kept permanent armies. In a republic, the citizens volunteered for service in local militias that defended their communities and their nation. The Second Amendment, in this reading, is a "relic of the American Revolution"[64] and simply forbids the national government from disarming the local militias. It does not involve a constitutional right to tote weapons.

Those who favor this view generally emphasize public safety and gun control. They argue that America's high homicide rate reflects the easy availability of rapid-fire, high-capacity weapons—in 2021 alone, guns were used in 20,726 murders and more than 27,000 suicides.[65] Gun control sentiment grows after terrible events like the slaughter at Robb Elementary School in Uvalde, Texas, in 2022.

The Palladium of All Liberties?

Proponents of gun rights read the same constitutional sentence very differently. As Justice Scalia explained, the Second Amendment has two parts—a preface about militias and a clause that really matters, declaring that "the right . . . to keep and bear arms shall not be infringed." Many see the right to bear arms as the most important right of all—"the palladium of the liberties of the republic," as Justice Joseph Story put it back in 1833 (a palladium is something that secures). "When all else fails," declared Charlton Heston, actor and longtime honorary president of the National Rifle Association, "it is the one right that prevails. . . . It is the one right that allows rights to exist at all."[66]

The Supreme Court has moved decisively over the last fifteen years to defend gun rights. In 2008, the Court struck down a District of Columbia rule that

Guns on Campus

Should Colleges Allow Concealed Carry?

The Second Amendment's ambiguous "right to bear arms" guarantee has been a source of much debate, almost since the Bill of Rights was originally introduced. College campuses historically have enjoyed low homicide rates.[67] However, after a shooting at Virginia Tech in 2007 left thirty-two people dead, political science major Chris Brown founded Students for Concealed Carry to lift bans on campuses. When the Supreme Court extended gun rights in 2022, it continued to permit legal restrictions in specific places—like college campuses. The issue remains highly charged across the nation.

The map shows which states allow concealed carry, which ban it, and which leave it up to the campuses to decide.

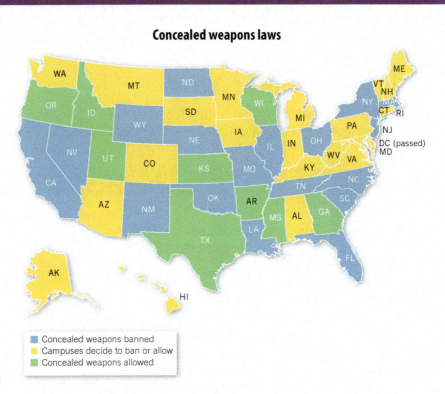

Concealed weapons laws

- Concealed weapons banned
- Campuses decide to ban or allow
- Concealed weapons allowed

THINK ABOUT IT

What policies have most states adopted on this issue before the Supreme Court stepped in? Do you see trends among the more liberal states of the Northeast or the more conservative states of the South?

Do students carrying concealed weapons make your campus safer? Or less safe? Why?

Source: National Conference of State Legislatures

restricted guns in people's homes. In 2010, in *McDonald v. Chicago*, the Court finally *incorporated* the Second Amendment.[68] For the first time, the constitutional right to bear arms applied to state and local governments.

The *McDonald* decision seemed to make it more difficult for cities and states to regulate weapons—but in the following years, most state and local restrictions were upheld. In the wake of a Parkland High School mass shooting in 2018, Florida's governor signed into law the most significant gun restrictions in that state in decades.

That all changed in 2022, when the Court, in *New York State Rifle & Pistol Association v. Bruen*, struck down New York State's gun law. The state had granted licenses to carry firearms only to people who could "demonstrate a special need." The court ruled that no one should have to justify their need for such a basic constitutional liberty—all citizens enjoyed the essential right to arm themselves in self-defense. States may enact conditions: licensing, background checks, training requirements, or gun-free zones like schools or churches. But the court's action vastly expanded access to firearms in states that had tried to limit them.[69]

Few rights issues have split Americans like the Second Amendment. Conservative and rural Americans generally defend gun rights, which they view as deeply rooted in American culture and essential to personal protection. Liberals fear carnage: Domestic disputes turn deadly, children kill their friends, and urban neighborhoods become combat zones. Mass shootings—and major Supreme Court rulings—keep this issue on the political agenda. Public opinion has remained largely consistent on this issue, with 66 percent of the public calling for stricter gun controls—compared to only 8 percent who would like to see fewer controls. (see Chapter 7).[70]

THE BOTTOM LINE

» Some critics see the Second Amendment as an outmoded defense of citizen militias.

» Others see it as a vital individual right—perhaps even the most important right in the entire Constitution.

» In 2010, the Supreme Court incorporated the right to bear arms as an essential individual right. For a dozen years after, state and local restrictions were largely upheld in lower courts . . . until the Court's 2022 decision that curbed state authority to restrict concealed carry.

 # The Rights of the Accused

The Bill of Rights places special emphasis on protecting people accused of crimes. Four amendments (Fourth, Fifth, Sixth, and Eighth) together list thirty-one different rights for those who face police action or criminal charges. No other civil-liberties issue gets as much attention in the Constitution. Protecting the accused involves another balancing act. On one hand, the courts must restrain law enforcement and defend the constitutional freedoms that define America. Yet the government must also protect public safety. After vastly expanding the rights of the accused in the 1960s, the courts—in step with Congress, presidents of both parties, and most states—now tilt firmly toward law enforcement. However, American incarceration rates are the world's highest and especially affect minority communities—leading to bipartisan calls for a renewed emphasis on rights. Sustained protest might just tilt the balance back against harsh criminal justice practices.

In this section, we examine the most important (and controversial) protections one at a time. As you read, think about the trade-offs between safe streets and civil liberties.

The Fourth Amendment: Search and Seizure

The Fourth Amendment protects people from government officials bursting into their houses.

> *The right of the people to be secure in their persons, houses, papers, and effects, against unreasonable searches and seizures, shall not be violated, and no Warrants shall issue, but upon probable cause, supported by Oath or affirmation, and particularly describing the place to be searched, and the persons or things to be seized. . . .*

British officials in the 1770s ransacked colonial homes, searching for weapons or smuggled goods. The Fourth Amendment prevents that from happening. Justice Louis Brandeis described it as "the right to be left alone—the . . . right most valued by civilized men."[71] The police may not enter a home unless they go before a judge and explain why they suspect that evidence of a crime can be found in a specific place. The judge determines whether there is "probable cause" to issue the warrant. It sounds simple, but there are large gray areas (see Figure 5.1).

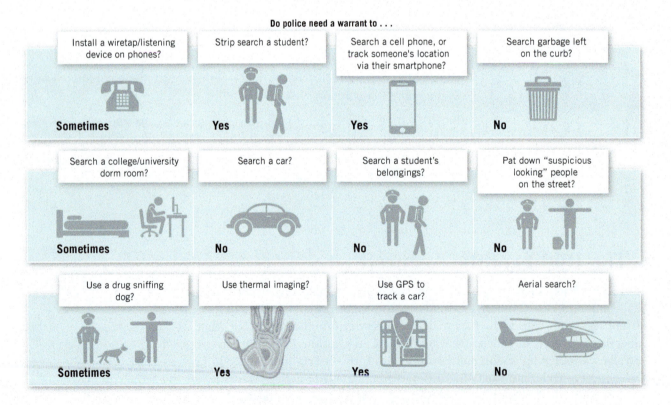

Do police need a warrant to . . .

| Install a wiretap/listening device on phones? | Strip search a student? | Search a cell phone, or track someone's location via their smartphone? | Search garbage left on the curb? |
| Sometimes | Yes | Yes | No |

| Search a college/university dorm room? | Search a car? | Search a student's belongings? | Pat down "suspicious looking" people on the street? |
| Sometimes | No | No | No |

| Use a drug sniffing dog? | Use thermal imaging? | Use GPS to track a car? | Aerial search? |
| Sometimes | Yes | Yes | No |

● **FIGURE 5.1** *When are search warrants required?*

The landmark search and seizure case began in 1957 with a tip that Dollree (Dolly) Mapp was hiding a bombing suspect in her apartment. In addition, the police suspected she had illegal gambling paraphernalia. The police knocked at her door, but she refused to let them in. They eventually broke the door down, and when she demanded to see a warrant they waved a piece of paper—not a warrant—in the air. In searching her apartment for the bombing suspect or the gambling material, the police discovered a suitcase of pornography—illegal at the time. Mapp was convicted on obscenity charges. The Supreme Court threw out the conviction and, in *Mapp v. Ohio* (1961, decided 6–3), devised the **exclusionary rule**: Evidence obtained in an illegal search may not be introduced in a trial. Even evidence that clearly proves someone is guilty of a crime may not be used if it was improperly obtained.

Exclusionary rule: The ruling that evidence obtained in an illegal search may not be introduced in a trial.

Twenty years later, President Ronald Reagan (1981–89) urged both Congress and the courts to abolish the rule. Supreme Court Chief Justice John Roberts, then a young Justice Department attorney, wrote the memos supporting Reagan's criticism. During the Reagan years, the courts began making exceptions to the exclusionary rule. For example, in 1984, police arrested Alberto Leon when they discovered a large quantity of illegal drugs in his possession. Their warrant had expired, but the Supreme Court made a "good faith" exception and permitted the drugs to be introduced as evidence.[72] In 2009, Chief Justice Roberts wrote (in a 5–4 opinion) that there was no need to exclude evidence if the police had violated a suspect's Fourth Amendment rights because of "isolated negligence."[73]

In 2011, the Supreme Court crossed an important threshold. It permitted officers to break into a house without a warrant. The officers in the case knocked, identified themselves, and heard movements that sounded like the destruction of evidence of drug use. Only one justice dissented. This ruling would, wrote Justice Ruth Bader Ginsburg, seriously curtail the use of warrants by police. Writing for the majority, Justice Samuel Alito took a hard line. Residents who "attempt to destroy evidence have only themselves to blame." In later cases, however, in 2016 and 2022, the Court ruled that evidence would have to be excluded "if there were flagrant police misconduct." In short, the courts have loosened—but not eliminated—the exclusionary rule.[74]

The Fifth Amendment: Rights at Trials

The Fifth Amendment lists a long series of rights focused largely on criminal trials. Consider them one clause at a time.

> *No person shall be held to answer for a capital, or otherwise infamous crime, unless on a . . . indictment of a Grand Jury.*

Before the government can prosecute, it must persuade a jury. A **grand jury** does not decide on guilt or innocence but only on whether there is enough evidence for the case to go to trial. The grand jury meets secretly and hears only from the prosecutor; as a New York judge once quipped, a decent prosecutor should be able to get a grand jury to "indict a ham sandwich."[75] As the Supreme Court has never incorporated the grand jury, this provision does not apply to the states. After the grand jury indicts, a petit (or small) jury of six to twelve individuals hears the case, weighs the evidence, and delivers a verdict.

Grand jury: A jury that does not decide on guilt or innocence but only on whether there is enough evidence for the case to go to trial.

> *. . . nor shall any person be subject for the same offense to be twice put in jeopardy of life or limb.*

Double jeopardy: The principle that an individual cannot be tried twice for the same offense.

An individual cannot face **double jeopardy**, or be tried twice for the same offense. ("Jeopardy of life and limb" refers to the old colonial practice of punishing people by lopping off an ear or damaging other limbs.) Without this provision, the government could simply keep trying people over and over.

Despite this prohibition, individuals sometimes face multiple trials. They can be tried on different charges, tried in federal court after being acquitted in state court, and—if they are acquitted on criminal charges—sued for damages. In a famous case, former football star O. J. Simpson was acquitted of murdering his wife and her companion, only to lose a civil judgment for damages to the victims' families.[76]

> *. . . nor shall be compelled in any criminal case to be a witness against himself.*

The Constitution aimed to protect citizens from torture and coerced confessions. The liberal Warren Court affirmed this right by requiring police officers to inform suspects that they have the right to remain silent, now known as the **Miranda warnings**, after *Miranda v. Arizona* (1966). Any evidence acquired before the warning would not be admissible in court. The ruling created an enormous outcry. Richard Nixon used *Miranda* in the 1968 presidential campaign as evidence that the United States had grown "soft on crime." Congress passed a law to get around the ruling, which the Court eventually struck down.[77]

Miranda warnings: A set of rights that police officers are required to inform suspects of, including the right to remain silent.

Over the past forty years, the courts have limited the *Miranda* rights—permitting confessions made to a police officer posing as another inmate (1990), carving out an exception for public safety (1984), limiting the rules when defendants take the stand in their own defense (1970), and blocking a defendant from suing a police officer who failed to provide a Miranda warning (2022). But the right, somewhat watered down, remains a central protection.[78]

The popular controversy subsided long ago, and Miranda warnings have become "part of national culture," as Chief Justice Rehnquist put it. Cop shows end with the police nabbing the criminal while intoning, "You have the right to remain silent." Some defense lawyers claim, half seriously, the phrase is now so familiar that what defendants actually hear is "We've caught you, and you're in big trouble now."

The Sixth Amendment: The Right to Counsel

The Sixth Amendment guarantees a speedy and public trial decided by an impartial jury. It includes another important provision, the right to counsel:

> *In all criminal prosecutions, the accused shall . . . have the assistance of counsel for his defense.*

The Supreme Court weighed in on this issue in an explosive case known as the Scottsboro Boys trial. In 1931, nine young Black men riding a freight train in Alabama were accused of raping two white women. Although the charges were false (one woman immediately recanted), angry mobs gathered, and eight of the young men were rushed through trials and condemned to death. In *Powell v. Alabama* (1932), the Court ruled that, at least in a capital case (a case that could end in the death penalty), the defendants are entitled to lawyers, who must be given enough time to meet with their clients and prepare their case. The Scottsboro case was a civil rights breakthrough for another reason: None of the Black men unfairly accused of raping a white woman were executed—though seven of the nine spent years in jail.

In 1963, the Court expanded the right to counsel to all felony cases (a felony is a crime punishable by at least one year in prison). Clarence Gideon, a Florida drifter, was allegedly caught breaking into a poolroom from which he had stolen beer, soft drinks, and change out of the jukebox. When he came to trial, he demanded a lawyer, but the Florida court denied the request. Gideon was convicted and sentenced to five years, but from his jail cell, working with legal texts, he scrawled an appeal. Astonishingly, his plea made it all the way to the Supreme Court. In *Gideon v. Wainwright* (1963), the Supreme Court ruled that the Sixth Amendment required the provision of a lawyer to defend those who cannot afford one. With a competent lawyer, Gideon was acquitted.[79] A network of public defenders soon spread across the country.

● *The Scottsboro Boys, with their attorney Samuel Leibowitz.*

In 2012, the Court increased the scope of the right to competent counsel by holding that defendants have a constitutional right to effective attorneys during plea bargain negotiations (in a 5–4 ruling). Today, almost all federal (97 percent) and most state (94 percent) felony charges involve a plea bargain, in which the defendant pleads guilty in exchange for a lighter sentence without actually going through a formal trial. With American courts clogged by arrest backlogs, this is one way to get the cases through the system.[80]

In practice, the right to counsel is growing difficult to maintain. The public is reluctant to spend tax revenues on lawyers who defend poor men and women accused of crimes. Public defenders face huge caseloads and small salaries—a Department of Justice study reported legal aid attorneys handle as many as nine hundred felony cases per year.[81] At the state and local level, the caseload is also overwhelming. One study reported that public defenders in many states had on average five minutes to confer with each client; some clients only got a minute of their overwhelmed lawyer's time. As with many federalist policies, states also differ in how well they support the public defender's office, with South Dakota and Pennsylvania providing no state funds to ensure the right to counsel.[82] Publicly funded criminal defense remains an essential—and endangered—part of civil liberty and American justice.

The Eighth Amendment: Fines and Death Penalty

The Eighth Amendment prohibits the federal government from imposing excessive fines or bail.

> *Excessive bail shall not be required, nor excess fines imposed. . . .*

In 2019, the Court incorporated this right, extending it to state governments in *Timbs v. Indiana*. In 2013, Tyson Timbs pleaded guilty to selling $225 of heroin and was sentenced to house arrest and $1,200 in fines. In a civil action, however, the state of Indiana also seized his $42,000 Land Rover—bought with funds from his father's life insurance policy—saying that Timbs had used it to commit crimes. The practice, known as civil forfeiture, enables law enforcement to seize drugs, cash, and other property. Many departments have come to rely on these funds. The federal Drug Enforcement Administration, for example, collects around a half-billion dollars a year from civil forfeiture.[83] The Supreme Court ruled unanimously that taking the Land Rover was excessive—challenging what has become a familiar practice across the country. States must now abide by this Eighth Amendment clause.

The Eighth Amendment also introduces the question of capital punishment.

Cruel and unusual punishment . . . shall not be . . . inflicted.

Is execution cruel and unusual punishment? Around the world, 108 nations have abolished (or never had) the death penalty—including all the nations of Western Europe, where it is considered a violation of human rights. While the United States executed more than 225 people in the past decade, executions are now plummeting. Twenty-six states have either abolished the death penalty or put a moratorium on all executions, and in the last five years (2018 through 2022) nine states executed a total of eighty-three people—a third of them in Texas and most others in Deep South states or convicted of federal crimes. Even so, thousands of men and women have been sentenced to death and are waiting on death row (see Figure 5.2). Most Americans (60 percent) support the death penalty—even though they acknowledge that Black people are more likely to be executed (56 percent).[84]

Proponents hold that some crimes are so terrible that justice demands capital punishment. It brings closure to grieving families. It may deter future murders (although there is no definitive evidence). Moreover, they argue, some criminals are so dangerous that they should be executed to protect other prisoners, prison officials, and the general public.

Opponents respond that killing people is immoral and that no government should be given the power to "play God." Because social systems are imperfect, some—perhaps many—innocent people will be executed. The system is tilted against people of color; Black people make up 12 percent of the population but, from year to year, between a quarter and half of those who are executed. In 2022, 41 percent of the inmates on death row were Black and another 14 percent

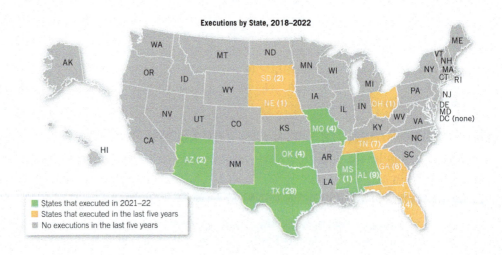

FIGURE 5.2 *Map of state executions in the United States. The federal government has executed thirteen prisoners in the past five years. (Death Penalty Information Center)*

Executions by State, 2018–2022

- States that executed in 2021–22
- States that executed in the last five years
- No executions in the last five years

were Latino. Repeated studies have shown that in capital cases, the race of the victim is a crucial matter—members of minority groups accused of murdering white people are the most likely to receive the death penalty.[85]

In 1972, the Supreme Court halted all executions, arguing that state laws were so vague that similar cases produced different outcomes. "The death standards are cruel and unusual," wrote Justice Potter Stewart in *Furman v. Georgia*, "the same way that being struck by lightning is cruel and unusual"—meaning that death sentences seemed to be meted out randomly. Thirty-five states drafted new capital punishment laws using *Furman* as a guide. In 1976, the Court again permitted executions to go forward—when state statutes included clear criteria to guide judge and jury in weighing death sentences.[86]

Beginning in 1992, a network of law students and their professors began to use DNA evidence to review capital cases. Working together as the "Innocence Project," they have documented false convictions of over 375 inmates, more than half of whom were convicted of capital crimes. All those exonerated have now been released, but the search for flawed convictions continues to turn up terrible mistakes.[87] The Project has received more than sixty-five thousand letters or emails from prisoners insisting that they did not commit the crimes for which they were convicted.

The Court has imposed additional death penalty limits. It has ruled that it is "cruel and unusual" to execute people convicted of crimes other than murder, striking down five state laws that allowed execution for child rape (2008). It has forbidden the execution of mentally ill individuals (2002) and of juvenile offenders (2005). In a much-discussed case, however, the Court ruled that lethal injections did not constitute cruel and unusual punishment despite the claim that they caused "an intolerable risk of pain" (2007).[88] This issue has become more pronounced in recent years, as sodium thiopental—a sedative injected into prisoners

WHAT DO YOU THINK?

End the Death Penalty?

Many citizens call for ending the death penalty. Is capital punishment a form of "cruel and unusual punishment" and therefore banned by the Eighth Amendment?	**No.** Some crimes are so terrible that they require this punishment. Justice demands it. It brings closure to the victims' families. American public opinion supports it. If there is a deterrent effect, executing criminals might save innocent lives. Some criminals are so hardened that they pose a safety threat to other prisoners, to prison officials, and to the public. Finally, multiple safeguards are in place to guarantee that innocent people are not executed.	**Yes.** It is time for the United States to join the other advanced democracies. Executions are unfair and are meted out primarily to poor and Black or Latino defendants accused of killing white victims. No government should have this power. Killing is morally wrong, and two wrongs do not make a right. Furthermore, it is impossible to ensure that no innocent people will be killed. The deterrent effect has not been proven. Tellingly, the American Medical Association refuses to let physicians participate in administering the death penalty.

before the fatal drug, which diminishes prisoners' pain—is no longer allowed by its manufacturers to be used in administering the death penalty. Substitute sedatives, charged Justice Sotomayor, leave inmates "exposed to what may well be the chemical equivalent of being burned at the stake." Nonetheless, in a widely watched 2022 case, the Court permitted execution of an Alabama man by lethal injection to proceed.[89]

THE BOTTOM LINE

» The Bill of Rights places special emphasis on the rights of those accused of crimes. Even so, American incarceration rates are the highest in the world.

» The police may not search or seize without a warrant (with minor exceptions); they must inform suspects of their right to remain silent; and the accused have a right to legal counsel. The courts have widened the right to counsel, but it is often limited by a lack of funding for public defenders.

» Under current interpretation, capital punishment is not considered "cruel and unusual punishment." However, the number of executions has been falling.

» Between 1962 and 1968, the Supreme Court vastly expanded the rights of the accused. Recent Court decisions have tilted the balance back toward law enforcement.

 # Terrorism, Noncitizens, and Civil Liberties

USA Patriot Act: Legislation that sought to enhance national security, passed in the aftermath of the September 11, 2001, terrorist attacks.

After the terrorist attacks on September 11, 2001, Congress passed the **USA Patriot Act**. In the fear and emotion of the terrible moment, only a few criticized the legislation. The act enhanced security by removing restrictions on law enforcement. Loosening restrictions, however, means limiting rights. The Patriot Act, the broader campaign against terrorism, and continued terror acts around the world have revived a long-standing national debate: How do we balance civil liberties and public safety?

Contacts with Forbidden Groups

The federal government enhanced rules that bar Americans from offering aid to terrorist organizations. For example, since 9/11, 238 Americans have been arrested for assisting ISIS, a terrorist organization that posted grisly beheading videos as recruitment tools.[90] Although the law forbids aiding terrorist organizations, expressing general support for such an organization is protected speech.

Drawing the line between public safety and free speech remains hotly contested. For now, U.S. courts permit the government to prosecute web postings if they provide funding or other specialized assistance to terrorist groups. What do you think? Is there an obvious balance between protecting free speech and fighting terrorism?

Domestic terrorism: Use of violent criminal acts by American citizens to advance ideological goals, often aimed at minority groups.

Domestic Terrorism

Although post-9/11 anti-terror efforts initially focused on Al Qaeda, ISIS, and other international terrorist groups, **domestic terrorism** also poses a serious threat to public order.

American terrorists, often white nationalists, generate violence against minority groups. How far can the government go in monitoring, silencing, and disarming them? Once again, the familiar question: Where is the line between protecting rights (to privacy, free speech, and bearing arms) and keeping citizens safe?

Tragic examples keep occurring. In May 2022, an eighteen-year-old man became incensed over a conspiracy known as "replacement theory"—the strange idea that American elites were replacing native-born white Americans with immigrants, Black Americans, and Jews. He drove three hours to a Buffalo supermarket and murdered ten people and wounded three others. Eleven of the victims were Black. The killer was tried in U.S. courts as a domestic terrorist, and the House of Representatives passed a "Domestic Terrorism Prevention Act," which ultimately failed in the Senate. The Biden administration's high-profile "National Strategy for Countering Domestic Terrorism" promises in its opening paragraphs to "address the threat" of domestic terrorism while "safeguarding bedrock American civil liberties."[91] As you know by now, there are no easy answers to balancing liberties and protecting public safety.

The Rights of Noncitizens

The war on terror prompted many questions around a more general theme: What are the constitutional rights of noncitizens? A substantial body of case law, going back to the nineteenth century, extends most basic constitutional rights to noncitizens—if someone is stopped by the police, for example, they have the same Miranda rights whether they are citizens, legal immigrants, or people without documentation. State governments may not pass laws that single out immigrants and discriminate against them.

There is one major difference, however: Immigration laws apply to noncitizens and, in that context, the procedural standards are different and ruled by the immigration laws themselves. There are still some rights—the right to remain silent and the right to legal counsel—but they are far more restricted.

During both the Trump and Biden administrations, images of children trying to cross the U.S.-Mexico border, often kept separate from their families, aroused public concern. And raised a still more complicated issue: How does the

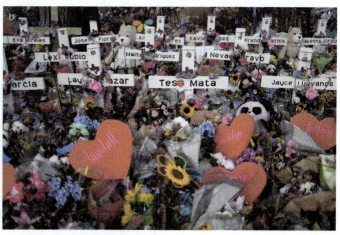

● *Memorial for victims of a domestic-terror attack at a Buffalo, New York, supermarket (a) and an elementary school in Uvalde, Texas (b). Terrorist attacks and mass shootings raise the question of how to balance national security and public safety with privacy rights, free speech, and the right to bear arms.*

Constitution apply to immigrants not yet in the United States (standing before a customs agent at the airport, for example)? The courts will be grappling with that and other thorny questions about noncitizen rights for a long time to come.

THE BOTTOM LINE

» The response to 9/11 and subsequent terrorist attacks created a debate about the balance between civil liberties and public safety.

» Domestic terrorism also poses complex challenges for public authorities. Does a hate-filled post on Reddit or other private Internet channel qualify as potential terrorism, and therefore deserve prosecution?

» Most constitutional rights apply to noncitizens. However, rights are also governed by immigration laws that offer more limited rights.

Conclusion: The Dilemma of Civil Liberties

Since 2020, a new civil-liberties concern has marked the nation's response to the COVID-19 pandemic. Should Americans be required to wear masks? Receive vaccinations, and then booster shots? The issue quickly became politicized, with some insisting on their personal liberty to avoid vaccination or to enter stores, restaurants, and other public or private spaces without a mask.[92] Medical professionals and most political leaders insisted that vaccination and masking were the best way to slow the spread of COVID-19. As with so many civil-liberties disputes, the matter wound up in court.[93]

How should the government balance its duty to keep the public safe, or to uphold moral standards, with its responsibility to protect civil liberties? This is one of the most important issues facing American democracy today. If we tilt too far toward combating terrorism or outlawing practices considered socially unacceptable, Americans will lose the liberties that have defined the nation since 1776. If we tilt too far the other way, the nation may be vulnerable to pandemics and international or domestic terror attacks, or lose its moral core.

Getting the balance right is a major challenge, for at least two reasons. First, civil-liberties rules are affected by larger cultural norms, which shift over time. Conservative federal courts thwarted Franklin D. Roosevelt's efforts to secure liberties for some historically dispossessed groups. Thirty years later, the liberal Warren Court expanded liberties dramatically, under liberal (LBJ) and conservative (Nixon) presidents alike. In the present day, a 6–3 Supreme Court conservative majority means some liberties—like the right to privacy—are again defined more narrowly. Want to enshrine a liberty not historically guaranteed, or incorporate a basic right not yet extended to the states? Your success might just depend on the era you live in.

Second, as we have seen across this chapter, the courts take the lead in protecting rights. But it is elected public officials who define the policies that the courts weigh. Ultimately, the balance between communal needs and individual rights is in voters' hands.

Isn't that exactly where it belongs? No. Recall the Supreme Court's judgment in 1943 when it reversed its earlier decision and protected Jehovah's Witnesses: "The very purpose of a Bill of Rights was to withdraw certain subjects from the vicissitudes of political controversy, to place them beyond the reach of majorities and officials and to establish them as legal principles to be applied by the courts." A core point of civil liberties is to protect the rights of individuals—even if it means overruling the majority of the country.

CHAPTER SUMMARY

★ Civil liberties are the limits we put on governing bodies (and the majorities that elect them) so that individuals can exercise their rights and freedom. Disputes are usually resolved by the courts and guided by the Bill of Rights.

★ The Bill of Rights did not apply to the states until the Fourteenth Amendment required that *no state* could deprive any citizen of life, liberty, or property.

★ The Supreme Court applied the Bill of Rights to the states, one right at a time. It began in 1897 (no taking property without compensation) and continued (so far) through 2019 (protection from excessive fines). This process is known as *incorporation*.

★ The Court discovered a right to privacy implicit (in the shadows) in the First, Third, Fourth, Fifth, and Ninth Amendments. The Court applied the right to privacy to strike down laws banning abortion. In *Roe v. Wade*, the Court issued a rule prohibiting states from interfering during the first trimester. In *Planned Parenthood v. Casey*, the Court replaced the rule with a standard forbidding laws that put "an undue burden" on the right to privacy. In 2022, the Court overruled itself and struck down any right to abortion. However, it did not strike down the right to privacy itself. At least not yet.

★ The Court extended privacy rights to same-sex couples by striking down anti-sodomy laws in 2003.

★ The Constitution includes two religious restrictions on government. The establishment clause bans the government from establishing (or favoring) a religion. In one view, this means separating church and state. For many years, the three-part Lemon test guided judicial decisions in cases involving religion. In 2022, the Court struck down the test and replaced it with "historical practices and understandings." Bottom line: Government may not promote one religious view over another.

★ The Constitution also forbids government from interfering with religious practice (the free exercise clause). The courts traditionally required a compelling government interest for imposing a burden—the Sherbert test. In 1990, the Court shifted and required only that the government action be neutral and that it apply to everyone. Congress, state governments, and religious groups pushed back and the courts have quietly returned to the traditional Sherbert test.

★ Free speech is crucial to democracy, and the Court gives it a privileged position—even against angry public opposition to flag-burning, cross-burning, or homophobic displays at military funerals. Free speech can be curtailed if it poses a "clear and present danger." Today, the Court requires the danger to be both imminent and likely to occur. There are limits to free speech involving hate speech (when "fighting words" are involved), student speech, commercial speech, and obscenity.

★ Some critics see the Second Amendment as an outmoded defense of citizen militias. Others see the right to bear arms as an important individual right—perhaps the most important liberty in the Constitution. In 2010 and again in 2022, the Supreme Court ruled it an essential constitutional right.

★ The Bill of Rights places special emphasis on the civil liberties of those accused of crimes. Even so, American incarceration rates are the highest in the world. The police may not search or seize without a warrant, they must inform suspects of their right to remain silent, and the accused have a right to legal counsel. Under current interpretation, capital punishment is not considered "cruel and unusual punishment"—but policy appears to be changing and only seven states are responsible for 90 percent of state executions in the past five years.

★ Tough new civil-liberties questions have arisen in recent years. Should restrictions on government actions be relaxed in the case of potential terrorist attacks? Do noncitizens deserve the same protection of liberties, given immigration laws that limit some rights? What about Americans who refuse to wear masks or get vaccinated during a global pandemic? These issues are debated widely in public, by governing officials, and in the courts—and they raise anew the classic question: Who are we?

KEY TERMS

Accommodation, p. 144	Fighting words, p. 151	Miller test, p. 155
Civil liberties, p. 134	Free exercise clause, p. 143	Miranda warnings, p. 162
Clear and present danger, p. 148	Grand jury, p. 161	Prior restraint, p. 154
Domestic terrorism, p. 166	Hate speech, p. 147	Selective incorporation, p. 137
Double jeopardy, p. 162	Imminent lawless action, p. 148	Strict separation, p. 144
Establishment clause, p. 143	Judicial rules, p. 141	Symbolic expression, p. 149
Exclusionary rule, p. 161	Judicial standards, p. 141	USA Patriot Act, p. 166

STUDY QUESTIONS

1. What are civil liberties? How are they different from civil rights?

2. In *Barron v. Baltimore*, the Supreme Court ruled that the Fifth Amendment did not protect a landowner if a state government took his property. Why?

3. Describe how the Bill of Rights was applied to the state governments. First, describe the constitutional amendment that directly addressed the states. Then describe the process of incorporation by which the Supreme Court applied the Bill of Rights to the states.

Bonus: Are there any civil liberties in the Bill of Rights that you think should be added to the "incorporated" list?

4. Describe how the Supreme Court declared the right to privacy. Discuss the case from a pragmatist's and an originalist's perspective. Would you vote to maintain the right to privacy? Or would you overrule the precedent? Explain your reasoning.

5. Describe the three-part Lemon test for determining whether a state action violates the establishment clause. The late Justice Scalia was highly critical of the Lemon test. What was his view? Do you agree or not? Explain why.

6. Sometimes the Court permits a racist to burn a cross—and sometimes forbids it. Explain the reasoning in each case. Do you agree with the Court's distinction, or would you rule differently?

7. There are two interpretations of the Second Amendment right to bear arms. Describe each. Which do you support? Why?

8. The Supreme Court gives free speech a "privileged position" among the rights in the Bill of Rights. What does that mean? How does the Court justify that position?

9. Feminist scholars argue that privileging free speech in pornography cases actually undermines free speech. What is their argument? Do you agree or disagree? Explain why.

10. Should the government monitor online forums known to be frequented by hate groups, to track those who openly discuss acts of domestic terror? If so, what action should public officials take when someone posts about potential terror acts?

6

THE STRUGGLE FOR CIVIL RIGHTS

SHEVRIN JONES'S VOICE cracked as he implored his colleagues in the Florida State Senate to vote down a bill that would prohibit classroom discussion about sexual orientation and gender identity. Jones is a Black man who came out as gay after his brother died in 2018. "I don't think y'all understand how much courage it takes," he told his fellow senators, as they discussed the "Parental Rights in Education Bill"—dubbed by opponents as "Don't Say Gay" legislation. Despite Jones's plea, the bill passed the Florida Senate, 22–17, and was triumphantly signed into law by Republican Governor Ron DeSantis in March 2022.

Laws like the one in Florida are sweeping through conservative legislatures. All reflect the same fears: Liberal teachers are twisting young minds by discussing sexual identity and gender change or promoting the idea that racism is institutionalized in American law and society. An academic idea known as **critical race theory** explores the ways racial hierarchy has been built into U.S. politics and economics. The topic has now been oversimplified and thrust into the political storm.

Critics, like Senator Shevrin Jones, call out the new wave of laws as just another effort to stir up fear and resentment—especially toward Black Americans and LGBTQ+ youth. They see one more battle line in the long American quest for civil rights.

This chapter reviews that epic story of civil rights. It is a distinctly American topic for three reasons: The United States has always included a diverse and changing population. The nation was founded on a soaring aspiration—all people are created equal. And, at the same time, the United States developed a booming economy (in both the South and North) on the labor of enslaved people.

Who are we? A profoundly diverse nation, founded on the idea that all people are "created equal" and "endowed" with "unalienable rights" including "life, liberty and the pursuit of happiness." We are also a nation that often fails to live up to its founding vision.

Civil rights are the freedom to fully participate in the life of the community—to vote in elections; to enjoy public facilities, such as parks; and to take full advantage of economic opportunities, like good jobs. People face discrimination when they are denied opportunities because of their

In this chapter, you will

 Explore the seven steps to winning civil rights in the United States.

 Review the experience of Black people in America that set the pattern for civil rights.

 Assess women's quest for economic and political rights.

 Examine the political experience of Latinos, Asians, and Native Americans.

 Consider the civil rights of other groups, including people with disabilities and LGBTQ+ individuals.

Critical race theory: A scholarly tradition that analyzes the way racial hierarchy is organized into American laws and institutions; has recently come under political fire as overly negative and pessimistic about the American experience.

● *Florida Senator Shevrin Jones, who is gay, tears up as he asks fellow lawmakers to vote down legislation that forbids discussion of sexual orientation and gender identity in schools.*

Civil rights: The freedom to participate in the full life of the community; to vote, use public facilities, and exercise equal economic opportunity.

race, sex, gender, ethnicity, religion, disabilities, age, or other personal characteristics. Once citizens have won their rights, public attention shifts to protecting them. We covered those protections—known as civil liberties—in Chapter 5. The long battle to win civil rights is the most powerful and enduring tale in American history. It reveals the deepest truths about the United States and its values. It tells us who we are—and who we strive to be.

The most visible political battle in American history has turned on racial justice. Black Americans blazed the civil rights trail: fighting slavery, resisting segregation, and challenging white supremacy. Their victories, like winning the Fourteenth Amendment (discussed in the last chapter), secured fresh rights for all Americans.

Many other groups have also fought long and hard for rights. The first Spanish settlers (in Florida and New Mexico) arrived long before any English speakers. And the first people, the Native Americans, had been on the land for some fifteen thousand years before any Europeans arrived at all. Women, Latinos, Asian Americans, Native Americans, people with disabilities, and the LBGTQ+ community all have long, rich, sometimes frustrating histories that we'll explore in the pages that follow.

In this chapter, we focus on groups one at a time, but, as Senator Shevrin Jones illustrates, many people reach for rights in multiple ways: He is both Black and gay. Some women face workplace discrimination as both women and people of color. The fight for civil rights is multilayered and complicated. Scholars who study identities and inequality call the mix **intersectionality**. Ultimately, across the political spectrum, liberals and conservatives generally agree on one thing: The quest for civil rights reflects the highest aspirations of the American dream.

Intersectionality: How different social identities like race, gender, and sexual orientation mix to create patterns of privilege and discrimination.

 ## Winning Rights: The Political Process

Discrimination usually stretches back through time and seeps into the ways powerful people see others: Even the Declaration of Independence calls Native Americans "merciless savages." White people justified enslavement of Black Americans by pretending that they were inferior beings. Men took responsibility for the supposedly "weaker" sex and limited women's participation in economic and political life. Psychiatrists defined homosexuality as an illness. All these perspectives diminished and repressed people.

How do things change? Through a battle for civil rights. Each civil rights campaign has its own unique history. However, the efforts usually involve the following stages—not necessarily in order.

Seven Steps to Political Equality

1. *A group defines itself.* In the first step toward civil rights, a group embraces its shared identity and redefines itself. Groups reject the old, often-demeaning labels that were thrust upon them and adopt a new name: Negroes, Miss, queers, and cripples became African Americans, Ms.,

BY THE NUMBERS Civil Rights

Zero Number of Black mayors in 1965

>600 Number of Black mayors in 2022[1]

1 Percentage of southern students who attended integrated schools eight years after *Brown v. Board of Education* (ruling in 1954)

91 Percentage of southern students who attended integrated schools eight years after the passage of the Civil Rights Act of 1964

404 Millions of dollars in annual funding for the Equal Employment Opportunity Commission (EEOC), which enforces federal laws against job discrimination and harassment

8 Billions of dollars in annual funding for Immigration and Customs Enforcement (ICE)

18 Number of Hispanic/Latino members of Congress in 2000

52 Number of Hispanic/Latino members of Congress in 2022

27 Percentage of Black Americans who report "a great deal" or "a fair amount" of confidence in the police, 2022

56 Percentage of white Americans who report "a great deal" or "a fair amount" of confidence in the police, 2022[2]

Zero Number of same-sex marriages legally performed in the United States, 2003

543,000 Number of same-sex married households in the United States, 2020[3]

How far have we come in achieving civil rights for all people? How far do we have to go?

LGBTQ+ individuals, and persons with disabilities. The change reflects a new self-consciousness—and often a sense of pride.

2. *The group challenges society.* The next step involves entering the political arena and demanding rights. Civil rights campaigns often go beyond normal politics and include marches, demonstrations, riots, and creative protests such as kneel-ins before segregated churches; or, in 2020, "die-ins," where marchers knelt or laid on the ground for eight minutes and forty-two seconds to honor George Floyd.[4]

3. *The stories change.* Civil rights always involve a contest over the stories that a society tells about a group. Why does the United States discriminate

against people in the first place? Because the majority portrays them as dangerous, inferior, or helpless. Winning rights requires changing the story. As you read about efforts to secure rights—past and present—be alert to the many different stories we tell about the groups in our society.

4. *Federalism comes into play.* Civil rights politics splashes across local, state, and federal governments. Because many minority groups are concentrated in certain states and regions, discrimination often begins on the local level. Furthermore, state and local officials control many of the policies that affect civil rights: education, law enforcement, and voting rules. For example, federal government officials (on the Supreme Court and Congress) broke racial segregation in the South. In other cases, states and localities first introduced reforms: Before the Nineteenth Amendment established women's suffrage nationally, women won voting rights in western states.

5. *The executive branch often breaks the ice.* Presidents can issue executive orders (rules that have the force of law but do not require congressional approval), creating opportunities and momentum for a civil rights campaign. President Truman desegregated the U.S. military in 1948, and President Obama extended protections for gender identity in 2014.

6. *Congress passes monumental legislation.* Typically, it is Congress that passes the great changes that finally secure civil rights and echo through history. The Fourteenth Amendment to the Constitution, ratified in 1868, still dominates every effort to win rights. The Civil Rights Act of 1964 profoundly changed the quest for civil rights in the United States. The Americans with Disabilities Act, enacted in 1990, was a landmark for people with disabilities.

7. *It all ends up in court.* The courts are the ultimate arbiters of civil rights. Individuals and groups challenge laws they consider unjust. Judges consider what the Constitution requires and weigh the laws, rules, regulations, and private actions for what is permissible and what is not. Different justices with different judicial philosophies often read the Constitution very differently—making the courts a major battleground for civil rights. The Supreme Court of one era (1973) ruled that the Constitution guaranteed a woman's right to an abortion; the Court today (2022) declared that it did no such thing (in the *Dobbs* decision introduced in Chapter 5).

● *Lucretia Mott, who helped organize the Seneca Falls (New York) convention for women's rights, is attacked by a mob of angry men. Women who challenged their own subordination faced violence in the nineteenth century.*

Notice how many moving parts there are in the reform process. We have already seen why this is so: American government is unusually fragmented, marked by overlapping actors and institutions all balancing one another. That usually makes it difficult to change deep social norms such as racial or gender discrimination. Reformers must win over many different power centers—state legislatures, Congress, governors, the judiciary, the media, and the public.

The March to Civil Rights

We can view the history of civil rights in two ways. Some observers see a steady march toward a deeper and richer American equality. One hundred twenty years ago, Black people faced down violent white supremacists—in the North as well as the South—with little assistance from fellow citizens or the government. Sixty years ago, Black and Latino citizens could not vote, and most professions were closed to them. Today, Black Americans are CEOs of Fortune 500 companies and head elite academic institutions—and one recently served two terms as U.S. president. Forty years ago, only one woman in American history had won a U.S. Senate seat in her own right. Today, the Senate includes 24 women and the U.S. House more than 125—the most in history. Twenty years ago, same-sex marriage was illegal, sodomy was a crime, homosexuality was listed as a sexual disorder in medical manuals, and LGBTQ+ people had scant protections against discrimination in schools and workplaces. Today, gay marriage and sex are legally protected, and the Supreme Court bans workplace discrimination on the basis of gender and sexual identity. From this perspective, the American promise faces many obstacles but marches steadily on.[5]

Other observers, however, believe that there is nothing inevitable about civil rights. Sometimes rights expand; sometimes they contract. Black people scaled many barriers, but still face resistance to getting jobs, living in many neighborhoods, achieving a good education, or winning fair treatment from police or courts. Asian Americans have won citizenship rights but still face twisted stereotypes—ranging from "model minority" to COVID-19 pandemic carriers. Anti-Asian hate crimes tripled in 2021 alone. And, still, in most places, most hate crimes target Black people. In some cities, like Chicago, hate crimes against gay people also rose recently.[6] There is nothing inevitable about American equality, say proponents of this perspective, and citizens should never take it for granted.[7]

As you read this chapter, ask which view seems most accurate to you: Has the United States advanced consistently toward greater civil rights for all? Or is this notion a myth, given unsteady progress toward equality and justice? Whatever your answer, continue to ask: What can and should we do to ensure fair treatment for everyone?

How the Courts Review Cases

Sooner or later, most civil rights disputes end up in court. Opponents of the "Parental Rights in Education" (or "Don't Say Gay") bill in Florida immediately declared they would sue to stop the legislation. When someone claims that a law violates their civil rights, the court places the case into one of three categories: suspect, quasi-suspect, and nonsuspect. Where do those categories come from? From the language in the Constitution and the long history of civil rights case law.

Suspect Categories.   Any legislation involving *race, ethnicity, religion,* or *alienage* (immigration status) faces **strict scrutiny**. The Supreme Court is primed to strike down any law that targets a race or ethnicity or religion, unless there is a very strong reason for doing so. The Court will ask: Is there a *compelling government interest* in singling out a race, immigration status, or ethnicity? For example, during World War II, the federal government forced Japanese Americans into internment camps. The internees sued and the Supreme Court ruled that, yes, in this case the war gave the government a "compelling interest" to intern an entire ethnic group despite the Constitution's explicit protection of racial and

Strict scrutiny: The standard by which courts judge any legislation that singles out race or ethnicity.

● *Marine Sargent Sheena Adams (left), Marine Lance Corporal Kristi Baker (middle), and Navy sailor and Hospital Corpsman Shannon Crowley (right) pose at their forward operating base in Afghanistan in 2010. A civil rights effort helped lift the ban on women in combat in 2013. Since 2016, women can perform all combat jobs—including joining the Navy SEALs.*

ethnic groups. This was a dramatic error and, in 2018, the Court itself acknowledged its mistake (we'll discuss the case in Chapter 16).[8]

Quasi-Suspect Categories. In 1976, women's advocates won a special category for gender cases: **quasi-suspect.** Any legislation—federal, state, or local—that introduces sex-based categories has to rest on an *important state purpose.* This is not as strong a test as a *compelling* interest, but it is still a powerful barrier to gender discrimination. For example, in 1996 the Court ruled that excluding women from the Virginia Military Institute (VMI), a state-funded school, did not serve an important state purpose. VMI had to open its doors to women cadets or forgo state funding.

Quasi-suspect category: A legal standard that requires governments to have an important state purpose for any legislation that singles out sex or gender. This is not as strong as the **suspect category,** which requires strict scrutiny.

Nonsuspect Categories. Other categories do not face special scrutiny—at least not yet. Legislation based on age, sexual orientation, gender identity, or physical disabilities simply has to have some rational connection between the legislation and a legitimate government purpose. This is the weakest test, but it can still bar discrimination. Using this test, for example, the Court ruled that there was no rational basis for a Colorado constitutional amendment that forbade any protection for LGBTQ+ people.[9]

In 2018, a federal judge in Seattle ruled against the Trump administration's ban on transgender people serving in the military. In this case, the judge ruled that transgender individuals deserve the highest form of protection and, for the first time, applied *strict scrutiny* (the first category we described) to the ban. Will the Supreme Court accept this lower court change and move LGBTQ+ related cases up to a different level? Stay tuned![10]

This threefold division is the framework for civil rights law. As with almost everything else in American government, politics produced these categories. Groups argued, lobbied, demonstrated, and sued to win stricter scrutiny.

THE BOTTOM LINE

» The battle for civil rights generally involves seven characteristics. The group seeking rights must define itself, challenge society, and change the way it is viewed. The contest for rights spills across all branches of government and involves states, the executive, Congress, and the courts.

» Courts interpret charges of discrimination using three standards: suspect, quasi-suspect, and nonsuspect.

Race and Civil Rights: Revolt Against Slavery

On a hot summer day in Ferguson, Missouri, a police officer confronted a Black man accused of stealing some cigarillos from a convenience store. Reports differ about what happened next, but there is no doubt how it ended: Officer Darren Wilson fired twelve bullets at Michael Brown. The Ferguson police then left his body bleeding on the street for four hours. The next day's vigils soon turned to protests and ultimately into a movement: "Black Lives Matter."

In the following months, a shocking series of images flashed before the public: A video of Eric Garner wrestled to the ground on Staten Island, New York, and choked to death as he gasped, "I can't breathe." In Baltimore, Maryland, police arrested Freddie Gray and chained his legs in the back of a police wagon; a week later he was dead of a severed spinal column because police neglected to secure him safely in the van. In Baton Rouge, Louisiana, Alton Sterling was shot to death by police after being pinned to the ground for illegally selling CDs outside a convenience store. In Chicago police shot seventeen-year-old Laquan McDonald as he walked away from them. The incidents were not new, given a terrible history of Black Americans' lives cut short, before and since.[11] But now the incidents were caught on video; one after another, they went viral—and with each the movement grew. Beneath the protests lay a profound message: A century and a half after slavery was abolished, many Americans are still not equal (Figure 6.1).

Black people came to America chained in the holds of slave ships, sold at auction, separated from their families, and killed for challenging their oppressors. After emancipation, leaders of the Black community were systematically murdered by the thousands to keep the entire population subordinated to white people. Over time, people of color faced a long roster of repression: lynching; voting restrictions that almost completely disenfranchised them in the South; restricted access to jobs, housing, schools, hospitals, hotels, and restaurants in both the North and South. Each injustice was sanctioned by government officials.

Black people fighting against racial bias developed the tactics that other groups would use in their own battles for civil rights. Black movements forged the laws, amendments, and judicial doctrines that opened the door to civil rights across society.

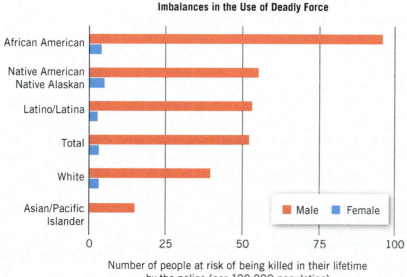

Imbalances in the Use of Deadly Force

Number of people at risk of being killed in their lifetime by the police (per 100,000 population)

● **FIGURE 6.1** *Deadly force imbalances by ethnic group. A recent analysis suggests that about 96 Black men per 100,000 are at risk of being killed by the police—more than twice the risk relative to white men.*

The battle for racial justice included three powerful crusades: one in the nineteenth century, one in the twentieth, and one today. As you read about the past, think about what has changed (a lot!) and what remains to be done.

The Clash over Slavery

Enslaved people were permitted to have churches, and in the early nineteenth century, religion offered leadership, organization, and a powerful message. Black leaders drew on the Christian Bible to compare Africans to the Israelites, bound in slavery but waiting for deliverance to freedom. By the middle of the nineteenth century, the dream of freedom had become a kind of religious faith in the slave quarters.[12] Three additional forces precipitated a national crisis over slavery: a moral crusade for abolition, economic interests, and political calculations.

Abolition: A nineteenth-century movement demanding an immediate and unconditional end to slavery.

Abolition.   An **abolition** movement rose up, branded slavery sinful, and demanded its immediate end. The abolitionists were unusually diverse for the time; the movement's leadership included women and people of color (most famously, Frederick Douglass). It was small and considered radical, but its newspapers and pamphlets created a furious reaction. Many Americans—in both the South and North—feared the abolitionists would incite enslaved people to rebellion. Most people preferred to ignore the issue.

Economics.   It was impossible to avoid the slavery question for a fundamental economic reason. As the United States spread west, every new settlement prompted the same question—would it be slave or free? Most Northerners opposed slavery on the frontier for a simple economic reason—they felt that the spread of slavery robbed them of the opportunity to settle into new lands. Southerners insisted that slavery needed to spread into new states to survive—or the South would fall into economic ruin. At the same time, the entire economic system—in both the South and the North—profited from enslaved people.[13]

Missouri Compromise: An agreement to open southern territories west of the Mississippi to slavery while closing northern territories to slavery.

Politics.   Because the federal government controlled territories until they became states, the question—slave or free?—constantly haunted Congress. Given that every state has two senators, an equal number of free and slave states permitted the South to defend its "peculiar institution." The enslaved people (who each counted as three-fifths of a person for the purposes of representation—as we saw in Chapter 3) gave southern states an additional thirty-six seats in the House of Representatives.

The Senate negotiated the tensions with a series of shaky compromises. The **Missouri Compromise** of 1820 drew a line through the Louisiana Territory (see Figure 6.2). All new states and territories north of the line except Missouri would be free; everything south of the line would be open to slavery. In 1845, as Americans moved west, Congress extended the line to include Texas. In 1850, California wanted to enter the Union as a free state. The solution was the **Compromise of 1850**, which permitted California to enter as a free state and turned the decision about slavery in Kansas and Nebraska over to the residents—a policy known as popular sovereignty.

Compromise of 1850: A complicated compromise over slavery that permitted some territories to vote on whether they would be slave or free and permitted California to enter the Union as a free state. It also included a hugely controversial fugitive slave law forcing Northerners to return Black men and women into bondage.

Dred Scott v. Sandford.   In 1857, the Supreme Court announced a shattering decision that upset all the careful compromises. An enslaved person named Dred Scott sued for his freedom. He argued that he had been taken to live in a free territory before returning to Missouri and that, as a result, he should be free. Chief Justice Roger Taney ruled that Scott was not free, because neither the territories nor the

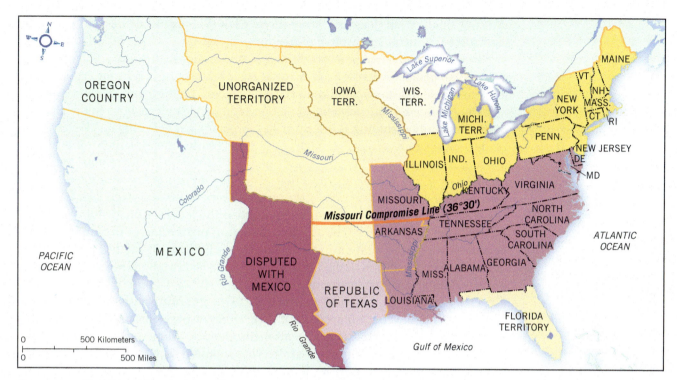

● **FIGURE 6.2** *The Missouri Compromise—all new American territory below the line would permit slavery; all above (except Missouri) would be free.*

federal government had the power to limit slavery or give a Black man rights. What about the Missouri Compromise? Unconstitutional, ruled Taney. Popular sovereignty? Also unconstitutional. The ***Dred Scott v. Sandford*** decision ruled that no territory could restrict slavery, much less elevate Blacks to citizenship.

The *Dred Scott* decision created a political crisis. The Republican Party rose to national prominence by explicitly rejecting the decision. In 1860, Abraham Lincoln won the presidency on a platform that flatly opposed the extension of slavery into any territories. When Lincoln won, southern states began withdrawing from the United States, and the Civil War erupted. In the four years from 1861 to 1865, more people lost their lives than in all the other American wars combined. From the blood and ashes arose a second American founding.

The Second American Founding: A New Birth of Freedom?

In his Gettysburg Address, President Lincoln announced "a new birth of freedom" and declared that the United States had been "conceived in liberty and dedicated to the proposition that all men are created equal." Lincoln expressed a view of self-government that the Declaration had not fully embraced, and the Constitution had rejected: "Government of the people, by the people, for the people."[14] With this simple declaration, Lincoln rewrote the American idea of freedom.

Lincoln's bold innovation was institutionalized in four documents. In 1863, Lincoln's **Emancipation Proclamation** freed enslaved people—but only in areas that were still rebelling. Ironically, Lincoln freed enslaved persons in the states where he had no power to enforce his decree. The enslaved people themselves, however, bolted by the thousands toward the Union Army and transformed it, as one historian wrote, into "a reluctant dragon of emancipation."[15] When the Civil

Dred Scott v. Sandford: A landmark Supreme Court decision holding that Black men could not be citizens under the Constitution. A national uproar followed.

Emancipation Proclamation: An executive order issued by President Abraham Lincoln that declared the enslaved people in all rebel states to be free.

War was finally over, Congress wrote three "Civil War amendments" that gave full legal force to Lincoln's new birth of freedom.

The *Thirteenth Amendment*, ratified in 1865, abolished slavery but included a fateful loophole: Slavery was abolished "except as a punishment for crime." The modern criminal justice system would be built, in part, on the foundation of slavery.

The *Fourteenth Amendment*, ratified in 1868, made anyone born in the United States, crucially including formerly enslaved persons, a U.S. citizen. We have already seen the most crucial passage of the Fourteenth Amendment, for it is at the heart of American civil liberties (described in Chapter 5): *No state shall "deprive any person of life, liberty or property without due process of law; nor deny to any person . . . the equal protection of the laws."* Through this language, as we saw in Chapter 5, the Fourteenth Amendment applied the federal Constitution and the Bill of Rights to the states. The key phrase—**equal protection of the laws**—would become a core legal weapon in the battle for civil rights. It might be the single most important addition to the Constitution in the last two hundred years. It bans any law designed to harm a group.

The *Fifteenth Amendment*, ratified in 1870, guarantees that voting rights "shall not be denied . . . on account of race, color, or previous condition of servitude." Do you notice what is not mentioned? Gender. Women had reasoned that because they were citizens, their right to vote should not be "denied or abridged," but the Supreme Court rejected this interpretation in 1875.

Freedom Fails

What happened to the formerly enslaved people? The era after the Civil War began with soaring hopes. Black families torn apart during slavery joyously reunited. Black people formed communities, organized churches, voted, entered politics, and demanded respect from their former owners. Two Black men were elected to the U.S. Senate and twenty-one to the House of Representatives (all as Republicans—at the time, the party of civil rights).

However, Black empowerment met fierce resistance. Some white people were outraged when the freedmen no longer stepped aside on the sidewalks. They simply could not imagine racial equality. And the Civil War had also created terrible hardships for the entire South, Black and white. "Gaunt hunger wept beside bereavement," as sociologist W. E. B. Du Bois put it.[16]

Southern state and local governments reacted by passing *Black codes*. They used the loophole in the Thirteenth Amendment—people could be bound right back into servitude for violating the law. The Black codes featured all kinds of rules forbidding the formerly enslaved people to leave their jobs or move freely without permission. Freed Black people were stripped of rights such as voting, owning guns, and buying property. Legal restrictions were backed by terrorist groups (the most famous was the Ku Klux Klan, or KKK), which killed and intimidated the formerly enslaved people in the name of restored white supremacy.

Black Americans fought back. For example, Congressman Robert Smalls, a Black American naval hero from the Civil War, won election to the U.S. Congress five times. During his last reelection campaign, an armed white gang known as the Red Shirts disrupted a speech he was giving. When he took shelter in a local store, the Red Shirts opened fire, aiming to kill him. Word spread quickly and hundreds of Black men and women came running, some of them bearing their old military firearms. They routed the militia group, and rescued Congressman Smalls—who went on to win his reelection.[17]

For a time, Congress supported the former slaves. In an effort known as **Reconstruction**, it tried to rebuild the South around a vision of racial justice.

Equal protection of the laws: The landmark phrase in the Fourteenth Amendment that requires equal treatment for all citizens.

Reconstruction: The failed effort, pursued by Northerners and Southerners, to rebuild the South and establish racial equality after the Civil War.

Congress organized a Freedmen's Bureau to assist formerly en-slaved people. The Civil Rights Act of 1866 guaranteed Black Americans the same property rights as white Americans; the Civil Rights Act of 1875 limited private racial discrimination in hotels, restaurants, and theaters.

However, dreams of racial equality began to slip away. The Democrats—then the party of white supremacy—fiercely resisted racial equality, opposed all civil rights legislation (including the three amendments), and even denied that the freedmen and -women (as the formerly enslaved people were known) faced any vi-olence at all. Northern Republicans, weary of the conflict, withdrew armed forces from the South in 1877. Congress eventually repealed the laws that implemented the Civil War amendments (as soon as the Democrats came back to power). No national mechanism was left to enforce "the equal protection of the laws." In the Civil Rights Cases of 1883, the Supreme Court struck down the Civil Rights Act of 1875, ruling that Congress did not have the authority to stop private discrimination. It took eighty-nine years before the Civil Rights Act of 1964 would find a way around this barrier.[18]

By the 1890s, southern state governments (with the active encour-agement of Democratic leaders in the North) had gutted the Fifteenth Amendment right to vote. *Grandfather clauses* forbade people from voting if their grandfathers had not voted; obviously, if a person's grandfather had been an enslaved person, he had not been allowed to vote. *Poll taxes* required voters to pay a fee that most Black people could not afford. **Literacy tests** required voters to read and interpret any passage in the state constitu-tion. These new rules did what violence and intimidation had failed to accomplish—they drove Black people out of politics. African Americans have been the only group in any democracy, notes political scientist Richard Valelly, to enter the electorate and then be cast out all over again.[19] African Americans continued to fight for rights and freedom, but by the 1890s they did so with very few national allies.[20]

The white majority in the South built a system of segregation known as **Jim Crow**, named after minstrel shows in which white singers and dancers blackened their faces and pretended to be Africans. Jim Crow laws segregated the races. Black people could not go to white schools, play in most parks, visit the zoo (Thursday eventually became "Black day" at many zoos), eat at a white restaurant, stay in a white hotel, drink from a white fountain, go to a white hospital, pray in a white church, or vote.

The small Black population in the North also faced racial discrimination. They were squeezed into Black neighborhoods and faced violence for even wan-dering into the wrong neighborhoods. Most good jobs and professions were closed to Black men and women. And there were almost no Black political officials any-where in the North. Even so, northern segregation was more subtle and not built into the legal system in the same way as the Jim Crow laws.

In 1896, the Supreme Court ruled in ***Plessy v. Ferguson*** that there was noth-ing inherently discriminatory in requiring separate but equal facilities for the Black and white races. "If one race be inferior to the other socially," wrote the majority, "the Constitution of the United States cannot put them upon the same plane." In practice, the facilities were separate but not at all equal. A year later, in *Williams v. Mississippi,* the Supreme Court unanimously upheld the poll tax and literacy test, announcing that it was not convinced "that their administration was evil, only that evil was possible under them." The Court looked the other way as African Americans were driven right out of politics.[21]

● *During the Civil War, Robert Smalls commandeered a southern vessel, loaded with cannons, and sailed to freedom. He became an acting captain in the Union navy, and after the Civil War, bought the house in which he had once been held as an enslaved person. Smalls went on to represent South Carolina in the U.S. Congress for five terms.*

Literacy test: A requirement that voters exhibit an ability to read; in reality, a way to restrict Black suffrage.

Jim Crow: The system of racial segregation in the U.S. South that lasted from 1890 to 1965, and that was often violently enforced.

Plessy v. Ferguson: An 1896 Supreme Court case that permitted racial segregation.

● *College students, like those pictured here from Howard University in 1934 near the White House, joined thousands across the U.S. in protesting lynching during the 1880s–1940s. But despite more than two hundred attempts, Congress refused to outlaw the crime until 2022.*

The entire system of southern segregation was held in place by the raw brutality of lynching—the ritualized murders of Black men (and occasionally women) who had violated the codes. These murders were not crimes of mob passion but organized killings, with police directing traffic around the scene and white families posing for pictures around the victim's mutilated body. They served as a horrific way to enforce racial separation. The *Negro Year Book* recorded 1,799 Black people lynched between 1882 and 1920, although current historians now consider that a low estimate.[22] The white majority directed extraordinary fury at men and women who fell in love across the racial divide—interracial couples threatened the entire structure of segregation.[23]

How could the majority accept such repression? White supremacists repeated a false story about Black men's supposed sexual lust for white women. Novels, plays, and films portrayed dangerous Black men threatening white women and white culture. The story in its most blatant form provided the plot for one of the seminal works in cinematic history. *The Birth of a Nation* (1915) features lust-filled Black men, backed by federal troops, menacing white women until the KKK saves the day. In one of the film's last triumphant scenes, the Klan disarms the Black men and stops them from voting. Woodrow Wilson screened the movie in the White House, and it became one of the top-grossing films of all time. Biased cultural images like *The Birth of a Nation* justified—and even celebrated—the restoration of white supremacy; they also induced many Americans to look the other way as black rights were violated.[24]

By 1915, the dreams of equality had collapsed. But far from the headlines, change was beginning to take place. African Americans began to move out of the South, quietly planting seeds of the next civil rights movement.

THE BOTTOM LINE

» The clash over slavery eventually led Lincoln to redefine the American idea of self-rule: "government of the people, by the people, for the people."

» *Institutional changes* marked the rise and fall of civil rights. The president issued the Emancipation Proclamation, Congress passed the Civil Rights Acts, and the states ratified the Thirteenth, Fourteenth, and Fifteenth Amendments.

» The Fourteenth Amendment contains the crucial legal rule for civil rights: "No state shall . . . deprive any person of . . . the equal protection of the laws."

» Later, courts struck down some civil rights laws, Congress repealed laws implementing the Civil War amendments, and the states introduced segregation, which the Supreme Court accepted.

» However, it was *culture*—the terrible, false stories that white Americans told about their fellow citizens—that fixed the new legal chains in place by inducing the majority to ignore the violations of Black rights.

The Next Fight for Racial Equality

Before 1900, most Black Americans lived in the South. Beginning in the 1910s, however, many left and moved to jobs in the northern cities. Their journey is known as the **Great Migration**. By the 1950s, 40 percent of the Black population lived in the North. In city after city—Chicago, Philadelphia, East St. Louis, Tulsa, Detroit, and the list goes on—savage riots greeted the newcomers. Over time, public policies reinforced the discrimination: Government housing loans went only to white families, new highways crashed through Black neighborhoods, and urban renewal projects flattened Black neighborhoods.

While in the South Jim Crow continued to rule, in the North Black people could fight back with a weapon that they were denied in the South: They had the right to vote. By 1936, many African Americans switched parties to become Democrats, and they began to wield political influence again. However, they faced many challenges in the long fight for racial equality.

Great Migration: The vast movement of African Americans from the rural South to the urban North between 1910 and the 1960s.

Types of Discrimination

There are two types of discrimination. Legal discrimination—known as **de jure discrimination**—involves laws that explicitly deny civil rights. By the time the civil rights movement ended, around 1970, Americans had conquered de jure discrimination—an enormous achievement.

A second type of discrimination—known as "in fact" or **de facto discrimination**—exists without the support of explicit laws and is more subtly embedded in society. Segregated residential neighborhoods are an example; this type of discrimination can be much harder to address. Today, Americans argue about whether and where de facto restrictions still exist—and, if so, how to reverse them.

De jure discrimination: Discrimination established by laws.

De facto discrimination: More subtle forms of discrimination that exist without a legal basis.

The Modern Civil Rights Campaign Begins

In 1909, Black leaders formed the **National Association for the Advancement of Colored People**, or **NAACP**, and began fighting segregation. In 1941, they won the first executive order on race since Reconstruction. President Franklin Roosevelt signed an order barring racial discrimination by defense contractors and created the Fair Employment Practices Committee to ensure compliance. What pushed Roosevelt to act? Black leaders, led by A. Philip Randolph, threatened to organize a massive protest march on Washington just as the United States was gearing up to fight the racist Nazi regime in World War II.

Over one hundred thousand Black troops fought in the war only to be greeted by racism and violence when they returned home. They added their voices to the call for equality—and helped change the American cultural image of Black people. In 1948, Harry Truman, pushed by millions of northern Black voters who had joined his Democratic Party, desegregated the armed forces, making the military the first racially integrated federal institution in the United States.

National Association for the Advancement of Colored People (NAACP): A civil rights organization formed in 1909 and dedicated to racial equality.

The Courts

The NAACP also went to court and chipped away at Jim Crow laws enforcing segregation. Democratic President Franklin Roosevelt (1933–44) appointed eight Supreme Court justices during his twelve years in office. The result: a Court sympathetic to Blacks' civil rights claims. In 1944, the Supreme Court ended the all-white Democratic primary in *Smith v. Allwright*, rejecting the idea that a political party was a private organization and could discriminate if it wished to.[25]

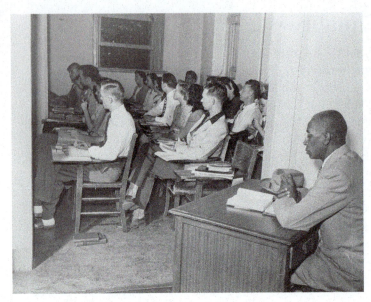

● *"Separate but equal" for George McLaurin meant a desk in the hallway. McLaurin, who was pursuing his Ph.D. at the University of Oklahoma, sued the university, and the Supreme Court ruled against segregated classes in graduate school.*

Brown v. Board of Education: The landmark Supreme Court case that struck down segregated schools as unconstitutional.

The Court struck down segregation in law schools and graduate schools—and then took a monumental step.[26]

In May 1954, in ***Brown v. Board of Education***, the Court ruled that segregated schools violated the equal protection clause of the Fourteenth Amendment. In public education, declared the Court, "the doctrine of separate but equal has no place." Separate facilities were inherently unequal.[27]

Brown v. Board of Education was part of a long-term legal strategy developed by Thurgood Marshall, a special counsel for the NAACP. Marshall decided to attack segregation in education. The first cases struck at the obviously unequal facilities, which led, eventually, to the direct attack on segregation's "separate but equal" education of Black and white children. Some of the cases preceding the *Brown v. Board of Education* decision are shown in Table 6.1.

Brown was a momentous decision. The follow-up to the ruling, however, was far less dramatic: Almost nothing changed. The Court did not impose a strong timetable or implementation plan. National officials did little to support *Brown*, and state and local leaders did much to oppose

TABLE 6.1 The Legal Road to *Brown v. Board of Education*

1938: *State of Missouri ex rel. Gaines v. Canada*	The Supreme Court ruled in favor of Lloyd Gaines, a Black student who had been refused admission to the University of Missouri Law School.
1948: *Sipuel v. Board of Regents of University of Oklahoma*	The Supreme Court ruled that Lois Ada Sipuel could not be denied entrance to a state law school solely because of her race.
1949: *Webb v. School District No. 90* (Kansas)	Authorities built a new elementary school near Merriam, Kansas, but forced Black children to attend an old and dilapidated school. The Kansas supreme court in 1949 ruled that equal facilities must be provided for all children. In this case, the issue was unequal facilities rather than segregation itself.
1950: *Sweatt v. Painter*	Texas hastily established a Black law school in a downtown basement (to avoid legal challenges by Black students). The Supreme Court ruled that the University of Texas Law School was vastly superior and had to admit a Black student, Herman Sweatt.
1950: *McLaurin v. Oklahoma State Regents*	The Supreme Court struck down the University of Oklahoma's requirement that a Black Ph.D. student could not sit with white students in the classroom, library, or cafeteria; he had to sit separately, even if that meant taking notes in the hallway outside the classroom.
1949–51: Five Different Cases Become *Brown v. Board of Education*	The Supreme Court bundled (or combined) five different cases into what was called simply *Brown v. Board of Education*. They were: 1949: *Briggs v. Elliott* (South Carolina); 1950: *Bolling v. Sharpe* (Washington, DC); February 1951: *Brown v. Board of Education* (Kansas); May 1951: *Davis v. Prince Edward County* (Virginia); October 1951: *Belton v. Gebhart Cases* (Delaware)
Source: National Archives	

it. A decade after *Brown*, less than 1 percent of the schools in the South had been desegregated.

Where desegregation did occur, the results could be explosive. The day before schools opened in 1957, Governor Orval Faubus came out against the desegregation of Central High School in Little Rock, Arkansas. The Arkansas National Guard turned away the nine Black high school students who tried to enter the school the next day.

The governor backed off in the face of a court order. But, when the African American students came back two weeks later, the National Guard had been replaced by what the *New York Times* called "a mob of belligerent, shrieking hysterical demonstrators" shouting racial epithets. President Dwight Eisenhower, a Republican, reluctantly dispatched the 101st Airborne to enforce the court order and desegregate Central High.

Elected officials throughout the South could not help but notice that Governor Faubus had become a local hero among whites and was returned to office for an unprecedented third term. Many white politicians reacted by staunchly fighting civil rights and desegregation. Years later, some white protesters would try and reconcile with the Black students they had jeered, and some local politicians would publicly regret what they had said and done. But it was clear at the time that, without political support, even a historic court decision like *Brown v. Board of Education* could neither crack segregation nor integrate the schools.

The Civil Rights Movement

What defeated segregation was not the Supreme Court or the paratroopers from the 101st Airborne, but ordinary American people who seized the moment and rose up. There had been scattered demonstrations throughout the country for years, but the organized movement began in Montgomery, Alabama, on a December afternoon in 1955.

Rosa Parks was riding the bus home after a long day at work. The white section filled up, and when a white man got on board, the driver called out that the white people needed another row. Everyone in the first Black row was expected to move. Parks refused to relinquish her seat and was arrested. This was not the first time someone had protested segregation—a quiet campaign had been flaring for two decades. But this time the local NAACP called a boycott of the Montgomery bus lines and put twenty-six-year-old Martin Luther King Jr. in charge. That night, King addressed thousands of people from the pulpit of the Holt Street Baptist Church: "We are determined here in Montgomery," he preached, "to work and fight until justice runs down like water, and righteousness like a mighty stream."[28]

● *Sixteen-year-old Elizabeth Eckford didn't know that there were escorts for the Black students who were integrating Little Rock's Central High School because her family had no phone. Elizabeth took the city bus, filed past the screeching adults, walked up to the guardsmen who blocked her way with raised bayonets, and then turned around and went back to the bus stop to sit, as the mob howled around her.*

A new civil rights campaign launched in the new legal setting established by *Brown v. Board of Education*. The decision itself did not create change. Rather, the decision enabled a movement that eventually led to landmark changes.

It took more than a year and direct intervention by the Supreme Court to desegregate the buses in Montgomery.

● The civil rights movement took courage. Here, protesters sitting at a whites-only lunch counter are taunted and doused with ketchup.

Freedom Riders: Black and white activists who rode buses together to protest segregation on interstate bus lines.

Free rider problem: A barrier to group or collective action arising because people who do not participate still reap the benefits.

But the pattern was set: The Court had opened the legal door. Protesters braved arrest, scorn, and violence to win change on the ground.

In February 1960, four Black college students from North Carolina A&T University sat at a white lunch counter and inspired a tactic that spread throughout the South. Within a year, seventy thousand people—Black and white—occupied segregated counters while onlookers jeered, poured ketchup on the sitters, and held cigarette lighters to the women's hair. From lunch counters, the sit-ins spread to movie theaters, parks, pools, art galleries, libraries, and churches.

In 1961, activists came up with a new tactic. Groups of young people rented Greyhound buses and drove as **Freedom Riders** to protest segregated interstate bus lines and terminals. The first bus was pursued by a "citizens' posse" and set ablaze. Angry men tried to hold the doors of the burning bus shut, and the students narrowly escaped—only to get a vicious beating with bats and pipes.[29]

Despite the protests, segregation *still* did not yield. The stalemate was finally broken in Birmingham, Alabama. Young marchers tumbled out of churches and walked, singing and clapping, straight into appalling police violence. Fire hoses sent them sprawling as police dogs snarled and snapped. Television blazed the images around the world. The police overreaction horrified the nation.

The Democratic Party at the time was divided between northern liberals and southern segregationists. The Kennedy administration was reluctant to embrace civil rights, fearing it would lose support from Southern Democrats. The images from Birmingham forced the issue, and the administration finally submitted strong civil rights legislation to Congress.

A major obstacle for all activists is what political scientists call the **free rider problem.** Civil rights protesters faced dog bites, criminal prosecution, and even death. Those who stood on the sideline reaped the same political benefits without any risks; they could have a free ride. Yet, in the early 1960s, hundreds of thousands of Americans ignored cost-benefit calculations and joined protests and marches.

● Freedom Riders narrowly escaped the burning bus—only to be beaten bloody.

Why did they put themselves in harm's way? Was it the idea of freedom? Their moral convictions? Or perhaps it was the communal exuberance of fighting for something larger than themselves. Have you joined in a Black Lives Matter or other protest? If so, you may have your own answer to this perennial political science question.

Congress and the Civil Rights Act

Despite the protests, Congress blocked civil rights legislation—as it had done many times in the past. This time, however, activists prevailed. In May and June 1963, a great wave of protests followed Birmingham. Media stories about demonstrations, violence, and arrests fostered a sense of crisis. The **1963 March on Washington** marked the high point of the peaceful protest movement: the entire nation watched Martin Luther King put aside his prepared text and declare, "I have a dream."

In November 1963, President Kennedy was assassinated, and action on civil rights became, as President Lyndon Johnson put it, a martyr's cause. The **Civil Rights Act of 1964** was powerful legislation. It forbade state and local governments from denying access to public facilities on the basis of race, color, religion, sex, or national origin. The law prohibited employers from discriminating on similar grounds, and barred discrimination in private motels, hotels, theaters, and other public accommodations. There would be no more "black Thursdays" at city zoos or whites-only water fountains. Congress relied on its constitutional authority over interstate commerce to forbid private businesses from discriminating—no more restaurants or hotels that served only whites.

Opponents sued, claiming that private businesses such as motels should be free to choose their own patrons. The Supreme Court ruled that because motels served people from other states, Congress could use its power over interstate commerce to stop owners from discriminating. Ollie's Barbecue in Birmingham, Alabama, did not have patrons from other states. However, in *Katzenbach v. McClung*, the Court ruled that because it received supplies through interstate commerce, it too fell under congressional jurisdiction. The era when traveling Black people had to sleep in their cars and seek out the few restaurants that would serve them—captured in the 2019 Oscar-winning movie *Green Book*—was finally over.[30]

The Civil Rights Act also empowered the federal government to withhold funds from segregated schools. In less than a decade the number of southern schoolchildren in integrated schools jumped from almost none to over 90 percent (see Figure 6.3). Today, court decisions on civil rights continue to cite this blockbuster legislation.

The following year, Congress passed the Voting Rights Act of 1965. This law protected the right to vote, struck down voter suppression tactics such as the literacy test, and empowered the attorney general and the U.S. District Court of Washington, DC, to weigh any voting change in suspect areas for its potentially discriminatory effect. The legislation effectively secured the Fifteenth Amendment guaranteeing the right to vote. Black people surged to the ballot boxes, and in their wake came Black elected officials (see Table 6.2). Over time, the number of elected African Americans skyrocketed—increasing 129-fold in forty years. Black people, who comprise over 12 percent of the American population, now make up 13 percent of the U.S. House, 10 percent of all state legislators, 3 percent of U.S. Senators, and 2 percent of governors.

1963 March on Washington: A massive rally for civil rights that included Martin Luther King's "I Have a Dream" speech.

Civil Rights Act of 1964: Landmark legislation that forbade discrimination on the basis of race, sex, religion, or national origin.

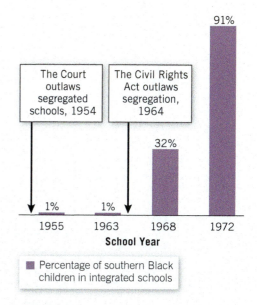

The Court outlaws segregated schools, 1954

The Civil Rights Act outlaws segregation, 1964

Percentage of southern Black children in integrated schools

● **FIGURE 6.3** *The Civil Rights Act of 1964—rather than the* Brown v. Board of Education *Supreme Court decision in 1954—led to rapid integration of southern schools.*

TABLE 6.2 Total Number of Black Elected Officials

	1964	1970	1980	1990	2022
Mayors	0	81	205	314	600 (est.)
Members of Congress	5	9	19	19	>60
Total Black elected officials in the United States	70	1,469	4,914	7,370	More than 10,500 (est.)

Sources: Congressional Research Service; African American Mayors' Association; Joint Center for Political Studies

The Rise of Black Nationalism

In the summer of 1964 alone, eighty civil rights workers were beaten in Mississippi, four were killed, and more than a thousand were arrested. Civil rights leaders like Dr. Martin Luther King had focused on the South and, through a long, difficult, patient strategy of peaceful protest, demanded basic rights in the face of terrible violence. Despite the agonizing pace, the strategy seemed to work. Shocking stories and images of murder, arson, beating, whipping, fire hoses, police dogs, and castrations drew many Americans to the moral cause. But there was an audience that the civil rights leaders had not reckoned with.

Young Black Americans in other parts of the country watched the implacable violence over simple things—a walk in the park, a seat at the lunch counter, a place in the pew. Yet they heard little about the troubles they faced outside the South. In Los Angeles, for example, the Black population grew from 63,000 in 1950 to 350,000 by 1965. Most Black Angelenos lived in dilapidated areas and were denied access to nicer ones. The state legislature responded with a Fair Housing Act in 1963, which would have limited racial discrimination in housing. The following year, however, opponents called a referendum on the reform and California voters buried it in a landslide, two to one.

The unrelenting violence in the South and discrimination everywhere else eventually provoked a backlash. Facing relentless hostility, harassment, and violence, many activists rejected nonviolent protest and seized instead on **Black power**—an idea that emphasized pride in Black heritage, the nurturing of Black interests, and the empowerment of the Black community to act on its own. The civil rights movement split over strategy: Some continued to follow King and his campaign of nonviolent protest. Others, most famously Malcolm X, thought it was time to recognize the inevitable: White Americans had rejected racial equality. It was time to stop being submissive and simply separate from them. Groups such as the Black Panthers armed themselves and vowed to answer violence with violence.

Eventually, years of frustration burst into urban riots—also known as insurrections—between 1964 and 1969. Watts, in Los Angeles, erupted in August 1965 (thirty-four deaths) the same week that the Voting Rights Act passed in Congress. Detroit, which had been the site of a terrible white riot in 1943, blew up again in July 1967 (with forty-three deaths). Most outbursts had a local cause—often incidents involving all-white police forces. White liberals who had energetically supported civil rights began to turn away from the movement. The era of civil rights gave way to a desire for "law and order"—a slogan that presidential candidate Richard Nixon used to great effect on the campaign trail in 1968.

Black power: A slogan that emphasized pride in Black heritage and the construction of Black institutions to nurture Black interests. It often implied racial separation in reaction to white racism.

THE BOTTOM LINE

» The NAACP won a series of cases against segregation, culminating in *Brown v. Board of Education;* however, implementation proved difficult.

» In the early 1960s, many men, women, and children—Black and white—organized in mass movements to turn the legal promise of the *Brown* decision into a practical reality. As the images from marches became more dramatic, surging public opinion pushed Congress to pass the Civil Rights Act of 1964 and the Voting Rights Act of 1965.

» Taken together, these institutional changes ended de jure segregation in the United States.

» The Black movement set the model for future civil rights campaigns by many other groups.

After the Southern Civil Rights Movement

After the strong challenge to de jure segregation, civil rights reformers faced the perplexing problems of pervasive de facto discrimination. When one of our Black students became a lawyer in Boston, the real estate agent shook her head and said, sadly, "Look, there are some nice neighborhoods I just can't show you." Protesters can kneel in front of a segregated church, but how do they challenge discrimination in housing and employment?

Martin Luther King had tried to deploy the southern movement's strategies in Chicago in January 1966. He led a housing drive and, as he walked through one suburb, he was brought to his knees when someone in the seething white crowd hurled a rock that hit him in the head. He later testified that he had "never seen—even in Mississippi and Alabama—mobs as hostile and hate-filled as I've seen in Chicago." On the other side, many young people thought King did not understand what had to be done to win a revolution. "I had preached to them about my dream," wrote a mournful King. "I had urged them to have faith in America and in white society." But in Chicago, his own people had booed him "because they felt we were unable to deliver on our promises."[31]

The civil rights movement had achieved extraordinary things. Black Americans could scarcely dream of becoming lawyers and mayors and judges before the movement began. Now incredible changes were stirring. At the same time, there remained then—as there remains today—an agonizingly long distance before achieving racial justice and equality.

Affirmative Action in the Workplace

In the 1970s, a new approach emerged to assist groups that had faced discrimination. **Affirmative action** involves direct, positive steps to increase the representation (especially in schools and workplaces) of groups that have faced discrimination in the past. The strategy started with race and then expanded to other forms of discrimination, such as those based on gender and ethnicity.

Affirmative action: Direct steps to recruit members of previously underrepresented groups into schools and jobs.

Disproportionate impact: The discriminatory effect of some policies, even if discrimination is not consciously intended.

In 1971, the Supreme Court propounded a doctrine called **disproportionate impact**. Companies could not hire or promote employees in ways that created "built-in headwinds for minority groups [that] are unrelated to measuring job capability." Companies who never hired women or had zero minority managers would be suspected of those "headwinds."[32]

Affirmative action raises difficult issues. The goal is *equality of opportunity*—giving each person the same chance to achieve success. Critics charge that affirmative action actually produces *equality of outcome* by reserving jobs or opportunities for individuals based on their race or gender. Proponents respond: How else can we make up for generations and generations of past discrimination? An obvious question confronted courts pursuing affirmative action: How long should the programs stay in place? How many years of affirmative action would make up for centuries of repression?

The question turned hot when politicians began to promote an idea that spread quickly: The programs were unfair to white men. By every measure (health, life expectancy, income, wealth, corporate offices, discrimination), white Americans do better than African Americans. And yet, the image of white male victims proved politically powerful.

The issue is so complicated because it mixes race and economics. Perhaps all populations that have historically been poor—rural white people as well as Black people, for example—should have some claim on affirmative action? As the economic pie shrank for those on the bottom (as we discussed in Chapter 2), the politics grew fiercer.

Affirmative action soon sparked a backlash and the Supreme Court began to narrow its use. In 1986, the Court warned that such programs could be used only in cases of "severe discrimination" and should not "trammel the interests of white employees."[33] By 1995, a more conservative Court rejected the entire idea of explicitly setting aside places for members of racial groups.[34]

In 2009, the New Haven, Connecticut, fire department began requiring a written exam for promotions. The top scorers on the test were all white. If the city accepted the test results, Black and Hispanic firefighters could sue under disproportionate impact, arguing that the test created "headwinds" unrelated to fighting fires. But when New Haven threw out the test results, white firefighters who had scored well sued. The Supreme Court agreed, 5–4, that New Haven should not have dismissed the results. The case is difficult because both sides have a good argument: The New Haven fire department needs diverse leadership, but ignoring the test results seems unfair to the individuals who did well.

Affirmative Action in Education

Civil rights advocates believed that if children from different races and ethnicities went to school together, they would shed the prejudices that marked their parents and grandparents. But because many children lived in single-race neighborhoods, local schools were inevitably segregated. One solution, known as **school busing**, aimed to achieve racial integration by driving students to other neighborhoods. Busing drew intense opposition and it declined after the 1980s. Observers still disagree over whether it was a successful effort to create a new generation that could move beyond racial divisions or social engineering that only whipped up racial animosity by using children to right old social wrongs.

School busing: An effort to integrate public schools by mixing students from different neighborhoods.

The battle spread to colleges and universities. Many schools tried to redress past discrimination by reserving places for members of minority groups. After all, argued college administrators, everyone benefits from a diverse student body.

These quotas too created a backlash. In one landmark case, a white man named Allan Bakke sued the University of California/Davis medical school for holding sixteen places in its entering class of one hundred for members of minority or economically disadvantaged groups. He had been rejected, he argued, despite having higher academic scores than some minority applicants who were accepted. The Supreme Court ruled in favor of Bakke, 5–4; setting an explicit quota, as the university had done, violated the equal protection guarantee of the Fourteenth Amendment. But the courts continue to permit universities to use race as one of many factors—a "plus factor"—in admitting a diverse student body.

In fall 2022, the Supreme Court heard a case brought by Harvard and UNC-Chapel Hill applicants claiming that efforts to enhance diversity are unfair to students with high test scores. The Court majority seemed poised to strike down affirmative action in admissions. Once again, two important values clash: On the one hand, Americans aim to reverse four centuries of white male privilege and honor the nation's commitment to embracing diversity; on the other, we aim to treat each person equally.[35]

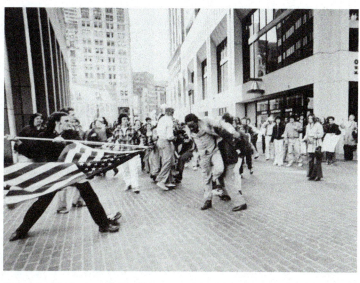

● *In cities like Boston, busing led to protests, riots, and even killings. In 1976, these protesters attacked Ted Landsmark, an African American attorney.*

WHAT DO YOU THINK?   Higher Education and Affirmative Action

What do we, as a society, owe to groups who have faced violence and discrimination for many generations? Consider higher education—the path to success in contemporary society. Which of the following positions would you support?

I favor affirmative action in college admissions.
Preferential admission for members of long-marginalized groups responds to many generations of discrimination. And it's good for everyone by promoting diversity—drawing on people from different backgrounds makes for a stronger community and a richer educational experience. It also builds a more equal society if races, classes, and genders interact and learn to work together in their formative years. Over time, affirmative action in education will help a whole generation look past ascriptive categories such as race, gender, and ethnicity.

I oppose affirmative action in college admissions.
Past discrimination does not justify special treatment now. In *Grutter v. Bollinger* (2003), the Supreme Court implied that the correct period should last roughly three generations, or sixty years (1965–2025). Although male students comprised 58 percent of the student body in the 1970s when affirmative action went into effect, they now make up only 41 percent.[36] Furthermore, affirmative action is tantamount to reverse discrimination against hard-working individuals. Education should have only one yardstick: merit!

● *During the initial peak of the BLM protests, in May 2020, the #BlackLivesMatter hashtag was tweeted 47.8 million times in one week.*

The Black Lives Matter Movement

As we saw earlier in this chapter, a new movement for Black civil rights, known as Black Lives Matter (BLM), sprang up after Michael Brown's death in 2014. Three years later, a mass white supremacist march in Charlottesville, Virginia, culminating in the death of a counter-protester, again drew national attention to the cause of racial equity. Still more urgent demands spread across America—and the globe—in 2020, following the killing of George Floyd by Minneapolis police. During the initial peak of the BLM protests, in May 2020, the #BlackLivesMatter hashtag was tweeted 47.8 million times in one week.[37] Many cities removed statues of Confederate generals and advocates of white supremacy, and many cities and states introduced criminal justice reforms—though the reform efforts dwindled in the face of rising crime rates.[38]

At the same time, the latest civil rights surge sparked an intense backlash. Politicians denounced those removing the statues as "cancel culture" and campaigned against Black Lives Matter. Senator Ron Johnson (R-WI) articulated a widespread feeling when he told a radio host that he would have been a lot more worried about the insurgents at the Capitol on January 6, 2021, if they had been "Black Lives Matter activists."[39] And in the 2022 midterms, many Republicans ran (with mixed success) against the specter of schools teaching critical race theory.

THE BOTTOM LINE

» To make up for past discrimination, legislatures and courts turned to affirmative action in the 1960s and 1970s. Employers and schools that had previously excluded Latinos, Native Americans, Black people, or women now set aside places for them.

» The courts initially sponsored affirmative action programs but are increasingly skeptical of any race-based categories, including those designed to ameliorate past injustice.

» A renewed push for Black civil rights that spread across the United States in more recent years continues—along with a backlash it has galvanized on the right.

Women's Rights

In the early nineteenth century, an American woman had no political rights. She could not vote, serve on a jury, or enter into a contract after marriage. Her husband controlled her property, her wages, and even her body. Husband and wife are one, mused Justice Hugo Black, and "that one is the husband."

Suffrage

The struggle for women's rights in the United States has been interconnected with the fight for racial equality. When women joined the abolition movement, they quickly grew frustrated by the barriers that confronted them. They could lecture to other women but not men (for that would be "promiscuous"); they could join abolitionist societies but not be elected officers.[40] The first American gathering for women's suffrage, the 1848 **Seneca Falls Convention**, grew directly out of staunch opposition to the gender barriers in the abolition movement.

In the 1870s, the women's movement gained momentum. The Women's Christian Temperance Union attacked alcohol as a cause of male violence against women. It championed voluntary motherhood (no more marital rape), suffrage for women, and decent wages. Two other groups focused on winning the vote. Led by Carrie Chapman Catt, the American Woman Suffrage Association emphasized winning voting rights state by state. The National American Woman Suffrage Association (NAWSA), galvanized by Alice Paul, fought for a constitutional amendment that would give every American woman the right to vote.

Success came first in the West, beginning with the Wyoming and Utah Territories, which granted women the vote in 1869 and 1870—partially because gender roles were less settled in those territories, partially because strong populist reform movements swept through the West. By 1916, women voted in every state of the West and Midwest except Texas and New Mexico. The issue remained contentious, however. Four northern states voted to reject suffrage during the 1916 presidential election; southern leaders remained strongly opposed for fear that women might reject segregation, marry across races, and—in their words—destroy "the Anglo Saxon race" (see Figure 6.4).[41]

During World War I, women took on new roles throughout the economy. Led by Alice Paul and NAWSA, they increased the pressure for suffrage. Paul was jailed for her activism. Eventually, President Woodrow Wilson grudgingly supported suffrage as a "wartime measure." The Nineteenth Amendment—giving women the right to vote—cleared Congress over stiff opposition in the Senate and was ratified by the states in 1920.

Although women had secured suffrage, voters did not send them to Washington for a long time. Montana elected the first woman to Congress, Jeanette Rankin, in 1916 (even before the amendment passed—again, western states were ahead of the curve). Still, fifty years later, only three women had been elected to the U.S. Senate for full terms, and after the 1970 election, there were eleven women in the House of Representatives (just 2 percent of that chamber). Then, during the 1970s–80s, the number of women officeholders soared—first on the local level and, by the 1990s, in Congress (see Figure 6.5).[42]

Despite these gains, the United States in 2022 ranks sixty-eighth worldwide in the percentage of women in its legislature (see Comparing Nations 6.1). In the United States, women are less likely than men to leap into the contest. The good news is that women who do run win just as often as men do. The 2020 elections marked a banner year for women candidates, as voters elected a record number

Seneca Falls Convention: The first convention dedicated to women's rights, held in July 1848 in Seneca Falls, New York.

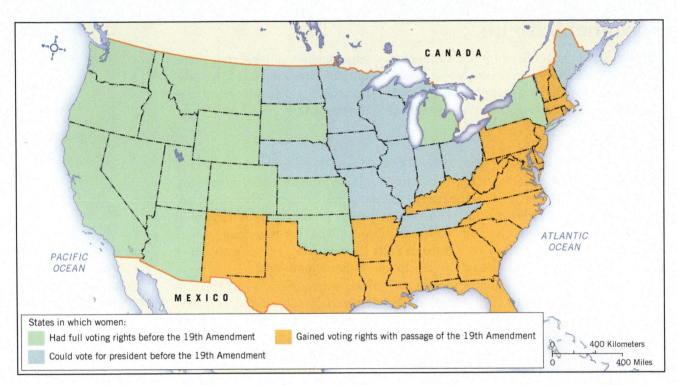

States in which women:

🟩 Had full voting rights before the 19th Amendment   🟧 Gained voting rights with passage of the 19th Amendment

🟦 Could vote for president before the 19th Amendment

● **FIGURE 6.4** *Before the Nineteenth Amendment, women had full voting rights in the West, limited rights in the Midwest, and almost none in the South and East. For women, winning the vote took a difficult political campaign that lasted more than eighty years.*

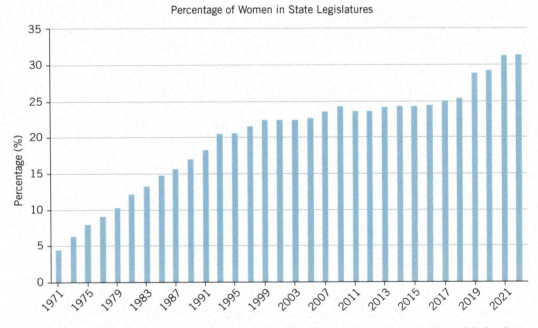

Percentage of Women in State Legislatures

● **FIGURE 6.5** *Number of women in state legislatures. Note the steep rise in the 1970s–80s and the leveling out after 1992—then rise again after 2018. (Center for American Women and Politics)*

of women. The 2022 midterms saw women expand their record-high presence in Congress and governor ranks. On the state level, women hold more than a quarter of elected offices and make up more than 40 percent of top appointees across the fifty states.[43]

COMPARING NATIONS 6.1	Percentage of Women in National Legislatures: Selected Countries	
	WORLD NATION % WOMEN IN RANK	LOWER (POPULAR) HOUSE
1	Rwanda	61.3
2	Cuba	53.4
4	Mexico	50.0
6	New Zealand	49.2
10	South Africa	46.5
37	France	37.3
46	United Kingdom	34.7
59	Canada	30.5
61	Israel	30.0
66	Iraq	28.9
68	United States of America	28.6
94	China	24.9
98	Ireland	23.1
118	Saudi Arabia	19.9
124	South Korea	18.6
129	North Korea	17.6
136	Russia	16.2
142	India	14.9
163	Japan	9.9
175	Iran	5.6
183	Papua New Guinea, Vanuatu, Yemen	0.0

Sixty-seven countries outdistance the United States in the percentage of women in national legislatures. Achieving balance is generally easier in a parliamentary system, where candidates are selected by the parties.
Source: Inter-Parliamentary Union; authors' compilation.

The Civil Rights Act of 1964: Unexpected Breakthrough

A breakthrough in the struggle for gender rights slipped into the Civil Rights Act of 1964. This landmark law, as we have seen, was designed to bar racial discrimination. Congressman Howard Smith, a segregationist from Virginia, proposed adding a single word—"sex"—to the legislation with the intent of making a mockery of the entire bill and killing it. There were loud guffaws from the men in the

House as he made his proposal; at the time, the idea of fighting sex discrimination seemed crazy. Most of the eighteen women members seized on the sarcastic suggestion as evidence of discrimination and it remained in the final bill. When the Civil Rights Act passed, it barred discrimination based on "race, color, religion, *sex*, and national origin."

At the time, no one predicted that the gender provision in the Civil Rights Act would have the same far-reaching consequences for gender rights as *Brown v. Board of Education* had for African Americans—but it did. As with the Supreme Court decisions on race, the Civil Rights Act merely opened the door to gender change. The women's movement had to seize the opportunity.

At first, officials ignored the gender provision. The **Equal Employment Opportunity Commission** (**EEOC**), which monitored compliance with the Civil Rights Act, considered it a "mischievous joke perpetrated on the floor of the House of Representatives." In response, a network of women organized the **National Organization for Women** (**NOW**), drawing directly on the tactics of the civil rights campaign—demonstrations, rallies, lobbying, and litigation.

Congress and the EEOC began to pay attention. In 1972, Congress passed federal education amendments that denied federal funds for programs that discriminated against women (Title VI) and that required equal athletic opportunities for men and women (Title IX). Underfunded women's sports programs began getting the same treatment as the men's varsity programs.[44]

Notice how a single piece of legislation can have far-reaching consequences. The next time you watch a women's basketball game on national television, thank Congressman Smith for dropping the word *sex* into the Civil Rights Act of 1964. Once again, legislation won by Black reformers empowered many Americans—in this case, women.

Equal Rights Amendment

The politics of civil rights spilled into other areas of gender politics. Feminists introduced an **Equal Rights Amendment** (**ERA**) in Congress every year between 1924 and 1972. The amendment was simple: "Equality of rights under the law shall not be denied . . . on account of sex." By 1972, it had become uncontroversial. Congress passed it by lopsided margins and within three years, thirty-four states had voted yes—just four states short of ratification. Then Phyllis Schlafly, a Republican activist, organized the STOP ERA movement. Schlafly argued that the ERA threatened traditional family life. "What the libbers don't understand," said Schlafly, is "that most women want to be a wife, mother, and homemaker."[45] (STOP stood for Stop Taking Our Privileges.) By **reframing the issue**, Schlafly halted the Equal Rights Amendment in its tracks. Forty-plus years later, four states—Indiana (ratified in 1977), Nevada (2017), Illinois

Equal Employment Opportunity Commission (EEOC): Federal law enforcement agency charged with monitoring compliance with the Civil Rights Act.

National Organization for Women (NOW): An organization formed in 1966 to take action for women's equality.

Equal Rights Amendment: An amendment, originally drafted by Alice Paul in 1923 and passed by Congress in 1972, that declared: "Equality of rights . . . shall not be denied or abridged . . . on account of sex." It fell short by three states.

Reframe the issue: To redefine the popular perception of an issue.

● *Not many of the cheering fans and players at the 2022 NCAA women's basketball championship realize how the Civil Rights Act changed their world.*

(2018), and Virginia (2020)—tipped the ERA past the three-quarters of states required to achieve a constitutional amendment—but the clock had run out in 1979. The debates (and the legal fights) continue.

The Courts

The women's movement also echoed the Black civil rights movement in targeting the courts. Led by Ruth Bader Ginsburg (later a Supreme Court justice until her death in 2020), advocates challenged discriminatory state laws, case by case. Because gender was a *nonsuspect category*, the courts upheld any state law that had some "rational connection to a legitimate state purpose." In a series of cases, culminating in *Craig v. Boren* in 1976, the Court lifted gender into a new category of *heightened scrutiny*—not as rigorous a test as the scrutiny the courts give racial classifications, but a more rigorous test than that applied to other social groups. Ironically, the case—a major victory for women's rights—involved men challenging an Oklahoma statute that set the drinking age for beer as eighteen for women and twenty-one for men.

The courts also applied the prohibition on gender discrimination in the Civil Rights Act to sexual harassment. In 1998, the Supreme Court expanded the protection by ruling that an employee did not have to prove a specific instance of sexual harassment if there was a hostile workplace environment, which might include sexual advances, lewd comments, or general attitudes. The Court ruled that even if employers were not aware of specific instances of harassment, they remained liable for the general culture of the workplace.

Women's advocates raised the issue of differential pay more than a century ago. Today, women working full time earn, on average, 84 percent as much as men—although the exact amount of the disparity is hotly disputed and varies depending on the methodology.[46] In a famous case, Lilly Ledbetter sued after a nineteen-year career as a supervisor with Goodyear Tire Company because she had been paid less than men in the same position. A jury found Goodyear guilty of pay discrimination, but the Supreme Court reversed the judgment by a 5–4 vote in 2007.[47] The majority ruled that Ledbetter should have sued within 180 days after Goodyear set her pay—long before she knew about the salary differential. In 2009, President Obama signed equal-pay legislation—known as the Lilly Ledbetter Act—that permits an employee to sue 180 days from her last paycheck (resetting the clock each time she gets a lower paycheck).[48]

Recent Supreme Court decisions have made it more difficult to sue businesses for gender discrimination. In an impactful case decided in 2011, the Court turned down a **class action** suit brought against Wal-Mart. The suit alleged that the company systematically discriminated against women by offering them less pay and fewer promotions. The Supreme Court ruled—once again by a 5–4 margin—that simply showing that women received less pay was not enough to prove discrimination. Rather, the plaintiffs (the women suing) needed to demonstrate a specific company-wide policy that set lower wages for all the women involved in the class action.[49]

Class action: A lawsuit filed on behalf of an entire category of individuals, such as all public housing residents in a state or all female managers in a large company.

Progress for Women—Into High Offices

There had never been a woman Supreme Court justice until Ronald Reagan named Sandra Day O'Connor to the bench in 1981; in 2023, four of the nine justices are women. In 1964, 7 percent of American women received bachelor's degrees (compared to 12 percent of men); by 2021, 59.5 percent of all college students in the United States were women (and just 40.5 percent were men).[50] There had never been

TABLE 6.3	Women CEOs of Fortune 500 Companies				
YEAR	2000	2010	2015	2020	2022
Women CEOs	3	15	23	37	74
Source: World Economic Forum					

a woman CEO of a Fortune 500 company until 1972. In 2022, the number was up to seventy-four, a major jump but still only 15 percent of the total (see Table 6.3).[51]

Gender politics raise provocative questions about social roles and power. What will it take to win genuine gender equality in the workplace? Conflicts turn on affordable childcare and expanded rights to maternity leave. On the pressures of caring for aging parents, which falls primarily on women (roughly a third of caregivers report negative impacts on their careers).[52] And on the more subtle matter of dress and behavior in the workplace—where women can be harassed for not conforming to long-established male-set norms.

Abortion

For many women, careers opened up when contraception became widely available in the early 1960s—women could decide when (and if) to have children. The Supreme Court protected those choices and prohibited states from interfering with contraception (with the *Griswold* decision, 1965) and abortion (*Roe v. Wade*, 1973). The Court rooted these decisions in the right to privacy. As we saw in Chapter 5, the *Dobbs* decision (2022) struck down *Roe v. Wade* (using scornful language about the reasoning behind *Roe*) and permitted states to ban abortions. What next? Could Congress ban abortions across the nation? Can conservative states return to an earlier era and regulate contraceptives? Watch the Court carefully in the years ahead.

#MeToo

Tarana Burke grew up poor in the Bronx and, as a child, suffered sexual abuse. Later, she began to counsel abused women and, in 2006, had a breakthrough idea: She started a movement called "metoo" designed to let abused women know they did not stand alone. In 2017, actress Alyssa Milano took up the fight and #MeToo exploded across the national (and the world) scene. Women exposed a long list of men as sexual harassers. Many stars—in politics, business, finance, and media—had behaved indecently, sometimes horrifically. The movement is both a bracing sign of progress and a harsh reminder that we remain a long way from gender equality.

● *Tarana Burke realized that abused women could be helped by standing together and founded the "metoo" movement.*

THE BOTTOM LINE

» In nineteenth-century law, women's political rights operated through their husbands. When women organized to win rights, they met with ridicule and violence.

» Women first won voting rights in the states—especially in the West and Midwest—before finally securing the Nineteenth Amendment, which guaranteed the right to vote regardless of gender.

» The Civil Rights Act of 1964 bars gender discrimination. As with the civil rights movement of the 1950s and 1960s, the women's movement organized to take advantage of legal changes. The law transformed American gender roles in political and professional life.

» Following *Roe v. Wade* in 1973 and the unsuccessful fight for the Equal Rights Amendment in the mid-1970s, gender politics became especially controversial, spilling into many other issues, including equal pay and the complexities of balancing work with caring for children and for aging parents.

» The Supreme Court opened a new era in sexual politics when it reversed *Roe v. Wade* in 2022 and renewed the debate over state laws facilitating and forbidding abortion.

» The #MeToo movement takes aim at sexual harassment and abuse and has spread across the nation—and the world.

Immigrants Help Build America

In addition to Black Americans and women, many other groups in the American mosaic have a rich history and legacy of civil rights. Each has been the focus of politics, of economics, of culture, and of national identity. Some groups, such as Latinos and Native Americans, have a North American history that long predates European settlers.

We can, unfortunately, only give you a brief introduction to the history and politics of the many other groups that are part of the civil rights legacy in the United States. But as we introduce them—and focus on the current issues they face—remember that each group has its own long and important history.

Latinos—A Rising Force in American Politics

Perhaps the most important group rising in American politics is not really a group at all. There are sixty-two million Latino or Hispanic Americans living in the United States, representing 19 percent of the total population and up from just 6.4 percent in 1980.[53] But many in the community describe themselves not as Latino but as Mexican American, or Dominican American, or Puerto Rican, or Cuban American. Americans from each country of origin have their own history, interests, and political issues. Nevertheless, taken as a single entity, Latinos may very well be the key to many U.S. electoral and policy outcomes today.

Barriers to Civil Rights. Latinos have long faced discrimination in the United States. They were already living in the Southwest—in Arizona, California, New Mexico, and parts of Colorado, Nevada, Utah, and Texas—before the United States took those lands from Mexico in 1848. As white settlers poured into the new territories, they often displaced Latino residents from their homes and farms. As the nation urbanized, Latinos were pushed into segregated schools, excluded from jobs, and barred from housing in white neighborhoods. They also faced hostility and violence.

During World War II, for example, some West Coast newspapers claimed (without merit) that California was undergoing a Mexican crime wave. In 1943, the animosity boiled into a riot. White soldiers and sailors poured through the streets of Los Angeles, pulling Mexican men and boys out of street cars, stores, and homes, assaulting them as the police stood by and looked the other way.

Today, despite enormous success in achieving the American dream, Latinos still face challenges. They are incarcerated at a much higher rate than white non-Hispanic Americans. They are more likely to be poor, less likely to have health insurance, and underrepresented in almost every political venue. The COVID-19 pandemic hit Latinos harder than most groups: They were four times more likely to be hospitalized than the general population and twice as likely to die. Despite all this, Latinos have a higher life expectancy than most other Americans—something that public health experts call the Latino paradox.[54]

Challenging Discrimination. Latino leaders have long tried to forge a political alliance across the many national groups that make up the population. They established the League of United Latin American Citizens (LULAC) in 1929. Like the NAACP, the organization fought segregation through lawsuits. In *Mendez v. Westminster*, decided in 1947, the Court struck down Latino school segregation in Orange County, California; the case was an important precursor to *Brown v. Board of Education*.

During the 1960s, young Latinos turned to activism. In 1968, high school and college students called a massive student strike that reverberated throughout the Southwest. The students pushed mainstream Latino organizations to fight more aggressively against discrimination; they challenged immigration policies that restricted movement across the Mexican border. Young people took a slur against Mexicans, *Chicano,* and turned it into a movement they labeled **Chicanismo**—a defiant pride in their heritage and culture.

At the same time, the **United Farm Workers** (**UFW**) organized the most vulnerable population—migrant workers who picked crops up and down the West Coast. The UFW became a symbol of Latino mobilization. Throughout the 1960s and 1970s, traditional organizations such as LULAC, activist students, and farm workers all challenged discrimination. Their efforts prepared the way for the entry of Latino elected officials into every level of government.

As you might expect, Hispanic politics are diverse and often depend on nationality, region, and even generation. For Mexican Americans, who are concentrated in the Southwest, the politics of immigration looms very large. In contrast, Puerto Ricans, the second-largest Hispanic population in the United States, are American citizens by birth; immigration issues are less relevant to them. Salvadorans, now the third-largest Latino group, face the problems of more recent immigrants—poverty, social integration, and community building. Cuban Americans offer still another contrast. They have high average incomes, generally do not share the same political concerns as most other Hispanic groups, and have traditionally voted strongly Republican—though Cuban youth now break evenly between the parties.[55]

Chicanismo: A movement expressing pride in Latino origins and culture in the face of discrimination.

United Farm Workers (UFW): An influential union representing migrant farm workers in the West.

Still, for all the diversity, Latinos are a very large group and, if unified, a central force in American elections. One of the major questions for the future of American politics: Might this very diverse population mobilize together for political action? Today, that question plays out amid two boisterous debates: immigration and language.

The Politics of Immigration

Despite their long heritage in the land, Latino politics is wrapped up with immigration. After all, Latinos have been the largest immigrant group in the past two decades.

Although the United States is an immigrant nation, the door to foreigners has historically swung from wide open to shut tight. Restrictions in the 1920s strictly limited immigration—President John Kennedy sadly noted forty years later that America no longer

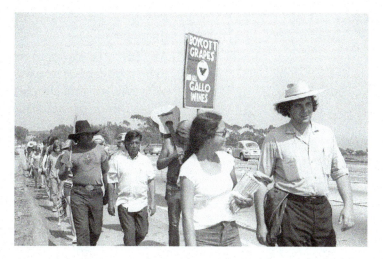

● The United Farm Workers' (UFW) 1,000 Mile March approaches Malibu, California, summer 1975. The march was a fifty-nine-day trek through central California organized by the UFW. Tens of thousands of farm workers marched by day and attended rallies in the evening. Their demands: better labor conditions on the ranches and an end to discrimination.

offered a beacon for immigrants. After his assassination, Congress lifted the restrictions, in 1965, and a new era of immigration began. Today, nearly one in seven American residents was born abroad.

Ancient Fears. Immigrants trigger fears that are repeated for every new group: They will undermine American values and culture; they will take away jobs; they will cling to their own languages; they will remain loyal to foreign countries; they don't share American values. All this was said about the Irish back in the 1840s—and they were also persecuted for being Catholics; in 1900, one U.S. senator justified a mob that killed eleven Italians after a jury exonerated them of murder, by arguing that Italians were natural criminals.[56] The sentiments grow stronger in periods of high immigration—from early in the nation to the present day.

Immigration by the Numbers. Between 2000 and 2021, the United States averaged a bit more than one million legal immigrants a year—that's one-fifth of the world's immigrants. Taken together, the people who were born abroad now number forty-seven million.[57] The rights of immigrants depend on their legal status.

Three Categories. Immigrant groups fall into three different categories with very different legal claims on civil rights.[58]

1. Those who were born in the United States or have become American citizens (roughly two-thirds of the Latino population) claim the same rights as any citizen. They are in the same protected legal category as Black Americans. Any law that singles them out is "suspect" and subject to strict scrutiny by the courts.

2. Foreigners who have not become citizens fall into a second category, which the U.S. government terms *resident alien*. They number approximately 13.5 million. They may work in the United States, and they pay taxes, but they cannot enjoy the benefits of citizenship: They may not vote in most elections

and many government safety-net programs exclude them for five years after their arrival.

3. An estimated eleven to twelve million people are not legally authorized to be residents. Most arrived on a temporary visa, got a job or fell in love, settled down, and simply remained after their legal time in the country expired. Undocumented individuals have limited constitutional rights and, when caught, are subject to immediate deportation—despite resistance by many state and local governments, as described in Chapter 4.[59]

Undocumented Individuals. The debate over people who are not legally authorized to be in the United States is especially intense. Some argue that they are a vital part of the American economy and society. Yet they live in fear of jail and deportation. As a result, many are wary of going to a hospital—even when they are seriously injured. They are afraid to visit their children's school, or even report crimes against them. Many Americans believe that simple decency requires that we bring these individuals out of the shadows and give them a path to legal status. They believe undocumented individuals should be able to obtain driver's licenses (eighteen states and the District of Columbia currently allow them to do so) and attend universities (Figure 6.6). And that no one should be denied basic rights—like healthcare.

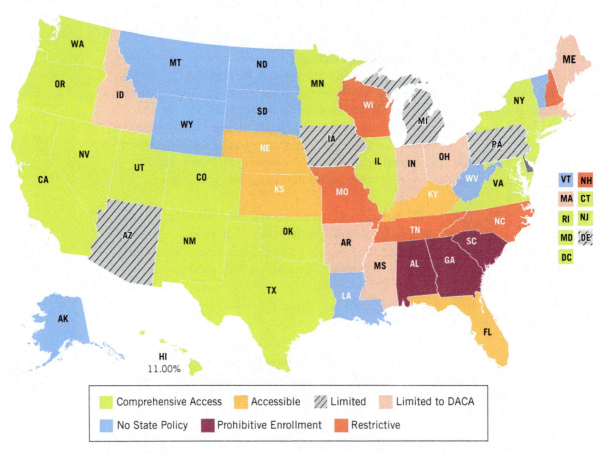

● **FIGURE 6.6** *Undocumented individuals and public higher education: The rules vary across the states—from open access to complete prohibition.*

Opponents respond that undocumented individuals have broken the law and should not be rewarded. They argue that it would be unfair to those who have waited patiently for years to receive authorization. They also fear that immigrants will take jobs and depress wages—particularly in occupations that do not require advanced education or training. Finally, they say, illegal immigration undermines the social cohesion, the sense of solidarity, within a society.

Immigration Policy

How should we set our immigration policy? How many people should we welcome? These questions often get drowned out by the raucous debates over hot-button issues like building a wall on the Mexican border or finding a path to citizenship for the undocumented individuals who arrived as children—known as Dreamers.

In 2012, President Obama signed an executive order that bypassed a deadlocked Congress and protected up to one million undocumented Dreamers. President Trump ended the program, arguing that the issue should be left to Congress—where a bill titled *Development, Relief, and Education for Alien Minors* (or DREAM) was first introduced twenty years ago but has never passed. President Joe Biden quickly resurrected the program, instructing administration officials to "preserve and fortify" it. The conflict goes on, in courts, in Congress, and across administrations.[60]

Too Many Immigrants? Or Too Few?   The debate over undocumented people often drowns out a more important matter. How many immigrants a year should the United States welcome? Again, there is a lively debate. Proponents argue that almost all population growth in the United States has come from immigration, and that this growth is essential for economic prosperity. The new arrivals, continue proponents, enrich America through their energy, skills, creativity, culture, and diversity.

On the other side, many people worry that too many immigrants will take jobs from the Americans who are already here; they will depress wages, overwhelm social programs, and change the culture. The United States will become a country they no longer recognize, fear the immigration skeptics.

Language Controversy: "Speak English!"   As long ago as 1752, Benjamin Franklin worried that there were so many Germans in Philadelphia that "instead of them learning our language, we must learn theirs or live as in a foreign country." In recent decades, Spanish language use has become a major issue. In 1974, the Supreme Court ruled in *Lau v. Nichols* that equal protection required schools to assist students whose primary language was not English. Many school districts established bilingual education programs.

Opponents worry that bilingual education divides the community, undermines traditional American culture, and disadvantages students who fail to learn English. Proponents (and many scholars) respond that, like every previous generation of immigrants, today's new Americans and, especially, their American-born children speak fluent English and that Spanish instruction cases the process.[61]

● More than 250 years after Benjamin Franklin expressed his concern, the owner of Geno's Steaks in Philadelphia announced that people should speak English (a) (although when Geno's son took over the business he removed the sign). While Geno's got the headlines, in many parts of the country, establishments routinely offer multilingual signs (b).

Latino Political Mobilization

Latino Americans face many challenges. About one in six lives below the poverty line—two times the rate for non-Hispanic whites.[62] They have less health insurance coverage and face tensions with law enforcement.[63]

When they turn to politics to address these vital concerns, Latinos face the issue we noted earlier: They come from many different nations, each with their own interests (see Figure 6.7). That returns us to the question we asked at the start of this section:

Is there a common political denominator across this diverse population?

Today, a pan-Latino movement seeks to find common ground and mobilize voters around issues that transcend any one country or group. Shared political influence, if Latinos seek to exercise it, figures to be formidable: The Latino population has grown three times faster than the general population in the last two decades. Latino leaders note that Mexican American voters moved California from solid Republican to decisively Democratic in the last twenty-five years.

In 2006, when the Republican-led Congress proposed tough new restrictions on undocumented individuals, massive demonstrations sprang up around the United States. In the past, Latino protesters had waved Mexican flags and symbols. This time, they marched under a sea of American flags. Researchers who were undertaking a major survey of Latino Americans at the time discovered that the protests made Latinos feel significantly more American.[64]

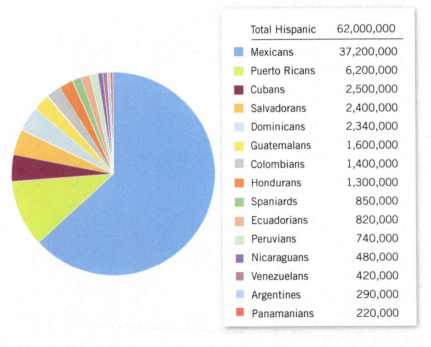

Total Hispanic	62,000,000
Mexicans	37,200,000
Puerto Ricans	6,200,000
Cubans	2,500,000
Salvadorans	2,400,000
Dominicans	2,340,000
Guatemalans	1,600,000
Colombians	1,400,000
Hondurans	1,300,000
Spaniards	850,000
Ecuadorians	820,000
Peruvians	740,000
Nicaraguans	480,000
Venezuelans	420,000
Argentines	290,000
Panamanians	220,000

● FIGURE 6.7 Countries of origin—Hispanics in America. Some two-thirds of Latinos who live in the United States were born here. This figure shows their national heritage. (Pew Research)

The surge in demonstrations reflects three key trends converging: the rapid growth of the Latino population, a sense of shared identity within that population, and an increasing identification with the American homeland. Still, the 2020 election was a reminder of Latino diversity. Donald Trump won Florida thanks in part to Latino support in Miami-Dade County. In Texas, too, Latinos started moving into the Republican camp. But, in Arizona, Joe Biden's win owed much to a large margin among Latino voters. In 2022, the mixed trend continued. Florida governor Ron DeSantis won more Latino votes than any previous statewide GOP candidate. In South Texas, however, Democrats won two of three House races in majority-Hispanic districts. Nationally, Democrats' share of Latino votes was higher than in 2020—and most high-profile Latino election winners were Democrats.

Across the last three elections, Latinos have voted roughly two to one for Democrats. Both parties are acutely aware of these numbers and the basic political reality: What happens in Latino politics will have enduring consequences for the future of American politics. And for the fate of the two parties.

Asian Americans—The Fastest-Growing American Population

Asian Americans are the third-largest minority in the United States after Black and Latino Americans and are, since 2000, the fastest growing—leaping up 81 percent (in contrast, Latinos grew 70 percent, Black Americans 20 percent, and whites not at all).[65] Asian Americans span a wide range of histories, cultures, and experiences. They describe themselves as Chinese American, Indian American, Vietnamese American, Korean American, Japanese American, and so on across many countries (see Figure 6.8).

As a group, Asian Americans have the highest education level and the highest median personal income of all American population groups. However, the statistics mask as much as they reveal, for Asian Americans range from Indian Americans with high income and education levels to Hmong from the mountains of Laos with income levels about one-third the U.S. average.

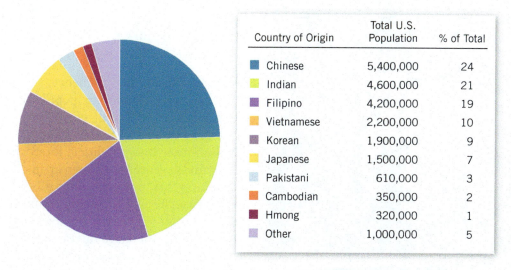

Country of Origin	Total U.S. Population	% of Total
Chinese	5,400,000	24
Indian	4,600,000	21
Filipino	4,200,000	19
Vietnamese	2,200,000	10
Korean	1,900,000	9
Japanese	1,500,000	7
Pakistani	610,000	3
Cambodian	350,000	2
Hmong	320,000	1
Other	1,000,000	5

● **FIGURE 6.8** *Countries of origin. The national identities of about twenty-two million U.S. residents whose heritage is Asian. (Pew Research)*

Facing Discrimination.   Asian people have a long history of negotiating the complicated American lines between "us" and "them." In 1882, Congress passed the Chinese Exclusion Act barring immigration and declaring Chinese people ineligible for citizenship. By 1917, Congress had extended the ban to "all natives of Asia including the whole of India." The California Alien Land Law of 1913 forbade "aliens ineligible for citizenship"—that is, Asian immigrants—from owning land. Each restriction came amid painful stereotypes. The Chinese were excluded because, as one California congressman put it, "his ancestors have bequeathed to him the most hideous immoralities."[66]

After the Japanese attack on Pearl Harbor in 1941, President Roosevelt ordered the army to round up Japanese Americans and place them in cold, miserable internment camps. They lost their liberty, jobs, property, and bank accounts. The Supreme Court upheld the internments. (More than seventy-five years later, the Supreme Court acknowledged its error and the governor of California apologized for the state's role.)[67]

The wartime camps marked only the most extreme case. Schools and neighborhoods were strictly segregated—giving rise to "Chinatowns." San Francisco established separate schools for Chinese Americans in the 1880s and maintained them until the *Brown* decision in 1954. Across the United States, Asian Americans found themselves straddling the racial binary of Black and white, particularly in the Jim Crow South.[68]

Perhaps the oddest cultural twist of all is the stereotype that emerged in the 1960s. Many Asian groups were perceived as the "model minority": a hardworking group that makes its own way without any demands for rights or privileges. It may seem that this is a "good" stereotype, but by reducing each person to nothing more than a member of a group, stereotypes demean individuals and stoke social tensions that erupt periodically. The spread of COVID-19 across America led to another surge of bullying and harassment, spurred in part by President Trump, who employed racist mockery like "Kung Flu" at public rallies.[69]

The past five years have seen a spike in hate crimes against people of Asian origin. Incendiary talk by irresponsible public figures, mixed with fears of COVID-19 and competition with China, appears to have stirred up bigotry. Almost half of all Asian Americans (45 percent) reported incidents ranging from racial slurs (like go back to your country) to fear of violence. And actual hate crimes have spiked, 339 percent in 2021 alone.[70]

Political and Cultural Influence.   The diverse Asian American population includes many different perspectives. Is there anything to tie the vast population into a united political interest? Slurs and violence have blown up in the past five years; does that forge a bond within and beyond the Asian community? While this remains to be seen, Asian Americans have migrated from the Republican Party (up until 1996) to the Democratic Party, and they voted two to one for President Biden in 2020.

● *South Korean K-pop band BTS performs in concert. Across music, anime, television, and movies, Asian cultural productions have had an enormous influence on American culture.*

The Census Bureau predicts that the Asian population will, taken together, form the largest American minority by 2060. Whether that prediction actually holds, a basic law of politics comes into play: As numbers rise, political influence follows.

And we can already see the exciting ripples in American society. Asian cultural productions have had enormous and rising influence—far beyond the Asian population. From K-pop to anime, from *Squid Games* and *Never Have I Ever* to *Drive My Car*, Asian sensibilities are influencing American culture in far-reaching ways.

THE BOTTOM LINE

» Latinos, the largest immigrant group, were for decades the fastest-growing population in the United States; the rate of increase has slowed in recent years. Asian Americans, the third-largest minority group in the United States, is now the fastest-growing population.

» Latinos and Asian Americans are diverse peoples with different national identities, histories, cultures, and concerns. Both groups have won civil rights advances—and suffered setbacks, as well as faced discrimination that continues to this day.

» A key political question is whether Latinos and Asian Americans can find common ground within their own respective populations and whether both groups can also forge ties with other groups around shared interests and concerns. If they do, they will become even more formidable political forces.

Native Americans

The original story of rights denied belongs to the native inhabitants of the United States. Before the Europeans arrived, an estimated ten million Indigenous people (also known as American Indians, Native Americans, and First Nations) lived on the land that would become the United States. As the colonists spread, they introduced deadly diseases, denied Indigenous peoples' sovereignty, fought bitter wars, and slowly pushed the tribes from their ancestral lands.

The Lost Way of Life

The darkest side of American expansion was "Indian removal." As European settlers moved west, native tribes were forced from their homelands. By the time the United States stretched from coast to coast, fewer than a million—less than 10 percent—of these original inhabitants remained.

Recent historians warn against simply seeing Native Americans as passive victims of American westward expansion. The Indians built their own empires and, at times, forced the white settlers to retreat. During King Philip's War (1675–78), natives destroyed or damaged one in five Massachusetts villages. (The war was named after the Native American leader Metacomet, known to the English as "King Philip.")

Between 1750 and 1850, the Comanches dominated economic and military life in the Southwest and pulled white settlers, Spanish colonies, and other tribes into what amounted to an imperial system.[71] Tecumseh (a Shawnee warrior) forged an alliance of Native American peoples across the Midwest to resist American expansion. But with much blood and conflict, the federal government had forced most of the Native Americans into reservations by the late 1800s.

On the reservations, Indians were pushed to adopt European lifestyles. The Dawes Act of 1887 divided reservation lands into individual parcels to destroy traditional ownership customs and encourage farming. Boarding schools educated and assimilated native children. By halting the transmission of cultural legacies, white officials hoped to "kill the Indian" and "save the man." Even Sitting Bull, famed Lakota seer and fierce opponent of white settlement, sent his son to be educated to ensure him a place in an uncertain future.[72]

Native Americans and the Federal Government

Domestic dependent nation: Special status that grants local sovereignty to tribal nations but does not grant them full sovereignty equivalent to that enjoyed by independent nations.

Native Americans have an ambiguous legal status. In 1831, the Supreme Court ruled that Indian tribes were **"domestic dependent nations"**—essentially, a separate people but without the rights of an independent nation. Native Americans were not considered citizens and were not protected by the Constitution until Congress passed the Indian Citizenship Act in 1924. Even today, their legal status remains ambiguous. About a quarter of the Native American population lives on or near tribal reservations, which are independent jurisdictions subject to federal but not state governments. These Indigenous people are both American citizens and members of self-governing independent lands.

The primary connection of Native Americans on reservations to American government is bureaucratic rather than electoral. The Bureau of Indian Affairs (BIA) is responsible for Native American issues. The early placement of the bureau offers a telling symbol: It was part of the Department of War. Later, Congress moved it to the Department of the Interior, whose chief purpose is to promote and protect natural resources and public lands.

The Struggle for Native American Civil Rights

Native Americans face poverty rates almost double the national rates: around 25 percent, compared to 13 percent for the nation as a whole. Life on the reservations is especially difficult. Most are in rural areas with few jobs or resources. Native Americans tend to suffer from low education levels, high infant mortality rates, and lower life expectancies.[73]

Native Americans' civil rights politics divides roughly into two camps. The *ethnic minority* perspective argues that Native Americans should engage American democracy and mobilize for rights and equality. The alternative is the separatist *tribal movement*, which advocates withdrawing from American politics and society and revitalizing Native American culture and traditions.

The 1960s civil rights protest movements spread to Native American activists.

● Assimilation of Native Americans, often forced, was official U.S. government policy well into the twentieth century. Pupils at Carlisle (Pennsylvania) Indian Industrial School, c. 1900.

Led by the American Indian Movement (AIM), tribes occupied the Bureau of Indian Affairs in Washington, DC, for six days in November 1972. They "captured" Alcatraz Island in San Francisco Bay and occupied the site of the infamous prison for nineteen months between 1969 and 1971. They seized control of the village of Wounded Knee on the Pine Ridge Indian Reservation, the site of a massacre of Indians in 1890, for seventy-one days; declared the reservation a sovereign nation; and exchanged occasional gunfire with federal marshals. During this Wounded Knee Incident, AIM brought its grievances before the United Nations General Assembly.

Native Americans and the Courts

As with their contemporaries in other civil rights struggles, Native Americans fought for legislation and sought judicial redress. In *United States v. Sioux Nation of Indians,* the Court ruled in 1980 that the federal government wrongly allowed lands reserved to the Sioux to be settled without purchasing them for fair market value. The settlement awarded, including a century's worth of interest, was approximately $105 million. Now totaling over $1 billion, the settlement remains unclaimed, as doing so would relinquish the Sioux Nation's claim to the disputed lands. In another closely watched case, the Supreme Court in 2018 let stand a lower court ruling that required Washington State to protect long-standing Native American fishing grounds, in a boost for tribal sovereignty. And a 2020 case, *McGirt v. Oklahoma,* was argued twice in the Supreme Court and resulted in a historic reaffirmation of tribal sovereignty over former reservation lands in eastern Oklahoma.[74]

In recent years, some tribes have used their exemption from state laws to create highly profitable gambling businesses and resorts. The Supreme Court ruled in 1987 that because tribes are considered sovereign entities, they are free from state prohibitions on gaming.[75] Around half of the 574 federally recognized tribes run casinos, generating more than $30 billion a year.[76] Whether this is a positive development—for the tribes, for the communities around them, and for the United States—is a matter of much dispute.

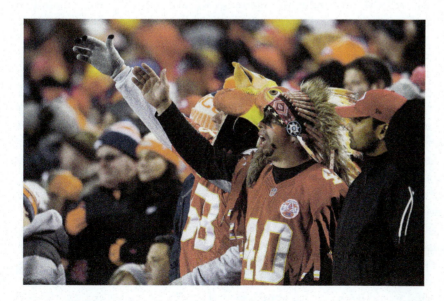

● *Kansas City Chiefs fans, some dressed in Native American headgear, routinely perform the "tomahawk chop" and fake Native chants. However, other teams have dropped long-standing names that were demeaning to Native Americans, including the Washington Redskins (now the Commanders), Cleveland Indians (Guardians), Dartmouth College Indians (Big Green), St John's Redmen (Red Storm) and Arkansas State Indians (Red Wolves).*

THE BOTTOM LINE

» Native Americans lost their way of life in the face of colonial settlers' diseases, armies, and forced removal.

» The Supreme Court gave American Indians a special status: a separate people without rights. Although they retain the special status, Native Americans became U.S. citizens in 1924.

» Native Americans support two different civil rights strategies: The ethnic minority approach argues for winning political rights and benefits. The tribal movement approach prefers to withdraw and to emphasize a separate Indian society and culture.

Groups Without Traditional Court Protections

Civil rights offer many American groups a powerful dream: organize and demand equal treatment. Two additional groups organized and won rights. Neither received special scrutiny from the courts. Neither appeared to be included in the Civil Rights Act of 1964. But each organized a civil rights campaign. Each has moved through the seven steps toward equality that we identified at the start of the chapter.

People with Disabilities

Before 1970, children in wheelchairs did not go to school, and most children with visual impairments never learned how to read. People with disabilities lived outside mainstream society. A political breakthrough came in an unnoticed provision that liberal congressional staff quietly dropped into an obscure bill. **Section 504** of the 1973 Rehabilitation Act borrowed language directly from the Civil Rights Act of 1964 and applied it to persons with disabilities: "No . . . handicapped individual . . . shall, solely by reason of his handicap, be excluded from participation in, or be denied the benefits of . . . any program or activity conducted by an executive agency." Suddenly, any university receiving federal funds—and all government agencies—had to accommodate people with disabilities.

Section 504 gave activists a political focus. When the government was slow to issue regulations, for example, people using wheelchairs staged sit-ins at regional offices and pushed the matter forward. Notice the dynamic: The political pattern resembles that followed by Black people after *Brown v. Board of Education* and feminists after the Civil Rights Act. Government action provided new legal rights; the group then organized and demanded further change.

Advocates went from requesting social benefits to demanding civil rights. The process culminated in 1990, when Congress passed the Americans with Disabilities Act (ADA). The ADA forbade companies of twenty-five or more employees from discriminating against people with disabilities. It also required companies to make "reasonable accommodations" for a wide range of disabilities.

Unlike racial discrimination, however, a business can avoid making accommodations if it would be expensive or inconvenient to do so. Courts constantly weigh the

Section 504: An obscure provision in a minor congressional act that required all institutions that received federal funds to accommodate people with disabilities.

costs and benefits. What is reasonable to require of a firm or a store or a university to accommodate special needs? Even with this delicate balancing of costs and access, the ADA created what amounts to a massive affirmative action program for people with disabilities. Public transportation, schools, shops, and businesses all must help facilitate a normal, mainstream life for people with special needs.

Sexual Orientation and Gender Identity

The movement for same-sex rights began with a riot. In June 1969, police raided a New York City gay bar named the Stonewall Inn. Traditionally, LGBTQ+ people had submitted to such raids as many felt shame over their own sexuality. But this time, the LGBTQ+ community smashed the conventions of the era. The civil rights movement had, in the past decade, inspired many different groups—including the men and women who defied this routine police raid.

● *President George H. W. Bush signs the Americans with Disabilities Act during a ceremony on the South Lawn of the White House on July 26, 1990. Activists took advantage of the new legal framework and won changes— just like the civil rights movement and the National Organization of Women had done in earlier generations.*

The Stonewall riot marks the moment that the LGBTQ+ community actively affirmed its identity. Coming out and disclosing sexual orientation became a major vehicle for raising political consciousness in the 1970s. In 1973, the American Psychiatric Association removed homosexuality from its list of mental disorders.

In the early 1980s, gay communities were devastated by a mysterious plague— AIDS. No one knew what the illness was or how it was transmitted—only that diagnosis meant death. The disease pushed gay groups into local politics. In every city, gay men and women organized and established links to the medical community, local governments, and social service networks.

Same-Sex Civil Rights. Few recent changes in American politics and culture are as dramatic as the transformation of same-sex civil rights. In 1993, newly elected Bill Clinton ran into a firestorm when he promised to open the military to gay men and women: Congress passed a law reaffirming the ban on gays in the military, and the Defense Department issued a special directive in support. Clinton managed to eke out a compromise policy, known as "don't ask, don't tell"—essentially, if gay soldiers did not tell anyone they were gay, they could keep their jobs. Seventeen years later, the Obama administration ended "don't ask, don't tell," in favor of a forthright affirmation of gays in the military; this time Congress passed a law in support. Changing cultural norms produced different outcomes in the White House and on Capitol Hill.

The same arc—from fierce resistance to broad acceptance—marked same-sex marriage. In 2000, Vermont recognized civil unions, legal arrangements that conferred some of the same rights and duties as marriage. The state erupted in protest. What happened next was a revolution in public opinion (covered in Chapter 7).[77] Approval of same-sex marriage leapt from 35 percent in 2001 to 70 percent in 2021.

Political institutions followed the revolution in public opinion. Massachusetts became the first state to permit same-sex marriage. Other states followed. The Supreme Court, in *Obergefell v. Hodges* (2015), narrowly (5–4) enshrined same-sex marriage as a national civil right. The majority held that both the Fourteenth Amendment's due process and equal protection clauses forbade the states from discriminating among couples on the basis of sexual orientation. Notice how the amendment, put in place to benefit formerly enslaved people after the Civil War, continues to offer broad protection against discrimination. But it took activism and public opinion, led by younger Americans, to achieve political change. Few civil rights areas—in politics, law, or public opinion—have evolved as quickly as this one.[78]

In 2020 the Supreme Court recognized LGBTQ+ rights with a blockbuster ruling. The Court went back to the Civil Rights Act, noted that it barred discrimination on the basis of sex, and ruled that the provision required equal treatment of LGBTQ+ people. "An employer who fires an individual merely for being gay or transgender defies the law," wrote Justice Neil Gorsuch for a 6–3 majority.[79]

The Conflicts Continue.   Still, many limits on rights remained. Although twenty-three states and Washington, DC, forbade employers from discriminating on the basis of sexual orientation or gender identity, one in three LGBTQ+ Americans (and three of five transgender individuals) reported facing discrimination. They faced bias in employment, housing, education, criminal justice, and public accommodations.[80] Moreover, eleven states passed legislation permitting social service agencies to deny LGBTQ+ couples or individuals the right to adopt children—most recently, Tennessee in 2020. President Trump moved to bar transgender people from serving in the U.S. military; the Biden administration removed the ban, but the back and forth illustrates the intense politics of the issue.

"Bathroom bills" mark another battleground in the movement for gay rights. In 2016 the city of Charlotte, North Carolina, passed an ordinance prohibiting businesses from discriminating against LGBTQ+ customers. The North Carolina legislature rushed through legislation that stopped the Charlotte action and, in particular, required individuals to use public bathrooms that match the biological sex on their birth certificate.[81] A major backlash arose in North Carolina. The NCAA relocated championship games, and companies such as PayPal and Adidas backed out of constructing facilities in the state; ultimately, the backlash cost the state $3.7 billion in lost revenues.

For a time, restrictive legislation slipped out of the news. Then a new wave of restrictions arose in conservative legislatures. For example, Tennessee passed a series of laws that rolled back LGBTQ+ rights—limiting classroom discussion of LGBTQ+ issues, introducing its own version of a bathroom bill, and excluding transgender girls from high school sports. This time, there was almost no pushback from the business community.[82]

Sports have become a particular flashpoint. When Lia Thomas, a transgender woman from the University of Pennsylvania, won the national swimming championship in the five-hundred-yard freestyle in 2022, many people cheered another national milestone—the first transgender college athlete to win a national championship. On the other side, however, two hundred protesters chanted their disapproval outside the swim center. Women were being shoved out of sports, they insisted, and they argued that Thomas should be swimming with the men.[83]

In effect, the battle pits one generation against another. Younger Americans are much more likely to accept transgender rights (and LGBTQ+ rights in general) as part of the new American landscape. Older, more conservative generations see it differently and push back against "woke" attitudes. We will explore these generational differences when we turn to public opinion in the next chapter.

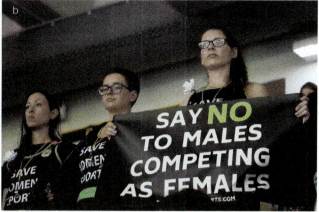

● *Lia Thomas, a transgender woman from the University of Pennsylvania, wins the national swimming championship in the five-hundred-yard freestyle in March 2022 (a). While many people cheered, others protested their disapproval outside the swim center (b).*

Who Faces Discrimination?

The People Disagree

There is a major difference between how Democrats and Republicans perceive discrimination. Most Democrats say there's "a lot" of discrimination against Muslims, Blacks, Hispanics, and LGBTQ+ individuals. In contrast, most Republicans do not think there's "a lot" of discrimination against any of those groups. But notice one of the groups that Republicans are most likely to identify as facing discrimination: Evangelical Christians.

Majorities of Americans say there is at least some discrimination against many different societal groups

% who say there is discrimination against each group in our society

	REP/ LEAN REP		DEM/ LEAN REP	
Black people	17	63	71	93
Muslims	20	67	55	88
Gays and lesbians	16	59	55	92
Hispanic people	12	60	45	89
Asian people	14	56	38	82
Women	11	53	32	84
Jews	18	63	22	73
Evangelical Christians	23	61		29
White people	26	63		20
Men	15	42		24

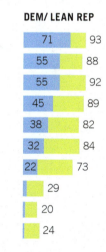

Source: Pew Research Center

THINK ABOUT IT

Where are the similarities between the parties?

....

What are the biggest differences between the parties?

....

In your view, which groups face the most discrimination?

THE BOTTOM LINE

» People with disabilities used an obscure bureaucratic rule to mobilize, and eventually won sweeping civil rights with the Americans with Disabilities Act. The goal is to mainstream people with disabilities as much as possible.

» LGBTQ+ communities have won important breakthroughs, driven in part by strong support from younger Americans. The Supreme Court ruled that states may not discriminate in the areas of employment or same-sex marriages. Still, LGBTQ+ Americans face challenges in education, housing, and other venues.

» The conflict over LGBTQ+ rights continues—with conservative legislatures passing legislation that restricts rights and more liberal legislatures seeking to protect those rights.

 # The Fight for Civil Rights Goes On

How close has the United States come to achieving racial equality and civil rights? A few key indicators measure how the past half-century of movements has changed America, and the distance remaining to full equal rights. Take election to the nation's highest office—the presidency. A Black man, Barack Obama, won the office twice—both times with a comfortable majority. A multiracial woman, Kamala Harris, is vice president. Pete Buttigieg is the first openly gay man to serve in the president's cabinet. But turn to the U.S. Senate: In the past 150 years, only five Black individuals have served a full Senate term—three of them (or 3 percent of the chamber) are serving today.

The original civil rights movement inspired a host of other groups—and provided them with new legal structures, such as the Civil Rights Act of 1964 and the Voting Rights Act of 1965. Yet the data—on poverty, employment, health, education, incarceration rates, and more—suggest that despite great progress, the struggle continues for many groups. Let's focus on the state of equality in three important areas: voting rights, socioeconomic well-being, and incarceration.

Voting Rights Today

The 2020 election ended with false claims of election fraud. Since then, states have rushed to act. Some made voting more difficult. Others have made it easier.[84]

Twenty-three states have added restrictions. For example, Texas added new ID requirements, introduced criminal penalties if people assist voters at the polls, forbade drive-through voting and extended voting hours, and gave partisan poll watchers more power.

The Supreme Court made restricting the vote easier in 2013 when it struck down the central requirement in the Voting Rights Act of 1965: States and counties that once denied Black people the vote were no longer required to "preclear" voting rights changes with the federal Justice Department. Chief Justice Roberts declared that the country had changed in the half-century since the rules went into place. If Congress discovered voting problems, it could target discrimination where it is still taking place. Within two hours of the ruling, Texas pushed through restrictive legislation previously forbidden by the Department of Justice. Twenty-three other states swiftly followed. Recall that the Constitution left most voting details to the states. Today, majorities in many states brazenly adjust the rules to keep their party in power.[85]

But that's only half the story. Even while some states were restricting access, twenty-five others were expanding it. For example, Virginia passed its own voting rights legislation (prohibiting discrimination in voting) and expanded voting hours and drop-off mailboxes. Nevada legislated voting by mail; every eligible voter will receive a ballot in the mail.[86]

In general, Democrats have tried to make voting easier, Republicans to make it more difficult. Each party believes it will gain from the changes it proposes. But are they correct? Do more voters mean bigger gains for Democrats? Some political scientists challenge the simple equation, calling it "the turnout myth" (see Chapter 10).[87]

Economic and Social Rights Today

Equality has many dimensions. Are Americans more equal when it comes to health, wealth, and social justice? Again, we find a mixed story: much progress and a long way left to go.

Health. In 1950, before the civil rights movement, white people lived over nine years (or 14 percent) longer than Black people. By 2019, that racial difference had fallen to under three years (less than 4 percent). Moreover, Asian and Hispanic Americans have a longer average life expectancy than white people (Table 6.4).

Income. Few groups in history have experienced a rise out of poverty as rapid as Black people between 1959 (55 percent in poverty) and today (19.5 percent in 2020). Still, for the entire half-century, the Black poverty rate has remained at nearly three times the white poverty rate (currently 8 percent). The percentage of Hispanic and Native Americans who live in poverty is significantly higher (Table 6.5).

For a different perspective, turn to the CEOs in America's five hundred largest corporations. As we saw earlier, there are seventy-four women in that corner office. There are also sixteen Latinos, ten Asian Americans, four Blacks, and no Native Americans. The number in 1995 for every one of these groups: zero. Although barriers remain in place, Americans of every description keep pushing the boundaries of civil rights.

TABLE 6.4 **Average Life Expectancy by Ethnic and Racial Group**

Asian American	86.3
Hispanic	82
White	78.6
Native American	77.4
African American	75
Source: Centers for Disease Control	

TABLE 6.5 **Percentage of People in Poverty, by Race**

Asian American	8
White	8.2
Hispanic	17
Black	19.5
Native American	25.4
Source: U.S. Census	

Blacks and Hispanics make up larger shares of prisoners than of U.S. population

U.S. adult population and U.S. prison population by race and Hispanic origin, 2018

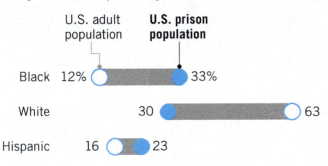

FIGURE 6.9 *Blacks and Latinos make up larger shares of prisoners than of the U.S. population. (Pew Research Center)*

The New Jim Crow: The idea that mass incarceration of Black people has the sweeping effects of Jim Crow discrimination laws. The term is the title of a book by Michelle Alexander.

Incarceration. One final twist to the American civil rights story introduces a new source of alarm. Black men are almost five times as likely to be in jail as white men. Latino men are also incarcerated at higher rates (see Figure 6.9). Is this "**The New Jim Crow**," as civil rights advocates have argued?

Some suggest that people of all races benefit from tough law enforcement. But most observers believe that the United States has gone too far in sending people to jail, especially for minor offenses. Studies have repeatedly suggested a racial bias throughout the criminal justice system, starting in the way Americans perceive criminals. For example, when subjects were asked to "imagine a drug user," 95 percent pictured a Black person. In reality, more than 65 percent of users are white people.[88] The images, and the incarceration rates, reflect subtle forms of racial and ethnic discrimination.

A formidable new front has opened in the long battle for civil rights. In this area, conservative and liberal groups have begun working together to reduce incarceration rates. Will their cooperation meet success? Now you have the tools to track this development!

THE BOTTOM LINE

» Voting rights remain a source of fierce political debate today.

» When we turn to health, poverty, and criminal justice, we find a familiar story: The United States has made great progress—and must overcome remaining limitations to achieve full civil rights.

 Conclusion: Civil Rights . . . By the People

Race. Gender. Latinos. Asians. Immigrants. Native Americans. People with disabilities. Sexual orientation. Transgender individuals. The struggle for civil rights—in many ways, the struggle to secure American ideals—spans the nation's history and engages every generation. We have seen how each group described here fought for civil rights. We also have seen how full civil rights remain something to fight for.

No American idea is more powerful than the idea of inalienable rights, and none generates more arguments. Government actions are crucial in advancing decisions about rights. One important lesson to draw from this chapter is that laws and court cases have far-reaching consequences. The 1964 Civil Rights Act, for example, ended de jure segregation, focused the women's movement, changed gender relations in schools and workplaces, inspired the disabilities rights movement, and guided the Supreme Court toward protecting LGBTQ+ rights; its influence continues even today.

The Supreme Court has been at the center of the storm across the last half-century of debates about civil rights. Liberals argue that the Court must ensure that past discrimination does not hobble future generations. Conservatives, in contrast, call on the judiciary to end programs that benefit some individuals simply because of race, gender, or any other factor.

America's civil rights movements marked an extraordinary attempt to overcome centuries of injustice, targeting minority and marginalized groups of all types. But did the nation do enough to give every member of society a genuine opportunity to succeed?

Ultimately, the power to make a change lies not with the Court or the Congress or the government, but with the people. The *Brown* decision became a significant force for change only after the civil rights movement sprang into action. Throughout this chapter, we have seen people transform the politics of rights— marching into violence in Birmingham in 1963 and across American cities in 2020, prodding a reluctant government to implement the gender provisions in the Civil Rights Act of 1964, waving American flags over immigrant rights in Chicago, holding sit-ins to hurry implementation of disability rules in Washington, and fighting for same-sex marriage when it seemed like an impossible dream. It was people who helped shape the meaning of legislation and of court decisions. Through their passion and their activism, Americans are constantly pushing the United States to live up to its founding ideals.

Each generation faces the same challenge: how to expand civil rights to deserving groups in ways that advance inclusivity for all. That challenge is what drew the two of us to political science. It is our own hope that the mostly young adults reading our book will, like so many Americans in the past, lead the United States toward greater civil rights.

CHAPTER SUMMARY

⭐ The battle for civil rights generally includes seven stages. A group seeking rights must define itself, challenge society, and change the cultural story. The contest for rights spills across the different levels of federalism and the different branches of government: The executive branch and state governments can break the ice, Congress is the key to enduring change, and the courts are the final arbiters of civil rights.

⭐ The Fourteenth Amendment contains the crucial legal rule for civil rights: "No state shall . . . deprive any person of . . . the equal protection of the laws."

⭐ A great mass movement featured ordinary men, women, and children turning the legal promise of the *Brown v. Board of Education* decision into practical reality. Protests eventually led to the Civil Rights Act of 1964 and the Voting Rights Act of 1965. The Black civil rights movement set the model for future civil rights campaigns by many other groups.

⭐ To make up for past discrimination, legislatures and courts turned to affirmative action in the 1960s and 1970s. The courts, and the public, have become increasingly skeptical of these programs.

★ Women first won voting rights in the states—beginning in the West—before finally securing the Nineteenth Amendment, which guarantees the right to vote regardless of gender.

★ The Civil Rights Act of 1964 bars gender discrimination. The women's movement organized to take advantage of these legal changes. The results transformed American gender roles in political and professional life.

★ Latinos, the United States' largest immigrant group, include many different national identities, histories, cultures, and concerns. A key political question is whether they will mobilize around shared interests and concerns. If they do, they will become a formidable force, poised to advance civil rights claims for "Dreamers" and other Latinos.

★ Asian Americans are the third-largest minority group in the United States and now comprise nearly 6 percent of the population. They are also a tremendously diverse group, misleadingly stereotyped as a "model minority."

★ Native Americans lost their way of life in the face of disease, armies, and settlers. The Supreme Court gave them a special status: a separate people without rights. Though they retain the special status, they became U.S. citizens in 1924.

★ People with disabilities leveraged an obscure bureaucratic rule, used it to mobilize, and eventually won the sweeping rights of the Americans with Disabilities Act.

★ LGBTQ+ communities have moved into mainstream politics. In 2020, the Supreme Court ruled that the Civil Rights Act of 1964 mandated equal treatment of gay and transgender people. Future cases will determine how far the ruling goes to strike down discrimination.

KEY TERMS

1963 March on Washington, p. 189
Abolition, p. 180
Affirmative action, p. 191
Black power, p. 190
Brown v. Board of Education, p. 186
Chicanismo, p. 202
Civil rights, p. 174
Civil Rights Act of 1964, p. 189
Class action, p. 199
Compromise of 1850, p. 180
Critical race theory, p. 173
De facto discrimination, p. 185
De jure discrimination, p. 185
Disproportionate impact, p. 192
Domestic dependent nation, p. 210

Dred Scott v. Sandford, p. 181
Emancipation Proclamation, p. 181
Equal Employment Opportunity Commission (EEOC), p. 198
Equal protection of the laws, p. 182
Equal Rights Amendment (ERA), p. 198
Freedom Riders, p. 188
Free rider problem, p. 188
Great Migration, p. 185
Intersectionality, p. 174
Jim Crow, p. 183
Literacy test, p. 183
Missouri Compromise, p. 180

National Association for the Advancement of Colored People (NAACP), p. 185
National Organization for Women (NOW), p. 198
The New Jim Crow, p. 218
Plessy v. Ferguson, p. 183
Quasi-suspect category, p. 178
Reconstruction, p. 182
Reframe the issue, p. 198
School busing, p. 192
Section 504, p. 212
Seneca Falls Convention, p. 195
Strict scrutiny, p. 177
United Farm Workers (UFW), p. 202

STUDY QUESTIONS

1. Name the seven steps involved in civil rights campaigns. Draw on the historical material in this chapter or your own reading/studies to describe: How did the steps work for Latino equality? For Black people? For LGBTQ+ people or people with disabilities? Which step seemed most important in each case?

2. Describe the Civil War amendments. Why was the Fourteenth Amendment so important? How has that amendment's promise of equality supported other group movements for civil rights over the nearly 150 years since it was passed?

3. What was Jim Crow legislation? What happened to Jim Crow practices? What does "The New Jim Crow" refer to in the present, and how has it fueled the Black Lives Matter movement?

4. Native American tribal nations have been described as "domestic dependent nations" since 1831. Should that ambiguous status be altered today in the name of enhanced rights, in your view?

5. Describe three effects of the Civil Rights Act of 1964.

6. What is affirmative action?
For further reflection: Write your own Supreme Court decision. Would you accept affirmative action in your college or university? Why or why not?

7. What is the Lilly Ledbetter Law?
For further reflection: Why do you think President Obama chose this to be the first law he signed as president?

8. How did LGBTQ+ people win civil rights? How would you sum up current discriminatory practices limiting gay rights? What policies to redress these, if any, would you enact?

9. Latinos and Asian Americans in the United States face a similar barrier to promoting their civil rights: Each group is made up of numerous national and cultural subgroups. How have Hispanics originally from Puerto Rico, Colombia, and Venezuela—or Asian Americans with roots in Shanghai, Manila, and Bombay—advanced movements for greater equity? How might they do so even more effectively in the future?

PUBLIC OPINION

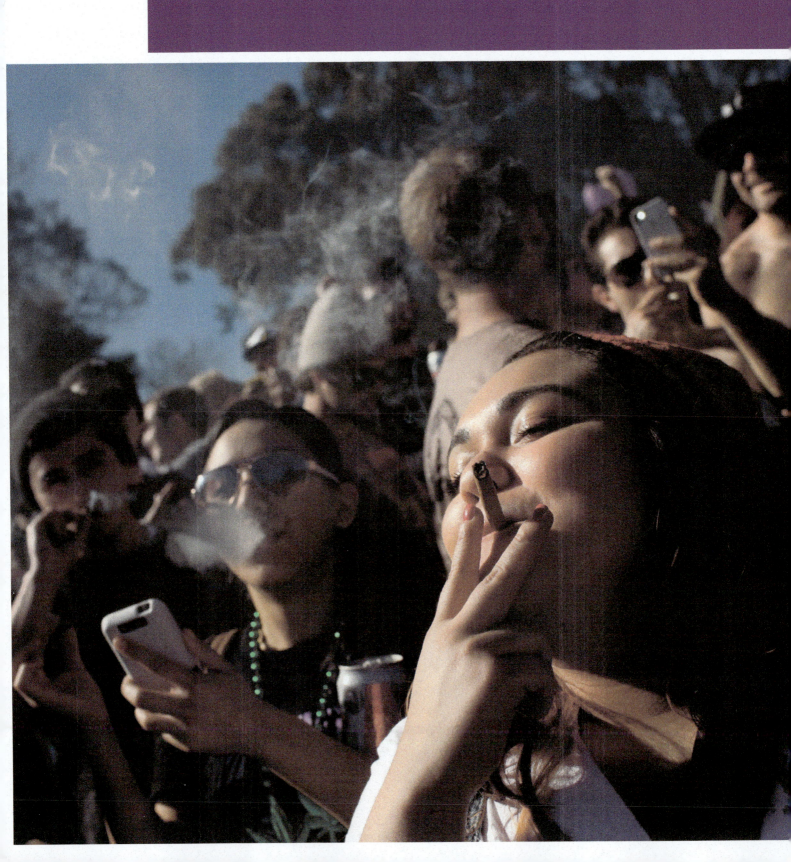

THE WAR ON DRUGS came down hard on Melissa Guzman in 2007. She was doing well as an insurance adjuster in Long Island, New York, when authorities arrested her husband, Eladio, for possessing marijuana with intent to sell. She bailed him out using the deed to her family house, but he was convicted and spent two years in jail. Her uncle also did jail time for a drug charge. Black and Latino individuals were much more likely to go to jail than whites. At the time, they made up 77 percent of those incarcerated on federal drug charges—and just 21 percent of the population.

Then, everything changed. New York legalized recreational marijuana and reserved one hundred retail cannabis licenses a year for people with marijuana-related convictions to make up for past injustice. The Guzmans applied for a license, joined the Latino Cannabis Association, and traveled to other cities to learn more about the business.[1]

How did the United States get from the war on drugs that arrested eight hundred thousand people a year on marijuana charges to legalized marijuana in thirty-nine states? The answer lies in public opinion. Twenty years ago, only one in four Americans supported legalizing marijuana. Then the number began to rise. Why? Because pollsters started asking a new generation with a very different outlook (Figure 7.1).

Younger respondents strongly support legalizing marijuana (70 percent in 2021). Even Republican Gen Zers agree (63 percent). That is a far cry from the oldest cohort, where more than half still disapprove. A new generation led the change in public opinion—and that led to new government policies.

Same-sex marriage reflects a similar story. Public approval leapt up from 31 percent in 2001 to 70 percent in 2021. Again, a new generation came along with different opinions and changed the results (Figures 7.2 and 7.3). As we saw in Chapter 6, state legislatures started approving same-sex marriage laws and in one courtroom after another, judges ruled that banning it violated the Fourteenth Amendment's guarantee of "equal protection under the law."[2]

However, strong public views do not always mean decisive government action. Take global climate change. Seventy-four percent of Americans believe there is clear evidence of global warming. Large majorities believe

In this chapter, you will

 Explore the sources of our opinions about public issues.

 Reflect on the role of public opinion in a democracy.

 Understand the uses of public opinion in politics and government.

 Explore how public opinion is measured.

● *Fifteen years ago, eight hundred thousand Americans were arrested for possessing marijuana. Now it is legal in thirty-nine states and approved for recreational use in nineteen (and rising). What changed? Public opinion. Why? A new generation came online. Here, people celebrate the decision to permit recreational use in Colorado.*

% who say marijuana should be legal for medical AND recreational use

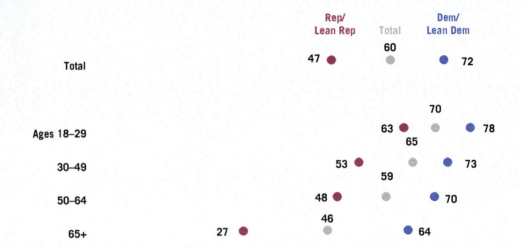

● **FIGURE 7.1** *Millennials and Gen Z set the pace. Growing support for legal marijuana reflects a change in public opinion between generations, with majorities of both younger Democrats and Republicans being supportive of legalization for medical and recreational use. (Pew Research)*

Do you think marriages between same-sex couples should or should not be recognized by the law as valid, with the same rights as traditional marriages?

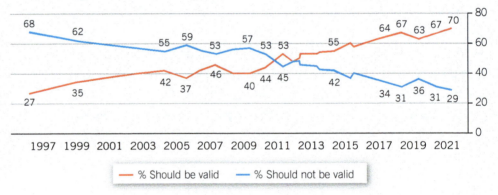

● **FIGURE 7.2** *Support for same-sex marriage has risen dramatically. (Gallup)*

Support for Gay Marriage, by Age Group, 2004–2021

% Saying same-sex marriages should be recognized by the law as valid

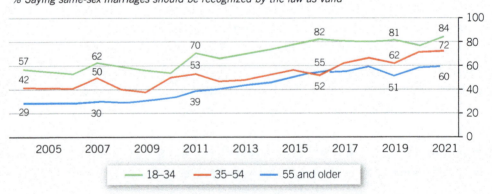

● **FIGURE 7.3** .... *with millennials and Gen Z setting the pace once again. (Gallup)*

something should be done. Yet until summer 2022, very little action occurred to combat climate change. The Trump administration rolled back environmental regulations, while Biden's first eighteen months in office saw little action. A timely switch by

Senator Joe Manchin (D-WVa.) enabled a climate bill to pass—a measure weaker than environmentalists hoped, however. Why didn't popular opinion translate into more sweeping action this time? Because Republican and Democratic Party members—and office holders—held passionate opinions on either side of the debate.[3]

By 2008, climate change had become a signature issue for each party. Republicans championed the fossil fuels industry, while Democrats called for tough action (even a Green New Deal). Perhaps the debate has been further influenced by the industry itself—five American companies have spent $3.6 billion over the past thirty years to frame the debate away from strong government action.[4] (We'll discuss the issue in Chapter 17.) Still, the groundwork for future action is in place. Here again, young voters in both parties are pressing for bolder action, just as they did for marijuana and same-sex marriage.[5] And, once again, younger people—across party lines—feel far more strongly than their older cohorts.

Finally, consider abortion. Here's another case where public opinion diverges from public policy. Three out of five Americans believe it should be legal, at least in some cases. And most people on both sides are somewhere in the middle: They would make some exceptions. But the debate itself is driven by the most intense: the small number of people who believe that abortion should be illegal in all cases, no exceptions (just 8 percent), versus those who believe it should be legal in all cases, no exceptions (19 percent) (Figure 7.4). The lesson: In politics, intensity matters.

Who are we? The world's oldest democracy. Public opinion takes us to the very heart of self-rule: The people's views are paramount in government. Isn't this exactly the way it should be?

Not necessarily. Remember that the Constitution limits direct popular rule through the Electoral College, lifetime appointment for federal judges, the system of checks and balances, and many other institutions. American government is designed to balance public opinion and the judgment of public officials. And even small minorities have many opportunities to act on their views—especially if they are organized and well funded.

No democracy can ignore its people for long. But public opinion raises a lot of tough questions: Can we trust the people to have informed opinions? Or are members of the public simply parroting their friends, or professional talking heads, or some vague idea that they may change tomorrow? What happens when the public is divided? How do we tell when public opinion is correctly measured?

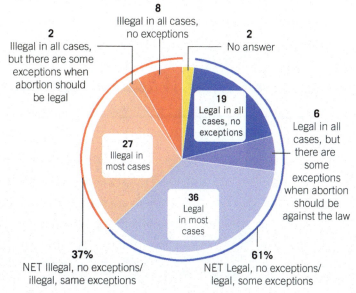

Majority of adults say abortion should be legal in some cases, illegal in others

% of U.S. adults who say abortion should be...

8 — Illegal in all cases, no exceptions

2 — Illegal in all cases, but there are some exceptions when abortion should be legal

2 — No answer

19 — Legal in all cases, no exceptions

6 — Legal in all cases, but there are some exceptions when abortion should be against the law

27 — Illegal in most cases

36 — Legal in most cases

37% NET Illegal, no exceptions/ illegal, same exceptions

61% NET Legal, no exceptions/ legal, some exceptions

● **FIGURE 7.4** *A large majority of adults say abortion should be legal in most cases. Note, however, the outlier positions that have dominated the political debate: only 19 percent saying abortion should be legal in all cases with no exceptions and only 8 percent saying it should be illegal in all cases with no exceptions. (Pew Research Center)*

BY THE NUMBERS Public Opinion

1788 Year that "public opinion" was first mentioned by a public official (in France)

37 Percentage of the American public who can name their U.S. House member[6]

46 Percentage of the "Silent Generation" (aged sixty-five and over) who approve of marijuana legalization

0.001 The authors' predicted probability that there will be no Social Security by the time the millennial generation retires[13]

55 Percentage of U.S. adults expressing support for the Black Lives Matter movement, September 2022[7]

67 Percentage of U.S. adults younger than thirty expressing support for the Black Lives Matter movement, 2022[8]

80 Percentage of millennials who expect that Social Security will provide no benefits by the time they retire[9]

38 Percentage of millennials who would prefer a smaller government providing fewer services

73 Percentage of millennials who expect a pay raise every year[10]

43 Percentage of the Silent Generation who expect a pay raise every year[11]

64 Percentage of the Silent Generation who would prefer a smaller government providing fewer services[12]

What role does public opinion play in democratic governments? What role should it play?

And even if we know precisely what the public thinks, perhaps politicians should do what they believe is the right thing, regardless of the polls.

These are the issues we discuss in this chapter. They all revolve around the most basic question in any democracy: How responsive should the government be to the people's views? And that goes back to the question we posed in the introduction: *Who governs?*

 ## Sources of Public Opinion

Public opinion is simply the sum of individual beliefs and opinions. Your views about how the United States should handle relations with Russia, whether to cut taxes or raise the minimum wage, whether sports betting should be legal, whether

abortion should be banned, and whether *The Walking Dead* is too violent for television—along with the views of everyone else in the country—make up public opinion. The central theme for this chapter: What role should your preferences play when public officials make policy? But before pondering that, we turn to a more basic question: Where do opinions come from?

Political Socialization

Why do white Americans trust the police more than Black or Latino Americans do? How come some of your friends—but not others—support a strong military? Why is one classmate a staunch Republican and another completely uninterested in politics? We call the many forces that shape our political attitudes and values **political socialization**.

Political socialization: The process by which individuals acquire their political values and outlooks.

President Lyndon B. Johnson (LBJ) once remarked, "Tell me where a man comes from, how long he went to school, and where he worships on Sundays, and I'll tell you his political opinions."[14] LBJ, a big-talking Texan, may have exaggerated a bit. And today, he'd have to add, "tell me where they get their news about politics." But basic life details are strong agents of socialization. And, yes, as Johnson claimed, they help predict where people stand. Let's look at some of the leading sources of political socialization.

Parents and Friends. Many people absorb the political attitudes of their parents and caregivers. Mark Losey, running for a U.S. House seat, told his audiences a typical story about how he chose his party: As a child he used to go walking on his grandfather's farm. On one of those walks, recalls Losey, he asked, "'Grandpa, are we Democrats or Republicans?' My grandpa, who grew up on a farm during the height of the Great Depression, paused. 'Before Roosevelt became president, our family almost starved to death,' he replied. Grandpa Wren is still a Democrat. So am I."[15]

Of course, some people—a minority—react against the attitudes they grew up hearing as children. Andrew LaGrone came from a family of very active Democrats—his grandmother had run for Congress. But when federal funding for his high school business club ran out, he said it "opened my eyes to fiscal conservatism." LaGrone shocked his family by becoming the head of the Nebraska College Republicans.[16] Social networks—friends and colleagues—exert a major influence in shaping public opinion. We tend to adopt views expressed by the people around us.

Education. Education is a key agent of socialization. Many of us were influenced by our teachers, going right back to kindergarten. Education marks one of the great political divisions to develop in recent years. In 1994, college graduates leaned Republican, 54 percent to 39 percent; a quarter-century later, in 2020, the numbers had flipped, with 56 percent of college graduates voting for Democrats like Joe Biden. Those with postgraduate experience go even more

● *Friends, pastimes, and public rituals all influence political socialization.*

Democratic—67 percent to 32 percent.[17] Education helps shape our political attitudes, but over time the effects on partisan politics tend to shift.

Gender. Gender also has a major effect on political views. Men are more likely to support nuclear power plants, fracking to extract natural gas, and testing products on animals. As these examples affirm, men lean Republican—and women Democratic. During the 2020 election, 55 percent of women went for Democrats, and 44 percent for Republicans. That 11-point difference was a lot lower than the eighteen-point gap in the previous election (and the 2022 midterms saw the gap shrink to eight points), but the gender difference has been present for a long time. If only women voted in American presidential elections, the sole Republican candidate who would have won in the last fifty years is Ronald Reagan in 1984. Of course, if only men voted, Republicans would win every time. You can see the point: Gender shapes political attitudes.[18]

Race. As we have already seen, race plays an enormous role in American politics and history. Black people are more likely to be regular churchgoers, more supportive of government spending on social services, and more Democratic. Racial identity figures prominently among African Americans (Figure 7.5). Roughly 90 percent of Black people identify as Democrats—a massive change from a century earlier when most voted Republican.

Latino Americans tend to be socially conservative on issues such as abortion but more liberal when it comes to government services. Most have trended strongly toward the Democratic Party, although in 2020 they were crucial in delivering Florida and Texas to Donald Trump. White Americans lean Republican—Democratic candidates for president have averaged just 39 percent of the white vote since 1980.

Religion. Religion shapes public opinion on core value questions—from support for SNAP (the Supplemental Nutrition Assistance Program, or "food stamps") to views about abortion. White evangelicals vote strongly Republican. And even though young white evangelicals have different views than older ones—especially on issues of sexual identity and immigration—they still trend strongly Republican. Catholic voters tend to be split. Black Protestants, Latino Catholics, Jews, and Muslims all trend decidedly Democratic.

Life Events. As we grow up, major events shape our outlooks. The plunge into a Great Depression (in the early 1930s), the attack on Pearl Harbor (in 1941), the assassination of Martin Luther King (1968), the 9/11 terrorist attacks (2001), the Great Recession of 2008, and the COVID-19 pandemic and Black Lives Matter protests of 2020–21—all can influence people, particularly young people who are just forming their political opinions. Each generation grows up with its own shared events, technologies, and expectations. For example, many analysts speculate that millennials and Gen Z are more skeptical toward capitalism because the recession of 2008—marked by bank bailouts and slow recovery—shaped their political outlook.[19]

Black adults are more likely than other groups to see their race or ethnicity as central to their identity

% in each group who say being _____ is extremely or very important to how they think about themselves

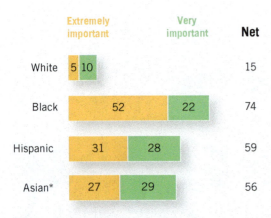

	Extremely important	Very important	Net
White	5	10	15
Black	52	22	74
Hispanic	31	28	59
Asian*	27	29	56

*Asians were interviewed in English only.

● **FIGURE 7.5** *Black Americans are more likely to say that race matters to them. But race is a powerful predictor of voting across citizen groups. (Pew Research, 2020)*

Democrats and Republicans on Climate Change

Far Apart or Coming Together?

Most Americans feel that global climate change is a problem. Six out of ten go so far as to say it's a "major threat." Yet, the Obama administration failed to get its climate plan through Congress, the Trump administration proudly announced the rollback of one hundred environmental regulations, and the Biden administration struggled against courts, fierce partisan divides, and Republican-led states to win strengthened environmental regulation—accomplished at last in August 2022.

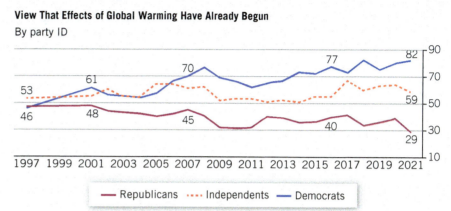

View That Effects of Global Warming Have Already Begun
By party ID

Republicans ···· Independents — Democrats

THINK ABOUT IT

Compare the two parties in 1997 and 2021; what are the most important changes?

What do you think those changes in public opinion will mean for the future of environmental regulation?

Source: Gallup

In sum, there is much truth in Lyndon Johnson's crack about understanding how a person votes. He just did not have enough variables to give a full account of political socialization. Family, friends, education, gender, race, generational context—tell us all those things and we can make a pretty good guess about where you stand politically. But today there's something even more powerful that tells us what people think.

Party

Party preference has become an even stronger predictor of individual opinions than factors such as race and religion. Most politically active Americans are aligned with either Democrats or Republicans and generally stay committed to their party (even if they call themselves independents, most stick to one party or the other). In recent years, the differences between the parties have grown on almost every issue.[20] Your party choice reveals more about your opinions than even strong demographic factors such as race and religion.

For a time, political scientists believed that elected officials were far more partisan than the public at large. Political scientist Morris Fiorina and his colleagues argued that, at least on cultural issues such as abortion, most Americans are moderates. More recent analysis, however, suggests that a major surge in partisan polarization has developed within the public.[21]

Self-Interest: Voting Our Pocketbooks

Some experts believe that economic self-interest matters most. According to this perspective, people with more money will vote for lower taxes, while people with less will vote to expand social programs.

In practice, economic interests are important, but they are only one factor among many. In a book entitled *What's the Matter with Kansas?*, liberal economist Thomas Frank pointed out that Kansas has some of the lowest average incomes in the country—but votes for a congressional delegation made up of Republicans who support cutting taxes and social programs. If these voters focused on their economic interest, argued Frank, they would be more likely to vote for Democrats. Recent studies, both of the entire U.S. and specific states such as Wisconsin, Mississippi, and Kentucky, have reached the same conclusion.[22] Still, most people vote their economic interests. Poorer Americans are more likely to affiliate with Democrats, while wealthy Americans' votes tend to go Republican (see Figure 7.6). Wallets are not everything—but they explain a lot.[23]

Elite Influence

Stop for a moment and think about whom you listen to when you make up your mind about an issue. Many people turn to friends and family. A series of studies, most notably by the political scientist John Zaller, suggests that people also look to **political elites**. Americans routinely receive signals from political leaders and embrace those that are consistent with their prior beliefs.[24]

Some people look up to "experts"—academics or media personalities such as Robin Roberts (on ABC), Lester Holt (NBC), or Harris Faulkner (Fox). Others follow very visible public figures such as Michelle Obama or Florida governor Ron DeSantis. And presidents generally have a large following.

Political elites: Individuals who control significant wealth, status, power, or visibility and consequently have significant influence over public debates.

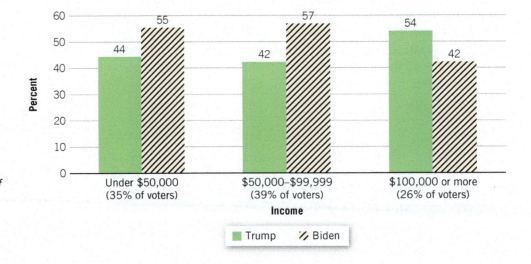

Total Family Income in 2019

● **FIGURE 7.6** *Exit poll results of 2020 election based on family income.*

Source: Roper Polls.

● *Robin Roberts (ABC) (a) and Harris Faulkner (Fox) (b) are among the most influential people in the news business.*

But few people have a following quite like the president of the United States. Presidents Obama and Trump were especially effective at moving their supporters—Donald Trump's tweets were followed by one in five adults and helped shape the opinions of both supporters and opponents.

Media

How do you learn about political events? From what you watch to whom you follow, your media network powerfully shapes your political views. We'll devote a chapter to the topic (Chapter 9). For now, just remember that the media is one of the factors that has changed most since Lyndon Johnson bragged about knowing how a person votes from their neighborhood, school, and church.

Wars and Other Focusing Events

Americans pull together during crises. Tragedy, terrorist attacks, and the start of wars generally produce consensus—and a spike in the government's approval ratings.

Wars inspire a strong sense of "we're all in this together," but that sentiment generally fades. After President Bush launched the Iraq War in March 2003, almost 80 percent of the public approved; four years later, approval for American involvement in Iraq had fallen to barely 30 percent.[25] Ninety percent initially supported the war in Afghanistan, but fifteen years later, large majorities said the war was a "mistake." The same backlash confronted every wartime president from Franklin Roosevelt (whose Democrats lost forty-five House seats during the World War II midterms) to Harry Truman (over Korea) and Lyndon Johnson (Vietnam).[26]

Most dramatic events have a similar, if smaller, effect on public opinion. When a bridge collapsed in Minnesota, or a drilling platform exploded causing a massive oil spill in the Gulf of Mexico, there was a spike in support for infrastructure

In general, do you feel that the laws covering the sale of firearms should be made more strict, less strict, or kept as they are now?

● **FIGURE 7.7** *Percentage of those who approve of enhanced gun controls spikes after shootings, such as the Uvalde, Texas, tragedy in 2022. Otherwise, a narrow majority tends to favor tighter controls. (Gallup)*

spending and environmental regulation—only to see both surges fade away. Occasionally, activists can use dramatic events, and the spike in public opinion, to win changes. When a shooting rampage in 2018 killed seventeen high school students in Parkland, Florida, their classmates mobilized, spoke out for gun control, and pushed the Florida legislature into taking action. Still, the general rule: Savvy political scientists discount the spikes in public opinion, knowing that the poll numbers almost always come back down again (Figure 7.7).

THE BOTTOM LINE

» Political socialization refers to the factors that shape our political opinions. These include family, friends, education, gender, race, religion, and major life events.

» Party identification has become the most reliable predictor of public opinion in recent years.

» Self-interest and political elites also influence political attitudes.

» How issues are framed can shift individual and collective views.

» Dramatic events, especially wars, also have a powerful role in shaping our opinions.

 ## Measuring Public Opinion

Opinion poll: Systematic study of a defined population, analyzing a representative sample's views to draw inferences about the larger public's views. Also termed *survey research.*

How do we know what the people are thinking? Professional polling firms such as Gallup and Rasmussen, major media organizations, partisan outfits, and academic research centers all jostle to provide the most up-to-date **opinion polls**. Candidates for office commission private polls to tell them how they are performing; presidents and governors retain pollsters to gauge public opinion on various policy items. Let's take a look at how reliable polls are designed, where not-so-good polls cut corners, and—most important—how to recognize each kind.

Polling Bloopers

Well-designed scientific polling techniques could have averted polling's first major embarrassment. Back in 1920, a magazine named the *Literary Digest* helped introduce the idea that polls could predict presidential elections. The magazine relied on postcards sent in by subscribers and boasted that it had never failed to predict the winner. Then, in 1936, the *Digest* forecast a lopsided defeat for incumbent President Franklin D. Roosevelt—who instead won the biggest landslide in a century. Why was the *Literary Digest* so far off base? Because its readers—who sent back the postcards—tended to be wealthy people who did not like President Roosevelt or his policies.

The biggest polling blooper of recent years? The 2016 presidential election. Scores of polls gave Hillary Clinton a solid lead. Reading the polls, experts pegged the probability of a Clinton victory at between 71 and 99 percent. Pollsters scrambled after the election to explain: How could their scientific predictions be so wrong? As the pollsters point out, they did predict the popular vote: Clinton won by 2.2 percent of the national vote—very close to the consensus prediction. But the polls were off in a few key states—upsetting predictions for the Electoral College results. In 2020, the polls again predicted a Democratic landslide, and the voters delivered a solid Democratic popular victory (a seven-million-vote margin). But, again, there was a very close Electoral College outcome thanks (again) to very close results in a few big states. The lesson: Polling is an inexact science. But some polls are better than others.[27]

Polling 101

Imagine that you are hired to conduct a public survey about the next mayoral election. Where do you start? You could ask a few friends in your American government class whom they plan to vote for, but that would not offer you a reliable way to predict the winner. Here is how to improve your poll.

The Random Sample. One foolproof way to predict the election would be to interview every voter. That would take years and cost too much. Instead, pollsters pick a **random sample**. They select individuals who reflect the entire population. All relevant people should have an equal chance of being interviewed. Otherwise, your results will be as misleading as the *Literary Digest* poll—skewed to the wealthy, or the young, or people who just happened to surf to your website.

Sampling Frame. If your poll is to accurately forecast public views, your survey respondents must reflect the population. That means they must mirror the population's *age, education, income, gender, race* or *ethnic group*, and many other factors that reflect who will vote in the mayoral election. Asking only your classmates would bias the poll toward college-educated and younger people. A good representative survey includes **demographic groups** in rough proportion to their presence in the population—that's what is known in the business as your **sampling frame**.

Refining the Sample. Do you want your poll to represent *all* city residents, or only those who will probably turn out and vote? Choosing **likely voters** will more accurately predict the outcome of most elections—but determining exactly who will turn out makes the pollster's job more difficult. One explanation for why

Random sample: A sample in which everyone in the population has an equal probability of being selected.

Demographic group: People sharing specific characteristics such as age, ethnicity/race, religion, or country of origin.

Sampling frame: A designated group of people from whom a set of poll respondents is randomly selected.

Likely voters: Persons identified as probable voters in an upcoming election. Often preferred by polling organizations, but difficult to specify with great accuracy.

pollsters got the 2016 election wrong: Their samples in key states were skewed toward people with higher education levels (who traditionally are more likely to vote).[28]

Timing.   Before you start knocking on doors or dialing numbers, consider the *timing* of your survey. When do you conduct the poll? If you do it during the day, people with jobs will be busy or away from home. If you conduct a survey on a Friday evening, younger residents are less likely to be home—skewing your results to older people's opinions.

Framing effects: The way the wording of a polling question influences a respondent.

Wording.   Once you have chosen your sampling frame and decided when to ask questions, you face an even more important concern: What exactly will you ask? If this were a chat with your classmates, you might ask simply, "Who do you support in the 2023 mayoral election?" But surveys must take into account **framing effects**: The *way* pollsters ask a question often influences the response.

For example, researchers from the Pew Research Center asked people to choose between a tax cut and "funding new government programs." The public overwhelmingly picked the tax cut, 60 percent to 25 percent. Then the pollsters adjusted the question and asked respondents to choose between a tax cut and funding for "programs on education, the environment, healthcare, crime fighting, and military defense." Now, 69 percent opted for the government programs and only 22 percent for the tax cut. The wording made all the difference. Slight rephrasing can dramatically change the results. Does government provide too much assistance to the poor? Only 6 percent say yes. Does government provide too much *welfare* (which is the same question with a new word)? Now, 40 percent say yes.[29]

Push poll: A poll question designed to get a certain result—often a negative campaign ad that masquerades as a regular opinion survey or a poll.

In other cases, these wording biases can be subtle. In obscure political races (other than president, governor, or large-city mayor), many survey respondents prefer the candidate who is named *first*, no matter what party or other identifying details are included in the question. A really good poll will pretest the questions to sniff out the subtle biases that creep in with different wordings. International polling also has grown more sophisticated (see Comparing Nations 7.1).

Lies, Damn Lies, and Polls.   Campaigns or advocacy groups often *want* to skew their survey results and use framing effects to their advantage. These surveys—which do not even pretend to be legitimate efforts to measure opinions—are termed **push polls**. Such "polls" are actually campaign advertisements masquerading as scientific surveys.

For example, in one conservative district, the pollster started by asking, "Did you know that [candidate name] repeatedly voted to use tax dollars to pay for abortions in the United States and in foreign countries?" (A more accurate statement would have simply noted that the candidate was pro-choice.) Then they asked if

Mocking bias in the polls.

COMPARING NATIONS 7.1   **Top Global Threats: Polling Around the World**

People in different nations worry about different things. In eight nations, from Canada to Sweden, the biggest concern is global climate change. In Denmark and Australia the threat of cyberattacks is the most concerning. And in the United States, Canada, and the UK the spread of infectious diseases is seen as a major threat. (*Pew Research Center, 2020*)

Majorities most consistently cite climate change, spread of infectious diseases as threats to their country: relatively few mention large-scale migration

% who say __ is a major threat to their country

Most common response · Second-most common response · Least common response

	Global climate change	The spread of infectious diseases	Terrorism	Cyberattacks from other countries	The spread of nuclear weapons	The condition of the global economy	Global poverty	Long-standing conflicts between countries or ethnic groups	Large numbers of people moving from one country to another
U.S.	62%	78%	69%	74%	65%	55%	56%	54%	35%
Canada	67	67	47	59	51	60	50	36	36
Belgium	70	69	68	61	59	56	55	46	39
Denmark	60	59	51	66	35	40	38	43	45
France	83	74	80	71	71	67	73	62	44
Germany	69	55	59	64	63	45	58	46	41
Italy	83	69	68	53	73	55	67	49	39
Netherlands	70	62	56	65	53	47	50	47	38
Span	83	78	74	59	71	76	73	48	49
Sweden	63	56	49	53	41	40	36	39	40
UK	71	74	65	63	50	65	51	50	39
Australia	59	68	45	70	46	61	42	41	41
Japan	80	88	77	83	87	74	51	59	38
South Korea	81	89	67	83	70	83	57	71	52
14-COUNTRY MEDIAN	70	69	66	65	61	58	53	48	40

people liked the candidate. Not surprisingly, a lot of people said "no." The opposition could then tout their rival's "falling" numbers. This, of course, was more an advertisement than a serious poll.[30]

Technology.   Pollsters began to notice a bias creeping into their surveys. To save time and money, most professional pollsters use *automated* dialing for landline calls. Machines dial dozens of numbers at once; when a caller answers, the "robo-dialer" transfers the call to a human surveyor. Can you see the problem? Of course! Seventy percent of all phone users rely exclusively on mobile phones—including most young people. Today, good polls have adjusted and call both landlines and cell phones.[31]

Sampling Error and Response Bias.   Finally, you have collected the raw data from all of your surveying. Time to tell the world about the details of your poll? Not so fast. You still need to determine your poll's "confidence interval," or **margin of sampling error**, a statistical measure of how accurate your results are based on the sample you took. A 3 percent margin of error means your results should be accurate—plus or minus 3 percent. By carefully designing their poll, national surveys are able to achieve only small errors with as few as one thousand respondents (see Figure 7.8).

Margin of sampling error: The degree of inaccuracy in any poll, arising from the fact that surveys involve a *sample* of respondents from a population, rather than every member.

Sampling size and sampling error

Margin of error (plus or minus)

40% — 35.9

30% — 24.7

20% — 20.0 17.3 15.4 14.0 13.0 12.1 11.4 10.8

10% — 7.5 6.2 5.4 4.5 4.4 4.1 3.8 3.6 3.4 2.4 2.0 1.7

0% —

Size of sample: 10 20 30 40 50 60 70 80 90 100 300 500 700 1,000 4,000

● **FIGURE 7.8** *Sampling errors decline with larger sample sizes; ask more people and you can be more certain of your results. (MEER Research)*

Response bias: The tendency of poll respondents to misstate their views—often to avoid "shameful" opinions such as sexism or racism.

Pollsters also must consider **response bias** in publicizing their findings. Studies show that some respondents purposely mislead pollsters. Response bias can reflect animosity toward pollsters or the all-too-human tendency to align with "acceptable" views. Survey questions that might elicit unpopular attitudes, such as racism or sexism, can lead respondents (consciously or unconsciously) to shift their answers in a more socially acceptable direction.

A classic example of response bias arose when Tom Bradley, the first Black mayor of Los Angeles, ran against a white candidate, George Deukmejian, for governor of California in 1982. Bradley had a comfortable double-digit lead in opinion surveys as Election Day approached—but lost the race. Today pollsters must be alert to what is now known as the Bradley effect: the possible inclination of some survey respondents to avoid appearing racist or racially motivated. Pollsters speculate there may have been "shy" Trump voters in 2016 and 2020—people reluctant to reveal that they supported Trump. Still another potential source of bias: Democrats may be more willing to respond to polls than Republicans.[32]

Sample size, framing effects, and margin of error: Account for all these, and you are well on your way to conducting a truly scientific public opinion survey. One important reason to understand the design of polls is so that you can distinguish the good from the bad. Table 7.1 summarizes some of the tips.

How Did They Do? After pollsters' poor performance in 2016, many reworked their methodology to take account of a changing electorate. The result in 2020? Another debacle. Most mainstream pollsters predicted a blue wave that would verge on a landslide for Joe Biden (the predicted margin averaged 8.5 percent), large Democratic gains in the House, a majority in the Senate, and new majorities in multiple state legislatures.

Once again, pollsters faced harsh questions when Biden won a close election and Republicans made major gains in the House, though Democrats did win four seats and control of the Senate. The back-to-back polling misfires in presidential elections were unprecedented. In the days after the election, some pollsters expressed concern about the fate of their industry itself.[33] And in 2022, polls predicting a "red wave" of GOP wins were wrong again.

| TABLE 7.1 | Tips on Reading Polls |

1. *Check out the margin of error.* A 3 percent margin of error means plus or minus 3 percent—turning a 50 percent approval rating into one that could be as low as 47 or as high as 53 percent. If the margin of error is too large (say, over 5 percent), then approach the poll with caution.

2. *What is the timing?* The further away from Election Day, the less meaningful the results.

3. *The random sample is the gold standard.* If the respondents chose themselves (by deciding to take the survey), then it may be fun to read . . . but it is probably not an accurate picture of the public.

4. *What is the sample size?* Be wary of polls that interview a small number of people. For a national poll, 1,000 to 1,500 respondents is typical. Too few respondents means a hefty margin of error.

5. *Compare across polls.* Because every poll has biases, read a range of polls, toss out the extreme findings, and average the rest. The media often headlines outlier polls that diverge from the pack—savvy political scientists put them right back in context by averaging them out.

WHAT DO YOU THINK?

Is Polling Bad for Democracy?

More than 375 surveys of Americans were conducted on the 2020 presidential election. Is that bad for democracy? *What do you think?*

Too much polling. Candidates who lead in the polls might use the bandwagon effect to convince undecideds to join them and thus unfairly influence the results of the election. Moreover, the media obsession with who's up and who's down drives out serious discussions of ideas and policies. In 2020, there was more than four times as much news coverage of the horse race than of policy stands.[34] We should focus less on the race and more on the issues.

Let a thousand polls bloom. Polls communicate the people's views and values to candidates and elected officials. As candidates assess how well they are doing in a given geographic region or with a demographic group, they hone and target their message, which becomes the campaign promises that they work to deliver once elected to office. Furthermore, the more polls, the less likely a candidate will be able to falsely claim they have a lead—and convince undecideds to join them.

Do Opinion Surveys Influence Us?

Might the profusion of poll numbers and types (see Table 7.2) also affect the decisions citizens make—including how to vote? Some evidence suggests that they may. Candidates who are leading in the polls sometimes pick up support from voters who were undecided or who weakly supported the opponent. The **bandwagon effect** in polling varies considerably from place to place and election to election. It can be exaggerated by media coverage.

Bandwagon effect: When people join a cause because it seems popular or support a candidate who is leading in the polls.

TABLE 7.2 Types of Polls

Benchmark polls	Conducted by a campaign as the race begins, these surveys provide a basis for comparison, or a "benchmark," for later polls.
Straw polls	Informal polls carried out by local party organizations or news outlets; they often involve actual (nonbinding) votes cast by party members. Media organizations (and the straw poll winners) tout the results, but they can be misleading.
Brushfire polls	Internal surveys conducted by a campaign once election season begins. They provide details about how a candidate is performing; if things are going poorly, the campaign can work to put out the bad news or "brushfire" (which burns hot and spreads fast).
Exit polls	Performed on Election Day, these surveys intercept voters as they exit the voting location. Media reporters often rely on exit polls to call results for one or the other candidate, even if ballots haven't been counted yet.

Boomerang effect:
The discrepancy between candidates' high poll ratings and election performance, caused by supporters' assumption that an easy win means they need not turn out.

A close cousin of polling's bandwagon effect is the **boomerang effect**. Here, a candidate who has been consistently ahead in opinion surveys underperforms on Election Day. Supporters see a big lead for their candidate, figure that he or she will win without any difficulty, and do not bother to vote.

WHAT DO YOU THINK?

Too Much Polling?

After reading all the material about polling, many of our students find themselves asking a simple question: Isn't there way too much attention given to polling? Given all the difficulties and miscues, are polls even worth having? As usual, there are two different views.

Polls give us a nuanced view of what the American people think. Voting offers us only crude choices between two candidates—often two people with many overlapping similarities and differences. Polls, especially polls over time, give us a much more nuanced view of what people think and desire. Isn't it essential to know when a majority supports the middle ground, especially as activists on both sides push for stronger policies? According to one author, it would be a "catastrophe for democracy" if there were no way to understand "what people think outside elections."[35]

Polls are unreliable guides to what the American people think. Campaigns use polls to micro-target groups rather than developing broad themes about government. The media touts the results and turns campaigns into horse races—announcing who had the best day and week and month on the basis of little bounces (sometimes phantom bounces). Leaders would have to find more robust ways to hear their constituents if they didn't have polls to fall back on. And they should. Polls are unreliable guides to what people really care deeply about.

Scrambling the issue further, some voters also appear to follow the *opposite* of the bandwagon effect. The **underdog effect** is invoked when a candidate losing in the polls performs better than expected. There is less empirical evidence for this phenomenon, though one study showed that candidates who told supporters they were "barely losing"—triggering the underdog effect—received 55 percent more donations than those reporting they were ahead in the polls.[36]

Underdog effect: Sympathy for a candidate behind in the polls, contributing to a higher-than-predicted vote total—and sometimes a surprise election victory.

THE BOTTOM LINE

» Scientific surveys have come a long way since their origins in 1936. Professionals now design well-specified polls that capture popular views with a high degree of accuracy in most cases.

» Indeed, poll results can affect public opinion, in ways ranging from the bandwagon effect to the underdog effect.

» Sampling errors, response bias, and other potential flaws inevitably confer a measure of uncertainty on any survey.

 ## Public Opinion in a Democracy

If the public is to have a meaningful role in governing, political leaders must listen to their views. But here is the uncomfortable question: Do the people know enough to shape government decisions? We have seen that the founders were wary of the public when they framed the Constitution. The question continues to provoke disagreement. Is the public rational and capable of self-government? Or are we, as political scientist David Sears argues, "an ignorant and easily duped electorate"?[37] Let's look at two different views.

Ignorant Masses

"The masses are asses!" insisted Walter Lippmann in his pathbreaking book *Public Opinion* (published in 1922). Lippmann, a well-known political journalist and cultural critic, dismissed the young "science" of public opinion as undeserving of the name. In his view, the typical American was distracted by celebrity shenanigans and minor scandals, rarely followed policy issues closely enough to understand the details, and yet readily offered up personal views on any topic. Paying attention to the uninformed masses was no way to run a country. Lippmann, along with many others, believed that governing involved technical decisions that were best left to well-trained experts.[38]

In 1960, four University of Michigan professors published a book that hit America like a thunderclap. Not only were most citizens uninformed, but even more damning, *The American Voter* described the scientific poll—the instrument widely used to capture public opinion by the 1950s—as all but useless. One of the authors, Philip Converse, later coined the term **nonattitudes** to describe the response of many Americans to polls. When people were asked the same questions at different times, they tended to change their answers—sometimes they came up with completely different answers. What's more, changes in their responses were random: People did not switch their positions in response to new information or

Nonattitudes: The lack of a stable perspective in response to opinion surveys; answers to questions may be self-contradictory or may display no consistency.

in changing contexts, but rather offered up different and even diametrically opposed views for no apparent reason.[39]

The American Voter shook the confidence in the value of both public opinion and the scientific methods used to measure it. If Americans spewed random thoughts in response to survey questions, what use were opinion polls? This perspective extends right down to the present. Titles of recent books repeat the old story: *Do Facts Matter?* Or, more pointedly, *Uninformed* and *Just How Stupid Are We?*[40]

Social science research echoes this pessimistic view, affirming that most people do not function as "rational actors" who seek and analyze information, weigh evidence, and choose candidates (or support policies) that advance their preferred views. People rationalize preconceived biases and may not even be aware of why they are making the choices they make.[41] In short, there are reasons to be skeptical about the people's wisdom in governing the nation.

Most Americans cannot answer basic questions about our political system. An annual survey discovered that in 2021, just 56 percent of adults could name the three branches of government—and that was up from 30 percent in 2014. Good news? Well, maybe. The Constitution Center has ascribed the rise to all the conflict between the branches.[42] Critics describe America as an "ignorant democracy." Popular whims and cleverly packaged slogans, they say, win out over serious political deliberation.[43] Public opinion, in this view, is a tool for manipulation by savvy message consultants and political marketers.

The Rational Public

Other commentators defend the American public. The alternative view was captured in a book-length response to *The American Voter* called *The Rational Public*. The authors, Benjamin Page and Robert Shapiro, agreed that yes, most voters were inattentive to policy issues and uninformed about political details. However, measured across large groups, public opinion moves in coherent, stable ways that signal shared views about policy issues.[44]

Although a single person may hold inconsistent or even self-contradictory notions, these are submerged in the collective outlook of tens of millions. Taken as a whole, the public can differentiate among alternative policies, in ways that accurately reflect its shared values and beliefs.

Information shortcuts:
Cues about candidates and policies drawn from everyday life.

Page and Shapiro argued that most of us use **information shortcuts** to arrive at reasonable judgments about politics and government. These shortcuts often derive from our direct personal experience. Homeowners grasp the importance of interest rate changes, and shoppers feel inflation's effect on rising prices. Both homeowners and shoppers develop an intuitive sense of the performance of the economy. Likewise, citizens notice the impact of other policy outcomes on their daily lives: Do trains or buses run on time? Does the mail arrive late? Does gas cost more than it did last month? Through a steady and often unwitting process of making everyday evaluations, voters and poll respondents can arrive at reasonably well-established positions on candidates or policy issues.

Is there any way to reconcile the two views: ignorant individuals on the one hand, a rational public on the other? The journalist James Surowiecki offered one solution, summarized by the title of his book: *The Wisdom of Crowds*. Even if any one individual does not have clear views, argued Surowiecki, a large crowd can add up to a rational public. In fact, a random collection of people is, in many cases, wiser than a group of experts.

Surowiecki built on the work by the French thinker Nicolas de Condorcet, who in the eighteenth century demonstrated that, although each member of a jury may not do much better than a coin flip in accurately judging guilt or innocence, taken as a whole the jurors are likely to reach a correct decision. Likewise, a group of people may include those that are ignorant about details or eccentric. However, if the group is big enough—at least a few dozen—and members feel free to speak their minds, they will zero in on a good collective decision. Often these are innovative, outside-the-box solutions. Experts, on the other hand, are typically trained in similar ways and are subject to **groupthink**: They tend to reinforce one another's existing prejudices.

Surowiecki illustrated his point by describing a nineteenth-century country fair in England. A prize was offered to whomever could guess the correct weight of a giant ox. Cattle experts weighed in with their informed guesses, but all were off the mark. More than eight hundred locals offered up guesses as well. Although no one hit the correct weight (1,198 pounds), an average of the crowd's collective estimate came out at 1,197—just one pound below the correct total, and closer than that offered by any of the agricultural experts.[45]

● How much does this ox weigh? Ordinary fairgoers' collective guess outperformed that of agricultural experts in a famous nineteenth-century contest—a testament to the wisdom of crowds.

The rise of **big data**—immense data sets that are too large for traditional software tools to process—may offer us a new kind of country fair wisdom. For example, we can now follow the spread of disease in real time simply by monitoring symptoms entered into search engines. Google tells us where a flu outbreak is rising long before the doctors and hospitals have collected the data and sent them to the Centers for Disease Control.

Of course, crowds are not always wise—they can turn into angry mobs, losing any semblance of rationality altogether. That is exactly why the Constitution has so many checks and balances. Recall the great question when we discussed the Constitution (in Chapter 3): Does American government have too many checks and balances? Or not enough?

Groupthink: The tendency among a small group of decision makers to converge on a shared set of views; can limit creative thinking or solutions to policy problems.

Big data: Immense data sets that are too large for traditional software tools to process.

THE BOTTOM LINE

» Since the founding era, some Americans have viewed public opinion as an unreliable, even dangerous, guide to government policymaking based in part on voter ignorance.

» Others argue that, in practice, a "rational public" is the best source of democratic decision making.

» One way to resolve these clashing views is to focus not on what individuals know about politics but on how many different popular views add up to the "wisdom of crowds."

 ## Public Opinion and Governing

The optimistic view about the crowd's wisdom restores traditional hopes about self-rule. However, if public opinion is to guide government, three conditions must be met.

1. The people must know what they want.
2. The public must clearly communicate its desires to political leaders.
3. Political leaders must pay attention to public views—and respond.

Each step is full of difficulties. Consider each in turn.

Do the People Know What They Want?

Most people (58 percent) want more regulation of big banks and financial institutions.[46] But what should Congress actually do? Limit CEOs' pay or multimillion-dollar Wall Street bonuses? Public opinion is divided. Regulate derivatives as we do stocks and bonds so that their trading is transparent? Maybe, or maybe not. The public may know what it wants in a general way. But it is up to political leaders to supply the policy specifics.

How Do the People Communicate Their Desires?

It is difficult for the people—even a clear majority—to convey their views to policymakers. None of our instruments for adding up and transmitting millions of people's views are particularly effective.

As we have seen, **survey research** can offer snapshots of public opinion on policy issues. However, polls have margins of error; they can be spun to advance partisan interests. They offer general impressions, not a guide to crafting policies and making decisions—as we just saw in the case of widespread public anger at Wall Street. And with so many competing polls, often with different results, it can be difficult to pin down what the public really wants. Still, sometimes forceful shifts in public opinion leap out from the polling cacophony and lawmakers get a clear message.

Of course, democracies also rely on elections. Candidates who win often claim they have a **mandate**: The people have spoken. But what exactly have they said? Every campaign offers a mix of different policies—often presented in general terms. Why did voters press Joe Biden's lever in the voting booths? Was it healthcare? Inequality? Immigration? Abortion rights? Climate change? Or were they simply casting a thumbs down on the Trump administration? Different voters voted for different reasons. Once again, successful leaders must take very general cues from the public and use them to design specific policies. And, of course, those plans must be further adjusted to negotiate the many checks and balances in the political process.

Do Leaders Respond to Public Opinion?

On the surface, the answer seems to be unambiguous: yes! Opinion surveys are everywhere, and politicians seem hooked on them. Every administration keeps a close eye on its **approval ratings**, and both allies and enemies tweet the upticks (and downdrafts) to rally supporters and raise money. American

Survey research: Systematic study of a defined population, analyzing a representative sample's views to draw inferences about the larger public's views. Also termed *opinion poll*.

Mandate: Political authority claimed by an election winner as reflecting the approval of the people.

Approval rating: A measure of public support for a political figure or institution.

● *Public opinion surveys alerted politicians to widespread anger at inequality and with big banks—but did not provide an answer for what to do about it.*

politicians spend more on pollsters, by far, than leaders of other nations—more than a billion dollars when you add up everyone running in a presidential year.

President Bill Clinton was said to poll on everything—including where to go on vacation.[47]

However, attention to public views does not necessarily mean that politicians slavishly follow the poll results. Polls are not telling President Biden how to think on an issue. Rather, polls guide political leaders in their efforts to persuade the public to embrace their own views—and criticize the opposition and their ideas.[48]

How does all this add up? Simple: Polls help set the **policy agenda**. Public opinion helps pick the topics that officials pay attention to in the first place. If the public thinks something is important, political leaders will usually respond.

Big changes in public opinion have an especially significant effect on elected leaders. Members of Congress and state legislatures are often reluctant to legislate in the face of strong popular opposition. When large numbers of us support or oppose an issue, politicians generally respond—as we saw in the chapter opening with legalizing marijuana and recognizing same-sex marriage.

Public opinion sometimes enables presidential actions that might otherwise be blocked. Theodore Roosevelt (1901–9) was a popular president, but he had to abandon his ambitious plans for a national system of protected forest in the eastern United States. His less popular successor, William Howard Taft (1909–13), signed the Forest Reserve Act into law. How did Taft succeed? After a massive forest fire known as the "Big Burn" raged across three western states and killed more than one hundred young firefighters, public opinion swung decisively in support of environmental protection. If you have hiked on the Appalachian Trail, vacationed in the Smoky Mountains, or gone leaf-peeping in New England, you have benefited from a program made possible by shifting public opinion.

Although collective public opinion matters, some groups matter more than others. As we have seen, pollsters target the opinions of likely voters—individuals they expect to participate in elections. Social movements, interest groups, and political parties can have a more direct influence on public policies. By participating in the political system, your voice is more likely to be heard.

In sum, the public's opinions—conveyed in many different ways—introduce new possibilities. Public officials hammer those general ideas into concrete policies. In a well-functioning republic, the people and public officials interact to make public policy.

Policy agenda: The issues that the media covers, the public considers important, and politicians address. Setting the agenda is the first step in political action.

THE BOTTOM LINE

» If public opinion is to guide politics, three conditions must be met: The public must know what it wants, its views must be effectively communicated, and leaders must pay attention.

» Even strong public opinion may not be specific enough to offer policy guidance.

» U.S. government officials devote more resources to polling operations than do top officials in other nations.

» Popular views can help set governing agendas. Polls most often guide officials in determining how best to win over the public to their policies. And occasionally, when a clear majority expresses its opinion, politicians follow suit.

Conclusion: Government by the People

Americans founded their nation on an inspiring idea: the consent of the governed. Lincoln put it beautifully, in his Gettysburg Address, when he prayed that "government . . . by the people shall not perish from the earth." But just how do we maintain those democratic dreams? They demand that public opinion guides—or at least influences—the government and that the people get involved in government affairs.

Public opinion surveys are the most widely used effort to understand the popular mind. Scientific techniques have refined polling, which sometimes yields remarkable accuracy, and sometimes not.

Below the debate about measuring the popular mind lies a question around the public's opinion itself. Is it uninformed, whimsical, and unreliable? Even the framers of the Constitution were skeptical. Others are more optimistic: Collective decisions—the wisdom of crowds—are often wiser than those made by well-trained experts.

Today, our smartphones, tablets, and laptops stream endless information, enabling each of us to instantly research any issue. But more information is not always better. An overabundance of choices and details tends to paralyze individual citizens, rather than empower them.[49]

The current torrent of polls, some of them carefully slanted by advocates or politicians, spews out reams of data. Politically attentive citizens (like you) and passionate advocates for a candidate or cause need to hone their skills at reading polls—drowning out the noise, picking the more accurate reflections of public sentiment.

Our sprawling intersection of politics and polls most often results in ambiguous public views. But, at times, massive shifts in public opinion influence officials' views and often lead to policy change. A rising generation's attitudes can decisively influence our public policies.

Ultimately, no public opinion poll can replace the central act of governance: elected leaders, with an eye to public sentiment (and all the surveys measuring their approval ratings), deciding what issues to promote and then voting "yes" or "no." On the issues where Americans are not sufficiently informed and uncertain, public officials have a major effect in setting the agenda, framing issues, and signaling popular views. They can take the lead in encouraging us to be better stewards of democracy.

CHAPTER SUMMARY

★ Scientific surveys have come a long way since the *Literary Digest* in 1936. Professionals now design well-specified polls that capture popular views with a high degree of accuracy. However, be cautious when reading polls, such as those without a well-defined sample (e.g., online surveys). Always pay attention to the margin of error when interpreting results.

★ Political socialization is the study of the forces that shape public opinion. The most important are

family and friends, race, gender, religion, economic interests, demographics, party affiliation, the view of political elites, and defining events such as war.

★ In a democracy, public opinion should guide the government. But are the people capable of self-rule? From the Constitutional Convention to contemporary social scientists, many experts consider public opinion to be uninformed and unreliable—and therefore a dangerous guide to decision making.

★ Others respond that the public, taken as a whole, is a rational, reliable source of government decisions. Even if individuals do not know much, there is wisdom in crowds.

★ The United States devotes more resources to polling operations than other nations. Polls have become the everyday mechanism for gauging public opinion. But while scientific techniques have made polls more accurate in some cases, rising costs, plummeting response rates, the difficulty of predicting turnout, and hostility to pollsters can all make polls miss.

★ Public officials generally balance public opinion with their own beliefs about the best decisions.

If they are seen as overly faithful to poll results, the paradoxical result may be that their approval rating falls. Polls often guide administrations, not in selecting a policy, but in determining how best to win over the public to their policies.

★ Popular views can be especially important in setting the agenda: If something seems important to the public (and the media), politicians respond. Congress, in particular, pays attention to spikes in public opinion. Presidents find it easier to get their policies passed when public opinion is strongly in favor of those policies.

KEY TERMS

Approval rating, p. 242
Bandwagon effect, p. 237
Big data, p. 241
Boomerang effect, p. 238
Demographic group, p. 233
Framing effects, p. 234
Groupthink, p. 241
Information shortcuts, p. 240

Likely voters, p. 233
Mandate, p. 242
Margin of sampling error, p. 235
Nonattitudes, p. 239
Opinion poll, p. 232
Policy agenda, p. 243
Political elites, p. 230
Political socialization, p. 227

Push poll, p. 234
Random sample, p. 233
Response bias, p. 236
Sampling frame, p. 233
Survey research, p. 242
Underdog effect, p. 239

STUDY QUESTIONS

1. "The masses are asses," wrote one observer of American politics. He was summarizing a perspective that public opinion is not a reliable guide to government. Why, exactly, do some say that public opinion is unreliable? Be sure to include the effect of *The American Voter*.

2. Other scholars insist that public opinion is a legitimate guide to government decision making. Summarize this alternative view, noting the argument made in *The Rational Public*.

3. For further contemplation: Which of these perspectives on public opinion seems more powerful to you? Do you believe the public is basically ignorant? Or collectively wise? (Yes, you may opt for a bit of both.) Defend your answer.

4. "Public officials must always balance public opinion with their own beliefs."

a) Explain why.
b) What problems face political leaders who *always* follow the polls in deciding what to do?
c) What problems face political leaders who *never* follow the polls in deciding what to do?
d) How can polls help leaders who already know what they want to do?

5. Define the following terms: push poll; sampling frame; margin of error; Bradley effect.

6. What does it mean to "frame an issue"? Illustrate using an issue in the headlines that interests you.

7. Given limitations on polling, can you imagine other ways that the public's opinion could best be conveyed to political leaders? (You'll encounter some alternatives in the next chapter as well.)

8 POLITICAL PARTICIPATION

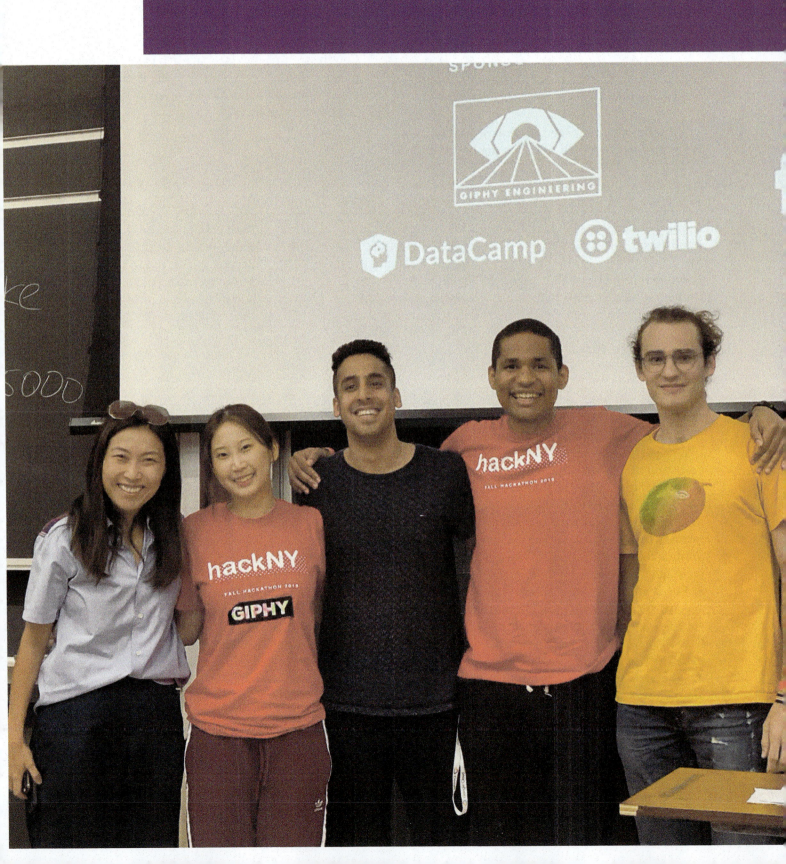

"WE MAKE THE WORLD BETTER!" College students from across the country arrived in New York for the seventeenth annual Hackathon. Some came in teams; others arrived solo and found their crews at the event. Then they got down to business: hacking toward a better world.

One group focused on impoverished schools in South Africa where students had cell phones but no textbooks. The hack team designed a system that provided education—including quizzes—through text messages. Another group developed a technology that might save people in school shootings with an image detection process that identified guns and texted everyone who was nearby to warn them of possible danger. A third team took on the problem of bots posing as real users on social media and skewing public perceptions. Their *redditBotAnalysis*—which took the prize for the most technical hack—constructed an algorithm that calculated the likelihood of bots overrunning a thread.

Almost a thousand miles away, in Janesville, Wisconsin, the Caldart sisters—Selame and Alemitu—exercised completely different political muscles. They marched with classmates to the state capitol in Madison to demonstrate support for gun control. "We marched fifty miles for something that we were passionate about," said Selame. "It's something I'll never forget."[1]

What do the marchers and the hackers have in common? They were participating in politics: They saw a problem, joined together with friends and strangers, and worked together to find a solution.

Who are we? Heirs of the revolutionary Americans who took to the streets and town centers to throw off British rule? A nation where every generation finds new ways to participate, sometimes violently? A country where thousands show up to political rallies to cheer long-shot candidates? A democratic nation that ranked around thirtieth in voter turnout among rich nations (a hundred million people did not bother to vote in 2016) and suddenly smashed recent turnout records in 2020 (nearly two-thirds of eligible voters cast ballots)?[2] We are all of these.

Americans have been leaping into politics since before there was a United States. Participation—getting directly involved in political life—takes many forms: You can work for a candidate, shout till you're hoarse at a campaign rally, join a protest, cast your vote, launch a political podcast, or design a

 In this chapter, you will

 Explore the long-standing paradox of America exhibiting strong *and* weak political participation.

 Learn the three types of participation: traditional politics, direct action, and civic engagement.

 Examine why people participate—and why many do not.

 Identify the benefits and drawbacks of online political engagement.

 Consider whether there can be too much popular participation in a democracy.

● *Hackers for social good. A group of participants pose with the organizer of the New York Hackathon.*

hack to improve life for others. Every era produces new spurs to participation—Black rights, women's rights, climate change, the right to life, or the age-old fear that "our" way of life is threatened by "them."[3] And each generation adds new ways to get involved, as the hackathon shows.

Political scientists call the latest formats, which are focused on software and social media, *clicktivism* or #politics. The concept burst on the scene as a new generation's form of political participation, only to run into a backlash sarcastically called "slacktivism"—activism for slackers. Former President Barack Obama dismissed it, saying, "That's not activism." But love it or hate it, a lot of participation (and a whole generation) is now online.[4]

Political participation reflects the most vibrant traditions in American politics—people solving problems, fighting injustice, and trying to build a better world. But there has always been a more dangerous side. Bigots band together and take up arms to attack others. People involved in protests (and counter-protests) lose their tempers and throw punches. Trolls swarm social media, generating hate and pain. Good, bad, and everything in between—welcome to the wide world of political participation.

Clicktivism: Democratic engagement in an online age: point your cursor or scan a QR code, click, and you have donated funds, "liked" a candidate, or (in some states) even cast your vote.

 # How We Participate

Political participation in the United States arises from a paradox. Sometimes Americans are highly engaged in politics. And sometimes, Americans are downright apathetic. This is especially true among voters under thirty (see Figure 8.1).

In this chapter, we explore the many pathways to participation in the political system. Some stretch back over two hundred years; others are new.

Think of an issue you care about—perhaps climate change or immigration reform or race relations (all top issues for Americans under thirty). How do you push for change? There are three different pathways to participate: traditional participation, direct action, and civic volunteerism.

Traditional Participation

Young voters (aged eighteen to twenty-nine) have been breaking records in recent years: the 2018 midterm and the 2020 presidential elections saw the highest turnout among young people in fifty years.[5] The trend continued in the 2022 midterms, with voters under thirty turning out at a pace similar to four years before. They also voted overwhelmingly Democratic (63–35 percent), contributing to the party's surprisingly strong showing.

When you vote, you're engaging in a form of **traditional participation**, getting involved in politics through formal government channels—organized by federal and state constitutions. Voting, working for a candidate, signing petitions, running for office, and contacting a member of Congress are all ways of becoming active (see Table 8.1).

Traditional participation: Engaging in political activities through the formal channels of government and society.

Voting.   Voting is the foundational political participatory act in any democracy. Yet despite record turnout, one in three eligible Americans did not turn out at the polls in the 2020 elections. Recall from Chapter 3 that the Constitution leaves

Political Participation

58.8 Percentage turnout of voting-age population, U.S. presidential election, 1940

24 Estimated number of politics-themed podcasts, 2004[7]

81 Percentage of Americans under age thirty expressing trust in U.S. government, 1961

52.8 Percentage turnout of voting-age population, U.S. presidential election, 1980

>850,000 Estimated number of politics-themed podcasts, 2021[8]

19 Percentage of American millennials and Gen Z expressing trust in U.S. government, 2022[10]

62 Percentage turnout of voting-age population, U.S. presidential election, 2020

44 Proportion of baby boomers who report volunteering when they were of college age

1 Rank of summer 2020 Black Lives Matter protest marches among largest protests in U.S. history[11]

1 Historical rank of 2020 presidential election for turnout of voters under thirty-five[6]

77 Proportion of U.S. college students who report volunteering for public service, including informal volunteering such as helping neighbors, 2019[9]

How is political participation changing? How are attitudes about political participation changing?

most election details up to the states. There are many subtle ways that a state can encourage (or discourage) voters by making it easier (or harder) to vote.

If you have voted, you know the basic drill. First, register to vote. Twenty-one states and the District of Columbia make the process much easier by permitting registration and voting on the same day. Oregon was the first state to automatically register voters.

Second, cast your vote. Only a few years ago, this meant arriving on Election Day at your assigned polling place. But today, all but four states permit early voting—and more than a third of the ballots are cast before Election Day. Seven states—Colorado, Hawaii, Oregon, Nevada, Utah, Vermont, and Washington—conduct their elections entirely by mail, and California has widespread mail balloting as well. If you do vote on Election Day, bear in mind that some states limit voting facilities—creating long lines, which discourage some voters. In November 2020, record turnout reached a sixty-year peak.

Do you consider yourself to be politically engaged or politically active?

Percent 18–29-Year-Olds Who Respond "Yes"

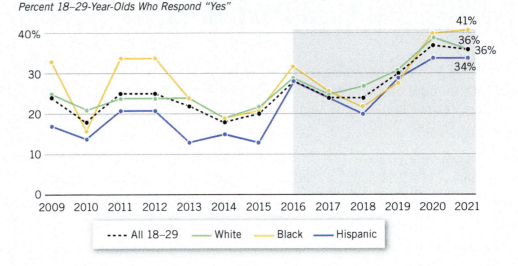

● **FIGURE 8.1** *Only 36 percent of eighteen- to twenty-nine-year-olds consider themselves to be politically engaged or politically active. But look how the number jumped between 2018 and 2020. Why do you think that is?*

TABLE 8.1	Rates of Traditional Political Participation

42 percent of Americans have expressed support for a campaign on social media.
29 percent of Americans have attended a political meeting on local, town, or school affairs.
23 percent have contacted an elected official in the past year.
13 percent have joined a group that tries to influence the public or government.
11 percent have attended a political rally or speech in the past year.
5 percent have worked or volunteered for a political party or candidate.
6 percent have donated to political campaigns.
1.4 percent donated $200 or more to political campaigns in 2020.
Source: Pew Research Center; opensecrets.org

The 2022 midterms, amid election experts predicting a drop in turnout, instead saw an overall turnout rate just below the 2018 level.

Once you get to the head of the line, you will encounter polling workers. They are usually unpaid volunteers—another form of political participation. They will direct you to a voting booth, often adorned with distinctive blue curtains. Inside, you find one of many different voting mechanisms. Some jurisdictions use touch screens; some states use voting machines with levers; and in others you mark paper ballots much as the first U.S. voters did in 1789 (although there were no curtains back then—everyone voted in public).

If many different offices are listed on the ballot, perhaps along with an issue referendum or two (which we discuss in Chapter 10), it might take you several minutes to work your way down the ballot and make all your choices. In local elections featuring just a handful of races, you may finish voting in thirty seconds or so. Either way, you have just participated in one of the great rituals of democratic participation.

In recent years, whispers of Election Day conspiracies have turned into shouts, amplified by former President Trump's claims about a stolen election in 2020—from rigged voting machines, to illegal immigrants voting, to boxes of ballots appearing mysteriously in the night. After multiple investigations across the states, and despite a long American history of cheating at the polls, there is almost no evidence of significant fraud in recent elections.[12]

● Celebrity endorsements can boost participation. Here, Kerry Washington campaigns for Joe Biden and Kamala Harris.

Still, state legislatures have been furiously responding to the fears. By the 2022 election, legislators in twenty-seven states had introduced over 200 measures designed to tighten up voting. On the other side, legislators in thirty-two states introduced some 400 bills to make voting easier.[13] Most of these bills did not pass, but they reflect the arguments on both sides: claims of a stolen election and counter-charges that the real danger lies in making it harder to vote. The 2022 midterms, featuring high turnout and few voting irregularities, affirm: Even amid highly politicized elections, the voting process today is largely secure.[14]

Electoral Activities. Beyond voting, Americans engage in other **electoral activities**. They volunteer to get out the vote for favorite candidates. They go to meetings and rallies. They post signs on their lawns and bumper stickers on their cars. They donate money (Figure 8.2).

Electoral activities: Public engagement in the form of voting, running for office, volunteering in a campaign, or otherwise participating in elections.

Political Voice. Political engagement continues after the election is over. More than one in five Americans contact a government official each year. They get in touch about potholes, immigration policy, inflation fears, or the school lunch menu.[15] Obviously, the key is finding the right official: Do not call the White House about potholes or the mayor's office about an international trade deal. To the surprise of many people, legislators—and especially members of Congress—devote considerable time to constituent inquiries. Go ahead and email your congressional representative. You'll get a response, and they'll keep tabs of the texts and messages. When elected officials don't hear about an issue, they are quick to say, "No one cares about that."

Political voice: Exercising one's public rights, often through speaking out in protest or in favor of some policy change.

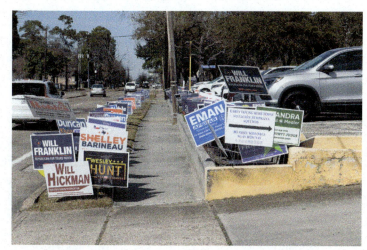

● Campaign signs line the streets outside a Spring Branch, Texas, polling location in 2022. Some jurisdictions make voting easy; others make it more difficult, resulting in long lines. And here's the secret: Big turnouts do not advantage either of the parties.

Americans are quick to express political opinions. On average, Americans exercise their **political voice** more often and more openly than citizens of many other countries.

Voted for political representatives with similar views	Signed petitions (including online)	Posted/shared on social media	Changed how they made product or service purchase decisions
Contacted & expressed opinions to political representatives	Participated in marches/rallies	Donated to relevant/ related organizations	Participated in protests

● **FIGURE 8.2** *Leading forms of political participation favored by eighteen- to twenty-nine-year-olds. (Case Foundation)*

They crowd into town meetings and, sometimes, shout at their elected officials. They contribute funds to challenge government programs in court. In addition, Americans express their voice through the market. Advocates on the left have boycotted companies who exploit workers or spoil the environment; today, conservatives are boycotting a long list of companies (BlackRock, Coca-Cola, Disney, Major League Baseball) for supporting efforts to slow climate change or criticizing laws that restrict voting, limit transgender rights, or make gun sales easier.[16]

Direct Action

Direct action: Participating outside of normal political and social channels through civil disobedience, demonstrations, and even riots.

When people feel that the traditional forms of participation are not working, they sometimes seek change outside of normal channels and take **direct action**. This is the world of demonstrations, marches, armed standoffs, and riots.

Protest politics can invoke the highest American aspirations. Or they can reflect nativism and prejudice. The goal is generally to call attention to a cause and to foster a movement around it. Of course, direct action can blur into electoral politics. Protests can foster political movements that then penetrate national institutions. For example, the record number of women candidates in the 2020 elections reflected an institutional change growing out of protests against sexism and gender inequity that inspired the #MeToo movement.[17]

Civil disobedience: Protesting laws one considers unjust by refusing to obey them—and accepting the punishment.

Occasionally, direct action goes further and violates the law—sometimes through proud acts of **civil disobedience**. Protesting slavery in 1849, Henry David Thoreau urged his countrymen: "If [the law] requires you to be the agent of injustice to another, then, I say break the law. Let your life be a counter friction to stop the machine." Martin Luther King picked up this theme in his cloquent letter from a Birmingham jail, where he explained to white liberals why Black Americans would break unjust laws rather than waiting quietly for reform.

Public Rallies

What Issues Draw People to Protest?

Nearly one in three people felt an urge to join a protest in recent years. What issues moved them? For liberals, it was abortion and women's rights, civil rights (especially racial equity), and voting rights. Conservatives protested over abortion, gun rights, COVID restrictions, and woke attitudes.

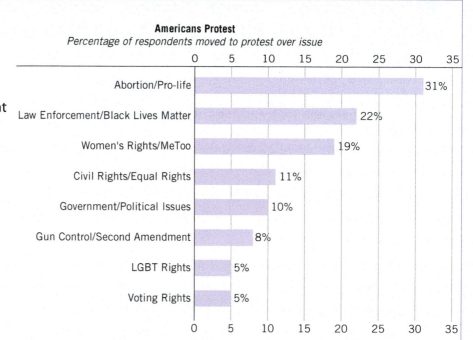

Americans Protest
Percentage of respondents moved to protest over issue

Issue	Percentage
Abortion/Pro-life	31%
Law Enforcement/Black Lives Matter	22%
Women's Rights/MeToo	19%
Civil Rights/Equal Rights	11%
Government/Political Issues	10%
Gun Control/Second Amendment	8%
LGBT Rights	5%
Voting Rights	5%

THINK ABOUT IT

As you look at this list, which issues do you think are most important?
....

Is there anything you'd like to see on the list that isn't there—something that arouses your passion enough to join a march or rally?
....

Is there anything on the list, or that should be on the list, that you predict will be a source of protests in the months ahead?
....

Now, look back at issue polls from the year you were born, or even just five years ago (both Pew and Gallup websites list these year by year). Which topics seemed most of interest then?
....

What has changed in the United States to explain the shift to this set of issues?

Source: Gallup

The line between traditional participation and direct action can blur. Recall that the First Amendment guarantees the right to assemble—although local authorities normally require a permit before people can march in the street. We label all marches and demonstrations direct action—whether the protesters have a permit (making their assembly legal) or not (making it civil disobedience).

WHAT DO YOU THINK?

Would You Have Protested?

Go back to the civil rights protests pictured in Chapter 6—young people at a sit-in are humiliated, those on a Freedom Bus beaten and almost burned alive. College students carried out the sit-ins and Freedom Rides. A question for you—one we often ask ourselves: **If you were in college between 1960 and 1962, would you have joined in?** It would have taken conviction, courage, and (for most students) a willingness to ignore parents horrified by the risks.

What would you have done? Explain why. Now consider the protests taking place on and off campuses today. How are they similar? How are they different? Have you taken part? Considered joining in? Explain why.

Direct action sometimes reflects the worst moments in American democracy. Sustained terrorism against Black people involved lynching in the South and violent rampages through Black neighborhoods in the North (described in Chapter 6). Today, protesters sometimes throw bricks, destroy property, and bash counterprotesters. Are they taking extreme action in response to repression? Recklessly endangering lives? Or both?

More often, great American rallies mark high points in our political history. Environmental activism offers a classic example. After millions of Americans

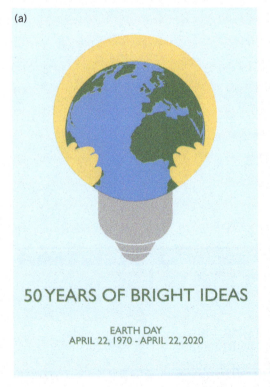

(a)

50 YEARS OF BRIGHT IDEAS

EARTH DAY
APRIL 22, 1970 - APRIL 22, 2020

(b)

● *Getting involved in politics comes in many forms. An Earth Day poster celebrates the fiftieth anniversary in 2020 (a), and a member of the Young America's Foundation (a conservative group) plants American flags in front of the U.S. Capitol in observance of 9–11 (b).*

gathered to promote cleaner air and water at the first Earth Day in April 1970, Congress passed major clean air legislation within a month, and a Clean Water Act soon after that. A series of "Rally for Life" marches in the 1980s–90s attracted more than seven hundred thousand. That type of political voice is a feature of American democracy that stretches back to the eighteenth century.

Civic Voluntarism

You can make a difference without plunging directly into politics. Many Americans—young, middle-aged, and seniors alike—volunteer for causes or donate money for local charities. These are forms of **civic voluntarism**—working together to address problems, often in one's own neighborhood, workplace, or school.

Civic voluntarism: Citizen participation in public life without government incentives or coercion, such as getting together to build a playground.

Civic voluntarism has long roots. When the French visitor Alexis de Tocqueville, whom we met earlier in this book, traveled through the United States in 1831–32, he was amazed by how often Americans got together to clear roads, build schools, or plan a civic celebration. Back home in France, he noted, the people would wait for the government authorities to act, while Americans just went ahead and did things without waiting for anyone's permission.[18]

The millennial generation became the most active in modern U.S. history to volunteer their time for worthy causes. The proportion of teenagers who volunteer has leveled off in recent years, but still stands at all-time highs.[19]

Voluntary engagement comes in many forms. People serve at a food bank, teach English as a second language, join a volunteer fire department, or help raise money for high school basketball uniforms. Many Americans respond to crowd-funding requests on sites such as Kickstarter, GoFundMe, and Indiegogo.

If you volunteer, you may think you're not being political at all. But this kind of activity tends to draw people into the common sphere. And once there, the payoff is clear. If you volunteer, you are more likely to vote, pay attention to political affairs, and otherwise engage in public life. As we saw in Chapter 1, successful democracies require a vibrant civic spirit.

The Participation Puzzle

Voter participation offers us a puzzle. American voting rates are usually low compared to other nations—under 60 percent in presidential elections and just 35 percent during the midterms. This is far behind Sweden (82 percent), Australia (80 percent), Israel (78 percent), Germany (69 percent), France (68 percent), or Mexico (65 percent). Then, suddenly, American participation surged: first in the 2018 midterm, then in the 2020 presidential election when 67 percent of Americans voted, then again in 2022. Is this a new trend? And which group rose the most? Voters under thirty, who increased their participation by around eleven points.[20]

Why did people vote in the last three elections but not before? First, the Donald Trump administration made the stakes seem high for both his supporters and his opponents. Voters turned out because they cared. Second, many states had been moving to make voting easier, especially in the wake of the COVID-19 pandemic.

Low **voter turnout** may reflect the barriers to voting that many states have erected over the years: registration requirements, the disenfranchisement of former felons, and so on. After all, rules can make it easier or more difficult for citizens to participate. Another key to voter turnout is *passion*. In 2022, states like Pennsylvania and Arizona, with high-profile Senate or governor races, voted at higher rates than in 2018 (when turnout set modern records). In states like West Virginia, with no statewide contest, turnout dropped to pre-2018 levels.

Voter turnout: A measure of which proportion of eligible voters actually cast a legitimate ballot in a given election.

Efforts to repress the vote have a long history rooted in national diversity itself. Northern officials tried to depress the immigrant vote, Southerners the Black vote. Mississippi was once so anxious about Black influence that it swept almost all voters out of the process—in 1938, the two million citizens of the state (49 percent of them Black) cast a total of only 35,439 votes for all five seats in Congress (under 1 percent of the adult population).[21] Limits in that era, like poll taxes and literacy tests, no longer exist. But critics still ask if a long legacy of suppressing the vote makes it easier to do so today. Here's the heretical idea: Perhaps government officials do not *want* the public involved in their work? After all, millions of new voters might shake up the status quo. Most democracies have a higher turnout than the United States. Some go so far as to *require* voting.[22] Of course, erecting barriers to traditional participation always invites the larger disruption of direct action.

Here's the fundamental question: Is the American system a miracle of mass participation? Or one designed to limit citizen access? Or, in the spirit of American federalism, is it a state-by-state patchwork of both?

THE BOTTOM LINE

» Traditional participation involves engaging politics through formal government channels. Voting is the most familiar form of traditional political participation.

» Americans participate in politics year-round. One in five contacts a public official in the course of a year.

» Direct action seeks immediate and sweeping change. It has a long legacy in the United States that goes back to its founding and includes some of the nation's great reform movements.

» Civic voluntarism is a form of engagement with public life that operates outside of government—but enhances democracy.

Why Do People Get Involved?

There's always a lot of people on the sideline. Whether it's an election, a boycott, or a riot—the way to win your goal is to get a lot of bystanders to pour in on your side. (If you're already winning, of course, you'll probably try to keep these unpredictable nonparticipants out of the action.) What makes some Americans more likely to jump into politics? Let's look at six major factors: background, friends, community, mobilization, government benefits, and historical context.[23]

Background

When researchers try to understand why certain people participate while others do not, they often look at factors related to personal background. These may include age, wealth, education, and race/ethnicity.

Age. Older people vote more often. Figure 8.3 shows voting rates for different American generations during midterm elections. Notice that *young* adults vote

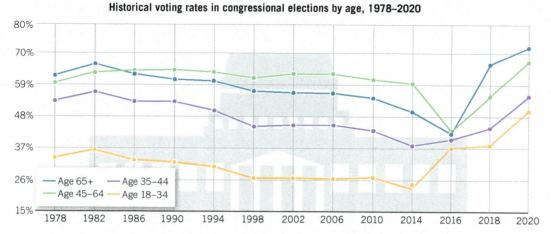

Historical voting rates in congressional elections by age, 1978–2020

● **FIGURE 8.3** *Voter turnout in congressional elections, by age. Notice how young people's participation soared between 2014 and 2020—and remained high (especially in contested states) in 2022. (U.S. Census Bureau, Current Population Survey)*

less. Even though younger people's participation flew up more recently, they still lag other age groups.

At the same time, many younger voters are likelier to try and influence politics through direct action. They are far more likely to engage politically online, to volunteer, and to protest. One Gen Z columnist summed it up: "For many [young Americans], protests seem like a more effective way to be heard than the ballot box."[24]

Wealth.   Income is another strong predictor: The higher your income, the more likely you are to get involved. That goes for all the traditional modes of participation, but especially political donations: Less than half of 1 percent of the population typically contributes over 70 percent of the total funds raised in presidential campaigns.[25]

Politics helps shape the size and scope of the wealthy class. In some eras, the political system facilitates vast differences in wealth—what Mark Twain called a "gilded age." These are the eras of relatively low taxes, weak oversight, and high (unregulated) finance. National resources flow to those at the very top. At other times, a backlash develops against growing inequality. In these egalitarian eras, national and state policies limit the accumulation of outsized wealth. However, in every era, wealthy people have more access to political leaders and more influence over politics.

Education.   Education also predicts political involvement—and education closely tracks income. The more education, the higher the voting levels. Less than 30 percent of people who did not finish high school normally vote in presidential elections, whereas citizens with a college degree are more than twice as likely to vote. In the past twenty years, as we saw in Chapter 7, a new divide has emerged: Well-educated voters have moved Democratic, less educated to the Republicans.[26]

Race/Ethnicity.   If we were writing this book fifteen years ago, we would have included another major reason for lower turnout: race. Traditionally, African Americans voted in lower numbers than white Americans. Gradually, however, the gap began to close, and in 2012, for the first time in U.S. history, Black people voted at a slightly higher rate than white people—thanks in part to intense support for Barack Obama. While the Black vote declined after that, it dramatically revived Joe Biden's campaign during the 2020 primaries.[27] Latinos and Asian

● *Votes, rallies, demonstrations, blogs, hacks, and even riots—participation in the United States takes many forms.*

Americans still vote at a lower rate than Black or white Americans: Under 50 percent of eligible voters in these communities cast ballots, for reasons researchers still debate.[28] As their overall numbers grow, however, Asian and Latino voters are becoming an increasingly important political force.

Friends and Family

Another way to predict whether someone will vote or volunteer is to find out whether their parents and closest friends do. On average, someone whose family or peers vote regularly is likely to do so as well.

But there is an even more powerful force than what your parents do: being *asked* by someone. Political science studies find that face-to-face encouragement is the most reliable route to political activity. Being asked to vote, even by a stranger, as long as it is in person, tends to get results.[29] This finding appears to hold for many forms of participation—and in many nations. Protesters are often part of personal networks, which have been greatly expanded thanks to smartphone technology enabling almost instantaneous social organization.[30]

Community

The type of community you live in also seems to make a difference. In some places, neighbors are more trusting and people are more likely to get involved—in local activities such as block watches or school fundraisers. Those types of communities also see higher voting rates. Social scientists call this spirit of embracing volunteerism and public participation **social capital**.

Communities with high social capital, where people tend to get together to do things, have happier, healthier residents. Why? Because engaging with others creates trust among citizens—and this finding seems to hold in nations around the world.[31] People who live in areas high in social capital are more deeply involved in book clubs, community gardens, sports leagues, and other activities; they spend more time connecting with one another than in places where people live more anonymously.

It may sound simple: A key to political participation is to live in a highly participatory community. But transforming a neighborhood into one with strong social

Social capital: Relations between people that build closer ties of trust and civic engagement, yielding productive benefits for the larger society.

capital—or sustaining civic connections once they exist—is no easy task. How might you help to cultivate a spirit of engagement in your surrounding community? And might online communities also foster social capital? What do you think?

In one neighborhood in the city of San José, Costa Rica, residents developed their own technique for boosting social capital. The neighborhood had experienced a sharp rise in crime. Residents got together and agreed to leave for work a few minutes earlier each morning, taking that extra time to greet and talk at least briefly with their neighbors. The practice became informally known as *El Ley del Saludo* (The Law of the Greeting), and it helped reduce crime markedly—as well as boost voting rates and other markers of political participation. Likewise, a low-income area of Detroit banded together and used social media to call out people dumping trash in their neighborhood. Once they began taking action, they found new ways to get involved: They painted vacant homes and started community gardens in the empty lots.[32]

● *Social capital in Detroit, where residents in low-income neighborhoods joined together to paint vacant homes.*

Political Mobilization

Party organizations have traditionally done the work of **political mobilization**. Both major parties remain powerful sources of encouraging millions of people to get involved—especially at election time. (We'll talk about political parties in Chapter 11.) In some cases, charismatic political figures are a source of mass mobilization. John F. Kennedy told Americans to "ask what they could do for their country" in the early 1960s and inspired young people to volunteer, organize, and demonstrate for civil rights. More than fifty years later, Donald Trump inspired many formerly apathetic white voters to vote, donate, and rally for his cause.

Today, there's a sharp twist to party mobilization known as **negative partisanship.** That's the impulse to get involved, not because someone inspires you, but because the other side offends or frightens you. Conservatives want to "own the libs," and liberals return the favor and flatly oppose Republican "nutjobs."

Interest groups and social movements also spur participation by rallying people to a cause. Groups like the National Rifle Association push gun rights, while Mothers Out Front fight for climate justice—both examples of **issue advocacy** campaigns.

Broader social movements like Black Lives Matter or the Tea Party Patriots also get people into politics. Movements always raise the same question: Are they focused on specific political changes (like the Tea Party) or are they more geared to changing public awareness for the cause (like Black Lives Matter)?[33]

In the eyes of professional political mobilizers—advocacy groups, campaign strategists, and other members of the enormous Washington, DC–based "political industry"—each of us is a potential resource. Activists constantly test ways to inspire people to sign a petition, write our congressional representatives, get out and vote, or otherwise engage politically (see Table 8.2).

Political mobilization: Efforts to encourage people to engage in the public sphere: to vote for a particular candidate (or donate money, work on the campaign, etc.) or to get involved in specific issues.

Negative partisanship: Participating in politics and forming opinions in opposition to a party one dislikes.

Issue advocacy: Organized effort to advance (or block) a proposed public policy change.

TABLE 8.2 How Mobilizers See Us

Political strategists and mobilizers have a language of their own. These are some of the terms you'll hear if you work in advocacy or campaign politics long enough.	
Grassroots	A movement for political reform that is sparked at the local level, from the ground up.
Astroturf	A movement for reform that appears to be grassroots but is actually run by political professionals.
Dog whistling	Using insider, "coded"—often racist—language that rouses some people but goes unnoticed by others (the analogy is from training dogs, which hear high-frequency whistles humans cannot).
Actorvist	A professional actor involved in political issue campaigns. Celebrities are often more successful than politicians—including presidents—at winning Americans' policy attention for their pet cause. Leonardo DiCaprio, for years a mainstay of the environmental movement; Oprah Winfrey, a passionate spokeswoman for gun control; and Bradley Cooper, who speaks out for U.S. military veterans, are among the many "actorvists" engaged in American policy mobilization efforts today.
Raptivist	A term describing rap artists who get involved in political causes: Chance the Rapper, Cardi B, and Kendrick Lamar are all examples.

Government Beneficiaries

A fifth factor encouraging participation in public life may strike you as odd at first glance: receiving government benefits. If, for example, you are covered by your parents' health insurance past age twenty-one or you receive a federally guaranteed student loan (which keeps interest rates low), you are a beneficiary. Receiving such support can boost active participation for years to come. Researchers have shown that when the government rewards service—as when returning soldiers receive free or discounted college tuition through the GI Bill—recipients are considerably more likely to get involved as volunteers and to exercise their public voice.[34]

However, not all government programs are alike. Programs that treat beneficiaries with dignity generate social capital. But programs aimed at people with lower incomes appear to depress political participation. Why? Public officials are far less courteous to these beneficiaries than to others.[35]

These spurs to participation all focus on individual factors. There is a larger backdrop to participation as well.

Historical Context

Major shifts in the economy and in politics affect both the intensity and favored types of participation. In the rural South during the 1950s, for example, an infestation of boll weevils (tiny insects that feed on cotton plants) devastated the cotton crop. Many Black subsistence farm workers, their livelihood gone, moved to cities (in both the South and the North) where they plunged into civil rights movements—and changed American politics.[36]

Context deeply influences opportunities for political engagement.[37]

● *Chance the Rapper speaks out about youth education in his native Chicago—and delivers a million-dollar check "for the kids." Some observers call him a "raptivist" (rapper + activist).*

During some historical periods, Americans have been more likely to engage in public life than at other times. For example, workers (in the 1930s) and students (1960s) flocked into direct action politics. Today—with Americans organizing across the political spectrum—we are in another high-participation moment, especially on college campuses.

THE BOTTOM LINE

» Participation in politics and government is influenced by personal factors: background characteristics, such as income and education; family and friends; communities and social capital; political mobilization; and receiving government benefits from programs that treat beneficiaries with respect (i.e., Social Security).

» Americans participate in political life at very different rates. A few engage passionately, a larger number are moderately engaged, and the majority are only sporadically involved. This contributes to the appearance of high *and* low participation in the United States.

» Political mobilization also is influenced by the larger social and historical context.

 ## What Discourages Political Participation?

Back to the participation puzzle noted earlier in this chapter. Americans engage at high rates in many forms of political activity—but lag other nations' voting rates. Then, in 2020, the American numbers jumped. In that election, the U.S. participation rate leapt up from thirtieth to fifteenth among active democracies (see Comparing Nations 8.1). But even in higher-turnout years like 2020 and 2022, tens of millions of eligible voters stay home. This section explores resistance to participating.

Political scientists used to try to shock their students by declaring, "Voting is a complete waste of time." They were channeling economist Anthony Downs's **paradox of voting**: Why bother taking all that time and energy when your vote is almost certainly not going to matter? Downs wondered why millions of apparently rational people bothered to troop to the polls every election. He could have said the same thing about joining a protest march or posting online.

Today, many political scientists flip the question. As we saw in the previous section, people get many benefits from participating: a sense of involvement, of duty performed, of belonging to a community. So, instead of asking why so many people bother to vote, we ask why don't *more* people vote, given the many benefits of participation?

Four broad reasons explain why people do not participate in political life: alienation, barriers to participation, complacency, and shifting mobilization patterns.[38]

Alienation

Alienation is a feeling of powerlessness, or an inability to control one's own political fate. Most alienated people ignore politics. When they get involved, it is usually not through traditional channels but through direct action—intense and even violent protest.[39] Younger people and recent immigrants tend to feel higher levels

Paradox of voting: For most individuals, the cost of voting (acquiring necessary information, traveling to polling site, and waiting in line) outweighs the apparent benefits. Economic theory would predict very low voter turnout, given this analysis.

COMPARING NATIONS 8.1   Voter Turnout in Selected Countries

Even in unusually high-turnout elections, the United States—the world's oldest democracy—ranks just fifteenth in voter turnout. Why?

In two of the top four countries, Australia and Belgium, voting is *compulsory*—required by law. In contrast, the United States requires two steps: registration and then voting. That makes the process more burden-some and depresses voter numbers in most years.

There is another reason that turnout is lower in the U.S.: It has only two par-ties (we'll explain why in Chapter 11); in contrast, Belgium has eighteen par-ties with representatives in the national legislature; Sweden and Denmark have eight and ten respectively. That makes it more likely that people can find a point of view that speaks to them. For example, in Sweden environmentalists vote Green, feminists vote Left Party, businesspeople vote Liberal, and populists fearful of immigrants turn to the Sweden Democrats. More people get excited about politics when there are more choices on the political menu.
Source: World Population Review/U.S. Census Bureau

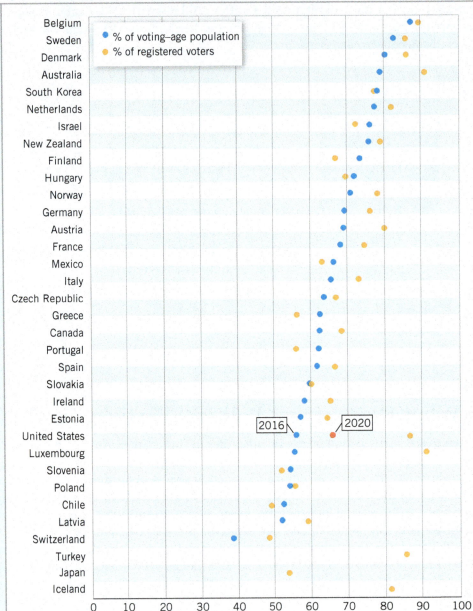

Voting-age population (VAP) and registered voter (RV) turnout are derived from different data sources, and consequently, VAP is lower than RV in some countries.

of alienation. Recently, alienation levels have soared among white men who failed to finish high school.

These findings raise a question: Do some groups feel alienated because they lack a history of participation? Remember, one predictor of whether a person will get involved in politics is whether their parents or peer group is actively engaged.

Or perhaps immigrants, minorities, and young people *want* to participate in politics and feel alienated because they are shut out?

The sheer number of elected offices (and of elections) might result in public disengagement, especially when campaigns feature seemingly endless negative advertisements.

Sharp partisan differences also play a role. The angry partisan debates—especially online—have led many Americans to dismiss all politics and politicians. The younger generation appears to be particularly uncomfortable with the high levels of conflict.[40]

● *Negative ad in the 2020 presidential race. Relentless attack-style politics can help mobilize highly partisan voters—while turning moderates away from participating.*

Finally, citizens may be alienated because they feel that national debates don't really address their problems. If you have gone door to door during a political campaign, you may have heard people—especially in less resourced neighborhoods—say something like, "Hey, it's not really going to affect my life, even if your candidate wins." They may believe that government officials only appease the rich and powerful—and ignore the issues that matter to ordinary people like growing inequality, a sense of being left behind, or the erosion of the nation's moral fabric.

Two candidates in both the 2016 and 2020 presidential races, Donald Trump and Bernie Sanders, channeled this alienation—and stunned political observers with their unexpected success. Trump's victory in 2016 was one of the great election upsets in American history.[41]

In countries with repressive political systems, alienation can become pervasive. Large majorities completely turn away from government and politics. Americans exhibit much lower levels of alienation than totalitarian regimes, but there's no denying its presence.

Looming changes in American society raise important questions about alienation. As the United States becomes a majority–minority country, will white voters tend to feel more alienated? How about poor and less-educated white voters who feel left behind and may blame others for their situation? On the other side, will minority groups feel more empowered? The 2018 and 2022 midterm elections and 2020 presidential contest, with the highest turnouts in a half-century, suggest that alienation can be overcome. One key to engaging previously alienated people: continuing to address their concerns through public policy (as you'll see in Chapter 17), after the election is over.

Institutional Barriers

When Will Walker, a young Black farmer, arrived to cast his vote in Tuscaloosa, Alabama, in 1964, he was first required by state law to pass a literacy test. None of the white voters streaming past Walker to the voting booths had to take the test. Walker shrugged and turned to the paper before him, brandished by an unfriendly poll worker. He had brushed up on his basic U.S. government facts, and he knew plenty about the various candidates running for election. Yet no amount of studying could have prepared Walker for questions like these:

- The electoral vote for president is counted in the presence of two governmental bodies. Name them: _____ and _____.

- The president is forbidden to exercise his or her authority of pardon in cases of _____.

- If the president does not wish to sign a bill, how many days is he or she allowed in which to return it to Congress for reconsideration? _____ days.
- At what time of day on January 2 each four years does the term of the president of the United States end? _____.

Will filled out as many of the twenty questions as he could; he did better than most political science majors might today. But he was turned away. Alabama allowed only Black voters with a perfect score to vote. The test wasn't really about literacy or intelligence. Rather, it was part of Jim Crow segregation (discussed in Chapter 6). Literacy tests were introduced across the South to keep Black citizens from voting. (And before that, they had been used in New England to keep the Irish from voting.) Once the literacy tests and other restrictions were put into place, Black voters were almost completely driven out of politics.

Most of these overtly racist obstacles to participation were eliminated during the 1960s. Nevertheless, some critics continue to point out structural barriers to participation in American public life, such as the disenfranchisement of individuals convicted of a crime, even after they have served their sentence.

The incentives and barriers to voting can be subtle: How difficult is it to register? Are there plenty of opportunities for early voting before Election Day, including on weekends? How long are the lines at polling places—and are polling locations plentiful and reasonably easy to reach?

Democrats have generally tried to make it easier to vote. States controlled by Democrats introduced same-day registration, long periods in which you can cast your ballot, and extensive online voting. Republicans in many states have moved the other way and tightened restrictions on voting. Some argue that more careful monitoring reduces fraud; others think that voting should be treated as a privilege—people should be willing to invest the time and energy. Republican-led states have introduced tougher identification requirements, limits on same-day registration, reductions in voting periods, and a purge of people from the list of registered voters who have not voted in six years.

Both sides believe they are boosting their own chances to win. More turnout, they think, helps Democrats. But here's the funny thing: It does not seem to be true. Many political scientists think the two parties are fighting over a myth.[42] High turnout does not seem to help one party over another, at least not anymore.

Still, there is one danger: If parties try to suppress specific groups—discouraging voters in the cities or subtly discriminating against Black citizens, for example—they could strip people of rights and tilt election outcomes. That's a present danger with a long, sad history in the United States.[43]

Complacency

Some people do not participate because they are satisfied with their lives. Without urgent problems they want solved, why bother to get involved? People run to join organizations (and pay the dues) when their values feel under threat. President Trump's election boosted membership in environmental organizations (their fundraisers reverberated with fears) but dampened support for gun groups (no threat). When Democrats get elected, or when mass shootings occur, renewed calls for gun control send the money flowing back to gun groups. Bad news has a silver lining, if you're raising money for a political cause.

Shifting Mobilization Pattern

Before the 1960s, political parties were Americans' main source of political mobilization. They focused on intensive door-to-door canvassing and targeted both the rich and the poor. Their emphasis was turning out as many people as possible.

Then social movements and interest groups leapt into politics and fought for consumer rights, the environment, morality, and other causes. In some ways, the rise of advocacy groups gave the public more leverage. But they tilted politics to the well-off who could write the checks that kept those organizations in business. Political sociologist Theda Skocpol noted that "Americans who are not wealthy or higher-educated now have fewer associations representing their values and interests, and enjoy dwindling opportunities for active participation."[44]

This shift from parties to advocacy groups as the main agents of political mobilization adds up to a **cycle of nonparticipation**. If people are so disengaged that they do not affiliate with either political party, party organizers are unlikely to reach out to them at election time—because they might vote for the wrong side.

Cycle of nonparticipation: Resistance by political parties to mobilizing disengaged Americans to vote—because their lack of involvement makes their allegiance to one or the other party suspect.

THE BOTTOM LINE

» Participation in civic life tends to vary by age, income level, and education.

» Several other factors have fueled a decline in Americans' political participation in recent years. These include alienation, barriers to participation, complacency, and shifting mobilization patterns.

Social Media, Big Data, and Gen Z

When the world went online, twenty-five years ago, politics changed. Social media made people both more and less involved in politics; it ushered in both opportunity and trouble. In some ways, we experience vibrant citizen participation and improved public policies. At the same time, social media yields deeply polarized communities, viral malice, and the rising power of tech companies.[45]

How Social Media Improves Democracy

First, optimists begin by pointing out how *active* online users are. People seek out news, follow links, and access a world of information (see Figure 8.4).

Second, people respond. You can swipe on a "Like" icon, comment on a social media post, or message a network of like-minded people. Democracies, when they are working well, *hear* their people. Social media gives individuals many opportunities to exercise their voice.

Third and related, the range of commentary has vastly expanded. Traditionally, political pundits formed a small circle of well-known personalities and authors. Today, if you have something to say, you can launch a podcast or TikTok political house, tweet to dozens or hundreds (or millions) of followers, or post news stories or opinions on your social media feeds. YouTube or TikTok videos and Instagram stories go viral all the time. People post petitions on change.org. Crowdfunding platforms like Kickstarter raise significant funds for civic and political causes.

Fourth, as we will see in Chapter 9, social media democratizes news production. Rather than wait for a news van and reporters, bystanders capture important events and upload them. Suddenly everyone sees a shooting, or an angry candidate blurt out a racial slur.

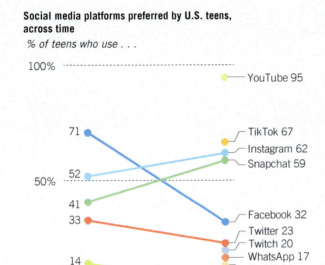

Social media platforms preferred by U.S. teens, across time

% of teens who use . . .

- YouTube 95
- TikTok 67
- Instagram 62
- Snapchat 59
- Facebook 32
- Twitter 23
- Twitch 20
- WhatsApp 17
- Reddit 14
- Tumblr 5

71
52
41
33
14

2014–15   2022

Note: Teens refer to those ages 13 to 17. Those who did not give an answer are not shown. The 2014–15 survey did not ask about YouTube, WhatsApp, Twitch and Reddit. TikTok debuted globally in 2018.

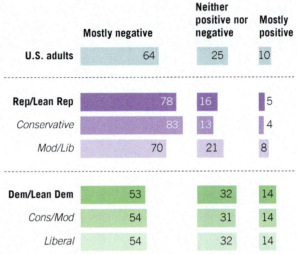

Views of social media as aiding or corroding political participation

% of Americans who view social media's effect on politics as . . .

	Mostly negative	Neither positive nor negative	Mostly positive
U.S. adults	64	25	10
Rep/Lean Rep	78	16	5
Conservative	83	13	4
Mod/Lib	70	21	8
Dem/Lean Dem	53	32	14
Cons/Mod	54	31	14
Liberal	54	32	14

Note: Those who did not give an answer are not shown.

● **FIGURE 8.4** *Most American teens (and adults) are online. The platforms they use change regularly, however (a). Social media's influence on political participation is much debated; most Americans view it as an overall negative (b).*

Fifth, politicians and parties (and media organizations) have more ways than ever to reach out. Texas politician and 2022 gubernatorial candidate Beto O'Rourke puts it simply: "If it's not on Instagram, it didn't happen."[46]

Finally, big data algorithms, powered by fast-expanding artificial intelligence (AI) machine learning, can deliver precisely targeted messages about issues and candidates to your social media feed or email inbox.

In sum, social media promotes active users, links people to one another, permits citizens to bypass the talking heads and make their own comments, and offers politicians a powerful tool to mobilize, connect, and collect. A wired and wireless world boosts American democracy.

How Social Media Challenges Democracy

At the same time social media introduces problems. The digital world poses three serious challenges to democracy: centralized control, din, and misinformation.[47]

Centralized Control. First, the social media universe imposes *central control*. It spreads the power of governments and a few corporations. "Facebook has more power in determining who can speak and who can be heard around the globe than any Supreme Court justice, any king or any president," noted law professor Jeffrey Rosen. Donald Trump's tweets dominated the media until Twitter froze his account in January 2021. Think about that: A private company cut off the president's favorite channel of communication to almost eighty million followers. Social media companies determine what speech violates their community standards, when to cooperate with security agencies, and how to monetize information about your shopping habits—or your political views.[48] Those AI algorithms also represent a dangerous potential for invading personal privacy.

Companies like Facebook collect enormous amounts of data. They claim to protect it, but many people do not trust them and think they threaten privacy in all kinds of ways: Law enforcement demands access. Companies gather personal information with every click and then sell it far and wide. Cybercriminals steal information and identities. Hackers aim to outrage people by pranking sites with unwelcome political memes or pornographic images. Agents—from foreign government trolls to high school geeks—try to hack the U.S. military millions of times *each day*.[49]

Din. Second, with billions of online sites, the sheer volume and variety of available information are mind-boggling. The resulting chaos and noise—known as **din**—can overwhelm participation as well as enhance it. Researching a specific topic often involves wading through a forest of hearsay, contradiction, malice, and deliberate misinformation.

Google this chapter's topic, "political participation," for example. As of 2023, we found more than eleven million online sources. Which ones provide valuable or even usable details about participation in the public sphere? Merely to scan each site for thirty seconds would take ten and a half years.

Din: Shorthand for the sheer volume of information and noise generated by online sources; can be a disincentive to participate politically.

Misinformation, Malice, and Trolls. Third, social media incubates lies, malice, and falsehoods. Rumors start and spread. Racism, anti-Semitism, misogyny, and character assassination all flourish. No, Hillary Clinton was not running a child-sex ring out of a Washington, DC, pizza parlor—though one man who saw that "news" online traveled from North Carolina, burst into Comet Ping Pong, and began firing his rifle at a locked closet to "save the children." A nutty story had metastasized online. The shooter went to jail, but TikTok users still buzz over "pizzagate." And the lies and malice only got worse.

In 2022, a young man whose head was filled with racist misinformation murdered ten people in a grocery store in Buffalo, New York. He had spent days surfing hard-right content. On BitChute he listened to a rant about the fall of the middle class. On Reddit and 4Chan he lurked in hate-filled chatrooms. Then mainstream sites—YouTube, Huff Post, and Medium—fed him lurid crime details as well as gun tutorials. And, in the end, he livestreamed his barbaric acts in real time. Social media channels (and spreads) domestic terrorism.[50]

Does Social Media Increase Political Participation?

Different observers add up the costs and benefits of social media in different ways. But optimists keep coming back to the same basic finding: Social media users are also more likely to participate in politics and engage in policy innovation than previous generations. Local government "hack-athons" invite residents to pitch their civic improvement ideas. Citizens use smartphones to publicize what their elected officials are doing.

What explains the connection between social media and participation? Perhaps individuals who are inclined to become involved in politics are more likely to be social media users. Or do people get engaged by what they see and hear online—and then act on it? Or is there a bandwagon effect—watching others comment on posts or joining groups stimulates individuals to jump in and do likewise? Whatever

● *Gen Z in politics. Students who survived a mass shooting at Parkland High School in Florida lead a mass demonstration for sensible gun control.*

Gen Z more likely than other generations to want an activist government

% saying government ...

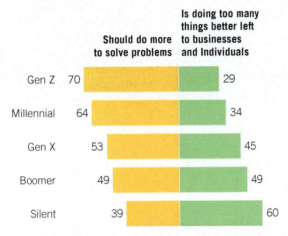

	Should do more to solve problems	Is doing too many things better left to businesses and Individuals
Gen Z	70	29
Millennial	64	34
Gen X	53	45
Boomer	49	49
Silent	39	60

● **FIGURE 8.5** *Gen Z is more likely than other generations to want an activist government, with 70 percent saying the government should do more to solve problems.*

How Millennials and Gen Z Participate

For a long time, political scientists fretted that millennials and Gen Z were not engaged by politics. Their voting numbers were low. They tended to shy away from political campaigns. They did not identify strongly with either party (over 40 percent identify as independents—more than any other age group).

Then, young people began to flock to the polls, and their voting numbers have risen faster than any other age group. Why didn't social scientists see this coming? They were looking in the wrong places. "This is not an apathetic bunch," concluded one recent study, "it's just that young people are engaging in civic life on their own terms, in their own way."[51] That means, for starters, that they are online and engaging with a web of peers. Young activists are less likely to focus on the large, well-organized, institutionally sanctioned political events like elections. They are more likely to mobilize for change in highly visible campaigns over an individual issue—most notably, gun reform, climate change, and racial justice.[52]

Millennials and Gen Z are also more likely to identify as liberals than any other generation. They are more willing to call for the government to address problems (Figure 8.5). Should we have a bigger government doing more things such as guaranteeing healthcare for all? Millennials and Gen Xers say "yes" (70 percent and 64 percent, respectively). Meanwhile, voters over sixty-five, who are enjoying the two largest government programs—Social Security and Medicare—say "no." Why?

On some policy issues, younger generations have distinctive views. For example, they are more likely to believe that climate change is due to human activity (Figure 8.6). They are also far more comfortable with changing sexual and gender norms; they are five times as likely to know someone who wishes to use gender-neutral pronouns (Figure 8.7), and largely accept friends coming out as LGBTQ+ or changing genders—although the level of acceptance is much higher among Democrats.[53]

As we saw in Chapter 7, millennials and Gen Z have already rewritten national attitudes on issues ranging from same-sex marriage (74 percent approval) to legalizing marijuana (70 percent approval). A strong majority (85 percent) believe undocumented immigrants should have a chance to become citizens.[54] Millennial and Gen Z political voices have already changed public policy—and will continue to do so.

In short, young America is diverse, is eager to build social capital by volunteering, and feels strongly about many political issues—as we saw at this chapter's opening. But, like many generations before them, they

Gen Z, Millennials, most likely to say climate change is due to human activity

% saying ...

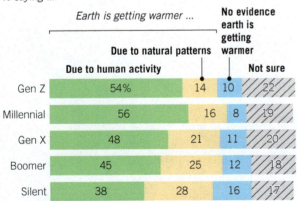

	Earth is getting warmer ...		No evidence earth is getting warmer	
	Due to human activity	Due to natural patterns		Not sure
Gen Z	54%	14	10	22
Millennial	56	16	8	19
Gen X	48	21	11	20
Boomer	45	25	12	18
Silent	38	28	16	17

● **FIGURE 8.6** *Gen Z and Millennials are most likely to blame humans for climate change, with 54 and 56 percent, respectively, saying climate change is due to human activity. Most older people deny it.*

Gen Zers are more likely to know someone using gender-neutral pronouns and more likely to say forms should offer gender options other than "man" and "woman"

% saying they personally know someone who prefers that others refer to them using gender-neutral pronouns

Gen Z	35
Millennial	25
Gen X	16
Boomer	12
Silent	7

% saying that when a form or online profile asks about person's gender it should include options other than "man" and "woman"

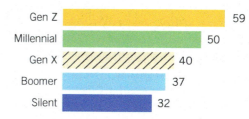

Gen Z	59
Millennial	50
Gen X	40
Boomer	37
Silent	32

● **FIGURE 8.7** *Gen Z is more likely to know someone using gender-neutral pronouns with 35 percent saying they personally know someone who prefers that others refer to them using gender-neutral pronouns. And 59 percent of Gen Zers believe that forms asking about gender should include options other than "man" and "woman." Again, this is mostly unknown territory for people over 60—the Boomer and Silent generations.*

participate in their own way: focused on single issues, tolerant of other people's identity, willing to accept more government action, leaning liberal, almost always online, and more racially and ethnically diverse than any generation in American history.

THE BOTTOM LINE

» Social media has changed the way Americans participate politically.

» The resulting activism and connection introduce both advantages and disadvantages.

» In some ways the activism empowers American democracy, but in other ways it challenges American politics through government and corporate control, din, and malice.

» Millennials and Gen Z have their own distinctive views and modes of participation.

 ## Conclusion: Revitalizing Political Participation

Participation is always in flux.

Rapid change reminds us of Ben Franklin describing the newly formed government back in 1787: "A republic, if you can keep it" (Chapter 1). Keeping the republic means constantly revitalizing the traditional channels of political participation. They are always changing—and every change brings new opportunities and many challenges.

Scan politics today and you'll find every kind of participation: massive demonstrations for social justice, venomous political feeds full of hate and lies, voting turnout that smashes recent records, an online generation that is more tolerant and more diverse than any previous generation, and a backlash to every item on this list.

People are participating more than ever. Can our institutions—our parties and our voting procedures—keep up? Some elections see very high turnout; others show widespread apathy. What might we do? Well, one thing would be to simply make voting easier. We could stop wrangling over the voting rules. Or, perhaps a more radical reform: Government requires you to wear a seatbelt or (in most states) use a motorcycle helmet. Maybe we should require everyone to vote as well. What do you think?

Americans today face the task of revitalizing the formal channels of participation. There is enormous political energy across the political spectrum—from fervent Trump supporters on the right to calls for social justice on the left. The key to the future lies in channeling that energy into everyday politics. Finding a way to make traditional politics vital and relevant is the key to "keeping the republic."

WHAT DO YOU THINK?

Should Voting Be Required by Law?

Americans, especially those under twenty-five, vote at relatively low rates. One proposal is to require voting (or pay a fine). Countries where voting is compulsory have much higher participation rates.	**Yes! A vibrant republic requires active participation by the people.** If everyone voted, elected officials would genuinely represent all the people. It would make our politics more inclusive. And it would avoid a grave danger: Apathetic people soon lose their rights and liberties.	**No! Voting is a privilege as well as a right.** People should inform themselves and take the extra effort to cast a vote. We shouldn't make voting too easy—it's probably a good thing if uninformed people stay home. It makes politics and governing more efficient.	**Not sure?** Today, political observers make arguments on both sides. Democrats are usually eager to expand voting. Republicans have increasingly been voting "no" on this issue. We hope you'll have a stronger, better-informed opinion by the time you've finished this book.

CHAPTER SUMMARY

★ Participation in civic and political life is a long-standing American tradition—helping, in the view of nineteenth-century visitors like Tocqueville, to distinguish the United States as a rising nation. Today, although Americans still exhibit higher levels of voluntarism than citizens of other countries, our rates of participation in politics and government have fallen to disturbing levels.

★ People participate in public life in three broad ways:

- First, by participating through traditional political mechanisms: voting, going to rallies, contributing to campaigns, contacting public officials.

- Second, by getting involved in direct action when traditional mechanisms seem unresponsive. This is the politics of demonstrations, protest movements, and even armed confrontations.

- Third, by contributing to civil society through volunteering and getting involved in the community.

⭐ Whether someone engages in civic life depends on both personal factors—those with politically active family members and close friends, or with higher education levels, are more inclined to participate—and political context. During periodic outbursts of direct participation, many people who might ordinarily stay on the sidelines are drawn to participate.

⭐ Another key to this push–pull of participation: Americans simultaneously get involved in civic affairs, especially in their local communities, and express high dissatisfaction with U.S. government institutions.

⭐ Traditionally, Americans have had low voting turnout—ranking about thirtieth among wealthy democracies. But in the 2018 and 2020 cycles, that's changed dramatically. Voting participation was extremely high. The 2022 election continued the high-turnout trend, especially in states with high-profile races.

⭐ Millennials and Gen Z vote in lower numbers than other generations. But in the last three elections they have started to vote in much higher numbers—breaking the record for youth voting in 2020.

⭐ Young Americans connect with others through social media, a force that is transforming political participation in fast-evolving (and, for the most part, poorly understood) ways.

⭐ Mass engagement in politics and other civic activities is the lifeblood of American democracy, helping to explain why analysts are so anxious to expand participation.

KEY TERMS

Civic voluntarism, p. 255
Civil disobedience, p. 252
Clicktivism, p. 248
Cycle of nonparticipation, p. 265
Din, p. 267

Direct action, p. 252
Electoral activities, p. 251
Issue advocacy, p. 259
Negative partisanship, p. 259
Paradox of voting, p. 261

Political mobilization, p. 259
Political voice, p. 251
Social capital, p. 258
Traditional participation, p. 248
Voter turnout, p. 255

STUDY QUESTIONS

1. This chapter describes three forms of political participation: traditional political participation, direct action, and civic volunteerism. Summarize each. Which do you think is most important? Why?
2. What are some of the benefits of participating in civic and political life? Why do so many Americans—especially younger people in their teens and twenties—choose not to participate through formal mechanisms?
3. Why do many Americans have a difficult time articulating a sense of the "public," compared to private life or affinity groups?
4. Describe the factors that encourage and discourage political participation.

5. Voter turnout is sometimes very low. At other times it is very high. Why?
6. Which features distinguish the millennial generation and Gen Z when it comes to participation in civic and political activities?
7. Do you consider social media sites a source of *enhancing* or *discouraging* participation in public life? Which evidence might you consider in support of your claim?
8. Artificial intelligence (AI) has improved policymaking by analyzing enormous data sets—including those built on millions of individual smartphone or Internet clicks. Are the privacy risks worth the policy gains, in your view?

9 MEDIA, TECHNOLOGY, AND GOVERNMENT

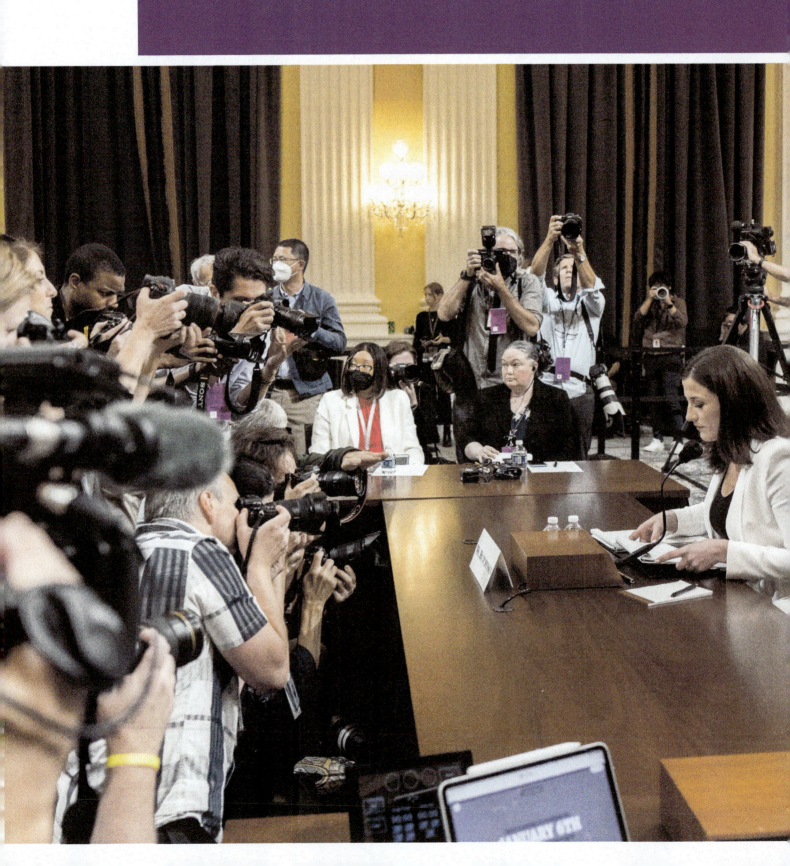

IN 1961, THE AMERICAN MEDICAL ASSOCIATION

enlisted actor Ronald Reagan to help fight President John F. Kennedy's health-care plan. Reagan cut a record (on vinyl) that the medical association sent (by snail mail) to every physician's home. "If this program passes," warned the future president, "one day we will awake to find that we have socialism. . . . We will spend our sunset years telling our children and our children's children what it was like in America when men were free." The record asked doctors' wives to invite their friends, serve coffee, play Reagan's message, and then write letters to Congress opposing government health insurance. Congress voted down the program, although another version passed four years later and is now known as Medicare.

In 1993, the Health Insurance Association of America aired television ads opposing President Bill Clinton's health plan. The ads featured "Harry and Louise," a pleasant middle-aged couple who were concerned that national health insurance would create a bureaucratic monster and wreck their healthcare. "They [the Washington bureaucrats] choose," intones a voice at the end of the ad. "You lose." Congress soon buried the Clinton health proposal. It took nearly two decades until a later president, Barack Obama, succeeded in getting a comprehensive healthcare plan passed, the Affordable Care Act (or "Obamacare").

In 2021–22, a small collection of "anti-vaxxers" spread doubt about COVID vaccines on social media platforms like Twitter, Instagram, Facebook, and TikTok. Public health experts piled up overwhelming evidence that vaccines were effective in combating a virus that killed more than a million Americans—by early 2022, the unvaccinated were ninety-seven times more likely to die of the disease than those who had been vaccinated and boosted.[1] One study found that just twelve influential people—including President Kennedy's nephew, Robert F. Kennedy Jr.—were responsible for the "vast majority" of online anti-vaccine "disinformation.[2] Thanks to social media, they reached some fifty-nine million people.

In every era, politicians have used available media technology to reach their audiences. In 1961, a recording went to elites who responded by mailing letters to Congress. In 1993, a TV ad ran in select markets and then spread further on television via pundits—and helped bring down a signature presidential initiative. Three decades later, a tweet or Instagram post instantly

In this chapter, you will

 Review the media's main contributions to American democracy.

 Learn how media coverage of politics is changing.

 Consider the democratic promises and pitfalls of social and mainstream media.

 Explore how the media is (and is not) biased.

 Understand the rules that channel the media into its current forms.

 Discover how U.S. media is distinctive.

 Assess how media coverage influences policymaking and elections.

● *The Media Frenzy. Photographers swarm witness Cassidy Hutchinson as she prepares to testify before a congressional committee investigating the January 6, 2021, attack on the Capitol.*

273

In interviews with The Defender, pilots injured by COVID-19 vaccines said despite a "culture of fear and intimidation" they are compelled to speak out against vaccine mandates that rob pilots of their careers — and in some cases their lives.

childrenshealthdefense.org
Exclusive: Pilots Injured by COVID Vaccines Speak Out: 'I Will Probably Never F...
In interviews with The Defender, pilots injured by COVID-19 vaccines said despite a "culture of fear and intimidation" they are compelled to speak out ...

● *From LP record albums (a) to Instagram posts (b) and tweets: Evolving media technologies have changed journalism—and American politics.*

reaches millions, generating reaction via social media and traditional channels (newspapers, radio, TV). Four major changes mark the evolution of media issue campaigns across more than fifty years:

- First, *information cascades faster and faster.* As media outlets multiply, consumers rush to keep up with the never-ending flood of news.

- Second, *today's media includes many more voices and formats.* Proliferating media options contribute to a more polarized public, as people follow sources that align with their interests or ideological outlook.

- Third, *social media permits the public to be much more active.* You can comment on a post or tweet more easily (and in more ways) than you could respond to a record in 1961 or a TV commercial in 1993. The public can act as media watchdogs and information providers, by recording and posting events via smartphones—supplying coverage formerly controlled by large media organizations.

- Finally, *social media enables the viral spread of misinformation.* Because any entity with a social media account can "say" virtually anything, malicious agents—foreign governments, automated "bots," pranksters, personal enemies—routinely spread false information and create chaos.

What is the media?[3] It is all the ways people obtain information about politics and the wider world: Instagram, television, TikTok or YouTube videos, podcasts, Facebook, newspapers, Snapchat posts, Reddit threads, blogs, Twitter feeds, and more. Media outlets are the major information bridge between citizens and government.

The successive rise of radio, television, the Internet, and social media each had a profound impact on American politics. Here's the biggest change: Fifty years ago, almost everyone heard the same newscast, agreed on the same facts, and took part in the same debate. Today, each position on the political spectrum tunes in to its own news source and links to its own network. People no longer agree on what happened.

What do you think about this great change? Does the proliferation of news sources enhance democracy by giving every perspective a voice? Diminish it by tilting the news and spreading lies? Or some of both?

Who are we? From the start of this book, we have seen that the United States is an immense, ongoing argument over political ideas. The media brings the people into political debates; it is the great link between leaders and citizens. The national media reflects America itself: raucous, fast-changing, multicultural, forceful, loud, and lucrative. It sparks intense policy debates at home. It broadcasts America to the world.

BY THE NUMBERS — The Media

$89 billion
Total revenue earned by U.S. newspapers, 2000

$17 billion
Total revenue earned by U.S. newspapers, 2022[4]

68 Percentage of Democrats who express trust in the U.S. media[5]

31 Percentage of independents who express trust in the U.S. media[6]

11 Percentage of Republicans who express trust in the U.S. media[7]

1 Rank of Barack Obama among most-followed Twitter accounts (132 million)

1 Rank of Charli D'Amelio among most-followed TikTok accounts (140 million)

32 billion
Total TikTok views of #blacklivesmatter-tagged videos, through June 2022

$500 million
Amount proposed in U.S. House bill to promote negative news coverage of China in global media outlets, to "counter China's misinformation campaign"[8]

8 Days after which the Russian government blocked access to Western media outlets such as Voice of America and BBC News following its invasion of Ukraine in 2022[9]

5.5 Estimated ratio of public relations (PR) professionals per journalist employed in the U.S.[10]

58 Percentage of reporters covering the Nebraska statehouse who are students—in high school or college[11]

How is news reporting changing? Is anything important lost about news reporting and publishing in the great transition from newspapers and network TV to digital platforms? What news sources do you trust? Why?

Media and American Democracy

Media outlets perform three essential functions in a democratic system: They provide information, act as a public watchdog, and help shape the political agenda. Let us take a closer look at all three.

Providing Information

First, media coverage *informs the public*. Without media bridging the gap, the public would be ignorant of most political events: Most of us cannot attend sessions of Congress, the Supreme Court, or our local city or town council—much less keep track of the thousands of policy issues and public problems that we face each year. When the media does its job well, we are more informed voters, more avid politics watchers, and more engaged citizens. And while social media enables proliferation of millions of voices, it is traditional national media sources—CNN and Fox News, the *New York Times* and *Wall Street Journal*, regional or local news organizations—that provide much of the content that Americans absorb.

Are there limits to this information-providing role? Imagine that you are a Republican with lots of Democratic friends. You come across a detailed news article that crushes one of their cherished beliefs. You send it to them with a snide comment—and what happens? Rather than changing their minds, the story strengthens what they already believe. New information rarely influences people who have strongly held opinions. Instead, new information reinforces existing views, regardless of the story's content.[12]

However, new items can have an impact on people who have not made up their minds. About a third of the public does not have strong political views and is less likely to follow the news. This group *is* open to influence by the media. Here is a paradox: The news media is most likely to influence the people who pay the least attention to it. Because this group does not follow politics and government very closely, only news stories with a **loud signal** are likely to reach them and influence their views.

Loud signal: Media stories with very broad coverage and an unambiguous message.

Watching Political Leaders

Second, the media is a **public watchdog**, scrutinizing government officials for mistakes, corruption, lies, and lawbreaking. Is a candidate misleading the public? Reporters keep careful score.

Public watchdog: Media coverage that alerts the public when a problem arises in politics or society.

The *Washington Post*'s fact checker examines politicians' words and ranks misstatements on a scale of one (mildly misleading) to four (a whopper) Pinocchios. Most politicians quietly walked back statements that got tagged with four Pinocchios—until President Trump came to office. He racked up more than twenty thousand false or misleading statements across four years in the White House, and almost gleefully repeated them when the *Post* ratings came out. That led the newspaper to add a new category: The "bottomless Pinocchio" marks a statement with three or four Pinocchios repeated at least twenty times. While Trump was an extreme case, most public figures exaggerate or shade the truth. For example, the *Post* slapped President Joe Biden with four Pinocchios for claiming that his inflation-fighting plan would save American households $500 annually off utility bills.[13]

Complaints about media coverage are nothing new, but serving as a watchdog for democracy has become especially difficult amid the politicization of news sources, disagreement over the facts, and shouts of "fake news." Journalists themselves worry that the rise of social media has diminished their profession. Three in four consider inaccurate news on social media platforms a "very big problem."[14] Even so, facts are stubborn and, over time, hard to evade. A sinking economy, a video of police brutality, or a war going badly can hurt incumbents—from mayors to presidents—regardless of how their followers spin it.

Shaping the Political Agenda

Editors and reporters have enormous influence on what Americans think *about*. Media executives listen to the political din and pluck out one or two stories to headline and a dozen others for the second tier. Those become the topics that politicians address, Congress investigates, talk shows debate, and you discuss and post and retweet. When an issue commands widespread attention, we say it is on the political agenda, also known as the **policy agenda**. The first step toward political action is to get your issue—homelessness, immorality, animal cruelty, whatever— onto the policy agenda, which often requires the attention of the news media.

Setting the agenda is one of the most important influences the news media has on American politics. Politicians, think tanks, interest groups, citizens, and experts all try to influence the agenda, but issues sometimes arise seemingly out of nowhere.

In May 2022, reports of a shortage of infant formula (a milk substitute fed to babies under a year old) in several U.S. states exploded into a major news agenda item. The shortage was due to COVID-related supply chain issues and the largest U.S. formula manufacturer temporarily shutting down production at its largest plant over safety concerns.[15] Eventually the shortage ended, but for several weeks baby formula was atop the policy agenda. As we will see in Chapter 17, getting onto the agenda is only the first step in responding to a problem.

Does the public attend to an issue because the media covers it? Or does the media cover an issue because the public is interested? In a classic study, two political scientists asked participants what issues they thought were most important. Then the researchers broke the participants into groups and, over four days, gave each group a tailored version of the nightly news emphasizing different issues—pollution, defense, inflation, and so forth. For the most part, the issues that the participants saw on the news became more important in their own minds.[16] When the media focuses on an issue, its importance—or salience—generally rises in public perception.

The media's focus on some stories and not others affects public perceptions of policy issues, political candidates, and public officials. This influence is known as **priming**. For example, because the Republican Party generally supports smaller government, stories about government incompetence prime the public to see the world through Republican eyes. Stories about the plight of the elderly or hard-working poor people prime voters to think along Democratic Party lines.

There are many ways to cover an issue, and each offers a slightly different perspective. When a media outlet emphasizes a particular slant, it is **framing** an issue. Consider how different outlets covered President Biden's national address following the terrible Robb Elementary School

Policy agenda: The issues that the media covers, the public considers important, and politicians address. Setting the agenda is the first step in political action.

Priming: Affecting public perceptions of political leaders, candidates, or issues by reporting on topics in ways that either enhance or diminish support.

Framing: The way an issue is defined; every issue has many possible frames, each with a slightly different tilt in describing the problem and highlighting solutions.

● *Issues can fly up the policy agenda when they are promoted by political leaders or interest groups—and amplified by media coverage. Or agenda items can arise from unexpected events—like a national shortage of infant formula.*

mass shootings in Uvalde, Texas, in May 2022. Conservatives watching Fox News heard Laura Ingraham condemn the president as "selfish" and conniving: Biden "spoke tonight because . . . in today's twisted world, it's considered perfectly appropriate to exploit the massacre of innocent little kids in order to try to turn around your own sagging poll numbers. . . . This attempt at political resuscitation on Biden's part, it's despicable." At an ABC studio nearby, the coverage emphasized the president's humanity and the symbols of his powerful office: "A clearly emotional President Biden spoke to the nation from the White House Roosevelt Room . . . about two hours after ordering, from Air Force One, that the flag flying above the White House be lowered to half-staff."[17] The same address, broadcast live to millions—and two dramatically different frames.

Often, media framing is invisible to the public because it reflects the dominant social values of the time. The issue of equality was once framed as a problem concerning white men: Could they achieve the American dream in an industrial system devoted to profits? Later, mass social movements reframed the issue as one that spoke directly to race, ethnicity, and gender. Today, it is often framed to emphasize the hurdles facing younger people—like college debt and diminished opportunities—as well as unequal treatment of Black Americans, especially at the hands of the police. Different times, different frames.

In short, framing defines the nature of the problem, organizes potential solutions, and, perhaps most important of all, sidelines alternative policies. A lesson all political leaders learn quickly: If you are not actively shaping the terms of debate, your opponents will. One academic article's title puts it perfectly: "Frame or Get Framed."[18] Media coverage plays a crucial role—often, *the* crucial role—in issue framing. One big question today: With hundreds of potential "framers" commenting across multiple platforms about every event, and sometimes adding entirely or mostly false spins, whose frame prevails?

THE BOTTOM LINE

» A vast change is underway in media formats, driven by rapid technological advancement.

» Media outlets continue to perform essential democratic functions: providing information, acting as "watchdogs" to protect the public trust, shaping what news is reported (agenda setting), setting the context for a topic (priming), and describing it in specific ways (framing). This work has grown more difficult amid regular "fake news" criticism and fast-multiplying outlets.

U.S. Media Today: Traditional Formats Are Declining

Media technology changes quickly, and each change remakes the connections between citizens and their leaders. The media affects the news we get, the arguments we hear, and the deliberations we engage in.

Where People Go for News

Your grandparents' choices were simple: Tune in or not. Fifty years ago, three national TV networks and the daily paper all delivered essentially the same news to an audience with few options for challenging (or even responding to) reporters' coverage. Most households subscribed to one newspaper. The networks delivered the news once a day. Today, there are choices galore. New technologies—and the giant Internet companies that invent and manage them—give Americans a host of options that challenge media, government, and society.

As Figure 9.1 shows, digital sources are replacing traditional media, but the media you consume depends on how old you are. Overall, some 40 percent of the public say they often get their news from television (split between cable, network, and local outlets), 33 percent from social media, and just over 20 percent from newspapers or their websites. Look, especially, at the breakdown by age. People over sixty-five overwhelmingly watch cable or network news (each over 50 percent) and consume local newspapers, in print or on the web (33 percent). In contrast, people under thirty turn to social media (41 percent), with YouTube and news websites coming next, at 27 percent each.

What are the implications of this shifting media world? Social media organizations such as Facebook or Instagram generally do not do their own reporting: They rely on traditional news sources, partisan sites, and public comments. Other media formats include podcasts, crowdfunded reporting, and multimedia platforms. Some, like the popular *Serial* podcasts, mix digital media and tell their stories with short videos, letters, maps, and other clues online. Contemporary media eliminate traditional gatekeepers such as producers and editors from deciding which issues receive priority coverage.

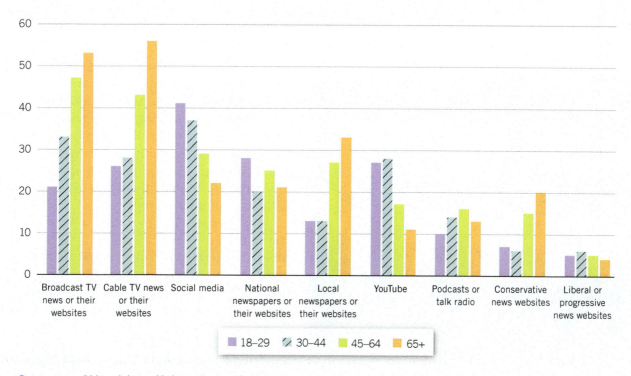

● **FIGURE 9.1** *Older adults are likely to rely on TV for their news, while adults under thirty are more likely to use social media to get their news. (YouGov/Economist poll, April 2022)*

What does this fast-changing landscape mean for the media, for politics, and for democracy? We can learn more by focusing on developments in each of the major media.

Newspapers and Magazines: Rise and Decline

Newspapers helped birth American democracy. The *Federalist Papers* (vital commentaries on our Constitution) first appeared as articles in the *New York Independent Journal*. George Washington subscribed to ten newspapers. His most famous statement, the Farewell Address, was actually a letter addressed to his "fellow citizens" and printed in the papers.

Mass media: Information and entertainment for broad popular audiences including newspapers, magazines, radio, and television.

In the 1830s, newspapers became the first **mass media**—just when the vote expanded to include all white men. Papers cost a penny and reflected the raucous, highly partisan, and often corrupt politics of the era. The *New York Herald* gave readers exactly what they wanted—murder, fire, suicide, and crime. The sensational journalism disgusted the old elites but made the *Herald* the most widely read newspaper in the world. One rival, the *New York Daily Tribune*, featured weekly articles by Karl Marx on European events.

Newspaper influence grew steadily. The Spanish-American War, in 1898, is known as the first media-driven war because banner headlines blamed Spain for sinking an American battleship in Havana Harbor (there was no evidence for the charge) and helped bully the McKinley administration into the conflict. By the turn of the twentieth century, there were more than 2,200 newspapers in the United States.[19] Even after the rise of radio and television, newspapers remained the major source for political information. A typical metropolitan newspaper ran seventy stories in a day, including national, local, and business news—add sports and society features and the total ran to more than a hundred. By contrast, the half-hour television news had time for only ten or twelve stories. Now, after more than two centuries at the center of the news media, the newspaper is waning, with news magazine circulation falling as well. The advertisers who once guaranteed profits have migrated to the Internet, and so have many readers—except for those over sixty-five.

The result is a dramatic decline in big-city newspapers. Newspapers have lost half their staff and 62 percent of their revenue since 2008.[20] Many simply stopped printing and moved online—or shut down altogether. Occasionally an "angel investor" comes along—Jeff Bezos, the Amazon founder, spent $250 million in 2013 to buy the *Washington Post*—but such investments are rare.

Local and state news, once a newspaper staple, has fallen on hard times. In Nebraska, Missouri, Virginia, and other states, more than a quarter of the reporters covering the statehouse are high school or college students—sometimes doing assignments for class.[21]

Radio Holds Steady

The first commercial radio stations began airing in the 1920s. President Franklin Roosevelt seized the new technology during

● *Franklin Roosevelt used a new medium—radio—to speak directly to citizens in their homes. One result: the rise of the personal presidency. As with social media today, a shift in media form helped introduce a change in politics.*

the Great Depression of the 1930s and delivered weekly radio addresses known as "fireside chats." The talks were informal, as if the president were talking to his listeners right by their own firesides. Hearing Roosevelt's voice personalized the relationship between Americans and their president. Indeed, political scientists link this development to the rise of the **personal presidency**.

The radio also gave new immediacy to wartime reports during World War II— and to baseball games. It accelerated the velocity of news and information. The medium made the nation, and the world, a smaller place. Radio's golden era lasted just thirty years. By the mid-1950s, television had become king. However, radio still has a role in national politics.

Conservative Talk. Conservative talk radio arose in the late 1980s after the Reagan administration cleared the way (we discuss the government connection later in this chapter). After Rush Limbaugh—a talented, pugnacious host— syndicated his daily talk show, a stream of fellow conservatives followed him onto the airwaves. Limbaugh pioneered the argument that became an article of conservative faith: The rest of the media is biased, so dial in here. Liberals tried to counter with their own talk shows, but their efforts largely foundered, perhaps because liberals are less likely to complain about media bias. One place to find political balance on radio: the satellite subscription service Sirius XM. Twenty channels are dedicated to politics—including large media outlets like CNN and Fox News.

Public Radio. Public radio has a large presence in the United States. National Public Radio's (NPR) audience is an estimated fifty-three million weekly, across both traditional and digital platforms.[22] Roughly 15 percent of NPR's funds come from the federal government, prompting ferocious criticism from conservatives, who argue that taxpayers should not be supporting "liberal" radio shows. Supporters respond that rural areas often have no other source of radio news. (Independent rating agencies have traditionally labeled NPR as "centrist"—though recent rankings have pegged it as "leaning left.")[23]

Podcasts. Podcasts are the fastest growing media format and offer a fresh source of news and investigative stories. Podcasts with the largest audience include the *Joe Rogan Experience*, which mixes news and entertainment; the *New York Times*'s daily update, *The Morning*; and *Crime Junkie*, which relies on the same formula that made the penny newspapers successful two centuries ago.[24] The rise of digital streaming radio—up from 15 percent of listening hours in 2013 to 40 percent today—has also helped keep radio relevant.

Television: From News to Infotainment

Television burst onto the American scene in the 1950s and revolutionized both entertainment and politics. President John F. Kennedy sensed TV's power and gave the first live press conference in February 1961. An incredible sixty-five million people—one in three Americans—tuned in. The young, charismatic president was a natural TV performer, and, once again, a new media technology intensified the link between the people and their president. Two networks, CBS and NBC, monopolized the television news business during the 1960s and 1970s. Interested Americans all watched the same version of the day's events, solemnly read during the evening news shows by celebrated anchors. ABC News rose in the latter 1970s to make it one of the "Big Three" networks. Then technology broke their monopoly.

Personal presidency: The idea that the president has a personal link to the public. Made initially possible by twentieth-century media.

Cable.   Cable stations began airing in the 1970s and attracted small slices of the network audience. They lingered on the fringe of the media until 1991, when an upstart named Cable News Network (CNN) remained on the ground during the Gulf War after the other broadcasters had fled. Viewers around the world watched the breakthrough live coverage of American rockets exploding into Baghdad, the capital of Iraq. CNN introduced a new model: It reported news all day long. No more waiting until 6 p.m. for the national network news. A new format was born: the twenty-four-hour news cycle. Thirty years ago, White House staff, and the reporters who covered them, all relaxed when the news cycle ended around 5 p.m. Today, the cycle never ends.

In 1996, Rupert Murdoch launched Fox News, a network with a conservative slant. As Republican viewers headed for Fox, other cable networks—most notably MSNBC—moved to the left and developed shows with a liberal spin. Eventually, cable channels filled every niche along the political spectrum—from *Hannity* on the right to the *Rachel Maddow Show* on the left. As households switched to cable, politicians began to speak only to members of their own party. President Biden bemoaned the polarization on cable TV in a 2022 news conference, warning that cable news would see declining viewers as a result.[25]

Is Biden right? As many American households "unbundle" cable services and remove news channels, cable TV has indeed seen ratings fall. Most cable channels are scrambling to keep audiences engaged by streaming their programs online, as well as posting clips and other content on social media.[26]

Infotainment.   As cable channels proliferated, the line between news and entertainment began to evaporate. Late-night talk shows got into the political act. Hosts gleefully lacerated the political losers of the day. Politicians, on both sides of the aisle, responded by lining up as on-air guests: Since Bill Clinton played his saxophone on the *Arsenio Hall Show* in 1992, every major presidential candidate has made the rounds.

Infotainment: The blurred line between news and entertainment.

Today news and entertainment, once strictly separate, have blurred into the hybrid known as **infotainment**. Overall, the TV picture reflects the state of the entire American media. A broadly shared view of the world, as interpreted by the nightly network news, has shattered. TV now runs the gamut from left to right and from formal news to frothy entertainment.

Scholars and media executives both raise the same alarm: The very idea of news—a report of events that occurred in the nation and the world—has shattered into entirely different accounts from different political perspectives. When Congress held high-profile hearings on the January 6 insurrection, reporters for mainstream media described the events in dramatic fashion. Most national TV networks carried the hearings live, with more than thirty million Americans tuning in. Reporters described testimony about "an unhinged former president" exhibiting "bizarre and violent behavior" while in the White House.[27] Fox News elected not to televise most of the hearings and dismissed them as "unfiltered propaganda" about a "forgettably minor

● *President Biden discusses gun control and the 2022 midterm election on Jimmy Kimmel's late-night show.*

outbreak" and "a TV smear campaign . . . a sham."[28] As the clash between outlooks grows louder and news merges into infotainment, a danger grows: Americans pay less attention, lose interest in politics, and stop participating.[29]

The Rise of Social Media

The Internet introduced one of the great communications revolutions in history. It was developed by a network of scholars, beginning in the 1960s, with primary funding from the U.S. Department of Defense, the National Science Foundation, and others. In 1995, less than 1 percent of the global population was online; three decades later, almost two-thirds of the world (5.3 billion people) has reliable Internet access.[30]

Until fifteen years ago, following politics online meant clicking on websites of mainstream media outlets. In 2006, a Harvard dorm-room startup, originally known as "The Facebook," morphed into the first social media platform, followed quickly by Twitter (later in 2006) and Instagram (2010). Political news accelerated to warp speed.

There is much to celebrate about engaging with political information online. You can click a Twitter link and read content from, say, the *Wall Street Journal*; post it with a comment on Instagram or TikTok; debate classmates in a Zoom chat room; and screen-share a YouTube clip posted by an eyewitness. The user, not an editor or producer, chooses the material. Users can respond, share, network, and learn more—often through multiformat platforms.

Worries About the News Media Today

Media analysts raise three concerns about media today. First, although social media platforms aggregate news and provide background, links, and multiple perspectives, most stories are still developed by traditional reporters. As large news organizations decline, there are fewer reporters to dig up the news. One report describes mainstream media organizations, with their large staffs of seasoned reporters, as a "few mountain springs of quality journalism." Some mainstream news organizations are thriving, but they now put their content behind paywalls. Most people (85 percent) do not choose to pay for this reporting. What information are they getting?[31]

Second, important stories get lost. Local media—newspapers, local TV news—always covered the "hot" topics (war, murder, and high school sports) along with less exciting civic issues (such as school board meetings and wetland controversies). Because everything was bundled together into one package, the popular stories paid for the civics lessons. As mainstream media, especially local newspapers, downsize staff and try to sell stories by the piece online, there may be no way to subsidize coverage on limited-interest (but very important) issues such as local education. This is especially true in rural areas—more than 1,800 American communities that now have no local news source, and are known as "news deserts."[32] A related concern: Traditional media must generate ever more dramatic headlines to keep up with the **"clickbait,"** dulling audiences' attention to complicated policy stories. Political scientists who study media report that this effect is particularly strong among the millennial and Gen Z generations.[33]

Clickbait: Alluring content online designed to encourage users to click on a link to explore further.

Third, traditional media included a variety of viewpoints. Conservative and liberal columnists tended to appear side by side on the op-ed page; pundits from left and right served on the same Sunday morning news show panel. Most Americans no longer receive this balanced news diet. Social media companies deploy algorithms (or individuals configure their social media feeds) to filter stories based on viewer preferences, emphasizing newsfeed items that fit a user's worldview.[34] The result: Each of us inhabits a shrinking "echo chamber," encountering mainly news that fuels our existing views and prejudices.

As diverse viewpoints disappear, **fake news**—stories that are made up, or twisted to promote a particular viewpoint—is on the rise. Malicious individuals, unwitting reposters, automatic bots, and troll farms all spread falsehood. Facebook removes more than six *billion* fake accounts from its site each year.[35] That makes it easy for politicians to dismiss any unwelcome news as "fake." (Many candidates for Congress in 2022, for example, ritually denounced Donald Trump's very real defeat in the 2020 presidential election as "fake news.") Americans express concern about misinformation both online and offline.[36] Of course, most do not believe that they are spreading fake news themselves (Figure 9.2).

Fake news: The deliberate spread of falsehood or misinformation, aided by proliferating social media sites; also a charge leveled by politicians against unfavorable stories.

Things to Cheer About the News Media Today

The rise of digital and social media, and other aspects of today's media landscape, has positive aspects as well. Social media turns us into activists. We all become potential news providers, and that, in turn, brings crucial stories out of the shadows.

Traditional news always awaited the arrival of a camera team or reporters. Now people record events on their phones, post to social media platforms, and watch their story go viral. Black activists had long complained about police practices. But when citizens whipped out their phones and began to record horrors that had rarely been captured by traditional news teams, Black Lives Matter exploded into a national movement.

Likewise, new technologies enable us to trace events that were much harder to track when people simply talked on landlines. The summer 2022 U.S. House Select Committee investigation into the January 6 insurrection, broadcast in prime time to an audience of tens of millions, featured scores of video clips of the Capitol rioting, along with public officials' texts or email trails that connected them to scandalous revelations, including that many House Republicans sought pardons from President Trump after their actions and posts that day.

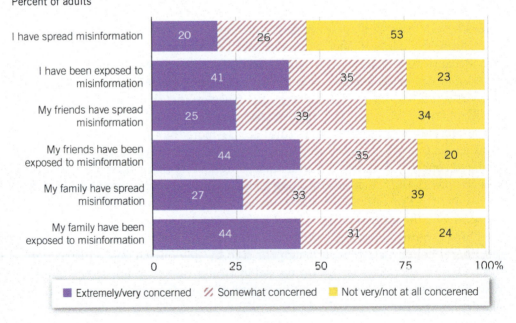

Many Americans are concerned about exposure to misinformation.
Percent of adults

● **FIGURE 9.2** *Proportion of Americans who are concerned about misinformation. (Associated Press/Pearson Institute/NORC).*

» Thirty years ago, a few outlets—three networks, a weekly news magazine, and the local newspaper—delivered roughly the same news. Today, media outlets cater to every perspective—left, right, and center. Americans no longer share a single source of news.

» Previous waves of rising "new" media—newspapers, radio, and television—changed the nature of news reporting and altered political institutions such as the presidency.

» Today all of these now-traditional institutions are in serious decline. Newspapers, news magazines, and network and local television are all losing ground as the place Americans go for news. Internet sources, especially social media platforms, are taking their place—especially among young people.

» The rise of social media raises several major concerns, including: Do the benefits—everyone's ability to contribute to "news" and increased transparency—outweigh losing traditional reporting sources and the rising incidence of "fake news"? Will these more democratic formats find large audiences, or are we too fragmented into individual niches? And can the news media invent revenue sources—besides paywalls that remove information from the mass public—that enable them to cover vital but sometimes obscured stories, especially about local issues?

Is the Media Biased?

Republicans have long complained about media bias, dating back to the 1964 presidential election when conservative GOP candidate Barry Goldwater handed out pins to reporters reading "Eastern Liberal Press."[37] The proliferation of news sources now makes those charges stick: There *is* a good deal of "fake news" circulating—on all points of the political spectrum.

But does that mean all media are suspect? Supporters of the major parties see it differently: 68 percent of Democrats have at least "a fair amount of trust" in the mass media (see Figure 9.3). On the other side, Republicans give the media a thumbs down: A bare 11 percent have confidence in it. Among Republicans, trust has fallen by nearly two-thirds since the 2016 election. Well, who is right? What *can* we say about bias in the media?

Are Reporters Politically Biased?

Conservatives are half right about the press corps' personal attitudes. Mainstream media reporters are less likely to identify as conservative (22 percent, in a 2020 study) than the national population (around 36 percent). Most call themselves independent, especially those in local media, where the number runs well above 60 percent.[38]

Scholars have searched for bias in campaign coverage and in the types of news stories that are aired. Most studies fail to show a systematic bias among mainstream media reporters. Perhaps reporters' views creep into their framing of

Americans' Trust in Mass Media, by Political Party

In general, how much trust and confidence do you have in the mass media—such as newspapers, TV, and radio—when it comes to reporting the news fully, accurately and fairly? A great deal, a fair amount, not very much, or none at all?

% Great deal/Fair amount

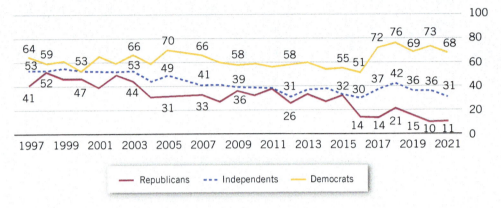

● **FIGURE 9.3** *Trust in U.S. media. Republicans have long been skeptical—but the numbers have plummeted since the 2016 election. More than half of Democrats have shown some trust across more than twenty years. (Gallup)*

which issues matter? Researchers find no reliable evidence to suggest that policy frames in mainstream media systematically favor liberal views. A detailed empirical study from 2020 was bluntly titled: "There Is No Liberal Media Bias in Which News Stories Political Journalists Choose to Cover." A more recent study found that reporters for mainstream outlets tend to exhibit a "centrist bias"—skewing neither liberal nor conservative, but featuring a "both sidesism"—including in their reporting experts representing both left- and right-wing views.[39]

What about the left-wing claim that corporate ownership encourages journalists to favor the status quo and avoid hard-hitting stories on poverty, marginalized people, or radical social movements? One well-known political science study found that news organizations that stood to benefit financially from legislation (the 1996 Telecommunications Act) covered the act more favorably than outlets realizing no financial gain. Other research demonstrates that newspapers tend to run content biased in favor of advertisers.[40] But a pervasive inclination to ignore less well-off Americans in favor of the wealthy and powerful? A raft of scholarship has turned up no such practice among mainstream media organizations. There *is* hard evidence of a much deeper bias that runs through the news media—the need to attract a larger audience. Media organizations' principal bias arises in their core purpose: attracting coverage and making money. Media outlets print or say or film with an eye to drawing an audience.

Profits Drive the News Industry

What does the media actually sell? The answer is not the news about politics or elections, or anything else. Media sells its audience to advertisers. As a result, the prime directive is to expand the audience. When ratings rise, the business prospers; when they fall, networks replace anchors and newspapers cut staff. As Sam Zell, former CEO of the media giant Tribune Company, bluntly said to his reporters: "You need to help me by being a journalist who focuses on what readers want and therefore generates more revenue."[41]

These financial realities give the traditional news media a strong incentive to pitch its own politics near the views of its audience. For the large networks, that means the political center, where most Americans have been most comfortable.[42]

Hence, people on both the left and right complain about bias; the center—where most stories are in fact pitched—*is* to the left of conservatives and to the right of liberals.

But as the large networks and national newspapers decline, every kind of media seeks its own audience. As the media fragments, conservatives go to conservative sources, liberals to liberal ones. The market forces that once drove news coverage to the center now push to the left and right (Figure 9.4).

Drama Delivers Audiences

Journalists find it relatively difficult to generate audience excitement about a school board meeting or a healthcare proposal. Miners trapped below the earth: *That* pulls people to their televisions and Twitter feeds. A good drama must have a narrative arc with a beginning, middle, and end. It should have a protagonist (the miners), pathos (anxious spouses and children), a villain (the coal company or government regulators), drama (will they be rescued before they run out of air?), an ending (tired but jubilant miners hugging their families), and a take-home message (we need to worry about mine safety).

Do not be fooled by the little moral lesson at the end of the episode. Real mine safety raises complicated—and potentially boring—policy issues that will not attract much of an audience. You can be sure that when the state legislature debates mine safety, the cameras and reporters will be off chasing the next hot story.

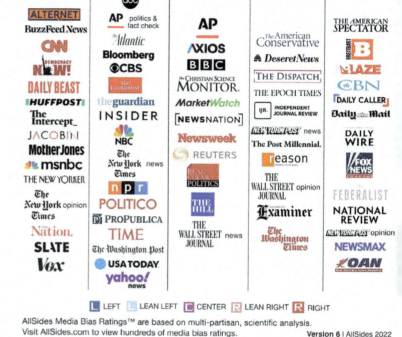

FIGURE 9.4 *Left, Right, and Center. The political slant of the top online media sources. How many have you read? (All Sides, 2022)*

Local news gets much of its drama from crime. A classic rule of thumb guides the local TV news: "If it bleeds, it leads." Many good things may have happened that day, but the lead story will feature the most grisly event. The images are familiar to the point of cliché—a breathless reporter live on the scene, yellow tape blocking the area, grim-faced cops or firefighters in the background, weeping relatives in a daze, and perhaps a blank-faced perpetrator blinking into the camera.

The need for drama also pushes every site and publication to hype its stories as major breaks. Stations—left, right, and center—report their news flashes and breaking news. It may come with a political spin, but the biggest pressure is to grab eyeballs for the advertisers.

The need for drama transforms election coverage as well. Election reporting rarely focuses on the issues—an audience turnoff. Instead, the dramatic spotlight is on the protagonists, their families, their strategies, their dirty tricks, and their blunders. Elections have a built-in narrative arc, just like every other drama: a *beginning* (the candidates throw their hats into the ring), an extended *middle* (who is ahead? who had the best week?), a *conclusion* (someone wins), and a *take-home message* (the loser had a fatal flaw that other candidates should avoid). Donald Trump brilliantly mastered the art of winning the media spotlight—his rivals struggled to get airtime. By 2020, that skill boomeranged on President Trump,

● *Conflict sells. In the wake of the death of George Floyd at the hands of Minnesota police, news outlets ran stories about protests and riots across the country. A burning building—here in Minneapolis—draws a lot more attention than a dozen peaceful protests.*

who found that grabbing the spotlight was no help amid a series of crises. Joe Biden surged into the presidency maintaining a relatively low profile, after turning the election into a referendum on Trump. During Biden's presidency, the tables turned again. A new media narrative featured a presidency imperiled by crises (rising crime rates, the frantic U.S. military pullout from Afghanistan, rampant inflation), culminating in a predicted 2022 midterm "red wave" of GOP gains. Instead, Biden's party performed well, calming Democrats' concerns that a weak president should not seek reelection in 2024.[43]

Political debates—whether about the environment, gun rights, education, or inflation—generally reflect the same pressure to build a narrative. Regardless of the issue, media coverage focuses on drama and conflict, heroes and villains, winners and losers. This tendency exacerbates media bias. For example, despite a dramatic drop in U.S. crime rates across the first two decades of this century, most Americans believed that crime was actually rising—and when crime ticked up in 2021–22, perceptions far outstripped reality.[44] The constant coverage, on local and national news alike (Fox News described American cities as "apocalyptic hellscapes" of crime in early 2022, for example),[45] misleads viewers to imagine that criminals are running rampant everywhere.

Click on your favorite news website. Can you see the dramatic narrative that frames the lead story? Pundits criticize media stories for lacking substance. However, as a student of political science, you have learned to examine the *institution* and its incentives. The media, seeking an audience to serve up to advertisers, covers whatever attracts the most attention. Simply calling for more serious coverage will not change the incentives built into the media market.

Investigative "Bias"

Other media biases have less to do with the market and more with the profession of journalism. Two are especially powerful: *skepticism* and *fairness*. Back in the early 1960s, Washington reporters were a small, white, male club with a code that winked at extramarital affairs in the White House or falling-down drunks in Congress. Then a series of events transformed the media's stance toward powerful men and women: The moral intensity of the civil rights movement, administration efforts to manipulate the press during the Vietnam War, and the **Watergate scandal** all made the old accommodations seem irresponsible. How could reporters go easy on segregationists or liars?

Watergate was especially significant in fostering skepticism. Reporters investigated a burglary of Democratic Party headquarters that led directly to the White House. President Nixon had secretly taped conversations in the Oval Office, and while pursuing the case of the botched burglary, the Supreme Court forced the release of the tapes. Their content stunned Americans. Now the public could hear their president order aides to "stonewall" the Watergate investigations. Even more shocking, the presidential tapes bristled with ethnic slurs, anti-Semitism, and foul language. (The newspaper transcripts were full of the notation "expletive deleted.")

Watergate scandal:
A failed effort in 1972 by Republican operatives to break into Democratic Party headquarters in the Watergate office complex in Washington, DC. President Nixon tried to cover up the event, eventually causing him to resign from the presidency.

In response, reporters redefined their roles. Rather than acting as chummy insiders, they became skeptics, aiming to pierce through official propaganda and find the hidden truth. Media emphasizing their "watchdog" function led relations between the press and politicians to turn more adversarial. Each time the members of the press felt misled by an administration, their skepticism grew. For example, George W. Bush insisted that Iraq owned dangerous weapons that threatened the United States. (It did not.) Barack Obama promised Americans, "If you like your health plan, you can keep it." (Not all could.) Media outlets kept a running tally of President Trump's false or misleading statements—beginning with the size of his inaugural crowd. In the new environment, the reporter's mission became uncovering lies and bad behavior.

The Fairness Bias

The effort to be fair introduces an unexpected bias. Reporters energetically try to present both sides of each issue. However, when issues do not have two equal sides, the effort creates the impression of a debate that does not exist. Companies that market tobacco, unhealthy foods, or toxic products, for example, have learned that they do not need to win the debate. They simply sponsor research and announce that there are two sides to the issue. The fairness bias then leads the media to report the two sides as equivalent—even if one of the sides was manufactured by an interested party.

Ultimately, political scientists' findings that mainstream media outlets are not politically biased clashes with the strongly held perception among conservatives that the media is organized against them. Nearly nine in ten Republicans say they don't trust mainstream media sources.[46] Rebuilding faith in the accurate flow of information that is essential to a free society: This is one of the great political challenges facing a rising generation of Americans.

WHAT DO YOU THINK?

Is the Media Objective? Should It Be?

After Congress repealed the fairness doctrine that forced media outlets to provide opposing viewpoints, some media sources began to cater to partisan audiences. Today, the only media organization trusted by more than 40 percent of Americans is the Weather Channel.[47] Many feel that the media is not doing a good job serving our democracy. Do you agree?	**Not enough objectivity.** Media organizations should serve as a platform for the expression of opposing views—vital to the democratic process. They also should do a better job of distinguishing facts from opinions to restore public trust in media—and other governing institutions.	**Enough objectivity.** Even though some media sources are partisan, people have access to a wide range of sources and viewpoints. I can gather a fuller picture of critical issues and arrive at a better interpretation of events by following multiple sources than by having someone else curate the facts for me.	**Too much objectivity.** Media reports too often bend over backward to give all sides a fair hearing. Journalists are very knowledgeable about politics; I want to hear their views, not just their "unbiased" recitation of facts and politicians' opinions.

THE BOTTOM LINE

» Both conservatives and liberals complain of media bias. However, the media generally reflects the centrist politics of its audience—which is to the left of conservatives and to the right of liberals.

» The media's deepest bias comes from its need to win ratings and appeal to advertisers. That puts an emphasis on drama, scandal, and conflict—exacerbating partisan political divisions.

» Media efforts to be objective and balanced can introduce their own biases, such as the effort to present two equal sides even if one is simply manufactured by an interested party.

 # How Governments Shape the Media

We have seen how technology constantly changes the media. Media reporting, in turn, changes politics. In this section, we examine how political rules shape the development of the media.

Democratic nations organize their media in three different ways: First, the *government can fund* media outlets. This **public ownership** model is familiar in many nations—but, for the most part, not the United States. Second, the government can *regulate* the media to ensure that it operates in the public interest. Third, the government can stand aside and let the *market* guide the media; the assumption of the market model is that private companies will give the people (and the advertisers) what they want.

Public ownership: A situation in which media outlets are run by the government and paid for by tax dollars.

The First Amendment Protects Print Media from Regulation

You have already encountered the primary political rule governing print media—the First Amendment: "Congress shall make no law . . . abridging the freedom of speech or of the press." As we saw in Chapter 5, the Supreme Court has been strict about forbidding government interference with the press. Compared to most peer nations, it is very difficult to censor news (a practice known as prior restraint), to convict someone of slander or libel (spoken or written lies), to restrict pornography, or to forbid hate speech. Reporters are also fierce in protecting their sources. A *New York Times* reporter, Judith Miller, went to jail for three months rather than reveal her source for a story about a CIA agent named Valerie Plame.[48]

Market forces and audience feedback impose the limits that do exist. American newspapers, paid for by local advertisers, generally reflect local mores. They are tame compared with, for example, the raucous English papers (it's much easier to sue for libel in England, as we discussed in Chapter 5). Web-based news outlets likewise reflect the outlook of their parent companies and of their audience. Social media consumers can respond swiftly to coverage they see as biased or inappropriate, through "comments" sections and by sharing or retweeting. When the gossipy site Gawker printed an article outing a gay Condé Nast executive, readers tweeted a torrent of objections, calling the story an unwarranted example of "gay shaming." Gawker soon removed the article.

Regulating Broadcasters

Radio and television fall into a separate category. They have been subject to government regulations from the start. As radio stations spread in the 1930s, their signals began to interfere with one another. In 1934, the Franklin Roosevelt administration created the Federal Communications Commission (FCC) to referee the industry. The agency was founded on a basic political philosophy: The airwaves belong to the public. The FCC would license stations on a given frequency—preventing signals from overlapping—but in exchange, stations were required to be "socially responsible." When a station secured or renewed its license, it had to show that it operated in the public's interest. When television emerged, the FCC expanded its jurisdiction to include it.

In 1949, the FCC issued an important regulation, the **fairness doctrine**. The fairness doctrine required radio and TV stations to give equal time to each side of a public issue. The rule reflected the era's expectations: sober, nonpartisan coverage of news and politics. Even though it was not strictly enforced, the fairness doctrine led stations to shy away from political controversies altogether; that way, they avoided the bother of achieving a balance.

In the 1980s, the Reagan administration challenged the entire idea of public responsibility enforced by regulatory agencies. It promoted a different political philosophy, viewing media as a private commodity rather than as a public good: End government regulations, they argued, and let consumers watch or hear whatever they want. The FCC repealed the fairness doctrine in 1983. The consequences were huge. Under the fairness doctrine, each talk show with a point of view had to be balanced by another talk show from the opposite perspective. A station that broadcast conservatives (such as Tucker Carlson, today) would be required to air an equal amount of liberal programming. Repealing the rule opened the door to the media landscape we have now: a rich and raucous menu of news and politics that reaches across the political spectrum.

Fairness doctrine: Regulation that required media outlets to devote equal time to opposite perspectives.

Regulating Social Media

Government regulation of social media is evolving as technology changes. TV and radio, as we saw above, are limited in their bandwidth—enabling government regulators to license the airwaves, and to place restrictions on what can be aired, even after the fairness doctrine was repealed. Social media posts have no bandwidth limitations—making their regulation much more difficult.

Why are some calling for government to step in? One main target is the algorithms used by social media companies to push often extreme, polarizing content to keep users scrolling as long as possible—driving up advertising dollars. Political science experts on social media note that "The more outrageous the content—the greater the profit opportunity."[49] Another, related concern is the sheer size of mega-firms like Meta (which owns Facebook, Instagram, and dozens of other technology companies).

Public officials could address the problems of extremist-fueling algorithms directly. Proposals before Congress would require media companies to adjust their algorithms to detect and flag false information. Social media firms insist that they are already doing so; Americans are mixed about whether they are doing enough. Should these giants be left alone to regulate themselves? Or should the federal government intervene and oversee them? (Figure 9.5).

A more powerful response: Break up the tech giants like Meta. Reformers designed anti-trust policy more than a century ago to stop powerful monopolies

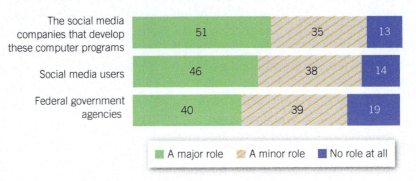

51% say social media companies should set standards for use of algorithms; 40% say federal agencies should

% of U.S. adults who say each of the following groups should play a major role in setting standards for how social media companies use computer programs to find false information on their sites

The social media companies that develop these computer programs: 51 (A major role), 35 (A minor role), 13 (No role at all)

Social media users: 46 (A major role), 38 (A minor role), 14 (No role at all)

Federal government agencies: 40 (A major role), 39 (A minor role), 19 (No role at all)

Legend: ■ A major role ▨ A minor role ■ No role at all

● **FIGURE 9.5** *Who should take the lead in regulating social media algorithms and finding false information? Notice how eight in ten people assign some role to all parties—the companies, the users, and the federal government. (Pew Trust Research, 2022)*

from dominating entire economic sectors. Today, leaders on both the left (like Senator Elizabeth Warren) and the right (Senator Ted Cruz) aim to turn anti-trust policy on the big media companies. Critics charge that the tech companies are too big, too dominant, and too powerful.

Worse, big tech gathers data (a *lot* of data) about you—ultimately to sell you things. But companies like Facebook or TikTok don't protect the personal information they collect. They have sold it to political consultants and shared it with law enforcement. To sum up opponents' fears: The big social media companies are part of the most extensive surveillance system in human history.

Local News: Most Trusted . . . and Fading Away?

Americans of all political backgrounds—left, right, center—trust their local news sources more than national outlets (Figure 9.6). Republicans are especially suspicious of national news, with trust levels tumbling to 5 percent by 2021.[50]

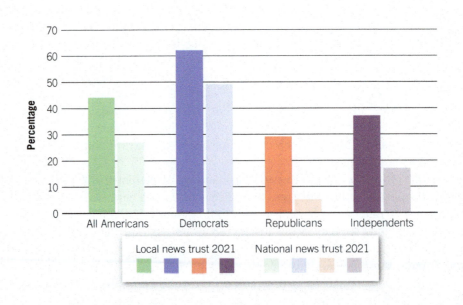

● **FIGURE 9.6** *Overall, 44 percent of Americans indicate trust in local media, seventeen percentage points higher than trust levels for national media (27 percent). (Gallup/Knight Foundation)*

Why do people trust the local news so much more than national outlets? Seventy-eight percent of respondents in one poll indicated that local news provides "information you need to get involved in your community," and 60 percent agreed that local reports supply "information you can use in your daily life." National media scored higher than local on only one dimension, "give enough attention to the important issues," by 32 percent to 28 percent.[51]

Local news may be more popular, but it's struggling. Nearly 2,200 local newspapers have closed in the past two decades, around a quarter of all the papers in the country. Similarly, many smaller independent radio stations have either been bought by giants like Clear Channel or gone out of business.[52]

Disappearing Local Outlets

The Collapse of Local Reporting

Americans trust local media more than national outlets, and rely on their hometown newspapers and TV stations to confirm what's happening in their own neighborhoods. However, changing business models are driving local newsrooms and TV studios to slash their workforce.

THINK ABOUT IT

With fewer reporters covering local stories, where can residents of "news deserts" turn for information?

....

If many Americans outside major metropolitan areas now rely on social media and Internet sites, what concerns does this trend raise?

....

How would you imagine Americans reversing this decline in town and city reporting?

Source: Report for America

THE BOTTOM LINE

» Democratic nations organize their media in three ways: government ownership, regulation, and markets. The United States has historically relied on the latter two models: regulation and markets.

» The First Amendment protects print media from most government regulation.

» Broadcast media in the United States was originally regulated by agencies such as the FCC, which imposed the fairness doctrine—a reflection of a less partisan era.

» The issue of control has become especially salient with the rise of the social network giants. Critics charge them with violating privacy, permitting malicious content, and stifling competition.

» Critics on both left and right have begun to suggest using anti-trust policy to break up the big tech companies.

» Deregulation, new technologies, and the rise of multiple media have created the spectrum of perspectives and views that mark American media today. Although local sources are more widely trusted than national, more and more communities have seen their newspapers close and local TV news hollowed out. This contributes to our partisan and conflicted politics.

 # Media Around the World

The American media is different from that of other nations. (Have you noticed how many times we have said that about American politics?) The "watchdog" tradition, combined with near-absolute freedom of the press to write or say what they wish, is stronger in the United States than in most other countries. Most nations also began with government-operated broadcast media—the one option the United States has barely pursued apart from small subsidies to public television (PBS) and radio (NPR). However, the differences may be eroding. The American media has gone global, and in some countries, leaders complain about the "Americanization" of their media—moving from public to private ownership.

Government-Owned Stations

When radio developed in the 1920s, leaders in many democratic nations worried about the new medium's potential power. What if demagogues seized the airwaves? Rather than leave radio and, later, television programming to private entrepreneurs, most democratic countries introduced public stations that were owned by the government and funded through taxes. To this day, the publicly owned BBC is the largest network in Britain, attracting 32 percent of the TV market; in contrast, the largest commercial network (ITV) draws 21 percent.[53] Most other democracies also have popular public stations; in many—Sweden, the Netherlands, Germany—they are cited by more than a third of the population as the most trusted source for news.[54] In 2022, the European Union and European Council provided monies to support the Public Broadcasting Company of Ukraine, in the face of Russian invasion and targeting of independent Ukrainian media.[55]

Now consider the United States, where public television draws barely 2 percent of the TV audience. Are there reasons to be concerned about private control of the airwaves in the United States? Or is this a fine example of the market at work? In many democratic countries, rising American-style commercial media has cultural figures concerned that the U.S. mix of infotainment and polarized news outlets will soon follow.[56]

Censorship

A different media model dominates authoritarian nations: The government directly controls the media and censors every story. Government censorship, limiting open information and political debate, has always been the tool of tyrants. Democracies can only operate with the free flow of ideas.[57]

Social media challenges the ability of authoritarian regimes to control information (see Comparing Nations 9.1). When the Internet is blocked, innovative networks can spring up to spread the news; new technologies permit people to receive content outside official channels. A key future question is whether (and how) citizens in authoritarian countries will successfully seize the democratic potential of digital media. Whatever the answer, the crucial link between media and popular government extends far beyond the United States to every nation.

COMPARING NATIONS 9.1   **Censorship Under Pressure?**

In advance of Russia's military invasion of neighboring Ukraine in February 2022, Russian premier Vladimir Putin stepped up pressure on domestic media, detaining as "foreign agents" reporters and editors critical of his regime. Russia's parliament passed a law soon after the invasion, allowing reporters who spread so-called fake news about Russia's military to be jailed for up to fifteen years. Brave journalists still denounced the war, most famously Marina Ovsyannikova, who disrupted a news broadcast with a sign denouncing the war in Ukraine.[58]

Along with stifling domestic media dissent, Putin's government sought to block Western news sources from reaching Russian masses. Media outlets around the world fought back: Scandinavian newspapers translated stories into Russian and posted them on social media; large outlets like the *New York Times* launched Telegram channels to provide Russians with access to their war coverage; and the U.S. government poured more than $5 million into funding virtual private networks (VPNs) that enabled Russians to evade censorship.[59]

● *Marina Ovsyannikova, an antiwar dissenter working at Channel One, Russia's most-watched news channel, bursts into the evening news with a sign condemning Vladimir Putin and the war in Ukraine. Ovsyannikova disappeared and supporters worried that she might be in jail—or dead. She eventually emerged and was fined 30,000 rubles (about 525 U.S. dollars).*

American Media in the World

American media industries have enormous reach. In one typical week in June 2022, *Jurassic World: Dominion* was the highest-grossing film in more than half the sixty-plus countries that report box-office receipts, including Norway, China, and Brazil; another twenty nations, including Bolivia, the United Arab Emirates, and Ukraine, were led by the animated animal-caper comedy *The Bad Guys*; the Disney hit *Doctor Strange in the Multiverse of Madness* led in Mexico, Germany, and New Zealand, among others; *Top Gun: Maverick*, the most popular movie worldwide in late May, was still on top in the United Kingdom and Japan; and the Viking thriller *The Northman* was box-office king in Egypt and Lebanon.[60] American television has a similarly wide influence, both in entertainment and in news. CNN is a staple on cable in virtually every corner of the world. The U.S. media model, with its emphasis on markets and consumer choice, has a major impact in both democracies and authoritarian nations.

Every nation has its own media style. Governments remain a major content provider (and regulator) in most industrial nations. Looking abroad illustrates how distinctive the U.S. model remains. Few other nations have organized a system of private entrepreneurs operating within a framework of very light (and heavily criticized) regulatory oversight.

THE BOTTOM LINE

» Rapidly changing media outlets link citizens to their politics around the world. An open media is vital to making democracy work.

» The American model of media as private enterprise is spreading. However, most other democracies retain more government regulation than the United States.

» Authoritarian nations censor their news reporters. Increasingly, social media is challenging government control of the news, but the censors are keeping pace.

The Media in Context: War, Terrorism, and U.S. Elections

Every aspect of the media's influence on politics is on display during two kinds of events: military conflicts and election campaigns. Many concepts we have discussed come together to shape the media coverage: framing issues, emphasizing drama, "infotainment," and the fragmenting of story lines in our social media age.

Covering Wars and Conflict

The NBC news team followed a young, clean-shaven military commander who was eager to show off his prize: He had captured an Iranian death squad working in Syria to prop up President Bashar al-Assad. This would be, they thought, a big story about Iranian involvement in the Syrian civil war. But as they drove into the countryside, their car was suddenly surrounded by gunmen toting AK-47s. The men dragged the team and their Syrian companions out of the cars, and threatened, terrorized, and beat them over the next days. Eventually, rebels seeking to rescue the journalists discovered their captive place. Of their party of nine, six got out alive. The team and their harrowing experience are part of an American tradition that goes back to the war with Mexico in 1846—and stretches forward to coverage of the Russian invasion of Ukraine.

Whenever the United States engages in (or supports) military conflicts, reporters are embedded with the troops. Mathew Brady's portraits of Civil War carnage helped establish photography's mass appeal; images from Vietnam spread doubts about that war. Conflict gives the media what it most looks for: drama. But questions

● CBS News reporter Holly Williams interviews Ukrainian soldiers fighting in eastern Ukraine. More than twenty members of the media were killed in the first three months of fighting, including a Fox News cameraman.

arise in every war about whether media is "sensationalizing" the conflict by providing gruesome images that grab the public eye—thereby reshaping perceptions of the war.

Inevitably, wartime coverage is controversial. Reporters try to tell audiences what's happening on the ground—aside from official accounts that are often spun for public relations. But it is not easy to get the story right: Wars are big, messy, and hard to assess standing on the battlefield. Do pictures of a firefight provide clarity? Or leave the wrong impression?

Moreover, reporters are embedded with troops, and their lives and livelihood are reliant on the men and women they are observing. They understandably bond with and admire the soldiers they cover. Can journalists be objective under these circumstances?

On the other hand, skeptical accounts can give "aid and comfort to America's enemies," as a U.S. general lamented darkly during the Vietnam conflict. Every war introduces horrors. In Vietnam, millions of people watched in revulsion as a South Vietnamese police chief strode into the camera's frame, pulled out his pistol, and shot a bound captive point-blank in the head. During the Iraq War, the media flashed horrific images of torture in a jail called Abu Ghraib. Do the images protect the United States by informing its citizens about the war? Or does it help the enemy by emphasizing terrible deeds and turning the public—at home and around the world—against the effort?

Media coverage of terrorist attacks—involving both foreign and domestic terrorists—raises similar questions about journalistic ethics. Some experts worry that extensive media coverage of terrorism may actually heighten the chance of a subsequent attack, as misguided individuals seek journalistic fame through terrible crimes. Should the Islamic State, for example, be given the media's "oxygen of publicity" for beheadings and other atrocious acts? How about white nationalist terrorists who murder people in the United States?

Political science research suggests that reporting inadvertently *does* lead to further terrorist acts. Separate studies of TV network and *New York Times* articles about terrorist attacks conclude that mainstream global coverage raises the

● *Stunning footage from the war zone. South Vietnamese police chief Nguyen Ngoc Loan strides into the television frame, lifts his firearm, and shoots a handcuffed Vietcong prisoner in the head (a). Americans torturing Iraqi prisoners at Abu Ghraib (b). Each image shocked Americans and turned public opinion against the wars.*

chances of another terrorist attack in relatively short order. The same appears to be true for school shootings and white nationalist violence.[61]

The Campaign as Drama

U.S. election campaigns involve political rather than armed conflicts, of course, but the media's influence is on display. As noted earlier, reporters cover electoral campaigns like horse races—obsessed with who will finish first. With the advent of digital media, the pace of information accelerates; one result is that now the coverage of presidential campaigns devotes much less time to the candidate's actual views. In 1968, the average clip of a candidate speaking on the news, called a **sound bite**, ran uninterrupted for over forty seconds. Today, the average clip has fallen to under eight seconds. After those few seconds, you might see the candidates gesture and move their lips: merely the backdrop for the anchor or pundit's analysis, which is often centered on (you guessed it!) why the candidate is winning or losing.

Candidates' own sound bites are increasingly compressed into Twitter or Instagram posts or seconds-long TikTok videos. Unlike earnest pundits or politicians, social media responses can be a lot less formal. One student offered the following take on Senator Jon Ossoff's (D-Georgia) solemn TikTok about climate change: "YAS DADDY JON."[62]

Throughout the campaign, reporters' antennae are always up for gaffes and hints of scandal. When one appears, the entire media throngs to it. Every speech and debate is carefully combed for blunders; sites such as "FactCheck.org" review all candidates' claims during stump speeches and debates. Does this media whirlwind really matter to election outcomes? The short answer: rarely. Effective campaigns develop rapid-response teams that deal with whatever crisis gusts through the media on that day. In fact, there is a school of thought which holds that virtually all news is good news. Free media amplifies candidates' messages or, at least, offers free publicity. It can also drown out their opponents.

Of course, candidates sometimes go too far. The youngest member in Congress, Representative Madison Cawthorn (R-NC), got all kinds of publicity for

Sound bite: A short audio clip; often refers to a brief excerpt from a politician's speech.

a series of antics. He accused his own Republican House colleagues of engaging in cocaine-fueled orgies; he was stopped twice for attempting to carry a loaded gun through airport security; and he decided to switch Congressional districts—and then switched back. All news was not good news in this case—after one term, voters chose another Republican to represent them.[63]

Candidate Profiles

Campaign coverage often features a powerful narrative. The media sketches a profile of each candidate—simplistic, exaggerated, and very hard to escape. That image then shapes future coverage. Once the portrait develops, it reverberates through the world of infotainment. Behavior that "fits" immediately gets airtime, reinforcing the narrative.

During the 2020 campaign, the media narrative about Donald Trump emphasized erratic decision making—especially after COVID hit the country. Any story that fit the narrative—the firing of a campaign director, an overly aggressive debate performance, funding problems during the campaign, misinformation about COVID—got maximum circulation. Stories that did not fit—a remarkable program to develop a COVID vaccine, the candidate's rising support in Latino communities—were overlooked. [64]

In contrast, Joe Biden won coverage for a low-key campaign that proved effective in debates and town halls, countering the Trump campaign's efforts to portray him as "Sleepy Joe" and "senile." Republicans renewed Trump-style attacks on Biden in the 2022 midterms—helping shape a media narrative of the president as *too* low-key: aging, out of touch. Again, however, the Biden approach proved effective with voters, as Democrats did far better than expected.

Campaigns respond to shrinking sound bites by creating visual images that will speak louder than the punditry. Waving flags, cheering crowds, or bales of hay down on the farm all convey images—regardless of media voiceovers. In Chapter 10, we discuss the extraordinary sums candidates spend on advertising to craft their images.

Social media have led to all kinds of changes in campaigning. Instagram, TikTok, Facebook, and Twitter give candidates a targeted way to circumvent the mass media and speak directly to supporters. Digital messaging creates a sense of movement, of belonging. It offers a way to mobilize supporters behind a cause without relying on traditional media coverage. Ironically, the mainstream media eagerly reports on successful social media campaigns—amplifying that success by publicizing it.

iammrbeat Mr. Beat (Matt Beat) · 6-11

If Sarah Palin wants to be elected to Congress, she has to get through Santa Claus first. #santaclausforcongress #santaclausvssarahpalin #herecomessantaclaus

♫ original sound - Mr. Beat (Matt Beat)

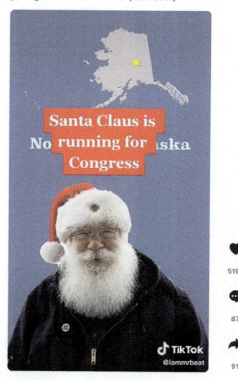

● *Would-be House members take to TikTok. Alaska tried a new ranked choice voting system in 2022 and attracted forty-eight candidates, including 2008 GOP vice presidential candidate Sarah Palin and a Democratic Socialist who changed his name to Santa Claus. When the votes were counted, Democrat Mary Peltola, who utilized social media effectively in the campaign, won the seat.*

THE BOTTOM LINE

» Reporting on war and terrorism has long attracted more viewers than almost any other political story. Ethical questions about the nature of media coverage continue to reshape editors' approaches to these dramatic stories.

» Media coverage of campaigns reflects the general patterns of the contemporary media. It emphasizes drama, conflict, and the horse race narrative.

» Campaigns attempt either to influence the media or to bypass it and speak directly to supporters, increasingly via social media. These efforts in turn become part of the mainstream media coverage.

Conclusion: At the Crossroads of the Media World

The media reflects the United States—and broadcasts it to the world. American media has many critics. Conservatives blast the mainstream media's liberal bias; progressives lament the stifling influence of corporate media ownership. Another complaint: Teenagers and twenty-somethings find it hard to filter the endless stream of news and information arriving from every social media corner. Remember what makes the American broadcast media unusual: It is and has always been a commercial enterprise. Whatever draws an audience survives and flourishes.

America's media reflects the nation and its people. The eighth-largest network in the United States is the Spanish-language Univision; six spots behind is Telemundo. In fact, the dozen Spanish-speaking networks on American television today boast a total of more than four hundred affiliates. Together, they reach more local stations than any one of the major networks. And the foreign-language media does not stop at Spanish. Depending on where you live in the United States, the giant cable provider Comcast offers as many as eighty-two foreign-language channels, and the Dish satellite menu includes more than 275 international stations in twenty-eight languages. Some seventy million Americans (including one of your authors) have at least one parent born abroad, and the media reflects that reality.

What else does the media tell us about who we are? Here is another important indicator: The ten largest religious networks have more than 350 affiliates. The largest, INSP (formerly the Inspiration Network), reaches an estimated eighty million households. By way of comparison, ESPN reaches eighty-four million.

As we have seen, television in every demographic is being squeezed by the Internet and social media. Netflix, for example, now has more than 220 million subscribers, and by some estimates will be the largest global "TV network" within the next few years. In this booming new category, as in much else, it is America's young people who are driving the change—pioneering new technologies and picking winners and losers among sites and applications.

What once appeared to be a digital divide is now shrinking, as Black and Latino youth catch up to white youth. In forums such as Twitter, they have nudged their way to the top among the young. The United States consumes programs in hundreds of languages. *Who are we?* A multinational and multicultural society, bustling with changes and beaming its images to the world—through television, cinema, blogs, Instagram posts, streaming Netflix, Hulu, and tweets.

Media critics lament the collapse of our national community. Every political side now has its own news shows. Americans do not just disagree about values—they do not even hear or see the same reality. Mainstream newspapers and networks are losing money, and as a result, their capacity to collect the news is declining. As the details about national and international events get sketchier, the void is filled by loud, ill-informed opinions. The entire news apparatus dashes after drama, conflict, and scandal. Important issues such as education, the environment, and healthcare are downplayed in this chase for an audience. To pessimists, today's media—fragmented, declining, sensationalist—exacerbates the conflicts in American politics.

In contrast, optimists see a thriving democracy in which people are active and engaged. Debates in Washington may be long and loud, but that only reflects an energetic nation undergoing tectonic change. As media outlets expand and go digital, people's choices grow richer. Today, the United States has a broad lineup of news, information, and analysis. Members of the traditional media try to present objective reports as best they can. Cable channels and radio stations get partisans excited about their ideas and their parties. And social media permits people, especially young people, to engage in political dialogue as never before. The media stirs up the best features of American politics: broad participation and strong opinions that leaders cannot help but hear.

CHAPTER SUMMARY

⭐ The media—and the stories editors and users choose to emphasize—helps set the political *agenda*, *prime* the electorate, and *frame* issues.

⭐ Media stories affect public opinion—primarily among people who do not have strong opinions. Because these people tend to pay less attention to the news, stories with clear signals (heavy coverage, a strong perspective) can change their views.

⭐ Media platforms have expanded from the traditional television, radio, and newspapers to include online news sites, podcasts, and social media.

⭐ Media technology changes very rapidly, and each change reshapes the connection between citizens and their leaders—a crucial criterion for democracy. A big question runs through this chapter: Does today's media strengthen or weaken American democracy?

★ News sources are changing. Newspapers, magazines, television, and radio are all facing very different business models, and rushing to fill the void with new formats such as on-demand streaming and podcasts. Online news is rising fast. Today, it is the number one source of news for people under thirty. The enormous number of news sources spans the political spectrum and blurs the line between entertainment and news.

★ Yes, the media is biased. Reporters in the mainstream press are less conservative than the general population, but they do not seem to tilt election coverage or other news. The deepest bias—across the entire news media spectrum—comes from the media's purpose: It is a business that needs an audience to generate revenue. Therefore, the news emphasizes drama, conflict, and scandal.

★ In most other democracies, the government ran the first radio and TV stations and still plays a large role in the media world, although commercial media is rising. In authoritarian countries, social media poses a threat to the old model of information control and press censorship.

★ Digital media is changing the nature of news and information. On the upside, users are more active. They can choose, respond, report, comment, critique, create, and share. Candidates and parties have new ways to connect. On the downside, the ready availability of online news has challenged the pay models of traditional print outlets, leading to an environment that facilitates the spread of rumors and even lies. All of this means that we as a society do not share the same news.

★ This influence gives media leaders considerable power over American politics. Whether that power is used for the public benefit is a much-debated question—perhaps most sharply when it comes to covering urgent topics such as war, terrorism, and election campaigns.

★ In many ways, the media reflects America. What we watch and hear tells us who we are.

KEY TERMS

Clickbait, p. 283
Fairness doctrine, p. 291
Fake news, p. 284
Framing, p. 277
Infotainment, p. 282

Loud signal, p. 276
Mass media, p. 280
Personal presidency, p. 281
Policy agenda, p. 277
Priming, p. 277

Public ownership, p. 290
Public watchdog, p. 276
Sound bite, p. 298
Watergate scandal, p. 288

STUDY QUESTIONS

1. Where do most Americans get their news—local television, network television, newspapers, or the Internet?

2. Which sources do millennial Americans and Gen Z rely on most for their news?

3. Name two problems most analysts see in the decline of the newspaper. Do you agree that these are problems? Why or why not?

4. How is the American media biased? Describe three of its biases.

5. How is the American media different from that of other nations?

6. Choose a news source and look at today's headlines. Can you find a "media narrative" in these stories? Do you see a narrative arc, drama, conflict, good guys, and bad guys? Can you come up with a more objective way to present the story?

7. Research a candidate for president, Congress, or governor during the 2024 primary election. What do they stand for? Now design a campaign commercial for that candidate. Put them in the best possible light using visuals and voiceovers. Post your creation on YouTube (hashtag us at #BTP).

8. Pick a big global story. Read its coverage in the *New York Times*. Now compare this coverage with that of two other sources: the *Wall Street Journal* and *Al Jazeera*. Identify at least one difference in the way the other two outlets covered the story.

CAMPAIGNS AND ELECTIONS

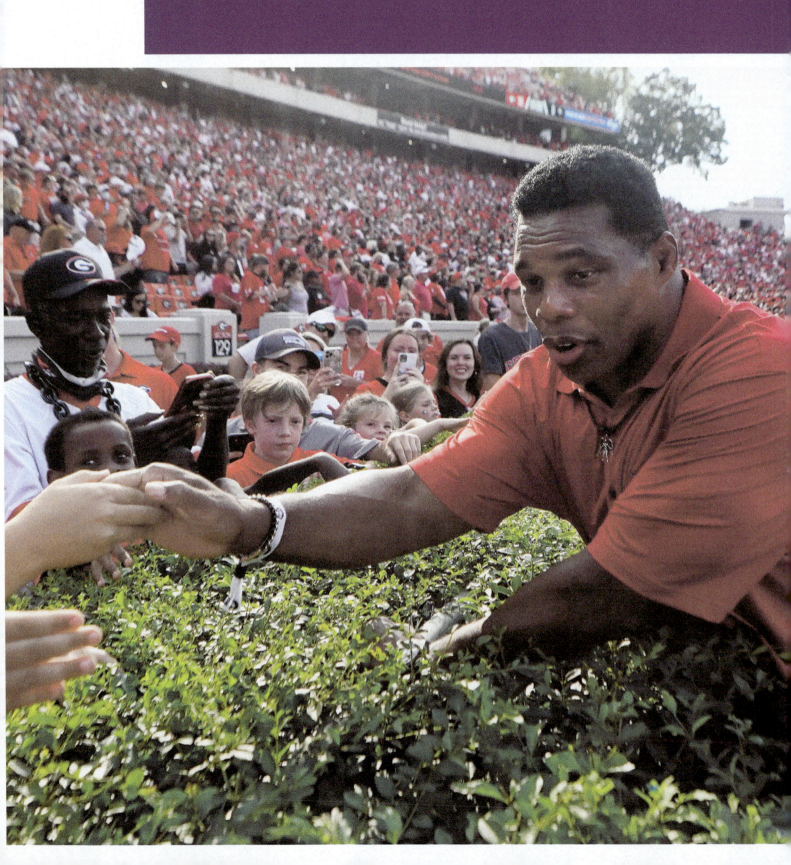

REPUBLICANS HAD NOT WON a single statewide race in Virginia in more than a decade, so Glen Youngkin was a long shot in the 2021 race for governor. But the rookie proved genial and effective on the campaign trail. It helped that he could draw on his wealth—he pumped $20 million into his campaign. And it also helped that Democratic President Joe Biden was low in the polls, giving the Republican a boost.

The Democratic candidate, former Governor Terry McAuliffe, tried to tie the Republican to Donald Trump (who lost the state by more than ten points in 2020). But Youngkin skillfully negotiated the Trump factor. On the one hand, he called it an honor when the former president endorsed him; on the other, he managed to skip every rally where Trump was involved and expressed discomfort when Republicans pledged allegiance to a flag that had flown at the January 6 insurrection.

During the campaign, Youngkin found an unexpected issue. He ignored the usual hot-button Republican topics—abortion, gun rights, crime—and emphasized parental control of schools. Youngkin lambasted critical race theory, a scholarly tradition that analyzes the way racial hierarchy is organized into American laws and institutions. Youngkin alleged that critical race theory was turning young people against their own country.

Democrats scoffed and called it a racist dog whistle—after all, critical race theory played almost no role in Virginia's schools. But Youngkin had hit a nerve. Parents were weary of COVID school shutdowns, and the campaign successfully stoked anxiety about a "woke" curriculum. McAuliffe, the Democrat, inadvertently highlighted the issue. Pressed about his own veto of a bill that would have required schools to tell parents about sexual content, McAuliffe responded, "I don't think parents should be telling schools what they should teach." That didn't sound right to a lot of people and underscored Youngkin's charge: Parents should take more control of their children's schools. In the end, the Republican won a close race (with 50.5 percent of the vote).

Youngkin entered office with the most diverse team in Virginia's history. Winsome Earle Sears, a Black woman originally from Jamaica, became

In this chapter, you will

 Learn what is distinctive (and what resembles other nations) about American elections.

 Examine how democratic American elections are today.

 Discuss the influence of money in elections.

 Explore presidential and congressional campaigns.

 Identify the keys to a successful campaign for Congress.

 Consider proposed election reforms.

● *Herschel Walker, boosted by an endorsement from Donald Trump, campaigns at a football game in Alabama. Walker won the Republican primary and pushed Senator Raphael Warnock to a runoff in December, won by Warnock—one of several Democrats to knock off Trump-endorsed challengers.*

lieutenant governor, and Jason Miyares became the first Latino attorney general of the state. Both had solid conservative records as well.

What's next? Another election, of course. That's the thing about American campaigns: There's always a new election coming up. Republicans, eager to win Congress back from the Democrats in 2022, looked to the Virginia Republicans as one path to success: racially diverse conservatives, outspoken about culture war matters (like critical race theory), and carefully negotiating a relationship to Donald Trump, who still stirs passionate feelings—for and against.

Across the nation, Republicans lined up their candidates. Some made a marked contrast to the Youngkin model. In Pennsylvania, a TV personality, Mehmet Oz (known as Dr. Oz), leapt into the Republican primary. Oz, once an innovative heart surgeon, had become a television personality touting discredited fears (apple juice will kill you) and cures (green coffee cures obesity, and hydroxychloroquine prevents COVID). Medical journals blasted him, Columbia University cut ties, but an endorsement from Donald Trump boosted him to the Republican nomination.[1]

Trump also endorsed Herschel Walker, a former football star (who had once played for a team that Trump had owned), for the U.S. Senate race in Georgia. Walker won the primary and challenged incumbent Democrat Reverend Raphael Warnock in a race that featured two Black men in what had been, until very recently, a deeply Republican state.

In Ohio, J. D. Vance—a Yale Law graduate and venture capitalist—became a full-throated Trump supporter and won the former president's endorsement. On the campaign trail, Vance drew on working-class roots, documented in his bestselling *Hillbilly Elegy*. He minced no words with working-class Ohio when he spoke about people who refused to work—like his own parents.[2]

Donald Trump further complicated the midterm races when he hinted broadly at his candidacy for the 2024 presidential election, before the 2022 midterm elections. Analyses of the GOP's poor 2022 outcome—despite forecasts of a "red wave" of Republican wins, based on an inflation-plagued economy and low approval ratings for President Biden—placed major blame on Trump. Although Vance won in Ohio, Oz and Walker were among numerous Trump-backed candidates to lose. Unlike most previous midterms, when a sitting president's party loses seats in Congress and statehouses, Biden's Democrats essentially broke even in the House and Senate and netted two governor's seats.

Some political scientists suggest that campaigns barely matter. More fundamental factors—such as the economy and the sitting president's approval rating—determine who wins the election. Not the hyped-up, media-saturated, roller-coaster campaign.

Yes, those factors matter a great deal. Amid bad economic news, Republicans who focused their campaigns on gas prices and other markers of high inflation—and avoided "Stop the Steal" talk about the 2020 election—won in many states. Two sitting

● *Democrat Stacey Abrams and Republican Brian Kemp in a rematch for the Georgia governor's race. In 2018 Abrams electrified Democrats and came within a hairsbreadth of winning. In 2022, on the other hand, Kemp stuck to messages about the sagging economy, and won easily.*

governors, Ron DeSantis of Florida and Brian Kemp of Georgia, stuck to economic messages and won by comfortable margins over strong challengers, for example. Yet despite the economy, Democrats won many races by emphasizing issues like abortion—and their opponents' weaknesses. Campaigns are essential to who wins and loses. This chapter will show you how and why.[3]

Who are we? A people of campaigns and elections. Americans vote more often and for more officers—on every level of government—than the citizens of most nations. Through elections, Americans choose leaders, guiding philosophies, programs and policies, and the nation's attitude toward the rest of the world.

And for the last twenty years, it's been a roller coaster. Since 2000, the Senate has changed hands five times, the House four times, and the White House four times. That's more flux than at any other time in American history. On the state level, things tend to be a little more stable—except in swing states. In 2022, Democrats flipped party control of the GOP-held Senate seat in Pennsylvania and held on narrowly in Senate races in Arizona, Nevada, New Hampshire, and Georgia— otherwise, especially with J. D. Vance's win in Ohio, the Senate would have flipped a sixth time.

Amid all the upheaval, the question we asked in the first chapter of this book is especially important for campaigns and elections: Is the American voting system really representative of the people? Should it better reflect popular views? Or perhaps, as some of the founders thought, American electoral machinery should be *less* sensitive to the whims of public opinion.[4]

BY THE NUMBERS Campaigns and Elections

1797–1807 Years in which American women first voted (in New Jersey)

1920 Year in which women in all states could vote

80 Percent of white (non-Hispanic) population in 1980

58 Estimated percent of (non-Hispanic) white population in 2025

61 Average percentage of white (non-Hispanic) vote for Republican presidential candidates since 1980

5 Number of times the Senate has flipped party hands since 2000

11 Percentage point jump in voting by eighteen- to twenty-nine-year-olds between 2016 and 2020

1.6 Percentage of U.S. House incumbents who lost in 2020

36.7 Percentage of voting-age population who turned out for midterm elections in 2014

47 Percentage of voting-age population who turned out for midterm elections in 2018

66 Percentage of voting-age population who turned out for presidential election in 2020

20 Percentage of Americans satisfied with national campaign finance laws (2020)[5]

Who participates in campaigns and elections, and how does that influence our democratic process?

How Democratic Are American Elections?

Time, place, and manner clause: The constitutional clause that delegates control of elections to the state governments.

The Constitution sidestepped a crucial matter: who votes and how. It left the election details—the **"time, place, and manner"**—up to the states. Every state builds its own electoral process. For example, felons can vote from jail in Maine, only after they have passed through parole and probation in Texas, and almost never in Mississippi. Politics generally plays a major role as states write and rewrite their voting rules. We can evaluate how well elections enhance popular rule by focusing on four dimensions: frequency, breadth, voting barriers, and the role of money.

Frequent and Fixed Elections

One way to hold public officials accountable is to require them to face the public frequently. The United States schedules elections for national office more often than most other democratic countries. House members are chosen every two years, presidents every four, and senators every six. Add state and local elections (many mayors and governors are elected in odd-numbered years, with no national election), and there is never a year in the United States without major elections.

In parliamentary democracies, the prime minister generally decides when to hold an election as long as there is at least one within a set period, usually five years (see Comparing Nations 10.1). In contrast, American national elections are on a fixed date (chosen back in 1845)—politicians do not have the luxury of deciding when to stand before the people. On the first Tuesday after the first Monday in November of every even-numbered year, Americans elect all House members and a third of the Senate; every fourth year, they elect a president. Special elections are held if an office holder dies or resigns, and each state sets the date of the primary elections that determine which candidates represent a political party for each office. The timing and frequency tilts U.S. elections in a more democratic direction.

Do you see any drawbacks to frequent elections? All that campaigning consumes a great deal of time, money, and energy. House members are always running for reelection. As a Canadian prime minister once remarked, "In your system, you guys campaign for 24 hours a day, every day for two years. You know, politics is one thing, but we have to run a government."[6]

Over 520,000 Elected Officials

Not only are American elections unusually frequent, but also an enormous *number* of positions are elected—from presidents to municipal drain inspectors. The United States was the first nation to choose its chief executive—and later judges—by popular election. Today, thirty-nine states elect judges (87 percent of all state judges). No other country elects judges, as they are supposed to be above politics. Critics charge that fundraising and campaign promises compromise the impartiality of state judges. But elections remain the American way.

To get a feel for the numbers, see Table 10.1, which lists elected officials in Iowa City, Iowa. Count them up: There are fifty-eight elected officials for some 77,000 residents.

COMPARING NATIONS 10.1	Election Timetables for National Government	
How does the United States compare to other selected advanced democratic countries in election frequency?	**FREQUENCY**	**GOVERNMENT BODY**
	2 years	**U.S. House of Representatives**
	3 years	House of Representatives in Australia, New Zealand, El Salvador
	4 years	Parliaments in Argentina, Costa Rica, Germany, Japan, South Korea, Switzerland; **U.S. president**; president and lower chamber of legislature in Brazil
	5 years	Parliament in Ireland; president in South Korea; congress in Peru; *maximum term* for prime minister (and parliaments) in Canada, Denmark, France, Italy, United Kingdom, many others
	6 years	Argentinian, Australian, and **U.S. senators**
	8 years	Senators in Brazil and Chile

TABLE 10.1	Who Do You Vote for in Iowa City?

NATIONAL OFFICIALS	
1 U.S. president	
2 U.S. senators from Iowa	
1 U.S. representative from Iowa's Second District	

IOWA STATE OFFICIALS	
1 governor	
1 lieutenant governor	1 secretary of state
1 attorney general	1 state treasurer
1 agriculture secretary	1 state auditor
1 state senator	1 state representative
7 Iowa Supreme Court justices (appointed for one year by governor, then must win a public "retention election" every eight years)	

COUNTY OFFICIALS	
1 supervisor	1 sheriff
1 treasurer	1 attorney
1 auditor	1 recorder

TOWNSHIP/CITY OFFICIALS (IOWA CITY IS BOTH A CITY AND A "TOWNSHIP")	
1 clerk	
3 trustees	
7 school board members	
4 education agency directors	
7 city council members (who in turn elect one member as Iowa City mayor)	
9 agriculture extension members	
1 soil and water conservation commissioner	

From Anchorage, Alaska, to Zapata, Texas, more than 520,000 officials stand for election at the local, state, and national level. That's one measure of democracy in action. Is this a good way to give the people influence over government? Or does it make informed judgment impossible by overwhelming them with too many choices? What do you think?

Barriers to Voting

The 2020 election drew the highest voter turnout in a century. But false cries of fraud after the election created a wave—or more accurately, two waves—of state legislation (Figure 10.1). Led by Texas and Georgia, nineteen states passed thirty-three stringent voting laws. They restricted early voting, demanded photo IDs (that can discriminate against people without driver's licenses), continue to forbid felons from voting even after they've done their time (currently in eleven states),

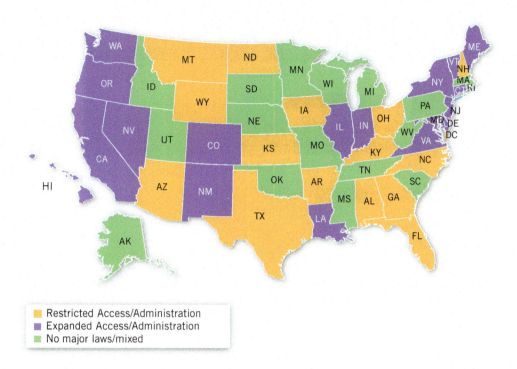

Restricted Access/Administration
Expanded Access/Administration
No major laws/mixed

● **FIGURE 10.1** *Starting in 2021, many states responded to the 2020 elections with laws that expanded access to voting, while others passed legislation that restricted access.*

and shifted election administration in ways that could make it more partisan. In the 2022 midterms, more than 175 "election deniers" won various races, including U.S. Senate and House seats. But candidates in battleground states like Arizona, Michigan, and Pennsylvania who ran for governor, secretary of state, or other offices that certify election results were nearly all defeated. "Stop the Steal" turns out to have been a losing slogan with a majority of voters in more than 100 midterm contests—including most of those where administering elections was on the ballot.

On the other side, twenty-seven states responded to the 2020 election with laws that enhanced voter access. They expanded mail voting (twenty-seven states), increased in-person early voting (twenty-seven states), simplified voter registration (twenty states), and permitted former felons to vote (eight states).

The point: It's all up to the states. Some encourage voting, while others raise barriers. Why? Usually, the majority party protects itself by adjusting the voting rules—a tendency that goes all the way back to the first American elections in the late eighteenth century.[7] However, the two parties may be fighting over a collective

WHAT DO YOU THINK?

Are There Too Many Elective Positions?

Yes, there are too many elective positions.	**No, we need to encourage people to vote more often.**
The public is asked to vote too often. Few voters can learn about so many races. The United States should appoint more experts to handle the technical aspects of government.	Reducing the number of elected officials would be unhealthy for our democracy. Voting permits the people to hold their public officials directly accountable. It's the best check on government officials.

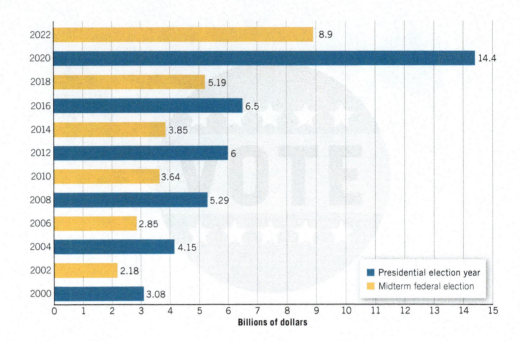

● **FIGURE 10.2** *The cost of national elections (inflation-adjusted dollars). (Open Secrets)*

myth. They believe that Democrats are more likely to win with higher turnout. As we saw in Chapter 8, however, recent work in political science suggests that this is not the case.[8]

Financing Campaigns: The New Inequality?

Immense sums flow through U.S. elections, triggering another set of fears. Does money tilt the process?

Too Much Money?   The price tag for 2020's races for president and Congress surpassed $14.4 billion (Figure 10.2); at $8.9 billion, 2022 set a record for midterms. Those billions raise a perennial question: Is there too much money in American political campaigns?

Many critics say yes. Public officials on every level devote enormous amounts of time and energy to raising money. As a result, critics fear that wealthy people may be able to buy influence—and bury candidates and political issues that they do not like. Polls consistently show overwhelming majorities want to reduce the role of money in U.S. elections. In 2002, Congress responded with the Bipartisan Campaign Reform Act (known as McCain–Feingold), which limited the amounts individuals, corporations, and organizations could give.

Bipartisan critics pushed back. Both Senate Majority Leader Mitch McConnell (R-KY) and the left-leaning American Civil Liberties Union argued that supporting campaigns is a form of free speech. The Supreme Court has largely accepted this perspective. In *Citizens United v. Federal Elections Commission*, the Court ruled (5–4) that the free speech clause of the First Amendment protects corporations, unions, and other groups who wish to support candidates or causes. In *McCutcheon v. Federal Elections Commission*, the Court struck down limits on the total donations an individual can make (again 5–4). The law still limits how much you can give an individual candidate running for office, but not how much you spend overall by donating to parties, donating to multiple candidates, and on issue ads.[9]

There was no great outcry over these Court decisions. Americans oppose the rising tide of campaign cash, but for most, the issue is not a high priority. Think about those campaign numbers in context: The $14.4 billion spent on all national contests in 2020 was twice what Americans spend at McDonald's each year, and three-quarters of annual spending on pornography. What do you think? Is contributing to campaigns a citizen's right? Or is it handing our democracy over to the wealthy?

Democracy for the Rich?   Do wealthy individuals or organizations dominate elections—perhaps even squeezing out the people's influence? There are three major concerns.

First, does one party get an advantage? Some organized groups do contribute mainly to one party. Labor unions back Democrats (by a ten-to-one margin, in recent elections), and some industries—such as oil and gas companies—largely support Republican candidates. But most business sectors traditionally split their donations about evenly between the two major parties; overall, in 2020, corporate donors split some $4 billion close to evenly, favoring Democratic candidates by $2.05 billion to $1.95 billion for Republicans. Most corporate sectors wanted a seat at the table in both parties. Republicans are regularly described as the party friendlier to business, but the figures across the past quarter-century do not bear this out.[10]

Second, incumbents generally overwhelm their challengers. In 2020, sitting senators amassed $15.5 million on average. Their opponents scraped together just $884,000. In 2022, the five costliest Senate races together topped $1.3 billion in spending. Perhaps that's one reason that reelection rates in 2020 and 2022 remained very high in both the Senate and the House—most incumbents won in landslides. Such lopsided funding has a big impact, not in the headline presidential contest and big contested Senate races, but down the ballot in the lower-profile congressional and state-level races—which receive less media attention.[11]

Third, critics worry that the need to raise funds—always more and more money—makes office holders especially sensitive to their funders. Big donors confidently chuckle that they are "buying a seat at the table"—they can always get in the door to talk to elected officials. Mick Mulvaney, who was White House Chief of Staff and director of the Office of Management and Budget in the Trump administration, put it bluntly when he was in Congress, saying, "If you're a lobbyist who never gave us money, I didn't talk to you."[12] Still, research has not yet found a systematic link between contributions and political influence.[13]

In sum, campaign money does not seem to matter much in high-profile races—such as the presidency—when both sides will get their message across. It is farther down the ballot, in less visible races, where money counts. Incumbent members of Congress rarely face well-financed opposition. Few other democracies reelect their legislatures in such overwhelming numbers—thanks, at least in part, to the vast sums that incumbents raise.

Major Donors: Easier to Give.   OK, you have made your fortune and you want to contribute to your favorite candidate. What are your options? First, many corporations and advocacy groups organize **political action committees (PACs)** to donate to candidates. PACs, which must include fifty or more contributors, may legally contribute $10,000 to any one candidate—$5,000 for the primary campaign,

Political action committee (PAC): An organization of at least fifty people, affiliated with an interest group, that is permitted to make contributions to candidates for federal office.

Super PACs: Organizations that raise and spend unlimited amounts of money to promote a candidate or publicize a cause. However, they may not directly contribute to a candidate or coordinate with a campaign.

$5,000 more for the general election. But if you give to the national parties, you can go up to $109,500 per year.

Want to contribute more? The **super PAC** was born in 2010 after the Supreme Court struck down laws limiting "independent" political spending by corporations and unions (in *Citizens United v. FEC*). Super PACs, formally known as "independent expenditure-only committees," may raise unlimited sums from virtually any source—business firms, unions, or individuals—and spend as much as they like to openly support or oppose political candidates. Unlike traditional PACs, they are not supposed to directly contribute to or coordinate with the candidate's political campaigns. But that rule is difficult to enforce as close associates generally run the super PACs lined up behind a candidate.[14]

Despite all this, Shaun McCutcheon, a conservative Alabama businessman, was frustrated by the campaign finance laws that capped his overall donations. In *McCutcheon v. FEC*, the Supreme Court agreed (5–4) to lift the cap. The law still limits how much you can give an individual candidate, but not how much you spend overall by donating to parties and outside groups. The top ten donors in 2022 gave a total of some $540 billion—about 61 percent of it to Republicans.

The Court's rulings left a patchwork of regulations. No one may contribute more than $2,800 to any individual candidate—the primary and general election are treated separately, so $5,600 to a candidate is the overall limit. You may not contribute more than $5,000 to an old-fashioned PAC (not to be confused with super PACs, which have no limits). One way around that limit is through **bundling**: convincing colleagues and friends to donate at or near the maximum amount, and then delivering all the checks together.

Bundling: A form of fundraising in which an individual persuades others to donate large amounts that are then delivered together to a candidate or campaign.

527 groups: Organizations that raise and spend unlimited amounts for "issue advocacy" but are forbidden to coordinate their efforts with any candidate or campaign.

Still another source of campaign-related funds are **527 groups**. These are named for the section of the U.S. tax code that regulates them; 527 groups are forbidden from advocating directly on behalf of any candidate's election. However, they can accept and spend unlimited amounts for "issue advocacy." They may not explicitly support or oppose a candidate, but the ads they run can be indirectly supportive—or scathing. "Senator Jones is a tree killer who hates the environment" is an acceptable message for a 527 group; "Vote against Senator Jones" is not.

PACs, super PACs, bundlers, 527s: In the 2020 campaign, these outside groups spent just under $3 billion—nearly twice as much as four years before. Each innovation raises a fresh round of questions about democracy and campaign spending. As the limits on campaign spending are eliminated, one very wealthy individual can essentially fund a presidential candidate through the primaries.

All this money has swamped another reform: public financing. During presidential primaries, party nominees who raise $5,000 in small donations ($250 or less) in each of twenty states qualify for federal matching funds—a lump sum ($103.7 million in 2020). There's one catch. If they accept the money, they must limit their total spending. In 2008, candidate Barack Obama declined public funds and badly outspent Republican John McCain, who accepted them and was barred from raising further funds. Since then, no presidential candidate has accepted public financing for a general election.

Money in Elections

The New Rules

Since 2010, Supreme Court rulings in *Citizens United v. FEC, McCutcheon v. FEC*, and others have weakened the limits on campaign contributions and enabled super PACs to emerge. Although per-candidate and per-PAC limits still exist, the caps on the number of candidates or PACs a donor can contribute to have been lifted.

THINK ABOUT IT

How has the amount of money a single donor can contribute to candidates, party committees, PACs, and super PACs changed?

....

How does the lifting of caps affect wealthy donors who hedge their bets by contributing to multiple candidates?

....

How will this affect elections and democratic representation overall?

Sources: Washington Post *and Center for Responsive Politics*

		2010	**2020**
Candidates	Limit for each candidate	House and Senate candidates $5,200 each	House and Senate candidates $5,600 each
	Limit for all candidates in an election cycle	**YES** Total possible contribution: $48,600	**NO LIMIT** By giving each candidate the maximum amount, one donor could contribute $2,620,800
Party committees	Limits	$74,600	$1,194,400
PACs	Limit for each PAC	$5,000 each	$5,000 each
	Limit for all PACs	**YES** Total possible contribution: $74,600	**NO LIMIT** By giving each PAC the maximum amount, one donor could contribute $Millions
Number of super PACs		0	Over 2,300

Does contributing funds to a legislator "buy" anything valuable for donors? Should the system be changed to reduce the influence of monetary contributions? Or is spending money on campaigns a vital form of free speech? These are among the essential complexities of American campaigns.

THE BOTTOM LINE

» Are American elections truly democratic? Americans vote more often and for more offices than the citizens of most other democracies. But they also face barriers to voting in many states.

» The most familiar question today focuses on the role of money in election campaigns. PACs, super PACs, and 527s have become fixtures in national elections.

» Recent court decisions have significantly expanded the ability of wealthy donors and outside groups to contribute large sums.

 # Presidential Campaigns and Elections

The presidency is the greatest electoral prize—and winning it is brutal. Running is expensive, exhausting, and often humiliating. Yet, in every presidential race, dozens take up the challenge.

Who Runs for President?

One-time candidate Morris "Mo" Udall, who ran in 1976, said afterward, "You have to be a little crazy to run for president." The U.S. Constitution merely requires that candidates be "natural born" American citizens (e.g., from birth, not later nationalized), aged thirty-five years or older, who have resided in the country for fourteen years or more. This was the rule that Donald Trump seized on when he began attacking President Obama in 2011: "He doesn't have a birth certificate," Trump told *Good Morning America*. The claims were fictitious (Obama was born in Hawaii), but they made Trump a star among people who opposed the Obama presidency.[15]

Serious presidential candidates generally have experience as elected officials—and in the last half-century, both parties have nominated candidates with one of three offices on their résumé—vice president, governor, or senator. The last president to have come directly out of the House of Representatives? James Garfield in 1880. Businesspeople with no experience in public office? None ever won the presidency—until Donald Trump in 2016 (Table 10.2).

The Three Phases of Presidential Elections

Presidential campaigns involve distinct stages—the nomination process, the party convention, and the general election. Each stage requires very different political strategies, played out amid the white-hot lights of global media coverage.

Winning the Nomination.   The grueling process begins with the invisible primary (also known as the money primary). Candidates toss their hat in the ring and then build an organization, compete in televised debates, and scramble for media attention. Before the first vote was cast in the 2020 race, eighteen candidates had already dropped out—doomed by low poll numbers, anemic fundraising, or weak debate performances.

TABLE 10.2 The Presidents' Résumés

YEAR	WINNER	PREVIOUS POSITION	LOSER	PREVIOUS POSITION
1960	John Kennedy	Senator	Richard Nixon	Vice president (1953–61)
1964	Lyndon Johnson	Vice president (1961–63)	Barry Goldwater	Senator
1968	Richard Nixon	Vice president (1953–61)	Hubert Humphrey	Vice president (1965–69)
1972	Richard Nixon	Incumbent	George McGovern	Senator
1976	Jimmy Carter	Governor	Gerald Ford	Vice president/incumbent
1980	Ronald Reagan	Governor	Jimmy Carter	Incumbent
1984	Ronald Reagan	Incumbent	Walter Mondale	Vice president (1977–81)
1988	George H. W. Bush	Vice president (1981–89)	Michael Dukakis	Governor
1992	Bill Clinton	Governor	George H. W. Bush	Incumbent
1996	Bill Clinton	Incumbent	Bob Dole	Senator
2000	George W. Bush	Governor	Al Gore	Vice president (1993–2001)
2004	George W. Bush	Incumbent	John Kerry	Senator
2008	Barack Obama	Senator	John McCain	Senator
2012	Barack Obama	Incumbent	Mitt Romney	Governor
2016	Donald Trump	Real estate developer, Reality TV star	Hillary Clinton	Secretary of State, Senator, First Lady
2020	Joe Biden	Vice president (2009–17), Senator	Donald Trump	Incumbent

Next, the candidates run the gauntlet of state contests. Traditionally, Iowa always kicks off the process. Iowans vote in a **caucus**, where activists in each precinct meet to select delegates who will vote for a candidate. Here's an opportunity to break out of the pack—or suffer an unexpected setback. In the 2020 Iowa Democratic caucus, confusion over new rules and virtual technologies—meant to make the often-byzantine caucus system more accessible to voters—resulted in a three-week delay before results were announced. Vermont Senator Bernie Sanders and national-stage newcomer Pete Buttigieg, mayor of South Bend, Indiana, finished in a dead heat. But attention had long since moved on to other states, leaving a big question mark: Will Iowa hold on to its first-mover status in the 2024 presidential contest?

The chaos in 2020 sharpened criticism many Democrats had long been making: Iowa is mostly white (90.1 percent), has a large rural population (the twelfth most rural state), and has become a Republican stronghold, so why should it lead off? In April 2022, the Democratic National Committee stripped Iowa of its first-in-the-nation status but gave it the opportunity to reapply (if it could respond to the question of diversity). Watch to see if the Democrats pick a more racially and economically diverse state for 2024.[16]

Next, on to New Hampshire's *primary*. In a **closed primary**, only party members go to the polls and vote for a nominee. In an **open primary**, voters can participate in either party's elections. New Hampshire's primary is semi-closed, because

Caucus: A local meeting of voters to select candidates to represent a political party in a general election or to choose delegates who select candidates at a convention.

Closed primary: A vote cast by party members to select candidates to represent the party in the general election.

Open primary: A vote cast by any eligible voter to select candidates to represent the party in the general election.

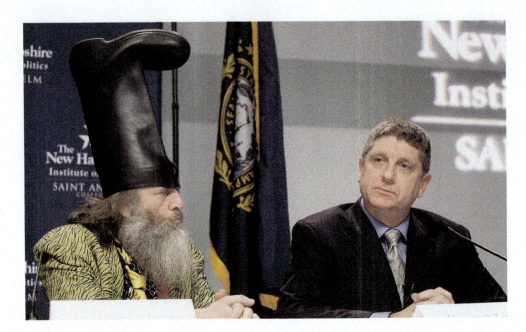

● *After placing fourth in New Hampshire's 2016 Democratic primary, repeat presidential candidate Vermin Supreme (not his real name) barely registered in the much more crowded 2020 field. Supreme's campaign promises included a pony for every American household, time-travel research, and federal preparation for a possible zombie apocalypse.*

independents may vote in either party's primary. New Hampshire can either confirm Iowa's front-runners or reshuffle the race by anointing a new leader. In 2020, with Iowa still frantically recounting caucus results, New Hampshire Democrats gave Senator Sanders the victory by three thousand votes over Mayor Buttigieg. Minnesota Senator Amy Klobuchar, catching the momentum wave, finished third. Former Vice President Joe Biden, after lackluster debate performances, finished a distant fifth. Pundits declared his candidacy over, and began pondering how a Sanders–Trump race would shape up in fall 2020, especially after Sanders won Nevada's caucuses by a whopping 26 percentage points.

WHAT DO YOU THINK?

Why Iowa and New Hampshire?

Beginning over a year before each presidential election, politicians, campaign advisors, and the media descend on two small states. By tradition, Iowa's caucuses and New Hampshire's primary are the first two presidential contests—giving them an outsized influence in the process. The Democratic National Committee is reassessing whether to continue starting the election in these two states. What would you advise them: Should they continue to have such an important say in choosing the president?

Yes.
Small states like these test the candidates' abilities through one-on-one meetings with small groups—a very different challenge than the mass media campaigns reliant on heavy fundraising that follow in the large states. These small states reveal the men and women behind the slick advertisements. I would stick with them.

No.
Iowa ranks thirty-first in population and is 90 percent white; New Hampshire forty-second in population and 93 percent white. Two highly unrepresentative states eliminate many candidates before any large state has had a chance to vote. I would begin with more diverse states.

After Iowa and New Hampshire, candidates face contests in many states, each with its own rules, norms (some states tolerate more negativity than others), and methods (endorsements matter more in some, issues like farmer support or border security in others). Candidates hopscotch the country trying to amass delegates while raising money—until **Super Tuesday**, when both parties schedule multiple elections on a single date. Party leaders hope to have a winner by Super Tuesday so that the nomination process does not drag on too long and damage the eventual nominee. In 2020, Joe Biden achieved a swift turnaround in his fortunes, winning South Carolina's primary thanks especially to African American support, and then cleaning up on Super Tuesday: Biden won nine contests, including in delegate-rich Texas, North Carolina, and Virginia, while Sanders came out on top in just three states.

Both parties require that a winning candidate attract a majority of the convention delegates. In 2020, the magic number was 1,237 for Republicans and 2,382 for Democrats. The parties assign each state a number of delegates based on state population and party loyalty in the last election. In the 2020 Democratic race, for example, Texas had 228 delegates and Vermont 16.

Democrats have generally employed a system of **proportional representation**, allocating delegates based on the proportion of the vote a candidate wins. In the past, Republicans used a **winner-take-all** system, under which the winning candidate receives all the delegates for that state. In 2016, however, the GOP primaries required proportional representation until mid-March, when states could choose to allocate all their delegates to the outright winner (seven states did so). Why all this rigmarole? Republican Party activists wanted a process that did not get decided too soon—before their candidate had been fully tested (as happened with John McCain in 2008)—but they did not want the contest to drag out so long as to damage the winner (Mitt Romney in 2012).

The traditional rules are clear: Primary season candidates must make strong first impressions; compete well in state after state; avoid errors or outrageous statements in a dozen or more debates; and manage a campaign team that, as the contests continue, can swell to thousands of people. They also tend to carefully calibrate their issue positions. Though Donald Trump broke many of those rules in his unorthodox 2016 run to the Republican nomination, Joe Biden ran a largely traditional campaign in 2020 (even amid a pandemic).

Watch the jockeying among potential GOP presidential candidates in the run-up to 2024: Are they back to the usual approach or extending Trumpism by offering dramatic, often highly provocative public statements and assembling a campaign team of newcomers, shutting out the party professionals? Or perhaps we are seeing a bit of both, with Trump himself taking his unorthodox approach and others going back to more traditional campaign teams?

In his three campaigns for president, Donald Trump broke all the rules. Normally, candidates run stronger to the left (for Democrats) or the right (Republicans) during the primaries. That's because those who turn out tend to be more ardent party members. For the general election, candidates tack to the center to appeal to independents and less committed voters. Not Trump. He constantly doubled down on a base strategy, addressing his most enthusiastic supporters. Across the political spectrum, Bernie Sanders also found surprising success speaking to the Democratic base. Though he never won the party nomination, he energized his mainly young, progressive supporters. For all their differences, Trump and Sanders shared one attribute: Each, in a very different way, conveyed authenticity to an electorate deeply cynical about politics and politicians.

Super Tuesday: The date on the presidential primary calendar when multiple states hold primaries and caucuses.

Proportional representation: The allocation of votes or delegates on the basis of the percentage of the vote received; contrasts with the winner-take-all system.

Winner-take-all: The candidate winning a simple majority (or, among multiple candidates, a plurality) receives all electoral votes or primary delegates; sometimes called "first-past-the-post."

Organizing the Convention. Political party conventions showcase the party's presidential nominee on a national stage; they also gather party insiders from across the United States for several days of meetings and celebration. Advocacy groups and corporate interests flock to the conventions as well. Everyone jockeys to be noticed by a potential future president and his or her closest advisors.

When it works well, the convention can provide the nominee an **electoral bounce**, a temporary boost in the polls. A star-studded Democratic convention in 2016 gave Hillary Clinton a bounce, vaulting her into a lead she never relinquished in the polls—until Donald Trump won the election. In 2020, the COVID-19 pandemic forced both conventions to become much smaller virtual events and neither offered the candidate much advantage.[17]

The General Election. After the convention, campaigns shift into overdrive. With just three months between the convention and Election Day, every hour matters. Campaigns scramble to stage media events, blast the opposing candidate, tweet, post, and meet with donors.

General elections usually feature debates between the nominees, although Republicans have cast doubt on their participation in 2024. Pundits scrutinize the performances, search for gaffes, and report the overnight polls. The truth, however, is that most viewers have already made up their minds and debates normally have only a slight impact on the race.

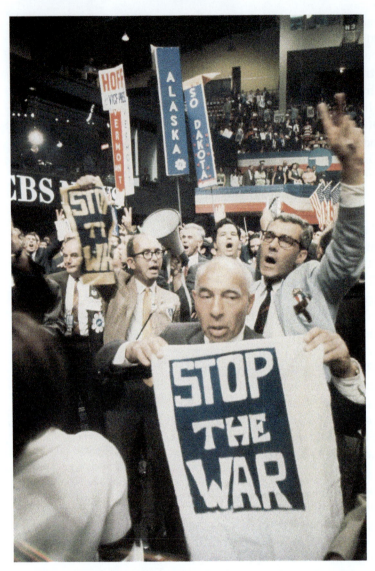

● *Chicago—1968 Democratic National Convention: Angry protests both in and outside the hall created an image of disarray and crisis. This convention symbolized the collapse of the old Democratic coalition. Republicans would take the White House in five of the next six elections.*

Winning Presidential Elections

Electoral bounce: The temporary spike in the polls that follows an event such as a party's national convention.

Both in 2016 and in 2020, U.S. intelligence services reported that Russian meddlers had run a sophisticated operation seeking to tilt the election to Donald Trump. The Russians spread disinformation through Internet trolls, hacked the computer systems of both major parties, and in 2016 leaked the emails of Democratic leaders online ahead of the Democratic National Convention.[18] Most analysts, however, are skeptical that Russian social media or cyber activities influenced the results of either election.[19] What factors did—and do—influence who wins presidential races? Along with the candidates themselves—their speeches, gaffes, debate performances, and responses to the unexpected—a variety of factors help determine the winner.

The Economy. Bill Clinton's headquarters in 1992 featured a famous whiteboard reminding campaign staffers: "It's the Economy, Stupid." If the economy is performing poorly, the party holding the presidency suffers. Many reasons help explain Joe Biden's electoral success in 2020, but tough economic times—after COVID-19 closed businesses and left tens of millions jobless—is high on the list. The message many Republicans ran on in the 2022 midterms? It's still the economy, stupid.

Demographics. Once upon a time, each party worked to build a winning coalition by relying on its base of likely supporters and reaching out to undecided groups in the middle. After the 2012 election, the Republican Party did an "autopsy" to explain why it had lost the presidency and slipped (minus two seats) in the Senate. Major conclusion: The party failed to appeal to growing ranks of millennials and minorities, especially Hispanics. In 2016, Republican primary voters spurned that advice and turned to a candidate who shouted

● Over seventy million Americans tuned into the Kennedy and Nixon debate in 1960—launching the age of televised campaigning. The more charismatic Kennedy won the White House by the slimmest of margins—0.001 percent.

out the perils of immigration and disparaged immigrants. When Trump tried a similar tack in 2020, though, it backfired. Instead an elderly white male, Joe Biden, racked up huge margins among Black voters (an estimated 87 percent of the vote), Hispanics (66 percent), Asians (63 percent), and under-thirty voters (62 percent).

But a warning sign for Democrats: In many key districts, Latinos have begun to defect to the Republicans—part of a working-class (non-college-educated) movement that is spreading across the electorate. In the 2022 midterm elections, that warning grew even louder in some states, like Florida. Nationwide in 2022, Latino voters still supported Democrats by a nearly two-to-one margin.

War and Foreign Policy. Most Americans pay far more attention to domestic issues, especially those that touch their pocketbooks, than foreign ones. Occasionally, however, foreign policy issues become pivotal, especially when the nation is at war. In 2004, for example, the 9/11 attacks—which had occurred three years earlier—helped George W. Bush win reelection. In 2020, Joe Biden—who had extensive foreign policy experience—repeatedly criticized Trump foreign policy in terms like "reckless," "haphazard," and "dangerously incompetent."[20] About one in three voters reported paying attention to foreign policy. That figure may come back to haunt Biden, who faces the debacle of leaving Afghanistan—but won praise for his response to Russia's Ukraine invasion (see Chapter 18).[21]

Domestic Issues. Every presidential candidate has a list of favorite programs and strategies. Bill Clinton discussed education, energy, Medicare, and Medicaid so often that his staff started calling his campaign E2M2. Donald Trump promised job creation, a hard line on immigration, and a strong nationalist trade policy—the United States would not be pushed around anymore. Joe Biden led with restoring economic growth, infrastructure, racial equity, and combating climate change. The candidates' issue preferences are important, not because they will decide the election (highly unlikely), but because they set the agenda for the presidency.[22]

The Campaign Organization. One truism that every would-be president knows is that it is essential to assemble a team of talented, loyal advisors capable of charting a plan for victory. Building a large, multistate organization—often from scratch—is a titanic job that tests every candidate's executive skill.[23] In both 2016 and 2020, Donald Trump bucked the norm: He relied on his own instincts and the advice of a small circle—despite Republican pleas that he defer to seasoned political managers. Joe Biden went back to the traditional campaign apparatus of seasoned experts and eager young foot soldiers.

Parties Matter. Donald Trump won 94 percent of Republican men and 91 percent of GOP women in 2020, testifying to the force of party attachment in a partisan era (see Chapter 11). Even a candidate that blasted many of the party's traditional policy positions still commanded the loyalty of the vast majority of Republicans. Joe Biden was helped to victory by winning an even higher proportion of Democrats—94 percent—as party loyalty continues to harden on both sides.

The Electoral College and Swing States. Because almost all states are winner take all, presidential elections usually hinge on a small number of states. Democrats know they will win in New York and California. Republicans know they will sweep most of the Deep South. Both parties compete to win swing states—states that might go either way in a race—to amass 270 Electoral College votes. Swing states keep changing. In 2020, election analysts had by midsummer identified six key swing states: Arizona, Florida, Michigan, North Carolina, Pennsylvania, and Wisconsin. In the end, Biden won four of the six (all but Florida and North Carolina) and shocked most observers by squeaking to victory in Georgia as well.[24]

In 2016, Hillary Clinton won by 2.9 million popular votes: 48.2 percent of the popular vote to Trump's 46.1 percent. So how did Trump win? Razor-thin margins in three states—Michigan (10,700 votes out of 4.7 million cast), Wisconsin (22,000 votes out of 4 million), and Pennsylvania (44,000 out of 6 million)—gave the Trump campaign all forty-six Electoral College votes and the presidency. In 2020, Biden won by more than seven million popular votes. But the outcome was close, once again, because he too won a series of swing states by razor-thin margins.

Why does the Electoral College seem to benefit Republicans who keep it close even while losing the popular vote by millions of voters? In part, because rural states have a small advantage (as we saw in Chapter 3, every state gets three Electoral College votes no matter how small). In addition, Democrats rack up huge margins in the cities. Republicans are more efficiently (at least for maximizing Electoral College votes) spread out over rural and suburban America (Figure 10.3). But a warning sign to Republicans: The suburbs have been moving into the Democratic column—the shifting suburban vote was the difference between victory (in 2016) and defeat (in 2020).

Many reformers (especially Democrats) criticize a system that regularly makes the popular vote loser the president. What might we do? The simplest fix would be to simply allocate each state's Electoral College vote to match its popular vote. Trump got 38 percent of the vote in New York, so he should get 38 percent (or eleven votes) in the Electoral College. That would have another advantage: Force candidates to campaign across the country instead of focusing all their time, energy, and money on a handful of swing states.

But here is a crucial historical point: The states regularly evolve. Forty years ago, California was reliably Republican, Texas Democratic. American politics is fluid, dynamic, and always changing. The 2020 changes in Latino voters (toward

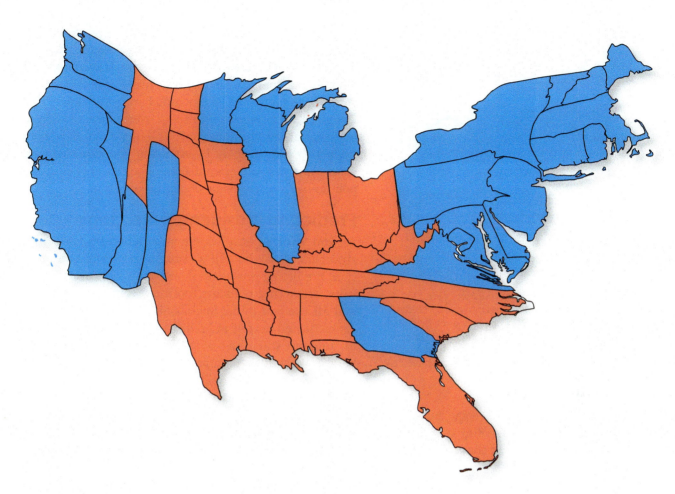

● **FIGURE 10.3** *The electoral map in 2020 with state size morphed to show size of Electoral College vote. Blue is Democrat, Red Republican. (Mark Newman)*

Republicans) and suburban voters (toward Democrats) are just the latest twists in the constant evolution of political attitudes.

Finally, one of the biggest factors is always the same: the people who do not show up. Despite record turnout in 2020, eighty million people did not vote. Why? Twenty-nine percent cited troubles registering; forty-three percent did not like the candidates or did not care enough about politics. All those nonvoters, especially in a close election, could be a blockbuster source of change if a candidate or a party could fire them up.[25]

That Elusive Winning Recipe. There is no sure recipe for winning a presidential election. They occur so rarely—the 2020 contest was only the nineteenth since World War II—and involve such an immense array of influences that journalists, historians, and political scientists spend years trying to draw lessons from each campaign.

In 2020, demographics mattered (Figure 10.4). In the wake of Trump's defeat in 2020, a great question hangs over the Republican Party's future: Will they find a way to reach out to minority and younger voters as those populations grow? In 2020, the white vote, which typically breaks Republican, fell from 70 percent (in 2016) to 66.7 percent of eligible voters—still a majority, but a steadily diminishing one. Meanwhile, voters who lean Democratic grew: Hispanic voters rose from 11 to 13 percent of all voters, Asian voters held steady at 5 percent, and Black voters

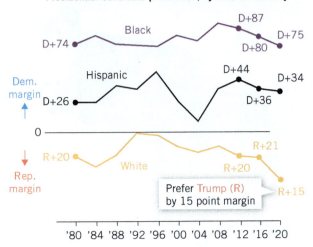

Presidential candidate preference, by race or ethnicity

● **FIGURE 10.4** *Demographics helps tell the story of the 2020 race—and other recent presidential elections. Note that Biden racked up huge margins among Black and Latino voters, while Trump's advantage among whites dropped from 21 to 15 points. But a warning to Democrats: some groups of Latino voters are slowly moving to the Republicans. Will that trend continue? (Pew Research Center)*

dropped from 13 to 12 percent. Overall, those changes helped boost the Democratic Party's presidential chances.

Changing demographics pose a major challenge for both political parties. Historically, two-thirds of Hispanic voters have supported Democratic Party candidates. Will Democrats continue to win them over on issues such as undocumented immigration? Or can Republicans continue to make inroads by stressing economics, moral values, and the American dream? The future of electoral politics lies in these rising demographic groups.[26]

Predicting Presidential Elections

Do you want an easy way to start a conversation with strangers? Ask who will win the next presidential election. Predicting presidential outcomes is a national pastime, attracting pollsters, political scientists, pundits, and all the rest of us. Social scientists have developed sophisticated models to predict the outcome on the basis of fundamentals long before the election. Some even believe that all the campaign excitement is irrelevant: Mathematical models will pick the winning party.

What goes into a model? Each has a slightly different recipe, but most political science models emphasize the economy; whether the country is at peace; presidential approval; and fatigue with the party in power—on that last point, no party has controlled the White House for more than two consecutive terms in the last seventy-six years.

How did the political science models do in 2020? See Table 10.3: Since President Trump ended up with 46.9 percent of the vote, five of the political science models came within 2 points; only two of them came within 1.5 points. That may not seem like a great track record, but average out all the models, and they almost score a direct hit: within 0.004—just under a half percentage point.

TABLE 10.3 Political Science Models Predict the 2020 Election

FORECASTER	PERCENTAGE OF TWO-PARTY VOTE TRUMP WILL WIN	PERCENTAGE POINTS BY WHICH THE MODEL MISSED (0 = PERFECT)	PREDICTED WINNER
Michael Lewis-Beck and Charles Tien, *Political Economy Model*	43.3	4.3	Biden
Robert Erikson and Christopher Wlezien, *Leading Economic Indicators*	45.0	2.6	Biden
Jay DeSart, *Long-Range State Level*	45.2	2.4	Biden
FiveThirtyEight.com	45.4	2.2	Biden
Peter Enns and Julius Lagodny, *State Presidential Approval/State Economy*	45.5	2.1	Biden
J. Scott Armstrong and Andreas Graefe, *PollyVote*	47.9	–0.3	Biden
Andreas Graefe, *Issues and Leaders*	48.6	–1.0	Biden

TABLE 10.3	*(continued)*		
FORECASTER	**PERCENTAGE OF TWO-PARTY VOTE TRUMP WILL WIN**	**PERCENTAGE POINTS BY WHICH THE MODEL MISSED (0 = PERFECT)**	**PREDICTED WINNER**
Thomas Gruca and Thomas Rietz, *Iowa Electronic Markets*	49.9	–2.3	Biden
Andreas Murr and Michael Lewis-Beck, *Citizen*	50.4	–2.8	Trump
Brad Lockerbie, *Prospective*	55.2	–7.6	Trump
Source: PS: Political Science and Authors' Compilation.			

THE BOTTOM LINE

» Presidential elections, despite their grueling intensity and duration, attract many aspirants every four years.

» Nearly all serious candidates for the presidency are experienced politicians. No candidate without any experience in the public sector had ever won the presidency—until Donald Trump.

» The three phases of the campaign—the nominating process, party conventions, and the general election—require different political strategies.

» Election outcomes are influenced by many factors: the economy, wars, organization, party loyalty, demographics, and the Electoral College. Add the roles of accident and luck, and election outcomes are often difficult to predict.

Congressional Elections

In contrast to the focus on two presidential candidates, congressional elections feature a colorful kaleidoscope of races across the country. Every two years, all 435 House districts hold an election, with an additional thirty-three or thirty-four Senate seats in play as well. It's a political junkie's dream.

Candidates: Who Runs for Congress?

Almost anyone can seek a seat in Congress. In the last two elections, candidates have included a leader of the Proud Boys militia, a whiskey distiller, three former sheriffs, a documentary filmmaker, seven ordained ministers, a former mixed martial arts fighter, and thirty-six supporters of the wacky QAnon conspiracy. As Table 10.4 shows, there are few limits on candidacy.

But winning is not easy. The average House race costs some $1.7 million; to make it to the Senate, you will need on average $13 million (depending on where you're running, of course).[27] Most candidates spend hours on the phone most workdays raising money. The personality traits that inspire candidates to run for Congress—self-confidence, leadership ability, and interest in politics—increase as people move up the political ladder.

TABLE 10.4	Requirements for Running for Congress
Age	Successful House candidates must be at least twenty-five years old to take office; senators must be at least thirty.
Citizenship	House candidates must have been a U.S. citizen for at least seven years; Senate candidates for at least nine.
Residence	Candidates must live in the state, though not necessarily the House district, where they are seeking election.

The median net worth of House and Senate members in 2020 was approximately $1 million (meaning half are above, half below).[28] However, congressional races attract relatively few top American business leaders, wealth holders, or celebrities—there are not many Mark Zuckerbergs, Elon Musks, or Oprahs in Congress. And when the famous or wealthy mount a run, they do not always win. Cleveland, Ohio, businessman Mike Gibbons spent more than $8 million of his own money seeking the Republican nomination for Senate in 2022 and lost—though he saved a significant sum compared to David Trone, who spent $13 million on a failed House campaign in 2016. (Rep. Trone won the next time around, in 2018.) World Wrestling Entertainment CEO Linda McMahon spent $100 million on her two failed Senate races in 2010 and 2012—although the publicity helped make her President Trump's head of the Small Business Administration.[29]

Each time one party targets a Senate candidate, the other party matches it. The price tag for Pennsylvania's Senate race in 2022 topped $375 million, smashing all prior records. Even little Maine's 2020 Senate race cost more than $200 million. The results reflected what political scientists have long found: Money alone rarely swings high-profile congressional elections. But with 468 races, the big money makes it hard to challenge most incumbents.[30]

If neither money nor celebrity guarantees a seat, here is a more promising shortcut to Congress: Be related to a member. One in eight members of Congress has a relative who already served (including twenty members who hold their parent's seat).

● Frederick Frelinghuysen, New Jersey delegate to the Continental Congress (1779) and later U.S. senator (1793–1796) (a). Frederick's great-great-great nephew Rodney Frelinghuysen served in the U.S. House from 1995 to 2018 (b). He was the sixth Frelinghuysen to represent New Jersey in Congress.

Since 1947, there usually has been a Kennedy in office in Washington—most recently, Congressman Joe Kennedy (D-MA), though he lost his Senate race in 2020. Other families—Bush, Adams, Roosevelt, Clinton—have built dynasties over the years.[31]

Still, political amateurs dominate each crop of new candidates challenging sitting members of the House for their seat. Typically, about one in six of these challengers is an elected official, usually from the state legislature; another 10 percent or so serve in nonelected government positions—often as former congressional staff. The remaining three-quarters are new to government service and often inspired by an issue or a cause. Senate candidates, because they run statewide, tend to be more experienced, and most are political veterans.

● A new generation: 2020 saw the largest number of women ever run for and win election to Congress. Here, California Republican Young Kim, who narrowly lost to Democrat Gil Cisneros in 2018 and then beat him by a razor-thin margin in a district that went for Democrat Joe Biden by 10 points. In 2022, redistricting forced Kim into a new district, where she won again. She is one of the most effective fundraisers in Congress.

Women on average are just as likely as men to win elections to Congress, but the parties were slower to recruit them as candidates, often because they were less eager to run. When they do run, they are more likely to draw primary challengers. In 2022, there were 125 women in the House (up from 88 four years ago) and 26 in the Senate—a bit more than a quarter of all members.[32]

Members of large minority groups (Blacks, Latinos, and Asian Americans) tend to run for Congress less often than white people. As we saw in Chapter 5, their ranks are slowly growing, especially in the House Democratic Caucus. The 117th Congress includes the most nonwhite members in history.

Talent and experience are vital in congressional races. Party leaders know that recruiting skilled candidates gives them an advantage—in both the election and in governing. How well Congress carries out its work depends on the ability of its members.

The Power of Incumbency

Talk to sitting members of Congress about reelection, and you will see the worry wash over their faces. House and Senate officeholders face a more volatile American electorate than they did a quarter-century ago: Voters are less predictable and harder to reach through traditional advertising. Now that virtually every utterance is digitally preserved, candidates have to be more careful about what they say.

Despite this more treacherous electoral environment, most incumbent House and Senate members fare very well in their quest for reelection. Fewer than ten House incumbents lost their general election in 2022, a typical number.

At first glance, this **incumbency advantage** is a mystery. As we explore in Chapter 13, Americans overwhelmingly give Congress a thumbs down. In June 2022, approval ratings for Congress sagged to 16 percent. Not the lowest on record but pretty dismal. What did the voters do? They voted most of the rascals right back in. Incumbents won some 95 percent of the races (see Figure 10.5).

What explains these consistently high incumbent success rates? For one thing, members have become very skilled at running *against* Congress. They

Incumbency advantage: The tendency for members of Congress to win reelection in overwhelming numbers.

● **FIGURE 10.5** *Senate (top) and House (bottom) reelection rates, 1966–2022. (Center for Responsive Politics)*

position themselves as reasonable individuals fighting against a dysfunctional institution—a position known as Fenno's paradox (named after a much-loved political scientist). And the way Congress operates—stalemate on the big issues, lots of little favors to constituents—makes the stance an easier sell. "I'm for expanding aid to needy children," say liberal members, "but I can't get it past the Republicans on Capitol Hill. Oh, and how about that new aquarium I funded?" GOP members tell a similar story.[33]

And back to money. Most congressional races feature very well-funded incumbents running against underfunded challengers. In short, members are attentive to constituents, raise a great deal of money, and already have staff and name recognition. Most win reelection. Here is the paradox: People despise Congress but defend their own representatives.[34]

Patterns in Congressional Elections

Midterm elections: National elections held between presidential elections, involving all seats in the House of Representatives, one-third of those in the Senate, thirty-six governorships, and other positions.

Midterm loss: The president's party typically loses congressional seats during the midterm elections.

Here's another familiar pattern: In most **midterm elections**, the president's party loses congressional seats—termed **midterm loss**. In the last forty midterm elections (going back to 1938), the president's party picked up seats in either chamber of Congress only five times—and only a few seats each time. In contrast, the president's party lost double-digit House seats eight of twelve times. In 2022's midterms the trend was upset, as Democrats lost only a handful of House seats and picked up one in the Senate (see Table 10.5). Remarkably, every Senate incumbent who stood for reelection won—the first time that has happened since 1914.

Another intriguing pattern involves elections when America is at war. Although we might expect voters to rally around the flag and support the president's party during wartime, in fact, the opposition usually wins seats in the congressional elections following a war's outbreak. Presidents Woodrow Wilson (World War I), Franklin Roosevelt (World War II), Harry Truman (Korea), Lyndon Johnson (Vietnam escalation), and George H. W. Bush (Gulf War) saw

| TABLE 10.5 | Midterm Congressional Election Results, 1970–2022 |

ELECTION YEAR	PRESIDENT	SEAT GAIN HOUSE	SEAT GAIN SENATE
2022	Biden (D)	R+5	**D+1**
2018	Trump (R)	D+41	**R+2**
2014	Obama (D)	R+13	R+9
2010	Obama (D)	R+63	R+6
2006	G. W. Bush (R)	D+30	D+6
2002	G. W. Bush (R)	**R+8**	**R+2**
1998	Clinton (D)	**D+5**	(No change)
1994	Clinton (D)	R+54	R+8
1990	G. H. W. Bush (R)	D+8	D+1
1986	Reagan (R)	D+5	D+8
1982	Reagan (R)	D+26	(No change)
1978	Carter (D)	R+15	R+3
1974	Ford (R)	D+48	D+3
1970	Nixon (R)	D+12	**R+1**

*The president's party has won seats in a midterm election only five times (indicated in **bold**) in the past fifty years. (Figures for 2022 are current as of November 15, 2022.)*

their parties suffer big losses in the first election after war was declared. George W. Bush (Iraq War) beat the cycle for two years, but then his party lost the House and Senate, as well as the presidency.

Redrawing the Lines: The Art of the Gerrymander

Fifty-one Democrats in the Texas House fled the state and holed up in Oklahoma. Legislative leaders called the Texas Rangers, the Federal Aviation Administration, and the Department of Homeland Security to "round 'em up and bring 'em home." What was going on?

Republicans had won control of the Texas legislature, and they immediately whipped out their red pens to redraw the congressional districts. Democrats claimed that Republicans were unfairly stacking the districts to ensure Republican winners—just as the Democrats traditionally did. Because they were going to lose a vote that they considered unfair, the Democrats fled the state to deny the majority a quorum (the number of members a legislature needs to have present to do official business). Sure enough, they eventually limped home and lost the vote over redistricting—and five House seats in the next election.

Redrawing congressional districts can have a significant impact on who gets elected (Figure 10.6). How does this work?

The House of Representatives has been fixed at 435 members for over a century. Every ten years, the census measures American population shifts, determines

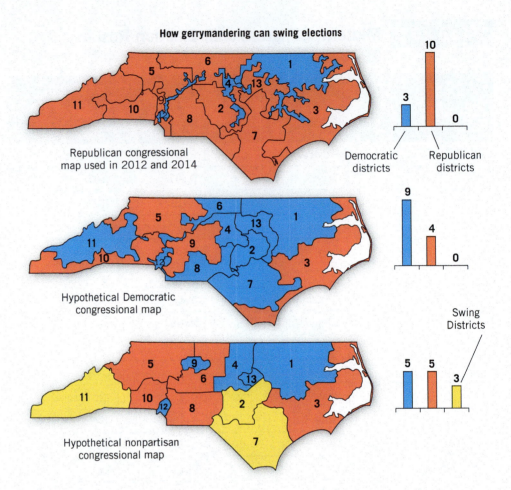

How gerrymandering can swing elections

Republican congressional map used in 2012 and 2014

Democratic districts | Republican districts

Hypothetical Democratic congressional map

Hypothetical nonpartisan congressional map

Swing Districts

FIGURE 10.6 *Both parties eagerly redraw the lines. Here, three versions in North Carolina yield completely different congressional delegations. (Daily Kos)*

Reapportionment:
Reorganization of the boundaries of House districts, a process that follows the results of the U.S. census, taken every ten years. District lines are redrawn to ensure rough equality in the number of constituents represented by each House member.

Gerrymander: Redrawing an election district in a way that gives the advantage to one party.

which states have gained or lost population, and **reapportions** House seats. In 2020, Texas gained two new seats; Florida, North Carolina, Montana, Colorado, and Oregon each gained one. Meanwhile, New York, California, Illinois, and West Virginia all lost a seat.

When populations shift, states redraw their election districts, a process called redistricting. Sometimes two U.S. House representatives will find themselves running against one another when their districts are combined.

In a **gerrymander**, the party in control of the state legislature draws the lines to help itself. See Figure 10.7 for a hypothetical example. Imagine a state called PoliSciLand that has two districts that are 100 percent Republican (A and B) and one district that is 100 percent Democratic (C): PoliSciLand sends two Republicans and one Democrat to Congress. Then an enterprising Republican on the redistricting committee says, "Hey, we're the majority in this PoliSciLand legislature. Let's redraw the congressional districts our way."

Check out the result: By drawing the district lines horizontally instead of vertically, Republicans take the Democratic district and split its voters into three different congressional districts. Instead of one district with 100 percent Democratic voters and two that are 100 percent Republican, PoliSciLand now has three districts, each 33 percent Democratic and 66 percent Republican. Without changing a single vote, our imaginary PoliSciLand state now has three House Republicans . . . and no Democrats.

The term *gerrymandering* goes back to 1812, when Massachusetts Governor Elbridge Gerry signed a bill that redrew the districts to help his party. One of Gerry's new districts looked like a salamander, which at that time was seen as

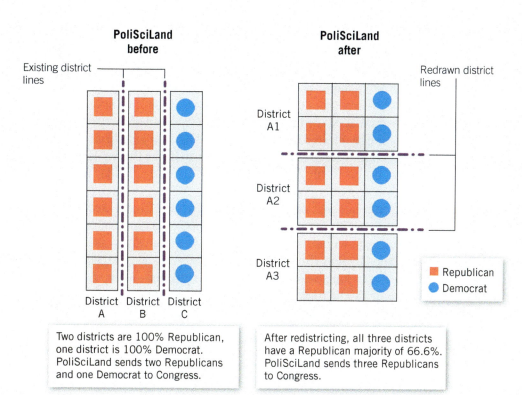

PoliSciLand before

Existing district lines

District A   District B   District C

PoliSciLand after

Redrawn district lines

District A1

District A2

District A3

■ Republican
● Democrat

Two districts are 100% Republican, one district is 100% Democrat. PoliSciLand sends two Republicans and one Democrat to Congress.

After redistricting, all three districts have a Republican majority of 66.6%. PoliSciLand sends three Republicans to Congress.

● **FIGURE 10.7** *How gerrymandering works—a hypothetical case of highly political redistricting.*

a sort of mythical dragon. "Gerry" + "salamander" = "gerrymander," and a great American contribution to the art of politics was born.

Today, with sophisticated information technology, state legislatures can carefully craft political boundaries. Two main techniques are "packing," or placing all the like-minded voters into one district, and "cracking," or spreading them out so that they form a minority in many districts. Because Democratic voters are crowded into cities, they are easy to pack. Our imaginary PoliSciLand cracked the Democratic district.

Savvy political observers carefully watch who wins the state legislatures in the round years ("10," "20," "30," . . .), because those results determine the majority that gets the job of redrawing the lines after the census numbers are announced. This is especially difficult if your state is losing population. An additional layer of confusion arose with the 2020 census, with data collection—crucial to an accurate snapshot of the population—delayed by the COVID-19 pandemic. Trump officials appear to have systematically undercounted undocumented individuals, quite possibly costing Texas, Florida, and Arkansas an additional seat.[35]

Redistricting processes in most states (even without a pandemic to contend with) are messy

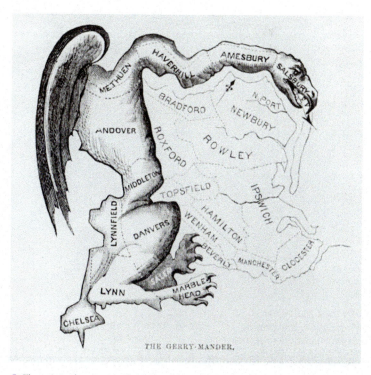

THE GERRY-MANDER.

● *The original gerrymander: Massachusetts, 1812.*

and politically charged. Many results look at least as bizarre as the original gerry-mander. Both political parties have perfected the practice, although Republicans have become masters of the art in multiple states. In Wisconsin, Democrats won every statewide office and a majority of the statewide vote in 2018, but thanks to ger-rymandering, won only thirty-six of the ninety-nine seats in the state assembly.

The 2022 midterms will be the first to use the latest round of gerrymanders. In Florida, Governor DeSantis rejected the legislature's redistricting map and proposed his own, which resulted in a congressional delegation that has twenty Republicans and eight Democrats—in an evenly divided state. Redistricting enabled a pickup of three GOP seats before any voters headed to the polls. What's lost are swing seats: There are only about 30 seats (out of 437) that don't lean to either party. But for all the complaints about Republicans, the Democrats appear to have come out of the latest district drawing wars with a very slight advantage (about six seats).[36]

As you can see, the election contest for House seats and state legislative seats usually begins in earnest—long before anyone starts running—when the state leg-islature sits down to draw the district. That has led some observers to quip that Congress selects their voters rather than voters selecting Congress.

Nonpartisan Districting and Minority Representation

Does all this seem unfair to you? Some reformers would like to put the whole process of drawing electoral districts into the hands of a nonpartisan commission that would divide states into natural communities and not tilt to any political side. California passed a law to do just that after the 2010 census—as have other states since (Figure 10.8). State legislative districts were redrawn by a "Citizens' Redistricting Commission" rather than by elected politicians, who naturally seek to protect their personal and partisan interests. The result was compact, contiguous districts faith-ful to existing geographic communities—and a lot of angry legislators at the state and U.S. House levels, who had to scramble to figure out their new district lines.

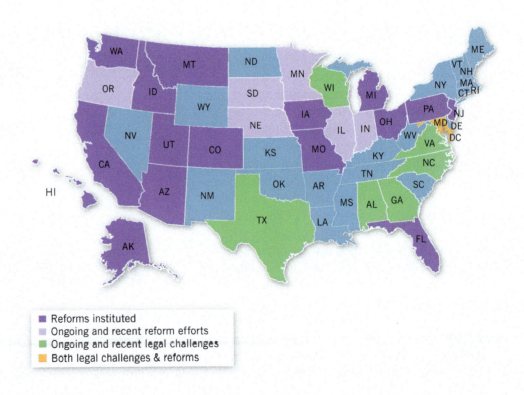

FIGURE 10.8 As gerry-mandering becomes more bare-knuckle, more states have moved toward nonpartisan commissions. (Reclaim the American Dream)

- Reforms instituted
- Ongoing and recent reform efforts
- Ongoing and recent legal challenges
- Both legal challenges & reforms

Guidelines generally direct redistricting commissions to keep racial and ethnic communities intact. In the past, some states used gerrymanders to create majority–minority districts—packed with Black voters. For Black Democrats, it was an anguishing call because it split two sides of their political identity: It delivered more Black representatives, but fewer Democrats.

As with so many American political disputes, redistricting and minority representation often wind up in court. In 2018, a Supreme Court majority held that courts should "presume" that states are acting in "good faith" and not aiming to suppress minority votes. Four liberal justices dissented and two saw "undeniable proof of intentional discrimination."[37]

The Supreme Court's ruling hardly ended litigation in this area. In 2020 alone, courts wrestled with minority representation and redistricting in multiple

---

COMPARING NATIONS 10.2 **American Parties in Context: How Would They Look in Europe?**

The U.S. Republican Party went far to the right of English conservatives, the Tories, in the 1980s (under Reagan); and then shifted right again with the Tea Party rebellion (in 2009–10). At that point, the Democrats were substantially closer to English Tories than the Republicans.

Then, starting in 2009, under President Obama, the Democrats moved back to the left, looking more like a typical European left party (though considerably to the right of the French socialists or the English Labour Party). And even with the leftward shift, the Democrats *still* lie closer to the English conservatives than to the Republican Party.

Source: Manifesto Project

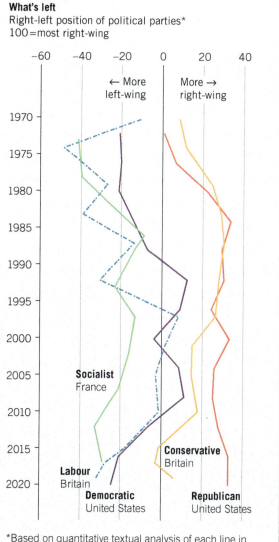

What's left
Right-left position of political parties*
100 = most right-wing

← More left-wing   More → right-wing

Socialist France

Conservative Britain

Labour Britain

Democratic United States

Republican United States

*Based on quantitative textual analysis of each line in party manifestos

states—Louisiana, North Carolina, Pennsylvania, and New York. These and other cases continued to wind their way through federal and state courts, even as the clock ticked down to Election Day.[38]

Presidents. Senate. House. Governors. Across every office, the two parties compete. Each charges the other with being out of touch and extreme. To see how the parties compare to the major parties in other nations, see Comparing Nations 10.2.

THE BOTTOM LINE

» Every two years, all 435 House seats and a third of the Senate seats are up for election.

» Very few restrictions govern who may run.

» House and Senate incumbents have powerful built-in advantages when running for reelection.

» The president's party generally loses House and Senate seats during midterm elections.

» Decennial redistricting of House seats can result in some strangely shaped—and politically motivated—districts, known as gerrymanders.

» Both parties gerrymander. In 2010, Republican control over state legislatures led to election districts that gave the Republicans an advantage in the House of Representatives.

» As the 2020 census results become clearer, a new wave of redistricting—and court cases—is mounting. Despite aggressive gerrymanders in Florida and Texas, Democrats may emerge with a small, incremental benefit.

 # Congressional Campaigns

Congressional candidates continue to navigate a changing political landscape, with the rise of social media, the influx of ever-greater sums of money into elections, and other developments. In this section, we examine how these trends are shaping the way candidates run for Congress.

Candidate-Centered Elections

In most democracies, political parties run campaigns—mobilizing voters and choosing slates of candidates to run under the party banner. Ask a classmate from another country who runs the government back home, and they will usually respond with a party name: Tories, or Socialists, or Liberal Democrats. Not in the United States. Over the past four decades, Americans have shifted to **candidate-centered elections**. Candidates themselves decide to run, raise money, grab airtime, and organize their own campaigns.

Why is the United States so different from other major democracies? It hasn't always been. Once upon a time the party bosses in many states quietly picked the candidates (puffing on cigars in smoke-filled rooms).[39] But primaries spread in

Candidate-centered elections: A system in which individual candidates decide to run, raise their own money, and design their own strategy—as opposed to party systems, in which political parties play these roles.

the 1970s. They required candidates for most offices to win a primary election. Anyone can leap in and run—undermining the party's ability to pick candidates. As social media expanded, candidates broke free from party databases, outreach, and fundraising.[40] Individual candidates now control their own destiny—deciding to run, raising their own money, choosing their issues, and organizing their team.

However, another trend limits a candidate's independence from the parties. As partisanship has risen, the party faithful who eagerly vote in low-turnout primaries has grown increasingly intolerant of moderates in the middle. Republicans who vote for a tax increase or Democrats willing to compromise on environmental standards have become endangered political species. Gerrymandered districts reinforce the trend by creating **safe districts**—where voters are likely to vote for one party over another by a large (safe) majority. Legislators are safe from the other party, but not from activists in low-turnout primaries who charge that the legislators have betrayed the party's values.

Safe district: A district consisting of voters who have historically voted for one party over the other by a large majority.

How to Run for Congress

Now that you know about campaigns and elections, are you ready to run your own race for Congress? It won't be easy, but following our advice will increase your chances. Here are our four keys to winning a congressional election—*money, organization, strategy,* and *message.* Even if you are not planning to run, remember these as you watch congressional races unfold in the next election.

Key 1: Money. First, you will need funds to mount a legitimate challenge—up to $2 million in many House districts and five to ten times that if you are running for the Senate. Where does all the money go? Advertising (on social media, TV, and direct mail) takes a big chunk, followed by database and demographic data, consultants, offices, phone banks, computers, and lawn signs. Unless you are wealthy, you are going to have to constantly "dial for dollars." Your staff will prepare **call lists**, leaving you to spend your days desperately filling your war chest.

Call list: A long list of potential donors who candidates must phone.

To boost your chances of winning and reduce the cost of campaigning, you may want to wait and run for an **open seat**—one with no incumbent running because of a member's retirement. Taking on an incumbent costs more each election cycle. Along with raising money, savvy newcomers find ways to get lots of media attention.

Open seat: A seat in Congress without an incumbent running for reelection.

Key 2: Organization. You also will need a well-constructed team to run for Congress. Somebody has to recruit and train your speechwriters, fundraisers, social media coordinators, and supportive community leaders. Back before the era of candidate-centered politics, parties took care of that work. Today, challengers like you usually have to create an organization from scratch.

There is a side benefit to assembling a talented campaign organization. Political insiders see hiring established pollsters, media experts, and so forth as the sign of a competitive campaign. Funders, recognizing a possible winner, will start directing more money your way. Although most new congressional candidates publicly decry the "professionalization" of campaign politics, almost all of them hire established members of the Beltway insiders' club.

If you're running for Congress, you will also want to make sure you know what your advisors are talking about. Table 10.6 includes a few insider terms from the campaign trail.

Key 3: Strategy. A fat bankroll and seasoned organization cannot compensate for a common rookie mistake—the lack of a well-conceived campaign strategy. Uncertainty is a central fact in every election, given fast-shifting political winds,

TABLE 10.6 Campaign Lingo

Robocall	Automated phone call used to contact thousands of voters; often features a recorded message by the candidate or a popular party personality—or an attack on the opponent.
Advance team	Campaign staffers who arrive at the site of major events ahead of time to organize the site and build crowds.
Field/GOTV	The staff and volunteers who engage one-on-one with the public to encourage them to vote.
Retail campaigning	Attracting supporters or votes one by one, through door-to-door visits or small meetings.
Wholesale campaigning	Reaching hundreds or thousands at once through a speech, targeted advertisement, or robocalls.
Oppo	Conducting research on the opposition to identify weakness.
Text-to-donate	Use of text messages to donate funds to a campaign. Tightly regulated by the Federal Election Commission: For example, donations to any one candidate are limited to $50 per phone billing period.

opponents' moves, and the power of unexpected events. Incumbents tend to stick to the strategy that worked the last time. Challengers must invent a strategy that plays well to their political and personal strengths.

Two elements of successful congressional campaign strategies are vital: building a coalition of supporters and connecting with voters. Every state or district includes local business leaders, political activists, religious leaders, and spokespeople for identity groups. Strategically attracting some of them is essential. A coalition-building strategy also targets broader groups likely to vote for a party's candidate.

During the 1980s and 1990s, House Republican candidates in district after district forged coalitions of conservative, middle-aged, white, Protestant, relatively affluent voters. They broke through and took (and held) the House for the first time in sixty years. By 2006, this reliable lineup had fragmented in many places, and Democrats won forty-seven of forty-eight contested House seats to retake control of the chamber. In 2010, a new Republican coalition, now fueled by Tea Party activists, featuring a larger proportion of lower-income, disaffected white voters, and animosity toward President Obama, regained control of the House. By 2018, the House was back in Democratic hands in the usual backlash against a Republican president, this time Trump. And in 2022, back it went once again, a reaction against Biden. Notice how fast the winds shift in contemporary electoral politics. If you're unhappy about the results, just wait a bit. If recent years are a guide, the backlash will soon begin.

Candidates primarily reach voters through the media. Candidate strategies need to include plenty of high-profile events—speeches, press conferences, visits to hospitals or nursing homes—that attract media coverage. If you cannot build crowds because of your low **name recognition**, you may resort to more creative approaches—bring in a local celebrity. Anything for airtime!

Name recognition: An advantage possessed by a well-known political figure, a political celebrity.

You also will need a smart social media strategy and brand identity. Instagram, tweets, Google banner ads, clever TikToks—all these are essential to grab eyeballs for your campaign.

But don't forget old-fashioned politicking. Knocking on someone's door and meeting face to face is still the best way to win votes. As a House challenger in 1974, Bill Clinton announced his intention to "shake every hand in the district." Clinton lost that race but employed the strategy in his next race for Arkansas governor, which he won. "I'd go to the store," reported one local, "there was young Bill Clinton. Go to the movies—there he was at the entrance, hand out. Eventually I told him I'd vote for him if I just didn't have to shake his hand anymore!"[41]

Sadly, there's another effective strategy: **negative campaigning**. This usually involves strewing seeds of doubt in voters' minds about your opponent's policy positions, ethics, and character. Much as you may find this strategy repugnant, many argue that "going negative" works. However, recent work in political science suggests that negative ads may not change many minds or actually win elections. The effect of all advertising, positive or negative, seems to decay quickly.[42]

Still, the proportion of negative ads grows. You can expect that the other side's opposition researchers will portray you in the least flattering light possible. The point is not to change people's minds but to discourage the weaker supporters on the other side—going negative is thought to keep them home on Election Day.

Negative campaigning: Running for office by attacking the opponent.

Key 4: Message.   Finally, you have to give people a good reason to vote for you. Candidates with a clear, powerful message sometimes topple better-financed and more elaborately organized opponents. In 2014, an unknown economics professor with a shoestring budget ($200,000) named David Brat upset House Majority Leader Eric Cantor. In 2020, a young former middle school principal, Jamaal Bowman, upset thirty-two-year House veteran Rep. Eliot Engel (D-NY). Both long-shot candidates had the same message: Their opponents had lost touch with the district. In 2018, Brat himself lost to a candidate, Abigail Spanberger, with a clear message: women and healthcare.

In the relatively rare case that a first-time challenge like yours is victorious, what can you expect as a freshman member of Congress? What comes next?

A *new campaign*, starting immediately. For House members, the next election looms just two years away. Senators have a more relaxing six years—but must run statewide, which in high-population or sprawling states is very time consuming. The legendary House Speaker Sam Rayburn told each incoming House freshman class that "a member of Congress can be elected by accident, but seldom reelected by accident." Voters back home will watch a first-term member especially closely, as will colleagues on Capitol Hill.

As a sitting representative or senator, you may join your colleagues in denouncing Washington as corrupt and in need of reform. That message gives incumbents a quick-shot electoral boost, but it has corroded Americans' support for their national legislature in recent decades. And this decline in support raises an important concluding question: Is the American electoral system in need of reform? And if so, how?

● *The newly elected Republican members of Congress, 2021. The old ritual lined up new members from both parties—yet another casualty of the partisan wars.*

THE BOTTOM LINE

» To run successfully for Congress, follow a few vital steps: Raise sufficient funds (and then raise more), organize a talented team, develop a strategy that plays to your strengths, and hone your message.

» If you win, you become a freshman. Well done! Now, start running all over again—your reelection campaign has begun.

Conclusion: Reforming American Elections

Does the U.S. electoral system work? In this chapter we highlighted a variety of concerns—from gerrymanders to incumbency rates to the influence of money in politics. Is it a problem that we keep sending the same representatives back to Congress, up to 98 percent of the time? Is it a problem that big spenders often win elections? Many reforms have been proposed. Here we focus on four.

Start with *gerrymanders*. We could try to end partisan battles over legislative districts by asking neutral panels to draw the lines—nine states do so for congressional districts, fourteen for state legislators. The goal: rational, compact, community-based districts that don't tilt to either party. The proposals always face the same challenges: Can we really trust the experts to find truly neutral districts? Indeed, is there any such thing? Iowa has tried to address the objections by giving the job to a nonpartisan panel and then forwarding the plans they draw up to the state legislature for an up or down vote. This reform debate heats up every time either party draws another outrageously biased district.

Second, turn to the way we elect the president. Over the years, the *Electoral College* has come in for a lot of criticism. In two of the last five elections, the candidate who lost the popular vote went into the White House. Moreover, the presidential election campaign shrinks to fit a small number of swing states. If you're in New York (safely Democratic) or Utah (Republican), you won't get any attention from either campaign. One simple fix: Push the states to split their electoral vote based on popular-vote share. Candidates who win a third of the popular vote could get a third of the electoral votes. Remember, states set the rules—and each could make this change for itself.

Next comes *money*. Do we really want our legislators spending hours each day, every day, raising funds? Do we want them piling up so much cash that no one can afford to run against them? Does it make sense to permit a single wealthy donor to fund a presidential candidate right through the presidential primaries? And even though political scientists have not found anything like direct "pay-to-play" schemes—contributing to a campaign for a policy payoff after the election—big donors certainly enjoy personal access to their representatives, and perhaps subtle forms of influence, especially over small issues (e.g., items in the tax code), which are difficult to measure.[43]

What reforms could we try? The simplest is simply to forbid anonymous donations (known as "dark money"). Let the public know exactly who is funding that oppo (negative research) shop.

● *Complaints about corporate influence go far back in American history. In 1889, cartoonist Joseph Keppler suggested that large corporate trusts were the real "bosses of the Senate." (a) The Senate of that era was eventually reformed. Does ours need reform as well? Here senators arrive for work sporting "snazzy jumpsuits" emblazoned with the names of their big corporate donors (b).*

A more ambitious proposal would limit and regulate campaign spending. And, going even further, many reformers call for publicly financed elections, in which the government provides equal funding to each candidate and permits small donations from the public. (Most other advanced democracies run elections this way.) Public financing would create a much more even playing field between incumbents and challengers. Several states—including Arizona, Connecticut, and Maine—have tried publicly funding statewide elections. In fact, many states are eager to experiment with campaign finance—using those laboratories of democracy to test different approaches (as we discussed in Chapter 4).[44]

Campaign finance reform polls well, but it also has strong critics. If a candidate excites you, why shouldn't you be able to support them as much as you like? Shouldn't corporations be permitted to fight for issues that matter to them—like lower taxes, fewer regulations, or access to abortions?

For now, the Supreme Court has taken the campaign finance debate almost entirely out of politics—striking down laws on both the national and the state level. The Court majority defines spending as speech—protected by the First Amendment (see Chapter 5). But the issue remains controversial in both jurisprudence and in politics. A more liberal court would put campaign finance back into political play.

How about *term limits*? The president (and governors of thirty-six states) are limited to two terms. Why not limit members of Congress to, say, twelve years of service? Here, many political scientists are skeptical. The problem with this reform is that good legislating takes skill. Term limits clear out legislators just when they have learned how to become effective.[45] Although twenty-one states instituted term limits on state legislators, starting in the 1990s, six have rolled them back—with others considering the move. The reform did introduce fresh faces, but the turnover had an unexpected downside. Seasoned lobbyists—no term limits for them—stepped in to "guide" the steady flow of rookie legislators. Still, proponents of the reform reply that incumbents become most skilled at staying in office—term limits would open Congress to novel ideas and talent.

These are four of the most popular reform ideas. Individual states have tried versions of each, but we still have partisan gerrymandering in most states, a winner-take-all Electoral College (with two exceptions, Maine and Nebraska), few (and declining) limits on campaign spending, and no term limits for Congress. In the end, the vast majority repeatedly win reelection to a partisan Congress that often bogs down in stalemate—and receives worse grades than almost any other institution in American life.

Is the system broken? Do the Electoral College, the barriers to voting, the role of money, and partisan gerrymanders derail majority rule too extensively? Or is American electoral politics doing what it has always done: giving a raucous people their voice while muddling through just fine? We will look at this issue from different angles when we study Congress in Chapter 13 and the presidency in Chapter 14.

Whether the system needs reform or not, campaigns and elections provide avenues to participation for the many groups in American society. Despite all the barriers and problems, repeated waves sweep new people, new voices, and new ideas into office. Each generation of Americans decides whether to shake up the system of campaigns and elections or to leave things in place. Every election brings new excitement, new voters, and new ideas into American politics: 2020 saw a surge of victories for women and people of color, and a repudiation of President Trump's divisive policies. New faces elected in 2022 include the first-ever Gen Z House member, 25-year-old Maxwell Frost (D-Fla.). American campaigns and elections may have many problems—but they have created a regular source of innovation and change in Washington, DC.

We are especially proud of our many students who have run (and won!) seats in state legislatures and in Congress. We hope that you get engaged too. After reading this chapter, you should better understand the challenges we face. And that engaging in elections remains the only way to ensure government by the people.

CHAPTER SUMMARY

★ Elections define democracies. They give the people a say over who governs them.

★ A key question in this chapter is: Are American elections democratic enough?

★ American electoral systems are unique because:

- We vote on a huge number of offices—over 520,000.

- We vote often compared to other nations.

- Federal elections for the House of Representatives take place every even-numbered year.

- Across the U.S. there are significant elections held every year.

★ The Constitution puts the states in charge of running elections, instructing them to manage "the time, place, and manner." But it is silent on crucial matters—such as who has the right to vote.

★ In the last sixty years, all presidents have had one of just three jobs on their résumés: vice president, governor, or senator. Donald Trump became the first president in American history with no public sector experience.

★ The road to the White House passes through three stages: primaries, the party convention, and the general election.

★ The most familiar question about American democracy today involves the role of money in election campaigns. PACs, super PACs, and 527s have become fixtures in national elections.

★ The only constitutional limits to running for Congress are age, citizenship, and residency in the state.

★ Winning a race for Congress takes money, organization, strategy, constituent service, name recognition, and a good knowledge of the district.

★ Every ten years, the state legislatures redraw their congressional districts to keep up with changes in the population. The *gerrymander* is a district that is redrawn to help one party.

★ Across time, some striking patterns have emerged in congressional elections: The president's party loses seats in the midterm elections, results have grown more volatile (with the party in power shifting often), and war spells trouble for the president's majority.

KEY TERMS

527 groups, p. 314
Bundling, p. 314
Call list, p. 335
Candidate-centered elections, p. 334
Caucus, p. 317
Closed primary, p. 317
Electoral bounce, p. 320
Gerrymander, p. 330

Incumbency advantage, p. 327
Midterm elections, p. 328
Midterm loss, p. 328
Name recognition, p. 336
Negative campaigning, p. 337
Open primary, p. 317
Open seat, p. 335
Political action committee
(PAC), p. 313

Proportional representation, p. 319
Reapportionment, p. 330
Safe district, p. 335
Super PACs, p. 314
Super Tuesday, p. 319
Time, place, and manner clause, p. 308
Winner-take-all, p. 319

STUDY QUESTIONS

1. Describe the limits that the Constitution places on popular participation in elections. Which one federal office could people originally vote for directly? Which people were generally not permitted to vote?
2. For further study: Is the American system of elections democratic enough for the twenty-first century? Defend your position by pointing to features that make it more (or less) democratic.
3. Describe the American system of campaign finance. What are PACs? How about super PACs? What influence did the *McCutcheon v. FEC* Supreme Court decision have on the system?
4. For further study: What is campaign finance reform? Make an argument for or against campaign

finance reform. If possible, explain how recent research supports your argument.
5. Describe the three stages of a U.S. presidential campaign. What were highlights of each stage during the 2020 contest?
6. You have decided to run for Congress. What four things will your campaign need to be successful?
7. What is negative campaigning? Why do candidates rely on it so heavily?
8. Consider this: If you were running for Congress, would you use negative campaign ads against your opponent? Why or why not?
9. Describe three reforms that have been suggested for U.S. campaigns and elections. Now, pick one and argue informedly for or against it.

11 POLITICAL PARTIES

CONGRESSMAN RON MACHTLEY, a moderate Republican from Rhode Island, enjoyed playing basketball in the House gym. Washington was a lonely place, with his friends and family back home, and the games were a great way to relax. One day in the early 1990s, a couple of serious-looking men came up to him with a blunt message from the rising Republican leader, Newt Gingrich (R-GA): "You're playing with the enemy—Democrats. No more basketball." Gingrich believed that Republicans had grown too comfortable in the minority, where they had languished for most of the last sixty years. The path back to power, he believed, required fire and resolve.[1]

Machtley was stunned. Until recently, Democrats and Republicans would battle it out during the day and then adjourn to bourbon and tall tales at night. Members of the two parties worked together to craft important laws. The Senate passed the Civil Rights Act (1965) thanks, in part, to Northern Republicans; five years later, Congress passed the Clean Air Act, a blockbuster environmental bill, almost unanimously (there was only one negative vote), and it was signed into law by Republican President Richard Nixon. In 1997, the Republican congressional majority worked with Democratic President Bill Clinton to extend health insurance to seven million children.

Cross-party majorities were not unusual because there was as much difference *within* each party as there was between the parties. The Democratic Party appealed to very conservative Southerners and very liberal Northerners; Republicans also stretched across the political spectrum. In the early 1990s, almost as many Republicans (86 percent) as Democrats (93 percent) agreed that the "nation needed stricter environmental laws and regulations."[2]

Those days are over. Liberals sorted themselves overwhelmingly into the Democratic Party, conservatives went to the Republicans, and now **partisanship** touches every aspect of politics—even over whether to wear face masks to protect others during a deadly pandemic.

The difference between parties is greater than any of the other divisions in American politics: greater than differences in race, income, education, religion, or gender. Today, Democrats continue to support strong environmental regulations, but the number of Republicans who do so has dropped by

In this chapter, you will

 Learn about the role parties play in governing America.

 Explore the two-party system and compare it to parties in other nations.

 Analyze a great paradox: Why Americans like parties . . . but don't like partisanship.

 Trace the history of parties in the United States.

 Investigate the organization and ideas of the parties and why people identify with one party (or why they don't).

 Reflect on the strength of parties and whether the United States has grown too partisan.

Partisanship: Taking the side of a party or espousing a viewpoint that reflects a political party's principles or position on an issue.

● *Nancy Pelosi, the Democratic leader in the House (known as the Speaker) rips up a copy of President Trump's State of the Union speech in February 2020 while the president is still speaking. Before the speech Pelosi had extended her hand and President Trump had refused to shake it. Until recently, party leaders were courteous to one another even when they disagreed. Not anymore.*

nearly fifty points since 2000. A wide divide has opened on almost every issue, leading most engaged Democrats (70 percent) to say Republicans make them "afraid," "angry," and "frustrated"—and similar majorities of Republicans believe Democrats will ruin the country.

Today, most Americans live near, hang out with, date, and marry people with similar political views. More than seven out of ten Democrats across the United States would refuse to date someone who voted for Trump. And that's just as well, since six out of ten party members would be unhappy if their children married across the party divide.[3] One study found that 15 percent of Republicans and 20 percent of Democrats believed the country would be better off if a large number of opposing partisans "just died."[4]

National party divisions are stronger today than they have been for at least a century (see Figure 11.1). A major focus of this chapter: Is that a bad thing? Does intense disagreement make it harder to govern? Is it splitting the country apart, as most people believe? Or might it actually enhance the people's voice by giving Americans a real choice between clashing principles and policies?[5]

Political party: A group that shares political principles and is organized to win elections and hold power.

Unlike almost every other institution we discuss in this book, **political parties** are not mentioned in the Constitution. Why? Because the founders despised them. President George Washington warned against parties as "destructive," "frightful," and "fatal." Thomas Jefferson, who helped organize the first party (against national government), offered the most memorable zinger: "If I could not get to heaven but with a party, I would not go there at all."[6]

The deep corruption of the nineteenth-century political parties seemed to justify the founders' fears (cynical politicians half-jokingly urged supporters, "Vote early, vote often"). By the mid-1800s, the two political parties—the rival engines of democracy—were the largest and most influential organizations in the nation. Corrupt or not, nineteenth-century Americans discovered they could not run a democratic republic without parties. Today, parties shape national elections, congressional votes, policy decisions, judicial rulings, state government, and our own political opinions.

Who are we? A deeply partisan people who helped invent the modern political party. Parties provide a vital link between Americans and public officials. Many Americans form lifelong party attachments, fear the other party, and yet are quick to denounce partisanship.

As partisan divides over political values widen, other gaps remain more modest

Average gap in the share taking a conservative position across 10 political values, by key demographics

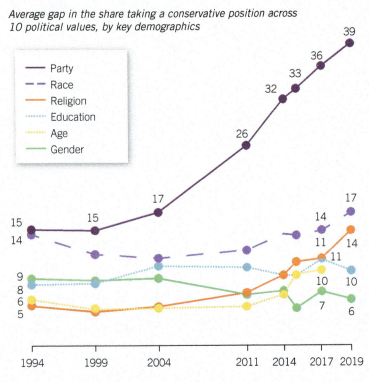

FIGURE 11.1 *Knowing what political party you vote for predicts your values and political opinions more than anything else about you. More than your education, your race, your gender, or your religion. Pay special attention to the change over the last twenty years. (Pew Research Center)*

BY THE
NUMBERS Political Parties

28 Percentage of Americans who identified as Democrats and as Republicans in 2022[7]

42 Percentage of Americans who identified as independents in 2022[8]

80 Percentage of people who say they are independents but almost always vote for one party[9]

71 Percentage of Republicans who say they believe Trump won reelection in 2020 (although he did not)[10]

3 Percentage of Democrats who say they believe Trump won reelection in 2020 (although he did not)[11]

17 Percentage of Asian voters who identified as (or lean toward) Republicans in 2020[12]

10 Percentage of Black voters who identified as (or lean toward) Republicans in 2020[13]

29 Percentage of Hispanic voters who identified as (or lean toward) Republicans in 2020[14]

53 Percentage of white voters who identified as (or lean toward) Republicans in 2020[15]

39 Percentage of college graduates who identified as Democrats in 1994[16]

53 Percentage of college graduates who identified as Democrats in 2020[17]

Zero Total number of parties (other than Republican or Democratic) getting at least one electoral vote in the last fifty years

What groups support each party today? Why do so many people call themselves independents and yet consistently vote with one party?

Political Parties and the U.S. Government

The Democratic congressman was blunt. "When President Obama was elected, the Republicans did everything to defeat everything—every single thing—he proposed." Well, it worked. The Republicans won control of Washington. Suddenly, Democrats were in the opposition and what did they do? Blocked Trump proposals, and it worked again—Democrats briefly won back control of both chambers in 2020. The cycle continued. One Congressman we talked to summed it up beautifully: "The electoral incentives for both parties are clear: Block the opposing party, denounce them as inept, come back into the majority."[18]

In the first two Biden years, there were flickers of bipartisanship. Nineteen Senate Republicans voted with Democrats on an infrastructure bill, ten for gun control, and three to confirm Justice Ketanji Brown Jackson to the Supreme Court. The slow return of a truce between the parties? Probably not.

After 2020, the tension between the parties ramped up even further. Most Republicans (71 percent) believe former President Trump's reelection falsehoods. Many ran for office (and, in 2022, nearly 200 won) on those claims; in contrast, just 3 percent of Democrats question the election results. And beneath the election claims lies animosity. Some political scientists worry that the mutual animosity is eroding our political institutions to the point that some party members would choose winning power over free and fair elections.[19]

The partisan conflict might tempt you to agree with President George Washington: Do we really need parties? The answer is "yes." We need parties that work. Let us see why.

What the Parties Do

Love them or hate them, political parties are an essential part of American government. They are responsible for five major jobs: championing ideas, selecting candidates, mobilizing voters, organizing the government after elections, and integrating new voters into the political process.

Parties Champion Ideas.   U.S. politics reverberates with ideas, as we saw in Chapter 2, and every candidate takes a position on scores of issues. How do voters keep all these positions straight? In effect, parties create a brand that gives people an easy way to find candidates who roughly share their views. If you strongly support environmental activism, a path to citizenship for undocumented immigrants, robust social programs, a woman's right to choose, a tax on the wealthy, limits on gun purchases, public radio, and high-speed rail, you are probably a Democrat. If, on the other hand, you care more about lowering taxes, reducing the size of government, deporting undocumented immigrants, supporting traditional families, and outlawing abortion, you are probably a Republican. Do you prefer to mix and match from the lists? You tend to be an independent who belongs to neither party—though political scientists know that four out of five independents are not really independent—they regularly vote for one party.[20]

At the same time, parties—and what they represent—are always evolving. Every election introduces new ideas and goals. Candidate Donald Trump challenged many traditional Republican views—he opposed free trade agreements, defended Russia's government, opposed military action, mocked past Republican presidents, and insisted that elites had "flourished" while factories closed. Despite the many breaks with the past, President Trump won support (and often adulation) from a sky-high 90 percent of Republican Party members. By his race for reelection in 2020, Trump had rewritten the Republican Party playbook and had made himself the central force in the party.

Across the aisle, Joe Biden had spent his long career as a moderate eager to work with Republicans. But as he campaigned for president, he began to draw on proposals from the left side of the party—like a tax on the wealthy and relief from student debt. In contrast to the Republicans, who sometimes resemble a fervent unified movement, Democrats include different (often clashing) interests and perspectives from the political center to the progressive left.

Parties Select Candidates.   Parties choose the candidates who will run for election. Democrats began with a record twenty-nine contenders for president in 2020 and voted, state by state, until they had selected Joe Biden as their candidate.

The parties also sponsor candidates far beyond Washington. They select candidates to run for office at every level of government except local government, which sometimes relies on **nonpartisan elections**.

Parties Mobilize Voters.   Party leaders work to get people to vote for their candidates. The parties raise money, hire consultants, craft advertisements, take polls, and organize social media campaigns. They also try to suppress the other side's votes through negative advertising. And party affiliation does tend to enhance political participation—especially among the young. Americans aged eighteen to thirty years tend to be far more involved if they describe themselves as Republicans or Democrats—in contrast to those who call themselves independents.[21]

Parties Organize Governing Activity After the Election.   Once the election is over, each party works to enact its programs. Leaders set agendas, line up votes, and organize their teams in Congress (as we will see in Chapter 13), in presidential administrations (as we will see in Chapter 14), and in state governments (as we saw in Chapter 4). After the 2022 election, Republicans controlled twenty-three state governments (governor and legislature), Democrats controlled fourteen, and thirteen were split between the parties.

Parties Help Integrate New Groups into the Political Process.   Parties are important agents of **political socialization**, drawing groups into politics. Savvy party leaders are always looking for overlooked groups they can rally to their cause. Barack Obama inspired Black Americans, who turned out at higher rates than white Americans for the first time in American history in 2012.[22] In 2016, Donald Trump galvanized white males without a college degree—who had felt abandoned by both Democrats and Republicans. Four years later, Joe Biden appealed to independents who had previously voted at lower rates. Over the years, parties have reached out to immigrants (usually Democrats), evangelical Christians (Republicans), young voters (both parties, depending on the era), high-tech entrepreneurs, and every other group you can imagine. Parties link 260 million voting-age Americans to their elected leaders.

Political parties provide an efficient, effective solution to these five issues.[23] Is there anything especially distinctive about the American **party system**? Yes: The United States is unusual because it relies on just two major parties.

Two-Party America

In January 2023, all 435 members of the House of Representatives, ninety-eight out of one hundred senators, and all fifty governors were either Democrats or Republicans. Why is the United States so resolutely devoted to the number "two" when it comes to party politics?

Perhaps this two-party tradition rests on American ideas (see Chapter 2). Democrats and Republicans often take different sides in the great American debate over ideas. For example, Republicans see liberty as freedom from

Nonpartisan election: An election in which candidates run as individuals, without any party affiliation. Many towns and cities feature nonpartisan elections.

Political socialization: Education about how the government works and which policies one should support; provided by parents, peers, schools, parties, and other national institutions.

Party system: The broad organization of U.S. politics comprising the two main parties, the coalition of supporters backing each, the positions they take on major issues, and each party's electoral achievements.

● *Parties socialize new groups into politics. Few presidents inspired as much fervor among evangelicals as Donald Trump. Here, evangelicals greet the president at a 2020 rally in Miami (a) and Barack Obama supporters celebrate his presidential reelection in 2012 (b). For the first time in history, Black voters voted at a higher rate than white voters when Obama ran for president.*

government coercion, while most Democrats emphasize "freedom from want" and support government programs that will ensure everyone has the basics.

As you know by now, institutions reinforce ideas. In this case, the winner-take-all electoral rules, described in Chapter 10, keep third parties out. The Libertarian or the Green Party may amass a great many votes, but even a party that wins 20 percent of the national vote and does not win an outright majority in any state gets zero votes in the Electoral College. The same goes in Congress. If a party does not win an outright majority in any district, it comes up with zero seats.

In contrast, most other democracies operate multiparty systems. Proportional representation systems give a party that wins 20 percent of the vote roughly 20 percent of the seats in the legislature. A French sociologist named Maurice Duverger drew the conclusion: American-style elections (often described with a horse-racing metaphor, "first past the post") generally yield a two-party system, while proportional representation produces many parties.

The result is simple and dramatic: The rules push every group to join one of the two major parties. When candidates decide to break out of the two-party system, they are accused of being "spoilers"—throwing the election to the opposing party that does not share their philosophy at all.

Consider the 2000 presidential election. In Florida, Republican George Bush beat Democrat Al Gore by a scant 537 votes (out of almost 6 million cast). But Green Party candidate Ralph Nader pulled in more than 97,000 (mostly liberal) votes. Bush's 0.001 percent margin gave him all 25 electoral votes in Florida and made him president. Disappointed Democrats blasted Ralph Nader for drawing just enough liberals to throw the election to the Republicans.

The same thing happened to the Republicans in 2020. On Election Day, Senator David Perdue easily won the Senate race in Georgia by over eighty-eight thousand votes—more than 2 percent. But because a Libertarian candidate drew a smattering of (mainly conservative) votes, Perdue missed an outright majority by a whisker (0.3 percent) on Election Day (Georgia rules require 50 percent to win) and then lost in a runoff two months later, throwing not just the Georgia seat but the entire Senate over to the Democrats. Experiences like these reinforce the institutional lesson: Work within the two parties.

Other institutional forces reinforce the two-party system. State laws determine who gets on the ballot, and they often make it very difficult for minor party candidates. In Florida, for example, a candidate for major office (governor, senator) must collect 144,419 notarized signatures simply to get on the ballot. And if you're running for president, you'll need a stack of signatures in every state. Without an organized party, a big wallet, and a battery of lawyers, it's almost impossible to get on the ballot in all fifty states.

The advantage of America's two-party system: It is predictable and stable. In nations with many parties, each election is followed by negotiations among the parties trying to form a majority. Germany has three parties in the ruling coalition (including the environmentally minded Green Party).

Die Partei is a satirical party in Germany. Their campaign poster mocks the political discussion ("Bla, Bla,…") and makes outlandish promises: "If you vote for us, we will execute the 100 richest Germans." The party won two seats in the European Parliament in 2019, receiving over nine hundred thousand votes.

Spain has five. And Israel sent voters to the polls three times in one year before leaders were able to cobble a coalition of eight parties; when just one legislator bolted the coalition (in June 2022), the administration collapsed and the Israelis had to go back to the polls yet again.

There also are disadvantages to two-party dominance in the United States.[24] For starters, it is less representative. In 2020, over 15 percent of the voters in Massachusetts voted for Republican congressional candidates. Is it fair to end up with nine Massachusetts Democrats—and no Republicans—in Congress?

Voters in Germany or Japan or other proportional representation systems generally have more choices for national or local office; people passionate about a cause—immigration, the environment, religion, racial justice, free markets, women's rights—can often find a party devoted to their cause (see Comparing Nations 11.1). And when those parties enter a governing coalition, they can make sure their issue stays alive.

Did Americans *ever* make room for additional parties? The answer is simple: no! It's always been two.

Third Parties in American Politics

Theodore "Teddy" Roosevelt is one of the most colorful figures in U.S. political history: a military hero who suffered from asthma and a big-game hunter who adopted an orphaned bear cub (giving rise to the familiar "teddy bear"). When Roosevelt came out of retirement to run as a Progressive Party candidate, he became one of only two third-party presidential candidates to come in second—but he still got clobbered by Woodrow Wilson, who won 435 electoral votes to Roosevelt's 88.

Table 11.1 lists all third-party presidential contestants who gained more than 5 percent of the popular vote or more than ten electoral votes since 1848. It is a short list, without a single candidate who came close to winning. And most third parties lasted just one term (or four years) at the national level. Roosevelt's Progressive Party, for example, elected some fifteen members to Congress and spearheaded important reforms but dissolved within four years.

COMPARING NATIONS 11.1   **Organizing Electoral/Governing Systems**

The international community features many different party arrangements. There are subtle differences among all nations, but a few main organizational styles tend to predominate, and each produces a different style of party politics.

Multiparty systems: The vast majority of the world's countries are governed along multiparty lines, from India to Italy and Japan to Tokelau, a tiny group of Pacific islands with about 1,400 inhabitants and three political parties. A coalition of two or more parties, with frequently shifting alliances and complex power-sharing arrangements, usually forms a government in multiparty systems.

Two-party systems: The United States is the largest two-party state; other examples are Jamaica and Malta. Elsewhere, as in the United Kingdom and Spain, two parties have dominated, but third parties occasionally join in governing coalitions.

Single-party systems: Only seven formal single-party states, in which only one party is allowed to contest national elections, exist today, ranging from China to Eritrea. Another forty-plus countries feature "single-party dominance" systems, in which minor parties are allowed but one powerful party wins national elections.

Nonpartisan systems: Today, some Persian Gulf states—the United Arab Emirates, Oman, and Kuwait—outlaw political parties and officially run on a "nonpartisan" basis, though a traditional tribal family rules in each of the three nations. A few Pacific island nations also are nonpartisan, partly because their populations are so small. Many urban governments in the United States are nonpartisan—a legacy of anticorruption crusades from the early twentieth century.

TABLE 11.1   **The Road to Nowhere: The Most Successful Third-Party Presidential Contenders, 1840–2023**

ELECTION	THIRD-PARTY CANDIDATE(S), PARTY	PERCENTAGE OF POPULAR VOTE (NO. OF ELECTORAL VOTES)
1856	Millard Fillmore, American (Know-Nothing) Party (Anti-immigrant)	22.0 (8)
1860	John Breckinridge, Constitutional Democratic Party (Pro-slavery) John Bell, Constitutional Union Party (Conservatives looking to compromise on slavery)	18.2 (72) 12.6 (39)
1892	James Weaver, People's Party (Populists fighting the rich and powerful)	8.5 (22)
1912	Theodore Roosevelt, Progressive Party (Progressive) Eugene Debs, Socialist Party (Socialist)	27.4 (88) 6.0 (0)
1924	Robert La Follette, Progressive Party	16.6 (13)
1948	Strom Thurmond, States' Rights (Dixiecrat) Party (Pro-segregation and anti–civil rights)	2.4 (39)
1968	George Wallace, American Independent Party (Pro-segregation and anti–civil rights)	13.5 (45)
1980	John Anderson, National Unity Party (Liberal Republicans making a last stand)	6.6 (0)
1992	Ross Perot, United We Stand Party (Anti–free trade, nationalist)	18.9 (0)
1996	Ross Perot, Reform Party (Anti–free trade, nationalist)	8.4 (0)

On the state level, third parties have done slightly better. In 2022, a few dozen members of the Libertarian Party—including one state legislator—and more than one hundred Green Party members hold elected office (out of 520,000 elected officials—see Chapter 10).[25] Since 1990, only a handful of states have elected third-party governors: Perhaps the best-known was Jesse Ventura, a former professional wrestler (known as "The Body") who rode his blend of outsized personality and blunt common sense to the Minnesota governor's mansion as a Reform Party candidate in 1998. In the last quarter-century, four other states have elected governors outside the major parties: Alaska (1990, 2014), Connecticut (1990), Rhode Island (2010), and Maine (1994, 1998). All four winners were independents rather than representatives of third parties.

● *Wrestler-turned-governor Jesse Ventura, a member of the Reform Party.*

Despite their history of electoral failure, minor parties make valuable contributions. They open the process to alternative views, give dissidents a voice, and expand civic engagement. Third-party movements have often injected strong and controversial views into the major parties. They fought for the abolition of slavery, the direct election of senators, gender equality, laws eliminating child labor, the prohibition of drinking, the income tax, limits on immigration, and smaller government.[26] They also fought for racial segregation and white supremacy. When a third-party cause becomes popular, one of the major parties tends to adopt it—as they did with every issue in the previous sentences.

THE BOTTOM LINE

» America's two-party style has endured for over two hundred years, with Democrats and Republicans as the main standard-bearers since 1856.

» The election rules explain the dominance of the two parties.

» Third parties arise periodically to challenge two-party dominance, but none has ever managed to break through.

 ## America's Party Systems: Origins and Change

Political parties are always evolving. Every few decades the entire U.S. party system changes: new issues, new winners, new (or renewed) parties, and new ways of winning elections. We can identify at least six distinctive "party systems"

stretching across American history. As you'll see, today's system has lasted longer than any other. That leads many observers to predict that big changes are just around the corner—or perhaps quietly underway.

Beginnings: First Party System (1789–1828)

Early Americans tried to avoid political parties. But they disagreed on a crucial issue: How strong should the central government be? Politicians who supported strong government became identified as Federalists and those for states' rights and limited national power became Democratic–Republicans. Political parties were born.

George Washington led the Federalists to win two unanimous elections (there was no campaign) and then announced he would not accept a third term. John Adams, Washington's vice president, won the third election.

In 1800, Democratic–Republican candidate Thomas Jefferson won a bitter victory over President John Adams. This was the first contested election, and the first time the White House changed party hands. For the rest of the first party period, the Democratic–Republicans dominated national politics, winning the next six presidential elections and controlling Congress for all twenty-four years (see Table 11.2). The Federalists bitterly noted that Jefferson had won by carrying

---

TABLE 11.2 | **Overview of the Six Party Systems**

Notice that the sixth party system—our own—is distinctive in one way: No party dominates. This is especially true in recent times. Democrats have an edge in the presidency, while Republicans have an edge in the House and Senate. Like every system, this one will likely end—perhaps with one party taking control. But which party?

	YEARS IN CONTROL					
	PRESIDENT		**HOUSE**		**SENATE**	
	FEDERALIST	**DEMOCRATIC–REPUBLICAN**	**F**	**DR**	**F**	**DR**
1. 1789–1828	12	28	8	26	12	22
	DEMOCRAT	**NATIONAL REPUBLICAN/ WHIG**	**DEM**	**NR/WHIG**	**DEM**	**NR/WHIG**
2. 1829–1860	24	8	24	8	28	4
	DEMOCRAT	**REPUBLICAN**	**DEM**	**REPUB**	**DEM**	**REPUB**
3. 1861–1896	8	28	6	30	14	22
4. 1897–1932	8	28	10	26	6	30
5. 1932–1968	28	8	32	4	32	4
6. 1969–present						
a) 1969–1992	4	20	24	0	18	6
b) 1993–2024	20	12	10	22	14*	16*

In 2001, Jim Jeffords of Vermont switched parties, from Republican to Democratic, placing the Senate in Democratic hands till Republicans won it back in the 2002 midterm election.

Note: As of early December 2022, the Senate outcome awaited a Georgia runoff election. Senate figures as of 2022.

the slave states, whose Electoral College count was inflated by adding three-fifths of a vote for each slave (discussed in Chapter 3). In fact, slaveholders held the presidency for most of the next forty years.

Ironically, the first party system featured widespread distrust of party politics. George Washington struggled, through the first two administrations, to project a nonpartisan image. The idea did not last long. Party newspapers were soon showering opponents with insults that would make modern politicians blush. Politics occasionally turned deadly. Aaron Burr, a Democratic–Republican who served as Jefferson's first vice president, despised Hamilton and his Federalist followers. On a hot July morning in 1804 the two fought a duel and Burr killed Hamilton, further hobbling a Federalist Party already in decline. The party limped along until 1816, but after 1800 it never won a presidential election or controlled a chamber of Congress.

The first party system set a durable pattern: two main parties contesting elections and building coalitions. One party (in this case, the Democratic–Republicans) dominated until evolving rules swept in a new constellation of parties, ideas, and supporters—in short, a new party system.

Rise: Second Party System (1828–1860)

When Andrew Jackson won the presidency in 1828, some twenty thousand Democrats (many angling for government jobs) swarmed into Washington for his inauguration. Supreme Court Justice Joseph Story spoke for the old-style gentry: "The reign of King Mob seemed triumphant."[27] What he was really seeing was the birth of modern party politics.

In just three decades, political parties had evolved into a form that we would recognize today. Party competition grew fierce, voting rights expanded to most white males, and enthusiastic party members threw themselves into politics.

The birth of modern politics and "the rise of the common man" came with serious downsides: Free Blacks were stripped of the right to vote (90 percent of African Americans were still slaves, but Black men with property in the North had eagerly voted). And elected officials dispensed jobs to their followers as the "spoils of office"—a corrupt patronage system of government (discussed in Chapter 15).[28]

Party names changed. The Federalists had vanished. Jefferson's old Democratic-Republicans split into two factions in the 1820s. Supporters of Andrew Jackson became Democrats; Jackson's enemies organized a rival party and called themselves the "Whigs," named after a British party that opposed royal tyranny.

Democratic platforms favored small farmers, rising urban workers, and local control. They embraced immigrants (and stuffed ballots in their hands soon after they landed). Democrats pursued a genocidal removal of Native Americans, plunged into war with Mexico, and increasingly became identified as the southern and pro-slavery party. Whigs favored a stronger government that would knit the country together through canals, railroads,

● Irish and German immigrants, identified by the type of liquor they prefer— whiskey or beer respectively. In the background, a serious election-day brawl. This nativist critique of urban (Democratic) voters during the second party period implies that immigrants will destroy American democracy.

the distribution of federal lands to settlers, and other infrastructure projects. They supported business and manufacturing, opposed Indian removal, fought to limit the influence of immigrants, and included a northern faction intent on resisting slavery's expansion.

There was no federal safety net during this pre–Civil War period. Democratic Party officials, especially in urban areas, often provided basic services in exchange for votes—the basis for the urban party machines that would grow extremely powerful by the late 1800s.

Both parties foundered on the question of slavery. Neither, however, could duck the issue. As the United States spread west, every new territory and state raised the same terrible question: Should slavery be permitted to spread?

Democrats had a direct answer: Leave it to the states and the territories. Whigs were divided: Those from the South fought for the expansion of slavery; those from the North opposed it—and the issue exploded the party. Out of the Whigs' demise a new party system arose—and clarified the future of slavery in the United States.[29]

War and Reconstruction: Third Party System (1860–1896)

Abraham Lincoln helped form a new party—the antislavery Republican Party. The Republicans strongly supported free labor (which today we call capitalism) and insisted that new western settlements should be free of slavery (free soil), because slavery's expansion would undermine the people's right to work for themselves (free labor). After Lincoln won the presidential election of 1860, the southern states feared the end of slavery, and the nation soon entered the Civil War.

During the war, Lincoln skillfully deployed the Republican Party on behalf of the Union forces. He drew on party members to recruit soldiers, name officers (party connections helped), negotiate for war supplies, and sell war bonds to finance the war effort. With no similar party apparatus in the South, Confederates faced a much more difficult task.[30]

After winning the war, northern Republicans again drew on the party to try and rebuild the nation. "Radical Republicans" promoted Black rights, helping to boost many former enslaved people into Congress and statehouses under the Republican banner. Democrats, the party of white supremacy in this era, denounced Reconstruction's "excesses" and often resorted to violence and racism to limit the freedom of the former enslaved people to travel, to vote, or to seek employment.

● Reconstruction set off a fierce political contest in the South. Here, Black men from all walks of life line up to vote: a laborer (with a mallet in his pocket), a businessperson, a soldier (there were two hundred thousand Black men fighting in the Union army by the end of the war), and a farmer. In most cases, the Black voters went Republican. White supremacists joined the Democratic Party; they resorted to terrible violence and caricatures to tell a false story that Black men were not ready for freedom and should be stripped of the vote.

Republicans dominated elections between 1860 and the midterm election of 1874, when the Democrats broke through and took back the House. By then, each party had a strong regional identity. Democrats controlled the former Confederate states, which became known as "the Solid South" because they reliably voted Democratic—after they violently drove Black Americans out of politics and restored white supremacy. Republicans grew strongest in the Northeast and the Midwest. Elections were decided by a whisker. After 1872, the presidency changed hands with each election, and two (of five) winners lost the popular vote but won in the Electoral College—something historians considered remarkable until it happened again in the current era (in 2000 and 2016).

During the 1870s and 1880s, large numbers of European and Asian immigrants streamed into the cities, where municipal governments featured well-developed **party machines**—powerful political organizations. Managed by **party bosses**, the machines provided immigrants with such basic services as food, shelter, jobs, contacts, and a sense of belonging. In exchange, the party (Democrats controlled the machines in most cities, Republicans in some others) could count on a block of all-important votes once immigrants became naturalized citizens. The machines grew notorious for bribery and corruption. In some places they paid men to vote, stuffed ballot boxes, permitted repeat voters, and engaged in brawls on Election Day.

The western lands joined the Union as solid Republican states, and party leaders no longer needed to scrape for Black Republican votes in the South. They stood aside as the Democratic politicians across the South stripped Black people of most rights, including the right to vote and hold office (see Chapter 5).

THE BOSS STILL HAS THE REINS

● *Cartoonist Thomas Nast mocks one corrupt politician, Boss Tweed, at the reins of New York's democracy.*

Party machine: A hierarchical arrangement of party workers, often organized in an urban area to help integrate immigrants and minority groups into the political system. Most active in the late nineteenth and early twentieth centuries.

Party boss: The senior figure in a party machine.

Business and Reform: Fourth Party System (1896–1932)

In 1892, the radical Populist Party swept out of the West and took five states and over a million votes. Shortly after the election, which the Democrats won, a terrible economic depression hit the country. In the 1894 midterm, the Democrats lost 116 seats—the biggest drop ever. In the 1896 presidential election, the Populists joined the Democrats to challenge the status quo but were defeated by Republicans, who had become the "millionaires' party." However, after President William McKinley was assassinated in 1901, his vice president, Theodore Roosevelt, stepped into the White House, challenged the "millionaires' club," and began to sponsor reforms.

The great debates of the fourth party system featured support for the status quo and business on the one side and pressures for political and economic equality (championed by reformers, known as Progressives) on the other. Should women be given the vote? Should the government regulate emerging corporate giants, such as Standard Oil or the Central Pacific Railroad? Should judges be elected? How about senators? On the state level, should the government regulate child labor? Should it limit the workday for men and women? To the Progressive reformers, led by Theodore Roosevelt, the answers were yes! yes! and yes!

● *One policy both parties agreed on for most of the fourth party system: prohibiting the sale of alcohol. The 1920s became a boom time, marked by rising new industries such as advertising, automobiles, electricity, and illegal liquor. These upstanding citizens mock the law that they are breaking. In 1929–30, the economy collapsed, taking down Prohibition—and the entire "fourth party system" as well.*

New Deal: Broad series of economic programs and reforms introduced between 1933 and 1936 and associated with the Franklin Roosevelt administration.

Grand Old Party (GOP): Long-standing nickname for the Republican Party; ironically, bestowed early in the party's history, in the 1870s.

This period also focused on the question of whether liquor should be prohibited. More than one in six Americans had been born abroad; drinking became associated with immigrants, big cities, political corruption, and spousal abuse. During World War I, a constitutional amendment whipped through Congress and the nation, and America banned the sale of alcohol beginning in 1920. A wave of crimes associated with illegal liquor rocked the cities, while rural districts went dry with little complaint (or violence). Business leaders bitterly complained that Prohibition—a massive national effort to change American habits—was creating an era of big government.[31]

Depression and the New Deal: Fifth Party System (1933–1968)

Another President Roosevelt, Teddy's distant cousin Franklin, helped define the fifth party system. The Great Depression (1929–41) unhinged party politics, crippling a Republican Party now associated with business elites and economic incompetence.

Roosevelt came to office after three years of economic misery and frankly blamed the "unscrupulous money changers" and "self-seekers"—the old "millionaires' club"—for the nation's "dark days." Roosevelt's **New Deal** focused on jobs, infrastructure, government aid to the elderly (Social Security), temporary assistance for the needy (unemployment insurance and welfare), and new federal government agencies to manage it all. Roosevelt's Democratic Party reaped the electoral rewards, reshaping party coalitions.

The Democratic Party coalition included an unusual mix of interests: the Solid South, which insisted on segregation; the big-city machines with their ethnic supporters; labor unions (the Democrats sponsored legislation that permitted the movement to grow); farmers, who saw agricultural prices rise during these years; and, starting in 1936, Black people in the North.

Black Americans had been loyal to the Republican "**Grand Old Party**" (**GOP**) since Lincoln signed the Emancipation Proclamation. From the party's free-soil origins in 1856 up through the 1920s, the GOP was the party of civil rights. Republican governments in the western states gave women the vote long before the Nineteenth Amendment extended it to women in Democratic strongholds. But after 1900, the Republican Party had stopped fighting for Black rights. White supremacy made the task difficult, and they had enough votes in the North and West to dominate politics. Now, Roosevelt's employment programs, along with the first, tentative efforts to reduce racial segregation, won many northern Black voters to the Democratic Party.

However, there was now a tension at the heart of the Democratic Party. Liberals, labor unions, and Black people pressured the party to expand social programs and civil rights; southern Democrats struggled to rein in social programs that were going to Black people and fought hard for segregation. Democrats kept the coalition together—and hung onto their national majority—for another thirty years, but as they became known as the party of civil rights, white southern voters shifted to the GOP. As the Democratic coalition began to crumble, a new generation of Republicans rose up with fresh ideas for America.

The Sixth Party System: Parties at Parity (1969–Present)

President Richard Nixon (1969–73) and, later, Ronald Reagan (1981–89) developed a "southern strategy" to win middle-class white votes. They emphasized small business, limited government, and a more market-oriented vision. The Republican Party always had a conservative wing, but now this wing rose to dominance.

By 1981, Republican President Ronald Reagan launched a direct assault on the fifth party system through a powerful new conservative mantra: Government is not the solution to our problems. Instead, said the rising Republican coalition, government is the *source* of the problem. During the 1980s, the parties lined up in their now-familiar ways: On economic and social issues alike, Democrats leaned left, Republicans right. There was also a racial alignment: People of color and immigrants became important to the Democratic Party; Republicans relied largely (averaging 88 percent of their voters) on whites.

Republicans controlled the fourth party period and Democrats the fifth. The current party era introduces something new: Neither party is in control. Instead, very close elections swing party control back and forth. The new era, the sixth party system, is the era of very close elections. And with very close elections, as we saw again in 2020 and 2022, comes bitter partisanship.

The most influential president of this period was Ronald Reagan and his new pro-market, antigovernment philosophy. Eventually, even Democrats began to abandon their old New Deal philosophy and echo Reagan. Democratic President Bill Clinton announced that "the era of big government is over."[32] A long period of splits *within* each party—Democrats housed both northern/western liberals and southern conservatives; Republicans had a strong liberal wing alongside conservatives—ended during the 1990s, as each party purged moderates and settled into a single dominant identity.

Perhaps the United States will experience close elections for a long time to come. However, this sixth party period is already one of the longest-lived. Political historians are watching carefully to see if one party or the other is poised to break away, establish dominance, and start a new party era. Perhaps the demographic rise of the millennial and Gen Z generations will eventually herald a new progressive era, unraveling the sixth party system's coalitions. After all, these are the most diverse and the most left-leaning generations, perhaps ever. What do you think?

Why the Party Period Matters

Why should we care what party system we are in? Because a new party system means new politics—and new national rules. Coalitions of voters, ideas, and political leaders determine how America is governed. Will we tackle climate change? Will we adopt universal health insurance? Will tax cuts encourage businesses to apply the savings to hiring new workers? Will we round up and deport undocumented people—or give them a path to citizenship? Will we make it easier for people to vote—or more difficult? Will we protect LGBTQ+ rights—or take rights away? These and many other decisions depend on the party—and the ideas—in power.

Does the 2020 Election Suggest a New Party System?

| What do the results of recent national elections tell us about the immediate future of the party system? Is one party poised to establish dominance for a long period of time? | **Yes.** With Joe Biden's presidential victory, Democratic candidates have won the popular vote in seven of the last eight elections—the second-best sustained streak in U.S. history. And while Republicans have won back Congress, for now, the Republican Party is too reliant on older white voters to come to dominance. The future will be Democratic. | **Probably not.** Republicans still control a majority of state houses and governorships, and as they proved during the Obama presidency, control of at least one chamber of Congress is enough to frustrate most legislative proposals. Control of the political system continues to swing back and forth. We've had an unprecedented twelve flips of Senate, House, or White House since 2000; expect more of the same ahead. | **No.** Democrats may now briefly control the presidency, but Republicans have a narrow House advantage, control more states, and (as a rural party) have a huge institutional advantage in both the Senate and the Electoral College. Elections are still won and lost by a hair. And time will tell about the rise of mostly Democratic younger voters—in any case, it has not yet materialized in sufficient numbers to declare a new enduring majority. |

THE BOTTOM LINE

» Two main parties have always dominated U.S. party politics—and since 1856, they have been the same two, Republicans and Democrats.

» The two parties—and the contest between them—regularly reboot the party system. Each change in party system means a change in the voters who make up each party and the ideas that inspire them.

» We count at least six party systems since the founding of the United States. The latest, which began in 1969, is marked by very close elections.

» Political historians are watching closely for the rise of the next party system.

 ## Party Identification . . . and Ideas

Party identification: Strong attachment to one political party, often established at an early age.

Many Americans feel strongly attached to their party. That attachment is called **party identification**, and it deeply affects how individuals see politics. Where do party identities and differences come from? And exactly who belongs to each party?

Building Party Identification

As we saw in Chapter 7, political socialization and party loyalty often start with family and include demography—race, gender, age, and so on. The Democratic Party is younger. Men break Republican, women Democratic (see Figure 11.2), a trend accelerated by the *Dobbs* Supreme Court decision in 2022.[33] The Republican Party is mostly white; the Democratic Party is increasingly diverse. Indeed, political scientists argue that underlying contemporary partisanship is a fierce identity politics—with white identity on the right and multicultural identity on the left. From these identities emerge views on immigration, social welfare policies, and the federal government itself.[34]

However, few party traits are permanent. We saw Black voters move from solid Republican to solid Democratic between 1936 and 1964. And, more recently, Latinos have surged toward the Republicans, going from 28 percent Republican in 2016 to 38 percent Republican in 2020.[35] The 2022 midterms were mixed, with record Latino majorities in Florida for Republican Governor Ron DeSantis but continued Democratic strength among Latino voters in South Texas and Arizona. Latinos still vote heavily Democratic (almost two to one), but here's the takeaway: Groups often change allegiance over time. Both parties will woo Latino voters in future elections, for they form a large and important constituency.

Other traits also matter. Urban dwellers are Democrats, suburbanites have been drifting from Republican to Democratic, and rural voters are staunch Republicans. White evangelicals and Mormons are strong Republicans, secular people Democrats. Even personality seems to matter. Some studies find that people who exhibit more "openness" (eagerness to explore new experiences) are more likely to be Democrats. Those who measure high in "conscientiousness" (strong sense of duty, discipline, impulse control) tend to be Republicans.[36] Think about your own personality: Does it fit with this recent political psychology theory?

Another influence on party affinity comes down to the political moment when voters form attachments. Certain times seem to carry magic for a political party—John Kennedy's 1960 election drew millions into strong identification as Democrats, as Ronald Reagan's election in 1980 did among Republicans. Millennial politics were shaped by the harsh realities of the 2008–9 recession, and Gen Z by the 2020–21 COVID-19 lockdowns, economic downturn, and renewed calls to end systemic racism.

Although political historians are always alert to a sea change, no mass shift in party identification has shown up for the last three decades. Current poll numbers show that approximately 28 percent of the electorate identifies as Democratic and 28 percent as Republican. Recently, we saw a surge in independents who are weary of both parties—at 42 percent, their numbers are larger than either party.[37] Why? The intense conviction among the party faithful may make others less willing to

A study in contrasts: Republican and Democratic strengths and weaknesses in party identification

% of registered voters in each group who identify as ...

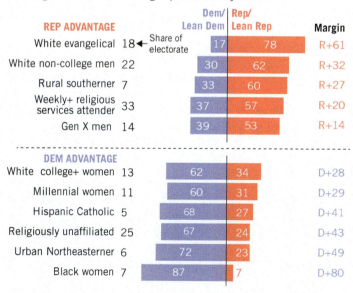

		Dem/ Lean Dem	Rep/ Lean Rep	Margin
REP ADVANTAGE				
White evangelical	18 ← Share of electorate	17	78	R+61
White non-college men	22	30	62	R+32
Rural southerner	7	33	60	R+27
Weekly+ religious services attender	33	37	57	R+20
Gen X men	14	39	53	R+14
DEM ADVANTAGE				
White college+ women	13	62	34	D+28
Millennial women	11	60	31	D+29
Hispanic Catholic	5	68	27	D+41
Religiously unaffiliated	25	67	24	D+43
Urban Northeasterner	6	72	23	D+49
Black women	7	87	7	D+80

● **FIGURE 11.2** *Party demographics. White, male, older evangelical voters are more likely to vote Republican, while Black, Asian, female, young, and urban voters are more likely to vote Democratic. (Pew Research Center)*

Does Personality Predict Party Affiliation?

Consider your own personality and party preference. Does recent political science research help predict your views—and the views of the people around you?	**Yes.** I believe that Democrats are generally more likely to seek new experiences and Republicans are more likely to emphasize duty and discipline.	**No.** I think there are different traits that explain party identification. (Please specify which traits you think matter most.)	**Interests, not personality.** I don't believe personality predicts politics. We are rational creatures pursuing our own self-interest regardless of personality.

identify themselves. Still, most independents vote faithfully for one party or the other and feel just as strongly about the shortcomings of the other party. As noted above, fewer than one in five Americans are true independents.[38]

Still, one factor may be slowly shifting the balance toward the Democratic Party: When Ronald Reagan whipped Jimmy Carter in the 1980 presidential election (489 to 49 in the Electoral College), the electorate was almost 90 percent white. As of 2020, the percentage of the electorate that considers itself white is estimated to be down to around 72 percent—and falling. That's big news because the Republican Party is dominated by people who identify as white. Even with the recent increase of Latino voters, Republican voters were 85 percent white; in contrast, only three out of five Democratic voters identify as white.

Of course, groups shift parties. Still, the demographic trend seems to contain an urgent message for the Republican future: Diversify the base.[39]

The Power of Party Attachment

Party identification shapes three key aspects of public involvement: voting/political participation, "filtering," and ideology.

Voting/Participation. Party identity is a very strong predictor of your voting habits. In 2020, for example, 94 percent of Democrats voted for Biden, while 93 percent of Republicans voted for Trump. Analysts measuring the strength of party attachment find that strong partisans tend to be very loyal **straight-ticket voters**, sticking with their party's candidates right down the ballot. Their opposite? **Split-ticket voters**, who make their choices candidate by candidate.

Voting rates are higher among those with strong party identification. Nearly 150 million voters (almost two-thirds of eligible voters) cast a ballot in the 2020 election. The key to every election is turning out the party's **base voters**—those who deeply identify with the party—while winning over some independents. Conventional wisdom used to hold that independents were in the middle. Not anymore. Today, most lean strongly toward either the Democratic or the Republican Party.[40]

Filtering. Party identification also plays a *filtering* role. Filters choose what signals in the media environment people are liable to accept or reject. As one political

Straight-ticket voter: Votes for the same party for all offices on a ballot.

Split-ticket voter: Votes for at least one candidate from each party, dividing his or her ballot between the two (or more) parties.

Base voters: Party members who tend to vote loyally for their party's candidates in most elections.

scientist wrote, "People tend to project favorable characteristics and acceptable issue positions onto the candidates of the party they favor."[41] In a set of experiments, social scientists asked respondents to rate a generic series of political candidates based on photos and detailed biographies. Each was sometimes described as a Democrat, sometimes as a Republican, and sometimes as an independent. The study found that self-identified Democrats preferred the candidates described as "Democrats," and the Republicans preferred "Republicans." The candidate's policy positions, race, gender, and family background were all less important than party label.

Ideology.   The parties take divergent views on issue after issue. This creates the polarization we described at the start of the chapter. Until very recently, the party split was clear and easy to identify: Should we provide government support to people who cannot take care of themselves? Democrats say yes (75 percent); Republicans say no (only 28 percent). Do U.S. institutions and laws need rebuilding because they are biased against racial and ethnic minorities? Progressive leftists agree (71 percent); committed conservatives don't (5 percent). Do you believe that God hears and answers your prayers? Republicans are more likely to say yes (54 percent) than Democrats (32 percent). On all these indicators, differences between the parties have more than doubled in the past fifteen years.

However, in recent years, the party lines on some policy issues have grown murky. Both the Trump and Biden administrations won major relief packages to combat COVID. And some populist Republicans feel that the economic system is biased and that the rich should pay higher taxes. Does this signal a sea change in attitudes? Or a blip during the crisis? Time will tell.[42]

Negative Partisanship.   Many party members are united by one especially intense feeling: They don't like the other party (Figure 11.3). The rival party, they believe, endangers the country. In fact, Republicans say that Democratic voters don't even "sincerely believe the Democratic Party is best for the country." Democrats say the same about Republicans by a slightly lower margin (72 percent to 58 percent, respectively).[43]

Why has **negative partisanship** grown so rapidly in the last three decades? Partly because the party members themselves have grown so different: urban versus rural, mostly white versus multicultural, strongly religious versus more secular. It's also because elections have become so close; people running for office stir up animosity to animate supporters. And different populations get their political information from entirely different sources—with deeply slanted social media groups replacing the newspapers and mainstream news reports. Of course, negative partisanship turns off many people, which might be why 42 percent of the population identifies as independent even if they generally vote for the same party.

Negative partisanship: Participating in politics and forming opinions in opposition to a party one dislikes.

Americans really don't like the other party

Percentage of Republicans and Democrats who have a "very unfavorable" view of the other party.

● FIGURE 11.3 *Party members grow more negative toward the other party; note the big increase in "very unfavorable" after 2018. Views toward their own party? They are drifting down too. (Pew Research Center)*

Of course, even with the growing intensity of party ideology, no party is a monolith. Each includes multiple factions with different—sometimes very different—ideas. Moreover, both parties are now in flux, with some factions rising while others fade away. Let's take a look at the factions within the parties today.

Growing Partisanship—On Core Issues

How Do Republicans and Democrats Divide?

Notice how the members of different parties take very different views on two questions at the start of this book: What does (and should) government do? And who are we?

THINK ABOUT IT

Summarize how each party sees the issues of government aid, environmental quality, and immigration. Where do you stand on these issues? Why? Can you describe how those with the opposite view would respond to your own arguments?

Do you think it's important to try and overcome these divisions? Why or why not? What might be done to minimize the divide on this issue? Suggest some possible steps.

% who say ...

Government should do more to help reduce poverty

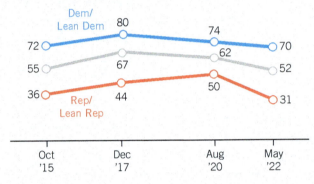

I'm worried a great deal about the environment (global warming, pollution, etc.)

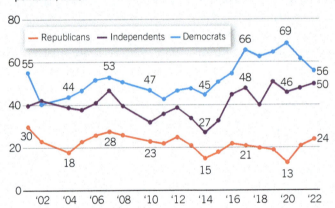

Immigration to the U.S. should be reduced

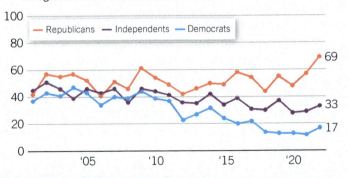

Source: Gallup, Pew Research Center

Republican Factions

Republicans are often lumped together as conservatives, but significant differences exist. Consider six distinct, if overlapping, Republican factions.

American Nationalists or Trumpists. These people feel left behind by economic and cultural changes. They are skeptical of elites in both parties, believing that they have turned their back on true Americans—and on America itself. They are strong nationalists: They vehemently oppose immigration; reject international trade deals that, as they see it, send American jobs overseas; and are dubious about alliances that commit the United States to obligations abroad. They are suspicious of "deep state" government institutions: from public health bureaucracies to the FBI. Former President Donald Trump vividly defined this wing of the party and remains its chief rallying point (Trumpists still believe the 2020 election was stolen). Nationalists cheer when he is politically incorrect—precisely because it so offends people who they dismiss as arrogant elites.[44]

Religious Traditionalists. Some conservatives support a return to what they consider America's Christian origins. Traditionalists oppose abortion, affirmative action, same-sex marriage, and LGBTQ+ rights; they firmly oppose transgender rights and believe that gender identity is permanently fixed at birth. They have a deep following among Protestant evangelicals but also build alliances with conservative Catholic intellectuals like Supreme Court Justices Amy Coney Barrett and Samuel Alito. They generally support school prayer, gun rights, and restrictions on immigration. Some view the Bible as a guide to social and political life that is every bit as important as the Constitution. This faction overlaps with the Populist nationalists.

Fiscal Conservatives. This faction has a clear enemy: big government. They support tax cuts and oppose spending on social programs. They wish to restrict the federal bureaucracy, cut entitlement programs like Social Security and Medicare, and push many federal programs off to the states, which can then decide whether to continue or to cut them (see Chapters 4 and 17).

Libertarians. Libertarians defend individual liberty and fight government intrusions into people's lives. Most libertarians are passionate advocates of free markets. Libertarians reject federal involvement in education, environmental regulations, transportation, healthcare, old-age pensions—you get the idea. That may sound conservative, but because libertarians oppose all government, they are also liberal on social issues. They think government has no business deciding whether you can have an abortion, smoke marijuana, or gamble. They believe you should marry whomever you like, or identify with whatever gender you wish. This faction was shaken by the rise of Donald Trump, but it has a long legacy in the party and is likely to be back.[45]

Neoconservatives. Neoconservatives support strong U.S. intervention to spread democracy and free markets globally. The "neocons" believe that America should exercise its military muscle to help improve the world. Donald Trump fiercely opposed this perspective, which was already tarnished by the long wars in Iraq and Afghanistan. But this outlook has deep intellectual roots and, aided by Russia's invasion of Ukraine, is coming back.[46]

● *Each party has factions. Here are two delegates to the Libertarian National Convention in 2020 (a) and leaders of the Lincoln Project—moderate Republicans who urged party members to vote against President Trump (b). Only one in ten Republicans followed their advice in 2020.*

Moderates.   Moderates, a once-proud GOP faction, tend to be fiscally conservative but will consider tax increases along with spending cuts and are willing to compromise with Democrats to get things done.[47] One-fifth of Republicans describe themselves as moderates, but they face scorn from many Republicans who dismiss moderates as RINOs: Republicans in Name Only.

Democratic Factions

Democrats also include very different groups. Today, 13 percent label themselves conservative, 51 percent moderate/Establishment, and 28 percent liberal or progressive.[48]

Progressives.   Sporting names like Our Revolution and Justice Democrats, Progressive groups occupy the left of the Democratic spectrum. Progressives are wary of corporate power and focused on fighting economic inequality. They are strong environmentalists, embrace universal healthcare, support immigrant rights, advocate for a woman's right to reproductive freedom, champion LGBTQ+ rights, and are committed to movements like #MeToo and Black Lives Matter. As millennials and Gen Z move into politics, they have increased the importance of progressive politics. Are they the voice of the Democratic future? About 12 percent of Democrats identify as Progressives now.

The Civil Rights Caucus.   Many Democratic Party members trace their political commitment to the civil rights movement—past and present. They stand with groups that have historically faced discrimination, especially racial minorities, recent immigrant communities, and women. They build "rainbow" coalitions, fight against discrimination, support social programs, and join in declaring sanctuary cities. Older members of this group saved Joe Biden's candidacy with strong support in 2020. While a close look at elections data suggests some divergence between Black and Latino voters (as well as young and old members), this faction works hard to bridge the divides.

Organized Labor.   Unions were once a dominant force in the Democratic Party—supplying money, votes, and ground game—but their influence has diminished along with the unions themselves. Unions support jobs programs, infrastructure projects, and workers' rights. Labor tends to oppose globalization and free trade, and they sometimes break with progressives on environmental issues and on immigration policies. As labor unions have declined, white working-class people have moved Republican.[49]

Centrists. In the 1990s, some centrist Democrats embraced a "Third Way" between the left progressives in the party and Republican conservatives. For example, they sought to reduce the number of abortions while legally protecting women's right to choose. They sought to balance environmental protection with "smart growth." Moderates remain important to Democrats because they can compete in Republican areas—in suburbs and conservative-leaning states.[50] Today, more than a third of self-identified Democrats call themselves centrists. The centrists are fiscally conservative and wary of major government initiatives like ambitious action on climate change. They introduce a major split within the Democrats that bubbles up to the surface every time the party comes to power. In an urban-oriented party, this faction remains a minority voice, moderating the party agenda rather than setting it. Still, when Democrats win (or maintain, as in 2022) power in Congress, it's because moderates have surged in more conservative swing states, leading to intense debates within the party.

● *Each party has factions. Progressives Alexandria Ocasio-Cortez (a) and Jamaal Bowman (b) shot into public prominence by defeating long-standing and powerful party members who'd served for decades.*

Why so many factions—ten across two parties? Because the parties each have millions of members with many different viewpoints and opinions. Add variations across states and regions, and the perspectives multiply. At the same time, of course, parties are always evolving, and different factions rise to the surface at different times: Today, national populists (among Republicans) and progressives (Democrats) are feeling especially emboldened. The crucial point: Parties are always boisterous combinations of views. Are you unmoved by every single one of these ten perspectives? Then you are a true independent!

Organizing the Parties

With so many factions, running a party is a complicated job. The work falls on three different groups: the party organization, the party in government, and the party in the electorate. As with most American institutions we have studied in this book, each of these groups has a national, a state, and a local dimension. By now you will recognize the classic feature of American political institutions: a very complicated organizational chart.

The Party Bureaucracy. The central organization for both parties is a national committee—the Republican National Committee (RNC) and the Democratic National Committee (DNC). These committees raise funds for the party, coordinate election strategies, decide which local races to fund, organize a national convention every four years, and prepare the **party platform**—the party's statement of purpose and its position on issues. In 2020, the Republicans surprised us by declining to publish a new platform for the first time since 1840. Instead, they endorsed the previous platform and focused attention on Donald Trump: "The Republican Party . . . will continue to support the President's America First agenda."[51]

The committees also issue and enforce the party's rules for primary elections, from the presidential level downward. Important members of the DNC and RNC include the state party chairs and vice chairs, who are the most faithful activists in each party.

Party platform: The written statement of a party's core convictions and issue priorities. Generally revised every four years, in time for the national party convention.

Party organization: The portion of a political party that includes activists, state/local leaders, and affiliated professionals such as fundraisers and public relations experts.

Traditionally, leaders of the **party organization** are anonymous insiders that oversee the primary process. During the 2016 primaries, Bernie Sanders charged that the DNC was openly siding against him. A blockbuster email trove, published by WikiLeaks (the result of a Russian intelligence hack), seemed to prove him right, as high-level staffers wrote things such as "he's never going to be president." With their behind-the-scenes activity exposed, DNC Chair Debbie Wasserman Schultz and other staffers resigned in disgrace. In 2020, the Democrats were more successful in balancing their liberal and moderate factions—perhaps because they were out of power and united in opposition to President Trump.

● Joe Biden (a) and Donald Trump (b) accept their nominations at respective party conventions in 2020.

Party in Government. The **party in government** gets all the recognition. These are the government officials in each party—elected leaders, appointed officers, individuals running for political office, and their staffs. The party in government struggles to enact the policies they support—and to stop their rivals from enacting theirs.

There is a constant struggle for influence within each party in government. Presidents usually command their own party—Joe Biden is the face of the Democratic Party, though he shares the spotlight with Nancy Pelosi, who has guided the Democrats in the House for almost two decades. But beware: If public approval ratings within the party fade, presidents can face challengers. For the party that does not control the White House, the contest is wide open. Sometimes, former presidents maintain influence—as Donald Trump does despite losing his reelection bid in 2020. Congressional leaders, governors, and presidential candidates all vie to put their own stamp on the party.

Party in the Electorate. What is left after the party organization and officeholders? We are! Each party's followers make up the **party in the electorate**.

The Big Tent. The media generally focuses on the famous party names. Political parties thrive, however, when all their elements—organization, officeholders, and public supporters—work together. That means sharing the same message, getting enthused about shared principles, and even embracing the party symbols—right down to the bumper stickers.

American federalism makes unanimity difficult. Local officials run the party in each state. Democrats in a conservative state like Alabama often have more in common with many Republicans in their own state than they do with liberal Democrats in San Francisco or New York. The same is true for moderate Republicans in New York or Massachusetts, compared to red-state colleagues in Oklahoma.

Party organizations always make tactical calculations: Do they put their resources in a few swing states that they have a good chance of winning in the next election cycle? Or should they spread their resources across many states—even long shots—with the hope of slowly building up their party in places where it does not often win?

Federalism pushes each of the two major parties to adopt a "big tent" approach: spread themselves more widely, embrace followers of divergent views, and hope any resultant ideological muddle does not turn off too many party members. However, many party members reject the big tent approach and insist on sticking to their political principles—which often makes for tumultuous politics (and multiple factions) within each party.

Party in government:
The portion of a political party's organization that comprises elected officials and candidates for office.

Party in the electorate:
The largest (and least organized) component of a political party, drawn from the public at large: registered members and regular supporters.

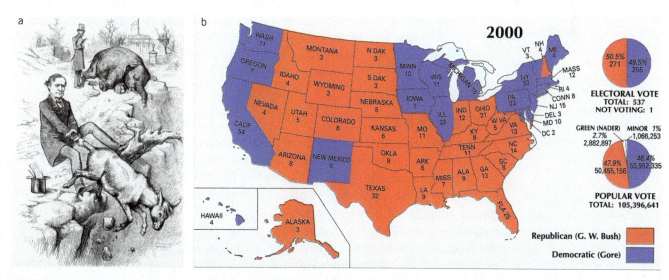

● Cartoonist Thomas Nast began drawing the Republican Party as an elephant and the Democrats as a donkey in the 1870s—in this comment on the election of 1880, the Democratic donkey is on the verge of plunging into financial chaos while the Republican elephant is either sleeping or dead (a). Since 2000, the parties are also known as blue (Democratic) and red (Republican). That's because the major broadcast networks used these colors to indicate whether GOP candidate George W. Bush (red) or Democratic nominee Al Gore (blue) had won a state (b).

THE BOTTOM LINE

» A substantial majority of voting-age Americans identify strongly with one of the two major parties. Others declare themselves independents—their numbers have been rising.

» Our powerful sense of party identification is a result of many factors, including parental influence, political context, and even personality type.

» Party identification in turn helps shape our voting patterns, the ways we filter political information, and our bedrock ideas about politics and government.

» Each party features several ideological factions, with most politically aware Americans aligning with one or two of these.

» Each party includes three groups: the party organization, the party in government, and the party in the electorate.

Party Competition . . . and Partisanship

Parties began to lose their influence over politics and government in the mid-1960s. Interest groups muscled in on party territory, mobilized voters, and shaped issue positions. Americans began to identify with movements and organizations—civil rights, environmentalism, the right to life, and libertarianism. The parties floundered. By the 1970s and 1980s, political observers were publishing books such as *The Party's Over* and *The Decline of American Political Parties*.[52] The central role of parties in organizing elections also slipped, with the rise to greater prominence of the "candidate-centered election" as we saw in Chapter 10. Political scientists warned that there was not enough partisanship in the American system—if the parties became too much alike, they could not offer the voters a meaningful choice.

Parties Rise Again

Just as political analysts pronounced the parties dead, their revival began. During the 1980s, changing congressional rules shifted power from committee chairs back to party leadership, strengthening the parties in Congress. A huge influx of money into politics further revitalized party organizations, buoyed by the widespread adoption of political action committees (PACs) in the 1980s, "527" committees in the 2000s, and super PACs in the 2010s (see Chapter 10). The DNC and RNC, along with the congressional campaign organizations, became the chief recipients of campaign funds—and directed them in turn to candidates, who became more dependent on the parties as a result.

The parties also became ideologically purer. Each party was now organized around a clearer set of ideas and principles. And, again, the parties attracted different people from different places: a largely white, native, rural party against a largely multicultural, pro-immigrant, urban party. Each side could concentrate on defeating its foes rather than on negotiating the differences within its own ranks.

Partisanship Intensifies

Today, the two parties are thriving, contesting very close national elections. Since 2000, the presidency has changed party hands four times, the Senate five times, and the House four times—that's an unprecedented twelve changes across eleven elections (including presidential elections and midterms). Americans have never seen so many razor-close elections. All that back and forth has made parties more important and partisanship more intense (see Table 11.3).[53]

In the past, partisan differences on Capitol Hill were blurred by factions within each party. Democrats were so bitterly divided over civil rights that they could barely hold a **party caucus** during the 1950s and 1960s. Today, those differences within the parties have almost disappeared. Party factions remain, as we saw earlier, but party members are far less diverse in their views. The strongest divisions are now between the two parties. By 2010, every single Republican in the U.S. Senate was to the right (in terms of voting record) of even the most conservative Senate Democrat. For the first time, ideological conflict in both the House and the Senate breaks down perfectly along party lines. This partisan divide makes

Party caucus: A meeting of all House or Senate members of one or the other main party, usually to discuss political and policy strategies.

TABLE 11.3	**Party Control of U.S. National Institutions**		
Twelve changes of control in eleven elections is an unprecedented level of turnover.			
ELECTION YEAR	**CONTROL OF PRESIDENCY**	**PARTY IN CONGRESSIONAL MAJORITY (SIZE OF MAJORITY)**	
		SENATE	**HOUSE**
2000	**R (Bush)**	R (1—vice president)* **May 2002: D (1 seat)****	R (9 seats)
2002	R (Bush)	**R (2 seats)**	R (24 seats)
2004	R (Bush)	R (10 seats)	R (29 seats)
2006	R (Bush)	**D (2 seats)**	**D (37 seats)**
2008	**D (Obama)**	D (19/20 seats)	D (79 seats)
2010	D (Obama)	D (6 seats)	**R (49 seats)**
2012	D (Obama)	D (10 seats)	R (34 seats)
2014	D (Obama)	**R (8 seats)**	R (60 seats)
2016	**R (Trump)**	R (4 seats)	R (47 seats)
2018	R (Trump)	R (2 seats)	**D (36 seats)**
2020	**D (Biden)**	**D (1—vice president) ***	D (30+ seats)***
2022	D (Biden)	D (2 seats)****	**R (~2 seats)******

Note: Boldface indicates a change in party control.
* When the Senate is divided 50-50, the vice president breaks ties, giving control of the Senate to the party who holds the White House. This happened in both 2000 and 2020.
** In May 2001, Senator Jim Jeffords switched from Republican to Democratic, flipping the Senate until the next election.
*** The Democrats won four seats in the 2020 election, splitting the chamber 50-50.
**** 2022 results were still being tallied as this book went to press.

the political contest—over ideas, programs, and even the meaning of America—louder and angrier than it has been in more than a century. Perhaps, again, the ideological divide is intensified by identity—Republicans skew white; Democrats tilt toward diversity. In the House of Representatives, for example, 70 percent of the Republicans are white males. Across the aisle sit the Democrats: just 33 percent white males.[54]

Who influences whom? Are partisan officials fanning the flames of party difference among the public? Or do activists within each party push their leaders to take stronger positions against the opposition? Or perhaps media outlets such as Fox News and MSNBC, catering to conservatives and liberals, respectively, have driven the people into their party corners? And maybe that process has been intensified by social media? The answer is probably yes to all four questions.[55]

Should we worry about the rise in partisan differences? Does it make governance worse? Might it even threaten democracy itself? Public opinion surveys repeatedly report popular dismay at partisan disagreement.

Some political scientists break with popular wisdom and argue that the fears of partisan breakdown are exaggerated: American government—with its checks, balances, and federalism—was designed to move incrementally. Delay is part of the normal process. **Divided government** (when at least one house of Congress is controlled by a party different from that occupying the White House) has always been loud, divisive—and unexpectedly productive.[56]

Moreover, even if the result is gridlock, isn't it better that people fight passionately for solutions they believe in? Strong partisans inject new ideas into politics. They upset the comfortable status quo. When Donald Trump first blustered onto the political scene, policymakers in both parties were all in on international free trade; the powerful response Trump generated upset the economists' comfortable assumptions and forced political leaders to take another look at the costs more clearly. Likewise, partisans on the left demand "a green New Deal," a campaign against inequality, a fight for racial justice, or fairness for LGBTQ+ individuals (and couples). Strong views, sum up the pro-partisan thinkers, help shake up the comfortable assumptions and the old coalitions.

Today, more and more political scientists are coming around to a more pessimistic view. The parties clash over almost everything and on every level of government. Divided government increasingly yields political paralysis. Dangerous results radiate out in many directions. In the past decade, political standoffs led to three government shutdowns (for a total of fifty-four days and at the cost of over $7 billion—all introduced by Republicans).

Gridlock in Congress drives power to the executive branch, upsetting the carefully devised separation of powers that helps advance compromises in American policymaking—compromises already hard to come by because of . . . hyperpartisanship. For example, even when Congress rejected the border wall, the Trump administration went ahead and started building—to loud cheers from supporters.

Gridlock in Congress also erodes another constitutional check: the authority of the Supreme Court. The parties stack the Supreme Court and try to win through litigation what they can't win through legislation. In the 2021–22 session alone, a newly conservative court struck down *Roe v. Wade* and abortion rights (putting the right to privacy at risk), rejected New York's gun control law, and hobbled the Environmental Protection Agency's effort to fight global warming. In the past, strong courts have been tempted to overreach. The winners celebrate their victories, while the party losing in the courts—today, the Democrats—decry

Divided government:
Periods during which at least one house of Congress is controlled by a party different from the one occupying the White House.

the politicians in robes. What are the consequences for a branch of government that was never designed to be at the center of the nation's controversies? (See Chapter 16.)

Even if divided government worked in the past, today's partisan intensity may be driving people away from the parties. On the one hand, 2020 marked the highest voter turnout in 120 years. On the other hand, the ranks of people unwilling to identify with either party keep growing.[57]

Which side is right? For now, be aware that there are two sides to the argument about whether rising partisanship is harming American government. However, as the debates go on, social scientists—like the general public—tilt increasingly toward the pessimistic perspective.[58]

● Senators Mitt Romney (R-UT) and Kyrsten Sinema (D-AZ) confer during a hearing on U.S. economic responses to the coronavirus pandemic. In a polarized age, moments of cross-party comity are much rarer than before—though they still occur, especially on such urgent issues.

WHAT DO YOU THINK?

Should We Be Trying to Diminish Partisanship?

Partisanship is growing faster in the United States than in most other democracies. We have two parties with very different political agendas about climate change, immigration, LGBTQ+ rights, healthcare, and on and on. Worse, they each sometimes paint the other as a threat to democracy. What do you think of the partisanship that dominates our political life? Should we try to diminish it?

Yes, partisanship is harmful.
It leads to paralysis and extremism. It tempts public officeholders—like governors and presidents—to dangerously expand their powers. Worse, it is turning people off from politics, a problem for any democracy in the long run. Sensible people in each party could and should find common ground, as Congress did when it came together to pass infrastructure legislation in 2021 and gun control legislation in 2022.

No, partisanship is healthy.
Our intense partisanship originates from compelling ideas and close elections. These arguments are useful and part of the democratic process. We should encourage intense views and strong arguments—that's what introduces innovative ideas. Difficult times call for bold new solutions, and we will never get those if the political class constantly shuffles to the middle. People who oppose what's happening today can have an impact where it counts tomorrow—at the ballot box!

Maybe.
Some partisanship is useful, but today the parties are taking disagreement too far. Every branch of government must be a mix of strong ideas and compromise.

THE BOTTOM LINE

» After declining thirty-five to forty-five years ago, the main political parties are now both thriving—and are highly competitive. Recent national elections have featured narrow margins of victory in presidential races and frequent shifts in party control.

» This competition has helped fuel a rise in partisan differences, evident among both national policymakers and the U.S. public.

» Is partisanship good for American government? Traditionally, many political scientists thought it was. Today, more agree with the public: The intensity of the conflict, they fear, is weakening our institutions.

 # Conclusion: A Party System Ripe for Reform?

Calls for reforming the U.S. party system are as old as the system itself. George Washington and other founders called for an end to partisan spirit before parties even arose. Yet parties swiftly became vital to American government. Now the party spirit that the founders feared may indeed have grown excessive—though political scientists still debate the matter. What should we do? Here are three of the most commonly voiced proposals:

1. Proportional Representation

As we saw earlier, America's winner-take-all system elects the highest vote recipient in each of 435 single-member House districts—and that reduces to almost zero the number of House or Senate members who are not from one of the two major parties. A proportional representation system provides minor parties with representation equivalent to their electoral support. You would soon have representatives of the environmental party, pro-immigration party, anti-immigration party, and libertarians. Would this kind of change be a good thing?

Supporters believe that moving to proportional representation would give voters more choices, possibly increasing voter turnout. It would enhance policymaking by ensuring that a wider spectrum of options is considered, better reflecting the nation's ideological and civic diversity. Many advocates predict that more women and minority-group representatives could be elected.[59]

2. Reduce the Barriers to Third-Party Competition in Elections

If not a wholesale switch to a proportional representation system, why not make it easier for minor parties to be listed on the ballot? Why not let them join major-party candidates onstage in debates? Multiple parties might reduce the level of conflict and force groups to compromise and reach out across party lines. They might bring change and fresh ideas into American politics.

On the other hand, perhaps the two parties have effectively managed the head-spinning diversity of America. Opening the floodgates to numerous minor parties might make it even more difficult to achieve consensus.

3. Reduce Partisanship in Government

Reformers promoting this approach sometimes call for a "postpartisan" American politics. They worry that hyperpartisanship is eroding American democracy itself. But what to do about it? Ideas include limiting negative campaigning, reducing the role of outside advocacy groups in campaigns, and adopting public financing. None of these ideas have gotten much traction—in part because the Supreme Court has struck down most of the efforts.

But there is another path out of our partisan conundrum: elections. Historically, when one party breaks through and becomes the clear majority party, it sets the political pace. The minority party (grudgingly) accepts the majority's basic principles and goes along with popular proposals. The real roots of hyperpartisanship: ten years of very close elections. Eventually, the voters may solve the problem.

Here is a slightly different way to think about parties and partisanship. Consider the rich history of party politics in America that we have traced across six party systems. Those 230 years have often seen a spirit that the Greeks called *agonistic*—a willingness to disagree with your adversaries while acknowledging their views as legitimate. This spirit means engaging wholeheartedly in a process of debate. In a democracy, successful political ideas must not just be rationally sound. We must also contest them, and we do this through party competition. Perhaps *stronger* parties, providing clear alternatives and articulating "core commitments" in a forthright way, are an antidote to our current gridlock and hyperpolarization.[60]

After all, the United States has always been a nation based on ideas—and intense disagreements about what they mean. The great debate that now occupies the parties has been going on for more than two hundred years. The important goal is that as many citizens as possible all join in. The greatest dangers come not from strongly held views but from apathy among the people. Increased public apathy and indifference to politics and government, in the long run, might be the greatest risk of our charged partisan times.

CHAPTER SUMMARY

★ America's two-party style has endured for over two hundred years, with Democrats and Republicans its main standard-bearers since 1856.

★ The foundational American ideas and the organization of our elections help explain the dominance of the two parties.

★ Third parties arise periodically to challenge two-party dominance, but none has ever managed to break through.

★ The system of two parties—and the contest between them—is regularly rebooted through the birth of new party systems. Each change in the party system means a change in the voters making up each party and the ideas that inspire them.

★ Historians count at least six party systems since the U.S. founding: the Federalist era, the Jacksonian era, Civil War and Reconstruction, the era of rising business and Progressive reform, the New Deal, and (beginning in the early 1970s) a contemporary period of roughly equal balance between the two major parties.

★ A substantial majority of voting-age Americans identifies strongly with one of the two major parties. Others declare themselves independents.

★ A powerful sense of party identification is a result of many factors, including parental influence, political context, and even personality type.

★ Party identification in turn helps shape our voting patterns, the way we filter political information, and our bedrock ideas about politics and government.

★ Each party features several ideological factions, with most politically aware Americans aligning with one or two of these.

★ Republicans include religious traditionalists, American nationalists/Trumpists, fiscal conservatives, libertarians, neoconservatives, and moderates.

Democratic factions include progressives, the civil rights caucus, organized labor, and centrists.

★ Each major party must work to unite under one "big tent" their key figures and followers. These include the *party in government* (elected politicians, their staffs, and affiliated political professionals), the *party organization* (party chairs, the national committees, and the state party leaders), and the *party in the electorate* (the millions of people who identify with the party).

★ American parties are highly decentralized: State and local party leaders largely run their own organizations, independent of national headquarters.

★ Most Americans—and many social scientists—believe that partisanship is affecting the quality of American government. The intensity of the conflict, they believe, will weaken our institutions.

★ Perhaps a long period of deep conflict will have this type of dangerous effect. However, strong debates are healthy in a democracy. Remember, the United States is a nation based on ideas—and intense disagreements about what they mean. The great debate that now occupies the parties has been going on for more than two hundred years. The important thing is that as many citizens as possible join the debate.

KEY TERMS

Base voters, p. 360
Divided government, p. 370
Grand Old Party (GOP), p. 356
Negative partisanship, p. 361
New Deal, p. 356
Nonpartisan election, p. 347
Partisanship, p. 343

Party boss, p. 355
Party caucus, p. 369
Party identification, p. 358
Party in government, p. 366
Party in the electorate, p. 367
Party machine, p. 355
Party organization, p. 366

Party platform, p. 366
Party system, p. 347
Political party, p. 344
Political socialization, p. 347
Split-ticket voter, p. 360
Straight-ticket voter, p. 360

STUDY QUESTIONS

1. What are the two main reasons American politics is usually limited to two political parties? Do you find these reasons persuasive, or can you imagine others?

2. What is proportional representation?

3. For further contemplation:

   a) Would you support introducing proportional representation in Congress?

   b) What would be the effects of this switch?

   c) Explain why these effects would help or harm American democracy.

4. Describe four functions that parties serve in the American electoral process.

5. What are the three separate parts of the party organization? Explain what each part is responsible for.

6. Choose any past party system in American history.

   a) Describe the era.

   b) Which party, if any, dominated the era?

   c) What replaced the party system you have chosen? (If you chose the present era, do you see any signs that this system is ending?)

7. What is party identification? Name three factors that influence party identification.

8. Describe three factions in each political party today.

9. For further contemplation:

   a) What does partisanship mean?

   b) Explain why many Americans worry about partisanship.

   c) Some suggest the fears of partisanship may be exaggerated. Do you agree with this suggestion or not? Explain why.

12 INTEREST GROUPS

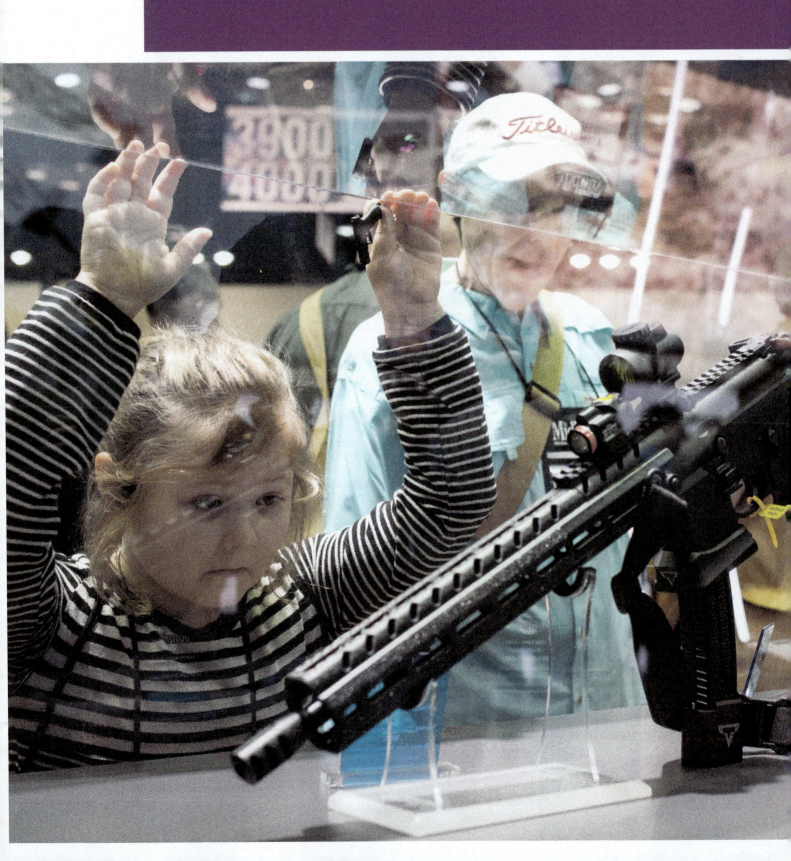

YOU HAVE BEEN HIRED as a new congressional staffer—and today is your first day at work on Capitol Hill. (Congratulations!) You arrive during a wildly busy legislative season. The office is bustling, and nobody has time to get you oriented. In fact, you barely know where you are assigned to sit . . . and now the legislative director has asked you to prepare a detailed analysis of "no peck," or at least that's what you heard her say. A sympathetic colleague explains that she meant "NOPEC," which Google tells you is the No Oil Producing and Exporting Cartels Act. Your diligent Internet search shows only that the bill might be introduced next year. And your analysis is due by tomorrow morning.

Where to begin?

Quick, call the Congressional Research Service, the research arm of Congress. They're glad to help you out, they say—but it will take a few weeks. *Weeks*? You have hours, at best.

You feel like slinking out of the office before anyone notices and fleeing Washington altogether. Then salvation arrives on your desk, in the form of an elegantly bound, meticulously researched report on NOPEC. All the details you need on international oil cartels and U.S. energy production—which House and Senate members are pushing what views, the politics involved, even the technical details—are laid out clearly. As you both weep and laugh with relief, you wonder: Who *wrote* this? You look around to thank your angel of an officemate. Not here, your colleagues smile: over on **K Street**. An interest-group lobbyist sent it directly to you. As this chapter shows, that elegant, informative, and timely report is at the heart of what interest groups do in Washington.

Interest groups have become so central to American government that it is difficult to imagine our system without them. At the same time, lobbyists and the interest groups they represent consistently receive among the lowest approval ratings of any professionals, in or out of politics: 5 percent approval, in Gallup's most recent survey.[1]

Who are we? We are a nation of too many lobbyists and special interests. Or are interest groups also positive contributors to American democracy? Pause and consider: How many interest groups work on *your* behalf? None, you say? Or perhaps one or two advocate for causes you care about—such as the environment or tax relief or the Catholic Church? In fact, like most Americans, you are represented by dozens of groups—pushing for clean air,

 Learn what interest groups do in American government—and how they do it.

 Trace the historical roots of interest-group activity, and see how lobbyists have changed.

 Examine the multiple roles that lobbyists play.

 Reflect on the benefits and drawbacks of interest groups in the U.S. system—and whether they wield too much power.

K Street: A major street in downtown Washington, DC, that is home to the headquarters for many lobbying firms and advocacy groups—and thus synonymous with interest-group lobbying.

● *The annual meeting of the National Rifle Association (NRA) typically draws about seventy-five thousand members. Here a little girl looks at a Sig Saur weapon displayed during a meeting in Indianapolis. Interest groups like the NRA occupy an important role in U.S. politics and government.*

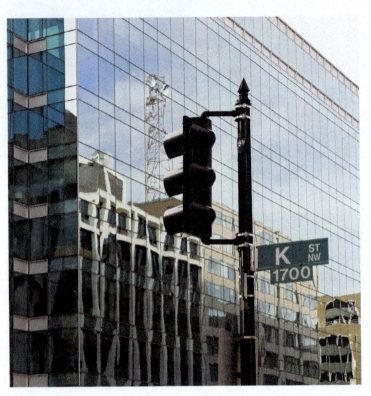

● *"K Street," where many lobbying firms locate their offices in the nation's capital, has become shorthand for interest-group power.*

safe food, affordable federal student loans, and most everything else you care about. Your college or university likely has representatives who lobby to promote the school's concerns—at the state capitol and in Congress. Your student fees or tuition may help pay for their work. Even your favorite subject, political science, has a national association based in Washington, DC, with several advocates on staff. Whether you know it or not, you are a participant in our "interest-group society."[2]

More than two centuries ago, in the *Federalist Papers*, James Madison warned that interest groups—he called them "factions"—were the "mortal disease" that had always killed off popular government. His solution? *Increase* the number of interest groups. That way, none would become too powerful, and they would have to work together to accomplish anything. Increase the number of groups? That is one piece of advice the United States has certainly taken.

Special interest: A pejorative term, often used to designate an interest group whose aims or issue preferences one does not share.

Concern about **special interests** has surged periodically since Madison published his famous warning. Jacksonian Democrats, Progressives, New Dealers, 1960s radicals, Bernie Sanders supporters, and Donald Trump voters: Groups across U.S. history expressed a fear that a few groups (usually big business) were getting fat off the rest of us. The outcry obscures a basic truth: Interest groups are not just "them"—they are us.

Who are we? The United States is a society of interest groups that are woven into the fabric of our politics. The central puzzle in this chapter is whether their influence saps American government of its vigor and fairness—as many people believe—or whether interest groups sustain and even enhance American democracy. Or perhaps they do both.

🏛 Interest-Group Roles in American Politics

President Ulysses Grant used to go over to the Willard Hotel, two blocks from the White House, for a nice brandy and cigar. But when he walked through the hotel's lobby, he was swarmed by people trying to influence him. "Those damn lobbyists," he complained. Today, making an impact on policy is a bit more complicated than

BY THE NUMBERS | Interest Groups

>5 Million National Rifle Association members, according to their website

33 Percentage of registered lobbyists who serve only public interest clients

710,000 Total dollars spent on lobbying by Miami-Dade County, 2021[5]

90,000 Estimated number of professionals lobbying the U.S. government

7.5 Billions of dollars in U.S. federal and state lobbying expenditures, 2021[6]

58 Percentage of former (nonretired) members of the 115th Congress (2017–19) who now work as Washington lobbyists[3]

28 Number of nationally active transgender-rights interest groups, 2022[4]

128,973 Average lobbyist's salary in the U.S. in 2022[7]

373 Estimated number of Obama White House staff who left for lobbying positions[8]

280 Estimated number of former lobbyists who worked in the Trump administration, 2017–20[9]

As you read through these examples, is interest-group lobbying more or less pervasive in American government than you imagined? Why?

pushing through the crowd at a fancy hotel and shoving a petition into the president's hand. Now, the job is done by interest groups.

What does it take to become an interest group? Dozens of lobbyists swarming around Capitol Hill? Inside connections galore? A million motivated supporters? It is much simpler: We define an **interest group** as *an organization whose goal is to influence government.*

Notice two important elements in that definition. The first is *organization*: A collection of wheat farmers begins to resemble an interest group only when they meet regularly to discuss and manage their concerns. The second is *influence government*: Plenty of organized groups have no contact with public officials. When those wheat growers join the American Farm Bureau Federation and press Congress for subsidies to keep crop prices stable, then they are an interest group.

Interest group: An organization whose goal is to influence government.

● World-class surfers push policymakers for clean beaches and coasts.

At least two hundred thousand interest groups are active in American politics—local, state, and national. About three-quarters of those are public advocacy or citizen groups; the remainder represents private (usually corporate) interests. For example, AARP is a public advocacy group that represents nearly forty million Americans over age fifty. It hires lobbyists to press government officials on issues of interest to seniors, such as healthcare. It also provides financial services, insurance, hotel discounts, and information. Financial Services Forum, a private lobbying association focused on banking, claims a much smaller membership: the CEOs of eight giant financial services firms, including Goldman Sachs, JP Morgan Chase, and Bank of America.

How does lobbying work? Imagine that you've joined a lobbying firm and you've been put in charge of an important account—surfers "rising up" for clean coastal waters. You'll have three different jobs to do: informing your group's members, communicating to policymakers, and mobilizing support for your positions.

Informing Members

First, interest groups inform their members about what's going on. The United States is an enormous nation with a sprawling government. Ordinary people can't possibly keep up with all the policies percolating through the system. The lobbyists' job is to keep interest-group members up-to-date on the many things that concern them. If you represent surfers, you'll tell them about a regulation in the Interior Department to open waters to oil drilling; a proposal in Congress to create a national park off the coast of California; the latest environmental regulations on waste treatment plants; and a slew of court cases that will affect clean water. The interest group will also inform its members how it's trying to affect the outcomes in each case (sometimes adding a plea for more funds). In short, interest groups provide one of the major links between government and the public. Once you sign up with a group, information will flow your way . . . through TikTok, Facebook, and other social media.[10]

Communicating Members' Views

Second, interest groups *communicate what members think to government officials.* Or to put it more directly, they try to win policies that their group members favor—clean beaches, unfettered access to firearms, marijuana reform, more generous student loans, and so on. How? Interest groups may meet directly with these officials, but often they gain access by hiring **lobbyists**. Put simply, a lobbyist is a person who engages with government officials on behalf of a cause or issue. Plenty of people try to influence government—like college students, who fan out across their state capital for an annual "Lobby Day," asking legislators to oppose higher student fees or appropriate more funding for science labs. Professional lobbyists are paid by clients to influence lawmakers, with an advantage: They know their way around Washington or the state capital. They know who to talk to and when to talk to them.

> **Lobbyist:** A person who contacts government officials on behalf of a particular cause or issue.

Take the public health concerns over vaping, for example. President Trump announced that his administration would take "very, very strong action" on teenage vaping by banning flavored e-cigarettes. Vaping companies like Juul, with allies in the tobacco industry and anti-government regulation groups, mounted a furious lobbying campaign featuring Trump voters appealing directly to the president on Twitter and on news shows favored by the president. The campaign caught the president by surprise. Trump postponed the ban and blasted his health advisors for failing to inform him that his own supporters strongly opposed their health proposal. Ultimately, under the Biden administration, the Food and Drug Administration essentially banned Juul—a ban that a court immediately put on hold.[11]

However, most lobbying is far less dramatic. In fact, lobbyists are most effective working on very narrow issues, far below the media radar, like a tweak in a trade regulation at the Department of Commerce. Why? Because politicians and policymakers have strong positions on high-profile issues—like regulating tobacco or firearms or oil companies. It's a lot easier to get what you want if no one else has even heard of the issue you're lobbying for.

Mobilizing the Public

Third, interest groups *mobilize the public*: They encourage groups of people to act politically. Lobbyists develop social media alerts, TV ads, and urgent direct-mail postcards, all meant to provoke action.

Many Americans care deeply about abortion policy, for example. Most are not satisfied with voting every two years for candidates who share their position. Pro-life and pro-choice groups offer members frequent opportunities to *do something* on this issue. Interest-group mobilization happens on many issues, from food safety to corporate espionage. Contributing funds, writing letters, organizing rallies and protests, exchanging ideas with others of similar views, and winning audiences with policymakers: Interest groups facilitate all these means of political participation.

For example, AARP mobilizes its members to communicate their views to government on a wide range of issues affecting seniors, from Social Security benefits to disability insurance.[12]

● *Elena Hung, executive director of Little Lobbyists, speaks at a "welcome back Congress" rally calling for an urgent focus on caregiving in 2021.*

In 2003, President Bush tried to add a new prescription drug benefit to Medicare; Democrats and conservative Republicans in Congress both opposed the bill and had the votes to block the legislation on Capitol Hill. Then AARP with its forty million members threw its weight behind the bill, and it squeaked through the House by a single vote.

How well do interest groups represent your concerns? If you care about something that is already on the government agenda, groups are likely promoting your views in Washington. For example, some two dozen groups advancing transgender rights have sprung up as the issue gained prominence. More obscure topics—and less powerful interests—have a harder time getting heard. However, if you have strong opinions about a policy that seems to be overlooked, do not despair. American political history is full of "crackpots" who believed in outlandish things—ending segregation, putting airbags in every car, slashing personal income-tax rates, cleaning polluted rivers—that eventually won out.

Indeed, through their work informing members, communicating views to political officials, and mobilizing the public, interest groups play an important role in democratic societies.

What Do Interest Groups Do for Democracy?

Around now, many of our students say something like, "Wait a minute—are all those interest groups a *good* thing?" Well, there's a hot debate about that.

Pluralism: An open, participatory style of government in which many different interest groups negotiate government policies.

A traditional view, known as **pluralism**, holds that the key to American democracy is an open political process in which a lot of groups come forward and represent many different interests. If every group that really cares about an issue makes itself heard, then government policies should roughly reflect public desires. No single set of interests dominates our system, pluralists believe; instead, all the different groups push and compromise and hammer out a decision. It may not be fast or hyper-efficient, but it is fair: Every interest gets a voice in the process. In effect, we have a democracy of groups. You might recognize this as an update on James Madison's argument in *Federalist No. 10* (described in the introduction to this chapter): The answer to the problem of interest groups is—more interest groups.

Hyperpluralism: The collective effect of the vast number of interest groups in slowing the process of American democratic policymaking.

Two pessimistic theories respond to the pluralists. Many Americans fear that the proliferation of interests and groups bogs down the entire system: Political scientists call this **hyperpluralism**. Any time a group promotes a policy change—education reform, a new highway, privatizing Social Security, or fighting global warming—there is always another group to oppose it because they do not want to pay the cost or fear harm to the environment. The result: stalemate. In sum, the immense buildup of lobbyists in Washington and state capitals leads to policy gridlock—or, as one scholarly article puts it, "vicious, street-fighting hyperpluralism."[13]

Power elite theory: The view that a small handful of wealthy, influential Americans exercises extensive control over government decisions.

Others fear just the opposite: not too many groups in the political process, but too few. As one political scientist famously put it, "The flaw in the pluralist heaven is that the heavenly chorus sings with a strong upper-class accent." The wealthy can sponsor more powerful interest groups and more well-connected lobbyists than anyone else. **Power elite theory** pictures a group of wealthy Americans who dominate the political system at a far more fundamental level than all of those interest groups.

Years ago, corporations and military leaders (especially military contractors) were thought to sit atop politics. Today, the power elite view focuses on multibillionaires with their deep pockets and global reach. They wield influence not just in Washington, DC, but in political capitals and financial centers around the world that no ordinary interest group can hope to match.[14]

For example, in 2022, Elon Musk, the CEO of Tesla, launched a bid to take over Twitter for $44 billion financed by his own wealth and funds from a consortium of seven banks. Musk was outspoken about his plans: He said he would emphasize free speech on the platform, which had blocked President Trump from his favorite means of communication. Note the power dynamics. Congress, the courts, and the public are not the ones weighing the complicated issue of free speech versus harmful lies (about the 2020 election). Rather, the decision about whether the former president of the United States may communicate with eighty million followers could hang on a billionaire tycoon and seven banks.[15]

● *Power elite theory: The richest person in the world (as of October 2022) is a lot more influential than you.*

One political science analysis of Washington interest-group spending came up with numbers that gave new life to the elitist perspective. Professional lobbying, these researchers wrote, is dominated by business: 53 percent of the lobbying organizations and 72 percent of the expenditures represent business interests. In contrast, public interest groups account for 5 percent of lobbyist spending. And groups supporting less privileged people employ just 2 percent of the lobbyists in Washington.[16]

Which view—pluralist, hyperpluralist, or power elite—is correct? In different situations and in different settings, all capture part of the political process. Yes, the powerful often get what they want, but not always. After all, they are often divided among themselves. Even small groups pursuing improbable causes sometimes break through and shake up the system—as we've seen in almost every chapter of this book. And most people who watch politics, especially in Washington, DC, are impressed by the sheer number of groups, pushing and hauling and checkmating each other. (Notice, that stalemate introduces its own political bias: It protects those who are already getting what they want and do not need help from government programs.)

In short, there is at least some truth to each of these views. For now, you understand the central issue: Interest-group behavior adds up to something important—the distribution of power in American politics. This theme takes us right back to the question we posed at the start of the book: *Who governs in America?*

THE BOTTOM LINE

» Interest groups, or organizations that seek to influence government, employ lobbyists to pursue benefits for their clients or membership.

» Groups serve their members by communicating political information to them, analyzing and relating members' views to policymakers, and mobilizing people to act politically.

» A long debate continues among pluralist, hyperpluralist, and power elite theorists about whether the collective public is well represented by interest groups and who wields power in America.

Types of Interest Groups

How well are collections of Americans—truck drivers, or political science students, or Latinos, or CEOs, or people experiencing homelessness—represented in the interest-group system? To answer that, you have to understand the different types of interest groups, and who they represent.

Political scientists divide the teeming world of interest groups into three main categories: *economic* groups; *citizen* groups, which advance public interest causes (as they see them) like climate change or religious liberty; and *intergovernmental* groups, where one government agency lobbies another. Texas and New York have lobbyists in Washington; and the White House has lobbyists working Congress. (Wait a minute: The *White House* has to lobby other parts of government? Read on!)

Economic Groups

Economic groups seek financial benefits for their members. Sometimes, they simply promote the interests of a single corporation; we call this category *business lobbyists* (see Table 12.1). For example, Amazon has 111 registered lobbyists (and spends more than $20 million a year on lobbying). If that seems like a lot, just think of all the different policy areas that touch a firm like Amazon: worker safety regulations, minimum-wage policy, high-tech patents, cybercrime, Department of Defense contracts, anti-trust policy (especially after some activists began to suggest breaking up the company), immigration policy (Amazon hires engineers and other experts from all over the world), and the list goes on. *Business* lobbyists don't necessarily try to influence politics in *all* these areas. Instead, many of these lobbyists stay busy simply making sure that their company is not caught unawares by a change that might cost them millions.

Labor groups represent workers from nearly all large industries in the United States. The largest is the National Education Association (NEA), which claims 3 million members, most of them public school teachers. Next largest, at 1.9 million members, is the Service Employees International Union (SEIU), representing many service industries such as healthcare, hospitality (e.g., hotels and restaurants), and public employees. Both the NEA and SEIU, like other labor groups,

TABLE 12. 1 **Types of Interest Groups**

CATEGORY	PRIMARY PURPOSE	EXAMPLE
Business groups	Seek economic benefits for a company or firm	Amazon (111 total lobbyists; some in house, some in specialty firms)
Labor groups	Seek economic benefits for labor union members	National Education Association (3 million members)
Trade or private associations	Seek economic benefits for businesses or professionals in a given sector	American Petroleum Institute (oil and gas company members)
Citizen groups; also called public interest groups	Organize and mobilize like-minded individuals around a shared passion, political viewpoint, or cause	Sierra Club, Christian Coalition
Intergovernmental groups	Advocate for one level or branch of government to another	National Governors Association

run education and political-engagement programs. But their greatest focus is on higher pay and better benefits for their members. This effort mainly targets employers, but they also lobby government—primarily on regulations affecting working conditions, such as higher minimum wage or safety improvements. They also fight legal challenges to unions and union organizing.

Third, **trade associations** represent companies or professionals in a specific sector. The American Petroleum Institute represents oil and gas companies: It lobbies for tax benefits, opposes regulations, fights to maintain government subsidies to its members, resists initiatives designed to reduce global climate change, and supports international trade deals on behalf of 625 companies. To join the American Architects Association, one must be—you guessed it—an architect; similarly, lawyers join the American Bar Association and doctors the American Medical Association, and political scientists join the American Political Science Association (yes, there are reduced rates for student members). Although these groups are well known, many associations are obscure: Take a guess at what PATH International represents. Others may use a name that masks their purpose: A few years ago, an association called Citizens for Better Medicare spent millions of dollars lobbying for changes to Medicare, the national program that covers health insurance for people over sixty-five. Eventually reporters figured out that the "citizen" members were actually drug companies, health insurers, and large hospitals looking for higher reimbursements.

Oh, and did you guess what PATH stands for? It's the Professional Association of Therapeutic Horsemanship—professionals who provide equine therapy to children and adults.

> **Trade association:** An organized group representing individuals and businesses that belong to the same industry.

Citizen or Public Interest Groups

What about the rest of us? Hundreds of thousands of *citizen groups*, also called *public interest groups*, cover the political spectrum, representing every conceivable issue and group. The National Alliance to End Homelessness, for example, is a Washington group whose national conference each year (on, you guessed it, Lobby Day) attracts hundreds of supporters from across the United States. Single-issue organizations, such as People for the Ethical Treatment of Animals (PETA), fit into this category. So do those established to promote a political viewpoint, such as the American Conservative Union.

Citizen groups do not have a built-in constituency (in contrast, most lawyers join the American Bar Association) and so must work hard to recruit and retain members. Many arise around an issue high on the policy agenda: When the Trump administration pulled out of the international Paris Agreement to fight climate change, for example, hundreds of citizen groups joined mayors and governors (of both parties), religious groups, Native American tribes, and more than 2,200 businesses and 353 universities to lobby under the #WeAreStillIn banner.[17] Public interest organizations all face the same problem: Why would a rational person join a group, pay dues, and spend time in meetings when others are willing to do the work? After all, everyone gets the benefits of clean air or consumer safety—whether they pitched in or not. Scholars call this the *free rider* problem—why pay your dues when you can enjoy the ride for free? (You might remember we raised this problem discussing who joined the civil rights demonstrations in Chapter 6: Why put yourself at risk when you can reap the benefits even if you stand on the sidelines?)

Log on to the website of any public interest group—Greenpeace or the National Rifle Association (NRA) or Habitat for Humanity, which builds homes

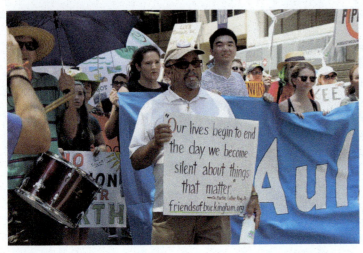

● *Citizen groups lobby across the country. Here, a Virginia group opposes a proposed power station in a historically Black community (they won the battle). Pluralists point to groups like this and conclude that American democracy is alive and well.*

for needy people around the globe. Alongside the rhetoric about global warming or the right to bear arms, you will see major swag available. Tote bags, curated trips to Yosemite, gun-safety videos, teddy bears, travel mugs—all free or discounted for joining.

In political science terms, these **material benefits** are vital to sustaining citizen groups. All that swag helps attract new members, whose dues keep the lights on and lobbyists on board. Others join because they feel moved by the cause—by being part of something bigger than their own individual interests. Social scientists, as usual, have a name for this kind of motivation: **expressive benefits**—the group expresses values that its members share, such as social justice or individual freedom. Black Lives Matter, not long after its original founding, organized as a lobbying group and continues to draw people who care intensely about racial justice—an expressive benefit.[18]

Still other people may join an interest group for **solidarity benefits**. Think of your own experience as a Girl Scout or fraternity member: It can feel very powerful to be part of the group. Interest-based organizations tap into that feeling and engage members based on shared social fellowship.

Trade associations are subsidized by their sponsoring firms. Members of the American Petroleum Institute, for example, pay annual dues based on the size of their organization, starting at $2,000 and rising to tens of thousands of dollars. Citizen groups are partly supported by members, but their dues are much less, averaging around $18. Larger donations might come from foundations, government grants, or wealthy individuals, who are called "angels" in the interest-group world.

The best-known angels are big-spending donors who usually align with one or the other political party. Richard Uihlein, a billionaire midwestern businessman, sponsors Republican candidates for all levels of office, and spent well over $60 million in the 2020 and 2022 elections. An "angel" on the other political side, George Soros, has funneled millions of dollars into liberal advocacy groups, from America Coming Together to MoveOn.org. In our highly polarized politics, angels such as Soros and Uihlein face bitter criticism from partisans on the other side.

Intergovernmental and Reverse Lobbying

Here's one of the oddest features of the American system: Public officials also act like interest groups. They aim to influence other public officials by engaging in **intergovernmental lobbying**. For example, the White House maintains a legislative affairs office, staffed by former House and Senate staffers, that negotiates with Congress. Even the president needs lobbyists!

State and local governments also have Washington offices. They lobby the president, Congress, and the bureaucracy. And like oil companies and doctors, they too have a national association. The National Governors' Association (NGA) includes all fifty states' governors—conservative and liberal alike. They all share an interest in federal funding, so they make their voices heard at the White House, in Congress, and throughout the federal bureaucracy. Cities lobby too.

Material benefits: Items distributed by public interest groups as incentives to sign up or remain a member.

Expressive benefits: Values or deeply held beliefs that inspire individuals to join a public interest group.

Solidarity benefits: The feeling of shared commitment and purpose experienced by individuals who join a public interest group.

Intergovernmental lobbying: Attempts by officials in one part of the government to influence their counterparts in another branch, or at a different (state or local) level.

Reverse lobbying: Attempts by government officials to influence interest groups on behalf of their preferred policies.

Over six hundred mayors pack the Conference of Mayors' gatherings in Washington, DC, each year, often addressed by the president and other top leaders.

Government officials also lobby interest groups, termed **reverse lobbying**. Before they introduce proposed legislation, for example, both executive and legislative leaders hold closed-door meetings with key interest groups to line up supporters. Sometimes they negotiate the details of the legislation because early compromises can diffuse future battles. At the same time, if the details become public, opponents will decry the special deals cut behind closed doors.

For example, President Obama used this approach to health reform when his advisors privately met with groups representing the insurance industry, pharmaceutical companies, hospitals, physicians, and other primary stakeholders. The negotiations helped reduce the interest-group battle over the Affordable Care Act. When the details became public, however, the Republicans (and most of the media) charged that Obama and Democratic allies had "bought off" these groups.

Michael B. Hancock ✓
@MayorHancock
Follow

Mayors are the ones implementing legal marijuana. We know what works & what doesn't. Teaming up w/ @MarkFarrellSF, @MayorJenny, @LibbySchaaf, @tedwheeler & @mayorheidi in a first-of-its-kind coalition to help cities, states & Congress prepare for legalization #MayorsMJCoalition

The Government for Responsible U.S. Cannabis Policy Coalition will push for Congress and the Administration to take action.

#MayorsMJCoalition

● *Intergovernmental lobbying in action. Urban leaders announce a "cannabis coalition" to defend state marijuana laws in Congress and the White House.*

THE BOTTOM LINE

» Interest groups come in several types: Those pursuing primarily *economic* concerns include business and labor groups, along with trade and professional associations.

» *Citizen* groups include those promoting broad causes (consumer rights, civil liberties) and single-issue advocates such as PETA, as well as ideological groups.

» Governments also lobby each other, as well as engaging in "reverse lobbying"—working with interest groups to advance desired aims.

 ## Interest Groups Past and Present

America's interest-group society has deep roots in our history. The First Amendment is among the most familiar American political creeds. Freedom of religion, speech, press, and assembly are all ingrained in the national mind. Most schoolbooks do not mention the final clause of that amendment, however: the right to "petition the government for a redress of grievances." In other words, the first amendment in the Bill of Rights guarantees . . . the right to lobby.

After the Constitution was ratified in 1789, the first Congress gathered—and so did petitioners seeking benefits: "After each legislative day, hogsheads of wine and port poured freely at sumptuous meals of mutton, pork, duck, and turkey. Dinner linens are snowy white; the cutlery is burnished & English, and the check was paid by the wealthy merchants of the day."[19] These merchants were among the original economic interest groups in American politics.

As far back as the 1750s, journalists lining the halls outside Britain's House of Commons were called "lobbyists." In the early 1830s, New York, the "Empire State," had the largest population and most business activity. Albany, the capital, was a constant target of privilege seekers, who became known as "lobby-agents." President Andrew Jackson, or someone on his White House staff, shortened this to "lobbyist" and hurled it pejoratively at national bankers. The name stuck and spread to anyone seeking to influence government.

1960s Advocacy Explosion

Although economic interest groups have a long history in the United States, the number of professional lobbyists remained at a few dozen for a century, and then gradually rose to perhaps two hundred by the 1950s. Public interest groups also arose during this period, but because they were organized around a specific objective—banning liquor sales or winning benefits for Civil War veterans—the enthusiastic membership melted away once the legislative battles were done. Writing in 1963, a group of seasoned political scientists concluded, "When we look at the typical lobby, we find its opportunities to maneuver are sharply limited, its staff mediocre, and its typical problem not the influencing of Congressional votes but finding the clients and contributors to enable it to survive at all."[20]

Then the old ways changed. Demonstrations for civil rights and against the Vietnam War roused massive numbers of Americans in the latter 1960s and 1970s. Spirited public engagement spread to other areas: women's rights, the environment, consumer rights, access to healthcare, protecting life, restoring the traditional family.

These movements required organizers to channel all that public passion to attain results. Enter professional public interest lobbyists. Advocacy groups such as the Sierra Club and the NAACP had existed for decades; now they expanded both their membership and political activities. As Washington churned out regulations, political and economic life became more complex—requiring a guide to explain all the intricate new rules to small businesses, farmers, local officials, and others. Enter the expert insider lobbyists. Big corporations, the target of many of these new rules (Make safer products! Increase gas mileage! Protect worker safety!), realized they needed louder voices in Washington as well. Enter the corporate lobbyists. Their demands also cascaded: Lower our taxes! Cut regulations! Protect us from competition! Help us create jobs!

The result of all this expanded public, government, and lobbying activity: an **advocacy explosion**. After the mid-1960s, the number of professional, full-time lobbyists swelled into the thousands (see Comparing Nations 12.1). Critics who already feared interest-group power were doubly alarmed by the growth of an elaborate "politics industry" in Washington, DC.

Advocacy explosion: A vast and relatively swift increase in interest groups active in Washington, DC, beginning in the mid-1960s.

Not Your Grandparents' Lobbyists

For many Americans, the mental portrait of a lobbyist involves a potbellied, middle-aged white man swapping yarns with his old pal the congressman. That

---

COMPARING NATIONS 12.1 **The Spread of American-Style Lobbying**

Though other countries also ramped up legislative volume and complexity during the 1960s, none has anything like America's interest-group society. Parliamentary democracies in Europe and Asia organize public and private interests into a few "peak groups," whose representatives sit with national officials to slice up the pie—deciding formally how much business and labor should get. These groups are often financed by the government and work more like collaborative partners than multiple opposing sides in a legislative scrum.

This political style leaves far fewer openings for interest groups. As a result, only the United States features lobbying *firms*, filled with hundreds of lawyer-lobbyists and their staffs. European observers long disdained them as "the American problem." But the European Union (EU) has changed all that. Today, there are some twenty-five thousand lobbyists spending $3.6 billion to try to influence EU policy. The list is headed by familiar American names: Google, Facebook, and many of the large U.S. lobbying firms. Washington's "dark arts" have arrived in Europe, lamented *The Economist,* an English weekly.[21] Ironically, the United States is exporting what may be the least popular feature of American government.

---

stereotype may fit an earlier era, but it's way out of date. Lobbying today is an entirely different enterprise. For starters, women now make up nearly half of Washington lobbyists and increasingly dominate social issue areas like healthcare and consumer rights.[22] Let's meet a few lobbyists—new school and old school.

Consider Pablo Chavez, a self-professed video game geek whose idea of a good time was programming. When Chavez became Google's top lobbyist in Washington, even the most traditional DC outlets took notice. *Roll Call*, a journal for congressional insiders, commented that the new Google chief had grown from a "policy nerd" into "a sophisticated leader on the government relations side." And a venerable Washington thinktank, the *Brookings Institution,* expanded the point: "Millennials Are on the Frontlines of Political and Cultural Change in America"—and that includes lobbying. It's all a far cry from the backslappers of an earlier era.[23]

If you ran into Ashley Solle on campus, you might think she was still a political science major at the University of Michigan. Ashley began her career as an intern at organizations fighting for immigrant children and international refugee resettlement. Then she joined a Washington lobbying firm, *Lobbyit.* Her first clients included Advocates for Wild Equines (AWE)—an organization devoted to the protection of wild horses and burros in the West. When the Department of the Interior planned to cull the herd, AWE led the protests and hired Lobbyit to help fight for their cause. Since Solle works for a lobbying firm, she has dozens of different clients—from nonprofit groups like AWE to trade associations like the Association of Woodworking and Finishing.[24]

Now meet Tom Dobbins, who served as president of the American Composites Manufacturers Association for thirteen years. ACMA represents

● *Even wild horses have their interest group—and their lobbyists. The Advocates for Wild Equines (AWE) lobby on behalf of stallions like the one shown here.*

only firms that make composites: everything from high-tech fiberglass boat hulls to carbon-reinforced materials that support our skyscrapers. Dobbins is a trade association lobbyist, working for a collection of firms in the same type of business. But he's not part of the old backslapping fraternity either. When he recently looked back on his years as president, he pointed to the most important part of his job—finding common ground among the firms in his business. He was especially proud of his role in creating a research institute and in helping hash out industry standards.[25]

Notice our three lobbyists each do a different kind of lobbying: Pablo Chavez directs lobbying for a single firm. Ashley Solle is in a lobbying firm and works for a lot of different kinds of clients seeking representation in Washington. And Tom Dobbins worked for an association of multiple firms in one industry; since tobacco farmers or trial lawyers or composites manufacturers share common interests in Washington, it makes sense to have a single association lobby for their concerns. But none of these individuals looks or sounds anything like the antiquated image of a Washington insider.

After working for a single firm or a trade association for a few years, many lobbyists go into business for themselves, representing a range of clients (usually in one issue area, though some high-profile lobbyists work across fields). These independent lobbyists are known in Washington-speak as "hired guns," though most of them hate that term (see Table 12.2 for a list of other terms associated with Washington lobbying).

TABLE 12.2 Washington Lobbying

Drop	Set of brochures and position papers left behind by a lobbyist after visiting a legislator's office.
Fly-in	A series of Washington meetings, usually on Capitol Hill, organized by lobbyists for their out-of-town clients.
Bird-dogging	Posing tough questions to an elected official, often at a public event. Advocacy groups often engage in this tactic to advance their cause and win attention.
Spilling the Tea	Lobbyists traffic extensively in gossip: Today's rumor could be introduced as a bill tomorrow. When younger lobbyists and Capitol Hill staffers exchange the latest political gossip, they say they are "spilling the tea."
Rainmakers	Lobbyists adept at raising funds for politicians or causes; when they collect large sums, they are said to be "making it rain."
Social Butterflies	There is a social side to lobbying work as well. One interest-group representative we know starts his weekdays in Longworth Cafeteria, on the House side of Capitol Hill. Strategically located at a central table, he greets the stream of members and staffers as they pick up a morning coffee or bagel, exchanging the latest political gossip.
Third House	In Washington, as well as many state capitals, lobbyists are viewed (not necessarily positively) as a co-equal "third branch" of government, given their expertise and access.

Interest-Group Lobbyists in Action

Another Monday morning in Washington, DC: All over the capital, lobbyists are starting their workweek. Some head straight to Capitol Hill to catch up with any staffer (or, ideally, Senate or House member) they might bump into. Others gather in boardrooms for breakfast with lobbyists sharing similar interests—protecting Social Security or promoting family values—to review the week's urgent legislation. Some flick through their Twitter or Instagram feeds, sifting the latest opinions and posting a few of their own. And several dig into an ongoing political research project, gulping coffee to break through the morning fog.

Lobbyists' Multiple Roles

Lobbyists wear many different professional hats. Some interest groups are large enough to hire specialists—staff members dedicated to researching policy issues or developing media advocacy campaigns. Lobbying firms also hire outside scientists, consultants, and other experts to assist them. But most Washington representatives juggle several roles: It's all part of the job.

Researchers. The typical interest-group representative spends significant time every day studying political trends, monitoring government programs, and analyzing policy information.

As giant appropriations bills make their way through Congress and the White House each year, groups working on budget and tax policy prepare detailed briefing books for each House and Senate office. (Remember the story at this chapter's opening: Those overworked congressional staffers often depend on clear, unbiased information from lobbying groups.)

Such research work can be very expensive. Between 2001 and 2014, the American Petroleum Institute, a trade group for the oil and natural gas industry, spent some $36 million on a single study refuting the link between cancer and benzene, which is a colorless gas that is part of automobile exhaust (as well as cigarette smoke). Despite the effort, benzene is still classified and regulated as a human carcinogen linked to leukemia.[26]

Witnesses. Most congressional committee hearings feature testimony—on both sides—from the interest groups most concerned about the issue. Executive agencies convene similar gatherings on how to implement a law, again featuring lobbyist experts. Even more lobbyists are in the audience at congressional hearings, following every utterance and move. Experienced Washington eyes can watch this

● Lobbyists work at all levels of government. Here, they watch state Senate floor action on a television kiosk in St. Paul, Minnesota.

crowd—a questioning look to a senator's aide here, a note passed to a witness there—and predict whether the committee will approve the legislation under discussion.

Position Takers. Washington representatives for various groups routinely issue statements outlining their organization's position on important legislation. Each January, for example, the U.S. Chamber of Commerce—which represents more than two million businesses—holds a press conference to announce the group's main goals for the coming legislative season. Even more frequently, the AFL-CIO, representing more than sixty labor unions, posts a "Working People Weekly List" of leading issues they are lobbying on in Washington and state capitals.

Coalition Builders. Affiliated groups often band together in **lobbying coalitions**, allowing them to share information and split the job of contacting lawmakers. Although quantum computers—machines that rely on quantum mechanics to solve complex problems—won't exist in marketable form for years, a lobbying coalition is already seeking U.S. government support and funding. The Quantum Industry Coalition, as of 2022, comprised twenty-three groups, including major industry players such as IBM and Google, as well as smaller start-up companies like EeroQ and ColdQuanta.

Grassroots Campaign Builders. Join an interest group, and you will receive a steady stream of appeals to write your representative or senator: to balance the budget, to stop teen smoking, to recognize Palestine as a nation, to protect wild horses, and so on. Interest groups mount these **issue campaigns** as part of their attempts to attract public support from across the country. They try to create the image of a powerful grassroots movement. If they are too obvious about it, opponents will mock their efforts as **"astroturf lobbying"**—industrial-grade fake grass with no roots at all.

Lobbying coalition: A collection of lobbyists working on related topics or a specific legislative proposal.

Issue campaign: A concerted effort by interest groups to arouse popular support or opposition for a policy issue.

Astroturf lobbying: An attempt by interest groups to simulate widespread public engagement on an issue.

Nonprofits Lobby?

For many citizen groups, the very word "lobbying" has a dirty connotation: "cutting shady deals with sleazy characters," as one report put it. Few public interest leaders think of themselves as lobbyists. "Well, I guess they're calling me lobbyist," chuckled one physician as he testified in favor of expanding healthcare coverage to more low-income people in Montana. He thought of himself as a reformer, not a lobbyist. The lesson of this chapter: You can be both.[27] Cleaning up a river, providing social services to immigrants, seeking English-only laws, or advocating for tax reform—they all require lobbying.

Even ordinary citizens get into the act. Senator Susan Collins (R-Maine) was on the fence about whether to support her party's push to repeal Obamacare. Party leaders put terrific pressure on her to go along with repeal. But then, she began to hear from her constituents. For the first time in her long career, people walked up to her in the Portland Airport and cheered her for her position. "People were thanking me, over and over again," she later recalled. They kept saying the same thing: "Stay strong, Susan!" In the end, buttressed by her constituents' views, Senator Collins ignored her own party leaders and voted against repeal—ending the bill's chance of success.[28] Her reputation as an independent who heard her constituents helped her win easy reelection in 2020 in what had been expected to be a very close race.

THE BOTTOM LINE

» Lobbyists perform a wide range of roles, from researchers to social butterflies.

» Private sector lobbyists can represent a single firm or a trade association, or set up in business for themselves as independent lobbyists.

» Citizens' groups are often loath to engage in "lobbying," but they must to succeed.

 ## Interest Groups and the Federal Branches of Government

The traditional model of Washington power brokers depicted a closed process dominated by **iron triangles**—tight, durable links among powerful interest groups, congressional committee chairs and their staff, and administrative officials.

Consider one example: *farm subsidies*. For decades, many American farmers—growing crops from corn to tobacco—have received price supports, or subsidies worth millions of dollars, from the U.S. government. Critics charge that this practice is a huge giveaway of taxpayer dollars. Agricultural experts explain that weather and other uncertainties endemic to farming make a system of crop insurance and production management necessary. During the 2018–19 farm bill reauthorization, farm subsidies were targeted for cuts. Legislators in both parties pointed to the need to rein in spending, but when the smoke cleared and the bill was signed into law, the price supports remained.[29]

In traditional accounts, a classic iron triangle explains the staying power of farm subsidies (Figure 12.1). Congressional members and staffers on the House and Senate agriculture committees have close relationships with lobbyists for farm groups, thanks in part to the many farmers in those members' home states. The lobbyists encourage their congressional friends to appropriate funds for the Department of Agriculture. Farm lobbyists establish connections with Department of Agriculture officials well aware of their power to help deliver the congressional funding their programs require. If these officials balked at implementing subsidies, they might find their congressional appropriation cut the following year—so they keep the programs humming along. The combination of executive branch, legislative branch, and lobbyists—the iron triangle—is all but unstoppable.

Iron triangle: The cozy relationship in one issue area between interest-group lobbyists, congressional staffers, and executive branch agencies.

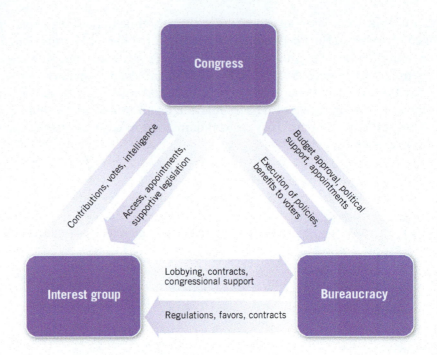

Congress

Contributions, votes, intelligence

Access, appointments, supportive legislation

Budget approval, political support, appointments

Execution of policies, benefits to voters

Interest group

Lobbying, contracts, congressional support

Regulations, favors, contracts

Bureaucracy

● FIGURE 12.1 *Iron triangle: The classic image of interest-group power features a close relationship between Congress, interest groups, and federal government bureaucracy.*

Farm policy, given its long-established players, may be the last vestige of an old system. Iron triangles proliferated around Washington into the 1960s, given the relatively closed environment of national policymaking. The subsequent "advocacy explosion" initially brought more lobbyists into closer contact with Capitol Hill staffers, which ensured the triangles' survival for a while.

Rise of the Issue Network

Over the past forty years, iron triangles have largely given way to a very different image of more open **issue networks**. A flood of new lobbyists representing more and more positions, in addition to the growing numbers of congressional staffers, has broken apart the cozy triangles. Political scientist Mark Peterson charts a "radical change" beginning in the 1980s, as triangles dissolved into a "far more diverse and open system" that featured "looser, less stable, less predictable, and more diverse patterns of interaction and decision."[30]

Issue network: Shifting alliances of public and private interest groups, lawmakers, and other stakeholders all focused on the same policy area.

One feature that helped to strengthen iron triangles and also undergirds issue networks: Washington actors often serve sequentially as policymakers, lobbyists, and formal party officials—a phenomenon termed the **revolving door**. More than half of current lobbyists passed through the "door"—they formerly worked in Congress or the White House.[31]

Revolving door: The tendency of many Washington lobbyists to move from government work (e.g., as a congressional or White House advisor) to lobbying and back again.

Figure 12.2 illustrates an example of an issue network focused on telecommunications policy. Notice how much more complicated than a simple triangle this network is. Welcome to the life of a Washington lobbyist today! To negotiate these networks—to faithfully represent members and attract new clients—modern interest-group representatives cannot count on a few reliable contacts with the chair of a congressional committee and a handful of bureaucrats. Instead, they must cultivate connections across Capitol Hill and in multiple executive departments and agencies. They also may have to master the byzantine ways of the judicial branch.

Government regulators
FCC, FTC, state utility commissioners, FAA (e.g., antenna/tower heights), Homeland Security and Defense Deptartment (national security telecomm issues), relevant House/Senate committees

Public interest groups
"Digital freedom" (e.g., TechFreedom), consumer protection groups like Free Press, expanded tech access (Media Access Group), ACLU (free speech), Benton Foundation (works on telecomm and media issues)

Telecommunications industry
Telecomm giants like Comcast, TV networks, broadband providers, infrastructure firms (e.g., cell towers), satellite providers, digital marketing firms, global firms like those in the Asia-Pacific Advanced Network (APAN), dozens more trade associations, and hundreds of lobbyists. Spending on telecomm lobbying topped $115 million in both 2021 and 2022.

Financial firms
The billions of dollars moving through the telecomm sector attracts financial companies as well: Harbinger Capital, a hedge fund, spent more than $3 million lobbying on telecomm in 2022, and the Japanese holding company SoftBank Corp. spent nearly as much.

High-tech industry
More than 600 Silicon Valley/internet companies lobby on telecomm issues, from high-profile (Amazon, Apple) to little-known (ZTE, a Chinese telecomm firm, spends millions annually on U.S. federal lobbying).

● **FIGURE 12.2** *Issue Network. Today, scholars see a more extensive network of actors influencing policy than the classic iron triangle. Here, the issue network that influences telecommunications policy. (Authors' compilation based on Berry and Wilcox)*

Interest Groups and the Courts

Iron triangles and issue networks portray interest groups engaging with the two elective branches, Congress and the presidency. What about the courts, which—as you will see in Chapter 16—have a major role in federal and state policymaking? By law and custom, interest groups have almost no access to Supreme Court justices and very little connection to other federal (or senior state) judges. But interest groups still manage to weigh in on judicial decision making, even without seeing judges in person to make their case. They do so in three main ways.

Lobbying on Judicial Confirmations. One way to shape court decisions is to influence the central players—to help determine who gets *appointed* as Supreme Court or federal judges. Each federal judge is approved by the Senate. That process used to be routine—Justice Ruth Bader Ginsburg, like most of her predecessors, was confirmed by a large Senate margin in 1993. Her replacement, Amy Coney Barrett, saw a highly partisan confirmation process that ended in a 51–49 vote. Today, every Supreme Court nomination immediately prompts a multimillion-dollar confirmation fight. Interest groups spend heavily on public campaigns to influence the presidents who choose judges and the senators who confirm—or block—a president's choice. In the 2020 confirmation battle over Justice Barrett, conservative groups spent over $30 million in support, while progressive groups like Demand Justice spent record amounts in opposition.[32]

The battle is not surprising. Justice Barrett's one-vote confirmation victory led promptly to the Supreme Court's reversal of *Roe v. Wade*.

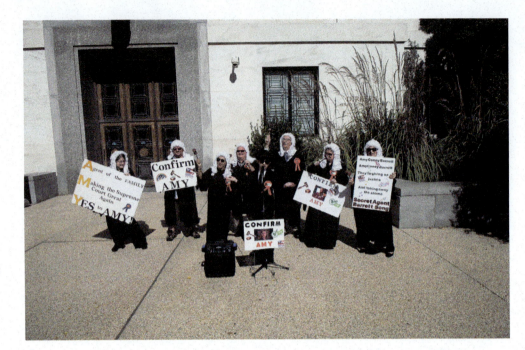

● Interest groups squared off over Amy Coney Barrett's nomination to the Supreme Court, spending millions of dollars in support or opposition. Shown here, supporters with the organization Public Advocate of the United States demonstrate in favor of Barrett's confirmation.

Filing *Amicus Curiae* (Friend of Court) Briefs. Groups interested in a pending case are permitted to—and sometimes invited by a court to—write up legal memos, or "briefs," arguing their position on the case. Major cases attract dozens of such documents: In 2021–22, when the Supreme Court reviewed Maine's ban on using public funds at religious schools (covered in Chapter 15), hundreds of groups and individuals filed fifty-six amicus curiae briefs.

Sponsoring Litigation. It can be very expensive to take a case to court. Researching the relevant issues, paying the lawyers, and pursuing litigation through multiple appeals can cost millions of dollars. Interest groups often take up a legal cause, contributing both money and expertise. When the Supreme Court agreed to review, in 2022–23, a civil-liberties case involving a wedding website designer who refuses business from gay couples, challenging a Colorado law that prohibits businesses from discriminating against LGBTQ+ people, interest groups such as the American Civil Liberties Union (liberal) and the Federalist Society (conservative) provided substantial expertise and financing.

THE BOTTOM LINE

» Lobbyists working in specific areas sometimes still form "iron triangles" with congressional staff and executive branch officials.

» More fluid "issue networks" featuring lobbyists as central players increasingly characterize today's complex policymaking environment.

» Interest groups also lobby the judicial branch by funding confirmation battles, filing *amicus curiae* briefs, and financing litigation.

Interest Groups and Power

Should Americans worry that interest groups are intimately involved in the details of policymaking, writing bills, and shaping legislative outcomes? Senator Henry F. Ashurst, an Arizona Democrat, once admitted bluntly: "When I have to choose between voting for the people or the special interests, I always stick to the special interests. They remember. The people forget."[33] If members of Congress are voting with or otherwise directly influenced by lobbyists, this unelected set of central actors deserves our close scrutiny—and perhaps alarm.

Political scientists lack hard evidence about interest groups' power: Did this bill pass because lobbyists said it should, or did it pass regardless of all their politicking? Instead, we fall back on typical measures of what matters in national politics: *numbers* and *money*. Washington insiders gauge the status of a White House agency or a special congressional committee based partly on how many staff it has. If interest groups are spending a lot to influence lawmakers, their financial input may be a clue to the return their clients are getting on their investment.

How many lobbyists work in Washington? Around 12,200 professionals registered as congressional lobbyists in 2021, but that number represents a fraction of the total. Lobbyists can avoid registering if they spend less than 20 percent of their time on "lobbying activities," a loosely defined term. Although legal penalties apply to those failing to disclose lobbying work, not one criminal case has ever been filed under this law. One interest-groups expert offers a figure closer to 100,000 based on all the grassroots advocates, political consultants, trade association representatives, and others who can claim to be under the 20 percent threshold.[34]

Tens of thousands of lobbyists, all chasing members of Congress and their staffs, as well as White House and executive branch officials—many commentators see these numbers as decisive evidence of interest-group influence. Interest groups are increasingly active in state and local government as well. Companies that used to focus on Washington are diversifying: Google had lobbyists in just two states in 2006; by 2015 they had expanded to thirty states, and through lobbying coalitions like the Internet Association they now reach all fifty states.[35]

Ultimately, if you measure the influence of interest groups by simple numbers, then this sector is certainly powerful. Do the numbers suggest an ability to win policy goals? Not necessarily. As lobbying networks become denser, there are more interest groups on every side, and it becomes easier to block legislation than to advance it.[36] That "veto power" underscores how central interest-group lobbyists have become to national, state, and local government. But the widespread notion that lobbyists are writing bills and getting them passed: No research substantiates that claim.

Interest Group Spending

Interest groups big and small, from Wall Street financial interests to California almond growers, spend some $8.5 billion each year attempting to influence Washington policymaking. This does not include spending on political campaigns or on state and local lobbying expenses, an issue discussed later in this chapter.

This $8.5 billion figure is inexact. Official Senate and House records indicate that *registered* lobbyists reported spending $3.77 billion on lobbying activities in 2021 (see Figure 12.3). Because many of those seeking to influence Congress never bother to register, analysts estimate that total spending is about 2.5 times the reported amount.[37]

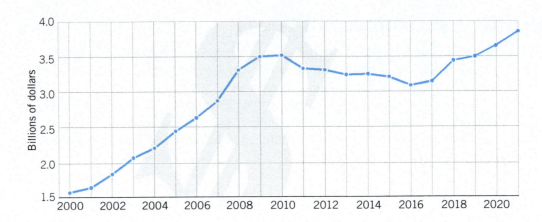

● **FIGURE 12.3** *Trends in spending by registered lobbyists, 2000–2021, in billions of dollars. (Center for Responsive Politics)*

Clients of private groups and members of public groups together provide those billions of dollars, which are spent on lobbyists' salaries, research costs (remember that neatly bound report!), the expense of running a Washington office, travel, and so forth. Table 12.3 lists the top-spending interest-group clients for 2021. Of the

TABLE 12.3 **Biggest-Spending Lobbying Clients, 2021**

LOBBYING CLIENT	TOTAL AMOUNT SPENT
U.S. Chamber of Commerce	$66,410,000
National Assn. of Realtors	$44,004,025
Pharmaceutical Research & Manufacturers of America	$30,406,000
Business Roundtable	$29,120,000
Blue Cross/Blue Shield	$25,176,385
American Hospital Assn.	$25,140,934
Meta	$20,070,000
American Medical Assn.	$19,490,000
Amazon.com	$19,320,000
American Chemistry Council	$16,640,000
Raytheon Technologies	$15,390,000
National Assn. of Manufacturers	$15,300,000
Lockheed Martin	$14,401,911
NCTA—The Internet & Television Assn.	$14,010,000
AARP	$13,680,000
Boeing Co.	$13,450,000
Comcast Corp.	$13,380,000
Biotechnology Innovation Organization	$13,290,000
Verizon Communications	$13,240,000
CTIA	$12,430,000

Source: Center for Responsive Politics

various sectors represented (healthcare, oil/gas, etc.), most of these big spenders are corporate interests. Does that confirm the "power elite" view? Or is it merely a waste of money because business appears to lose plenty of policy battles? Or is it really money spent on keeping businesses informed, avoiding surprises, and supporting allies? (Remember: One of the things interest groups do is inform their clients on what's happening right across Washington.)

When an issue of importance to a group or industry arises in Washington, affected groups tend to boost their spending. Amazon was already devoting millions to its lobbying efforts when, in 2017–18, the Trump administration considered raising tax rates for online retail and U.S. Postal Service shipment costs. Amazon expanded its lobbying team, and by 2021, it had built up a lobbying team more than 100 strong, spending tens of millions of dollars to engage federal and state/local officials.[38]

Some analysts look at annual growth in lobbying spending and conclude that it proves interest groups' extensive political influence. But the truth is more complicated. We might ask, for example, what Amazon and other e-commerce companies got for all their spending. An Internet sales tax that Amazon and fellow online retailers strenuously opposed was, at the last minute, pulled out of the 2018 spending bill over President Trump's objections. Eventually the Supreme Court stepped in and ruled that the states may tax Amazon and other online retailers. The next time you buy something, look for the charge and remind yourself: The intergovernmental lobbyists from the states beat the corporate lobbyists from Amazon.[39]

Our conclusion about the billions in spending by lobbying groups: It probably did not influence many votes. On a high-profile issue such as Internet taxation, most members of Congress have very strong views. Seasoned politicos can predict most of the votes before the debate even begins. What are the lobbyists spending funds on, then? They are supporting the members who agree with them, or trying to "soften up" the few members who might be persuadable on this topic. If members need facts for their speeches, lobbyists are there to provide background. That is why, in our story at the beginning of the chapter, that invaluable report landed on your desk.[40]

A clearer sign of lobbying heft may be a barely visible adjustment in a policy or specific bill. Energy companies, for example, successfully pushed to include an "offset program" in climate change legislation that allowed them to invest in projects to remove carbon dioxide from the atmosphere if they were unable to meet reduced emissions targets. This technical policy change underlines an important truth: The more obscure the provision, the better the chances of winning it. The less the public is aware of a topic, the more room Congress has to deliver favors.

Regulating Interest Groups

All this talk of influence leads to questions about how interest groups are regulated. What are lobbyists forbidden to do in pursuit of their policy goals? For a long time, the answer was "not much." Until 1946, there were no real limits on lobbying, though out-and-out bribery—clearly exchanging votes for money or other favors—was prohibited. That year, Congress passed the **Federal Regulation of Lobbying Act**, which required lobbyists seeking to influence Congress to *register* with a special office (now done online every three months) and *report each client* and how much that client paid. Can you spot the loophole in the 1946 act? It didn't put any restrictions on lobbying itself; lobbyists were free to pass on glitzy watches and glamorous vacations to their congressional friends.

Federal Regulation of Lobbying Act: The initial U.S. statute spelling out requirements on lobbyists active in Congress, which was passed in 1946.

Tech Lobbying Interests

How Do Interests Expand as Companies Grow?

Many companies, especially in the technology area, announce as they grow that they will remain out of politics. Yet, most tech companies spend much more on lobbying, as shown in the graph.

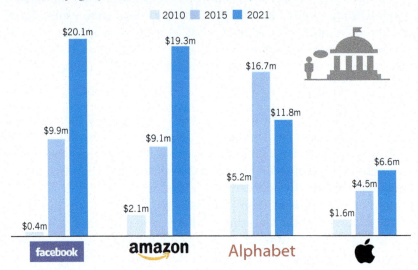

Tech Giants Ramp Up Lobbying in Face of Antitrust Scrutiny
Annual lobbying expenditures of selected tech companies in the U.S.

2010 2015 2021

facebook: $0.4m, $9.9m, $20.1m
amazon: $2.1m, $9.1m, $19.3m
Alphabet: $5.2m, $16.7m, $11.8m
(Apple): $1.6m, $4.5m, $6.6m

* excl. some subsidiareis

Sources: Senate Office of Public Records, Center for Responsive Politics

---

Ted Cruz @tedcruz · May 30, 2019
Here's something I don't say often: on this point, I AGREE with @AOC Indeed, I have long called for a LIFETIME BAN on former Members of Congress becoming lobbyists. The Swamp would hate it, but perhaps a chance for some bipartisan cooperation?

> **Alexandria Ocasio-Cortez** @AOC · May 30, 2019
> If you are a member of Congress + leave, you shouldn't be allowed to turn right around&leverage your service for a lobbyist check.
>
> I don't think it should be legal at ALL to become a corporate lobbyist if you've served in Congress.
>
> At minimum there should be a long wait period.
> twitter.com/Public_Citizen...
> Show this thread

💬 4.4K   🔁 9.3K   ♡ 64.9K   ⬆️

● *Two very different members of Congress—ultra-conservative Texas Senator Ted Cruz and leading young liberal New York Congresswoman Alexandria Ocasio-Cortez ("AOC")—share a Twitter moment about the need to limit the "revolving door" between Capitol Hill and K Street.*

Tighter restrictions on gift giving were imposed in 1995 and 2007. More comprehensive lobbying-reform proposals seem to be announced after every election. Both newly elected President Trump (in 2016) and newly elected House Speaker Pelosi (in 2019) promised reforms. The bipartisan efforts to reduce interest-group influence—for example, by forbidding former members of Congress to lobby their ex-colleagues for a specified time period—failed to pass.[41] Today, interest groups continue to sponsor trips for members of Congress or state legislators; the "revolving door" between Capitol Hill or the White House and K Street continues to turn; and most of those seeking to influence government officials find loopholes that permit them to get away without even registering.

Over in the executive branch there has been more action but with limited consequences. When President Trump came into office, he signed an executive order permitting former lobbyists to work in the White House but forbidding those who left the administration from lobbying the government for five years; on his last day in office, Trump revoked the five-year ban he'd introduced at the beginning.[42] On his first day in office, President Biden signed his own executive order imposing a ban on lobbyists working in the White House (for two years) or top administration officials turning into lobbyists (for the duration of the administration). Even so, liberal lobbyists were soon flourishing, leading one liberal to sound the familiar alarm: "Beware, Lobbyists."[43]

THE BOTTOM LINE

» Because of the difficulty of measuring interest-group influence in government, researchers turn to metrics such as a lobbying firm or interest group's number of lobbyists and how much they spend on lobbying.

» Regulations on interest-group activity are relatively limited in the United States. They have periodically been tightened, but extensive loopholes remain.

Are Interest Groups Bad or Good for America?

Americans remain deeply cynical about the work of interest groups in our national polity, even as we write checks to groups promoting the causes we care about or show up for "Lobby Day" at our state capitol. What is wrong with interest-group activity in American government? Let's look at the worries, as well as some possible upsides.

Four Concerns About Interest Groups

Throughout this chapter we have explored the question of influence—how much say lobbyists have in national politics. Here we summarize four primary concerns, raised at various points in this chapter.

1. Corruption. The close connections between lobbyists and federal lawmakers arouse concerns about the unfair advantage enjoyed by lobbyist insiders over ordinary citizens. As we saw earlier, interest groups devote some $8.5 billion annually to influence national policymaking and help direct hundreds of millions more to campaigns for Congress and the presidency. Does this add up to corruption at the core of American government?

Paul Manafort would fit right into a nineteenth-century lobbyist's portrait: well connected, high living . . . and thoroughly corrupt. Manafort was a Washington pioneer, combining lobbying, public relations, and campaign consultancy under one roof. He represented arms dealers and foreign dictators, including the Philippines' Ferdinand Marcos, Ukraine's Victor Yanukovych, and Jonas Savimbi of Angola, collecting millions in unreported fees. Manafort never bothered to register as a foreign lobbyist, and was sentenced in 2019 to ninety months in federal prison for "subverting lobbying laws" overseas along with related crimes.[44]

2. Division and Hyperpluralism. Critics also worry about interest groups' divisive influence. Former Harvard president Derek Bok wrote that "America no longer seems diverse; it seems divided into innumerable special interests . . . gray power, gay power, red power, black power; the sun belt and the frost belt; environmentalists and hard hats; industrial groups, professional groups, educational groups: all more conscious of their rights, all more aware of their claims on the rest of society."[45]

Bok's view taps into an old debate about whether individual preferences add up to the "public good." Does any collective interest transcend the self-focused demands of specific interest groups? Alexis de Tocqueville praised Americans' tendency to form voluntary associations to achieve political ends. Modern public interest groups, however, seem like pale shadows of the lively civic bodies Tocqueville applauded.

A related concern, introduced earlier in this chapter, is "hyperpluralism": the fear that the crush of lobbyists hinders decisive political action. One after another, idealistic people flock to Washington, DC, with each new administration; a few years later, they start to exit, bitterly complaining about how the sheer volume of interest-group activity made it hard to get anything done.

3. Accountability. America's leaders are accountable to the people, thanks to our frequent national elections. Interest-group lobbyists face no such public accountability, despite their significant roles in influencing debates and policymakers. No lobbyist is elected by the people, and few legal controls regulate their activities. Moreover, negative issue campaigns by interest groups appear to enhance cynicism among the public about "bureaucracy," corroding the government's accountability.[46]

4. Unequal Representation. Interest groups bring public concerns before national officials. Yet not all segments of the population are equally represented. There are a lot of barriers to representation—it takes money and organization to get through all the noise. Not surprisingly, the powerful get a much louder voice. Political sociologists Theda Skocpol and Vanessa Williamson summarized the concern: "Over the past few decades, attentive and well-resourced business lobbying organizations [have] gained enormous influence." They point to four ways that business wins: They influence what issues come up for debate in Washington; they block key provisions in legislation as it goes through Congress; they insert crucial phrases in laws that do get through; and they influence the rules taking place in administrative agencies (a process we'll describe in Chapter 15).[47]

Though blatantly corrupt acts such as Manafort's may be rare, according to this view the real scandal is not in lavish trips or fancy meals. Instead, the U.S. political system may face a more fundamental problem: The proliferation of interest groups and lobbyist bias tilts democracy toward the wealthy and the powerful.

These four arguments constitute a sobering critique, fueling the pressure for reform that has occupied Congress for years. It led many Americans to cheer Donald Trump's call to "drain the swamp." Joe Biden offered a wonky Democratic version of the same idea when he promised an overhaul of legislation guiding lobbyists. Taken together, the worries return us to the question of democracy itself: Have special interests usurped government by the people?

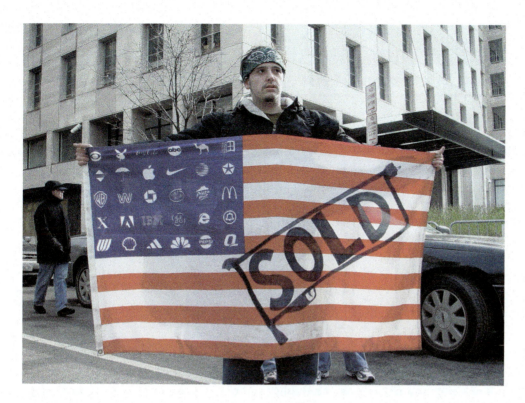

● *Do interest groups representing large corporations have greater access—and therefore power—than other groups? Notice the familiar corporate brands, from media companies to big banks, that have eclipsed the fifty states on the flag.*

Four Defenses of Interest Groups

There is another side of the story—one you don't often hear. Early in this chapter we looked at how interest groups may be useful to you as a member of a group. Might they also benefit our political system? Here are four arguments in their favor.

1. More Democratic Representation.   Pluralists hold that the proliferation of interest groups, and their links with public officials, helps make American politics more democratic. The expanded number of groups translates into better representation of a wide range of interests. Not *all* interests, however: People seeking assistance from government typically must possess some combination of resources, organization, and a favorable political context.[48] Even so, advocates' ability to negotiate the system—and connect directly to lawmakers and party leaders—means that many Americans and their interests are well represented today.

2. Communication and Information.   Conveying citizen views to officials and providing the population with information about government activities are essential features of any democratic polity. Such two-way communication is facilitated by constant exchanges between interest groups and the members or private clients they represent.[49] Thanks to technological advances in communication, as well as innovative tactics developed in part by interest groups, any interested citizen has vast quantities of information available with only a few swipes or clicks.

Likewise, Capitol Hill and the executive branch are inundated with lobbyists describing public (and corporate) views—permitting lawmakers to analyze more information and hear more points of view before reaching a decision. Additional information and new perspectives can inform both public and official preferences, thus enhancing the democratic deliberative process.

WHAT DO YOU THINK?

How Much Influence Should Interest Groups Have in American Government?

	Less influence.	About the same amount.	More influence.
Think about the four concerns and the four defenses described in this section and about our discussion of influence a few pages back. Then ask yourself: How much influence *should* interest groups have in American government?	Interest groups and lobbyists are a serious problem for democracy and good government, and their influence must be limited—or the power elite will continue to control politics and policy in America.	Madison's observation long ago still holds: Limiting groups' ability to form and seek influence is worse than the excesses of lobbying influence. We should, however, vigorously enforce existing regulations on lobbying.	Despite their poor reputation, interest groups enhance democracy and good government. As pluralists rightly note, when the public wants something from government, interest groups help us obtain it.

3. Mobilizing and Organizing the Public. America's mass political parties originally came into existence to mobilize the vast number of white male voters entering the system after the expansion of suffrage. Parties still play an important mobilizing role, but their work is supplemented by interest groups. Issue advocacy appears to spur at least modest increases in voter turnout. It also may encourage more participation in other respects, as citizens are inspired to write members of Congress and otherwise get involved. In our social media age, interest groups help connect the public with issues that arouse their passions and register their views.[50]

4. Stability. The flip side of hyperpluralism—in which the thicket of lobbyists slows down our separated-powers system of policymaking—is *stability*. One virtue of the U.S. system, in some eyes, is its remarkable longevity. Over 230 years after the Constitution was ratified, we see relatively few changes in our basic structures of national government.

James Madison's fundamental concern about factional influence led him to recommend the proliferation of interests, preventing any handful of powers from gaining enduring control over public policy. The legacy of that view exists today: Interest-group activity is so extensive, featuring strong positions on every side of most issues, that the American policymaking system inches along very slowly. It is difficult to mount sweeping new policy programs, or even pass major legislation, given the army of lobbyists and formal party leaders seeking to rewrite, add amendments to, or kill outright most bills.

In summary, the interest-group story is a paradoxical one. One principal result of all the heaving and pushing, effort and striving, by thousands of lobbyists in Washington may be greater stability in government. Whether the four benefits described here outweigh the dangers we described earlier is the ultimate puzzle of interest groups and democracy. The answer depends on what you value most. Are you eager to see fundamental change? This chapter gives you another reason why it happens very rarely in American politics. If, on the other hand, you value stability and are wary of rapid changes, then the interest-group system is for you!

THE BOTTOM LINE

» Critics of interest groups in American governance variously claim that they are corrupt, are too numerous, lack accountability, and/or enjoy access to lawmakers that ordinary citizens usually can't achieve.

» Supporters of interest groups respond that they enhance democratic representation, help communicate popular views to public officials (and in turn report on government actions to their members), mobilize people for action, and that their sheer numbers enhance the stability and predictability of American government.

Conclusion: Interest-Group Influence Revisited

We end with a final question: How might we better tap the potential *benefits* of lobbying while minimizing the dangers? If national policymakers work to keep the political process open and transparent, their efforts can enable more groups to gain access—and to help ensure something like a level playing field for all of us.

Could interest groups themselves enhance their contributions to democratic governance? Aware that *information* is at the heart of lobbying activities, two political scientists suggested a central clearinghouse that collects details on the flood of interest-group activity—allowing the public to access more of the information that interest groups provide to Congress and other policymakers.[51] The "OpenSecrets" database maintained by the Center for Responsive Politics allows instantaneous access to all lobbyist registrations and spending details; LobbyView is a related tool, created by a political scientist in 2018, that provides dynamic visual details of lobbying activity.

Public officials also can strive to ensure that the least well-off sectors of our society—typically those poorly represented by interest groups—receive enhanced representation. As you have seen throughout this book, some Americans are uneasy about a government that stitches together a patchwork safety net of welfare benefits, healthcare, and other essential services for people down on their luck. The powerful and the wealthy have plenty of voices looking after their concerns in Washington. A fair system can ensure that groups supporting the least powerful will get the sanction and resources needed to make our interest-group society one that embraces every member.

CHAPTER SUMMARY

⭐ Interest-group lobbying has long been a vital feature of U.S. government and politics. Lobbyists are deeply engaged across our policymaking system, and groups have sprung up to represent virtually every professional, personal, and identity-based interest, providing their members with information about federal policies and conveying those members' concerns to Washington. Yet Americans continue to hold lobbyists in very low regard.

★ Public anxiety centers on interest groups' reputed power to affect policymaking. Groups spend billions of dollars each year to advance their views, and lobbyists swarm over Washington (and state capitals) in vast numbers. It is not clear, however, what all this activity adds up to.

★ Although critics insist that lobbyist influence in shaping government outcomes is extensive, political science research has not turned up definitive evidence in support. And the proliferation of groups on all sides of most issues tends to mean that even if one sector (e.g., business) gains the upper hand in Washington, the pendulum eventually swings to the other side, and other sectors (e.g., public interest groups) win a string of policy victories. Lobbyists are most likely to win on obscure matters that few people notice.

★ A long history of interest-group involvement in American national and state politics was punctuated by an "advocacy explosion" that began in the 1960s. In recent years, interest-group representatives have been getting younger—and many more women have entered the lobbying profession. Today, lobbyists perform a wide range of roles, from testifying on policy issues before Congress to acting as full-service "concierges" on behalf of their private or public interest clients. Advocacy or membership groups have a harder time retaining members and must appeal to a mix of benefits: material, solidarity, and expressive.

★ Interest groups are active in all three branches of government; in each, they both seek and provide information—the currency of politics. They also work on (and help finance) political campaigns and are closely intertwined with the leadership of both the Republican and the Democratic Parties.

★ The central presence of interest groups in the halls of government has led—across U.S. history—to calls for reform, including banning lobbyists altogether. At least partly balancing the dangers that interest groups pose is a set of benefits they provide, including boosting democratic representation and contributing to the long-lived stability of American politics and governance.

KEY TERMS

Advocacy explosion, p. 388
Astroturf lobbying, p. 392
Expressive benefits, p. 386
Federal Regulation of Lobbying Act, p. 399
Hyperpluralism, p. 382
Interest group, p. 379
Intergovernmental lobbying, p. 386

Iron triangle, p. 393
Issue campaign, p. 392
Issue network, p. 394
K Street, p. 377
Lobbying coalition, p. 392
Lobbyist, p. 381
Material benefits, p. 386
Pluralism, p. 382

Power elite theory, p. 382
Reverse lobbying, p. 386
Revolving door, p. 394
Solidarity benefits, p. 386
Special interest, p. 378
Trade association, p. 385

STUDY QUESTIONS

1. What is an interest group, and what are their main roles in the American political system? What are the different types of interest groups? How did the groups (and the lobbyists they employ) proliferate so widely in American national politics?

2. Name the three main theories about the effects of interest groups (pluralism, for example, is one). Describe each.

3. After reading the chapter, which of the theories in Question 2 seems to you most accurate? Justify your answer.

4. Describe the traditional iron triangle. Explain the issue network that has now replaced it in large part.

5. What is the free rider problem? Name three types of benefits that interest groups provide to overcome the free rider problem.

6. Describe three ways that interest groups try to affect Supreme Court decisions.

7. One of the most important elements to lobbying success is gathering information. Explain how and why.

8. Describe four primary concerns about interest groups (summarized at the end of the chapter). Anything missing from that list, in your view?

9. Describe four defenses of interest groups. Are there any you would add, based on your reading?

10. Researchers have not made much headway in specifying interest-group influence. Can you imagine any better ways to accurately measure lobbyists' influence on American policymaking?

11. Think of the interest group that represents you the best. Is it a group that works on a specific issue, such as gun control or lower taxes? Or is it one representing a specific "identity" group, as in women or Latinos or LGBTQ+ people? Or is it a geographically based organization, concerned with the interests of Texans or New Englanders or mountain states residents? Or, perhaps, is the group organized around a partisan or ideological perspective? Why is that group your preferred representative?

12. What do you think the effects might be of the trend toward younger and more women lobbyists? Can you imagine any changes in how lobbyists do their work or the effect of interest groups on the policy system?

13 CONGRESS

CONGRESSMAN ANTHONY GONZALEZ got to the Capitol Building at dawn on January 6, 2021. "Wow," muttered the Ohio Republican when he saw all the buses clogging the streets. President Trump's "Stop the Steal" rally, scheduled for later in the day, was going to be huge.[1] As the crowds grew outside, Congress started a traditional and symbolic routine: certifying the winner of the presidential election. But this time, the old routine blew up.

Paul Gosar, a Republican from Arizona, rose in the House and claimed that hundreds of thousands of votes had been stolen in his state. While he was talking, Capitol police quietly walked into the chamber and escorted the presiding officers out of the room.

After the leadership had been whisked away, the rest of the members learned that the Capitol Building had been breached by a mob. "We have tear gas in the Rotunda," shouted a police officer, referring to the grand space under the congressional dome. "There are gas masks under your seats," he continued. Most of the members had no idea that the masks were there or how to put them on. Ruben Gallego (D-AZ), a marine veteran, leapt onto a table at the front of the room and demonstrated how to use the masks. The lawmakers could now hear banging and screams right outside their chambers.

Then a gunshot—one of the mob, Ashli Babbitt, had been shot dead as she tried to break in. Terrified members began to call and text their families. Blunt Rochester, a Democrat from Delaware, dropped to her knees and prayed. "You need to get out now," shouted an officer. The members hurried nervously from the chamber—some locked themselves in their offices, turned furniture into barricades, and huddled with their staff as the crowd banged on the doors and taunted them.[2]

It took most of the day, but eventually, the crowd was driven out. Bomb-sniffing dogs, their paws covered in leather boots to protect them from the broken glass, combed through the Capitol Building. Members from both parties went back to work and certified the election—eight Republicans in the Senate who had originally opposed certification now changed their minds and duly voted with the Democrats to approve Biden's victory.

After that explosive day, Congress remained deeply divided. Democrats were furious that even after all the violence, 138 (or 65 percent) of the Republicans in the House and six (12 percent) in the Senate refused to certify the results, even though many quietly admitted that they knew the election

In this chapter, you will

 Learn what Congress does—and how it is changing.

 Reflect on how well Congress represents the people.

 Examine the internal workings of Congress.

 Consider the importance of skilled congressional leadership.

 Think about the problems that face Congress—and some possible solutions.

● *A new Congress is sworn into office on January 3, 2021— and three days later chaos ensued.*

had not been stolen.[3] But now the divisions weren't just between the parties. They also ran deep within the parties.

For Republicans, the insurrection caused a split. One week after the riot, ten House Republicans voted to impeach Donald Trump for inciting insurrection and seven Republican senators voted to convict him. On the other side of the Republican divide, members defended Trump and fiercely denounced the turncoats. The division within the party ran right through the congressional session and into the 2022 primary elections. Conservatives who accepted the 2020 results fought conservatives who did not. The deniers knocked off the moderates in primary after primary. But, in the 2022 midterms, deniers did badly. The Republican caucus swung back to traditional conservatives.

Across the aisle, the Democrats had won control in 2022: a small majority in the House, a miniscule majority in the Senate (50-50, but the vice president breaks ties), and a Democratic president. The victory only exposed their own divisions.

The Biden administration proposed two massive spending bills: a $1.2 trillion infrastructure bill (with money for highways, trains, broadband Internet, and repairs to neighborhoods divided by past construction projects) and a $3.5 billion Build Back Better Plan (including $500 billion for climate change and $400 billion for childcare and preschool). In the Senate, Democrats and Republicans came together and passed the infrastructure bill with nineteen Republicans joining all fifty Democrats. The more liberal Build Back Better package, however, was blocked by the two most conservative Democrats. In the House, progressive Democrats responded to the impasse over Build Back Better by blocking the infrastructure bill; they would vote for it only after the Senate agreed to pass Build Back Better. The two senators refused to yield. Finally, in November, with Democratic leaders applying maximum pressure (and after the Republican candidate won easily in the Virginia governor's race), the House voted to pass the infrastructure bill. Six progressive Democrats voted no; the legislation was saved by thirteen Republicans (out of 213) who defied the House Republican leadership and voted yes.

Eight months later, negotiations among Democrats unexpectedly yielded a new version of Build Back Better (now tagged the Inflation Reduction Act)—with the climate money but not the childcare. The legislation squeaked through without a single Republican vote in either chamber. This time, progressive members simply went along.

Welcome to Congress, where today every move is marked by deep, bitter partisanship. Notice how the big division *between* the parties is complicated by smaller splits *within* them.

Many political scientists consider Congress "the broken branch of government." The legislature, in this view, does not address national problems, passes few important laws, fails to properly oversee the government, and has let its own process break down.[4] Extreme partisanship is not what the founders intended—they imagined careful deliberation (without any parties at all).

But Congress still lies at the heart of the national government. Big changes require laws and crises require congressional action. Despite all the worries and criticism, the two parties did compromise their way to the infrastructure package (with 14 out of 219 House Republicans voting yes), gun controls (5 Republican votes), and a boost to the semiconductor industry (24 Republican votes). Do these bills signal a rising spirit of cooperation? Two parties pulling back from the partisan brink? Or rare exceptions for a dysfunctional branch of government? After all, only a very small number of Republicans crossed over to vote aye with the Democrats.

Who are we? A vibrant people deeply divided by our political attitudes. The parties carry that division right into Congress. This chapter raises an urgent question about the American legislature: Is it indeed the "broken branch," unable to address the problems we face? Or should we see it in a more positive light as a place where our clashing ideas—about politics, about national problems, about America itself—get a full hearing? Where a minority can often stop action it opposes? And where, despite all the barriers, important bills still get negotiated (or watered down) and passed?

BY THE NUMBERS Congress

18 Percentage of Americans who approved of Congress, summer 2022[5]

55 Percentage of Americans who approved of Congress, fall 1998

1.2 Percentage of all 12,645 bills proposed in the 117th Congress (2021–22) that became law[6]

96 Proportion of U.S. House members with a college degree, 2022

45 Number of Chinese National Congress members who are billionaires

5.0 Percentage of all 14,692 bills proposed in the 96th Congress (1979–80) that became law[7]

136 Number of nonwhite members of Congress, 2022

63 Number of nonwhite members of Congress, 2001

Zero Number of U.S. House or Senate members whose net worth reaches half a billion

174,000 Annual salary, in dollars, for members of Congress

223,500 House Speaker's annual salary in dollars

7 Number of House and Senate committees investigating executive branch spending of $5 trillion in coronavirus relief funds.

Members of Congress collectively look more like the nation they represent, churn out many bills and conduct major investigations each year, and are paid far less while in office than leaders in other fields. Yet public approval ratings for Congress have never been lower. How do you explain Americans' disdain for Congress?

🏛 Introducing Congress

The Constitution places Congress at the center of American government. The document's first and longest article provides a detailed accounting of legislative organization and authority (Table 13.1).

This is a formidable set of powers. Congress soon after the founding seized its constitutional authority, and for most of American history it ruled. After the Civil War, President Andrew Johnson brooded in the White House while Congress passed bill after bill redefining the nation, including the postwar constitutional amendments declaring equality and guaranteeing the former slaves a right to vote—ideas that President Johnson (and, at the time, the Democrats) bitterly opposed. A half-century later, when Senator Warren Harding won the presidential election of 1920, one of his old Senate buddies told him to "sign whatever bills the Senate sends you . . . and don't send bills for the Senate to pass."[8]

By the middle of the twentieth century, however, Congress had become increasingly deferential to the White House and the courts. Congress has the constitutional power to declare war, but has not formally done so since World War II in 1942. Today, the nation looks first to the president to manage the economy, deploy troops, respond to crises, conduct foreign affairs, and address policy problems. And it turns to courts to break logjams. Immigration, abortion, election rules, and even the fate of Obamacare: Congress failed to act. Presidents leapt in with executive orders (which we'll cover in Chapter 14). The Supreme Court made strong rulings settling controversies.

Even when Congress does act decisively, the credit often goes to the White House. Most Americans call the Affordable Care Act "Obamacare," and credit President Trump for the 2017–18 tax cut, even though Congress worked out most of the details on each.

Still, Congress remains a vital institution of American government. Presidents may command more public attention, but they need cooperation from the House and Senate to advance their policies. We judge presidents in part on whether their programs win approval from Congress, as you will see in Chapter 14. Moreover, Congress's importance extends far beyond the vital responsibility of lawmaking.

TABLE 13.1 Constitutional Powers of Congress

From Article 1, Section 8 (unless otherwise noted).*
Financial. Power to raise revenue through taxes and borrowing, pay national debts, "provide for the common defense and general welfare," and regulate trade and commerce among the American states and with other countries.
Legal. Power to establish U.S. citizenship laws, regulate bankruptcy laws, issue U.S. money, punish counterfeiters, establish a patent system ("to promote the progress of science and useful arts"), fix national weights/measures standards, and enact laws subject to presidential approval. Impeach presidents and federal judges.
Institutional. Power to organize the judicial and executive branches, establish a postal system (Article 2, Sec. 2), set up and control the national capital (Washington, DC, since 1797), admit new states, and exercise control over U.S. territories (Article 3, Sec. 3). Alter or amend the time, place, and manner of states' election laws related to congressional elections (Article I, Sec. 4).
National defense. Power to declare war; regulate rules for prisoners of war; and raise and fund the U.S. Army, Navy, Department of Homeland Security (since 2002), and other defense and intelligence forces.
Additional congressional powers are provided by constitutional amendment. For example, the Thirteenth (1865), Fourteenth (1868), and Fifteenth (1870) Amendments authorize Congress to enforce African Americans' civil rights, as you read in Chapter 6.

As much as any other actor or institution in U.S. government, it is Congress that answers the question, *Who are we?*

Two Chambers, Different Styles

Like most other national legislatures, Congress is bicameral, comprising two "houses" or chambers. Legend has it that Thomas Jefferson, who had been in Paris during the Constitutional Convention, asked George Washington why the Constitution established two chambers. "Why," responded Washington, "do you pour your tea into the saucer?" "To cool it," replied Jefferson. "Just so," returned Washington, "we pour House legislation into the senatorial saucer to cool it." Whether the exchange actually took place, it neatly captures the traditional contrast between House and Senate.[9]

The two chambers each reflect a different American value introduced in Chapter 2. The much larger House reflects direct democracy, and, because it is far more centralized, it can respond quickly to constituent demands. At the same time, Americans are suspicious of their government. Enter the senators, who each have a lot more leverage and plenty of tools to slow legislation down.

The House of Representatives includes 435 members, divided among the states based on population size, along with 6 nonvoting delegates from Washington, DC, Puerto Rico, Guam, and other U.S. territories. All House members serve two-year terms, and each represents a district of approximately 730,000 people (the Constitution originally specified districts of 30,000).

The House is organized around a relatively clear set of rules and procedures. The majority party wields centralized control through a powerful leadership team. The Republicans held the majority in the 115th Congress (2017–18) and the Democrats in the 116th and 117th (2019–22). Republicans appeared poised to take back the leadership in the **118th Congress** (2023–24). The leader of the majority party becomes Speaker of the House and controls which issues reach the **floor**—if they can control all the factions in the party.

The Senate is made up of one hundred members, two from each U.S. state, each elected for a six-year term. The Republicans won the Senate majority in 2014 (after eight years in the minority). In 2020, Democrats grabbed it back by winning four seats and vaulting into a 50-50 tie; Democratic Vice President Kamala Harris breaks ties in the Senate, giving the Democrats a one-vote edge. The Democrats clung to their narrow majority in 2022. This is a remarkable amount of churning, with neither party able to maintain its majority for long. While the turnover affects both chambers, the result in the Senate is to increase the independence of individual senators. Back in the nineteenth century, an old truism (attributed to Mark Twain) declared "every senator a little king."[10] To this day, each senator possesses a remarkable degree of autonomy, especially compared to the average House member. Any senator—even the most junior—is able to halt the entire body's consideration of a bill merely by placing a **legislative hold** on it.

For example, the Senate must vote to approve every U.S. ambassador nominated by the president. Normally, this is a routine formality. Cassandra Butts, an experienced government official, was proposed in 2014 as new ambassador to the Bahamas. She excitedly awaited confirmation. Months, then years, passed. First Senator Ted Cruz (R-Texas) put a hold on all State Department nominations because he was upset about a U.S. treaty with Iran. Then Senator Tom Cotton (R-AR) put holds on Butts as well as two other proposed ambassadors. What troubled Senator Cotton? A complaint about a Secret Service leak of private

118th Congress: The Congress elected in November 2022, meeting in 2023–24. The first Congress met in 1789–90. Each Congress is elected for two years and numbered consecutively.

Floor: The full chamber, either in the House of Representatives or the Senate. A bill "goes to the floor" for the final debate and vote, usually after approval by one or more committees.

Legislative hold: An informal way for a senator to object to a bill or other measure reaching the Senate floor. The action effectively halts Senate proceedings on that issue, sometimes for weeks or longer.

● *Traditionally, filibusters meant talking and talking to block action. Here, members get a bit of sleep during the filibuster of the Civil Rights Act of 1964 that began on March 30 and went on (and on) until June 10—sixty working days. Eventually, twenty-seven Republicans (out of thirty-three) joined forty-four Democrats to break the filibuster.*

Filibuster: Rule unique to the U.S. Senate that allows any senator to hold the floor indefinitely and thereby delay a vote on a bill to which he or she objects. Ended only when sixty senators vote for cloture.

information, unrelated to Butts or the Bahamas. Cotton wanted the administration's attention, so he did what any senator can: bring the body to a halt with a one-man veto.[11]

The hold is an extreme example of a **filibuster**—a peculiar feature of the U.S. Senate. In 1806, the Senate reorganized its rules and did not include a provision for ending debates. That meant the Senate could not act until everyone was finished talking—a loophole in the rules that permitted a minority from stopping legislation by talking it to death. The term arises from a Dutch word for "freebooter," or pirate: in politics, someone who was "pirating" legislative proceedings by holding up action. At first, filibusters were very rare. One of the first, in 1890, defeated a bill designed to protect the right to vote among Black people in the South. By the 1950s, there was an average of one filibuster in each congressional session—usually to stop civil rights legislation. They used to be dramatic affairs—senators had to keep talking till the Senate agreed to give up and move on to other legislation. The rules changed in the 1970s, and now senators quietly (often secretly) announce a legislative hold. It takes sixty votes (three-fifths of the chamber) to break a filibuster, and thanks to intense partisanship, the three-fifths vote has become the new normal for getting most legislation through the Senate—the other side filibusters almost every major bill. There have been more than one thousand filibusters in the past twelve years, which is roughly as many as there had been in the previous ninety years.

Is the Senate too good at the task of "cooling legislation"? The Senate only functions with some degree of cooperation between the two parties. The presiding officer must ask for "unanimous consent" to bring any item to the floor for consideration; a single objection derails the matter and it takes sixty votes to get it back on track. Cooperation between the two parties, essential for getting around the filibuster or hold, has diminished—the tone in the once courtly Senate now increasingly resembles the partisan House.[12]

Congress has not passed a budget in time for the start of the fiscal year since 1997. Across the United States, schoolteachers, police officers, state health officials, and everyone else dependent on federal funding has to wait for agonizing months while the Senate and House miss deadline after deadline amid partisan wrangling. Imagine trying to plan for a new school year or organize a Mars launch with no certainty about your available resources. Do we need a more nimble and responsive government as America navigates crises at home and around the world? Or is the senatorial function of slowing things down more important than ever?

As the filibuster has become the default option for important bills, progressive Democrats have begun to press for its elimination. In July 2020, former President Obama called it "a Jim Crow relic." The practice has already been eliminated for court appointments, military base closures, arms sales, and some fiscal matters. Now, say many progressives, it should be scrapped entirely—let the majority get things done. Since every state gets two senators regardless of its population, the chamber overrepresents rural minorities: Senators representing just 17 percent of the American population can shut down any proposed law. What we've developed, critics conclude, is an intense case of minority rule.[13]

WHAT DO YOU THINK?

Senate Filibusters and Legislative Holds

	Yes.	No.	Not sure.
Recent presidents have joined a long line of critics demanding the Senate end its distinctive filibuster rule.[14] Should senators be allowed to hold up legislative initiatives indefinitely, or at least until their opposition can round up sixty votes to stop their stalling action? What do you think?	Filibusters and holds ensure independence and protect minority rights. They also require the majority to work with the minority, forcing bipartisanship in a partisan era. Finally, slowing government down is often a good idea.	The sixty-vote rule makes a mockery of simple majority rule and causes gridlock, slowing policymaking to a crawl. If Congress fails to act, authority will flow to other branches of government—like the unelected courts. It is time to rewrite Senate rules and end the filibuster and legislative hold.	You may want to ponder this question as you read the rest of the chapter; we will return to this theme.

Opponents, mainly Republicans at present, respond with a cautious, "Be careful what you wish for," especially as the party in the majority so regularly becomes the minority these days. Traditionalists also argue that the filibuster forces the two parties to work together; it would be sad to sacrifice that ideal to partisan warfare. What do you think?

House and Senate: Unique Roles for Each

The Constitution also grants each branch unique authority. The Senate has sole power to review presidential appointments—the Constitution calls it "advice and consent." For example, each nominee for federal courts must win confirmation by the Senate. Here is another place where some political scientists see a broken branch: When the Republicans took control of the Senate, they refused to vote on Democratic President Barack Obama's nominations—blocking seventy-three appointees in 2016 alone. That left a great many vacancies for President Trump, who during his first term successfully appointed one out of four federal judges. Joe Biden kept up that pace when Democrats had control of Congress. By keeping control of the Senate in 2022, Democrats were able to keep appointing judges. The new informal rule: Presidents can only appoint judges when their party controls the Senate.[15]

Why did neither party use the filibuster to slow down judicial appointments when their rivals controlled the White House? Because filibusters are no longer allowed for judicial appointments. When the Democrats were in power, they put the filibuster rule aside for lower court nominations. When Republicans regained control of the Senate and the White House, they expanded the exception to cover Supreme Court appointments (see Chapter 16). As you can see, both parties have edged toward removing the filibuster rule for things they care most about.

The Senate also has authority over treaties. The president negotiates treaties with other countries and, according to the Constitution, the Senate must approve them by a two-thirds majority. Sixty-seven votes is a very high bar in today's partisan politics—only very popular treaties make it through. As discussed in Chapter 14, presidents have found ways around this provision—more than 90 percent of international agreements today never make it to the Senate. As you can see, the constitutional processes do not work very well under the pressure of extreme partisanship. Again, a broken branch? Or a reflection of the voters' will? In either case, stalemate in Congress leads to more power in the presidency and the courts.[16]

The House also has its own distinctive authority. All budget measures must originate in the House (because until 1913 it was the only chamber elected directly by the public; now both are). The House holds the power to impeach public officials—including the president. After the House impeaches an officeholder, the Senate holds a trial and decides whether to remove him or her.

THE BOTTOM LINE

» Congressional powers, as granted under the Constitution, are extensive and very clearly defined.

» America's Congress is bicameral: The House has 435 members (plus six nonvoting members) who are elected every two years. The one hundred senators serve six-year terms.

» The House and Senate work together in many areas, most notably passing legislation; each chamber has distinctive powers as well, such as the Senate's sole authority to approve presidential appointments and treaties.

» The two chambers of Congress reflect different national priorities. Populists appreciate the responsive House; advocates of stability embrace the more deliberate Senate, where rules like the filibuster and hold make it more difficult to pass legislation.

» Less legislation and more partisanship have Congress watchers debating: Is this a broken branch of government?

🏛 Congressional Representation

Members of Congress represent their constituents in multiple ways. They must live in the same state or district, which is known as *geographic* representation. But Congress represents more than geography—it is meant to reflect people's beliefs and backgrounds. How well does today's Congress represent America and Americans? That depends on the kind of representation we are considering.

Does Congress Reflect America?

A half-century ago, every senator was white. Only two Black members sat in the House of Representatives. Today, Congress more closely resembles the country it represents—in some respects.

Congressional caucus:
A group of House or Senate members who convene regularly to discuss common interests; they may share political outlook, race, gender, or geography.

Race.   As Figure 13.1 shows, the Congressional Black Caucus, one of several **congressional caucus** groups, has grown to include over fifty-eight members

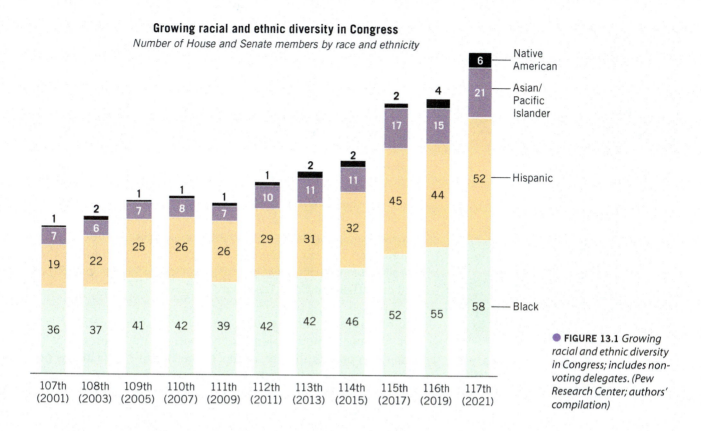

Growing racial and ethnic diversity in Congress
Number of House and Senate members by race and ethnicity

● **FIGURE 13.1** *Growing racial and ethnic diversity in Congress; includes non-voting delegates. (Pew Research Center; authors' compilation)*

(including two nonvoting representatives from Washington, DC, and the Virgin Islands). Among House Democrats, nearly one in four representatives is Black. Latinos have more recently broken into Congress, leaping from eleven members in 1990 to fifty-two members today. There are twenty-one Asian Americans (including Pacific Islanders) and six Native Americans in Congress.

Despite the growth, Congress has a long way to go before it reflects America. Overall, only 25 percent of the House and just 9 percent of the Senate are members of racial minorities—compared to 42 percent of the population. And the two parties offer very different profiles. In 2022, 47 percent of House Democrats identified as racial minorities (16 percent in the Senate), while the number for Republicans was 9 percent (House) and 6 percent (Senate).

Gender. Jeannette Rankin (R-MT) was the first woman elected to the House, in 1916. She fought for women's suffrage, Prohibition, and workers' rights during her first term. Many years later, in 1941, Rankin returned to the House for a second term (by then, there were six other female members). As a confirmed pacifist, she was one of fifty members to vote against U.S. entry into World War I, and the only member to vote against declaring war on Japan after the attack on Pearl Harbor in 1941.

Among historically underrepresented groups, the number of women in Congress has risen most rapidly. The House had twenty female members in 1966, thirty by the late 1980s, and 127 in 2022—that's just under 30 percent of the total. Twenty-four women served in the Senate. Despite the rise, as we saw in Chapter 6, the United States ranks low among legislatures worldwide on the percentage of women in the larger national chamber (our House). Some nations *require* a certain percentage of women. That is easier to do in a parliamentary system,

● *Representative Jeannette Rankin (R-MT), the first woman in Congress. She was first elected in 1916—before the Nineteenth Amendment legally enfranchised women in all states.*

where political parties choose the candidates, than in the United States, where candidates declare themselves and run in primary elections for the nominations.

The two parties offer very different profiles. Forty-one percent of Democrats, versus 14 percent of Republicans, in the House identified as female. However, Republicans may be catching up—they doubled the number of women in their ranks in 2021.

Religion.   The religious makeup of Congress has also changed dramatically over the last half-century. Until recently, the body was overwhelmingly Protestant. Today, Catholics make up nearly a third of Congress (reflecting their proportion of the population); Jews make up 5 percent of the House and 8 percent of the Senate (more than two times their percentage in the population); there are seventeen Mormons, four Muslims, two Buddhists, one Hindu, and one atheist in Congress today.[17]

Profession and Education.   In other ways, Congress does not reflect the population. Lawyers make up 1 percent of the American population but a third of the House—a far higher percentage than in other nations. Every senator and 94 percent of the House membership has graduated from college, compared to just 38 percent of the population. Only about one in ten Americans has attended graduate school, compared to 70 percent of Congress. On the other hand, the newly elected members of Congress have something in common with most people: 40 percent never before held political office.

Descriptive Versus Substantive Representation.   All this raises a critical question about the importance of *descriptive representation*—the idea that representatives reflect their constituents' race, ethnicity, gender, age, national origin, and so on. Is it important that your representatives look like you and have the same background?[18]

A completely different way to see representation is to ask whether the representative pursues my interests effectively. We call that *substantive representation*. If you are a conservative, evangelical woman who deeply believes in the right to life, you were probably not thrilled when Nancy Pelosi (a liberal who strongly supports abortion rights) was the most powerful person in the House of Representatives. She represents you descriptively (you are both women) but not substantively (you don't share the same ideas or policy preferences). You might say that Speaker Pelosi does not represent your interests at all. And here's a thorny matter that political scientists argue about: Are substantive representation (she understands my interests) and descriptive representation (she looks like me) linked to one another? Do you need to be a woman to really understand women's interests? What do you think?[19]

Trustees and Delegates

Each member of Congress—in fact, every representative in any organization—faces the same conundrum: Do what you think is right? Or do what your constituents want?

Who Really Represents You?

Which do you consider more important—descriptive or substantive representation?	**Descriptive representation.** Race, ethnicity, gender, sexual orientation, and/or class are crucial to political representation. Someone cannot really speak for me if they have not experienced the world as I have.	**Substantive representation.** It doesn't matter if someone looks like me as long as they effectively represent my views. Someone who does not share my policy priorities and political outlook is not going to represent me well.	**Not sure.** There may be no right answer to this question. Political theorists have long argued about which to emphasize. Think about how you might *combine* these two positions.

Do the Right Thing. One view holds that representatives owe us their best judgment. They sit in the House or Senate, with considerably more information than their constituents. Just like your doctor, your lawyer (and, some would say, your political science professor!), your House and Senate members' job is to pursue what is best for you. And if you disagree with the result, you can always vote for their opponent in the next election. This perspective, as we saw in Chapter 3, is known as the *trustee* view of representation.

On a lot of issues, members of Congress must rely on their (or their staff's) expertise and judgment. Constituents often have no strongly held views. Most people do not care whether their senators voted to approve the president's choice for deputy undersecretary of commerce, or whether their House member supports a technical corrections bill updating an obscure law.

Do What the People Want. Another view holds that true representation involves House or Senate members faithfully following popular preferences. A lot of choices before Congress have to do with basic values. You do not need more information to know how you feel about the right to own guns, whether healthcare is a universal human right, or who won the last presidential election. A legislator, according to this view, should take voting instructions directly from his or her constituents. This is the *delegate* view of representation.

What Should Members Do? Political scientists recognize that the rules help tilt individuals one way or another (here is the institutional perspective again).[20] When the constitutional framers required members of the House to run every two years, they favored the delegate view: Pay close attention to the people or you will be out of a job. Each senator has six years between elections; the rules practically instruct them to be trustees, to act as they think best.

What ultimately makes for good representation? The theoretical answer is simple: *Representatives effectively pursue their constituents' substantive interests.* The trick comes in figuring out what those interests are and promoting them through the complicated legislative process. Eventually, at election time, the people judge whether their members of Congress effectively pursued their interests. To political scientists, this is how a well-operating representative system works.

What Do Members *Actually* Do? This theorizing barely registers with most members of the House and Senate. They come to Congress with a clear perspective that informs nearly all of their important votes. They rarely spend time pondering what stance to take on abortion rights or on climate change. The answers are part of their basic philosophy, forged years before they arrived in Congress.

At least on large, visible issues, they know what they believe. However, a great outcry from the constituency over an issue will often moderate a member's strongly held views. If all the phone calls and emails are tilting to one side, members will be reluctant to act—it's a lot safer to do nothing and blame the other members for an unpopular outcome.

THE BOTTOM LINE

» Members of the House and Senate represent Americans in multiple ways. These include:

1. *Geographic representation*: Constitutional election rules say members must live in the state or district they represent.
2. *Descriptive representation*: Does the assembly resemble the people?
3. *Substantive representation*: Do members of Congress effectively pursue constituent interests?

» Along with these different styles of representation, members can act as delegates or trustees. Representatives can faithfully follow what the people want or do as their political experience, instincts, and core principles dictate.

Getting to Congress—and Staying There

How do members of Congress spend their days? From occasional glimpses of C-SPAN, you might picture Congress as a feast of debates, but members of the House and the Senate spend little time on the floor. Table 13.2 displays the typical workweek of a member of the House, taken from a survey. Not a lot of time left for quietly contemplating the major issues of the day, is there? One classic political science study suggests that the "electoral connection" occupies members of Congress more than anything—they spend so much time and energy getting reelected that we might think of American politics as a permanent campaign.[21]

The Permanent Campaign

Congress members spend extensive time on the campaign trail. House members face the voters every two years—more frequently than other national legislators. Even senators, with a more comfortable six years between races, must keep their campaign operation, especially fundraising, humming along. In Table 13.2, notice that the members spend as much time raising money as they do on committee meetings or floor action. They sit in a little cubicle with an assistant who contacts potential supporters. One retiring member of Congress spoke for many of his

TABLE 13.2 **Average Division of Time of a U.S. House Member**

Meeting with staff (mostly in Washington)	19 percent
Meeting with constituents (mostly in district)	19 percent
Ceremonial events (in district; some in Washington)	13 percent
Fundraising calls/meetings	11 percent
Committee meetings (hearings, member meetings)	8 percent
Floor action (votes, debates, morning business)	7 percent
Office work (email, reading, legislative drafting)	6 percent
Informal talks (with colleagues, lobbyists, media)	6 percent
Caucus meetings (all-party or subgroup gatherings)	5 percent
Other (miscellaneous)	5 percent

Source: Congressional Management Foundation

colleagues when he said he quit because he could not face that call room for another day. He also reckoned he had attended 1,600 fundraising events in sixteen years—one every two working days, year in and year out.[22]

Does this constant pressure to attract donations discourage members of Congress, or potential candidates, from running? As we saw in Chapter 10, most representatives stay in office a long time. And when a seat in either chamber opens because of retirement or death, a long list of office seekers from both parties is usually ready to run.

Home Style: Back in the District

New members of Congress—and most long-serving representatives and senators, for that matter—spend a lot of time back in their district or state. Often they are returning home to families who have decided to stay in Seattle or St. Louis or Scranton rather than making the move to Washington. Today, more than one hundred House members, most of them conservative Republicans, proudly refuse to settle into a Washington residence and, instead, sleep on a cot in their office. Most members leave Capitol Hill on Thursday evenings and only return on Monday evening or even Tuesday morning, unless House or Senate votes are scheduled on a Friday or Monday.

Back home in their constituency, members are kept hopping. District staff line up events for them to attend every morning, afternoon, and evening. Members spend this time meeting with constituents, giving talks about Washington issues (and hearing plenty of advice about how to do things better), cutting ribbons on new ballparks or office buildings or schools, visiting with local party leaders and elected officials, and raising funds for their next election. And even when Senators and House members are in Washington, many hold virtual town meetings with constituents—reflecting the high premium members place on staying in touch.

These meetings inform members about their constituents' main concerns and hopes. They signal empathy with their needs. And, despite all the money and the media in politics, there is nothing as effective as personal communication.

That's why most members will cheerfully meet with your class or team or whatever group you are part of. Try it out yourself: Make an appointment with your own member of Congress and say what's on your mind.[23]

While the home style makes our government more accessible, it comes at a cost.

A Government of Strangers

In the past—before jets, advanced technology, and modern campaigns—members of Congress lived in Washington. Senators or representatives worked together during the day and socialized during evenings and weekends. In fact, a bar for members, called the Hole in the Wall, was located between the House and Senate chambers.

Today, most legislators are not in Washington long enough to get to know one another. They dash in, spend three days packed with congressional business, and dash back home. This schedule makes it harder for Congress to get things done, because it is now a collection of strangers. The complicated legislative process is made more difficult by the lack of personal relations. The result: more control in the leaders' hands.

Why do members insist on rushing home each week, and scheduling virtual meetings from Washington with their constituents? Because it helps them win reelection—an ever-present concern. In fact, when political scientists build models to explain and predict congressional behavior, they sometimes assume that reelection is a member's primary or even only goal.[24] We think this is an exaggeration. Many members are genuinely pursuing their political ideals. When one Democrat from a conservative district balked at passing Obamacare, he told us that the president came over to Capitol Hill, looked him in the eye, and said: "Before you vote, ask yourself, why did I come here?" He voted aye—and then lost his seat in the next midterm. Like our friend, people in Congress sometimes take risky votes on principle. But there is no getting around the basic fact: The pressure for reelection significantly shapes congressional behavior.[25]

THE BOTTOM LINE

» Members of Congress are always running for office. Fundraising takes up a particularly large amount of time and attention.

» Members pay special attention to their home style: Most go back to their constituency every week—compressing normal congressional business into the period from Tuesday through Thursday.

» Congress has become an institution of strangers who do not know one another. Most members focus intensely on reelection.

Congress at Work

When members of the House and Senate do gather in Washington, they have a staggering to-do list: managing the nation's legislative business, investigating executive branch activities, staging public hearings about everything from auto safety to U.S. aid to Zimbabwe. And, of course, raising money for reelection. How—and where—do they accomplish all that work?

The City on the Hill

The huge Capitol Building is perched on an actual hill; its majestic marble dome dominates the Washington skyline. Traditionally, no building in the District of Columbia except the Washington Monument may be taller. The Capitol Building is also the heart of a small city within a city. Six grand office buildings house the members and their staff; the newer buildings feature offices the size of basketball courts. Three ornate structures house the Library of Congress, which has mushroomed from Thomas Jefferson's personal book collection into the largest library in the world.

This City on the Hill also includes a dozen restaurants, two gyms, a chapel, a bank, a post office, and a warren of "hideaways": small unmarked offices for the personal use of senior members. Add another half-dozen staff "annex" buildings, several elegant townhouses rented most nights for fundraising events, a small high school for congressional pages—young men and women who scurry around the House and Senate floor running errands for members—and even a subway, to shuttle the members back and forth between their office buildings and the congressional chambers.

Citizens of the City: Members and Staffers

Inhabitants of this "city" include the 541 members of Congress, along with more than 22,000 staff members, who range from well-paid senior policy experts to summer interns; a police force of 250 members; and the U.S. poet laureate, a Congress-appointed position whose occupant receives a beautiful office in the Library of Congress. And do not forget the thousands of lobbyists. It all adds up to a very busy place.

How much are members paid? As of 2022 the rate is $174,000 for House and Senate members, a figure frozen since 2009.[26] That is a little over three times what the average American makes (see Table 13.3). Leaders earn a slightly higher salary; the House Speaker is the highest paid at $223,500. Constituents frequently complain that congressional salaries are too high. Note, however, that comparable leaders in other areas—from business managers to academic deans—are paid much more.

Congressional staff members are a major presence in this company town. Until 1893, most members of the House had no staff support; beginning in 1891, senators were allotted one part-time staffer, paid $6 per day. As Congress became more professional, it saw a steady increase in assistants, researchers, committee experts, legal counsel, and the like. By the 1990s, House and Senate staff leveled off at around twenty-seven thousand; the number has since declined to about twenty-two thousand.

Each House and Senate member has a chief of staff, a legislative director, a press secretary, a scheduler, and a host of other office staffers, including legislative correspondents who handle the huge volume of constituent requests that pour into each member's office. Many college graduates take entry-level positions (like legislative correspondents) because there are many opportunities to move up quickly. We have both worked on Capitol Hill—it is an exciting job for the young men and women, many of them right out of college, who dominate staff positions.

In addition, each summer, thousands of college students descend on Capitol Hill to work, usually without pay. Interning is not a glamorous activity, but congressional offices hum with excitement and offer a ringside seat on one of the

TABLE 13.3	Annual Average Salaries by Profession, 2021
CEO, top 500 company	$14.5 million
NBA player	$7.5 million
NFL rookie minimum salary	$660,000
U.S. president	$400,000
Surgeon	$294,520
Senior U.S. executive branch official (capped since 2010)	$199,700
Member of Congress	**$174,000**
Lawyer	$148,030
Pharmacist	$125,690
Aerospace engineer	$122,970
Personal financial advisor	$119,960
Political science professor	$100,640
Web developer	$81,320
Elementary school teacher	$64,870
Plumber	$62,250
Child/family social worker	$54,880
Home health aide	$29,260

Sources: Associated Press; Sporting Intelligence; Bureau of Labor Statistics (September 2022 report); U.S. Office of Personnel Management

● When Congressman Elijah Cummings died in office, his daughters endorsed a long-time staff member, Harry Spikes, to replace him. He lost the primary and the district is now represented by Kweisi Mfume.

most fascinating institutions in the world. But notice the problem: Taking an unpaid position is a lot easier for people who are well-off. When Alexandria Ocasio-Cortez (D-NY) arrived in Congress in 2019, she saw the problem immediately. Most staffers (63 percent) were unpaid interns. She pledged to pay every intern $15 an hour.[27] That helped boost a movement and, today, most interns are paid (on average, $1,612 for a seven-week stint in the House).

New staffers arriving on the Hill soon hear the most common question: not "What do you do?" but "Who are you with?" Working for a congressional leader, a committee chair, or a nationally known figure can catapult even new staffers up the Washington pecking order. Many staff members feel a rush when an important bill they helped craft passes or when they prepare their boss to succeed on a major news show—or when their member gets a call from the White House and goes over to meet with the president.

Buzzing with Action: Life on Capitol Hill

Capitol Hill life runs on a distinct rhythm. Congress usually remains in session, apart from holidays, from the beginning of January through early August; members return after Labor Day and rush to finish for the year in early October during election (even-numbered) years, because they are anxious to focus on their campaigns. In nonelection years, the session lasts longer—the Senate passed a COVID relief bill on December 21 (2020) and Obamacare did not go through until late at night on December 24 (2009). When in session, the Hill buzzes with action, especially when members are in residence Tuesday through Thursday. Staffers work late into the night, while lobbyists and media swarm around the Capitol.

Members of Congress know that they stand in the vortex of history. Every move—such as the deep bow made by clerks carrying House bills to the Senate and vice versa—reflects a legacy that may stretch as far back as the Virginia House of Burgesses, which first convened in 1619. In fact, new members of Congress make a candlelight visit to that historical site as part of their orientation.[28]

Minnows and Whales: Congressional Leadership

When Lyndon Johnson (D-TX) served as Senate majority leader in the 1950s, he divided colleagues into two camps: "whales," who could influence landmark legislation, and "minnows," who dutifully followed others. Most "whales" are chairs of important committees or part of the formal leadership structure.

In the past, the House and Senate featured very different leadership styles. The House was the more partisan branch, perhaps because the whole body is up for election every two years. The Speaker exerted tight control over the action in the House. The smaller, more collegial Senate—where any member can request a hold and bring the entire body to a halt—traditionally required patient, consensus-minded leadership. Majority leaders did not so much lead as manage Senate procedures, cajoling and pleading proud senators to move legislation along. There's still a lot of truth to those differences, although the Senate has slowly become more like the partisan House.

House Leadership

Democrats and Republicans each choose a party leader from their ranks. Every two years, when a new Congress opens, the majority party votes its leader to the top post in Congress, the **Speaker of the House**. The Speaker serves as the chamber's chief administrator while also leading the majority party.

Speaker of the House: The chief administrative officer in the House of Representatives.

The Speaker rules on procedural issues, chooses members for committees, assigns legislation to committees, and "maintains order and civility"—although civility is increasingly difficult to sustain. The Speaker also sets the House's agenda and determines which bills are considered and when. Speakers negotiate with the Senate and executive branch. And they help manage the Rules Committee, which sets the terms of the debate for every piece of legislation that reaches the House floor. Speakers sometimes work with Rules to hold the majority together or derail opposition on important votes.

The role of the House Speaker changed in the late 1980s when a new generation of Republican rebels burst onto the scene. In 1989, Congressman Newt Gingrich of Georgia became one of the House leaders (the minority whip, responsible for corralling Republican votes), and blasted his party colleagues for becoming too comfortable in the minority, where they had languished for most of the last sixty years. Get tough and even nasty, he urged his colleagues.[29]

For example, when the cable TV channel C-SPAN put cameras in the House, any member could speak to the empty chamber after hours. The cameras were fixed on the dais, so viewers did not see that there was no one else in the room. Pretending he was addressing a crowded chamber, Gingrich rose and denounced fifty-one Democrats for believing that America was "stupid" and its allies "rotten and corrupt." Gingrich pretended that the absent Democrats were too cowed or too callow to object to his rant. An outraged Democratic Speaker, Tip O'Neill, confronted him for "the lowest thing I've seen in my 32 years in Congress." The Republicans snapped right back and rebuked O'Neill for being derogatory to another member—the first Speaker to be censured in almost two centuries. The young rebels who had gathered around Gingrich gave him a standing ovation at the end of the episode.[30]

But the Republicans remained restless. Gingrich and the three Republican leaders who followed him each retired or were swept aside in the next twelve years—largely for not being conservative enough. Democrats stuck with Nancy Pelosi throughout the same period. But the job had become overtly partisan on both sides of the aisle. Why are things so heated? Because unlike earlier eras, when one party controlled the House for decades at a time, both sides have a realistic shot of winning in each election. The chance of victory inspires each to remain ready for war—rather than cooperate with the other side to get things done. In the last twenty years, the House and Senate have each switched hands four times—an unprecedented amount of turnover.

The leadership team in the House must constantly juggle two very different goals: smoothly running the House and winning the looming election (and with a vote every two years, there is always a looming election).[31]

The House majority leader is the second in command, acting as the majority party's floor manager, negotiator, and spokesperson. The majority leader also serves as the Speaker's eyes and ears, tracking party members' actions and preferences. Steny Hoyer (D-MD) held this position going into the 118th Congress.

The number-three position is the majority whip. Whips are responsible for party discipline—tracking where the members stand and rounding up votes. The term *whip* comes from the British Parliament, which borrowed the term from fox hunting, where the "whipper-in" kept hounds together—and yes, they did the job by cracking whips. The majority whip leads a team of nine deputy whips, each responsible for members from a different region.

The minority generally has the same leadership structure, with one big difference: no Speaker. The top-ranking Republicans in the 117th Congress are Minority Leader Kevin McCarthy (R-CA) and Minority Whip Steve Scalise (R-LA).

House whips often have to be creative. Back in the 1970s, Minority Whip Leslie Arends (R-IL) needed one

● Control over the Congressional process has increasingly flowed toward party leaders—here, Nancy Pelosi, Democratic Speaker of the House, and Mitch McConnell, Republican majority leader in the Senate.

more GOP vote to win an important agriculture bill. One Ohio Republican, knowing the bill was unpopular with his constituents, simply flew home. When Arends discovered his crucial vote was missing, he called an Ohio radio station and persuaded the DJ to repeatedly announce, "If anybody spies Representative Jones . . . tell him he's supposed to be in Washington tomorrow for an important vote." Jones flew back and sheepishly voted with his fellow Republicans.

Senate Leadership

The Senate takes all the difficulties involved in managing the House—and multiplies them. Senate rules, such as the filibuster and the hold, give each individual senator a great deal of autonomy. The Senate leadership must turn to personal skills, especially an ability to negotiate with colleagues.

The senators elect a majority leader—currently Chuck Schumer (D-NY). However, the Senate leader does not even formally preside over the chamber. The Constitution gives that job to the vice president. Most vice presidents show up only for ceremonial occasions. However, the vice president breaks ties in the Senate and with the Senate evenly split between the parties, Vice President Kamala Harris broke 26 ties in her first twenty months on the job (2021–22)—the third most tie-breaking votes in history (and just five short of the all-time record set in the 1820s).

When the vice president is not there, the **president pro tempore**—usually the longest-serving member of the majority—presides over formal Senate gatherings. Otherwise, every senator takes a turn presiding over the body, each serving a half-hour stint. A staff member stands by the presiding member's side, helping him or her to negotiate the complex rules. The rules are incredibly complicated—and errors could give one party or the other an advantage—so the staff experts have a little pedal that permits them to mute the microphone if the presiding senator gets mixed up. The first time Senator Hillary Clinton (D-NY) presided, she said it was "the most difficult thing I'd ever done in politics."[32]

President pro tempore:
Majority party senator with the longest Senate service.

Senate whips from both the majority and minority parties serve the same functions as in the House—though they have a tougher job owing to the Senate's individualistic ways. So does the Senate majority leader, who chooses which policies will be considered on the chamber's floor, usually in consultation with the minority leader, who either agrees or indicates that the item faces a filibuster or a hold. When that happens, the majority leader normally passes over it and moves to the next item on the agenda.

Committees: Workhorses of Congress

Senator Orrin Hatch (R-UT), chair of the Senate Finance Committee, blasted Senator Lamar Alexander (R-TN), chair of the Senate Health, Education, Labor and Pensions (HELP) Committee. Alexander was trying to craft a bipartisan plan to shore up the Affordable Care Act, which Hatch wanted to repeal because both Congress and the White House were in Republican hands (in 2017). But Hatch explained why he was really steamed: "He's stealing our jurisdiction." Translation: My committee should handle this issue, not his.[33]

Congressional lawmaking traditionally plays out mainly in committees. Committees draft legislation, sponsor hearings, and oversee the executive agencies under their jurisdiction—the Senate Committee on Agriculture, Nutrition and Forestry, for example, oversees the agencies that deal with agriculture.

TABLE 13.4	**Congressional Committee Types**
Standing committee	Permanent bodies, with fixed jurisdiction (Table 13.5 lists them all). House and Senate standing committees vary widely in prestige: The oldest are traditionally the most influential, though some newer ones (such as Intelligence, created after 9/11 in both chambers) deal with significant topics. Standing committees are further divided into multiple *subcommittees*, organized around areas of expertise, like agriculture, aging, and Indian Affairs.
Select committee	Created to investigate a particular issue; these exist for a defined period of time. Also called *special committees*. The British Parliament normally relies on this kind of committee.
Joint committee	Made up of both House and Senate members to address topics of continuing importance. These committees can remain in place for decades; the Joint Committee on Taxation has existed since 1971, for example. *Conference committees*, introduced later in this chapter, are temporary joint committees, created to consider a specific piece of legislation.

The committees also draft the budget for the agencies they oversee. Every year, the administration sends its priorities to Congress. Leadership duly assigns issues to committees, where chairs take those ideas and rethink them, rewrite them, pass some through to the floor, and let most die a quiet death.

Table 13.4 lists the types of congressional committees. Legislative committees were invented in the very early days of the United States; the British Parliament still has nothing like them. For decades, observers have called for reform. But the committees live on. Why?

The Enduring Power of Committees

There are two reasons committees have endured for so long: First, inertia—it is hard to remake Congress, given layers of tradition and complex rules. Second, in their own creaky way, committees work. Individual members devote extensive time to fundraising and constituents. The committee system permits busy members (and, crucially, committee staff) to become experts on a narrow range of topics—especially in the House, where members typically serve on one primary committee. Committees enable Congress to devise fairly sophisticated legislative solutions.

The committee system is yet another way American government separates powers. It leaves Congress with multiple centers of authority, slowing down the legislative process and making it harder for the public to follow. But the division of labor allows an institution—with distracted, busy members—to accomplish more. By dividing the labor of its members, the 117th Congress was able to enact 157 laws, review over two thousand nominations (to positions like executive branch leadership roles and federal judgeships), and approve three treaties in its two years.

The standing committees (see Table 13.5) provide a main avenue to send favored services, or "pork," home to a representative's district. Tom Delay was a brawling Republican leader known as "the Hammer." But, sometimes, during a tight vote, he would pay a quiet visit to Jack Murtha, a powerful Democrat on the Appropriations Committee who oversaw defense spending. The committee's **earmarks**—money spent in members' districts—meant a lot of people owed Murtha favors. Although Delay and Murtha rarely agreed, the earmarks made it possible to wheel and deal. Members of the Appropriations

Earmark: A legislative item, usually included in spending ("appropriations") bills, that directs Congress to fund a particular item in one House member's district or a senator's state.

TABLE 13.5	House and Senate Permanent Standing Committees

U.S. HOUSE COMMITTEES	U.S. SENATE COMMITTEES
Agriculture	Agriculture, Nutrition, and Forestry
Appropriations	Appropriations
Armed Services	Armed Services
Budget	Banking, Housing, and Urban Affairs
Education and Labor	Budget
Energy and Commerce	Commerce, Science, and Transportation
Ethics	Energy and Natural Resources
Financial Services	Environment and Public Works
Foreign Affairs	Finance
Homeland Security	Foreign Relations
House Administration	Health, Education, Labor, and Pensions
Judiciary	Homeland Security and Governmental Affairs
Natural Resources	Intelligence (Permanent Select)
Oversight and Reform	Judiciary
Rules	Rules and Administration
Science, Space, and Technology	Small Business and Entrepreneurship
Small Business	Veterans' Affairs
Transportation and Infrastructure	
Veterans' Affairs	
Ways and Means	

Committee—which decides how U.S. funds are spent—are informally called "cardinals," like the ruling cadre in the Vatican. In 2011, Congress banned earmarks, which made dealmaking even harder. But in 2021, the Democrats (with considerable help from Republicans) brought back the practice. While some fiscal reformers decried the return of pork, many Congress watchers quietly cheered. Beneath the partisan bluster there could be a bit of dealmaking—"you scratch my back, I'll scratch yours." The cardinals are back in business.[34]

The committee system makes Congress far more efficient. But there is also a harsher reality. Committees fragment Congress into small fiefdoms, hide action from public view, and make it relatively easy to do favors for well-placed constituents (a tax break or a phone call to get a pesky regulator to back off). The fragmentation also makes it still more difficult to pass major legislation or to address large national problems. Only about 6 percent of the bills and proposals assigned to committees ever make it to the floor.

The organization of Congress raises, once again, the dilemmas of American democracy: Does the bias against action frustrate the popular will or simply reflect the American wariness of government (or perhaps both)? What do you think?

Committee Assignments

After the 2022 election, many House members found excuses to check in with the 118th Congress's presumed Speaker: Along with fond holiday wishes, they were jockeying for preferred committee assignments. The Speaker is a key player in assigning members (and chairs) to each committee—a vital decision, given all the power committees wield. Each party votes on members' committee assignments, and seniority remains a vital factor in determining chairs, but all decisions are made with the Speaker's blessing. Over in the Senate, the decision involves more give-and-take but ultimately rests in the majority leader's hands. Minority party assignments are recommended by minority leaders in both chambers.

Members compete to join the most influential committees. Once they are on a committee, representatives and senators often stay for many years—gaining power and influence and aspiring to become chair. Traditionally (but not always), the chair is the longest-serving committee member. Members generally seek to join committees that reflect the concerns of their district. When political scientist David Price (D-NC) won a seat in Congress, his colleagues at Duke University wondered how his committee assignment would reflect his expertise. Price, already a savvy politician, requested a seat on the House Banking (now Financial Services) Committee because his district has a strong banking and financial service sector.[35]

Each committee has its own process. Each has its own political slant. Committees can bury a bill, completely rewrite it, report out an unrealistic version, or boost the chances of success with a strong bill. However, as we have seen, on major matters, leaders in both the House and Senate have consolidated their authority thanks to the fierce conflict between the parties. Jurisdictional squabbles can erupt into battles for influence between committees with overlapping responsibilities. The House and the Senate each have different committees for Homeland Security, Intelligence, and Foreign Affairs. Since legislation goes to every committee with jurisdiction on the topic, all three committees often write different versions of the same bill. The overlapping authority means multiple committees wrestling to shape the same legislation. See Comparing Nations 13.1 to find out how this legislative process differs in other countries.

COMPARING NATIONS 13.1   A Unique U.S. Committee System

The American style of multiple committees claiming jurisdiction is very unusual. When the British Parliament considers major environmental or tax legislation, it forms a special committee to craft the law—and the majority party in the House of Commons follows the lead of the prime minister, who it elected to his or her post.

In Japan, the bureaucracy writes laws and the Diet (Japan's national legislature) passes them—no subset of Diet committee members examines and rewrites legislation.

In Germany, most legislation is drawn up by the chancellor (or executive) and forwarded to the *Bundesrat* (or upper house), which has six weeks to comment. The bill then goes back to the executive for rewriting and is submitted to the *Bundestag* (the lower and more powerful chamber).

Only in the United States do we have this scrum of committees, clashing with one another throughout the process.

THE BOTTOM LINE

» Congress resembles a small city. Its residents include the 541 members of Congress, twenty-two thousand staff members, and an army of lobbyists. The city includes its own amenities, traditions, and slang.

» House leadership includes a Speaker, majority and minority leaders, and ten whips. Successful leaders in the House impose discipline on their party members. The Senate allows far more individual action. Party leaders and whips have fewer institutional tools with which to impose discipline.

» Congressional committees are the workhorses of Congress. They have proved efficient and adaptable over the years. However, the committee system also fragments Congress, hides action from public view, accommodates constituents seeking individual favors, and makes it difficult to pass major legislation.

How a Bill Becomes a Law

Congressional lawmaking can be boiled down to five words: *Complex process. Difficult to win.* The last decade saw thousands of bills submitted each year (see Figure 13.2). How many made it all the way through the process to become law? Less than 3 percent. Compare the Ninety-Fourth Congress (from 1975) to recent years: There were many more laws, but today's legislation packs more items into big bills.

Why even bother pursuing legislative wins? There are other ways to make policy. As we will see in subsequent chapters, presidents can issue executive orders (Chapter 14), bureaucrats can write regulations (Chapter 15), and activists can go to the courts (Chapter 16). But nothing else has the status of an act of Congress. They generally produce the most enduring changes, partially because the same process that makes laws so difficult to pass makes them difficult to repeal. That's why bills keep coming despite the long odds.

Americans complain about the nation's failure to address global climate change. Or systemic racism. Or our broken public education system. Or our inability to ensure net neutrality, or pay down the national debt. Pundits explain these failures by invoking "American attitudes" or "American culture" or "powerful lobbyists." Here is a more accurate explanation: Congressional rules make it very hard to do any of these things—even when a majority of legislators (and the nation) are in support. What happens when a bill is proposed? Read on.

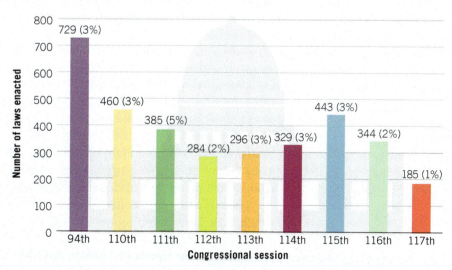

● **FIGURE 13.2** *Laws enacted in each Congress (with the percentage of all proposals that made it into law): 117th as of October 15, 2022. (GovTrack)*

TABLE 13.6	Examples of Creative Legislative Titles	
COVID-19 Stop Calling Americans Maliciously (SCAM) Act (2020)	Prohibit texts or phone calls for deceptive acts or practices, such as fraudulent fundraising for COVID victims or peddling false "cures."
Clarifying Lawful Overseas Use of Data (CLOUD) Act (2018)	Allow U.S. law enforcement (with a judge's subpoena) to obtain American citizens' private data from servers anywhere in the world.
EGO (Eliminating Government-Funded Oil-Painting) Act (2013)	Bans federal funding of official portraits of government officials.
Personal Responsibility in Consumption Act (2006)	Immunizes fast-food companies against lawsuits by obese consumers.
What Really Happened Act (2002)	Requires instant TV replay in all major sports.

Note: Only the second of these bills—the CLOUD Act—passed.

Drafting a Bill

Anyone can petition Congress to consider a bill, but only members of the House and Senate have the right to introduce one. Every piece of legislation needs at least one primary sponsor, whose name is publicly inscribed on the first page. Major bills are often referred to by the sponsors' names, with some creative exceptions (see Table 13.6).

Bills can feature any number of co-sponsors, or members who agree to have their names listed as supporters. The main sponsors usually try to sign on many members, especially powerful ones such as committee chairs, as co-sponsors. A loose rule of thumb: The more co-sponsors a bill has, the higher the likelihood of passage.

Anything can be introduced as legislation—no matter how outlandish. Former Congressman Ron Paul (R-TX) once introduced a bill mandating that the Treasury buy a one-inch-wide strip of land stretching down the middle of the United States from Canada to Mexico. All goods or people crossing that line would be charged a toll, declared Representative Paul. All other taxes and government fees would be eliminated. The bill did not make it out of committee. But, like many bills, it stood as a symbol and a rallying cry—in this case, for libertarians who oppose government taxation.

Bills' sponsors rarely write the legislation themselves. Some bills include language taken from state legislation, or even other countries' parliaments. Congressional members "borrow" legislative language from each other, adapting colleagues' bills for their own use. Most serious bills go to the experts at the House or Senate Office of Legislative Counsel and the Congressional Research Service (CRS) for drafting help. Bill drafters also consult outside sources, including executive branch officials, lobbyists, and academics. And members copy themselves; as each new session begins, congressional offices participate in a time-honored ritual: dust off and reintroduce bills that failed last time.

There is a fine art to bill drafting. Writing legislation necessitates major political choices. How much money should we ask for in spending bills? How far can we change current laws? Do we test existing constitutional limits? Many bills include bargaining chips—provisions the sponsors might negotiate away to win over the skeptics. Legislation to reduce average elementary school class sizes might also promise healthier lunches in all public schools. When the serious bargaining starts on Capitol Hill, that line may be dropped to satisfy budget hawks worried about costs or the sugar lobby protecting donut and cola makers. Fuzzy language sometimes helps avoid disagreement, but drafters are also aware that if the law passes, it may very well end up involved in litigation, which puts a premium on clarity and precision.

Once the bill is drafted and the co-sponsors have signed on, it is ready for the next step: submission.

Submitting the Bill

The more traditional Senate typically introduces bills as the legislative day opens, around noon on Tuesdays, Wednesdays, and Thursdays. Let's peek inside the chamber.

The presiding officer taps their gavel, bringing the stir of conversation to a halt. Members pause as the Senate chaplain recites a prayer. A swirling bustle breaks out as the chaplain concludes. Routine administrative motions (such as approving records of the previous day's proceedings) are followed by morning-hour statements—short speeches that celebrate home state achievements. A constituent is turning one hundred years old, or a softball team has won the state title, or a popular political science professor is retiring from the state university.

Watch closely: A senator snaps their fingers. A page (usually a high school student trained for this role) dashes down the aisle, takes the senator's document, and places it in a flat wooden tray beside the bill clerk. The clerk writes a number on the first page (bills are numbered serially, starting each session with S.1), notes the senator's suggestion for committee referral, and places it in a tray. That night it is printed. A bill has been born!

The House is less ritualized, in keeping with its democratic spirit. Representatives carry proposed bills themselves down to the rostrum. They hand their legislation to the clerk or drop it in a mahogany box, called the "hopper." From there, bills are delivered to the Speaker's office, where they are assigned a number—starting each session with H.R. 1—and referred to committee.

Committee Action

As we have seen, committees are the congressional workhorses. The House leadership normally assigns each bill to committees with authority (or jurisdiction) over the area affected by the proposed legislation. Major legislation can go to as many as six different committees. Once they are assigned a bill, the committees perform four major tasks.

1. Hold Hearings on Policy Topics. Witnesses submit written testimony for staff members and reporters; unless they are senior government officials or celebrities, they are limited to a five-minute presentation at the **committee hearing**. When they begin, a little green light goes on; at the four-minute mark, a yellow light goes on. At five minutes, a red light blinks. Nervous rookies stop mid-sentence; veterans ignore the lights and talk serenely on—until the chair bangs the gavel.

The staff assembles a list of who is testifying at each hearing. Witnesses generally include White House officials and cabinet heads—whose testimony has to be cleared with the Office of Management and Budget (OMB; introduced in Chapter 14 as "the agency that says no"). At many hearings, officials try to stick to their authorized script while critical Senate or House members pummel them, knowing full well

Committee hearing:
A way for committees to gather information and gauge members' support as legislative policymaking gets underway. Hearings usually feature witnesses who submit testimony, make an oral presentation, and answer questions from members of Congress.

● *Celebrity congressional witnesses include ... Elmo! Elmo "testifies," with the help of music industry executive Joe Lamond, before the House Education Appropriations subcommittee in support of funding for school music programs. When he finished, Elmo tried to eat the microphone.*

that the government witness cannot express any views that were not cleared by the OMB.

Celebrities are popular witnesses, attracting media attention to what might otherwise be a low-profile event. Angelina Jolie has appeared before Congress five times on international aid issues; Kourtney Kardashian spoke to the Senate about safety measures in the cosmetics industry; writer Ta-Nehisi Coates advocated before a House Judiciary subcommittee on reparations for Black Americans given the nation's legacy of slavery; and actress Sophia Bush testified in 2021 on countering some Americans' hesitancy to be vaccinated for COVID. More often, witnesses include interest-group lobbyists, think tank experts, academics (your authors have testified multiple times), and pollsters reporting public opinion on the issues.

Hearings also can get tough. When the CEOs of three big U.S. automakers went to Congress looking for a bailout, their trouble began when Representative Brad Sherman (D-CA) needled them about flying to Washington on corporate jets while claiming that their companies faced bankruptcy.

Rep. SHERMAN:	I'm going to ask the three executives here to raise their hand if they flew here commercial.
Mr. MULALLY [Ford CEO], Mr. WAGONER [GM], Mr. NARDELLI [Chrysler]:	(No response.)
Rep. SHERMAN:	Second, I'm going ask you to raise your hand if you're planning to sell your [private] jet . . . and fly back commercial.
Messrs. MULALLY, WAGONER, NARDELLI:	(No response.)
Rep. SHERMAN:	Let the record show no hands went up.
Rep. ACKERMAN:	It's almost like seeing a guy show up at the soup kitchen in high-hat and tuxedo. . . . I mean, couldn't you all have downgraded to first class or jet-pooled or something to get here?

Other members asked the CEOs if they would give up their hefty compensation packages and work for $1 a year. Nardelli, the Chrysler chairman, declined with a muttered, "I'm good." The CEOs learned their lesson: When they next testified before Congress, they rode to Washington in cars manufactured by their company.

Committee markup session: A gathering of a full committee to draft the final version of a bill before the committee votes on it.

2. Prepare Legislation for Floor Consideration. Committees are the primary source of policy development in Congress. Members and committee staff rewrite bills in **committee markup sessions**, when the committees work through the proposed legislation, line by line. The result, called a "chairman's mark," is hot property among lobbyists and public advocates. It contains the details of a rising piece of legislation.

Following markup, the committee holds a vote on whether to report a bill to the full House or Senate. When the Senate Finance Committee took up a $1.5 trillion tax reform bill in November 2017, it considered 355 amendments over four days—incorporating nearly one hundred before voting to approve by a party-line vote of 14–12. All that work in just one Senate committee—and remember that at least one other committee is usually negotiating another version of the same legislation—in this case Senate Budget, which plowed through several dozen more amendments before voting 12–11 to send an amended bill to the Senate floor.

If a bill is voted down in committee—not reported, in Congress-speak—it is usually dead. Those voted through by a narrow margin will probably face a tough time on the floor, and the Speaker or majority leader may decide never to bring the closely divided measure up for a vote.

3. Kill Legislation.   Of the more than four thousand bills referred to the forty House and Senate standing committees each year, only about one in eight sees any action. Some bills are proposed just to satisfy voters or score political points and have no chance of passing. Others make a symbolic point; committees usually bury them swiftly. Well into modern times, bills often died in committee without any public acknowledgment of how members voted. A key reform of the 1970s required all committees to keep full records of important votes.

4. Exercise Oversight.   Congress's work is not done after a law passes. House and Senate committees also monitor the executive branch, making sure cabinet departments and agencies perform their roles properly. This can be a high-stakes activity: Oversight hearings investigate scandals, review major issues such as cybersecurity and protection against terrorism, and evaluate presidential appointees. Committees also continue to monitor the programs that they have passed: Is the agency spending its budget properly? Are people benefitting from the program as promised?

That's the usual process—but today, important bills often leap over the process. When it came time to respond to COVID-19, Trump administration officials met with the Republican Senate leaders and hammered out a bill. Democratic leaders blocked the bill until some of their issues could be addressed. The two parties bargained in front of the media—each accused the other side of playing politics during a crisis. Once they had struck a bargain, the legislation went directly to the floor. Is this a violation of the old processes? Or a sign that this eighteenth-century institution is catching up to our faster era?

Floor Action

The next stop: the House or Senate floor, where the entire chamber votes. Once a bill gets there, its chance of becoming law soars. More than half the bills that make it to the floor get

● *When the House and Senate pass different versions of a bill, it goes to a House-Senate conference where the differences are hammered out. Here, members are negotiating the 2017 tax reform bill.*

enacted. But your bill might have a long wait—leaders rarely call up a bill until they think they have the votes to win.

Getting to the Floor.   Floor procedures in the House and Senate are very different. Senate bills come out of committee and go on a "business calendar" worked out by the majority and minority leaders. Only bills that receive **unanimous consent**—agreement by all senators—are brought to the floor. One "nay" and the bill goes on hold until the majority can round up sixty votes.

In the House, majority party leaders exert more control over which issues make it to the floor. They may start by rewriting the legislation—sometimes because multiple committees have passed different bills. Or sometimes, the leaders rewrite to win more support and get the measure through.

Next, it's on to the House Rules Committee, which hammers out rules for this particular bill. For example, may members add amendments and, if so, what kind? Each bill has its own set of rules in the House. The Rules Committee is tilted to favor the majority party and works closely with the Speaker. When the cameras are on, minority members sometimes offer amendments that the rules don't permit—and then charge that they are being muffled. Good media politics, but it does not affect the bill on the floor of the House.

The Senate, in contrast, allows virtually unlimited consideration on the floor; amendments keep on coming from all sides. Even bills that make it on to the calendar can get stuck before going to the floor. There may be a logjam slowing things down. Or one chamber might wait if the bill is less popular in the other. Bills are sometimes bottled up in the Senate by the "unanimous consent" requirement. Achieving 100 percent agreement to allow a bill to come up for a vote often involves elaborate negotiations.

On the Floor.   Eventually a bill's moment on the floor arrives. Supporters hope their measure will be taken up in the House and Senate around the same time, knowing that legislation often makes it only through one chamber during a session—another death sentence for a bill. In the 117th Congress (2021–22), bills to protect electoral integrity, update the Voting Rights Act, forbid discrimination on the basis of sexual orientation and gender identity, bolster the right to unionize, and protect Dreamers (undocumented individuals who came to the United States as young children) sailed through the House only to die in the Senate.

Floor action in both chambers follows roughly the same procedures. First, a bill is assigned a floor manager—usually the main sponsor, but on big issues, the chair of the committee that reported the bill. The managers run the show, handling amendments as they come up and controlling the time for debate. Majority and minority party members each have a specific number of hours and minutes to discuss the legislation, determined in the Senate by agreement between party leaders and in the House by the Rules Committee.

Then the political maneuvers really start. In both the House and Senate, floor action involves

Unanimous consent: A Senate requirement, applied to most of that body's business, that all senators agree before an action can proceed.

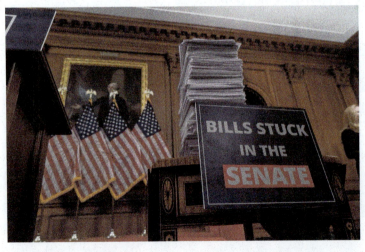

● Even when the same party controls both chambers (as the Democrats did in 2021 23), the well disciplined House is quicker to pass legislation than the independent-minded Senate with its filibuster. The difference becomes even starker when the chambers are in different party hands. Here, the House sends a message to frustrated constituents: The gridlock is not our fault.

amendments, procedural moves, and eventually a final vote—all accompanied by a lot of talk. Members rarely change any votes with their eloquence. But floor speeches are not empty oratory. Congress watchers know that who chooses to speak, and what they say, matters. "I rise to support H.R. 835" is very different from "I rise to thank my good friend for introducing this excellent bill, H.R. 835; I have just a few questions about it." Each statement offers valuable clues about the likely outcome. Whips listen especially closely and adapt their floor strategies to secure a majority in support of party-approved amendments and the final vote for passage.

The real audience for much of the speechmaking is the constituency back home, eager to see their representatives fight for (or against) an issue. Increasingly, members get frustrated with one another—leading to a new phrase in the lexicon of politics, *Constitutional Hardball*: "things a judge might let you get away with" (because it does not violate the Constitution), "but that your mother never would" (because it violates the norms of good behavior).[36]

House rules permit leaders to introduce creative strategies to get their legislation through. They can extend the time allocated for debate (while a few more arms are twisted). They sometimes permit members to vote "yes" on multiple contradictory motions knowing only one (the last vote, or the one with the most votes) will really count; this procedural antic permits members to tell angry constituents, "Don't blame me; I voted for that bill" (yes, they did—but they also voted against it when it really counted).

Senate leaders, far from inventing new rules, are more likely to breathe a sigh of relief just to steer a bill past the potential member holds and simply get it to the floor. There, a related danger lurks: the filibuster. A senator (or group of senators) may halt all activity in the chamber by refusing to yield the floor; the only way to stop her or him is through a **cloture vote**, which requires the approval of three-fifths of the Senate—sixty votes.

Today, most Senate business requires a cloture vote—another change introduced by high partisanship. Between 1927 and 1960, there were only eighteen efforts to break a filibuster—or cloture filings, as they are called. Not a single one succeeded. As you can see in Figure 13.3, the effort to invoke cloture grew more common in the 1970s (which averaged thirty-two filibusters every

Cloture vote: The Senate's only approved method for halting a filibuster or lifting a legislative hold. If sixty senators—three-fifths of the body, changed in 1975 from the original two-thirds—vote for cloture, the measure can proceed to a vote.

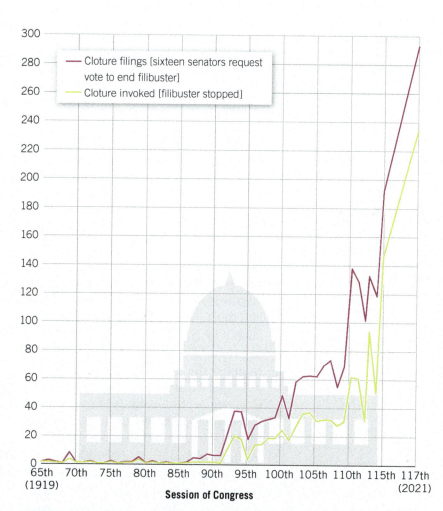

● **FIGURE 13.3** *Cloture votes are called to end a filibuster or hold. When the majority gets 60 votes, the filibuster ends. Notice how they used to be rare events. Now, each session features more. The 113th Congress (2013–14) broke the all-time record for cloture votes. Now we get a new record every session, with 318 for the 117th Congress (2021–22). (U.S. Senate)*

two-year session); it became a common tactic in the 1990s and 2000s. Both Democratic and Republican majorities averaged seventy-two cloture filings (seeking to break a filibuster or lift a hold) each session. The Republican minority (2007–15) broke all filibustering records and Democrats averaged 161 cloture filings a session. By the 117th Congress (2021–22), Republicans filed more than 300 cloture motions. Again, this minority party roadblock is the new normal for most bills in the Senate: It now takes sixty votes to get most things through.

The Vote

Once all the amendments have been voted down or adopted, the time for speeches has expired, and the leadership reckons it has a winning majority, the chamber votes. On uncontroversial matters, leaders in the House call for a **voice vote.** But some votes are judged important enough to require a **roll-call vote.** In the Senate, a clerk still calls the roll alphabetically, scrolling through senators by last name, with each responding "yea" or "nay" (or "present," if they wish to abstain). There were 880 Senate roll calls in the 117th Congress (2021–22). Because the much larger House would take hours to vote if it proceeded in this way, roll calls are now done electronically. Representatives use a voting device about the size of a credit card that they plug into kiosks located around the House chamber.

Roll-call votes on major bills (and judicial appointments in the Senate) are among the most important public acts a member of Congress performs. These votes attract a great deal of attention from constituents, lobbyists, the media, and potential campaign opponents—who might use an unpopular vote to attack an incumbent.[37]

Conference Committee

Legislation must pass the Senate and House in identical form to be ready for presidential action. If different versions of a bill pass—and technically a single comma in a five-hundred-page bill counts as a "difference"—a **conference committee** must reconcile them. These special sessions, made up of lawmakers from both chambers, provide a golden opportunity for disgruntled members or attentive lobbyists to revisit a bill. Interested parties who failed to get a favorite item included during committee or floor action now have another chance. "An apple and an orange could go into conference committee," lamented President Ronald Reagan, "and come out a pear."[38] No joke: The conference can write a significantly new bill, though sections that were the same in House and Senate versions cannot be altered in conference.

House-Senate conferences, if successful, yield a single version of a bill. Each chamber then has an "up-or-down" floor vote—no further amendments permitted. Opponents in the Senate may launch yet another filibuster, hoping to win over new members who object to the compromises made with the House. If the majority beats the filibuster in the Senate and a majority of both houses votes in favor, the bill has passed Congress.

In recent years, however, the two chambers have increasingly negotiated with one another prior to passage in a process known as "ping pong." That yields bills that are identical on House and Senate floors, eliminating the need for conference committees. The number of conferences has declined dramatically—from more than fifty a session (in the 1990s) to seven in the 115th Congress, two in the 116th

Voice vote: A congressional vote in which the presiding officer asks those for and against to say "yea" or "nay," respectively, and announces the result. No record is kept of House or Senate members voting on each side.

Roll-call vote: A congressional vote in which each member's vote is recorded, either by roll call (Senate) or electronically (House).

Conference committee: A special House-Senate committee that must reconcile differences between the two chambers' versions of the same bill.

Congress, and just one in the 117th (as of July 1, 2022). The decline reflects the growing power of the leaders in both chambers. Again, the question arises: Is this a breakdown of traditional congressional norms? Or much-needed modernization to speed up the process?[39]

Presidential Action: Separated Powers Revisited

Even after all that, legislation still faces another hurdle. No bill becomes law until the president takes action, usually by signing it (without the president's signature, bills also become law within ten days of congressional passage, if Congress remains in session). On important issues, a signing ceremony often takes place in the White House Rose Garden. Presidents sign multiple copies of the bill, handing out pens to the original sponsors and other high-ranking congressional members in attendance.

Presidents can also **veto** legislation. Here is yet another place a bill can falter. If the president says no, Congress has one more shot at passing the legislation. It is a high bar, though. To deny or override a veto, both chambers need a two-thirds majority: At least sixty-seven senators and 291 members of the House have to say no to the president. Only in this way can a bill become law without presidential approval. Figure 13.4 summarizes the process of how a bill becomes law.

Veto: The constitutional procedure by which a president can prevent enactment of legislation passed by Congress.

Vetoes are rare and seldom come as a surprise. The president's team negotiates with each chamber every step of the way. President Trump only vetoed eight bills in his sole term, and, after two years, President Biden vetoed none—a number that is not likely to rise after the Republicans failed to win both chambers in the 2022 midterms.

The media covers every step of this complicated process if the bill is important—and when there's a public outcry, a lot of votes can suddenly change. A quiet public also speaks volumes. We once asked a member from California if he was worried about a vote that seemed to go against the latest public opinion surveys. His answer: "Nope. I didn't hear from a single person on that one."

THE BOTTOM LINE

» Passing a law is difficult. Why bother? Because legislation remains the central act of American domestic government. Important laws have far-reaching consequences.

» Thousands of bills are introduced in Congress each year. Most proposed legislation (97 percent) never gets through the process to become law.

» Congressional committees are traditionally the central actors in legislative policymaking, holding hearings and marking up (or deleting) bills to prepare them for floor action.

» Today, leadership plays a more active role in crafting legislation.

» Floor procedures are intricate. Even after passage, a bill may still face a conference committee or a presidential veto.

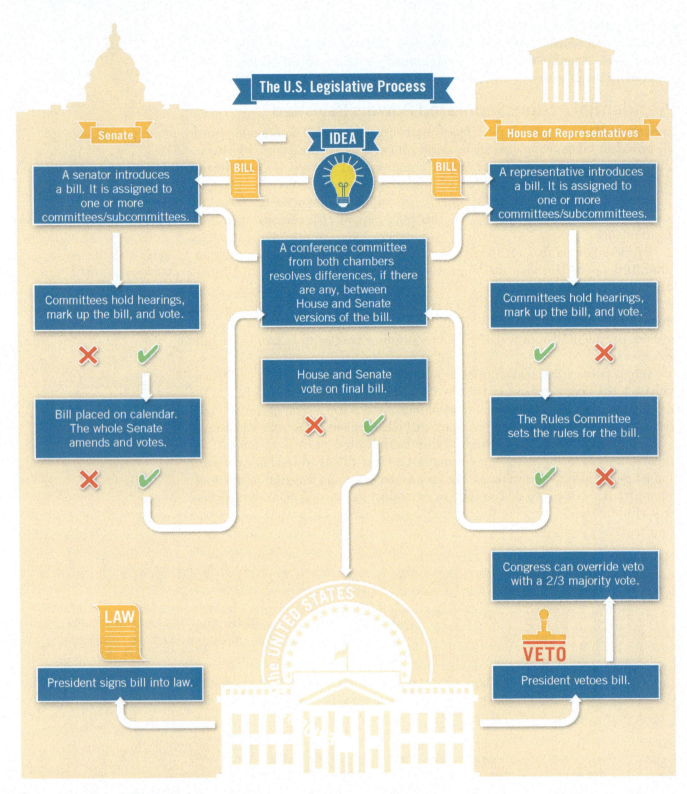

The U.S. Legislative Process

Senate

IDEA

House of Representatives

BILL

BILL

A senator introduces a bill. It is assigned to one or more committees/subcommittees.

A representative introduces a bill. It is assigned to one or more committees/subcommittees.

A conference committee from both chambers resolves differences, if there are any, between House and Senate versions of the bill.

Committees hold hearings, mark up the bill, and vote.

Committees hold hearings, mark up the bill, and vote.

House and Senate vote on final bill.

Bill placed on calendar. The whole Senate amends and votes.

The Rules Committee sets the rules for the bill.

Congress can override veto with a 2/3 majority vote.

LAW

VETO

President signs bill into law.

President vetoes bill.

The UNITED STATES

● **FIGURE 13.4** *How a bill becomes a law.*

Why Is Congress So Unpopular?

You might think Congress, the "people's branch," would be more popular than the other parts of the government. After all, you can meet your member of Congress a lot more easily than the president or Supreme Court justices. But it's not even close—for a half-century, polls have reported that Congress is the least popular branch—and, usually, by a large margin. Today, Congress is less popular than at any other time in modern history and less popular than, well, almost anything—including the Internal Revenue Service, dog poop, zombies, and hipsters (see Figure 13.5).[40] And yet, as we saw in Chapter 10, Americans reelect over 90 percent of their representatives, year after year. Why?

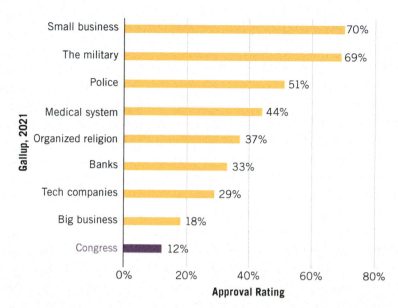

● **FIGURE 13.5** *At the bottom: Public approval of Congress, compared to other institutions. (Gallup)*

Constituents tend to like their own representatives and senators, who receive far higher approval numbers than Congress as a whole. And individual members have become adept at raising money (to drive off talented challengers) and running against the Congress they serve in. But what makes the institution itself so unpopular? The public dislikes both partisan fighting and gridlock. Let us look more carefully at each complaint.

Partisan Polarization in Congress

Congress has exhibited partisan differences since its origins. Strong party disputes, fueled by regional and racial divisions, led nineteenth-century members to carry swords, pistols, or Bowie knives into chambers. Following a rousing anti-slavery speech by Senator Charles Sumner of Massachusetts in 1856, a southern House member, Preston Brooks, slipped onto the Senate floor and beat Sumner unconscious with a cane. Sumner was unable to resume his Senate duties for nearly three years, while Brooks became a hero in South Carolina. One historian calls the Congress of that era a "field of blood."[41] Recent combat in Congress has been limited mainly to words.

During the 1950s and 1960s, large Democratic majorities in both chambers masked differences—mostly between southern conservatives and liberals from other regions of the country—within the Democratic caucus. Conflict between the parties rose during the 1980s, as Republicans gained congressional seats. When the GOP won control of the Senate in the 1980s and challenged Democrats for control of the House after 1990, the fault lines between the parties cracked open.[42]

The proportion of House votes in which a majority of Democrats voted against a majority of Republicans increased by more than 50 percent during the 1990s and early 2000s.[43]

● *Congressional partisanship, Civil War era–style. A northern cartoonist vividly renders the 1856 caning of Senator Sumner.*

Or, to see the same thing from another angle, the number of members who voted with their party majority went from roughly 65 percent before 1990 to above 90 percent in 1990—and remain even higher today. The big fights used to be within the parties—each had liberals and conservatives. Now they are between the parties, which are divided by both principles (Republicans are conservative) and demographics (Republicans are more likely to be white rural-dwelling males).[44]

The titles of recent books about Congress underscore the point: *Fight Club Politics*; *The Broken Branch*; *They Don't Represent Us*; *Insufficient Representation: The Disconnect Between Congress and Its Citizens*; and, by a House member, *Drain the Swamp: How Washington Corruption Is Worse Than You Think.*[45]

Partisan Polarization

How Has It Changed over Time?

Democrats and Republicans in Congress have grown further apart today than they were at any time in the last fifty years.

Republicans have moved further to the right than Democrats have to the left
Average ideology of members, by Congress

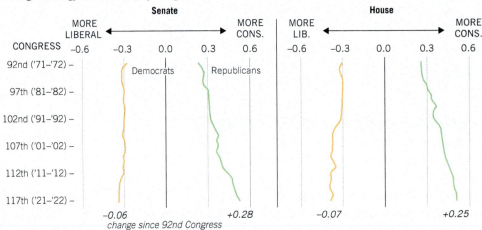

Note: Data exclude nonvoting delegates, as well as lawmakers who officially served but (due to illness, resignation or other factors) didn't have a scorable voting record for a given Congress. Party categories include independents who caucused with that party. Members who changed parties (or became independents) during a Congress were classified according to the status they held the longest during that Congress. For most of the 116th Congress, Rep. Justin Amash of Michigan was either an independent or a Libertarian, and didn't caucus with either major party.

THINK ABOUT IT

How has that gap changed since 1970?

Would you criticize the Republicans for becoming more conservative? Or cheer them for standing up for what they believe in?

How about the Democrats? Are they being reasonable? Or are they afraid of their own principles?

Think about the issues you really care about—perhaps global warming or the right to bear arms. Do you want to see candidates compromise or fight hard for their positions?

Source: Pew Research Center

WHAT DO YOU THINK?

Is a Partisan Congress a Good Thing?

Should Congress seek more cross-party agreement? The answer may not be so obvious—especially if you view politics in terms of principles, not merely the pursuit of self-interest. Today's "partisan" Congress features a significant ideological divide between conservative Republicans and progressive Democrats. Partisanship helps guide how members pursue the goals they believe in and try to persuade the public. What do you think?

Yes, a partisan Congress is a good thing.
It permits the public to choose between very different political philosophies. For decades, both parties in Congress had largely indistinguishable positions. Now, Republicans favor increased deportation of undocumented people, more parental guidance over education, rolling back same-sex marriage, and limiting transgender rights. On the other side, progressive Democrats press for climate justice, a higher minimum wage, childcare for working families, and a restoration of the right to choose. If parties are too moderate, people don't have a real choice.

No, Congress has gotten too partisan.
The parties may disagree with one another, but they do not reflect the views of most Americans. Most people are moderates who do not feel well represented by the strong party views that fail to listen to the other side. More important, rising partisanship hampers cooperation necessary for Congress to pass important legislation and respond to the American public's preferences. Congress should seek compromises in the national interest.

It depends.
Context matters. For example, in times of economic suffering, people should put aside their political philosophy (whether pro- or anti-government) and pass legislation for relief. But on other matters (such as abortion, gun control, LGBTQ+ rights, or immigration) members should stick to their principles.

There are two perspectives on polarization. One view suggests that it comes from a simple fact: Parties are now almost completely sorted by ideology for the first time in modern history—Republicans have moved steadily to the right over the past quarter-century, and Democrats have been swinging to the left. Others see "asymmetrical polarization": The Republicans, inspired by a fiery conservative movement, are the ones who have moved further right.[46]

Divided Government

The headlines about Congress are partisanship, gridlock, and lost authority. Why? One familiar answer—divided government.[47] That's when the parties split control of the three elected branches

● *Public disapproval of Congress.*

of national government—House, Senate, and presidency. In the last fourteen years, each party has controlled all three for just two years each. For many years, political scientists discounted the effects of a split in party control: "Divided we govern," we said. Party division, we believed, led to more effective lawmaking.[48] But as the partisanship grew, the stalemate deepened. More recent studies are more in line with conventional wisdom: Divided government leads to gridlock and policy stalemate.[49] We have seen one result throughout the chapter: a "virtual disappearance of regular order in Congress"—that is, bipartisan lawmaking, through committees, according to long-established norms. Instead, each party falls in line around their leaders, who demand discipline while they look to the next election.[50]

THE BOTTOM LINE

» Congress has grown more partisan. Today, the parties themselves are more ideologically consistent. This makes for sharper conflict, but it also gives people clearer choices.

» Does divided government lead to more gridlock? Political scientists argued in the past that it does not, but today partisanship makes it harder for Congress to address America's problems.

Some Popular Reforms—and Their Limits

Should we care that Americans do not like Congress? Many observers—and thoughtful members—worry that continued public disapproval will erode the effectiveness of Congress as an institution. Some worry that laws will compel less attention, respect, and obedience if the institution passing them is seen as corrupt or hapless. Others worry that the high-decibel disagreements will discourage talented young people from considering a congressional career (as either staffers or members). Still another danger: A deadlocked Congress will permit power to leak into the executive branch, which will increasingly make policy on its own. We will explore that worry in Chapter 14.

Each year, reformers propose various fixes to improve Congress. We have already discussed two such reforms: increasing third parties and imposing term limits (see Chapter 10). Here we discuss two other popular reforms: limits on lobbyists and public education about what Congress really does.

Limit Lobbyists

Many Americans favor efforts to reduce the influence of lobbyists. In Chapter 12 we saw lots of reforms, including banning the gifts and meals that lobbyists once gave to members. Both reform packages were greeted with yawns from the public: Congressional approval ratings actually dropped after each was implemented.

Remember James Madison's surprising conclusion from *Federalist #10*: Because groups inevitably promote their own interests, liberty is best protected when many groups pursue their interests out in the open. That way, the different interests will check one another and people will have a choice among a great many perspectives. The solution to special interests: more special interests.

Madison could not have imagined the vast array of interests swarming over Capitol Hill today. But, as discussed in Chapter 12, one person's special interest is another's cherished protector of a vital program. Lobbyists represent virtually everyone. And they link together our vast public and the complicated structures of national governance.

Even so, congressional organization—with its arcane ways, complicated processes, and multiple committees and subcommittees—creates many opportunities for special interests to quietly win favors and block initiatives they do not like. The problem is not their power over the big issues, on which members have strong views and votes are in the limelight, but in the minute details or obscure items to which few pay attention, even though millions of dollars can be gained or lost with a few strokes of a legislator's pen. The concern many Americans have is simple: Wealthy and powerful Americans, supported by lobbyists, bend the system and get their way.

How to limit such deals and favors? Perhaps James Madison had the best answer. When energy companies seek special benefits, environmental groups blow the whistle (and vice versa); when public hospitals push higher pay for CEOs, taxpayer groups challenge their arguments. Perhaps the solution to the problem of interests really is more interests. That would mean reforming the way Congress does business—to make sure that a wider array of interests are heard on every issue. And reforming campaign finance to diminish the influence of money. Those reforms might be more effective than the effort to eradicate lobbying itself.

Educate the Public

Some reform proposals include an earnest plea for better education about Congress. Many Americans do not know their House member's name and cannot begin to explain how bills become law. Perhaps with a little more knowledge, the public would be more sympathetic.

Or maybe not. Political scientists John Hibbing and Elizabeth Theiss-Morse argued, on the other side, that Americans' real problem with Congress is not lack of knowledge. The underlying problem is deeper: Americans dislike logrolling and bargaining, committees and bureaucracy, political partisanship and interest groups. All that bickering and backstabbing and self-interest turn people off. Or, to put it differently, concluded Hibbing and Theiss-Morse, many Americans disapprove of some of the core features of democracy in practice. Although Americans love democracy in the abstract and demand transparency in politics, we do not enjoy watching the congressional process playing out with all its messy give-and-take.[51]

The Real World of Democracy

This chapter has tried to make clear how difficult, complex, and often muddled congressional policymaking is. Our ultimate goal is to increase your appreciation for the messiness of democracy, as carried out in the people's branch. Maybe the national legislature's bargaining, partial solutions, noisy debates, horse trading, and compromising faithfully reflect a diverse, divided, sometimes raucous American public. Congress is, on balance, the most open, transparent institution in our system of government. It is also inevitably full of flaws and limits—just like the humans it serves.

Why, in the end, are people's opinions of Congress so dismal? Perhaps the public laments how hard it is to get legislative results from Congress despite glowing campaign promises. Or perhaps it is discomfort with the essential realities of democracy: partisan bellowing, stops and starts, compromises that satisfy no one fully. Part of the fault also lies with the individual members who glide to reelection, year after year, by vehemently criticizing the institution they serve in.

THE BOTTOM LINE

» Some popular reforms propose limiting the influence of lobbying groups in Congress. And limiting the power of money.

» Others emphasize the importance of educating the public, so that Americans can exercise greater oversight and develop a deeper understanding of the workings of Congress.

» We recommend a different education: Learn to love the messy, convoluted, give-and-take that marks legislating in a diverse democratic nation.

Conclusion: Congress and the Challenge of Governing

Congress, as an institution, does some important things very well—representatives and senators are remarkably adept at looking after individuals who request help. Direct constituent service, at home in the district and state, is often superb. That is one reason reelection rates are so high.

But as our individual needs have become better supported, Congress has grown less capable of solving big societal problems—such as immigration, healthcare, crime, inequality, wage stagnation, climate change, stubborn racism, or the byzantine tax code. By any measure, Americans' collective aspirations are at least as important as our personal concerns. The overarching question throughout this chapter is whether the U.S. Congress has lost its ability to achieve big collective aims, or whether it still muddles through—more or less as the constitutional framers, with all their checking and balancing, intended.

In the past, Congress has certainly proven capable of broad achievements. Medicare and Social Security, to take two of the largest congressional programs, have cut the rate of poverty among elderly Americans by more than half and provided seniors with generous health benefits. The Civil Rights Act of 1964 created a framework of citizen rights that is still opening the door to groups more than a half-century later.

Genuine democratic, popular government can be chaotic, muddled, and sometimes repugnant. But it is essential. Our representatives in Congress must find a way to continue to fulfill their democratic duties. The people's branch will have to find a way to govern effectively—and to win back popular approval—if American democracy is to flourish in the future.

CHAPTER SUMMARY

⭐ Congress has become intensely partisan because the parties are more ideologically consistent and evenly matched. This makes for sharper conflict, but gives voters clearer choices.

⭐ Americans debate whether Congress still works the way it is supposed to, slowly addressing problems, or whether it has become "the broken branch."

⭐ America's Congress is bicameral: The House of Representatives contains 441 members (435 voting; six others represent territories such as Puerto Rico) elected every two years; in the Senate, one hundred senators—two from each state—serve six-year terms.

⭐ The two chambers of Congress reflect different national priorities. Populists appreciate the responsive House; advocates of stability embrace the more deliberate Senate.

★ Members of the House and Senate represent Americans in multiple ways. These include:

> ★ *Geographic representation*: Constitutional election rules say members must live in the state or district they represent.

> ★ *Descriptive representation*: Does the assembly look like the people?

> ★ *Substantive representation*: Do members of Congress effectively pursue constituent interests?

★ Members of Congress run constantly for office. Fundraising takes up a particularly large amount of time and attention. Members pay special attention to their home styles: Most go back to their constituency every week—compressing normal congressional business into the period from Tuesday through Thursday.

★ Congress is increasingly an institution of strangers who do not know one another well.

★ Congressional leadership in the House includes a Speaker, majority and minority leaders, and ten whips. Successful House leaders impose discipline on their party members. In the Senate, party leaders and whips have fewer institutional tools with which to keep members in line.

★ With rising partisanship, congressional party leaders have more authority. And they sometimes bypass regular order.

★ Congressional committees have proved efficient and adaptable over the years, preparing legislation and conducting oversight of the executive branch. However, the committee system also fragments Congress, hides action from public view, enables well-placed constituents to win individual favors, and makes it difficult to pass major legislation.

★ Floor procedures are another intricate part of the legislative process. Once passed, legislation may still face a conference committee, a presidential veto, or both.

★ The difficult path to legislation raises a key question about Congress: Should we cheer the slow-moving process as a way to limit government? Or should we worry that the institution is not up to addressing America's vital problems?

KEY TERMS

118th Congress, p. 413
Cloture vote, p. 437
Committee hearing, p. 433
Committee markup session, p. 434
Conference committee, p. 438
Congressional caucus, p. 416

Earmark, p. 428
Filibuster, p. 414
Floor, p. 413
Legislative hold, p. 413
President pro tempore, p. 427
Roll-call vote, p. 438

Speaker of the House, p. 425
Unanimous consent, p. 436
Veto, p. 439
Voice vote, p. 438

STUDY QUESTIONS

1. Discuss the following reforms:
   a) There should be public financing for all congressional elections, even if that means raising taxes.
   b) The Senate filibuster and legislative hold should be abolished.
   c) There should be more limits on lobbyists' access and/or influence.

2. How did Congress lose so much power to the president? Are there ways to get some of that power back? Should power be more balanced between the two branches?

3. Describe three major differences between the House and Senate. How do the differences affect whether members see themselves as delegates (pursuing their constituents' interests) or trustees (doing what they think is in constituents' best interest)?

4. Why is Congress today so partisan? Can you think of ways to reduce partisanship? Are there any advantages to drawing strong partisan lines between Republicans and Democrats?

5. Should it be easier to pass laws through Congress? What, if any, benefits do all the checks and balances provide?

6. Why is Congress so unpopular with the American people? In your view, does Congress deserve its low approval ratings?

7. Suggest and defend a reform for improving Congress.

THE PRESIDENCY

GEORGE WASHINGTON, the first president of the United States, faced a problem. He had to persuade thirteen independent-minded states to think of themselves as one unified nation. Washington decided to foster unity by touring the new country. He set out with assistants, slaves, horses, and dogs. As the party approached each town, the president mounted a great white steed and cantered handsomely into the cheering throngs, his favorite greyhound trotting at his side. Washington named the dog Cornwallis, after the British general who surrendered to end the Revolutionary War. Poor Cornwallis the greyhound died while touring the southern states, but his name reminded the people that they were part of a proud and independent nation. Everywhere Washington went the people greeted their president with ringing bells, cheers, songs, speeches, parades, and flags. The crowds felt, at least for a day, like Americans.[1]

Who are we? Each president offers a different answer. Washington was a great president, not because of his domestic programs or foreign policies—at the time, critics were scathing about both. Instead, Washington embodied the new nation. He articulated the country's ideals, introduced new ideas, and shaped the powers of his office. Washington represented America—both to Americans and to the world. All presidents do the same, some more successfully than others.

The president's role is difficult partly because Americans rarely agree about who we are. The United States are often the *Un*-United States. Washington took enslaved people on his unity tour. He kept people in bondage throughout his presidency. Didn't slavery violate the new nation's ideals? Many Americans knew that it did. In fact, President Washington shuffled the men and women he held in bondage in and out of Philadelphia, the capital city, to get around a Pennsylvania law that declared all enslaved people free after six months. Even a great president did not represent all Americans—or their hopes and dreams.[2] Fast forward to modern times. When Donald Trump took the presidency, Democrats demonstrated with chants of "not my president," and danced in the streets

In this chapter, you will

 Review how the Constitution defines the presidency.

 Focus on presidential power.

 Learn what presidents do.

 Reflect on presidential popularity—and greatness.

 Consider the personal side of the office.

 Tour the Executive Office of the president, and meet the team around a president.

● *Presidents define us: President Joe Biden managed an unusual string of legislative victories—highlighted by a trillion-dollar infrastructure bill (with nineteen Republican votes in the Senate), a gun safety measure (fifteen GOP votes), and a breakthrough climate measure (zero Republican votes). And the midterm elections, which usually run strongly against the party in the White House, saw no large anti-Biden backlash. Still, after two years, Biden's approval ratings remained low—at about 42%.*

when Trump lost in 2020. Republicans returned the favor, with sitting GOP members of Congress mocking President Joe Biden as "senile," "incoherent and confused," and "not up to the challenge of being president of the United States." By his second year in office, more than 90 percent of Republicans disapproved of Biden's performance as president.[3]

Some 230 years after Washington's tour, newly inaugurated President Biden signed multiple executive orders on his first day in office: He reversed the ban on immigration from Muslim nations, fortified protection for Dreamers (undocumented immigrants brought to the United States as children), rejoined the Paris Agreement on fighting climate change, added new environmental protections, and aimed to end discrimination on the basis of gender identity and sexual orientation. These orders all reversed orders signed by his predecessor, Donald Trump. Many constitutional experts read these executive orders as emblematic of swelling presidential power.[4] Like George Washington, both Biden and Trump were redefining the president's role.

But there is another way to see presidential power. Presidents are enmeshed in a complex institutional web. Both Trump and Biden soon faced judicial decisions limiting presidential power. Is there a way around the courts? Yes: Both presidents also went to Congress to enact their policies through new laws—each met both success and failures in the legislature.[5]

The ultimate test, of course, is always the next election. The voters rejected President Trump's expansion of presidential authority and he lost his bid for reelection. The White House swung back to the Democrats. Two years later, in the 2022 midterms, the voters surprised the pundits and voted to continue the status quo—without a large swing to either party.

Today, the presidency raises precisely the same question the delegates debated at the Constitutional Convention: How much authority should the president wield? From Washington's tour to Trump's bans and Biden's plans, the presidency reflects the same three themes:

> *The president personifies America.* More than any other individual, presidents tell us who we are—and what we are becoming. As Americans grow more partisan, this traditional role becomes more challenging.
>
> *The president injects new ideas and themes into American politics.* Our discussion of Congress emphasized the institutional rules of the game; the presidency puts more focus on individuals and ideas.
>
> *The president has enormous powers—at least on paper.* That authority, and how presidents use it, returns us to the fundamental question: Is the presidency too powerful for a democratic republic? Or is the office too weak to do what Americans demand of it? Perhaps the same president can be both too strong and too weak. Keep this question of authority in mind as you read the chapter.

The Presidency

1 Length, in months, of the shortest presidency (William Henry Harrison)

Zero Number of presidents older than Joe Biden when elected

4 Number of cabinet members, 1789 (President Washington)

145 Length, in months, of the longest presidency (Franklin D. Roosevelt)

1872 Year in which the first woman (Victoria Woodhull) ran for president

15 Number of cabinet members, 2023 (President Biden)

2 Number of presidents younger than Barack Obama when they were elected (Theodore Roosevelt and John F. Kennedy)

4 Number of presidents who were sons or nephews of prior presidents (John Quincy Adams, Benjamin Harrison, Franklin D. Roosevelt, George W. Bush)

33 Estimated percentage of presidents who have had extramarital affairs.

138 Number of times presidents have committed U.S. troops to military actions abroad since 1973 (as of November 2022)[6]

1 Number of presidents to hold a patent (Abraham Lincoln, for an invention to free boats trapped on a sandbar)

Who do Americans elect to the highest office—and how representative are they?

 ## Defining the Presidency

Time travelers from the nineteenth century would easily recognize today's Senate or Supreme Court. However, the modern White House would stun them. The presidency is the branch of the federal government that has changed the most over the decades.

Up until eighty years ago, Americans could walk right in the front door of the White House and greet the president. In 1829, during President Andrew Jackson's inauguration, supporters mobbed the mansion and forced the president to climb out a window for his own safety; aides placed tubs with whiskey and orange juice on the lawn to lure the crowds outside. When William Henry Harrison won the presidency in 1840, so many men milled about the White House hoping to get a

● *Different eras. After Andrew Jackson's inauguration, supporters mobbed into the White House and almost crushed the President—aides put whiskey punch on the lawn to draw the crowds outside (a). In 2021, entertainers like Jennifer Lopez (b), Lady Gaga, Garth Brooks, and poet Amanda Gorman wowed the crowd at President Biden's inaugural ceremony at the U.S. Capitol.*

government job that the president-elect could not find an empty room to meet with his cabinet.

Today, there are no more throngs in the White House. Presidents have redefined their roles and renegotiated their powers. The presidency is a different institution. In part, all the changes arise because each president has the opportunity to reshape the office. One reason the presidency is so fluid lies in the job description. By now, you know where to look for that: the Constitution.

Defined by Controversy

The Constitutional Convention's delegates faced three tough questions when they defined the presidency (for more detail, see Chapter 3). First, *should the United States even have a president?* Traditional republics feared executive power. The founders feared the English king was too powerful, but also worried that the state governments did not have enough executive power and were too feeble to govern effectively. Their job was to find a happy medium. In the end, they selected a single president and established simple qualifications for the post: a natural-born citizen at least thirty-five years old who had lived in the United States for at least fourteen years.

Second, *how long should the president serve?* The delegates at the Constitutional Convention considered terms of four, six, seven, eight, eleven, and fifteen years. Alexander Hamilton passionately argued that presidents should be elected for life—an elected king. They settled on four years, with no limit on the number of terms. Washington would set a precedent when he stepped down after his second term, dazzling his contemporaries by walking away from power. For a century and a half, American presidents followed Washington's example and served no more than two terms—until Franklin D. Roosevelt broke the pattern and won four elections between 1932 and 1944. The Twenty-Second Amendment, ratified in 1951, six years after Roosevelt's death, bars presidents from serving more than two terms.

Third, *how should the United States choose its president?* Delegates to the convention feared that the public did not know enough, that the state legislatures were too self-interested, and that Congress would become too powerful if given the task of appointing the executive. They finally settled on a roundabout method, the

Electoral College, which you encountered in Chapter 10: The states each get electoral votes equal to the members in their congressional delegation. Who would elect the electors? The convention simply left the matter to the states (see Chapter 3).

Political scientists and pundits still debate the Electoral College because it distorts the popular vote. Even very close popular votes often look lopsided in the Electoral College. Ronald Reagan got 50.7 percent (in a three-way race) in 1980, yet the Electoral College made these contests look like a rout, with Reagan taking a whopping 91 percent of the Electoral College vote.

More important, the Electoral College has put the popular vote loser in the White House in two of the last four presidencies. If the candidate with the most popular votes took the White House, Democrats would have won every presidential election but one (2004) in the past thirty-five years. Major population centers—New York, Los Angeles, Houston—are all but ignored during presidential elections because they are in states that safely give majorities (and all their Electoral College votes) to one party or the other.[7]

The President's Powers

Article 2 of the Constitution, which defines the presidency, seems puzzling at first glance. Article 1 meticulously lists everything Congress is empowered to do: The instructions run for fifty-two paragraphs. In contrast, Article 2 says very little about who the president is or what the president does. Thirteen short paragraphs define the office. This vague constitutional mandate is one reason the office keeps evolving.

The Constitution is especially terse when it gets to the heart of the presidency: the powers and duties of the chief executive. It grants the president a limited number of **expressed powers**, or explicit grants of authority. Most are carefully balanced by corresponding congressional powers. Table 14.1 summarizes this balance.[8]

The president draws real authority from a simple phrase at the end of the section: "Take care that the laws be faithfully executed." Congress votes on legislation and then sends it to the executive branch to put into effect. In other words, Congress grants **delegated powers** to the president. For example, Congress passes legislation that aims to improve hospital care. It delegates power to the executive branch, which issues detailed rules saying that hospitals will receive lower federal payments if patients develop infections after surgery. Vague laws increase the discretion of the executive branch that puts them into effect.

Presidents claim a third source of authority: **inherent powers**. These are not specified in the Constitution or delegated by legislation, but are implicit in the

Expressed powers: Powers the Constitution explicitly grants to the president.

Delegated powers: Powers that Congress passes on to the president.

Inherent powers of the presidency: Powers assumed by presidents, often during a crisis, on the basis of the constitutional phrase "The executive power shall be vested in the president."

TABLE 14.1 The President's Expressed Powers

The president is commander-in-chief of the army, navy, and state militias. But Congress has the power to declare war, set the military budget, and make the rules governing the military.
The president can grant pardons and reprieves for offenses against the United States.
The president can make treaties (with the approval of two-thirds of the Senate), appoint ambassadors (with the advice and consent of the Senate), and select Supreme Court justices and other officers (again, with Senate approval).
The Constitution also authorizes presidents to appoint executive officers and solicit their opinions, and requires presidents to report on the state of the Union.

THE BIG STICK IN THE CARIBBEAN SEA

● *President Theodore Roosevelt, who entered the White House in 1901, combined diplomacy and military might—"speak softly," he summarized, "and carry a big stick."*

Executive agreements: International agreements made by the president that do not require the approval of the Senate.

Executive privilege: Power claimed by the president to resist requests for authority by Congress, the courts, or the public. Not mentioned in the Constitution but based on the separation of powers.

vague Article 2 phrase, "The executive power shall be vested in a president." During crises, presidents have often seized on "inherent" authority. During the Civil War, for example, President Lincoln took a series of unprecedented military actions with no clear legal basis. He imposed censorship, ordered a naval blockade, and issued orders while Congress was not in session. After the 9/11 terrorist attacks on the United States, President Bush exercised inherent powers to engage in foreign surveillance, to detain enemy combatants without hearings, and to authorize coercive interrogation (which critics called torture). The president's claim of inherent powers is not the last word on the matter. Congress may pass legislation in response, and the Supreme Court often weighs whether the president has overstepped the constitutional boundaries of executive authority.

Modern presidents have expanded presidential power in many ways. As we shall see later in this chapter, presidents regularly issue executive orders, negotiate **executive agreements** with other nations, and claim **executive privilege**—all ways of bypassing Congress. Throughout this chapter we review subtle ways that presidents have expanded their power.

The result is a very fluid definition of presidential power. Presidents regularly renegotiate the limits of the office through their actions at home and abroad. Crises generally expand the presidential role. More than any other institution, the presidency is a constant work in progress. The arc of presidential history begins with a vague constitutional grant of power that has grown through the years.

This discussion brings us back to the question we posed at the start of the chapter: Has the president become too powerful? We turn to that question in the next section.

COMPARING NATIONS 14.1	Chief Executives' Power
Although presidents have expanded their authority over time, chief executives in parliamentary systems, those used in most other democracies, typically are granted these powers. U.S. presidents might long to exercise any of these.	A *legislative majority*: Since parliament usually selects the executives, they can expect a party majority or (in multiparty systems) a majority coalition.
	The executive does not face a *separation of powers*. Parliament will generally approve the executive's legislation.
	Emergency decree powers: Executives' authority is greatly expanded in national emergencies (and they typically get to decide what counts as an "emergency").
	Partial (line-item) veto: Prime ministers and other foreign leaders are able to strip out individual legislative provisions that they find objectionable.
	Exclusive right to *introduce certain types of legislation*, especially budgets.
	The ability to *dismiss the legislature* and call new elections.

THE BOTTOM LINE

» Presidents serve a four-year term and can run for reelection once.

» They are elected indirectly, via the Electoral College.

» The president has three types of powers: *expressed* in the Constitution, *delegated* by Congress, and *inherent* in the role of chief executive.

» In theory, Congress passes laws and the president executes them. In reality, presidents constantly negotiate the limits of their power—which often expands during crises.

Is the Presidency Too Powerful?

The constitutional framers wrestled with the same issue we debate today: *power.* How much authority do presidents need to protect the nation and get things done? When does the office's reach violate the idea of limited government?

An Imperial Presidency?

During George Washington's national tour, a few Americans fretted about his nine stallions, gold-trimmed saddles, personal attendants, and all that adulation. Washington, they whispered, was acting more like a king than the president of a homespun republic. They were articulating a constant American theme: The president has grown too mighty. Flash forward two centuries.

When President Biden visited Brussels in 2022, hundreds of Secret Service agents arrived in advance and military cargo planes hauled in more than fifty support vehicles, including an ambulance stocked with the president's blood type and four of the of the presidential limousines known as "The Beast," measuring eighteen feet and weighing some eight tons—thanks to thick armored plating and bulletproof windows. As many as a thousand staff members accompanied President Biden, including his personal chef. Today, American presidents travel like emperors.[9]

● President Biden takes off from Los Angeles aboard Marine One—surrounded by support aircraft, including an identical second helicopter to confuse would-be attackers. Today, presidents travel like emperors.

What happens when a weaker individual becomes president? Washington's successor, President John Adams, did not have to worry about cheering crowds. Critics mocked the chubby second president as "His Rotundity." Adams attracted so little attention that he regularly swam naked in the Potomac River (until a female reporter allegedly spied him, sat on his clothes, and demanded an interview). Even Adams, however, aroused widespread fears about executive power when he signed the Alien and Sedition Acts, which gave presidents and their teams broad powers to deport "dangerous aliens" and punish "false, scandalous, and malicious" speech. The president seemed to be trampling the First Amendment by silencing criticism.

Many presidents have stretched the limits of the office. One approach, the **unitary executive theory,** defends the expansion of power. This view contends that the Constitution puts the president in charge of executing the laws, and therefore no one—not Congress, not the judiciary, not even the people—may limit presidential power when it comes to executive matters. Many executive decisions demand swift, decisive, and sometimes secretive action. Only an empowered president, the argument goes, can make those instantaneous calls.[10]

The unitary executive theory is controversial. Arthur Schlesinger Jr., a celebrated historian, warned of an **imperial presidency**. Very powerful presidents, he feared, become like emperors: They run roughshod over Congress, issue secret decisions, unilaterally deploy force around the world, and burst past the checks and balances limiting presidential power. Critics worry that imperial features have slowly become part of the presidency itself. Republicans bitterly argued that the Obama administration's overreach embodied the imperial presidency. Democrats said the same about the Trump administration. President Biden began his campaign promising a reset to a more traditional role—but immediately heard from supporters who demanded bold action to address the nation's many problems. Soon after, Republican critics echoed past complaints about presidential abuse of power.

Many contemporary scholars echo this fear of presidential power: As Congress grows more deadlocked, suggested political scientist Francis Fukuyama, supporters cheer when presidents act decisively—even if it pushes the boundaries of presidential power. Power appears to be flowing steadily to the president. One political scientist recently fretted about a presidency of "edicts and coups."[11]

At issue are two vital principles: We need a president who is strong enough to lead the country and face our problems. But if presidents become too strong, we lose our republican form of government. This is a deep paradox of American politics: *We need powerful leaders; we fear powerful leaders.*

A Weak Office?

At the same time, the presidency can sometimes seem very weak. Every modern president has complained about his inability to get basic goals accomplished. Congress, the courts, the opposing political party, the media, interest groups, and bad luck can all humble a president. Since 1960, only four (of eleven) presidents have completed two full terms. What kind of "imperial" presidency is that?

Presidents often appear weakest when they wrestle with domestic issues. Even under the best of circumstances, as we saw in Chapter 13, it is difficult to get major legislation through Congress. The president nominally runs the executive branch, but the bureaucracy is immense and often difficult to control—and cabinets are staffed by officials the Senate must approve. Introducing changes through the American political process is extremely difficult, even for the savviest presidents.

Unitary executive theory: The idea that the Constitution puts the president in charge of executing the laws and that therefore no other branch may limit presidential discretion over executive matters.

Imperial presidency: A characterization of the American presidency that suggests it is demonstrating imperial traits, and that the republic is morphing into an empire.

For a case study of a weak presidency, take Jimmy Carter. Congressional relations turned frosty early in his term after Carter unexpectedly vetoed a spending bill. Carter's major legislative proposals stalled on Capitol Hill. Then the economy soured: interest rates spiraled toward 20 percent, and unemployment topped 10 percent. Gas prices soared, forcing customers in some regions to wait in long lines at gas stations.

Carter did not seem to have an answer to all the woes besetting the nation. A mischievous editor at the *Boston Globe* captured one reaction to Carter's speech when he designed a mock headline, "Mush from the Wimp." By mistake, the headline ran in the *Globe*'s first edition.[12] A few months later, militant Iranian students took fifty-three Americans hostage at the U.S. embassy in Tehran and held them for 444 days. A weak president seemed to be completely overwhelmed by events all around him.

President Trump made progress on many of his goals: he rolled back environmental regulations, cut taxes, restricted immigration from Muslim countries (and cut overall immigration to a quarter of its previous levels), won conservative court appointments, and created a COVID vaccine in record time. Even so, he struggled to get much of his agenda through Congress: He failed to repeal Obamacare (by a single vote in the Senate), to change the immigration laws, to slash federal spending, or to significantly roll back the federal bureaucracy (or the deep state, as he called it). Trump relied on various mechanisms—executive orders, redeploying funds, declaring emergencies, and going to court—to get around Congress and push his agenda forward.

President Biden, across his first two years, experienced the same mix of success and failure. He won legislation on COVID relief, infrastructure spending, microchip development, gun control, climate change, and health reforms. Biden also reversed many of Trump's achievements (and added a few of his own, like student debt relief) through executive orders—a symbol of the presidency as muscle-flexing that was often limited by the courts.

Back and forth goes the debate. Is the president getting too powerful and breaking free from popular control—both formal institutional limits and more subtle norms? Or do presidents need more power and authority if they are to effectively govern a superpower in the twenty-first century? To answer these questions, let us take a closer look at just what presidents do.

THE BOTTOM LINE

» Americans want a powerful president; simultaneously, Americans fear a powerful president.

» The executive branch has grown far stronger over time, especially when it comes to foreign policy.

» The presidency relies on legislation, executive orders, and other methods to get things done.

» In significant ways, presidential power also is limited, especially when it comes to solving domestic problems.

What Presidents Do

Over time, presidents have taken on many jobs. Some are described in the Constitution. Others arise organically during national crises. Presidents seize still other powers as they jockey for political advantage. By now, the president has accumulated an extraordinary number of hats (and helmets). Some of the roles listed in this section are actual titles, conferred in the Constitution ("Commander-in-Chief," for example). Others are informally applied to presidents, based on powers they have acquired over time.

Commander-in-Chief

The Constitution lays it out simply: "The president shall be the Commander-in-Chief of the Army and Navy of the United States and the militia of the several states." Congress declares war and presidents manage it.

For many years, the United States had a small standing army and called men and women to service in wartime. After each war, the army quickly demobilized. This approach reflected classical theory. In great republics like Athens and Rome, citizens took up arms when enemies loomed and then returned home when the crisis had passed—just as George Washington had done during the American Revolution. Peacetime armies were, according to the traditional perspective, a recipe for empire or monarchy.

This tradition changed after World War II, when the United States faced off against the Soviet Union in the Cold War. An army of around 250,000 (after World War I) grew into a force of over two million and spread across the globe. Back in 1835, Tocqueville mused that the Constitution gave the president "almost royal prerogatives which he has no occasion to use." Now the occasion had arrived, and the president's power grew.[13]

Today, America's active-duty force numbers over 1.4 million, with another 845,000 in reserve (Figure 14.1). Military spending fell sharply between 2011 and 2015—partially because of troop reductions in Iraq and Afghanistan—and then began to rise again in 2016, topping $800 billion in 2023. And that does not include the Department of Veterans Affairs, the Department of Homeland Security, intelligence agencies, and other related efforts. The military operates about 750 installations around the globe. In short, the commander-in-chief oversees the

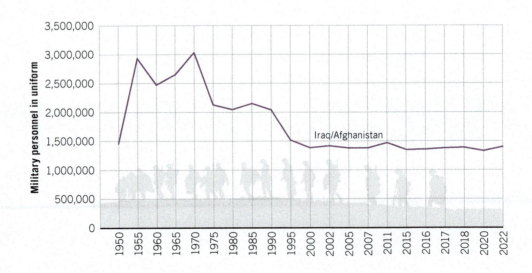

● FIGURE 14.1 *The military grew to three million individuals at the height of the cold war (1950 to 1970), then settled at just under 1.5 million people over the last thirty years. Note how recent wars in Iraq and Afghanistan did not increase the number of Americans in uniform. (Historical Statistics/Statistical Abstracts and US Department of Defense)*

world's largest fighting force. That role, by itself, makes the president one of the most powerful individuals in the world.

Meanwhile, checks on the commander-in-chief have faded. The Constitution authorizes Congress to declare wars, but since the nuclear age dawned in 1945, presidents have rarely waited for Congress to act. Facing the doomsday threat of nuclear missiles, military response time is measured in minutes—too fast for congressional deliberation, or so many people believe.

In an effort to regain some of its authority, Congress passed the War Powers Act (1973). The act permitted the president to send American forces into combat "in case of a national emergency created by an attack on the United States . . . or its armed forces." When presidents deploy troops, however, they must notify Congress within forty-eight hours and gain its approval within sixty days. In practice, presidents have unilaterally deployed troops and treated the War Powers Act with contempt. Even when they sometimes do turn to Congress, it is very difficult to vote no when Americans are in combat.[14]

Presidential powers have always waxed during wartime. Franklin D. Roosevelt's attorney general once quipped, "The Constitution has not greatly bothered any wartime president."[15] Three developments have further increased the president's military authority: America's powerful military machine, always poised for deployment; new technologies, such as drones, that permit presidents to target enemies around the globe; and perceptions of perpetual threat—first from the Soviet Union, then from terrorists, and most recently from Russia and China.[16]

Presidents are deeply engaged by their military role. They traditionally start each day with a security briefing—a dense intelligence report—that reviews all the dangers stirring around the world. They are surrounded by a large national security staff. And—the great symbol of our nuclear age—presidents are never more than a few feet away from "the football."

If you see the president in person, or a wide-angle shot on television, you can glimpse a military officer standing about twenty feet away and clutching a medium-size black briefcase, known as "the football." What is in the bag? The answer is classified, but over the years the public has learned that it is a mobile communications center locked into the American nuclear arsenal. Every minute of every day, the American president is steps away from a kit that would enable him or her to launch an attack that could obliterate any nation from the face of the earth.

Top Diplomat

The Constitution gives presidents the lead role in foreign affairs. Presidents and their international advisors set an overall framework

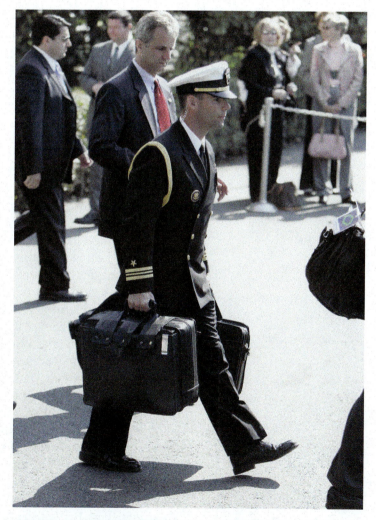

● *A uniformed officer with "the football"—a briefcase that contains launch codes for the nuclear arsenal. The football is never more than a few feet away from the president.*

Who Should Deploy American Troops?

The Constitution gives Congress the power to declare war and makes the president commander-in-chief. However, Congress has not declared war since 1941—the start of World War II. Since then, the United States has fought wars in Korea, Vietnam, the Persian Gulf, Kosovo, Afghanistan, Iraq, Syria, and more—without a congressional declaration. The War Powers Act only requires the president to seek approval sixty days after committing troops. Should the president have the power to dispatch troops without prior authorization from Congress?

Yes. Today, dangers arise in minutes, not months. Enemies have sophisticated weapons that can threaten the United States or its allies at any time. New surveillance techniques alert the executive about terrorists planning an operation, troops massing on a border, or unusual communications patterns. In the modern world, the United States cannot afford to leave decisions to deploy military power to the slow, partisan, very public congressional process.

No. The founders were clear that decisions over war and peace should be debated in Congress. This is one of the most important roles that Congress has and a public debate is crucial for democracy. Open public debate, caution, and the ability to hear all sides are just as important—perhaps even more important—than speed when it comes to deploying troops. Besides, giving the presidents this power makes it too easy to deploy America's powerful arsenal. Anyone who feels this section of the Constitution is out of date must follow the rules and propose a constitutional amendment.

for the U.S. role in the world. Some administrations emphasize international alliances; they work closely with foreign powers and build multinational institutions. Others prefer to go it alone—they ignore the United Nations and are reluctant to sign treaties for fear that they will bind the United States to foreign governments.

Foreign policy crises differ vastly from everyday domestic politics. Passing laws is a long, complicated process full of compromise and constraint. During international crises—hostage situations, terrorist attacks, the outbreak of war, or simply international negotiations—all eyes turn toward the president and his team. Often presidents must make fast decisions with immediate consequences. As Russian troops massed on Ukraine's border in February 2022, President Biden decided to share secret U.S. intelligence on likely Russian moves with Ukraine's leaders, U.S. allies, and then the media. When Russia invaded Ukraine, Biden was swift to denounce the act and delivered $9.8 billion in military aid in just six months.[17]

Foreign diplomacy is not just about trouble spots. The State Department manages more than 305 embassies, consulates, and diplomatic missions around the world. Presidents must hash out American relations with nearly two hundred nations that range from "special friends" to distant allies to avowed enemies. Intricate questions arise about how to approach each country: Should the president shake hands with our nation's enemies? Every smile or snub sends a diplomatic message. A president sets the tone and the policy for all these relationships.

Many presidents make minor blunders. When the newly elected President Obama met then–British Prime Minister Gordon Brown for the first time, the English press howled about "humiliation." Brown had given Obama a valuable pen carved from the timbers of a nineteenth-century British warship; Obama's gift was a pile of DVDs. In contrast, President Trump stunned allies and violated the polite language of classical diplomacy. He attacked the prime minister of Canada as "very dishonest and weak" and canceled a trip to "nasty" Denmark when its prime minister dismissed the idea of selling Greenland to the United States.[18] President Trump fundamentally reoriented foreign policy to serve what he argued was the economic best interests of the United States.

After World War II, American leaders from both parties built a web of alliances to promote Western and— sometimes—global interests: military alliances such as NATO, economic agreements to lower tariffs and facilitate free trade, and special accords on issues like climate change (the Paris

● *President Biden and the limits of personal diplomacy. Across forty years as an elected official, Biden connected personally with many world leaders. But his long association with Russian President Vladimir Putin, pictured here at a U.S.-Russia summit in 2021, did not improve relations between the two nations.*

Climate Accords). Promoting his America First policy, President Trump bluntly questioned whether many of these institutions serve U.S. interests.[19] President Biden, facing an international landscape altered by his predecessor, moved swiftly to repair alliances, reaffirm trade agreements, and restore treaties—an effort aided, as we shall see in Chapter 18, by unity among democratic countries in opposition to Russia's invasion of Ukraine. Still, there is a new wariness toward the United States in many capitals around the world as leaders wonder whether the renewed cooperation will last.

The First Legislator

The Constitution includes presidents in the legislative process. It authorizes them to *recommend measures* for Congress's "consideration," report to Congress *information on the state of the Union*, and *veto legislation* they oppose.

Recommending Measures. Until modern times, presidents generally avoided legislative affairs. In 1840, William Henry Harrison devoted his inaugural address—the longest and dullest in history—to denouncing the insatiable love of power creeping into the presidency. He pledged to honor congressional authority by avoiding legislative involvement. Dwight Eisenhower (1953–61) was the last president to try to leave legislation to Congress. His cabinet officers complained, and before long Eisenhower was recommending measures—and blasting Congress when it failed to approve them.

Today, presidential candidates define the legislative agenda. President Joe Biden's campaign priorities—economic stimulus for Americans reeling from two years of the COVID pandemic, addressing climate change, gun safety, and building bridges, broadband connections, and other U.S. infrastructure—were the main measures tackled by Congress across his first two years in office. Congressional leaders have their own lists.

But unexpected issues constantly spring up and sometimes press the administration in a new direction. Inflation, fueled by supply chain backlogs and Russia's invasion of Ukraine, soared to forty-year highs in 2022. The Biden administration recommended measures to lower costs of everything from energy to prescription drugs; as one headline blared, "Biden Aide Says Inflation Fight Can Advance if Congress Helps."[20] Presidents can help set Congress's agenda but cannot automatically push bills to passage—especially when the president's popularity sags.

State of the Union.   The Constitution invites the chief executive to report on the state of the Union "from time to time." Today, the "SOTU," as insiders term it, is an annual event, delivered with great fanfare before Congress, Supreme Court justices, cabinet members, and a national television audience. The speech announces the president's legislative program for the year.

Following the SOTU address, each program undergoes a second round of debates within the administration: Does it really fit our budget? Can we make it work smoothly? Did Congress cheer or yawn when the boss rolled it out? What was the public reaction? Most policies have friends and enemies in the administration—and if you get your favorite idea funded, I may not get mine. The process is a bureaucratic version of a knife fight. Proposals that survive go up to Capitol Hill, where they face the long, complicated congressional process we described in Chapter 13.

Presidential "Batting Average."   Only members of Congress can formally propose a law, so presidents rely on supporters in each chamber to submit their bills. The White House has a congressional liaison team to negotiate and cut deals. Generally hidden from public view, the liaison is a key role in the modern presidency. No matter how talented a liaison might be, frustration inevitably sets in. To the executive branch, legislators seem overly parochial as they focus on their states and districts. Still, most presidents quickly learn the same lesson: Work closely with Congress. Managing relations with House and Senate members is one of the most important presidential skills.

One measure of a president's success is their "batting average"—how many of their bills get through (Table 14.2). There are many different ways to keep score: successful passage as a proportion of all the bills the president endorses, of the most important bills, or of bills that the other party opposes. You can see that when the same party controls the White House and Congress, known as unified government, the batting average is much higher, usually around .800. When the opposition party controls Congress (divided government), the average usually falls below .500. Some political scientists have argued that divided government makes for a more effective legislative process. But notice how divided governments have been yielding less agreement in recent years. President Trump enjoyed the highest batting average in the past seventy-five years when both chambers were Republican—nosing out President Obama's first term when both chambers were Democratic. The lowest score in the past seventy-five years? President Trump's 13 percent, after the Democrats took back the House of Representatives.

Of the presidents since World War II, President John F. Kennedy signed the most legislation in his first year (684). Both Presidents Trump and Biden signed fewer than one hundred bills in their first years: Trump preferred executive orders to lobbying Congress, and the 117th Congress under Biden put multiple items in massive spending bills rather than passing separate pieces of legislation.[21]

Veto power: The presidential power to block an act of Congress by refusing to sign and returning it to Congress with objections.

Override: The process by which Congress can overcome a presidential veto with a two-thirds vote in both chambers.

Veto.   When Congress passes a law, presidents have the authority to sign or **veto** it (*veto* means "I forbid" in Latin). As we saw in the last chapter, a veto blocks the legislation unless two-thirds of both chambers vote to **override** it, a very high

| TABLE 14.2 | Presidential Batting Average: Measuring the Proportion of Congressional Bills on Which the President Took a Position That Passed |

PRESIDENT	PARTY	YEARS IN OFFICE	CONGRESSIONAL CONTROL	PERCENTAGE OF CONGRESSIONAL VOTES SUPPORTING PRESIDENT'S POSITION
Ronald Reagan***	R	1981–86	Mixed control (R Senate, D House)	67.4
Ronald Reagan**	R	1987–89	Democrats control Congress	45.4
George H. W. Bush**	R	1989–93	Democrats control Congress	51.8
Bill Clinton*	D	1993–94	Democrats control Congress	86.3
Bill Clinton**	D	1995–2000	Republicans control Congress	48.1
George W. Bush*	R	2001–6	Republicans control Congress	80.9
George W. Bush**	R	2007–8	Democrats control Congress	43.0
Barack Obama*	D	2009–10	Democrats control Congress	92.0
Barack Obama***	D	2011–14	Mixed control (D Senate, R House)	52.8
Barack Obama**	D	2015–16	Republicans control Congress	35.7
Donald Trump*	R	2017–18	Republicans control Congress	93.4
Donald Trump***	R	2019–20	Mixed control (R Senate, D House)	13
Joe Biden*	D	2021–22	Democrats control Congress	97.3 (for 2021)

President's party controls Congress.
**Opposition party controls Congress.*
***Congress split.*

bar. Presidents have ten days to return the legislation to Congress with a message explaining why they have rejected it. If the president does nothing, the bill becomes law in ten days—unless the congressional session has expired and the president's inaction kills the legislation, a move known as a "pocket veto."

The veto is a formidable weapon. In the last eighty years, presidents have rejected more than 1,400 bills. Congress managed to override just sixty times, a congressional "batting average" of 4 percent. Recently the veto has become a more partisan weapon, as conflict between the parties has escalated. Franklin D. Roosevelt, Harry Truman, and Jimmy Carter all flourished the veto pen against a Congress controlled by their own party; in their first two years, the three presidents struck down seventy-three, seventy-four, and nineteen, respectively. In contrast, presidents over the past thirty years—Clinton, Bush, Obama,

● *Across the ideological divide: President Ronald Reagan (a Republican) and Speaker of the House Tip O'Neill (D MA) negotiate the budget. "Maybe Tip and I told too many Irish stories," wrote Reagan in his diary after a long dinner together.*

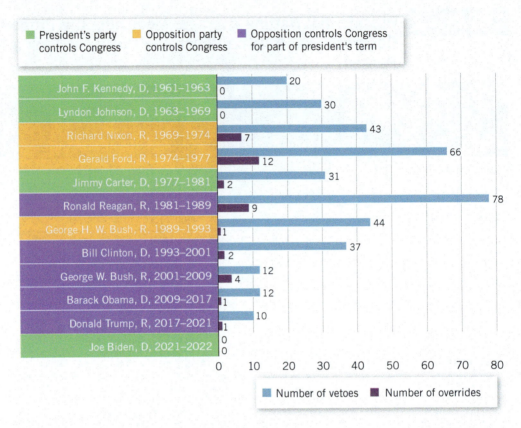

FIGURE 14.2 *Presidential vetoes and overrides. Note that vetoes were far more common thirty years ago, even when the same party controlled Congress and the White House. Congress rarely manages to override a presidential veto. (U.S. Senate)*

Trump, and Biden—have been far more sparing in their use of their veto power (see Figure 14.2).

A president's veto rarely comes as a surprise. As Congress works on a law, the president's congressional liaisons are ever present. Administration officials may threaten a veto to shape the legislation in ways they prefer. When negotiations get especially intense, the president can also go public and challenge individual members or Congress as a whole—in an effort to move the legislators along. Congressional leaders in turn can threaten to bury another bill the president wants or defy a president to veto popular bills. After all the back and forth, presidents have developed yet another strategy: They can voice their displeasure while signing bills into law.

Signing Statements.   Bill signing has become a great Washington ritual, especially for popular legislation. Congressional sponsors flank the president, who has a big pile of pens to hand out to the program's key supporters while cameras capture the smiling moment.

● *President Biden signs a $1.2 trillion infrastructure bill into law—surrounded by administration officials and congressional leaders of both parties.*

In recent decades, presidents have increasingly issued **signing statements** as they sign a bill into law. These statements may offer their administration's interpretation of the law—one sometimes at odds with Congress's expressed ideas.

Chief Bureaucrat

As chief bureaucrat, the president has the powers to make appointments and issue executive orders.

Appointments. The Constitution gives the president the power to appoint the men and women of the executive branch of government, subject to confirmation by the Senate. President Washington took the top officers of the major departments and organized them into a cabinet to advise him. By 1800, the executive branch comprised five departments and two hundred officeholders.[22]

Today, the executive branch includes fifteen departments and 2.7 million employees—a number that has leveled off in recent years; add the military, and the executive branch tops four million. Presidents appoint some four thousand **political appointees** who direct the executive agencies; the rest are **civil servants** who stay on from one administration to the next (all discussed in Chapter 15).

The Trump administration shattered one record: Ten cabinet secretaries were fired or resigned in the first three years. By one count, 92 percent of the Trump administration's top staff—the A team—had left or been fired before the end of his single term; that's nearly 650 departures of the top 700-plus positions. In more than 150 cases, the Trump team simply never nominated anyone for top jobs across cabinet departments. (We'll explore this issue in Chapter 15.) The administration's supporters cheered the full-throttle, take-no-prisoners approach to governing. Others worried that large organizations like cabinet agencies suffer when there is rapid turnover at the top.[23] When the COVID-19 pandemic hit the United States, for example, the lack of experienced leadership in multiple agencies—from Homeland Security (which had five directors in three years) to the Food and Drug Administration (where the director turned over just as the epidemic hit the United States)—created frustrating delays in getting reliable tests, ordering equipment, and deploying resources. When President Biden took office, he appointed 319 senior civil-service officers in his first three months—more than twice the rate of any of his predecessors; even so, after 20 months, the administration had not yet filled 226 of its top 800 positions.[24]

Executive Orders. As chief executive, presidents wield powers that do not need to go through Congress. They can sign **executive orders**, with the force of law, setting guidelines for federal agencies. Most executive orders specify the details needed to implement acts of Congress. Some are simply instructions for operating the executive branch: setting up a new council or office, for example. Others involve controversial decisions. They can be issued with fanfare or executed secretly. Recent executive orders include securing LGBTQ+ rights, embracing science to combat climate change, prohibit U.S. companies' investment in Russia, forgiving some student loans, and strengthening access to affordable healthcare.

Some presidential scholars suggest that executive orders are unconstitutional—the Constitution never mentions them. However, courts generally permit the orders as part of the "inherent powers" of the presidency.[25] Before the Biden administration, the Supreme Court had struck down only eleven executive orders—five of Franklin Roosevelt's, two of Bill Clinton's, one of Barack Obama's, and three of Donald Trump's—out of more than fourteen thousand going back to the Washington administration.

Signing statements: Written presidential declarations commenting on the bill that is being signed into law—often including criticism of one or more provisions.

Political appointees: Top officials in the executive agencies, appointed by the president.

Civil servants: Members of the permanent executive branch bureaucracy who are employed on the basis of competitive exams and keep their positions regardless of the presidential administration.

Executive order: A presidential declaration, with the force of law, that issues instructions to the executive branch without any requirement for congressional action or approval.

Contemporary administrations had been issuing between thirty and forty executive orders a year. President Trump averaged fifty-five orders per year, the most since Jimmy Carter forty years earlier. The Trump administration used executive orders to undo Obama's executive orders on immigrants brought to the United States as children, the "Dreamers" (at least temporarily blocked by the Supreme Court); to alter regulations for Obamacare; to cap refugees coming to the United States; to stop immigration from specific (mainly Muslim) nations; to ban transgender people from the military (overruled by the Supreme Court); to restrict environmental reviews on infrastructure projects; to form (and then disband) a voter fraud commission; and to bar tax authorities from imposing penalties on clergy members who endorse political candidates. After President Biden took over in 2021, he continued the high pace, averaging more than sixty executive orders per year—many of them overturning orders of his predecessor.

Some observers charge that, once again, Congress is steadily losing authority. Presidents—from both parties—use a traditional form of executive power to expand the scope of their office. More and more, worry the critics, they bypass Congress and make policy from the White House—and Congress, marked by partisan stalemate, has been slow to respond.[26] There is, however, an inherent weakness in governing by executive order: They are much easier for an incoming administration to repeal and replace than an act of Congress.

Economist-in-Chief

Economic authority is one item the Constitution definitely does *not* grant the president. It places the power of the purse—taxing, spending, borrowing, and regulating commerce—firmly in congressional hands. However, during the Great Depression of the 1930s, the Roosevelt administration seized responsibility for putting the nation back to work, launching one recovery program after another. "Take a method and try it," insisted Roosevelt. "If that fails, try another. . . . Above all try something."[27]

The idea soon took root: The president was responsible for a healthy economy. The year after Roosevelt died, Congress legislated the Council of Economic Advisers (CEA) to help presidents oversee the economy. Today, the president and a small army of officials monitor economic conditions. White House economists vet every plan and proposal for its impact on American prosperity; they help formulate policy on almost every issue—taxing, spending, trade deals, and the projected costs of a new federal holiday. Every new administration crowds more economists into its ranks. Presidential popularity and, as we saw in Chapter 10, the party's chances of holding onto the office in the next election are heavily influenced by economic conditions.

During the Biden administration's first year, in 2021, the U.S. economy grew 5.7 percent—the fastest increase since 1984. As always, credit went to the administration in power. Partly the economic boom owed to nearly $6 trillion in government stimulus spending, as the nation began to recover from COVID shutdowns. President Biden took a visible role as the American economy's chief steward, publishing a *Wall Street Journal* op-ed that claimed, "When I took office, the economy had stalled." He cheered his administration's performance on deficit reduction and dramatic declines in unemployment as leading "the most robust recovery in modern history."[28]

Even as Biden wrote, however, economic conditions were shifting fast, with inflation—higher prices for goods and services—spiraling upward at a rate not seen in nearly forty years. By summer 2022, Americans' outlook on the economy was dismal, hitting a new low in a national survey of economic sentiment that

Executive Orders Issued, Total and Per Year

Which Presidents Relied Most on This Power?

All presidents issue executive orders. Notice that the three presidents who issued the most orders include two progressive reformers (Roosevelt, Wilson) and a conservative trying to reduce the role of government (Coolidge).

Some executive orders simply direct agencies in implementing laws that Congress has passed. Others introduce new programs that Congress refused to pass.

THINK ABOUT IT

Should presidents hold this autonomous power to act through executive orders, or does it violate the spirit (and perhaps the letter) of the Constitution?

Does a gridlocked Congress make the practice necessary? Or will it lead to an overly active government?

Source: Statista

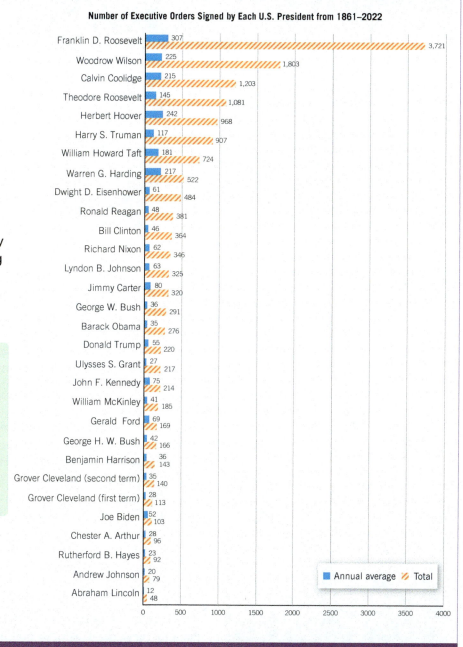

Number of Executive Orders Signed by Each U.S. President from 1861–2022

President	Annual average	Total
Franklin D. Roosevelt	307	3,721
Woodrow Wilson	225	1,803
Calvin Coolidge	215	1,203
Theodore Roosevelt	145	1,081
Herbert Hoover	242	968
Harry S. Truman	117	907
William Howard Taft	181	724
Warren G. Harding	217	522
Dwight D. Eisenhower	61	484
Ronald Reagan	48	381
Bill Clinton	46	364
Richard Nixon	62	346
Lyndon B. Johnson	63	325
Jimmy Carter	80	320
George W. Bush	36	291
Barack Obama	35	276
Donald Trump	55	220
Ulysses S. Grant	27	217
John F. Kennedy	75	214
William McKinley	41	185
Gerald Ford	69	169
George H. W. Bush	42	166
Benjamin Harrison	36	143
Grover Cleveland (second term)	35	140
Grover Cleveland (first term)	28	113
Joe Biden	52	103
Chester A. Arthur	28	96
Rutherford B. Hayes	23	92
Andrew Johnson	20	79
Abraham Lincoln	12	48

went all the way back to the early 1950s. Why the dramatic reversal? High oil and food prices tied to the Russian invasion of Ukraine in early 2022 and continuing problems with global supply chains—how goods move around the world—tied to COVID interruptions. But good, bad, or in between—the president gets credit or blame for an economy that is often beyond the president's control.

The president as head of state. President Bill Clinton and First Lady Hillary Clinton wear traditional kente cloth as they wave to thousands of cheering Ghanaians. With them is then-president of Ghana, Jerry Rawlings.

The Head of State

Most nations have a ceremonial head of state who stands above partisan politics and represents the nation. The king of England, the emperor of Japan, and the president of Israel all play this nonpolitical role while their prime ministers make the policies that govern their countries. Citizens of the British Isles do not need to check their political affiliation when they sing "God Save the King"—Charles III represents them across the political spectrum. In contrast, the presidents of the United States play both roles. They stand for the nation even while they fight for one party.

Presidents spend a lot of time in their ceremonial role. They throw out the first pitch during the World Series, spare a turkey every Thanksgiving, light the White House Christmas tree and menorah, smash a bottle of champagne across the bow of a new aircraft carrier, congratulate national heroes, host championship sports teams, and embody America every time the Marine Corps Band plays "Hail to the Chief." When presidents travel abroad, they generally try to represent all Americans, not just their party or their supporters. The problem is that this role often clashes with the next one, the party leader.

Party Leader

George Washington repeatedly warned the country against political parties and the strife they bring. However, by his second term, rival parties were not so quietly emerging and they eventually thrust yet another role onto the president: party leader. This role sharpens the tension we described in the last section. There is a very fine line between leading the nation (and standing for everyone) and leading the Republicans (which means defeating Democrats).

Can anything tamp down the partisan conflict? Yes: The secret ingredient is fear. When a president grows very popular, opponents will often go along out of fear that the voters might punish them if they do not. Presidents who get more votes in a district than a House member, or more votes in the state than a senator, can be very persuasive—as long as their poll numbers remain high.

The Bully Pulpit: Introducing Ideas

President Theodore Roosevelt was bursting with ideas, opinions, exhortations, and warnings. He called the presidency itself a "bully pulpit" (today we might say "awesome brand multiplier"). Roosevelt knew that an active president has the country's ear, an opening to introduce and promote new ideas.

Most presidencies are marked by a few big ideas. In his inaugural address, John F. Kennedy called the nation to public service. "Ask

Theodore Roosevelt takes full advantage of his bully pulpit.

not what your country can do for you," said Kennedy. "Ask what you can do for your country." As the second-youngest president in history (after Theodore Roosevelt), Kennedy projected youthful energy and vigor. The president's ideas seemed part and parcel of the man himself. Ronald Reagan championed a very different idea when he called government the source of our national problems; individuals pursuing the American dream and trying to get rich were, he declared, the real source of national vitality. Successful presidents arrive in office with powerful ideas—and persuade the public to embrace new visions of our political life.

A sign of a fading party is a cupboard bare of ideas. When Jimmy Carter won the White House in 1976, a member of his transition team wrote a strange memo. The new administration, he said, must educate its appointees about President-elect Carter's "goals and philosophy." The Democrats of that era were so vague about their ideas that the president's staff thought it necessary to instruct its troops about what their new leader stood for—even after a long election campaign.[29]

"The power of the presidency," as political scientist Richard Neustadt famously put it, "is the power to persuade."[30] Neustadt was thinking about the president persuading members of the Washington establishment, but the role involves much more. Persuasion involves the ability to put something new before the public, the power to take an unfamiliar notion and get the whole nation to talk about it. Throughout this book, we have focused on the power and importance of ideas in American politics. The presidency is the institution best geared to inject new ideas into our great national conversation.

The Impossible Job

How can anyone juggle so many different presidential roles? The honest answer is that no one can. Even great presidents cannot handle all their jobs well all of the time. Still, this is what we demand of our chief executive.

Each presidential role requires different strengths and skills. No person will have them all. The bully pulpit can help: Bold ideas bring together the many threads of this huge task. They make a presidency coherent. Without that, presidents may seem overwhelmed by the job, skittering from one task to another without a broader sense of purpose or vision.

Finally, note one theme that runs through every role: Presidential authority has grown in every aspect of the office. The president's many roles are one more way to measure the swelling power and importance of the office. That brings us back again to the central paradox of the executive: The presidency grows ever more powerful, yet the role has grown so large that no one person can perform every aspect of it well.

THE BOTTOM LINE

» The president wears many hats and helmets. Some are specified in the Constitution. Others have developed over time.

» Presidential roles include commander-in-chief, top diplomat, first legislator, head bureaucrat, economist-in-chief, head of state, and party leader. Presidents also are uniquely situated to introduce new ideas—tying together these many different roles.

» The president's authority has expanded over time in every one of these roles. And yet it is difficult to do so many different things effectively.

Presidential Leadership: Success and Failure in the Oval Office

Presidents try to manage perceptions of their performance. They address the public, use (and bypass) the media, schedule eye-catching events, and rely on polls to hone their message. How do we know if they have succeeded? We will examine three different measures of presidential achievement: polls, historical rankings, and the great cycles of political time.

Managing the Public

As the only nationally elected official (excepting the vice president, who is elected as a package with the president), presidents develop a relationship with the people, which they cultivate by **going public**—directly addressing citizens to win support. Each new form of communication—radio, television, social media—shifts the way presidents go public.

John F. Kennedy demonstrated the full power of the media when he held the first live, televised press conference in February 1961. It was a smash hit, with sixty-five million viewers; Kennedy's approval ratings climbed to 75 percent and stayed high for sixteen months. Kennedy had shifted how presidents connect to the public: People saw him, heard him, and related to him directly. Few people gave Donald Trump much chance in the 2016 Republican primary, much less the general election. What did they overlook? His savvy in going public and dominating media coverage.

Today, presidents continue to look for ways to connect with Americans. They give campaign speeches before large crowds—even when the next election is years away. They speak directly to the camera from the Oval Office. Their office tweets supporters. You can follow them on social media. Each of these actions is an effort to win the public over—sometimes for a specific policy, sometimes for a broad presidential agenda.

Presidents deploy an entire office that directs their public outreach—and their strategies are always changing. Presidents constantly balance going public with playing "the inside game"—quietly working with Congress and the bureaucracy to get things done. Which is more effective? That depends on the time and circumstance. But every president—going public or playing the inside game—works to shape public perceptions.[31]

Images are often more important than words. Presidents hug disaster victims, play basketball with the troops, or wave to cheering throngs. The image can turn negative in an instant. President Johnson playfully lifted his beagle by the ears in front of the press (cruel!). President Ford slipped and fell in public (clumsy!). President George H. W. Bush threw up at a state dinner in Japan (you can imagine!). In a complicated world, a single picture can distill popular perception. Images have an impact—positive or negative—when they seem to reveal the president's true strengths or weaknesses. The key point is simple: *Presidents constantly try to manage their image in the public eye.*[32]

Our 24/7 media era, described in Chapter 9, complicates the effort to touch the public. Today the sheer volume of information flowing through the media means that only the most important events will command attention for long. The president's message now requires constant repetition, amplification, and—to grip viewers—a touch of novelty and drama. Going public is a rapidly changing art form.

Going public: Directly addressing the public to win support for oneself or one's ideas.

● *Lyndon Johnson lifting his beagle by the ears. The president was trying for a lighthearted moment but quickly felt the backlash from outraged pet lovers.*

The White House runs a sophisticated polling operation that guides its outreach efforts. The president's daily schedule frequently includes briefings from the administration's pollster. The president's team scrutinizes the findings, not to develop new policies but to recalibrate the ways it presents its message. President Trump proved especially adept at bending the news cycle with his tweets—to the delight of some and the chagrin of others.[33] President Biden's social media messages are much more disciplined, but (perhaps as a result) attract far fewer followers.

Some political scientists caution that it is very difficult to move public opinion. The bully pulpit is most powerful, suggested political scientist George Edwards, when presidents recognize and exploit changes that are already in the political air.[34]

WHAT DO YOU THINK?

Go Public or Play the Inside Game

| Pick an issue you care about: immigration or climate change or something else. Now, what would you advise the president to emphasize? | **Go public.** In this era, presidencies are almost like social movements— keep your supporters mobilized. | **Play the inside game.** To really make progress, you have to work quietly with individual members of Congress and the bureaucracy. | **Do both.** Of course, every president does both, but on most issues they must stress one or the other. |

Approval Ratings

Every week, another wave of polls reports how Americans view the president's performance. These are used widely, inside and beyond Washington, as a rough barometer of the administration's success. Any one poll can be misleading (as we saw in Chapter 7), but if you eliminate the outliers—the occasional polls that are much higher and lower than the others—and scan the rest, you will have a snapshot of the administration's ratings that are reverberating through the media and around Washington.

A president riding high in the polls finds governing easier. Members of Congress watch the president's popularity in their own states and districts and think twice about opposing them. As the president's approval sinks, criticism rises. Congressional allies back away. Press coverage turns sour. The late-night talk shows serve up an extra dose of mockery.

Most administrations run through polling cycles; no president stays above 50 percent approval for an entire term. Average out differences across administrations and roughly the same pattern generally emerges: high approval scores at the start, usually above 60 percent; a slow decline that bottoms out midway through the second year (see Figure 14.3); a gradual ascent and peak toward the end of the fourth year. With luck, it rises above 50 percent in time for reelection. Then a dip after reelection and a rise at the end.[35]

Dramatic events create spikes in approval (or disapproval). The two highest ratings on record reflected boosts for George H. W. Bush after a quick, dramatic victory in the First Gulf War, and for his son George W. Bush after he responded

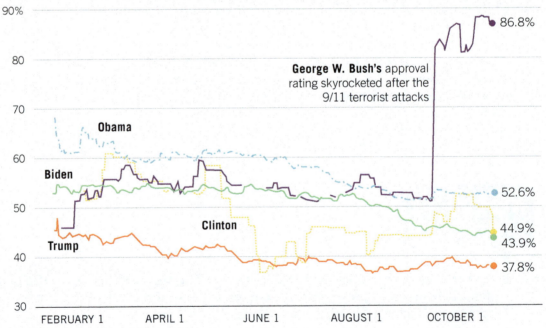

Job Approval Ratings for Presidents' First Nine Months in Office, 1993–2021

George W. Bush's approval rating skyrocketed after the 9/11 terrorist attacks

86.8%
52.6%
44.9%
43.9%
37.8%

The first data point for each president reflects when there was enough polling data to produce an average. Polling data for Biden runs through October 20, 2021.

● **FIGURE 14.3** *A repeating pattern: Public approval generally declines during a president's first nine months. Note the exception: George W. Bush's approval skyrocketed after the 9/11 terrorist attacks. (FiveThirtyEight)*

to terrorist attacks on the World Trade Center in September 2001 by standing defiantly on the rubble with a bullhorn, surrounded by cheering firefighters and cleanup crews.

Each Bush peaked at an 89 percent approval rating in Gallup polls. Such spikes in popularity are usually temporary. A year after his military triumph, George H. W. Bush's approval rating had fallen below 40 percent, and he lost his reelection campaign. The younger Bush narrowly won reelection but ended his time in office tied for the lowest ratings of all modern presidents after a full term.

Recently, the cycles have grown less pronounced. President Trump, for example, remained stuck between roughly 38 percent and 44 percent approval—an unusually narrow band. His approval numbers among Republicans remained sky high—and forestalled any Republican primary opposition; but his overall approval

● George W. Bush visits the scene of the 9/11 World Trade Center attack. The dramatic days following the attack drove President Bush's approval ratings to one of the highest levels recorded by Gallup. They soon fell back down again.

ratings remained low—43 percent as people went to the polls in November—and he lost his reelection race to Joe Biden. Trump's low point came after the January 6, 2021, Capitol insurrection, when his ratings fell to 34 percent. President Biden began at a high of 57 percent, fell under 50 percent in late July 2021, and remained stuck in the 40s—quite close to the Trump average—for more than a year.

Polls offer immediate public feedback, but they do not reflect an administration's historical importance or long-term success. For that we can turn to a different type of poll.

Presidential Greatness

Back in 1948, historian Arthur Schlesinger Sr. asked a panel of historians to rank the presidents. Their choice for the top three: Abraham Lincoln, George Washington, and Franklin D. Roosevelt.

Poll after poll followed—we list four different versions in Table 14.3. In each, a different panel of historians and political scientists ranks the presidents in order from great to failed.

Liberals and conservatives rarely disagree about how the presidents rank. Ronald Reagan is an exception, though his ratings from left-leaning scholars have climbed in recent polls. Such agreement returns us to the question: What makes a great president?

There are plenty of answers. President Harry Truman said that all the great presidents were especially decisive. Political scientists Marc Landy and Sidney Milkis suggested that great presidents redefine the presidency. Our view is that great presidents redefine America; they reshape the way the nation sees itself. Or, to put it slightly differently, *great presidents tell us who we are*. Their definitions of America resonate with the public and endure over time.[36]

TABLE 14.3 Rating the Presidents

Here are the results of four independent polls by historians and political scientists (you can find dozens of them). Historian Arthur Schlesinger polled historians in 1948; his son Arthur Schlesinger Jr. repeated the exercise with historians and political scientists in 1996; the United Kingdom Center for the United States Presidency (USPC) provided rankings from a foreign scholarly perspective; and C-SPAN conducted a survey in 2021.

	POLITICAL PARTY	SCHLESINGER (1948)	SCHLESINGER JR. (1996)	USPC (2011)	C-SPAN (2021)
George Washington	Federalist	2	2	3	2
John Adams	Federalist	9	11	12	15
Thomas Jefferson	Dem-Repub.	5	4	4	7
James Madison	Dem-Repub.	14	17	14	16
James Monroe	Dem-Repub.	12	15	13	12
John Q. Adams	Dem-Repub.	11	18	20	17
Andrew Jackson	Democratic	6	5	9	22
Martin Van Buren	Democratic	15	21	27	34
William H. Harrison	Whig	—	—	—	40
John Tyler	Whig	22	32	37	39
James K. Polk	Democratic	10	9	16	18
Zachary Taylor	Whig	25	29	33	35
Millard Fillmore	Whig	24	31	35	38
Franklin Pierce	Democratic	27	33	39	42
James Buchanan	Democratic	26	38	40	44
Abraham Lincoln	Republican	1	1	2	1
Andrew Johnson	Democratic	19	37	36	43
Ulysses Grant	Republican	28	24	29	20
Rutherford Hayes	Republican	13	23	30	33
James Garfield	Republican	—	—	—	27
Chester Arthur	Republican	17	26	32	30
Grover Cleveland	Democratic	8	13	21	25
Benjamin Harrison	Republican	21	19	34	32
William McKinley	Republican	18	16	17	14
Theodore Roosevelt	Republican	7	6	5	4
William H. Taft	Republican	16	22	25	23
Woodrow Wilson	Democratic	4	7	6	13
Warren Harding	Republican	29	39	38	37
Calvin Coolidge	Republican	23	30	28	24
Herbert Hoover	Republican	20	35	26	36
Franklin D. Roosevelt	Democratic	3	3	1	3

TABLE 14.3 (continued)					
	POLITICAL PARTY	SCHLESINGER (1948)	SCHLESINGER JR. (1996)	USPC (2011)	C-SPAN (2021)
Harry Truman	Democratic	—	8	7	6
Dwight D. Eisenhower	Republican	—	10	10	5
John F. Kennedy	Democratic	—	12	15	8
Lyndon B. Johnson	Democratic	—	14	11	11
Richard Nixon	Republican	—	36	23	31
Gerald Ford	Republican	—	28	24	28
Jimmy Carter	Democratic	—	27	18	26
Ronald Reagan	Republican	—	25	8	9
George H. W. Bush	Republican	—	24	22	21
Bill Clinton	Democratic	—	20	19	19
George W. Bush	Republican	—	—	31	29
Barack Obama	Democratic	—	—	—	10
Donald Trump	Republican	—	—	—	41

Greatness in Context: The Rise and Fall of Political Orders

Presidents are not masters of their destiny. The times make the presidents as much as presidents make the times. Individual presidents fit into national cycles of politics and power. Presidential scholar Stephen Skowronek described each presidency as part of a great historical pageant: the rise and fall of **political orders**. A political order is a set of ideas, institutions, and coalitions that dominates an era.[37] In Skowronek's telling, orders rise and fall in three steps. Every president fits somewhere in the cycle.

Political order: The set of institutions, interests, and ideas that shape a political era. Great presidents reconstruct the framework, launching a new order.

Step 1: A New Order Rises. Outstanding leaders take over the presidency and shake up the political system. An Abraham Lincoln, Franklin D. Roosevelt, or Ronald Reagan introduces a fresh philosophy of government. He leads a political party with new allies and new ideas into power. The public responds enthusiastically to this bold break with old political ways.

Step 2: The Order Refreshed. Every governing coalition eventually grows tired. The great president who boldly articulated its themes is gone. Many of the original goals are won. New problems arise that have nothing to do with the philosophy that fired up the party in the first place. The ideas begin to look out of date; the great coalition begins to unravel. If a party is lucky, a new leader will come along and infuse the party with a fresh variation of the old philosophy, renewing the aging order.

Step 3: The Old Order Crumbles. No order lasts forever. Over time, the party finds its ideas increasingly irrelevant. The old order feels outdated, a political dinosaur.

Every president comes to Washington with fresh hope and promise. Political historians look back and see that each operates within a cycle. Some (Lincoln, Roosevelt, Reagan) take office as the head of a new coalition with fresh ideas. If the rival party comes to power when the order is still strong, they will usually bend to its assumptions and general outlook. Others come to Washington at the end of an era (Herbert Hoover, Jimmy Carter). They face a far more difficult governing challenge. To some extent, the rankings we see in Table 14.3 reflect each president's place in political time.

Political historians are already speculating about Donald Trump and Joe Biden's places in the historical cycle. Did Trump create a new order different from what went before, reinventing what it is to be a Republican? Was Biden the last of a dying order—or refreshing an order begun by Barack Obama, whom Biden served as vice president? What do you think?

THE BOTTOM LINE

» Presidents try to manage public perceptions of the job they are doing. They get immediate feedback from polls. A president's place in history, however, does not emerge right away.

» Great presidents change the way Americans see themselves. They change what government does. They forge a new answer to the question, *Who are we?*

» Individual presidents don't completely control their own destiny. They operate in the historical cycle of political orders.

The Personal Presidency

In at least one respect, the presidency is very simple: It is always about one individual. At the heart of the enterprise stands a person with strengths and weaknesses, quirks and foibles. The personalities of our presidents have imprinted their administrations in many ways, big and small.

Presidential Style

James Madison was just a bit over five feet tall and weighed less than one hundred pounds. He wore tall hats to add height, dressed entirely in black, and never owned more than one suit at a time. He was both diminutive and timid. Early historians blasted him for his cautious leadership during the War of 1812. But scholars have warmed to Madison. Historians now believe that the war helped define America as a united nation. Madison was guided by a fierce attachment to the Constitution that he had drafted. Who better than a small, shy, modest man in black to avoid too much "personality" in the presidency?

Or take some darker personal qualities . . .

Secluded in his hideaway office across the street from the White House, the fireplace crackling as the air conditioner hummed, Richard Nixon scribbled on yellow legal pads into the night. He was brilliant—and paranoid. Nixon usually dealt directly with just four or five aides; their job was to keep others away from the boss. Sitting alone, writing away on his yellow pads, he dreamed up remarkable ideas.

At the time, the United States was locked in a cold war with two great communist powers, Russia and China. Nixon calculated that our two enemies were bitterly opposed to one another. He negotiated secretly with China. When the Russians discovered the thaw between China and the United States, they feared being left out. They too pursued closer relations with the United States. Nixon had invented a way to ratchet down the bitter cold war by playing off our enemies against one another.

Nixon also cooked up a national health insurance plan that serves as a model (for Democrats) to the present day. But, sitting alone and often drinking heavily into the night, he also stoked the personal demons that ultimately cost him the White House.

Or consider a very different political genius . . .

Ronald Reagan loved to tell stories. He told them to make a point, to deflect people from saying things he did not want to hear, to reorient a conversation that was going the wrong way, or, well, just because he loved telling them. "He could drive you crazy [telling] . . . the same stories over and over again," reported Congressman Dan Rostenkowski (D-IL). "He really made no show whatsoever of listening to arguments. . . . He saw reality not as a thing to bow to, but a thing that could be changed and shaped."[38]

Was it really true that, during World War II, army bureaucrats granted Reagan's unit permission to destroy a warehouse full of useless files, "provided copies are made of each paper destroyed"? Who knows? The parable was irresistible: Government bureaucracies choke the life out of any enterprise.[39]

Such tall tales went to the heart of Reagan's successes and failures as president. He focused on parables rather than policies. His airy indifference to the analytic world of evidence and arguments freed him to repeat his handful of moral lessons, impressing them on American discourse. Such tales helped him reframe American politics in terms of a more rugged individualism that scorned handouts and collective action. He made it work because he wrapped that individualism in a nostalgic vision of America.

Madison's republican simplicity, Nixon's brilliance and paranoia, and Reagan's pointed storytelling and gauzy vision of American free enterprise all shaped the way they governed and the mark they left. This kind of territory used to be the province of historians and anthropologists, not political scientists. But we know that it is vital to acknowledge—and study—the personal dimension of the presidency.[40]

The Burden of the Office

For another truth about the presidency, compare photographs of almost any president at the start and then at the end of their

● *Ronald Reagan: This sunny, folksy, patriotic, old-fashioned storyteller introduced a new conservative era.*

● *Young man, older man: Barack Obama as president-elect and late in his presidency.*

time in office: It is an exhausting job that takes a visible toll on the incumbents. Fourteen presidents and former presidents died during the twentieth century; eleven passed away prematurely. Presidents before they take office usually appear young, handsome, and smiling; by the time they step down, they often look care-worn and gray.[41]

These morbid health statistics remind us that the Oval Office houses a vulnerable human being. Presidents get sick, take dubious drugs, get drunk, overeat, have affairs, contemplate suicide, fret about ailing parents, and burn with insecurities. None can escape the human condition. All wrestle with an extremely difficult job.

Presidents are usually very politically and personally talented—or they would not have gotten to the White House. As with all people, however, they have strengths and weaknesses, skills and blind spots.[42] Confronting these personal limits returns us to a central question of this chapter: Has the presidency developed too much power for any one person to handle?

THE BOTTOM LINE

» Although presidential scholars generally focus on ideas and institutions, the presidency also has an important personal dimension.

» All presidents exhibit a distinctive personal style.

» Presidents are limited human beings with strengths and weaknesses. That is precisely why the Constitution located the office in an intricate system of checks and balances.

The President's Team: A Tour of the White House

When Herbert Hoover moved into the Oval Office in 1929, he presided over a presidential staff of four administrative assistants, plus thirty-six typists, clerks, and messengers. That was it. No speechwriter, no press secretary, no congressional liaison; no chief of staff, no drug czar, no budget director. Today, the presidency is more than a person or an idea or a party. It is a bureaucracy staffed by thousands of people.

The Political Solar System: Presidential Appointments

Every time a new president is elected, hopes spread across the country. University professors who have always dreamed of government service, college students who worked on the campaign, business executives looking for a plum position on their résumé, and supporters who believe the president-elect will make America a better place: All want to work for the new administration.

To get a job in the executive branch, do not start by being modest. You must campaign. One executive angling to be a senior Treasury Department official some years back tasked four subordinates to do nothing but promote his name to the team in charge of selecting top appointees (yes, he got the job).

Let us take a tour of the offices working directly for the president. A crucial opening point: Power is always measured by proximity to the Oval Office. The executive branch is like the solar system, with the president as the sun and everyone else rotating around him. The most impressive thing you can say in Washington, DC: "When I was talking to the president yesterday. . . ." Most people who work for the president are in an orbit somewhere past Pluto: They never get any face time. Let us look at who does.

The Vice President

Traditionally, the vice president's primary job was to stand in the wings in case the president died. That awful transition has happened eight times in American history, four times by murder. There were at least four more close calls: Assassins fired point-blank at Andrew Jackson (the gun jammed), Franklin D. Roosevelt (the shooter missed the president and killed the mayor of Chicago), Gerald Ford (a bystander grabbed the gunwoman's arm, diverting the shot), and Ronald Reagan (the bullet lodged less than an inch from his heart).

Besides standing by in case of catastrophe, vice presidents preside over the Senate and cast a vote in case of a tie. (With a Senate split 50-50 during President Biden's first two years, Vice President Kamala Harris broke more Senate ties than all but two other vice presidents.)

Otherwise, a vice president's responsibilities are entirely up to the president. For a long time, the role was meager. Senator Daniel Webster rejected the vice presidential nomination in 1848 with an acid comment: "I do not choose to be buried until I am really dead."[43] Bad move: Webster would have become the thirteenth president when Zachary Taylor died in the White House. Franklin D. Roosevelt's first vice president, John Nance Garner, offered an infamous assessment of the post when he said the job was "not worth a pitcher of warm piss."[44]

The weak vice presidency continued well into the twentieth century. Harry Truman had barely met with President Roosevelt when FDR's death in 1945 catapulted him into the Oval Office. "Boys," he said when he met the press the next day, "if you ever pray, pray for me now." In 1960, reporters asked President Eisenhower

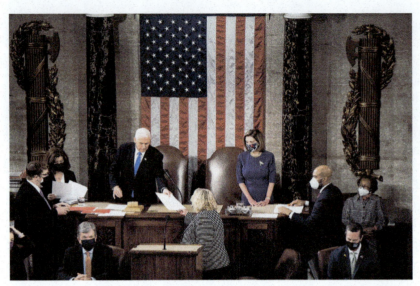

January 6, 2021. Vice President Mike Pence carries out a ceremonial vice presidential duty: presiding over the electoral-vote count for president. This time, President Trump called on him to break with all precedent and block certification of Joe Biden's Electoral College victory. Pence refused amid an attack on the Capitol unprecedented in U.S. history.

what ideas Vice President Nixon had contributed after eight years in the post. "If you give me a week," quipped the president nastily, "I might think of one."[45]

The vice presidency became important during the Carter administration (1977–81). From Carter through Trump, six of eight presidents were Washington outsiders who had never held a federal job; every newcomer chose an experienced Washington hand as his vice president, relying on them as advisors, envoys, and (in Mike Pence's case) fundraisers. Slowly, vice presidents gathered the emblems of power: a seat at cabinet meetings (1950s), an office in the White House (1970s), a vice presidential jet (Air Force 2, in the 1970s), a growing staff, and—perhaps most important in status-obsessed Washington—regular meetings with the president.[46]

The Cabinet

Members of the cabinet have two primary roles: They run executive branch departments, and they meet to discuss policy with the president in cabinet meetings. Once the cabinet served as a president's governing team. Washington's initial cabinet had four members. Today, there are fifteen members; add the vice president and other important presidential staff officers, and meetings are too large to serve as a real decision-making body. We discuss the cabinet, and the hundreds of thousands of federal bureaucrats who work under cabinet secretaries in the executive agencies, in Chapter 15.

In most administrations, a handful of cabinet officers rise above the rest and shape administration policy. Political scientists call them the "inner cabinet": usually, the secretaries of state, defense, the treasury, and justice—precisely the quartet in Washington's original cabinet. Most other cabinet secretaries operate far from the centers of power. Departments such as Transportation and Energy have vital roles to play. But unless the "outer cabinet" secretaries have personal connections, they are rarely part of a president's closest circle of advisors.

Cabinet secretaries often come to see issues from the perspective of their own bureaucracy rather than that of the administration or the party. After all, they are surrounded by tens of thousands of employees who do a lot of work with limited resources and look to the secretary to champion their causes. Richard Nixon's close advisor John Ehrlichman groused that the administration chose solid, budget-cutting conservatives to run the cabinet departments, and then watched them run off and "marry the natives"—a sarcastic way of saying they saw things through the eyes of their departments, pushing for big budgets and more personnel.[47] President Biden, aiming to secure loyalty across the bureaucracy, placed seasoned professionals in executive departments—many of whom had, like Biden, served in the Obama administration. He also removed an unprecedented number of President Trump's appointments to independent agencies, such as the National

Labor Relations Board general counsel and the head of the Social Security Administration.[48]

Presidents must manage the tension between senior cabinet officials and the circle of presidential advisors in the White House. At one cabinet meeting during the Carter years, the secretary of Housing and Urban Development summed up her frustration by blurting out: "We can move government forward by putting phones in the White House staff offices and then using them." Translation: No one in the White House even returns my phone calls. The president's inner circle had shifted from the cabinet to the White House staff.[49]

The Executive Office of the President

Influence over government policy has leaked steadily into the **Executive Office of the President** (**EOP**), made up of agencies that help a president manage the president's daily activities. These administrators and advisors surround the chief executive. President Franklin D. Roosevelt organized the EOP in 1939; it now has about 1,800 employees. Many are experts who stay on from one administration to the next. Presidents who have been most adamant about expanding the EOP are conservatives frustrated that the cabinet agencies did not pursue their values. Richard Nixon created or revamped four of the EOP offices; Ronald Reagan added three more. Today, every president—left, right, or center—relies on them.

Table 14.4 illustrates the offices in the EOP. The list reflects the hats and helmets that the president wears. Organizing a new EOP office or an office within

Executive Office of the President (EOP): The agencies that help the president manage daily activities.

TABLE 14.4 Offices in the Executive Office of the President, 2022

OFFICE	YEAR ORGANIZED	ORGANIZED BY
White House Office	1939	F. D. Roosevelt
Council of Economic Advisers	1946	Truman
National Security Council	1947	Truman
Office of Intergovernmental Affairs	1955	Eisenhower
Office of the U.S. Trade Representative	1963	Kennedy
Council on Environmental Quality	1969	Nixon
Office of Management and Budget	1921/1971	Harding/Nixon
Office of Public Engagement (formerly Office of Public Liaison)	1974	Ford
Office of Science and Technology Policy	1976	Ford
Office of Administration	1977	Carter
Office of National Drug Control Policy	1988	Reagan
National Space Council	1989	Reagan
Domestic Policy Council (formerly Office of Policy Development)	1970/1993	Nixon/Clinton
National Economic Council	1993	Clinton
Homeland Security Council	2001	G. W. Bush
Office of Domestic Climate Policy	2021	Biden
Office of the National Cyber Director	2021	Biden
Gender Policy Council	2021	Biden

the White House Office is one way for administrations to signal the things they consider most important. George W. Bush added an office for his faith-based initiatives; Barack Obama, reflecting the high-tech/information age, created an Office of Digital Strategy, which was closed by his successor Donald Trump. Trump, the first businessman in the White House, created an Office of American Innovation—which was shuttered early in the Biden administration. Biden went on to add three new offices to the EOP: an Office of Domestic Climate Policy, to analyze and address climate change; an Office of the National Cyber Director, responsible for managing U.S. cybersecurity policy; and a Gender Policy Council, to advance gender equity and equality in U.S. federal policymaking.

In the EOP, a familiar clash gets especially intense. On one hand, most EOP employees are experts on specific issues—immigration, global trade, or the budget. On the other, they have to serve each president's political philosophy (not to mention furthering his reelection prospects). Slowly, the balance between these goals has tipped toward politics.[50] Let us visit the most important offices in the EOP.

The Office of Management and Budget (OMB).   This is the most powerful agency in the executive branch—known (not very fondly) as "the agency that says no." The OMB uses its authority over the federal budget to manage the entire executive branch. During the Reagan administration, the agency acquired its most powerful weapon—**central clearance**: the power to review and "clear" (or okay) anything a member of the administration says or does in public. All members, from the defense secretary to an analyst in the Small Business Bureau, must submit every speech they make, opinion piece they write, congressional testimony they deliver, and policy they propose to the OMB for its approval. Until they get the OMB's nod, they may not say or publish a word.

The OMB vets every administration proposal. When Congress passes a bill, the OMB coordinates various White House officials' recommendations about signing or vetoing the legislation. Officials at the OMB often get the last word as well. Imagine how frustrating it must be for energetic new secretaries to take over their departments, only to learn they must clear all their formal statements and policy proposals with the budget office.

Before the Nixon administration organized the OMB in 1971, fiscal control was much looser. President Lyndon Johnson famously low-balled his economic estimates. One day, instructing a young senator from Massachusetts named Ted Kennedy, Johnson warned him not to let economic projections slow down his favorite bills and illustrated the point with Medicare. "The fools [at the Bureau of the Budget] had to go projecting [Medicare] down the road five or six years, and when you project it the first year it runs $900 million," Johnson told Kennedy.[51] Those anticipated costs, complained LBJ, cost him votes in Congress; he advised the new senator to stop economists from interfering with important proposals. Today, the OMB requires cost-benefit analyses for all White House policy moves. The era of simply suppressing cost estimates is long past. The formal rules now empower an economic perspective. Still, every savvy political operator knows plenty of ways to massage the numbers.[52]

The Council of Economic Advisers (CEA) and National Economic Council (NEC).
Meet two more groups of economists. Both councils and their chairs keep an eye on the whole economy, private as well as public. CEA staff perform economic analyses for the president: unemployment predictions, productivity measurements, economic forecasts, and much more. Think of the CEA as an in-house

Central clearance: The OMB's authority to review and "clear" (or approve) anything a member of the administration says or does in public.

economics think tank for the president. NEC officials also pay close attention to economic trends and policies; their role is to *coordinate* economic policymaking in the White House, convening meetings of several key advisors (including the CEA head) to recommend a presidential administration's economic policy direction.

The National Security Council (NSC). The NSC brings together the powerful officers who make national security policy: secretaries of state, defense, energy, and the treasury (economists again); the chair of the Joint Chiefs of Staff; and others who the president selects. The national security advisor directs the council and must work for consensus across all the different perspectives and formidable personalities: diplomatic, military, and economic. In some administrations, the national security advisor is as influential as the secretaries of state or defense.

The Heart of Power: The White House Office

Our tour ends at the heart of power. The White House Office is part of the Executive Office of the President, but it also stands apart. This group of four hundred or so advisors, aides, and associates work directly for the president, most of them in the West Wing. At the center sits the **Chief of Staff**, the president's gatekeeper, traffic cop, and coordinator. Other important offices include the communications team, White House counsel (the president's official lawyer), and legislative affairs staff.

Chief of Staff: The individual responsible for managing the president's office.

Until recently, the two parties organized their White House Office very differently from one another. Franklin D. Roosevelt set a mixed example for future Democrats: creative chaos. Roosevelt surrounded himself with gifted intellectuals, gave them overlapping tasks, and let them freelance from issue to issue. Many Democratic administrations tried to mimic Roosevelt. John F. Kennedy valued broad-minded intellectuals and encouraged them to weigh in on any subject. So did Bill Clinton; early in his administration, staffers would jump in and out of meetings and conversations regardless of their assigned tasks. The bull sessions went on deep into the night.

In contrast, Republicans traditionally liked clearly defined organization and tasks. You would find no vague or dotted lines on their personnel tables. Republican executives usually modeled their organization on the military or traditional business: crisp lines of authority flowing from the president to the Chief of Staff. Everyone had a clearly defined role.

Now, that has all changed. The Obama White House was tightly organized—almost Republican in style; Joe Biden's White House is similarly arranged along highly disciplined lines. In contrast, President Trump thrived on creative chaos—encouraging aides and confidantes to drop by the Oval Office, hiring and firing White House officials at an unprecedented clip, encouraging aides to argue (and even scream) in front of him, and assigning tasks to trusted associates regardless of their background.[53]

No matter the style, the Chief of Staff makes the White House run. They direct traffic through the president's office, oversee the schedule, sum up the decisions that are made, and follow up to see that those decisions are understood and implemented. The position requires a strong, talented, smooth, competent administrator familiar with the levers of power. And they must have the president's confidence. In the past, some presidents tried to act as Chief of Staff (Jimmy Carter) or to bring in a political neophyte (Bill Clinton chose his pal Mack McLarty, who he'd known since kindergarten); chaos followed. Someone has to follow up each meeting and summarize what has been decided. Otherwise, everyone remembers something different. Again, President Trump broke the record: four chiefs in four years. His creative chaos left him in charge. The other extreme is equally dangerous. If the Chief of Staff seems arrogant, aloof, or rude, the White House loses support and cooperation.

The White House staff is like a little village, full of odd folkways and habits that reflect the way the president wishes to run the country. For example, Ronald Reagan put special emphasis on his speechwriting team; they spent hours watching tapes of his past speeches to learn his rhythms and his way of thinking. The president reworked their draft speeches with great care. Reagan's successor, George H. W. Bush, thought the president should speak more plainly and rejected all the attention on crafting speeches. He demonstrated the new order by stripping the speechwriting team of its White House Mess (dining hall) privileges. The village recognized a major demotion.

When a new president comes to town, attention focuses on the cabinet selections. The wise observer knows to track more subtle appointments to the White House Office. After all, no matter how brilliant the secretary of labor or how experienced the secretary of health and human services, they will have to rely on unseen advisors in the White House to convey their ideas, programs, and problems to the president. The route to influence—the path to "yes" on any program—usually runs through the White House Office staff.

Unlike the high-ranking members of the cabinet agencies, most EOP staffers are not subject to Senate confirmation. They are elected by no one, overseen only by the Chief of Staff, and often have regular access to the president's ear. Should the president's advisors, rather than the experienced cabinet secretaries confirmed by the Senate, run the executive branch? Again, we confront the fundamental issue: power and control versus democracy and enhanced accountability. Perhaps granting authority to White House staff makes the whole federal leviathan more responsive to the will of the people. Most democracies are, ultimately, ruled by experts. American government is run in part by men and women with a sharp eye on winning the next election.

One final feature of the White House staff strikes most newcomers: Its members are young—much younger than the staff running other governments, large corporations, universities, or major nonprofit organizations. Cabinet secretaries with years of experience often complain that their access to the president is governed by millennials and Gen Zers in their twenties and thirties.

The First Spouse

One team in the White House Office does not fit any traditional political category: the office of the president's spouse. Traditionally, the First Lady role was simply that of hostess. Jackie Kennedy joked that "first lady" sounded like a prized racehorse.[54]

Eleanor Roosevelt, perhaps the most famous first spouse, pioneered a new role: the First Lady as activist. Eleanor was a powerful liberal voice, a popular symbol of the New Deal, and a forceful advocate for Franklin and his policies. In effect, she became a one-woman campaign for liberal social policy. A *New Yorker* cartoon captures the First Lady's spirit of tirelessly campaigning for social and labor reform. Deep underground, two sooty coal miners stop their labors as one remarks with surprise: "For gosh sakes, here comes Mrs. Roosevelt!"

WHAT DO YOU THINK?

Do Presidents Need Such a Large Staff?

The Executive Office of the President (EOP) now houses more than 1,800 staff members, from economic and foreign policy advisors to communications specialists. All answer directly to the president and his top aides; most do not require Senate confirmation. By comparison, President Lincoln had four personal assistants, and when Franklin D. Roosevelt took office ninety years ago, he had a staff of thirty-six. Does the modern presidency require such a large staff?	**Yes, absolutely.** Given the office's immense range of responsibilities, presidents need reliable, trustworthy experts and assistants to analyze intelligence and economic data, to assess overseas threats, and to help manage public perceptions of the president. In fact, it's surprising there isn't more support (Congress, after all, has more than twenty-five thousand staffers).	**No—start staff cuts immediately.** Modern technology could make the presidency far more efficient. If CEOs can run major companies with far fewer staff reporting to their office, and other sectors are able to function with far fewer personnel, so could the White House.	**Not sure.** The huge array of presidential staff reportedly work incredibly hard, and the White House certainly has a plateful of duties. But perhaps the large staff reflects too much power in the executive? If Congress reasserted its traditional powers, we could cut back the EOP army.

Few First Spouses were as active or committed as Eleanor Roosevelt, but she set a pattern of policy engagement that her successors have followed. Lady Bird Johnson chose "beautification" of American cities and highways as her policy focus. Nancy Reagan became a spokesperson for the war on drugs. Mrs. Reagan was the first to achieve that mark of status, an office in the West Wing. Bill Clinton assigned his wife, Hillary, the signature policy initiative of his presidency, national healthcare reform. In fall 1993, Hillary Clinton's performance in a series of congressional hearings drew praise from both parties; it did not save the health plan but signaled the start of her own political career—and established a new ceiling for First Ladies' contributions to presidential action.

Michele Obama focused her White House years on children—her "Let's Move!" campaign targeted

● *First Lady Dr. Jill Biden, a longtime educator, has an extensive public-service record, emphasizing literacy and breast health.*

childhood obesity, her "Reach Higher!" encouraged every student in America to finish high school, and her "Let Girls Learn!" aimed to inspire adolescent girls around the world to get a good education. Melania Trump focused on children as well; her "Be Best" program centered on child well-being, cyber-bullying, and opioid abuse. Jill Biden, a longtime community college educator, continued to teach during her husband's terms as president and vice president—becoming the first spouse of a president to work outside the White House. Her focus as First Lady is on supporting military families, advancing educational opportunities for all Americans, and early detection and prevention of breast cancer.

Political scientists—especially those interested in gender and power—have begun to pay particular attention to the role of the First Spouse.[55]

THE BOTTOM LINE

» Each president directs a massive organization—the executive branch of the federal government.

» Cabinet secretaries manage the complex executive branch bureaucracies, but only a few have influence in the White House.

» Over time, executive branch policymaking has migrated from the cabinet to the Executive Office of the President—the network of offices that help the president manage the government.

» The president's innermost circle is the White House Office. These close advisors—often relatively young—include the Chief of Staff, speechwriters, the legislative liaison, and the office of the First Spouse.

 ## Conclusion: The Most Powerful Office on Earth?

In 2021, President Biden took office, bursting with ideas and campaign promises—and raising, once again, a fundamental question about the presidency. Biden's initial acts were mostly executive orders, rather than sweeping legislation co-created with Congress. While Biden reshaped the domestic and foreign policy landscape, presidential orders can be easily overturned by a successor—just as President Trump had done to President Obama's orders, and as Biden, in turn, did to President Trump's.

The presidency is a far more powerful office than it was a century ago. Has it grown too powerful for a republic? Or is it too hobbled to carry out the mandate of the public? Perhaps it is most accurate to say that the same president can be both too powerful and too weak, depending on the issue, the circumstances, and the incumbent. The Biden Administration, with a tiny majority in the Senate (just one vote) saw individual senators dictate policy. Still, with control of both chambers in Congress it managed to get a great deal done in its first two years. As you watch the administration after the midterm elections, ask yourself: Is the presidency too powerful? Or not powerful enough?

As partisanship has grown, it pulls the president two ways—as leader of a party on the one hand, and as a representative of the nation on the other. Long-standing norms have traditionally helped balance these two roles, including a basic civility toward political opponents, deference to judges and courts, respect for a free press, and adherence to the rules, written and unwritten.[56] Strong democracies rely not just on formal laws, as Alexis de Tocqueville put it, but also the "reason and mores" that limit power and guide behavior.[57] These practices have been under stress in recent years. Once they are broken, they may be hard to reestablish.

Who are we? The president offers us an answer—actually, several different answers. Americans seek a powerful, confident figure at their government's center. At the same time, we fear strong executives and hem them in with a labyrinth of checks and balances. We want our collective democratic voice ringing in the ears of our national leaders, but also want our security protected in ways that may require secrecy and fast, decisive choices. We are a people who demand small government, yet complain when every need is not speedily met by the executive branch. We are a complicated, diverse, paradoxical people—just like the presidency that reflects and serves us.

CHAPTER SUMMARY

★ *The president personifies America.* More than any individual, the president tells us who we are— and what we are becoming.

★ *The president injects new ideas into American politics.* Our discussion of Congress emphasized the institution and the rules of the game; the presidency puts more focus on individuals and ideas.

★ The president has three types of powers: those expressed in the Constitution, those delegated by Congress, and those inherent in the role of chief executive.

★ The executive branch has grown far more powerful over time, especially when it comes to foreign policy.

★ The office of the president constantly raises the same fundamental question: *Is the president too powerful for a democratic republic? Or is the office too weak to accomplish what Americans demand of it?* We may also consider whether the president is both too strong and too weak at the same time.

★ The president wears many hats and helmets. Presidential roles include commander-in-chief, top diplomat, first legislator, head bureaucrat, economist-in-chief, head of state, and party leader. The president's authority has grown in every one of these many roles. At the same time, it is difficult for one person to do so many different things effectively.

★ Presidents try to manage public perceptions of the job they are doing by going public and getting feedback from polls. Individual presidents do not completely control their own destiny. They operate in the historical cycle of *political orders*.

★ The presidency always has a personal dimension. Presidents are limited human beings with strengths and weaknesses. That is precisely why the Constitution located the office within an intricate system of checks and balances.

★ Over time, executive branch policy has flowed from the cabinet secretaries to the Executive Office of the President—the network of offices that help the president manage the government.

★ The president's innermost circle is the White House Office. These close advisors—who are often relatively young—include the Chief of Staff, speechwriters, the legislative liaison, and the office of the First Spouse.

KEY TERMS

Central clearance, p. 482
Chief of Staff, p. 483
Civil servants, p. 465
Delegated powers, p. 453
Executive agreements, p. 454
Executive Office of the President (EOP), p. 481

Executive order, p. 465
Executive privilege, p. 454
Expressed powers, p. 453
Going public, p. 470
Imperial presidency, p. 456
Inherent powers of the presidency, p. 453

Override, p. 462
Political appointees, p. 465
Political order, p. 475
Signing statements, p. 465
Unitary executive theory, p. 456
Veto power, p. 462

STUDY QUESTIONS

1. Some people have suggested changing the president's term to one seven-year term without the possibility of reelection. How would that proposal shift the incentives that currently face a first-term president?
2. Why is the Constitution considerably more vague about presidential than congressional powers? What problems—and benefits—does that ambiguity create?
3. What do you think: Is the president too strong or too weak? Defend your opinion.
4. Name seven different roles the president plays. Which do you consider the most important right now? How well do you think the president is carrying out this role today?
5. How well do you think President Biden "goes public"—appeals to the American public to support his policies? Do *you* respond positively to his speeches and legislative requests?
6. Should presidents care about their approval ratings from the American public? Why or why not?
7. Explain how presidents help Americans understand (and define) who we are. What does the president tell the world about the kind of nation and people we are?

8. Explain the role of the Office of Management and Budget (OMB). What does this agency do? What perspective was it designed to bring to policy debates?

9. Describe the role of the First Spouse. Despite getting involved in policies, spouses are often more popular than their presidential partners. Why do you think that is so?

10. Describe the three stages of every political order. Where do you think we stand today in the great cycle of presidential political time?

15 BUREAUCRACY

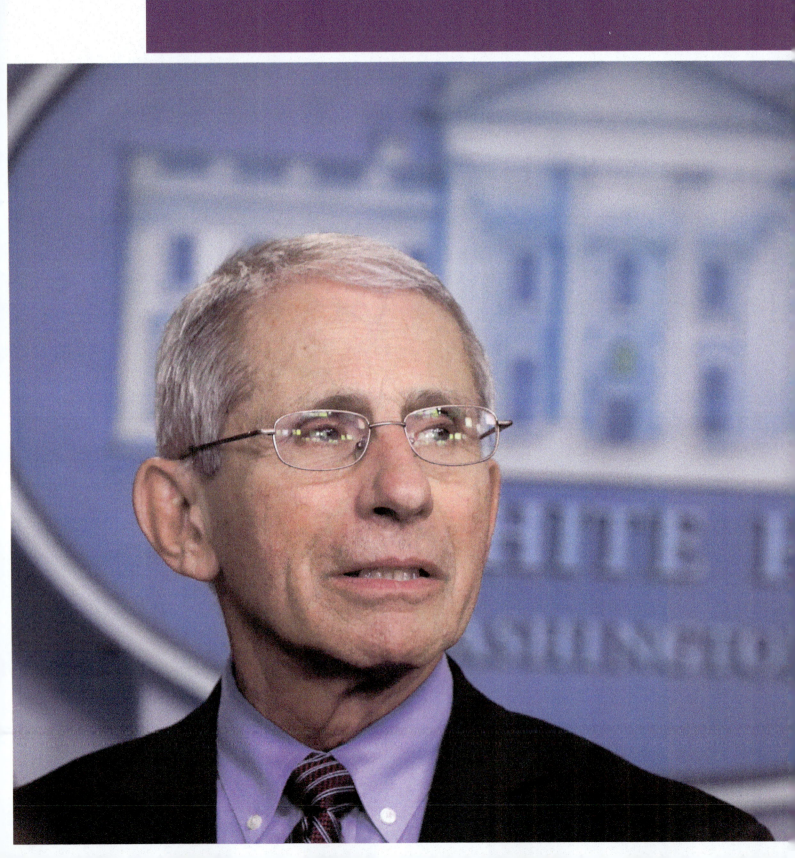

MOST PEOPLE HAVE NEVER HEARD OF BARDA

(the Biomedical Advanced Research and Development Authority), but when COVID hit the United States, that bureaucracy deployed $10 billion in the race to develop a vaccine. The Commanding General in the Army Acquisition Corps (most people haven't heard of that either) ran the operation; the Food and Drug Administration (FDA) provided technical assistance; and two cabinet secretaries—Defense, Health and Human Services—anchored the oversight board. Together, these bureaucrats, working with the Trump administration and private industry, shattered all speed records for vaccine development, and saved countless lives.

Here's a story you don't hear very often: Bureaucrats save the day. But it happens all the time. Firefighters charge into a burning building, meteorologists warn about a looming hurricane, Secret Service agents throw their bodies into the line of fire, health researchers trace disease vectors, and your mail carrier shows up every weekday regardless of the weather. These employees of federal, state, or local governments—all bureaucrats—share a mission: helping the public.

Bureaucrats helping? Most Americans hate the bureaucracy and, by a large margin, agree that "unelected or appointed officials in the federal government have too much influence in determining federal policy."[1] That makes it easy for politicians to bash the bureaucrats. Ted Cruz (R-TX) called them "locusts."[2] President Obama promised to eliminate programs that do not work in his first inaugural address, and President Trump routinely blasted a "deep state" of federal bureaucrats allegedly poised to thwart him at every turn.

This chapter tells a different story about the federal bureaucracy. Yes, we'll look at the critiques—and the important points they make. But we also present the other side. Bureaucrats, often working in partnership with the private sector, perform vital, sometimes life-saving services. You rely on federal bureaucrats almost every hour of every day.

Moreover, a closer look suggests that the public agrees. The criticism of bureaucrats melts away when pollsters ask about specific agencies. The Post

 Learn how the federal bureaucracy developed, how it is meant to work, and why programs and processes sometimes fail.

 See how federal agencies do their job.

 Examine the different types of agencies that comprise the public service.

 Consider who—if anyone—controls the massive, sprawling federal bureaucracy.

 Review possible reforms—and affirm what works well in our bureaucracy.

● *Dr. Anthony Fauci, Director of the National Institute of Allergy and Infectious Diseases since 1984, became a celebrated figure during his daily COVID-19 briefings from the White House in 2020. Eventually, he found himself in the eye of the political storm: celebrated by Democrats and attacked by Republicans, before stepping down at the end of 2022. Dr Fauci is just one member of a government bureaucracy that provides essential services—and now finds itself under partisan fire.*

Office gets a thumbs up from 91 percent of the public; 77 percent approve of the Census Bureau, 73 percent affirm Health and Human Services, and even the tax-collecting Internal Revenue Service (IRS) weighs in with a 65 percent approval.[3] In fact, every corner of the bureaucracy ranks higher in the public's esteem than Congress (19 percent), the Supreme Court (25 percent), or the president (39 percent).

Even so, the same rising partisanship that has transformed Congress and the presidency has struck the bureaucracy. As we'll see, both administrative agencies and individual bureaucrats—like Dr. Anthony Fauci—are now in the middle of the political storm.

Who are we? In many ways, a country of bureaucrats: U.S. national departments and agencies employ 2.8 million civilians (4.2 million if you count the military).[4] More than nineteen million Americans work for state and local governments. These numbers add up to over twenty-three million people on government payrolls—one in every ten working-age adults. What's more, the federal bureaucracy resembles the population it serves more than any other branch of government (Figure 15.1). Remember that Congress is overwhelmingly white, male, and middle-aged; all presidents have been male, and, except for Barack Obama, they have all been white. But the bureaucracy is far more diverse.

Does its diversity make the bureaucracy more representative? Not necessarily. One of the great challenges every national bureaucracy faces is how to synchronize its work with the people's will. A vital question for this chapter: How can a bureaucracy of 2.8 million unelected federal workers govern democratically? An efficient and effective federal bureaucracy is essential to good government. But the bureaucracy runs on expertise; democracy operates on the people's will. The enduring dilemma raised in this chapter: How do we make the two—the experts and the people—work together?

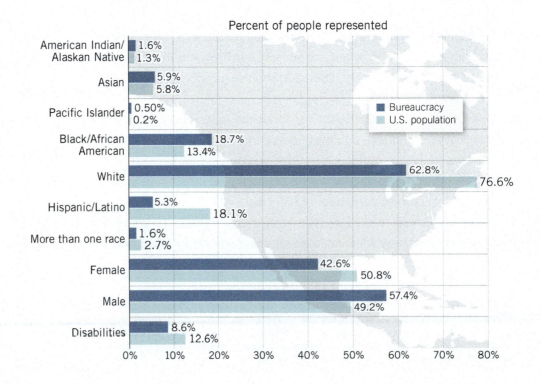

● **FIGURE 15.1** *U.S. civilian bureaucracy demographic characteristics. Notice which groups are overrepresented relative to the population and which are underrepresented. (U.S. Census)*

The Trump administration illustrates the tension. It came to Washington eager to shake up American government and immediately ran into a bureaucratic wall: rules, rules, rules. The president soon discovered that announcing (or tweeting) a policy change had to be followed by a rigorously defined process.

The Biden administration entered with far more expertise in bureaucratic rule-making but ran headlong into its own obstacle: a skeptical Supreme Court that, as we'll see in Chapter 16, knocked down many of its proposed rules.

How does that rulemaking process work? Read on!

BY THE NUMBERS ## The Bureaucracy

7 Number of departments during the Theodore Roosevelt administration (1905)

15 Number of cabinet departments, U.S. executive branch, 2022

66 Number of official independent agencies/commissions, such as the CIA or Postal Service[5]

4.2 Number of workers, in millions, in the federal bureaucracy including military

247 Number of workers, in thousands, in Japanese military

5.3 Estimated "hidden workforce" of federal contractors and grantees, in millions[6]

33.1 Percentage of federal bureaucracy workforce who are active-duty military

37 Number of women, in U.S. history, who have headed cabinet-level departments

2 Number of women who headed cabinet-level departments before 1975

146,757 Maximum annual salary in dollars earned by a civil servant (GS-15, top of scale), 2022

17.5 Miles of hallways in the largest U.S. federal building, the Pentagon

64 Average layers of upper management in large U.S. cabinet departments

The federal bureaucracy was modernized in the 1890s. How has it changed over the century and a quarter since?

🏛 How the Bureaucracy Grew

Almost three million people. How did the bureaucracy get so large in a nation that is skeptical of government? This section tells you how the bureaucracy grew, what it is supposed to look like, and some of the ways it falls short.

Birth of the Bureaucracy

In the nineteenth century, political parties were the largest and most powerful organizations in America. They handed out government jobs as political prizes. Men (and later, women) obtained their posts—as officers in the army, postmasters in rural towns, or tax collectors in ports—because they helped politicians win elections. When George Washington Plunkitt, a colorful New York Irishman, decided to enter politics, he went to the local party boss with a marketable commodity: votes. He got his start in politics by delivering the votes of all his friends and neighbors.[7]

This system was inefficient, unfair, and corrupt. Senator William Marcy, another New Yorker, gave the system its name when he declared, "To the victor belong the spoils." Giving jobs to political friends became known as the **spoils system**.

Reformers fought for years to break this corruption. Jobs, they insisted, should be distributed on the basis of merit, not political connections. These good-government advocates championed **universalistic politics**: a government of impartial rules that apply equally to everyone. That ideal was the basis for bureaucratic government in the United States.[8]

The party leaders defended their spoils system and scoffed at the reformers as "namby-pamby goody-goody gentlemen" (they eventually shortened the insult and just called them "goo-goos").[9] Then a shocking event changed the politics. A crazed office seeker assassinated President James Garfield in 1881. Now the reformers had a martyr for their cause. The spoils system, they said, had caused the president's murder. Popular outcry pushed a reluctant Congress to pass the **Pendleton Civil Service Act** (1883), which required the federal government to hire well-qualified individuals, who took exams to achieve their posts. It was the first step toward building the civil service—another name for the bureaucracy—that runs the government today.

Spoils system: A system in which government jobs are given out as political favors.

Universalistic politics: A government that is run according to transparent rules, impartially applied.

Pendleton Civil Service Act: The law that shifted American government toward a merit-based public service.

Reformers fighting for a more efficient government had a big advantage: There were jobs that needed doing. As American society and economy grew more complex, the spoils system (which rewarded political operators even if they were completely unqualified for their posts) failed to answer national needs. Five forces pushed the United States toward a more efficient bureaucracy.

War. Each time the United States mobilized for war the bureaucracy grew. The Civil War (1861–65) exposed the political hacks who had become officers through the spoils system as incompetent and dangerous. After that, each war spurred a search for competent administrators and well-organized offices. After each war, government kept doing some of the new

● *James Garfield is assassinated in the Baltimore train station by a paranoid job seeker. Reformers blamed the spoils system and used the tragedy to introduce the civil service.*

jobs it had taken on. The number of civilian employees doubled during World War I and tripled during World War II. World War II, more than any other force in American history, created the large national bureaucracy we have today.[10]

Morality.   The U.S. government has long actively regulated public morality. Enforcing moral rules required the creation of increasingly sophisticated agencies. For example, the effort to outlaw all liquor (under Prohibition, which lasted from 1920 to 1933) created a powerful new law enforcement agency in the Department of the Treasury.[11]

Economics.   Over time, the federal government assumed responsibility for the economy. This created many new government offices—commissions designed to regulate business (starting in 1887 with efforts to manage the giant railroads); the Federal Reserve, intended to stabilize banking (created in 1913 after a series of financial panics); and a host of offices and agencies in response to the Great Depression (in the 1930s).

Geography.   The United States spread rapidly across the continent. Keeping the far-flung nation together required a more sophisticated postal service (including, briefly, the famous Pony Express), new forms of transportation, the distribution of public lands to homesteaders, and repeated war against Native Americans.

Race and Ethnicity.   Slavery and civil rights constantly engaged the federal government—leading, most dramatically, to the Civil War and the Reconstruction-era occupation of southern lands by the federal army. Likewise, shifting immigration policies, often based on ethnicity (the Chinese Exclusion Act of the 1880s, for example), required a huge network of federal officials deciding who was permitted to settle in the United States.[12]

Toward Efficiency.   Each of these forces—war, morality, economics, geography, and race/ethnicity—pushed the United States toward more efficient national bureaus and agencies. The Pendleton Act of 1883 laid the cornerstone for the civil service that developed into a professional national bureaucracy by 1900 (after the Spanish-American War). After World War II (1939–45), the country developed many of the agencies that govern America to this day—although each administration right up to the present has tinkered with the lineup of cabinet departments and independent agencies, as we will see.

The Bureaucratic Model

What is a bureaucracy supposed to look like? The German social scientist Max Weber (1864–1920) reduced it to five characteristics that, in theory, mark all modern bureaucracies—including the American civil service. As we consider each, remember that this is how the bureaucracy is *supposed* to operate, not how it always does.[13]

"Your Honor, this woman gave birth to a naked child!"

● Late nineteenth-century moral reformer Anthony Comstock and his quest to stamp out any signs of smut. His effort helped build a sophisticated postal bureaucracy.

Hierarchy. All bureaucracies have a clear chain of command. Each individual reports to the person above them all the way up to the president—or the queen, or the CEO, or the university chancellor. Every individual along the chain has well-defined superiors and subordinates. Weber noted that the desire to move up the ladder makes most individuals sensitive to their superior's orders. In this way, the efforts of thousands of people can be coordinated.

Figure 15.2 shows the hierarchy of the U.S. Department of Energy (DOE), starting with the cabinet secretary and moving down through elaborate subsets of assistants, deputies, and associate administrators. This chart lists only the top fifty-six positions, but some fifteen thousand people work in the agency (and another forty thousand or more work under contracts with the DOE). The principle of hierarchy allows leaders to coordinate the work of all their subordinates.

Division of Labor. Bureaucracies divide up complex programs and assign each piece to an individual or a group. Members of the agencies become experts at their own specialized tasks. The hierarchy coordinates all the specialists into a smoothly working operation. For example, the division of labor permits the State

● **FIGURE 15.2** *Organizational chart for the Department of Energy. (U.S. Department of Energy)*

Department to have specialists in each region of the globe; they speak the languages and understand local cultures.

Fixed Routines.   Rather than making things up as they go along, bureaucrats are expected to follow well-specified codes of conduct called standard operating procedures (SOPs).

Have you ever applied for a passport or unemployment compensation? If you do, you face a sequence of forms, sometimes bewildering details, and multiple visits to different offices. This is bureaucratic routine in action, designed to treat everybody the same way. If you have been stopped for speeding, recall the routine that police officers follow, from requesting your license and registration to checking for outstanding warrants. That's a fixed routine too, and each step in the SOP has a purpose.

Equal Rules for All.   The ideal is always the same in a bureaucracy: The rules apply equally to everyone. In the spoils system, it was all about who you knew. In contrast, the bureaucratic official is not supposed to care whose daughter you are or what special story you have to tell.

Technical Qualifications.   Because bureaucracies operate on the basis of expertise, people get their jobs only on the basis of their qualifications. For example, consider Figure 15.2. You will find an Advanced Research Projects Agency (ARPA-E), which supports research into the origins of the universe, at the top of the second column from the right. George Washington Plunkitt got his job by rounding up votes for New York's Democratic Party; in contrast, the ARPA-E staff got their jobs thanks to their scientific expertise.

Bureaucratic Pathologies

These five characteristics look good on paper. However, bureaucracies often work very differently in practice.

Almost everyone has an annoying bureaucrat story. You may have experienced one in dealing with your university: for example, "You cannot take this course until you take that one"—even though you took one just like it at another school—or "You can't register until you've paid your tuition"—even though you paid it last week. People who deal with the federal government regularly experience this type of bureaucratic error and are familiar with the annoying chorus: You filed the wrong form, stood in the wrong line, or are forbidden to receive a benefit for which you actually qualify.

Here's a telling example: Starting in 2010, eight-year-old Mikey Hicks, an ordinary American boy with no ties to terrorism, was pulled out of line and interrogated every time he and his family

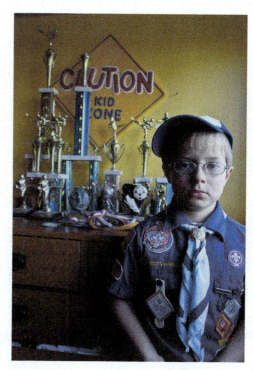

● *A threat to national security? Mikey Hicks was subjected to intense questioning every time he flew—thanks to a glitch in the no-fly list. Bureaucratic pathologies include a deep reluctance to break established routines.*

boarded a plane. The Transportation Security Administration (TSA) explained that his name was on the agency's no-fly list (because a real suspect had a similar name). Despite his family's complaints, it took the TSA months to remove Mikey from the list. And while the TSA agents were grilling Mikey, a *real* terrorist, Umar Farouk Abdulmutallab, boarded a Northwest Airlines flight and unsuccessfully tried to blow it up. No one asked him any questions, even though two months earlier, his father, a prominent businessperson, had reported that his son was training at an Al Qaeda camp for terrorists in Yemen.

Why do these errors happen? Because every feature of the ideal bureaucracy has its potential downside, known as **bureaucratic pathologies**. Familiar pathologies include the following:

Bureaucratic pathologies:
The problems that tend to develop in bureaucratic systems.

- **Rote.** Some bureaucrats slavishly follow familiar standardized routines despite new developments. The failure to adjust (often accompanied by the excuse of "I'm just doing my job") can lead to problems, even tragedies. When members of an organization get too used to following SOPs, they avoid responsibility—and potential blame—by hiding behind their assigned routines.

- **Imperialism.** Bureaucracies compete just like private companies. They want bigger budgets and better staffs. This status seeking can lead them to grow too big and to resist interference by "outsiders" (sometimes including Congress and the White House).

- **Turf war.** Agencies often find that they are doing overlapping jobs. This replication leads to tensions about who is responsible for what. For example, there are at least eighteen intelligence agencies in the federal government. Agencies such as the FBI and CIA view each other as competitors and often refuse to share vital information with the competition.

- **Lack of coordination.** Even agencies skilled at doing their own job may lack mechanisms for cooperating with other agencies. That is because their routines are internal to the agency and do not apply to other organizations. If the agencies are imperialistic or fighting a turf war, the problem can become acute.

- **Clientelism.** Sometimes an agency develops routines that favor some constituents over others. For example, if the Department of Agriculture sends out complicated forms to qualify for loans, they will favor agricultural corporations (which have bookkeepers and administrative assistants) over small family farms that do not have time to fill in fifty-page forms. The bias may not be intentional, but it is built into the SOPs. And because the most powerful clients—the big farms—don't complain, the routine continues.

● *Farmers rally with members of Congress on the Capitol steps. Close ties between "Big Ag"—giant agribusiness operations—and the U.S. government arouses complaints: an example of the bureaucratic pathology termed* clientelism.

Mikey ran into the problem of *rote*. Once his name was on the watch list, the agency kept running through its routine and questioning him. Because the agency would face serious trouble if it crossed a real terrorist off the list, the routine for removing names is slower, with more checkpoints and approvals, than the routine for adding a name. Why did the real terrorist slip through? Here, the problem was a *lack of coordination*, compounded by a *turf war*: Different security agencies competing for resources failed to communicate. Umar Farouk Abdulmutallab's father contacted one agency, which neglected to pass the information to another.

In popular culture, the story of bureaucratic pathology often eclipses every other aspect of the subject. This is a mistake. We could not run the military, deliver the mail, operate an airport, process Social Security checks, predict the weather, or battle a pandemic without bureaucratic agencies. The key question for all governments—for all organizations, including your college or university—is this: How do we produce the benefits of bureaucracy while minimizing the pathologies?

The Democratic Dilemma

Bureaucracies do not fit easily with democracy. Democracy is rooted in mass public engagement. Citizens express their opinions about what officials should do. Congress and the presidency are essentially democratic institutions because their authority comes directly from the people (at least, the people who vote).

In contrast, bureaucratic authority comes not from the people, but from officials' expertise. Deputy secretaries of civilian radioactive waste management in the Energy Department rely on their highly specialized knowledge. Engineering specialists with the Air Force have the expertise and training to build airfields, buildings, and runways. Meteorologists at the National Oceanic and Atmospheric Administration (known as NOAA) monitor scientific weather data. None of these jobs involves public opinion or securing the most votes.

The difference between elected office and bureaucratic posts creates a clash of cultures. Democracy flows up from the people. Bureaucracy, when it runs properly, operates on the basis of specialized information, often organized top-down. An enduring challenge for American government is how to manage the tension between these two polarities.

Before considering democratic controls on the bureaucracy, we turn to a more detailed look at what bureaucrats actually do.

THE BOTTOM LINE

» Before the bureaucracy's rise, government jobs were distributed as spoils, or political rewards. Reformers challenged this system and eventually built a national bureaucracy.

» The ideal bureaucracy has five characteristics: hierarchy, division of labor, fixed routines, equal rules for all, and technical expertise.

» Bureaucracies are prone to pathologies: sticking too closely to a routine, fighting over turf, favoring some clients over others, and refusing to coordinate. These are all exaggerations of the very features that make bureaucracies efficient.

» Because they rely on specialized expertise and information, bureaucracies pose a dilemma for democratic governance, which relies on popular opinion.

🏛 How Bureaucracies Work

After Congress passes a law or the president issues an executive order, the bureaucracy puts it into effect. Sometimes this work involves routine administrative action: Congress appropriates funds for Social Security checks, and bureaucratic workers at the Social Security Administration issue the checks. Just as often, implementing laws and executive orders requires complicated judgments because inevitably there are gaps in the law. Sometimes Congress sidesteps difficult questions to avoid a conflict or an unpopular decision; sometimes the laws or executive orders are vague because they were written in a hurry or amended at the last minute; and sometimes legislation requires technical details that Congress leaves to the bureaucratic experts. In each of these cases, the bureaucracy follows a well-established process for putting a law into practice.

The process is extremely important. When officials in the Trump administration tried to introduce changes to programs (like immigration rules, environmental regulations, or the way the census was conducted), they discovered that they could not simply issue a new policy overnight. Instead, each change had to follow a well-organized procedure. Opponents of the Trump administration could (and did) go to the courts to block any changes that missed a step. For example, when the administration tried to rescind the Dreamers program (which protected immigrants without papers who had come to the United States as children), the Supreme Court issued a dramatic ruling: Yes, the administration had the authority to change the program, but it could not do so until it went through the proper procedures.[14]

Putting a law into practice involves two different procedures: First, the administration hammers out the *rules*. Then it *implements* them.

Rulemaking

Rulemaking showcases classic bureaucratic principles in action: a fixed process with multiple steps always carried out the same way (Figure 15.3). First, the agency studies the law and proposes a "rule" that spells out how the new program will operate; the details must make it clear to the thousands of businesses and individuals exactly what they are required to do. For example, in 2021 President Biden, building on a law passed in 1980, announced that goods purchased by the federal government—from desks to helicopter windscreens—would have to be built from components that were at least 75 percent made in America.[15]

That sounds simple enough, right? Wrong. Defining "made in America" is not easy. If a radio built in Ohio uses foreign oil for its plastic casing, what percentage of the product is built in America? How about a Texas firm that builds a PC using imported steel for its disk drive casing? Multiply those questions across the $600 billion worth of goods

Agency employees draft proposed regulation

⬇

OMB approves

⬇

Proposed regulation published in Federal Register

⬇

Public comments

⬇

Agency prepares final rules and impact analysis

⬇

OMB approves

⬇

Final rules published in Federal Register and go into effect in 30 days

⬇

Affected interest can sue or go back to Congress and, if successful, agency starts back at step one

● **FIGURE 15.3** *Rulemaking in practice. Government rulemaking showcases classic bureaucratic principles in action: a fixed process with multiple steps always carried out in the same way. Any executive order that does not follow precisely this path will be blocked by the courts. (Office of Management and Budget)* purchased by the federal government each year, and you can see that public officials are going to have to give American industry very carefully defined rules to follow. The bureaucracy's job is to spell out all the details and instruct American businesses and government purchasers how to reach that 75 percent threshold without violating any other existing rules or laws. The same goes for every federal rule, whether it is lowering drug prices paid by Medicare (which pays health costs for people over sixty-five) or defining how refugees should be treated at the southern border.

Public officials do all that by following a very precise routine. They begin by drafting a regulation that lays out precisely how to calculate the percentage of a product that is made in America.

After the agency has drafted its rule, it sends the proposed rule to the Office of Management and Budget (OMB) for approval. (Recall from our tour of the White House in the last chapter that the OMB has the power of central clearance—it can say "no" to almost anything.) After the OMB gives its okay, the agency publishes the **proposed rule** in a publication called the *Federal Register,* the daily journal of the federal government. Anybody who is interested can comment.

Proposed rule: A draft of administrative regulations published in the *Federal Register* for the purpose of gathering comments from interested parties.

Who reads the *Federal Register*? In theory, any citizen can read it just by going online. Of course, most people are blissfully unaware it exists. Lobbyists and lawyers, on the other hand, pore over the *Federal Register* like it's a hot new novel.

The day we wrote this chapter, for example, the *Federal Register* included proposed rules on hazard analysis for animal food (from the Food and Drug Administration), energy conservation standards for furnaces (the Energy Department), air worthiness standards for Boeing Airplanes (from the Federal Aviation Administration), and emissions standards for hazard pollutants in paint stripping products (the Environmental Protection Agency).[16]

You can be sure that lawyers and lobbyists from Purina Pet Food, Addison Heating and Cooling, Boeing, and Sherman Williams Paint manufacturers bombarded the agencies with comments and questions (each comment is also published in the *Federal Register,* usually with a response from the agency). Environmental and consumer groups also join the conversation. The details of the proposed rule and the comments are highly technical.

The agency reviews all the public comments and makes changes—a process that can take months or even years—and then hammers out a **final rule**, along with an analysis of the likely impact of the new rule. Back it goes to the OMB, which has thirty days to review the final rule. Then the final rule is published in the *Federal Register.* Thirty days later, the regulation goes into effect. The final rule is not necessarily the end of the process, however. An individual citizen, group, or corporate firm objecting to the result can sue the agency for misinterpreting Congress's intent. Or, increasingly, for overstepping its authority.

Final rule: The rule that specifies how a program will actually operate.

In practice, lobbyists for the industry negotiate with the agency as proposed and final rules are written. They offer advice or threaten to sue. Experts in the agency decide when to call the industry's bluff. Consumer groups often jump in as well and try to balance industry views. Once in a while, when a rule taps into a broader controversy, this debate spills over into the public eye.

Each year, all the updated rules published in the *Federal Register*—usually more than three thousand—are published together with a set of permanent administrative rules guiding the bureaucracy's practice and performance. This massive document is known as the *Code of Federal Regulations.*

Next time the White House tweets or an executive agency announces a new policy, you will know that it is just the beginning of the process. What comes next

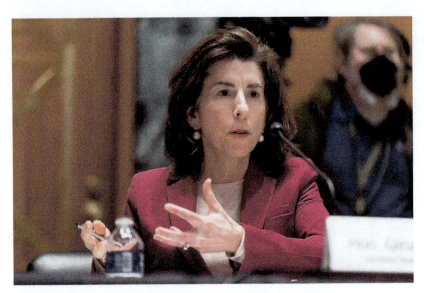

● Secretary of Commerce Gina Raimondo testifies about the department rules designed to increase broadband access in rural areas—one of the thousands of rules required to implement the bipartisan $1.2 trillion infrastructure plan.

is the whole list we just described: proposed rules, comments, final rules, and quite possibly lawsuits.

Apart from occasional flash points, rulemaking takes place far from the public eye. Congress gets plenty of media coverage when it considers legislation. But negotiations over rules take place in the shadows, where only the most informed experts understand what is going on. This hidden debate shapes every law, executive order, and public policy. It may be technical, but it involves everyone in the country.

Now you can see the importance of our central question about democracy: How can the public possibly control these battles that occur deep in the bureaucratic leviathan? Read on.

Implementation

After the rules are in place, bureaucracies implement the new policies. Farmers' pesticides have to be inspected, nuclear power plants regulated, GI Bill benefits delivered, or medical care provided to veterans.

Street-level bureaucrats:
Public officials who deal directly with the public.

Who does this work? General policies are formulated in the higher administration, but **street-level bureaucrats**, those who interact directly with the public, actually run the programs on the ground. Street-level bureaucrats include police officers, teachers, poultry plant inspectors, public health officials (and, if you're at a public university, your professors and TAs). They have a great deal of discretion in implementing policies. For example, the police officer may let you off with a warning, write you a ticket, or cuff you and haul you down to the station.

Consider a more complicated case. The Women, Infants, and Children program (WIC) provides vouchers for meals to low-income families with children. On the national level, Congress debates WIC funding and the administration determines eligibility criteria. On the local level, street-level bureaucrats constantly make judgment calls. For example, one person was ill and missed the application deadline—give her the benefit card anyway, allowing her to buy food? Another family has broken the rules again and again, but if they are cut off from the program, the children will suffer. Street-level bureaucrats constantly decide what to do—giving them enormous influence over how the program actually works. Program beneficiaries quickly learn about the power of the bureaucrats they see again and again.

● Street-level bureaucrat in action: A nurse measures the height of a five-year-old during a physical examination in a Child Health Center in Denver, Colorado.

Implementation is the last step in a long process. The president and/or members of Congress proposed the law; the House and Senate passed it; the courts upheld it; and the bureaucratic agency proposed draft rules, gathered comments, and published final rules in the *Federal Register*. Bureaucrats are active at every stage in the process. For example, they shape proposed programs by suggesting legislative language to allies in Congress and testifying before congressional committees that are considering the law.

Sometimes executive bureaucrats develop close alliances with members of Congress as well as with interest-group lobbyists. A specialist in the Environmental Protection Agency (EPA) might spend years working with green members of Congress, along with the environmental groups and industries most affected by the regulations. Experts at the Bureau of Alcohol, Tobacco, Firearms, and Explosives connect frequently with gun makers and members of Congress

Regulating Health Systems

Do We Have Too Many Regulations?

Health systems must comply with hundreds of regulatory requirements issued by state and federal bureaucratic agencies. These regulations are designed to ensure patient safety and compliance with a wide expanse of policies. The judiciary and Congress also affect the regulation, providing oversight.

THINK ABOUT IT

Identify three institutions that create regulations for health systems and note which types of regulations they issue. Are you surprised that any of the agencies are involved in healthcare regulation?

Some argue that our health system is too heavily regulated—restricting medical innovation and driving up costs. What do you think: Are there areas of our public health system that should be more or less strictly regulated?

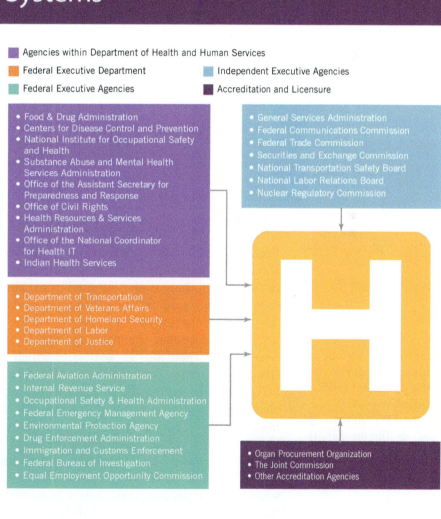

- ■ Agencies within Department of Health and Human Services
- ■ Federal Executive Department
- ■ Independent Executive Agencies
- ■ Federal Executive Agencies
- ■ Accreditation and Licensure

- Food & Drug Administration
- Centers for Disease Control and Prevention
- National Institute for Occupational Safety and Health
- Substance Abuse and Mental Health Services Administration
- Office of the Assistant Secretary for Preparedness and Response
- Office of Civil Rights
- Health Resources & Services Administration
- Office of the National Coordinator for Health IT
- Indian Health Services

- General Services Administration
- Federal Communications Commission
- Federal Trade Commission
- Securities and Exchange Commission
- National Transportation Safety Board
- National Labor Relations Board
- Nuclear Regulatory Commission

- Department of Transportation
- Department of Veterans Affairs
- Department of Homeland Security
- Department of Labor
- Department of Justice

- Federal Aviation Administration
- Internal Revenue Service
- Occupational Safety & Health Administration
- Federal Emergency Management Agency
- Environmental Protection Agency
- Drug Enforcement Administration
- Immigration and Customs Enforcement
- Federal Bureau of Investigation
- Equal Employment Opportunity Commission

- Organ Procurement Organization
- The Joint Commission
- Other Accreditation Agencies

Source: American Hospital Association

who care about guns. Some criticize these arrangements as too cozy (recall the iron triangles discussed in Chapter 12). In any case, the bureaucracy is not walled off from other actors in government. It is part of the process all along the way.

The bureaucracy affects every aspect of our lives. It inspects the food you eat; monitors the air you breathe; negotiates the trade rules that governed the importation of your T-shirt; regulates seat belts, airbags, and the crash-resistant frame of your car; oversees your student loans; and awards your professors grants to study topics ranging from elections to Maya Angelou's poems to nanotechnology. Almost everything you do today has been touched, one way or another, by bureaucracies implementing policies that were once proposed rules in the *Federal Register*.

THE BOTTOM LINE

» Once a law is passed or an executive order is signed, the program goes to the bureaucracy to be put into effect.

» Bureaucrats propose rules, publish them in the *Federal Register*, gather comments, rewrite the rules, and publish the final version. The law or executive order is now in effect.

» At every step of the process, lawyers and lobbyists interact with the bureaucracy; this interaction engages experts far from the political limelight.

» Bureaucratic officials take part in every step of the political process—from proposing legislation to putting it into effect.

 ## How the Bureaucracy Is Organized

Each presidential administration names the heads of the government bureaucracy—about four thousand people known as political appointees. The Senate approves the highest-ranking twelve hundred or so cabinet secretaries, their assistants and deputies, ambassadors, and other top figures. Their role: steer their agencies in the direction charted by the president and the voters.

Under these four thousand appointees toil some 2.8 million **civil servants** who work at their jobs regardless of which party occupies the White House.[17] Imagine the tensions when a rookie political appointee (often a campaign official) arrives eagerly touting the new president's philosophy to an office of career officials. Those long-serving bureaucrats usually have far more expertise than the political appointee who has just been named their boss. The civil servants know that before long (on average, less than three years), the eager new appointee will move on, to be replaced by another. The civil servants are acutely aware of the rules, regulations, and SOPs that guide their agency. They literally tell their new bosses what they can do, how they should do it, and what proposed actions could land them in trouble because they fall outside the rules, clash with another agency's mission, or raise a sore point with a powerful member of Congress.

Over the years, civil servants have built up a vocabulary of their own, often caricatured as "bureaucratese"—the cautious, cover-your-backside language of

Civil servants: Members of the permanent executive branch bureaucracy who are employed on the basis of competitive exams and keep their positions regardless of the presidential administration.

TABLE 15.1	Bureaucracy Buzzwords
Bureaucrat: You need to be more proactive.
Meaning: You should have protected me from myself.
Bureaucrat: We want you to be the executive champion of this project.
Meaning: I want to be able to blame you for my mistakes.
Bureaucrat: We need to syndicate this decision.
Meaning: We need to spread the blame if it backfires.
Bureaucrat: I see you involved your peers in developing your proposal.
Meaning: One person couldn't possibly come up with something this stupid.
Bureaucrat: Our agency is going through a paradigm shift.
Meaning: We have no idea what we've been doing, but in the future we shall do something completely different.
Bureaucrat: Value-added.
Meaning: Expensive.
Source: H. George Frederickson, Up the Bureaucracy.

experts with lifetime positions who provide more than $3 trillion worth of federal services every year. Table 15.1 includes some humorous examples. Master these lines, and you will be ready for a job in the executive branch!

The federal government's organizational chart includes four types of agencies: cabinet departments, autonomous bureaus, independent regulatory agencies, and the bureaucracy's service organizations. Let us take a closer look at each.

The Cabinet Departments

President George Washington's cabinet had just four departments: State, Treasury, War (now called Defense), and the Office of the Attorney General (now the Justice Department). Over time, presidents added new departments until the cabinet reached its current size of fifteen. Table 15.2 lists each department, the year it was founded, and total employees. Notice how the military dominates the government's personnel count. The Department of Defense houses some 2.2 million employees, including the people in uniform, and manages some 750 facilities sitting on thirty million acres around the world; no other organization in the United States, and few in the world, comes close.

Because State and Treasury are the two oldest departments, the secretaries of state and the treasury always sit on either side of the president in cabinet meetings. The younger the agency, the farther away from the president the secretary sits. (Each position is indicated by a silver plaque on the back of the chair, with the department's founding date.) In every formal event, the leaders of the oldest departments enter first, while the secretary of the newest department (currently Homeland Security) brings up the rear. The secretary of state is fourth in line to take over the presidency, followed by each cabinet secretary—again in the order the agencies were founded.

TABLE 15.2 **U.S. Executive Bureaucracies**

DEPARTMENT (WITH YEAR OF FOUNDING)	CURRENT EMPLOYEES (AS OF 2022)
State 1789	77,243
Treasury 1789	95,922
Defense 1789	763,778 civilians; 1.4 million uniformed military
Justice 1789	117,390
Interior 1849	67,799
Agriculture 1862	93,807
Commerce 1903	50,907
Labor 1913	16,855
Health and Human Services (originally 1953; "Health, Education, and Welfare")	87,626
Housing and Urban Development 1965	7,792
Transportation 1966	53,795
Energy 1977	14,595
Education 1979	4,116
Veterans Affairs 1989	426,007
Homeland Security 2002	211,336
OTHER LARGE FEDERAL AGENCIES	
Social Security Administration	59,707
Environmental Protection Agency	14,788
National Aeronautics and Space Administration	18,108
General Services Administration	11,689
U.S. Postal Service (a semi-independent federal agency since 1971)	566,431
Executive Office of the President (detailed in Chapter 14)	1,869
Total Civilian Federal Service **Total Including Military**	**2,772,688** **4,216,486**
Estimated number of federal contractors and grantees	**Between 5 and 6 million** (depending on who's counting)

Source: Congressional Research Service, June 2022; OSHA, March 2022; individual agency reports.

The Challenge of Governing.   Nominating cabinet secretaries and other bureaucratic leaders is part of the fanfare of a new administration. The president sings the nominee's praises and the media speculates about fresh policy directions. Then the difficulties begin. Imagine that you are in the secretary's shoes: Here are the hurdles you will face.

First, you must go before the Senate for confirmation. In the increasingly partisan Washington environment, any past indiscretion, even a controversial tweet, may force you to withdraw. If all goes well, you take office when the president does, on a cold Washington day in late January.

Next, you select your staff—your team is not yet in place. The presidential transition group sends you boxes of résumés. You pick names for your deputies, your assistants, and the leaders of the dozens of offices in your agency; some you know, others the president's advisors recommend, and still others look especially impressive on paper. Now send your selections over to the White House for a thumbs up. Because White House staffers may have their own favorites, you must negotiate your choices. The FBI examines every nominee's background, which can sometimes take months. After that, each nominee goes to the Senate for confirmation.

If you are lucky, the White House does not ask a thousand questions, nothing embarrassing turns up in the FBI's detailed check, and no senator objects to the appointment. You might then have your political appointees in place after you've been on the job for seven months or so.

However, if you get caught in a bottleneck—at the White House, with the FBI, or in Congress—it can be a year or more before members of your team are in place. Remember, there are fifteen cabinet departments—in addition to dozens of federal agencies—and all are scrambling to get their people through the neck of the bottle. In September 2001, President George W. Bush did not yet have most of his security team in office when the terrorists attacked on September 11, eight months after Inauguration Day.

After five hundred days in office, the Biden administration had just half of its top 800 officials in place. Almost 150 were waiting for congressional action, while more than 100 had still not officially been named. But this is not unusual. After four years, the Trump administration still had not filled half of its positions in Homeland Security.[18] As Washington has grown more partisan, the confirmation process has become more difficult.

The next hurdle: running an organization you know very little about. Cabinet secretaries usually do not have any experience with the many facets of their department. Secretary of Labor Marty Walsh was a popular Boston mayor. But he had no experience with mine safety and health, or labor statistics, or international labor affairs—all departments now under his direction. When a new administration comes to town, a huge to-do list awaits the new executives, who are usually negotiating a new organization with few of their team members in place.

Cabinet Meetings. Fifteen department heads gather around a White House conference room table with the president, vice president, and as many as ten additional senior leaders. Who are those other "senior leaders"? Each president names a set of positions as "cabinet-level"—for example, the CIA Director and the White House Chief of Staff. Along with the department heads, this group attends cabinet meetings and receives special briefings.[19]

Does the whole group—department secretaries plus additional cabinet-level officials—serve as a president's central advisory team? No. There are too many of them. With twenty-five or more people around the table, plus dozens of staff lining the walls behind them, it is hard to have a serious discussion (see Chapter 14).

The Rotating Bureaucracy. The turnover at the top of the U.S. bureaucracy is unique. No other democracy works this way. No private company, nonprofit organization, or university routinely asks thousands of outsiders to take over for three or so years and then step aside and make way for a new crop of leaders. Yet the political appointees scrambling to catch up are in charge of a huge bureaucratic

---

COMPARING NATIONS 15.1   Parliamentary Systems

Countries with parliaments—such as England, South Africa, Japan, or Israel—are different from the U.S. system when it comes to bureaucratic leadership. In all these nations, senior members of the legislature become ministers, the equivalent of cabinet secretaries in the United States. Notice the contrast: Legislative leaders from the majority party also lead the bureaucracy.

Each ministry has two heads. The elected minister drawn from parliament represents the public and sets the policy goals; the other leader is a career civil servant (often called the director general), who provides technical expertise and continuity across the years. Both these positions are highly prestigious—in England, an effective director general of an important ministry often earns a knighthood.

Some parliamentary systems result in coalition governments. Seven parties together form the majority in the government of Spain. The different parties bargain for control of Spain's government ministries—the defense ministry is in the hands of a

legislator from the Socialist Workers' Party; the head of the left Podemos Party is vice president for environment/sustainability; and a member of the Catalan party runs the universities.

In other nations, no one sends in a résumé to become a department head—you have to win an election to parliament and work your way up the party hierarchy. There is no long confirmation process, no hostile congressional committees overseeing the bureaucracy, no checks and balances between the executive and legislative branches. The civil service is extremely prestigious. Successful civil servants can climb to the top of the ministry—rather than always working for a new set of senior appointees rotating in after each presidential election.

In the United States, the Constitution bars members of Congress from taking "any civil office"—to join the bureaucracy or the judiciary, they must resign their House or Senate seat. The founders, as always, insisted on checks and balances.

---

leviathan. Thousands of civil servants toil away at the agency's tasks, working from one administration to the next even as new agency directors come and go.

Management consultants would run screaming from the room if you suggested setting up a business in this way. We cannot look to the Constitution for justification because it does not mention cabinet departments, much less an entire bureaucracy. Many political scientists, however, think the bureaucracy works reasonably well. The civil service does its job. And the political leadership, for all the problems we just described, takes over with a definite philosophy, based on a president's ideas. The Biden team, like the Trump and Obama teams before them, came to Washington with a distinctive point of view.

The Trump administration was unusual, replacing more than one-third of its own top officials (and two cabinet secretaries) in the very first year. The Biden administration has gone back to the traditional way, replacing less than a quarter of that number (and no cabinet secretaries) (Figure 15.4).[20]

Pairing a suitable philosophy with skilled political leadership can make a real difference in an agency's management. An example is the Federal Emergency Management Agency (FEMA), which responds to natural disasters. President Bill Clinton named a talented FEMA

● *President Biden (on the right in the middle) meets with his cabinet. Fifteen cabinet department heads, ten other high-ranking officials, and eighteen senior staffers—way too many for a serious policy discussion.*

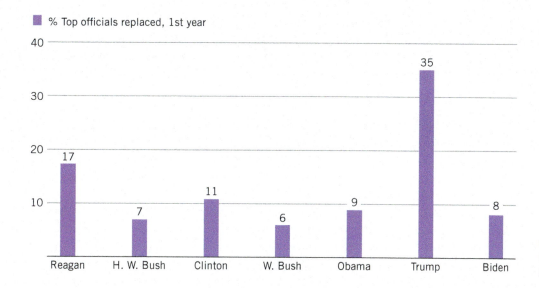

■ % Top officials replaced, 1st year

● **FIGURE 15.4** *Senior officials replaced during first year of presidency.*

director, James Lee Witt, who transformed the agency into a decentralized, authority-sharing, proactive outfit. When floods hit the Midwest in 1993, FEMA won applause for its swift, well-organized assistance.

When the George W. Bush administration came to office, FEMA was on its list of target agencies. From a conservative perspective, FEMA had become *too* proactive. The Bush administration restored the old FEMA policies and installed an inexperienced (but politically connected) campaign donor, Michael Brown, as director.

The changes led to political disaster. In part owing to the restoration of a rules-bound, hierarchical structure, and in part to Brown's inexperience as a leader, FEMA responded feebly to Hurricane Katrina, a massive storm that flooded New Orleans in 2005. The media depicted widespread desperation: More than 1,800 people lost their lives in the storms and subsequent flooding—with scant federal response. Director Brown lost his job, and President Bush's popularity ratings tumbled.

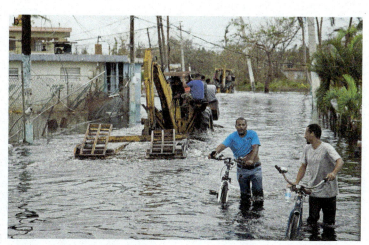

● *Federal Emergency Management Agency's (FEMA) response to disasters poses a challenge for every White House. When administrations fail to appoint experienced managers, troubles follow. Two notoriously slow responses: (a) Hurricane Katrina in New Orleans (in 2005) and (b) Hurricane Maria in Puerto Rico (2017).*

The FEMA example illustrates another important point about the federal bureaucracy. Calling for smaller government sounds promising on the campaign trail. However, each nook and cranny of the sprawling government establishment has a job to do; almost all deliver services that people rely on. That responsibility makes cutting government agencies difficult in practice.

The Cabinet and Diversity. Like the bureaucracy they lead, the fifteen secretaries increasingly reflect the American public. Table 15.3 shows the number of women and minority members in the cabinet over time. Until the mid-1960s, just two women had served in the cabinet in all of American history—and not a single Black, Latino, Asian, or Native American person.

The dramatic change that began in the 1970s reflects the social revolution that swept the nation over one generation. During the first two hundred years of American history, only three women and two Black people were appointed as heads of executive departments. Since the 1980s, every president has appointed a diverse set of secretaries that reflects the nation, although some presidents have put more emphasis on diversity than others.

Other Agencies

Nearly three-quarters of the federal bureaucracy—about 1.9 million civilians— works in the cabinet departments. Three other categories of federal workers each offer a different twist on the bureaucracy.

Executive Agencies. Independent executive agencies have more specific assignments than the cabinet departments. The Environmental Protection Agency, for

TABLE 15.3 Demographic Makeup of Presidential Cabinet Department Heads

PRESIDENT	WOMEN	MINORITIES	CABINET OFFICERS NAMED DURING ADMINISTRATION	YEARS
All presidents to 1963	2	0	—	1789–1963
Johnson	0	1	25	1963–68
Nixon	0	0	31	1969–74
Ford	1	1	22	1974–76
Carter	4	1	22	1977–80
Reagan	3	2	33	1981–88
G. H. W. Bush	3	3	21	1989–92
Clinton	5	10	30	1993–2000
G. W. Bush	6	8	34	2001–8
Obama	8	10	32	2009–16
Trump	3	3	24	2017–20
Biden	5	4	15	2021–22

example, is entirely focused on one tough job: overseeing the environment. In contrast, a cabinet agency like the Department of the Interior has responsibilities that include—among many other things—supervising Native American affairs, national parks, geological surveys, oceans and energy, and surface mining.

The more than thirty independent executive agencies perform a wide range of tasks. They land astronauts on the moon (NASA), send Americans around the world to perform service projects (the Peace Corps), gather intelligence about other nations and groups (CIA), manage the banking system (the Federal Reserve), and investigate violations of civil rights in the workplace (Equal Employment Opportunity Commission).

The U.S. Postal Service became a cabinet agency in 1792. Some 180 years later, in 1971, the post office became an independent agency of the U.S. federal government—operating without direct federal subsidy. The Postal Service has over half a million employees (down from nearly eight hundred thousand in 1999) and 250,000 vehicles; it is the second-largest federal bureaucracy after the Defense Department.

Independent Regulatory Commissions. In the 1880s, farmers and small business complained bitterly that they were at the mercy of the railroads and their arbitrary freight rates. The farmers pleaded for government controls. However, reformers faced a problem. Wealthy, powerful railroad owners dominated the state legislatures and Congress. How could consumers be protected against these "robber barons"? Reformers organized a regulatory agency, the Interstate Commerce Commission (ICC), that would operate separately from Congress and the White House. Reformers hoped that the agency's independence would permit it to regulate industry—free from corrupting lobbyists and politics. That reform set the organizational template for a new kind of agency, independent regulatory commissions.

Today, there are fourteen independent regulatory commissions performing many different jobs, from overseeing elections to protecting consumers (Figure 15.5). All are designed to be independent from the political branches. The reformers' dream, beginning with the Interstate Commerce Commission, was that the commissions would rely on modern management methods rather than politics to guide regulatory policy.

Each agency issues regulations, enforces laws, and settles disputes—essentially combining legislative, executive, and judicial powers in one agency. A set of commissioners, nominated by the president and confirmed by the Senate, runs the agency for a fixed term that does not overlap with the president's term—still another way to minimize political influence.

You probably recognize the reformers' naiveté: Independent agencies are no less political than any other branch of government. As we saw when we examined rulemaking, regulating an industry inevitably involves back-and-forth negotiations between regulators and the industry. Moreover, to understand an industry well enough to monitor its activities, regulators need relevant expertise. Commissioners are frequently drawn from the ranks of the regulated industry. Ironically, the effort to keep the regulatory commissions independent of Congress and the White House has left them *more* susceptible to industry influence; there are fewer countervailing interests to argue the other side. For decades, critics have charged that the independent regulatory agencies are "captured" or "acquired" by the industry and simply do its bidding.

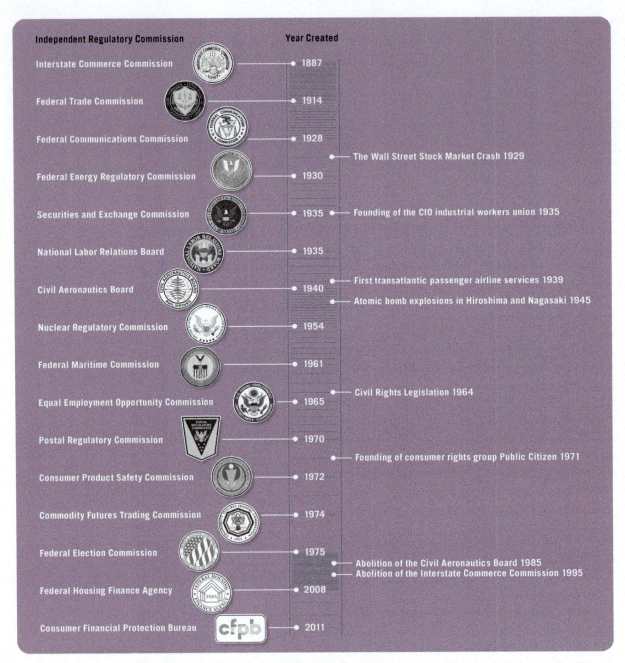

Independent Regulatory Commission   **Year Created**

Interstate Commerce Commission — 1887

Federal Trade Commission — 1914

Federal Communications Commission — 1928

Federal Energy Regulatory Commission — 1930
— The Wall Street Stock Market Crash 1929

Securities and Exchange Commission — 1935
— Founding of the CIO industrial workers union 1935

National Labor Relations Board — 1935

Civil Aeronautics Board — 1940
— First transatlantic passenger airline services 1939
— Atomic bomb explosions in Hiroshima and Nagasaki 1945

Nuclear Regulatory Commission — 1954

Federal Maritime Commission — 1961

Equal Employment Opportunity Commission — 1965
— Civil Rights Legislation 1964

Postal Regulatory Commission — 1970
— Founding of consumer rights group Public Citizen 1971

Consumer Product Safety Commission — 1972

Commodity Futures Trading Commission — 1974

Federal Election Commission — 1975
— Abolition of the Civil Aeronautics Board 1985
— Abolition of the Interstate Commerce Commission 1995

Federal Housing Finance Agency — 2008

Consumer Financial Protection Bureau — 2011

● **FIGURE 15.5** *Congress creates independent regulatory commissions in response to stock market failures, the rise of new technologies, or other emerging needs.*

Regulatory capture:
The theory that industries dominate the agencies that regulate them.

There is no escaping the politics that pervade the independent regulatory agencies. Still, the "**regulatory capture**" argument is often overstated. Consumer groups also lobby, provide information to, and sue the agencies. Moreover, the civil servants who run the agencies often work hard to achieve their institution's goals—and express pride in its independent stance.[21]

In the past forty years, a new generation of reformers has promoted *deregulation*—abolishing these agencies and letting free-market competition protect consumers. The original ICC was dismantled in 1995. The Civil Aeronautics Board, a regulatory commission that oversaw (and some would say protected) the airline industry was abolished in 1985, with good and bad consequences for consumers—frequent-flyer programs, fewer airlines, fewer direct flights to smaller cities, and huge fluctuations in fares.

Today, conservatives have targeted many of these regulatory agencies—especially the Consumer Financial Protection Bureau created by the Obama administration in the wake of the recession of 2008–9. In 2020 the Supreme Court declined to knock down the agency, although it permitted the president (then, Donald Trump) to take direct control over the commission.[22]

Deregulation brings us full circle. Once, farmers and small business pleaded for relief from predatory markets. Now, a new generation of reformers offers a solution to problems with the regulatory agencies: Return to the markets.

An Army of Their Own. A small support army maintains and services the massive office buildings housing the executive branch. Imagine the job of supplying 2.8 million workers—not to mention hiring, paying, reviewing, promoting, and sometimes firing them. These details require still another type of institution in the American bureaucracy: independent **central service agencies**, most notably the Office of Personnel Management (OPM) and the General Services Administration (GSA).

Central service agencies: The organizations that supply and staff the federal government.

Want to work for the U.S. government? The OPM manages the giant "USAJobs" website, which lists hundreds of thousands of federal bureaucracy job openings each year. Your application will be screened by OPM staff. If you are hired, your employment materials (pay level, vacation time details, and health benefits) will come from them. And when you decide to leave government service, the OPM determines the government pension you have accumulated.

While you are a government employee, the GSA manages all the details of maintenance and supply. Your building just got painted? The GSA did the work—or hired and supervised the company that did it under contract. Do you need a shipment of forest fire–fighting helicopters (for the National Park Service) or a secure smartphone (at the OMB)? The GSA is your one-stop shopping spot.

Private contractors: Private companies that contract to provide goods and services for the government.

Private Contractors. The final category of government employees does not work directly for the government. They come from private companies that provide goods and services under contract to the government. **Private contractors** now perform many jobs that once were handled directly by government employees. For example, the military increasingly relies on private firms to provide meals, transportation, security services, and even commando teams. For the first time in American history, there were more private contractors (over 200,000) than uniformed military personnel (about 190,000) in the war zones in both Iraq and Afghanistan. (Compare to the Vietnam War, where the ratio of uniformed soldiers to private contractors was an estimated fifty-five to one.[23])

● *U.S. private security contractors in Iraq investigating the site where a military bus was damaged by a roadside bomb. An ever-expanding world of private contractors supports American military forces worldwide—and performs nearly every type of government service, from collecting trash to monitoring trade agreements.*

Besides war-related services, private companies provide a full range of government services, including homeland security, international diplomacy, prison management, and garbage collection.

Why contract out government services? Three main reasons: First, private companies, foundations, and nongovernmental organizations often have special skills and resources they can bring to a job. Second, they lobby hard for the business. And third, Americans critical of the bureaucracy often assert that private companies work better and cheaper.

In practice, private contractors sometimes do a better job than the public sector, but at other times they charge more for inferior services. For better or for worse, private contracting in government is here to stay. The key to making it work is ensuring that government officials maintain careful oversight of the work that is done for hire.[24]

Executive branch agencies and commissions all face leadership challenges similar to those faced by the cabinet departments. The appointment process is cumbersome and complicated by politics. New appointees scramble to learn the bureaucratic ropes, even as the to-do list piles ever higher—and meanwhile the administrative team takes months or even years to get into place.

How can the nation's agencies operate effectively when their leaders are on the way in and just learning the ropes, or are on the way out and operating as lame ducks? For an answer, we need to confront the complicated question of just who is in charge of the American bureaucracy.

THE BOTTOM LINE

» The federal bureaucracy includes five different types of agencies. The fifteen cabinet departments, forming the largest group, employ roughly 1.9 million civilians.

» The president appoints a small number of executives; the rest are members of the permanent civil service. The cabinet has grown far more diverse in the past twenty-five years.

» The cabinet and other appointed executives provide political direction; the civil servants provide expertise and continuity.

» Among the many challenges to a smoothly functioning system is the time—often more than a year—that it takes a new administration to get its leadership team in place.

» The government includes four other types of bureaucracies: Executive agencies focus on one type of issue, such as environmental quality; independent regulatory commissions oversee specific industries; central service agencies staff and supply the entire bureaucracy; and private contractors are licensed to provide goods and services for the government. Different types of agencies face different political problems and challenges.

Who Controls the Federal Bureaucracy?

Managing four million civilian bureaucrats and military personnel, and over five million private contractors,[25] is a daunting leadership responsibility—and a giant management headache. It is also crucial for democracy. Self-rule requires mastering the bureaucracy. But who is in charge? Traditional answers include the people, the president, Congress, and the interest groups. Recently, the courts have stepped in and taken a more active role.

Finally, there is a popular perspective championed by former President Donald Trump and many conservatives: A sprawling bureaucracy that relies on experts is fundamentally at odds with the people, who rely on common sense. Political leaders like Trump are eager to rethink the entire bureaucracy. Let's look at each of these perspectives.

The People

In a democracy, the federal government must ultimately respond to the people. Most executive departments trumpet something like "We Serve the People" on their websites. However, real popular control faces a core problem: Much of what the bureaucracy does is too technical for direct public engagement.

How does the IRS compute tax penalties for S corporations that wrongly elect to amortize anticipated losses with write-downs? What is the maximum engineering pendular sway ratio on truss-style bridges? Does the chemical compound bisphenol-A, widely used in plastics, leach into bottled drinking water—and if so, how dangerous is it to public health? Few Americans have the time or knowledge to develop opinions about such matters. We need someone to act on our behalf.

The President

In theory, the president controls the bureaucracy. The Constitution is clear on this issue: "The executive Power shall be vested in a President of the United States of America." The president is the bureaucrat-in-chief. The form of bureaucratic control that follows from this declaration is known as **overhead democracy**: The people elect presidents, who, through their appointees, control the bureaucracy from the top.

In practice, most presidents have been frustrated in their efforts to manage the millions of people under their command. Harry Truman put it famously when he commented on his successor, General Dwight D. Eisenhower: "He'll sit here and he'll say 'Do this!' and 'Do that!' *And nothing will happen.* Poor Ike, it won't be a bit like the army. He'll find it very frustrating."[26]

When presidents appoint directors of the executive branch, they quickly discover that the bureaucracy has its own preferences, processes, and routines. Before long, many executives begin to see the world through the eyes of their agencies—rather than from the perspective of the White House.

After four years of butting heads with federal agencies, the Trump administration hit upon a bold executive action: Create an entirely new classification of federal employees who would have no civil service protection—they would serve at the discretion of the president. Known as *Schedule F*, the plan would permit an administration to turn any policymaking role into a political appointment.

Overhead democracy: A system by which the people elect the president, who, through their appointees, controls the bureaucracy from the top.

The Trump Administration never implemented Schedule F, the courts never reviewed it, and the Biden administration promptly revoked it. In its original form it may not have passed legal scrutiny. After all, Congress created the Civil Service and it probably cannot be revoked by executive action.

Still, Schedule F offers populists opposed to the national bureaucracy a clear plan. Former President Trump has emphasized the plan at rallies. A conservative Congress might agree with a future administration and write it into law. It all sounds highly technical, but watch carefully. Schedule F bids to be the biggest change in the federal bureaucracy—and one of the most important in American governance—since 1883 when the merit system first went into place.[27]

Congress

Although bureaucrats "belong" to the executive branch, the legislative branch wields a surprising amount of authority over them. Congress shapes the bureaucracy in four primary ways.

- **Funding.** Most important, Congress funds nearly all executive branch programs because it determines the federal budget. If Congress does not like a bureaucratic proposal, or if an agency head falls out of favor with a powerful subcommittee, that program or department may find its budget slashed.

- **Oversight.** Congress has formal power to supervise the executive branch. Policing department and agency actions is normally a routine operation—making sure that funds are properly expended or that programs achieve their stated goals. But Congress can extend its oversight authority by launching major investigations of executive branch actions. When the other party controls Congress, agency heads can expect an uncomfortable grilling when they appear before congressional committees.

- **Authorization.** Congress often has to reauthorize laws after a specified number of years. Although recent administrations have increasingly relied on executive orders, Congress wields the power to amend programs or even deny their reauthorization.

- **Reorganization.** Finally, Congress can change the structure and nature of executive branch organizations. Recently, for example, some House Democrats proposed to eliminate the Immigration and Customs Enforcement (ICE) agency, while Republicans contemplated plans to shift several programs, such as a revised H1-B visa program for skilled workers, from the Department of Labor to the Department of Education—and possibly even merge the two departments into one.[28]

These four sources of power add up to extensive congressional influence. Agency heads and cabinet secretaries are often more responsive to Congress—with its power of the purse and oversight authority—than to the president. Bureaucratic leaders regularly lobby Congress for additional funding or authority. They also frequently complain, however, about congressional "micromanagement."

Political scientists view the relationship between Congress and the bureaucracy through **principal-agent theory**. This approach analyzes how a principal (in this case, Congress) hires an agent (the bureaucracy) to do a job. The problem arises when the agent has much more information than the principal. How do you control a bureaucracy when there is "information asymmetry," that is, when "they" know a lot more than "you" do? The answer: Make sure their interests are the same as yours. Many scholars suggest that although Congress cannot possibly supervise everything the bureaucracy does, the power of its weapons—especially

Principal-agent theory: Details how policymakers (principals) control the actors who work for them (agents)— but who have far more information than they do.

funding and oversight—leads bureaucratic officials, by and large, to conform to congressional wishes.[29] Put differently, the fear of being hauled before a congressional panel and threatened with loss of funding is enough to make bureaucrats worry about congressional intent and desires.

Congressional power also is circumscribed, of course. The power to shape or influence the bureaucracy is still a far cry from the power to command it. And today the deep stalemate of a partisan Congress makes many of its oversight tools far more difficult to wield.

Interest Groups

Interest groups closely engage bureaucrats as they administer the laws. As we saw in Chapter 12, lobbying groups comment extensively on proposed rules. They offer information about the needs and capacity of the affected industry. As bureaucrats finalize rules and implement programs, they routinely engage industry representatives, whose cooperation may be necessary to make the program work smoothly. Officials in the bureaucracy, trade groups, and consumer alliances often share expertise and interests. Over time, close relations may develop, making lobbyists influential in the day-to-day operations of the executive agencies. Interest groups—often fighting among themselves—have many ways to challenge overzealous regulators: They can go public with complaints, enlist friends in Congress, or sue. The result is another set of influences on bureaucrats in action.

Bureaucratic Autonomy

Partly because they have so many would-be masters, bureaucrats wind up with considerable autonomy in how they do their work. Many civil servants have strong views about their field, whether it is protecting the environment, enforcing civil rights laws, or keeping the homeland safe. They also have an interest in increasing their own autonomy—applying their best judgment to the problems they face.

Some federal bureaucrats themselves call attention to abuses within their department or agency. These happen enough that there is a term for a worker—public or private—who reports corruption or fraud: **whistleblower**. In many cases, permanent civil servants blow the whistle on fraudulent or misbehaving political appointees higher up in the department or agency.

Whistleblower: A federal worker who reports corruption or fraud.

Finally, the street-level bureaucrats—the officials who deal directly with the public—often exercise a great deal of discretion. From the top to the bottom, bureaucracies tend to seek autonomy from their many masters. That, in turn, has generated a powerful critique.

Challenging the Experts. Today, many attack the bureaucracy as a "deep state" that pursues its own interests regardless of the people and their elected representatives. The attack echoes an old American theme: The massive bureaucracy relies on experts—economists, health specialists, foreign language specialists—who make decisions based on their training and skills; they are, fundamentally, at odds with the people, who rely on common sense. And they often make mistakes that common sense could have avoided, for example, pursuing free trade that hollows out American cities, blundering into wars, or botching COVID testing by clinging to unrealistic laboratory standards.

President Trump and some of his advisors made this a major theme of his presidency, and it soon spread far beyond the president's circle. During the COVID lockdowns, politicians ranging from Senator Rand Paul (R-KY) to Governor Ron DeSantis (R-FL) criticized scientists like Dr. Anthony Fauci as narrow, arrogant, and even destructive. They insisted that the idea of closing schools, requiring

" I really believe red tape is the future!"

Dukelow

● *Who controls the federal bureaucracy? Agencies follow their operating procedures and are acutely aware of what they can and can't legally do. Like every organization, they pursue their own self-interest. This can be extremely frustrating to presidents who want to institute fundamental change, and an endless source of mockery.*

masks, and mandating vaccinations violated the very idea of freedom and failed to strike a proper balance between promoting health and a robust economy.[30]

Across the party divide, Democrats praised and admired Fauci and the health team for fighting to save lives. They responded that misinformation was mixing with the populist critique and that in heavily Republican districts vaccine hesitancy was higher than the rest of the country—as were the death rates.[31]

Despite the fury, neither Congress nor the White House has ever made much progress rolling back the supposed deep state. After all, the experts in the many agencies perform vital tasks. Each crisis has Americans turning to the agencies that can help formulate a response. Still, the Trump administration—with its Schedule F—broke new conceptual ground in trying to bring the bureaucracy into line with its political goals.

Major questions doctrine: Conservative legal doctrine that limits administrative discretion by holding that administrative agencies need explicit authorization from Congress before deciding issues of major importance.

The Courts Step In.   Recently, the Supreme Court has begun to take on the public regulation and administration of the bureaucracy by promulgating a new approach that conservative scholars have called the **major questions doctrine**: A regulatory agency may not make regulatory judgments on important matters unless Congress has given it clear, statutory language authorizing the agency's regulatory actions.[32]

When, for example, the EPA promulgated a rule pushing utilities to move from coal to cleaner forms of energy such as wind and solar, the Court ruled that it could not do so without a clear mandate from Congress. As Congress is mired in stalemate, such mandates are not likely. In a concurring opinion, justice Neil Gorsuch was blunt: This was a response "to the explosive growth of the administrative state since 1970."[33]

Chevron doctrine: Principle of judicial review that requires courts to defer to federal agencies' interpretation of ambiguous congressional statutes.

This is a sharp break with traditional judicial doctrine, codified in *Chevron v. Resources Defense Council* (1984). The **Chevron doctrine** instructs courts to defer to an administrative agency's interpretation of a statute—especially where the statute is ambiguous.[34] The Court again in June 2022 revisited the Chevron doctrine of deference to the bureaucracy in a case involving Medicare reimbursements for prescriptions. This time the Court simply ignored the *Chevron* case, ruling against Medicare.

Where do the West Virginia and Medicare cases leave the bureaucracy as it makes rules on everything from Wall Street to climate change? And what about the fight against climate change more generally? Keep a close eye on the new conservative court majority (discussed in Chapter 16) as it challenges bureaucratic authority in the years ahead.

Democracy Revisited

Many agents—the president, Congress, courts, and interest groups—exert some control over the bureaucracy. Each does so on behalf of others: The White House tries to speak for the national public, Congress for voters in a state or district, courts to defend injured parties or protect the Constitution, and interest groups on behalf of clients who range from business to environmentalists to the civil

WHAT DO YOU THINK?

Change Versus Stability: Should We Have More Politically Appointed Bureaucrats?

Presidents often complain that "the bureaucracy" is unresponsive to their goals. Career civil servants—hired long before a new administration sweeps into office—owe their loyalty to the department or agency they serve, not to the current president or the appointed head of their bureau. Is this tension a problem for good governance?

Yes. "Deep state" equals gridlock. Career bureaucrats can be a drag on innovation, which our government desperately needs to keep up with a twenty-first-century economy and global political crises. When bureaucrats block the goals of an elected president, they are acting against the popular will. I would vastly increase the proportion of *appointed* civil servants, following the practice in other democratic countries. We should simplify the process for appointing new officials so that each administration can introduce a new team and change the direction of public policy.

No. Leave the experts in charge. The complex demands of governing our trillion-dollar federal bureaucracy require technical expertise and seasoned experience. Career bureaucrats have been a central feature of the executive branch for well over a century. They are controlled by democratic norms—responding to leaders who are approved by the Senate and appointed by the president. Besides, with all the problems of political gridlock and getting a team into place, the permanent bureaucracy provides stability and is key to the American government's ability to function and adapt.

rights community. Bureaucrats try to maximize their own discretion to do what they think is best. The Supreme Court has moved to limit that discretion, returning power to a Congress that, bogged down in stalemate, does not seem ready to exercise it. Do all these clashing forces add up to democratic control?

The answer is yes and no. At times, these different forms of democratic control offer a rough kind of popular oversight. Administrations that focus on delivering services can have considerable success; presidents who seek to change the direction of federal policy sometimes succeed; congressional oversight often improves responsiveness. But these levers of democratic control are all blunt instruments. Effectively using them takes hard work and constant attention. In the next section, we examine three reform proposals that might strengthen popular control.

THE BOTTOM LINE

» In a democracy, the public must ultimately control the government bureaucracy. The question is how.

» Different actors exert some influence over the bureaucracy: the president (who names the leaders), Congress (through funding and oversight), and interest groups.

» Bureaucrats still operate with considerable autonomy, especially those at the "street level."

» The conservative majority on the Supreme Court has begun to target that administrative autonomy.

Reforming the Bureaucracy

Americans ask a great deal of the bureaucracy, but—as reported at this chapter's start—they do not like it much. Let us look at the usual criticisms and then explore some solutions.

Critiques

Three major sources of disapproval focus on cost, inertia, and public mistrust.

Cost. Critics complain about the high cost of the bureaucracy and its programs. As a proportion of America's gross domestic product (GDP), however, the cost of the bureaucracy—as well as the number of federal bureaucrats—has remained generally steady over the past forty years. And although every politician has a story to tell about waste or fraud, most bureaucratic programs have a substantial constituency who rely on the service they provide. The bureaucratic agencies meet real needs, which is one reason elected officials find them difficult to cut.[35]

Inertia. American politics and culture are in constant motion. In our restless, innovative nation, the slow, rule-bound, hierarchical bureaucracy never seems to keep up. Many examples illustrate government organizations that are out of touch with a changing nation. Why do NASA flights, such as the space shuttle, always take off from Florida, despite uncertain weather and a growing population potentially endangered by crashes? Because an obscure 1950s rule prohibited the flight of test aircraft west of the Mississippi River. Once bureaucratic routines are set, they are hard to change.

Inertia also comes from clashing political desires. For example, the government is prohibited—again by bureaucratic regulations—from purchasing knives, forks, and spoons from abroad. Employees on State Department business are prohibited from flying aboard non-American airlines. It is often less expensive, however, to buy foreign goods or to fly on international carriers. Why don't bureaucratic rules shift to accommodate this reality? Because multiple political constituencies demand different things. Congress, reflecting many voices, insists on both efficient purchasing policies *and* "buying American."

Clashing rules reflect different goals and values: We want to spread government contracts around the country, ensure social equity, stimulate new kinds of American products and services, and support American producers. These desires can clash with one another—and with the need for lower costs or faster services. Which priority deserves the most weight? The effort to choose among them is what democracy is all about. It is a debate that never ends.

Another, more troubling, problem is the increasing difficulty of recruiting the "best and the brightest" to government service. Individuals tapped for senior positions face the long process—and, often, hardball politics—we have described: Eager appointees linger in limbo for months waiting for a senator to lift their "hold." Then they must generate an extraordinary paper trail to pass security clearance; for example, these busy people must report every trip they took abroad in the last ten years. The media will jump on any past indiscretion. And, after all these hurdles, appointees arrive on the job and discover that civil service pay scales have only inched up in recent years.

Perhaps the real challenge is something unexpected: how to make government service more attractive to more people.

Public Mistrust. Politicians from both parties bash the bureaucracy. Republican Ronald Reagan announced that "government is not the solution to our problem" and declared, "It is time to make [bureaucrats] stand by our side, not ride on our back." Democrat Bill Clinton declared, "The era of big government is over."

Fueling public mistrust of bureaucrats are scandals and mistakes, many covered in detail by a 24/7 media mix of headlines, punditry, blogs, and tweets. In an institution as large as the federal bureaucracy, occasional examples of error, corruption, and fraud are inevitable. After all, government officials are human, just as prone to personal flaws and errors as anyone else. But in an environment of constant bureaucracy bashing, the bad news is far more prominently reported than are bureaucratic achievements, which only reinforces the general image of a corrupt, lazy bureaucracy riding "on our backs."

Proposed Reforms

The bureaucracy's reputation for being expensive, slow-moving, and scandal-ridden has attracted a long history of reform efforts. Let us consider four popular proposals.

Open Up the System.   One thing we can do is make the bureaucracy more transparent. Sunshine laws, which require public hearings and citizen input, open bureaucratic debates to public view. The **Freedom of Information Act** (**FOIA**) extends citizen access to agency and department deliberations. Any individual or news organization may file a FOIA request to see an unreleased government document (the legislation created a new verb, "to FOIA" a document). Today, every federal agency has its own website that tries to explain what it is doing.

Bureaucratic officials sometimes resist these efforts. Concerns have been raised about the potentially chilling effect on communication by politically motivated FOIA requests: As one headline asked, "Is the Freedom of Information Act Stifling Intellectual Freedom?"[36] Advocates of greater openness push for more access. Many government agencies drag their feet in response to a FOIA request.

Some have genuine security concerns. Others resent the time and effort it takes to ensure transparency. And many simply want to protect themselves from criticism.

More Efficiency!   Efforts to increase bureaucratic efficiency are as old as American government itself. Almost every administration tried to find ways to cut delays, reduce costs, and make the bureaucracy operate more smoothly, more like a business.

But here's the difference. Most businesses have a simple goal: maximize returns for investors. In contrast, bureaucratic agencies have many constituencies with multiple goals. For example, if the Department of Agriculture focuses on farmers and helps to maintain price levels, complaints will arise from consumers (high prices), environmentalists (disappearing topsoil), and even foreign governments (protections may violate free trade). Efficiency *sounds* good. However, government officials are called on to juggle many different

Freedom of Information Act (FOIA): A 1966 law that facilitates full or partial disclosure of government information and documents.

● *Businesswoman turned bureaucrat. Lillian Salerno, who ran a successful healthcare business, joined the Department of Agriculture in 2009 to manage a rural-development program providing some $30 billion annually in grants and low-interest loans to farmers in rural America.*

● *A San Francisco postal worker. Many conservatives have sought for years to "privatize" the U.S. Postal Service—hand its functions over to private companies like FedEx and UPS. What do you think: Would this be an improvement?*

goals: They have to be fair, responsive, and objective; focus on the national interest; and attend to international trade rules. Being efficient at one goal often clashes with being efficient at another.

Restore the Original Constitutional Logic. In theory, Congress passes laws and the bureaucracy implements them. In practice, Congress has become bogged down in stalemate, and each administration pursues its goals through administrative agencies. The Trump administration emphasized cracking down on undocumented individuals, building a wall on the southern border, and homeland security. The Biden administration came into office pursuing completely different goals.

One method for solving this problem, from conservative legal theory, is to rein in the administrative discretion. Executive agencies may pursue only what the law (in other words, what Congress) explicitly instructs them to do. No legal mandate, no administrative action.

Critics charge that this violates long-standing court doctrine—the Chevron deference approach—and amounts to nothing less than a conservative court's recipe for paralysis. It hobbles government, they argue, and offers no realistic alternative to getting things done. We cannot meet the challenges of global climate change—or a host of other problems—without administrative discretion. The battle between these perspectives is heating up. What do you think?

Privatization. If the bureaucracy seems slow and inefficient, perhaps private companies can do the job better, as discussed earlier in this chapter.

Private firms often can do a job for less. But the savings are at least partly offset by the need for government supervision. What happens when private companies—worrying about the bottom line and returning money to their investors—cut corners or violate rules?[37]

The benefits of privatization are still debated. Research in this area suggests that *competitive contracting* (requiring more than one bid from outside contractors who want to provide government services) can save money and boost quality. However, the most important calculation, one often overlooked by reformers, is factoring in a way for government officials to supervise the private contractor. Careful oversight is a critical dimension of making privatization work.[38]

THE BOTTOM LINE

» Critics of the bureaucracy focus on cost, inertia, and public mistrust.

» Solutions include sunshine reforms, reinventing government to make it more constituent friendly, and privatizing some of its functions.

Conclusion: The Real Solution Lies with You

President Kennedy came to office amid a burst of idealism and declared, "Ask not what your country can do for you—ask what you can do for your country." Inspired by the young president, the early civil rights movement, and the general optimism of the era, many college graduates streamed into public service. Today, fewer Americans are attracted to government service.[39] Can this trend change? What would draw *you* into working for the government?

The ultimate answer to the problems of bureaucracy, we believe, lies in the interest and commitment of a new generation. We are deeply concerned that people like you and your classmates— a well-educated group interested in political science—will bypass government altogether.

What is the problem? Politicians from both parties take shots at the bureaucracy. They freeze pay, downsize departments, and disparage millions of professionals. A closer look suggests that the bureaucracy performs many jobs we need and value, from managing our national finances to predicting the weather to defending the United States. Ultimately, our government—our democracy—is only as good as the bureaucracy that puts public policy into effect. And this brings us back to your generation's commitment to public service, and what might attract *you* to work in the name of bettering American democratic governance.

● *Wanted: a few good bureaucrats!*

CHAPTER SUMMARY

★ Within the executive branch, the U.S. federal bureaucracy does a vast amount of work in governing the country—and more closely resembles the nation's population than any other segment of our national government. However, Americans express deep ambivalence about our bureaucracy, generally rating it very low in opinion polls.

★ The American bureaucracy was established in reaction to the spoils system, dominant between 1828 and 1901. A merit-based hiring system has been in place for more than a century since.

★ In theory, all bureaucracies share five characteristics: hierarchy, division of labor, fixed routines, equal rules for all, and technical qualifications.

★ Bureaucrats in the United States, as in other countries, perform a wide range of functions—from managing the nation's defense and national economy to providing nutrition assistance and tax cuts. The bureaucracy is specifically charged with implementing the laws passed by Congress and signed by the president. This typically involves an administrative rulemaking process, as well as actual delivery of services and carrying out of programs.

★ Since the 1930s, the federal bureaucracy has grown to more than four million employees—two-thirds civilians and one-third active-duty military. This growth has occurred despite anti–"big government" sentiment among Americans; helping to overcome this sentiment have been the twin forces of war and enforcing morality.

★ Organizing such a sprawling set of cabinet departments and agencies, populated by civil servants and political appointees, is an immense job.

★ It is not readily apparent who is in charge of managing the bureaucracy. Many different players have a role, including the public, the president, Congress, and interest groups. The result of all those masters: Bureaucrats have considerable discretion in how they work.

★ This freedom can lead to serious tensions between Americans' democratic ideal of representative accountability and an unelected, often *unaccountable* workforce of civil servants.

★ Public disapproval of the bureaucracy arises from different complaints. Our executive bureaucracy costs too much, say some critics; others argue that bureaucratic inertia makes it difficult to respond to policy crises. A stream of well-reported scandals influences Americans' perceptions of our bureaucracy, driving up mistrust.

★ Reform efforts include enhancing the transparency of bureaucratic practices, reinventing government to improve responsiveness and reduce layers of management, and carefully privatizing government services.

KEY TERMS

Bureaucratic pathologies, p. 498
Central service agencies, p. 513
Chevron doctrine, p. 518
Civil servants, p. 504
Final rule, p. 501
Freedom of Information Act (FOIA), p. 521

Major questions doctrine, p. 518
Overhead democracy, p. 515
Pendleton Civil Service Act, p. 494
Principal-agent theory, p. 516
Private contractors, p. 513
Proposed rule, p. 501
Regulatory capture, p. 512

Spoils system, p. 494
Street-level bureaucrats, p. 502
Universalistic politics, p. 494
Whistleblower, p. 517

STUDY QUESTIONS

1. Is the U.S. federal bureaucracy too large? Do we need four million people working for the government—in addition to several million more hired under federal contracts? If you would like to see a smaller bureaucracy, where do you think we should start cutting workers?

2. Who *should* run the bureaucracy, in your view? Do bureaucrats have too much discretion in how they perform their duties? What are the respective merits of a "street-level" or "top-down" management style? And should presidents (or Congress, or interest groups, etc.) have more authority than they currently wield to exert their will on the bureaucracy?

3. What is a street-level bureaucrat? Give three examples. Some political scientists argue that, in effect, they use their discretion to make policy as much as the legislatures and leaders at the top of the bureaucracies. Do you agree? Why or why not?

4. Let's say you have just learned about some unsavory doings in your bureaucratic agency or department. Do you blow the whistle—that is, report the problem? Or do you keep quiet, knowing your job could be in danger? What factors would affect your decision?

5. Based on what you now know about the U.S. bureaucracy, should we mount a major push for reform? What type(s) of reforms would be most useful? Or are the various agencies and processes, such as rule-making, of the bureaucracy working pretty well the way they are?

6. What is the major questions doctrine? When the Supreme Court uses it to rein in administrative agencies, it argues that it is restoring constitutional balance. Critics say that the Court is making it impossible to address urgent problems like global climate change. Who do you think is right? Why?

7. Given your expanded knowledge of the bureaucracy, are you more or less likely to be interested in working in an executive office like the Treasury Department or EPA? Does this seem like a promising way to exercise your civic spirit? Why or why not?

16 THE JUDICIAL BRANCH

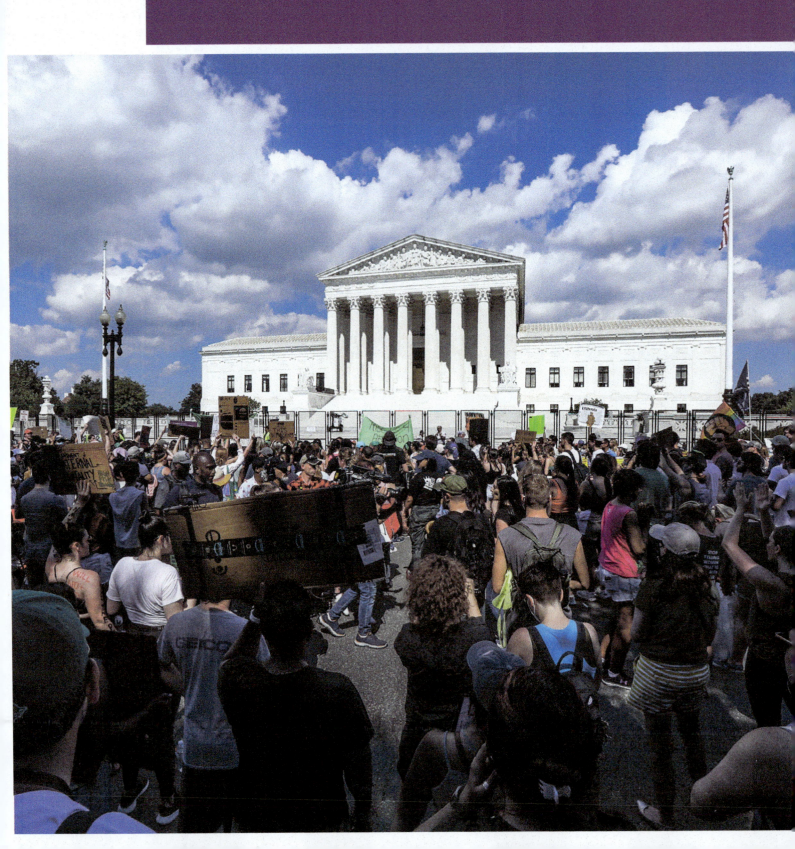

JUNE IS ALWAYS A GOOD TIME to visit the Supreme Court. There's usually high drama when the term comes to an end and the justices announce their rulings. In 2022, the Court's decisions rocked the legal world. Conservatives won a series of judgments that are likely to define American politics for years to come.

In its most momentous decision—*Dobbs v. Jackson Women's Health Organization*—the 6–3 majority held that *Roe v. Wade* (1973), protecting the right to an abortion, was "egregiously wrong" and "exceptionally weak." The Constitution includes no right to an abortion, concluded the majority, and states are free to ban the procedure. One justice, Clarence Thomas, pushed further and in a separate opinion suggested that states should be permitted to ban contraception and same-sex marriage—because all were built on the same legal foundation: a right to privacy. None of the other justices were willing to go that far. At least not yet.

The response was tumultuous. Republicans celebrated. "The Court has corrected a terrible legal and moral error," said Republican Senate leader Mitch McConnell. "This historic ruling will save countless innocent lives," added House Republican leaders.[1] Democrats denounced the ruling. "What century are they in?" asked President Joe Biden, who added, "We cannot allow an out-of-control Supreme Court working in conjunction with extremist elements of the Republican Party to take away freedoms and our personal autonomy."[2]

Three members of the Supreme Court dissented "with sorrow for this court, but more, for the many millions of American women who have today lost a fundamental constitutional protection" that they had enjoyed for almost fifty years.[3]

Overruling *Roe v. Wade* would have been momentous all by itself, but the Court had more blockbuster rulings to announce. It knocked down a long-standing New York law that required people to show "proper cause" before the state would issue them a license to carry concealed guns. In *New York State Rifle and Pistol Association v. Bruen,* the Court majority ruled that citizens should not need to explain why they wanted a firearm. What state restrictions were permissible? The majority suggested that the state could do background and mental health checks, require training, and forbid firearms

 Consider how the law reflects the American people—and our national culture.

 Learn how the judicial system operates.

 Examine the courts' role in American politics.

 Explore the inner workings of the Supreme Court.

 Reflect on how judges decide cases.

 Review landmark judicial cases.

 Weigh proposals for reforming the court system.

In this chapter, you will

● *Abortion supporters and opponents gather on the Supreme Court's marble steps, following the* Dobbs v. Jackson Women's Health Organization *decision overturning* Roe v. Wade. *Court rulings on a half-dozen major issues each year reshape American politics and government—quite an achievement for the "least dangerous branch."*

in schools. But the decision meant a lot more guns—and a lot of controversy. "We're already dealing with a major gun violence crisis," responded New York Governor Kathy Hochul.[4]

In another decision, the Court also seemed to revolutionize administrative procedures when it struck down a rule announced by the Environmental Protection Agency (EPA). The rule, which had not yet gone into effect, limited greenhouse gas emissions by pushing fossil fuel companies to shift toward renewable energy sources (we described the case, *West Virginia v. EPA*, in Chapter 15). The Court ruled that Congress did not explicitly authorize that effort, and so the EPA could not pursue it. Conservatives cheered a limitation on the federal bureaucracy; liberals glumly responded that Republicans had defeated American efforts to address global climate change.

Two more landmark cases dealt with the separation of church and state. In Bremerton, a small town in Washington State, a high school football coach used to pray on the field after games. The school district forbade the practice. The Supreme Court (again, 6–3) ruled that the district had violated the coach's free speech and freedom to exercise religion. The minority responded that the coach was a role model and that his very visible prayer would make students feel pressured to join in—a public establishment of religion forbidden by the Constitution (*Kennedy v. Bremerton School District*, discussed in Chapter 5).[5] The Court had, in essence, created a new standard for judging the separation of church and state. Instead of asking whether a government action has a secular purpose or endorses religion (the Lemon test; see Chapter 5), the Court now asks whether a government action fits with "historical practices and understandings" about the establishment of religion.

In still another religious case, the Court ruled that Maine could not exclude religious schools when it established a tuition program for private schools. Providing funds to religious schools was not the same as establishing a religion; the Court minority responded that the state would be sending funds to schools that restricted enrollment based on sexual orientation, gender identity, and religion (*Carson v. Mankin*, also discussed in Chapter 5).

Notice the remarkable assertion of power represented across these decisions. An angry president, the majority in Congress, state lawmakers, environmental scientists—all were powerless (at least temporarily) before the Court. How did nine, mostly elderly, unelected figures come to hold such extraordinary sway over the government? How does that fit with democratic norms? During the battle to ratify the Constitution, Alexander Hamilton predicted that the judiciary "will always be the least dangerous" and "the weakest" branch of government. It has "no influence" over "the sword" (the president controls the army) or "the purse" (Congress is in charge of the budget).[6] Yet over time, the U.S. judiciary has accumulated sweeping authority. It negates laws, rules, and regulations that violate the Constitution—as the Court majority interprets it.

We have seen the great reach and power of the Supreme Court throughout this book. For example, it swept away hard-won congressional agreements (like the Missouri Compromise) and protected the rights of those enslaving people to settle in every territory, regardless of what the people of that territory wanted (in *Dred Scott*, 1857); it first permitted segregation (*Plessy v. Ferguson*, in 1896) and then rejected it (*Brown v. Board of Education*, 1954); it swept away a network of state laws prohibiting abortion (*Roe v. Wade*, 1973) and then overruled itself and let the states reassert those prohibitions (*Dobbs v. Jackson Women's Health Organization*). And the list of major rulings goes on.

The previous two chapters, on the presidency and on the bureaucracy, asked if and how each still fits into a democratic framework. The question becomes even more pointed for the federal courts. Unelected officials wield the power to overrule the long, hard democratic process of forging legislation in both Washington and the states.[7] The founders believed that the more political branches of government—the president and Congress—needed to be checked by the courts. Has that check now grown too powerful? Is it used too often?

Still, the Supreme Court also sits within the intricate system of checks and balances. The other branches, the states, and the agencies can all push back. For example, when the Court ruled that Maine could not exclude religious schools from its subsidies (in *Carson v. Mankin*), state officials amended their anti-discrimination laws. Institutions that accept state funds may not discriminate based on sexual identity and sexual orientation. The two Christian schools that had filed the suit in the first place reported that they would forego the funds rather than accept LGBTQ+ students. The last word? No, only the latest word in a long debate.

American government includes a more fundamental check. The Constitution gives Congress the power to shape the federal judiciary. Congress responded to the *Dred Scott* decision by adding a tenth justice (in 1863), squeezed the number down to seven members (in 1866), and, finally, returned it to nine (in 1869). Today, progressives have begun to press for fundamental changes. And the prospect, once barely imaginable, may be enhanced by the Court's own standing, which has now fallen to the lowest point since polling began more than a half-century ago.

Who are we? A nation founded on the world's oldest constitution, which directly or indirectly governs almost every aspect of our collective life. The courts apply the Constitution to the problems we face. Over time, the Court has become increasingly active in striking down acts of Congress and state legislatures. Too active? That's a critical question for our republic.

We begin with the basics. What kind of institution is the court system? How does it make decisions? How did it amass so much power over American politics, government, and daily lives? Throughout we will pose the same fundamental query: Does the American political system effectively balance the authority of elected officials and lifetime judges? And can an institution that was designed to be nonpartisan—that draws its authority from the people's deference and respect—survive for long in the eye of the American partisan storm?

The answer starts with the basic character of the American people: *Who we are.*

BY THE NUMBERS

The U.S. Judiciary

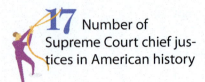

17 Number of Supreme Court chief justices in American history

4 Number of Supreme Court chief justices since 1953

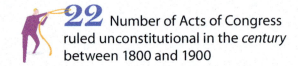

16.5 Average number of years a Supreme Court justice served before retiring, 1790–1954

25.4 Average number of years a Supreme Court justice served before retiring, 1970–2022

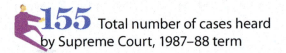

22 Number of Acts of Congress ruled unconstitutional in the *century* between 1800 and 1900

38 Number of Acts of Congress ruled unconstitutional in the *decade* between 2012 and 2022[8]

155 Total number of cases heard by Supreme Court, 1987–88 term

67 Total number of cases heard by Supreme Court, 2021–22 term

90 Percentage of defendants in federal criminal cases who plead guilty and never go to trial[9]

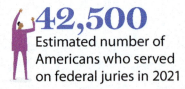

42,500 Estimated number of Americans who served on federal juries in 2021

1.4 Estimated number, in millions, who served on juries in state or local courts[10]

100 Total number in millions of cases filed in state courts[11]

How has the character and role of our judicial system changed over time?

🏛 Who Are We? A Nation of Laws . . . and Lawyers

The United States relies on courts to resolve more matters than most nations. The result is a deeply legalistic political culture.

Embracing the Law—and Lawsuits

Litigation: The conduct of a lawsuit.

Lawsuits, or **litigation**, are a near-constant feature of American public life. The annual U.S. criminal caseload includes thirty-five to forty million cases filed in state courts. Traffic violations add another fifty-five million cases. Federal courts open about four hundred thousand new cases a year (notice that federal cases equal about 1 percent of the volume in state courts). Another three-quarters of a million cases enter bankruptcy courts. Add all of these up, and the United States approaches one hundred million legal actions a year. And that is before we get to all the cases heard in specialized federal courts.

Courts are the primary sites for settling both private and public disputes. Advocacy groups, private citizens, and corporations go to court as a "first-strike" option. Litigation is an essential part of the rule-making process (discussed in Chapter 15). Business competition spills into the courts. Most other industrial nations rely more on **mediation** in noncriminal cases; citizens also are more likely to defer to civil servants. In contrast, Americans sue. Only a few other nations—most notably, Great Britain and Denmark—have as many suits per capita as the United States does.

Americans are not only a people of litigation but also a people of lawyers, with 1.3 million lawyers (around 800,000 in active practice). That number has risen fourfold since 1960, six times faster than population growth. The nation now has one lawyer for every 250 people—far outstripping the United Kingdom (one in every 401), India (one in every 1,200), France (one in 1,403), and every other nation (see Comparing Nations 16.1). As early as 1835, Alexis de Tocqueville could comment, "There is hardly any political question in the United States which does not, sooner or later, turn into a judicial one."[12]

Mediation: A way of resolving disputes without going to court, in which a third party (the mediator) helps two or more sides negotiate a settlement.

Trust in Courts

Traditionally, lawyers and courts enjoyed high prestige. Tocqueville described early nineteenth-century lawyers as democracy's natural aristocrats and noted that the American people trusted them. Not anymore.

Today, the courts struggle to maintain their reputation (Figure 16.1).[13] One big challenge is managing the conflicts that a polarized political system thrusts on the judiciary. For example, after Justice Scalia died in 2016, President Obama nominated Merrick Garland to the Supreme Court. The Republican-controlled Senate refused to hold hearings on the grounds that a presidential election was approaching—although nine months remained before the vote. When he won the

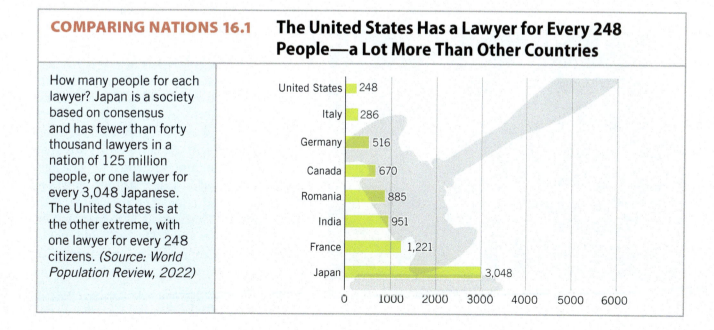

COMPARING NATIONS 16.1   **The United States Has a Lawyer for Every 248 People—a Lot More Than Other Countries**

How many people for each lawyer? Japan is a society based on consensus and has fewer than forty thousand lawyers in a nation of 125 million people, or one lawyer for every 3,048 Japanese. The United States is at the other extreme, with one lawyer for every 248 citizens. *(Source: World Population Review, 2022)*

Country	People per lawyer
United States	248
Italy	286
Germany	516
Canada	670
Romania	885
India	951
France	1,221
Japan	3,048

Confidence in the U.S. Supreme Court

"Now I am going to read you a list of institutions in American society. Please tell me how much confidence you yourself have, in each one—a great deal, quite a lot, some, or very little. The U.S. Supreme Court"

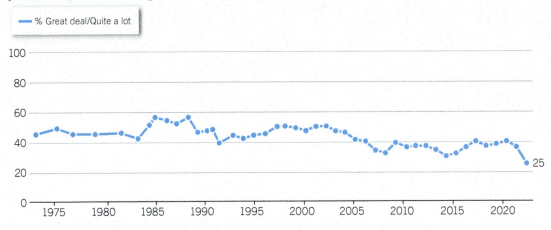

● **FIGURE 16.1** *The Supreme Court's approval rating hit an all-time low in 2022. For Democrats, the approval rating is down to 13 percent. Even a majority of Republicans are skeptical, with just 38 percent saying they have confidence in the Court. What happens to the Court's authority when the people's respect for it vanishes? (Gallup)*

election, Donald Trump nominated and the Republican Senate quickly confirmed conservative Neil Gorsuch. Approval rose 15 percent among Republicans and fell 10 percent among Democrats.[14] Four years later, liberal Ruth Bader Ginsburg died just weeks before the 2020 election. President Trump immediately nominated a conservative, Amy Coney Barrett, who was quickly confirmed without a single Democratic vote. Smart politics? The growing politicization of an institution that was designed to stand above politics? Or both?

Recent polls register the problem: The Supreme Court has fallen to an all-time low in public esteem—only 25 percent of the public approves. For the first time in polling history, the Court comes in below the president and is moving toward congressional territory (rock bottom of all American institutions, as we saw in Chapter 13). Here's the most important question: The Court relies on respect for the law. What happens to the Court's authority when that respect vanishes?

Courts in American Culture

Images of law and lawyers run through American culture, with the image alternating between heroism and cynicism. In *To Kill a Mockingbird*, Gregory Peck's Atticus Finch wins the Black community's respect when he passionately defends a Black man unjustly accused of rape: "In our courts all men are created equal," he proclaims at the film's climax. "That's no ideal to me. That is a living, working reality." The book and movie's racial idealism reflected the optimism of the early 1960s—though all that idealism did not protect the Black hero from being murdered (shot seventeen times, no less) by prison guards.

● *Michael B Jordan and Jamie Foxx portray real-life figures in a stirring scene from the film* Just Mercy. *Images of law in popular culture are a longtime American staple.*

Julia Roberts played another legal heroine, the real-life Erin Brockovich, a clerk without any legal training whose indefatigable work led to a major environmental lawsuit against Pacific Gas and Electric for contaminating the water supply of Hinkley, California. Laura Dern won accolades for her portrayal of a divorce lawyer in *Marriage Story*. And in *Just Mercy*, Michael B. Jordan played Bryan Stevenson, a civil rights lawyer who worked to free wrongly condemned death row prisoners. Images of law as a kind of crusade—for racial equity, environmental protection, or criminal justice—reflect and reinforce images of political idealism.

In American culture, as in politics, the courts are a place where our highest ideals are on display—and where we simultaneously fear that corruption runs rampant. We will return at chapter's end to proposed reforms of the legal system. First, let's explore how that system works in practice.

THE BOTTOM LINE

» The United States relies on courts and litigation more than most other nations—a political reality reflected in both its number of lawsuits and its number of lawyers.

» Trust in the Supreme Court has fallen to an all-time low in recent years, as the Court now seems to reflect the intense partisanship of the era.

» Law continues to play an important role in American popular culture, which portrays it in both idealistic and cynical terms.

 # Organizing the Judicial Branch

The Constitution offers detailed instruction for Congress (Article 1) and vague rules for the executive branch (Article 2). The judiciary gets the least attention of all. The Constitution vests judicial power in the Supreme Court without specifying the number of justices it should include and empowers Congress to design the rest of our federal court system. This is an important point: Congress has the authority to reorganize the judiciary—a power that grows more tempting as the courts seem to become more partisan. This section examines how the courts are now organized. As usual, there is a distinctive look to how Americans run this branch of government.

Divided We Rule

By now you know the story: When Americans see government power, they divide it. Two chambers of Congress, with layers of committees and subcommittees; an executive branch split into departments, agencies, commissions, and White House offices; and a federalist "super-swirl cake" of national, state, and city officials all cooperating, competing, and overlapping. Well, you guessed it: Court powers also are divided.

Most other nations feature a single unitary system of courts. In contrast, the United States exhibits *judicial federalism*: There are separate federal and state court systems, and each is further divided, in most cases, into three layers (see Figure 16.2). Lower courts conduct trials, appellate courts hear appeals, and a supreme court in both state and federal systems renders a final verdict. The national Supreme Court is the ultimate arbiter for all cases that involve the Constitution

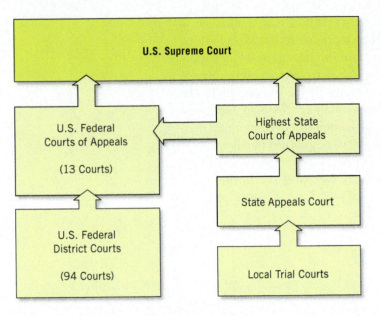

U.S. Supreme Court

U.S. Federal Courts of Appeals

(13 Courts)

U.S. Federal District Courts

(94 Courts)

Highest State Court of Appeals

State Appeals Court

Local Trial Courts

● **FIGURE 16.2** *Organization of the U.S. courts system.*

or federal law. Millions of cases are filed each year; around ten thousand appeals reach the Supreme Court, which only accepts and hears about seventy. That leaves a great deal of authority to the lower ranks of the judiciary.

State and Local Courts

Local trial and state appeals courts are the workhorses of the judiciary, handling most of the nontraffic cases in the United States each year. State courts are responsible for all cases that arise under state law; they rule on everything from antitrust disputes to murder cases, from medical malpractice to marijuana possession. Every state organizes its judicial system in its own way—so there is considerable variation around the nation.

The first stop in most cases is a state trial court (in which lawyers present evidence and witnesses testify to the facts of a case). Appeals usually are handled in state appellate courts (which focus on questions of law and whether the law was correctly applied). Appeals courts generally consist of an appellate court and then a court of final appeal, generally known as the state supreme court. Appeals from the top state courts may be heard by the U.S. Supreme Court. Many landmark cases originate—and sometimes are settled—in state courts. *Dred Scott* (which defended the spread of slavery and gave the country a major push toward the Civil War), *Roe v. Wade* (which struck down a Texas law banning abortion), and *Bush v. Gore* (which halted the recount of disputed presidential ballots in Florida in 2000) all began in state courts. However, these were exceptions. Very few of the millions of state cases ever reach a federal judge, as these cases did.

Judicial Selection

Interested in becoming a state judge? There are surprisingly few formal criteria for selection. You may not even need a law degree: twenty-two states and the federal courts require no formal training before judges start hearing cases.

Judicial Selection in the States. Most state judges first make their name as lawyers, though many come from government or academic positions. If you plan to lobby a governor to ensure your judicial appointment, make sure you pick the right state: Only seventeen states authorize their governor to select judges, and two leave selection to the state legislature. Most states (thirty-one) *elect* judges. Judges' terms range across the states, from two to fourteen years, and are usually renewable.

The idea of electing judges is controversial. After all, the courts are meant to be above partisan politics, protecting rights and weighing evidence without political pressures. Elections, say the critics, undermine the courts' ability to stand up for the rights of unpopular minorities. Moreover, campaign contributions and campaign promises could lead to bias and even corruption on the state benches. Former Supreme Court Justice Sandra Day O'Connor was an especially vocal critic of electing judges; she called judicial campaigns "tawdry and embarrassing."[15] Still, the United States is the land of five hundred thousand elected officials.

WHAT DO YOU THINK?

How Should States Select Their Judges?

Which of these three approaches to judicial selection in the states seems most persuasive to you?	**Let the people vote.** The people are the best guardians of their own welfare. Let them decide who their justices should be. No matter how courts are organized, it is naive to think that politics can be kept out of the equation. Today, 84 percent of the public thinks that justices sometimes let their own political views influence their rulings. Because politics is inevitable, the public should have a direct voice in judicial selection.[16]	**Appointment by a governor.** A state governor (with the advice and consent of the state senate) will have valuable information about the candidates and can keep better track of which justice is doing a good job. It also avoids the problems introduced by elections: campaigning, fundraising, potential corruption, and the temptation to win votes by making promises that could later compromise the court.	**Establish merit committees.** Courts must be above politics. They must defend the rights of minorities and unpopular views. The only way to ensure such fairness is to let impartial commissions select judges. The commission's nominees can then be voted up or down by the legislature.	**Unsure.** You will probably develop a stronger opinion on this question by the end of the chapter.

The American ideal—government by the people—leads many states to insist that judges stand before the public. After all, argue proponents, the last repository of rights and justice in a democracy ought to lie with the people themselves.

Judicial Selection to the Federal Bench. The president appoints federal judges and they are confirmed by the Senate. They hold their office for life. Until recently, the Senate routinely approved nearly all judicial appointments, sometimes with very little scrutiny. Then partisanship caught up with the bench. In today's Congress, the opposition party regularly challenges judicial nominations—slowing them down in the hope that their party will take the presidency and fill the empty seats. When the Republicans gained the Senate in 2014, they applied the brakes to the Obama administration's judicial appointments. By 2016, the administration's last year, almost three hundred positions were vacant. Because the Republicans maintained control of the Senate, the Trump administration had great success filling the judiciary with conservative appointees. By ending the filibusters for judicial nominees, the Senate confirmed 226 judges—28 percent of the federal bench in Trump's one term (Figure 16.3). Republican leaders were explicit about their aims: Transform the judiciary from the high court on down.[17]

Trump appointed nearly as many federal appeals court judges as Obama—in half the time. Biden was off to a fast pace as well.

Federal judges appointed by each president

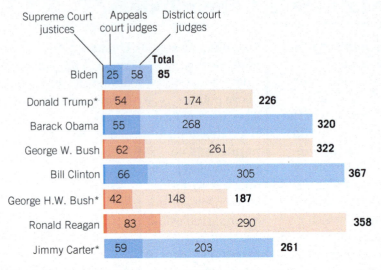

	Supreme Court justices	Appeals court judges	District court judges	Total
Biden	25	58		85
Donald Trump*	54	174		226
Barack Obama	55	268		320
George W. Bush	62	261		322
Bill Clinton	66	305		367
George H.W. Bush*	42	148		187
Ronald Reagan	83	290		358
Jimmy Carter*	59	203		261

*Served one term. Biden figure through October 2022.
Note: Excludes judges confirmed to certain specialized or territorial courts. Judges confirmed to multiple positions, such as those first appointed to a district court and later elevated to an appeals court, are counted separately for each position, but only once in each president's total.

● **FIGURE 16.3** *The number of federal judges appointed by each administration. As partisanship rises, more issues end up making the race to appoint sympathetic judges increasingly important.*

President Joe Biden came to office with a new Democratic majority in the Senate and set an even faster pace. In his first twenty-two months, the Senate had confirmed eighty-five federal justices and fifty-six more nominations were before the Senate (by October 15 of his second year). As long as the party in the White House controls the Senate, the fast pace of judicial appointments is likely to be continued. But when the opposition takes over, the approval process slows down or stops completely. A large backlog will develop and await a break in the partisan logjam or the next time the Senate and the White House are in the same party hands. Given the stakes, with political decisions slipping from Congress to the judiciary, the federal selection process may be even more political than judicial elections on the state level.

The Federal Courts in Action

Federal courts hear three types of cases. First, they handle crimes that violate federal laws, issues that involve federal treaties, and cases touching on the Constitution. Examples range from the dramatic to the mundane: terrorism, immigration, organized crime, civil rights, patents, insider trading, and flag burning. Second, they decide disputes that spill across state lines—for example, interstate drug trafficking and conflicts between parties in different states (when at least $75,000 is involved). Finally, after state courts have ruled on a case, the parties can appeal to the federal courts—if a federal issue is involved.

Most federal cases begin in one of the ninety-four **district courts**, which together house 677 judges. Every state has at least one district court, and the larger states (like California and Texas) have as many as four. District courts determine the facts of the case (did John Smith try to blow up a federal building?), build a record detailing the evidence, and then apply the law to reach a ruling. Cases at this level are heard by a single district judge.

Above the ninety-four district courts are thirteen federal appellate courts, known as **circuit courts**. A party that loses in district court can appeal to this next level. Three circuit court judges hear each case, usually to determine whether the district court made the correct ruling. They rule on the basis of the record established on the lower level; there is no jury and no cross-examination. Some 180 judges serve on these circuit courts, collectively ruling on nearly sixty thousand cases in a typical year. As with the district courts, the majority of circuit courts are organized geographically (with the exception of two, which are organized by issue) and referred to by their number (see Figure 16.4). Appeals from Ohio, for example, go to the Sixth Circuit Court of Appeals, based in Cincinnati. Some types of cases (like those involving patents or international trade) go directly to a court known as the U.S. Court of Appeals for the Federal Circuit. Like district court

District courts: The first level of federal courts, which hear the evidence and make initial rulings.

Circuit courts: The second stage of federal courts, which review cases decided in district courts and uphold or reverse those decisions.

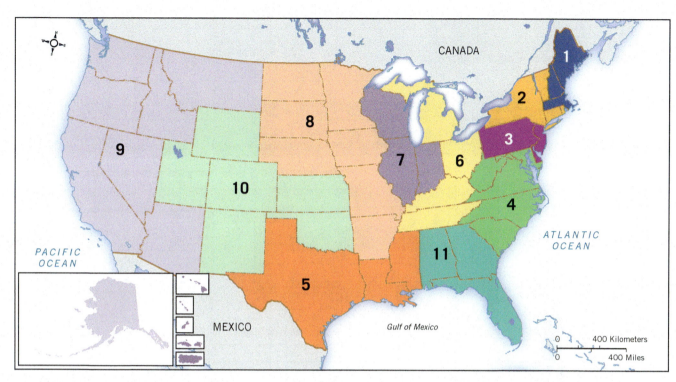

● **FIGURE 16.4** *The federal circuit courts. In addition, there are two courts, one for Washington, DC, and one for specialized cases, that are not shown here. (Federal Judicial Center)*

judges, those on circuit courts are nominated by the White House and subject to Senate confirmation.

The federal courts just described—Supreme, circuit, and district—are sometimes called Article III courts. Can you guess why? Because they spring from Article III of the Constitution. The next section turns to the other federal courts.

Specialized Courts

The federal judiciary also includes a set of specialized courts, each covering a specific subject such as military justice, tax disputes, terrorism, and bankruptcy. These courts' workload rises and falls with larger societal changes: bankruptcy claims, for example, soared to 1.5 million (during the Great Recession), settled at an average of 782,000 a year (between 2016 and 2019), and then tumbled to a very low 414,000 in 2021 (in the aftermath of COVID-19).

The president appoints (and the Senate confirms) judges to all of these courts. Unlike the judges in Article III courts, however, they do not serve for life. Bankruptcy judges, for example, serve renewable fourteen-year terms; federal magistrates, who handle certain types of civil trials, are appointed to renewable eight-year terms.

The U.S. military runs its own separate court system, which addresses breaches of justice by members of the armed forces. These courts became a source of controversy in recent years after President George W. Bush called for military tribunals to try defendants charged with terrorism against the United States, many of whom were being held as enemy combatants in Guantánamo Bay, Abu Ghraib, and other detention centers around the globe. The Obama administration at first suspended the military trials, but after Congress resisted moving the trials to civilian courts, the administration reinstated the tribunals with some changes in their rules. In rare cases, tribunals are permitted under the Constitution.

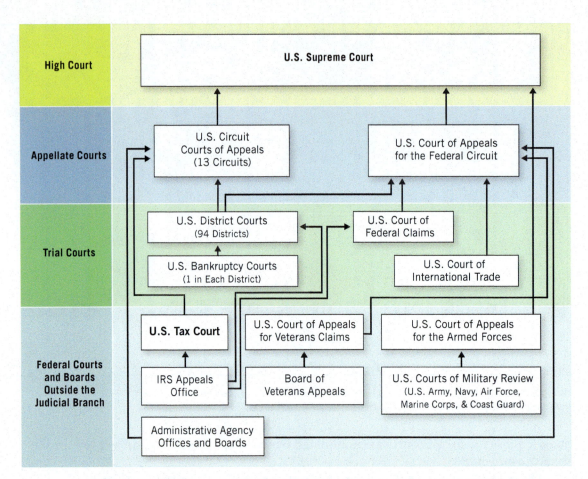

● **FIGURE 16.5** *Special courts within the federal system. A more detailed snapshot of the federal system illustrates that it is, in reality, far more complicated than the simple tripartite system of district courts, circuit courts, and the Supreme Court.*

The last large-scale use of military tribunals occurred after World War II, to try Nazi war criminals.[18]

Together, these specialized courts, ranging from bankruptcy to military, constitute something of a "third judiciary" alongside state and federal courts. Overall, specialized courts provide a further example of the complexity characterizing the divided, fragmented U.S. judicial branch—as Figure 16.5 vividly demonstrates.

Diversity in the Federal Judiciary

Do federal judges reflect America's population? No. Or at least not yet. Slow change began in 1973: That was the last year when every newly appointed judge was a white male. Since then, every administration, except the Trump administration, has added to the diversity of the federal courts (Table 16.1). The appointments during the Trump administration were 84 percent white and 76 percent male. The Biden administration, in contrast, has emphasized diversity more than any prior administration. In its first eighteen months, it appointed the first LGBTQ+ woman to the court of appeals, the first Muslim American to the federal judiciary, and ten Black women to the federal bench—including the first Black woman on the Supreme Court.[19]

Still, there is a way to go before the federal judiciary reflects the population. Seventy-one percent of judges identify as white non-Hispanic (compared to 63 percent of the population) and two out of three are male. Today, 12.4 percent of

| TABLE 16.1 | **How Presidents Compare on Racial and Ethnic Diversity of Appointed Judges** | | | | | | |

PRESIDENT	JUDGES	WHITE	BLACK	HISPANIC	ASIAN	OTHER	% BLACK/HISPANIC
Biden	84 (first 20 mos.)	29	21	14	11	9	42
Trump	226	189	9	9	13	6	7
Obama	324	208	58	31	18	0	36
G. W. Bush	324	266	24	30	4	0	18
Clinton	372	282	61	23	5	1	24
Bush	188	169	11	8	0	0	10

Source: Brennan Center for Justice; American Constitution Society

federal judges are Black (closely reflecting the percentage of the population), 9 percent are Hispanic (compared to 18.7 percent of the population), 5 percent are Asian American (again, roughly reflecting the population), and five justices are Native American (one-half of 1 percent).

Does it make a difference if the judge presiding over a federal case is female or Latino? Supreme Court Justice Sonia Sotomayor suggested that it did, ten years before she was appointed to the court. "I would hope that a wise Latina woman," Sotomayor said, "with the richness of her experience would more often than not reach a better conclusion than a white male who hasn't lived that life." Her autobiography vividly describes Sotomayor's distinctive childhood as a Puerto Rican girl living in New York City and filled in some of those details. Her perspective on how personal experience might inform judicial decisions provided cause for reflection—and also raised controversy. Former House Speaker Newt Gingrich claimed that a white male judge making a similar claim on behalf of white men would be forced to resign.[20]

Does background make a difference? Sometimes. Research suggests that Black judges are more likely to vote in favor of affirmative action,[21] more likely to find violations of the Voting Rights Act,[22] more likely to side with LGBTQ+ claimants, and more likely to accept Black defendants' claims of police misconduct.[23]

WHAT DO YOU THINK?

Identity on the Bench

| Do you agree with Justice Sotomayor's comment that a person's life experience can deeply inform his or her judgment about politics, culture, and other matters? | **Agree.** Everyone inevitably brings his or her personal experience to bear in making important decisions, and justices are no different. That's why diversity on the bench is so important. | **Disagree.** Judges should rule on the basis of law. Their background is irrelevant and (just like their political views) should not cloud sound legal judgment based on the laws and the facts of a case. |

Black judges are also 10 percent more likely to be overturned. Likewise, women on the bench rule somewhat differently from male judges in gender-related cases. Women are roughly 10 percent more likely to find discrimination—as are male judges if they are serving on a panel with a female judge.[24]

THE BOTTOM LINE

» State courts handle the vast majority of cases. Nearly all states divide their judiciary into three levels: trial courts, appeals courts, and a state supreme court. A majority of U.S. states elect their judges.

» Federal courts rule on cases involving constitutional questions, federal laws, and federal treaties. They are divided into ninety-four district courts, thirteen appeals courts, and the Supreme Court.

» Federal justices are selected by the president and confirmed by the Senate, and hold their position for life. Party polarization in Congress has created intense competition over judgeships, which increasingly reflect the diverse U.S. population.

» Numerous additional federal courts handle everything from bankruptcy to military matters.

The Court's Role

Alexander Hamilton's assurance that the judiciary would play a minor role in American government did not last long. John Marshall, the longest-serving chief justice in U.S. history—he held the office from January 1801 to July 1835—helped establish the U.S. courts as unusually powerful. How did Marshall do it?

Judicial Review

The breakthrough came in the landmark case of *Marbury v. Madison,* in which Marshall asserted that the Supreme Court has the authority to overrule any act of Congress that violates the Constitution.

The case arose after John Adams lost the 1800 election and, during his final hours as president, made "midnight appointments" that installed his supporters in judicial positions. The new president, Thomas Jefferson, came to office with very different political views and vehemently opposed the last-minute appointments. Jefferson directed his secretary of state, James Madison, to destroy the appointment letters—including one naming William Marbury as justice of the peace for the District of Columbia. The Judiciary Act of 1789, which had established the position, referred some cases (those involving writs of mandamus, or direct orders to government officials) directly to the Supreme Court. Marbury duly petitioned the Court to order Madison to deliver his commission. This action constituted a high-stakes early test of the Court's authority.

Marshall and his fellow justices faced a trap. If the Court ruled in favor of Marbury, the recently elected President Jefferson would ignore the Court—and diminish its importance in the new federal government. In fact, neither Jefferson nor Madison, the party being sued, even bothered to show up at the Court for the case. They assumed the Court would rule against them and planned to ignore the decision. Marshall found an ingenious way around Jefferson's defiance and vastly expanded the Court's role in American governance.

Led by Marshall, a unanimous Court ruled that Congress, in drafting the Judiciary Act of 1789, had erred in granting the Supreme Court the direct authority (or "original jurisdiction") to decide the question. The Constitution implied that the Supreme Court should rule on such cases only on appeal from the lower courts. However, the Constitution was silent on what would happen if Congress passed a law that clashed with the Constitution. Marshall filled in the blank with a dramatic move: "It is emphatically the province and duty" of the Court, wrote Marshall, to judge "if a law be in opposition to the Constitution." With that, Marshall established the court system's mighty power of **judicial review**—even though that authority is never mentioned in the Constitution itself.

● *John Marshall denied Marbury's suit and, in the process, asserted the power of the Supreme Court to strike down acts of Congress when they violated the Constitution.*

The Court decided the case by striking down Section 13 of the Judiciary Act of 1789—the section that referred writs of mandamus directly to the Supreme Court. Since Section 13 was the basis of Marbury's petition, the Court ruled that it had no constitutional authority to force the administration to deliver the petition. President Jefferson opposed Marshall's clever move, vigorously denouncing the "despotism" and "oligarchy" by which unelected officials "usurp[ed]" control of the Constitution from elected ones. But what could Jefferson do? In asserting the Court's power, Marshall had sided with the president and denied Marbury his petition. Jefferson had no way to defy a case he had won. By apparently relinquishing power, Marshall permanently strengthened the federal judiciary.[25]

Judicial review: The Court's authority to determine whether legislative, executive, and state actions violate the Constitution and overrule those that do.

Marshall deftly addressed a basic issue in American government, with profound implications that reverberate to the present day. When there is doubt about what the Constitution holds or implies, the Supreme Court continues to claim that it makes the call.[26]

Activism Versus Restraint

The Supreme Court was slow to wield the power it had asserted. It did not overrule another act of Congress for fifty-four years, until the notorious *Dred Scott* decision struck down the Missouri Compromise and declared that Black people were "so far inferior that they had no rights which the white man was bound to respect."[27] That decision brought the issue of slavery to a boil in 1857 and established a pattern: Many of the most intense disputes in American politics wind up decided in court.

The judiciary has stepped up the pace at which it overrules Congress (see Figure 16.6). In the 150 years following *Marbury*, it struck down just twenty-two federal laws; in the thirty years between 1990 and 2020, it struck down sixty-six, including laws designed to limit flag burning, guns near schoolyards, child pornography, violence against women, barriers to voting, limits on gambling, and same-sex marriage.

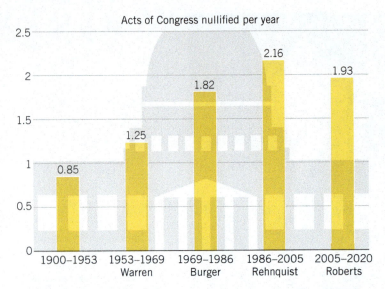

Acts of Congress nullified per year

Period	Value
1900–1953	0.85
1953–1969 Warren	1.25
1969–1986 Burger	1.82
1986–2005 Rehnquist	2.16
2005–2020 Roberts	1.93

● **FIGURE 16.6** *Acts of Congress nullified by the Supreme Court. (Journal of Legal Metrics)*

Today, the Supreme Court is embroiled in many intense debates in addition to the five described just above. May Congress limit campaign contributions? May it restrict firearms? What statutory limit should apply to members of the U.S. military charged with rape? Can the White House regulate emissions from power plants to combat climate change? May universities practice affirmative action in admissions? Can governments mandate vaccines for their workers? As the Court addresses each of these topics, the questions are often removed from the realm of public opinion and the jurisdiction of elected officials and settled by nine justices.

At the same time, the Court sometimes puts issues back into political play. When it withdrew the right to abortion, fifty states scrambled to forbid, regulate, or protect the procedure.

The Supreme Court also reviews state and local statutes. This power can be wielded without any subtle maneuvering. The Constitution's "supremacy clause" declares that "this Constitution and the laws of the United States . . . shall be the supreme Law of the Land" (Article 6). The Judiciary Act of 1789, which established the federal court system (yes, the same act that created William Marbury's position), granted the Court authority to enforce the supremacy clause and to strike down state laws that clash with the Constitution or with federal statutes. The judiciary has been more active on this level, striking down state actions at about six times the rate it overturns federal laws. Over time, federal courts have declared some 1,100 state and local laws unconstitutional and ruled that more than another two hundred state and local laws were preempted by federal law. Historic cases overruled state laws that established segregation, outlawed abortion, established school prayer, limited private property rights, or forbade same-sex marriage.

● *Legal! The Court struck down a federal law that banned sports gambling in most states.*

The growing number of rulings that strike down legislation raises an enduring question: How energetic should courts be in reviewing cases? Judicial activists take a vigorous approach to reviewing the other branches of government and believe that the courts must be vigilant in protecting rights. Between the 1950s and the 1970s, liberal activists were in the Supreme Court majority. During this period, the Court struck down segregation, forbade school prayer, and found a right to privacy in the penumbra (or shadow) of the Constitution (see Chapters 5 and 6 for a discussion of these cases). Today the balance of power has swung to conservatives. Now, some of the conservative justices are eager activists, ready to overturn precedents that clash with their judicial outlook.

Judicial restraint holds, on the contrary, that the courts should overturn the elected branches of government reluctantly and as a last resort. The terms *activism* and *restraint* are easily politicized. Conservatives bitterly attacked liberal **judicial activism** during the civil rights era of the 1950s to early 1970s; as the courts turned conservative, however, liberals began to criticize activist judges for overruling the will of the people's representatives.

Underlying the debate about activism lies a more basic question: How should justices read the law (or the Constitution) when they interpret it? One view, which we've called *pragmatism*, suggests that judges should treat the Constitution as a living and evolving document. Judges inevitably (and correctly) interpret the Constitution in light of their own era and experience. This perspective is also referred to as the "living Constitution" (see Chapter 3).

A second perspective, *originalism*, encourages judges to try to understand the original meaning of the document. What did the Constitution writers intend when they wrote the Constitution? What did Congress intend when they wrote the legislation before the Court? This can be a difficult path to follow—it requires deep historical knowledge and, sometimes, a bit of guesswork about just what was on James Madison's mind, for example.

A more recent version of originalism is called **textualism** and is focused on the plain meaning of the legal text and nothing else. Many textualists don't worry about original intent. To them, it's all right there, in the sentences before the judge. When the question of discrimination against LGBTQ+ individuals came before the Supreme Court, conservative Justice Neil Gorsuch read the text of the Civil Rights Act—which forbids discrimination based on "race, color, religion, sex, or national origin"—and concluded that the language forbids sexual discrimination and so LGBTQ+ rights must be protected.

As we noted in Chapter 3, the difference between these positions is less stark than it might appear. The Constitution can be ambiguous, and a nimble analysis is often required to apply it to a contemporary case—as Marshall illustrated when he first asserted the right of judicial review. Even staunch originalists and textualists regularly disagree with one another about the Constitution's meaning and how it applies in any individual case.

The Judicial Process

The judiciary's role goes far beyond weighing constitutionality. Legal cases constantly raise the question of how a law should be applied in a specific dispute. We saw this in Chapter 15, in the case of the bureaucratic rule-making process. If lobbyists do not like new regulations for inspecting poultry slaughterhouses, they can go to court and claim that the regulatory agency has mistaken what Congress intended when it authorized those inspections. Ultimately, the court has to rule on what Congress meant to do—perhaps in the distant past. Or, for the textualists, what it wrote into law. Because lawsuits are a regular feature of policymaking, federal courts stay busy interpreting the intent of the other branches.

Often there is no legislative record or executive action to settle a case. The American colonists introduced an English system known as **common law**. Common law (also known as *case law*) is a system of law developed by judges in deciding cases over the centuries. Because legal judgments should be consistent from case to case, each time a court settles a case it sets a **precedent** that will guide similar cases in the future. Over the years, the common law offers a rich legal heritage to guide judges in settling disputes. In countries without a common

Judicial restraint: Reluctance to interfere with elected branches, only doing so as a last resort.

Judicial activism: A vigorous or active approach to reviewing the other branches of government.

Textualism: A mode of legal interpretation that focuses on the plain meaning of the Constitution or the legal document.

Common law: A system of law developed by judges in deciding cases over the centuries.

Precedent: Judicial decisions that offer a guide to similar cases in the future.

law tradition, such as France, judges may not rule unless there is a statute or regulation to guide them.

American courts handle two different kinds of cases. **Civil law** handles cases between two parties. William Marbury sues James Madison for his commission; a celebrity files a defamation suit against a tabloid for spreading malicious gossip; a major corporation sues a local pizza chain for copying its corporate logo. **Criminal law** involves cases in which someone is charged with doing something prohibited by the government, such as stealing private property, assaulting another person, or secretly arranging with a competitor to set higher prices (an "antitrust" violation).

Civil law: Cases that involve disputes between two parties.

Criminal law: Cases in which someone is charged with breaking the law.

The party who complains—Marbury, the slandered celebrity, or the government charging an alleged criminal—is called the **plaintiff**; the party who is sued is the **defendant**. In court cases, the plaintiff is listed first and the defendant second; thus, the case is called *Marbury* (the plaintiff) *v.* (for versus) *Madison* (the secretary of state who did not deliver the commission). When a party loses in a lower court, it becomes the plaintiff on appeal; that is why you see case titles such as *Dobbs v. Jackson Women's Health Clinic* (the lower court drew on precedent and ruled that there was a right to abortion and so Dobbs, a state official, became the plaintiff on the appeal) or *West Virginia v. EPA* (the lower court ruled for the EPA clean air regulations and West Virginia became the plaintiff).

Plaintiff: The party who brings the action in a lawsuit.

Defendant: The party who is sued in a court case.

Too Much Power?

Should nine unelected, lifetime appointees wield this much power in a twenty-first-century democracy? Add to that the more than 850 circuit and district court federal judges, also all appointed to their posts by the president for life: How can we say "the people" rule over the judicial branch?

In other nations, elected branches make vital decisions about environmental protection, gun rights, immigration rules, and other urgent questions (see Comparing Nations 16.2). In the United States, courts are major players in resolving these issues . . . and other issues in almost every policy realm.

American courts profoundly shape our politics. Critics left, right, and center worry, as a recent book suggests, that the judiciary has become the "most dangerous branch," reversing Alexander Hamilton's *Federalist* assurance.[28] At the same time, other experts flag the long-standing checks on courts' power.

COMPARING NATIONS 16.2   Power of the Judiciary

Judges in other advanced democracies rarely exercise anything like the influence that American courts have over government and politics. In Japan, for example, the judiciary is widely viewed as a rubber stamp for executive and legislative decisions, almost never questioning (much less reversing) decisions of the other branches. The United Kingdom goes even further: The doctrine of "parliamentary sovereignty" holds that when Parliament passes a statute, it cannot be overturned in court. Canada abandoned parliamentary sovereignty in 1982 and granted the federal courts fuller judicial review powers; those are only rarely used, however, and the parliament can still overturn the courts' ruling. In Germany, the Supreme Constitutional Court has the power to review all legislation for adherence with the Constitution; it even has the authority to ban a political party (like the Nazi Party) if it moves to deny the rights of others. Yet the German high court does not take cases from lower courts on appeal—its role is solely as a constitutional court. Finally, less democratic nations generally place their power in the executive—their courts do not have the authority to challenge executive decisions. In its extensive authority to reshape public policies and other acts of the executive and legislative branches, the U.S. judiciary stands alone.

... Or Still the "Least Dangerous" Branch?

Although the courts are undeniably powerful, every institution faces limits. The courts operate with four restraints.

First, the federal courts have *no electoral base*. Their prestige and mystique are balanced by a lack of democratic authority. This has made some past courts careful about confronting elected officials. For example, the Supreme Court delayed its ruling in *Brown v. Board of Education* (striking down segregated schools) for almost two years while the justices struggled to reach unanimity. Chief Justice Earl Warren felt that such an important case should have the backing of all nine members because a major decision that went against popular opinion could harm the Court's authority and prestige. Today, political scientists wonder if the Court's bold decisions on highly partisan matters—abortion, firearms, global warming, and much more—will erode the Court's most precious asset, popular respect and deference.

Second, courts have relatively *limited resources* compared to other units of government. Senators generally command more than fifty staff members and can call on the Congressional Research Service and the Government Accountability Office: Each has hundreds of experts who can study any question a member might raise. In contrast, most federal judges have only two or three clerks—young staffers, usually fresh from law school, with little judicial experience—who serve them for less than a year. Supreme Court justices, whose decisions can shape the course of government for generations, have at most four clerks, who serve for a year or occasionally two.

The courts also command small budgets. The Supreme Court operates on an annual budget of around $140 million a year. The entire federal judiciary—thirteen circuit courts, ninety-four district courts, and the Supreme Court—receives about $8.6 billion annually. That is roughly 1/100th of the annual U.S. defense budget.

Third, courts are *reactive decision makers*. Executive branch agencies or legislators can tackle problems and devise solutions. Courts await disputes; cases must come to them. True, most major issues eventually do wind up before the courts—but, unlike the other branches, the courts do not define the problem or shape the question that is being disputed.

Finally, the courts must rely on other branches for *enforcement*. The Court rules. Other actors—in and out of government—implement the decisions. The Supreme Court could strike down school desegregation; it could not, however, enforce that decision by sending troops to Little Rock or cutting the budgets of schools that refused to comply. In fact, the *Brown* decision was blocked for years by intransigent state and local officials (until civil rights protests finally moved Congress to pass the Civil Rights Act). President Andrew Jackson made this point dramatically. When the Supreme Court struck down a Georgia law, because the state had no "dominion" over the Cherokees, he allegedly said, of the chief justice: "John Marshall has made his decision, now let him enforce it."[29]

Now you have a handle on how the courts both have expanded their power and operate under long-standing constraints. *What do you think*: Is the judiciary the guarantor of American constitutional rights? Or an outmoded throwback to an earlier, more elitist age? To explore further, let's look behind the scenes at the inner workings of the Supreme Court.

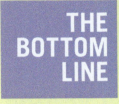

THE BOTTOM LINE

» Chief Justice John Marshall asserted the courts' authority to review acts of Congress to ensure that they fit with the Constitution in *Marbury v. Madison*. The Judiciary Act of 1789 authorized the Supreme Court to review state laws.

» For more than a century, the Court rarely struck down acts of Congress, but it began to do so at a quicker pace after the 1970s.

» *Activists* believe in a vigorous judiciary that scrutinizes the other branches; judicial *restraint* holds that courts should intervene rarely and reluctantly.

» The vital question regarding the judiciary remains the same one that Chief Justice Marshall and President Jefferson crossed swords over more than two centuries ago: Is the Court acting in ways that are indispensable to democracy? Or is it acting in ways that threaten it?

 ## The Supreme Court and How It Operates

Tucked away at the top of the majestic marble Supreme Court building on East Capitol Street, among all the justices' offices and conference rooms and libraries lined with leather law books, is . . . a small basketball court. Known as the "highest court in the land," the facility is used exclusively by Supreme Court insiders: the justices' clerks, both current and former; a few staff members; and occasionally even one of the justices. We can imagine the basketball court as symbolic of the Supreme Court itself: exclusive, little known, and open to a tiny membership for a lifetime.

Hearing Cases

The Supreme Court is in session for approximately nine months each year, traditionally opening on the first Monday in October. The justices are generally out of public view, except when the Court meets to hear *oral arguments*—the presentation of a case that the Court has agreed to review. Arguments are usually scheduled on Monday, Tuesday, and Wednesday mornings. If you are visiting Washington, DC, on a day when oral arguments are occurring, do attend. These fascinating sessions are free and open to the public, on a first-come, first-served basis with only fifty available seats. (We recommend that you get to the Court early to wait in line; bring something to read—perhaps this book!)

Supreme Court oral arguments do not resemble the courtroom scenes on TV. Rather than lawyers making dramatic arguments or cross-examining witnesses, the Supreme Court features nine justices as the sole audience: no jury, no witnesses. Any case that the Supreme Court agrees to hear has usually been thoroughly aired by at least one lower court. Normally, cases are heard in one hour, and each side's lawyer—called the "counsel" in Court-speak, regardless of whether it is one lawyer or many—is granted thirty minutes to make his or her best argument.

The justices usually interrupt the presenting lawyer almost immediately with questions, some supportive and others combative. They may also deliver mini-speeches of their own; no lawyer ever dares interrupt a Supreme Court justice, even if the lawyer's thirty minutes is slipping away. No photos or video are allowed, so sketches are the most accurate depiction. The Court posts a transcript of oral arguments later that day and releases audio of the week's arguments on Fridays—you can check the audio of two big cases we've discussed (on abortion and the EPA) in the endnotes.[30]

Before the hearing, both sides submit written briefs spelling out the details of their argument. Other interested parties may submit their own briefs endorsing the side they favor. The outside contributions are known as *amicus curiae* (Latin for "friend of the court") briefs. A creative, well-written *amicus curiae* brief, researchers have found, may well wind up being included in a justice's written opinion on the case.[31]

Are oral arguments important? Perhaps not. Justice Clarence Thomas told one interviewer that they influence his colleagues "in five or ten percent of the cases, maybe, and I'm being generous there." Chief Justice John Roberts once added, "The judges are debating among themselves and just using the lawyers as a black-board."[32] What matters far more are the written briefs that the counsel submit.

● *The Supreme Court hears* Dobbs, *the abortion case, in June 2022. The chief justice sits at the center; the seats closest are occupied by justices with the most seniority; the most recent appointees sit at the two ends. From left: Kavanaugh, Kagan, Alito, Thomas, Chief Justice Roberts, Breyer, Sotomayor, Gorsuch, Barrett. For the 2023 term, Justice Ketanji Brown Jackson will take her place all the way on the right. Only sketches like this one of the Court are permitted; no photographs or TV coverage is allowed.*

Amicus curiae: A brief submitted by a person or group who is not a direct party to the case.

Selecting Cases: Formal Requirements

How do the justices decide which cases to hear? Losing parties in lower courts are permitted, depending on the nature of the case, to file a petition with the Supreme Court stating the facts of the case and setting out detailed arguments as to why the Court should hear it. The petitions are split up among the justices and their clerks; on selected Fridays, the justices meet to choose the cases they will hear. At least four judges have to vote to hear a case for it to make it to the Supreme Court; that requirement is known as the **rule of four**.

When the justices agree to hear a case, the Supreme Court issues a *writ of certiorari* (legal-speak for "to be informed") demanding the official record from the lower court that heard the case. Roughly ten thousand petitions are filed with the Supreme Court each year, and some seventy or eighty are accepted—less than 1 percent. How do cases make it into that elite group? That remains one of the great mysteries of American government. The Court never gives any formal explanation for why it decides to grant certiorari to this case and not that one.

Formally, a case must meet three conditions before it is even eligible for the Supreme Court—or any other court, for these requirements apply at all judicial levels. The case must involve a *legitimate controversy,* that is, an actual dispute between two parties. Supreme Court justices do not deal with hypothetical matters; no federal court offers "advisory opinions" based on something that might someday happen.

Second, the parties bringing a case must have *standing:* They must prove an actual harm (or imminent harm) to receive a hearing. Merely being distressed or concerned about a far-off environmental disaster's effect is not enough to bring a lawsuit; you must prove that the oil spill directly affects your livelihood (or your health or your property).

Rule of four: The requirement that at least four Supreme Court judges must agree to hear a case before it comes before the Court.

Finally, if the Court's proceedings will no longer affect the issue at hand, it is considered moot—irrelevant—and the case is thrown out. A famous exception comes from *Roe v. Wade*, in which a federal district court dismissed the case as moot because the plaintiff, "Jane Roe" (real name: Norma McCorvey), had already delivered her child. The Supreme Court rejected this view, noting that the typical length of legal appeals processes meant that pregnancies would usually conclude too soon for a court decision to be reached.

Selecting Cases: Informal Factors

Thousands of cases each year meet the standards—controversy, standing, and mootness. Informally, we can identify four additional factors that help predict whether a case is more or less likely to be accepted by the Court.

First, the Supreme Court is more inclined to hear a case when two lower courts decide the legal question differently (usually two federal courts, but sometimes federal and state). Different rulings in similar cases require a resolution.

Second, justices are inclined to grant certiorari to cases in which a lower court decision conflicts with an existing Supreme Court ruling. In 1989, the Court ruled in *Penry v. Lynaugh* that a death sentence was sometimes permissible for criminals under the age of eighteen. More than a decade later, the Missouri Supreme Court declared that the death penalty for nonadults was "cruel and unusual punishment," citing a recent Supreme Court ruling that struck down capital punishment for mentally disabled people. The Supreme Court agreed and, in *Roper v. Simmons*, reversed its own 1989 decision.

Third, the Supreme Court is more likely to look favorably on cases that have significance beyond the two parties involved. Rarely does a sexual harassment case reach the Supreme Court because this area of law is relatively settled. But when Paula Jones brought such a suit against President Bill Clinton, the Court agreed to hear *Clinton v. Jones* because the case tested the larger question of whether a sitting U.S. president is required to defend himself against a lawsuit while in office. (Yes, the Court ruled; it allowed Jones's lawsuit to proceed—and set off a cascade of events that rocked the Clinton presidency and led the House of Representatives to impeach him—although the Senate voted against removing him from office.)

Fourth, the Supreme Court is especially likely to hear a case when the U.S. government is a party. Almost half of the Court's caseload involves the solicitor general, the attorney who represents the Justice Department before the Supreme Court. Historically, the solicitor general had a "home court advantage" and usually won cases for its client, the federal government. Not anymore. President Obama's legal team won just 52 percent of the time—the lowest score in at least a century. Until the Trump administration won just 47 percent of its cases—the worst of any modern president.[33] Biden's solicitor general had a 67 percent success rate in 2021–22.

These criteria increase the odds of making it to the Supreme Court—but even a case that meets all four may be passed over. Again, the Court's decision on whether to grant certiorari to any particular case remains shrouded in mystery.

For the cases that the Court agrees to hear, oral arguments are scheduled (primarily on Monday, Tuesday, and Wednesday mornings) from early October through late April. The Court then issues decisions in all cases that it heard during the session: as we saw in the chapter opening, usually on weekday mornings in June. Those days are very exciting—and, for those involved in a case's outcome, very anxious—occasions. No one knows when the Court will hand down a decision in a given case, nor is there a set time period in which the justices must reach a decision. However, the Court generally decides all the cases it has heard during the term before the summer recess begins.

Conference Sessions and Written Decisions

What do the justices do when they are not on the bench hearing oral arguments? There is plenty of work to occupy them. Justices are engaged writing opinions (usually with substantial assistance from their clerks, who prepare drafts and discuss details with their boss), deciding which cases to hear in the future, and reading briefs for upcoming oral arguments. And, most intriguing of all, the justices meet in conference.

Supreme Court conferences, which typically take place on Thursday or Friday afternoons, are closed to everyone except the justices—even their clerks stay out. Justices sit around a conference table; by tradition, the most junior justice sits nearest the door, opening it only to allow a staff member to wheel in carts piled with materials for the next case under consideration. The Supreme Court's most significant collective decisions take place in conference.

Justices discuss the cases they have heard, indicate their votes, and the chief justice, if he is in the majority, assigns the job of writing the **majority opinion**; otherwise, the senior member of the majority assigns the job. The majority opinion is the official statement of the Court. Any justice who wishes to can issue a **concurrent opinion** explaining why he or she voted in favor of the majority outcome—different justices come to the same conclusion for different reasons. Justices who disagree about the outcome write a **dissent** indicating why they voted against the majority. Some dissents become celebrated or form the basis for a future judicial shift in thinking.

In May 2022, someone shattered the protocol. For the first time in history, a draft opinion was leaked and published in *Politico*.[34] Samuel Alito's majority opinion striking down a right to abortion in *Dobbs v. Women's Health* made headlines and rocked national politics. "This was a singular and egregious breach of . . . trust," declared a shaken Chief Justice Roberts. "Absolutely appalling." He directed the Marshal of the Court to investigate, but nothing came of it.[35] Who did it? Among the most often repeated theories: A liberal hoped that a wave of indignation might slow down the majority; or a conservative wanted to lock in the majority and make it more difficult for justices to compromise. Just one thing's for sure: The leak is just one more sign of the politicization of an institution that was not designed for politics.[36]

Though justices are generally publicity averse, they do make public appearances. They typically address law schools or legal conferences. Some justices speak at less formal events, especially after the year's session ends in June. The late Ruth Bader Ginsburg became a cultural icon and was the subject of a documentary (*RBG*), a *Saturday Night Live* parody, a feature film (*On the Basis of Sex*), and a meme, *The Notorious RBG*. The website

Majority opinion: The official statement of the Supreme Court (or a district court, since they also have multiple justices).

Concurrent opinion: A statement that agrees with the majority opinion.

Dissent: A statement on behalf of the justices who voted in the minority.

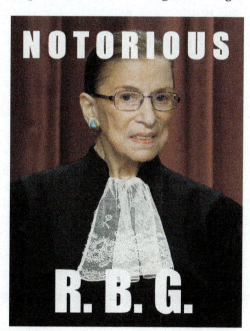

● Supreme Court Justice and feminist icon Ruth Bader Ginsburg as meme—the notorious R.B.G.—a play on rapper Biggie Smalls, aka The Notorious B.I.G. Her death and quick replacement by conservative justice Amy Coney Barrett tilted the Court into a new alignment. A conservative 5–4 line-up with Justice Roberts moderating Court opinions became a 6–3 conservative supermajority. What's next? So far, monumental decisions galore.

SCOTUS Map (www.scotusmap.com) tries to track all such appearances, although they are not formally announced by the Court or the individual justices. Whatever the topic, however, all justices maintain a strict norm of not publicly discussing cases before the Court.

Supreme Court Clerks

Supreme Court clerks, usually recent law school graduates, exercise a remarkable amount of influence. They help the justices write opinions and reach decisions, and they initially screen the thousands of certiorari petitions that reach the Court each year.

Though the process is kept strictly secret, the clerks reject many of the petitions, choosing a smaller set of a few hundred potential cases for the justices' consideration. Remember: These cases can shape American government in powerful ways. And a small group of unelected people in their twenties often influence whether a case will reach the Court.

Are you interested in serving as a Supreme Court clerk? It is a hard job to win. Out of more than one thousand applicants each year, only a handful—less than three dozen—will achieve this post. After completing your law degree (JD), you would generally serve one year in a lower court clerkship for a district court judge or in a state supreme court. During that year, you would apply to a specific Supreme Court justice's chambers, although some aspirants apply to all nine to maximize their chances of being selected. As with other jobs, if you make it through the initial screening, you'll be invited in for an interview, first with the clerks, then with one of the justices. Those interviews are reputedly among the toughest going: Former Justice Scalia, for example, subjected his clerkship candidates to a "Scalia grilling" that covered, as one said afterward, "the law—all of it."[37]

Should you receive the congratulatory call, prepare to join one of the most exclusive clubs in American government. Supreme Court clerks who elect to stay in public service often go on to important posts or become professors at top law schools. If you decide instead to go into private practice, you will be a hot commodity: "Court clerk bonuses" to sign with a law firm competing for your talents run to around $400,000.

Confirmation Battles

In March 2016, Justice Antonin Scalia suddenly died. Scalia was a powerful conservative voice on the court. President Barack Obama nominated Merrick Garland. Thirty years ago Garland, like most respected jurists, would have been approved, perhaps unanimously. Not anymore. In 2016, the Senate was in Republican hands and Senate Majority Leader Mitch McConnell refused to consider any nomination—"all null and void." Since there were just eight months to the next election, McConnell explained, this selection should be in the hands of the people. When Donald Trump won the presidency, a solid conservative, Neil Gorsuch, took the seat. A liberal majority had been narrowly averted.

Four years later, just weeks before the 2020 election, Ruth Bader Ginsburg died. Ginsburg was the liberals' Scalia—and a powerful intellectual leader. Now, the arguments about letting the people decide were tossed aside. The Republican Senate rushed through Amy Comey Barrett, a former professor from Notre Dame with a strong conservative philosophy, and in the process fundamentally changed the Court alignment of the previous decades: The 5–4 conservative tilt became a 6–3 conservative supermajority. The blockbuster cases described at the start of the chapter—every one of them decided 6–3—flowed from the new power alignment.

Enraged liberals insisted that the legitimacy of the Court itself would suffer from this kind of hardball. Perhaps they are right, but given the immense influence wielded by Supreme Court justices, confirmations have been fierce partisan contests for decades. Each opening ignites national campaigns, and political uproars, all designed to influence the Senate Judiciary Committee, which holds hearings on a nominee and issues a recommendation to the Senate.

Nomination politics first turned overtly partisan in 1987, when President Ronald Reagan nominated Robert Bork to the Court. Bork certainly seemed qualified: He was a national authority on antitrust law; he had served under President Nixon as solicitor general, representing the U.S. government in cases before the Supreme Court; and he had been acting attorney general and a circuit court judge.

● Supreme Court nominee Robert Bork testifying at his confirmation hearing. His nomination was a watershed in the politicization of the Court. Before Judge Bork, the major focus was on competence; now, the focus is on political perspectives.

However, Bork was also a no-apologies conservative who would replace Justice Lewis Powell, a moderate "swing vote." Liberal groups mobilized to oppose the nomination; Democratic senators, led by Ted Kennedy, criticized what they called "Robert Bork's America." And Robert Bork was tough minded and outspoken in his views (and the last nominee to speak in anything but vague platitudes).

After twelve days of hearings, the Senate defeated the nomination, fifty-eight to forty-two. What surprised observers was the swift rise of organized opposition based not on the candidate's qualifications, but on his judicial philosophy. Conservatives coined a new word to describe the phenomenon: *Borking*. They have returned the favor. Every Court appointment now faces a partisan nomination fight: packed hearings, demonstrations (pro and con), intense media coverage, public opinion polls serving up regular updates on how the nominee fares in the public view, and millions of dollars of statewide ads to influence key Senate votes (see Table 16.2).

● Reversing their "no hearings during an election year" position of four years before, Senate Republicans rushed Amy Coney Barrett (a) through the hearings process. Democrats howled "Unfair!" but Republicans had the majority . . . and the power. Two years later, Ketanji Brown Jackson (b) was confirmed with something that was becoming scarce—three votes from the (Republican) opposition.

TABLE 16.2 Supreme Court Nominations and Confirmations

Nomination votes have gotten closer over the years. As partisanship rose through the 1990s, the Court grew politicized, unanimous votes disappeared, and hearings became more contentious. Debates become especially heated when a swing vote—like Justice Kennedy—is up for replacement. It is much easier to replace a liberal with a liberal or a conservative with a conservative.

JUDGE	AGE AT TIME OF APPOINTMENT	APPOINTED BY (PRESIDENT)	SELECTED FROM	YEAR	SENATE VOTE		PUBLIC OPINION	
					YES	NO	YES	NO
Ketanji Brown Jackson	51	Biden	U.S. Court of Appeals	2022	53	47	66	34
Amy Coney Barrett	48	Trump	U.S. Court of Appeals	2020	52	48	42	46
Brett Kavanaugh	53	Trump	U.S. Court of Appeals	2018	50	48	46	45
Neil Gorsuch	49	Trump	U.S. Court of Appeals	2017	54	45	48	35
Elena Kagan	50	Obama	U.S. Solicitor General	2010	63	37	44	34
Sonia Sotomayor	55	Obama	U.S. Court of Appeals	2009	68	31	56	36
Samuel Alito	55	G. W. Bush	U.S. Court of Appeals	2006	58	42	54	30
John Roberts	50	G. W. Bush	U.S. Court of Appeals	2005	78	22	60	26
Stephen Breyer	55	Clinton	U.S. Court of Appeals	1994	87	9	—	—
Ruth Bader Ginsburg	60	Clinton	U.S. Court of Appeals	1993	96	3	53	14
Clarence Thomas	43	G. H. W. Bush	U.S. Court of Appeals	1991	52	48	58	30
Anthony Kennedy	51	Reagan	U.S. Court of Appeals	1988	97	0	—	—
Robert Bork	43	Reagan	U.S. Court of Appeals	1987	42	58	38	35

The rise of partisan confirmations is not surprising. A single vote makes the difference on a host of issues: the rights to privacy and abortion, gun control, criminal justice, campaign finance, immigration, healthcare reform, the rights of terrorism suspects—and the list goes on. Small wonder that the debates over each new justice get so heated, especially when a nominee's political philosophy differs from his or her predecessor. Longtime Court watchers decry this politicization: "The least dangerous branch," they affirm, was not designed to be in the eye of the political hurricane.

THE BOTTOM LINE

» The Supreme Court generally hears cases on the basis of petitions requesting a review of lower court decisions. Four justices have to vote to hear a case before it becomes part of the 1 percent that comes before the Court.

» To be heard in federal court, a case must meet criteria involving controversy, standing, and mootness. Other factors that make it more likely that the case will be heard include the scope of the question, a clash between lower courts or between a lower court and previous Supreme Court decision, and requests from the solicitor general.

» Cases involve oral arguments, written briefs, and conferences with only the justices present. If in the majority, the chief justice assigns a majority opinion; others write concurring or dissenting opinions for the record.

» Confirmation to the federal bench—and especially to the Supreme Court—was once a polite affair that largely involved questions of competence. Today, confirmations are some of the most charged events on the political calendar. This discord raises an important question: How does the polarization that surrounds the Court affect its own workings—and its standing with the public?

 # Judicial Decision Making and Reform

How do judges reach their decisions in a case? Social scientists emphasize four different perspectives.

The Role of Law

In traditional theory, justices decide cases on the basis of the legal facts, as laid out in the documents submitted. They read the law, consider the intent of those who framed it, and place the case in the context of both the Constitution and prior decisions. As Chief Justice John Roberts put it at his confirmation hearing, "Judges are like umpires. Umpires don't make the rules; they apply them. . . . My job is to call balls and strikes."[38] Over the last decade, the Supreme Court has ruled unanimously about 40 percent of the time (and in some sessions, as much as 60 percent of the time). The justices often agreed on the law and applied it. According to long-established principle, justices generally abide by the precedents set in previously decided cases. This is known as **stare decisis** (literally, "stand by the things decided"). Even justices who bring a new philosophy to the Court will often try to reassure anxious senators at their confirmation hearings that stare decisis will protect the law from abrupt changes.

Stare decisis: Deciding cases on the basis of previous rulings or precedents.

This view of decision making amounts to a long-standing and useful myth. The Court has reversed itself 237 times—more than it has struck down acts of Congress. The abortion ruling in 2022 shows just how politically significant a single turnaround can be. And on most of the high-profile cases, rulings tend to reflect the political division on the Court. In the 2021–22 session, unanimous rulings fell to 30 percent of the judgments. The most common vote was 6–3 (see Figure 16.7).

● **FIGURE 16.7** *In the previous decade, unanimous decisions (9–0) were most common. Not anymore. For the first time, in 2021–22, the most common outcome on the Supreme Court was 6–3, reflecting the philosophical divide between the justices. (Scotusblog .com)*

The reality is that legal cases are often ambiguous. Applying the Constitution more than two centuries after its passage is rarely simple or straightforward. Political scientists who study Supreme Court decisions have found another perspective with greater analytic power.

Ideology and Partisanship

Ideology provides a more accurate guide to the judicial mind. Political scientists have found that the justices' beliefs are the most powerful predictor of how they will vote, especially on difficult cases. Some studies look at the justices' party identification, others at their ideology prior to confirmation, and still others at the views of the presidents who appointed them. No matter how ideology is measured, one study after another suggests a strong relationship between the justices' beliefs and their votes (see Figure 16.8). In brief, we can predict the justices' votes over time with considerable accuracy, based on their political orientation.[39]

As Figure 16.8 displays, the Supreme Court features six members on the conservative side (Chief Justice Roberts, Thomas, Alito, Gorsuch, Kavanaugh, and Barrett) and three reliable liberals (Breyer [retired in 2022], Sotomayor, and Kagan). Of course, justices evolve over time. And Chief Justice Roberts (and Justice Kavanaugh) are moving toward the middle—perhaps the swing voters of the future.

Ideology lines up with the judicial philosophy we discussed earlier. *Pragmatists* (who see the Constitution as a living, changing document) will approach cases differently from *originalists* (who believe we must interpret the document's text literally) or textualists.

Likewise, activists may be quicker to strike down acts of Congress, state laws, and court precedents. Conservatives charged liberal justices with being overly activist during the Warren Court (1953–69); today, liberals repeat the complaint about conservative justices. The judges insist that they are not acting ideologically. But their judicial philosophies strongly predispose them to align with positions that reflect one or the other parties, as the march of 6–3 decisions indicate. Ultimately, simple political perspective—liberal versus conservative—is one of the most effective ways of explaining how justices rule.

The public now shares the scholarly view about how justices decide. In recent polls, as we saw earlier in this chapter, a full 84 percent of the public suggested that Supreme Court justices "sometimes let their ideological views influence their decision."[40] The idea that the Court often rules on the basis of politics poses a dilemma for our democratic system. The Court is designed to stand above politics, to interpret and explain the rules without partisan consideration. That is the reason justices are selected for life. When they rule on the basis of political ideology—and are widely seen as doing so—they raise a problem for the legitimacy of this increasingly powerful institution.

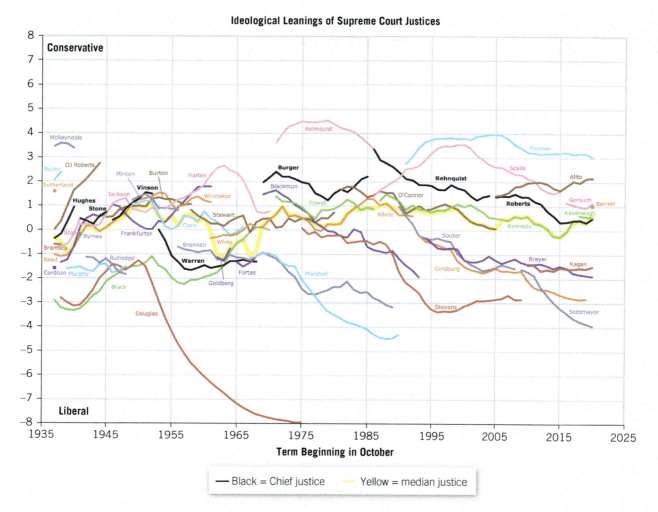

Ideological Leanings of Supreme Court Justices

- Black = Chief justice
- Yellow = median justice

● **FIGURE 16.8** *Ideological leanings of Supreme Court justices over the past ninety years. Notice that Thomas lines up as one of the three most conservative justices since 1935 with Alito close behind. On the other side, Sotomayor's record stands as one of the most liberal. Also note Roberts and Kavanaugh clustering near the middle—perhaps offering swing votes in the future.*

Collegiality and Peer Pressure

A third factor shaping Court decisions is *collegiality,* or to put it more bluntly, *peer pressure.* Justices spend a lot of time together, hearing cases and discussing their decisions. They exert influence on one another. Persuasion is a traditional feature of Court discussions; justices appear to change positions in many cases based on legal arguments and personal appeals of colleagues. They also may change their votes for strategic reasons—trading votes in different cases.[41]

This is a factor that is less important today. Past generations engaged in more give and take—in the 1950s and 1960s, at least one justice would switch his vote in about half of all cases.[42] Today, justices appear to be more settled in their convictions. And many Court watchers think the *Dobbs* opinion on abortion was leaked to avoid just this kind of give and take.

Another angle on the idea of "peer pressure" arises from the larger legal community. A few hundred people—law professors, law students, legal bloggers, congressional members, committee staff for the House and Senate Judiciary Committees, and interest-group activists—make up the attentive audience for most judicial decisions. The audience's judgment about a specific judicial opinion

How Americans View the Supreme Court

Party Members See It Differently Today

Americans are divided over their view of the Supreme Court. Back in 2017, Democrats, Republicans, and independents all gave the court a 40 percent approval rating. Today, there's a wide gap between party members, but all are negative.

Source: Gallup

Confidence in the U.S. Supreme Court, Recent Trend, by Political Party

"Now I am going to read you a list of institutions in American society. Please tell me how much confidence you yourself have in each one—a great deal, quite a lot, some, or very little. The U.S. Supreme Court" (% Great deal/Quite a lot)

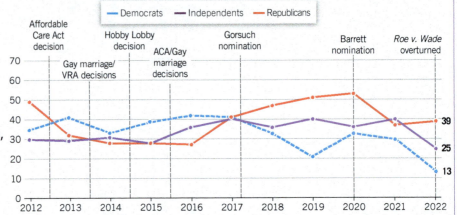

— Democrats   — Independents   — Republicans

Affordable Care Act decision
Gay marriage/ VRA decisions
Hobby Lobby decision
ACA/Gay marriage decisions
Gorsuch nomination
Barrett nomination
Roe v. Wade overturned

THINK ABOUT IT

How have party differences shifted over time?

How have court decisions affected this view?

How have views changed since the appointment of Justices Kavanaugh in 2018 and Barrett in 2020?

Does the conviction that judges rule on the basis of ideology require us to rethink the way we appoint the justices or how the Court operates? Or is it desirable in our party-polarized age that justices exhibit strong viewpoints as so many politicians and ordinary citizens do today, thereby better representing the public?

---

can be laudatory or scathing.[43] Once again, this factor has diminished. Today that audience is itself divided along partisan lines. Liberal and conservative justices come from different legal circles with different philosophies. The fractured legal communities reinforce the partisan divide.

Institutional Concerns

Finally, some justices do appear to think about the interests of the Court as an institution. They spend many years on the bench and worry about the standing of the Court—before public opinion, a hostile Congress, or a skeptical executive. As we saw earlier, Justice Marshall carefully considered the role and standing of his institution as he crafted his complicated opinion in *Marbury v. Madison*. Some recent studies underscore the importance of this perspective. Justice Roberts increasingly reflects this attitude. In *Dobbs*, for example, he joined the conservatives to uphold the Mississippi law strongly restricting abortion, but would have avoided the larger tempest by not explicitly overturning *Roe v. Wade*.

THE BOTTOM LINE

» Four different perspectives help explain how justices make their decisions.

» First, we should pay attention to their own explanation: They follow precedent and the facts of the case.

» Political scientists often find that ideology is the best predictor of justices' decisions in the long run. Recently, the public also has taken this view, which poses a dilemma for American governance: An institution designed to be above politics is increasingly seen as essentially political.

» Two final factors also play a role in judicial decision making: collegiality and institutional protection.

 # Nineteen Cases You Should Know

The history of American Court cases includes a long list of famous—and occasionally infamous—decisions. You have already encountered some in our discussion of civil liberties (Chapter 5) and civil rights (Chapter 6). We introduced five more at the opening of this chapter. If you take a course in constitutional law (or decide to attend law school), you will study cases by the hundreds. All are part of American *jurisprudence,* or the study of law. Here we list nineteen cases that every student of American government ought to be familiar with, organized chronologically. The ones we have covered elsewhere in this book are briefly described here only to refresh your memory. We have left one place blank in the top twenty. Think about the other cases you have encountered in this and other chapters and join the conversation: Which case would *you* add to our "A list"? Are there any you would subtract?

1. *Marbury v. Madison* (1803)

Without Chief Justice Marshall's momentous decision, we might not have judicial review—or courts so deeply engaged in U.S. government and policymaking. You read about this case earlier in this chapter.

2. *McCulloch v. Maryland* (1819)

Recall from Chapter 4 that this case, in which Marshall denied a state right to tax a national bank, was a significant Court affirmation of national power. This advanced the "dual federalist" balance between the states and federal government that Marshall ardently sought.

3. *Dred Scott v. Sandford* (1857)

As tensions mounted over the spread of slavery into the West, Chief Justice Roger Taney inserted the Supreme Court squarely into the middle of the debate. Writing for a 7–2 Court majority, Taney ruled that Dred Scott, a Missouri slave who was taken to a free state and later back to Missouri, was still a slave. He might have stopped there. Remember, one cannot sue without *standing,* and slaves, by definition, did not have standing.

● *Chief Justice Roger Taney (a), who served on the Court from 1836 to 1864, authored the* Dred Scott *decision—often described as the worst decision in Court history. Dred Scott, an enslaved person (b), sued for his own freedom and that of his two daughters, arguing that he had been taken to Illinois and the Wisconsin Territory, both free areas. The Court rejected his bid for freedom, 7–2.*

The Court, however, went on to rule that Congress did not have the power to prohibit slavery in the territories. Taney continued, in passages that are shocking to read today, that Blacks were "beings of an inferior order and altogether unfit to associate with the white race." They were not and could never become U.S. citizens. The bottom line: Slavery could not be restricted in any western territory.[44] Many constitutional historians choose *Dred Scott* as the worst Supreme Court decision in American history (for more details, see Chapter 6).

4. *Santa Clara Co. v. Southern Pacific Railroad* (1886)

Santa Clara Co. v. Southern Pacific Railroad was a complex tax case, decided unanimously without much notice—but it reverberates through our politics still. California forbade corporations from deducting their debts from their taxable property. The Court ruled that California had acted improperly because corporations should be treated as persons and afforded the Fourteenth Amendment right of equal protection. The case established a precedent—later expanded—that vastly enhanced the power of corporations. By 1938 Justice Hugo Black would complain that the Fourteenth Amendment had been written "to protect weak and helpless human beings," and not to "remove corporations in any fashion from the control of state governments." A decade later, Justice William O. Douglas added: "The *Santa Clara* case becomes one of the most momentous of all our decisions. . . . Corporations were now armed with constitutional prerogatives." The bottom line: *Santa Clara* set a precedent that, with time, gave corporations all the legal benefits of individual citizens. The legal theory in *Santa Clara* helped inform the Court when it struck down campaign finance laws (in *Citizens United* and other recent cases).[45]

5. *Plessy v. Ferguson* (1896)

The Civil War resulted in freedoms for Black Americans, codified in three constitutional amendments (the Thirteenth, Fourteenth, and Fifteenth). After the turbulent period of Reconstruction, the South (followed, if less blatantly, by other sections of the United States) set about reasserting second-class status for African Americans. Across the region, state legislatures passed explicit laws mandating segregated facilities.

In 1890, a Louisiana statute required that railroads maintain separate cars for Black and white ticket holders—it was part of a network of laws pushing Black people into second-class citizenship. Homer Plessy deliberately challenged the law by refusing to move to the "colored car" on an East Louisiana Railroad train. The case eventually reached the Supreme Court, where Plessy's lawyers argued that the segregation violated his Fourteenth Amendment rights. (Remember that the Fourteenth Amendment guaranteed to all Americans "equal protection under the law.") The Court rejected Plessy's argument and upheld Louisiana's law, cementing the infamous doctrine of "separate but equal" for nearly sixty years (until *Brown v. Board of Education* in 1954). The decision permitted racial segregation, and in the next ten years, the Jim Crow system was put firmly into place with the Supreme Court's blessing.

The sole dissenting justice, John Marshall Harlan (note his first and middle names), wrote a blistering critique of the decision, predicting accurately that *Plessy* "will prove as infamous" as the *Dred Scott* case and insisting that the Constitution was "color blind." After the decision was handed down, Homer Plessy pled guilty to the violation and paid a $25 fine (for more details, see Chapter 6).

● *Keith Plessy and Phoebe Ferguson, descendants of the two men named in the famous case, became friends and formed a foundation to promote innovative ways of studying civil rights. The battle for civil rights is passed on from generation to generation. Now it is in your hands.*

6. *Lochner v. New York* (1905)

The rise of mass industry and manufacturing in the late nineteenth century bred strong demands for worker protection. Several states passed laws limiting working hours and banning child labor. New York State's worker protections, passed in 1897, included a "Bakeshop Act" that prohibited anyone from working more than ten hours a day, or sixty hours a week, in a bakery.

Joseph Lochner, a bakery owner in Utica, was fined for requiring employees to exceed the sixty-hour weekly limit. He took his case to court, insisting that the Fourteenth Amendment protected his right to establish free contracts with his workers, independent of state influence.

Two New York courts denied Lochner's appeals. In a 7–2 ruling, the Supreme Court reversed the New York decisions, holding that the Bakeshop Act was an invalid exercise of the state's power. The decision ushered in a thirty-year **Lochner era**, during which courts repeatedly struck down state economic and labor regulations, including minimum wage laws, in the name of individual economic liberty. Governments could not interfere with the private right to contract by introducing worker protections.

In dissent, Justice Oliver Wendell Holmes wrote: "The Fourteenth Amendment does not enact Mr. Herbert Spencer's *Social Statics*"—that is, society should not operate by survival of the fittest.

Lochner era: A period from 1905 to 1937, during which the Supreme Court struck down laws (e.g., worker protection or minimum wage laws) that were thought to infringe on economic liberty or the right to contract.

7. *Muller v. Oregon* (1908)

Oregon limited the number of hours women could work. Whereas *Lochner* ruled that the state could not regulate men's hours, the Court chose to treat women differently. The Court ruled that "the difference between the sexes does . . . justify a different rule respecting a restriction of the hours of labor." The concern about "healthy mothers" justified state intervention.

Louis Brandeis defended the law with an innovative strategy. He disposed of the legal arguments in two pages and then compiled page after page of data—health statistics, medical evidence, the experience of other nations. From that time forward, this kind of statistical brief, brimming with data, would be known as a "Brandeis brief."

● *Lawyer Louis Brandeis, later a Supreme Court justice, relied on social science data to win* Muller v. Oregon. *To this day, we call an argument that emphasizes social science research rather than legal argument a "Brandeis brief."*

Clear and present danger: Court doctrine that permits restrictions of free speech if officials believe that the speech will lead to prohibited action such as violence or terrorism.

The case is particularly important for gender readings of the law. Yes, women won labor protections, but notice how: The case supported the idea that a woman was different from a man and, more to the point, that her role as child bearer and mother was more important than her role as worker.

8. *Schenck v. United States* (1919)

Charles Schenck, the secretary of the U.S. Socialist Party, printed and distributed leaflets expressing opposition to a U.S. military draft during World War I. Schenck was convicted under the Espionage Act of aiding the enemy during wartime. Insisting that he was exercising his First Amendment free speech rights, Schenck took his appeal to the Supreme Court.

One of the Court's most prolific (and quotable) justices, Oliver Wendell Holmes Jr., wrote the decision for a 9–0 majority that upheld Schenck's conviction. For the first time, the Court formally marked out boundaries around protected speech: As Holmes wrote, words presenting a "clear and present danger" were legitimate subjects of legislative prohibitions, just like you cannot scream fire in a crowded building. The **clear and present danger** test guided the Court for fifty years, until it was rewritten in 1969. Recall that a "test" is a general principle designed to guide future Court decisions on a topic (for more details, see Chapter 5).

9. *National Labor Relations Board v. Jones and Laughlin Steel Corporation* (1937)

Jones and Laughlin was the nation's fourth-largest manufacturer of steel—an industry that had very aggressively opposed unionization. The company fired ten workers who tried to launch a union, and was sued by the National Labor Relations Board for violating the Wagner Act of 1935, which protected the right to unionize. The company responded that the Wagner Act violated the Constitution. The lower courts both agreed that precedent was on the company's side.

In a 5–4 decision, Chief Justice Charles Evans Hughes reversed the lower court decisions and held that Congress had the power, under the interstate commerce clause, to regulate the company's treatment of its workers. This decision broadly expanded congressional power to regulate economic matters. It meant that the Court—by a one-vote margin—would accept New Deal legislation. We can understand the enormous scope of this ruling when, three decades later, Congress used its authority over interstate commerce to outlaw segregation in hotels and restaurants (with the Civil Rights Act of 1964, discussed in Chapter 6).

Along with another case, *West Coast Hotel Company v. Parrish* (also decided 5–4 in 1937), the courts now permitted legislatures to regulate relations between business and workers. The cases meant the end of the Lochner era. Today, conservative judicial activists are eager to roll back congressional use of the interstate commerce power. Some even call for a return of the Lochner era.

10. *Korematsu v. United States* (1944)

Strict scrutiny: A form of judicial review that requires the government to have a "compelling government interest" for any law that singles out race or ethnicity.

During World War II, an executive order by President Roosevelt forced Japanese Americans out of their homes and into hastily constructed internment camps. Fred Korematsu, a California native, was arrested for defying the order. The Court ruled 6–3 that the need to defend against espionage during wartime justified the order—and its violation of equal protection. The case was one of the first to adopt **strict scrutiny** of government actions: The Court is primed to strike down any law that singles out a race or ethnicity unless there is a very strong reason for doing so (see Chapter 6 for discussion). In this case, the Court ruled, the government's action met the standards of strict scrutiny.

The case was always infamous for its mistreatment of Japanese Americans. It became even more so when legal historian Peter Irons, researching a book about the internment, discovered that the solicitor general had suppressed crucial information. A report from the Office of Naval Intelligence had concluded that there was no evidence that Japanese Americans were disloyal or acting as spies. In 1983, a federal district court in California used the new information to vacate (or void) Korematsu's conviction. To many people, including Fred Korematsu himself, the case stands as an enduring warning. War breeds fear that can threaten civil liberties. Korematsu drew on his own experience to file an *amicus* brief in a case involving the legal rights of enemy combatants held in Guantánamo Bay. The Court formally reversed the precedent of *Korematsu* in 2018 in *Trump v. Hawaii*—a landmark case that upheld the Trump administration's ban on new visas from selected, mostly Muslim, countries.

● *Fred Korematsu refused to enter a Japanese internment camp. Today, his lifelong fight on behalf of civil liberties is commemorated by the "Fred Korematsu Day of Civil Liberties and the Constitution."*

11. *Brown v. Board of Education* (1954)

This watershed unanimous decision declared that segregating schools for Black and white children violated the equal protection clause of the Fourteenth Amendment. As Supreme Court Justice Earl Warren put it, "Separate schools are inherently unequal." The decision boosted the civil rights movement and paved the way for an end to legal segregation. It overturned *Plessy v. Ferguson*, case number 5 above (for more details, see Chapter 6).

12. *Gideon v. Wainwright* (1963)

Clarence Gideon was accused (unjustly, as it eventually was proved) of a minor theft from a Florida pool hall. Lacking funds to hire a defense attorney, Gideon represented himself at his trial—a relatively common practice into the early 1960s. He was swiftly convicted, but he appealed his sentence based on the state's failure to provide him with a competent defense lawyer.

The Supreme Court held that Gideon was wrongly convicted and ordered a new trial. The *Gideon* legacy: Anyone charged with a serious criminal offense has the right to an attorney.[46] Moreover, the state must provide a lawyer to any defendant unable to afford legal counsel. *Gideon* was the first in a series of landmark judicial decisions upholding the rights of defendants in criminal proceedings, including the so-called *Miranda rights* to counsel during police questioning. Recently, the Court has strengthened the right to counsel, holding that it applies to plea bargain cases in which a defendant is offered a deal: Plead guilty, avoid a trial, and receive a lighter sentence (for more details, see Chapter 5).

13. *Roe v. Wade* (1973)

The *Roe v. Wade* decision, written by Justice Harry Blackmun, struck down a Texas statute outlawing abortion—and expanded the personal right to privacy under the Constitution. This right, wrote Blackmun, is "fundamental" and "broad enough to encompass a woman's decision whether or not to terminate her pregnancy." The *Roe* decision became one of the great dividing lines in American politics and a litmus test for most federal judicial nominations. For years, the Court appeared to be divided. Four justices seemed ready to overturn *Roe*, four eager to defend it, and one—Justice Kennedy—in the middle, balancing a right to privacy with a state's interest in limiting abortions. When Amy Comey Barrett joined the Court, the critics finally had their majority and struck down *Roe v. Wade*.

14. *United States v. Nixon* (1974)

This case revolved around the Watergate break-in and the historic political debate that ensued. President Nixon refused to turn over audiotapes of White House conversations, along with other requested materials, to the special prosecutor investigating Watergate, on the grounds of "executive privilege," a sweeping claim of presidential immunity. In a unanimous 8–0 decision, Chief Justice Warren Burger (appointed by Nixon five years earlier) upheld the doctrine of executive privilege but concluded that presidents could not invoke it in criminal cases to withhold evidence. Nixon acquiesced—and resigned as president a month later.

15. *Bush v. Gore* (2000)

High drama surrounded a recount of some of Florida's disputed ballots in the 2000 presidential election, stretching well past the November 7 election date. On December 8, Florida's Supreme Court ordered a manual recount of ballots; George W. Bush's lawyers, fearing this would result in an advantage for Vice President Gore, appealed the decision to the U.S. Supreme Court. The Court, acting with unusual speed because of the urgency of the issue—a presidential election hung in the balance—halted the recount the very next day. Two days later, on December 11, the Court scheduled time to hear from both sides' lawyers. Less than twenty-four hours later, Chief Justice Rehnquist handed down a 5–4 ruling that no constitutionally valid recount could be completed by Florida's December 12 deadline for certifying election results. The long presidential contest of 2000 was over. George Bush won Florida's twenty-five electoral votes and, with them, the presidential election.

16. *Citizens United v. Federal Elections Commission* (2010)

Citizens United, a conservative nonprofit group, distributed a film criticizing presidential candidate Hillary Clinton. Their action violated campaign finance rules (it was too close to the presidential primary) and the Federal Election Commission stopped them. The group sued and the Court ruled, 5–4, that independent political spending by groups or corporations was a form of free speech. The case is discussed in Chapter 10.

17. *National Federation of Independent Business v. Sebelius* (2012)

This decision took on two controversial features of the Obama administration health reform law (the Affordable Care Act, or ACA). The ACA required all Americans to buy health insurance or face a fine (paid with their income taxes); it also expanded Medicaid, a joint federal and state program, to cover all Americans under sixty-five who were poor or near poor (the federal government would pay 90 percent of the costs).

Can the federal government require individuals to carry health insurance? Proponents said yes: Congress has the power to regulate interstate commerce (see case number 9, *National Labor Relations Board v. Jones and Laughlin Steel Corporation*). Chief Justice Roberts and the four conservative justices ruled that Congress does *not* have the power under interstate commerce to require that people buy health insurance. Then, very dramatically, the chief justice broke with the conservatives and ruled that Congress does have the power to tax—and that the ACA constitutes a tax. The Obama reform was upheld. However, Roberts got Supreme Court watchers buzzing. Remember, conservatives have long wanted to curtail the congressional use of interstate commerce. Was Roberts handing conservative jurisprudence a victory, perhaps a return to the Lochner era that conservatives have been calling for, even while upholding the Obama healthcare law?

Time will tell. In the other part of the case, the Court ruled 7–2 that Congress could not change the rules of the Medicaid program and require states to expand their program. It could only offer the funds and encourage the states to participate. Was this, wondered analysts, a new rollback of the federal government's power over federalism? Again, time will tell. The true scope of a case like this often takes years to reveal itself.

18. *Obergefell v. Hodges* (2015)

John Arthur was dying of ALS and his husband, Jim Obergefell, wanted the death certificate to list him as the surviving spouse. However, Ohio law did not recognize same-sex marriage (the couple had been wed in Maryland) and the state attorney general defended the state ban. In *Obergefell*, a narrowly divided Court ruled (5–4) that denying marriage licenses to same-sex couples violated the due process and the equal protection clauses of the Fourteenth Amendment. The ruling, authored by Justice Kennedy, required every state to accord same-sex marriages all the rights and conditions that accompany opposite-sex marriages.

Four different dissenting opinions criticized the majority for stretching the Fourteenth Amendment, for breaking with precedent, and for taking a controversial issue out of the hands of the voters. Again, Justice Kennedy's retirement and Justice Ginsburg's death raise the question of how future decisions might affect this ruling.

19. *Dobbs v. Jackson Women's Health Organization* (2022)

The 6–3 majority overruled *Roe v. Wade.* The Court permitted states to outlaw abortions. We discussed the ruling in Chapter 5 and the opening to this chapter.

The Nineteen Cases—and the Power of the Court

The list of cases illustrates the wide range of questions addressed in U.S. federal courts. There are issues affecting civil rights and liberties (*Dred Scott, Plessy, Korematsu*), federalism and nationhood (*McCulloch, National Federation of Independent Business*), criminal charges (*Gideon*), First Amendment freedoms (*Schenck*), business regulation (*Lochner, National Labor Relations Board, National Federation of Independent Business*), elections (*Bush v. Gore*), gender (*Muller, Roe, Obergefell, Dobbs*), and separated powers (*Nixon*). These cases illustrate the formidable reach of the judiciary in American politics and government.

Many of these cases were very controversial when decided—and some remain disputed today. Such controversy returns to the question we have asked throughout the chapter: Does the Supreme Court (and do courts in general) overstep democratic boundaries when ruling on such momentous political matters? How deferential should they be to the people's representatives? Each case introduces a different type of judgment call—not just on the substance of the case but on the scope of the Court's authority.

WHAT DO YOU THINK?

Name Another Landmark Case

Why didn't we take our list to a nice round number? To leave room for your choice. Think about the many cases we have already discussed in this book—perhaps including the major 2022 decisions opening this chapter. Then pick one that you would add to the list: What would it be?

Hint: Some cases frequently seen as landmarks include *Loving v. Virginia* (which struck down bans on interracial marriage); *Miranda* (the right to remain silent; see Chapter 5); *Tinker* (student free speech; see Chapter 5); *Mapp v. Ohio* (limiting unlawful searches; see Chapter 5), or *Bakke* (affirmative action; see Chapter 6). And *West Virginia v. EPA*, introduced at the start of this chapter. Now it is your turn. Choose a case, add it to the list, and explain why you consider it a landmark.

THE BOTTOM LINE

» A few judicial decisions become landmark decisions, significantly reshaping American politics and society.

» We have listed nineteen of the most important Supreme Court decisions across more than two centuries. Are there any you would add—or subtract?

 ## Improving the Judiciary

An independent judiciary has deep roots in both our colonial English heritage and the classical liberal tradition (as you saw in Chapter 2). Yet despite its appetite for litigation, the public also expresses concerns about our legal system. Four common criticisms are cost, bias, judicial power, and the dangers of corruption.

Criticisms

First, the costs associated with America's litigious society have become a source of widespread discontent, especially among conservatives. U.S. companies spend an estimated $24 billion annually on litigation costs, and although an exact estimate across society is difficult to measure, Americans collectively spend more than $400 billion annually responding to and adjudicating lawsuits.[47]

Second, the U.S. legal system is sometimes perceived as biased. The Black Lives Matter movement, especially in the wake of George Floyd's death at the hands of a Minneapolis police officer, is rooted in charges about inequitable criminal justice and policing practices. Two-thirds of Americans (including 86 percent of Black people) believe that citizens should be able to sue police for misconduct and excessive use of force.[48]

The power of the legal system is a third source of critique. This concern partly owes to our fear of winding up in court, especially as a defendant. The legendary U.S. federal judge Learned Hand wrote in 1926, "As a litigant, I should dread a lawsuit beyond almost anything short of sickness and death."[49] If Judge Hand, after forty-three years as a federal judge, was made anxious by the law's power, imagine how most nonlawyers feel.

Finally, critics cite the power of the Supreme Court majority to decide the important questions in the political system. Congress has become bogged down in stalemate. The White House changes hands and one administration's executive actions are reversed by the next administration. The courts have, slowly but surely, filled the vacuum. Although Democrats, now in the minority, are more dissatisfied (recall that only 13 percent approve of the Court), observers across the political spectrum worry about the power in judicial hands.

Ideas for Reform

How to respond to widespread calls for reform of the judicial system? When Joe Biden entered the White House, he named a commission to think about reforming the Supreme Court. Its final report added to a growing list of ideas for reforming the judiciary.[50] Here we list four.

Policing Reforms. Calls echoed across summer/fall 2020 protests to "Defund the Police!" This slogan covered a sprawling set of reforms—some of which have been instituted in specific cities and towns (remember, in the U.S. federalist system, many matters including policing are under state or local control). Some of the most widely supported reforms include retraining police in nonviolent alternatives to deadly force, a federal database to track officers accused of misconduct, and granting power to civilian (nonpolice) oversight boards to investigate and discipline misconduct by police.[51]

More Resources.   Another reform proposal would grant the courts more resources. The American judiciary faces a "quiet crisis" in attracting talented judges. One reason is a long-term decline in judges' pay, which has fallen dramatically relative to that of other professionals. In 1969, district court judges earned a substantially higher salary than their academic counterparts at Harvard, the highest-paying law school. Today they make half as much as senior professors—and barely a third as much as law school deans.

We also have seen that the U.S. court system runs on a very small budget, relative to that of other governing institutions. State courts stagger under the volume of cases—and cope by using strategies like pushing through plea bargains in the vast majority of criminal cases, again raising charges of bias as we saw in Chapters 5 and 6. Public defenders have impossible caseloads. The tensions of underfunding run throughout the court system. Perhaps courts should receive more resources. On the federal level, it may also be worth thinking about developing a research capacity to evaluate the potential impact of court rulings.

Term Limits.   Judicial term limits (often proposed as eighteen years) would help address the fear of "unelected judges" overruling the elected branches, for justices would cycle off the Supreme Court with each election. After their term, justices could move to the appellate bench—satisfying the constitutional requirement of lifetime appointment. Judicial term limits may reduce the battles that surround judicial appointments, especially to the Supreme Court. Forty-year-old justices would no longer sit on the bench for three decades or more.

Term limits would still keep the Court insulated from political tumult—eighteen years is a long time—while providing for a regular circulation of new judges with fresh perspectives. One version of this proposal would permit the president to nominate a Supreme Court justice (and the Senate to confirm) every two years so that the Court would always balance new ideas and experienced hands. Would you support or oppose such an innovation? What do you think?

Shift Authority to Congress.   Some scholars believe Congress should have the authority to modify Court precedents—essentially sharing the power to interpret the Constitution. After taking the oath of office, President Abraham Lincoln argued that American policy could not be "irrevocably fixed by decisions of the Supreme Court" for, if it were, "the people would cease to be their own rulers." Of course, the Court decides the case between the two parties in a suit. But Congress might revise the Court's general policies. In *Federalist 81*, Alexander Hamilton took the same view, suggesting that Congress "may prescribe a new rule for future cases" even if it violates Court precedent. As we have seen, the Court asserted the power to interpret the Constitution. Perhaps that power should now be shared with Congress.[52]

President Biden's commission on the Supreme Court devoted a chapter to this kind of reform. Among the ideas: Require that major Court decisions be made by more than a simple majority vote, which would mandate that justices persuade one another across ideological divides. Or permit legislative overrides to judicial decisions. While these reforms are not likely in the short run, their rise suggests a growing unease with the power that the Court now wields on the major political questions of our time.

THE BOTTOM LINE

» The courts face four popular criticisms: cost, bias, power over individual lives, and influence over American politics.

» Reform proposals popular with a majority of Americans include a set of policing reforms, as well as more resources for the judicial branch—in both the state and the federal courts—especially to help alleviate overcrowded dockets of criminal cases.

» Other often proposed reforms include term limits for federal judges and shifting some authority for deciding important constitutional matters back to Congress.

Conclusion: Democracy and the Courts

Courts wield an unusual amount of influence in the United States—far more than courts in most other nations, and perhaps too much in a modern democratic society. At the same time, there are clear limits to judicial power—from the reactive nature of the judicial process to the courts' reliance on others to implement decisions. Expanding resources and imposing term limits could modernize the judiciary and enhance this "least dangerous" branch's ability to serve American government by doing what they do at their best: faithfully reflecting—and consistently enforcing—the constitutional rules that guide our public life.

Reforms can only go so far. The powerful role of the courts in a democracy will always be vexing for a simple reason: The courts are designed to serve as a check, ultimately, on the majority. The courts, when they are acting properly, stop the people and their representatives from violating the Constitution or from harming minority rights. However, as the many cases discussed in this chapter indicate, what exactly the Constitution means is often a highly controversial matter. Further, with the benefit of hindsight, we see that the Court has interpreted the Constitution in ways that reduce rights in cases like *Dred Scott, Plessy, Korematsu,* and many others.

As a result, the courts always face a delicate balance between enforcing the Constitution (as a majority on the Court sees it) and deferring to democracy (and the majority of the country).

CHAPTER SUMMARY

★ The judiciary has a central place in U.S. government and politics—as well as in our legalistic national culture.

★ Americans express uneasiness about their judicial system, despite their faith in the rule of law.

★ Compared to other advanced democratic nations, U.S. courts possess a great deal of influence over our politics and government. This owes primarily to the power of judicial review, asserted long ago by Chief Justice John Marshall. Once again, Americans found a way to separate and fragment power—continuing the work begun in the Constitution.

⭐ Alongside their uncommon influence, courts are hemmed in by restrictions such as limited resources, stare decisis requirements, and their lack of an electoral base (at the federal level).

⭐ The judiciary has affected a vast range of areas through its authority to interpret the Constitution, from religion and race to economic regulations and even presidential election outcomes. This impact is evident in a set of landmark cases—each of which has aroused great controversy, leading to renewed calls for limits on judicial activism. The originalist and pragmatist schools of thought have very different views of what constitutes such "activism."

⭐ The Supreme Court marks the pinnacle of judicial—and constitutional—authority in the United States. Its operations, often carried out behind closed doors, are the subject of fascinated speculation: How do nine justices decide? The leading theories: They follow the rule of law, they are guided by their ideology, they are moved by peer pressure, and they are concerned about the institution of the courts.

⭐ Given the combination of the power of the courts and Americans' uncertainty about how that power should be wielded, a set of reforms is put forth each year. Three, in particular, deserve careful attention: a collection of policing reforms, limits on Supreme Court justices' current life terms, and the possibility of rewarding the judiciary's expansive responsibilities with more resources.

KEY TERMS

Amicus curiae, p. 547
Circuit courts, p. 536
Civil law, p. 544
Clear and present danger, p. 560
Common law, p. 543
Concurrent opinion, p. 549
Criminal law, p. 544
Defendant, p. 544

Dissent, p. 549
District courts, p. 536
Judicial activism, p. 543
Judicial restraint, p. 543
Judicial review, p. 541
Litigation, p. 530
Lochner era, p. 559
Majority opinion, p. 549

Mediation, p. 531
Plaintiff, p. 544
Precedent, p. 543
Rule of four, p. 547
Stare decisis, p. 553
Strict scrutiny, p. 560
Textualism, p. 543

STUDY QUESTIONS

1. Should the judiciary have less power in American government and politics? If so, how would you propose restraining judicial authority in practice?
2. The Supreme Court now includes four women, three members of historically underrepresented groups, and four white males. It also includes six Roman Catholics. Should we be attentive to this sort of descriptive representation? Should the courts look like the rest of the population or does it not matter? And what about religion? Should we care about the religious preferences of Supreme Court justices?
3. Do Supreme Court clerks—and other federal judges' clerks—have too much influence, given their relatively young ages and inexperience? Should they serve for longer than one year, given the importance of the work they do? Should the courts have larger and more professional staff? Why or why not?
4. Should we mandate more transparency for judicial operations—should we televise Supreme Court oral arguments or require that Court conferences be transcribed and publicized? Are there any benefits to the secrecy that characterizes the federal judiciary?
5. Do any of the reforms raised at the end of this chapter appeal to you? Why or why not? Might reforms of the judiciary be most successful if offered as a package? (Combining term limits, which appeal to critics of judicial activism, with higher judicial pay and more resources for the courts might make term limits palatable to current and future judges.)
6. Should the federal judiciary be the last line of defense in protecting Americans' constitutional rights and liberties? Why or why not? And if not, what other institution or group of people should have this responsibility? Be specific: How would another actor or group protect rights and liberties better than federal judges, and ultimately the Supreme Court, do today?

"WE ARE THE ECONOMY!" chanted the protesters, gathered outside Federal Reserve headquarters in Washington, DC, where "the Fed" was considering a hike in interest rates.

Fast-rising prices had left low-income Americans worried about paying the rent, eviction from their apartments, increasing food prices, hunger, and the cost of gasoline.[1] Grabbing a bullhorn, one protester bellowed, "Policymakers, do something! Do something that helps *us*!"[2]

But what to do? Democratic leaders, clinging to power in advance of the 2022 midterm elections, proposed an ambitious $2 trillion package of assistance to low-income households. The aid package, known as Build Back Better, triggered a loud debate in Congress that reflected a fundamental choice over public policy: Support low-income Americans? Or trust markets to sort out the damage? Every Republican and a single Democrat opposed Build Back Better—enough to sink the plan in the Senate. Their argument: The proposed law would only fuel inflation and make everything worse. (Eventually, a revised lower-cost version passed.)

At the very same time, policymakers at the Federal Reserve Board were quietly making another set of choices: raise interest rates to combat inflation, even if it risked a recession. Government bodies—ranging from Congress to little known economic agencies—hammer out different policies in different ways. Each decision reflects basic values about politics, economics, and society. As you'll see throughout this chapter, the policies passed in Washington, state governments, or city councils have immense effects on people's daily lives.

As the protesters at the Fed sought to remind public officials, many policy changes in recent years have made inequality worse. The "wealth gap" between the highest and lowest earners in the United States has never been wider.[3] That didn't happen by chance: Public policy influences nearly all aspects of American lives, including inequality across income, racial, and other divides.

Each policy debate involves competing values—reducing inequality versus market freedom, for example. Each takes place in the context of unexpected events: Pandemics, changing economic conditions, rising and falling markets, shifting political attitudes, and new presidential administrations. All affect policy outcomes. The Biden administration pushed, especially in

In this chapter, you will

 Trace the five stages of public policymaking.

 Review the history of U.S. social policy.

 Assess what counts as good policy, including claims of fairness and economic efficiency.

 Learn how the federal budget process drives much of our domestic policymaking.

 Consider how U.S. policymaking could be reformed, including through a racial equity lens.

● *Soaring gas prices in the wake of Russia's invasion of Ukraine helped fuel U.S. inflation at rates not seen for forty years. Public policymakers debated solutions—but the complex, slow-moving American policy system makes it hard to address crises swiftly or comprehensively.*

its early months, to reduce inequality—in part by requiring executive branch officials to consider policy decisions through a racial-equity lens. Every policy debate also focuses officials across all levels of government on the same fundamental question: *What should government do?* In other words, what public policies should we make?

Who are we? One answer: We are what we do. We are the sum of our policies. In some ways, Americans are best described in terms of the policies we enact—and those that we reject or abandon. Why do we provide hefty government subsidies to farmers growing corn, dairy, and beef, but virtually none to growers of fruits and vegetables? Why do we imprison one in nine young Black men? Why do we closely regulate sex but not violence in movies? Why do we control privately owned land to protect spotted owls and flying squirrels? Why do some states (like Louisiana) permit higher levels of pollution than others (like California)? These and thousands of other policy decisions contribute to the kaleidoscopic portrait of the United States.

All the actors introduced in this book—interest groups, Congress, the media, executive branch officials, the courts, the public, the media, and more—come together to create public policy. Here we will look at domestic policymaking, and in Chapter 18 we will turn to foreign policy. As we will see, budgets and finance have become a central feature of the policy process. Moreover, it is impossible to discuss policy without considering the larger economic and social context. That means weighing the costs and the benefits of every proposal and program.

Finally, recall the core American ideas we explored in Chapter 2. Public policies give those ideas concrete form. Should we ensure that everyone has access to healthcare or a basic national wage (positive liberty!)? Or simply leave people to use their own income to buy health insurance—or anything else they may want (negative liberty!)? How do we actually make these kinds of choices in the U.S. governing system? That's what you'll learn in this chapter.

 ## Public Policymaking in Five (Not-So-Easy) Stages

Think about an issue you care about: clean drinking water, infant mortality, the minimum wage, abortion, gun control. Public policy examines how government officials address (or duck) these issues—by regulating pollutants, encouraging prenatal care, or enacting gun control measures. Policies take many forms: laws, regulations, presidential executive orders, court rulings, funding formulas (determining who gets how much), and even cultural norms.

Making domestic policy is an elaborate process, involving five overlapping stages (Figure 17.1) We organize our trip through the public policy system by exploring each of these in turn; however, in the real world, the different stages don't always line up in a nice, neat order.

BY THE NUMBERS ## U.S. Public Policy

214 Number of laws passed, 117th Congress (2021–22), as of November 15, 2022

906 Number of laws passed, 80th Congress (1947–48), labeled the "Do-Nothing Congress" by President Truman

3,280 Number of new federal regulations introduced during first year in office, Trump administration

3,257 Number of new federal regulations introduced during first year in office, Biden administration

90 Percentage of federal rules reviewed by the Office of Management and Budget (OMB) that are required to include a cost-benefit analysis, 2018–21[4]

2.4 Spending, in trillions of dollars (estimated), on Social Security, Medicare, and Medicaid in 2023

9 Percentage of Americans aged sixty-five and over living in poverty, 2022[5]

29 Percentage of Americans aged sixty-five and over living in poverty, 1966[6]

40 Percentage decrease in U.S. teenagers using drugs, past three years[7]

13.7 million Estimated number of Americans behind on rent or mortgage payments, June 2022[8]

274 Number of U.S. universities offering an accredited degree program in public policy and administration, 2023[9]

How has the volume of U.S. policymaking activity—laws passed, regulations issued, government dollars spent—changed over time? And what are some of the results?

1. Agenda Setting

Policymaking does not begin until public officials see a problem they need to address.

Of many potential issues, a few rise onto the policy agenda. They get there thanks to political speeches, media attention, political rallies, interest groups, and late-night talk shows. Some issues come up regularly. Others seem to rise out of nowhere—and often fade away just as fast.

Focusing event: A major happening, often of crisis or disaster proportions, that attracts widespread media attention to an issue.

Policy agenda: The issues that the media covers, the public considers important, and politicians address. Setting the agenda is the first step in political action.

For example, no one outside public health circles had thought much about masking mandates—until the COVID pandemic. Once masks were scientifically established as a promising source of prevention, healthcare experts ardently recommended them. Mask mandates spread across schools, universities, businesses, nonprofits, government offices, the U.S. military, and sports leagues. Then a counter-movement developed, fed partly by libertarians ("Don't tread on me!" became "Don't require me to mask!"). Donald Trump eventually endorsed the demonstrators who staged mask burnings and other protests. Democrats in Congress and in state governments introduced bills to require masking; Republicans were virtually united in opposition (see Figure 17-2). The Biden administration's national mask mandate was challenged—and partially overturned—in federal court. America's deep partisan divide was evident again, tied to a health measure proven to save people from a potentially fatal virus. In political science terms, the mask mandate and protests in response were a **focusing event** that took the tension between public health and personal liberty and put it squarely on the national agenda.

Focusing events shape **policy agendas**. There's always fierce competition to set the agenda because the policy system can digest only a few priorities at any time. As Table 17.1 shows, the policy agenda changes across the years—even month to month. Notice how COVID and racial issues were at the top of the public's list in 2020. Two years later, as the pandemic abated and the urgency around race following George Floyd's death faded as well, both issues had fallen out of the top ten, listed as top problems by just 1 and 2 percent of Americans. Meanwhile, concerns about inflation, economic problems, gun violence (see next section), and crime shot to the top.

Policy agendas are difficult to pin down, as issues burst suddenly into Americans' collective consciousness . . . or fade away. Although mass shootings are depressingly familiar in the United States, the tragedy in Uvalde, Texas, in 2022, when nineteen children and two teachers were killed at Robb Elementary School, propelled guns back onto the policy agenda. Polling revealed the most support for controlling gun violence (59 percent) versus protecting gun rights (35 percent) in

2021 State Mandated School Mask Policies*

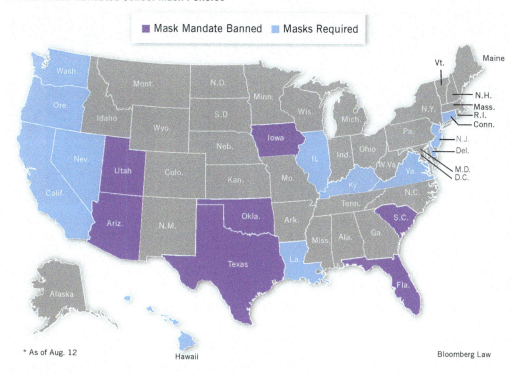

■ Mask Mandate Banned ■ Masks Required

* As of Aug. 12

Bloomberg Law

● **FIGURE 17.2** *State Policies on Masks in Schools, 2021. Mask mandates in some states were countered by bans on mandates in others. This map shows the policies as students returned in 2021: eleven states mandated masks in public schools—and seven states forbade mandates in schools. States on both sides overruled local authorities and school boards. (Bloomberg Law)*

TABLE 17.1 **Comparison of Top National Agenda Items, Two Years Apart**

MOST IMPORTANT PROBLEM FACING THE COUNTRY, SUMMER 2020	PERCENTAGE MENTIONING IN 2020	MOST IMPORTANT PROBLEM FACING THE COUNTRY, SUMMER 2022	PERCENTAGE MENTIONING IN 2022
The government/poor leadership	21	High cost of living/inflation	18
Coronavirus/disease	20	The government/poor leadership	18
Race relations/racism	19	Economy in general	13
Economy in general	8	Guns/gun control	8
Unifying the country	4	Crime/violence	6
Lack of respect for one another	4	Fuel/oil prices	5
Gap between rich and poor	3	Immigration	5
Healthcare	3	Unifying the country	5
Ethics/morals/religious/family decline	3	Ethics/morals/religious/family decline	4
Police brutality	2	Poverty/hunger/homelessness	3
Source: Gallup			

a decade.[10] Within weeks of the tragic event, Congress had passed its most significant gun control legislation since 1994. As with so many U.S. policy disputes, the new restrictions are winding their way through the courts.

You get the idea. Nothing happens until people are talking about an issue, government officials are springing into action, and the media are spinning headlines:

● *As President Biden discussed the new law strengthening gun control on the White House lawn in 2022 (a), he was interrupted by Manuel Oliver (b), whose son was killed during a mass shooting at Parkland High School in Florida four years before. Mass shootings often serve as tragic focusing events, propelling gun violence up the policy agenda.*

The policy has hit the agenda. Getting something on the agenda means thinking big—you need to get everyone talking about the issue. Once it's on the agenda, the question changes: Before policymakers take action, they have to define the problem and find a solution. That moves us to the next stage.

2. Framing

Translating agenda items into proposed policy solutions means answering a series of questions. What are the root causes of the problem? How bad a problem *is* this? And, of course, what policy moves might solve it? What should we do, if anything? Most agenda issues involve framing questions such as these (discussed in Chapter 9). Different people will come up with different answers.

Consider an example from education policy. Every three years, a representative sample of fifteen-year-olds from around the world sits for exams in reading, math, and science. When the latest results were released, American secondary school students finished far behind their counterparts from many other advanced countries. Poor school performance dominated local and national conversations. Everyone agreed: Scores had to improve.

The test results (a focusing event) placed the issue on the agenda. Then the debate over defining, or *framing*, the problem began. Was the American school year too short? The curriculum too easy? Are calls to replace unionized teachers who remain in classrooms despite poor results a step toward reform, or unfair assaults on the dedicated professionals working hard in public schools?

And who should decide: Is education—or, for that matter, any public problem—best addressed on a national or local level? Would national solutions reduce inequity or merely amount to federal government meddling? These different ways of framing issues, also called *problem definition*, have big consequences: They help determine which policy responses the government considers. As issues are framed and reframed, policy actors translate their preferred solutions into legislation, propelling policymaking to a third stage.

3. Policy Formation

Now it's time to adapt (or discard) the solution. Formulating policies is a sprawling process. Congress, state legislatures, or city councils get down to all the activities you read about in Chapter 13: drafting bills, holding hearings, and hammering out compromises in committee meetings and floor debates. Executive branch experts weigh in—all the way up to the president if the issue is sufficiently high profile (recall Chapters 14 and 15). Advocacy groups and industry lobbyists swarm around lawmakers (as we saw in Chapter 12). Judicial rulings reshape the policy debate (see Chapter 16). And pundits opine through podcasts, online publications, social media, the blogosphere, and TV talk shows (Chapter 9). Every aspect of the political system comes together in formulating public policies.

Analyzing Policy, Ex Ante. Competing ideas, rhetorical displays, deft procedural moves, power plays: These underpin policy formation in every society. Recently, more technical work has entered the process. Policy analysis involves projecting a proposed policy's costs and benefits—ex ante, or before it passes and goes into effect. Such assessment efforts are a central feature of contemporary policymaking.

One familiar approach projects the **cost effectiveness** of proposed policies. Analysts compare several policy alternatives that deliver the same overall benefit to determine which one does so at the *lowest cost*. Imagine that a local government decides to repaint the town hall. Different painting companies bid for the job. Presumably they all provide the same basic service, perhaps with minor differences in paint color or warranty. City officials can compare these similar vendors based on proposed costs and ask which provides the most cost-effective service.

Most policy decisions are a lot more complicated than painting a building. Typically, a proposal's *benefits*, along with the costs, must be taken into account. To do so, every side deploys its own technical studies as they push for their preferred solution. Each of the past three presidents, for example, has recommended an increase in the federal gasoline tax. For thirty years, the national gas tax has remained at 18.4 cents per gallon, after slowly rising over the preceding sixty years from a penny per gallon. (Although, as inflation spiraled upward in 2022, President Biden proposed a three-month "gas tax holiday"—reducing the 18.4 cent tax to zero during the summer.[11]) To illuminate the likely effects of a gas tax hike—and to estimate an ideal level for an increase—experts perform a **cost-benefit analysis.** Such evaluations are carried out by trained analysts, some of them working in government and others in academia, lobbying firms, or think tanks.

The first step in a cost-benefit analysis is to list all the expected costs of a policy proposal, as well as all the expected benefits. Before submitting a proposed gas tax increase, White House or congressional or private sector analysts identify primary categories of cost and main areas of benefit. The results are summarized in Table 17.2.

Researchers then "monetize," or assign dollar values to, these costs and benefits, using mathematical formulas. In the gas tax example, the estimated *costs* of a higher tax are around 78 cents per gallon: 54 cents for the increased price of services (such as higher costs of goods transported by truck) and 24 cents in direct costs to drivers. Seems like a pretty steep cost to add to each gallon of gas. Well, the predicted *benefits* are considerably higher. Adding together the estimated savings yields a $1.81 benefit per gallon, as Table 17.3 shows.

According to the cost-benefit analysis, national gas taxes could be raised by just over a dollar per gallon ($1.81 in benefits, minus the 78-cent cost). From the perspective of economic effectiveness, society would be better off. Benefits include environmental improvements, public health (fewer accidents, more time saved), and reduced payments for imported oil. One more beneficiary, if the tax passed,

Cost effectiveness: The projected costs of a proposed policy, as revealed by a relatively simple study.

Cost-benefit analysis: A more complex study of the projected costs and benefits associated with a proposed policy.

TABLE 17.2 Gas Tax Costs/Benefits

GAS TAX COSTS
Direct cost of the tax to drivers (those in rural areas, and with lower incomes, would be hardest hit)
Higher price of services dependent on transportation, such as shipping goods by truck
GAS TAX BENEFITS
Reduced urban air pollution (thereby improving public health)
Reduced CO_2 emissions (slowing the pace of climate change)
Reduced U.S. dependence on imported oil
Diminished traffic congestion (saving drivers time)
Reduced traffic accidents (because people drive less or switch to mass transit)

TABLE 17.3 Cost-Benefit Valuation of a Proposed Gas Tax

COSTS OF GAS TAX	VALUE*	BENEFITS OF GAS TAX	VALUE*
Direct cost to drivers	$0.24	Public health (reduced air pollution)	$0.43
Transportation services	$0.54	Climate (reduced CO_2 emissions)	$0.13
		Reduced oil imports	$0.11
		Time saved (less traffic)	$0.58
		Reduced accidents	$0.56
TOTAL	**$0.78**		**$1.81**

Values are estimated per gallon of gas.
Source: Authors' calculation, combining several existing models

would be the federal Treasury, which could apply new tax dollars to infrastructure improvement, including transportation funding.

Of course, each step of the process requires judgment calls. When the Trump administration did a cost-benefit valuation for regulating greenhouse gas emissions, they calculated the price of spewing carbon into the air at $1 to $7 a ton—making the cost of regulation too high, for it would only save a few dollars a ton. Biden administration economists reworked the assumptions and bumped the carbon-emissions price all the way up to $51 per ton—roughly where it had been before Trump took office. Whenever you see any cost-benefit regulation, look carefully to see how the analyst is totaling up the costs and benefits.[12]

From Cost-Benefit Analysis to Politics. Cost-benefit and other ex ante evaluations are widely used in policymaking. Yes, there is plenty of room for interpretation in the analysis. And you are now savvy enough to know the political reality: Even the best analyses do not determine policy. When Presidents Obama, Trump, and Biden each floated separate proposals to significantly raise the gas tax, the plan met with immediate opposition from antitax conservatives. Partly due to such opposition and partly due to rising gas prices in each administration, the plan was quietly shelved.

Political considerations regularly overcome even a clearly positive policy analysis. And political interests who oppose a policy can be expected to charge in with their own cost-benefit analyses that—surprise—bolster their own position. Notice the trend: Policy debates and even loud arguments are carried on partially through dueling technical studies.[13]

If the swirling politics and institutions align just right, a metaphorical **policy window** opens.[14] Might a new policy be launched? There is no guarantee of success. Of the several thousand bills and measures introduced in Congress each year, only two hundred or so make it into the statute books. Policy windows rarely stay open for long. Advocates who tinker with their policies for too long find that their window of opportunity has slammed shut. Seasoned policy wonks long ago learned the lesson: When opportunity strikes, move fast.

Policy window: A figurative description of the opportunity—often brief, measured in days or weeks rather than years—to pass a bill in Congress or a state legislature.

4. Policy Implementation

When a new law makes it onto the books, policymaking passes to the implementation stage. As you read in Chapter 15, this process takes place in the shadows—far from public view. During policy formation, televised congressional hearings, White House speeches, and cliffhanger congressional votes keep the media whirring and the attentive public engaged. Afterward, however, the media glare dims. The implementation of national policies is primarily handled by the executive bureaucracy, far from public view. Does this shift in visibility mean that the work of policy implementation is less politicized?

Many political thinkers used to think so. Back in 1887, political scientist Woodrow Wilson wrote that "administrative questions are not political." They were, he said, "a technical science." Wilson learned how wrong he had been when he became president thirty years later.[15]

Implementing public policy is highly political. Implementation involves two main steps: working out the law's specifics, primarily through the rulemaking process introduced in Chapter 15, and then delivering government services or enforcing new regulations. Both these steps attract intense interest—and, inevitably, political fighting—from the communities most affected by the policy change.

Rulemaking Revisited.   Once a law passes and the bureaucracy gets to work, politics is still front and center in this more obscure rulemaking phase. As you will recall from Chapter 15, each aspect of a new law requires a separate rule, and each rule is spelled out in painstaking detail. For example, one part of the Affordable Care Act (ACA, or Obamacare) mandates that dependents up to age twenty-six remain eligible for health insurance through their parents; the previous cutoff age was eighteen, or twenty-one for students enrolled in college. In the ACA as written by Congress, this requirement was spelled out in only a couple of sentences. However, the Department of Health and Human Services rule specifying details—who was eligible, under what circumstances, penalties for violation, and so forth—ran to more than twenty-five single-spaced, tiny-print pages in the *Federal Register*.[16] Each of those pages shapes the policy in major and minor ways.

With such room for maneuvering, complaints abound. Some charge that interested parties have too much influence in designing the rules. Others complain that agencies move too slowly to protect the public or, alternately, that they impose rules too quickly to permit proper review by interested parties. The average environmental rule during the Obama administration took fifty-four days—an agonizing wait for some, unacceptably fast for others.[17] Then the Trump administration came along and eliminated more than one hundred of the environmental rules passed under Obama. President Biden returned the favor, restoring environmental protection regulations in dozens of cases. Conservatives rejoiced when the Supreme Court rebuked the Environmental Protection Agency (EPA) in a 2022 decision, declaring that the EPA's regulatory zeal outstripped its congressional warrant.[18] Liberals had their turn to cheer when the Inflation Reduction Act, passed on a party-line vote in August 2022, met the Court's objection by explicitly giving the EPA the authority to regulate greenhouse gases.[19] Republicans promised to go back to the courts.

Ultimately, as we saw in Chapter 15, rules have to be carefully specified. Poorly worded or legally dubious rules are likely to be challenged successfully in court, as the Trump administration repeatedly discovered to its chagrin.[20] Still, a clear trend is emerging: More and more policy battles—over everything from environmental regulations to cryptocurrency rules to gun control—are taking place in the shadowy corners of the rulemaking process (see Figure 17.3).

Remember this key lesson from our discussion of public policy implementation. As with all steps in the policy process, rulemaking involves political battles alongside the technical details. Once the final rule setting out a policy's details has been issued, it is time to carry out the policy. Governments implement policies in different ways.

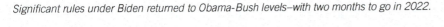

Significant rules under Biden returned to Obama-Bush levels—with two months to go in 2022.

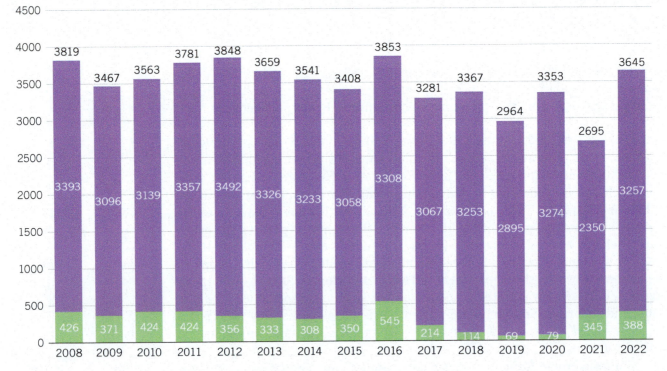

● **FIGURE 17.3** *Rules and "Significant Rules" in the Federal Register, by Year. "Significant" rules represent meaningful changes in policy, such as a rule to allow oil and gas drilling on federal land. Note that, although overall rulemaking kept pace during the supposedly anti-regulatory Trump years (2017–20), there were far fewer significant rules than in ordinary times, under both Republican and Democratic administrations. (Federal Register)*

Top-Down Delivery. As the American national government stepped up its level of domestic policy activity following World War II, delivery of public services was established as a "top-down" process. Confident in the wake of victory, American and British architects of the new science of public policy proclaimed that the executive branch, working from clear goals and strategies, could deliver government services in a coherent, transparent manner. They saw cabinet secretaries and agency heads as firmly in charge of the process. Lower-level bureaucrats and "policy clients" (the people government was serving) were mainly concerned with *compliance*, or doing what they were told to do.

● When the Food and Drug Administration (FDA) receives reports about possibly dangerous food products like Fudgeamentals and Walmart brand fudge in 2022, the agency, along with the Department of Agriculture, supervises a national top-down recall.

Many policy planners still promote this top-down model of delivering government benefits and services. It can work when a policy is relatively simple, with clear, well-specified goals that are not difficult to meet. Imagine a national ban on sales of a food product found to be tainted by potentially fatal bacteria, for example. A high-ranking figure, such as the secretary of agriculture or the head of the Food and Drug Administration, issues a public warning. Government inspectors ensure that the dangerous product is removed from grocery shelves, law enforcement officials investigate the cause of the outbreak, and prosecutions may follow. The public's role is simple: Avoid the tainted product. The policy aim is clear, as are the lines of authority.

As you know well by now, governing is rarely so straightforward. Most issues involve many interested actors, leading to struggles over jurisdiction—and making top-down control of policymaking impossible much of the time. Six different House committees considered a proposal to enhance housing options for low-income Americans in 2021; the Senate took up no fewer than seven bills on the same topic during the 117th Congress (2021–22). Meanwhile President Biden issued two major executive orders on housing: one, soon after taking office, to advance racial equity in public housing, and a second in summer 2022 to make rents more affordable during the inflationary spiral in housing costs.[21]

Policy goals can be ambiguous or confusing ("enhance access to affordable and integrated policy options"), slowing executive bureaucrats' ability to enact new regulations or hand out services. Our federalist system, described in Chapter 4, does not help matters by creating multiple levels of jurisdiction. Authorities are frequently stymied in their attempts to police pot growers, for example, given all the conflicting local, state, and federal regulations governing medicinal marijuana—especially with nineteen states and Washington, DC, permitting recreational marijuana use (see Figure 17.4).[22]

Bottom-Up Delivery. For complicated policies, "bottom-up" provisions of public services or regulations can be more effective than top-down efforts to command and control outcomes. Bottom-up service delivery starts with street-level

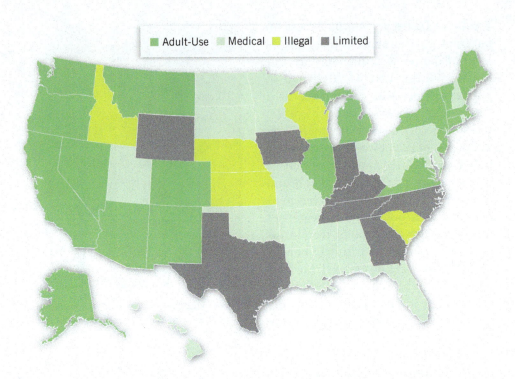

Adult-Use   Medical   Illegal   Limited

● **FIGURE 17.4** *Marijuana policy in the states, as of summer 2022. A series of conflicting federal (including Congress, executive agencies, and courts) and state policy decisions has left this area a patchwork—illustrating the complexity of policy implementation. (National Cannabis Industry Association)*

bureaucrats, introduced in Chapter 15; recall that these officials work directly with recipients of government benefits. Examples include the physician's assistant at a public hospital providing care and advice to new mothers, the air-traffic controller who guides your flight in safely for landing, and the immigration official who asks to see your papers.

All these policy providers and regulators work directly with the public, and they can exercise discretion in making decisions. Certainly, a hierarchy is still in place, with cabinet secretaries and agency heads at the top. But when street-level officials are allowed a measure of autonomy, or input into decision making, government services are sometimes delivered more efficiently and regulations are put in place with less disruption. These street-level actors may even ignore superiors' orders and do what they consider best, based on their experience.

Is this democracy in action—or bureaucracy run amok? Well, often both. Think of resident assistants (RAs) in college and university dormitories. Although vice presidents and deans set official policies for dorm residents, RAs—who are usually students themselves—are directly aware of the needs and concerns of residents on their hall or floor. Academic studies have chronicled how these "street-level" RAs bring their personal experience and knowledge of individual students to improving the implementation of residence-hall rules and benefits.[23] Sometimes this may mean bending university regulations to make sure the residents' needs are served; occasionally, those rules are later revised as a result of an RA's suggestion. At other times, however, the RAs might discriminate against people on the basis of race, gender, or sexual orientation. They might reap confusion by misinterpreting university guidelines or playing favorites with their friends.

The same thing happens across the federal bureaucracy: Street-level employees who are directly aware of a policy's effects may change their practices to make sure a program performs effectively. Or they might favor some clients over others or practice subtle forms of discrimination. One classic study showed how public officials were courteous to recipients of some programs (such as Social Security for people over sixty-five) and rude and intrusive to beneficiaries of others (poor mothers on public assistance).[24] The fiery debate that followed George Floyd's murder in 2020 was all about the bottom-up behavior of street-level bureaucrats—in this case, the police.

For every program and policy, the debate continues. When is it most effective to build uniform top-down policies? And when bottom-up? Who benefits and who is harmed? Just a few of the many questions that well up as we hammer out our public policies.

5. Policy Evaluation and Feedback

Once a solution has been formulated, passed into law, and implemented, is our policymaking story over? Not at all. We still have to figure out if it actually works.

This is the stage of policy evaluation. Does a school-lunch program need tweaking in practice because its benefits are not reaching many kids? Should we abandon an ineffective government effort to reduce tax fraud and try something else? Policy evaluators analyze how well a policy is meeting its stated goals.

Policymaking proceeds in a context of uncertainty: Even armed with technical, ex ante studies, no one can be sure how a policy will play out in practice. Policymakers (and interest groups) perform ex post (Latin for "after the event") studies to measure success or failure, and perhaps make adjustments. The studies may put new policies on the agenda and start the process all over again.

Ex Post Policy Evaluations. Ideally, evaluators would track every new government benefit or regulation to see how well it works. Because of resource constraints, that does not happen, but many policies are subjected to at least occasional ex post evaluations. These generally follow a prescribed sequence. An evaluator compares a policy program to the original goals that Congress and executive branch rule makers had in mind. The evaluator could be a government agency, an academic or think tank analyst, an interest group, a court-appointed independent authority, or sometimes every one of these at the same time. The evaluator collects and assesses relevant information, using data if it is available; makes a judgment about program effectiveness; and issues recommendations.[25]

At best, these steps add up to a reasonably objective analysis. If a policy is performing in line with its designers' goals, it should be left alone. If not, a good ex post evaluation will point out how the policy could be improved. But policymaking is rarely that straightforward.

When a law is introduced, advocates fight hard to frame it positively, advance the legislation through Congress, and win the president's signature. Many of them remain engaged during the rulemaking process to make sure it is rolled out as they expected. Now imagine an ex post evaluation that suggests the policy is not working well. These supporters probably will not agree that their extensive efforts were in vain. Instead, they may criticize the evaluation for flawed methodology and commission a competing review. Likewise, in the face of a positive evaluation, the opposition—which fought against the new policy all the way from framing to rulemaking—rarely gives up and admits that its criticisms were wrong. They leap in with their own evaluation.

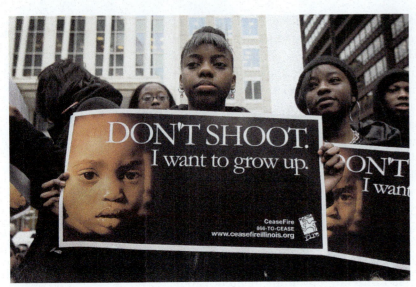

● *Evaluating anti-gang policies. Cure Violence, initially a controversial policy that was widely adopted after ex post evaluations demonstrated some success. Scientific evaluations of the program continue.*

A Case in Point: Gang Violence. The apparently simple evaluator's question—Does the policy work?—is rarely answered in a clear way. Take the issue of reducing gang violence. Some policymakers have argued for years that we must "fight fire with fire." Boost the police presence, including intrusive stop-and-frisk policies; toughen the penalties for gang crimes; come down hard, even on first convictions, with long sentences, in harsh prison conditions.

A few years ago, a different idea surfaced. David Kennedy, a criminal justice professor, introduced a program called Ceasefire (since renamed Cure Violence). Cure Violence organized "call-ins"—meetings that brought together suspected young gang members with community leaders, ex-gang offenders, religious figures, prosecutors, and police. Organizers offered the youth in attendance counseling, job leads, and an opportunity to talk frankly without fear of reprisal. At the same time, the youth were warned that any hint of violent activity in the future would result in widespread arrests. Not only the offenders but also their network of associates would be hauled into court as well.[26]

Cure Violence has been implemented in dozens of cities, both large ones such as Boston, New York, and Chicago, and smaller places like High Point, North Carolina, and Erie, Pennsylvania. The program has won widespread attention; President Biden visited a program site in Queensbridge, New York. However, evaluators have reached mixed conclusions about how well Cure Violence works.[27] By some measures, such as reducing violent crime during the first few weeks after implementation, Cure Violence appears preferable to tough police tactics. By other metrics, the program seems to have made little difference. Rates of youth unemployment in some neighborhoods have hardly changed, nor have longer-term trends in violent crime. Faced with mixed messages, should a mayor invest in Cure Violence in response to the spread of youth gangs? Policy evaluation, like much else in U.S. policymaking, is as much an art as a science.

Policy Feedback. New policies, once implemented, do not just play out in a vacuum. They in turn shape and constrain future policymaking. Scholars term this process *policy feedback*.

A program that distributes benefits will attract loyal supporters who will push for its extension. Lawmakers seeking to reform or cancel the program (perhaps based on an ex post evaluation) can find their efforts thwarted by these grateful recipients. More subtly, as a policy is rolled out, actors of various types will adapt to the policy, making it difficult to change. Bureaucrats get organized to administer a benefit; businesses rework their economic forecasts to account for a new regulatory framework. Political scientist Paul Pierson described these tendencies as **path dependence**: Once a policy is established, possibilities for reform or change are constrained by the "path" it has followed through implementation and service delivery.[28]

Path dependence: Social science term for how policymakers' choices are shaped by institutional "paths" that result from policy choices made in the past.

A classic example of a policy with powerful feedback effects is Social Security, passed in 1935. Social Security achieved far-reaching effects. It lifted many people over age sixty-five out of poverty and, in the process, attracted the fierce loyalty of beneficiaries. Senior citizens feel that they have earned their right to receive old-age government benefits—by paying payroll taxes in their working years. Millions of Americans organize their investment decisions and retirement planning around the path created by Social Security. Indeed, roughly half of retired Americans in 2022 had almost no other source of income.[29] This makes Social Security virtually untouchable by policymakers.

THE BOTTOM LINE

» U.S. policymaking involves five stages. Policies do not proceed neatly from one to the next, but the "stages" idea is a useful way of distinguishing among different actions carried out by policy officials.

» The first of these stages is agenda setting, whereby concerns receiving widespread attention become policy issues.

» A second stage is problem definition and framing, featuring debates about how to describe an issue and which solutions are most viable.

» A third stage is policy formation, a process of legislative and executive activity to develop the policy idea in concrete terms.

» A fourth stage is policy implementation, marked by rulemaking and service delivery.

» A fifth stage includes evaluation and policy feedback, steps that help determine whether a policy works—and that often start the debate all over again.

U.S. Social Policy

Public policy comes in many forms, as you can see from the many examples in this chapter.

Fiscal policy has to do with financial matters; we delve into it later in this chapter. *Foreign policy* covers topics like wars, defense, diplomacy, and trade agreements, discussed in Chapter 18. Most other issues are grouped together as *social policy,* or policies that address people's well-being. Health, housing, education, employment, poverty reduction, criminal justice, child welfare, and old-age security: All these areas make up social policy. So do controversial topics such as abortion, same-sex marriage, racial and gender equity, and recreational drug use.

Compared to industrialized Western European countries, the United States was slow to adopt modern social policies. Germany provided old-age insurance as far back as 1883, and Great Britain did so in 1911. The United States did not establish a similar policy (Social Security) until Franklin Roosevelt's New Deal in 1935. Almost all wealthy democracies enacted universal health insurance starting in the 1880s; the United States still does not guarantee healthcare to all its citizens. And after the Supreme Court's *Dobbs* decision in 2022, the United States joins Poland as the only wealthy democratic nation that does not support a right to abortion.

Why has American social policy been more limited? There are at least four traditional arguments. First, some point to individualism and resistance to big government.

Second, others argue that the difference lies in American institutions. It's very difficult to get high-profile reforms through Congress; for many years, the Supreme Court struck down social policies on both the federal and state level (recall the Lochner era described in Chapter 16). Congress, courts, checks and balances, federalism: American institutions make big policy changes difficult to win—even if they are popular.

A third perspective suggests that the deep racial and ethnic divisions running through American history have split the working class and made it more difficult to foster a culture of solidarity.

Finally, some political scientists point out that the United States spends just as much on social welfare policies as other countries—but generally focuses benefits on the middle class and elderly rather than the poor. Which is right? We believe there is merit in all these perspectives. Which is most important? What do you think?[30]

Wars and Social Policy

Wars and their aftermath were the source of most major social policy advances during the first century and a half after the Constitution was ratified. The Revolutionary War inspired the earliest state-level efforts to administer organized benefits. In New York, for example, a "Committee on Superintendence of the Poor" was created to aid people who lost their homes during the fighting. After the Civil War, national government benefits flowed to soldiers and their families. The first old-age pensions were provided to Union army veterans during the late nineteenth century. Their mothers, widows, and children later received some state support, including monthly welfare payments and regulations on child labor—the sons and daughters of soldiers who died in combat should not be forced to work, the argument went.[31]

A more recent instance of a war-related policy is the GI Bill, passed in 1944 to reward American troops returning from World War II with a heavily subsidized college education. The bill's designers expected that soldiers themselves would benefit from attending college; a secondary hope was that U.S. labor markets would be able to adjust gradually to millions of newly returned soldiers as universities absorbed many of the veterans.

What policymakers did not expect is that American higher education would be transformed by the GI Bill, as colleges and universities expanded to meet the needs of 4.4 million soldiers turned students—many of them with fewer family resources than the traditionally better-off young men and women who attended U.S. colleges before 1945. Moreover, many GI Bill beneficiaries, political scientist Suzanne Mettler demonstrated, went on to become unusually civic-minded Americans.[32] College attendance continued to grow in subsequent years, aided by a host of new government programs (policy feedback again!) stretching from Pell Grants and low-interest student loans, both established in the 1960s, to the American Opportunity Tax Credit, passed in 2010 and extended in 2018, and COVID-era student loan forgiveness programs extended in 2022 by the Biden administration.

War's domestic equivalent is grave economic hardship, and the Great Depression, starting in 1929, helped lead to more extensive federal social policies, many arising from Franklin Roosevelt's New Deal. Among the numerous social programs run or financed by the U.S. government today, three of the longest lived and most extensive deserve special attention.

Old-Age Insurance: Social Security

Social Security provides Americans of retirement age—who have lived in the United States for at least five years—with a monthly stipend. The minimum age for Social Security was recently raised to sixty-six years for those born before 1954, rising gradually to sixty-seven for those born in 1955 and after. Social Security payments vary with income: A worker who retires in 2023 making $50,000 a year would currently receive around $1,911 per month. The original act also created an unemployment insurance program (more on that later), paid benefits to disabled workers and their families, and offered financial assistance to low-income families with children. One constant over the years: Social Security's financing comes from a payroll tax on all eligible workers and their employers.

The Social Security Act initially excluded many occupations from the program, limiting benefits (and payroll-tax contributions) primarily to white males. In subsequent years, such jobs as teachers, nurses, domestic helpers, librarians, and farmers were added, effectively creating the first universal social policy in American history. Although the program began small—with only fifty-three thousand beneficiaries when it was implemented in 1937—it grew rapidly. In 2021, Social Security paid more than $1.1 trillion to more than seventy million workers, supported by payroll taxes from more than 170 million employees. At roughly 5 percent of the nation's **gross domestic product (GDP)**, Social Security is the largest single federal government program.

Although the old-age benefits provided by Social Security have helped lift many seniors out of poverty, anxious voices sound alarms about paying for the program, especially as the huge baby boomer generation retires and receives benefits. How urgent is the problem? Many moderates and conservatives argue that the inexorably rising costs pose an economic risk in the long run. Liberals accuse conservatives of exaggerating the threat, and argue that relatively small adjustments (increasing the retirement age, raising taxes, tinkering with benefits) will fix the problem. Once again we have a framing debate, over whether rising Social Security costs pose an economic risk to the country.

Gross domestic product (GDP): The value of all the goods and services produced in a nation over a year. For 2022, the U.S. GDP is an estimated $24.8 trillion.

● *Ida May Fuller, the first recipient (in 1940) of a monthly Social Security check for $22.54. That check would be worth roughly $477 in today's economy.*

Whatever the extent of the problem, the system remains extremely difficult to change. Efforts to introduce fundamental reforms generally go down in flames. Strong public support for Social Security has given rise to a colorful metaphor borrowed from electrified train lines: Touch the "third rail" surging with electricity, say railroad workers, and you will receive a fatal shock. Well, Social Security is the "third rail of American politics": Touching the program can be politically fatal.

Unemployment Benefits

As the Great Depression stretched into the 1930s, some thirty-four million Americans (more than a quarter of the 122 million population) lived in households with no full-time wage earner. Across the United States, unemployment rates reached shocking levels, topping out at 80 percent of able-bodied adults in Toledo, Ohio. In 1932, Wisconsin became the first state to provide cash assistance to temporarily jobless residents. Three years later, the Social Security Act included a provision for joint federal-state unemployment benefits, funded like old-age insurance through a payroll tax on employees. States administer the program, with federal oversight and funding assistance. Under serious pressure from the Roosevelt administration (which threatened to add additional Supreme Court justices), the high court approved the federal program.

When COVID-19 shut down the American economy in 2020, the ranks of the unemployed soared to levels not seen since the Great Depression of the 1930s. Within two months, forty million people found themselves unemployed. The Trump administration and Congress quickly passed a series of aid packages worth over $2 trillion to help businesses and workers (equal to more than 15 percent of the entire economy before the shutdowns). In the first days of the crisis, few politicians stopped to fret about the expansion of big government. A second aid package proved more difficult to win, but eventually passed once President Biden took office. The results were positive: Unemployment rates fell to their lowest point in three decades. During the latter half of 2021 and most of 2022, U.S. employers reported more job openings than job seekers overall. Inflation's rise eventually cooled off the hot economy, but unemployment remained relatively low compared to the high inflation years of the late 1970s to early 1980s.

As the Biden administration and Congress wrestled with high inflation, social policy

● *Recalling "poor relief" in the Great Depression (a), food banks expanded their support during the economic devastation accompanying the COVID pandemic of 2020 (b). During both episodes, new federal social policies were created at a rapid clip.*

debates often invoked young Americans. How, policymakers asked, would the COVID-inspired economic crisis, coming on the heels of the Great Recession less than a decade earlier, affect young Americans already skeptical of free market capitalism?[33]

Health and Disability: Medicare/Medicaid

In the early 1960s, America was the wealthiest nation in the world, but barely half of the nation's seniors had health insurance. Even with Social Security, an estimated third of those over sixty-five lived in poverty, often because of the cost of healthcare.

Democrats had been pressing for government health insurance since the 1940s—first for all Americans (in the 1940s), then for people over sixty-five (starting in the 1950s). Critics defeated the proposals, year after year. During the 1964 election, Republican candidate Senator Barry Goldwater mocked what he considered health insurance handouts to the elderly: "Having given our pensioners their medical care in kind, why not food baskets, why not public housing accommodations, why not vacation resorts, why not a ration of cigarettes for those who smoke and of beer for those who drink?"[34]

Lyndon Johnson's landslide victory over Goldwater swept more than forty liberals into Congress on his coattails. Medicare was the first bill on the congressional agenda in 1965—and won by large margins in both chambers. Within a decade, seniors had gone from the sickest and neediest cohort in the United States to the healthiest (compared to seniors in other nations) and the best off. As with old-age and unemployment benefits, Medicare was financed through a payroll tax on employees. And as with Social Security, the program grew rapidly after it was implemented in 1966. Today, nearly sixty-five million Americans receive Medicare benefits.

As the battle over Medicare raged in 1965, conservatives introduced an alternative proposal to provide health insurance to low-income and disabled dubbed "Medicaid." They reasoned that a program for the poor, managed by the states, would be smaller and less expensive. At the very last minute, the Johnson administration pulled an unexpected maneuver and passed *both* Medicare and Medicaid. Each state was encouraged (but not required) to establish a Medicaid program of its own; Arizona was the last state to sign on, in 1982. Over time, a variety of additional benefits were added to Medicaid, including dental and nursing home coverage. Today Medicaid serves some eighty million Americans, up from fewer than seventy million just five years ago. The Affordable Care Act permitted states to expand eligibility to everyone near the poverty line—making Medicaid one of the largest health insurance programs in the world.[35]

Unlike other large American entitlement programs, Medicaid is a "means-tested" program: Only people below a certain income threshold are eligible. States set the income level, and (note federalism in action yet again) there are huge differences. For example, in Texas, only families making less than $3,654 (for a single mom with two kids) are eligible—that's 16 percent of the **federal poverty line**. In Connecticut, families who make ten times as much ($36,848, or 160 percent of the poverty line) qualify for the program.

The Affordable Care Act (or Obamacare) aimed to make eligibility the same in all states. Everyone who made less than $30,000 (or 138 percent of the poverty line) would now be covered by Medicaid. The Supreme Court's historic 2012 decision to uphold the ACA as constitutional, described in Chapter 16, also rejected the

Federal poverty line: The annually specified level of income (separately calculated for individuals and families) below which people are considered to live in poverty, and eligible for certain federal benefits. For 2022, the poverty line is set at $27,750 for a family of four.

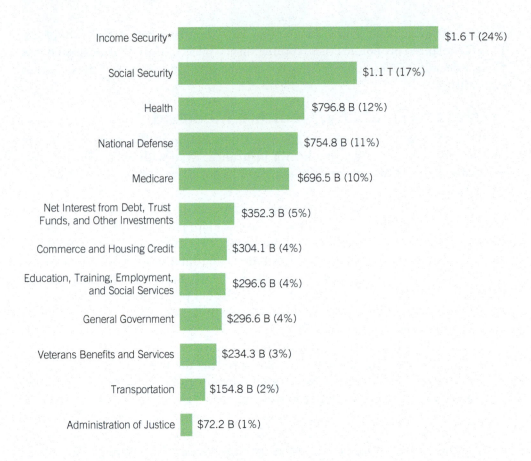

Income Security* $1.6 T (24%)

Social Security $1.1 T (17%)

Health $796.8 B (12%)

National Defense $754.8 B (11%)

Medicare $696.5 B (10%)

Net Interest from Debt, Trust Funds, and Other Investments $352.3 B (5%)

Commerce and Housing Credit $304.1 B (4%)

Education, Training, Employment, and Social Services $296.6 B (4%)

General Government $296.6 B (4%)

Veterans Benefits and Services $234.3 B (3%)

Transportation $154.8 B (2%)

Administration of Justice $72.2 B (1%)

● **FIGURE 17.5** *FY 2022 Federal Budget, largest programs. *The Economic Impact Payments (stimulus payments; $569.5B) issued in response to the COVID-19 pandemic and Child Tax Credit Payments ($79.0B) are reported as "Income Security."*

Entitlement program: A government benefit program whose recipients are *entitled* by law to receive payments. Social Security, Medicare, and Medicaid are the three largest.

universal Medicaid funding requirement. Instead, each state may decide whether it will adopt the standard. Thirty-nine states and the District of Columbia have decided to expand Medicaid. Taken together, Medicare and Medicaid pay for more than one-third of all American healthcare costs.

These three **entitlement programs**—Social Security, Medicare, and Medicaid—dominate the federal budget (Figure 17.5). And they lie at the heart of one of America's most important policy debates. For liberals, the entitlement programs are the building blocks of a fair society and a limit to rampant inequality. They help provide aging and low-income Americans a decent life. But, from the liberal perspective, the problem is that the entitlement programs are tilted to the old. Everyone should be assured of healthcare and a basic income level, they argue—not just people over sixty-seven. Most liberals vote against tax cuts because they make it harder to finance (and expand) these entitlement programs. You might recognize this perspective from Chapter 2—positive liberty.

Some conservatives call these three programs the "original sin" of big government. As long as these popular programs exist, the United States will be saddled with a massive federal government spending trillions of dollars—no matter what other programs are cut. Worse, as the baby boomers retire, the programs will grow—Medicare alone will serve nearly eighty million people and its costs will reach an estimated $1.5 trillion by the late 2020s. We can't afford it, say conservatives, and even if we could, people should not be so reliant on the federal government in the first place.

The debate continues. Are these programs the down payments toward a just society, as liberals insist? Or a terrible burden that saps American self-reliance, as conservatives fear? What do you think?

WHAT DO YOU THINK?

Should We Expand or Contract Social Security and Medicare?

	Yes, EXPAND	No, LIMIT these	Leave these pro-
Social Security and Medicare are two of the most fiercely debated U.S. government programs. Some argue for expanding them: Right now, they are focused on people in their latter sixties. Why not include people of all ages who need help (for example, by offering Medicare to everyone)? Others fear that the programs already cost too much, require high taxes, and permit people to rely on big government rather than saving for themselves. What do you think?	**Medicare to cover people of all ages.** Expand Social Security pensions to give all Americans a basic and decent minimum. The United States taxes less than most other wealthy nations and confronts a lot more inequality. Use these programs as the building blocks of a more just and fair society. Roll back recent tax cuts so all Americans have a decent life and reasonable healthcare.	**programs.** Their costs are out of control and are quickly outpacing the taxpayers' ability to fund them. Rather than expand, we must find ways to shrink them. We could raise the eligibility age of Social Security and Medicare to seventy—after all, people live longer today than when the program was started more than fifty years ago. Brave politicians should try to limit (and perhaps someday eliminate) these programs. People, young and old, should rely on themselves.	**grams alone.** Either way, the political fallout would be too big. Small changes (like higher payments to people who wait longer to take the benefits) are enough to keep the programs stable.[36]

THE BOTTOM LINE

» Social policymaking in the United States is typically more controversial, and features less expansive coverage, than social policymaking in other advanced industrial nations.

» Wars, along with severe economic downturns, have been major sources of expansions in American social policies across U.S. history.

» Three large social programs—old-age insurance, or Social Security; unemployment insurance; and health/disability benefits, or Medicare and Medicaid—are especially significant in U.S. politics and government.

 ## Economic Policymaking: Fiscal and Monetary Policy

Many Americans judge their leaders first and foremost on economic performance. Despite a sexual affair with an intern, a major health plan that crashed, impeachment, and considerable chaos, Bill Clinton easily won reelection and left office a popular president. Why? The economy was booming. On the other hand, Clinton's predecessor, George H. W. Bush, after the Gulf War (1990–91) enjoyed the highest popularity rating in modern history. Barely a year later, an economic downturn sank Bush's public opinion ratings and left him a one-term president. Likewise, Trump administration officials panicked when COVID-19 thrust the U.S. economy into a deep recession; the president fell behind in the polls, replaced his campaign leaders, and strove to reassure Americans that the downturn would be short-lived. Trump, like George H. W. Bush, was out of office after one term.

The government tries to manage the $24 trillion American economy in two different ways. Government decisions about taxing and spending—generally managed through the budget process described in the following sections—is termed **fiscal policy**. The actions of central banks to control the money supply—directly affecting unemployment and inflation rates—is known as **monetary policy**. Let us look at each in turn.

Fiscal Policy

Well into the twentieth century, the U.S. government's fiscal policy was described as "laissez-faire," a French term meaning "leave it alone." Most presidents and congressional leaders sought to balance the (relatively small) federal budget, with limited tax or spending authority. That approach changed during wartime, when military needs drove tax collections and spending temporarily much higher.

During the Great Depression, national economic devastation led Franklin Roosevelt and his advisors to actively manage fiscal policy. Ambitious New Deal programs were funded through government spending on an unprecedented scale. The resulting budget deficits—federal funds flowing out much faster than tax revenues coming in—reflected a Keynesian approach to national economic policy, named for the influential British and later American economist John Maynard Keynes. Keynes recommended "pump-priming" during economic downturns: When consumers and businesses stop spending, the government should start. Pour government funds into a faltering economy and cut taxes, argued Keynes, and that will give people enough cash (and confidence) to get the economy moving.

Following close on the Depression came World War II, which resulted in a great spike in government spending. At the height of the war in 1943, the federal deficit reached an all-time high of 30 percent of GDP. The booming economy appeared to prove Keynes right. Postwar American policymakers, brimming with confidence about their ability to manage the economy, adopted active taxing and spending policies. Inequality fell. The economy grew. Across Democratic and Republican control of the White House and Congress, fiscal policy has continued to serve as a means of securing the general welfare of the American public.

The parties traditionally differ on which fiscal levers to pull. Facing an economic downturn, Democrats are more likely to favor expanded spending—hence the large stimulus packages passed early in both the Obama and Biden presidencies, each designed to rescue the national economy from the brink of disaster. Republicans generally prefer tax cuts, on the argument that the economy benefits as consumers spend more of the windfall.[37] Hence party leaders, including President Trump, praised the 2017 tax cut as fueling economic growth through 2018. But when the economy crashed due to COVID-19 business closures, it was Republicans who shaped the first massive rescue package. Amid crisis, both parties resembled New Dealers. Before long, however, each party reverted back to form.[38]

Fiscal policies sound technical and boring—loud arguments over changes to tax and spending levels. But few policy areas are so fraught with consequences. Recent battles include government shutdowns, filibusters, and warnings of

Fiscal policy: Taxing and spending policies carried out by government, generally in an effort to affect national economic development.

Monetary policy: Actions of central banks, which in the United States culminate in the Federal Reserve, designed primarily to maximize employment and moderate inflation.

impending doom. Members of Congress from both parties regularly lament that the U.S. budget process is "broken"—the budget almost never gets passed before the start of the fiscal year (see Chapter 13). That's all the more alarming during economic downturns.[39]

Monetary Policy

Following the collapse of the venerable Lehman Brothers investment bank in fall 2008, with other giant financial institutions tottering, the U.S. government leapt into action. The main actors were not presidents or congressional leaders, but more obscure figures: the Federal Reserve chairman, the treasury secretary, and the chair of the Federal Reserve Bank of New York. And the economic tools they applied had nothing to do with increasing (or cutting) taxes or spending: Instead, the conversation was about liquidity and the national money supply.[40]

These experts were deploying monetary policy in response to the gravest financial crisis in seventy-five years. By manipulating the national money supply and interest rates, they aimed to increase employment while holding inflation (the rate at which the price of goods and services rises) in check. Although the White House and Congress are the chief institutional architects of fiscal policy, monetary shifts are carried out by central bankers: In the United States, the main actor is the Federal Reserve System, comprising a headquarters in Washington, DC, along with twelve bank branches around the country. The current Federal Reserve (or "Fed," in Washington-speak) director is Jerome Powell.

The Federal Reserve can deploy several tools, such as buying Treasury securities and setting required dollar reserve levels that banks are required to hold, which allow them to influence interest rates. The Fed reduces interest rates to stimulate economic growth, making it easier for businesses to borrow money to expand production and hiring or invest in research and development. Likewise, individuals can borrow at lower interest rates to buy new homes or consumer goods. If, however, economic demand is growing too fast, or outside events—like the Ukraine-Russia war—are forcing prices sharply upward, as in 2022, the Fed raises interest rates to reduce inflationary pressures that raise prices and result in an economic slowdown.

Think of the Federal Reserve as performing an essential balancing act—enabling growth when the economy balks, but slowing things down to ease inflation as the economy heats up. As one writer famously put it, the Fed's job is to take away the punch bowl just as the party's heating up. But it's a tricky call: Move too quickly against inflation, and the Fed risks hurting economic growth—making life a lot harder for those on the economic bottom.

Again, the COVID-19 crisis led to unprecedented action. While the popular press focused on the trillion-dollar-plus bailout negotiated by the White House and Congress, the Fed was quietly pumping $4 trillion into

● *Though rarely recognized in public, Federal Reserve Chair Jerome Powell, recently sworn in for a second term through 2026, is a key figure in managing the nation's money supply—a central feature of U.S. economic policy.*

the financial sector. Two years later, the Federal Reserve bumped up interest rates five times in five months, putting the brakes on price increases. Because presidents are judged on economic performance, they often seek to influence Federal Reserve actions—but, like other parts of the bureaucracy, the agency prides itself on independence.

THE BOTTOM LINE

» The U.S. government employs both fiscal policy and monetary policy to affect the economy.

» Taxes and spending are the two main levers of fiscal policy. During economic downturns, Republicans prefer to enact tax cuts; Democrats favor spending programs.

» The Federal Reserve is the main architect of monetary policy. By adjusting interest rates and the national supply of money, the Fed works to affect inflation and unemployment.

 Economic Policymaking: The Federal Budget Process

Federal budget deficit:
The gap between revenues received by the national government (primarily through individual income and corporate taxes) and spending on all public programs.

People who oppose an idea always have a ready answer: "It may be a good idea, but we don't have the budget space." The bottom-line claim rests on a simple concern: the growing U.S. **federal budget deficit**—the gap between how much our national government spends and how much we take in through taxes and fees. As President Biden said when introducing his 2023 budget, "Don't tell me what you value. Show me your budget and I'll tell you what you value."[41] American values and ideas—what our nation and its leaders prioritize, what is left out, where support is growing or shrinking over time—are all reflected in the federal budget.

During economic downturns, deficits soar because the federal government takes in less revenue (people are being laid off and don't pay taxes) and spends more on unemployment, food support, and bailouts. During the "Great Recession" of 2009, the deficit roughly tripled, leaping to almost 10 percent of GDP. Five years later, it was down to its prerecession level. Conservatives continued to charge that the deficit, at $500 billion, was still too high; liberals responded that federal spending had been cut back too quickly, hampering the recovery. The coronavirus crisis repeated the pattern. The 2020 deficit swelled from $1 trillion (under 5 percent of GDP) to an estimated $3.2 trillion—or 15 percent of GDP, a post–World War II record. The following year, again featuring stimulus spending to combat COVID, the deficit was lower—$2.8 trillion—but still 12 percent of GDP, a level most economists view as unsustainable over time. With less pandemic spending required in 2022, the deficit returned to a more manageable $1 trillion. Budget hawks on Capitol Hill and around the United States continued to worry, however, about the cumulative effects of such a historically large deficit.[42]

Even at more normal levels, is the budget deficit a major problem? Social Security, Medicare, and Medicaid together cost $2.4 trillion (more than half of all federal spending). Some economists urge Americans to put their fiscal house in order by raising taxes or cutting spending. Others dismiss deficits as a minor problem; instead, they point out that deficits help get the nation through economic slumps and, once the economy is booming, deficits generally fall. Focus on the economy, they conclude, not on the deficits.

Whatever your view about deficits, American domestic policymaking is organized around the budget process. As a rising policy analyst, you have to know the basics of government budgeting. Budget politics involves three primary stages: the president's budget proposal, a congressional budget resolution and appropriations bills, and the final budget. These stages are established by two laws: the Budget and Accounting Act of 1921, passed in an age of much smaller American national government; and the Congressional Budget and Impoundment Control Act, passed in 1974 during a time of political turmoil and economic recession. The process begins with the White House (see Figure 17.6).

President's Budget Proposal

Since the 1921 Budget and Accounting Act, presidents kick off the process. The United States starts its **fiscal year** (**FY**) each October 1; FY 2023 began October 1, 2022. In early February, the White House submits a budget for the following fiscal year (beginning eight months later). This massive document proposes spending levels for thousands of different government programs. The process of assembling that February proposal begins many months earlier in the executive branch, with each cabinet department and federal agency compiling its spending requests. The Office of Management and Budget has the massive task of coordinating all these estimates; the Treasury Department chimes in with what it expects to receive in

Fiscal year (FY): In budget calculations, the "new year" beginning October 1 and ending the following September 30. Organized many decades ago for accounting purposes.

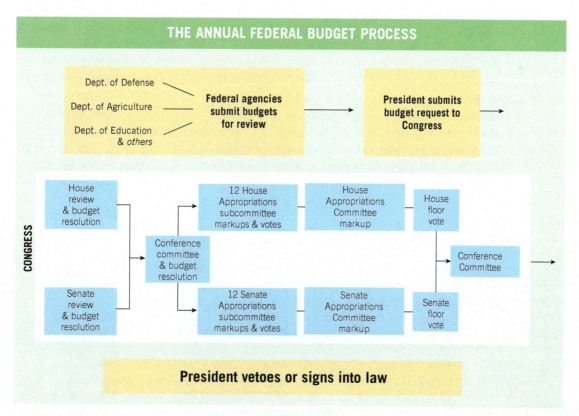

FIGURE 17.6 *The U.S. federal budget process. (House Budget Committee)*

taxes and other revenues. New presidential priorities are included as well. And the comprehensive document reflects the administration's goals. The Biden administration, for example, featured in its 2023 proposed budget funds to reduce crime and ease clogged global supply lines (enabling goods to move more readily to and from American ports and airports), to tackle climate change, and to cut health-care costs—paying for these and other spending hikes through tax reform, including a proposed new tax on billionaires.[43]

Unlike in most other countries, the president's budget proposal lacks any statutory authority (see Comparing Nations 17.1). Congress is free to ignore it completely, as it did with Joe Biden's in 2023 (and most Biden, Trump, and Obama budgets before that). But the proposal's release by the White House is still a major event. Advocacy groups howl when funding for their pet projects is cut (or not increased enough), and businesses jockey to minimize the costs of new regulations or taxes. Congressional committees with budget responsibilities schedule hearings to question cabinet heads and senior presidential aides, and media organizations compile helpful charts.

Congressional Budget Resolution

While executive branch analysts feed figures into the White House budget proposal, congressional budget experts create their own blueprint for spending and revenues, known as a **budget resolution**. Congressional budget resolutions are not binding laws, and do not require a presidential signature. Instead, they provide a general "sense of Congress" about budgetary expectations and are meant to guide the committees responsible for finishing the budget during summer and fall.

Budget resolution: A joint House-Senate creation that outlines targets for federal spending, revenue levels, and the resultant budget deficit (or surplus) for the coming fiscal year.

Budget resolutions are less detailed than the president's several-hundred-page proposal. They set out overarching spending expectations in nineteen broad categories, known as "budget functions." Budget committees in both the House and the Senate, created by the 1974 Congressional Budget and Impoundment Control Act, carry out the bulk of this work. Each committee spends several months assembling a budget resolution, which must pass the full chamber. Senate and House versions are inevitably different, and they must be reconciled in a conference committee. The joint outcome, formally known as a "concurrent budget resolution," is supposed to be approved by April 15 of each year. Owing to partisan differences and other political battles, these resolutions are almost always late. Over the past forty-five years, Congress has approved a budget resolution on schedule only six times. (Congress was not able to pass any budget resolution at all in more than half of the past twenty years.)

Reign of the Cardinals: Appropriations Committee Action

The two budget committees were created in 1974 to simplify the unwieldy process of creating a budget and funding government programs. Unfortunately, Congress left the old rules in place alongside the new ones. As a result, the budget process got more complicated, not less.

The Appropriations Committees in the House and the Senate are charged with specifying which departments and programs will get how much money. Recall from Chapter 13 that, because of their central role in spending decisions, members of Appropriations are informally known on Capitol Hill as "cardinals" after the high-ranking Vatican officials. The cardinals split budget authority into twelve separate jurisdictions (see Table 17.4).

Each of these twelve areas is assigned to a separate Appropriations subcommittee in the House and Senate. Each subcommittee handles budget planning for all policy areas under its jurisdiction. Some, such as Labor, Health and Human Services, and Education (known informally on the Hill as "Labor-H"), supervise thousands of individual programs. Appropriations' cardinals must remain attentive to the budget resolution blueprint, which is monitored by yet another set of budget "authorizing committees" in each chamber. If spending on all the programs in the Appropriations Committees' jurisdiction exceeds the total specified in the resolution, they must go back and make changes to bring it into line.

After a subcommittee approves its bill with program-by-program spending authorization, the measure must pass the full Appropriations Committee in that chamber. If successful, it heads to the House or Senate floor. Each of the appropriations bills attracts intense attention from House and Senate members, who try to add funding to their favorite programs. If an appropriations bill survives the floor

TABLE 17.4 **Appropriations Subcommittees: Areas of Jurisdiction**

Agriculture; Rural Development; Food and Drug Administration
Commerce; Justice; Science
Defense
Energy and Water Development
Financial Services and General Government
Homeland Security
Interior and Environment
Labor; Health and Human Services; Education
Legislative Branch
Military Construction and Veterans Affairs
State and Foreign Operations
Transportation; Housing and Urban Development

vote in its chamber, a House-Senate conference committee is all but inevitable. This step provides another opportunity for members seeking financial benefits for their district—or lobbyists pushing a client's pet provision—to weigh in. Once the two sides agree in conference, the identical version is voted on in both House and Senate and sent to the president for consideration.

Because they only deal with **discretionary programs**, which require legislative action to explicitly authorize spending, the twelve appropriations bills cover only about a third of all U.S. government spending. Compare the large entitlement programs we read about earlier: Social Security, Medicare, and Medicaid. These are considered *mandatory spending* because they are funded annually, based on a formula, without requiring Congress's reauthorization each year. Thus, a giant chunk of the U.S. federal budget, over $2 trillion, is essentially untouchable. Unless Congress elects to change the spending formula for a program such as Social Security, which would arouse anger from beneficiaries, those funds—with guaranteed annual increases to protect beneficiaries from inflation—flow automatically. The budget fights that make the headlines are over spending on the margins—they involve important but much smaller programs.

Appropriations bills are required to be signed by September 1. With the start of the fiscal year looming on October 1, federal agencies and departments have a month to finalize their plans for spending funds and delivering services. As with other deadlines in the budget process, this September 1 marker is far more often missed than hit: 1997 was the last time that all the appropriations bills were passed before the new fiscal year, a mark achieved only twice more (in 1989 and 1995) in the last half-century.

What happens when one or more bills are not approved? As the new fiscal year approaches, with spending decisions necessary before federal funds can begin flowing, Congress may combine all the outstanding appropriations measures into a single "omnibus" spending bill. This can be thousands of pages long, listing funding for as many as twelve thousand separate programs. It is unlikely that anyone will read every line, especially as this legislation is typically cobbled together with only days or even hours to spare before the September 30 end to the fiscal year.

More often than not in recent years, Congress fails even to pass an omnibus bill, leaving some areas unfunded as the new fiscal year opens. In that case, the president asks Congress to pass a **continuing resolution (CR)**, which keeps the dollars flowing—usually at the just-ended fiscal year's rate—for a specified period, usually two weeks or a month. In some years, Congress is forced to pass CR after CR. Otherwise, the government officially runs out of spending authority for discretionary programs and shuts down.

Fiscal 2022 offered a good snapshot of the new normal. Congress could not agree on a budget by the start of the fiscal year on October 1, 2021, and instead passed a continuing resolution covering seven weeks expiring December 3. (Even that CR was hotly debated, failing twice in the Senate before finally passing.) On December 2, as the midnight deadline approached, Congress passed another CR to fund the government for another nine weeks, squeaking through the House by just nine votes. A third continuing resolution passed in early March, as a huge omnibus spending bill moved toward passage—but Congress had to buy still more time, passing a fourth CR on March 9, adding a few more days until the budget finally passed and was signed by President Biden on March 11—six and a half months late. Three years before, the government had to shut down entirely for thirty-five days because Congress and the Trump administration—fighting over funding for the president's proposed border wall—could not even agree to pass a continuing resolution.

All big decisions are affected by the budget because every government action has significant financial implications. And because most budget decisions have winners and losers—more money for my program means less for yours—this is one of the most politically charged aspects of policymaking. Who gets what, when, and how? In the United States, we make those decisions in significant part through our budget process. Except, ironically, for the really big programs: Eligible people receive Social Security and hospitals receive Medicare payments, all required by law—and untouchable by the budget process.

Budgeting also underscores many of this book's basic lessons about politics and government. Separated powers slow the process by encouraging bargaining, battling, and compromise. Informal actors are deeply involved: Interest groups weigh in at both ends of Pennsylvania Avenue, while journalists and think tank experts spin their narratives of budgetary winners and losers. The central place of economic efficiency in policymaking is reinforced by a politics organized around budgeting. Cost-benefit calculations are made in monetary terms, after all. Ultimately, budgeting involves the fundamental choices that help define how we Americans see ourselves.

THE BOTTOM LINE

» The U.S. budget process, when on schedule, runs from early February through October 1 and encompasses a presidential proposal, a concurrent budget resolution, and appropriations bills.

» In practice, the process rarely runs on time, and various "fixes" like omnibus bills and continuing resolutions have been invented to keep the budget system functioning.

» Although the details can be obscure, budget battles in Washington are among the most dramatic features of U.S. policymaking because of the high stakes involved.

 # Making Good Policy

You now have a handle on how policymaking works, as well as an introduction to economic policies and our largest social programs. Here's the big question about the policy process: Does it produce desirable outcomes? That's a thorny issue because it's often not clear what counts as good policy. But three key considerations offer a guide.

- Is the proposed policy *feasible*? In other words: Can it attract enough votes in Congress to pass? Will the president sign? Is the bureaucracy capable of implementing it smoothly? And will it stand up to judicial scrutiny in the courts?

- Is the proposed policy *fair*? Is it the right thing to do? Does it correspond to widely held values such as equality and fairness? Or does it simply benefit one group, perhaps of powerful people, at the expense of others?

- Is the proposed policy *effective*? Do the expected benefits of the policy outweigh its estimated costs? Are there more *efficient*—faster or cheaper—ways to achieve the desired aims?

Each of these questions leads to hot debates that are rarely resolved before a policy goes into effect. But most high-profile policy proposals inspire sustained attention to these three dimensions: political (feasibility), moral (fairness/equity), and economic (effectiveness, usually measured in cost-benefit terms).

The first dimension is almost self-evident: A policy counts as politically feasible if it passes Congress and unfeasible if it fails to attract sufficient support. Of course, the next legislative session or Supreme Court ruling might result in a different decision. The moral and economic dimensions are where the sharpest contests over good domestic policy play out. Let us look at each.

Moral Policies: Justice or Democracy?

Some people—philosophers, regular citizens, politicians—say that the focus of public policy should be creating a *more just society*. In this view, we should judge a policy by considering whether it enhances equality, rights, and distributive justice—who is helped and who is harmed. If millions of Americans lack health insurance, some advocates argue that policymakers must provide it. Policy proposals to reform the healthcare system must keep the uninsured front and center—or so insist those who view public policy through the lens of justice.

Others might agree about the importance of emphasizing justice but throw up their hands at anyone's ability to decide what is truly egalitarian or fair. Instead, they argue, we should rely on democracy: Give a majority of the people what they want. Appealing though that sounds, recall from Chapter 7 that it is difficult to know what any group of Americans, much less the entire populace, wants to achieve. And America's constitutional foundation rests on protecting the minority's rights from the majority's opinion (as we discussed in Chapter 5). Around thirty million people lack health insurance; do we emphasize their rights? Or the 90 percent of all Americans—a very large majority—who do have health insurance? Some of them are dubious about paying more taxes or changing the healthcare system to help the minority in need. The answer eventually comes down to our basic values. Asking about the right thing to do quickly returns us to the fundamental question we have raised in every chapter: *Who are we*—as a nation and as a people?

Economically Efficient Policies

Faced with the difficulty of determining the most just policy or the majority opinion, some policy thinkers favor a different approach. Relying on neoclassical economic theory, this view recommends the most efficient system of delivering government services. Use an objective assessment, such as a cost-benefit analysis, to identify one policy option as preferable to another: Which provides public goods at the lowest cost? If there is a clear answer, go with that policy.

Better still, these economic theorists say, use our free enterprise system to maximize efficiency in our slow-moving, polarized policy system. Libertarian thinkers and their followers see markets as the most efficient way of organizing just about anything, and they are eager to apply that perspective to policymaking. Citizens should be given choices about the public programs and services they consume.

To illustrate, let's go back to health insurance. Instead of government support for uninsured people, how about creating a big market for health insurance and letting Americans' economic preferences drive their decisions? If some are cautious about health risks and willing to pay high premiums each month, that is their business. If others figure their chances of getting sick are minimal, there is no need to make them pay for insurance. Recent college graduates and low-income workers, for example, often prefer to spend on other things—and forego health insurance. Why not let them choose for themselves?

Many advocates of economic efficiency believe in *rational choice theory*, introduced in Chapter 1. Recall that this perspective takes individual rationality (or individual choices) to be the best basis for good public policy. Let people maximize their own self-interest; the majority—the largest group sharing an interest—will determine more or less desirable policy choices. Through market-style competitive pressures, as different companies or nonprofit organizations compete to provide services, their cost will come down, saving taxpayers money.

Although in practice Americans combine moral, majoritarian, and economic efficiency preferences, a belief in markets' guidance has been the dominant view among policymakers, especially conservatives, in recent years. One result is the privatization of public services, discussed in Chapter 15.

Yet the "contracting out" of government functions—turning them over to private firms—is increasingly controversial. As the $1.2 trillion infrastructure program, a Biden administration signature, moved toward congressional approval, progressives in the House and Senate slowed the bill over alarms that national assets like highways, airports, and bridges might be privatized.[44] Critics of this strategy continue to multiply, even as privatized services have spread across national, state, and local governments. Economic efficiency may be an appealing notion, but its dominance leaves many Americans uneasy. How do we know? Just head to the movies.

Capitalism Goes to the Movies

We know from opinion polls that many Americans say they prefer market-style decisions to "big-government" regulation. You might imagine that those preferences would show up in our most popular movies and books—those drawing the biggest audiences.

Instead, American popular culture displays a deep suspicion of the free enterprise system. *Avatar*, for example—the highest-grossing film ever—is at heart a morality fable about the dangers of corporate greed, as earth-based mining companies relentlessly pursue the not-so-subtly named mineral "unobtanium." And, the drawbacks of the capitalist system are at the heart of the second-highest-grossing film of all time, 2019's *Avengers: Endgame,* in which the superheroes' mighty foe Thanos seeks to control the universe through possessing a set of priceless stones. As one film review notes, Thanos represents "the destruction brought about by the reckless accumulation of power, capital, and profit."[45] In a still more recent Marvel blockbuster, *Thor: Love and Thunder,* the once peaceful fishing village of New Asgard has become a parody of capitalist excess, its quiet

● *Characters from* The Lego Movie 3, *released in 2023. The original* Lego Movie, *featuring an evil "Lord Business" bent on planetary dominance, is among the many onscreen blockbusters that express a clear concern about capitalism.*

Views on Policymaking

Do Americans Feel That U.S. Policies Are Beneficial?

Donald Trump took office promising to reduce the number of immigrants permitted into the United States. The Biden administration has worked to reverse course and welcome more immigrants. State policies vary widely, mostly along party lines.

Public opinion on the issue has been volatile, swinging between positions repeatedly in the last twenty years. Immigration policy raises a thorny set of questions: Who should get priority? Do we reunite families? Prioritize workers with needed skills? Offer a hand to refugees fleeing violence or persecution?

THINK ABOUT IT

How did attitudes toward immigration change during the height of the COVID pandemic (2020–21)?

....

Why did Republicans (red line on chart) express so much more dissatisfaction with immigration starting in 2021?

....

Look at the categories of people who the United States admits as immigrants. If you were in charge, would you keep the same percentages, or would you emphasize different qualifications when determining who the U.S. should admit as immigrants?

a

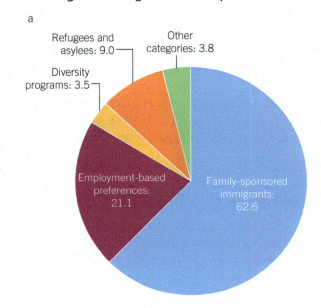

Refugees and asylees: 9.0
Other categories: 3.8
Diversity programs: 3.5
Employment-based preferences: 21.1
Family-sponsored immigrants: 62.6

b

Partisans' Dissatisfaction with Immigration Level in U.S.

% Dissatisfied

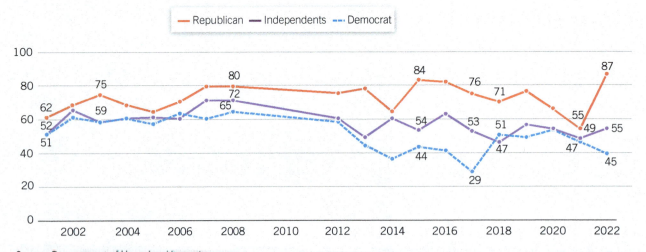

Source: Department of Homeland Security
Source: Gallup

communal streets now a riot of tourist-trap stores—including an ice cream shop cheekily named after the priceless stones Thanos sought.

Even animated films, aimed primarily at children, tell a similar story. The hugely popular *Lego Movie* features an ordinary working man turned hero who defeats the evil "Lord Business." What does popular culture have to do with policymaking? The evident appeal of these works testifies to the different values Americans hold simultaneously. Yes, many people are suspicious of big government, but many also question the benefits of big, unregulated markets. And the younger the generation, the higher the skepticism.

THE BOTTOM LINE

» Although everyone wants "good" public policies passed, Americans have a hard time agreeing on what constitutes those.

» Moral arguments about equality and fairness in policymaking have declined in recent years, as attention to economic efficiency as a measure of a policy's worthiness has grown.

» One article of faith among efficiency advocates is that privatizing government programs enables more cost-effective and higher-quality services. But concerns about markets sorting out public policies also are evident. Just take a look at many popular American movies as one indicator.

Reforming U.S. Policymaking

Most would-be reformers of U.S. domestic policymaking and budgeting address specific policies, from protecting against disastrous accidents at nuclear plants to reducing youth violence. Some reformers also work at the *system* level, seeking to alter the procedures or institutions that underlie policymaking.

Systemic Reform

Critics have suggested some systemic reforms that could increase the odds of better policy production. Term limits for members of Congress (and perhaps other federal officials) would rotate representatives and senators every six years or so, bringing a regular infusion of new blood to Washington. Perhaps the resultant sense of urgency—or the reduced need for campaign funds to run for multiple terms—would improve policymaking. Many political scientists respond that a Congress made up mostly of new and soon-departing members would lack institutional memory and legislative skills. Interest-group lobbyists likely would gain even more sway over policymaking than they already have.[46]

Other calls to streamline the slow-moving process of policy formation range from revising the Senate filibuster and legislative-hold rules, which effectively require sixty votes to advance any policy idea, to requiring Congress to spend five-day workweeks on legislative labors in Washington. As we saw in Chapter 13, most members of the House and Senate fly back home to their district or state every

Thursday afternoon, returning to the Capitol the following Tuesday—creating a "workweek" in Washington of less than three days.[47]

Political scientist Paul Light, echoing Alexander Hamilton in the *Federalist Papers*, noted the importance to good policymaking of a "government well executed." He warned that today's federal service, bogged down by lengthy hiring delays and difficulty motivating its workers, is too often a government *ill* executed. Light and fellow executive branch reformers call for a greatly streamlined hiring process, along with financial and other incentives designed to attract the "best and brightest" young Americans to work for the national government.[48]

Undergirding all these changes is a call for advancing racial equity in public policymaking, voiced by President Biden soon after taking office and promoted especially by progressives in Congress, policy-focused nonprofits, and academics. As Biden declared in an executive order: "We need to make the issue of racial equity not just an issue for any one department of government; it has to be the business of the whole of government." Reading through White House policy proposals, including far-reaching ones like the COVID stimulus package termed the "American Rescue Plan," attention to equity is consistently and prominently featured.[49]

Ambitious but manageable reforms such as these seem more achievable than a full-system overhaul. In the past decade, Congress has initiated internal reforms, such as an extensive gift ban and other ethics changes. Both the Trump and Biden administrations came into office proposing a major restructuring of the executive branch. Such sweeping organizational change is very hard to accomplish in a national capital featuring deeply rooted institutions.

Policy Entrepreneurs

The term "policy entrepreneur" identifies those who generate new ideas, help move them up policy agendas, translate them into workable proposals, and sometimes help implement them. These entrepreneurs are frequently young, often just out of college. They have not been part of the regular policymaking system long enough to be subject to "groupthink," the tendency to recycle familiar (and sometimes stale) ideas.

What do we know about these innovative individuals? They share some common characteristics. For one, policy entrepreneurs are willing to invest time and resources, often at the risk of their own comfort and financial well-being, in order to achieve policy changes. These innovators also tend to be talented storytellers, able to convey complex policy information through simplified stories and scenarios. Recall from Chapter 7 the importance of powerful narratives in successful policy framing. Third, policy entrepreneurs tend to be connected across the policy system through a network of entrepreneurs, diffusing policy ideas across towns, cities, and states.[50]

Policy entrepreneurs generally share a passion for reform regardless of age. After the mass shooting at Robb Elementary School in Uvalde, Texas, local students joined with national organizers (including former high school students who survived another infamous mass shooting, at Parkland High in Florida) to promote laws to reduce gun violence; their cause was joined by a group of Uvalde mothers who dubbed themselves the "Fierce Madres."[51] Another set of policy entrepreneurs, "climate kids," is a group of young Americans, aged nine to twenty, who, along with their nonprofit sponsor, Our Children's Trust, filed a lawsuit against the executive branch; they charged that policymakers in the White House had failed to protect the planet from the effects of climate change. As scientists first chronicled in 1979, human activity such as burning fossil fuels was causing warming temperatures, rising sea levels, and increasingly severe storms. The climate kids cited sober scientific warnings of the near-term global impact—with dangerously rising temperatures in the American Southwest, regular flooding in coastal cities like Miami, and tides wiping out entire nations like the Maldives.[52]

Over the years, American government has proved resistant to large-scale changes in individual policy areas—in part because the existing ways of carrying out policy have become institutionalized, reinforcing the status quo. Although this trend can be discouraging to would-be reformers, those who can pursue policies within a context of predictable rules (like "climate kids" using the courts to seek reduced carbon emissions) may achieve the most long-lasting reforms.

Even so, we have seen that mass movements—for civil rights or gender rights or taxpayers' rights—can generate deep changes in American politics. Incremental changes dominate, until new ways of thinking erupt onto the scene.

Eight Steps to Successful Policy Reform

Want to change an existing policy or persuade Congress to address a problem you care about? Put on your policy entrepreneur's hat and begin connecting to fellow innovators. Here are eight lessons—distilling much of what you have learned in this book—about how to best advance your policy goals.

Bring Passion.   To gain supporters across the decision-making community, it is essential both to have passion and to inspire it in others. Anti-abortion movement organizers believed fervently in their cause and promoted it for decades, appealing to national and state legislatures and executives while filing lawsuit after lawsuit. Their tectonic victory before the Supreme Court in 2022—which is rekindling passion on the pro-choice side—is testament to the power of sustained determination.[53] It's hard to get very far in the policy realm without passionate commitment to a plan or perspective.

Act Fast.   As we emphasized earlier, policy windows are typically open only briefly. With the financial system on the brink of failure in 2008, a handful of policymakers swiftly organized a bailout plan that may well have averted a global economic meltdown. They did it again in the "COVID spring" of 2020. Most advocates do not face decisions of that magnitude, but the ability to move quickly to take advantage of favorable contexts is still essential. The largest difference between the Obama health plan, which succeeded, and the Clinton health plan, which failed? Speed![54]

Bring a Plan.   James Madison is known as the "Father of the Constitution" not because he was the most effective orator or backslapper at the

● *Members of the "Network of Enlightened Women," a group of young conservatives, combine passion for specific causes with engaging symbols—two keys to policy success.*

Constitutional Convention. Madison was a shy, quiet man, but he had one vital asset: the Virginia Plan, which he had painstakingly worked out in advance of the convention. He traveled early to Philadelphia and strategically approached other members as they arrived in town. Once the convention opened, it adopted the Virginia Plan as its working document.

Mind the Symbols.   Simple, stark words and compelling visual depictions—the American flag, a hungry child, #MeToo, urban disorder, starving polar bears—are essential to successful policy framing. Across America in 2020, thousands of activists lay down on their stomachs, held hands behind their backs, and chanted, "I can't breathe" for nine minutes—a powerful reminder of George Floyd's final minutes under the knee of a Minneapolis police officer. Symbols like this one are essential ways to command the political agenda—in this case, for police reform and racial justice.

Have a Philosophy.   Symbols and stories help convey ideas, but reform must connect to an underlying philosophy to survive the policy process. Franklin Roosevelt articulated his guiding perspective at the height of the Great Depression in 1933, in his first inaugural address as president: "These dark days will be worth all they cost us if they teach us that our true destiny is not to be ministered unto but to minister to ourselves and to our fellow-men."[55] This idea—that government is a source of collective support, helping those down on their luck—was woven throughout all FDR's subsequent New Deal programs.

Go Public.   President Ronald Reagan, faced with a Democratic Congress's opposition to his tax reform proposal, successfully took his case to the American public. Few of us have as prominent a "bully pulpit" as President Reagan did (or his communication skills). But policy reformers who can connect with a wider audience are more likely to see an advance toward law.

Know the Rules.   When Lyndon Johnson was inaugurated as a new senator in 1949, he spent his first several weeks quietly at his desk on the Senate floor, following the action but never seeking recognition to speak. Johnson's aides, knowing his famously energetic style, worried that he had become depressed. Eventually Johnson explained brusquely, "I'm learning the rules."[56] LBJ went on to be perhaps the most effective Senate majority leader ever, in part because he knew the rulebook down to every loophole, variation, and exception.

Learn How to Lose.   The U.S. system is organized around fragmented power, rather than a unified system that promotes sweeping policy changes. Even the most talented advocate will rack up far more losses than wins in policy battles. To survive to fight another day, it is essential to accept defeat graciously and prepare to bounce back. Advocates for reducing gun violence lost most major policy battles between 1994, when the "Brady Bill" limiting purchases of semiautomatic rifles was passed, and 2022, when bipartisan legislation to restrict some gun purchases became law. Don't let temporary setbacks discourage you; instead, keep on pushing.

THE BOTTOM LINE

» System-wide policy change is frequently pursued by reformers, but it is very difficult to achieve in a United States that organizes its policymaking around separated powers.

» Policy entrepreneurs, drawn from all walks of life, seek innovative solutions for public policies. The most successful among them tend to develop compelling narratives about their preferred issue, are willing to risk creature comforts to pursue policy change, and develop networks to diffuse and test their ideas.

» Although novel policies are hard to get through the complex U.S. policy system, the contest over agenda setting and problem definition is relatively open. As in the business or the nonprofit sector, a persistent entrepreneur can realize rewards.

Conclusion: Policy Matters

As you go about your day today, recognize all the different ways you encounter the policy system. Notice the "USDA Organic" label on your breakfast cereal or yogurt container, along with all those government-mandated nutrition facts. Hopping in your car or on your bike? The cost of any gas you buy, the condition of the roads you travel on, the street signs you navigate by: All are the result of policy decisions, often hard-fought ones. Federal agencies license and manage the electromagnetic spectrum that you use to communicate by smartphone or watch TV, regulate the safety of the gym where you work out, and inspect (plus, moving to the state and local levels, charge tax on) the food you buy. Headed to class? Policy decisions determined the subsidy supporting you and the rates you pay on your student loans (and whether they may be forgiven after you graduate)—and if you attend a public college or university, they may have some say over the curriculum you study.

These are just a few of the ways in which public policy helps shape your daily experience. As a member of this vast but surprisingly accessible democracy, you have the ability (and now, we hope, the enhanced knowledge) to shape those policy decisions in turn. May you find a fulfilling role in the great continuing American experiment: government by the people.

CHAPTER SUMMARY

★ Public policymaking inevitably involves choices: Should the Fed raise interest rates to calm inflation, recognizing that Americans may lose jobs as a result? Can NASA launch a manned mission to Mars? Will President Biden open formerly protected lands to oil and gas drilling? Understanding those choices is the essence of politics and government in America.

★ Five stages mark the process of devising domestic policies. These are not a blueprint for action, but most policy achievements pass through all these.

★ Agenda *setting* describes the transformation of an idea into a policy issue as public attention expands.

★ Once a topic is on the agenda, it must be *defined*—what is this issue about?—and *framed:* How lawmakers and the public talk about an agenda item often determines whether it will move forward.

★ A third stage, *policy formation,* involves the legislative and executive activities that translate talk into concrete statutory language.

★ Once a policy has been passed into law, it must be *implemented*, involving rulemaking and then delivery of public services.

★ Finally, policies are *evaluated*; once implemented, they create a *feedback* process that affects future policymaking in that area.

★ The largest U.S. policy programs, in terms of spending and numbers of people served, are social policies such as Social Security, Medicare, Medicaid, and unemployment insurance.

★ The resistance to expansive social policy comes from four different sources: resistance to big government; the checks and balances organized into American institutions that make passing new programs difficult; racial and ethnic tensions that divide the working class; and a proclivity to spend money on the middle class. That same resistance makes it difficult to change programs once they are in place (remember Social Security is the third rail). And leads toward privatization—shifting public services to the private sector.

★ Heightened attention to fiscal and monetary policy, combined with harder economic times, has elevated the importance of budgeting in American politics and government. The federal budget process is a complicated, slow-moving machine, which rarely meets its key deadlines—largely because the financial stakes are so high.

★ Every stakeholder agrees on the importance of good public policies—but controversies will never end about what these are. Some measure "good" policy in moral terms of right and wrong; others prefer clearer metrics such as economic efficiency, using cost-benefit and related analyses.

★ Reform-minded groups and individuals seek change, both in the rules of the game (systemic changes) and in specific policy areas. Entrepreneurs who succeed tend to tell memorable stories, sacrifice comfort and resources to advance their policy efforts, and work collaboratively with fellow reformers. Engaging in the policy process, though it moves slowly and incrementally, can be immensely fulfilling.

KEY TERMS

Budget resolution, p. 594
Continuing resolution (CR), p. 596
Cost-benefit analysis, p. 575
Cost effectiveness, p. 575
Discretionary programs, p. 596
Entitlement program, p. 588

Federal budget deficit, p. 592
Federal poverty line, p. 587
Fiscal policy, p. 590
Fiscal year (FY), p. 593
Focusing event, p. 572

Gross domestic product (GDP), p. 585
Monetary policy, p. 590
Path dependence, p. 582
Policy agenda, p. 572
Policy window, p. 577

STUDY QUESTIONS

1. How do items get on the policy agenda?

2. Think of an issue you care about. How is it currently *framed* in national discussions about the issue? Would you frame it differently?

3. Why does policy formation—translating a topic from "good idea" into a bill ready for a congressional vote—typically take so long?

4. What is the difference between an ex ante and ex post policy evaluation? How are both useful in helping shape a government program?

5. Why are our largest entitlement programs—Social Security, Medicare, and Medicaid—so expensive? Bonus: If any/all strike you as *too* expensive, any recommendations for trimming benefits to save millions of dollars? And any public officials you could identify who would champion your politically risky idea?

6. Given a choice, would you emphasize managing the economy through fiscal policy (taxing and spending) or monetary policy (managed by banks, especially the Federal Reserve)? Defend your choice.

7. Why does Congress wind up passing continuing resolutions at the end of most budget years?

8. In your view, how important is balancing the U.S. budget?

9. What are at least two ways to determine whether a policy idea is worth pursuing (in other words, whether it is a good idea)? Do you prefer one approach to others?

10. If you could adopt a major reform to the American policymaking process, what would it be? (You may choose from among options in the last section of this chapter or propose your own.)

11. What qualities characterize successful policy entrepreneurs?

THE INVASION BEGAN IN THE EARLY MORNING HOURS. Russian armed forces began shelling Ukraine's eastern region as columns of Russian soldiers attacked—marking the first war between European nations in decades. U.S. alerts sped around the globe. President Biden immediately announced economic sanctions on Russia and his foreign policy team coordinated the response from the European Union, Japan, and other sympathetic nations.

For months the U.S. president had urged his Russian counterpart Vladimir Putin *not* to invade Ukraine; Biden's decision to share U.S. intelligence about Russia's military movements in advance of the invasion helped Ukrainian forces mount a focused, fierce resistance. In coming days and weeks, the U.S and its allies streamed weapons and financial aid into Ukraine.

As the war dragged on, the price tag for supporting Ukraine swelled past $10 billion. Indirect costs, especially a rise in gas and oil prices, exacerbated inflation, as we saw in Chapter 17. In some places, allies began to question the support for Ukraine. In response, President Biden insisted that supporting Ukraine "is not just the right thing to do. It is in our vital national interests to ensure a peaceful and stable Europe and to make it clear that might does not make right." Moreover, the president affirmed, "If Russia does not pay a heavy price for its actions . . . it will put the survival of other peaceful democracies at risk. And it could mark the end of the rules-based international order and open the door to aggression elsewhere."[1]

Biden's staunch defense of Ukraine in the face of Russian aggression invokes three core pillars of U.S. foreign policy—security, prosperity, and spreading American values. These are regularly called into question when the United States engages abroad, with friends and foes alike. Foreign policy defines American relations with external nations, groups, and problems. It involves countless decisions, large and small: what to do about nuclear threats from North Korea; whether to intervene in genocide; how to calibrate U.S. engagement in complex regions like the Middle East; how to manage immigration policies with more than one hundred countries; and whether and how to deploy military force. American foreign policies change the world. They also boomerang back home and change the United States.

In this chapter, you will

 Learn the three goals of American foreign policy: security, prosperity, and spreading American values.

 Analyze American attitudes toward world affairs.

 See who makes foreign policy and how.

 Take a bird's-eye view of American foreign policy in the past one hundred years.

 Examine recent U.S. foreign policy, influenced by the COVID-19 crisis, economic conflict with China, and the Russian invasion of Ukraine.

● *President Biden speaks at a weapons-manufacturing facility in Troy, Alabama, in May 2022. Biden stressed the importance of U.S.-made weapons to Ukraine's defense against Russian invasion. The American military has long been the world's largest and best-funded; the United States is also the #1 arms manufacturer and seller worldwide.*

Who are we? Foreign policy offers an important answer. What we do around the world broadcasts our values and our interests. Our international strategies and actions signal what we stand for as a nation. They also trigger intense arguments. Foreign policy debates raise a host of important questions: What are America's most fundamental interests? How should the nation pursue them? Should we act alone? Or rely on the web of alliances, partnerships, and relations with nations around the globe?

Foreign policy differs from everything you have read in previous chapters. The American political process is usually slow and full of checks and balances. In contrast, foreign policy often moves swiftly, the stakes are high, and the results—triumphs or disasters—can be immediately clear. The president has much wider powers over foreign policy than most other areas. Even so, there are always many different hands involved in shaping foreign policy.

Let's start with the three goals guiding foreign policy: national security, prosperity, and spreading American values. Sometimes, these goals clash with one another. As we describe each, think about which seems most important to you.

 # Foreign Policy Goal No. 1: Security

First, the United States must defend itself. *Security means protecting the nation and its values from external threats.* But what constitutes an external threat? Should policymakers focus on terrorists? Russia's expanding military? China's rising power? Rogue nations like North Korea? Or perhaps the greatest danger comes from climate change, or limits on natural resources. Different dangers require different strategies.

Military Primacy

Every administration, whether Democratic or Republican, seeks security through a powerful military. The United States spends as much on its armed forces as the other top nine nations combined (see Comparing Nations 18.1). Even these numbers understate total military spending: The Department of Homeland Security, intelligence agencies, and the Veterans Administration add more than $200 billion to the total.

A large military comes with a very high price tag. Why spend so much more than other nations? Because U.S. military strategy is based on the theory of **primacy**: Maintain an unrivaled military force that can overwhelm any enemy. Is this expensive doctrine necessary? That depends on how we see the world.

Basis for Primacy: Realism

Two main views of the U.S. role in the world have colored American foreign policy debates since the 1950s. **Realism** sees the world as dangerous, full of tough rivals competing for advantage. The best way to protect the nation is to maximize military and economic power. Realists see the international system as an anarchy—individual states struggle for dominance in a lawless international arena marked by the survival of the fittest. The only hope for peace and stability: Powerful states assume leadership and establish order.

Primacy: The doctrine asserting that the United States should maintain an unrivaled military.

Realism: A doctrine holding that nation-states seek to amass power to ensure their self-preservation.

BY THE NUMBERS Foreign Policy

 52
Percentage of U.S. federal budget spent on defense, 1960

 11
Percentage of U.S. federal budget spent on defense, 2023

5
Percentage increase in U.S. military spending since departure from Afghanistan, as of August 2021[2]

 38 U.S. military spending as a percentage of all global military spending, 2021[3]

14 China's military spending as a percentage of all global military spending, 2021[4]

28.4 Total combined economic activity of Japan, China, and Germany, in trillions of dollars, 2022

24.8 Total U.S. economic activity, in trillions of dollars, 2022

1
Rank of U.S. among world nations, strength of "soft power," 2021–22[5]

4
Rank of China among world nations, strength of "soft power," 2021–22[6]

 0.5 Percentage of gross domestic product (GDP), U.S. foreign aid, 1960

0.9 Percentage of GDP, U.S. foreign aid, 2021

1.5 Percentage of GDP, U.S. humanitarian, financial, and military aid to Ukraine, 2022

How does the United States' economic and military position compare to that of other nations? How has this changed over time?

As a result, realists emphasize international security threats around the world—terrorists, rivals, and rogue states. In an unstable world, say the realists, the United States must sustain a powerful military to use as a deterrent—and if necessary to deploy it against threats to American interests.

Realists debate what type of international order is most stable: unipolar (led by one nation), bipolar (led by two), or multipolar (with multiple powers). During the Cold War, the international order was bipolar (with the United States and the Soviet Union competing for dominance). The vital questions today: What type of international order is emerging? Will it prove stable? What effects will global pandemics and Russian aggression in Ukraine have?

COMPARING NATIONS 18.1   Military Spending Worldwide

The United States spends more on its armed forces than the other top nine nations combined *(Stockholm International Peace Research Institute)*

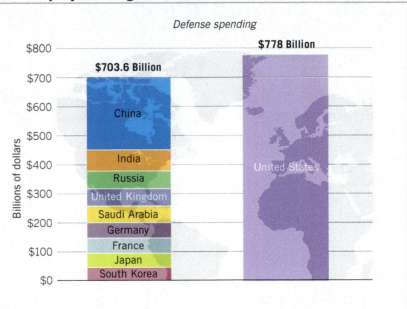

Defense spending

$778 Billion

$703.6 Billion

Billions of dollars

- $800
- $700
- $600 — China
- $500
- $400 — India
- $300 — Russia / United Kingdom
- $200 — Saudi Arabia / Germany
- $100 — France / Japan
- $0 — South Korea

United States

Liberalism: A doctrine that views nation-states as benefiting most from mutual cooperation, aided by international organizations.

Security trap: The idea that using military force creates multiple, often unforeseen, problems.

Realism offers a strong perspective that underpins the doctrine of primacy. Yes, it is expensive to maintain such a large army. But no other military has the same reach, and none can move as swiftly to respond to trouble around the globe. Realists insist that it is the price of security.

A Different View: Liberalism

A very different perspective agrees that the world can be a dangerous place—but insists that the best way for nations to secure peace and prosperity is to work together. **Liberalism** focuses on identifying common goals, building international organizations such as the United Nations, and exchanging cultural ambassadors— from rock stars to football teams. Together nations can create a world that moves beyond self-interest.

Liberal critics of the realist strain in U.S. foreign policy raise an alarming question: Could building such a large military make the United States *less* secure? Liberals identify three potential problems with military primacy.

First, they warn of a **security trap**: Using military force often produces a backlash. It humiliates other nations and leaves them more susceptible to anti-American sentiments.[7] When the United States deploys its military, civilians are inevitably killed—an estimated two hundred thousand civilians died during the invasion and occupation

● *Realists see a world bristling with threats. Here, North Korean troops on parade.*

of Iraq from 2003 to 2020.[8] Civilian casualties are not America's responsibility alone—but they are sobering.

Second, military primacy costs the United States close to $1 trillion a year. This high economic burden shifts spending from other priorities. Liberal thinkers argue that mutual engagement with other nations is more likely to foster increased trade and enhances everyone's economic well-being.

Finally, liberal thinkers are joined by conservatives in warning that too much emphasis on military power undermines liberty. As we saw in Chapter 2, Americans long feared that a large army would turn a republic into an empire. That critique evaporated during the Cold War. Facing communists armed with atomic bombs, America could not afford to worry about the problems posed by a standing army. Once communism fell, however, critics argued that it was time to downsize the military.

Those promoting cuts in military spending face the same problem we have seen in almost every chapter: entrenched institutions. Many local economies depend on military bases, military contractors, or military suppliers. It is always hard to cut any budget.[9]

Soft Power

Packed stadiums around the world shout out the words at Billie Eilish or Drake concerts. To foreign policy analysts, they are another way to spread American influence. Political scientist Joseph Nye calls it "**soft power**": Use culture and economics to persuade rather than coerce (hard power).[10]

Soft power: The influence a nation exerts through culture and commerce; a contrast to attempted influence through force.

Soft power is an important part of liberal foreign policy. As tourists began traveling again following the easing of COVID restrictions, the United States is again a leading world tourist destination. American music, movies, and television are everywhere (see Chapter 9). Locals line up outside Apple or Starbucks stores from Sydney to Shanghai. Sharing these cultural experiences forms bonds among people, which create a different type of security. In an annual ranking of nations' "soft power," the United States—which slipped out of the top five during the erratic Trump years—returned in 2021 to the top spot.[11]

Some critics abroad and at home push back, accusing the United States of cultural imperialism. However, most administrations rely on hard and soft power. The sharp question is how to balance the two. What do you think?

Foreign Aid and National Security

The United States is the largest foreign aid donor among wealthy democracies, in terms of resources expended: around $42 billion in 2021. Many Americans believe we spend far too much—and from the realist perspective, it is a drain on our economic resources. But there is another way to look at it. The United States devotes

● *Soft power: American lattes are welcome where the army is not. Here, in the heart of the Forbidden City (the imperial palace in Beijing), one of more than 5,400 Starbucks locations in China.*

COMPARING NATIONS 18.2   Spending on Foreign Aid

Top: The United States devotes more resources to foreign aid than any other wealthy democratic country. Bottom: Now, look at foreign assistance as a percentage of the gross national income (GNI), or total economy. The United States is low compared to other wealthy nations.

Twenty years ago, Organisation for Economic Co-operation and Development (OECD) nations agreed to reach a target of 0.7 percent of their income; as the chart shows, the United States is far from that level. Realists push allies to spend more on their military; liberals might respond by asking the United States to achieve targets for development assistance. Which would you advise the president to emphasize?
Source: OECD (https://bit.ly/3AWdk1C)

Official development assistance, net

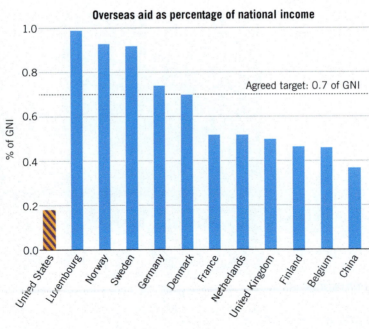

Overseas aid as percentage of national income

less than 1 percent of gross national income on humanitarian and development aid—less than a fifth of Sweden's percentage, and half as much as Japan or Canada (see Comparing Nations 18.2). Is this too much—or too little?[12]

Those with a more liberal view of America's role in the world believe that assisting other nations is an important path to security. It builds goodwill and helps lift nations out of the poverty that breeds extremism. Others counter that financial assistance only makes other nations dependent on "handouts." Moreover, foreign aid often flies straight into the pockets of the rich and the powerful. Whatever side you take, remember that foreign assistance forms a tiny part of U.S. spending.

THE BOTTOM LINE

» The first goal of American foreign policy is security.

» Two leading foreign policy views, realism and liberalism, differ sharply on how best to ensure security for Americans and allied countries.

» To pursue security, the United States deploys a large military and maintains a policy of primacy—the idea that no military power should rival ours.

» Liberal thinkers emphasize the importance of multinational cooperation, soft (or cultural) power, and foreign aid.

 # Foreign Policy Goal No. 2: Prosperity

The United States is a superpower because of its economy. In the long run, national power rests not on armies but on economic engines. The second goal of foreign policy: Keep that economic engine humming.

Back in 1960 the United States accounted for 40 percent of the world's economic output—and stood alone as a major international power. Today, American wealth accounts for roughly a quarter of the world's gross domestic product (GDP). That is still the world's largest economy, but some analysts believe the international order is turning multipolar. Growing centers of economic power in Asia and Europe may be challenging U.S. supremacy in the years ahead. When President Biden described China as America's "most serious competitor," he had economic primacy in mind.[13]

Economic Superpower or Nation in Decline?

At first glance, the United States certainly does not look like a country on the skids. The American economy is a third larger than China's, nearly five times larger than Japan's, five and a half times larger than Germany's (see Figure 18.1), and larger than 171 other nations *combined*. The American dollar is the international reserve currency—used in foreign trade and investment. And English has become the language of international affairs.

Although the U.S. economy remains by far the largest in the world, China is catching up. Its economy has been growing twice as fast—vaulting past Japan and increasing at a rate much higher than most developed countries. Two other areas with high growth could also be potential rivals: the European Union and India.[14]

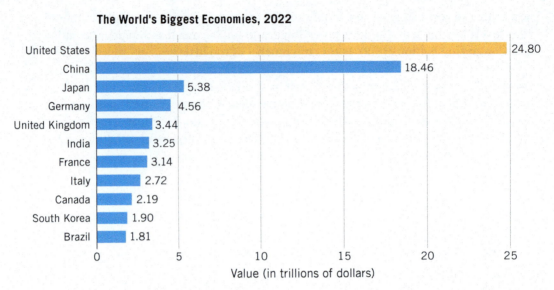

The World's Biggest Economies, 2022

Country	Value (in trillions of dollars)
United States	24.80
China	18.46
Japan	5.38
Germany	4.56
United Kingdom	3.44
India	3.25
France	3.14
Italy	2.72
Canada	2.19
South Korea	1.90
Brazil	1.81

● **FIGURE 18.1** *The United States is still the world's largest economy—though China has been catching up. (International Monetary Fund)*

Trade deficit: The financial gap arising when a nation imports (or buys) more goods from foreign nations than it exports (or sells) to them.

Another possible risk: The United States buys more from other nations than it sells to them. This imbalance, known as a **trade deficit**, has existed every year since 1975. Is it a problem? Economists differ. Some believe that the United States cannot continue buying more from other nations than it sells to them without eventual economic consequences; this was a major pillar of the Trump Administration's economic outlook. Others suggest that trade deficits can be a sign of strength—a strong dollar and a humming economy make foreign goods more affordable. And many specialists point out that the deficit is complicated by the vast global supply chains of American companies like Apple and General Motors, which make parts and goods in factories across the world—then "import" them to the United States.[15]

Political economists have also long worried that the United States is failing to invest in its *infrastructure*—its roads, train tracks, air terminals, and public transportation, as well as modern networks like 5G service. Travelers to Asia marvel at the sleek airports and railroads. Does the Chinese growth of the past decade mean that authoritarian governments are more efficient at organizing the economy than America's democracy is? The Biden administration's trillion-dollar domestic infrastructure improvement plan, passed by Congress in 2022, along with expanded infrastructure support for Latin America and other regions is in part an attempt to sustain American economic primacy through expanded networks for travel and trade.[16]

How do all of these concerns add up? Pessimists worry that other nations, especially China, will overtake the United States economically. Optimists disagree. The world's biggest economy can afford to buy more goods and services from around the world. It has been running both trade and budget deficits for the past fifty years, and the financial sky has not fallen. Yes, politicians bicker, but they do not diminish the energy of American inventors. American entrepreneurial genius has powered the information age through Microsoft, Apple, Google, Meta, Amazon, and the Internet itself. As the coronavirus pandemic begins to recede, the United States remains an economic powerhouse.[17]

Which is it: A nation in decline? Or an entrepreneurial dynamo still setting the global pace? Keep your own score in the years ahead by tracking just one measure of world power: the size of the American economy relative to the rest of the world.

Free Trade

For seventy years after World War II, U.S. administrations championed **free trade**—the idea that goods and services should move across international boundaries without government interference. Prior to the 1940s, most governments tried to protect their own industries by slapping tariffs on foreign goods—special taxes that made foreign competitors more expensive than local products. This practice is called **protectionism** because it is designed to protect local industries, like steel and aluminum, from foreign competition.

In theory, free trade helps businesses and consumers in every country, because it offers more choices and lower prices. If Detroit can make better cars at a lower price, consumers from Kansas to Kazakhstan should be able to buy them. And because a quarter of all American economic activity involves foreign trade, there is a lot of money on the table.

American policymakers pushed for both bilateral trade agreements with individual countries and, more important, multilateral treaties with many nations—the most important resulted in the **World Trade Organization (WTO)**, which oversees international trade rules. However, the costs and benefits are not evenly spread out. Over the past three decades many U.S. companies shifted operations overseas, leaving hundreds of thousands of American workers at least temporarily without jobs. Opposition to free trade deals began to grow. Between 1990 and 2016, presidents pressed free trade deals; in Congress Democrats generally opposed and Republicans supported them.[18]

President Trump led the Republicans in a sharp U-turn. He insisted on the renegotiation of trade deals, with neighboring allies like Mexico and Canada and competitors like China alike. Why? We will see in the next section.

Challenges to Free Trade

Almost every economics textbook repeats the same mantra: Free trade makes everyone better off. However, many Americans strongly disagree. Free trade faces four main challenges.

Cost. First, critics of free trade note that it is cheaper to produce goods in nations that pollute, outlaw unions, reject safety standards, and keep wages low. If global agreements are not carefully negotiated, jobs will flow to those nations—leaving their workers, the global environment, and the United States all worse off. Some Democrats in Congress, along with many liberal thinkers, suggest an alternative to free trade: **fair trade**—emphasize worker protections and environmental standards. Fair trade can be built into deals that reduce trade barriers. That way, say proponents, companies in different nations are competing under the same rules.

Social Displacement. Second, free markets cause social displacement, at least in the short run. Free trade in agriculture, for example, pushes small farmers in poorer nations such as Nigeria off their farms and into megacities like Lagos. What happens to the Nigerian farmer and his family when they lose their land? What happens to software engineers in Austin, Texas, who find their jobs migrating to Bangalore, India? Few nations have adequate policies to help workers who are displaced by international competition. Even if everyone is better off in the long run, as free traders argue, politics—and individuals—focus on troubles in the short run.

Free trade: Goods and services moving across international boundaries without government interference.

Protectionism: Efforts to protect local business from foreign competition.

World Trade Organization (WTO): An international organization that oversees efforts to open markets and promote free trade.

Fair trade: Trade agreements that include environmental and labor protections, so that nations do not receive unfair advantages by exploiting workers or harming the environment.

Volatile Markets. Third, as international markets have expanded to facilitate the huge sums involved in free trade, they have grown more volatile. The COVID pandemic's economic effects include disrupted supply chains—global trade crucially depends on reliable movement of goods worldwide—that lingered well into 2022, and Russia's attack on Ukraine shook markets in food and energy all over the world. Liberal economists such as Paul Krugman warn that free markets create a wild ride full of booms, bubbles, and busts; conservative thinkers have increasingly questioned once sacrosanct support for free trade as well.[19]

Protectionist Pushback. Fourth, American leaders have long championed free trade only until they ran into powerful American interests. When Washington helps U.S. farmers, it violates the rules of free trade that the government itself is championing. However, because few politicians are willing to take on the farm lobby or the rural states, American farm subsidies stay in place despite the different administrations' commitment to free trade.

Across his term, President Trump openly embraced protectionism. He charged that trade deals were "rigged."[20] U.S. trade wars, often launched by presidential directive, reversed years of Republican support for free trade. President Biden, while dialing back blatant protectionist policies including open trade wars, has emphasized Americans' middle-class economic concerns across his foreign policy priorities. Two years into his presidency, Biden had done little to signal a return to the strong free trade policies that long characterized American administrations.[21]

Almost all experts and most political leaders reject a return to protectionism. They point out that the current system is the result of intricately negotiated agreements in which both sides give and take. Now, however, opposition to those agreements has spread. On the left, critics argue that those deals have hurt workers and the environment; on the right, opponents charge that they have been a source of U.S. economic decline. Polls show continued general support for free trade among Americans, with Democrats *more* positive than in the past about free international trade, and Republicans less so (see Figure 18.2). But the days of unabashed free trade now seem over in both political parties.

Americans' Opinions About Foreign Trade

What do you think foreign trade means for America? Do you see foreign trade more as an opportunity for economic growth through increased U.S. exports, or a threat to the economy from foreign imports?

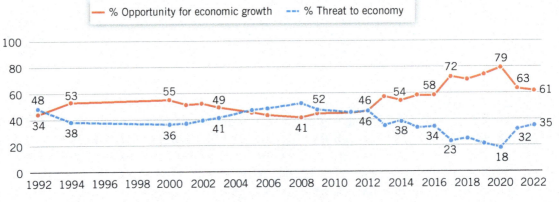

2000 and 2005 data are based on average of polls conducted during the year.

● **FIGURE 18.2** *Despite years of criticism of free trade by President Trump and his administration, and questions about free trade's efficacy from economists and political scientists, Americans remain supportive of this approach to international exchange. (Gallup, 2022)*

Energy

Foreign policymakers keep a close eye on energy supplies. The United States consumes just over twenty million barrels of oil a day, a quarter of the world total. It produces more than it uses, but because of supply chain and refinery issues, the United States imports about seven million barrels a day.

In 2021, demand for oil soared. Energy consumption returned to pre-COVID levels and Russia's invasion of Ukraine cut back the supply. The United States, with its large oil and gas industries, faced less economic pain than western and central European nations, deeply reliant on Russian gas. Still, Americans are reliant on oil from the Middle East—indeed, across the last thirty years the United States has fought three major wars in the region—which has an estimated 60 percent of the world's oil reserves. When Joe Biden traveled to the Middle East in summer 2022, expanded oil production and lower energy prices were high on his agenda.[22]

● *Clashing values in foreign policy. Joe Biden vowed to treat Saudi Arabian leader Mohammed bin Salman (known as MBS) as a "pariah" because of human rights violations, including the murder of a reporter for the Washington Post who wrote critically about MBS. When oil prices soared after Russia invaded Ukraine, Biden visited MBS to discuss boosting Saudi oil production—and greeted the Saudi leader warmly, with a "fist bump heard 'round the world."*

Economic Weapons

American officials use economic relations as carrots to reward other nations or as sticks to punish them—for attacking another country (the most extensive set of sanctions in modern history was applied to Russia in 2022), developing nuclear weapons, or hacking American elections. Economic sanctions include the following:

- A boycott, or refusing to buy goods or services from a country.

- An economic embargo, or restricting the flow of trade into a country. Sometimes the Navy or the Air Force enforces the embargo.

- Divestment, or refusing to invest in another country. Even local governments and private companies can use this strategy.

- Freezing assets, or seizing the bank accounts and other financial sources that foreign nationals have invested here. This strategy targets rulers and other elites in particular by stripping them of their foreign bank accounts.

- Finally, withholding foreign aid—if the country is receiving any.

Applying these economic sanctions is not easy because it requires building an international coalition—and sustaining it over time. If other countries refuse to go along, the United States may lose a market for its own goods without applying any real pressure. However, being the world's largest economy makes a difference; when the Trump administration renewed economic sanctions on Iran, overriding European objections, European firms discovered that the United States would punish them for violating the sanctions—few valued their Iran business over their American trade.[23]

One final problem: Economic weapons often hurt ordinary people long before they touch the rich and powerful. When sanctions pinch a nation's economy, it is the poor that go hungry. The wealthy (and the well connected) have more resources to ride out the hard time.

THE BOTTOM LINE

» A second primary goal of foreign policy is to protect prosperity. Economic strength is the ultimate source of power on the world stage.

» Today, the U.S. economy is the largest in the world—but many Americans and allies around the globe wonder: Will the United States maintain its economic strength relative to other nations?

» American economic policy has been guided by the pursuit of free trade—the removal of barriers to international commerce. Resistance has grown to free trade, especially among congressional Democrats (who support *fair* trade) and many Republicans (who embrace going it alone).

» International economic policy also focuses on protecting energy sources and using economic sticks and carrots to influence the behavior of other nations.

 ## Foreign Policy Goal No. 3: Spreading American Ideals

Most people believe that every nation's foreign policy goal can be simply described: blunt self-interest. However, explaining American action only in terms of power or prosperity misses something important.

In the very first inaugural address, delivered in 1789, President George Washington declared that the new nation had a special mission: "The sacred fire of liberty and the destiny of the republican model of government are . . . entrusted to the hands of the American people." This, he told his countrymen, might even be liberty's best and final chance. From the very start, Washington and other American leaders believed that the United States had a special role in the world—to champion liberty.[24]

American leaders often justify foreign policy action in terms of promoting values such as liberty and democracy. The United States entered World War I, said President Woodrow Wilson, because "the world must be made safe for democracy." America is "privileged to spend its blood," he continued, for "a universal dominion of right." More than a century later, a new president and his team insisted that the "Biden Doctrine" involved repaired alliances and renewed attention to universal values.[25]

American Exceptionalism

American exceptionalism:
The view that the United States is unique, marked by a distinct set of ideas such as equality, self-rule, and limited government.

Again and again, American leaders return to the idea that the United States has a unique duty to spread freedom, democracy, and peace to other nations. The belief that the United States plays a special role in world affairs is known as **American exceptionalism**. This does not mean that Americans ignore their own interests. America's deepest interest, according to this view, lies in promoting the peace, freedom, and democracy that will benefit all people.[26]

Is the United States really exceptional? Some observers warn that American exceptionalism is a dangerous myth. It can lead Americans to reduce complicated reality into a simple clash between good and evil. And it can blind American policymakers to other perspectives and interests.[27]

A faith in America's special destiny, whether it is truth or a myth, makes foreign policy more controversial. Political science research suggests that advancing democratic values and economic growth in underdeveloped countries helps everyone. According to the **theory of democratic peace**, nations with legitimate democratic governments do not go to war with each other.[28] The question raised by Americans and politically minded citizens around the world today: Can a United States facing eroding democratic norms at home continue to champion democratic values worldwide?

The View from Abroad

How do others see the United States? By the end of the Obama years, the United States

● *Nineteenth-century artists imagined a spirit of providential destiny that guided America. Here, America flies forward, the star of empire on her forehead with learning and technology in either hand, as Native Americans and wild beasts flee before the irresistible civilization. This painting, by John Gast, was widely copied and reprinted.*

was viewed far more favorably than other international powers. Subsequently, President Trump's "America First" outlook caused American approval to crash in many countries—especially those in Europe and North and South America— falling 50 percent overall (see Figure 18.3). However, a few nations did have confidence in President Trump's policies—most notably, the Philippines, Nigeria, and Israel.[29]

The debate continues about American values and their meaning for other nations. Even supporters, at home and overseas, fear American society is increasingly

Theory of democratic peace: Theory that strongly democratic nations are unlikely to engage in wars with one another.

WHAT DO YOU THINK?

Is America Exceptional?

	Yes.	No.	It depends.
Every nation is unique in many ways. But is the United States exceptional in fighting for the great values expressed in its Declaration of Independence?	The United States is exceptional in that it makes sacrifices to spread values such as freedom and democracy around the world. It does not ignore self-interest but equates it with the spread of liberty and democracy.	Americans may like to claim that they are acting purely on principle. But, like every other nation, the United States pursues its own self-interest. It is dangerous and misleading to insist that we are helping others when in reality we are helping ourselves.	Americans pursue their self-interest. They also pursue values such as democracy and rights. Some leaders get the balance right and are cheered around the world. Others are less effective. It depends on the leader and the situation.

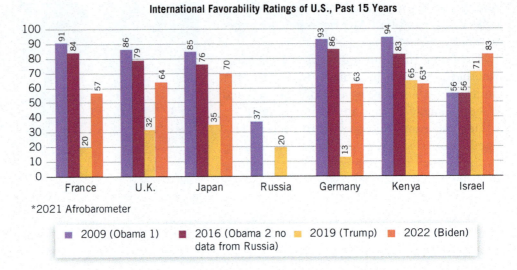

International Favorability Ratings of U.S., Past 15 Years

*2021 Afrobarometer

■ 2009 (Obama 1) ■ 2016 (Obama 2 no data from Russia) ■ 2019 (Trump) ■ 2022 (Biden)

● **FIGURE 18.3** *The Trump effect? U.S. favorability in most countries soared during the Obama years and plummeted during Trump's four years. The Biden administration claims that "America is back"—but how will other nations respond?*

unequal, marked by less opportunity and a growing gulf between rich and poor. The United States seems, to many observers, more fixed on hard-knuckled economic competition and amassing great wealth than on a genuine belief that all people are equal.

Despite Trump administration limits on immigration and the perils of COVID, in 2022–23, more immigrants are again crowding into the United States than into any other nation.[30] Even with tougher screening and strong anti-immigrant rhetoric by some national leaders, people stand in long lines to sign up for the lottery that will grant a few of them a visa and a green card. People even risk their lives to pursue the American Dream. If the United States is a nation in inexorable decline, then why are so many people fighting to move here?

In short, American values have played an important role in guiding American foreign policy. Today, new questions have risen: Are these values still vital—or are they beginning to fade? Can they inspire people around the world—or do they simply seem like rhetorical cover for American self-interest? Will the Biden administration move decisively away from Donald Trump's America First policies?

THE BOTTOM LINE

» The United States tries to spread its own values of democracy and freedom—sometimes creating goodwill, at other times a backlash. This is a rare goal for a nation's foreign policy.

» American standing in international polls plummeted in many countries after the election of Donald Trump, but returned with U.S. leadership in opposition to Russia's Ukraine invasion.

» Critics argue that the United States simply uses the language of values to pursue its self-interest. They see even the nation's talk of liberty as little more than a cover for unbridled capitalism and inequality. Yet, millions around the world still sign up eagerly for the lottery that will grant a few of them a visa and a green card.

Foreign Policy Perspectives

Every administration develops a foreign policy strategy by answering three key questions. Should the United States engage the world or withdraw from it? Do we go it alone or work with others? Which foreign policy goals and values are most important?

Engage the World? Isolationism Versus Intervention

President George Washington warned his countrymen to stay clear of foreign politics: "The great rule of conduct for us, in regard to foreign nations, is . . . to have . . . as little *political* connection as possible." In other words, the United States should limit itself to commerce. We can best promote our values simply by building an ideal society that other nations will admire and want to imitate.[31]

Many Americans hold a version of this view, now known as **strategic disengagement**.[32] While few politicians today embrace all-out **isolationism**—avoiding any involvement in other nations' affairs—some argue that the United States will remain strong and secure by limiting its involvement overseas, especially military activity.

Many people believe that the United States traditionally practiced isolationism. This is a myth. Right from the start, the United States exerted its muscle around the world. It battled the French navy in 1798, just ten years after the Constitution went into effect. It fought the Barbary Wars on the north coast of Africa beginning in 1801. (If you are familiar with the Marine Corps anthem, its "shores of Tripoli" refers to the Barbary Wars.) American forces entered Mexico ("the halls of Montezuma") five times between 1836 and 1848 before declaring war. By one count, the military deployed overseas 165 times before World War II.

For all the action, however, the United States maintained only a small standing army until the end of World War II. Then, locked in a Cold War with the Soviet Union, the country built an army ready to deploy anywhere around the globe at a moment's notice. The sheer size and sophistication of its military pushes the United States away from isolationism and toward internationalism.

Indeed, most contemporary foreign policy analysts opt for **internationalism**. They believe that America's interests are best protected by actively engaging the world. Both the United States and the world would be worse off, they argue, if the United States withdrew into its own borders. Americans must combat terrorism, confront Russian aggression, help contain an unpredictable North Korea, work to advance human rights—and the list goes on. This perspective insists that withdrawing from world affairs will allow problems to fester, enemies to multiply, and people to suffer.

Go It Alone or Act with Others?

Although the United States was rarely isolationist, through most of its history it acted

> **Strategic disengagement:** The doctrine that a nation should not interfere in other nations' affairs unless such involvement clearly advances its own interests.

> **Isolationism:** The doctrine that a nation should avoid all foreign policy commitments and alliances and withdraw from world affairs.

> **Internationalism:** The belief that national interests are best served by actively engaging and working with other nations around the world.

● To the shores of Tripoli: American foreign policy was interventionist right from the beginning. Here, marines lead the charge in Derna, Libya, in 1805 during the first Barbary War.

alone. President Washington broke the alliance with France that had helped win the Revolutionary War, and America did not enter another peacetime alliance for 150 years. Thomas Jefferson sternly warned the country, in his first inaugural address, not to get involved in "entangling alliances." This perspective is known as **unilateralism**—American foreign policy should be independent and self-sufficient. Unilateralists oppose treaties with foreign nations or international organizations because such agreements, they say, tie America down.

Unilateralism: A doctrine that holds that the United States should act independently of other nations. It should decide what is best for itself—not in coordination with partners and allies.

Multilateralism: A doctrine that emphasizes operating together with other nations to pursue common goals.

In the half-century following World War II, American policy changed. Facing a hostile Soviet Union armed with nuclear weapons and as the newly emerged leader of the Western world, American leaders insisted that the United States could no longer afford to go it alone. **Multilateralism** means acting together with other nations to pursue common goals. Those who support multilateralism believe we cannot solve global problems by ourselves. Fighting communism during the Cold War required concerted action. Likewise, only international cooperation can defeat terrorism, reverse climate change, secure prosperity, end starvation, stop ethnic killing, resist global pandemics, reduce the international traffic in drugs and sex, and end violence against women. Foreign policy officials who take an internationalist view are strong supporters of multilateralism.

The youngest adult population (aged 18–29) expresses a clear preference for multilateralism. That's because they engage the world: More than three times as many study abroad than did members of Generation X twenty-five years ago.[33] They are also more likely to travel abroad than previous generations. Those experiences show up in young Americans' support for foreign policy approaches that emphasize cooperation among nations.

One especially pressing issue that cannot be solved through a unilateral, isolationist approach is the spread of nuclear weapons. Five nations openly possess them (the United States, England, France, Russia, and China). Four others are thought to have developed them (India, Pakistan, North Korea, and Israel). A small number of foreign policy experts argue that the spread of these weapons makes wars less likely, because either side can annihilate the other.[34] Most observers believe the opposite: As nuclear weapons spread to less stable nations, they are more likely to be used and to fall into the hands of extremist groups. In the words of a past U.S. secretary of defense under President Bill Clinton, "Today, the danger of . . . a nuclear catastrophe is greater than it was during the Cold War and most people are blissfully unaware of

● Ukrainian president Volodymyr Zelensky faced overwhelming odds on the battlefield with Russia—including a nuclear-weapons threat by Vladimir Putin. But this inexperienced leader rallied his nation and won the respect of Western leaders. Shown here, Zelensky stands in the center with (from left to right) German Chancellor Olaf Scholz, French President Emmanuel Macron, Italian Prime Minister Mario Draghi, and Romanian President Klaus Iohannis.

this fact."[35] American foreign policy must work around the globe to avoid this nightmare scenario.

Vladimir Putin, as Russian losses mounted in Ukraine, issued a not-so-veiled threat to retaliate with nuclear weapons if Western nations sent troops into action in Ukraine. Five years earlier, President Trump warned North Korea "of fire and fury like the world has never seen" if it continued to threaten others and develop nuclear weapons.[36] Trump then offered an unprecedented initiative: meeting North Korean leader Kim Jong-Un in a summit focused on containing the dangers of a nuclear nightmare. But by 2020, after a second failed summit, Kim had openly acknowledged a return to nuclear-weapons testing.

Today, another threat looms: cyberweapons. Russia, China, and North Korea have turned cyberweapons (developed in the United States) on Western nations, threatening power grids, governments, banks, and more. To combat these cyber-threats, vulnerable Western nations may find it more effective to cooperate rather than go it alone.[37]

Four Approaches

As you can see, Americans have a lot to balance in making foreign policy—three overarching goals, isolation versus action, and unilateralism versus multilateralism. How do we bring together these competing priorities? Over time, Americans have generally divided into four different camps. Each approach emphasizes different foreign policy goals. Each is named after a famous statesman who helped define it.[38]

Wilsonians believe that American values should be the core consideration guiding foreign policy. Fighting a war to make the world safe for democracy, as Woodrow Wilson urged America to do during World War I, is the classic Wilsonian move.

Hamiltonians believe that American foreign policy should focus on protecting American prosperity. Named after Alexander Hamilton, the first secretary of the treasury, this approach emphasizes making economic deals that benefit the United States. Hamiltonians favor big business and accept big government to advance American economic benefits worldwide. To them, military intervention should always be weighed not against vague values such as freedom or morality, but against hard-headed analysis: Is the action in America's economic interest?

Jeffersonians focus on freedom and democracy at home. Building a large military and deploying it around the world threatens the American ideals of local and democratic government. Jeffersonians are nervous about the military–industrial complex and its corrosive effect on American freedom. President Thomas Jefferson warned that international alliances would "entangle" the nation in foreign wars and power politics. Modern Jeffersonians firmly believe in *strategic disengagement.*

Jacksonians believe that the United States should simply focus on its own security and well-being. It should worry about itself and let other nations do the same. Jacksonians are skeptical of foreign aid, indifferent to international diplomacy, and slow to support foreign action. However, they put special emphasis on honor. Once the military is deployed, they insist on total victory. Of the four traditions, the Jacksonians are most likely to be chanting, *"USA! USA!"*

WHAT DO YOU THINK?

Foreign Policy Perspectives

It is time for you to pick a perspective that ties foreign policy together. Where do your values lie? With which of the following do you most identify?

I am a Wilsonian.	I believe that American foreign policy must rest on American values and work with other nations to secure them.
I am a Hamiltonian.	I believe that the business of America is advancing business and otherwise maximizing economic gain.
I am a Jeffersonian.	I prefer to worry about democracy on the home front.
I am a Jacksonian.	I believe that the only criteria for foreign action are American security and American prosperity.
None of these choices seem right.	Feel free to develop a different perspective. You can emphasize some other goal of American foreign policy. Or mix and match from these.

Source: Adapted from Walter Russell Mead

THE BOTTOM LINE

» Three decisions guide foreign policy: First, policymakers must choose between strategic engagement (only get involved in a global conflict or alliance when it clearly advances the U.S. national interest) or internationalism (engagement with the world).

» Second, policymakers must choose whether to act unilaterally (go it alone) or multilaterally (in alliance with other nations).

» Third, policymakers put it all together with an overall perspective: Wilsonians focus on values, Hamiltonians on economics, Jeffersonians on democracy at home, and Jacksonians on defending American security and well-being.

 # Who Makes Foreign Policy?

What is misleading about the following media headlines?

- "American Foreign Policy Is Not Ready for Climate Change"
- "South Korea Seeks to Balance Relations with China, United States"
- "India's Gamble in Afghanistan"

They all describe nations as if they were *unitary actors*, or individuals with minds of their own. Every chapter in this book has told another story. The United

States constructs politics out of many perspectives, interests, institutions, and arguments. So does every other nation. Foreign policy emerges out of negotiation. Several major players have a seat at the table when American foreign policy is made.

Congress

The Constitution carefully balances responsibility for foreign policy between Congress and the president. Congress has the power to declare war, to set the military's budget, and to ratify treaties. These responsibilities worked fine in a slower world. In the early nineteenth century, the Americans defeated the English in the Battle of New Orleans because word had not filtered back across the Atlantic that a peace treaty had already ended the War of 1812.

Today, response time can be measured in minutes rather than weeks or months. As the decision clock sped up, defense—and, more generally, foreign policy—shifted away from Congress to the White House. Congress has not declared war since 1941, despite major wars in Korea (where thirty-six thousand Americans died), Vietnam (another fifty-eight thousand), the Persian Gulf, the Balkans, Afghanistan, and Iraq. Congress is divided, slow to act, uneasy about taking risks, focused on domestic issues, and always running for reelection. For all these reasons, it has let control of foreign policy slip to the executive branch.

In 1973 Congress tried to reassert some control by passing the **War Powers Act**, which requires presidents to win congressional permission for military action after troops are in the field for no more than sixty days. Presidents often ask Congress for support before they commit troops (see Chapter 14 for details). And when wars drag on and grow unpopular, Congress asserts itself: It holds hearings, rallies opposition, and squeezes the budget.

> **War Powers Act:** Legislation passed in 1973 to increase congressional involvement in undeclared wars. It requires Congress to approve military action undertaken by the president in no more than sixty days.

The Constitution requires the Senate to ratify international treaties with a two-thirds vote—a very high bar in our partisan era. To get around the requirement, presidents sign *executive agreements* with other nations; these have the same legal effect as formal treaties but do not require the two-thirds vote. *Legislative executive agreements* pass with a simple majority, as any other legislation. A *sole executive agreement* is simply signed by the president without any congressional approval at all.

The Constitution also makes Congress responsible for confirming top foreign policy appointments. Again, partisan politics has slowed this process in recent years.

In short, Congress has evolved from a partner to a type of check on executive foreign policymaking. The executive branch crafts the policies. It then must win over Congress for funding, legislation, confirmations, and cooperation. In effect, Congress pushes back when presidential policies become unpopular.

The President

The president commands the military, negotiates treaties, rallies Americans during crises, and oversees relations with more than two hundred nations. Each administration defines America's stance toward the world. Presidents and their team decide whether, when, where, and how to intervene around the globe. They balance foreign policy with domestic priorities and political calculations. President George W. Bush committed the United States to war in Afghanistan; Presidents Obama and Trump expanded American military presence; and President Biden made the difficult decision to end the war—injuring his standing at home and with some allied countries.[39]

Recent administrations have demonstrated the enormous power inherent in the president's foreign policy role. Ironically, modern presidents have more authority and less experience. Early presidents all had a rich foreign policy background. Most recent presidents have arrived in the White House with no foreign policy experience at all (see Table 18.1). Trump's 2016 victory came, in part, from a great wave of distrust toward Washington insiders. In contrast to recent presidents, Joe Biden has a great deal of foreign policy experience: He served on the Senate Foreign Relations Committee for three decades and then helped shape foreign policy as vice president for eight years.

Although presidents take the lead, they have many partners in conducting international affairs. One key to presidential success is wisely managing the enormous foreign policy bureaucracy. Each office in the pyramid does a

TABLE 18.1   Presidents' Foreign Policy Experience

The first six presidents had extensive foreign policy experience. Of the most recent presidents only two, George H. W. Bush and Joe Biden, had any foreign policy experience at all.

	SECRETARY OF STATE	OTHER DIPLOMATIC OR INTERNATIONAL POLICY CABINET POST	CHIEF U.S. REPRESENTATIVE TO GREAT BRITAIN	CHIEF U.S. REPRESENTATIVE TO OTHER MAJOR POWER	COMMANDED U.S. FORCES IN WAR
FIRST SIX PRESIDENTS					
George Washington					X
John Adams		X	X	X	
Thomas Jefferson	X	X		X	
James Madison	X				
James Monroe	X	X	X	X	
John Quincy Adams	X	X	X	X	
MOST RECENT PRESIDENTS					
Jimmy Carter					
Ronald Reagan					
George H. W. Bush		X		X	
Bill Clinton					
George W. Bush					
Barack Obama					
Donald Trump					
Joe Biden		X			

different job and sees the world in its own way. Together, however, the collection of long-serving foreign policy experts in the executive branch was famously dubbed "The Blob" by Benjamin Rhodes, a national security advisor to President Obama. Here's a more detailed description of The Blob: A "bipartisan foreign policy elite that believes maintaining the United States' global dominance is essential to ensuring American safety and international peace."[40]

The State Department

The State Department, the first cabinet agency established under the Constitution, is responsible for managing diplomatic relations with more than two hundred nations. State is responsible for negotiating treaties, distributing foreign assistance, and managing daily contact with other nations.

State Department officers are trained in understanding other nations and cultures. They learn foreign languages, live abroad, and favor diplomatic solutions—usually multilateral ones. The department is sometimes accused of being out of step with majority American opinion, which can favor strategic disengagement. Critics often have a bit of sarcastic fun with the location of the State Department's headquarters—an area of Washington, DC, known as Foggy Bottom.

This skepticism leads to a serious problem: The State Department is chronically underfunded. Its offices around the world lack key personnel. Many observers (as well as foreign policy officers talking off the record) worry that the United States is shortchanging its diplomatic efforts by underfunding the State Department. They warn that American neglect of statecraft means ceding the crucial area of diplomacy to rivals like China—which are taking full advantage of American indifference.[41]

The Department of Defense

The Department of Defense (DOD) manages the military. It is the largest organization in government and the largest employer in the United States. The DOD is responsible for nearly two million active-duty and reserve military personnel, 715,000 civilian employees,[42] and troops deployed in more than 150 nations from Turkey to Djibouti. They are all led by the secretary of defense, who is always a civilian. The department is housed in a huge five-sided office building known as the Pentagon.

The DOD makes military calculations, toting up risks and threats, assets, and strategy. Not surprising, Defense Department officials see the world very differently than the State Department; a familiar Washington lament bemoans the failure of these two important cabinet offices to coordinate with one another.

Two problems haunt the Department of Defense. First, the massive bureaucracy is bound up in red tape and very slow to change.[43] Second, the military is divided by rivalry between the services. The Army, Navy, Air Force, and Marine Corps are all eager to deploy their own tactical assets during military operations. These tensions can create such confusion that, in one notorious case, a Marine involved in the invasion of Grenada had to use a pay phone back to the Pentagon to request a supporting artillery strike.[44] The chairman of the Joint Chiefs of Staff, a military figure, is charged on behalf of the president and secretary of defense with coordinating the branches—a tall order, given rivalries among them.

Intelligence

The United States has a large and complicated intelligence community. More than eighteen different agencies and offices gather information from around the world. The best known is the Central Intelligence Agency, which is responsible for foreign intelligence. However, the Departments of State, Defense, Energy, and the Treasury all have their own foreign intelligence operations, as do the military branches. The Federal Bureau of Investigation is responsible for domestic intelligence, which often has to be coordinated with information from abroad.

In theory, each intelligence office and agency monitors a different spectrum of threats. In reality, they have overlapping jurisdictions and act as rivals (a familiar theme in the foreign policy bureaucracy, sometimes counteracted by "The Blob"). They are slow to share information or communicate. There is a standard answer to turf wars like the one in the spy community: Create a new agency and charge it with coordinating all the others. In 2004, after hearings into the 9/11 terrorist attacks exposed the chaos, Congress created a director of national intelligence charged with bringing order to American intelligence. Did this mandate impose coordination or simply inject one more voice into the contest? Answer: Both.

The National Security Council

The National Security Council is part of the Executive Office of the President. It brings the most important foreign policy officers together to advise the president. The council includes the president and the vice president, along with the secretaries of state, defense, and homeland security. It also includes the director of national intelligence, the head of the Joint Chiefs of Staff (the top military officer), and others who the president may name. This is one of the most high-powered groups in a city of high-powered groups. Very different perspectives and personalities come together to hammer out major foreign policy decisions.

Other Executive Agencies

A great many other bureaus and agencies engage in foreign policy. The president's economic team plays an important role. The Office of the U.S. Trade Representative negotiates trade deals. The Commerce Department leads business groups abroad. The Department of Homeland Security brings together a host of agencies ranging from the Coast Guard to the Immigration Service. Each agency and office pushes to define foreign policy problems. Each seeks to put its own spin on America's approach to the world.

Interest Groups and the Public

Organized groups play an active role in U.S. foreign policymaking—far more so than in most other nations. On high-profile issues such as trade agreements, every side mobilizes and lobbies. Some groups focus support for specific countries, while others lobby for specific causes: Human rights groups and Christian organizations that are concerned about religious persecution in other nations are among the most familiar interest groups on Capitol Hill.

Groups are most effective at exerting influence on low-profile issues. Cherry growers or health insurance companies can often persuade policymakers to slip favors into a law or regulation. It is much harder to affect high-profile issues because policymakers are usually committed to their positions. In these cases, interest groups assist officials who are already on their side by arming them with information, elegant PowerPoint presentations, and social media posts (see Chapter 12).

Foreign governments are also very active in lobbying U.S. officials, as we saw in Chapter 12. As Russia's military buildup on the Ukraine border proceeded in 2021–22, lobbyists for the Ukrainian government made more than ten thousand contacts with White House officials and congressional staff—more than three times as many as the next most active country, Saudi Arabia.[45]

Public opinion and the media can also have a powerful impact. Public preferences on foreign policy tend to remain stable over time, and

● *Activists also play a role in American foreign policy. Here, Nadia Murad tells a rapt Senate hearing on the Islamic State (IS): "I was raped and sold and was abused [by IS] but I was lucky." Her mother and six brothers were all killed in one day.*

issues like healthcare or jobs attract more attention than diplomatic maneuvers or trade.[46] Once in a while, however, a foreign policy issue moves to the forefront of American politics: The Biden administration's reputation among the public was shaped in part by the end of the war in Afghanistan and by its response to the Russian-Ukrainian war. The media plays it up and the public leaps in with opinions. The administration—or its opponents—can keep the issue at the top of the newsfeeds.

Wars are the most common major events, and they often follow a cycle. At first, the American majority rallies around the flag and throws its support to the president and the troops. Initial antiwar demonstrations get scant media attention. Over time, especially if the war bogs down or its purpose grows murky, as in Vietnam or Iraq, the public turns against the action. It becomes a major story. Even small antiwar protests make the news. Congress begins to stir, holding hearings and scrutinizing appropriations. Public outcry, fanned by media coverage, makes unpopular wars difficult to prosecute. Though—as the Biden administration learned the hard way in Afghanistan—even long-lasting, unpopular conflicts are difficult to end gracefully.

Fragmentation or Success?

The policies produced by these many agencies, offices, legislators, and groups—all pulling and hauling and scrambling for influence—are typical of American government. It is chaotic, messy, unpredictable, open—and often democratic. Yet there is always the foreign policy difference: At any point in the process, the president can make a decision and break the stalemate—deploy the Navy, issue a warning, embrace one foreign leader and challenge another, sign an executive agreement with one nation, abruptly end an agreement with another. Strong presidents have considerable leverage. Despite the messy process, U.S. foreign policy has been relatively successful through much of the nation's history. The United States emerged victorious and more powerful than ever from World War I, World War II, and the Cold War.

The great question about the foreign policy process today is one that we have raised in many other contexts. Does the fragmented, wide-open American policy scramble capture a democratic energy that forces policymakers to see things from many different perspectives? Or does it leave too much power in the hands of the president?

Global Corruption and U.S. Foreign Policy

The NGO "Transparency International" assesses nations based on their levels of corruption, ranking them from 100 (very clean and yellow on the map) to 0 (highly corrupt and dark red on the map). In 2021, the United States scored a 67, ranking it twenty-seventh (tied with Chile) and well below the world's least corrupt countries, such as Denmark, Finland, and New Zealand, with scores of 88.

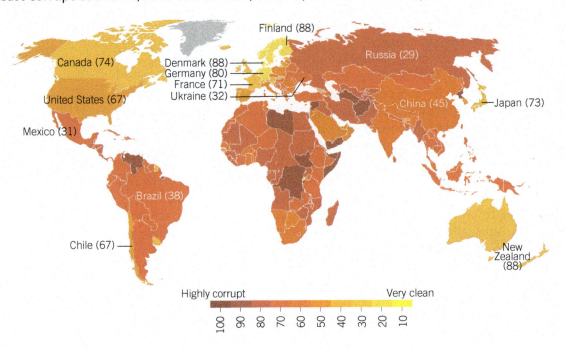

THINK ABOUT IT

Some liberals suggest that the United States should enter into alliances only with "clean" countries, not those with human rights violations, fraudulent elections, and other instances of corruption. Does such an attitude seem desirable? Why or why not?

....

Some realists argue that the world is a dangerous place, and the United States should form alliances and sign treaties based on our self-interest and power balancing. Do you agree? Why or why not?

....

In the 2021 ratings, the United States dropped out of the top twenty-five least corrupt countries for the first time. What factors might have contributed to that change?

THE BOTTOM LINE

» Although we often talk about nations as if they had a single interest, many different individuals and institutions shape foreign policy.

» Congress and the presidents were originally foreign policy partners. During the Cold War, the checks and balances diminished. Today, the president takes the lead and Congress offers a check.

» The most important executive agencies in foreign policymaking are the State Department, the Defense Department, and the National Security Council.

» Other important foreign policy influences include intelligence agencies such as the CIA, economic bureaus like the Office of the U.S. Trade Representative, interest groups, corporations, foreign governments, the media, and the public.

» The key question about American foreign policy: Is the messy, fragmented system swirling around the president an effective way to generate new ideas? Or is it too chaotic for the 2020s? Or both?

 # Adding All of It Up: Grand Strategies in U.S. History

American leaders create an overall framework to meet the challenges of the time. Their **grand strategy** includes everything from a military doctrine to ways of seeing and interpreting the world. The United States has adopted then moved away from four main grand strategies over the past century. Once a strategy is in place it can be very difficult to change—until a dramatic event breaks up the old order. Today, many different interests and forces struggle to shape a new grand strategy for our time.

Grand strategy: An overarching vision that defines and guides a nation's foreign policy.

Standing Alone (1918–1939)

World War I was horrific. The fighting bogged down in trenches in eastern France, and hundreds of thousands of men died moving the battle line back and forth a few miles. After Europeans on both sides had bled their armies for three years, the United States entered the war and quickly tipped the balance. At least from the American perspective, the United States led England and France to victory over Germany and Austria.

President Woodrow Wilson championed a new international order after the war. The United States would spread democracy to every nation and join with other countries in a collective security organization called the League of Nations. Wilson's dreams were, he said, "to correct the evil" and to "purify ... every process of our common life."[47]

Wilson's highly moral and multilateral vision met with furious opposition. Many Americans were scornful of the European leaders who had blundered into the terrible war. Some became isolationists and wanted nothing more to do with international affairs. Many others became unilateralists. They were willing to act abroad, but only on American terms. They would not permit the League of Nations—or any other international organization—to make decisions for the United States. In November 1918, the Republicans won both houses of Congress, and when President Wilson refused to compromise on his multilateral approach, Congress voted down his peace treaty and refused to join the League of Nations.

In the years following World War I, the American grand strategy was simple: The United States would intervene, unilaterally, only when its own interests were threatened. The United States sent ships and troops around the world—to Russia (during and after the Bolshevik Revolution), Mexico, Panama, Turkey, China, and many other places. It almost always acted independently and minded its own interests.

The Cold War (1945–1991)

When World War II began in 1939, many Americans wanted nothing to do with another foreign war. "America first," they said. On December 7, 1941, Japan attacked the naval base at Pearl Harbor, sank eleven ships, and killed 2,400 men. On that day, the era of standing alone ended.

Less than four years later, large swaths of Europe and Asia lay in rubble. A mind-numbing number of people were dead (estimates vary from thirty-eight to seventy million). When the war ended, in September 1945, the only rival to the United States was the Soviet Union, whose armies occupied the nations of Central Europe. Many observers warned that the Soviets were poised to extend their control. If anyone was going to lead the free world against the Soviet Union, it had to be the United States.

Containment: American Cold War strategy designed to stop the spread of communism.

The Truman administration decided to accept the Soviets' current sphere of influence but to oppose every effort to expand it, a policy known as **containment** (see Figure 18.4). The crucial test came in February 1947. The Democratic administration asked a Republican Congress to pour funds into Greece and Turkey to

U.S. Forces in Europe (1945–2020) Historical View

● **FIGURE 18.4** *U.S. Troop Strength in Europe Since 1945. For fifty years, the United States, operating with its allies (through the North Atlantic Treaty Organization, or NATO), focused on containing the Soviet Union by stationing troops in Europe and elsewhere. Now renewed Russian aggression has U.S. European forces on the rise again. (U.S. European Command; U.S. Department of Defense)* stop them from turning to communism. Legend has it that the chair of the Foreign Relations Committee, Senator Arthur Vandenberg (R-MI), promised to support Truman but gave him a word of advice about rallying the nation: "You are going to have to scare the hell out of the American people."[48] Truman proceeded to do just that in a famous speech before Congress: Regimes of "terror and oppression," said Truman, "exploiting human want and misery" menace the world.[49]

Although the United States retained economic and military primacy, it joined with other nations in **multilateral organizations** dedicated to opposing communism and spreading democracy and capitalism. It broke with its unilateral past to help establish multiple organizations: the United Nations (formed in 1945), the Organization of American States (OAS, 1948), and the North Atlantic Treaty Organization (NATO, 1949). Senator Vandenberg gave the era its famous slogan when he quipped that American party politics "stopped at the water's edge." In other words, Democrats and Republicans would no longer disagree (at least, not too loudly) about international affairs.[50]

Multilateral organization: An international organization of three or more nations organized around a common goal.

All the same, the era posed new and difficult questions for American leaders. Should the United States support brutal dictators if they joined us in fighting communists? Should it resist popular democratic movements if they seemed to tilt toward communism? Where and when should we send troops? Each of these questions eventually escalated into an angry debate. Conservatives defended the fight against "the Evil Empire," as some of them dubbed the Soviet Union. Liberals began to charge that an increasingly knee-jerk fight against the fading threat of communism was leading the United States to repress democratic movements around the world.

The debate grew heated. However, with thousands of American and Soviet missiles still threatening a nuclear holocaust, the Cold War framework remained in place—until Soviet communism suddenly collapsed.

The New World Order (1989–2001)

Around the world, people gaped at the incredible television footage in November 1989. Germans were clambering onto the Berlin Wall and ripping it apart. For almost thirty years, the wall—running through Berlin and separating communist Germany from democratic Germany—had been the symbol of the Cold War. Communist guards had shot people trying to leap to freedom. President John Kennedy had looked out at the wall and declared, "All free [people], wherever they may live, are citizens of Berlin." Ronald Reagan had stood on the same spot and challenged the Soviet leader, "Mr. Gorbachev, tear down this wall." Now the East German guards watched awkwardly, uncertain what to do, as the delirious mob tore it down themselves. Within two years, the entire Soviet empire collapsed. The framework that had guided American foreign policy for more than fifty years was suddenly irrelevant. What next?

President George H. W. Bush proclaimed "a new world order." He touted an active, multilateral march toward free markets and democracy. On his right, a group of so-called "neoconservatives" began to press for a more muscular foreign

● *One of history's turning points: Jubilant Berliners climb the Berlin Wall as communism collapses. Suddenly, American foreign policymakers needed an entirely new grand strategy.*

policy. The United States should use its unchallenged military strength to make the world more peaceful, democratic, and secure, this group argued. If allies did not want to get on board, they should just get out of our way.

The War on Terror (2001–2009)

The 9/11 attacks killed almost three thousand people. The attacks shut down American institutions from coast to coast—financial markets in New York, Disney World in Florida, the great arch in St. Louis, and air travel across American airspace (for five days). In the stunned aftermath, the George W. Bush administration constructed a formidable new foreign policy framework. To define the attacks as a crime would have brought in the American justice system. Instead, the administration declared them an act of war and responded with a "war on terror." That choice changed America's role in the world.

The War on Terror targeted terrorists, nations that harbored terrorists, and any organizations that assisted terrorists. Opponents charged that a war on terror would become an endless conflict against an amorphous foe and would, in the long run, weaken the United States by undermining its bedrock values—liberty and the rule of law (we discussed this debate in Chapter 5, on civil liberties).

During the Cold War, the United States operated on the theory of *deterrence:* build a military so overpowering—including nuclear weapons—that other nations will be afraid to attack. Deterrence is aimed at other governments. However, the strategy does not work with extremists who are willing to sacrifice their lives for a cause.

Preemptive war: The effort to attack hostile powers before they launch attacks. Highly controversial because it sanctions striking first.

What can be done against such fanatics? President George W. Bush proclaimed a strategy of **preemptive war**. As the president explained it at West Point, "Deterrence—the promise of massive retaliation against nations—means nothing against shadowy terrorist networks with no nation or citizens to defend." The United States, he continued, had to eliminate threats "before they emerge."[51]

In responding, often preemptively, to terrorist threats, the United States launched long and costly wars in Afghanistan and Iraq; it launched air strikes or sent special forces into Libya, Syria, Yemen, Cameroon, and many other hot spots. However, in tackling terrorist threats, conventional means of warfare, such as invading another country, prove less effective than policing measures, such as gathering intelligence and punishing criminal behavior.

In the aftermath of the terrorist attacks on 9/11, the administration and Congress created the Homeland Security Act, which set in motion one of the largest government reorganizations since the creation of the Department of Defense in 1947. The act created the Department of Homeland Security, which has more than 210,000 employees and twenty-four subordinate agencies ranging from Immigration and Customs Enforcement (ICE) to the Secret Service protecting the president. Related legislation, the USA Patriot Act, gave police and security personnel far more latitude to monitor, search, and detain suspects both abroad and at home.

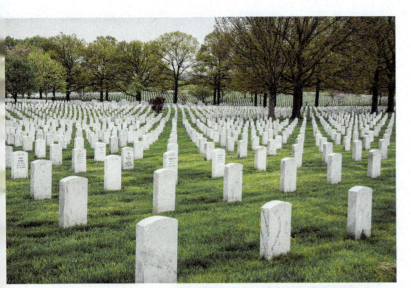

● *Arlington National Cemetery holds the remains of soldiers from every American war. It reminds us that foreign policy reflects America's deepest values and convictions—and often calls for the nation's greatest sacrifices.*

The War on Terror agencies live on, as part of the national bureaucracy and as voices in foreign policy debates. The Obama administration, however, stopped using the term "War on Terror," and lowered the rhetorical temperature. Fighting terror—with intelligence, drone strikes, and special forces—remained important but no longer defined the United States' role in the world.

THE BOTTOM LINE

» The United States forged four grand strategies in the twentieth century: It stood alone and acted unilaterally (1918–39), it led the democratic nations in multilateral coalitions during the Cold War (1945–91), it debated a new world order after the Cold War (1991–2001), and it launched a war on terror (2001–09).

Conclusion: The Next Grand Strategy

Today, American grand strategy is up for grabs. The Obama administration developed a modest foreign policy strategy with four interlocking components: maintain American military and economic primacy ("The Blob" consensus); reduce American military commitments; operate through international organizations ("lead from behind," said the president); and pivot toward Asia.[52]

President Trump came to office with a strong "America First" attitude: realist, deeply impatient with international organizations, and ready to reset relations with undemocratic enemies. Though generally unpopular—in early 2020, Americans rejected Trump's foreign policy by a two-to-one margin in polls[53]—the centralization of global decisions in the White House meant Trump was largely free to act. Immigration, ties with traditional allies including NATO, climate accords, trade deals: On all these and more Trump departed from the Obama grand strategy.[54]

Trump's turbulent foreign policy left many American allies uncertain about the nation's continued commitments. President Biden's foreign policy strategy appears to mix elements of his predecessors: a return to Obama-style multilateralism, reflected in the United States rejoining the Paris Accords on climate change and the World Health Organization, as well as organizing the coalition of nations opposing Russia's actions in Ukraine. At the same time, however, Biden's hallmark "foreign policy for the middle class" at home in the United States has strong echoes of Trump's "America First" economic theme.[55]

How will it all add up? As you reflect on the options, go back to the goals of American foreign policy. Any grand strategy must successfully protect national security, enhance economic well-being, and reflect American values. As you can see, the national discussion about how best to accomplish these goals points in completely different directions—from going it alone to engaging the world and collaborating with others.

No matter what you would choose, remember the basic truth: The next American foreign policy strategy will—like all the past ones—reflect American ideals and values. It will answer the same question raised in every chapter of this book, the deepest question of American politics: *Who are we?*

WHAT DO YOU THINK?

Building a New Grand Strategy

Following the COVID-19 pandemic, American leaders are looking for a new grand strategy in international affairs. We need to organize around a set of ideas—and signal them to the world. What is the most important thing to include?

Emphasize cooperation.
The world faces many kinds of difficulties: global public health, climate change, rogue regimes (like North Korea), terrorism, unfair economic competitors, and Russian flaunting of Ukraine's self-determination. The best approach: Negotiate multilateral agreements that enlist many countries in addressing problems that no nation, no matter how rich or powerful, can solve alone. No nation will get everything it wants, but working together would be best for everyone.

America first.
The United States is the richest and most powerful nation in the world. In pursuit of multilateral agreements, it has permitted other, weaker nations to take advantage. Even if all nations benefit from free trade, the United States has still seen loss of its manufacturing base—hurting the nation and its communities in the long run. Moreover, the world is a dangerous place with many actors who respond only to direct threats of force. This will mean scaling back some ambitions—such as ending global warming—but, even there, we can lead by example.

Mix and match.
A successful doctrine has to be flexible and apply in many kinds of situations. Can you think of a way to combine these two? Or is there some other priority encountered in this chapter—perhaps American values, or Hamiltonian foreign policy—that you would include in your grand strategy?

CHAPTER SUMMARY

★ Foreign policy explores how America engages the world. Is the United States the richest and most powerful country, prepared to lead the world, or is it a declining superpower that should restore its own society to health?

★ The three goals of U.S. foreign policy are security, prosperity, and spreading American values. These three goals sometimes conflict.

★ The United States spends as much on its military as do other leading powers combined. Primacy suggests that it should act with unparalleled power. The security trap suggests that an effort to achieve and maintain primacy builds resentments and resistance. Soft power leads instead through culture and values.

★ The United States is responsible for a fifth of the world economy and is the largest economy in the world. However, China's economic growth rate in recent years has been much higher than that of the United States. The rivalry between the United States and China is growing.

⭐ U.S. economic policy for decades revolved around free trade—reducing barriers to trade between nations. Today, free trade meets resistance.

⭐ American policymakers face two basic choices: isolationism versus active engagement with the world; unilateralism (going it alone) versus multilateralism (working with other nations in organizations and associations).

⭐ Congress originally shared foreign policy with the executive branch, but today prime responsibility has shifted to the executive. However, foreign policy is best understood in light of domestic policy, as the outcome of many agencies and groups pushing for their own interests and advantage.

⭐ Twentieth-century grand strategies included standing alone (1918–39), primacy in a coalition of anticommunist nations (1946–89), the search for a new world order (1991–2001), and the War on Terror (2001–09); a new consensus is up for grabs.

⭐ One key question of contemporary foreign policy is whether war makes the United States more secure or whether pursuing security has compromised American values and harmed America's stance in the world.

KEY TERMS

American exceptionalism, p. 620
Containment, p. 634
Fair trade, p. 617
Free trade, p. 617
Grand strategy, p. 633
Internationalism, p. 623
Isolationism, p. 623
Liberalism, p. 612

Multilateralism, p. 624
Multilateral organization, p. 635
Preemptive war, p. 636
Primacy, p. 610
Protectionism, p. 617
Realism, p. 610
Security trap, p. 612
Soft power, p. 613

Strategic disengagement, p. 623
Theory of democratic peace, p. 621
Trade deficit, p. 616
Unilateralism, p. 624
War Powers Act, p. 627
World Trade Organization (WTO), p. 617

STUDY QUESTIONS

1. Name the three foreign policy goals that the United States pursues. Discuss the relative importance of each goal. If you had to stress one, which would it be?
2. What do you consider the most important threat to American security? Would it be a traditional threat like foreign enemies, a recent phenomenon like the COVID-19 pandemic, or a longer-term problem such as global climate change? Explain your thinking.
3. What is free trade? Describe the difference between free trade and fair trade.
4. Describe "American exceptionalism." Do you consider it a truth, a myth, or something in between? Defend your answer.
5. Define strategic disengagement and internationalism. Pick one perspective and defend it.

6. Define unilateralism and multilateralism. Which position makes more sense to you? Explain why.
7. List a few main ways that U.S. foreign policy changed with the shifts in presidential administrations, first from Obama to Trump and then from Trump to Biden. In your view, does the U.S. president have too much power to change American foreign affairs? Too little? About the right amount?
8. We described four approaches to foreign policy: Wilsonian, Hamiltonian, Jeffersonian, and Jacksonian. Describe each. Defend the one that most appeals to you.
9. What four grand strategies did the United States pursue in the twentieth century? Describe each.
10. If you had to design a grand strategy for today, what would you emphasize?

The Declaration of Independence

When in the course of human events, it becomes necessary for one people to dissolve the political bands which have connected them with another, and to assume, among the powers of the earth, the separate and equal station to which the Laws of Nature and of Nature's God entitle them, a decent respect to the opinions of mankind requires that they should declare the causes which impel them to the separation.

We hold these truths to be self-evident, that all men are created equal, that they are endowed by their Creator with certain unalienable Rights, that among these are life, liberty and the pursuit of happiness. That to secure these rights, governments are instituted among men, deriving their just powers from the consent of the governed; that whenever any form of government becomes destructive of these ends, it is the right of the people to alter or to abolish it, and to institute new Government, laying its foundation on such principles and organizing its powers in such form, as to them shall seem most likely to effect their safety and happiness. Prudence, indeed, will dictate that Governments long established should not be changed for light and transient causes; and, accordingly, all experience hath shown, that mankind are more disposed to suffer, while evils are sufferable, than to right themselves by abolishing the forms to which they are accustomed. But when a long train of abuses and usurpations, pursuing invariably the same object evinces a design to reduce them under absolute despotism, it is their right, it is their duty, to throw off such government, and to provide new guards for their future security. Such has been the patient sufferance of these colonies; and such is now the necessity which constrains them to alter their former systems of government. The history of the present King of Great Britain is a history of repeated injuries and usurpations, all having in direct object the establishment of an absolute tyranny over these States. To prove this, let facts be submitted to a candid world:

He has refused his assent to laws, the most wholesome and necessary for the public good.

He has forbidden his governors to pass laws of immediate and pressing importance, unless suspended in their operation till his assent should be obtained; and, when so suspended, he has utterly neglected to attend to them.

He has refused to pass other laws for the accommodation of large districts of people, unless those people would relinquish the right of representation in the legislature, a right inestimable to them and formidable to tyrants only.

He has called together legislative bodies at places unusual, uncomfortable, and distant from the depository of their public records, for the sole purpose of fatiguing them into compliance with his measures.

He has dissolved representative houses repeatedly, for opposing with manly firmness his invasions on the rights of the people.

He has refused for a long time, after such dissolutions, to cause others to be elected; whereby the legislative powers, incapable of annihilation, have returned to the People at large for their exercise; the State remaining in the mean time exposed to all the dangers of invasion from without, and convulsions within.

He has endeavored to prevent the population of these States; for that purpose obstructing the laws for naturalization of foreigners; refusing to pass others to encourage their migrations hither, and raising the conditions of new appropriations of lands.

He has obstructed the administration of justice, by refusing his assent to laws for establishing judiciary powers.

He has made judges dependent on his will alone, for the tenure of their offices, and the amount and payment of their salaries.

He has erected a multitude of new offices, and sent hither swarms of officers to harass our people, and eat out their substance.

He has kept among us, in times of peace, standing armies without the consent of our legislatures.

He has affected to render the Military independent of, and superior to, the civil power.

He has combined with others to subject us to a jurisdiction foreign to our constitution and unacknowledged by our laws; giving his assent to their acts of pretended legislation:

For quartering large bodies of armed troops among us;

For protecting them, by a mock trial, from punishment for any murders which they should commit on the inhabitants of these States;

For cutting off our trade with all parts of the world;

For imposing taxes on us without our Consent;

For depriving us, in many cases, of the benefits of Trial by Jury;

For transporting us beyond Seas to be tried for pretended offences;

For abolishing the free System of English Laws in a neighbouring Province, establishing therein an Arbitrary government, and enlarging its Boundaries so as to render it at once an example and fit instrument for introducing the same absolute rule into these colonies;

For taking away our charters, abolishing our most valuable laws, and altering fundamentally the forms of our governments;

For suspending our own legislatures, and declaring themselves invested with power to legislate for us in all cases whatsoever.

He has abdicated government here, by declaring us out of his protection and waging war against us.

He has plundered our seas, ravaged our coasts, burnt our towns, and destroyed the lives of our people.

He is at this time transporting large armies of foreign mercenaries to complete the works of death, desolation and tyranny, already begun with circumstances of cruelty and perfidy scarcely paralleled in the most barbarous ages, and totally unworthy the head of a civilized nation.

He has constrained our fellow citizens taken captive on the high seas to bear arms against their country, to become the executioners of their friends and brethren, or to fall themselves by their hands.

He has excited domestic insurrections amongst us, and has endeavored to bring on the inhabitants of our frontiers, the merciless Indian savages, whose known rule of warfare, is an undistinguished destruction of all ages, sexes and conditions.

In every stage of these oppressions we have petitioned for redress in the most humble terms; our repeated petitions have been answered only by repeated injury. A prince whose character is thus marked by every act which may define a tyrant, is unfit to be the ruler of a free people.

Nor have we been wanting in attentions to our British brethren. We have warned them from time to time of attempts by their legislature to extend an unwarrantable jurisdiction over us. We have reminded them of the circumstances of our emigration and settlement here. We have appealed to their native justice and magnanimity, and we have conjured them by the ties of our common kindred to disavow these usurpations, which, would inevitably interrupt our connections and correspondence. They, too, have been deaf to the voice of justice and of consanguinity. We must, therefore, acquiesce in the necessity, which denounces our separation, and hold them, as we hold the rest of mankind, enemies in war, in peace friends.

We, therefore, the representatives of the United States of America, in general Congress, assembled, appealing to the Supreme Judge of the world for the rectitude of our intentions, do, in the name, and by the authority of the good people of these colonies, solemnly publish and declare, that these united colonies are, and of right ought to be free and independent states; that they are absolved from all allegiance to the British Crown, and that all political connection between them and the state of Great Britain, is and ought to be totally dissolved; and that, as free and independent states, they have full power to levy war, conclude peace, contract alliances, establish commerce, and to do all other acts and things which independent states may of right do. And for the support of this declaration, with a firm reliance on the protection of Divine Providence, we mutually pledge to each other our lives, our fortunes and our sacred honor.

The Constitution of the United States of America

We the People of the United States, in Order to form a more perfect Union, establish Justice, insure domestic Tranquility, provide for the common defence, promote the general Welfare, and secure the Blessings of Liberty to ourselves and our Posterity, do ordain and establish this Constitution for the United States of America.

Article I

Section 1

All legislative Powers herein granted shall be vested in a Congress of the United States, which shall consist of a Senate and House of Representatives.

Section 2

The House of Representatives shall be composed of Members chosen every second Year by the People of the several States, and the Electors in each State shall have the Qualifications requisite for Electors of the most numerous Branch of the State Legislature.

No Person shall be a Representative who shall not have attained to the Age of twenty five Years, and been seven Years a Citizen of the United States, and who shall not, when elected, be an Inhabitant of that State in which he shall be chosen.

Representatives [and direct Taxes]* shall be apportioned among the several States [which may be included within this Union, according to their respective Numbers, which shall be determined by adding to the whole Number of free Persons, including those bound to Service for a Term of Years, and excluding Indians not taxed, three fifths of all other Persons].** The actual Enumeration shall be made within three Years after the first Meeting of the Congress of the United States, and within every subsequent Term of ten Years, in such Manner as they shall by Law direct. The Number of Representatives shall not exceed one for every thirty Thousand, but each State shall have at Least one Representative; and until such enumeration shall be made, the State of New Hampshire shall be entitled to choose three, Massachusetts eight, Rhode-Island and Providence Plantations one, Connecticut five, New York six, New Jersey four, Pennsylvania eight, Delaware one, Maryland six, Virginia ten, North Carolina five, South Carolina five, and Georgia three.

When vacancies happen in the Representation from any State, the Executive Authority thereof shall issue Writs of Election to fill such Vacancies.

The House of Representatives shall choose their Speaker and other Officers; and shall have the sole Power of Impeachment.

---

* Modified by the Sixteenth Amendment.
** Negated by the Fourteenth Amendment.

Section 3

The Senate of the United States shall be composed of two Senators from each State, chosen [by the Legislature thereof]* for six Years; and each Senator shall have one Vote.

Immediately after they shall be assembled in Consequence of the first Election, they shall be divided as equally as may be into three Classes. The Seats of the Senators of the first Class shall be vacated at the Expiration of the second Year, of the second Class at the Expiration of the fourth Year, and of the third Class at the Expiration of the sixth Year, so that one third may be chosen every second Year, [and if Vacancies happen by Resignation, or otherwise, during the Recess of the Legislature of any State, the Executive thereof may make temporary Appointments until the next Meeting of the Legislature, which shall then fill such Vacancies].**

No Person shall be a Senator who shall not have attained to the Age of thirty Years, and been nine Years a Citizen of the United States, and who shall not, when elected, be an Inhabitant of that State for which he shall be chosen.

The Vice President of the United States shall be President of the Senate, but shall have no Vote, unless they be equally divided.

The Senate shall choose their other Officers, and also a President pro tempore, in the Absence of the Vice President, or when he shall exercise the Office of President of the United States.

The Senate shall have the sole Power to try all Impeachments. When sitting for that Purpose, they shall be on Oath or Affirmation. When the President of the United States is tried, the Chief Justice shall preside: And no Person shall be convicted without the Concurrence of two thirds of the Members present.

Judgment in Cases of Impeachment shall not extend further than to removal from Office, and disqualification to hold and enjoy any Office of honor, Trust or Profit under the United States: but the Party convicted shall nevertheless be liable and subject to Indictment, Trial, Judgment and Punishment, according to Law.

Section 4

The Times, Places and Manner of holding Elections for Senators and Representatives, shall be prescribed in each State by the Legislature thereof; but the Congress may at any time by Law make or alter such Regulations, except as to the Places of chusing Senators.

[The Congress shall assemble at least once in every Year, and such Meeting shall be on the first Monday in December, unless they shall by Law appoint a different Day.]***

Section 5

Each House shall be the Judge of the Elections, Returns and Qualifications of its own Members, and a Majority of each shall constitute a Quorum to do Business; but a smaller Number may adjourn from day to day, and may be authorized to compel the Attendance of absent Members, in such Manner, and under such Penalties as each House may provide.

---

* Changed by the Seventeenth Amendment.
** Modified by the Seventeenth Amendment.
*** Changed to January 3 by the Twentieth Amendment.

Each House may determine the Rules of its Proceedings, punish its Members for disorderly Behaviour, and, with the Concurrence of two thirds, expel a Member.

Each House shall keep a Journal of its Proceedings, and from time to time publish the same, excepting such Parts as may in their Judgment require Secrecy; and the Yeas and Nays of the Members of either House on any question shall, at the Desire of one fifth of those Present, be entered on the Journal.

Neither House, during the Session of Congress, shall, without the Consent of the other, adjourn for more than three days, nor to any other Place than that in which the two Houses shall be sitting.

Section 6

The Senators and Representatives shall receive a Compensation for their Services, to be ascertained by Law, and paid out of the Treasury of the United States. They shall in all Cases, except Treason, Felony and Breach of the Peace, be privileged from Arrest during their Attendance at the Session of their respective Houses, and in going to and returning from the same; and for any Speech or Debate in either House, they shall not be questioned in any other Place.

No Senator or Representative shall, during the Time for which he was elected, be appointed to any civil Office under the Authority of the United States, which shall have been created, or the Emoluments whereof shall have been increased during such time; and no Person holding any Office under the United States, shall be a Member of either House during his Continuance in Office.

Section 7

All Bills for raising Revenue shall originate in the House of Representatives; but the Senate may propose or concur with Amendments as on other Bills.

Every Bill which shall have passed the House of Representatives and the Senate, shall, before it become a Law, be presented to the President of the United States: If he approve he shall sign it, but if not he shall return it, with his Objections to that House in which it shall have originated, who shall enter the Objections at large on their Journal, and proceed to reconsider it. If after such Reconsideration two thirds of that House shall agree to pass the Bill, it shall be sent, together with the Objections, to the other House, by which it shall likewise be reconsidered, and if approved by two thirds of that House, it shall become a Law. But in all such Cases the Votes of both Houses shall be determined by yeas and Nays, and the Names of the Persons voting for and against the Bill shall be entered on the Journal of each House respectively. If any Bill shall not be returned by the President within ten Days (Sundays excepted) after it shall have been presented to him, the Same shall be a Law, in like Manner as if he had signed it, unless the Congress by their Adjournment prevent its Return, in which Case it shall not be a Law.

Every Order, Resolution, or Vote to which the Concurrence of the Senate and House of Representatives may be necessary (except on a question of Adjournment) shall be presented to the President of the United States; and before the Same shall take Effect, shall be approved by him, or being disapproved by him, shall be repassed by two thirds of the Senate and House of Representatives, according to the Rules and Limitations prescribed in the Case of a Bill.

Section 8

The Congress shall have Power

To lay and collect Taxes, Duties, Imposts and Excises, to pay the Debts and provide for the common Defence and general Welfare of the United States; but all Duties, Imposts and Excises shall be uniform throughout the United States;

To borrow Money on the credit of the United States;

To regulate Commerce with foreign Nations, and among the several States, and with the Indian Tribes;

To establish an uniform Rule of Naturalization, and uniform Laws on the subject of Bankruptcies throughout the United States;

To coin Money, regulate the Value thereof, and of foreign Coin, and fix the Standard of Weights and Measures;

To provide for the Punishment of counterfeiting the Securities and current Coin of the United States;

To establish Post Offices and post Roads;

To promote the Progress of Science and useful Arts, by securing for limited Times to Authors and Inventors the exclusive Right to their respective Writings and Discoveries;

To constitute Tribunals inferior to the supreme Court;

To define and punish Piracies and Felonies committed on the high Seas, and Offences against the Law of Nations;

To declare War, grant Letters of Marque and Reprisal, and make Rules concerning Captures on Land and Water;

To raise and support Armies, but no Appropriation of Money to that Use shall be for a longer Term than two Years;

To provide and maintain a Navy;

To make Rules for the Government and Regulation of the land and naval Forces;

To provide for calling forth the Militia to execute the Laws of the Union, suppress Insurrections and repel Invasions;

To provide for organizing, arming, and disciplining the Militia, and for governing such Part of them as may be employed in the Service of the United States, reserving to the States respectively, the Appointment of the Officers, and the Authority of training the Militia according to the discipline prescribed by Congress;

To exercise exclusive Legislation in all Cases whatsoever, over such District (not exceeding ten Miles square) as may, by Cession of particular States, and the Acceptance of Congress, become the Seat of the Government of the United States, and to exercise like Authority over all Places purchased by the Consent of the Legislature of the State in which the Same shall be, for the Erection of Forts, Magazines, Arsenals, dock-Yards, and other needful Buildings;—And

To make all Laws which shall be necessary and proper for carrying into Execution the foregoing Powers, and all other Powers vested by this Constitution in the Government of the United States, or in any Department or Officer thereof.

Section 9

The Migration or Importation of such Persons as any of the States now existing shall think proper to admit, shall not be prohibited by the Congress prior to the Year one thousand eight hundred and eight, but a Tax or duty may be imposed on such Importation, not exceeding ten dollars for each Person.

The Privilege of the Writ of Habeas Corpus shall not be suspended, unless when in Cases of Rebellion or Invasion the public Safety may require it.

No Bill of Attainder or ex post facto Law shall be passed.

[No Capitation, or other direct, Tax shall be laid, unless in Proportion to the Census or enumeration herein before directed to be taken.]*

No Tax or Duty shall be laid on Articles exported from any State.

No Preference shall be given by any Regulation of Commerce or Revenue to the Ports of one State over those of another; nor shall Vessels bound to, or from, one State, be obliged to enter, clear, or pay Duties in another.

No Money shall be drawn from the Treasury, but in Consequence of Appropriations made by Law; and a regular Statement and Account of the Receipts and Expenditures of all public Money shall be published from time to time.

No Title of Nobility shall be granted by the United States: And no Person holding any Office of Profit or Trust under them, shall, without the Consent of the Congress, accept of any present, Emolument, Office, or Title, of any kind whatever, from any King, Prince, or foreign State.

Section 10

No State shall enter into any Treaty, Alliance, or Confederation; grant Letters of Marque and Reprisal; coin Money; emit Bills of Credit; make any Thing but gold and silver Coin a Tender in Payment of Debts; pass any Bill of Attainder, ex post facto Law, or Law impairing the Obligation of Contracts, or grant any Title of Nobility.

No State shall, without the Consent of the Congress, lay any Imposts or Duties on Imports or Exports, except what may be absolutely necessary for executing its inspection Laws: and the net Produce of all Duties and Imposts, laid by any State on Imports or Exports, shall be for the Use of the Treasury of the United States; and all such Laws shall be subject to the Revision and Control of the Congress.

No State shall, without the Consent of Congress, lay any Duty of Tonnage, keep Troops, or Ships of War in time of Peace, enter into any Agreement or Compact with another State, or with a foreign Power, or engage in War, unless actually invaded, or in such imminent Danger as will not admit of delay.

Article II

Section 1

The executive Power shall be vested in a President of the United States of America. He shall hold his Office during the Term of four Years, and, together with the Vice President, chosen for the same Term, be elected, as follows:

Each State shall appoint, in such Manner as the Legislature thereof may direct, a Number of Electors, equal to the whole Number of Senators and Representatives to which the State may be entitled in the Congress: but no Senator or Representative, or Person holding an Office of Trust or Profit under the United States, shall be appointed an Elector.

[The Electors shall meet in their respective States, and vote by Ballot for two Persons, of whom one at least shall not be an Inhabitant of the same State with

---

* Modified by the Sixteenth Amendment.

themselves. And they shall make a List of all the Persons voted for, and of the Number of Votes for each; which List they shall sign and certify, and transmit sealed to the Seat of the Government of the United States, directed to the President of the Senate. The President of the Senate shall, in the Presence of the Senate and House of Representatives, open all the Certificates, and the Votes shall then be counted. The Person having the greatest Number of Votes shall be the President, if such Number be a Majority of the whole Number of Electors appointed; and if there be more than one who have such Majority, and have an equal Number of Votes, then the House of Representatives shall immediately choose by Ballot one of them for President; and if no Person have a Majority, then from the five highest on the List the said House shall in like Manner choose the President. But in choosing the President, the Votes shall be taken by States, the Representation from each State having one Vote; a quorum for this purpose shall consist of a Member or Members from two thirds of the States, and a Majority of all the States shall be necessary to a Choice. In every Case, after the Choice of the President, the Person having the greatest Number of Votes of the Electors shall be the Vice President. But if there should remain two or more who have equal Votes, the Senate shall choose from them by Ballot the Vice President.]*

The Congress may determine the Time of choosing the Electors, and the Day on which they shall give their Votes; which Day shall be the same throughout the United States.

No Person except a natural born Citizen, or a Citizen of the United States, at the time of the Adoption of this Constitution, shall be eligible to the Office of President; neither shall any Person be eligible to that Office who shall not have attained to the Age of thirty five Years, and been fourteen Years a Resident within the United States.

In Case of the Removal of the President from Office, or of his Death, Resignation, or Inability to discharge the Powers and Duties of the said Office, the Same shall devolve on the Vice President, and the Congress may by Law provide for the Case of Removal, Death, Resignation or Inability, both of the President and Vice President, declaring what Officer shall then act as President, and such Officer shall act accordingly, until the Disability be removed, or a President shall be elected.

The President shall, at stated Times, receive for his Services, a Compensation, which shall neither be increased nor diminished during the Period for which he shall have been elected, and he shall not receive within that Period any other Emolument from the United States, or any of them.

Before he enter on the Execution of his Office, he shall take the following Oath or Affirmation:—"I do solemnly swear (or affirm) that I will faithfully execute the Office of President of the United States, and will to the best of my Ability, preserve, protect and defend the Constitution of the United States."

Section 2

The President shall be Commander in Chief of the Army and Navy of the United States, and of the Militia of the several States, when called into the actual Service of the United States; he may require the Opinion, in writing, of the principal Officer in each of the executive Departments, upon any Subject

---

* Changed by the Twelfth and Twentieth Amendments.

relating to the Duties of their respective Offices, and he shall have Power to grant Reprieves and Pardons for Offences against the United States, except in Cases of Impeachment.

He shall have Power, by and with the Advice and Consent of the Senate, to make Treaties, provided two thirds of the Senators present concur; and he shall nominate, and by and with the Advice and Consent of the Senate, shall appoint Ambassadors, other public Ministers and Consuls, Judges of the supreme Court, and all other Officers of the United States, whose Appointments are not herein otherwise provided for, and which shall be established by Law: but the Congress may by Law vest the Appointment of such inferior Officers, as they think proper, in the President alone, in the Courts of Law, or in the Heads of Departments.

The President shall have Power to fill up all Vacancies that may happen during the Recess of the Senate, by granting Commissions which shall expire at the End of their next Session.

Section 3

He shall from time to time give to the Congress Information of the State of the Union, and recommend to their Consideration such Measures as he shall judge necessary and expedient; he may, on extraordinary Occasions, convene both Houses, or either of them, and in Case of Disagreement between them, with Respect to the Time of Adjournment, he may adjourn them to such Time as he shall think proper; he shall receive Ambassadors and other public Ministers; he shall take Care that the Laws be faithfully executed, and shall Commission all the Officers of the United States.

Section 4

The President, Vice President and all civil Officers of the United States, shall be removed from Office on Impeachment for, and Conviction of, Treason, Bribery, or other high Crimes and Misdemeanors.

Article III

Section 1

The judicial Power of the United States shall be vested in one supreme Court, and in such inferior Courts as the Congress may from time to time ordain and establish. The Judges, both of the supreme and inferior Courts, shall hold their Offices during good Behaviour, and shall, at stated Times, receive for their Services a Compensation, which shall not be diminished during their Continuance in Office.

Section 2

The judicial Power shall extend to all Cases, in Law and Equity, arising under this Constitution, the Laws of the United States, and Treaties made, or which shall be made, under their Authority;—to all Cases affecting Ambassadors, other public Ministers and Consuls;—to all Cases of admiralty and maritime Jurisdiction;—to Controversies to which the United States shall be a Party;—to Controversies between two or more States;—[between a State and Citizens of another State];—between Citizens of different States;—between Citizens of the same State claiming

Lands under Grants of different States, [and between a State,] or the Citizens thereof, [and foreign States, Citizens or Subjects].*

In all Cases affecting Ambassadors, other public Ministers and Consuls, and those in which a State shall be Party, the supreme Court shall have original Jurisdiction. In all the other Cases before mentioned, the supreme Court shall have appellate Jurisdiction, both as to Law and Fact, with such Exceptions, and under such Regulations as the Congress shall make.

The Trial of all Crimes, except in Cases of Impeachment, shall be by Jury; and such Trial shall be held in the State where the said Crimes shall have been committed; but when not committed within any State, the Trial shall be at such Place or Places as the Congress may by Law have directed.

Section 3

Treason against the United States, shall consist only in levying War against them, or in adhering to their Enemies, giving them Aid and Comfort. No Person shall be convicted of Treason unless on the Testimony of two Witnesses to the same overt Act, or on Confession in open Court.

The Congress shall have Power to declare the Punishment of Treason, but no Attainder of Treason shall work Corruption of Blood, or Forfeiture except during the Life of the Person attainted.

Article IV

Section 1

Full Faith and Credit shall be given in each State to the public Acts, Records, and judicial Proceedings of every other State. And the Congress may by general Laws prescribe the Manner in which such Acts, Records and Proceedings shall be proved, and the Effect thereof.

Section 2

The Citizens of each State shall be entitled to all Privileges and Immunities of Citizens in the several States.

A Person charged in any State with Treason, Felony, or other Crime, who shall flee from Justice, and be found in another State, shall on Demand of the executive Authority of the State from which he fled, be delivered up, to be removed to the State having Jurisdiction of the Crime.

[No Person held to Service or Labour in one State, under the Laws thereof, escaping into another, shall, in Consequence of any Law or Regulation therein, be discharged from such Service or Labour, but shall be delivered up on Claim of the Party to whom such Service or Labour may be due.]**

Section 3

New States may be admitted by the Congress into this Union; but no new State shall be formed or erected within the Jurisdiction of any other State; nor any State be formed by the Junction of two or more States, or Parts of States, without the Consent of the Legislatures of the States concerned as well as of the Congress.

---

* Altered by the Twelfth Amendment.
** Repealed by the Thirteenth Amendment.

The Congress shall have Power to dispose of and make all needful Rules and Regulations respecting the Territory or other Property belonging to the United States; and nothing in this Constitution shall be so construed as to Prejudice any Claims of the United States, or of any particular State.

Section 4

The United States shall guarantee to every State in this Union a Republican Form of Government, and shall protect each of them against Invasion; and on Application of the Legislature, or of the Executive (when the Legislature cannot be convened), against domestic Violence.

Article V

The Congress, whenever two thirds of both Houses shall deem it necessary, shall propose Amendments to this Constitution, or, on the Application of the Legislatures of two thirds of the several States, shall call a Convention for proposing Amendments, which, in either Case, shall be valid to all Intents and Purposes, as Part of this Constitution, when ratified by the Legislatures of three fourths of the several States, or by Conventions in three fourths thereof, as the one or the other Mode of Ratification may be proposed by the Congress; Provided that no Amendment which may be made prior to the Year One thousand eight hundred and eight shall in any Manner affect the first and fourth Clauses in the Ninth Section of the first Article; and that no State, without its Consent, shall be deprived of its equal Suffrage in the Senate.

Article VI

All Debts contracted and Engagements entered into, before the Adoption of this Constitution, shall be as valid against the United States under this Constitution, as under the Confederation.

This Constitution, and the Laws of the United States which shall be made in Pursuance thereof; and all Treaties made, or which shall be made, under the Authority of the United States, shall be the supreme Law of the Land; and the Judges in every State shall be bound thereby, any Thing in the Constitution or Laws of any State to the Contrary notwithstanding.

The Senators and Representatives before mentioned, and the Members of the several State Legislatures, and all executive and judicial Officers, both of the United States and of the several States, shall be bound by Oath or Affirmation, to support this Constitution; but no religious Test shall ever be required as a Qualification to any Office or public Trust under the United States.

Article VII

The Ratification of the Conventions of nine States, shall be sufficient for the Establishment of this Constitution between the States so ratifying the Same.

The Word, "the," being interlined between the seventh and eighth Lines of the first Page, the Word "Thirty" being partly written on an Erazure in the fifteenth Line of the first Page, The Words "is tried" being interlined between the thirty second and thirty third Lines of the first Page and the Word "the" being interlined between the forty third and forty fourth Lines of the second Page.

Attest William Jackson Secretary

Done in Convention by the Unanimous Consent of the States present the Seventeenth Day of September in the Year of our Lord one thousand seven hundred and Eighty seven and of the Independence of the United States of America the Twelfth In witness whereof We have hereunto subscribed our Names,

G°. WASHINGTON
Presidt and deputy from Virginia

Delaware
Geo: Read
Gunning Bedford jun
John Dickinson
Richard Bassett
Jaco: Broom

Maryland
James McHenry
Dan of St Thos. Jenifer
Danl. Carroll

Virginia
John Blair
James Madison Jr.

North Carolina
Wm. Blount
Richd. Dobbs
Spaight
Hu Williamson

South Carolina
J. Rutledge
Charles Cotesworth
Pinckney
Charles Pinckney
Pierce Butler

Georgia
William Few
Abr Baldwin

New Hampshire
John Langdon
Nicholas Gilman

Massachusetts
Nathaniel Gorham
Rufus King

Connecticut
Wm. Saml. Johnson
Roger Sherman

New York
Alexander Hamilton

New Jersey
Wil: Livingston
David Brearley
Wm. Paterson
Jona: Dayton

Pennsylvania
B Franklin
Thomas Mifflin
Robt. Morris
Geo. Clymer
Thos. FitzSimons
Jared Ingersoll
James Wilson
Gouv Morris

Articles

In addition to, and Amendment of the Constitution of the United States of America, proposed by Congress, and ratified by the Legislatures of the several States, pursuant to the fifth Article of the original Constitution.

(The first ten amendments to the U.S. Constitution were ratified December 15, 1791, and form what is known as the "Bill of Rights.")

Amendment I

Congress shall make no law respecting an establishment of religion, or prohibiting the free exercise thereof; or abridging the freedom of speech, or of the press; or the right of the people peaceably to assemble, and to petition the Government for a redress of grievances.

Amendment II

A well regulated Militia, being necessary to the security of a free State, the right of the people to keep and bear Arms, shall not be infringed.

Amendment III

No Soldier shall, in time of peace be quartered in any house, without the consent of the Owner, nor in time of war, but in a manner to be prescribed by law.

Amendment IV

The right of the people to be secure in their persons, houses, papers, and effects, against unreasonable searches and seizures, shall not be violated, and no Warrants shall issue, but upon probable cause, supported by Oath or affirmation, and particularly describing the place to be searched, and the persons or things to be seized.

Amendment V

No person shall be held to answer for a capital, or otherwise infamous crime, unless on a presentment or indictment of a Grand Jury, except in cases arising in the land or naval forces, or in the Militia, when in actual service in time of War or public danger; nor shall any person be subject for the same offence to be twice put in jeopardy of life or limb; nor shall be compelled in any criminal case to be a witness against himself, nor be deprived of life, liberty, or property, without due process of law; nor shall private property be taken for public use, without just compensation.

Amendment VI

In all criminal prosecutions, the accused shall enjoy the right to a speedy and public trial, by an impartial jury of the State and district wherein the crime shall have been committed, which district shall have been previously ascertained by law, and to be informed of the nature and cause of the accusation; to be confronted with the witnesses against him; to have compulsory process for obtaining witnesses in his favor, and to have the Assistance of Counsel for his defence.

Amendment VII

In Suits at common law, where the value in controversy shall exceed twenty dollars, the right of trial by jury shall be preserved, and no fact tried by a jury, shall be otherwise re-examined in any Court of the United States, than according to the rules of the common law.

Amendment VIII

Excessive bail shall not be required, nor excessive fines imposed, nor cruel and unusual punishments inflicted.

Amendment IX

The enumeration in the Constitution, of certain rights, shall not be construed to deny or disparage others retained by the people.

Amendment X

The powers not delegated to the United States by the Constitution, nor prohibited by it to the States, are reserved to the States respectively, or to the people.

Amendment XI

Passed by Congress March 4, 1794. Ratified February 7, 1795.

Note: Article III, Section 2, of the Constitution was modified by Amendment XI.

The Judicial power of the United States shall not be construed to extend to any suit in law or equity, commenced or prosecuted against one of the United States by Citizens of another State, or by Citizens or Subjects of any Foreign State.

Amendment XII

Passed by Congress December 9, 1803. Ratified June 15, 1804.

Note: A portion of Article II, Section 1, of the Constitution was superseded by the Twelfth Amendment.

The Electors shall meet in their respective states and vote by ballot for President and Vice-President, one of whom, at least, shall not be an inhabitant of the same state with themselves; they shall name in their ballots the person voted for as President, and in distinct ballots the person voted for as Vice-President, and they shall make distinct lists of all persons voted for as President, and of all persons voted for as Vice-President, and of the number of votes for each, which lists they shall sign and certify, and transmit sealed to the seat of the government of the United States, directed to the President of the Senate;—the President of the Senate shall, in the presence of the Senate and House of Representatives, open all the certificates and the votes shall then be counted;—The person having the greatest number of votes for President, shall be the President, if such number be a majority of the whole number of Electors appointed; and if no person have such majority, then from the persons having the highest numbers not exceeding three on the list of those voted for as President, the House of Representatives shall choose immediately, by ballot, the President. But in choosing the President, the votes shall be taken by states, the representation from each state having one vote; a quorum for this purpose shall consist of a member or members from two-thirds of the states, and a majority of all the states shall be necessary to a choice. [And if the House of Representatives shall not choose a President whenever the right of choice shall devolve upon them, before the fourth day of March next following, then the Vice-President shall act as President, as in case of the death or other constitutional disability of the President.—]* The person having the greatest number of votes as Vice-President, shall be the Vice-President, if such number be a majority of the whole number of Electors appointed, and if no person have a majority, then from the two highest numbers on the list, the Senate shall choose the Vice-President; a quorum for the purpose shall consist of two-thirds of the whole number of Senators, and a majority of the whole number shall be necessary to a choice. But no person constitutionally ineligible to the office of President shall be eligible to that of Vice-President of the United States.

Amendment XIII

Passed by Congress January 31, 1865. Ratified December 6, 1865.

Note: A portion of Article IV, Section 2, of the Constitution was superseded by the Thirteenth Amendment.

---

* Superseded by Section 3 of the Twentieth Amendment.

Section 1

Neither slavery nor involuntary servitude, except as a punishment for crime whereof the party shall have been duly convicted, shall exist within the United States, or any place subject to their jurisdiction.

Section 2

Congress shall have power to enforce this article by appropriate legislation.

Amendment XIV

Passed by Congress June 13, 1866. Ratified July 9, 1868.

   Note: Article I, Section 2, of the Constitution was modified by Section 2 of the Fourteenth Amendment.

Section 1

All persons born or naturalized in the United States, and subject to the jurisdiction thereof, are citizens of the United States and of the State wherein they reside. No State shall make or enforce any law which shall abridge the privileges or immunities of citizens of the United States; nor shall any State deprive any person of life, liberty, or property, without due process of law; nor deny to any person within its jurisdiction the equal protection of the laws.

Section 2

Representatives shall be apportioned among the several States according to their respective numbers, counting the whole number of persons in each State, excluding Indians not taxed. But when the right to vote at any election for the choice of electors for President and Vice-President of the United States, Representatives in Congress, the Executive and Judicial officers of a State, or the members of the Legislature thereof, is denied to any of the male inhabitants of such State, being twenty-one years of age,* and citizens of the United States, or in any way abridged, except for participation in rebellion, or other crime, the basis of representation therein shall be reduced in the proportion which the number of such male citizens shall bear to the whole number of male citizens twenty-one years of age in such State.

Section 3

No person shall be a Senator or Representative in Congress, or elector of President and Vice-President, or hold any office, civil or military, under the United States, or under any State, who, having previously taken an oath, as a member of Congress, or as an officer of the United States, or as a member of any State legislature, or as an executive or judicial officer of any State, to support the Constitution of the United States, shall have engaged in insurrection or rebellion against the same, or given aid or comfort to the enemies thereof. But Congress may by a vote of two-thirds of each House, remove such disability.

Section 4

The validity of the public debt of the United States, authorized by law, including debts incurred for payment of pensions and bounties for services in suppressing

---

* Changed by Section 1 of the Twenty-sixth Amendment.

insurrection or rebellion, shall not be questioned. But neither the United States nor any State shall assume or pay any debt or obligation incurred in aid of insurrection or rebellion against the United States, or any claim for the loss or emancipation of any slave; but all such debts, obligations and claims shall be held illegal and void.

Section 5

The Congress shall have the power to enforce, by appropriate legislation, the provisions of this article.

Amendment XV

Passed by Congress February 26, 1869. Ratified February 3, 1870.

Section 1

The right of citizens of the United States to vote shall not be denied or abridged by the United States or by any State on account of race, color, or previous condition of servitude.

Section 2

The Congress shall have the power to enforce this article by appropriate legislation.

Amendment XVI

Passed by Congress July 2, 1909. Ratified February 3, 1913.

Note: Article I, Section 9, of the Constitution was modified by Amendment XVI.

The Congress shall have power to lay and collect taxes on incomes, from whatever source derived, without apportionment among the several States, and without regard to any census or enumeration.

Amendment XVII

Passed by Congress May 13, 1912. Ratified April 8, 1913.

Note: Article I, Section 3, of the Constitution was modified by the Seventeenth Amendment.

The Senate of the United States shall be composed of two Senators from each State, elected by the people thereof, for six years; and each Senator shall have one vote. The electors in each State shall have the qualifications requisite for electors of the most numerous branch of the State legislatures.

When vacancies happen in the representation of any State in the Senate, the executive authority of such State shall issue writs of election to fill such vacancies: Provided, That the legislature of any State may empower the executive thereof to make temporary appointments until the people fill the vacancies by election as the legislature may direct.

This amendment shall not be so construed as to affect the election or term of any Senator chosen before it becomes valid as part of the Constitution.

Amendment XVIII

Passed by Congress December 18, 1917. Ratified January 16, 1919. Repealed by Amendment XXI.

Section 1

After one year from the ratification of this article the manufacture, sale, or transportation of intoxicating liquors within, the importation thereof into, or the exportation thereof from the United States and all territory subject to the jurisdiction thereof for beverage purposes is hereby prohibited.

Section 2

The Congress and the several States shall have concurrent power to enforce this article by appropriate legislation.

Section 3

This article shall be inoperative unless it shall have been ratified as an amendment to the Constitution by the legislatures of the several States, as provided in the Constitution, within seven years from the date of the submission hereof to the States by the Congress.

Amendment XIX

Passed by Congress June 4, 1919. Ratified August 18, 1920.

The right of citizens of the United States to vote shall not be denied or abridged by the United States or by any State on account of sex.

Congress shall have power to enforce this article by appropriate legislation.

Amendment XX

Passed by Congress March 2, 1932. Ratified January 23, 1933.

Note: Article I, Section 4, of the Constitution was modified by Section 2 of this amendment. In addition, a portion of the Twelfth Amendment was superseded by Section 3.

Section 1

The terms of the President and the Vice President shall end at noon on the 20th day of January, and the terms of Senators and Representatives at noon on the 3d day of January, of the years in which such terms would have ended if this article had not been ratified; and the terms of their successors shall then begin.

Section 2

The Congress shall assemble at least once in every year, and such meeting shall begin at noon on the 3d day of January, unless they shall by law appoint a different day.

Section 3

If, at the time fixed for the beginning of the term of the President, the President elect shall have died, the Vice President elect shall become President. If a President shall not have been chosen before the time fixed for the beginning of his term, or if the President elect shall have failed to qualify, then the Vice President elect shall act as President until a President shall have qualified; and the Congress may by law provide for the case wherein neither a President elect nor a Vice President shall have qualified, declaring who shall then act as President, or the manner in which one who is to act shall be selected, and such person shall act accordingly until a President or Vice President shall have qualified.

Section 4

The Congress may by law provide for the case of the death of any of the persons from whom the House of Representatives may choose a President whenever the right of choice shall have devolved upon them, and for the case of the death of any of the persons from whom the Senate may choose a Vice President whenever the right of choice shall have devolved upon them.

Section 5

Sections 1 and 2 shall take effect on the 15th day of October following the ratification of this article.

Section 6

This article shall be inoperative unless it shall have been ratified as an amendment to the Constitution by the legislatures of three-fourths of the several States within seven years from the date of its submission.

Amendment XXI

Passed by Congress February 20, 1933. Ratified December 5, 1933.

Section 1

The eighteenth article of amendment to the Constitution of the United States is hereby repealed.

Section 2

The transportation or importation into any State, Territory, or Possession of the United States for delivery or use therein of intoxicating liquors, in violation of the laws thereof, is hereby prohibited.

Section 3

This article shall be inoperative unless it shall have been ratified as an amendment to the Constitution by conventions in the several States, as provided in the Constitution, within seven years from the date of the submission hereof to the States by the Congress.

Amendment XXII

Passed by Congress March 21, 1947. Ratified February 27, 1951.

Section 1

No person shall be elected to the office of the President more than twice, and no person who has held the office of President, or acted as President, for more than two years of a term to which some other person was elected President shall be elected to the office of President more than once. But this Article shall not apply to any person holding the office of President when this Article was proposed by Congress, and shall not prevent any person who may be holding the office of President, or acting as President, during the term within which this Article becomes operative from holding the office of President or acting as President during the remainder of such term.

Section 2

This article shall be inoperative unless it shall have been ratified as an amendment to the Constitution by the legislatures of three-fourths of the several States within seven years from the date of its submission to the States by the Congress.

Amendment XXIII

Passed by Congress June 16, 1960. Ratified March 29, 1961.

Section 1

The District constituting the seat of Government of the United States shall appoint in such manner as Congress may direct:

A number of electors of President and Vice President equal to the whole number of Senators and Representatives in Congress to which the District would be entitled if it were a State, but in no event more than the least populous State; they shall be in addition to those appointed by the States, but they shall be considered, for the purposes of the election of President and Vice President, to be electors appointed by a State; and they shall meet in the District and perform such duties as provided by the twelfth article of amendment.

Section 2

The Congress shall have power to enforce this article by appropriate legislation.

Amendment XXIV

Passed by Congress August 27, 1962. Ratified January 23, 1964.

Section 1

The right of citizens of the United States to vote in any primary or other election for President or Vice President, for electors for President or Vice President, or for Senator or Representative in Congress, shall not be denied or abridged by the United States or any State by reason of failure to pay poll tax or other tax.

Section 2

The Congress shall have power to enforce this article by appropriate legislation.

Amendment XXV

Passed by Congress July 6, 1965. Ratified February 10, 1967.

Note: Article II, Section 1, of the Constitution was affected by the Twenty-Fifth Amendment.

Section 1

In case of the removal of the President from office or of his death or resignation, the Vice President shall become President.

Section 2

Whenever there is a vacancy in the office of the Vice President, the President shall nominate a Vice President who shall take office upon confirmation by a majority vote of both Houses of Congress.

Section 3

Whenever the President transmits to the President pro tempore of the Senate and the Speaker of the House of Representatives his written declaration that he is unable to discharge the powers and duties of his office, and until he transmits to them a written declaration to the contrary, such powers and duties shall be discharged by the Vice President as Acting President.

Section 4

Whenever the Vice President and a majority of either the principal officers of the executive departments or of such other body as Congress may by law provide, transmit to the President pro tempore of the Senate and the Speaker of the House of Representatives their written declaration that the President is unable to discharge the powers and duties of his office, the Vice President shall immediately assume the powers and duties of the office as Acting President.

Thereafter, when the President transmits to the President pro tempore of the Senate and the Speaker of the House of Representatives his written declaration that no inability exists, he shall resume the powers and duties of his office unless the Vice President and a majority of either the principal officers of the executive department or of such other body as Congress may by law provide, transmit within four days to the President pro tempore of the Senate and the Speaker of the House of Representatives their written declaration that the President is unable to discharge the powers and duties of his office. Thereupon Congress shall decide the issue, assembling within forty-eight hours for that purpose if not in session. If the Congress, within twenty-one days after receipt of the latter written declaration, or, if Congress is not in session, within twenty-one days after Congress is required to assemble, determines by two-thirds vote of both Houses that the President is unable to discharge the powers and duties of his office, the Vice President shall continue to discharge the same as Acting President; otherwise, the President shall resume the powers and duties of his office.

Amendment XXVI

Passed by Congress March 23, 1971. Ratified July 1, 1971.

Note: Amendment XIV, Section 2, of the Constitution was modified by Section 1 of the Twenty-Sixth Amendment.

Section 1

The right of citizens of the United States, who are eighteen years of age or older, to vote shall not be denied or abridged by the United States or by any State on account of age.

Section 2

The Congress shall have power to enforce this article by appropriate legislation.

Amendment XXVII

Originally proposed Sept. 25, 1789. Ratified May 7, 1992.

No law, varying the compensation for the services of the Senators and Representatives, shall take effect, until an election of representatives shall have intervened.

APPENDIX III

THE FEDERALIST PAPERS

By Alexander Hamilton, James Madison, John Jay

The debate over ratifying the Constitution in 1787–8 was very close, especially in New York. To persuade the people of the state, Hamilton, Madison, and Jay wrote eighty-five newspaper essays arguing for ratification. Three of the most influential, reproduced here, are Federalist Papers 1, 10, and 51.

FEDERALIST No. 1

General Introduction
For the Independent Journal. Saturday, October 27, 1787

HAMILTON
To the People of the State of New York:

AFTER an unequivocal experience of the inefficacy of the subsisting federal government, you are called upon to deliberate on a new Constitution for the United States of America. The subject speaks its own importance; comprehending in its consequences nothing less than the existence of the UNION, the safety and welfare of the parts of which it is composed, the fate of an empire in many respects the most interesting in the world. It has been frequently remarked that it seems to have been reserved to the people of this country, by their conduct and example, to decide the important question, whether societies of men are really capable or not of establishing good government from reflection and choice, or whether they are forever destined to depend for their political constitutions on accident and force. If there be any truth in the remark, the crisis at which we are arrived may with propriety be regarded as the era in which that decision is to be made; and a wrong election of the part we shall act may, in this view, deserve to be considered as the general misfortune of mankind.

This idea will add the inducements of philanthropy to those of patriotism, to heighten the solicitude which all considerate and good men must feel for the event. Happy will it be if our choice should be directed by a judicious estimate of our true interests, unperplexed and unbiased by considerations not connected with the public good. But this is a thing more ardently to be wished than seriously to be expected. The plan offered to our deliberations affects too many particular interests, innovates upon too many local institutions, not to involve in its discussion a variety of objects foreign to its merits, and of views, passions and prejudices little favorable to the discovery of truth.

Among the most formidable of the obstacles which the new Constitution will have to encounter may readily be distinguished the obvious interest of a certain class of men in every State to resist all changes which may hazard a diminution of the power, emolument, and consequence of the offices they hold under the State establishments; and the perverted ambition of another class of men, who will either hope to aggrandize themselves by the confusions of their country, or will flatter themselves with fairer prospects of elevation from the subdivision of the empire into several partial confederacies than from its union under one government.

It is not, however, my design to dwell upon observations of this nature. I am well aware that it would be disingenuous to resolve indiscriminately the opposition of any set of men (merely because their situations might subject them to suspicion) into interested or ambitious views. Candor will oblige us to admit that even such men may be actuated by upright intentions; and it cannot be doubted that much of the opposition which has made its appearance, or may hereafter make its appearance, will spring from sources, blameless at least, if not respectable—the honest errors of minds led astray by preconceived jealousies and fears. So numerous indeed and so powerful are the causes which serve to give a false bias to the judgment, that we, upon many occasions, see wise and good men on the wrong as well as on the right side of questions of the first magnitude to society. This circumstance, if duly attended to, would furnish a lesson of moderation to those who are ever so much persuaded of their being in the right in any controversy. And a further reason for caution, in this respect, might be drawn from the reflection that we are not always sure that those who advocate the truth are influenced by purer principles than their antagonists. Ambition, avarice, personal animosity, party opposition, and many other motives not more laudable than these, are apt to operate as well upon those who support as those who oppose the right side of a question. Were there not even these inducements to moderation, nothing could be more ill-judged than that intolerant spirit which has, at all times, characterized political parties. For in politics, as in religion, it is equally absurd to aim at making proselytes by fire and sword. Heresies in either can rarely be cured by persecution.

And yet, however just these sentiments will be allowed to be, we have already sufficient indications that it will happen in this as in all former cases of great national discussion. A torrent of angry and malignant passions will be let loose. To judge from the conduct of the opposite parties, we shall be led to conclude that they will mutually hope to evince the justness of their opinions, and to increase the number of their converts by the loudness of their declamations and the bitterness of their invectives. An enlightened zeal for the energy and efficiency of government will be stigmatized as the offspring of a temper fond of despotic power and hostile to the principles of liberty. An over-scrupulous jealousy of danger to the rights of the people, which is more commonly the fault of the head than of the heart, will be represented as mere pretense and artifice, the stale bait for popularity at the expense of the public good. It will be forgotten, on the one hand, that jealousy is the usual concomitant of love, and that the noble enthusiasm of liberty is apt to be infected with a spirit of narrow and illiberal distrust. On the other hand, it will be equally forgotten that the vigor of government is essential to the security of liberty; that, in the contemplation of a sound and well-informed judgment, their interest can never be separated; and that a dangerous ambition more often lurks behind the specious mask of zeal for the rights of the people than under the forbidden appearance of zeal for the firmness and efficiency of government. History will teach us that the former has been found a much more certain road to the introduction of despotism than the latter, and that of those men who have overturned the liberties of republics, the greatest number have begun their career by paying an obsequious court to the people; commencing demagogues, and ending tyrants.

In the course of the preceding observations, I have had an eye, my fellow-citizens, to putting you upon your guard against all attempts, from whatever quarter, to influence your decision in a matter of the utmost moment to your welfare, by any impressions other than those which may result from the evidence of truth. You will, no doubt, at the same time, have collected from the general scope of them, that they proceed from a source not unfriendly to the new Constitution. Yes, my countrymen, I own to you that, after having given it an attentive consideration, I am clearly of opinion it is your interest to adopt it. I am convinced that this is the safest course for your liberty, your dignity, and your happiness. I affect not reserves which I do not feel. I will not amuse you with an appearance of deliberation when I have decided. I frankly acknowledge to you my convictions, and I will freely lay before you the reasons on which they are founded. The consciousness of good intentions disdains ambiguity. I shall not, however, multiply professions on this head. My motives must remain in the depository of my own breast. My arguments will be open to all, and may be judged of by all. They shall at least be offered in a spirit which will not disgrace the cause of truth.

I propose, in a series of papers, to discuss the following interesting particulars:

THE UTILITY OF THE UNION TO YOUR POLITICAL PROSPERITY—THE INSUFFICIENCY OF THE PRESENT CONFEDERATION TO PRESERVE THAT UNION—THE NECESSITY OF A GOVERNMENT AT LEAST EQUALLY

ENERGETIC WITH THE ONE PROPOSED, TO THE ATTAINMENT OF THIS OBJECT—THE CONFORMITY OF THE PROPOSED CONSTITUTION TO THE TRUE PRINCIPLES OF REPUBLICAN GOVERNMENT—ITS ANALOGY TO YOUR OWN STATE CONSTITUTION—and lastly, THE ADDITIONAL SECURITY WHICH ITS ADOPTION WILL AFFORD TO THE PRESERVATION OF THAT SPECIES OF GOVERNMENT, TO LIBERTY, AND TO PROPERTY.

In the progress of this discussion I shall endeavor to give a satisfactory answer to all the objections which shall have made their appearance, that may seem to have any claim to your attention.

It may perhaps be thought superfluous to offer arguments to prove the utility of the UNION, a point, no doubt, deeply engraved on the hearts of the great body of the people in every State, and one, which it may be imagined, has no adversaries. But the fact is, that we already hear it whispered in the private circles of those who oppose the new Constitution, that the thirteen States are of too great extent for any general system, and that we must of necessity resort to separate confederacies of distinct portions of the whole. This doctrine will, in all probability, be gradually propagated, till it has votaries enough to countenance an open avowal of it. For nothing can be more evident, to those who are able to take an enlarged view of the subject, than the alternative of an adoption of the new Constitution or a dismemberment of the Union. It will therefore be of use to begin by examining the advantages of that Union, the certain evils, and the probable dangers, to which every State will be exposed from its dissolution. This shall accordingly constitute the subject of my next address.

PUBLIUS

FEDERALIST No. 10

The Same Subject Continued (The Union as a Safeguard Against Domestic Faction and Insurrection)
From the Daily Advertiser. Thursday, November 22, 1787.

MADISON

To the People of the State of New York:

AMONG the numerous advantages promised by a well constructed Union, none deserves to be more accurately developed than its tendency to break and control the violence of faction. The friend of popular governments never finds himself so much alarmed for their character and fate, as when he contemplates their propensity to this dangerous vice. He will not fail, therefore, to set a due value on any plan which, without violating the principles to which he is attached, provides a proper cure for it. The instability, injustice, and confusion introduced into the public councils, have, in truth, been the mortal diseases under which popular governments have everywhere perished; as they continue to be the favorite and fruitful topics from which the adversaries to liberty derive their most specious declamations. The valuable improvements made by the American constitutions on the popular models, both ancient and modern, cannot certainly be too much admired; but it would be an unwarrantable partiality, to contend that they have as effectually obviated the danger on this side, as was wished and expected. Complaints are everywhere heard from our most considerate and virtuous citizens, equally the friends of public and private faith, and of public and personal liberty, that our governments are too unstable, that the public good is disregarded in the conflicts of rival parties, and that measures are too often decided, not according to the rules of justice and the rights of the minor party, but by the superior force of an interested and overbearing majority. However anxiously we may wish that these complaints had no foundation, the evidence, of known facts will not permit us to deny that they are in some degree true. It will be found, indeed, on a candid review of our situation, that some of the distresses under which we labor have been erroneously charged on the operation of our governments; but it will be found, at the same time, that other causes will not alone account for many of our heaviest misfortunes; and, particularly, for that prevailing and increasing distrust of public engagements, and alarm for private rights, which are echoed from one end of the continent to the other. These must be chiefly, if not wholly, effects of the unsteadiness and injustice with which a factious spirit has tainted our public administrations.

By a faction, I understand a number of citizens, whether amounting to a majority or a minority of the whole, who are united and actuated by some common impulse of passion, or of interest, adversed to the rights of other citizens, or to the permanent and aggregate interests of the community.

There are two methods of curing the mischiefs of faction: the one, by removing its causes; the other, by controlling its effects.

There are again two methods of removing the causes of faction: the one, by destroying the liberty which is essential to its existence; the other, by giving to every citizen the same opinions, the same passions, and the same interests.

It could never be more truly said than of the first remedy, that it was worse than the disease. Liberty is to faction what air is to fire, an aliment without which it instantly expires. But it could not be less folly to abolish liberty, which is essential to political life, because it nourishes faction, than it would be to wish the annihilation of air, which is essential to animal life, because it imparts to fire its destructive agency.

The second expedient is as impracticable as the first would be unwise. As long as the reason of man continues fallible, and he is at liberty to exercise it, different opinions will be formed. As long as the connection subsists between his reason and his self-love, his opinions and his passions will have a reciprocal influence on each other; and the former will be objects to which the latter will attach themselves. The diversity in the faculties of men, from which the rights of property originate, is not less an insuperable obstacle to a uniformity of interests. The protection of these faculties is the first object of government. From the protection of different and unequal faculties of acquiring property, the possession of different degrees and kinds of property immediately results; and from the influence of these on the sentiments and views of the respective proprietors, ensues a division of the society into different interests and parties.

The latent causes of faction are thus sown in the nature of man; and we see them everywhere brought into different degrees of activity, according to the different circumstances of civil society. A zeal for different opinions concerning religion, concerning government, and many other points, as well of speculation as of practice; an attachment to different leaders ambitiously contending for pre-eminence and power; or to persons of other descriptions whose fortunes have been interesting to the human passions, have, in turn, divided mankind into parties, inflamed them with mutual animosity, and rendered them much more disposed to vex and oppress each other than to co-operate for their common good. So strong is this propensity of mankind to fall into mutual animosities, that where no substantial occasion presents itself, the most frivolous and fanciful distinctions have been sufficient to kindle their unfriendly passions and excite their most violent conflicts. But the most common and durable source of factions has been the various and unequal distribution of property. Those who hold and those who are without property have ever formed distinct interests in society. Those who are creditors, and those who are debtors, fall under a like discrimination. A landed interest, a manufacturing interest, a mercantile interest, a moneyed interest, with many lesser interests, grow up of necessity in civilized nations, and divide them into different classes, actuated by different sentiments and views. The regulation of these various and interfering interests forms the principal task of modern legislation, and involves the spirit of party and faction in the necessary and ordinary operations of the government.

No man is allowed to be a judge in his own cause, because his interest would certainly bias his judgment, and, not improbably, corrupt his integrity. With equal, nay with greater reason, a body of men are unfit to be both judges and parties at the same time; yet what are many of the most important acts of legislation, but so many judicial determinations, not indeed concerning the rights of single persons, but concerning the rights of large bodies of citizens? And what are the different classes of legislators but advocates and parties to the causes which they determine? Is a law proposed concerning private debts? It is a question to which the creditors are parties on one side and the debtors on the other. Justice ought to hold the balance between them. Yet the parties are, and must be, themselves the judges; and the most numerous party, or, in other words, the most powerful faction must be expected to prevail. Shall domestic manufactures be encouraged, and in what degree, by restrictions on foreign manufactures? are questions which would be differently decided by the landed and the manufacturing classes, and probably by neither with a sole regard to justice and the public good. The apportionment of taxes on the various descriptions of property is an act which seems to require the most exact impartiality; yet there is, perhaps, no legislative act in which greater opportunity and temptation are given to a predominant party to trample on the rules of justice. Every shilling with which they overburden the inferior number, is a shilling saved to their own pockets.

It is in vain to say that enlightened statesmen will be able to adjust these clashing interests, and render them all subservient to the public good. Enlightened statesmen will not always be at the helm. Nor, in many cases, can such an adjustment be made at all without taking into view indirect and remote considerations, which will rarely prevail over the immediate interest which one party may find in disregarding the rights of another or the good of the whole.

The inference to which we are brought is, that the CAUSES of faction cannot be removed, and that relief is only to be sought in the means of controlling its EFFECTS.

If a faction consists of less than a majority, relief is supplied by the republican principle, which enables the majority to defeat its sinister views by regular vote. It may clog the administration, it may convulse the society; but it will be unable to execute and mask its violence under the forms of the Constitution. When a majority is included in a faction, the form of popular government, on the other hand, enables it to sacrifice to its ruling passion or interest both the public good and the rights of other citizens. To secure the public good and private rights against the danger of such a faction, and at the same time to preserve the spirit and the form of popular government, is then the great object to which our inquiries are directed. Let me add that it is the great desideratum by which this form of government can be rescued from the

opprobrium under which it has so long labored, and be recommended to the esteem and adoption of mankind.

By what means is this object attainable? Evidently by one of two only. Either the existence of the same passion or interest in a majority at the same time must be prevented, or the majority, having such coexistent passion or interest, must be rendered, by their number and local situation, unable to concert and carry into effect schemes of oppression. If the impulse and the opportunity be suffered to coincide, we well know that neither moral nor religious motives can be relied on as an adequate control. They are not found to be such on the injustice and violence of individuals, and lose their efficacy in proportion to the number combined together, that is, in proportion as their efficacy becomes needful.

From this view of the subject it may be concluded that a pure democracy, by which I mean a society consisting of a small number of citizens, who assemble and administer the government in person, can admit of no cure for the mischiefs of faction. A common passion or interest will, in almost every case, be felt by a majority of the whole; a communication and concert result from the form of government itself; and there is nothing to check the inducements to sacrifice the weaker party or an obnoxious individual. Hence it is that such democracies have ever been spectacles of turbulence and contention; have ever been found incompatible with personal security or the rights of property; and have in general been as short in their lives as they have been violent in their deaths. Theoretic politicians, who have patronized this species of government, have erroneously supposed that by reducing mankind to a perfect equality in their political rights, they would, at the same time, be perfectly equalized and assimilated in their possessions, their opinions, and their passions.

A republic, by which I mean a government in which the scheme of representation takes place, opens a different prospect, and promises the cure for which we are seeking. Let us examine the points in which it varies from pure democracy, and we shall comprehend both the nature of the cure and the efficacy which it must derive from the Union.

The two great points of difference between a democracy and a republic are: first, the delegation of the government, in the latter, to a small number of citizens elected by the rest; secondly, the greater number of citizens, and greater sphere of country, over which the latter may be extended.

The effect of the first difference is, on the one hand, to refine and enlarge the public views, by passing them through the medium of a chosen body of citizens, whose wisdom may best discern the true interest of their country, and whose patriotism and love of justice will be least likely to sacrifice it to temporary or partial considerations. Under such a regulation, it may well happen that the public voice, pronounced by the representatives of the people, will be more consonant to the public good than if pronounced by the people themselves, convened for the purpose. On the other hand, the effect may be inverted. Men of factious tempers, of local prejudices, or of sinister designs, may, by intrigue, by corruption, or by other means, first obtain the suffrages, and then betray the interests, of the people. The question resulting is, whether small or extensive republics are more favorable to the election of proper guardians of the public weal; and it is clearly decided in favor of the latter by two obvious considerations:

In the first place, it is to be remarked that, however small the republic may be, the representatives must be raised to a certain number, in order to guard against the cabals of a few; and that, however large it may be, they must be limited to a certain number, in order to guard against the confusion of a multitude. Hence, the number of representatives in the two cases not being in proportion to that of the two constituents, and being proportionally greater in the small republic, it follows that, if the proportion of fit characters be not less in the large than in the small republic, the former will present a greater option, and consequently a greater probability of a fit choice.

In the next place, as each representative will be chosen by a greater number of citizens in the large than in the small republic, it will be more difficult for unworthy candidates to practice with success the vicious arts by which elections are too often carried; and the suffrages of the people being more free, will be more likely to centre in men who possess the most attractive merit and the most diffusive and established characters.

It must be confessed that in this, as in most other cases, there is a mean, on both sides of which inconveniences will be found to lie. By enlarging too much the number of electors, you render the representatives too little acquainted with all their local circumstances and lesser interests; as by reducing it too much, you render him unduly attached to these, and too little fit to comprehend and pursue great and national objects. The federal Constitution forms a happy combination in this respect; the great and aggregate interests being referred to the national, the local and particular to the State legislatures.

The other point of difference is, the greater number of citizens and extent of territory which may be brought within the compass of republican than of democratic government; and it is this circumstance principally which renders factious combinations less to be dreaded in the former than in the latter. The smaller the society, the fewer probably will be the distinct parties and interests composing it; the fewer the distinct parties and interests, the more frequently will a majority be found of the same party; and the smaller the number of individuals composing a majority, and the smaller the compass within which they are placed, the more easily will they concert and execute their plans of oppression. Extend the sphere, and you take in a greater variety of parties and interests; you make it less probable that a majority of the whole will have a common motive to invade the rights of other citizens; or if such a common motive exists, it will be more difficult for all who feel it to discover their own strength, and to act in unison with each other. Besides other impediments, it may be remarked that, where there is a consciousness of unjust or dishonorable purposes, communication is always checked by distrust in proportion to the number whose concurrence is necessary.

Hence, it clearly appears, that the same advantage which a republic has over a democracy, in controlling the effects of faction, is enjoyed by a large over a small republic,—is enjoyed by the Union over the States composing it. Does the advantage consist in the substitution of representatives whose enlightened views and virtuous sentiments render them superior to local prejudices and schemes of injustice? It will not be denied that the representation of the Union will be most likely to possess these requisite endowments. Does it consist in the greater security afforded by a greater variety of parties, against the event of any one party being able to outnumber and oppress the rest? In an equal degree does the increased variety of parties comprised within the Union, increase this security. Does it, in fine, consist in the greater obstacles opposed to the concert and accomplishment of the secret wishes of an unjust and interested majority? Here, again, the extent of the Union gives it the most palpable advantage.

The influence of factious leaders may kindle a flame within their particular States, but will be unable to spread a general conflagration through the other States. A religious sect may degenerate into a political faction in a part of the Confederacy; but the variety of sects dispersed over the entire face of it must secure the national councils against any danger from that source. A rage for paper money, for an abolition of debts, for an equal division of property, or for any other improper or wicked project, will be less apt to pervade the whole body of the Union than a particular member of it; in the same proportion as such a malady is more likely to taint a particular county or district, than an entire State.

In the extent and proper structure of the Union, therefore, we behold a republican remedy for the diseases most incident to republican government. And according to the degree of pleasure and pride we feel in being republicans, ought to be our zeal in cherishing the spirit and supporting the character of Federalists.

PUBLIUS

FEDERALIST No. 51

The Structure of the Government Must Furnish the Proper Checks and Balances Between the Different Departments.
For the Independent Journal. Wednesday, February 6, 1788.

MADISON
To the People of the State of New York:

TO WHAT expedient, then, shall we finally resort, for maintaining in practice the necessary partition of power among the several departments, as laid down in the Constitution? The only answer that can be given is, that as all these exterior provisions are found to be inadequate, the defect must be supplied, by so contriving the interior structure of the government as that its several constituent parts may, by their mutual relations, be the means of keeping each other in their proper places. Without presuming to undertake a full development of this important idea, I will hazard a few general observations, which may perhaps place it in a clearer light, and enable us to form a more correct judgment of the principles and structure of the government planned by the convention.

In order to lay a due foundation for that separate and distinct exercise of the different powers of government, which to a certain extent is admitted on all hands to be essential to the preservation of liberty, it is evident that each department should have a will of its own; and consequently should be so constituted that the members of each should have as little agency as possible in the appointment of the members of the others. Were this principle rigorously adhered to, it would require that all the appointments for the supreme executive, legislative, and judiciary magistracies should be drawn from the same fountain of authority, the people, through channels having no communication whatever with one another. Perhaps such a plan of constructing the several departments would be less difficult in practice than it may in contemplation appear. Some difficulties, however, and some additional expense would attend the execution of it. Some deviations, therefore, from the principle must be admitted. In the constitution of the judiciary department in particular, it might be inexpedient to insist rigorously on the principle: first, because peculiar qualifications being essential in the members, the primary consideration ought to be to select that mode of choice which best secures these qualifications; secondly, because the permanent tenure by which the appointments are held in that department, must soon destroy all sense of dependence on the authority conferring them.

It is equally evident, that the members of each department should be as little dependent as possible on those of the others, for the emoluments annexed to their offices. Were the executive magistrate, or the judges, not independent of the legislature in this particular, their independence in every other would be merely nominal.

But the great security against a gradual concentration of the several powers in the same department, consists in giving to those who administer each department the necessary constitutional means and personal motives to resist encroachments of the others. The provision for defense must in this, as in all other cases, be made commensurate to the danger of attack. Ambition must be made to counteract ambition. The interest of the man must be connected with the constitutional rights of the place. It may be a reflection on human nature, that such devices should be necessary to control the abuses of government. But what is government itself, but the greatest of all reflections on human nature? If men were angels, no government would be necessary. If angels were to govern men, neither external nor internal controls on government would be necessary. In framing a government which is to be administered by men over men, the great difficulty lies in this: you must first enable the government to control the governed; and in the next place oblige it to control itself. A dependence on the people is, no doubt, the primary control on the government; but experience has taught mankind the necessity of auxiliary precautions.

This policy of supplying, by opposite and rival interests, the defect of better motives, might be traced through the whole system of human affairs, private as well as public. We see it particularly displayed in all the subordinate distributions of power, where the constant aim is to divide and arrange the several offices in such a manner as that each may be a check on the other—that the private interest of every individual may be a sentinel over the public rights. These inventions of prudence cannot be less requisite in the distribution of the supreme powers of the State.

But it is not possible to give to each department an equal power of self-defense. In republican government, the legislative authority necessarily predominates. The remedy for this inconveniency is to divide the legislature into different branches; and to render them, by different modes of election and different principles of action, as little connected with each other as the nature of their common functions and their common dependence on the society will admit. It may even be necessary to guard against dangerous encroachments by still further precautions. As the weight of the legislative authority requires that it should be thus divided, the weakness of the executive may require, on the other hand, that it should be fortified. An absolute negative on the legislature appears, at first view, to be the natural defense with which the executive magistrate should be armed. But perhaps it would be neither altogether safe nor alone sufficient. On ordinary occasions it might not be exerted with the requisite firmness, and on extraordinary occasions it might be perfidiously abused. May not this defect of an absolute negative be supplied by some qualified connection between this weaker department and the weaker branch of the stronger department, by which the latter may be led to support the constitutional rights of the former, without being too much detached from the rights of its own department?

If the principles on which these observations are founded be just, as I persuade myself they are, and they be applied as a criterion to the several State constitutions, and to the federal Constitution it will be found that if the latter does not perfectly correspond with them, the former are infinitely less able to bear such a test.

There are, moreover, two considerations particularly applicable to the federal system of America, which place that system in a very interesting point of view.

First. In a single republic, all the power surrendered by the people is submitted to the administration of a single government; and the usurpations are guarded against by a division of the government into distinct and separate departments. In the compound republic of America, the power surrendered by the people is first divided between two distinct governments, and then the portion allotted to each subdivided among distinct and separate departments. Hence a double security arises to the rights of the people. The different governments will control each other, at the same time that each will be controlled by itself.

Second. It is of great importance in a republic not only to guard the society against the oppression of its rulers, but to guard one part of the society against the injustice of the other part. Different interests necessarily exist in different classes of citizens. If a majority be united by a common interest, the rights of the minority will be insecure. There are but two methods of providing against this evil: the one by creating a will in the community independent of the majority—that is, of the society itself; the other, by comprehending in the society so many separate descriptions of citizens as will render an unjust combination of a majority of the whole very improbable, if not impracticable. The first method prevails in all governments possessing an hereditary or self-appointed authority. This, at best, is but a precarious security; because a power independent of the society may as well espouse the unjust views of the major, as the rightful interests of the minor party, and may possibly be turned against both parties. The second method will be exemplified in the federal republic of the United States. Whilst all authority in it will be derived from and dependent on the society, the society itself will be broken into so many parts, interests, and classes of citizens, that the rights of individuals, or of the minority, will be in little danger from interested combinations of the majority. In a free government the security for civil rights must be the same as that for religious rights. It consists in the one case in the multiplicity of interests, and in the other in the multiplicity of sects. The degree of security in both cases will depend on the number of interests and sects; and this may be presumed to depend on the extent of country and number of people comprehended under the same government. This view of the subject must particularly recommend a proper federal system to all the sincere and considerate friends of republican government, since it shows that in exact proportion as the territory of the Union may be formed into more circumscribed Confederacies, or States, oppressive combinations of a majority will be facilitated: the best security, under the republican forms, for the rights of every class of citizens, will be diminished: and consequently the stability and independence of some member of the government, the only other security, must be proportionately increased. Justice is the end of government. It is the end of civil society. It ever has been and ever will be pursued until it be obtained, or until liberty be lost in the pursuit. In a society under the forms of which the stronger faction can readily unite and oppress the weaker, anarchy may as truly be said to reign as in a state of nature, where the weaker individual is not secured against the violence of the stronger; and as, in the latter state, even the stronger individuals are prompted, by the uncertainty of their condition, to submit to a government which may protect the weak as well as themselves; so, in the former state, will the more powerful factions or parties be gradually induced, by a like motive, to wish for a government which will protect all parties, the weaker as well as the more powerful. It can be little doubted that if the State of Rhode Island was separated from the Confederacy and left to itself, the insecurity of rights under the popular form of government within such narrow limits would be displayed by such reiterated oppressions of factious majorities that some power altogether independent of the people would soon be called for by the voice of the very factions whose misrule had proved the necessity of it. In the extended republic of the United States, and among the great variety of interests, parties, and sects which it embraces, a coalition of a majority of the whole society could seldom take place on any other principles than those of justice and the general good; whilst there being thus less danger to a minor from the will of a major party, there must be less pretext, also, to provide for the security of the former, by introducing into the government a will not dependent on the latter, or, in other words, a will independent of the society itself. It is no less certain than it is important, notwithstanding the contrary opinions which have been entertained, that the larger the society, provided it lie within a practical sphere, the more duly capable it will be of self-government. And happily for the REPUBLICAN CAUSE, the practicable sphere may be carried to a very great extent, by a judicious modification and mixture of the FEDERAL PRINCIPLE.

PUBLIUS

APPENDIX IV

Presidential Elections, Congressional Control, 1789–2020

KEY: Party abbreviations: Dem = Democrat | DemRep = Democratic Republican | Fed = Federalist
IndRep = Independent Republican | NatRep = National Republican | Rep = Republican

Election Year	Presidential Candidates	Political Party	Electoral Vote	Percentage of Popular Vote	Control of Congress	
					House	Senate
1789	George Washington	None	69	No Popular Vote	Fed	Fed
	John Adams	--	32			
	Others	--	35			
1792	George Washington	None	132	No Popular Vote	DemRep	Fed
	John Adams	--	77			
	Others	--	55			
1796	John Adams	Fed	71	No Popular Vote	Fed	Fed
	Thomas Jefferson	DemRep	68			
	Thomas Pinckney	Fed	59			
	Aaron Burr	DemRep	30			
	Others	--	48			
1800	Thomas Jefferson	DemRep	73	No Popular Vote	DemRep	DemRep
	Aaron Burr	DemRep	73			
	John Adams	Fed	65			
	C. C. Pinkney	Fed	64			
1804	Thomas Jefferson	DemRep	162	No Popular Vote	DemRep	DemRep
	C. C. Pinkney	Fed	14			
1808	James Madison	DemRep	122	No Popular Vote	DemRep	DemRep
	C. C. Pinkney	Fed	47			
1812	James Madison	DemRep	128	No Popular Vote	DemRep	DemRep
	De Witt Clinton	Fed	89			
1816	James Monroe	DemRep	231	No Popular Vote	DemRep	DemRep
	Rufus King	Fed	34			
1820	James Monroe	DemRep	231	No Popular Vote	DemRep	DemRep
	John Q. Adams	IndRep	1			
1824	John Quincy Adams*	DemRep	84	30.5	Pro Adams / Pro Jackson (at midterm)	Pro Jackson
	Andrew Jackson	DemRep	99	43.1		
	Henry Clay	DemRep	37	13.2		
	W. Crawford	DemRep	41	13.1		
1828	Andrew Jackson	Dem	178	56.0	Pro Jackson	Pro Jackson
	John Q. Adams	NatRep	83	44.0		
1832	Andrew Jackson	Dem	219	55.0	Pro Jackson	Opposition / Pro Jackson
	Henry Clay	NatRep	49	42.0		
1836	Martin Van Buren	Dem	170	50.9	Dem	Dem
	William H. Harrison	Whig	73	36.7		
1840	William H. Harrison**	Whig	234	53.1	Whig / Dem (at midterm)	Whig
	Martin Van Buren	Dem	60	46.9		
1844	James K. Polk	Dem	170	49.6	Dem / Whig (at midterm)	Dem
	Henry Clay	Whig	105	48.1		
	James Birney	Liberty (Abolition)	0	2.3		
1848	Zachary Taylor**	Whig	163	47.4	Dem	Dem
	Lewis Cass	Dem	127	42.5		
	Martin Van Buren	Free Soil	0	10.0		
1852	Franklin Pierce	Dem	254	50.9	Dem / Opposition (at midterm)	Dem
	Winfield Scott	Whig	42	44.1		

* Lost the popular vote, won the Electoral College and became president

** Died in office

A-30

Election Year	Presidential Candidates	Political Party	Electoral Vote	Percentage of Popular Vote	Control of Congress	
					House	**Senate**
1856	James Buchanan	Dem	174	45.4	Dem	
	John Fremont	Rep	114	33.0		Dem
	Millard Fillmore	American (Know Nothing)	8	21.6	Rep (at midterm)	
1860	Abraham Lincoln	Rep	180	39.8		
	Stephen Douglas	Dem	12	29.5		
	John Breckinridge	Dem	72	18.1	Rep	Rep
	John Bell	Constitutional Union	79	12.6		
1864	Abraham Lincoln**	Rep	212	55.0	Rep	Rep
	George McClellan	Dem	21	45.0		
1868	Ulysses Grant	Rep	214	52.7	Rep	Rep
	Horatio Seymour	Dem	80	47.3		
1872	Ulysses Grant	Rep	286	55.6	Rep	Rep
	Horace Greeley	Dem	66	43.9	Dem (at midterm)	
1876	Rutherford Hayes*	Rep	185	48.0	Rep	Rep
	Samuel Tilden	Dem	184	51.0	Dem	Dem (at midterm)
1880	James Garfield**	Rep	214	48.3	Rep	
	Winfield Hancock	Dem	155	48.2		Rep
	James Weaver	Greenback-Labor	0	3.4	Dem (at midterm)	
1884	Grover Cleveland	Dem	219	48.5		
	James Blaine	Rep	182	48.2	Dem	Rep
	Benjamin Butler	Greenback-labor		11.8		
1888	Benjamin Harrison*	Rep	233	47.8	Rep	Rep
	Grover Cleveland	Dem	168	48.6	Dem (at midterm)	Rep
1892	Grover Cleveland	Dem	277	46.0	Dem	Dem
	Benjamin Harrison	Rep	145	43.0		
	James Weaver	People's (Populist)	22	8.5	Rep (at midterm)	Rep (at midterm)
1896	William McKinley	Rep	271	51.0	Rep	Rep
	William J. Bryan	Dem	176	45.5		
1900	William McKinley**	Rep	292	51.7	Rep	Rep
	William J. Bryan	Dem	155	45.5		
1904	Theodore Roosevelt	Rep	336	56.4	Rep	Rep
	Alton Parker	Dem	140	37.6		
1908	William H. Taft	Rep	321	51.6	Rep	Rep
	William J. Bryan	Dem	162	43.1		Dem
1912	Woodrow Wilson	Dem	435	41.8		
	Theodore Roosevelt	Progressive	88	27.4	Dem	Dem
	William H. Taft	Rep	8	23.2		
	Eugene Debs	Socialist	0	6.0		
1916	Woodrow Wilson	Dem	277	49.2	Rep	Dem
	Charles Hughes	Rep	254	46.1		
1920	Warren Harding	Rep	404	60.0	Rep	Rep
	James Cox	Dem	60	34.6		

* Lost the popular vote, won the Electoral College and became president

** Died in office

**KEY: Party abbreviations: Dem = Democrat | DemRep = Democratic Republican | Fed = Federalist
IndRep = Independent Republican | NatRep = National Republican | Rep = Republican**

Election Year	Presidential Candidates	Political Party	Electoral Vote	Percentage of Popular Vote	Control of Congress — House	Control of Congress — Senate
1924	Calvin Coolidge	Rep	382	54.1	Rep	Rep
	John Davis	Dem	136	28.8		
	Robert La Follette	Progressive	13	16.6		
1928	Herbert Hoover	Rep	444	58.2	Rep	Rep
	Alfred Smith	Dem	87	40.8	Dem (at midterm)	
1932	Franklin Roosevelt	Dem	472	57.3	Dem	Dem
	Herbert Hoover	Rep	59	39.6		
1936	Franklin Roosevelt	Dem	523	60.8	Dem	Dem
	Alfred Landon	Rep	8	36.4		
1940	Franklin Roosevelt	Dem	449	54.7	Dem	Dem
	Wendell Wilkie	Rep	82	44.8		
1944	Franklin Roosevelt**	Dem	432	52.8	Dem	Dem
	Thomas Dewey	Rep	99	44.5	Rep (at midterm)	Rep (at midterm)
1948	Harry Truman	Dem	303	49.5	Dem	Dem
	Thomas Dewey	Rep	189	45.1		
	Strom Thurmond	States Rights	39	2.4		
1952	Dwight Eisenhower	Rep	442	55.2	Rep	Rep
	Adlai Stevenson	Dem	89	44.5	Dem (at midterm)	Dem (at midterm)
1956	Dwight Eisenhower	Rep	457	57.4	Dem	Dem
	Adlai Stevenson	Dem	73	42.0		
1960	John F. Kennedy**	Dem	303	49.9	Dem	Dem
	Richard Nixon	Rep	219	49.6		
1964	Lyndon Johnson	Dem	486	61.1	Dem	Dem
	Barry Goldwater	Rep	52	38.5		
1968	Richard Nixon	Rep	301	43.4	Dem	Dem
	Hubert Humphrey	Dem	191	42.7		
	George Wallace	American	41	13.5		
1972	Richard Nixon	Rep	521	61.3	Dem	Dem
	George McGovern	Dem	17	37.3		
1976	Jimmy Carter	Dem	297	50.1	Dem	Dem
	Gerald Ford	Rep	240	48.0		
1980	Ronald Reagan	Rep	489	51.0	Dem	Rep
	Jimmy Carter	Dem	49	41.0		
	John Anderson			6.6		
1984	Ronald Reagan	Rep	525	58.8	Dem	Rep
	Walter Mondale	Dem	13	41.0		Dem (at midterm)
1988	George H. W. Bush	Rep	426	53.4	Dem	Dem
	Michael Dukakis	Dem	111	46.0		
1992	Bill Clinton	Dem	370	43.0	Dem	Dem
	George H. W. Bush	Rep	168	37.4	Rep (at midterm)	Rep (at midterm)
	Ross Perot	--	0	18.9		
1996	Bill Clinton	Dem	379	49.2	Rep	Rep
	Robert Dole	Rep	159	40.7		
	Ross Perot	Reform	0	8.4		
2000	George W. Bush*	Rep	271	47.8	Rep	Rep
	Al Gore	Dem	266	48.4		
	Ralph Nader	Green	0	2.7		

* Lost the popular vote, won the Electoral College and became president
** Died in office

Election Year	Presidential Candidates	Political Party	Electoral Vote	Percentage of Popular Vote	Control of Congress	
					House	Senate
2004	George W. Bush	Rep	286	50.7	Rep	Rep
	John Kerry	Dem	251	48.2	Dem (at midterm)	Dem (at midterm)
2008	Barack Obama	Dem	365	52.8	Dem	Dem
	John McCain	Rep	173	45.6	Rep (at midterm)	
2012	Barack Obama	Dem	332	50.5	Rep	Dem
	Mitt Romney	Rep	206	47.9		
2016	Donald Trump*	Rep	306	46	Rep	Rep
	Hillary Clinton	Dem	232	48	Dem (at midterm)	
2020	Joe Biden	Dem	306	51.3	Dem	Rep
	Donald Trump	Rep	232	46.9		

* Lost the popular vote, won the Electoral College and became president

Glossary

118th Congress: The Congress elected in November 2022, meeting in 2023–24. The first Congress met in 1789–90. Each Congress is elected for two years and numbered consecutively.

527 groups: Organizations that raise and spend unlimited amounts for "issue advocacy."

1963 March on Washington: A massive rally for civil rights that included Martin Luther King's "I Have a Dream" speech.

Abolition: A nineteenth-century movement demanding an immediate and unconditional end to slavery.

Accommodation: The principle that government does not violate the establishment clause as long as it does not confer an advantage on some religions over others. (See "strict separation.")

Advocacy explosion: A vast and relatively swift increase in interest groups active in Washington, DC, beginning in the mid-1960s.

Affirmative action: Direct steps to recruit members of previously underrepresented groups into schools and jobs.

American exceptionalism: The view that the United States is uniquely characterized by a distinct set of ideas such as equality, self-rule, and limited government.

Amicus curiae: A brief submitted by a person or group who is not a direct party to the case.

Approval rating: A measure of public support for a political figure or institution.

Astroturf lobbying: An attempt by interest groups to simulate widespread public engagement on an issue.

Bandwagon effect: When people join a cause because it seems popular or support a candidate who is leading in the polls.

Base voters: Party members who tend to vote loyally for their party's candidates in most elections.

Bicameral: Having two legislative houses or chambers—such as the House and the Senate.

Big data: Immense data sets that are too large for traditional software tools to process.

Bill of Rights: The first ten amendments to the Constitution, listing the rights guaranteed to every citizen.

Black power: A slogan that emphasized pride in Black heritage and the construction of Black institutions to nurture Black interests. It often implied racial separation in reaction to white racism.

Block grants: National government funding provided to state and local governments with relatively few restrictions or requirements on spending; programs to block grants marked a trade-off for state officials: more authority, fewer funds.

Boomerang effect: The discrepancy between candidates' high poll ratings and election performance, caused by supporters' assumption that an easy win means they need not turn out.

Brown v. Board of Education: The landmark Supreme Court case that struck down segregated schools as unconstitutional.

Budget resolution: A joint House-Senate creation that outlines targets for federal spending, revenue levels, and the resultant budget deficit (or surplus) for the coming fiscal year.

Bundling: A form of fundraising in which an individual persuades others to donate large amounts that are then delivered together to a candidate or campaign.

Bureaucratic pathologies: The problems that tend to develop in bureaucratic systems.

Call list: A long list of potential donors who candidates must phone.

Candidate-centered elections: A system in which individual candidates decide to run, raise their own money, and design their own strategy—as opposed to party systems, in which political parties play these roles.

Caucus: A local meeting of voters to select candidates to represent a political party in a general election or to choose delegates who select candidates at a convention.

Central clearance: The OMB's authority to review and "clear" (or approve) anything a member of the administration says or does in public.

Central service agencies: The organizations that supply and staff the federal government.

Checks and balances: The principle that each branch of government has the authority to block the other branches, making it more difficult for any one branch or individual to exercise too much power. This system makes passing legislation far more difficult in the United States than in most other democracies.

Chevron doctrine: Principle of judicial review that requires courts to defer to federal agencies' interpretation of ambiguous congressional statutes.

Chicanismo: A defiant movement expressing pride in Latino origins and culture in the face of discrimination.

Chief of staff: The individual responsible for managing the president's office.

Circuit courts: The second stage of federal courts, which review the trial record of cases decided in district court to ensure they were settled properly.

Civic voluntarism: Citizen participation in public life without government incentives or coercion, such as getting together to build a playground.

Civil disobedience: Protesting laws one considers unjust by refusing to obey them—and accepting the punishment.

Civil law: Cases that involve disputes between two parties.

Civil liberties: The limits on government that allow people to freely exercise their rights.

Civil rights: The freedom to participate in the full life of the community—to vote, use public facilities, and exercise equal economic opportunity.

Civil Rights Act of 1964: Landmark legislation that forbade discrimination on the basis of race, sex, religion, or national origin.

Civil servants: Members of the permanent executive branch bureaucracy who are employed on the basis of competitive exams and keep their positions regardless of the presidential administration.

Class action: A lawsuit filed on behalf of an entire category of individuals, such as all public housing residents in a state or all female managers in a large company.

Classical republicanism: A democratic ideal, based in ancient Greece and Rome, that calls on citizens to participate in public affairs, seek the public interest, shun private gain, and defer to natural leaders.

Clear and present danger: Court doctrine that permits restrictions on free speech if officials believe that the speech will lead to prohibited action such as violence or terrorism.

Clicktivism: Democratic engagement in an online age: point your mouse or scan a QR code, click, and you have donated funds, "liked" a candidate, or (in some states) even cast your vote.

Closed primary: A vote cast by party members to select candidates to represent the party in the general election.

Cloture vote: The Senate's only approved method for halting a filibuster or lifting a legislative hold. If sixty senators—three-fifths of the body, changed in 1975 from the original two-thirds—vote for cloture, the measure can proceed to a vote.

Commerce clause: The constitutional declaration (in Article 1, Section 8) empowering Congress to regulate commerce with foreign nations, between states, and with Indian tribes.

Committee hearing: A way for committees to gather information and gauge members' support as legislative policymaking gets underway. Hearings usually feature witnesses who submit testimony, make an oral presentation, and answer questions from members of Congress.

Committee markup session: A gathering of a full committee to draft the final version of a bill before the committee votes on it.

Common law: A system of law developed by judges in deciding cases over the centuries.

Compact: A mutual agreement that provides for joint action to achieve defined goals.

Compromise of 1850: A complicated compromise over slavery that permitted some territories to vote on whether they would be slave or free and permitted California to enter the Union as a free state. It also included a strict—and hugely controversial—fugitive slave law forcing Northerners to return Black men and women into bondage.

Concurrent opinion: A statement that agrees with the majority opinion.

Concurrent powers: Governmental authority shared by national and state governments, such as the power to tax residents.

Confederation: A group of independent states or nations that yield some of their powers to a national government, although each state retains a degree of sovereign authority.

Conference committee: A special House-Senate committee that must reconcile the differences between the two chambers' versions of the same bill.

Congressional caucus: A group of House or Senate members who convene regularly to discuss common interests; they may share political outlook, race, gender, or geography.

Conservatives: Americans who believe in reduced government spending, personal responsibility, traditional moral values, secure borders, and a strong national defense. Also known as right or right-wing.

Constitution: A statement of fundamental principles that governs a nation or an organization.

Containment: American Cold War strategy designed to stop the spread of communism.

Continuing resolution (CR): A congressionally approved act required when no national budget has been passed before the start of a new fiscal year. This extends spending at current levels for a prescribed period of time.

Cooperative federalism: Also called marble cake federalism, a system of mingled governing authority, with functions overlapping across national and state governments.

Cost-benefit analysis: A more complex study of the projected costs and benefits associated with a proposed policy.

Cost effectiveness: The projected costs of a proposed policy, as revealed by a relatively simple study.

Covenant: A compact invoking religious or moral authority.

Criminal law: Cases in which someone is charged with breaking the law.

Critical race theory: A scholarly tradition that analyzes the way racial hierarchy is organized into American laws and institutions; has recently come under political fire as overly negative and pessimistic about the American experience.

Cycle of nonparticipation: Resistance by political parties to mobilizing disengaged Americans to vote—because their lack of involvement makes their allegiance to one or the other party suspect.

De facto discrimination: More subtle forms of discrimination that exist without a legal basis.

Defendant: The party who is sued in a court case.

De jure discrimination: Discrimination established by laws.

Delegated powers: Powers that Congress passes on to the president.

Delegate representation: Representatives follow the expressed wishes of the voters.

Democracy: A form of government in which the people hold power, either by acting directly or through elected representatives.

Demographic group: People sharing specific characteristics such as age, ethnicity/race, religion, or country of origin.

Devolution: The transfer of authority from the national to the state or local government level.

Diffusion: The spreading of policy ideas from one city or state to others; a process typical of U.S. federalism.

Din: Shorthand for the sheer volume of information and noise generated by online sources; can be a disincentive to participate politically.

Direct action: Participating outside of normal political and social channels through civil disobedience, demonstrations, and even riots.

Direct democracy: A form of government in which all laws and rules are made directly by the citizens, rather than through elected representatives.

Discretionary programs: Nonentitlement program spending, subject to the decision ("discretion") of Congress each year.

Disproportionate impact: The effect some policies have of discriminating, even if discrimination is not consciously intended.

Dissent: A statement on behalf of the justices who voted in the minority.

District courts: The first level of federal courts, which actually try the cases. Each decision is based not on a statute but on previous judicial decisions.

Divided government: Periods during which at least one house of Congress is controlled by a party different from the one occupying the White House.

Domestic dependent nation: Special status that grants local sovereignty to tribal nations but does not grant them full sovereignty equivalent to that enjoyed by independent nations.

Domestic terrorism: Use of violent criminal acts by American citizens to advance ideological goals, often aimed at minority groups.

Double jeopardy: The principle that an individual cannot be tried twice for the same offense.

Dred Scott v. Sandford: A landmark Supreme Court decision holding that Black men could not be citizens under the Constitution of the United States. It created a national uproar.

Dual federalism: Also called layer cake federalism, the clear division of governing authority between national and state governments.

Earmark: A legislative item, usually included in spending ("appropriations") bills, that directs Congress to fund a particular item in one House member's district or a senator's state.

Economic equality: A situation in which there are small differences in wealth among citizens.

Electoral activities: Public engagement in the form of voting, running for office, volunteering in a campaign, or otherwise participating in elections.

Electoral bounce: The temporary spike in the polls that follows an event such as a party's national convention.

Electoral College: The system established by the Constitution to elect the president; each state has a group of electors (equal in size to that of its congressional delegation in the House and the Senate). Today, the public in each state votes for electors, who then vote for the president.

Emancipation Proclamation: An executive order issued by President Abraham Lincoln that declared the enslaved people in all rebel states to be free.

Entitlement program: A government benefit program whose recipients are *entitled* by law to receive payments. Social Security, Medicare, and Medicaid are the three largest.

Equal Employment Opportunity Commission (EEOC): Federal law enforcement agency charged with monitoring compliance with the Civil Rights Act.

Equality: All citizens enjoy the same privileges, status, and rights before the law.

Equal opportunity: The idea that every American has the same chance to influence politics and achieve economic success.

Equal outcome: The idea that citizens should have roughly equal economic circumstances.

Equal protection of the laws: The landmark phrase in the Fourteenth Amendment that requires equal treatment for all citizens.

Equal Rights Amendment (ERA): An amendment, originally drafted by Alice Paul in 1923, passed by Congress in 1972, and ratified by thirty-five states, that declared: "Equality of rights . . . shall not be denied or abridged . . . on account of sex."

Establishment clause: The First Amendment principle that government may not establish an official religion.

Exclusionary rule: The ruling that evidence obtained in an illegal search may not be introduced in a trial.

Executive agreement: An international agreement made by the president that does not require the approval of the Senate.

Executive Office of the President (EOP): The agencies that help the president manage daily activities.

Executive order: A presidential declaration, with the force of law, that issues instructions to the executive branch without any requirement for congressional action or approval.

Executive privilege: Power claimed by the president to resist requests for authority by Congress, the courts, or the public. Not mentioned in the Constitution but based on the separation of powers.

Expressed powers: Powers the Constitution explicitly grants to the president.

Expressive benefits: Values or deeply held beliefs that inspire individuals to join a public interest group.

Fairness doctrine: Regulation that required media outlets to devote equal time to opposite perspectives.

Fair trade: Trade that emphasizes the inclusion of environmental and labor protections in agreements so that nations do not receive unfair advantages by exploiting workers or harming the environment.

Fake news: The deliberate spread of falsehood or misinformation, aided by proliferating social media sites; also a charge made by politicians facing unfavorable stories.

Federal budget deficit: The gap between revenues received by the national government (primarily through individual income and corporate taxes) and spending on all public programs.

Federalism: Power divided between national and state government. Each has its own sovereignty (independent authority) and its own duties.

Federal poverty line: The annually specified level of income (separately calculated for individuals and families) below which people are considered to live in poverty, and eligible for certain federal benefits. For 2022, the poverty line is set at $27,750 for a family of four.

Federal Regulation of Lobbying Act: The initial U.S. statute spelling out requirements on lobbyists active in Congress, which was passed in 1946.

Fighting words: Expressions inherently likely to provoke violent reactions and not necessarily protected by the First Amendment.

Filibuster: Rule unique to the U.S. Senate that allows any senator to hold the floor indefinitely and thereby delay a vote on a bill to which he or she objects. Ended only when sixty senators vote for cloture.

Final rule: The rule that specifies how a program will actually operate.

First Continental Congress: A convention of delegates from twelve of the thirteen colonies that met in 1774.

Fiscal policy: Taxing and spending policies carried out by government, generally in an effort to affect national economic development.

Fiscal year (FY): In budget calculations, the "new year" beginning October 1 and ending the following September 30. Organized many decades ago for accounting purposes.

Floor: The full chamber, either in the House of Representatives or the Senate. A bill "goes to the floor" for the final debate and vote, usually after approval by one or more committees.

Focusing event: A major happening, often of crisis or disaster proportions, that attracts widespread media attention to an issue.

Framing: The way an issue is defined; every issue has many possible frames, each with a slightly different tilt in describing the problem and highlighting solutions.

Framing effects: The way the wording of a polling question influences a respondent.

Freedom: The ability to pursue one's own desires without interference from others.

Freedom of Information Act (FOIA): A 1966 law that facilitates full or partial disclosure of government information and documents.

Freedom Riders: Black and white activists who rode buses together to protest segregation on interstate bus lines.

Free exercise clause: The First Amendment principle that government may not interfere in religious practice.

Free rider problem: A barrier to group or collective action arising because people who do not participate still reap the benefits.

Free trade: Goods and services moving across international boundaries without government interference.

Full faith and credit clause: The constitutional requirement (in Article 4, Section 1) that each state recognizes and upholds laws passed by any other state.

Gerrymander: Redrawing an election district in a way that gives the advantage to one party.

Gift ban: A regulation that eliminates (or sharply reduces the permitted dollar amount of) gifts from interest groups to lawmakers.

Going public: Directly addressing the public to win support for oneself or one's ideas.

Grand jury: A jury that does not decide on guilt or innocence but only on whether there is enough evidence for the case to go to trial.

Grand Old Party (GOP): Long-standing nickname for the Republican Party; ironically, bestowed early in the party's history, in the 1870s.

Grand strategy: An overarching vision that defines and guides a nation's foreign policy.

Grants-in-aid: National government funding provided to state and local governments, along with specific instructions about how the funds may be used.

Great Migration: The vast movement of Black people from the rural South to the urban North between 1910 and the 1960s.

Gross domestic product (GDP): The value of all the goods and services produced in a nation over a year. For 2022, the U.S. GDP was an estimated $24.8 trillion.

Groupthink: The tendency among a small group of decision makers to converge on a shared set of views; can limit creative thinking or solutions to policy problems.

Hate speech: Hostile statements based on someone's personal characteristics, such as race, ethnicity, religion, or sexual orientation.

Hyperpluralism: The collective effect of the vast number of interest groups in slowing the process of American democratic policymaking.

Imminent lawless action: Updated Court doctrine; restrictions on free speech only permitted if officials affirm a credible threat that dangerous illegal actions—such as acts of terror or assault—are an immediate and probable danger.

Imperial presidency: A characterization of the American presidency that suggests it is demonstrating imperial traits, and that the republic is morphing into an empire.

Incorporation: The process by which the Supreme Court declares that a right in the Bill of Rights also applies to state governments.

Incumbency advantage: The tendency for members of Congress to win reelection in overwhelming numbers.

Indentured servant: A colonial American settler contracted to work for a fixed period (usually three to seven years) in exchange for food, shelter, and transportation to the New World.

Individualism: The idea that individuals, not the society, are responsible for their own well-being.

Information shortcuts: Cues about candidates and policies drawn from everyday life.

Infotainment: The blurred line between news and entertainment.

Inherent powers: Powers that, although neither specified nor implied by the Constitution, are necessary for the president or Congress to fulfill their duties.

Inherent powers of the presidency: Powers assumed by presidents, often during a crisis, on the basis of the constitutional phrase "The executive power shall be vested in the president."

Initiative: A process in which citizens propose new laws or amendments to the state constitution.

Institutions: The organizations, norms, and rules that structure government and public action.

Interest group: An organization whose goal is to influence government.

Intergovernmental lobbying: Attempts by officials in one part of the government to influence their counterparts in another branch, or at a different (state or local) level.

Internationalism: The belief that national interests are best served by actively engaging and working with other nations around the world.

Intersectionality: How different social identities like race, gender, and sexual orientation mix to create patterns of privilege and discrimination.

Iron triangle: The cozy relationship in one issue area among interest-group lobbyists, congressional staffers, and executive branch agencies.

Isolationism: The doctrine that a nation should avoid all foreign policy commitments and alliances and withdraw from world affairs.

Issue advocacy: Organized effort to advance (or block) a proposed public policy change.

Issue campaign: A concerted effort by interest groups to arouse popular support or opposition for a policy issue.

Issue network: Shifting alliances of public and private interest groups, lawmakers, and other stakeholders all focused on the same policy area.

Jim Crow: The system of racial segregation in the U.S. South that lasted from 1890 to 1965, and that was often violently enforced.

Judicial activism: A vigorous or active approach to reviewing the other branches of government.

Judicial restraint: Reluctance to interfere with elected branches, only doing so as a last resort.

Judicial review: The Court's authority to determine whether legislative, executive, and state actions violate the Constitution and overrule those that do.

Judicial rules: Hard-and-fast boundaries between what is lawful and what is not.

Judicial standards: Guiding principles that help governments make judgment calls.

K Street: A major street in downtown Washington, DC, that is home to the headquarters for many lobbying firms and advocacy groups—and thus synonymous with interest-group lobbying.

Legislative hold: An informal way for a senator to object to a bill or other measure reaching the Senate floor. The action effectively halts Senate proceedings on that issue, sometimes for weeks or longer.

Legislative referral: The state legislature puts a proposal up for a popular vote.

Liberalism: A doctrine that views nation-states as benefiting most from mutual cooperation, aided by international organizations.

Liberals: Americans who value cultural diversity, government programs for the needy, public intervention in the economy, and individuals' right to a lifestyle based on their own social and moral positions. Also known as left or left-wing.

Libertarians: Americans who are strong proponents of negative liberty and aim to reduce all government to a minimum.

Likely voters: Persons identified as probable voters in an upcoming election. Often preferred by polling organizations, but difficult to specify with great accuracy.

Literacy test: A requirement that voters exhibit an ability to read; in reality, a way to restrict Black suffrage.

Litigation: The conduct of a lawsuit.

Lobbying coalition: A collection of lobbyists working on related topics or a specific legislative proposal.

Lobbyist: A person who contacts government officials on behalf of a particular cause or issue.

Lochner era: A period from 1905 to 1937, during which the Supreme Court struck down laws (e.g., worker protection or minimum wage laws) that were thought to infringe on economic liberty or the right to contract.

Loud signal: Media stories with very broad coverage and an unambiguous message.

Major questions doctrine: Conservative legal doctrine that limits administrative discretion by holding that administrative agencies need explicit authorization from Congress before deciding issues of major importance.

Majority opinion: The official statement of the Supreme Court (or district courts, since they also have multiple justices).

Mandate: Political authority claimed by an election winner as reflecting the approval of the people.

Margin of sampling error: The degree of inaccuracy in any poll, arising from the fact that surveys involve a sample of respondents from a population, rather than every member.

Mass media: Information and entertainment for broad popular audiences including newspapers, magazines, radio, and television.

Material benefits: Items distributed by public interest groups as incentives to sign up or remain a member.

Median: A statistical term for the number in the middle or the case that has an equal number of examples above and below it.

Mediation: A way of resolving disputes without going to court, in which a third party (the mediator) helps two or more sides negotiate a settlement.

Mercantilism: An economic theory according to which government controls foreign trade to maintain prosperity and security.

Midterm elections: National elections held between presidential elections, involving all seats in the House of Representatives, one-third of those in the Senate, thirty-six governorships, and other positions.

Midterm loss: The president's party loses congressional seats during the midterm elections. This has occurred in most midterm elections.

Millennials: Americans born between 1983 and 2001. Though very large (some eighty million people) and diverse, millennials tend to share certain characteristics, including political outlook.

Miller test: Three-part test for judging whether a work is obscene (if it has all three, the work loses First Amendment protection).

Miranda warnings: A set of rights that police officers are required to inform suspects of, including the right to remain silent.

Missouri Compromise: An agreement to open southern territories west of the Mississippi to slavery while closing northern territories to slavery.

Monetary policy: Actions of central banks, which in the United States culminate in the Federal Reserve, designed primarily to maximize employment and moderate inflation.

Motor voter law: Passed in 1993, this act enables prospective voters to register when they receive their driver's license.

Multilateralism: A doctrine that emphasizes operating together with other nations to pursue common goals.

Multilateral organization: An international organization of three or more nations organized around a common goal.

Name recognition: An advantage possessed by a well-known political figure, a political celebrity.

National Association for the Advancement of Colored People (NAACP): A civil rights organization formed in 1909 and dedicated to racial equality.

National Organization for Women (NOW): An organization formed in 1966 to take action for women's equality.

Necessary and proper clause: The constitutional declaration (in Article 1, Section 8) that defines Congress's constitutional authority to exercise the "necessary and proper" powers to carry out its designated functions.

Negative campaigning: Running for office by attacking the opponent.

Negative liberty: Freedom from constraints or the interference of others.

Negative partisanship: Participating in politics and forming opinions in opposition to a party one dislikes.

New Deal: Broad series of economic programs and reforms introduced between 1933 and 1936 and associated with the Franklin Roosevelt administration.

New federalism: A version of cooperative federalism, but with stronger emphasis on state and local government activity versus national government.

New Jersey Plan: Put forward at the Constitutional Convention by the small states, this plan left most government authority with the state governments.

The New Jim Crow: The idea that mass incarceration of Black people has the sweeping effects of Jim Crow discrimination laws. The term is the title of a book by Michelle Alexander.

New media: On-demand access to information through digital devices that increasingly feature interactive participation with content.

Nonattitudes: The lack of a stable perspective in response to opinion surveys; answers to questions may be self-contradictory or may display no ideological consistency.

Nonpartisan election: An election in which candidates run as individuals, without any party affiliation. Many towns and cities feature nonpartisan elections.

Open primary: A vote cast by any eligible voter to select candidates to represent the party in the general election.

Open seat: A seat in Congress without an incumbent running for reelection.

Opinion poll: Systematic study of a defined population, analyzing a representative sample's views to draw inferences about the larger public's views. Also termed *survey research.*

Originalism: A principle of legal interpretation that relies on the original meaning of those who wrote the Constitution.

Overhead democracy: A system by which the people elect the president, who, through their appointees, controls the bureaucracy from the top.

Override: The process by which Congress can overcome a presidential veto with a two-thirds vote in both chambers.

Paradox of voting: For most individuals, the cost of voting (acquiring necessary information, traveling to polling site, and waiting in line) outweighs the apparent benefits. Economic theory would predict very low voter turnout, given this analysis.

Partisanship: Taking the side of a party or espousing a viewpoint that reflects a political party's principles or position on an issue.

Party boss: The senior figure in a party machine.

Party caucus: A meeting of all House or Senate members of one or the other main party, usually to discuss political and policy strategies.

Party identification: Strong attachment to one political party, often established at an early age.

Party in government: The portion of a political party's organization that comprises elected officials and candidates for office.

Party in the electorate: The largest (and least organized) component of a political party, drawn from the public at large: registered members and regular supporters.

Party machine: A hierarchical arrangement of party workers, often organized in an urban area to help integrate immigrants and minority groups into the political system. Most active in the late nineteenth and early twentieth centuries.

Party organization: The portion of a political party that includes activists, state/local leaders, and affiliated professionals such as fundraisers and public relations experts.

Party platform: The written statement of a party's core convictions and issue priorities. Generally revised every four years, in time for the national party convention.

Party system: The broad organization of U.S. politics comprising the two main parties, the coalition of supporters backing each, the positions they take on major issues, and each party's electoral achievements.

Path dependence: Social science term for how policymakers' choices are shaped by institutional "paths" that result from policy choices made in the past.

Pendleton Civil Service Act: The law that shifted American government toward a merit-based public service.

Personal presidency: The idea that the president has a personal link to the public. Made initially possible by twentieth-century media.

Plaintiff: The party who brings the action in a lawsuit.

Plessy v. Ferguson: An 1896 Supreme Court case that permitted racial segregation.

Pluralism: An open, participatory style of government in which many different interest groups negotiate government policies.

Policy agenda: The issues that the media covers, the public considers important, and politicians address. Setting the agenda is the first step in political action.

Policy window: A figurative description of the opportunity—often brief, measured in days or weeks rather than years—to pass a bill in Congress or a state legislature.

Political action committee (PAC): An organization of at least fifty people, affiliated with an interest group that is permitted to make contributions to candidates for federal office.

Political appointees: Top officials in the executive agencies, appointed by the president.

Political culture: The orientation of citizens of a state toward politics.

Political elites: Individuals who control significant wealth, status, power, or visibility and consequently have significant influence over public debates.

Political equality: All citizens have the same political rights and opportunities.

Political mobilization: Efforts to encourage people to engage in the public sphere: to vote for a particular candidate (or donate money, work on the campaign, etc.) or to get involved in specific issues.

Political order: The set of institutions, interests, and ideas that shape a political era. Great presidents reconstruct the framework, launching a new order.

Political party: A group that shares political principles and is organized to win elections and hold power.

Political socialization: Education about how the government works and which policies one should support; provided by parents, peers, schools, parties, and other national institutions.

Political voice: Exercising one's public rights, often through speaking out in protest or in favor of some policy change.

Populists: Americans who believe the rich and powerful have captured the government and seek to win back government to help the common people.

Positive liberty: The ability to pursue one's goals, which requires basic resources and power.

Power elite theory: The view that a small handful of wealthy, influential Americans exercises extensive control over government decisions.

Pragmatism: A principle of legal interpretation based on the idea that the Constitution evolves and that interpretations of the Constitution must be framed in the context of contemporary realities.

Precedent: A judicial decision that offers a guide to similar cases in the future.

Preemption: The invalidation of a U.S. state law that conflicts with federal law.

Preemptive war: The effort to attack hostile powers before they launch attacks. Highly controversial because it sanctions striking first.

President pro tempore: Majority party senator with the longest Senate service.

Primacy: The doctrine asserting that the United States should maintain an unrivaled military.

Priming: Affecting public perceptions of political leaders, candidates, or issues by reporting on topics in ways that either enhance or diminish support.

Principal-agent theory: Details how policymakers (principals) control the actors who work for them (agents)—but who have far more information than they do.

Prior restraint: Legal effort to stop speech before it occurs.

Private contractors: Private companies that contract to provide goods and services for the government.

Progressive federalism: Approach that gives state officials considerable leeway in achieving national programs and goals.

Proportional representation: The allocation of votes or delegates on the basis of the percentage of the vote received; contrasts with the winner-take-all system.

Proposed rule: A draft of administrative regulations published in the *Federal Register* for the purpose of gathering comments from interested parties.

Protectionism: Efforts to protect local business from foreign competition.

Public ownership: A situation in which media outlets are run by the government and paid for by tax dollars.

Public–private partnership: A government program or service provided through the joint efforts of private sector actors (usually businesses) and public officials.

Public watchdog: Media coverage that alerts the public when a problem arises in politics or society.

Push poll: A form of negative campaigning that masquerades as a regular opinion survey. They usually feature unflattering information about an opponent.

Quasi-suspect category: A legal standard that requires governments to have an important state purpose for any legislation that singles out sex or gender. This is not as strong as the suspect category, which requires strict scrutiny.

Racial profiling: A law enforcement practice of singling out people on the basis of physical features such as race or ethnicity.

Random sample: A sample in which everyone in the population (sampling frame) has an equal probability of being selected.

Rational choice theory: An approach to political behavior that views individuals as rational, decisive actors who know their political interests and seek to act on them.

Realism: A doctrine holding that nation-states seek to amass power to ensure their self-preservation.

Reapportionment: Reorganization of the boundaries of House districts, a process that follows the results of the U.S. census, taken every ten years. District lines are redrawn to ensure rough equality in the number of constituents represented by each House member.

Reconstruction: The failed effort, pursued by Northerners and Southerners, to rebuild the South and establish racial equality after the Civil War.

Referendum: An election in which citizens vote directly on an issue.

Reframing the issue: To redefine the popular perception of an issue.

Regulatory capture: The theory that industries dominate the agencies that regulate them.

Republic: A government in which citizens rule indirectly and make government decisions through their elected representatives.

Reserved powers: The constitutional guarantee (in the Tenth Amendment) that the states retain government authority not explicitly granted to the national government.

Response bias: The tendency of poll respondents to misstate their views frequently to avoid "shameful" opinions that might appear sexist or racist.

Reverse lobbying: Attempts by government officials to influence interest groups on behalf of their preferred policies.

Revolving door: The tendency of many Washington lobbyists to move from government work (e.g., as a congressional or White House advisor) to lobbying and back again.

Roll-call vote: A congressional vote in which each member's vote is recorded, either by roll call (Senate) or electronically (House).

Rule of four: The requirement that at least four Supreme Court judges must agree to hear a case before it comes before the Court.

Safe district: A district consisting of voters who have historically voted for one party over the other by a large majority.

Sampling frame: A designated group of people from whom a set of poll respondents is randomly selected.

School busing: An effort to integrate public schools by mixing students from different neighborhoods.

Second Continental Congress: A convention of delegates from the thirteen colonies that became the acting national government for the duration of the Revolutionary War.

Section 504: An obscure provision in an minor congressional act that required all institutions that received federal funds to accommodate people with disabilities.

Security trap: The idea that using military force creates multiple, often unforeseen, problems.

Selective incorporation: The extension of protections from the Bill of Rights to the state governments, one liberty at a time.

Self-rule: The idea that legitimate government flows from the people.

Seneca Falls Convention: The first convention dedicated to women's rights, held in July 1848 in Seneca Falls, New York.

Signing statements: Written presidential declarations commenting on the bill that is being signed into law—often including criticism of one or more provisions.

Social capital: Relations between people that build closer ties of trust and civic engagement, yielding productive benefits for the larger society.

Social democracy: The idea that government policy should ensure that all are comfortably cared for within the context of a capitalist economy.

Social equality: All individuals enjoy the same status in society.

Soft power: The influence a nation exerts through culture and commerce; a contrast to attempted influence through force.

Solidarity benefits: The feeling of shared commitment and purpose experienced by individuals who join a public interest group.

Sound bite: A short audio clip; often refers to a brief excerpt from a politician's speech.

Speaker of the House: The chief administrative officer in the House of Representatives.

Special interest: A pejorative term, often used to designate an interest group whose aims or issue preferences one does not share.

Split-ticket voter: Votes for at least one candidate from each party, dividing his or her ballot between the two (or more) parties.

Spoils system: A system in which government jobs are given out as political favors.

Stare decisis: Deciding cases on the basis of previous rulings or precedents.

Straight-ticket voter: Votes for the same party for all offices on a ballot.

Strategic disengagement: The doctrine that a nation should not interfere in other nations' affairs unless such involvement clearly advances its own interests.

Street-level bureaucrats: Public officials who deal directly with the public.

Strict scrutiny: A form of judicial review that requires the government to have a "compelling government interest" for any law that singles out race or ethnicity.

Strict separation: The strict principles articulated in the Lemon test for judging whether a law establishes a religion. (See "accommodation.")

Sunshine laws: Laws that permit the public to watch policymakers in action and to access the records of the proceedings.

Supermajority: An amount higher than a simple majority (50 percent plus one)—typically, three-fifths or two-thirds of the voters.

Super PACs: Organizations that raise and spend unlimited amounts of money to promote a candidate or publicize a cause. However, they may not directly contribute to a candidate or coordinate with a campaign.

Super Tuesday: The date on the presidential primary calendar when multiple states hold primaries and caucuses.

Supremacy clause: The constitutional declaration (in Article 6, Section 2) that the national government's authority prevails over any conflicting state or local government's claims, provided the power is granted to the federal government.

Survey research: Systematic study of a defined population, analyzing a representative sample's views to draw inferences about the larger public's views. Also termed *opinion poll*.

Symbolic expression: An act, rather than actual speech, used to demonstrate a point of view.

Textualism: A mode of legal interpretation that focuses on the plain meaning of the Constitution or the legal document.

Theory of democratic peace: Theory that strongly democratic nations are less prone to engage in wars with one another.

Time, place, and manner clause: The constitutional clause that delegates control of elections to the state governments.

Trade association: An organized group representing individuals and businesses that belong to the same industry.

Trade deficit: The financial gap arising when a nation imports (or buys) more goods from foreign nations than it exports (or sells) to them.

Traditional participation: Engaging in political activities through the formal channels of government and society.

Trustee representation: Representatives do what they regard as being in the best interest of their constituents—even if constituents do not agree.

Unanimous consent: A Senate requirement, applied to most of that body's business, that all senators agree before an action can proceed.

Underdog effect: Sympathy for a candidate behind in the polls, contributing to a higher-than-predicted vote total—and sometimes a surprise election victory.

Unfunded mandate: An obligation imposed on state or local government officials by federal legislation without sufficient federal funding support to cover the costs.

Unicameral: Having a single legislative house or chamber.

Unilateralism: A doctrine that holds that the United States should act independently of other nations. It should decide what is best for itself—not in coordination with partners and allies.

Unitary executive theory: The idea that the Constitution puts the president in charge of executing the laws and that therefore no other branch may limit presidential discretion over executive matters.

Unitary government: A national polity governed as a single unit, with the central government exercising all or most political authority.

United Farm Workers (UFW): An influential union representing migrant farm workers in the West.

Universalistic politics: A government run according to transparent rules, impartially applied.

USA Patriot Act: Legislation that sought to enhance national security, passed in the aftermath of the September 11, 2001, terrorist attacks.

Veto: The constitutional procedure by which a president can prevent enactment of legislation passed by Congress.

Veto power: The presidential power to block an act of Congress by refusing to sign—and returning it to Congress with objections.

Virginia Plan: Madison's plan, embraced by the Constitutional Convention delegates from larger states; this plan strengthened the national government relative to state governments.

Voice vote: A congressional vote in which the presiding officer asks those for and against to say "yea" or "nay," respectively, and announces the result. No record is kept of House or Senate members voting on each side.

Voter turnout: A measure of which proportion of eligible voters actually cast a legitimate ballot in a given election.

War Powers Act: Legislation passed in 1973 to increase congressional involvement in undeclared wars. It requires Congress to approve military action undertaken by the president in no more than sixty days.

Watergate scandal: A failed effort in 1972 by Republican operatives to break into Democratic Party headquarters in the Watergate office complex in Washington, DC. President Nixon tried to cover up the event—eventually causing him to resign from the presidency.

Whistleblower: A federal worker who reports corruption or fraud.

Winner-take-all: The candidate receiving a simple majority (or, among multiple candidates, a plurality) receives all electoral votes or primary delegates. Sometimes called "first-past-the-post."

World Trade Organization (WTO): An international organization that oversees efforts to open markets and promote free trade.

Notes

Chapter 1

1. Computed from Gallup Polls using the first poll released in February from 2013 t0 2022 (Using the first October poll across the past 10 years yields an even lower average of 17.6.), https://bit.ly/3taB258.
2. *Dred Scott v. Sandford*, 60 U.S. (19 How) 393 (1857).
3. For a classic statement of this view, see G. William Domhoff, *Who Rules America Now* (New York: McGraw Hill, 2006); for a recent book warning about dynastic wealth, see Thomas Piketty, *Capital and Ideology,* trans. Arthur Goldhammer (Cambridge, MA: Harvard University Press, 2020). A suggestion that wealth/inequality may not be so concentrated is in "Economists Are Rethinking the Numbers on Inequality," *The Economist*, November 28, 2019, https://econ.st/39C8JBz.
4. For an influential statement of the conservative perspective, see Milton and Rose Friedman, *Free to Choose: A Personal Statement* (New York: Harcourt, 1980).
5. John Gerring et al., "Who Rules the World? A Portrait of the Global Leadership Class," *Perspectives on Politics* 19, no. 4 (2019): 1079–97. Lawrence R. Jacobs and Theda Skocpol, eds., *Democracy and Inequality* (New York: Russell Sage, 2005).
6. Harold D. Lasswell, *Politics: Who Gets What, When, and How*, rev. ed. (New York: Smith Books, 1990).
7. Roger Sherman, quoted in James Madison, *Notes of Debates in the Federal Convention*, ed. Adrienne Koch (New York: Norton, 1987), 39.
8. For a fine overview, see Eleanor Ostrom, *Understanding Institutional Diversity* (Princeton, NJ: Princeton University Press, 2005).
9. Philip Tetlock, *Expert Political Judgment: How Good Is It? How Can We Know?* (Princeton, NJ: Princeton University Press, 2005). On 2022 outcome, see Philip Bump, "Why Was the Midterm Result Such a Surprise?" *Washington Post*, November 9, 2022, https://wapo.st/3UGsz5a.

10. Ronald Reagan, "Inaugural Address," January 20, 1981, Yale Law Library Avalon Project, https://bit.ly/34jjYia.
11. Alexis de Tocqueville, a young French aristocrat, spent nine months traveling around the United States in 1831–32 and published a book on his observations, *Democracy in America*. It is one of our favorite books on America and on democracy. Many of his observations remain fresh today; no matter where you are on the political spectrum, you will find insights to challenge your views. For good introductions to civic engagement, see Robert Putnam, *Bowling Alone* (New York: Simon & Schuster, 2000); Eric Klinenberg, *Palaces of the People* (New York: Random House, 2018).
12. Pew Research Center, "Public Trust in Government," June 6, 2022, https://pewrsr.ch/3vkptts.
13. Paul Frymer, *Building an American State: The Era of Territorial and Political Expansion* (Princeton, NJ: Princeton University Press, 2017).
14. Michael Lind, *Land of Promise: An Economic History of the United States* (New York: HarperCollins, 2012), 205.
15. Pew Research Center, "Public Holds Broadly Favorable Views of Many Federal Agencies, Including CDC and HHS," April 9, 2020, https://pewrsr.ch/3DYhAOl.
16. Figures on discretionary spending are calculated by the Congressional Budget Office. For updated analyses, see cbo.gov.
17. *Dobbs v. Jackson Women's Health Organization*, No. 19–1392.
18. Organisation for Economic Co-Operation and Development (OECD), "Revenue Statistics," https://stats.oecd.org/Index.aspx?DataSetCode=REV.
19. Suzanne Mettler, *The Submerged State* (Chicago: University of Chicago Press, 2011); Christopher Howard, *The Hidden Welfare State* (Princeton, NJ: Princeton University Press, 1997); Jacob Hacker, *The Divided*

Welfare State (New York: Cambridge University Press, 2002).
20. Joint Committee on Taxation, "Estimates of Federal Tax Expenditures for Fiscal Years 2019–2023," JCX-55-19 (Washington, DC: Joint Committee on Taxation, 2020).
21. David Blumenthal and James Morone, *The Heart of Power: Health and Politics in the Oval Office* (Berkeley: University of California Press, 2009), chap. 3.
22. Suzanne Mettler, *The Government-Citizen Disconnect* (New York: Russell Sage Foundation, 2018).
23. For a description, see James A. Morone, *Hellfire Nation: The Politics of Sin in American History* (New Haven, CT: Yale University Press, 2003).
24. Miriam Jordan and Robert Gebeloff, "Amid Slowdown, Immigration Is Driving U.S. Population Growth," *New York Times*, February 5, 2022, https://www.nytimes.com/2022/02/05/us/immigration-census-population.html.
25. Andrew Daniller, "Two-Thirds of Americans Support Marijuana Legalization," Pew Research Center, November 19, 2019, https://pewrsr.ch/34lGmHy.
26. Roberta Katz, Sarah Ogilvie, Jane Shaw, and Linda Woodhead, *Gen Z, Explained: The Art of Living in a Digital Age* (Chicago: University of Chicago Press, 2021), esp. 39–68.

Chapter 2

1. Alice Sparberg Alexious, *Jane Jacobs: Urban Visionary* (New Brunswick, NJ: Rutgers University Press, 2006); Jane Jacobs, *The Death and Life of Great American Cities* (New York: Random House, 1961).
2. Richard Wike and Janell Fetterolf, "Global Public Opinion in a Time of Democratic Anxiety," Pew Research Center, Dec. 7, 2021, https://pewrsr.ch/3E5IZ0w.
3. Wike and Fetterolf, 2021 (see chap. 2, note 2).

4.   Board of Governors of the Federal Reserve System, "Distribution of Wealth in the U.S. Since 1989," https://www.federalreserve.gov/releases/z1/dataviz/dfa/distribute/table/.

5.   For this and preceding note: Alexandre Tanzi and Michael Sasso, "Richest 1% of Americans Close to Surpassing Wealth of Middle Class," *Bloomberg News*, November 9, 2019, https://bloom.bg/3laAnLw.

6.   American Association for the Advancement of Science, "Survey: Most Americans Want Government Commitment to Reduce Inequality," April 27, 2020, https://bit.ly/3cCTXuD.

7.   Simon Schama, *Rough Crossings: Britain, the Slaves, and the American Revolution* (New York: Harper-Collins, 2006).

8.   Emily Silverman, Emily Davies, Steve Thompson, and Ian Duncan, "'Freedom Convoy' Spinoff Rallies in Md. with About 1,000 Vehicles and Plans to Drive Around the Capital Beltway," *Washington Post*, March 5, 2022, https://www.washingtonpost.com/dc-md-va/2022/03/05/peoples-convoy-protest-hagerstown/.

9.   The classic statement comes from Isaiah Berlin, "Two Concepts of Liberty," reprinted in *Liberty*, ed. Henry Hardy (Oxford: Oxford University Press, 2002), 166–17.

10.   Samuel Huntington, *American Politics: The Promise of Disharmony* (Cambridge, MA: Harvard University Press, 1981).

11.   Samuel Huntington, *American Politics: The Promise of Disharmony*, rev. ed. (Cambridge, MA: Harvard University Press, 1983); Rogers Smith, *Civic Ideals: Conflicting Visions of Citizenship in U.S. History* (New Haven, CT: Yale University Press, 1997); Mary Frances Berry, *History Teaches Us to Resist: How Progressive Movements Have Succeeded in Challenging Times* (Boston: Beacon Press, 2018).

12.   Quoted in James A. Morone, *The Democratic Wish: Popular Participation and the Limits of American Government* (New Haven, CT: Yale University Press, 1998), 54.

13.   Thomas Jefferson, "Response to the Citizens of Albemarle," February 12, 1790; First Inaugural Address, March 4, 1801. Jefferson's first inaugural address offers the best summary of what we now call Jeffersonian democracy.

14.   James Madison, *Federalist* no. 10. The quote is from Roger Sherman, recorded in "Madison's Notes of Debates," in *The Federal Convention and the Formation of the Union*, ed. Winston Solberg (Indianapolis, IN: Bobbs Merrill, 1958), 84–85.

15.   Michael Kammen, *People of Paradox* (New York: Knopf, 1972), 31.

16.   Alexis de Tocqueville, *Democracy in America*, trans. George Lawrence (Garden City, NY: Doubleday, 1969), 1:60, 89; James Bryce, *The American Commonwealth* (London: Macmillan, 1888), 3:267.

17.   Steven Levitsky and Daniel Ziblatt, *How Democracies Die* (New York: Crown Books, 2018).

18.   Charles Postel, "If Trump and Sanders Are Both Populists, What Does Populism Mean?," *The American Historian* (Organization of American History), n.d., https://bit.ly/3tozHaQ. For a historical perspective, see James A. Morone, *Republic of Wrath: How American Politics Turned Tribal from George Washington to Donald Trump* (New York: Basic Books, 2020), chap. 5.

19.   John Kingdon, *America the Unusual* (New York: St. Martin's Press, 1999), 1.

20.   See the essays in Keith Banting and Will Kymlicka, *The Strains of Commitment: The Political Sources of Solidarity in Diverse Societies* (New York: Oxford University Press, 2017).

21.   Martin Luther King Jr., Speech given at Ohio Northern University, January 11, 1968, https://www.onu.edu/mlk/mlk-speech-transcript.

22.   On the rise and fall of solidarity/empathy and counterbalancing force of individualism, see Stanley Feldman, Leonie Huddy, Julie Wronski, and Patrick Lown, "The Interplay of Empathy and Individualism in Support for Social Welfare Policies," *Political Psychology* 41, no. 2 (2020): 343–62.

23.   Milton Friedman, *Capitalism and Freedom* (Chicago: University of Chicago Press, 1962).

24.   The original statement of this theory is by Louis Hartz, *The Liberal Tradition in America* (New York: Harcourt, Brace, and World, 1955).

25.   See Noel Ignatiev, *How the Irish Became White*, 2nd ed. (New York: Routledge, 2009).

26.   Franklin quotes taken from *Poor Richard's Almanac*; see http://www.ushistory.org/franklin/quotable/.

27.   James Truslow Adams, *The Epic of America* (New York: Taylor and Francis, 1938), xx.

28.   Clinton quoted in Jennifer Hochschild, *Facing Up to the American Dream* (Princeton, NJ: Princeton University Press, 1995), vi, 18. The White House, "Remarks by Vice President Harris at the S. Carolina Democratic Party Palmetto Dinner," June 10, 2022, https://bit.ly/3BAY7TI.

29.   Gordon Wood, *The Radicalism of the American Revolution* (New York: Knopf, 1992), 369.

30.   Emmanuel Saez, "Striking It Richer: The Evolution of Top Incomes in the United States," updated working paper (February 2020), https://bit.ly/3d1tlDR.

31.   Thomas Piketty, *Wealth and Inequality* (Cambridge, MA: Harvard University Press, 2020).

32.   Roosevelt quoted in James Morone, *Hellfire Nation* (New Haven, CT: Yale University Press, 2004), 347.

33.   On evangelicals, see articles in *Praxis Journal* (https://journal.praxislabs.org/); Tom Krattenmaker, *The Evangelicals You Don't Know: Introducing the Next Generation of Christians* (Rowman and Littlefield, 2013).

34.   Wim Van Lancker and Zachary Parolin, "COVID-19, School Closures, and Child Poverty: A Social Crisis in the Making," *Lancet Public Health* 5, no. 5 (2020): E243–44.

35.   Figures from Samuel J. Abrams et al., "AEI Survey on Community and Society: Social Capital, Civic Health, and Quality of Life in the United States," February 2019, https://bit.ly/3cYR5IO.

36.   Linley Sanders, "In 2022, Do Americans Still Believe in the American Dream?" YouGov America survey, July 14, 2022, https://bit.ly/3BJl5bJ.

37.   Tocqueville, *Democracy in America*, 1:9.

38.   Hugh Brogan, *Alexis de Tocqueville: A Life* (New Haven, CT: Yale University Press, 2007), 352.

39.   "Gini Coefficient by Country," *World Population Review*, https://worldpopulationreview.com/country-rankings/gini-coefficient-by-country.

40.   Tocqueville, *Democracy in America*, 2:558.

41.   John Winthrop, "A Model of Christian Charity" (Sermon delivered aboard the *Arbella*, 1630), Collections of the Massachusetts Historical

Society, Boston, 1838, 3rd series, 7:31–48.

42. Scott Detrow and Barbara Sprunt, "'He Thinks Division Helps Him': Biden Condemns Trump's Protest Response," NPR, June 2, 2020, https://www.npr.org/2020/06/02/867671792/biden-tocondemn-trumps-protest-responsein-speech.

43. Gallup, "Religion," 2020, http://www.gallup.com/poll/1690/religion.aspx.

44. Jeffrey Jones, "How Religious Are Americans?," Gallup, December 23, 2021, https://news.gallup.com/poll/358364/religious-americans.aspx. Frank Newport, "Millennials' Religiosity Amidst the Rise of the Nones," Gallup, October 29, 2019, https://bit.ly/3fEynIc.

45. Eileen W. Lindner, ed., *Yearbook of American & Canadian Churches* (Washington, DC: National Council of Churches, 2013).

46. Pew Research Center, "In U.S., Decline of Christianity Continues at Rapid Pace," October 17, 2019, https://pewrsr.ch/3hGljnb.

47. Thomas Jefferson, "Letter to the Danbury (Connecticut) Baptists," Library of Congress collection, www.loc.gov/loc/lcib/9806/danpost.html.

48. For details—and citations in this section—see Morone, *Republic of Wrath*.

49. See, for example, Beth Lew-Williams, *The Chinese Must Go: Violence, Exclusion, and the Making of the Alien in America* (Cambridge, MA: Harvard University Press, 2015).

50. Clifford Geertz, *The Interpretation of Cultures* (New York: Basic Books, 1973).

51. James A. Morone, "Is There an American Political Culture?," in *The Devils We Know: Us and Them in America's Raucous Political Culture* (Lawrence: University of Kansas Press, 2014), 1–30.

52. Madison, *Federalist* no. 10.

Chapter 3

1. William G. Howell and Terry M. Moe, *Relic: How the Constitution Undermines Effective Government* (New York: Hachette, 2016).

2. Edmund Burke, "Speech to the Bristol Electors," in *Representation*, ed. Hannah Pitkin (New York: Atherton Press, 1969), 175–76.

3. See James A. Morone, *The Democratic Wish* (New Haven, CT: Yale University Press, 1998), chap. 1.

4. Robert Middlekauff, *The Glorious Cause* (New York: Oxford University Press, 1982), 74.

5. Bernard Bailyn et al., *The Great Republic: A History of the American People* (Boston: Little, Brown, 1977), 256.

6. Middlekauff, *Glorious Cause*, 223–28, quotation on 226.

7. Joseph J. Ellis, *The Cause: The American Revolution and Its Discontents* (New York: W. W. Norton, 2021).

8. See teapartypatriots.org. On "tea party of the left," see, e.g., Andrew Marantz, "Are We Entering a New Political Era?," *New Yorker*, May 24, 2021, https://bit.ly/3i4daKJ.

9. David Hackett Fischer, *Liberty and Freedom: A Visual History of America's Founding Ideas* (New York: Oxford University Press, 2005), 95–96.

10. Randy Barnett, "The Declaration of Independence and the American Theory of Government," *Harvard Journal of Law & Public Policy* 42, no. 1 (2019): 23.

11. See David Hackett Fischer, *Washington's Crossing* (New York: Oxford University Press, 2004), 384–85.

12. Gordon Wood, *The Creation of the American Republic* (Chapel Hill: University of North Carolina Press, 1969).

13. Rogan Kersh, *Dreams of a More Perfect Union* (Ithaca, NY: Cornell University Press, 2001).

14. Quoted in Gordon Wood, *Empire of Liberty* (New York: Oxford University Press, 2009), 14.

15. George Washington, Circular Letter of Farewell to the Army, June 8, 1873.

16. Richard Beeman, *Plain, Honest Men: The Making of the American Constitution* (New York: Random House, 2009), 3–7, 12.

17. Leonard Richards, *Shays's Rebellion: The American Revolution's Final Battle* (Philadelphia: University of Pennsylvania Press, 2002).

18. Beeman, *Plain, Honest Men*.

19. James Madison, "Madison's Notes of Debates," in *The Federal Convention and the Formation of the Union*, ed. Winston Solberg (Indianapolis, IN: Bobbs Merrill, 1958), 84–85.

20. Madison, "Madison's Notes," 81.

21. Madison, "Madison's Notes," 81.

22. Madison, "Madison's Notes," 122 (quotes); also see David Brian

Robertson, *The Constitution and America's Destiny* (New York: Cambridge University Press, 2005), 139.

23. Luther Martin, "Letter on the Federal Convention of 1787," American Constitution Society, https://bit.ly/3fNos8G.

24. Robertson, *Constitution and America's Destiny*, 140.

25. Mara Liasson, "Democrats Increasingly Say American Democracy Is Sliding Toward Minority Rule," NPR, June 9, 2021, https://n.pr/3pWIjEx.

26. Francis Fukuyama, "American Political Dysfunction," *American Interest*, November/December 2011, https://bit.ly/2MQLxTS; Sarah Repucci, "From Crisis to Reform," Freedom House, Summer 2021.

27. Max Farrand, ed., *The Records of the Federal Convention of 1787*, rev. ed. (New Haven, CT: Yale University Press, 1966), 3:179.

28. Beeman, *Plain, Honest Men*, 335. On slavery in early America, see also Wendy Warren, *New England Bound* (New York: Norton, 2016).

29. Emily A. Vogels et al., "Americans and 'Cancel Culture,'" Pew Charitable Trusts, May 19, 2021, https://pewrsr.ch/3MLvQwS.

30. Beeman, *Plain, Honest Men*, 333.

31. See James A. Morone, *The Democratic Wish* (New Haven, CT: Yale University Press, 1998), chap. 1.

32. Madison, "Madison's Notes."

33. Catherine Thorbecke, "The U.S. Dollar Could Go Digital," CNN Business, March 11, 2022, https://cnn.it/3t66G4A.

34. Ford in *Congressional Record*, 116 (1970), 11913.

35. *United States v. Windsor*, 570 U.S. 744 (2013) struck down key portions of the Defense of Marriage Act; *Obergefell v. Hodges* 576___ (2015) guaranteed the right of same-sex couples to marry.

36. Herbert Storing, *What the Anti-Federalists Were For: The Political Writings of the Opponents of the Constitution* (Chicago: University of Chicago Press, 1981).

37. Drew DeSilver, "The Polarization in Today's Congress," Pew Research Center, March 10, 2022, https://pewrsr.ch/3I9L2jY; Lilliana Mason, *Uncivil Agreement: How Politics Became Our Identity* (Chicago: University of Chicago Press, 2018).

38. Wood, *Radicalism of the American Revolution*.

39. To track which parts of the Bill of Rights have been incorporated and therefore apply to state/local governments, see the Cornell Law Institute's helpful list, at https://bit.ly/3ik0NdX.
40. "Ceremonies Mark Constitution Day," *New York Times*, September 17, 1923, 11.
41. Thomas Jefferson, "Letter to Samuel Kercheval, July 12, 1816," in *The Works of Thomas Jefferson*, ed. Paul Leicester Ford (New York: Putnam's Sons, 1905), 12:13–14.
42. Robert Dahl, *How Democratic Is the American Constitution?*, 2nd ed. (New Haven, CT: Yale University Press, 2003).

Chapter 4
1. Jose Antonio Vargas, *Dear America: Notes of an Undocumented Citizen* (New York: Dey Street/William Morrow, 2018), 103–4.
2. Hans Schattle, "Moral Visions of Sanctuary Across the Great Divides in Contemporary Political Philosophy," *Globalizations* (2021), DOI: 10.1080/14747731.2021.1902037.
3. Jonathan Stempel, "New York Sues Trump Administration over 'Punitive' Ban from Traveler Program," Reuters, February 10, 2020, https://reut.rs/3hQjRyE.
4. Congressional Research Service, "Federal Workforce Statistics Sources: OPM and OMB" (updated each October), https://bit.ly/3dTsrL7. Figure includes some seven hundred thousand civilian members of the Department of Defense.
5. For updated state and local government employment figures, see the Bureau of Labor Statistics' "occupational employment statistics" site, at https://www.bls.gov/oes/home.htm.
6. BLS site (see chap. 4, note 5).
7. Megan Brenan, "Americans' Trust in Government Remains Low," Gallup, September 30, 2021, https://bit.ly/3A0h4xA; Lee Rainie, Scott Keeter, and Andrew Perrin, "Trust and Distrust in America," Pew Research Center, July 22, 2019, https://pewrsr.ch/2vnybeu.
8. Justin McCarthy, "Americans Still More Trusting of Local Than State Government," Gallup, October 8, 2018, https://bit.ly/2uvB24w; Rainie et al., 2019 (see chap. 4, note 7).
9. McCarthy, 2018 (see chap. 4, note 8).
10. The Supreme Court affirmed Dillon's rule in *Hunter v. Pittsburgh*, 207 U.S. 161 (1907).

11. Edward Banfield and James Q. Wilson, *City Politics* (Cambridge, MA: Harvard University Press, 1967), 65.
12. Danielle Muoio Dunn, "It's a Global Phenomenon—Now New York is Poised to Lead the Nation in Congestion Pricing," *Politico*, September 3, 2022, https://politi.co/3hfQRVg.
13. David Brian Robertson, *Federalism and the Making of America* (New York: Routledge, 2012); Jacob M. Grumbach and Jamila Michener, "American Federalism, Political Inequality, and Democratic Erosion," *Annals of the American Academy of Political and Social Science* 699:1 (2022): 143–55.
14. From Justice Brandeis's dissenting opinion in *New State Ice Co. v. Liebmann*, 285 U.S. 262, 311 (1932).
15. Steven Levitsky and Daniel Ziblatt, *How Democracies Die* (New York: Crown, 2018), 2.
16. Neal D. Woods, "An Environmental Race to the Bottom? 'No More Stringent' Laws in the American States," *Publius* 51:2 (2021): 238–261; Yacouba Kassouri, "Fiscal Decentralization and Public Budgets for Energy RD&D: A Race to the Bottom?" *Energy Policy* 161 (2022): 112761.
17. Morone, *Hellfire Nation*, part 3 (see chap. 2, note 51).
18. Dirksen quoted in Richard P. Nathan, "Updating Theories of American Federalism," in *Intergovernmental Management for the Twenty-First Century*, ed. Timothy Conlan and Paul Posner (Washington, DC: Brookings Institution Press, 2008), 15.
19. Heather K. Gerken and Joshua Revesz, "Progressive Federalism: A User's Guide," *Democracy Journal* 44, Spring 2017, https://bit.ly/3tff0Ou.
20. Ursula Hackett, "Federalism," in Gillian Peele, et al., eds., *New Developments in American Politics* 9 (New York: Palgrave Macmillan, 2022).
21. See the "We're Still In" declaration: https://www.wearestillin.com.
22. Abbe Gluck and Thomas Scott-Railton, "Affordable Care Act Entrenchment," *Georgetown Law Journal* 108: 495–578, (2020).
23. See James A. Morone and David Blumenthal, "The Arc of History Bends Toward Coverage: Health Policy at a Crossroads," *Health Affairs* 37, no. 3 (2018): 351.
24. *McCulloch v. Maryland*, 17 U.S. 316 (1819).

25. Benedict Anderson, *Imagined Communities* (New York: Verson, 1983). Anderson explains that every nation faces the same issue, that they are all "imagined communities."
26. David Waldstreicher, *"In the Midst of Perpetual Fetes": The Making of American Nationalism, 1776-1820* (Chapel Hill: University of North Carolina Press, 1997).
27. Harris Mylonas and Maya Tudor, "Nationalism: What We Know and What We Still Need to Know," *Annual Review of Political Science* 24 (May 2021): 109–32.
28. Samuel Goldman, *After Nationalism: Being American in an Age of Division* (Philadelphia: University of Pennsylvania Press, 2021).
29. Michael Feola, "'You Will Not Replace Us': The Melancholic Nationalism of Whiteness," *Political Theory* 49:4 (2021): 528–553; Luis Noe-Bustamante, "Asian American Concerns Over Threats, Attacks," Pew Research Center, May 9, 2022, https://pewrsr.ch/3tcdY5N.
30. Tocqueville, *Democracy in America*, 1:61–70. For a modern perspective, see Anthony M. Pellegrino et al., "Picturing New Notions of Civic Engagement in the U.S.," in *Youth Voices, Public Spaces, and Civic Engagement*, ed. Stuart Greene, Kevin J. Burke, and Maria K. McKenna (New York: Routledge, 2016), 25–49.

Chapter 5
1. *Matal v. Tam*, 582 U.S. ___ (2017).
2. Adam Liptak, "Supreme Court Strikes Down Law Barring Vulgar Trademarks," *New York Times*, June 24, 2019, B3.
3. *Schenck v. United States* 249 U.S. 47 (1919).
4. See, for example, Pavlos Vasiliopoulous et al., "Emotions, Governmental Trust, and Support for the Restriction of Civil Liberties During the Covid-19 Pandemic," *European Journal of Political Research* 61, no. 1 (2022). 1–35
5. *New York Times*/Siena College Research Institute survey (2022), https://bit.ly/390FKLK.
6. Death Penalty Information Center, "Executions Overview" (as of May 2022), https://bit.ly/3MSKYIa.
7. Death Penalty Information Center, "Executions Overview" (as of May 2022), https://bit.ly/3MSKYIa.

8. Reporters Without Borders, 2022 (see chap. 5, note 8).

9. Reporters Without Borders, "World Press Freedom Index," May 2022, https://rsf.org/en/index.

10. Reporters Without Borders, 2022 (see chap. 5, note 8).

11. Shawn Francis Peters, *Judging Jehovah's Witnesses: Religious Persecution and the Dawn of the Rights Revolution* (Lawrence: University Press of Kansas, 2000).

12. The two cases are *Minersville School District v. Gobitis*, 310 U.S. 586 (1940), and *West Virginia State Board of Education v. Barnette*, 319 U.S. 624 (1943).

13. Tocqueville, *Democracy in America*, 252 (see chap. 2, note 12).

14. *Barron v. Baltimore*, 32 U.S. 243 (1833).

15. *The Slaughter-House Cases*, 83 U.S. 36 (1873); *United States v. Cruikshank*, 92 U.S. 542 (1876).

16. *Palko v. Connecticut*, 302 U.S. 319 (1937).

17. If you're interested in reading more on any of the cases we discuss, see Lee Epstein, Kevin T. McGuire, and Thomas G. Walker, *Constitutional Law for a Changing America*, 12th ed. (Washington, DC: CQ Press, 2023).

18. For a description of the fears that led to the prohibitions, see Morone, *Hellfire Nation*, chap. 8 (see chap. 2, note 51).

19. *Dobbs v. Jackson Women's Health*, No. 19–1392 (2022).

20. "Abortion Policy in the Absence of Roe: State Laws and Policies," *Guttmacher Institute*, July 1, 2022, https://bit.ly/3WMkUUL.

21. Marc A. Thiessen, "Watch Out, Democrats. The Abortion Ruling May Help Republicans," *Washington Post*, May 5, 2022, https://wapo.st/3sjwjxK.

22. Thomas Jefferson, "Letter to the Danbury Baptist Association," January 1, 1802, https://www.loc.gov/loc/lcib/9806/danpre.html.

23. *Everson v. Board of Education*, 330 U.S. 1 (1947).

24. *Engel v. Vitale*, 370 U.S. 421 (1962).

25. *Lamb's Chapel v. Center Moriches Union Free School District*, 508 U.S. 384 (1993).

26. *Kennedy v Bremerton School District*, No. 21-418 (2022).

27. Lee Epstein and Eric Posner, "The Roberts Court and the Transformation of Constitutional Protects for Religion: A Statistical Portrait," *The Supreme Court Review* 315 (2022).

28. *Carson v. Makin*, 20-1088 (2022); *Ramirez v. Collier*, 21-5592 (2022); *Shurtleff v. City of Boston*, 20-1800 (2022).

29. In *Good News Club v. Milford Central School*, 533 U.S. 98 (2001), the Court ruled 6–3 in favor of the club, allowing them to meet on school grounds.

30. *Employment Division, Department of Human Resources of Oregon v. Smith*, 494 U.S. 872 (1990).

31. *Burwell v. Hobby Lobby Stores*, 573 U.S. 682 (2014).

32. *Fulton v. City of Philadelphia*, 593 U.S. ___ (2021).

33. *Holt v. Hobbs*, 574 U.S. 352 (2015).

34. The decision that explicitly adopted a preferred position for free speech was *Brandenburg v. Ohio*, 395 U.S. 444 (1969), discussed later in this section.

35. John Stuart Mill, *On Liberty* (New York: Penguin Classics, 1982), 103. Oliver Wendell Holmes expressed a powerful faith in the marketplace of ideas in his dissent in *Abrams v. United States*, 250 U.S. 616 (1919).

36. Knight Foundation, "Free Expression in America Post-2020," 2022, https://kng.ht/3KVICH2.

37. *Dobbs v. Jackson Women's Health*, No. 19–1392 (2022).

38. For a discussion and context, see Morone, *Republic of Wrath*, chap. 1 (see chap. 2, note 36).

39. *Gitlow v. New York*, 268 U.S. 652 (1925). Gitlow, the socialist author of a left-wing manifesto, was convicted, but in the process the courts incorporated free speech.

40. *Brandenburg v. Ohio*, 395 U.S. 444 (1969). For a fine discussion, see Harold Sullivan, *Civil Rights and Liberties* (Upper Saddle River, NJ: Pearson Prentice Hall, 2005), chap. 2.

41. See Rebecca Barrett-Fox, *God Hates: Westboro Baptist Church, American Nationalism, and the Religious Right* (Lawrence: University of Kansas Press, 2016).

42. Adrienne LaFrance, "Facebook Papers: 'History Will Not Judge Us Kindly,'" *The Atlantic*, October 21, 2021, https://bit.ly/3LdZnxD.

43. Valerie Strauss, "A Sobering New Finding on Americans' Civic Knowledge," *Washington Post*, September 17, 2021, https://wapo.st/3FuKqpA.

44. *Virginia v. Black*, 538 U.S. 343 (2003).

45. *Texas v. Johnson*, 491 U.S. 397 (1989).

46. Corey Brettschneider, *When the State Speaks, What Should It Say?* (Princeton, NJ: Princeton University Press, 2012).

47. All death penalty figures from Cornell Law School, Cornell Center on the Death Penalty Worldwide project, http://www.deathpenaltyworldwide.org.

48. *Chaplinsky v. New Hampshire*, 315 U.S. 568 (1942).

49. Burton Caine, "The Trouble with the Fighting Words Doctrine: *Chaplinsky v. New Hampshire* Is a Threat to First Amendment Values and Should Be Overruled." *Marquette Law Review* 88, no. 3 (2004): 441–562.

50. David Hudson, "80 Years Ago the Supreme Court Introduced 'Fighting Words,'" *FIRE* (March 9, 2022), https://bit.ly/3fRWrgn.

51. *Tinker v. Des Moines Independent Community School District*, 393 U.S. 503 (1969).

52. *Bethel School District No. 403 v. Fraser*, 478 U.S. 675 (1986); *Hazelwood School District v. Kuhlmeier*, 484 U.S. 260 (1988).

53. *Mahanoy Area School District v. B.L.*, 594 U.S. ___ (2021).

54. See the summary in Jennifer Miller, "What College Students Really Think About Cancel Culture," *The Atlantic*, May 2022, https://bit.ly/3G7ptkM.

55. *Uzuegbunam v. Preczewski*, 592 U.S. ___ (2021). For details, see Adam Liptak, "A College's 'Free Speech Areas' Face Supreme Court Review," *New York Times*, March 8, 2021, https://nyti.ms/3O6MJ5p.

56. *New York Times Company v. United States*, 403 U.S. 713 (1971).

57. Bob Egelko, "S.F. Judge Dissolves His Wikileaks Injunction," *San Francisco Chronicle*, March 1, 2008, https://bit.ly/3tcgKbc.

58. Michael S. Schmidt and Adam Goldman, "Ashley Biden's Diary Was Shown at a Trump Fundraiser. Weeks Later, Project Veritas Called Her," *New York Times*, March 23, 2022, https://nyti.ms/3NxKgk5.

59. *United States v. Stevens*, 130 U.S.C. 1577 (2010).

60. Catharine MacKinnon, "Pornography, Civil Rights, and Speech," in *Constitutional Law and American Democracy*, ed. Corey Brettschneider (New York: Wolters Kluwer, 2011), see note 10, 661–70.

61. *Ashcroft v. Free Speech Coalition* (00–795) 535 U.S. 234 (2002) struck down the first statute; *United States v.*

Williams, 553 U.S. 285 (2008) upheld the second.

62. Devin Dwyer, "Fact Check: Judge Ketanji Brown Jackson Child Porn Sentences 'Pretty Mainstream,'" ABC News, March 22, 2022, https://abcn .ws/3wJGcGu.

63. Joshua A. Geltzer and Neal K. Katyal, "The True Danger of the Trump Campaign's Defamation Lawsuits," *The Atlantic,* March 11, 2020, https://bit.ly/2Ac1OCi.

64. Seth Lipsky, *The Citizen's Constitution: An Animated Guide* (New York: Basic Books, 2009), 222.

65. Chip Brownlee, "Gun Violence in 2021: By the Numbers," *The Trace,* May 27, 2022, https://bit.ly/ 3vYxuED.

66. Charlton Heston quoted in "Charlton Heston Rips Media," *Chicago Tribune,* September 12, 1997; *District of Columbia v. Heller,* 554 U.S. 570 (2008).

67. Joseph Story, *Commentaries on the Constitution of the United States* (Boston: Hilliard, Gray, 1833), 3:746.

68. *District of Columbia v. Heller,* No. 478F 3d 370 (2008); *McDonald v. Chicago,* 561 U.S. 742 (2010).

69. *New York State Rifle & Pistol Association v. Bruen,* No. 20-843 (2022).

70. "America's Gun Culture—in Seven Charts," BBC News, 2022, "https:// www.bbc.com/news/world-us-canada-41488081; "Guns," *Gallup Polls,* June 22. 2022, https://news .gallup.com/poll/1645/guns.aspx.

71. *Olmstead v. United States,* 277 U.S. 438 (1928).

72. *United States v. Leon,* 468 U.S. 897 (1984).

73. *Herring v. United States,* 555 U.S. 135 (2009).

74. *Kentucky v. King,* 131 U.S. 865 (2011); *Utah v. Strief,* 579 U.S. ___, 136 S. Ct. 2056 (2016); *Thompson v. Clark,* No. 20-659 (2022).

75. Linda Monk, *The Words We Live By: Your Annotated Guide to the Constitution* (New York: Hyperion, 2003), 165.

76. The Supreme Court reaffirmed the constitutionality of trying a suspect in both state and federal court in a 2019 case, *Gamble v. U.S.,* 587 U.S. ___ (2019).

77. *Dickerson v. United States,* 530 U.S. 428 (2000).

78. *Illinois v. Perkins,* 496 U.S. 292 (1990); *New York v. Quarles,* 467 U.S. 649 (1984); *Harris v. New York,* 401 U.S. 222 (1970); *Vega v. Tekoh,* No. 21-499 (2022).

79. Anthony Lewis, *Gideon's Trumpet* (New York: Vintage, 1989).

80. *Missouri v. Frye,* 132 U.S. 55 (2012); Emily Yoffe, "Innocence Is Irrelevant: This Is the Age of the Plea Bargain," *The Atlantic,* September 2017, https://bit.ly/3zTVdIj.

81. U.S. Department of Justice, "Access to Justice," http://www .justice.gov/atj/file/788166/download.

82. Richard A. Oppel Jr. and Jugal K. Patel, "One Lawyer, 194 Felony Cases, and No Time," *New York Times,* January 31, 2019, https:// nyti.ms/2B5lZCr; Andrew Cohen, "The Right to An Attorney: Theory v. Practice," Brennan Center, December 20, 2021, https://bit.ly/3NwrMAa.

83. "DEA Asset Forfeiture," United States Drug Enforcement Administration, https://www.dea.gov/dea-asset-forfeiture.

84. "Most Americans Favor the Death Penalty Despite Concerns About Its Administration, *Pew Research,* June 2, 2021, https://www.pewresearch.org/ politics/2021/06/02/most-americans-favor-the-death-penalty-despite-concerns-about-its-administration-/.

85. The Death Penalty Information Center has put together a useful clearing house of data, https:// deathpenaltyinfo.org/racedeath-row-inmates-executed-1976?scid=5& did=184.

86. For a list of executions by state and region since 1976, see https:// deathpenaltyinfo.org/ numberexecutions-state-and-region-1976.

87. For an updated list of inmates whose crimes have been exonerated by Innocence Project efforts, see https://www.innocenceproject.org/ dnaexonerations-in-the-united-states/.

88. *Kennedy v. Louisiana,* 554 U.S. 407 (2008); *Atkins v. Virginia,* 536 U.S. 304 (2002); *Roper v. Simmons,* 543 U.S. 551 (2005); *Baez v. Rees,* 271 S. W. 3d. 207 affirmed (2007).

89. *Hamm v. Reeves,* 595 U.S. __ (2022); Sotomayor in *Glossip v. Gross,* 576 U.S. 863 (2015).

90. As of March 2022. Data updated by George Washington University's "Extremism Tracker," at https:// extremism.gwu.edu/isis-america.

91. National Security Council, *National Strategy for Countering Domestic Terrorism* (Washington, DC: NSC, 2021).

92. See, e.g., Jack Kelly, "A Consequence of COVID-19 Could Be a Loss of Civil Liberties—Resulting in

Career Restrictions," *Forbes,* April 24, 2020, https://bit.ly/2ZdVLFQ.

93. Lawrence O. Gostin and Meryl Chertoff, "Lockdowns, Quarantines, and Travel Restrictions, During COVID and Beyond: What's the Law, and How Should We Decide?" *Health Affairs Blog,* April 16, 2021, DOI No.: 10.1377/hblog20210322.450239.

Chapter 6

1. James Wright, "Nation's Black Mayors Meet in D.C. to Address Common Challenges," *Washington Informer,* May 4, 2022, https://bit .ly/3QWIU4a.

2. Jeffrey M. Jones, "In US, Black Confidence in Police Recovers from 2020 Low," Gallup, July 14, 2021, https://bit.ly/3tiA4E2.

3. "Who Is Living Together? Same-Sex Couples in the United States," U.S. Census Bureau, November 2019, https://bit.ly/2SQqBCw.

4. E.g., "Protesters Stage a Die In to Protest the Death of George Floyd," *Boston Globe,* June 5, 2020, https:// bit.ly/2BJSxSo. The 8:42 timing was initially (and erroneously) reported as the length of time a police officer kept his knee on Floyd's neck, killing him.

5. Samuel Huntington, *American Politics: The Promise of Disharmony* (Cambridge, MA: Harvard University Press, 1981).

6. Kimmy Yam, "Anti-Asian Hate Crimes Increased 339 Percent Nationwide Lat Year, Report Says, *NBC News,*" February 14, 2022.

7. Smith, *Civic Ideals* (see chap. 2, note 7).

8. *Korematsu v. United States,* 323 U.S. 214 (1944); overruled in *Trump v. Hawaii,* 585 U.S 218 (2018).

9. *Pierce v. Society of Sisters,* 268 U.S. 510 (1925); *Romer v. Evans,* 517 U.S. 620 (1996).

10. Lyle Denniston, "Constitutional Milestone on Transgender Rights," *Constitution Daily,* April 16, 2018, https://bit.ly/3DLSLEE.

11. Ta-Nehisi Coates, *Between the World and Me* (New York: Spiegel and Grau, 2015); Ishmael Reed, "America's Criminal Justice System and Me," *New York Times,* June 22, 2020, https://nyti.ms/3WKVd7b.

12. W. E. B. DuBois, *The Souls of Black Folk* (New York: New American Library, 1982), 220.

13. See Sven Beckert and Seth Rockman, eds., *Slavery's Capitalism: A New History of American Economic*

Development (Philadelphia: University of Pennsylvania Press, 2016).

14. Garry Wills, *Lincoln at Gettysburg* (New York: Simon & Schuster, 1992).

15. C. Vann Woodward, *The Burden of Southern History*, 3rd ed. (Baton Rouge: University of Louisiana Press, 1993), 72.

16. W. E. B. Du Bois, *The Souls of Black Folk: Essays and Sketches* (Chicago: McClurg and Co.: 1903), 16.

17. Morone, *Republic of Wrath*, part II (see chap. 2, note 36).

18. *The Civil Rights Cases*, 109 U.S. 3 (1883).

19. Richard Valelly, *The Two Reconstructions* (Chicago: University of Chicago Press, 2004), 2.

20. See, e.g., Le'Trice D. Donaldson, *Duty Beyond the Battlefield: African American Soldiers Fight for Racial Uplift, Citizenship, and Manhood, 1870–1920* (Carbondale: Southern Illinois University Press, 2020).

21. *Plessy v. Ferguson*, 163 U.S. 537 (1896); *Williams v. Mississippi*, 170 U.S. 213 (1898).

22. Jessie Parkhurst Guzman, *The Negro Yearbook* (Tuskegee, AL: Tuskegee Institute, 1947); Philip Dray, *A Lynching at Port Jervis: Race and Reckoning in the Gilded Age* (New York: Farrar, Straus, & Giroux, 2022).

23. Peggy Pascoe, *What Comes Naturally: Miscegenation Law and the Making of Race in America* (New York: Oxford University Press, 2008).

24. Daniel P. Franklin, *Politics and Film: The Political Culture of Film in the United States* (Lanham, MD: Rowman and Littlefield, 2006).

25. *Smith v. Allwright*, 21 U.S. 649 (1944).

26. *Morgan v. Virginia*, 328 U.S. 373 (1946); *Sweatt v. Painter*, 339 U.S. 629 (1950); *McLaurin v. Oklahoma*, 339 U.S. 637 (1950).

27. *Brown v. Board of Education*, 347 U.S. 483 (1954).

28. Taylor Branch, *Parting the Waters* (New York: Simon & Schuster, 1988), 203.

29. See Raymond Arsenault, *Freedom Riders: 1961 and the Struggle for Racial Justice* (New York: Oxford, 2006).

30. *Heart of Atlanta Motel Inc. v. United States*, 379 U.S. 241 (1964); *Katzenbach v. McClung*, 379 U.S. 294 (1964).

31. Martin Luther King, *Where Do We Go from Here: Chaos or Community?* (New York: Harper and Row, 1967) (I had preached); Andrew Kopkind, "Soul Power," *New York Review of Books*, August 24, 1976; Zelizar, *Fierce Urgency*, 230 (never seen).

32. *Griggs v. Duke Power Co.*, 401 U.S. 424 (1971).

33. *Sheet Metal Workers v. EEOC*, 478 U.S. 421 (1986).

34. *Adarand Construction v. Peña*, 515 U.S. 299 (1995).

35. *University of California v. Bakke*, 438 U.S. 265 (1978); *Fisher v. University of Texas at Austin et al.*, 579 U.S. 14–981 (2016); Richard D. Kahlenberg, "The Affirmative Action That Colleges Really Need," *The Atlantic*, October 26, 2022, https://bit.ly/3DSzeTk.

36. Maria Carrasco, "Record Numbers of Men 'Give Up' On College," *Inside Higher Education*, September 8, 2021, https://bit.ly/3QBzqex.

37. Monica Anderson et al., "#BlackLivesMatter Surges on Twitter After George Floyd's Death," Pew Research Center, June 10, 2020, https://pewrsr.ch/3E3TOQz.

38. Weihua Li and Humera Lodhi, "Which States Are Taking on Police Reform After George Floyd?," The Marshall Project, June 18, 2020, https://bit.ly/2ZBfHTc.

39. Tom McCarthy, "Republican Senator Says He Would've Been Afraid Had the Capitol Rioters Been BLM Activists," *The Guardian*, March 14, 2021, https://bit.ly/3hlPpAJ.

40. Abby Kelly Foster, quoted in Morone, *Hellfire Nation*, 166 (see chap. 2, note 51).

41. Morone, *Republic of Wrath*, chap. 5 (see chap. 2, note 36).

42. On this history and developments for women officeholders since, see Julie Dolan, Melissa M. Deckman, and Michele L. Swers, *Women and Politics: Paths to Power and Political Influence*, 4th ed. (Lanham, MD: Rowman & Littlefield, 2021).

43. For updated figures on women serving in federal and state office, see Center for American Women and Politics, Rutgers University, https://cawp.rutgers.edu/facts.

44. Daiquiri J. Steele, "IX at 50," *Social Education* 86.3 (2022): 216–219.

45. Donald Critchlow, *Phyllis Schlafly and Grassroots Conservatism* (Princeton, NJ: Princeton University Press, 2005), chap. 9.

46. "The Simple Truth About the Gender Pay Gap," American Association of University Women, 2020, https://bit.ly/2urCe9w. Megan Wisniewski, "What Is the Gender Wage Gap in Your State?" U.S. Census Bureau, March 1, 2022, https://bit.ly/3fXZeo6.

47. *Ledbetter v. Goodyear Tire & Rubber Co.*, 550 U.S. 618 (2007).

48. Steven J. Vodanovich and Deborah E. Rupp, *Employment Discrimination* (New York: Oxford University Press, 2022), ch. 6 ("Sex-Specific Workplace Discrimination").

49. *Wal-Mart Stores Inc. v. Dukes*, 603 F. 3d 571, reversed (2011).

50. Carrasco, 2021 (see chap. 6, note 36).

51. Katharina Buchholz, "How Has the Number of Female CEOs in Fortune 500 Companies Changed Over the Last 20 Years?" *World Economic Forum*, March 10, 2022, https://bit.ly/3IPqvTT.

52. Abha Bhattarai, "Caring for Aging Parents, Sick Spouses Is Keeping Millions Out of Work," *Washington Post*, April 4, 2022, https://wapo.st/3EhVKpQ.

53. Cary Funk and Mark Hugo Lopez, "A Brief Statistical Portrait of U.S. Hispanics," Pew Research Center, June 14, 2022, https://pewrsr.ch/3AY2I2e.

54. Aaron Klein and Ember Smith, "Explaining the Economic Impact of COVID-19: Core Industries and the Hispanic Workforce," *Brookings Institution Policy Brief* (2021), 1–18.

55. Anthony Man, "Poll Shows Generational, Political Divides Among Cuban-Americans," *South Florida Sun-Sentinel*, February 1, 2019, https://bit.ly/3c4TW3k.

56. Honorable Henry Cabot Lodge, "Lynch Law and Unrestricted Immigration," *North American Review* 152 (1891): 602–12.

57. On immigration history, see Smith, *Civic Ideals* (see chap. 2, note 7); Daniel Tichenor, *Dividing Lines: The Politics of Immigration Control in America* (Princeton, NJ: Princeton University Press, 2002). On immigration polls, see "Immigration/Border Security," Polling Report, 2020, https://bit.ly/2TdvaWa.

58. For recent immigration data, see Migration Policy Institute, "Migration Information Source," https://bit.ly/2xjUpMD.

59. Updated estimates of resident aliens and undocumented immigrants are provided monthly by the Department of Homeland Security, at https://bit.ly/3K8TuCE.

60. Eileen Sullivan, "Appeals Court Says DACA Is Illegal but Keeps Program Alive for Now," *New York Times,* October 5, 2022, https://nyti.ms/3WKMv95.

61. Sarah C.K. Moore, *A History of Bilingual Education in the U.S.: Examining the Politics of Language Policymaking* (Bristol, UK: Channel View, 2021).

62. Emily A. Shrider et. al., "Income and Poverty in the United States," U.S. Census Bureau (Sept. 2021), https://bit.ly/3PrRbwn.

63. Mohammad Moslimani, "Deportation a Concern for Many U.S. Latinos," Pew Research Center, February 14, 2022, https://pewrsr.ch/3RKcKdj.

64. Heather Silber Mohamed, "Can Protests Make Latinos 'American'? Identity, Immigration Politics, and the 2006 Marches," *American Politics Research* 41, no. 2 (2013): 298–327.

65. Abby Budiman and Neil G. Ruiz, "Key Facts About Asian Americans, A Growing and Diverse Population," Pew Research Center, April 29, 2021, https://pewrsr.ch/3tfe2BR.

66. Smith, *Civic Ideals,* 361 (see chap. 2, note 7).

67. Anagha Srikanth, "California Lawmakers Apologize for Japanese Internment 78 Years Later," *The Hill,* February 20, 2020, https://bit.ly/2w0bT2u; *Trump v Hawaii* 585 U.S 218 (2018).

68. Lon Kurashige, *Two Faces of Exclusion: The Untold Story of Anti-Asian Racism in the United States* (Chapel Hill: University of North Carolina Press, 2016).

69. Yeonjung Jane Lee and Sophia B. Kim, "Standing Against Anti-Asian Racism in America," *Health and Social Work* 47:3 (2022), 157–159.

70. Luis Noe-Bustamante et al., "A Majority of Asian Americans Say Violence Against Asians is Increasing in the U.S.," Pew Research Center, May 9, 2022, https://pewrsr.ch/3RQVPFR.

71. Pekka Hämäläinen, *The Comanche Empire* (New Haven, CT: Yale University Press, 2008).

72. Hämäläinen, 2008 (see chap. 6, note 71).

73. Arohi Pathnak, "How the Government Can End Poverty for Native American Women," CAP, October 22, 2021, https://ampr.gs/3FZ2Oco; Dedrick Asante-Muhammad, Esha Kamra, Connor Sanchez, Kathy Ramirez, and Rogelio Tec, "Racial Wealth Snapshot: Native Americans," National Community Reinvestment Corporation, February 14, 2022, https://bit.ly/3WLGY1X.

74. *Sharp v. Murphy,* 875 F.3d 896 (2020); *McGirt v Oklahoma,* No. 18-9526 (2021).

75. *California v. Cabazon Band of Mission Indians,* 480 U.S. 202 (1987).

76. Martin Harris, "Tribal Casinos in the U.S.," PlayUSA, Mar. 31, 2022, https://bit.ly/3v4HzzB.

77. Justin McCarthy, "Record-High 70% in U.S. Support Same-Sex Marriage," Gallup, June 8, 2021, https://bit.ly/3A2WcpH.

78. Hye-Yon Lee and Diana C. Mutz, "Changing Attitudes Toward Same-Sex Marriage," *Political Behavior* 41 (2019): 701–22.

79. *Bostock v. Clayton County, Georgia,* No. 17–1618 (2020).

80. Miriam Smith, "LGBTQ Politics in Anglo-American Democracies," in *The Oxford Handbook of Global LGBT and Sexual Diversity Politics,* ed. Michael A. Bosia, Sandra M. McEvoy, and Momin Rahman (New York: Oxford University Press, 2020); Steven Peck, "The Criminal Justice System and the LGBTQ Community: An Anti-Queer Regime," *Themis: Research Journal of Justice Studies and Forensic Science* 10 (2022), 103–132.

81. Michael Lipka, "Americans Are Divided Over Which Bathrooms Transgender People Should Use," *Pew Research Center,* October 3, 2016, https://pewrsr.ch/3hmxE4h.

82. Jeremiah J. Castle and Kyla K. Stepp, "Partisanship, Religion, and Issue Polarization in the United States: A Reassessment," *Political Behavior* 43 (2021): 1311–1335; Ronald Brownstein, "Want to Understand the Red-State Onslaught? Look to Florida," *The Atlantic,* March 10, 2022, https://bit.ly/3EiwZtG.

83. Katie Barnes, "Amid Protests, Penn Swimmer Lia Thomas Becomes First Known Transgender Athlete to win Division 1 National Championship," ESPN, March 17, 2022, https://es.pn/3WPbMiw.

84. Masood Farivar, "How U.S. Voting Laws Have Changed Since 2020," *VOA,* November 3, 2022, https://bit.ly/3fRFVNj. For regular updates on state changes, see Voting Rights Lab's "State Voting Rights Tracker," https://bit.ly/3UJJSlU.

85. *Shelby County v. Holder,* 557 U.S. 193 (2013); Allan Lichtman, *The Embattled Vote in America* (Cambridge, MA: Harvard University Press, 2018); Morone, *Republic of Wrath* (see chap. 2, note 36); *Abbot v. Perez,* 17–586 (2018).

86. Benjamin Swasey, "Map: See Which States Have Restricted Voter Access, and Which States Have Expanded It," NPR, September 7, 2021.

87. Daron Shaw and John Petrocik, *The Turnout Myth* (New York: Oxford University Press, 2020).

88. Marina Sheriff, "Testimony: Public Hearings on the Rockefeller Drug Laws, Special Housing Units, and Transitional Services for Inmates," New York Civil Liberties Union, May 4, 2001; U.S. Substance Abuse and Mental Health Services Administration, "2018 National Survey on Drug Use and Health," August 2019.

Chapter 7

1. "After Pot Conviction, NY Couple Plans for Legal Dispensary," AP Newswire, April 26, 2022, https://www.independent.co.uk/news/ap-new-york-cannabis-long-island-dominican-republic-b2065391.html.

2. Hannah Fingerhut, "Support Steady for Same-Sex Marriage and Acceptance of Homosexuality," Pew Research Center, May 12, 2016, http://pewrsr.ch/2ajmvN7; a 2016 update from Gallup: "In Depth: Topics A to Z: Marriage," http://bit.ly/1iiDKeI.

3. Coral Davenport and Eric Lipton, "How G.O.P. Leaders Came to View Climate Change as Fake Science," *New York Times,* June 3, 2017, A1; Emily Holden, "How the Oil Industry Has Spent Billions to Control the Climate Change Conversation," *The Guardian,* January 8, 2020; Holly Fuong and Geoffrey Skelley, "Do Democrats and Republicans Agree on Anything About Climate Change and Immigration?" *FiveThirtyEight,* September 29, 2022, https://53eig.ht/3StC0Ew.

4. "Emily Holden, "How the Oil Industry Has Spent Billions to Control the Climate Change Conversation," *The Guardian,* January 8, 2020, https://bit.ly/3hrPWBd.

5. Cassidy DiPaola, "Young Voters Want Biden to Act on Climate and Fossil Fuel Industry Accountability," Data for Progress, March 28, 2022, https://bit.ly/3UIsG0i.

6. Philip Bump, "Americans Are More Aware of Who Represents Them Than You Might Assume," *Washington Post,* October 27, 2022, https://wapo.st/3E3Ui9l.

7. Tori DeAngelis, "Support for Black Lives Matter Remains Stable," American Psychological Association, January 2022, https://www.apa.org/monitor/2022/01/numbers-black-lives.

8. DeAngelis, 2022 (see chap. 7, note 7).

9. Aegon, "The New Social Contract: Future-Proofing Retirement," March 1, 2022, https://bit.ly/3E2utX9.

10. David Tinsley, "U.S. Labor Market: Changing for the Better?" Bank of America Institute, May 25, 2022, https://bit.ly/3AdxZwN.

11. Mark Perna, "Younger Workers Say Show Us the Money—And They Mean Business," *Forbes*, February 11, 2020, https://bit.ly/3hBdvYs.

12. Vianney Gómez and Andrew Daniller, "Younger U.S. Adults Less Likely to See Big Differences Between the Parties or to Feel Well Represented by Them," Pew Research Center, December 7, 2021, https://pewrsr.ch/3hDnOvb.

13. Why? Because older people vote, and politicians are very unlikely to withdraw benefits from highly mobilized voters. Republicans are unlikely to threaten the program because seniors are their most staunch supporters—and are focused on protecting Social Security; Democrats are not likely to because they consider it an important program. In short, the political support for Social Security is very strong. Despite forty years of repeating that the program will soon collapse (despite no real evidence for that claim), the program enjoys robust support from both parties.

14. Michael Jackman, ed., *Crown's Book of Political Quotations* (New York: Crown Books, 1982), 181.

15. Mark Losey, "Why I Am a Democrat," Democratic-Underground.com, http://bit.ly/oHsB2C.

16. Leanne Italie, "Democratic Families Deal with the Shock of Children Going Republican," *Washington Times*, August 28, 2012, https://bit.ly/3aX5PIP.

17. Joshua Zingher, "Diploma Divide: Educational Attainment and the Realignment of the American Electorate," *Political Research Quarterly* 75:2 (2022): 263–77.

18. Janie Velencia, "The 2018 Gender Gap Was Huge," *FiveThirtyEight*, November 9, 2018, https://fivethirtyeight.com/features/the-2018-gender-gap-was-huge/.

19. Maitane Sardon, "A Guarded Generation: How Millennials View Money and Investing," *Wall Street Journal*, March 13, 2020, https://www.wsj.com/articles/the-recession-left-millennials-loaded-with-debtand-cynical-11583956727.

20. Larry Bartels, "Under Trump, Democrats and Republicans Have Never Been More Divided—On Nearly Everything," *Washington Post*, May 21, 2020, https://wapo.st/2Yxsu9o.

21. James N. Druckman et al., "Affective Polarization, Local Contexts, and Public Opinion in America," *Nature Human Behavior* 5 (2021): 28–38; Nolan McCarty, *Polarization: What Everyone Needs to Know* (New York: Oxford University Press, 2019).

22. William W. Franko and Christopher Witko, "Class, Policy Attitudes and U.S. Presidential Voting in the Post-Industrial Era," *Political Research Quarterly* 75:3 (2022); Jacob S. Hacker and Paul Pierson, *Let Them Eat Tweets: How the Right Rules in an Age of Extreme Inequality* (New York: Live-right, 2020). On states, see Katherine J. Cramer, *The Politics of Resentment: Rural Consciousness in Wisconsin and the Rise of Scott Walker* (Chicago: University of Chicago Press, 2016); David K. Jones, "Health Reform in the South: Re-Tracing Robert F. Kennedy's Steps in Mississippi and Kentucky," *World Medical & Health Policy* 9, no. 2 (2017).

23. Andrew Gelman, *Red State, Blue State, Rich State, Poor State: Why Americans Vote the Way They Do* (Princeton, NJ: Princeton University Press, 2009).

24. John Zaller, *The Nature and Origins of Mass Opinion* (New York: Cambridge University Press, 1992).

25. Bruce Drake, "More Americans Say U.S. Failed to Achieve Its Goals in Iraq," Pew Research Center, June 12, 2014, http://pewrsr.ch/1lsN29q.

26. Steven Shepard, "Trump's Challenge: A Wall of Public Skepticism on Afghanistan War," Politico, August 21, 2017, http://politi.co/2szdFWo.

27. A good overview is in Spencer Kimball, "2016 Presidential Statewide Polling—A Substandard Performance: A Proposal and Application for Evaluating Pre-election Poll Accuracy," *American Behavioral Scientist*, October 12, 2017, https://doi.org/10.1177/0002764217735622.

28. Courtney Kennedy, et al., "Confronting 2016 and 2020 Polling Limitations," Pew Research Center Methods (2021).

29. Jonathon P. Schuldt, Sungjong Roh, and Norbert Schwarz, "Questionnaire Design Effects in Climate Change Surveys," *Annals of the American Academy of Political and Social Science* 658, no. 1 (2015): 71.

30. Jon Coupal, "Pernicious Push Polls Pervert Politics," *Orange County Register*, May 19, 2018, https://www.ocregister.com/2018/05/19/pernicious-push-polls-pervert-politics/.

31. Amnon Cavari and Guy Freedman, "Survey Nonresponse and Mass Polarization: The Consequences of Declining Contact and Cooperation Rates," *American Political Science Review* (2022).

32. Natalie Jackson, Michael S. Lewis-Beck, and Charles Tien, "Pollster Problems in the 2016 U.S. National Election: Vote Intention, Vote Prediction," *Italian Journal of Electoral Studies* 83, no. 1 (2020): 17–28; John G. Bullock and Gabriel Lenz, "Partisan Bias in Surveys," *Annual Review of Political Science* 22 (2019): 325–42.

33. Aaron Zitner, "What Went Wrong with the Polls This Year?," *Wall Street Journal*, November 4, 2020, https://www.wsj.com/articles/whatwent-wrong-with-the-polls-this-year-11604536409.

34. Richard Thomas and Allaina Kilby, "US Election: Horse-Race Reporting Is Media Gold But Democratic Poison," *The Conversation*, October 3, 2020, https://bit.ly/33HQLwo.

35. David A. Graham, "The Polling Crisis Is a Catastrophe for Democracy," *The Atlantic*, November 4, 2020, https://www.theatlantic.com/ideas/archive/2020/11/polling-catastrophe/616986/.

36. Anastasia Leontiou, Georgios Manalis, and Dimitrios Xefteris, "Bandwagons in Costly Elections: The Role of Loss Aversion," SSRN Paper (2022), https://ssrn.com/abstract=3970025.

37. David O. Sears, "An Ignorant and Easily Duped Electorate?," *Perspectives on Politics* 15, no. 1 (2017): 137–41.

38. Walter Lippmann, *Public Opinion* (New York: Harcourt, Brace, 1922). On the movement to govern through technical expertise, see Morone, *The Democratic Wish*, chap. 3 (see chap. 2, note 8).

39. Angus Campbell et al., *The American Voter* (New York: Wiley, 1960).

40. Jennifer L. Hochschild and Katherine Levine Einstein, *Do Facts Matter? Information and Misinformation in American Politics* (Norman: University of Oklahoma Press, 2015); Arthur Lupia, *Uninformed: Why People Seem to Know So Little About Politics and What We Can Do About It* (New York: Oxford University Press, 2016); Rick Shenkman, *Just How Stupid Are We? Facing the Truth About the American Voter* (New York: Basic Books, 2008).

41. Christopher H. Achen and Larry M. Bartels, *Democracy for Realists: Why Elections Do Not Produce Responsive Government* (Princeton, NJ: Princeton University Press, 2016); Love Christensen, "How Does Uncertainty Affect Voters' Preferences?" *British Journal of Political Science* 52:3 (2022): 1186–1204.

42. Annenberg Public Policy Center, "Americans' Civics Knowledge Increases During a Stress-Filled Year," September 14, 2021, https://www.asc.upenn.edu/news-events/news/americans-civics-knowledge-increases-during-stress-filled-year.

43. Ilya Somin, *Democracy and Political Ignorance*, 2nd ed. (Stanford, CA: Stanford University Press, 2016).

44. The classic statement of this position comes from the dean of public opinion research, V. O. Key, *Public Opinion and American Democracy* (New York: Knopf, 1967); Benjamin I. Page and Robert Y. Shapiro, *The Rational Public: Fifty Years of Trends in Americans' Policy Preferences* (Chicago: University of Chicago Press, 1992).

45. James Surowiecki, *The Wisdom of Crowds* (New York: Doubleday, 2004), xii.

46. Clare Williams, "Polling Suggests Support Among Voters for Harsher Wall Street Messaging," *Morning Consult*, December 7, 2018, https://morningconsult.com/2018/12/07/polling-suggests-support-among-voters-for-harsher-wall-street-messaging/.

47. John F. Harris, *The Survivor: Bill Clinton in the White House* (New York: Random House, 2005), 331.

48. Lawrence R. Jacobs and Robert Y. Shapiro, *Politicians Don't Pander: Political Manipulation and the Loss of Democratic Responsiveness* (Chicago: University of Chicago Press, 2000).

49. Barry Schwartz, *The Paradox of Choice: Why More Is Less* (New York: Harper Perennial, 2004).

Chapter 8

1. Hanne Post, "Spring 2018 Student Hackathon Recap," *Hack New York*, https://bit.ly/2G0biTI (for subsequent versions, including ingenious efforts to track COVID-19 spread and address structural racism, see https://hackny.org/); Emily Badger and Claire Cain Miller, "How the Trump Era Is Molding the Next Generation of Voters," *New York Times*, April 1, 2019, https://nyti.ms/388yeZ6.

2. Turnout remained high in 2022; see Kati Perry et al., "Where Voter Turnout Exceeded 2018 Highs," *Washington Post*, November 11, 2022, https://wapo.st/3O2tQl6. On recent turnout history: Drew DeSilver, "Turnout In U.S. Has Soared in Recent Elections but by Some Measures Still Trails That of Many Other Countries," Pew Research Center, November 1, 2022, https://pewrsr.ch/3AaIP6K.

3. Ashley Jardina, *White Identity Politics* (Cambridge: Cambridge University Press, 2019).

4. Yevgeniya Li, Jean-Grégoire Bernard, and Markus Luczak-Roesch, "Beyond Clicktivism: What Makes Digitally Native Activism Effective?" *Social Media & Society* 7:3 (2021): 1–22.

5. Younger voters turned out at record rates in 2022 as well: Ashley Lopez, "Turnout Among Young Voters Was the Second Highest for a Midterm in Past 30 Years," *NPR*, November 10, 2022, https://n.pr/3E65Lp2. On Gen Z/millennial voters generally, see "Dispelling Myths About Youth Voting," CIRCLE: Center for Information and Research on Civic Learning and Engagement, Tufts, https://bit.ly/3Oa9DKb.

6. DeSilver, 2022 (see chap. 8, note 2).

7. Doc Searls, "DIY Radio with PODCasting," *Doc Searls's IT Garage* (blog), September 28, 2004, https://bit.ly/2SX5GO2.

8. "Podcast Stats & Facts," Podcast Insights, January 2021, https://bit.ly/2HTuvnx.

9. Case Foundation, *Millennial Impact Report 2019* (Washington, DC: Case Foundation, 2019).

10. Pew Research Center, "Public Trust in Government," June 6, 2022, https://pewrsr.ch/3ALBwC1.

11. Larry Buchanan, Quoctrung Bui, and Jugal K. Patel, "Black Lives Matter May Be the Largest Movement in U.S. History," *New York Times*, July 3, 2020, https://nyti.ms/2YDeqev.

12. Andrew Eggers, Haritz Garro, and Justin Grimmer, "No Evidence for Systematic Voter: A Guide to Statistical Claims About 2020," *Proceedings of the National Academy of Science*, November 2, 2021, https://www.pnas.org/doi/10.1073/pnas.2103619118. "The Myth of Voter Fraud," Brennan Center for Justice, https://bit.ly/3UJSskQ.

13. Farivar, 2022 (see chap. 6, note 84); Brennan Center, "Voting Laws Roundup: May 2022," May 26, 2022, https://bit.ly/3B8hNxQ.

14. Carrie Cordero, "How Cybersecurity Saved U.S. Democracy," *Horizons* 20 (2022): 12–23. Rosalind S. Helderman, Patrick Marley, and Tom Hamburger, "Why GOP Efforts to Cry Foul Fizzled This Time," *Washington Post*, November 9, 2022, https://wapo.st/3NV7Ngj.

15. "The Public, the Political System, and American Democracy," Pew Research, April 26, 2018, https://www.pewresearch.org/politics/2018/04/26/10-political-engagement-knowledge-and-the-midterms/.

16. Pete Schroeder, "How Republican-Led States Are Targeting Wall Street with 'Anti-Woke' Laws," *Reuters*, July 6, 2022, https://reut.rs/3KLfwMn.

17. Lee Ann Banaszak and Holly J. McCammon, "Women's Activism from Electoral Campaigns to Protest Action: Into the Next 100 Years," in *100 Years of the Nineteenth Amendment*, ed. Holly J. McCammon and Lee Ann Banaszak (New York: Oxford University Press, 2018), 356–70.

18. Tocqueville, *Democracy in America*, 1:189–95 (see chap. 2, note 12).

19. Laura Hanson Schlachter, "Civic Engagement and Volunteering," *AmeriCorps Research & Evaluation*, December 2021, https://bit.ly/3hwazwj.

20. Estimates of the Gen Z vote in 2020 range from 8% to 11%. See DeSilver, 2022 (chap. 8, note 2); William H. Frey, "Turnout in 2020 Election Spiked Among Both Democratic and Republican Voting Groups," Brookings Institution, May 5, 2021, https://brook.gs/3g4xKgL.

21. Peter Augustine Lawler, "Days of Apathy," *American Enterprise Review,* November 1, 1997, 22–24.

22. Emilee Booth Chapman, "The Distinctive Value of Elections and the Case for Compulsory Voting," *American Journal of Political Science* 63, no. 1 (2019): 101–12.

23. "The 2018 World's Most Generous Countries Report," Gallup, https://bit .ly/397UW58.

24. Chloe Vassot, "Young People Believe Activism Can Help. But Voting?," *Boston Globe*, July 15, 2020, https://bit.ly/2D0Qdr0.

25. Center for Responsive Politics, "OpenSecrets: Donor Demographics" [2022; updated regularly], https://bit .ly/3TSuRyT.

26. Joshua Zingher, "Diploma Divide: Educational Attainment and the Realignment of the American Electorate," *Political Research Quarterly* 75:2 (2022): 263–77.

27. Lyn Ragsdale, "The Obama Legacy in American Electoral Participation," in *Looking Back on President Barack Obama's Legacy*, ed. Wilbur C. Rich (New York: Springer, 2019), 25–46.

28. Gabriel R. Sanchez, Luis Ricardo Fraga, and Ricardo Ramírez, *Latinos and the 2016 Election* (East Lansing: Michigan State University Press, 2020); Natalie Masuoka, Kumar Ramanathan, and Jane Junn, "New Asian American Voters: Political Incorporation and Participation in 2016," *Political Research Quarterly* 72, no. 4 (2019): 991–1003.

29. Donald P. Green and Alan S. Gerber, *Get Out the Vote: How to Increase Voter Turnout*, 4th ed. (Washington, DC: Brookings Institution Press, 2019).

30. John B. Holbein and D. Sunshine Hillygus, *Making Young Voters: Converting Civic Attitudes into Civic Action* (New York: Cambridge University Press, 2020).

31. Robert Putnam, *Making Democracy Work: Civic Traditions in Modern Italy* (Princeton, NJ: Princeton University Press, 1993); Ashutosh Varshney, *Ethnic Conflict and Civic Life: Hindus and Muslims in India* (New Haven, CT: Yale University Press, 2002).

32. Mark Guarino, "How Organic Farming and YouTube Are Taming the Wilds of Detroit," *Washington Post*, November 14, 2015, https://wapo .st/3A3kfF3.

33. Doug McAdam and Karina Kloos, *Deeply Divided: Racial Politics and Social Movements in Post War America* (New York: Oxford University Press, 2014); on identity politics and Democrats, see collected essays in "E Pluribus Unum: The Fight over Identity Politics," *Foreign Affairs* 98 (2019): 160ff; Perry Bacon Jr., "Why Identity Politics Could Be Good Politics for Democrats," *FiveThirtyEight*, April 2, 2019, https://53eig.ht/3akOLed.

34. Suzanne Mettler, *Soldiers to Citizens: The GI Bill and the Making of the Greatest Generation* (New York: Oxford University Press, 2005).

35. Joe Soss, *Unwanted Claims* (Ann Arbor: University of Michigan, 2002).

36. Mark Harvey, *Celebrity Influence: Politics, Persuasion, and Issue-Based Advocacy* (Lawrence: University Press of Kansas, 2018).

37. Doug McAdam, *Political Process and the Development of Black Insurgency, 1930-1970*, 2nd ed. (Chicago: University of Chicago Press, 1999).

38. Donald E. Klingner and Charles S. Bullock III, "Topic: Voting Rights and Public Participation," *Public Integrity* 21, no. 3 (2019): 358–68.

39. Miguel de Oliver, "Emporia and the Exclusion Identity: Conservative Populist Alienation in the USA," *International Journal of Politics, Culture, and Society* 35:1 (2022): 153–178; Hanes Walton Jr., Robert C. Smith, and Sherri L. Wallace, *American Politics and the African American Quest for Universal Freedom* (New York: Routledge, 2017), esp. 77–79.

40. Neslihan Kevser Çevik, "The Millennial Generational Style: New Global Political and Economic Orientations," *Journal of Economy, Culture & Society* 65:1 (2022): 29–46.

41. Gary C. Jacobson, "The Triumph of Polarized Partisanship in 2016: Donald Trump's Improbable Victory," *Political Science Quarterly* 132, no. 1 (2017): 9–41.

42. Daron Shaw and John Petrocik, *The Turnout Myth: Voting Rates and Partisan Outcomes in American National Elections* (New York: Oxford University Press, 2020); Knight Foundation, *The 100 Million Project*, February 18, 2020, https:// knightfoundation.org/reports/ the-100-million-project/.

43. On the long history of institutional barriers, the classic is Alexander Keyssar, *The Right to Vote: The Contested History of Democracy in the United States* (New York: Basic Books, 2000). See, more recently, Michael Waldman, *The Fight to Vote* (New York: Simon and Schuster, 2017).

44. Theda Skocpol, "Voice and Inequality: The Transformation of American Civic Democracy," *Perspectives on Politics* 2, no. 1 (2004): 14.

45. Sam Bestvader et al., "Politics on Twitter," Pew Research Center, June 16, 2022, https://pewrsr.ch/3BcuTKz; Emily Kubin and Christian von Sikorski, "The Role of (Social) Media in Political Polarization: A Systematic Review, *Annals of the International Communication Association* 45:3 (2021): 188–206.

46. Hannah Murphy and Demetri Sevastopulo, "Why US Politicians Are Turning to Instagram," *Financial Times,* February 21, 2019, https:// on.ft.com/3ciqHKG.

47. See Simon Lindgren, *Digital Media and Society,* 2nd ed. (New York: Sage, 2021); Matthew Hindman, *The Myth of Digital Democracy* (Princeton, NJ: Princeton University Press, 2009).

48. See, e.g., Cass R. Sunstein, *#Republic: Divided Democracy in the Age of Social Media* (Princeton, NJ: Princeton University Press, 2018).

49. Frank Konkel, "Pentagon Thwarts 36 Million Email Breach Attempts Daily," *NextGov* (blog), January 11, 2018, https://bit .ly/2kcWcfg.

50. Steven Lee Myers and Steven Thompson, "Racist and Violent Ideas Jump from Web's Fringes to Mainstream Sites," *New York Times*, June 1, 2022, https:// nyti.ms/3G9ydJ1; Cecilia Kang and Sheera Frenkel, "'PizzaGate Conspiracy' Theory Thrives Anew in the TikTok Era," *New York Times*, June 27, 2020, https:// nyti.ms/3E4ITGx; Nicholas Snell et al., "Assessing Online Media Reliability: Trust, Metrics and Assessment," *Proceedings SPIE 11013, Disruptive Technologies in Information Sciences II*, June 2019. See also Saul Levmore and Martha C. Nussbaum, eds., *The Offensive Internet* (Cambridge, MA: Harvard University Press, 2010).

51. John Palfrey and Urs Grasser, *Born Digital* (New York: Basic Books, 2016), 230.

52. "Millennials More Democratic in Their Leaned Party Affiliation Than Older Generations," Pew Research Center, June 2, 2020, https://pewrsr. ch/2D0pvyH. Roberta Katz, Sarah Ogilve, Jane Shaw, and Loinda

Woodhead, *Gen Z Explained: The Art of Living in a Digital Age* (Chicago: University of Chicago Press, 2021).
53. Anna Brown, "Deep Partisan Divide on Whether Greater Acceptance of Transgender People is Good for Society," *Pew Research Center*, February 11, 2022, https://pewrsr.ch/3UQMi2s.

Chapter 9

1. D'Angelo Gore, "Latest CDC Data: Unvaccinated Adults 97 Times More Likely to Die from Covid-19 Than Boosted Adults," *Annenberg Public Policy Center: FactCheck.org.* February 9, 2022.
2. Erum Salam, "Majority of Covid Misinformation Came from Twelve People, Report Finds," *The Guardian*, July 17, 2021, https://bit.ly/3POajW0.
3. Properly speaking, *media* is the plural of *medium*—usually defined as the way we convey something. We use the term *media*—meaning mass communication—as a singular noun in keeping with the way the language is evolving.
4. This and previous statistic: Congressional Research Service, "Stop the Presses? Newspapers in the Digital Age" (Washington, DC: CRS Reports, 2022).
5. Megan Brenan, "Americans' Trust in Media Dips to Second Lowest on Record," Gallup, October 7, 2021, https://bit.ly/3t5Wskj.
6. Brenan, 2021 (see chap. 9, note 5).
7. Brenan, 2021 (see chap. 9, note 5).
8. Lee Harris, "Congress Proposes $500 Million for Negative News Coverage of China," *American Prospect*, February 9, 2022, https://bit.ly/3M7kv90.
9. Reuters, "Russia Blocks Access to BBC and Voice of America Websites," March 4, 2022, https://reut.rs/3NO4C8W.
10. Elahe Izadi, "The New Journalism—And the PR Firms Behind It," *Washington Post*, June 4, 2021, https://wapo.st/3GzcTLn.
11. Carrie Blazina, "In Some States, Students Account for a Large and Growing Share of Statehouse Reporters," Pew Research, May 19, 2022, https://pewrsr.ch/3xmnGpn.
12. Nassim Nicholas Taleb, *Black Swan: The Impact of the Highly Improbable* (New York: Random House, 2010).
13. Glenn Kessler, "Meet the Bottomless Pinocchio, a New Rating for a False Claim Repeated Over and Over Again," *Washington Post*, December 10, 2018, https://wapo.st/3GOFegU; Glenn Kessler, "Biden's Fantastical Claim of $500 in Annual Utility Savings," *Washington Post*, June 2, 2022, https://wapo.st/3NPmBLY.
14. Greg Burns, "Journalists Give Thumbs Down to Social Media," *Northwestern Medill Research*, February 9, 2022, https://bit.ly/3HkSTwc.
15. Derek Thompson, "What's Behind America's Shocking Baby Formula Shortage?," *The Atlantic*, May 12, 2022, https://bit.ly/3xb5OMP.
16. Shanto Iyengar and Donald R. Kinder, *News That Matters: Television and Public Opinion*, 2nd ed. (Chicago: University of Chicago Press, 2010).
17. Caleb Ecarma, "On Fox News, Calls for Militarizing Schools Abound While Gun Reform Shunned," *Vanity Fair*, May 25, 2022, https://bit.ly/3GV0PUP; Libby Cathey, Adam Carlson, and Armando Garcia, "Biden Addresses Nation on 'Horrific' School Shooting: 'We Have to Act,'" ABC News, May 24, 2022.
18. David Bach and Daniel J. Blake, "Frame or Get Framed," *California Management Review* 58, no. 3 (2016): 66–87.
19. Reliable historical counts of U.S. newspapers appear in Mathew Gentzkow, Jesse M. Shapiro, and Michael Sinkinson, "United States Newspaper Panel," Inter-University Consortium for Political and Social Research, https://bit.ly/2JpIcxK.
20. Elizabeth Grieco, "Fast Facts about the Newspaper Industry's Financial Struggles as McClatchy Files for Bankruptcy." Pew Research Center, February 14, 2020, https://pewrsr.ch/3WXTTxO; "Newspaper Fact Sheet, Pew Research Center, June 29, 2021, https://www.pewresearch.org/journalism/fact-sheet/newspapers/.
21. Carrie Blazina, "In Some States, Students Account for a Large and Growing Share of Statehouse Reporters," Pew Research Center, May 19, 2022.
22. "NPR Selects Take 1 for Transcription Services in 3-Year Deal," *InBroadcast: Industry News*, no. 124 (May 2022), https://bit.ly/39kPIZ1.
23. "Media Bias Ratings," *Allsides*, June 2022, https://bit.ly/2m62i5l.
24. The fifty podcasts drawing the largest audiences are updated quarterly by Edison Podcast Metrics, at https://bit.ly/3zpmWkF.
25. Dominick Mastrangelo, "Biden Says Cable News Industry 'Heading South,'" *The Hill*, January 19, 2022, https://bit.ly/3NLzPdi.
26. Philip Bump, "Is There a Viable Cable News/Streaming Audience?," *Washington Post*, April 21, 2022, https://wapo.st/3aKefH8.
27. Maggie Haberman, "Cassidy Hutchinson Stuns with Testimony About Trump on Jan. 6," *New York Times*, June 28, 2022, https://nyti.ms/3NBxZKX.
28. Tucker Carlson, "The Truth of What Happened on Jan. 6 Is Still Unknown," Fox News, June 9, 2022, https://fxn.ws/3aa7ej7; Sean Hannity, "We Are Suffering Through Yet Another Anti-Trump Smear," Fox News Flash, June 9, 2022, https://fxn.ws/3ulI3kt.
29. Ira Bruce Gaultney, Todd Sherron, and Carrie Boden, "Political Polarization, Misinformation, and Media Literacy," *Journal of Media Literacy Education* 14:1 (2022): 59–81.
30. Data from Internet World Stats, https://www.internetworldstats.com/stats2.htm.
31. Michael Luo, "The Fate of the News in the Age of the Coronavirus," *New Yorker*, March 29, 2020, https://bit.ly/2ZBnekJ.
32. Rob Garver, "Effort to Save Local Journalism Inches Toward Enactment," *Voice of America*, December 8, 2021, https://bit.ly/3xBhcTu.
33. Johanna L. Dunaway and Doris A. Graber, *Mass Media and American Politics*, 11th ed. (Washington, DC: CQ, 2022), 176, 440.
34. See, e.g., Matteo Cinelli et al., "The Echo Chamber Effect on Social Media," *PNAS* 118 no. 9 (2021): 1–8.
35. Richard L. Hasen, *Cheap Speech: How Disinformation Poisons Our Politics—And How to Cure It* (New Haven, CT: Yale University Press, 2022). Facebook's parent company Meta reports quarterly on fake-news removal; see, e.g., Guy Rosen, "Community Standards Enforcement Report, 1Q 2022," Meta, May 17, 2022, https://bit.ly/3xC2Nq8.
36. Mazhar J. Awan et al., "Fake News Data Exploration and Analytics," *Electronics* 10, no. 19 (2021): 2326–41.
37. Nicole Hemmer, "Attacking the Press for Liberal Bias Is a Staple of Republican Campaigns—And It All Began in 1964," CNN, February 29, 2020, https://cnn.it/3MGgSHg.
38. Hans J. G. Hassell, John B. Holbein, and Matthew R. Miles,

"There Is No Liberal Media Bias in Which News Stories Political Journalists Choose to Cover," *Science Advances* 6, no. 14 (2020): 1–8; see U.S. proportion of conservatives in Lydia Saad, "U.S. Political Ideology Steady; Liberals, Moderates Tie," Gallup, January 17, 2022, https://bit.ly/3xFSaCJ.

39. Hassell, "There Is No Liberal Media Bias." On centrism, Nader Elhefnawy, "Toward a Fuller Understanding of Media Bias: The Role of Centrist Ideology," SSRN Paper, 2022, https://bit.ly/3aYKQt5.

40. Martin Gilens and Craig Hertzman, "Corporate Ownership and News Bias: Newspaper Coverage of the 1996 Telecommunications Act," *Journal of Politics* 62, no. 2 (2000): 369–86; Graham Beattie et al., "Advertising Spending and Media Bias: Evidence from News Coverage of Car Safety Recalls," NBER Working Paper No. 23940, October 2017.

41. Zell speaking on *Last Week Tonight with John Oliver*, YouTube, August 7, 2016, https://bit.ly/2M6SK1M.

42. See Elhefnawy, "Toward a Fuller Understanding of Media Bias."

43. Isaac Chotiner, "Did the Press Create Donald Trump?," *Slate*, March 22, 2016, http://slate.me/22u0KjM; Reid J. Epstein and Jennifer Medina, "Should Biden Run in 2024? Democratic Whispers of 'No' Start to Rise," *New York Times*, June 11, 2022, https://nyti.ms/3MJiaRR.

44. Matthew Manning et al., "What Matters More, Perceived or Real Crime?," *Social Indicators Research*, April 2022. See also Elaine Tyler May, *Fortress America: How We Embraced Fear and Abandoned Democracy* (New York: Basic Books, 2017).

45. Max Boot, "On Crime, Democrats in Danger of Being Mugged by Reality," *Washington Post*, February 1, 2022, https://wapo.st/3tti1va.

46. Jessica R. Collier, Gina M. Massulo, and Marley Duchovnay, "Conservative News Audiences: A Lack of Media Trust and How They Think Journalism Can Improve," in *The Future of the Presidency, Journalism, and Democracy*, ed. Robert E. Gutsche (New York: Routledge, 2022).

47. Lindley Sanders, "Trust in Media 2022," *YouGov America*, April 5, 2022, https://bit.ly/3mFEEJ9.

48. Lloyd C. Gardner, "The Challenge of Journalism and the Truth in Our Times: James Risen, Judith Miller, and National Security Planning," in *Whistleblowing Nation,* ed. Kaeten Mistry and Hannah Gurman (New York: Columbia University Press, 2020), 297–326.

49. Michael A. Cusumano, David B. Yoffie, and Annabelle Gawer, "Pushing Social Media Platforms to Self-Regulate," *Regulatory Review*, January 3, 2022, https://bit.ly/3OeVIkY.

50. Sarah Fioroni, "Local News Most Trusted in Keeping Americans Informed About Their Communities, *Knight Foundation*, May 19, 2022, https://kng.ht/3EqHXxq.

51. Ibid.

52. https://www.cjr.org/local_news/local_reporters_decline_coverage_density.php.

53. Figures from Julia Stoll, "Television Industry in the United Kingdom: Statistics and Facts," *Statista*, October 6, 2021, https://bit.ly/39uSkUk.

54. Ipsos European Public Affairs, "Eurobarometer News & Media Survey 2022" (November 2022), https://bit.ly/3EsnXut.

55. Council of Europe, "Grant to Support Operations of Public Broadcasting Company of Ukraine," May 16, 2022, https://bit.ly/3HsAJZG.

56. Timothy Neff and Victor Pickard, "Funding Democracy: Public Media and Democratic Health in 33 Countries," *International Journal of Press & Politics* (2022), https://doi.org/10.1177/19401612211060255.

57. Cristina Corduneanu-Hici and Alexander Hamilton, "Selective Control: The Political Economy of Censorship," *Political Communication* (2022), doi:10.1080/10584609.2022.2074587.

58. Shuvraijt Das Biswas, "In Russia Journalists Brave Censorship, Criticize Putin's War in Ukraine," *Opoyi Central*, May 20, 2022, https://bit.ly/3QulSCi.

59. Robert McMahon, "Russia Is Censoring Media on the War in Ukraine. Foreign Media Are Trying to Get Around That," Council on Foreign Relations, March 18, 2022, https://on.cfr.org/3Hwhj61; James Pearson and Christopher Bing, "U.S. Targets Russia with Tech to Evade Censorship of Ukraine News," Reuters, June 15, 2022, https://reut.rs/3NYOlOO.

60. The media analysis group IMDB publishes a weekly round-up of box-office totals, both in the U.S. and worldwide. See https://bit.ly/3MQW0gM for the latest totals—and notice how many U.S. films are on top around the globe.

61. Diana Zulli, Kevin Coe, Zachary Isaacs, and Ian Summers, "Media Coverage of the Unfolding Crisis of Domestic Terrorism in the United States, 1990–2020," *Public Relations Inquiry* 10, no. 3 (2021): 357–75; Ayten Gorgun Smith and Banu Baybars Hawks, "Ethical Journalism: News Coverage of Terrorism," *Journal of Management Practices, Humanities and Social Sciences* 3, no. 2 (2019): 58–64.

62. Anna P. Kambhampaty, "Securing the TikTok Vote," *New York Times Magazine*, March 22, 2022, https://nyti.ms/3xW8b7B.

63. David Morgan, "Republicans Oust Trump-Backed, Scandal-Plagued Congressman Madison Cawthorn," Reuters, May 18, 2022, https://reut.rs/3MY7TSe.

64. Elena Schneider and Zach Montellaro, "Trump's Cash Woes Mount as Biden Laps Him," *Politico*, October 21, 2020, https://politi.co/3jqJZ32.

Chapter 10

1. Timothy Caulfield, "Dr Oz Shouldn't Be a Senator—or a Doctor: His Brand of Misinformation Has Already Tarnished Medicine," *Scientific American*, December 15, 2021, https://www.scientificamerican.com/article/dr-oz-shouldnt-be-a-senator-or-a-doctor/; Jon C. Tilburt, Megan Allyse, and Frederic W. Hafferty, "The Case of Dr. Oz: Ethics, Evidence, and Does Professional Self-Regulation Work?," *AMA Journal of Ethics*, February 2017, https://bit.ly/2ZlTOl9.

2. Lisa Pruitt, "What Republicans Know (and Democrats Don't) About the White Working Class," Politico, June 24, 2022, https://politi.co/3tnNQoL; J. D. Vance, *Hillbilly Elegy: A Memoir of a Family and a Culture in Crisis* (New York: Harpers, 2017).

3. J. Alexander Branham and Christopher Wlezien, "Do Election Campaigns Matter? A Comparative Perspective and Overview," in Elizabeth Suhay, Bernard Grofman, and Alexander H. Trechsel (eds), *The Oxford Handbook of Electoral Persuasion* (New York: Oxford University Press, 2020), 184–200.

4. Achen, *Democracy for Realists* (see chap. 7, note 40).

5. David M. Primo and Jeffrey D. Milyo, *Campaign Finance and*

American Democracy: What the Public Really Thinks and Why It Matters (Chicago: University of Chicago Press, 2020).

6. "Americans' Satisfaction Levels," Gallup, January 2019, https://bit.ly/3fdBzcS.

7. Christopher Ingraham, "About 100 Million People Couldn't Be Bothered to Vote This Year," *Washington Post*, November 12, 2016, https://wapo.st/3ECExbb; Alexander Keyssar, *The Right to Vote* (New York: Basic Books, 2000).

8. Daron Shaw and John Petrocik, *The Turnout Myth: Voting Rates and Partisan Outcomes in American* National Elections (New York: Oxford University Press, 2020); Knight Foundation, *The 100 Million Project*, February 18, 2020, https://knightfoundation.org/reports/the-100-million-project/.

9. *Citizens United v. Federal Election Commission*, 558 U.S. 310 (2010); *McCutcheon v. Federal Election Commission*, 572 U.S. ___ (2014).

10. Graham K. Wilson, "Business and Politics in the United States," *The Political Quarterly* 93:2 (2022): 198–208; Paul Mulholland, "Campaign Contribution Data Show Finance Industry Split on Democrats and Republicans," Center for Responsive Government, October 28, 2022, https://bit.ly/3g1S5Dn.

11. "Open Secrets, "Incumbent Advantage, Senate Races 2021-2," https://www.opensecrets.org/elections-overview/incumbent-advantage; Jamie L. Carson, Joel Sievert, and Ryan D. Williamson, "Nationalization and the Incumbency Advantage," *Political Research Quarterly* 73, no. 1 (2020): 156–68.

12. James Hohmann, "The Daily 202: Mick Mulvaney's Confession Highlights the Corrosive Role of Money in Politics," *Washington Post*, April 25, 2018, https://wapo.st/2I0n1P0.

13. Alexander Fouirnaies and Anthony Fowler, "Do Campaign Contributions Buy Favorable Policies? Evidence from the Insurance Industry," *Political Science Research and Methods* 10:1 (2022): 18–32; Anthony Fowler, Haritz Garro, and Jörg Spenkuch, "Quid Pro Quo? Corporate Returns to Campaign Contributions," *Journal of Politics* 82, no. 3 (July 2020): 844–58.

14. "How Super PACs Run Campaigns," editorial, *New York Times*, April 27, 2015, A18.

15. Trump quoted in James Morone, *Republic of Wrath: How American Politics Turned Tribal from George Washington to Donald Trump* (New York: Basic Books, 2020), 22.

16. Brian Pfannenstiel, "DNC Panel Strips Iowa of Guaranteed First Vote for President; State Party Can Still Apply for Coveted Spot," *Des Moines Register*, April 13, 2022, https://bit.ly/3O0jC4J.

17. Gerhard Peters, "The Post-Convention Bounce in Voters' Preference," American Presidency Project, University of California-Santa Barbara (2022), https://bit.ly/3DYrwsm.

18. Vincent Charles Keating and Olivier Schmitt, "Ideology and Influence in the Debate over Russian Election Interference," *International Politics* 58:3 (2021): 757–771.

19. Alan Abramowitz, "Did Russian Interference Affect the 2016 Election Results?," *Sabato's Crystal Ball*, August 8, 2019, https://bit.ly/3XbffYX.

20. See, e.g., Brian Padden, "Biden Slams Trump on Russia Bounties in Foreign Policy Contrast," *Voice of America News*, July 3, 2020, https://bit.ly/2XldpHE.

21. Thomas Wright and Fred Dews, "Foreign Policy in the 2020 Election," Brookings podcast, October 9, 2020, https://brook.gs/2GMCo1q.

22. Stephen Ansolabehere, Jonathan Rodden, and James M. Snyder, "The Strength of Issues: Using Multiple Measures to Gauge Preference Stability, Ideological Constraint, and Issue Voting," *American Political Science Review* 102, no. 2 (2008): 215–32.

23. Dan Woods, "Building Tech at Presidential Scale," InfoQ, October 21, 2021, https://bit.ly/3CfBxjL; Jonathan Allen and Amie Parnes, *Lucky: How Joe Biden Barely Won the Presidency* (New York: Crown, 2021), esp. 179–201.

24. "2020 Electoral College Ratings," Cook Political Report, June 29, 2020, https://bit.ly/30nihxS.

25. For the classic analysis of the by-standers, see E. E. Schattschneider, *The Semisovereign People* (New York: Holt, Reinhardt, and Wilson, 1960). Katie Livingstone, "Nonvoters 2020: Counted Out," Medill School/NPR, December 15, 2020, https://bit.ly/3dOcfjc.

26. Todd C. Shaw, Kirk A. Foster, and Barbara Harris Combs, "Race and Poverty Matters: Black and Latino Linked Fate, Neighborhood Effects, and Political Participation," *Politics, Groups, and Identities* 7, no. 3 (2019): 663–72.

27. "Cost of Election," Open Secrets: Center for Responsive Government, https://bit.ly/3hDa1j9.

28. Karl Evers-Hillstrom, "Majority of Lawmakers in 116th Congress Are Millionaires," *OpenSecrets News*, April 23, 2020, https://bit.ly/3i3DB19.

29. Raymond Arke, "Linda McMahon, Trump Donor and Cabinet Member, to Head Pro-Trump Super PAC," *Open Secrets*, April 1, 2019, https://bit.ly/2UvoyFg.

30. Kenneth M. Miller, "Nationalized Congressional Finance: Evidence from 2018 and 2020," in John C. Green et al., eds., *State of the Parties 2022* (Lanham, MD: Rowman & Littlefield, 2022), 163–178.

31. On American "dynasties," see Stephen Hess, *America's Political Dynasties: From Adams to Clinton*, 2nd ed. (Washington, DC: Brookings Institution Press, 2016).

32. Congressional Research Service, "Women in Congress: Statistics and Brief Overview," July 7, 2022, https://sgp.fas.org/crs/misc/R43244.pdf; Jennifer Lawless and Richard Fox, *It Takes a Candidate: Why Women Don't Run for Office* (New York: Cambridge University Press, 2005).

33. Richard F. Fenno Jr., *Home Style: House Members in Their Districts* (New York: Longman Classics, 2002).

34. Ibid.

35. Editorial Board, "The Trump Census Sabotage Campaign May Have Backfired," *Washington Post*, June 2, 2022, https://www.washingtonpost.com/opinions/2022/06/02/census-undercount-trump-sabotage/.

36. Ryan Best and Aaron Bycoffe, "What Redistricting Looks Like in Every State," *FiveThirtyEight*, July 19, 2022, https://53eig.ht/3DVM192.

37. *Husted v. A. Philip Randolph Institute*, 584 U.S. ___ (2018).

38. Michael Li, Thomas Wolf, and Annie Lo, "The State of Redistricting Legislation," Brennan Center for Justice, June 23, 2020, https://bit.ly/3kbZr4l.

39. See David C. W. Parker, *The Power of Money in Congressional Campaigns* (Norman: University of Oklahoma Press, 2008).

40. For the classic account of candidate-centered politics, see Martin P. Wattenberg, *The Rise of Candidate-Centered Politics: Presidential Elections of the 1980s* (Cambridge, MA: Harvard University Press, 1991).

41. Gerald M. Pomper, *Voters, Elections and Parties: The Practice of Democratic Theory* (Piscataway, NJ: Transaction, 1988), 104. On traditional

campaigning in the age of AI, see Scott Neuman, "Campaign Signs Influence How We Vote More Than You Might Realize," NPR, October 1, 2022, https://n.pr/3GcBVSb.
42. Alessandro Nai and Jürgen Maier, "Is Negative Campaigning a Matter of Taste? Political Attacks, Incivility, and the Moderating Role of Individual Differences," *American Politics Research* 49:3 (2021): 269–281.
43. Clayton D. Peoples, "Campaign Finance and Policymaking: PACs, Campaign Contributions, and Interest Group Influence in Congress," *Sociology Compass* 7, no. 11 (2013): 900–913, doi:10.1111/soc4.12079.
44. Brandice Canes-Wrone and Nathan Gibson, "Does Money Buy Congressional Love? Individual Donors and Legislative Voting," *Congress and the Presidency* 46, no. 1 (2019): 1–27.
45. Craig Volden and Alan Wiseman, *Legislative Effectiveness in the United States Congress: The Lawmakers* (New York: Cambridge University Press, 2014).

Chapter 11

1. Machtley story reported by the congressman to one of the authors.
2. "Think Environmental Laws and Regulations Should Be Stricter," Pew Research Center, April 18, 2007, http://pewrsr.ch/2bCNp4U.
3. Anna Brown, "Most Democrats Who Are Looking for a Relationship Would Not Consider Dating a Trump Voter," Pew Research Center, April 24, 2020, https://pewrsr.ch/3rlmn6g; Erik Santoro and David E. Broockman, "The Promise and Pitfalls of Cross-Partisan Conversations for Reducing Affective Polarization," *Science Advances* 8:25 (2022). On climate change, Holly Fuong and Geoffrey Skelley, "Do Democrats and Republicans Agree on Anything About Climate Change and Immigration?" *FiveThirtyEight*, September 29, 2022, https://53eig.ht/3StC0Ew.
4. Nathan P. Kalmoe and Lilliana Mason, "Lethal Mass Partisanship: Prevalence, Correlates, & Electoral Contingencies," Paper presented at NCAPSA American Politics Meeting, January 2019.
5. Jennifer McCoy and Murat Somer, "Overcoming Polarization," *Journal of Democracy* 32:1 (2021): 6–21. Nolan McCarty, Keith Poole, and Howard Rosenthal, *Polarized America: The Dance of Ideology and Unequal Riches*, 2nd ed. (Cambridge, MA: MIT Press, 2016).

6. Thomas Jefferson to Francis Hopkinson, Paris, March 13, 1789, National Archive, http://founders.archives.gov/documents/Jefferson/01-14-02-0402. For Washington's text and an informed commentary, see Matthew Spalding and Patrick J. Garrity, *A Sacred Union of Citizens: George Washington's Farewell Address and the American Character* (Lanham, MD: Rowman & Littlefield, 1998).
7. Gallup, "Party Affiliation." July 30–August 12, 2022. https://news.gallup.com/poll/15370/party-affiliation.aspx.
8. Gallup, "Party Affiliation." July 30–August 12, 2022. https://news.gallup.com/poll/15370/party-affiliation.aspx.
9. https://www.pewresearch.org/politics/2019/03/14/political-independents-who-they-are-what-they-think/.
10. Lane Cuthbert and Alexander Theodoridis, "Do Republican Voters Really Believe Trump Won the Election of 2020? Our Research Suggests That They Do," *Washington Post: The Monkey Cage*, January 7, 2022, https://www.washingtonpost.com/politics/2022/01/07/republicans-big-lie-trump/.
11. Lane Cuthbert and Alexander Theodoridis, "Do Republican Voters Really Believe Trump Won the Election of 2020? Our Research Suggests That They Do," *Washington Post: The Monkey Cage*, January 7, 2022, https://www.washingtonpost.com/politics/2022/01/07/republicans-big-lie-trump/.
12. Data for next four items from "In Changing U.S. Electorate, Race and Education Remain Stark Dividing Lines," Pew Research Center, June 2, 2020.
13. "In Changing U.S. Electorate, Race and Education Remain Stark Dividing Lines," Pew Research Center, June 2, 2020.
14. "In Changing U.S. Electorate, Race and Education Remain Stark Dividing Lines," Pew Research Center, June 2, 2020.
15. "In Changing U.S. Electorate, Race and Education Remain Stark Dividing Lines," Pew Research Center, June 2, 2020.
16. Pew Research, "Democratic Edge in Party Identification Narrows Slightly," June 2, 2020, https://pewrsr.ch/3UOgziR.
17. Pew Research, 2020 (see chap. 11, note 16)
18. Congressman David Cicillini (D-RI), remarks at Brown University, Providence, RI, June 9, 2015.

On election deniers winning in 2022, see Adrian Blanco, Daniel Wolfe, and Amy Gardner, "Tracking Which 2020 Election Deniers Won, Lost In the Midterms," *Washington Post,* November 2022, https://wapo.st/3G4HguM.
19. Nathan P. Kalmoe and Lilliana Mason, "Lethal Mass Partisanship: Prevalence, Correlates, & Electoral Contingencies," Paper presented at NCAPSA American Politics Meeting, January 2019. On election deniers winning in 2022, see Adrian Blanco, Daniel Wolfe, and Amy Gardner, "Tracking Which 2020 Election Deniers Won, Lost In the Midterms," *Washington Post*, November 2022, https://wapo.st/3G4HguM.
20. Bruce Keith et al., *The Myth of the Independent Voter* (Berkeley: University of California Press, 1992); see also "Political Independents: Who They Are, What They Think," Pew Research Center, March 14, 2019, https://pewrsr.ch/2UnbYHm.
21. Laura Wray-Lake, Erin H. Arruda, and David A. Hopkins, "The Party Goes On: Young Adults' Partisanship and Political Engagement Across Age and Historical Time," *American Politics Research* 47, no. 6 (2019): 1358–75.
22. Jens Manuel Krogstad and Mark Hugo Lopez, "Black Voter Turnout Fell in 2016, Even as a Record Number of Americans Cast Ballots," Pew Research Center, May 12, 2017, https://pewrsr.ch/2VPb9W2.
23. John H. Aldrich, *Why Parties? The Origin and Transformation of Political Parties in America* (Chicago: University of Chicago Press, 1995).
24. See especially Teresa Amato, *Grand Illusion: The Myth of Voter Choice in a Two-Party Tyranny* (New York: New Press, 2009).
25. The Libertarian Party and Green Party websites: https://www.lp.org/elected-officials-2/; http://www.gp.org/officeholders.
26. J. David Gillespie, *Challengers to Duopoly: Why Third Parties Matter in Two-Party American Politics* (Columbia: University of South Carolina Press, 2012).
27. R. Kent Newmyer, *Supreme Court Justice Joseph Story: Statesman of the Old Republic* (Chapel Hill: University of North Carolina Press, 1985), 158.
28. For a picture of the spoils system, see Morone, *The Democratic Wish*, chap. 2 (see chap., note 8).
29. Daniel Walker Howe, *What Hath God Wrought: The Transformation of America, 1815–1848* (New York: Oxford University Press, 2007).

30. A good summary of this and related views is in Mark E. Neely Jr., *The Union Divided: Party Conflict in the Civil War North* (Cambridge, MA: Harvard University Press, 2002).

31. You can read all about Prohibition in Morone, *Hellfire Nation*, chaps. 9 and 10 (see chap. 2, note 51).

32. President William Jefferson Clinton, State of the Union Address, January 23, 1996, Washington DC, https://clinton2.nara.gov/WH/New/other/sotu.html (the era of big government is over); President Barack Hussein Obama, Inaugural Address, January 20, 2009, Washington DC, http://bit.ly/1VG1k9q (promising to end programs that do not work).

33. Amelia Thomson-DeVeaux and Meredith Conroy, "Women Have Swung Toward Democrats Since the *Dobbs* Decision," *Politico*, September 28, 2022, https://53eig.ht/3RxzAmR.

34. John V. Kane, Lilliana Mason, and Julie Wronski, "Who's at the Party? Group Sentiments, Knowledge, and Partisan Identity," *Journal of Politics* 83:4 (2021): 1783–1799; John Sides, Michael Tesler, and Lynn Valreck, *Identity Crisis: The 2016 Presidential Campaign and the Battle for the Meaning of America* (Princeton, NJ: Princeton University Press, 2018).

35. Data from "Behind Biden's 2020 Victory," Pew, June 30, 2021.

36. Alan S. Gerber et al., "Personality and Political Attitudes: Relationships Across Issue Domains and Political Contexts," *American Political Science Review* 104, no. 1 (2010): 111–33; Nicole Satherley, Chris G. Sibley, and Danny Osborne, "Ideology Before Party," *Social Psychology* 60:2 (2021): 509–523.

37. Pew Research Center, "As Partisan Hostility Grows, Signs of Frustration With the Two Party System" (August 2022), https://pewrsr.ch/3SwZCIy.

38. See endnote 20, above.

39. Patrick Fisher, "Generational Replacement and the Impending Transformation of the American Electorate," *Politics & Policy* 48, no. 1 (2020): 38–68; Leonardo Baccini and Stephen Weymouth, "Gone For Good: Deindustrialization, White Voter Backlash, and US Presidential Voting," *American Political Science Review* 115:2 (2021): 550–567.

40. Geoffrey Skelley, "Few Americans Who Identify as Independent Are Actually Independent,"

FiveThirtyEight (April 15, 2021), https://53eig.ht/3fzDHl3; Barbara Norrander, "The Nature of Crossover Voters," in *Routledge Handbook of Primary Elections,* ed. Robert G. Boatright (New York: Routledge, 2018), chap. 6.

41. Marjorie Randon Hershey, *Party Politics* in America, 18th ed. (New York: Routledge, 2021), 109.

42. On parties and polarization, see Nathan J. Canen, Chad Kendall, and Francesco Trebbi, "Political Parties as Drivers of U.S. Polarization, 1927–2018," Social Science Research Network (May 2022), https://bit.ly/3RxetRD. On government support, Pew Research Center, "Values and Expectations of Government," June 6, 2022, https://pewrsr.ch/3E9uJ8y; on rebuilding "racist" institutions, Pew Research Center, "Beyond Red vs. Blue: The Political Typology" (November 19, 2021), https://pewrsr.ch/3C1PS1G; on belief in God, Jeffrey M. Jones, "Belief in God Dips to 81%, A New Low," Gallup, June 17, 2022, https://bit.ly/3dUYfnJ.

43. Eric Plutzer and Michael Berkman, "American Not Only Divided but Baffled over What Motivates Their Opponents," *Mood of the Nation Poll,* McCourtney Institute for Democracy, Penn State, https://democracy.psu.edu/wp-content/uploads/sites/14/2020/08/Poll-Report-November-2018.pdf.

44. Greg Sargent, "A GOP's Remarkable Admission About Trump and Mueller," *Washington Post,* March 21, 2018; Gary C. Jacobson, "Donald Trump's Big Lie and the Future of the Republican Party," *Presidential Studies Quarterly* 51:2 (2021): 273–289.

45. Clark Neily, Walter Olson, and Ilya Somin, "Team Libertarian Report: Restoring the Guardrails of Democracy," George Mason Legal Studies Research Paper No. LS 22-22 (July 7, 2022); Andrew M. Koppelman, *Burning Down the House: How Libertarian Philosophy Was Corrupted by Delusion and Greed* (New York: St. Martin's Press, 2022).

46. Robert Tracinski, "Has the Invasion of Ukraine Made Us All Neoconservatives Now?" *Discourse,* March 4, 2022, https://bit.ly/3dTHE3W; W. James Antle III, "'New Right' Takes It Back to Old Pre-Neocon Roots, Starting With Ukraine," *Responsible Statecraft,* May 31, 2022, https://bit.ly/3fB7dHm.

47. Anthony Fowler et al., "Moderates," *American Political Science Review* (September 5, 2022), doi: 10.1017/S0003055422000818.

48. Pew Research Center, "The Democratic Coalition: A Snapshot," November 5, 2021, https://pewrsr.ch/3SJwZas.

49. Laura C. Bucci and Kevin Reuning, "The State of Labor in the Democratic Party Coalition," *Party Politics* 27:6 (2021): 1243–1253; Joan Williams. "How Biden Won (Enough of) the White Working Class," *Harvard Business Review*, November 10, 2020.

50. Chelsea N. Kaufman, "Where Are the Values Voters? Ideological Constraint and Stability Among Rural, Suburban, and Urban Populations in the United States," *Journal of Rural Studies* 88 (December 2021): 169–180.

51. Republican National Committee, *Resolution Regarding the Republican Party Platform,* https://bit.ly/3M6I0AH.

52. David S. Broder, *The Party's Over: The Failure of Politics in America* (New York: Harper & Row, 1972); Martin P. Wattenberg, *The Decline of American Political Parties, 1952–1980* (Cambridge, MA: Harvard University Press, 1985).

53. Byungkyu Lee, "Close Relationships in Close Elections," *Social Forces* 100:1 (2021): 400–425; Frances Lee, *Beyond Ideology: Politics, Principles, and Partisanship in the U.S. Senate* (Chicago: University of Chicago Press, 2009).

54. Drew DeSilver, "Polarization in Congress Has Roots That Go Back Decades," Pew Research Center, March 10, 2022, https://pewrsr.ch/3E5we7M.

55. See Ezra Klein, *Why We're Polarized* (New York: Avid Reader, 2020), chap. 1.

56. David R. Mayhew, *Divided We Govern: Party Control, Investigations, and Lawmaking, 1946–2002,* 2nd ed. (New Haven, CT: Yale University Press, 2005).

57. Pew Research, "Partisan Hostility" (2022), note 37 above.

58. Robert B. Talisse, *Sustaining Democracy: What We Owe to the Other Side* (New York: Oxford University Press, 2021); Lee Drutman, *Breaking the Two-Party Doom Loop: The Case for Multiparty Democracy in America* (New York: Oxford University Press, 2020);.

59. Soo-hyung Ahn, Jaechun Kim, and William Kang, "Low Female

Political Representation in the U.S.: An Institution-Based Explanation," *Journal of International and Area Studies* 26, no. 1 (2019): 65–88; see generally Douglas J. Amy, *Real Choices/New Voices: How Proportional Representation Elections Could Revitalize American Democracy* (New York: Columbia University Press, 2002).

60. The term *core commitments* and an extended argument on behalf of stronger parties are in Russell Muirhead, *The Promise of Party in a Polarized Age* (Cambridge, MA: Harvard University Press, 2014); Amber Hye-Yon Lee et al., "Negative Partisanship is Not More Prevalent Than Positive Partisanship," *Nature Human Behaviour* 6 (2022): 951–963.

Chapter 12

1. Lydia Saad, "Military Brass, Judges Among Professions at New Image Lows," Gallup, January 12, 2022, https://bit.ly/3fBfDhS.

2. Jeffrey M. Berry and Clyde Wilcox, *The Interest Group Society*, 6th ed. (New York: Routledge, 2018).

3. "Revolving Door: Former Members of the 115th Congress," OpenSecrets.org (2022), https://bit.ly/3C7SyL8.

4. The American Bar Association maintains an updated list of transgender rights organizations; see https://bit.ly/3SQX3AD.

5. "Client Profile: Miami-Dade County, FL," OpenSecrets.org, https://bit.ly/3f23Jsg.

6. Jonathan O'Connell and Anu Narayanswamy, "Lobbying Broke All-Time Mark in 2021 amid Flurry of Government Spending," *Washington Post*. March 12, 2022. Pete Quist and Dan Auble, "Layers of Lobbying," *OpenSecrets*, June 2, 2022, https://bit.ly/3RE9rmp.

7. "Regulatory Affairs Specialist" median salary, salary.com (September 26, 2022), https://bit.ly/3EeEG4D.

8. Conor McGrath, "President Obama's Regulation of Lobbying and Lobbyists," in *Interest Group Lobbying*, 273.

9. David Mora, "Update: We Found a Staggering 281 Lobbyists Who've Worked in the Trump Administration," ProPublica, October 15, 2019, https://bit.ly/2IyZoxS—this count was for the first two years of Trump's presidency (2017–18); the Center for Responsive Politics had identified another thirty-three administration appointees by early 2020.

10. Tine Ustad Figenschou and Nanna Alida Fredheim, "Interest Groups on Social Media: Four Forms of Networked Advocacy," *Journal of Public Affairs* 20, no. 2 (2019), https://doi.org/10.1002/pa.2012.

11. Nicole Karlis, "The E-Cig Industry Poured Money into Lobbying Prior to Trump's Reversal on Vaping Ban," *Salon*, November 18, 2019, https://bit.ly/2vFSGDN; Katherine Gammon, "US Bans Juul but Young Vapers Are Already Switching to Newer Products," *The Guardian*, June 26, 2022, https://bit.ly/3M4jb8l.

12. For more on how AARP (and other membership groups) wield influence, see Peter Murray, "The Secret of Scale," *Stanford Social Innovation Review*, Fall 2013, http://ssir.org/articles/entry/the_secret_of_scale.

13. Charles M. Cameron et al., "From Textbook Pluralism to Hyper-Pluralism: Interest Groups and Supreme Court Nominations, 1930–2017," *Journal of Law & Courts* 8:2 (2020): 301–332.

14. G. William Domhoff, ed., *Studying the Power Elite: Fifty Years of Who Rules America* (New York: Routledge, 2018).

15. "Elon Musk's Takeover Financing Deal Could Clip Twitter's Wings," *The Guardian*, May 7, 2022, https://www.theguardian.com/technology/2022/may/07/elon-musks-takeover-financing-deal-could-clip-twitters-wings.

16. Schattschneider, *Semisovereign People*, 35 (see chap. 10, note 19); Kay Lehman Schlozman, Sidney Verba, and Henry Brady, *The Unheavenly Chorus: Unequal Political Voice and the Broken Promise of American Democracy* (Princeton, NJ: Princeton University Press, 2012).

17. See https://www.wearestillin.com; as of fall 2022, more than 3,950 groups and leaders had signed on to this effort.

18. Jose A. Del Real, Robert Samuels, and Tim Craig, "How the Black Lives Matter Movement Went Mainstream," *Washington Post*, June 9, 2020, https://wapo.st/3dVhMOY.

19. Jeffrey H. Birnbaum, *The Lobbyists: How Influence Peddlers Work Their Way in Washington* (New York: Times Books, 1993), 8.

20. Raymond A. Bauer, Ithiel de Sola Pool, and Lewis Anthony Dexter, *American Business and Public Policy*, 2nd ed. (New Brunswick, NJ: Transaction, 1968), 34.

21. "Swamp in the Heart of Europe: The Power of Lobbyists Is Growing in Brussels and Berlin," *The Economist*, May 13, 2021, https://www.economist.com/business/2021/05/13/the-power-of-lobbyists-is-growing-in-brussels-and-berlin.

22. Timothy M. LaPira, Kathleen Marchetti, and Herschel F. Thomas, "Gender Politics in the Lobbying Profession," *Gender & Politics* (2019), https://bit.ly/2TNJZPE; Rogan Kersh, "Ten Myths About Health Lobbyists," in *Health Politics and Policy*, 5th ed., ed. James A. Morone and Daniel C. Ehlke (Stamford, CT: Cengage, 2014).

23. Matthew Murray, "Google's Top Lobbyist Shows It's Hip to Be a Nerd," *Roll Call*, June 11, 2010, https://rollcall.com/2010/06/11/googles-top-lobbyist-shows-its-hip-to-be-a-nerd; Brennan Hoban, "Millennials Are on the Frontlines of Political and Cultural Change in America," Brookings, 2018, https://brook.gs/2ILnCFD.

24. "Lobbyist Profile: Ashley Solle," Open Secrets, https://www.opensecrets.org/federal-lobbying/lobbyists/summary?cycle=2021&id=Y0000058101LLobbyit.com; "Meet the Team," Lobbyit.com. https://lobbyit.com/about/our-team/.

25. "A Tribute to Tom Dobbins," *Composites Manufacturing*, March 5, 2020, https://compositesmanufacturingmagazine.com/2020/03/a-tribute-to-tom-dobbins/2/.

26. Myron A. Mehlman, "Benzene, a Multi-Organ Carcinogen," *European Journal of Oncology* 13, no. 1 (2008): 7–19; "Fossil Fuel Companies Distorted the Science About the Dangers of Benzene," Union of Concerned Scientists, October 24, 2017, https://bit.ly/2lMZSp6; "Why Is Cancer Linked Benzene in so Many Personal Care Products?," *US News and World Reports*, February 24, 2022, https://www.usnews.com/news/health-news/articles/2022-02-24/why-is-cancer-linked-benzene-in-so-many-personal-care-products.

27. Fraser Nelson, David W. Brady, and Alana Conner Snibbe, "Learn to Love Lobbying," *Stanford Social Innovation Review* 5, no. 2 (Spring 2007): 57. Montana reformer from remarks made at *The Future of Health Care in America*, sponsored by the Mike Mansfield Center of Politics and Policy, University of Montana, 2013.

28. Quoted in Ian Prasad Philbrick and David Leonhardt, "How to Participate in Politics," *New York Times*, August 2020, https://nyti.ms/2BIqUJz.

29. Catherine Boudreau, "How Congress Killed Efforts to Slash Subsidies for Wealthy Farmers," Politico, August 20, 2018, https://politi.co/2MEPkHw.

30. Mark Peterson, "Congress in the 1990s: From Iron Triangles to Policy Networks," in *The Politics of Health Care Reform*, ed. James Morone and Gary Belkin (Durham, NC: Duke University Press, 1994), 108, 127.

31. Timothy M. LaPira and Herschel F. Thomas, *Revolving Door Lobbying* (Lawrence: University Press of Kansas, 2017); see also Michael E. Shepherd and Hye Young You, "Exit Strategy: Career Concerns and Revolving Doors in Congress," *American Political Science Review* 114, no. 1 (2020): 270–84.

32. Jordan Fabian, "Trump-Allied Groups Pour $30 Million into Barrett Confirmation," *Bloomberg News*, October 22, 2020, https://bloom.bg/3n6qw9J; Alex Gangitano, "Barrett Ad War Exceeds Kavanaugh Fight," *The Hill*, September 30, 2020, https://bit.ly/32q5hbk.

33. Paul F. Boller Jr., *Congressional Anecdotes* (New York: Oxford University Press, 1991), 122.

34. James Thurber estimate cited in Lee Fang, "Michael Cohen and the Felony Overtaking Washington," *New York Times*, June 18, 2018, https://nyti.ms/2JVNvBf; see also Herschel F. Thomas and Timothy M. LaPira, "How Many Lobbyists are in Washington? Shadow Lobbying and the Gray Market for Policy Advocacy," *Interest Groups & Advocacy* 6 (2017): 199–214.

35. On the shift to lobbying states, see Dante Chinni, "With Gridlock in Washington, Lobbyists Turn to Statehouses," *Wall Street Journal*, January 16, 2016. The Internet Association's "50-State Government Affairs Program" is described on the association's website, https://bit.ly/2ymRWnz.

36. Virginia Gray and David Lowery, "Interest Group System Density and Diversity: A Research Update," *International Political Science Review* 15, no. 1 (January 1, 1994): 5–14; on interest-group gridlock in state politics, see Trevor Culhane, Galen Hall, and J. Timmons Roberts, "Who Delays Climate Action? Interest Groups and Coalitions in State Legislative Struggles in the United States," *Energy Research & Social Science* 79 (2021): 102114.

37. See Lee Fang, "Where Have All the Lobbyists Gone?," *The Nation*, March 17, 2014.

38. "Amazon," Open Secrets, 2022, https://www.opensecrets.org/federal-lobbying/clients/summary?id=D000023883.

39. B. Derek Rose and John P. Barrie, "'Wayfair' One Year Later," *Bloomberg News*, October 23, 2019, https://bit.ly/2TS3VRz.

40. On who lobbyists "target," see Adam Newmark and Anthony J. Nownes, "All of the Above: Lobbying Allied, Undecided, and Opposing Lawmakers in Committee and on the Floor," *Political Research Quarterly* (2022), DOI 10.1177. On lobbying as risk management, see Mirzokhidjon Abdurakhmonov et al., "Strategic Risk and Lobbying: Investigating Lobbying Breadth as Risk Management," *Journal of Management* 48:5 (2022): 1103–1130.

41. James M. Strickland, "Nudging Lobbyists to Register with Online Registration and Grace Periods," in Arielle John, Rosemarie Fike, and Stefanie Haeffele, eds., *Nudging Public Policy: Examining the Benefits and Limitations of Paternalistic Public Policies* (Lanham, MD: Rowman & Littlefield, 2021), 119–143.

42. Andrew Sollender, "Trump Revokes Lobbying Ban He Signed at the Beginning of His Presidency," *Forbes* (January 20, 2021), https://bit.ly/3REnvMI.

43. Casey Michel, "Beware, Lobbyists: The Future of FARA Under a Biden Presidency," *Just Security*, April 9, 2020, https://bit.ly/3EfdCCl. For the Biden ethics commitments, see https://bit.ly/3e92pIQ

44. Sharon LaFraniere, "Paul Manafort's Prison Sentence Is 7½ Years," *New York Times*, March 13, 2019, https://nyti.ms/2IBRxQn.

45. Bok quoted in Ronald J. Hrebenar and Clive S. Thomas, "American Interest Group Politics in the 21st Century," paper, Western Political Science Association, Vancouver, Canada, March 20, 2009.

46. Poul A. Nielsen and Donald P. Moynihan, "How Do Politicians Attribute Bureaucratic Responsibility for Performance? Negativity Bias and Interest Group Advocacy," *Journal of Public Administration Research and Theory* 27, no. 2 (2017): 269–83.

47. Theda Skocpol and Vanessa Williamson, *The Tea Party and the Remaking of Republican Conservatism* (New York: Oxford University Press, 2012), 100–101.

48. For a good recent study of citizen groups' influence, in this case among organized groups of senior citizens, see Sarah F. Anzia, "When Does a Group of Citizens Influence Policy?," *Journal of Politics* 81, no. 1 (2019).

49. On lobbyists' role as information providers, see Adam J. Newmark, "Regulating Lobbying in the United States," in Cigler, Loomis and Nownes, *Interest Group Politics*, 229–43.

50. On voter turnout: Daniel E. Bergan et al., "Grassroots Mobilization and Voter Turnout in 2004," *Public Opinion Quarterly* 69, no. 5 (2005): 760–77. On social media connections: Sunstein, *#Republic*, chap. 11 (see chap. 8, note 48).

51. Lee Drutman and Christine Mahoney, "On the Advantages of a Well-Constructed Lobbying System: Toward a More Democratic, Modern Lobbying Process," *Interest Groups & Advocacy* 6, no. 3 (2017): 290–310.

Chapter 13

1. Jonathan Martin and Alexander Burns, *This Will Not Pass: Trump, Biden and the Battle for America's Future* (New York: Simon and Schuster, 2022), 191.

2. Martin and Burns, *This Will Not Pass*, 199.

3. See Adam Schiff (a Democratic congressman), *Midnight in Washington: How We Almost Lost Our Democracy and Still Could* (New York: Random House, 2021). Some members have confidentially told each of us the same thing: When we asked, "Do you really believe Trump won?," they shook their heads or said "no."

4. Quoted in Sheryl Gay Stolberg and Nicholas Fandos, "As Gridlock Deepens in Congress, Only Gloom Is Bipartisan," *New York Times*, January 27, 2018, A1; see also Thomas E. Mann and Norman J. Ornstein, *The Broken Branch: How Congress Is Failing America and How to Get It Back on Track* (New York: Oxford University Press, 2006). For a less critical view, see James M. Curry and Frances E. Lee, *The Limits of Party: Congress and Lawmaking in a Polarized Era* (Chicago: University of Chicago Press, 2020).

5. https://news.gallup.com/poll/1600/congress-public.aspx.

6. Govtrack, "Statistics and Historical Comparison," https://www.govtrack.us/congress/bills/statistics.

7. Govtrack, "Statistics and Historical Comparison," https://www.govtrack.us/congress/bills/statistics.

8. Robert A. Caro, *Master of the Senate: The Years of Lyndon Johnson* (New York: Knopf, 2002), 52. For a different view of Andrew Johnson, as an important president who, sadly, advanced arguments for white supremacy, see Jeffrey Tulis and Nicole Mellow, *Legacies of Losing in American Politics* (Chicago: University of Chicago Press, 2018), chap. 3.

9. Caro, *Master of the Senate*, 9.

10. For more along this line, see Mark Twain and Charles Dudley Warner, *The Gilded Age* (New York: Oxford University Press, 1996).

11. Frank Bruni, "An Obama Nominee's Crushed Hopes," *New York Times*, June 6, 2016, http://nyti.ms/2aC1OIG. On the rising use of filibusters and holds more generally, see Gregory Koger, "Partisanship, Filibustering, and Reform in the Senate," in *Party and Procedure in the United States Congress*, 2nd ed., ed. Jacob R. Straus and Matthew E. Glassman (Lanham, MD: Rowman & Littlefield, 2016), chap. 10.

12. Sean Theriault, *The Gingrich Senators: The Roots of Partisan Warfare in Congress* (New York: Oxford University Press, 2013).

13. David Sirota, "Just How Severe Will American Minority Rule Become?," *The Guardian*, March 26, 2021, https://bit.ly/3Enechg; Tim Lau, "The Filibuster Explained," *The Brennan Center for Justice*, April 26, 2021, https://www.brennancenter.org/our-work/research-reports/filibuster-explained.

14. Presidents Biden, Trump, and, as we saw, Obama have all sought to replace or scale back the filibuster. On Biden: Kelly Hooper, "Biden Says He Supports a Filibuster Carveout to Restore Abortion Rights," *Politico*, June 30, 2022, https://politi.co/3RCKQyA. On Trump: Stefan Becket, "Trump Calls for End to Filibuster," CBS News, July 29, 2017, https://cbsn.ws/3rDK0XW.

15. Sam Wice, "The End of the Senate Filibuster," *Yale Journal on Regulation* blog post, August 9, 2020, https://bit.ly/2QCUEoJ.

16. Jeffrey S. Peake, "The Decline of Treaties? Obama, Trump, and the Politics of International Agreements," 2018, SSRN, https://bit.ly/3judYYf; Sean Farhang, "Legislative Capacity & Administrative Power Under Divided Polarization," *Daedalus* 150:3 (2021): 49–67.

17. Katherine Schaefer, "The Changing Face of Congress in 7 Charts," *Pew Research*, March 10, 2021, https://www.pewresearch.org/fact-tank/2021/03/10/the-changing-face-of-congress/.

18. Jane Mansbridge, "Rethinking Representation," *American Political Science Review* 97, no. 4 (2003): 515–28.

19. On representation, the classic is Hannah Pitkin, *The Concept of Representation* (Berkeley: University of California Press, 1967). A good empirical study is Kenneth Lowande, Melinda Ritchie, and Erinn Lauterbach, "Descriptive and Substantive Representation in Congress: Evidence from 80,000 Congressional Inquiries," *American Journal of Political Science* 63 no. 3 (2019): 644–59.

20. A thoughtful treatment is in Daniele Caramani, "Will vs. Reason: The Populist and Technocratic Forms of Political Representation," *American Political Science Review* 111, no. 1 (2017): 54–67.

21. David R. Mayhew, *Congress: The Electoral Connection*, 2nd ed. (New Haven, CT: Yale University Press, 2004).

22. Chris Lee, "HBOs John Oliver Exposed the Absurd and Awful Ways Congress Members Raise Money," *Forbes Magazine*, April 4, 2016, https://fortune.com/2016/04/04/john-oliver-congress-fundraising-money/.

23. For the classic account, Richard Fenno, *Home Style: House Members in the Districts* (New York: Longman Classics, 2002).

24. See Jamie L. Carson and Jeffery A. Jenkins, "Examining the Electoral Connection Across Time," *Annual Review of Political Science* 14, no. 1 (2011): 25–46.

25. For a classic account of the traditional ways, see Donald R. Matthews, "The Folkways of the US Senate: Conformity to Group Norms and Legislative Effectiveness," *American Political Science Review* 53, no. 4 (December 1959): 1064–89. The Obamacare story as told to us by a (former) member of Congress.

26. Congressional Research Service, "Salaries of Members of Congress," August 8, 2022, https://bit.ly/3Cgd5NN.

27. Kaelan Deese, "Ocasio-Cortez Pitches Interns to Work for Her Instead of McConnell," *The Hill*, June 27, 2020, https://bit.ly/3lu0CNp.

28. We joined the new members for that trip during one orientation. Even the most jaded member was moved by the ritual.

29. Dov Grohsgal and Kevin M. Kruse, "How the Republican Majority Emerged," *The Atlantic*, August 6, 2019.

30. See Sean Theriault, *The Gingrich Senators: The Roots of Partisan Warfare in Congress* (New York: Oxford University Press, 2013), 23.

31. David E. Price, "Congressional–Executive Balance in an Era of Congressional Dysfunction," *PS: Political Science & Politics* 49, no. 3 (2016): 485–86, https://bit.ly/2EuFzty.

32. Carl Bernstein, *A Woman in Charge: The Life of Hillary Rodham Clinton* (New York: Knopf, 2007), 546–47.

33. Jennifer Haberkorn, "Two GOP Heavyweights Brawl over Obamacare Bill," Politico, September 17, 2017, https://politi.co/2QEcH4p.

34. On the real power over earmarks, see Christopher Berry and Anthony Fowler, "Cardinals or Clerics? Congressional Committees and the Distribution of Pork," *American Journal of Political Science* 60, no. 3 (July 2016): 692–708. On Murtha, see Ezra Klein, *Why We're Polarized* (New York: Avid Reader, 2020), 213.

35. Linda Greenhouse, "David E. Price; Professor in Congress Is Doing Homework on Theory and Reality," *New York Times*, February 11, 1988.

36. Mark Tushnet, "Constitutional Hardball," *John Marshall Law Review* 37, no. 2 (2004): 523–53, https://repository.jmls.edu/law-review/vol37/iss2/7/.

37. Political scientists also find roll-call votes compelling, in part as a handy data source (hundreds of votes each session, each with a clear yes/no alternative). Despite years of roll-call analyses and associated theories, we are not very good at predicting vote outcomes. Whips and other nose-counters in Congress perform better than academic models.

38. Gail Russell Chaddock, "In Congress, All Roads Lead to a Conference Room," *Christian Science Monitor*, August 4, 2003, https://bit.ly/2LjGv66.

39. Jonathan Lewallen, *Committees and the Decline of Lawmaking in Congress* (Ann Arbor: University of Michigan Press, 2020), esp. chap. 3.

40. "Congress Less Popular Than Toenail Fungus and Zombies," AllGov, October 10, 2013, https://bit.ly/34K8wfz.

41. Joanne Freeman, *The Field of Blood: Violence in Congress and the Road to Civil War* (New York: Farrar, Strauss and Giroux, 2018).

42. Juliet Eilperin, *Fight Club Politics: How Partisanship Is Poisoning the House of Representatives* (Lanham, MD: Rowman & Littlefield, 2007), 13.

43. Barbara Sinclair, *Unorthodox Lawmaking: New Legislative Processes in the U.S. Congress*, 3rd ed. (Washington, DC: CQ, 2007), 71.

44. See Morone, *Republic of Wrath* (chap. 2, note 36).

45. Eilperin, *Fight Club*; Mann, *Broken Branch*; Lawrence Lessig, *They Don't Represent Us: Reclaiming Our Democracy* (New York: Harper Collins, 2019); Patrick Fisher, *Insufficient Representation: The Disconnect Between Congress and Its Citizens* (Lanham, MD: Lexington Books, 2020); Ken Buck with Bill Blankschaen, *Drain the Swamp: How Washington Corruption Is Worse Than You Think* (Washington, DC: Regnery Publishing, 2017).

46. Matt Grossmann and David Hopkins, *Asymmetric Politics: Ideological Republicans and Group Interest Democrats* (New York: Oxford University Press, 2016); Danielle M. Thomsen, *Opting Out of Congress: Partisan Polarization and the Decline of Moderate Candidates* (New York: Cambridge University Press, 2017); Jacob S. Hacker and Paul Pierson, *Let Them Eat Tweets: How the Right Rules in an Age of Extreme Inequality* (New Haven, CT: Yale University Press, 2020).

47. See, e.g., Patricia A. Kirkland and Justin H. Phillips, "Is Divided Government a Cause of Legislative Delay?," *Quarterly Journal of Political Science* 13, no. 2 (2018): 173–206.

48. David R. Mayhew, *Divided We Govern: Party Control, Lawmaking, and Investigations, 1946–2002*, 2nd ed. (New Haven, CT: Yale University Press, 2005).

49. Stephen Ansolabehere, Maxwell Palmer, and Benjamin Schneer, "Divided Government and Significant Legislation: A History of Congress from 1789 to 2010," *Social Science History* 42, no. 1 (2018): 81–108; Donald A. Moynihan and Alasdair Roberts, "Dysfunction By Design? Trumpism as Administrative Doctrine," *Public Administration Review* 81:1 (2021): 152–156.

50. James M. Curry and Frances E. Lee, "What Is Regular Order Worth? Partisan Lawmaking and Congressional Processes," *Journal of Politics* 82, no. 2 (2020): 627–41.

51. Mann, *It's Even Worse Than It Looks*, 110 (chap. 11, note 47). See also Sarah Binder, *Stalemate: Causes and Consequences of Legislative Gridlock* (Washington, DC: Brookings Institution Press, 2003).

Chapter 14

1. Joseph Ellis, *His Excellency: George Washington* (New York: Random House, 2004), 194–95; see also Nathaniel Philbrick, *Travels with George: In Search of Washington and His Legacy* (New York: Viking, 2021).

2. Henry Wiencek, *An Imperfect God: George Washington, His Slaves and the Creation of America* (New York: Farrar, Straus and Giroux, 2003); Erica Armstrong Dunbar, *Never Caught: The Washingtons' Relentless Pursuit of Their Runaway Slave, Ona Judge* (New York: Atria, 2017).

3. Rep. Mike Rogers (R-AR), "Biden 'Senile,' 'Not Up to the Challenge,'" Press Release, February 9, 2022, https://bit.ly/3yjUm30; Sen. Rick Scott (R-FL), "The Most Effective Thing Joe Biden Can Do . . . Is Resign," Press Release, May 10, 2022, https://bit.ly/3HQNXzA.

4. See Kenneth Lowande and Jon C. Rogowski, "Presidential Unilateral Power," *Annual Review of Political Science* 24 (2021): 21–43; Corey Brettschneider, *The Oath and the Office: A Guide to the Constitution for Future Presidents* (New York: Norton, 2018).

5. Elizabeth Bomberg, "Joe Biden's Climate Change Challenge," *Political Insight* 13, no. 1 (2022): 30–33.

6. White House, "Letter to the Speaker of the House and President Pro Tempore of the Senate Regarding the War Powers Report," June 8, 2022, https://bit.ly/39YxfC0; National Archives, "War Powers Resolution of 1973," July 27, 2021, https://bit.ly/3buGQk6.

7. Alexander Keyssar, *Why Do We Still Have the Electoral College?* (Cambridge, MA: Harvard University Press, 2020); George Edwards, *Why the Electoral College Is Bad for America* (New Haven, CT: Yale University Press, 2011).

8. For a classic treatment of presidential power, see Richard Neustadt, *Presidential Power and the Modern Presidents: The Politics of Leadership from Roosevelt to Reagan* (New York: Free Press, 1990).

9. Belle de Jong, "Biden in Brussels: Presidential Visit Costs over €2,000 per Minute," *Brussels Times*, March 22, 2022, https://bit.ly/3OGSk2J.

10. Sollenberger, *The Unitary Executive Theory: A Danger to Constitutional Government* (Lawrence: University Press of Kansas, 2020); Stephen Skowronek, "The Conservative Insurgency and Presidential Power: A Developmental Perspective on the Unitary Executive," *Harvard Law Review* 122 (June 2009): 2070–103; Steven Calabresi and Kevin Rhodes, "The Structural Constitution: Unitary Executive, Plural Judiciary," *Harvard Law Review* 105 (April 1992): 1153–216.

11. Francis Fukuyama, *Political Order and Political Decay* (New York: Farrar, Straus, & Giroux, 2015); Arthur Schlesinger, *The Imperial Presidency* (New York: Houghton Mifflin, 1973); Benjamin Ginsberg, *The Imperial Presidency and American Politics: Governance by Edicts and Coups* (New York: Routledge, 2022).

12. Kirk Scharfenberg, "Now It Can Be Told: The Story Behind Campaign '82's Favorite Insult," *Boston Globe*, November 6, 1982.

13. Tocqueville, *Democracy in America*, 126 (see chap. 2, note 12).

14. Erica H. Ma, "The War Powers Resolution and the Concept of Hostilities," *Northeastern University Law Review* 13, no. 2 (2021): 519.

15. Francis Biddle, *In Brief Authority* (New York: Doubleday, 1962), 219.

16. H. R. McMaster and Gabriel Scheinmann, "U.S. Restraint in Russia and China Has Created an Unstable and Dangerous World," *Foreign Policy*, June 17, 2022, https://bit.ly/3P0Vyhl.

17. Anthony Blinken, Secretary of State, "One Billion in New Military assistance for Ukraine," *U.S. Department of State*, Press Release,

August 8, 2022. https://www.state
.gov/1-billion-in-new-u-s-military-
assistance-for-ukraine/; Aaron Blake,
"Biden Does a Victory Lap on Russia-
Ukraine Intelligence," *Washington
Post*, February 24, 2022, https://wapo
.st/3bC2EKL.

18. Dan Bilefsky and Catherine
Porter, "Trump's 'Bully Attack' on
Trudeau Outrages Canadians," *New
York Times*, June 10, 2018, A5; BBC
News, "Greenland: Trump Criticises
'Nasty' Denmark Over Cancelled
Visit," August 21, 2019, https://bit.ly/
3ewbgEA.

19. "Donald Trump Tells NATO
Allies to Spend 4% of GDP on
Defense—US President Suggests
Doubling 2% Spending Target," *The
Guardian*, June 11, 2018, https://
www.theguardian.com/world/2018/
jul/11/donaldtrump-tells-nato-allies-
to-spend-4-of-gdp-on-defence.

20. Tony Czuczka, "Biden Aide
Says Inflation Fight Can Advance if
Congress Helps," *Time*, June 19, 2022,
https://bit.ly/3P1Vk9U.

21. George C. Edwards III, "Was
Donald Trump an Effective Leader
of Congress?," *Presidential Studies
Quarterly* 51, no. 1 (2021): 4–34; Stef
W. Kight, "How Many Bills Congress
Has Passed So Far," *Axios*, March 8,
2022, https://bit.ly/3OHO2bF.

22. Leonard White, *The Federalists*
(New York: Macmillan, 1942).

23. Kathryn Dunn Tenpas,
"Tracking Turnover in the Trump
Administration," Brookings
Institution, January 2021, https://
brook.gs/2HX2fys; Matthew J.
Dickinson and Kate Reinmuth,
"Turnover, Loyalty and Competence
in the West Wing: The Trump
White House in Historical Context,"
Presidential Studies Quarterly 51:4
(December 2021): 763–780.

24. Alex Zhao and Daniel Lippman,
"Biden Races to Hire Senior Staff at
Drained Agencies," Politico, August
10, 2021, https://politi.co/3NLPrMV;
Charles F. Parker and Eric K.
Stern, "The Trump Administration
and the COVID-19 Crisis," *Public
Administration* (2022), DOI: 10.1111/
padm.12843.

25. Margit Cohn, *A Theory of the
Executive Branch: Tension & Legality*
(New York: Oxford University Press,
2021), esp. 149–63; Kenneth Mayer,
*With the Stroke of a Pen: Executive
Orders and Presidential Power*
(Princeton, NJ: Princeton University
Press, 2001).

26. Lowande and Rogowski,
"Presidential Unilateral Power."

27. For a description of Roosevelt's
approach, see James Morone, *The
Democratic Wish* (New Haven, CT:
Yale University Press, 1998), 131.

28. President Joe Biden, "My Plan
for Fighting Inflation," *Wall Street
Journal*, May 30, 2022, https://on.wsj
.com/3utuW0A.

29. Memo from Pat Caddell to
"Governor Carter," December 21, 1976,
Carter Library; see also see David
Blumenthal and James Morone, *The
Heart of Power: Health and Politics in
the Oval Office* (Berkeley: University
of California Press, 2009), 249.

30. Richard Neustadt, *Presidential
Power and the Modern Presidents*,
rev. ed. (New York: Free Press, 1991),
chap. 3.

31. Joshua M. Sacco and Kevin Coe,
*Presidential Communication and
Digital Democracy in Tumultuous
Times* (New York: Oxford University
Press, 2021).

32. Samuel Kernell, *Going Public*
(Washington, DC: CQ, 2007).

33. Stephen Macedo, "Lost in the
Marketplace of Ideas: Toward a New
Constitution for Free Speech After
Trump and Twitter?," *Philosophy and
Social Criticism* 48, no. 4 (2022):
496–514.

34. George Edwards, *On Deaf Ears:
The Limits of the Bully Pulpit* (New
Haven, CT: Yale University Press,
2003).

35. Frank Newport and Lydia Saad,
"Presidential Job Approval," *Public
Opinion Quarterly* 85, no. 1 (2021):
223–41.

36. Harry Truman, *Where the Buck
Stops*, ed. Margaret Truman (New
York: Warner Books, 1989), 371–72;
Marc Landy and Sidney Milkis,
Presidential Greatness (Lawrence:
University Press of Kansas, 2001).

37. Stephen Skowronek, *The
Politics Presidents Make: Leadership
from John Adams to Bill Clinton*
(Cambridge, MA: Harvard University
Press, 1997).

38. Peggy Noonan, *When Character
Was King* (New York: Penguin Books,
2001), 242–43, 245–49.

39. Blumenthal, *Heart of Power*, 293.

40. On personality theories, see
Michael Nelson, "The Psychological
Presidency," in *The Presidency
and the Political System*, 12th ed.
(New York: Sage Press, 2020),
199–228.

41. Mortality data from Robert
E. Gilbert, *The Mortal Presidency:
Illness and Anguish in the White
House* (New York: Fordham
University Press, 1998), 4–5.

42. Rose McDermott, *Presidential
Leadership, Illness, and Decision
Making* (New York: Cambridge
University Press, 2008).

43. Quoted in Jody C. Baumgartner,
"The Second Best Choice? Vice-
Presidential Candidates in the
Modern Era," in *White House
Studies Compendium*, ed. Anthony
J. Eksterowicz and Glenn P. Hastedt
(New York: Nova Science Publishers,
2008), 158.

44. Quoted in Elliot A. Rosen, "'Not
Worth a Pitcher of Warm Piss': John
Nance Garner as Vice President,"
in *At the President's Side: The Vice
Presidency in the Twentieth Century*,
ed. Timothy Walch (Columbia:
University of Missouri Press,
2007), 45.

45. Stephen E. Ambrose, *Eisenhower:
Soldier and President* (New York:
Simon & Schuster, 1990), 564.

46. Joel Goldstein, *The White
House Vice Presidency: The Path
to Significance, Mondale to Biden*
(Lawrence: University Press of
Kansas, 2016).

47. Richard J. Ellis, *The Development
of the American Presidency* (New
York: Routledge, 2012), 284.

48. Andrew M. Grossman and Sean
Sandoloski, "The End of Independent
Agencies? Restoring Presidential
Control of the Executive Branch,"
Federalist Society Review 22 (2021):
216–25.

49. Joseph Califano, *Governing
America: An Insider's Report from the
White House and the Cabinet* (New
York: Simon & Schuster, 1981), 431;
personal interview with the authors,
June 15, 2006.

50. For a fine description, see
Matthew Dickinson, "The Executive
Office of the President: The Paradox
of Politicization," in *The Executive
Branch*, ed. Joel Aberbach and
Mark Peterson (New York:
Oxford University Press,
2005), 135–73.

51. Johnson quoted in David
Blumenthal and James Morone, *The
Heart of Power: Health and Politics in
the Oval Office* (Berkeley: University
of California Press, 2009), 8.

52. For a marvelous case study of
"massaging the numbers," see Robert
Saldin, *When Bad Policy Makes Good
Politics* (New York: Oxford University
Press, 2017).

53. On Trump's leadership style
(and especially the combat between
aides), see David Blumenthal and
James A. Morone, *Whiplash: Health
Politics in the White House* (New

Haven, CT: Yale University Press, in preparation).

54. "The First Lady and Her Role," George W. Bush Presidential Library and Museum. https://bit.ly/3IAFAsu.

55. See the excellent treatment in Lauren A. Wright, *On Behalf of the President: Presidential Spouses and White House Communications Strategy Today* (Santa Barbara, CA: Praeger, 2016).

56. Julia R. Azari and Jennifer K. Smith, "Unwritten Rules: Informal Institutions in Established Democracies," *Perspectives on Politics* 10, no. 1 (March 2012): 37–55; Aurélia Bardon et al., "Disaggregating Civility: Politeness, Public-Mindedness and Their Connection," *British Journal of Political Science* (2022), DOI: https://doi.org/10.1017/S000712342100065X.

57. Tocqueville, *Democracy in America*, 122 (see chap. 2, note 12).

Chapter 15

1. "Public Troubled by 'Deep State,'" Monmouth University Polling Institute, March 19, 2018, https://bit.ly/2pvHOlF.

2. Cruz quoted in Stuart Shapiro, "Government Bureaucrats Are People Too," *The Hill*, November 12, 2015, https://bit.ly/1Sm9Khg; President Barack Obama, First Inaugural Address (see chap. 11, note 22).

3. "Public Holds Broadly Favorable Views of Many Federal Agencies, Including CDC and HHS," Pew Research Center, April 9, 2020.

4. Congressional Research Service, "Federal Workforce Statistics," June 28, 2022, https://bit.ly/3s74LuY.

5. The official U.S. government website, USA.gov, lists sixty-six agencies as of January 2023, at https://bit.ly/3TczHpU.

6. Paul C. Light, *The True Size of Government* (Washington, DC: Volker Alliance, 2017).

7. William Riordan, *Plunkitt of Tammany Hall: A Series of Very Plain Talks on Very Practical Politics* (New York: Penguin, 1995).

8. What inspired the term *bureaucracy*? The word comes from France where, beginning in the nineteenth century, executive offices were termed *bureaus*. French officials governed ("-cracy") through these rule-based organizations rather than the whims of a king or ruling family. Though Americans are more apt to use words like *agency* (Central Intelligence Agency) or *department* (Treasury Department), we have a few bureaus as well—the best known our FBI, the Federal Bureau of Investigation.

9. James A. Morone, *The Democratic Wish: Popular Participation and the Limits of American Government* (New Haven, CT: Yale University Press, 1998), 101.

10. James T. Sparrow, *Warfare State: World War II, Americans, and the Age of Big Government* (New York: Oxford University Press, 2012).

11. See Daniel Carpenter, *The Forging of Bureaucratic Autonomy: Reputations, Networks, and Policy Innovation in Executive Agencies* (Princeton, NJ: Princeton University Press, 2001); Morone, *Hellfire Nation* (see chap. 2, note 51).

12. Sue Fawn Chung, "Chinese Exclusion, the First Bureau of Immigration, and the 1905 Special Chinese Census," *Chinese America: History and Perspectives* (2018): 21–34.

13. Max Weber, "Bureaucracy," in *From Max Weber: Essays in Sociology*, ed. H. H. Gerth and C. Wright Mills (New York: Oxford University Press, 1946), 196–98.

14. The DACA/Dreamers program was still winding through the courts in late 2022. See Eileen Sullivan, "Appeals Court Says DACA Is Illegal but Keeps Program Alive for Now," *New York Times*, October 5, 2022, https://nyti.ms/3yPa7z0. Jonathan Adler, "Hostile Environment: Trump's EPA Is Having a Hard Time in Federal Court," *National Review*, October 15, 2018, 18–20.

15. Courtney Bublé, "Biden Administration Releases Made in America Proposed Rule," *Government Executive*, July 28, 2021, https://bit.ly/3ETqjTA.

16. *Federal Register*, July 6, 2022, https://www.federalregister.gov/public-inspection/search?conditions%5Bspecial_filing%5D=0&page=1.

17. This figure includes just under 500,000 U.S. Postal Service workers. Updated totals for federal workers available from the Office of Personnel Management, https://bit.ly/2Y7KmIB.

18. For regular updates of top executive positions filled/vacant, see the joint tracking effort of the *Washington Post* and Partnership for Public Service, at https://wapo.st/3Tt9qTj.

19. On the history of the presidential cabinet, see Lindsay M. Chervinsky, *The Cabinet: George Washington and the Creation of an American Institution* (Cambridge, MA: Harvard University Press, 2022).

20. Kathryn Dunn Tenpas, "Tracking Turnover in the Biden Administration," *Brookings Report*, October 2022, https://brook.gs/3EPBUmB. See also Eleanor L. Schiff, *Bureaucracy's Masters and Minions: The Politics of Controlling the U.S. Bureaucracy* (Lanham, MD: Lexington Books, 2020).

21. For a close-up look at one such official, Federal Maritime Commission head Dan Maffei, see Peter S. Goodman, "Can Global Shipping Be Fixed? One Regulator Will Try," *New York Times*, August 8, 2022, https://nyti.ms/3MHghqx.

22. *Seila Law LLC v. Consumer Financial Protection Bureau*, 591 US ___ (2020).

23. Naiomi Gonzalez, "An Assessment of the Private Military Industry and Its Role in the Iraq and Afghanistan Wars," *Real Clear Defense*, August 5, 2019, https://bit.ly/3dakMXH; Robert D. Peltz, "Blackwater Rising: The Legal Issues Raised by the Unprecedented Privatization of U.S. Military Functions," *University of Miami Law Review* 76 (2021–2022): 163–191.

24. Bert A. Rockman, "The Melting Down of Government: A Multidecade Perspective," *Governance* 30, no. 1 (2017): 29–35; Allison Stanger, *One Nation Under Contract: The Outsourcing of American Power and the Future of Foreign Policy* (New Haven, CT: Yale University Press, 2011).

25. Light, "The True Size of Government."

26. Truman quoted in Richard Neustadt, *Presidential Power* (New York: Free Press, 1990), 10.

27. Donald Moynihan: "Public Management for Populists: Trump's Schedule F Executive Order and the Future of the Civil Service," *Public Administration Review* (January–February) 2022, 174–178.

28. Glenn Thrush and Erica L. Green, "Trump to Propose Government Reorganization, Targeting Safety Net Programs," *New York Times*, June 21, 2018, A17.

29. Kenneth W. Abbott, "Competence Versus Control: The Governor's Dilemma," *Regulation & Governance* (2019), https://doi.org/10.1111/rego.12234.

30. See, for example, Mark Meadows, *The Chief's Chief* (St. Petersburg, FL: All Seasons Press, 2022), 56; Natashia Korecki and Sarah Owermohle,

"Attacks on Fauci Grow More Intense, Personal and Conspiratorial," Politico, June 4, 2021, https://www.politico .com/news/2021/06/04/fauci-attacks-personal-conspiratorial-491896.

31. Toby Bolsen and Risa Palm, "Politicization and COVID-19 Vaccine Resistance in the U.S.," *Progress in Molecular Biology & Translational Science* 188:1 (2022): 81–100.

32. "The Major Questions Doctrine," Congressional Research Service, April 6, 2022, https://crsreports.congress .gov/product/pdf/IF/IF12077.

33. *West Virginia v. Environmental Protection Agency (EPA)*, 597 US ____ 2022.

34. *Chevron U.S.A., Inc. v. Natural Resources Defense Council, Inc.*, 467 U.S. 837. On the 2022 Medicare case, and the Chevron doctrine generally, see James Romoser, "In an Opinion that Shuns Chevron, the Court Rejects a Medicare Cut for Hospital Drugs," *SCOTUS Blog*, June 15, 2022, https:// bit.ly/3CGK6mz.

35. "All Employees, Federal," US Bureau of Labor Statistics, https://fred.stlouisfed.org/series/ CES9091000001.

36. Emily Willingham, "Is the Freedom of Information Act Stifling Intellectual Freedom?," *Forbes*, November 21, 2015, https://bit.ly/ 2mzCbAE.

37. A good summary of privatization—including discussion of a $1 trillion public-private Trump administration infrastructure plan—is in Reed Karaim, "Privatizing Government Services," *CQ Researcher* 27, no. 43 (December 2017), https:// bit.ly/2A4Wa3M. For a more critical take, see Donald Cohen and Allen Mikaelian. *The Privatization of Everything: How the Plunder of Public Goods Transformed America and How We Can Fight Back* (New York: The New Press, 2021).

38. John Goodman and Gary Loveman, "Does Privatization Serve the Public Interest?," *Harvard Business Review*, November– December 1991, https://hbr. org/1991/11/doesprivatization-serve-the-public-interest.

39. 2020 figures at https://bit .ly/2KSUUn7. See also Danny Vinik, "America's Government Is Getting Old," Politico, September 27, 2017, https://politi.co/2SvATal; Jaclyn S. Piatak and Stephen B. Holt, *Public Service Motivation and Public Opinion: Examining*

Antecedents and Attitudes (New York: Cambridge University Press, 2021).

Chapter 16

1. Julia Shapero, "Republicans, Anti-Abortion Groups Celebrate Supreme Court Overturning Roe v. Wade," Axios, June 24, 2022, https:// bit.ly/3eHR0zY.

2. Thomas Franck and Spencer Kimball, "Biden Says Supreme Court Is 'Out of Control,' Orders HHS to Protect Abortion Access," *CNBC*, July 8, 2022, https://cnb.cx/3eLoD3O.

3. Adam Liptak, "In 6-3 Ruling, Supreme Court Ends Nearly 50 Years of Abortion Rights," *New York Times*, June 24, 2022, https://nyti .ms/3VA4CxX.

4. Adam Liptak, "Supreme Court Strikes Down New York Law Limiting Guns in Public," *New York Times*, June 23, 2022, https://nyti .ms/3F0F0Vb. For a description that cheers the rulings, see Zack Smith and Alex Phipps, "Five Monumental Cases That Highlighted the Supreme Court's 2021-2 Term," Heritage Foundation, July 8, 2022, https:// herit.ag/3ETy2kA.

5. *Kennedy v. Bremerton School District*, 597 U.S. ____ (2022).

6. Alexander Hamilton, *Federalist* no. 78.

7. Nikolas Bowie, "How the Supreme Court Dominates Our Democracy," *Washington Post*, July 16, 2021, https://wapo.st/3Dl1m2t.

8. Constitution Annotated, "Table of Laws Held Unconstitutional in Whole or Part by the Supreme Court," https://bit.ly/3Ty8duv.

9. John Gramlich, "Only 2 Percent of Federal Criminal Defendants Go to Trial and Most Who Do Are Found Guilty," Pew Research Center, June 11, 2019, https://pewrsr .ch/2XHzRZo.

10. National Center for State Courts, "Jury Management," 2020, https://bit .ly/3f6N5aY.

11. Quality Judges Initiative, *FAQs: Judges in the United States*, University of Denver, Institute for the Advancement of the American Legal System, no date, https://bit.ly/ 3glh0lk.

12. Tocqueville, *Democracy in America*, 1:270 (see chap. 2, note 11).

13. Stephen Jessee, Neil Malhotra and Maya Sen, "The Supreme Court is Now Operating Outside of American

Public Opinion," *Politico Magazine*, July 19, 2022, https://politi .co/3FcwhPR.

14. Justin McCarthy, "GOP Approval of Supreme Court Surges, Democrats' Slides," Gallup, September 28, 2017, https://bit.ly/3lTLiKg.

15. John Schwartz, "Effort Begun to End Voting for Judges," *New York Times*, December 23, 2009.

16. Pew Research Center, "Public's Views of Supreme Court Turned More Negative Before News of Breyer's Retirement," February 2, 2022, https://pewrsr.ch/3sccvMA.

17. Christine L. Nemacheck, "Trump's Lasting Impact on the Federal Judiciary," *Policy Studies* 42:6 (2021): 544–562; "Donald Trump Is Appointing Federal Judges at a Blistering Pace," *The Economist*, February 14, 2020, https://econ .st/3jS1x8u;.

18. In *Boumediene v. Bush*, 553 U.S. 723 (2008), the Supreme Court ruled that prisoners held in Guantánamo have habeas corpus rights and cannot be held without charges; in *Hamdan v. United States*, 696 F.3d 1238 (D.C. Cir. 2012), the Court ruled that military commission trials do not conform to U.S. law.

19. Russell Wheeler, "Biden's First Year Judicial Appointments—Impact," Brookings, January 27, 2022, https:// brook.gs/3s6C3L3; Madison Alder and Jasmine Ye Han, "Trump Nears Post-Nixon First: No Black Circuit Judges," *Bloomberg Law*, June 25, 2020, https://bit.ly/2W7eUbK; Carl Tobias, "President Trump's War on Federal Judicial Diversity," *Wake Forest Law Review* 54 (2019).

20. Charlie Savage, "A Judge's View of Judging Is on the Record," *New York Times*, May 14, 2009; Sonia Sotomayor, *My Beloved World* (New York: Vintage, 2013).

21. Stephen B. Burbank and Sean Farhang, "Politics, Identity, and Class Certification on the U.S. Court of Appeals," *Faculty Scholarship at Penn Law* no. 2095 (2020); Jonathan Kastellec, "Racial Diversity and Judicial Influence on Appellate Courts," *American Journal of Political Science* 57, no. 1 (2013): 167–83.

22. Allison P. Harris and Maya Sen, "Bias and Judging," *Annual Review of Political Science* 22 (2019): 241–59.

23. Nancy Scherer, "Blacks on the Bench," *Political Science Quarterly* 119, no. 4 (2005): 655–75; Darren Lenard Hutchinson, "*Who* Locked Us

Up? Explaining the Social Meaning of Black Punitiveness," *Yale Law Journal* 127 (2018): 2388–477.

24. Christina L. Boyd and Michael J. Nelson, "The Effects of Trial Judge Gender and Public Opinion on Criminal Sentencing Decisions," *Vanderbilt Law Review* 70 (2017): 1819–43.

25. Thomas Jefferson, "Letter to Justice Spencer Roane on the Limits of Judicial Review," in *Writings* (New York: Library of America, 1984), 1425–28.

26. See, e.g., Robert G. McCloskey and Sanford Levinson, *The American Supreme Court*, 6th ed. (Chicago: University of Chicago Press, 2016), esp. 302–12.

27. *Dred Scott v. Sandford*, 60 U.S. 393 (1857).

28. David A. Kaplan, *The Most Dangerous Branch: Inside the U.S. Supreme Court in the Age of Trump* (New York: Random House, 2019).

29. The case was *Worcester v. Georgia*, 31 U.S. (6 Pet.) 515 (1832).

30. Supreme Court of the United States, Docket Number 19–1392, *Dobbs v. Jackson Women's Health*, https://www.supremecourt.gov/oral_arguments/audio/2021/19–1392; or Docket Number 20–1530, *West Virginia v. EPA*, https://www.supremecourt.gov/oral_arguments/audio/2021/20–1530.

31. Kayla S. Canelo, "The Supreme Court, Ideology, and the Decision to Cite or Borrow from Amicus Curiae Briefs," *American Politics Research* 50:2 (2022): 255–264; Paul M. Collins Jr., Pamela C. Corley, and Jesse Hamner, "The Influence of Amicus Curiae Briefs on U.S. Supreme Court Opinion Content," *Law and Society Review* 49, no. 4 (December 2015): 917–44.

32. Adam Liptak, "Are Oral Arguments Worth Arguing About?," *New York Times: Sunday Review*, May 6, 2012; Tonja Jacobi and Matthew Sag, "The New Oral Argument: Justices as Advocates," *Notre Dame Law Review* 94 (2019): 1161–1208.

33. Lee Epstein and Eric Posner, "Trump Has the Worst Record at the Supreme Court of Any Modern President," *Washington Post*, July 20, 2020. Lee Epstein and Eric Posner, "The Decline of Supreme Court Deference to the President," *University of Pennsylvania Law Review* 166, no. 4 (March 2018): 829–60.

34. Josh Gerstein and Alexander Ward, "The Supreme Court Has Voted to Overturn Abortion Rights, Draft Opinion Shows," Politico, May 3, 2022, https://politi.co/3CKlOYS.

35. Chloe Folmar, "Chief Justice Roberts Calls Draft Opinion Leak 'Absolutely Appalling,'" *The Hill*, May 5, 2022, https://bit.ly/3ThWbpx.

36. Brad Mielk and Haley Yamada, "Who Leaked the Supreme Court Draft Opinion on Abortion?," ABC News, May 3, 2022, https://abcn.ws/3eLPb5b.

37. Randee Fenner, "Clerking at the Supreme Court," *Stanford Lawyer* 77 (Fall 2007): 7–9.

38. Senate Hearing 109–158, Hearing Before the Committee on the Judiciary, United States Senate 109 Congress (September 12, 2005), http://bit.ly/2aLRGSW.

39. See, e.g., Kevin Buckler and Elizabeth L. Gilmore, "Originalism, Pragmatic Conservatism, and Living Document Judicial Philosophies: Explaining Variation in U.S. Supreme Court Votes in Criminal Procedure Cases for the 1994–2004 Terms of Court," *American Journal of Criminal Justice* 42 (2017): 28–54, http://bit.ly/2aUoirR; see also Jeffrey Segal et al., "Ideological Values and the Votes of U.S. Supreme Court Justices Revisited," *Journal of Politics* 57, no. 3 (August 1995): 812–23 Tom S. Clark, B. Pablo Montagnes, and Jörg L. Spenkuch, "Politics from the Bench? Ideology and Strategic Voting in the U.S. Supreme Court" (June 2022), https://bit.ly/3z1BYvR.

40. See Pew Research Center (2022), endnote 16.

41. Richard Holden, Michael Keane and Matthew Lilley, "Peer Effects on the United States Supreme Court," *Quantitative Economics* 12:3 (2021): 981–1019;

42. Saul Brenner, "Fluidity on the Supreme Court, 1956–1967," *American Journal of Political Science* 90, no. 56 (1996): 90–107.

43. Frederick Schauer, "Incentives, Reputation, and the Inglorious Determinants of Judicial Behavior," *University of Cincinnati Law Review* 68, no. 3 (2000): 615–36.

44. *Dred Scott v. Sandford*, 60 U.S. 393 (1857).

45. Justice Black in *Connecticut General Life Insurance Co. v. Johnson*, 303 U.S. 77 (1938); William O. Douglas, "Stare Decisis," *Columbia Law Review* 49, no. 6 (1949): 735–58.

46. What constitutes a serious crime? In *Duncan v. Louisiana* (1968) the Court ruled that they were defined by the potential penalty—more than $500 in fines or six months in prison.

47. Statistia Research Department, "Litigation Spending by Large Companies in the U.S., 2015–2021," Statistia, July 6, 2022, https://bit.ly/3TxlIuE; Amicus Capital Group, "New Report Shows an Increase in Litigation Spending in the U.S.," December 16, 2021, https://bit.ly/3zm8ER9.

48. Carroll Doherty et al., "Majority of Public Favors Giving Civilians the Power to Sue Police Officers for Misconduct," Pew Research Center, July 9, 2020, https://pewrsr.ch/2ZjiOAf.

49. Learned Hand, "The Deficiencies of Trials to Reach the Heart of the Matter," *Lectures on Legal Topics* 3 (1926): 89, 105.

50. Presidential Commission on the Supreme Court of the United States, *Final Report*, December 2021, https://bit.ly/3VLIlgz.

51. Doherty, "Majority of Public Favors Giving Civilians."

52. Abraham Lincoln, First Inaugural Address, March 4, 1861; Roy Basler, ed., *The Collected Works of Abraham Lincoln*, vol. IV (New Brunswick, NJ: Rutgers University Press, 1953), 262–71, quoted at 268; Alexander Hamilton, *Federalist* no. 81; this argument is developed in Ryan Emenaker, "Repairing the Judicial Void: Modifying the Rights-Rescinding Court" (PhD diss., Political Science Department, Brown University, Providence, RI, 2019).

Chapter 17

1. Abha Bhattarai and Rachel Siegel, "Inflation is Making Homelessness Worse," *Washington Post*, July 3, 2022, https://wapo.st/3z3gpvg.

2. Jonnelle Marte, "Protesters Urge Fed to Remember That Big Rate Hikes Can Hurt Vulnerable Workers," *Bloomberg News*, June 14, 2022, https://bloom.bg/3yXCVWg; authors' firsthand observation.

3. Jermaine Toney and Cassandra L. Robertson, "Intergenerational Economic Mobility and the Racial Wealth Gap," *AEA Papers and Proceedings* 111 (2021): 206–10.

4. Office of Management and Budget, "Report to Congress on the Benefits and Costs of Federal Regulations," 2022 (updated annually at https://bit.ly/3OXGTnr).

5. United Health Foundation, "Public Health Impact: Poverty," 2022, https://bit.ly/3NYiJrF.

6. Congressional Research Service, "Poverty Among the Population Aged 65 and Over," Washington, DC: CRS, April 2021.

7. Deidre McPhillips, "Substance Use Among Teens Dropped Significantly in 2021," CNN, December 15, 2021, https://cnn.it/3cg1ftB.

8. Bhattarai and Siegel, "Inflation is Making Homelessness Worse."

9. "Data Report," National Association of Schools of Public Affairs & Administration, 2022, https://bit.ly/3c6Cz6L.

10. Domenico Montanaro, "Poll: Support for Controlling Gun Violence Hits Its Highest Point in a Decade," NPR, June 9, 2022, https://n.pr/3Pn75aU.

11. The White House, "President Biden Calls for a Three-Month Tax Holiday," June 22, 2022, https://bit.ly/3yzoDKf.

12. Juliet Eilperin and Brady Dennis, "Biden Is Hiking the Cost of Carbon. It Will Change How the U.S. Tackles Global Warming," *Washington Post*, February 26, 2021, https://wapo.st/3P4FcEL.

13. Cass R. Sunstein, "Some Costs & Benefits of Cost-Benefit Analysis," *Daedalus* 150, no. 3 (2021): 208–19.

14. Deborah Stone, *Policy Paradox: The Art of Political Decision Making*, 3rd ed. (New York: Norton, 2011).

15. Woodrow Wilson, "The Study of Administration," *Political Science Quarterly* 2, no. 2 (1887): 197–222.

16. Rogan Kersh, "Health Reform: The Politics of Implementation," *Journal of Health Politics, Policy, and Law* 36, no. 3 (2011): 613–23.

17. Lawrence Hurley and John McArdle, "Supreme Court Puts Spotlight on Speed of Rulemaking," *Environment & Energy News*, December 4, 2012, http://www.eenews.net/stories/1059973307.

18. Nadja Popovich et al., "The Trump Administration Rolled Back More Than 100 Environmental Rules. Here's the Full List," *New York Times*, January 20, 2021, https://nyti.ms/3yzAEzs; Nina Totenberg, "Supreme Court Restricts the EPA's Authority to Mandate Carbon Emission Reductions," NPR, June 30, 2022, https://n.pr/3awmCGS.

19. Lisa Friedman, "Democrats Designed Climate Law to Be a Game Changer. Here's How," *New York Times*, August 22, 2022, https://nyti.ms/3WY3tRr.

20. Neal Kataly and Joshua Geltzer, "Why Trump Keeps Losing at the Supreme Court," *The Atlantic*, June 20, 2020, https://bit.ly/3z0yb2j.

21. The White House, "Redressing Our Nation's and the Federal Government's History of Discriminatory Housing Practices and Politics," January 26, 2021, https://bit.ly/3O3rgtz; The White House, "President Biden Announces New Actions to Ease the Burden of Housing Costs," May 16, 2022, https://bit.ly/3O5iqv8.

22. Lucy Xiaolu Wang and Nicholas J. Wilson, "U.S. State Approaches to Cannabis Licensing," *International Journal of Drug Policy* 106 (2022): 103755; Rebecca L. Haffajee, Robert J. MacCoun, and Michelle M. Mello, "Behind Schedule—Reconciling State and Federal Marijuana Policy," *New England Journal of Medicine* 379 (2018): 501–4, DOI:10.1056/NEJMp1804408.

23. Emil Robert Mackey, *Street-Level Bureaucrats and the Shaping of University Housing Policy* (Fayetteville: University of Arkansas Press, 2008); Kristen A. Renn, "How Resident Assistants Understand and Enact Their Role in Student Success," *Journal of College and University Housing* 46, no. 2 (2020): 10–26.

24. Joseph Soss, *Unwanted Claims: The Politics of Participation in the US Welfare System* (Ann Arbor: University of Michigan Press, 2000).

25. Mark Bovens, Paul 't Hart, and Sanneke Kuipers, "The Politics of Policy Evaluation," in *Oxford Handbook of Public Policy*, ed. Michael Moran, Martin Rein, and Robert E. Goodin (New York: Oxford University Press, 2008), 320; also good is Kai Ruggieri et al., "Policy Evaluation and Behavioral Economics," in *Psychology and Behavioral Economics: Applications for Public Policy*, ed. Kai Ruggieri (New York: Routledge, 2021).

26. Anthony A. Braga et al., "Problem-Oriented Policing, Deterrence, and Youth Violence: An Evaluation of Boston's Operation Ceasefire," *Journal of Research in Crime and Delinquency* 38, no. 3 (2001): 195–225.

27. Shani A. Buggs, Daniel W. Webster, and Cassandra K. Crifasi, "Using Synthetic Control Methodology to Estimate Effects of a *Cure Violence* Intervention in Baltimore, Maryland," *Injury Prevention* 28 (2022): 61–67; Magdalena Cerda, Melissa Tracy, and Katherine M. Keyes, "Reducing Urban Violence," *Epidemiology* 29, no. 1 (2018): 142–50.

28. Paul Pierson, "When Effect Becomes Cause: Policy Feedback and Political Change," *World Politics* 45, no. 4 (1993): 595–628; for a recent overview of policy feedback and path dependence, see Joe Soss and Donald P. Moynihan, "Policy Feedback and the Politics of Administration," *Public Administration Review* 74, no. 3 (May/June 2014): 320–32.

29. Center for Budget & Policy Priorities, "Policy Basics: Ten Facts About Social Security," March 2022, https://bit.ly/3IzwYSF.

30. For a discussion of these theories, see James A. Morone, *The Devils We Know* (see chap. 2, note 43).

31. Theda Skocpol, *Protecting Soldiers and Mothers* (Cambridge, MA: Harvard University Press, 1995).

32. Suzanne Mettler, *Soldiers to Citizens: The G.I. Bill and the Making of the Greatest Generation* (New York: Oxford University Press, 2005).

33. R. Michael Holmes, David Andrew Waldman, Donald Siegel and Justin Pepe, "Declining Trust in Capitalism: Managerial, Research, and Public Policy Implications," *Academy of Management Perspectives* 37:1 (2023), DOI: 10.5465.

34. American Medical Association, "Goldwater–Johnson: Remarks," *Washington News* 189, no. 3 (July 20, 1964): 3.

35. Enrollment figures from Medicaid.gov, updated monthly; see https://bit.ly/3P590RQ. On the remarkable story of passage, see David Blumenthal and James A. Morone, *The Heart of Power: Health and Politics in the Oval Office* (Berkeley: University of California Press, 2009), chap. 5.

36. Pamela Herd et al., "A Targeted Minimum Benefit Plan: A New Proposal to Reduce Poverty Among Older Social Security Recipients," *RSF: The Russell Sage Foundation Journal of the Social Sciences* 4, no. 2 (February 2018): 74–90.

37. Dennis S. Ippolito, *Deficit Spending in the United States: Taxes, Spending, and Fiscal Discontent* (New York: Routledge, 2022). Another good contrast of Republican and

Democratic views of fiscal policy, especially of tax cuts, is in Alexander Hertel-Fernandez and Theda Skocpol, "Congress Makes Tax Policy," in *Congress and Policy Making in the 21st Century,* ed. Jeffrey A. Jenkins and Eric M. Patashnik (New York: Cambridge University Press, 2016), 137–61.

38. Ken Thomas and Darlene Superville, "Trump in Ohio Praises Tax Cuts for Growing Economy," *PBS News Hour,* February 5, 2018, https://to.pbs.org/2shj9oL.

39. Rep. Scott Peters et al. (twenty-four House members of both parties), "Letter on Bipartisan Budget Reforms," February 22, 2022, https://bit.ly/3Rr6NBX; Sen. Sheldon Whitehouse, "Senators Whitehouse and Enzi Offer Bipartisan Reforms to Fix Broken Budget Process," Senate Floor Remarks, October 31, 2019, https://bit.ly/32yz9mD.

40. For a good insider's recap of the crisis and monetary policy responses, see Timothy F. Geithner, *Stress Test: Reflections on Financial Crises* (New York: Random House, 2014), 258–387.

41. Sarah Ewall-Wice, "White House Unveils 2023 Budget, Calls for New Spending Aimed at Reducing Crime, Unclogging Supply Lines, and a New Tax on Billionaires," CBS News, March 28, 2022, https://cbsn.ws/3cbZfm6.

42. Martin Crutsinger, "US Budget Deficit Hits $2.77 Trillion in 2021, 2nd Highest," *U.S. News,* October 22, 2021, https://bit.ly/3uMLCjM; Alan Rappeport, "U.S. Budget Deficit Projected to Fall to $1 Trillion in 2022," *New York Times,* May 25, 2022, https://nyti.ms/3PoDLRl.

43. Office of Management and Budget, "Budget of the U.S. Government: Fiscal 2023," https://bit.ly/3RvO482.

44. Jessica Corbett, "Progressives Alarmed by Privatization Dub Infrastructure Deal 'A Disaster in the Making,'" *Common Dreams,* June 24, 2021, https://bit.ly/3AMN7lQ.

45. Elliott Dolan-Evans, "A Marxist Viewing of Avengers: Infinity War," *PPE Sydney,* September 27, 2018, https://bit.ly/2WyzstM.

46. See, e.g., Ashley Oravetz, "Congressional Term Limits: The Right Idea, The Wrong Numbers," *University of Dayton Law Review* 46, no. 1 (2020).

47. Livia Albeck-Ripka, "Why a California Congressman Has Proposed a Four-Day Workweek," *New York Times,* March 21, 2022, https://nyti.ms/3O13JcE.

48. Paul Light, *A Government Ill Executed: The Decline of the Federal Service and How to Reverse It* (Cambridge, MA: Harvard University Press, 2008).

49. Deputy Treasury Secretary Wally Adeyemo, "The American Rescue Plan: Centering Racial Equity in Policymaking," Department of the Treasury, September 2021, https://bit.ly/3z48ygV.

50. On policy entrepreneurship, see Lynn Ross, *Policy Entrepreneurship: A Guide to Shaping and Understanding Policy* (Washington, DC: Brookings Institution Press, 2016).

51. Silvia Foster-Frau and Teo Armus, "A Half-Century After One Movement, 'Fierce Madres' Call for Another," *Washington Post,* June 23, 2022, https://wapo.st/3uNdPHe.

52. Nancy Fitzgerald, "Eco-Anxiety: Kids Worried About Climate Change," *Optum,* April 5, 2022, https://bit.ly/3PaElm0; Katy Scott, "Can 'Climate Kids' Take on Governments and Win?," CNN, July 24, 2018, https://cnn.it/3PpKL0h.

53. Abigail Abrams, "The Battle over the Future of the Anti-Abortion Movement," *Time,* March 25, 2022, https://bit.ly/3RAyBUg.

54. On the difference between the Clinton and Obama plans, see Blumenthal and Morone, *Heart of Power.*

55. President Franklin Delano Roosevelt, First Inaugural Address, March 4, 1933, http://avalon.law.yale.edu/20th_century/froos1.asp.

56. Robert Caro, *Master of the Senate* (New York: Knopf, 2002), 151–53.

Chapter 18

1. Joseph R. Biden Jr., "What America Will and Will Not Do in Ukraine," *New York Times,* May 31, 2022, https://nyti.ms/3c6filu.

2. Jonathan Guyer, "Why the US Is Paying More for the Military After the Afghanistan War Is Over," *Vox,* December 22, 2021, https://bit.ly/3o4bJyV.

3. Alexandra Manolache, "World Military Expenditure Passes $2 Trillion for First Time," Stockholm International Peace Research Institute, April 25, 2022, https://bit.ly/3OedF2y.

4. The Stockholm International Peace Research Institute (SIPRI) is the best source of global defense spending percentages; for annual updates see https://www.sipri.org/databases/milex.

5. Brand Finance, "Global Soft Power Index 2022," March 15, 2022, https://bit.ly/3cgDVfv.

6. Brand Finance, "Global Soft Power Index 2022."

7. John Ikenberry, "The Security Trap," *Democracy: A Journal of Ideas* 1, no. 2 (Fall 2006, https://bit.ly/3ckrvDs; a more recent book-length study is Andrew W. Neal, *Security as Politics; Beyond the State of Exception* (Edinburgh: Edinburgh University Press, 2019).

8. For detailed figures, see https://www.iraqbodycount.org/.

9. Paul Pierson, "Increasing Returns, Path Dependence, and the Study of Politics," *American Political Science Review* 94, no. 2 (June 2000): 251–67.

10. Joseph Nye, *Soft Power: The Means to Success in World Politics* (New York: Public Affairs Books, 2004); see also Maria Repnikova, "The Balance of Soft Power: The American and Chinese Quests to Win Hearts and Minds," *Foreign Affairs* (July/August 2022), 44–51.

11. Brand Finance, "Global Soft Power Index 2022."

12. This figure excludes military aid. See James McBride, "How Does the U.S. Spend Its Foreign Aid?," Council on Foreign Relations, October 1, 2018, https://www.cfr.org/backgrounder/how-does-us-spend-its-foreign-aid.

13. President Joe Biden, "Remarks by President Biden on America's Place in the World," *The White House,* February 4, 2021, https://bit.ly/3Dq3oy6.

14. Husain Haqqani and Aparna Pande, "India's Economy Can't Compete with China's—And That Should Worry U.S. Policymakers," *The Hill,* July 13, 2022, https://bit.ly/3uTpKDx.

15. James McBride and Andrew Chatzky, "The U.S Trade Deficit: How Much Does it Matter?" *The Council on Foreign Relations.* March 8, 2019. https://www.cfr.org/backgrounder/us-trade-deficit-how-much-does-it-matter

16. Frida Ghitis, "Biden Aims to Challenge China in Latin America with B3W," *World Politics Review,* October 7, 2021, https://bit.ly/3Phmda8.

17. See Aaron L. Friedberg, "The Growing Rivalry Between America and China and the Future of Globalization," *The Strategist* 5, no. 1 (2022): 95–119; *The Economist*, "Will China's Economy Ever Overtake America's?" Sept. 6, 2022, https://econ.st/3eZV3b4.

18. An excellent history of U.S. trade policy is in Craig Van-Grasstek, *Trade and American Leadership: The Paradoxes of Power and Wealth from Alexander Hamilton to Donald Trump* (New York: Cambridge University Press, 2019).

19. Paul Krugman, *Arguing with Zombies: Economics, Politics, and the Fight for a Better Future* (New York: Norton, 2020); on the conservative side, see William Shearer and William Fletcher, *The Conservative Case Against Free Trade* (Warrenton, VA: Conservative Caucus Foundation, 2012).

20. See, e.g., Chad P. Bown and Douglas A. Irwin, "Trump's Assault on the Global Trading System," *Foreign Affairs* 98, no. 5 (2019), https://fam.ag/3eu3cOs.

21. On Biden and free trade, see James Bacchus, "Biden and Trade at Year One: The Reign of Polite Protectionism," CATO Institute Policy Analysis No. 926, April 26, 2022, https://bit.ly/3yPLnWF.

22. Andrew Ross Sorkin et al., "Biden, Oil, and the Middle East," *New York Times,* July 14, 2022, https://nyti.ms/3o6QBIs.

23. Moritz Pieper, "An Iran Nuclear Deal Without the United States? Chinese, European, and Russian Interests and Options After the U.S. Withdrawal from the Joint Comprehensive Plan of Action," in *Contemporary Issues in International Political Economy*, ed. Fu-Lai Tony Yu and Diana Kwan (New York: Palgrave Macmillan, 2019).

24. George Washington, "First Inaugural Address, in the City of New York," April 30, 1789, http://www.bartleby.com/124/pres13.html; see also Alexander Hamilton, *Federalist* no. 1.

25. Stephen M. Walt, "Biden Needs Architects, Not Mechanics, to Fix U.S. Foreign Policy," *Foreign Policy*, July 12, 2022, https://bit.ly/3Oc7YSU.

26. On foreign policy and American exceptionalism, see Thanassis Cambanis, "The End of American Exceptionalism: What the United States Should Learn from Its Peers," *Foreign Affairs* 99, no. 3 (2020); Karl W. Schweizer, "American Exceptionalism: Origins and Policy Implications," *The European Legacy* 27:7–8 (2022): 832–838.

27. Jeffrey Sachs, *A New Foreign Policy: Beyond American Exceptionalism* (New York: Columbia University Press, 2018).

28. For a recent summary of "democratic peace" debates in political science, see Nils Petter Gleditsch, "Toward a Social-Democratic Peace?," *Ethics & International Affairs* 34, no. 1 (2020): 67–75.

29. "Confidence in U.S. Presidents," Pew Research Center, January 7, 2020, https://pewrsr.ch/35MWPmG For regular updates on migration figures to the U.S. and other countries, see Migration Data Portal, at https://bit.ly/3F9167Z.

30. Jeanne Batalova, Brittany Blizzard, and Jessica Bolter, "Frequently Requested Statistics on Immigrants and Immigration in the United States," Migration Policy Institute, February 14, 2020, https://bit.ly/3fGtSOa. For regular updates on migration figures to the U.S. and other countries, see Migration Data Portal, at https://bit.ly/3F9167Z.

31. George Washington, Farewell Address: To the People of the United States, September 19, 1796, https://bit.ly/3MXmTRE.

32. See Carla Norrlof and William C. Wohlforth, "Is U.S. Grand Strategy Self-Defeating? Deep Engagement, Military Spending, and Sovereign Debt," *Conflict Management & Peace Science* 36, no. 3 (2019): 227–47.

33. Michael T. Nietzel, "Foreign Applications to U.S. Colleges and Study Abroad by Americans Rebound, New Report Shows," *Forbes*, June 23, 2022, https://bit.ly/3fYdWvF; "55 Study Abroad Statistics: Facts and Figures," *IvyPanda*. July 7, 2022, https://ivypanda.com/blog/46-study-abroad-statistics-convincing-facts-and-figures/.

34. Brent J. Talbot, "Getting Deterrence Right: The Case for Stratified Deterrence," *Journal of Strategic Security* 13, no. 1 (2020): 26–40; Kenneth Waltz, "Why Iran Should Get the Bomb," *Foreign Affairs*, July/August 2012.

35. William J. Perry, "The Risk of Nuclear Catastrophe Is Greater Than During the Cold War," *HuffPost*, January 20, 2016, https://bit.ly/3gyxEOi.

36. Bruce Cumings, "Obama, Trump, and North Korea," in *The United States in the Indo-Pacific,* ed. Oliver Turner and Inderjeet Parmar (New York: Palgrave Macmillan, 2020), 79–93.

37. David Sanger, *The Perfect Weapon: War, Sabotage and Fear in the Cyber Age* (New York: Crown, 2018); Julian E. Barnes and David E. Sanger, "Congress, Warning of Cybersecurity Vulnerabilities, Recommends Overhaul," *New York Times*, March 11, 2020, https://nyti.ms/2SVkRGW.

38. These categories are adopted from Walter Russell Mead, *Special Providence: American Foreign Policy and How It Changed the World* (New York: Routledge, 2001).

39. Amit Ayalon et al., "The United States Withdrawal from Afghanistan After Two Decades," *Strategic Assessment* 25, no. 1 (March 2022): 36–54.

40. Peter Beinart, "Is Biden's Foreign Policy Team the Best of 'The Blob'?," *New York Times*, June 2, 2022, https://nyti.ms/3Ocuc7k.

41. Kurt M. Campbell and Rush Doshi, "How America Can Shore Up Asian Order," *Foreign Affairs*, January 12, 2021, https://fam.ag/3c9gbK3.

42. Zoe Manzanetti, "2021 Military Active-Duty Personnel, Civilians by State," *Governing*, February 1, 2022, https://bit.ly/3uQIVh5.

43. Arita Holmberg and Aida Alvinus, "How Pressures for Change Challenge Military Organizational Characteristics," *Defence Studies* 19, no. 2 (2019): 130–48.

44. Blake Stilwell, "That Time a Soldier Used a Payphone to Call Back to the US to Get Artillery Support in Grenada," *We Are the Mighty*, April 16, 2016, https://bit.ly/32vl5KP.

45. Jonathan Guyer, "Inside Ukraine's Lobbying Blitz in Washington," *Vox*, July 5, 2022, https://bit.ly/3RFFgg5.

46. Thomas Gift and Jonathan Montem, "Media Misperception of Public Opinion on US Foreign Policy," *Foreign Policy Analysis* 17, no. 1 (2022), https://academic-oup-com.eres.qnl.qa/fpa/article/17/1/oraa015/5892796; Dina Smeltz, "Who Says Foreign Policy Doesn't Win Elections?," *Foreign Affairs* 98, no. 3 (2019), https://fam.ag/3fZwqvA.

47. Woodrow Wilson, "First Inaugural Address," March 4, 1913, https://bit.ly/3StObjK.

48. Robert Mann, *A Grand Delusion: America's Descent into Vietnam* (New York: Basic Books, 2002), 24.

49. President Harry Truman, "The Truman Doctrine: Address Before a Joint Session of Congress," March 12, 1947, Washington, DC.

50. Arthur Vandenberg, "American Foreign Policy" (In the Senate), January 10, 1945, https://bit.ly/3DrqiW4.

51. President George W. Bush, Graduation Address, United States Military Academy, June 1, 2002, https://bit.ly/3Fh9cv0.

52. Hal Brands, "Breaking Down Obama's Grand Strategy," *National Interest,* June 23, 2014; both Obama quotes are cited here: https://bit.ly/3TvGWJv.

53. Quinnipiac University Poll, "President Trump Approval Ratings," March 9, 2020, https://bit.ly/35YQrZQ.

54. Nicholas Kitchen, "Why American Grand Strategy Has Changed: International Constraint, and the Return of Realism," *Global Affairs* 6, no. 1 (2020): 87–104.

55. Walt, "Biden Needs Architects." See also Heidi Crebo-Rediker and Douglas Rediker, "A Real Foreign Policy for the Middle Class: How to Help American Workers and Project US Power," *Foreign Affairs* 101 (2022): 105–121.

Credits

Photos

About the Authors
xxiv: Gabby Salazar; xxiv: WFU/Ken Bennett

Chapter 1
2: Spencer Platt/Staff. Getty Images; 6: Larry McCormack, The Tennessean; 9: REUTERS/Eduardo Munoz; 10: MATTES René/hemis.fr via Getty Images; p. 11: AP Photo/Suzanne Plunkett; 12: Photo by Rajiv Perera on Unsplash; 12: Jim West/Alamy Stock Photo; 12: Shutterstock; 15: Dana Summers/The Orlando Sentinel/TCA; 18: bauhaus1000/Getty Images.

Chapter 2
24: Shutterstock; 27: Bettmann/Getty Images; 28: Universal History Archive/Universal Images Group via Getty Image; 32: "JEFF KOWALSKY/Getty Images"; 39: ASSOCIATED PRESS; 42: Win McNamee/Getty Images; Justin Sullivan/Getty Images; 43: MPI/Getty Images; 50: Danny Johnston/ASSOCIATED PRESS, Ian West/PA Archive/PA Images; 53: Tami Ruble/Alamy Stock Photo; 58: AP Photo/Josh Boak.

Chapter 3
62: Photo by Hank Walker/The LIFE Picture Collection via Getty Images; 66: Library of Congress Prints and Photographs Division, LC-USZC4-7155; 67: Twenty Brave Men, a National Guard Heritage Painting by Jackson Walker, courtesy the National Guard Bureau; 70: Image copyright © The Metropolitan Museum of Art. Image source: Art Resource, NY; 74: National Archives and Records Administration NAID 532935; 75: "Regulators" Artwork by Bryant White - www.whitehistoricart.com; 76: VCG Wilson/Corbis via Getty Images; 78: George Caleb Bingham, The County Election, 1852; 81: © Louis Glanzman; 86: Original Photographers: McPherson and Oliver; 95: Photo by Smith Collection/Gado/Getty Images; 96: Sara Krulwich/The New York Times/Redux; 100: "FatCamera/Getty Images."

Chapter 4
104: Homeland Security Photo/Alamy Stock Photo; 110: Sundry Photography/Alamy Stock Photo; 115: From American Government: Stories of a Nation, Scott F. Aberanthy. Sage Publications.; 118: Widening the Augusta Canal 1875, by Bernard Willington. Oil on canvas. Painted in 2006., Bettman/Getty Images, A 1949 Herblock Cartoon, © The Herb Block Foundation.; 124: Nick Anderson Editorial Cartoon used with the permission of Nick Anderson, the Washington Post Writers Group and the Cartoonist Group. All rights reserved.; 128: Bloomberg/Getty Images, Shutterstock.

Chapter 5
132: Suzi Pratt/Getty Images; 136: Nathan Benn/Corbis via Getty Image, Bettman/Getty Images; 141: Bill Clark/Getty Images; 142: AP Photo/David J. Phillip; 144: Boston Herald photo by Chris Christo ; 146: Shutterstock; 149: Brendan Hickey/Wikimedia Commons; 150: Shutterstock, AP Photo/Alaric Lambert, Mark Peterson/Redux, AP Photo/Elaine Thompson, File; 153: Clay Good/Zuma Press; 155: Bloomberg/Getty Images; 156: Getty Images, Getty Images; 163: Bettman/Getty Images; 167: Scott Olson/Getty Images, Alex Wong/Getty Images.

Chapter 6
172: ASSOCIATED PRESS; 176: Bettman/Getty Images; 178: Photo by Paula Bronstein/Getty Images; 1283: Everett Collection Historical/Alamy Stock Photo; 184: Beettman/Getty Images; 186: Bettman/Getty Images; 187: Bettmann/Getty Images; 188: Bettman/Getty Images, AP Photos/File; 193: The Soiling of Old Glory, StanelyForman Photos.com; 194: Stephanie Keith/Getty Images; 198: Shutterstock; 200: Photo by Gilbert Carrasquillo/GC Images/Getty Images; 203: Cathy Murphy/Getty Images; 206: AP Photo/Matt Rourke, Alamy; 208: Chicago Tribune/Getty Images; 210: Frontier Forts; 211: Cal Sport Media/Alamy Stock Photo; 213: ASSOCIATED PRESS; 215: Justin Casterline/Getty Images, ASSOCIATED PRESS.

Chapter 7
222: REUTERS/Robert Galbraith/File photo; AP Photo/Julio Cortez; 231: Eugene Gologursky/Getty Images, Roy Rochlin/Getty Images; 234: Copyright © 2006 Jake Fuller; 224: iStock.com/mamado; 242: AP Photo/Charlotte Observer, Diedre Laird.

Chapter 8
246: hackNY_____; 251: Photo by Jeffrey Camarati/Getty Images, Associated Press; 254: design by Melissa Wilkinson, Associated Press; 258: Nicholas Kamm/Getty Images; 259: Photo by Salwan Georges/For the Washington Post; 260: Timothy Hiatt/Getty Images; 267: Photo by Matt McCLain/The Washington Post via Getty Images.

Chapter 9
272: Anadolu Agency/Getty Images; 274: Ronald Reagan Speaks out Against Socialized Medicine LP Cover (1961), via Twitter; 277: Alamy; 280: AP Photo;

288: AP Photo/Julio Cortez; 295: AFP/Getty Images; 297: Getty Images; 198: AP Photo/Eddie Adams, File, Photo courtesy of Washington Post via Getty Images; 299: via iamrbeat TikTok.

Chapter 10

304: ASSOCIATED PRESS; 307: ASSOCIATED PRESS; 318: AP Photo/Cheryl Senter; 320: Bettman/Getty Images; 321: Time Life Pictures/Getty Images; 326: Hulton Archives/Getty Images, AP Photo/Mark J. Terrill; 327: Mark J Terrill/AP/Shutterstock; 331: Bettman/Getty Images; 337: Tom Williams/Getty Images; 339: GRANGER/GRANGER—All rights reserved., Cahle Cartoons/Monte Wolverton, Battle Ground, WA.

Chapter 10

311: Data Source: Voting Rights Lab. https://votingrightslab.org/showdown-2022-the-state-of-state-election-law-and-the-fights-ahead/; 333: Data Source: Manifesto Project.

Chapter 11

342: Bloomberg/Getty Images; 348: Joe Raedle/Getty Images; Mario Tama/Getty Images; 349: AP Photo/Michael Sohn; 351: LGI Stock/Corbis/VCG via Getty Images; 353: GRANGER/GRANGER—All rights reserved; 354: Photo by © CORBIS/Corbis via Getty Images; 355: www.CartoonStock.com; 356: Wisconsin Historical Society, WHS-9426; 364: SOPA Images/Getty Images; Photograph by Marget Long; 365: Alex Edelman/CNP/ZUMA Wire/Alamy Live News; Sipa US/Alamy Stock Photo; 366: Associated Press; Associated Press; 367: Shutterstock; United States Geological Survey, Public domain, via Wikimedia Commons; 371: Samuel Corum/Getty Images.

Chapter 12

376: Matthew Hatcher/SOPA Images/LightRocket via Getty Images; 378: Ken Howard/Alamy Stock Photo; 380: © 2022 Surfrider Foundation; 381: Paul Morigi/Getty Images; 383: Apex MediaWire/Alamy Stock Photo; 386: © Chesapeake Climate Action Network; 387: Michael Hancock twitter screen grab; 389: Photo by Missi Köpf: https://www.pexels.com/photo/black-horse-running-on-the-shore-6215840/; 392: Photo By DAVID BREWSTER/Star Tribune via Getty Images; 396: Bloomberg/Getty Images; 403: Jonathan McIntosh/Wikimedia Commons.

Chapter 13

408: Erin Scott/Getty Images; 414: U.S. Senate Historical Office; 418: FPG/Getty Images; 424: AP Photo/Julio Cortez; 426: Photo by Win McNamee/Getty Images; 435: C-SPAN screen grab; 436: Ken Cedeno/Sipa USA(Sipa via AP Images); 441: Bettman/Getty Images; 443: Cagle Cartoons/John Darkow, Columbia, MO.

Chapter 14

448: Drew Angerer/Getty Images; 452: National Archive/Newsmakers, Rob Carr/Getty Images; 454: GRANGER/GRANGER — All rights reserved; 459: AP Photo/Ringo H.W. Chiu; 461: Saul Loeb/Getty Images; 463: AP Photo/Ron Edmonds; 464: ZUMA Press, Inc./Alamy Stock Photo; 468: AP Photo/Greg Gibson; 468: Bettman/Getty Images; 471: Courtesy, LBJ Presidential Library; 473: AP Photo/Doug Mills; 477: Bettman/Getty Images; 478: Charles Omman-ney/Getty Images, Dennis Brack-Pool/Getty Images; 480: UPI/Alamy Stock Photo; 485: JIM WATSON/Getty Images.

Chapter 15

490: Photo by Alex Wong/Getty Images; 494: The Granger Collection, NYC – All rights reserved; 495: The Granger Collection, NYC – All rights reserved.; 497: FRED R. CONRAD/© The New York Times; 498: Photo by Michael Brochstein/Sipa USA(Sipa via AP Images); 502: Andrew Harnik/Getty Images; 502: Craig F. Walker/Getty Images; 508: American Photo Archive/Alamy Stock Photo; 509: David J. Philip/AFP/Getty Images, FEMA/Yuisa Rios; 513: Associated Press; 518: Colin Dukelow, © 2022 CartoonStock Ltd. All Rights Reserved; 521: Tom Fowlks/Vanity Fair; 522: David Paul Morris/Bloomberg via Getty Images; 523: The Granger Collection, NYC – All rights reserved.

Chapter 16

526: Anadolu Agency/Getty Images; 532: Andy Manis/AP; 541: The Granger Collection, NYC - All rights reserved.; 542: Photo by Glenn Pinkerton/Las Vegas News Bureau via Getty Images; 547: ASSOCIATED PRESS; 549: Artwork by: William J Hennessy Jr/CourtroomArt.com; 551: Mark Wilson/Getty Images; 551: Photo by CNP/Getty Images, WENN Ltd/Alamy Stock Photo, Shawn Thew/Bloomberg via Getty Images; 558: Library of Congress Prints and Photographs Division Washington, D.C. 20540 USA, Everett Collection/Shutterstock; 559: AP Photo/Bill Haber; 560: Photo by Fotosearch/Getty Images; 561: © Chris Stewart/San Francisco Chronicle.

Chapter 17

568: Shutterstock; 574: Chip Somodevilla/Getty Images, Chip Somodevilla/Getty Images; 579: Shutterstock; 582: Scott Olson/Getty Images; 585: AP Photo/Manuel Balce Ceneta; 586: Justin Sullivan/Getty Images, Scott Olson/Getty Images; 591: AP Photo; 603: Chip Somodevilla/Getty Images.

Chapter 18

608: Bloomberg via Getty Images; 612: AP Photo/Wong Maye-E; 613: Corbis Documentary/Getty Images; 619: Photo by Royal Court of Saudi Arabia/Handout/Anadolu Agency via Getty Images; 621: GRANGER/GRANGER — All rights reserved; 623: U.S. Marines Capture the Barbary pirate fortress at Derna, Tripoli, 27th April 1805 (w/c on paper), Waterhouse, C.H. (fl.1812)/Private Collection/Peter Newark Historical Pictures/Bridgeman Images; 624: Photo by Alexcy Furman/Getty Images; 631: Photo by JUNG YEON-JE/AFP via Getty Images; 635: Photo by Mark Wilson/Getty Images; 636: KAREN BLEIER/AFP/Getty Images.

Figures

Chapter 1

13: Created by OUP based on data from Pew; 14: Created by OUP based on data from usgovernmentspending.com; 16: OECD (2022), Tax revenue (indicator). doi: 10.1787/d98b8cf5-en (Accessed on 31 August 2022); 17: Created by OUP based on data from Pew Research Center and Washington Post; 19: Created by OUP using data from the U.S. Census Bureau; 20: Created by OUP based on data from Pew Research Center.

Chapter 2

32: (NYconstitution.org); 35: Pew Research Center; 37: Wide partisan gaps on many issues, but majorities in both parties prioritize a stronger economy. Pew Research Center, Washington, D.C. (February 2022). https://www.pewresearch.org/politics/2022/02/16/publics-top-priority-for-2022-strengthening-the-nations-economy/pp_2022-02-16_priorities_0-04a/; 41: World Values Survey; 46: Created by OUP based on data from Robert Frank, Falling Behind. University of California Press, 2007; Created by OUP based on data from Elizabeth Sawhill and John Morton, Economic Mobility: Is the American Dream Alive and Well? Economic Mobility Project, Pew Charitable Trusts; Larry Bartells, Unequal Democracy (Princeton, NJ: Princeton University Press/Russell Sage Foundation, 2008), Chap. 1; The Federal Reserve, Distributional Financial Accounts. Retrieved from: https://www.federalreserve.gov/releases/z1/dataviz/dfa/distribute/table/; 47: Source: World Inequality Database (WID.world); 55: Pew Research Center, Washington, D.C (Spring 2021). https://www.pewresearch.org/global/2021/10/13/diversity-and-division-in-advanced-economies/pg_2021-10-13_diversity_0-01/.

Chapter 3

68: Map by Miklos Pinther in Atlas of Great Lakes Indian History, edited by Helen Hornbeck Tanner. Copyright © 1987 by the University of Oklahoma Press, Norman. Reprinted by permission of the publisher., Map by Miklos Pinther in Atlas of Great Lakes Indian History, edited by Helen Hornbeck Tanner. Copyright © 1987 by the University of Oklahoma Press, Norman. Reprinted by permission of the publisher; 96: Article by Richard J. Werther. JOURNAL OF THE AMERICAN REVOLUTION © 2018.

Chapter 4

110: Tax Foundation; 111: Source: Cathryn Stout and Thomas Wilburn, Chalkbeat New York. https://www.chalkbeat.org; 122: Created by the Center for American Progress (www.americanprogress.org); 129: Lokal_Profil, CC BY-SA 2.5 <https://creativecommons.org/licenses/by-sa/2.5>, via Wikimedia Commons.

Chapter 6

204: © 2022 Higher Ed Immigration Portal. All rights reserved.; 215: Majorities of Americans say there is at least some discrimination against many different societal groups. Pew Research Center. https://www.pewresearch.org/fact-tank/2021/03/18/majorities-of-americans-see-at-least-some-discrimination-against-black-hispanic-and-asian-people-in-the-u-s/ft_2021-03-18_discrimination_04/.

Chapter 7

224: Republicans ages 65 and older far less likely than younger Republicans to support legalizing marijuana for medical and recreational use. Pew Research Center. https://www.pewresearch.org/fact-tank/2021/04/16/americans-overwhelmingly-say-marijuana-should-be-legal-for-recreational-or-medical-use/ft_2021-04-16_marijuana_03/, Data Source: Gallup, Inc. https://news.gallup.com/poll/1651/gay-lesbian-rights.aspx, Data Source: Gallup, Inc. https://news.gallup.com/poll/350486/record-high-support-same-sex-marriage.aspx; 225: Majority of adults say abortion should be legal in some cases, illegal in others. Pew Research Center. https://www.pewresearch.org/religion/2022/05/06/americas-abortion-quandary/pf_05-06-22_abortion-views_0_0/; 229: Data Source: Gallup, Inc. https://news.gallup.com/poll/343025/global-warming-attitudes-frozen-2016.aspx; 230: Data Source: "National Exit Poll for Presidential Results." CBS News, December 14, 2020. https://www.cbsnews.com/elections/2020/united-states/president/exit-poll/; 232: Created by OUP based on data from the Pew Research Center; 235: Majorities most consistently cite climate change, spread of infectious diseases as threats to their country; relatively few mention large-scale migration. Pew Research Center. https://www.pewresearch.org/global/2020/09/09/despite-pandemic-many-europeans-still-see-climate-change-as-greatest-threat-to-their-countries/pg_2020-09-09_global-threats_00-02/; 236: Created by OUP based on data from the Pew Research Center.

Chapter 8

250: Data Source: Harvard IOP Youth Poll. https://iop.harvard.edu/youth-poll/spring-2021-harvard-youth-poll; 253: Data Source: Gallup, Inc. https://news.gallup.com/poll/241634/one-three-americans-felt-urge-protest.aspx; 257: Created by OUP based on data from the Pew Research Center; 266: Growing share of Americans say they use YouTube; Facebook remains one of the most widely used online platforms among U.S. adults. Pew Research Center. https://www.pewresearch.org/internet/2021/04/07/social-media-use-in-2021/pi_2021-04-07_social-media_0-01/, Age gaps in Snapchat, Instagram use are particularly wide, less so for Facebook. Pew Research Center. https://www.pewresearch.org/internet/2021/04/07/social-media-use-in-2021/pi_2021-04-07_social-media_0-02a/; 268: On the Cusp of Adulthood and Facing an Uncertain Future: What We Know About Gen Z So Far. Pew Research Center. https://www.pewresearch.org/social-trends/2020/05/14/on-the-cusp-of-adulthood-and-facing-an-uncertain-future-what-we-know-about-gen-z-so-far-2/, On the Cusp of Adulthood and Facing an Uncertain Future: What We Know About Gen Z So Far. Pew Research Center. https://www.pewresearch.org/

social-trends/2020/05/14/on-the-cusp-of-adulthood-and-facing-an-uncertain-future-what-we-know-about-gen-z-so-far-2/; 269: On the Cusp of Adulthood and Facing an Uncertain Future: What We Know About Gen Z So Far. Pew Research Center. https://www.pewresearch.org/social-trends/2020/05/14/on-the-cusp-of-adulthood-and-facing-an-uncertain-future-what-we-know-about-gen-z-so-far-2/.

Chapter 9
279: YouGov/Economist Poll https://bit.ly/3md9Tep; 284: Data Source: Pearson Institute/AP-NORC Poll. 2021; 286: Data Source: Gallup, Inc. https://news.gallup.com/poll/355526/americans-trust-media-dips-second-lowest-record.aspx; 287: © AllSides.com 2022; 292: 51% say social media companies should play a major role in setting standards for use of algorithms to find false information; 40% say federal agencies should. Pew Research Center. https://www.pewresearch.org/internet/2022/03/17/ai-and-human-enhancement-americans-openness-is-tempered-by-a-range-of-concerns/ps_2022-03-17_ai-he_03-010/. Data Source: Source: Gallup/Knight Foundation. https://knightfoundation.org/articles/local-news-most-trusted-in-keeping-americans-informed-about-their-communities/; 293: Courtesy of Report for America.

Chapter 10
311: Data Source: Voting Rights Lab. https://votingrightslab.org/showdown-2022-the-state-of-state-election-law-and-the-fights-ahead/; 333: Data Source: Manifesto Project.

Chapter 11
361: Data Source: Boxell, Gentzkow, Shapiro. https://fivethirtyeight.com/wp-content/uploads/2020/10/drutman.NEGATIVE-PARTISANSHIP.0915.png?w=575.

Chapter 12
400: Statista. https://www.statista.com/chart/18792/annual-lobbying-expenditures-of-major-tech-companies-in-the-us/; 434: Photo by Scott J. Ferrell/Congressional Quarterly/Getty Image.

Chapter 13
442: Republicans have moved further to the right than Democrats have to the left. Pew Research Center. https://www.pewresearch.org/fact-tank/2022/03/10/

the-polarization-in-todays-congress-has-roots-that-go-back-decades/ft_22-02-22_congresspolarization_chamber_party_new1/.

Chapter 14
467: Statista. https://www.statista.com/statistics/1125024/us-presidents-executive-orders/; 472: FiveThirtyEight. https://fivethirtyeight.com/features/biden-has-lost-support-across-all-groups-of-americans-but-especially-independents-and-hispanics/.

Chapter 15
492: Office of Personnel Management; U.S. Census.; 496: US Department of Energy; 500: The Office of Management and Budget; 503: American Hospital Association; 509: Brookings Institution; 512 Provided by authors, created by OUP.

Chapter 16
532: Created by OUP; 532: Source: Gallup; 534: Created by OUP; 536: Pew Research Center. https://www.pewresearch.org/fact-tank/2021/01/13/how-trump-compares-with-other-recent-presidents-in-appointing-federal-judges/ft_21-01-07_trumpjudges_2/; 537: Created by OUP; 538: Created by OUP; 542: Created by OUP; 554: Angie Gou, As unanimity declines, conservative majority's power runs deeper than the blockbuster cases, SCOTUSblog, https://www.scotusblog.com/2022/07/as-unanimity-declines-conservative-majoritys-power-runs-deeper-than-the-blockbuster-cases/; 555: Randy Schutt, CC BY-SA 3.0 <https://creativecommons.org/licenses/by-sa/3.0>, via Wikimedia Commons; 556: Created by OUP, data from Gallup.

Chapter 17
573: Burbio. Retrieved from: https://www.bloomberg.com/news/articles/2021-08-13/school-mask-rule-clash-puts-heat-on-state-courts-to-steer-policy; 600: DHS Office of Immigration Statistics, Gallup, Inc. https://news.gallup.com/poll/389708/dissatisfaction-immigration-level-rises.aspx.

Chapter 18
616: Source: Pew Research/Ipsos; 618: Gallup, Inc. https://news.gallup.com/poll/390614/views-foreign-trade-nearly-back-pre-trump-levels.aspx; 632: Corruption Perceptions Index (2021) by Transparency International is licensed under CC BY 4.0. https://www.transparency.org/en/cpi/2021.

Index

Note: Page references followed by a *t* indicate table; *f* indicate figure; italicized references indicate illustrations or photos.

AARP. *See* American Association of
    Retired Persons
Abdulmutallab, Umar Farouk, 498
abolition, 74, *86*, 180
abortion, 6, 14–15, 31
    back-alley, 140
    *Dobbs v. Jackson Women's Health
        Organization*, 126*t*, 141–42,
        148, 200, 527, 549, 563
    Planned Parenthood v. Casey, 141
    pro-choice stance toward, 140–42
    pro-life stance toward, 140–42, 255
    public opinion on, 225, 225*f*
    Rally for Life marches against, 255
    Roe v. Wade, 126, 126*t*, 140–42, 200,
        527, 548, 561
    in states, 141
Abrams, Stacey, *307*
Abu Ghraib, Iraq, 297, *298*, 537
ACA. *See* Affordable Care Act
accommodation, 144–45
activist government, 268*f*
actorvist, 260*t*
ADA. *See* Americans with Disabilities Act
Adams, James Truslow, 45
Adams, John, 53, 352, 456, 474*t*, 628*t*
Adams, John Quincy, 474*t*, 628*t*
Advanced Research Projects Agency
    (ARPA-E), 497
advance team, 336*t*
advertising, 280, 286, 327
advice and consent, 415
advocacy explosion, 388
Advocates for Wild Equines (AWE),
    389, *389*
AFDC. *See* Aid to Families with
    Dependent Children
affirmative action, 191–93
Affordable Care Act (ACA), 39, 120,
    123, 273
    Supreme Court on, 562, 587–88
Afghanistan, 10–11, 231, 513
African Americans. *See also* Civil Rights
    Movement; National Association
    for the Advancement of Colored
    People
    for Biden, Joe, 321
    in cabinet, 410
    as CEOs, 177
    challenges facing, 174
    in Civil War, *183*
    Congressional Black Caucus, 416–17
    in court, 557–59
    death penalty and, 164

denied rights, 185
in digital divide, 301
as elected officials, 189, 190*t*
empowerment, resistance to, 182–84
enslaved population, 1790, 85*t*
Great Migration of, 185
Jim Crow and, 183
life expectancy, 217, 217*t*
lynching of, 184, *184*
mass incarceration of, 218, 218*f*
for Obama, B., *348*
percent in U.S. population, *20*
police using deadly force against, 179,
    179*f*, 194
poverty rate of, 217*t*
as protected legal category, 203
race and identity of, 228*f*
"replacement theory" and, 167
in Republican Party, fifth party sys-
    tem era, 356
at R. R. Moton High School, 63
voter suppression, 183, 213–14, 256
voter turnout, 257–58
white nationalist fears of, 128
age
    in political participation, 250*f*,
        256–57, 257*f*
    social media choice and, 266*f*
agenda setting, 571–74, 573*f*, 573*t*
aging populations, 19, *19*
agonistic spirit, 373
agriculture, *498*, 506*t*
    American Farm Bureau Federation,
        379
    farm subsidies, 393
    UFW, 202
AIDS, 213
AIM (American Indian Movement), 211
Alabama
    Birmingham, 188
    Montgomery, 187
    Powell v. Alabama, 138*t*, 162
Alaska, *153*, 299
Alexander, Lamar, 427
Alien and Sedition Acts, 148
alienation, 261–63
Alito, Samuel, 161, 363, *547*, 549, 552*t*, 554
Alphabet, *400*
AMA. *See* American Medical
    Association
Amazon, 280, 398*t*, *400*
Amendments, to U.S. Constitution, 64,
    91, 97–101, 99*t*, *100*. *See also spe-*
    cific amendment

America First, 636–37
American Association of Retired Persons
    (AARP), 379, 381–82, 398*t*
American Board of Customs, 69
American Chemistry Council, 398*t*
American colonies, 65–71
American Composites Manufacturers
    Association, 389–90
American Dream, 45–48, 46*f*, 72*t*,
    202, 622
American exceptionalism, 27,
    620–21, *621*
American Farm Bureau Federation, 379
American Hospital Association, 398*t*
American ideas
    American Dream, 45–48, 46*f*
    in Constitution, 64, 87
    in Declaration of Independence,
        26–27, 71–73, 72*t*
    democracy as, 8–9
    diversity as, 54–57, 72*t*
    equality, 48–51, *50*
    foreign policy spreading, 620–22
    individualism, 40–44, *42*, *43*, *44*
    "the land of the free," 28–29
    liberty, 14, 28–30, 72*t*
    limited government, 34–39
    negative liberty, 29–30, 36, 42, 50–51
    by the numbers, *26*
    positive liberty, 29–30, 50
    public policy and, 570
    religion, 51–54, 52*f*, *53*, 72*t*
    self-rule, 31–34
American Indian Movement (AIM), 211
American Medical Association (AMA),
    273, *274*, 398*t*
American nationalists, 363
American Opportunity Tax Credit, 584
American Petroleum Institute (API), 386
Americans for Prosperity, *58*
Americans with Disabilities Act (1990)
    (ADA), 212–13
The American Voter (Campbell,
    Converse, Miller, W., Stokes),
    239–40
American wealth, 6
amicus curiae, 395–96, 547
Anderson, John, 350*t*
Anti-Federalists, 92–95, *95*, 130
antigovernment sentiment, 17, 35
antitax sentiment, 16
anti-vaxxers, 273, *274*
API (American Petroleum
    Institute), 386

Appalachian Mountains, 68
appellate courts, 533–34, 536–37, 565
Apple, *400*
appointments, presidential, 465, 479
Appropriations Committees, 428–29,
    429t, 595–97, 595t
approval rating, of presidents,
    242–43, 472–73, 472f
Arends, Leslie, 426–27
Argentina, *66, 90, 129*
Arizona, 138t, 162
Arkansas, 187
Arkansas National Guard, 187
Arlington National Cemetery, *636*
Army Acquisition Corps, 491
ARPA-E (Advanced Research Projects
    Agency), 497
Arsenio Hall Show, 282
Arthur, Chester, *467, 474t*
Arthur, John, 563
Article 1, U.S. Constitution, 88–89, 114
Article 2, U.S. Constitution, 89–90
Article 3, U.S. Constitution, 90–91
Article 4, U.S. Constitution, 91
Article 5, U.S. Constitution, 91
Article 6, U.S. Constitution, 91, 115
Article 7, U.S. Constitution, 91
Articles of Confederation, 73–77, 80,
    83, 96f
Ashurst, Henry F., 397
Asian Americans
    attacks against, 128, *128*, 177
    challenges facing, 177
    in Congress, 417
    countries of origins, 207, 207f
    COVID-19 and, 208
    discrimination and, 208
    diversity of, 208
    Japanese Americans, 560–61
    life expectancy, 217t
    "model minorities" stereotype, 208
    police using deadly force against, 179f
    political and cultural influence of,
        208, 208–9
    poverty rate, 217t
    Trump, D.'s, racism towards, 208
    in U.S. population, *20*
assembly, rights of, 253
astroturf, 260t
astroturf lobbying, 392
Attucks, Crispus, 69
Australia, *90, 129, 614*
    citizen satisfaction in, *35*
    diversity acceptance in, *55*
    social mobility in, *47*
    voter turnout, *262*
Austria, *66, 262*
Avatar, 599
Avengers: Endgame, 599
AWE (Advocates for Wild Equines),
    389, *389*

Baby Boomers, 19, 268f, 269f
The Bad Guys, 296
Bakeshop Act, 559

Bakke, Allan, 193
balanced budget, *101*
balancing test, 145–46, *146*
bandwagon effect, 237
banks, 441f
Barbary Wars, 623, *623*
BARDA (Biomedical Advanced
    Research and Development
    Authority), 491
Barrett, Amy Coney, 141, 363, 395, *396*,
    532, *547*, 550, *551*, 552t, 554
Barron, John, 137
Barron v. Baltimore, 137
base voters, 360
"bathroom bills," 214
batting average, of successful bills,
    462, 463t
Battle of Monmouth, *74*
Battle of Yorktown, 28
Bedford, Gunning, 81
Beeman, William, 86
Belgium, *262, 614*
    citizen satisfaction in, *35*
    diversity acceptance in, *55*
Bell, John, 350t
Belton v. Gebhart Cases, 186t
benchmark polls, 238t
Berlin Wall, 635, *635*
Berry, Mary Frances, 30
best practices, 113
Bezos, Jeff, 280
bicameralism, 80
Biden, Ashley, 154–55
Biden, Jill, *485*, 486
Biden, Joe, 9, 45, *282*, 305, 317t, 358,
    369t, *448*
    African American, Latino support
        for, 321
    agenda of, 457, 461–62
    approval ratings of, 472f, 473
    Build Back Better Plan and, 410, 569
    cabinet of, 507–8, *508*, 510t
    on cable television and
        polarization, 282
    campaign promises of, 38
    clean energy policy and, 122
    climate change and, 122, 224–25
    digital central bank and, 89–90
    on domestic terrorism, 167
    Dreamers policy of, 205
    economy under, 466–67
    Electoral College totals of (2020), 83f
    EOP of, 482
    executive orders of, 450, *467*
    foreign policy of, 321, 460, 461, 628,
        628t, 637
    on gas tax, 575–76
    on immigration, 106
    Inauguration Day of, *452*
    Inflation Reduction Act and, 410
    infrastructure and, 410, 616
    judicial nominees of, 415, 536, 536f
    on lobbyists, 401, 402
    MBS and, *619*
    media profile of, 299
    midterms, 329t

misleading statements by, 276
multistate lawsuits filed under, 121f
partisanship and, 346
passing bills, 463t
presidential appointments of, 465,
    480–81
primaries of (2020), 317–19
Putin with, *461*
on racial equity, 602
religion and, 52
Republican disapproval of, 450
Russia's invasion of Ukraine and,
    608, 609, 619
Schedule F and, 516
signing statements, *464*
student loans and, 584
on Supreme Court rulings, 527
trade policy and, 618
travel of, 455, *455*
Trump, D., fighting election certifica-
    tion of, 3, 409–10
unfilled posts, 507
on Uvalde massacre, 277–78
vetoes, 439, 464, 464f
voter turnout of, 257
White House of, 483
big data, 241
big government, 13–14, 16, 268f,
    273, 357
big tent approach, 367
bilingual education programs, 205
Bill of Rights, 91, 115–16, 137, 138t.
        See also civil liberties; *specific
        amendments*
    ERA, 198–99
    Hancock's insistence on, 95
    on lobbying, 387
    Madison on, 97
    penumbras, emanations of, 139–42
    on rights of the accused, 159
    summary of, 97–98, 98t
    Supreme Court, incorporating, 159
bills
    becoming law, 440f
    committee action on, 433–35
    committee markup sessions, 434–35
    in conference committee, 438–39
    drafting, 432–33
    floor action on, *435*, 435–38, *436*, 437f
    introducing, 431f
    language of, 433
    omnibus spending, 596
    presidential batting average with,
        462, 463t
    roll-call, voice votes on, 438
    signing statements, *464*, 464–65
    submitting, 433
    titles of, 432t
    veto of, 439
Bingham, George Caleb, *78*
bin Salman, Mohammed (MBS), *619*
Biomedical Advanced Research
    and Development Authority
    (BARDA), 491
Biotechnology Innovation Organization,
    398t

bipartisanship, *371*, 410–11
bird-dogging, 390*t*
Birmingham, Alabama, 188
birtherism, 316
The Birth of a Nation, 184
birthright citizenship, 56
Black, Hugo, 143, 185, 195
Black Lives Matter, 6, 56, 179, 259, 284, 564
Blackmun, Harry, 561
Black power, 190
the Blob, 629
block grants, 120
Blue Cross/Blue Shield, 398*t*
Boebert, Lauren, 71
Boeing, 398*t*
Bok, Derek, 402
Bolling v. Sharpe, 186*t*
boomerang effect, 238
Bork, Robert, 551, *551*, 552*t*
Borking, 551, *551*
Boston, *193*
Boston Globe, 457
Boston Massacre, 56, 69–70, *70*
Boston Tea Party, 70
bottom-up delivery, 579–81
Bowdoin, James, 75–76
Bowman, Jamaal, 337, *365*
Bradley, Tom, 236
Brady, Mathew, 297
Brandeis, Louis D., 109–10, 160, 559, *560*
Brandenburg, Clarence, 148–49
Brandenburg v. Ohio, 148–49
Brat, David, 337
Brazil, *41*, *66*, *90*, 129, *129*, 616*f*
Breckinridge, John, 350*t*
Brennan, William J., Jr., 145, 150
Breyer, Stephen, *547*, 552*t*, 554
Briggs v. Elliott, 186*t*
Brockovich, Eric, 533
Brookings Institution, 389
Brooks, Preston, 441
Brown, Gordon, 460–61
Brown, Michael, 179, 194, 509
Brown v. Board of Education, 63, 186–87, 186*t*, 198, 219, 529, 545, 561
brushfire polls, 238*t*
BTS, *208*
Buchanan, James, 474*t*
Buddhists, 52*f*, 418
Budget and Accounting Act (1921), 593
budget resolution, 594–95
Buffalo, 167, *167*
Build Back Better Plan, 410, 569
bully pulpit, *468*, 468–69, 471, 604
bundling, 314
bureaucracy
    autonomy of, 517–18
    birth of, 494–95
    cabinet departments, 505–10, 510*t*
    civil servants in, 465, 504
    Congress and, 516–17
    control of federal, 515–19
    "deep state" and, 517–19
    in democracy, 499, 518–19

demographics of, 492, 492*f*
diversity of, 492, 492*f*
executive, 506*t*
executive agencies, 510–11
growth of, 494–99
in healthcare, *503*
hierarchy in, 496
implementing policies, 502–4
independent regulatory commissions, 511–13, 512*f*
inertia and, 520
interest groups and, 517
in iron triangle, 394*f*
language of, 505*t*
model, 495–97
by the numbers, 493
organization of, 504–14
overhead democracy and, 515
pathologies of, *497*, 497–99
president in, 456–57, 465, 515–16, 523
principal-agent theory on, 516–17
privatization of, 522
public mistrust of, 520–21
public opinion on, 491–92
race, ethnicity in, 495
reform, 520–22
rotating, 507–10, 509*f*
in rulemaking, 500–502, 500*f*
Schedule F and, 515–16
SOPs, 497
street-level, 502
Supreme Court on, 518
Trump, D., on, 522
Weber on, 495
whistleblowers in, 517
bureaucratic theory, 7, 7*t*
Bureau of Alcohol, Tobacco, Firearms and Explosives, 503–4
Bureau of Indian Affairs, 210–11
Burger, Warren, 562
Burke, Edmund, 68
Burke, Tarana, 200, *200*
Burr, Aaron, 353
Bush, George H. W., 317*t*, 635–36
    approval rating of, 472–73
    cabinet of, 510*t*
    economy and, 590
    executive orders of, *467*
    foreign policy experience, 628*t*
    judicial nominees of, 536*f*
    midterms, 329*t*
    multistate lawsuits filed under, 121*f*
    passing bills, 463*t*
    rating, 475*t*
    vetoes/overrides, 464*f*
Bush, George W., 53, 124, 231, 317*t*, 369*t*, 628*t*
    approval rating of, 472–73, 472*f*, *473*
    authorizing torture, 454
    cabinet of, 510*t*
    election of, 348
    EOP of, 482
    executive orders of, *467*
    Hurricane Katrina response, 509
    inherent powers exercised by, 454
    judicial nominees of, 536*f*

    midterms, 329*t*
    military tribunal, 537
    misleading statements by, 289
    multistate lawsuits filed under, 121*f*
    passing bills, 463*t*
    preemptive war strategy of, 636
    progressive federalism of, 120
    rating, 474*t*
    reelection of, 321
    security team of, 507
    vetoes/overrides, 463–64, 464*f*
Bush, Sophia, 434
Bush v. Gore, 534, 562
business, public approval of, 441*f*
business interest groups, 384, 384*t*
Business Roundtable, 398*t*
Buttigieg, Pete, 216, 317, 318
Butts, Cassandra, 413–14

cabinet, 480–81, 505–10, *508*, 509*f*, 510*t*
cable stations, 282
Caldart, Alemitu, 247
Caldart, Selame, 247
California
    Citizens' Redistricting Commission, 332
    Mexican Americans in, 206
    Robinson v. California, 138*t*
California Alien Land Law (1913), 208
call lists, 335
Calvinists, 43
Campaign for Innocent Victims in Conflict (CIVIC), 11
campaigns. *See also* congressional campaigns; presidential elections
    advertising in, 327
    financing, 312–15, *315*
    issue, 392
    lingo, 336*t*
    major donors to, 313–15, 338
    in midterms, 306–7
    negative, 337
    by the numbers, 308
    organizations, 322
    PACs in, 313–14, *315*
    for presidency, 316–24, *318*, *321*
    social media use in, 299
Campbell, Angus, 239–40
Canada, 186*t*, 262
    aging populations, *19*
    citizen satisfaction in, *35*
    Constitution of, *66*
    diversity acceptance in, *55*
    economy of, 616*f*
    foreign aid spending, *614*
    government of, *90*, 129, *129*
    social mobility in, *47*
    taxes, 15*f*
    women in legislature, *197*
"cancel culture," 153, 194
candidate-centered elections, 334–35
candidates
    for congressional office, 325–27, *326*, 326*t*, *327*
    political parties selecting, 347
Cantor, Eric, 337

Cantwell v. Connecticut, 138t
capitalism, 599, 601
Capitol, U.S., *10*
Capitol Hill, 423–25
Cardi B, 260t
Carlson, Tucker, 9, 291
cars, self-driving, *110*
Carson v. Mankin, 528, 529
Carter, Jimmy, 317t, 628t
    cabinet of, 510t
    executive orders of, *467*
    judicial nominees of, 536f
    lacking ideas, 469
    midterms, 329t
    rating, 474t
    Reagan, R., beating, 360
    vetoes/overrides, 463, 464f
    vice presidency under, 480
    weak presidency of, 457
case selection, 547–49
Catholics, 43, 56, 144, 146, 203, 418
Catholic Social Services (CSS), 146
Catt, Carrie Chapman, 195
caucus, 317, 369, 416–17
Cawthorn, Madison, 298–99
CBS, 281
CEA. *See* Council of Economic Advisers
Ceasefire, 582
celebrity endorsements, *251*
celebrity witnesses, 434, *434*
census, 68
Census Bureau, 492
central clearance, 482
central control, 266–67
central government, 34–35, 75, 77
Central High School, Little Rock, 187, *187*
Central Intelligence Agency (CIA), 511, 630
central service agencies, 513
centrists, 365
CEO. *See* chief executive officer
Chamber of Commerce, U.S., 398t
Chance the Rapper, *260*, 260t
Charlottesville, Virginia, 32, 194
Chavez, Pablo, 389–90
checks and balances
    in Constitution, 8–9, 37–38, 83–85
    Constitutional Convention creating, 83–85, 84f
    defining, 8
Chevron doctrine, 518
Chevron v. Resources Defense Council, 518
Chicago, Burlington, and Quincy Railroad Co. v. Chicago, 138t
Chicanismo, 202
chief executive officer (CEO), 49, 177, 200t
Chief of Staff, 483–84
child pornography, 156
Chile, 15f, *262*
China, 129, *129*
    economy of, 616, 616f
    foreign aid spending, *614*

on government taking care of poor, *41*
    women in legislature, *197*
Chinatowns, 208
Chinese Americans, 207–8
Chinese dream, *47*
Chinese Exclusion Act (1882), 56, 208
Christians
    Catholics, 43, 56, 144, 146, 203, 418
    demographics, 52f
    Evangelical, 145, 156, *348*, 359f
CIA. *See* Central Intelligence Agency
circuit courts, 536–37, 537f
citizen interest groups, 384t, 385–86, *386*
citizenship, birthright, 56
Citizens' Redistricting Commission, 332
Citizens United v. The Federal Elections Commission, 312, 314, 562
CIVIC (Campaign for Innocent Victims in Conflict), 11
civic voluntarism, 128, 255
Civil Aeronautics Board, 512–13, 512f
civil disobedience, 252–55
civil law, 544
civil liberties. *See also* freedom of speech; rights of the accused
    Bill of Rights and, 137
    civil rights and, 134–36
    Constitution and, 139–40
    COVID-19 and, 168
    defining, 134
    dilemma of, 168–69
    Fourteenth Amendment and, 135–37, 138t
    freedom of press, 153–57
    freedom of religion, 29, 53, 143–46
    as negative, 151
    by the numbers, 135
    purpose of, 136
    right to bear arms, 157–59, *158*
    right to privacy, 139–42
    rise of, 134–37
    terrorism and, 166–67, *167*
    around the world, 151
civil rights. *See also* Latinos; women's rights
    civil liberties and, 134–36
    de facto denial of, 185
    defining, 173–74
    de jure denial of, 185
    free rider problem and, 188
    judicial branch in, 176–78
    LGBT, *172*, 173, 213–15
    by the numbers, 175
    by the people, 218–19
    presidency in, 176
    race and, 179–84
    seven steps to winning, 174–76
    of women, serving in combat, *178*
Civil Rights Act (1866), 183
Civil Rights Act (1875), 183
Civil Rights Act (1964), 126, 135, 189, 189f, *198*, 198–99, 214, 218–19, 343

civil rights caucus, 364
Civil Rights Movement
    affirmative action and, 191–93
    Black power in, 190
    Brown v. Board of Education, 63, 186–87, 186t, 198, 219, 529, 545, 561
    Civil Rights Act (1866), 183
    Civil Rights Act (1875), 183
    Civil Rights Act (1964), 176, 189, 189f, 198–99, 218–19
    courage of, *188*
    Dred Scott v. Sanford, 180–81, 529, 541, 557–58, *558*
    Freedom Riders, 188, *188*, 254
    March on Washington (1963), 189
    NAACP in, 63, 185, 186–87
    post civil rights era, 191–94
    religion in, 53
    school busing in, 192
    Voting Rights Act (1965), 189, 213–14
civil servants, 465, 504
civil society, 12
Civil War, 87, 118, 137, 181–82, *183*, 354, 388, 454, 495
class action, 199
class hierarchy. *See also* economic inequality
    elite theory, 382–83
    in political campaigns, 312–15, 312f
    political elites, 230–31
classical republicanism, 92
Claus, Santa, *299*
Clean Air Act, 343
clean energy policy, 122, 122f
Clean Water Act (1972), 255
clear and present danger, 148, 560
clerks, Supreme Court, 550
Cleveland, Grover, *467*, 474t
clickbait, 283
clicktivism, 248
clientelism, 498
climate change, *9*
    federalism and, 121–23, 122f
    public opinion on, 223–25, 229, *229*, 268, 268f
    public policy and, 602–3
climate kids, 602–3
Clinton, Bill, 45, 213, 282, 317t, 548, 628t
    approval rating, 472f
    on big government, 357
    cabinet of, 510t
    economy and, 589–90
    executive orders of, *467*
    FEMA under, 508–9
    healthcare plan of, 273, 343
    judicial nominees of, 536f
    midterms, 329t
    multistate lawsuits filed under, 121f
    on opinion polls, 243
    passing bills, 463t
    presidential campaign, 320–21, 336
    rating, 474t
    with Rawlings, *468*
    vetoes/overrides, 463–64, 464f
    White House of, 483

Clinton, Hillary, 233, 267, 317*t*, *468*, 562
  Democratic convention and electoral
    bounce of, 320
  Electoral College loss of, 322
  as first spouse, 485
  in Senate, 427
Clinton v. Jones, 548
closed primary, 317–18
cloture vote, 437–38, 437*f*
Clyburn, James, 426
CNN, 282
Cold War, 53, 458, 634–35, 634*f*
collective decisions, 8, 241, 244
collegiality, 555–56
Collins, Susan, 392–93
colonies, American, 65–71
Colorado, 53, 138*t*
combat, women in, *178*
Comcast, 398*t*
Commander in Chief, 458–59
commerce clause, 114–15
Commerce Department, 506*t*
committee hearing, 433–34, *434*
committee markup session, 434–35
Commodity Futures Trading
    Commission, 512*f*
common law, 543
communalism, 47, 72*t*. *See also*
    solidarity
community. *See also* lesbian, gay, bisexu-
    al, and transgender communities
  individualism versus, 40–42
  in political participation, 258–59
compact, 65
compelling interest, 177–78
competent counsel, 163
competitive contracting, 522
complacency, 264
Compromise of 1850, 180
Comstock, Anthony, *495*
concealed carry, *158*
concurrent opinion, 549
concurrent powers, 116, 116*f*
Condé Nast, 290
Condorcet, Nicolas de, 240–41
Confederate flag, 150
confederation, 73, 108
conference committee, 438–39
conference sessions, 549–50
Congress, U.S., 38
  acts of, nullified by Supreme
    Court, 542*f*
  in amendments, to Constitution, 91
  Appropriations Committees,
    428–29, 429*t*, 595–97, 595*t*
  approval rating, 4
  average salaries, of members, 424*t*
  bills introduced to, 431*f*
  bureaucracy and, 516–17
  Capitol Hill, 423–25
  caucus, 416–17
  as city on a hill, 423–25
  in civil rights, 176
  committees, 427–30, 429*t*
  conference committee, 438–39
  Constitution on, 88–89, 412–16, 412*t*

COVID-19 relief package from, 435
  diversity of, 416–20, 417*f*
  education in, 418
  filibuster, *414*, 414–15, 437–38, 437*f*
  floor of, 413
  in foreign policy, 627
  freshman class, 337, *337*
  gender in, 417–18
  governing challenges, 446
  gridlock, 443–44
  interns, 423–24
  in iron triangle, 394*f*
  leaders, 425–27
  lobbyists and, 399–401, 444–45
  by the numbers, 411
  118th, 413
  overriding vetoes, 462–64, 464*f*
  partisan polarization of, 441–44, *442*
  policymaking by, 431–39, 431*f*, 432*t*,
    434, *435*, *436*, 437*f*, 440*f*,
    573–74, *600*
  powers of, 412*t*
  professions in, 418
  public opinion of, 441, 441*f*
  race in, 416–17, 417*f*
  reforming, 444–45
  relatives serving in, 326–27
  religion in, 418
  representation by, 416–20
  in separation of powers, 83–85, 84*f*
  staff, 423–25, *424*
  swearing in, *408*
  in War Powers Act (1973), 459, 460
  Washington, G., on, 413
Congressional Black Caucus, 416–17
Congressional Budget and
    Impoundment Control Act
    (1974), 594
congressional budget resolution, 594–95
congressional campaigns
  candidate-centered, 334–35
  home district visits in, 421–22
  message, 337
  money in, 335
  negative, 337
  organization, 335
  as permanent, 420–21
  strategy, 335–37
congressional caucus, 416–17
congressional elections
  candidates, 325–27, *326*, 326*t*, *327*
  incumbency in, 327–28, 328*f*
  midterms, 328, 329*t*
  minority groups in, 327
  war in, 328–29
  women in, 327, *327*
Congressional Research Service,
    432, 545
Connecticut, 34, 85*t*, 94*t*, 123, 138*t*, 192
Connecticut Compromise, 81–82
consenting adults, sex between, 142
conservatives, 17, 51
  definition of, 36
  fiscal, 363
  liberals on issues compared to, 37*f*, 38*t*
  on media bias, 285

  in pro-life movement, 140–42
  on radio, 281
  in Republican Party, 363
  on Supreme Court, 554
  on television, 282
Constitution, U.S. *See also* Articles of
    Confederation; Bill of Rights
  Amendments to, 64, 91, 97–101,
    99*t*, *100*
  on basic functions of government, 14
  on census, 68
  checks and balances in, 8–9, 37–38,
    83–85
  civil liberties and, 139–40
  colonial roots of, 65–71
  commerce clause, 114–15
  in comparative context, *66*
  on Congress, 88–89, 412–16, 412*t*
  defining, 63
  on federalism, 114–17
  Federalists, Anti-Federalists on,
    92–95
  final vote for, 94*t*
  full faith and credit clause, 116
  ideas in, *26*
  on immigration, 105
  institutionalizing American ideas,
    64, 87
  on institutions, 58
  as law, 91
  missing articles of, 92
  national authority in, 114–15, 116*f*
  necessary and proper clause, 115
  by the numbers, 64
  originalism and, 100, 102
  pragmatism and, 101, 102
  preamble to, 88
  on presidency, 89–90, 316, 458, 462
  ratification of, 91–96, 94*t*, *95*, 96*f*
  on relations between states, 91
  on self-rule, 31
  on shared power, 116–17
  on slavery, 86
  state authority in, 116–17, 116*f*
  supremacy clause in, 115, 542
  Supreme Court and, 90–91
  today, 101
Constitutional Convention, Philadelphia
    (1787), 5, 9, 88, 413, 450
  big versus small states, 79–82, 94
  Madison, J., at, *76*, 76–80, *81*
  national versus state government
    debate, 79
  on presidency, 83, 452
  public involvement, in government,
    78, 78–79
  secrecy around, 76–77
  separation of powers, 83–85, 84*f*
  slavery and, 85–87, 85*t*, *86*
  three-fifths compromise of, 85–86
  Washington at, 76, 83
"Constitutional Hardball," 437
Consumer Financial Protection Bureau,
    512*f*, 513
Consumer Product Safety Commission,
    512*f*

containment, 634–35
contested federalism, 117f, 119–20, 121f, 130
Continental Congress
    Annapolis Convention of, 76
    Articles of Confederation of, 74
    First, 70
    national meeting of, 76
    Northwest Ordinance, 75
    Second, 71
continuing resolution (CR), 596
contraception, 139–42
conventions, of political parties, 320, 320, 366
Converse, Philip, 239–40
Coolidge, Calvin, 467, 474t
Cooper, Bradley, 260t
cooperative federalism, 117f, 118, 118–19, 119t, 130
Cooper v. Harris, 126t
coordination, among levels of government, 113
corruption, 401–2, 632
Costa Rica, 36, 66
cost-benefit analysis, 575–77, 576t
cost-effectiveness, 575
Cotton, Tom, 413–14
Council of Economic Advisers (CEA), 466, 481t, 482–83
Council on Environmental Quality, 481t
counsel, right to, 162–63, 163
Court of Appeals, U.S., 536–37
the courts. See judicial branch; Supreme Court, U.S.
covenant, 65
COVID-19, 228, 255, 490
    Asian Americans and, 208
    civil liberties and, 168
    Congressional relief package for, 435
    economic crash from, 47, 466
    Federal Reserve actions and, 591–92
    grand strategy for, 637
    Latinos and, 202
    leadership experience and response to, 465
    lockdown protests, 33
    mask mandates and, 123, 168, 572, 573f
    national policies and, 115, 123
    partisanship and, 572
    state government responses to, 123
    supply chain issues related to, 277
    Trump, D., campaigning and, 299
    unemployment and, 586, 586–87
    vaccine development for, 491
    vaccine disinformation on, 273, 274
CR. See continuing resolution
Craig v. Boren, 199
Crime Junkie, 281
criminal justice system, 441f, 564–65
criminal law, 544
critical race theory, 173, 194
cross burning, 136, 149–50
crowdfunding, 255, 265
cruel and unusual punishment, 151, 164–65

Cruz, Ted, 292, 400, 413, 491
cryptocurrencies, 89–90
CSS (Catholic Social Services), 146
CTIA, 398t
Cuba, 197
culture, 57–59, 184
Cummings, Elijah, 424
Cure Violence, 582, 582
cycle of nonparticipation, 265
Czech Republic, 262

Dahl, Robert, 102
The Daily, 281
Davis v. School Board of Prince Edward County, 63, 186t
Dawes Act (1887), 210
deadly force, used by police, 179, 179f, 194
death penalty, 135, 151, 163–66, 164f, 548
Debs, Eugene, 350t
Declaration of Independence, 5, 96f
    enduring ideas in, 71–73, 72t
    Hancock signing, 27
    ideas of, 26–27, 87
    principles and grievances stated in, 71–73
    on rights, 26–27
    slavery and, 74
"deep state," 12, 517–19
de facto discrimination, 185
defendant, 544
Defense of Marriage Act (1996), 91
deficit, budget, 592
de Jonge v. Oregon, 138t
de jure discrimination, 185, 191
Delaware, 85t, 86, 94t, 186t
Delay, Tom, 428
delegated powers, 114, 116f, 453
delegate representation, 67–68
delegates, 76–77, 418–20
democracy
    as American idea, 8–9
    bureaucracy in, 499, 518–19
    defining, 5
    direct, 31–33, 32f
    limited government and, 38–39
    media in, 276–78
    opinion polls in, 237
    overhead, 515
    popular vote and, 4
    public opinion in, 239–43, 244
    satisfaction with, comparing nations, 35
    self-rule, 31–32
    social, 40–41
    social media challenging, 266–67
    social media improving, 265–66
    Supreme Court and, 4
    three sectors of society in, 12–13
    Tocqueville on, 35, 45
    wealth and, 312–15
Democracy in America (Tocqueville), 45, 48, 255
Democratic National Convention, 54, 320

Democratic Party, 34, 352t, 367. See also elections; party system; political parties
    affiliations, by income level, 230f
    centrists in, 365
    civil rights and, 188
    civil rights caucus in, 364
    on climate change, 225, 229, 229
    demographics of, 323–24
    European political parties compared to, 333
    factions of, 364–65
    on federalism, 124
    on marijuana use, 224f
    organized labor in, 364–65
    party identification of, 359–60, 359f
    progressives in, 364
    public opinion of, 362
    Republican Party on issues compared to, 37f, 38t
    on spending, 590
    symbols of, 367
    on trust in media, 286f
    views, of Republicans, 343–44, 441–44
    on voter laws, 264
    Watergate burglary of, 288
democratic peace, theory of, 621
democratic republic, 33
demographic groups, 233
demographics. See also diversity
    of Christians, 52f
    of civilian bureaucracy, 492, 492f
    of party identification, 359f
    of presidential cabinet department heads, 510t
    in presidential elections, 321, 323–24
    U.S., changing, 20
demonstrations, 31
Denmark, 15f, 36, 47, 66, 262, 614
Department of Agriculture, U.S., 393, 506t
Department of Defense, U.S., 14f, 506t, 629. See also military, U.S.
Department of Education, U.S., 506t
Department of Energy, U.S., 496, 496f, 499, 506t
Department of Health, Education, and Welfare, U.S., 506t
Department of Health and Human Services, U.S. (HHS), 506t
Department of Homeland Security, U.S., 9, 128, 465, 506t, 636
Department of Housing and Urban Development, 506t
Department of Justice, 506t, 548
Department of the Interior, U.S., 506t
Department of the Treasury, U.S., 505, 506t, 593–94
Department of Transportation, 506t
Department of Veterans Affairs, U.S., 506t
Depp, Johnny, 156
deregulation, 512–13
Dern, Laura, 533
DeSantis, Ron, 9, 173, 230, 332

descriptive representation, 418, 419
deterrence, 636
Detroit, *259*
devolution, 123
DiCaprio, Leonardo, 260*t*
Dickinson, John, 86
diffusion, 109–10
Diggs, Daveed, *96*
digital central bank, 89–90
Dillon's rule, 108
din, 267
diplomat, president as, 459–61, *461*
direct action, 252–55
direct democracy, 31–33, 32*f*
Dirksen, Everett, 119
disabled Americans
    Americans with Disabilities Act (1990), 212–13
    Medicaid and, 587–88
    Rehabilitation Act (1973), 212
    Section 504, 212
discretionary programs, 596
discrimination, 152, 174, 179
    Asian Americans and, 208
    challenging, 202–3
    Chinese Exclusion Act, 208
    de jure, 191
    against disabled people, 212–13
    employment, 214
    gender, 199
    against Latinos, 202–3
    by law enforcement, 218
    against LGBT communities, 214
    public opinion on, 215, *215*
    segregation, 185–90, *186*, 202
    severe, 192
disproportionate impact, 192
dissent, 549
district courts, 536
diversity
    as American idea, 54–57, 72*t*
    of Asian Americans, 208
    of bureaucracy, 492, 492*f*
    cabinet and, 410, 510*t*
    of Congress, 416–20, 417*f*
    in Declaration of Independence, 72*t*
    fear and, 56
    public opinion on, *55*
    in Supreme Court, 538–40, 539*t*
    urban design and, 25
divided government, 370–71
Dobbins, Tom, 389–90
Dobbs v. Jackson Women's Health Organization, 126*t*, 141–42, 148, 200, 527, 549, 563
Doctor Strange in the Multiverse of Madness, 296
dog whistling, 260*t*
Dole, Bob, 317*t*
domestic dependent nations, 210
domestic issues, in presidential campaigns, 321
Domestic Policy Council, 481*t*
domestic terrorism, 166–67, *167*
donkey symbol, *367*

"Don't Say Gay" legislation ("Parental Rights in Education Bill"), *172, 173*
double jeopardy, 162
Douglas, William O., 139–40
Downs, Anthony, 261
Draghi, Mario, *624*
Dreamers, 205
Dred Scott v. Sanford, 180–81, 529, 541, 557–58, *558*
Drive My Car, 209
drop, 390*t*
drug users, 218
dual federalism, 117–18, 117*f*, *118*, 119*t*, 130
Du Bois, W. E. B., 182
due process, 214
Dukakis, Michael, 317*t*
Duverger, Maurice, 348

earmarks, 428–29
Earth Day, 31, *254, 255*
East India Tea Company, 70
e-cigarettes, flavored, 381
Eckford, Elizabeth, *187*
economic equality, 49
economic inequality, 45–51, 46*f, 47, 50,* 257, 569–70
The Economist, 389
education
    affirmative action in, 191–93
    bilingual education programs, 205
    Brown v. Board of Education, 63, 186–87, 186*t*, 198, 219, 529, 545, 561
    of Congress members, 418
    critical race theory in, 173, 194
    Davis v. School Board of Prince Edward County, 63, 186*t*
    Department of Education, 506*t*
    Everson v. Board of Education, 138*t*
    Juneau-Douglas High School, *153*
    NEA, 384–85
    in political participation, 257
    in public opinion, 227–28
    on race, 111, *111*
    R. R. Moton High School, Virginia, 63
    youth, *260*
Edwards, George, 471
EEOC. *See* Equal Employment Opportunity Commission
Ehrlichman, John, 480
Eighteenth Amendment, 118
Eighth Amendment, 163–66
Eisenhower, Dwight, 6, 187, 461, 479–80
    executive orders of, *467*
    rating, 474*t*
    Truman on, 515
elected officials, 33, 309–11, 310*t*
elections. *See also* campaigns; congressional elections; presidential elections; voting
    barriers to voting, 310–12
    candidate-centered, 334–35
    certification of, *3*
    corporate influence in, *339*

Electoral College map, 2020, 83*f*
    expanding access to, 311*f*
    FEC on, 312, 314, 512*f*
    frequent and fixed, 308–9
    gerrymandering, 329–34, 330*f, 331, 331f, 332f*
    indirect, 78
    judicial, 534–35
    media coverage, 287–88, 298–99
    midterm, 306–7
    minority representation in, 332–34
    money in, 312–15, 312*f, 315,* 325–26
    nonpartisan, 347
    number of elected officials, 309–10, 310*t*
    by the numbers, 308
    PACs, super PACs in, 313–14, *315*
    popular vote and, 4
    reforming of, 338–40, *339*
    rules, 98
    third-parties in, 372–73
    time, place, manner clause and, 308
    timetables for, *309*
electoral activities, 251, 252*f*
electoral bounce, 320
Electoral College, 82–83, 83*f,* 322–23, 323*f,* 338, 453
electors, 82–83, 83*f*
elephant symbol, *367*
elitism, 7–8, 7*t,* 382
Emancipation Proclamation (1863), 181, 356
emergency decree powers, 454*t*
Employment Division v. Smith, 146
Engel, Eliot, 337
Engel v. Vitale, 144
English language, 205, *206*
entitlement programs, 588–89, 588*f*
enumerated powers, 114
environmental activism, 254–55
Environmental Protection Agency (EPA), 503, 506*t,* 528, 578
EOP. *See* Executive Office of the President
EPA. *See* Environmental Protection Agency
Equal Employment Opportunity Commission (EEOC), 198, 511, 512*f*
equality. *See also* racial equality
    as American idea, 48–51, *50*
    in Declaration of Independence, 72*t*
    defining, 48
    economic, 49
    political, 49, 174–76
    social, 48–49
equal opportunity, 50–51, 192
equal outcome, 50–51, 192
equal protection, 64, 205
equal protection of the laws, 182
Equal Rights Amendment (ERA), 198–99
Escobedo v. Illinois, 138*t*
Espionage Act (1917), 148, 560
establishment clause, 143–45, *144*
Estonia, *262*

Ethiopia, *129*
ethnicity, *20*, 495
European Union, 151, *333*
Evangelicals, 145, 156, *348, 359f*
Everson v. Board of Education, 138*t*
exclusionary rule, 161
executive agencies, 510–11, 630
executive agreements, 454, 627
executive authority, 82
executive branch. *See* presidency
executive bureaucracies, 506*t*
Executive Office of the President (EOP),
      481–83, 481*t*, 484,
      485, 506*t*
executive orders, 450, 454, 465–66, *467*
executive power, 89–90
executive privilege, 454
exit polls, 238*t*
expressed powers, 114, 453, 453*t*
expressive benefits, 386

Facebook, 149, 266, 266*f*, 273–74, 279,
      283, 292, *400*
FactCheck.org, 298
factions, 93
fairness, 597
fairness bias, 289
fairness doctrine, 291
fair trade, 617
faith in God, 72*t*
fake news, 284, 284*f*
family
      in political participation, 258
      in public opinion, 227
Family and Medical Leave Act
      (1993), 40
farming. *See* agriculture
farm lobbyists, 393–94
farm subsidies, 393
Faubus, Orville, 187
Fauci, Anthony, *490*, 492
Faulkner, Harris, 230, *231*
FBI. *See* Federal Bureau of Investigation
FCC. *See* Federal Communications
      Commission
FDA. *See* Food and Drug
      Administration
FEC. *See* Federal Election Commission
federal budget, 14*f*
      deficit, 592
      entitlement programs in, 588, 588*f*
      fiscal policy and, 590–91
      military in, 14, 458*f*
      OMB in, 433–34, 481*t*, 482, 500*f*,
            501, 593
      president proposing, 593–94
      process, 593*f*
Federal Bureau of Investigation (FBI),
      507, 630
Federal Communications Commission
      (FCC), 291, 512*f*
federal courts, 533–34, 536–37, 536*f*, 537*f*
Federal Election Commission (FEC),
      312, 314, 512*f*, 562
Federal Emergency Management
      Agency (FEMA), 508–9, *509*

Federal Energy Regulatory Commission,
      512*f*
federal government
      dual versus cooperative, 117*f*, 119*t*
      in immigration policy, 105–6
      interest groups and, 393–96, 394*f*,
            395*f*
      multistate lawsuits filed against, 121*f*
      Native Americans and, 210
      reducing, 123
      trust in, 108*f*
      unitary government compared to,
            129, *129*
Federal Housing Finance Agency, 512*f*
federalism, 79, 106
      big tent approach to, 367
      climate change and, 121–23, 122*f*
      connection, 125
      Constitution on, 114–17
      contested, 117*f*, 119–20, 121*f*, 130
      cooperative, 117*f*, *118*, 118–19, 119*t*, 130
      in the courts, 125–26, 126*t*
      Democrats, Republicans on, 124
      devolution in, 123
      dual, 117–18, *118*, 119*t*, 130
      eras of, 130
      forging, 107–8
      government authority in, 109–13
      healthcare and, 123
      individual rights protection, 109
      in interstate conflict, *115*
      issues in, 121–25, *124*
      judicial, 533–34
      lobbying in, 128
      local governments in, 123
      national government in, 117, *118*
      nationalism and, 112, 127–29
      national policy in, 112–13
      new, 120
      by the numbers, 107
      partisan, 120, 125
      political innovation in, 109–10
      progressive, 120
      as responsive, to citizen needs, 109
      state-level policy in, 109–10
      styles of, in U.S. history, 117*f*
      Supreme Court decisions on, 126*t*
      of Trump, D., 120
      unfunded mandates, 123
Federalist Papers (Madison, J.),
      32–33, 58, 93, 280, 382, 444
Federalists, 92–95, *95*, 130, 352–53, 352*t*
federal poverty line, 587
Federal Register, 501–4, 577, 578*f*
Federal Regulation of Lobbying Act
      (1946), 399
Federal Reserve, 511, 569, *591*, 591–92
Federal Trade Commission, 512*f*
FEMA. *See* Federal Emergency
      Management Agency
feminists, 155, 198
Fenno's paradox, 328
Ferguson, Missouri, 179
Ferguson, Phoebe, *559*
field/GOTV, 336*t*
Fierce Madres, 602

Fifteenth Amendment, 79, 182
Fifth Amendment, 137, 151, 161–62
fighting words, 151
filibuster, *414*, 414–15, 437–38, 437*f*
Fillmore, Millard, 350*t*, 474*t*
filtering, 360–61
filtration, 78
final rule, 501
financial powers, of Congress, 412*t*
Financial Services Forum, 379–80
Finland, 15*f*, *47*, 262, *614*
Fiorina, Morris, 230
First Amendment, 98, *100*. *See also* free-
      dom of speech
      establishment clause, 143–45
      on freedom of press, 153–57, 290
      freedom of religion in, 29, 53,
            143–46, *144*
      free exercise clause, 143, 145–46
      on lobbying, 387
      preferred position of, 147–48
      privacy and, 139
      right to assembly, 253
First Continental Congress, 70
first spouse, 484–86
fiscal conservatives, 363
fiscal policy, 583, 590–91
fiscal year, 593
527 groups, 314
flag-burning, 149–50, *150*
flavored e-cigarettes, 381
Fletcher, Benjamin, 34–35
floor, 413
floor action, *435*, 435–38, *436*, 437*f*
Florida, 53, 68*f*, 106, 123
      death penalty in, 135
      "Parental Rights in Education Bill,"
            172, 173
      Parkland, 159, 232, *267*, *574*, 602
      in 2000 presidential election, 348,
            534, 562
Floyd, George, *6*, 31, 194, *288*, 564, 572,
      581, 604
fly-in, 390*t*
focusing event, 572
FOIA (Freedom of Information Act), 521
folk religions, 52*f*
Food and Drug Administration (FDA),
      491, 579, *579*
"the football," 459, *459*
forbidden groups, contacts with, 166
Ford, Gerald, 317*t*, 329*t*, *467*
      attempted assassination against, 479
      cabinet of, 510*t*
      on impeachment, 90
      rating, 474*t*
      vetoes/overrides, 464*f*
foreign aid, 613–15, *614*
foreign policy, 583
      activists in, *631*
      America First, 636–37
      American ideals spread through,
            620–22
      of Biden, Joe, 321, 460, 461, 628,
            628*t*, 637
      Cold War, 634–35, 634*f*

Congress in, 627
corruption and, *632*
Department of Defense in, 629
economic weapons in, 619
energy in, 619
executive agencies in, 630
experience, of presidents, 628*t*
foreign aid in, 613–15
grand strategies, 633–37
importance of, 609–10
intelligence community in, 630
interest groups in, 630–31
liberalism, 612–13
military in, 610, *612*
National Security Council in, 630
by the numbers, 611
of Obama, B., 637
perspectives, 623–25, 626*t*
in presidential elections, 321
president in, 459–61, 627–29, 628*t*
for prosperity, 615–19
public opinion on, 631
realists, 610–12
for security, 610–15
soft power, 613, *613*
State Department in, 629
of Trump, D., 461
Fortune 500 companies, 177, 200*t*
Fourteenth Amendment, 63–64, 174, 186, 193
on citizenship, 56, 182
civil liberties and, 135–37, 138*t*
due process clause, 214
equal protection of the laws, 182
freedom of religion, 138*t*
incorporation, of Bill of Rights into, 138*t*
Supreme Court on, 558–59, 561, 563
Fourth Amendment, 160–61
Fox News, 278, 282
Foxx, Jamie, *532*
framing, 277–78, 574
framing effects, 234
France
aging populations, *19*
citizen satisfaction in, *35*
Constitution of, *66*
diversity acceptance in, *55*
economic equality in, 49
economy of, 616*f*
foreign aid spending, *614*
French and Indian War, *67*, 67–69, 68*f*
government of, *90*, 129, *129*
loans from, 75
religiosity in, 52
social mobility in, *47*
taxes, 15*f*
voter turnout, *262*
women in legislature, *197*
Frank, Thomas, 230
Franklin, Benjamin, 5, 45, *81*, 94, 205, 269
Frederick, Joseph, *153*
Freedmen's Bureau, 183
freedom, 11. *See also* liberty
defining, 29

idea of, changing, 30
positive versus negative liberty, 29
of press, 153–57, 290
of religion, 29, 53, 143–46, *144*
rights and, 30
from want, 29–30
Freedom of Information Act (1966) (FOIA), 521
freedom of speech, 29
on campus, 152–53
"cancel culture" and, 153, 194
in First Amendment, 133, 147–53, *153*
hate speech and, 133–34, 147–48
limits to, 149–53, 155–57
on social media, 149, 153, 154
students, 152–53
Supreme Court on, 133–34, 147–52
symbolic expression, 149–50
threats, intimidation and, 149–50
Freedom Riders, 188, *188*, 254
free exercise, 143, 145–46
free rider problem, civil rights and, 188
free riders, 385
"free speech zones," 153
free trade, 617, 618*f*
Frelinghuysen, Rodney, *326*
French and Indian War, 67–69, 68*f*
Friedman, Milton, 41–42
friends
in political participation, 258
in public opinion, 227
frontier life, 42–43
fugitive slaves, 86–87
Fukuyama, Francis, 456
Fuller, Ida May, *585*
full faith and credit clause, 116
Fulton v. City of Philadelphia, 146
Furman v. Georgia, 165

Gage, Thomas, 70
Gaines, Lloyd, 186*t*
Gallego, Ruben, 409
Gamble v. United States, 126*t*
gang violence, 582, *582*
Garfield, James, 316, 474*t*, 494, *494*
Garland, Merrick, 531–32, 550
Garner, Eric, 179
Garner, John Nance, 479
Garner, Tyron, *142*
Gast, John, *621*
gas tax, 575–76, 576*t*
Gawker, 290
GDP. *See* gross domestic product
Geertz, Clifford, 57
gender. *See also* women
of Congress members, 417–18
discrimination, 199
identity, 213–14, 268
intersectionality and, *174*
politics, 200
in public opinion, 228
gender-neutral pronouns, 268, 269*f*

Gender Policy Council, 481*t*
general election, 320
General Services Administration (GSA), 506*t*, 513
Gen X, 268*f*, 269*f*, 624
Gen Z, 20, 21, *267*, 268–69, 269*f*
geographic representation, 416
George III (king), *27*, 70, 72*t*, 73, 93
Georgia, 53, 85, 85*t*, 94*t*, *307*, 545
Germany, 36
aging populations, *19*
Berlin Wall, 635, *635*
citizen satisfaction in, *35*
Constitution of, *66*
diversity acceptance in, *55*
economy of, 616*f*
foreign aid spending, *614*
government of, *90*
on government taking care of poor, *41*
immigrants from, *353*
legislation in, 430
political parties in, 349, *349*
social mobility in, *47*
Supreme Constitutional Court in, 544
taxes in, 15*f*
voter turnout, *262*
Gerry, Elbridge, 78, 330–31
gerrymander, 329–34, 330*f*, *331*, 331*f*, 332*f*, 338
Gettysburg Address, 181, 244
Ghana, *468*
Gibbons, Mike, 326
Gideon, Clarence, 138*t*, 163, 561
Gideon v. Wainwright, 138*t*, 163, 561
gift ban, 400
Gingrich, Newt, 343, 425–26, 539
Gini coefficient, 49
Ginsburg, Ruth Bader, 161, 199, 395, 532, *549*, 549–50, 552*t*
Gitlow v. New York, 138*t*
Glanzman, Louis, *81*
Gobitas, Lillian, 136, *136*
Gobitas, Walter, *136*
going public, 470–71
golden opportunity, 42–43
Goldwater, Barry, 317*t*, 587
the Good News club, 145
Goodyear Tire Company, 199
Google, 397
GOP (Grand Old Party), 356. *See also* Republican Party
Gorbachev, Michael, 635
Gore, Al, 317*t*, 348, 534, 562
Gorsuch, Neil, 214, 532, 543, *547*, 550, 552*t*, 554
Gosar, Paul, 409
governing, public opinion in, 241–43, *242*
government. *See also* federal government; state government
amendments and, 98
beneficiaries, 260
benefits, 17*f*

government (*continued*)
  central, 34–35, 75, 77
  citizen satisfaction with, *35*
  as democratic republic, 33
  divided, 370–71, 443–44
  election timetables for, *309*
  engagement with, 17–18
  functions of, 14–15
  hidden, 16–17
  interest groups influencing, 378–79
  limited, 34–39
  local, 93, 123
  national, 34–35, 74–75, 79, 93, 117, *118*
  private industry and, 13–14
  public involvement in, *78*, 78–79
  Reagan, R., on, 11–12, 357
  sector, 12–13
  securing rights, 27
  setting rules, for society, 14–15
  shaping media, 290–93
  shutdown, 370
  spending, 14, 590
  taking care of poor, *41*
  Trump, D., on, 12
  trust in, 13*f*, 108*f*
  unitary, 107, 129, *129*
  U.S., compared to other democracies, *90*, 129, *129*
Government Accountability Office, 545
grandfather clause, 183
grand jury, 161
Grand Old Party (GOP), 356. *See also* Republican Party
grand strategies, 633–37
Grant, Ulysses, 378, *467*, 474*t*
granted powers, 115
grants-in-aid, 119
Grassley, Charles, 427
grassroots, 260*t*
Gray, Freddie, 179
Great Britain, *66*, *90*, 129, *129*. *See also* United Kingdom
  in French and Indian War, 67–69
  Parliament of, 83
  representation and, 67–68
  standing army of, 73
Great Depression, 39, 47
  New Deal and, 356, 583, 590
  poor relief in, *586*
  unemployment benefits and, 586
Great Migration, 185
greatness, presidential, 473–76, 474*t*
Great Recession, 228, 513
Greece, 15*f*, *35*, *262*
  diversity acceptance in, *55*
Green New Deal, 225
Green Party, 348
Greenpeace, 385
gridlock, 370–71, 519
Griswold v. Connecticut, 139–42, 200
gross domestic product (GDP), 493*f*, 520, 585, 588*f*, 590
groupthink, 241
Grutter v. Bollinger, 193

GSA. *See* General Services Administration
Guantánamo Bay, 537, 561
Gulf of Mexico oil spill, 231–32
Gulf War, 282
guns, 15
  on campus, *158*
  control, 31, 112–13, 572–73, *574*, 604
  in mass shootings, *167*, 264
  New York State Rifle & Pistol Association v. Bruen, 159, 527–28
  NRA and, 259, *376*, 386
  Parkland massacre, 159, 232, *267*, *574*, 602
  public opinion on, 232*f*
  rights, 112–13, 151, 157–59
  Uvalde massacre, *167*, 277–78, 572–73, 602
Guzman, Melissa, 223

habeas corpus, 89
Habitat for Humanity, 386–87
Hackathon, *246*, 247
hackers, *246*, 247, 266–67
Hamilton, 96
Hamilton, Alexander, *81*, 90, *96*, 353, 452, 528, 540, 565, 602
Hamiltonians, 625, 626*t*
Hancock, John, *27*, 69, 95
Hand, Learned, 564
Hannity, Sean, 282
happiness, pursuit of, 72*t*
Harding, Warren, 412, *467*, 474*t*
Harlan, John Marshall, 559
Harris, Kamala, 45, 216, 413, 427, 479
Harrison, Benjamin, *467*, 474*t*
Harrison, William Henry, 451–52, 461, 474*t*
Harvard University, 193
Hatch, Orrin, 427
hate speech, 133–34, 147–48, 150
Hayes, Rutherford, *467*, 474*t*
Health and Human Services, 492
healthcare, 16–17. *See also* Medicaid; Medicare
  ACA, 39, 120, 123, 273, 562, 587–88
  anti-vaxxers and, 273, *274*
  bureaucracy in, *503*
  federalism and, 123
  national, 58
  percent in federal budget, 14*f*
  plan, of Clinton, B., 273, 343
  plan, of Kennedy, John F., 273
  policy, 598–99
  reform, of Obama, B., 387
Heard, Amber, *156*
hearing cases, 546–47
heightened scrutiny, 199
Henry, Patrick, 11, 95, *95*
Heston, Charlton, 158
HHS (Department of Health and Human Services, U.S.), 506*t*
Hibbing, John, 445
Hicks, Mikey, *497*, 497–98
hidden government, 16–17

higher education, 193
Hillbilly Elegy (Vance, J. D.), 306
Hindus, 52*f*, 418
Hispanic Americans. *See* Latinos
history, 11, 30
Hobby Lobby Corporation, 146
Hochul, Kathy, 528
Holland, 75
Holmes, Oliver Wendell, 134, 148, 559
Holt, Lester, 230
Homeland Security Council, 481*t*
home rule, 108
Hoover, Herbert, 474*t*, 479
House of Representatives, U.S., 4, 38, 80, 81, 325–26. *See also* bills; Congress, U.S.
  conference committee, 438–39
  Constitution Article 1 on, 88–89
  diversity of, 417*f*
  division of time, by members, 421*t*
  floor action, *435*, 435–38, *436*, 437*f*
  floor of, 413
  House Rules Committee, 436
  impeachment by, 90
  leadership of, 425–27, *426*
  permanent standing committees, 428–29, 428*t*, 429*t*
  in separation of powers, 83–85, 84*f*
  Speaker of the House, 425–26, *426*
  whips, 425–26
  women elected to, 195–96
House Rules Committee, 436
Hoyer, Steny, 426
Hughes, Charles Evans, 560
Hulu, 301
Humphrey, Hubert, 317*t*
Hung, Elena, *381*
Hungary, 15*f*, *262*
Huntington, Samuel, 30
Hurricane Katrina, 509, *509*
Hurricane Maria, *509*
Hutchinson, Cassidy, *272*
Hutchinson, Thomas, 70
hyperpluralism, 382, 402

ICC. *See* Interstate Commerce Commission
ICE. *See* Immigration and Customs Enforcement
Iceland, 129, *129*, *262*
idealism, 32
ideas, 8–9, 26–27, 57–58, *58*. *See also* American ideas
identity
  gender, 213–14, 268
  intersectionality and, 174
  race and, 228, 228*f*
identity politics, 359
ideology, 361, 554, 555*f*
ignorant masses, 239–40
Illinois, 138*t*
immigrants, 30, 43
  ancient fears of, 56, 203
  categories of, 203–4
  Irish, German, *353*

Trump, D., on, 55–56, 321
undocumented individuals,
 204–5, 204f
U.S. as nation of, 18, 18–19
immigration
 Alien and Sedition Acts, 148
 American Board of Customs, 69
 Biden, Joe, on, 106
 Constitution on, 105
 federal authority over, 105–6
 Latinos and, 203–5, 206
 public opinion on, 268
 Trump, D., on, 105–6
Immigration and Customs Enforcement
 (ICE), 104, 105–6, 516, 636
impeachment, 84, 90
imperialism, 498
imperial presidency, 455, 455–56
implementation, of policies, 502–4,
 577–81, 579
implied powers, 115
important state purpose, 178
incarceration
 mass, 218, 218f
 U.S. rate of, 160
income growth, 46f
income tax rates, by state
 government, 110f
incorporation, 97–98, 137, 138t, 159
incumbency, 327–28, 328f
indentured servant, 65
independent court, 73
independent lobbyists, 390
independent regulatory commissions,
 511–13, 512f
independent states, 74
India, 66, 90, 129, 129, 197, 616f
Indiana, 163–64
Indian Citizenship Act (1924), 210.
 See also Native Americans
indirect elections, 78
individualism
 as American idea, 40–44, 42,
 43, 44
 community versus, 40–42
 in Declaration of Independence, 72t
 defining, 40
 negative liberty in, 42
 Republican national convention, 42
 roots of, 42–43, 43
 solidarity versus, 41, 42, 43, 44
individual rights, 109
individuals, 10–11
inequality, economic, 45–51, 46f, 47, 50,
 257, 569–70
infant formula shortage, 277
inflation, 568
Inflation Reduction Act, 410
information, 274, 276
information shortcuts, 240
infotainment, 282–83
infrastructure, 410, 616
"In God We Trust," 27, 53, 144
Ingraham, Laura, 278
inherent powers, 115, 453–54
initiatives, 32, 32f

Innocence Project, 165
INSP, 300
Instagram, 154, 265–66, 266f, 273–74,
 279, 283
institutional perspective, 58
institutional powers, of Congress, 412t
institutions, 9–10, 57–59, 369t, 556
interest groups, 10
 bureaucracy and, 517
 communicating members' views,
 380–81
 concerns about, 401–2, 403
 courts and, 395–96
 defenses of, 403–4
 economic, 384–85, 384t
 federal government and, 393–96,
 394f, 395f
 in foreign policy, 630–31
 history of, 387–90
 influence of, 404
 influencing government, 378–79, 381
 informing members, 380
 intergovernmental, 384t, 386–87, 387
 in iron triangle, 393–94, 394f
 lobbying by, 381, 381
 mobilizing the public, 381–82, 404
 by the numbers, 379
 power and, 397–401
 private, 379–80
 public, 384t, 385–86, 386, 388
 regulating, 399–401
 roles of, 378–83
 spending by, 397–99, 398f, 398t
 stability and, 404
 in telecommunications, 395f
 types of, 384–87, 384t
interests, 10
intergovernmental lobbying, 384t,
 386–87
Internal Revenue Service (IRS), 492, 515
internationalism, 623
internet. See also social media
 falsehoods on, 267
 in political participation, 265–68,
 266f
internment camps, 208, 560–61
interns, 423–24
intersectionality, 174
Interstate Commerce Commission
 (ICC), 511, 512f
Intolerable Acts (1774), 70
investigative bias, 288–89
invoking cloture, 437–38, 437f
Iohannis, Klaus, 624
Iowa, 310t, 317, 318
Iran, 197, 619
Iraq, 10–11, 53, 231, 282
 Abu Ghraib, 297, 298, 537
 private contractors in, 513, 513
 women in legislature, 197
Ireland
 Constitution of, 66
 immigrants from, 353
 taxes, 15f
 voter turnout, 262
 women in legislature, 197

Irish Catholics, 43, 56
Irons, Peter, 561
iron triangles, 393–94, 394f
IRS. See Internal Revenue Service
ISIS, 165
isolationism, 623, 633
Israel, 15f, 36, 90
 Constitution of, 66
 political parties in, 349
 voter turnout, 262
 women in legislature, 197
issue advocacy, 259
issue campaign, 392
issue networks, 394, 395f
Italians, 203
Italy, 15f, 66, 262, 616
 citizen satisfaction in, 35
 diversity acceptance in, 55
 social mobility in, 47

Jackson, Andrew, 353, 388, 451, 452,
 474t, 479, 545
Jackson, Ketanji Brown, 156, 346, 551,
 552t
Jacksonians, 625, 626t
Jacobs, Jane, 25
January 6, 2021 insurrection, 272,
 282–84, 409–10
Japan, 36, 262
 aging populations, 19
 citizen satisfaction in, 35
 Constitution of, 66
 diversity acceptance in, 55
 economic equality in, 49
 economy of, 616f
 foreign aid spending, 614
 government of, 90, 129, 129
 on government taking care of
 poor, 41
 judiciary in, 544
 legislation in, 430
 religiosity in, 52
 social mobility in, 47
 taxes, 15f
 wealth in, 49
 women in legislature, 197
Japanese Americans, 208, 560–61
Jay-Z, 260t
Jefferson, Thomas, 76–77
 Democratic-Republican Party of,
 352–53
 on direct democracy, 31–33
 foreign policy experience, 628t
 Marbury v. Madison and, 540–41
 on political parties, 344
 rating, 474t
 on separation of church and state, 53,
 72t, 143–44
 as slave owner, 73, 352–53
 Washington, G., and, 413
Jeffersonians, 625, 626t
Jehovah's Witnesses, 136, 136, 142, 169
Jews, 52f, 418
 "replacement theory" and, 167
Jim Crow, 9, 183, 185, 208, 218,
 254, 264

Joe Rogan Experience, 281
Johns, Barbara, *62*, 63
Johnson, Andrew, 412, *467*, 474*t*
Johnson, Lady Bird, 485
Johnson, Lyndon Baines, 227, 229, 231,
    317*t*, 425, *471*
    cabinet of, 510*t*
    executive orders of, *467*
    Medicare and, 482, 587
    rating, 474*t*
    as Senate majority leader, 604
    vetoes/overrides, 464*f*
Johnson, Ron, 194
joint committees, 428*t*
Jones, Paula, 548
Jones, Shevrin, *172*, 173–74
Jordan, Michael B., 532, *532*
judicial activism, 543
judicial branch, *526*
    appellate courts, 533–34,
      536–37, 565
    circuit courts in, 536–37, 537*f*
    in civil rights, 176–78
    district courts in, 536
    diversity in, 538–40, 539*t*
    elections, 534–35
    in enforcement, 545
    federal courts in, 533–34,
      536–37, 536*f*
    federalism in, 125–26, 126*t*
    interest groups and, 395–96
    limited resources of, 545
    by the numbers, 530
    organizing, 533–40, 534*f*
    in popular culture, *532*, 532–33, *549*,
      549–50
    power of, 528–29, 544–45
    reform of, 564–65
    role of, 540–45
    salaries of, 565
    selecting judges, 534–36
    Senate approving nominees to, 415
    in separation of powers, 83–85, 84*f*
    specialized courts in, 537–38, 538*f*
    stare decisis, 553
    state and local courts, 534
    term limits, 565
    trust in, 531–32, 532*f*
judicial federalism, 533–34
judicial restraint, 543
judicial review, 541
judicial rule, 141
judicial standard, 141
Judiciary Act (1789), 540–42
Juneau-Douglas High School, *153*
Jurassic World: Dominion, 296
jurisprudence, 557
justice, 598
Just Mercy, 532, 533

Kagan, Elena, *547*, 552*t*, 554
Kansas, 186*t*, 230
Kansas City Chiefs, *211*
Kansas v. Garcia, 126*t*
Katzenbach v. McClung, 189
Kavanaugh, Brett, 552*t*, 554

Kemp, Brian, *307*
Kennedy, Anthony M., 552*t*, 561
Kennedy, David, 582
Kennedy, Jackie, 484
Kennedy, Joe, 327
Kennedy, John F., 188, 203, 259, 317*t*,
    359, 635
    approval rating, 470
    bully pulpit, 468–69
    on civil service, 523
    executive orders of, *467*
    healthcare plan of, 273
    inaugural address, 468–69
    rating, 474*t*
    televised debate, *321*
    on television, 281
    vetoes/overrides, 464*f*
    White House of, 483
Kennedy, Robert F., Jr., 273, *274*
Kennedy, Ted, 482, 551
*Kennedy v. Bremerton School
    District*, 528
Keppler, Joseph, *339*
Kerry, John, 317*t*
Keynes, John Maynard, 590
Kickstarter, 265
Kim, Young, *327*
Kim Jong-Un, 625
Kimmel, Jimmy, *282*
King, Martin Luther, Jr., 228
    on civil disobedience, 252
    hostility against, 191
    "I am my brother's brother," 41
    "I have a dream," 31, 189
    Letters from a Birmingham Jail
      by, 252
    in March on Washington (1963), 189
    on Montgomery bus boycott, 187
    nonviolence and, 190
Kingdon, John, 40
King Philip's War, 209
kings, 34–35
King v. Burwell, 126*t*
Klobuchar, Amy, 318
Klopfer v. North Carolina, 138*t*
Korea. *See* North Korea; South Korea
Korematsu, Fred, 560–61, *561*
Korematsu v. U.S., 560–61, *561*
K-pop, *208*, 209
Krugman, Paul, 618
K Street, 377
Ku Klux Klan, 149–50, 182, 184

Labor Department, 506*t*
labor interest groups, 384–85, 384*t*
lack of coordination, in bureaucracy, 498
Lafayette, Marquis de, 127
La Follette, Robert, 350*t*
LaGrone, Andrew, 227
Lamond, Joe, *434*
Landsmark, Ted, *193*
Landy, Marc, 473
language, 205, *206*, 260*t*
Latino Cannabis Association, 223
Latinos, *20*
    American dream of, 202

    for Biden, Joe, 321
    challenges faced by, 177
    in Congress, 417
    countries of origin, 206*f*
    COVID-19 and, 202
    death penalty and, 164
    in digital divide, 301
    discrimination against, 202–3
    immigration politics, 203–5, 206
    language and, 205, *206*
    life expectancy, 217*t*
    mass incarceration of, 218, 218*f*
    police using deadly force against, 179*f*
    political mobilization of, 206–7
    poverty rate of, 217*t*
    as protected legal category, 203
    protesters, 206
    as rising force in U.S., 201–3
Latvia, *262*
Lau v. Nichols, 205
"law and order" slogan, 190
The Law of the Greeting (*El Ley del
    Saludo*), 259
Lawrence, John Geddes, 142, *142*
Lawrence v. Texas, 141–42, *142*
lawsuits, 530–31
    multistate, 121*f*
lawyers, per capita, 531
layer cake, dual federalism as, 117–18,
    117*f*, 130
Lazarus, Emma, 56
League of Nations, 633
League of United Latin American
    Citizens (LULAC), 202
Ledbetter, Lilly, 199
legal powers, of Congress, 412*t*
legislation. *See* bills
legislative branch. *See* Congress, U.S.
legislative-executive agreements, 627
legislative hold, 413, 415
legislative referral, 32
legislatures
    bicameral, 80
    state, 75, *197*
    Texas, 329
    unicameral, 80
    women elected to, 195–96, *197*
legitimate controversy, 547
Lego Movie, 601
The Lego Movie 3, *599*
Lehman Brothers, 591
Leibowitz, Samuel, *163*
the Lemon test, 144
Lemon v. Kurtzman, 144
Leon, Alberto, 161
lesbian, gay, bisexual, and transgender
    (LGBT) communities
    "bathroom bills" and, 214
    on campus, 152
    civil rights, *172*, 173, 213–15
    discrimination against, 214
    intersectionality and, 174
    in military, 213
    right to privacy, 142, *142*
    same-sex marriage, 91, 213–14, 223,
      224*f*, 268

El Ley del Saludo (The Law of the Greeting), 259
LGBT communities. *See* lesbian, gay, bisexual, and transgender communities
libel, *156*, 156–57
liberalism, 612–13
liberals, 17, 51
    conservatives on issues compared to, *37f*, 38t
    definition of, 36
    on Supreme Court, 554
    on television, 282
    youth as, 268–69
Libertarian Party, 348, 351, 363
libertarians, 36, 363
liberty. *See also* civil liberties
    as American idea, 14, 28–30, 72t
    in Declaration of Independence, 72t
    negative, 29–30, 36, 42, 50–51
    positive, 29–30, 50
liberty tree, *28*
Libya, 623, *623*
life, liberty, and pursuit of happiness, 72t
life, liberty or property, 182
life events, in public opinion, 228–29
life expectancy, U.S., 217t
Light, Paul, 602
likely voters, 233
Limbaugh, Rush, 281
limited government
    as American idea, 34–39
    conservatives, liberals, libertarians, and populists on, 36
    in Declaration of Independence, 72t
    democracy and, 38–39
    government action versus, 37–38
    origins of, 34–35
Lincoln, Abraham, 474t, 565
    on common values, 128
    election of, 181
    executive orders of, *467*
    Gettysburg Address, 181, 244
    in Republican Party, 354
    on slavery, 87, 354
Lincoln Project, *364*
lingo, campaign, 336t
LinkedIn, 266f
Lippman, Walter, 239
literacy tests, 183
Literary Digest, 233
litigation, 396, 530–31
Little Lobbyists, *381*
Little Rock, Arkansas, 187
lobbying. *See also* interest groups
    by Amazon, 398t, *400*
    American-style, spreading, 389
    astroturf, 392
    Bill of Rights on, 387
    clients, biggest-spending, 398t
    coalitions, 392
    courts, 395–96
    Federal Regulation of Lobbying Act (1946), 399
    gift ban on, 400

    by interest groups, *376*, 381, *381*
    intergovernmental, 384t, 386–87
    on judicial confirmations, *395*, *396*
    K Street, 377
    by nonprofits, 392–93
    power elite theory and, 382–83
    reverse, 386–87
    special interests, 378
lobbyists, 381, *381*
    Biden, Joe, on, 402
    EPA and, 503
    farm, 393–94
    hyperpluralism and, 402
    independent, 390
    limiting, 444–45
    Manafort, 401–2
    number of, Washington, 397
    as position takers, 392
    registered, 397, 398f
    reporting to Congress, 399–401
    as researchers, 391
    in revolving door, 394
    supporting litigation, 396
    Supreme Court and, 395–96, *396*
    Trump, D., on, 400–402
    as witnesses, 391–92
Lobbyit, 389
local government, 93, 108f, 123
local media, 292–93, 292f, *293*
Lochner era, 559
Lochner v. New York, 559
Locke, John, 72, 72t
Lockheed Martin, 398t
Los Angeles, 190
Losey, Mark, 227
loud signal, 276
LULAC (League of United Latin American Citizens), 202
Luxembourg, *47*, *262*, *614*
lynching, of African Americans, 184, *184*

Machtley, Ron, 343
Macron, Emmanuel, *624*
Maddow, Rachel, 282
Madison, James, 280
    on Bill of Rights, 97
    at Constitutional Convention, *76*, 76–80, *81*
    on factions, 378, 404
    Federalist Papers by, 32–33, 58, 93, 382, 444
    foreign policy experience, 628t
    Marbury v. Madison, 90–91, 540–41, 544, 557
    rating, 474t
    style of, 476
    Virginia Plan of, 79–81, 603–4
magazines, 280
Mahanoy Area School District v. B.L., 152
Maine, 53
majority, will of, 31
majority-minority country, U.S. becoming, 263

majority opinion, 549
major questions doctrine, 518
Malcolm X, 190
Manafort, Paul, 401–2
Manchin, Joe, 9
mandate, 242
Mapp, Dollree, 138t, 161
Mapp v. Ohio, 138t, 161
marble cake, cooperative federalism as, 117f, 118–19, 119t, 130
Marbury, William, 540–41
Marbury v. Madison, 90–91, 540–41, 544, 557
March on Washington (1963), 31, 189
Marcos, Ferdinand, 401
margin of sampling error, 235, 237t
marijuana, 15, 112, 113, *222*, 223, 224f, 268, 579, 580f
marriage. *See* same-sex marriage
Marriage Story, 533
Marshall, John, 90–91, 125–26, 540–41, *541*, 545, 557
Martin, Luther, 81
Marx, Karl, 280
Maryland, 81, 85t, 94t, 125, 138t, 557
mask mandates, 123, 168, 572, 573f
Mason, George, 86, 95
Massachusetts, 85t
    Boston Tea Party, 70
    gerrymander, 330–31, *331*
    Puritans landing in, 18
    Quakers banned from, 51
    in ratification, of Constitution, 94t, 95
    Shays's Rebellion, 75, 75–76, *76*
mass incarceration, 218, 218f
mass media. *See also* new media
    FCC on, 291, 512f
    newspapers as, 280
    radio as, *280*, 280–81
    television as, 281–83
mass shootings, *167*, 264, 277–78
material benefits, 386
Mayflower Compact, 65, *66*
MBS (Mohammed bin Salman), *619*
McAuliffe, Terry, 305
McCain, John, 314, 317t, 319
McCarthy, Kevin, 413, 426
McCauley, Mary Ludwig Hays, *74*
McConnell, Mitch, 312, *426*, 427, 527, 550
McCulloch, James William, 125, 557
McCulloch v. Maryland, 125, 557
McCutcheon v. Federal Elections Commission, 312, 314
McDonald, Laquan, 179
McDonald v. Chicago, 138t, 159
McGirt v. Oklahoma, 211
McGovern, George, 317t
McKinley, William, 355, *467*, 474t
McLaurin, George, *186*
McLaurin v. Oklahoma State Regents, 186t
McMahon, Linda, 326

media. *See also* mass media; new media; social media
  in American democracy, 276–78
  Americanization of, globally, 294
  campaign drama, 298–99
  candidate profiles in, 299
  censorship, 295
  at crossroads, 300–301
  digital sources of, 279, 279f, 300–301
  election coverage in, 287–88, 298–99
  framing by, 277–78
  government shaping, 290–93
  information in, 276
  local, 292–93, 292f, 293
  loud signal in, 276
  market forces on, 290
  by the numbers, 275
  objectivity of, 289
  priming by, 277
  public ownership of, 290
  as public watchdog, 276–77, 289
  regulating, 290–92, 292f
  shaping policy agenda, 277, 277–78
  technology, 273–75, 300–301
  Telecommunications Act of 1996, 286
  traditional formats, declining, 278–84, 279f, 283
  Trump, D., gaining attention from, 287–88
  trust in, 286f
  war, terrorism coverage, 296–98, 297
  around the world, 294–96
media bias
  drama, conflict and, 287–88, 288
  fairness, 289
  investigative, 288–89
  profits and, 286–87, 287f
  public opinion on, 285–86, 286f
  of reporters, 285–86
median, 49
mediation, 531
Medicaid, 14, 17, 31, 120, 123, 587–88
Medicare, 39, 124
  in federal budget, 14
  growth of, 587–89
  Johnson, L. B., and, 482, 587
mercantilism, 69
Meta, 291, 398t
#MeToo movement, 6, 200, 252
Mettler, Suzanne, 17, 17f, 584
Mexican-Americans, 206
Mexico, 262
  border with, 71
  on government taking care of poor, 41
  taxes, 15f
  war with, 353
  women in legislature, 197
Michigan, 106
midterm elections, 306–7, 328, 329t
midterm loss, 328
Milano, Alyssa, 200
military, U.S.
  in Cold War, 634f
  Commander in Chief of, 458–59

in federal budget, 14, 458f
in foreign policy, 610, 612
gay men, women in, 213
spending, 612
tribunal, 537–38
military-industrial complex, 6
Milkis, Sidney, 473
Mill, John Stuart, 147
millennials, 21, 267, 268–69, 268f, 269f, 389
Miller, Judith, 290
Miller, Warren, 239–40
Miller test, 155
Miller v. California, 155
millionaires' club, 355
Minersville School District v. Gobitis, 136
minimum wage, 31
Minneapolis, 154
Minnesota, 351
minority representation. *See also* diversity
  in elections, 332–34
  in presidential cabinet, 510t
minutemen, 70–71
Miranda, Lin-Manuel, 96
Miranda rights, 162, 167, 561
Miranda v. Arizona, 138t, 162
Miranda warnings, 162
misinformation, 267, 274, 284, 284f
Mississippi, 141, 183, 256
Missouri, 53, 135, 179, 186t, 548
Missouri Compromise, 180, 181f, 541
Miyares, Jason, 306
mobilization, 259, 260t, 264–65, 381–82, 404
moderate Republicans, 364
Mondale, Walter, 317t
monetary policy, 590–92
money. *See also* economic inequality; wealth
  in congressional campaigns, 335
  in elections, 312–15, 312f, 315, 325–26, 338–39
  of major donors, 313–15, 338
Monroe, James, 474t, 628t
Montana, 195
Montesquieu, Charles-Louis de Secondat de, 84
Montgomery, Alabama, 187
morality, government regulation of, 495
Mothers Out Front, 259
Mott, Lucretia, 176
movies, 296, 599, 601
MSNBC, 282
Muller v. Oregon, 559–60, 560
multilateralism, 624
multilateral organization, 635
multiparty systems, 350
multistate lawsuits, 121f
Mulvaney, Mick, 314
Murad, Nadia, 631
Murdoch, Rupert, 282
Murphy v. NCAA, 126t
Murtha, Jack, 428
Musk, Elon, 383, 383
Muslims, 52f, 418, 450

NAACP. *See* National Association for the Advancement of Colored People
Nader, Ralph, 348
name recognition, 336
Napoleon, 68f
NASA. *See* National Aeronautics and Space Administration
Nast, Thomas, 355, 367
Natick Indians, 69
National Aeronautics and Space Administration (NASA), 506t, 511
National American Woman Suffrage Association (NAWSA), 195
national anthem protests, 150
National Association for the Advancement of Colored People (NAACP), 63, 138t, 185, 186–87
National Association of Manufacturers, 398t
National Association of Realtors, 398t
national authority, in Constitution, 114–15, 116f
national defense powers, of Congress, 412t
National Economic Council (NEC), 481t, 482–83
National Education Association (NEA), 384–85
National Federation of Independent Business v. Sebelius, 126t, 562
national government, 34–35, 74–75, 79, 117, 118
National Governors' Association (NGA), 386
nationalism
  American, 127–29
  double-edged sword of, 127–28
  federalism and, 112, 127–29
  rise of, 127
  white, 128, 130
National Labor Relations Board, 512f, 560
National Labor Relations Board v. Jones and Laughlin Steel Corporation, 560
National Oceanic and Atmospheric Administration (NOAA), 499
National Organization for Women (NOW), 198
national policy, 112–13
National Public Radio (NPR), 281, 294
National Rifle Association (NRA), 259, 376, 385
National Security Agency (NSA), 154
National Security Council (NSC), 481t, 483, 630
National Space Council, 481t
Native Americans, 18, 30, 45
  AIM, 211
  BIA and, 210–11
  colonial era wars with, 66, 67, 67–69
  in Congress, 417
  federal government and, 210
  forced assimilation of, 210
  French and Indian War, 67, 67–69
  genocide, 353

Indian Citizenship Act (1924), 210
King Philip's War, 209
life expectancy, 217t
lost way of life, 209
Natick Indians, 69
police using deadly force against, 179f
poverty rate of, 210, 217t
religious practices, 145–46
rights, denied, 210
Sioux Nation, 211
Supreme Court and, 211
Wounded Knee incident, 211
NATO. See North Atlantic Treaty
    Organization
NAWSA (National American Woman
    Suffrage Association), 195
Nazism, 151
NBC, 281
NCTA the Internet & Television
    Association, 398t
Ndiaye, Pap, 129
NEA (National Education Association),
    384–85
Near v. Minnesota, 138t, 154
NEC. See National Economic Council
necessary and proper clause, 89, 115
negative campaigns, 337
negative liberty, 29–30, 36, 42, 50–51
negative partisanship, 259, 361, 361f
Negro Year Book, 184
neoconservatives, 363
Netflix, 300
Netherlands
    citizen satisfaction in, 35
    Constitution of, 66
    diversity acceptance in, 55
    foreign aid spending, 614
    loans from, 75
    social mobility in, 47
    voter turnout, 262
Network of Enlightened Women, 603
Neustadt, Richard, 469
neutrality test, 146
Never-Trump faction, 364
New Deal, 119, 356, 560, 583, 590
new federalism, 120
New Hampshire, 85t, 94t, 95,
    317–18, 318
New Haven, Connecticut, 192
New Jersey, 85t, 94t
The New Jersey Plan, 80–81
New Jim Crow, 218
new media. See also Internet; social media
    clickbait in, 283
    data from, 284
    fake news, 284, 284f
    information in, 274
    misinformation on, 284, 284f
    public activity in, 274
    rise of, 283
newspapers
    advertising, 280, 286
    decline of, 279f, 280, 283
    freedom of press, 153–57
    as mass media, 280
New World Order, 635–36

New York, 34, 79, 94t, 95
    enslaved population in, 85t
    Gitlow v. New York, 138t
    Lochner v. New York, 559
    New York City, 25, 108
    September 11, 2001, 166, 228, 473,
        507, 636
New York Daily Tribune, 280
New York Herald, 280
New York Independent Journal, 280
New York State Rifle & Pistol Association
    v. Bruen, 159, 527–28
New York Times, 154–55, 155, 187, 281,
    290, 295
    on media coverage, of terrorism,
        297–98
New Zealand, 15f, 129, 129
    citizen satisfaction in, 35
    Constitution of, 66
    diversity acceptance in, 55
    social mobility in, 47
    voter turnout, 262
    women in legislature, 197
Nextdoor, 266f
NGA (National Governors'
    Association), 386
Nguyen Ngoc Loan, 298
Nineteenth Amendment, 79, 195, 196f
Ninth Amendment, 139
Nixon, Richard, 317t, 343, 476–77
    cabinet of, 510t
    executive orders of, 467
    "law and order" slogan of, 190
    midterms, 329t
    on Miranda rights, 162
    on Pentagon Papers, 154
    rating, 474t
    resigning, 90
    southern strategy, 357
    televised debate, 321
    U.S. v. Nixon, 561–62
    vetoes/overrides, 464f
    Watergate scandal, 288
NOAA (National Oceanographic and
    Atmospheric Administration), 499
nomination process, in presidential elec-
    tions, 316–19
nonattitudes, 239–40
non-citizens, rights of, 167–68
nonpartisan districting, 332–34, 332f
nonpartisan election, 347
nonpartisan systems, 350
nonprofits, 392–93
nonsuspect categories, 178, 199
nonviolence, 190
North Atlantic Treaty Organization
    (NATO), 461, 634f, 635
North Carolina, 85t, 94t, 95, 126t, 127,
    138t, 188, 214, 330f
North Korea, 197, 612, 625
The Northman, 296
Northwest Ordinance, 75
Norway, 40–41, 262, 614
"no taxation without representation," 73
NOW (National Organization for
    Women), 198

NPR. See National Public Radio
NRA. See National Rifle Association
NSA (National Security Agency), 154
NSC. See National Security Council
Nuclear Regulatory Commission, 512f
Nye, Joseph, 613

OAS (Organization of American
    States), 635
Obama, Barack, 216, 317t, 369t, 492,
    550, 628t. See also Affordable
    Care Act
    African-American support for, 348
    approval ratings, 472f
    birtherism and, 316
    Brown, G., and, 460–61
    burden of office, 478
    cabinet of, 510t
    campaign spending, 314
    climate change policy and, 122
    on diversity as American idea, 54
    Dreamers policy of, 205
    EOP of, 482
    executive orders of, 467
    foreign policy, 637
    health care reform, 387
    inaugural address of, 491
    judicial nominees of, 415, 535, 536f
    midterms, 329t
    misleading statements by, 289
    multistate lawsuits filed under, 121f
    passing bills, 463t
    progressive federalism of, 120
    rating, 474t
    Republican opposition to, 345
    vetoes, 463–64, 464f
    voter turnout for, 257
    White House of, 483
Obama, Michelle, 230, 485–86
Obamacare. See Affordable Care Act
Obergefell, Jim, 563
Obergefell v. Hodges, 126t, 213–14, 563
obscenity, 155–56
Ocasio-Cortez, Alexandria, 9, 365,
    400, 424
O'Connor, Sandra Day, 199, 534
Office of Administration, 481t
Office of Domestic Climate Policy, 481t
Office of Intergovernmental Affairs, 481t
Office of Management and Budget (OMB),
    433–34, 481t, 482, 500f, 501, 593
Office of National Cyber Director, 481t
Office of National Drug Control
    Policy, 481t
Office of Personnel Management
    (OPM), 513
Office of Public Engagement, 481t
Office of Science and Technology, 481t
Office of U.S. Trade Representative, 481t
Ohio, 138t, 148–49, 161
oil, 568
O'Keefe, James, 155
Oklahoma, 43, 135, 186t, 199, 211
Oliver, Manuel, 574
OMB. See Office of Management and
    Budget

omnibus spending bill, 596
Onaodowan, Okieriete, *96*
118th Congress, 413
O'Neill, Tip, 426, *463*
open carry, 112–13
open primary, 317–18
open seat, 335
opinion polls, 232
    bandwagon effect in, 237
    bias in, *234*
    bloopers, 233
    boomerang effect in, 238
    Clinton, B., on, 243
    in democracy, 237
    framing effects in, 234
    participation in, *234*
    push polls and, 234–35
    random samples in, 233*t*
    reading, 237*t*
    refining sample in, 233–34
    response bias in, 236
    sample size of, 236*f*, 237*t*
    sampling error in, 235, 236*f*
    sampling frame in, 233
    technology and, 235
    threats to, globally, *235*
    types of, 238*t*
    underdog effect in, 239
    wording of, 234
OPM (Office of Personnel
    Management), 513
oppo, 336*t*
oral arguments, 546–47
Oregon, 145–46
    de Jonge v. Oregon, 138*t*
    Muller v. Oregon, 559–60, *560*
Organization of American States
    (OAS), 635
organized labor, 364–65
originalism, 100, 102, 543
O'Rourke, Beto, 266
Ossoff, Jon, 298
Our Children's Trust, 602–3
Oval Office, 479
overhead democracy, 515
overrides, veto, 462–64, 464*f*
Ovsyannikova, Marina, 295, *295*
Oz, Mehmet, 306

PACs. *See* political action committees
Page, Benjamin, 240
Pakistan, *47*
Palin, Sarah, *299*
Papua New Guinea, *197*
paradox of voting, 261
"Parental Rights in Education Bill"
    ("Don't Say Gay" legislation),
    172, 173
Paris Climate Accord, 122, 461
Parker v. Gladden, 138*t*
Parkland, Florida, 159, 232, *267*,
    574, 602
Parks, Rosa, 187
parliamentary systems, 508
Die Partei, *349*
partial veto, 454*t*

participation. *See* political participation
partisanship
    COVID-19 and, 572
    in federalism, 120, 125
    in gerrymandering, 329–32
    in gridlock, 443–44
    negative, 259, 361, 361*f*
    polarization and, 441–44, *442*
    political parties in, 343–44, 344*f*,
        368–73
    reducing, 371, 373
    in Senate, 369
    of Supreme Court, 370–71, 554, 555*f*
party boss, 355, *355*
party caucus, 369
party identification, 358, 373
    building, 359–60, 359*f*
    Democratic factions, 364–65
    demographics of, 359*f*
    filtering, 360–61
    in ideology, 361
    negative partisanship and, 361, 361*f*
    party organization and, 365–67
    personality and, 360
    power of, 360–62
    Republican factions in, 363–64
    in voting, 360
party-in-government, 366–67
party in the electorate, 367
party machine, 355
party organization, 365–67
party platform, 366
party system, 347
    fifth, 356–57
    first, 352–53
    fourth, 355–56
    new, after 2020 presidential election,
        358
    overview, of six party systems, 352*t*
    reforming, 372–73
    second, 353–54
    sixth, 357
    third, 354–55
Patent and Trademark Office, U.S., 133
Paterson, William, 81
PATH (Professional Association of
    Therapeutic Horsemanship), 385
path dependence, 582
Patriot Act (2001), 166, 636
Paul, Alice, 195
PBS (Public Broadcasting System), 294
Peace Corps, 511
Pearl Harbor, Hawaii, 208, 228
Peck, Gregory, 532
peer pressure, 555–56
Pell Grants, 584
Pelosi, Nancy, *342*, 400, 413, 425,
    426, *426*
Peltoa, Mary, 299
Pence, Mike, 3, *342*, *480*
Pendleton Civil Service Act (1883), 494
Pennsylvania, 51, 85*t*, 94*t*. *See also*
    Constitutional Convention,
    Philadelphia
    Minersville, 136
    Philadelphia, 76–77, 148

Penry v. Lynaugh, 548
Pentagon Papers, 154
People for the Ethical Treatment of
    Animals (PETA), 385
Perdue, David, 348
Perot, Ross, 350*t*
personal presidency, 281, 476–78
Peru, 129, *129*
PETA (People for the Ethical Treatment
    of Animals), 385
Pew Research Center, 234
peyote, 145–46
Pharmaceutical Research &
    Manufacturers, 398*t*
Philadelphia, 76–77, 146, 148
Pierce, Franklin, 474*t*
Pine Ridge Indian Reservation, 211
Pinterest, 266*f*
Pitcher, Molly, *74*
"pizzagate," 267
plaintiff, 544
Plame, Valerie, 290
Planned Parenthood v. Casey, 141
Pledge of Allegiance, 53, *128*, 144
Plessy, Homer A., 183, 558–59
Plessy, Keith, *559*
Plessy v. Ferguson, 183, 529, 558–59,
    559, 561
pluralism, 7–8, 7*t*, 382, 404
pocket veto, 463
podcasts, 279, 281
Pointer v. Texas, 138*t*
Poland, *262*
polarization, 441–44, *442*
police
    deadly force used by, 179, 179*f*, 194
    protests for reform of, 6, *6*, 31, *288*,
        564–65
policy. *See also* Congress, U.S.; foreign
    policy; public policy
    agenda, 243, *277*, 277–78, 571–74
    window, 577
political action committees (PACs),
    313–14, *315*, 368
political appointees, 465
political campaigns. *See* campaigns;
    elections
political culture, 57–59
political decision-making, 8–11
political elites, 230–31
political equality, 49, 174–76
political industry, 259
political innovation, 109–10
political institutions, 57–59
political mobilization, 259, 260*t*,
    264–65, 381–82, 404
political orders, 475–76
political participation
    age in, 250*f*, 256–57, 257*f*
    alienation from, 261–63
    civic volunteerism, 128, 255
    community in, 258–59
    complacency against, 264
    direct action, 252–55
    discouraging, 261–65
    education in, 257

friends and family in, 258
by Gen Z, *267*, 268–69
by government beneficiaries, 260
historical context for, 260–61
institutional barriers to, 263–64
internet, social media in,
 265–68, *266f*
leading forms of, *252f*
by millennials, *267*, 268–69
mobilization in, 259, *260t*
by the numbers, 249
race in, 257–58
traditional, 248–52, *250t*
voter turnout, 255–56
voting, 248–51, *251*
wealth in, 257
political parties. *See also* Democratic
 Party; party identification; party
 system; Republican Party
 affiliations, by income level, *230f*
 beginnings, 352–53
 candidates of, 347
 championing ideas, 346–47
 competition between, 368–71
 controlling national institutions, *369t*
 conventions, 320, *320*, *366*
 demographics, *359f*
 in Europe, *333*
 in gerrymandering, 329–32
 Jefferson on, 344
 by the numbers, 345
 organizing, 365–67
 partisanship and, 343–44, *344f*,
 368–73
 president, as leader of, 468
 in presidential elections, 321
 in public opinion, 229–30
 in Reconstruction, 354–55
 socialization by, 347, *348*
 symbols of, *367*
 third parties, 349–51, *350t*, *351*
 two-party tradition, 347–50
 Washington, G., on, 344, 468
political socialization, *227*, 227–29,
 347, *348*
political voice, 251–52
politics
 defining, 8
 disagreements in, 5
 of education on race, 111, *111*
 engagement in, 21
 ideas in, 57–58, *58*
 industry, 388
 media technology in, 273–75
 of religion, 53–54
 of slavery, 180
 universalistic, 494
Polk, James, *474t*
polls. *See* opinion polls
poll taxes, 183
poor relief, *586*
popular movements, *9*
popular vote, 4
populists, 36
pork, 428–29
pornography, 155–56

Portugal, *262*
positive liberty, 29–30, 50
Postal Regulatory Commission, *512f*
Postal Service, U.S., 492, *506t*, 511, *522*
post civil rights era, 191–94
postpartisanship, 373
poverty, 217, *217t*
 economic inequality, 45–48, *46f*, *47*
 government assistance for, *41*
Powell, Jerome, 591, *591*
Powell, Lewis, 551
Powell v. Alabama, *138t*, 162
power, theories of, 7–8, *7t*
power elite theory, 382–83
pragmatism, 102, 543
prayer, in school, *100*
preamble, to Constitution, U.S., 88
precedent, 543
preemption, 124
preemptive war, 636
presidency
 appointments by, 465, 479, 480–81
 approval ratings, 472–73, *472f*
 batting average, of successful bills,
 462, *463t*
 as bully pulpit, *468*, 468–69, 471
 burden of, 477–78, *478*
 in bureaucracy, 456–57, 465,
 515–16, 523
 cabinet of, 480–81
 campaigning for, 316–24, *318*, *321*
 checks and balances on, 83–85, *84f*
 in civil rights, 176
 as Commander in Chief, 458–59
 Constitutional Convention on, 83, 452
 Constitution on, 89–90, 316, 458, 461
 defining, 451–54
 as economist in chief, 466–67
 Electoral College in, 453
 Electoral College map (2020), *83f*
 EOP, 481–83, *481t*, 484, 485
 executive authority of, 82
 executive orders, 450, 454,
 465–66, *467*
 executive privilege of, 454
 expressed powers of, *453t*
 as first legislator, 461–65
 first spouse, 484–86
 foreign policy in, 459–61,
 627–29, *628t*
 going public, 470–71
 greatness, 473–76, *474t*
 as head of state, 468
 images of, *470*, *471*
 imperial, *455*, 455–56
 as impossible job, 469
 length of, 452
 managing public, 470–71
 nuclear weapons and, 459, *459*
 by the numbers, 451
 Oval Office, 479
 as party leader, 468
 personal, 281, 476–78
 in political orders, 475–76
 powers of, 449, 453–54, *453t*, 486–87
 presidential style, 476–77, *477*

 in proposed federal budget, 593–94
 rating the presidents, *474t*
 résumé for, 316, *317t*
 in separation of powers, *84f*
 signing statements, *464*, 464–65
 State of the Union address, *343*, 462
 as top diplomat, 459–61, *461*
 unitary executive theory, 456
 veto power, 439
 vice president, 479–80
 weak, 456–57
 White House Office, 483–84
presidential elections
 campaign organizations, 321
 campaigns and, 316–24, *317t*, *318*,
 320, *321*, *323f*, *324t*
 caucuses, primaries, 316–19
 of Clinton, B., 320–21, 336
 demographics in, 321, 323–24
 domestic issues in, 320
 economy in, 320–21
 Electoral College in, 322–23, 338
 Electoral College map (2020), *323f*
 Florida (2000), 348
 general election, 320
 new party system and, 358
 nonparticipation in, 323
 party conventions in, 320, *320*, *366*
 political parties in, 321
 predicting, 324, *324t*
 Super Tuesday in, 319
 swing states in, 322–23
 third-party candidates in,
 349–51, *350t*
 three phases of, 316–20
 war, foreign policy in, 321
 winning, 320–24
 winning nomination, 316–19
president pro-tempore, 427
Price, David, 430
primaries, 316–19
priming, 277
principal-agent theory, 516–17
prior restraint, 154–55, *155*
privacy, 139–42
private contractors, *513*, 513–14
private industry, 13–14
private life, 12
privatization, of federal programs, 522,
 522
problem definition, framing as, 574
pro-choice, 140–42
profession, of Congress members, 418
Professional Association of Therapeutic
 Horsemanship (PATH), 385
progressive federalism, 120
Progressive Party, 349, 355
progressives, 364
Project Veritas, 154–55, *155*
pro-life, 140–42, 255
pronouns, gender-neutral, 268, *269f*
property rights, 151
proportional representation, 319, 372
proposed rule, 501
protectionism, 617
Protestants, 418

protests
  COVID-19 lockdown, *33*
  issues drawing, 253, *253*
  Latinos and, 206
  national anthem, *150*
  for police reform, 6, *6*, 31, *288*,
      564–65
Public Broadcasting System (PBS), 294
public financing, 314
public interest, 10
public interest groups, 384*t*, 385–86,
    386, 388
public involvement, in government, *78*,
    78–79
public opinion. *See also* opinion polls
  on abortion, 225, *225f*
  on bureaucracy, 491–92
  on climate change, 223–25, 229, *229*,
      268, *268f*
  communicating, 242
  on Congress, 441, *441f*
  on criminal justice reform of, 564–65
  in democracy, 239–43, 244
  of Democrats, Republicans, *362*
  on discrimination, 215, *215*
  on diversity, *55*
  in economic inequality, 49–50
  education in, 227–28
  on environmental protections, 243
  family and friends in, 227
  on foreign policy, 631
  on free trade, *618f*
  gender in, 228
  of Gen Z, 268–69
  governing and, 241–43, *242*
  on government taking care of
      poor, *41*
  on gun control, *232f*
  on immigration, 268
  leaders responding to, 242–43
  life events in, 228–29
  mandate, 242
  on marijuana, 223, *224f*, 268
  measuring, 232–39, *234*, *235*, *236f*
  on media bias, 285–86
  of millennials, 268–69
  by the numbers, 226
  on policymaking, *600*
  political party in, 229–30
  political socialization in, *227*, 227–29
  race in, 228, *228f*
  religion in, 228
  on same-sex marriage, 223, *224f*, 268
  on satisfaction, with democracies, *35*
  sources of, 226–32
  on Supreme Court, *532f*, *556*
  survey research and, 242
  timing of, 234
  on U.S. from abroad, *622f*
  wars, terrorist attacks in, 231
Public Opinion (Lippman), 239
public ownership, of media, 290
public policy. *See also* foreign policy
  agenda setting, 571–74, *573f*, 573*t*
  American ideas and, 570
  bottom-up, 579–81

climate change and, 602–3
cost-benefit analysis of, 575–77
cost effectiveness of, *575*
economic, 589–97
entrepreneurs, 602–3
evaluation, feedback on, 581–83
ex post evaluations, 581
Federal Register and, 577, *578f*
fiscal, 590–91
five stages of, 570–83, *572f*
focusing event, 572
formation, 574–77
framing, 574
healthcare, 598–99
implementation, 577–81, *579*
importance of, 605
losses and, 604
making good policy, 597–601
monetary, 590–92
by the numbers, 571
racial equality and, 602
reforming process, 601–4
social, 583–89
symbols and, 604
top down, 579, *579*
window, 577
public-private partnership, 13
public watchdog, media as, 276–77, 289
Puritans, 18, 51, 65
push polls, 234–35
Putin, Vladimir, 295, *461*, 625

Quakers, 51
Quantum Industry Coalition, 392
quasi-suspect categories, 178

race, *20*
  in bureaucracy, 495
  civil rights and, 179–84
  of Congress members, 416–17, *417f*
  critical race theory, 173, 194
  education on, 111, *111*
  identity and, 228, *228f*
  intersectionality and, 174
  in political participation, 257–58
  in public opinion, 228, *228f*
  of Trump, D., voters, 228
  urban design and, 25
  white nationalism and, 128
race to bottom, 113
racial equality. *See also* Civil Rights
    Movement; Native Americans;
    Supreme Court, U.S.
  affirmative action in, 191–93
  Biden, Joe, and public policy on, 602
  fight for, 185–90
  Freedom Riders for, 188, *188*, 254
  March on Washington (1963)
      for, 189
  NAACP for, 63, 138*t*, 185, 186–87
  religious opponents of, 53
  in school busing, 192
racial inequality. *See also* discrimination
  Jim Crow laws, 9, 183, 185, 208, 218,
      254, 264
  segregation, 185–90, *186*, 202

racial profiling, 218
racial segregation, 63–64
radio
  conservatives on, 281
  FCC on, 291
  fireside chats, of Roosevelt, F.,
      280, 281
  government-owned, 294
  as mass media, *280*, 280–81
  NPR, 281
Raimondo, Gina, *502*
rainmakers, 390*t*
Rally for Life, 255
Ramos, Anthony, *96*
Randolph, A. Philip, 185
Randolph, Edmund, 79–80, 82
Randolph, William, 95
random sample, 233, 237*t*
Rankin, Jeanette, 195, 417, *418*
raptivist, *260*, 260*t*
RAs (resident assistants), 580
ratification, of U.S. Constitution, 91–96,
    94*t*, *95*, *96f*
rational choice theory, 10, 599
The Rational Public (Page and Shapiro),
    240
Rawlings, Jerry, *468*
Rayburn, Sam, 337
Raytheon Technologies, 398*t*
Reagan, Nancy, 485
Reagan, Ronald, 199, 228, 317*t*, 360,
    628*t*, 635
  AMA and, 273, *274*
  attempted assassination against, 479
  block grants and, 120
  Bork nomination, 551
  bully pulpit of, 604
  cabinet of, 510*t*
  on conference committee, 438
  election of, 453
  on exclusionary rule, 161
  executive orders of, *467*
  against FCC regulations, 291
  on fifth party system, 357
  on government, 11–12, 357
  judicial nominees of, *536f*
  midterms, 329*t*
  multistate lawsuits filed
      under, 121*f*
  new federalism of, 120
  O'Neill with, *463*
  passing bills, 463*t*
  rating, 474*t*
  southern strategy, 357
  style of, 477, *477*
  vetoes/overrides, *464f*
realism doctrine, 610–12
reapportionment, 330
Reconstruction, 182–83, *354*,
    354–55, 495
red/blue party colors, *367*
Redcoats, 67, 69
Reddit, 266*f*, 274
redditBotAnalysis, 247
Red Shirts, 182
referendum, 32, *32f*

Reform Party, 351
reframing the issue, 198–99
registered lobbyists, 397, 398f
regulation
    of broadcasters, 291
    government, 495
    independent regulatory commis-
        sions, 511–13, 512f
    of interest groups, 399–401
    of media, 290–92, 292f
regulatory capture, 512
Rehabilitation Act (1973), Section
    504, 212
Rehnquist, William, 126, 162
religion. *See also* Christians
    in American colonies, 65
    as American idea, 51–54, *53*, 72t
    of Congress members, 418
    establishment clause and,
        143–45, *144*
    freedom of, 29, 53, 143–46, *144*
    free exercise clause and, 143, 145–46
    politics of, 53–54
    in public opinion, 228
    separation of church and state, 53,
        72t, 144–45, 528
    teaching, *53*
    types of, 52–53, 52f
religiosity, 52
Religious Freedom Restoration Act
    (1993) (RFRA), 146
religious traditionalists, 363
"replacement theory," 167
representation
    Congressional, 416–20
    delegate, 67–68, 418–20
    descriptive, 418, 419
    substantive, 418, 419
    taxation without, 73
    trustee, 68, 418–20
    violations, of right of, 73
republic, 8, 21, 269
    defining, 5, 32
    self-rule and, 32–33
Republican National Committee
    (RNC), 366
Republican national convention, *42*
Republican Party, 34, *304*, 352t, 367.
    See also elections; party system;
        political parties
    affiliations, by income level, 230f
    American nationalists/Trumpists
        in, 363
    autopsy, after 2012 election, 321
    Biden, Joe, and disapproval of, 450
    on climate change, 225, 229, *229*
    conservatives in, 363
    Democratic Party on issues com-
        pared to, 37f, 38t
    demographics of, 323–24
    European political parties compared
        to, *333*
    factions of, 363–64
    on federalism, 124
    as GOP, 356
    libertarians in, 363

Lincoln in, 354
    on marijuana use, 224f
    moderates in, 364
    Obama, B., and opposition of, 345
    party identification of, 359–60, 359f
    public opinion of, *362*
    southern strategy of, 357
    on spending, 590
    symbols of, *367*
    tax bill, 435, *435*
    Tea Party and, 336
    Trump, D., on, 346
    on trust in media, 286f
    views, of Democrats, 343–44, 441–44
    voter restrictions of, 264
    white support for, 323
Republicans in Name Only (RINOs),
    364, 410
reserved powers, 115–16, 116f
resident alien, 203–5
resident assistants (RAs), 580
resources, equalizing, 113
response bias, 236
retail campaigning, 336t
revenge porn, 156
revenue, 75
Revere, Paul, 69–70, *70*
reverse lobbying, 386–87
Revolutionary War, 28, *28*, 30, 34, 45,
    67, 70–71
    organized benefits in, 584
    supplying, 75
    women in, 74, *74*
revolving door, 394
RFRA (Religious Freedom Restoration
    Act), 146
Rhode Island, 65, 75, 79, 85t, 94t, 95
Rhodes, Benjamin, 629
rights. *See also* Bill of Rights; civil
        liberties; civil rights; women's
        rights
    amendments extending, 98
    of assembly, 253
    to bear arms, 157–59, *158*
    in Declaration of Independence,
        26–27
    economic, social, 217–18
    freedom and, 30
    government securing, 27
    incorporating, 97–98, 137, 159
    individual, 109
    of Native Americans, denied, 210
    of non-citizens, 167–68
    privacy, 139–42
    property, 151
    of undocumented individuals, 204–5
rights at trials, 161–62
rights of the accused
    Bill of Rights on, 159
    death penalty and, 151, 163–66, 164f
    right to counsel, 162–63, *163*
    search and seizure rights, 160–61
RINOs (Republicans in Name Only),
    364, 410
RNC (Republican National Committee),
    366

Roberts, John, 126, 161, *547*, 549, 552t
    on ACA, 562
    on judges, as umpires, 553
    on oral arguments, 547
    as swing vote, 554
    on voting rights, 216–17
Roberts, Julia, 533
Roberts, Robin, 230, *231*
Robinson v. California, 138t
robocall, 235, 336t
Rochester, Blunt, 409
Roe v. Wade, 126, 126t, 140–42, 200,
    527, 548, 561
Roll Call, 389
roll-call vote, 438
Romney, Mitt, 317t, 319, *371*
Roosevelt, Eleanor, 484
Roosevelt, Franklin D., 29–30, 47, 168,
    185, 231, 233, 459, 474t
    attempted assassination
        against, 479
    cooperative federalism of, 118–19
    death of, 479
    EOP under, 481
    executive orders of, *467*
    FCC under, 291
    in fifth party system, 356
    fireside chats of, *280*, 280–81
    guiding perspective of, 604
    internment camps of, 208
    New Deal, 590
    vetoes, 463
    White House of, 483
Roosevelt, Theodore, 243, *467*, 474t
    on bully pulpit, 468, *468*
    expanding presidential authority,
        454
    Progressive Party and, 349, 350t
    reforms under, 355
Roper v. Simmons, 548
Rosen, Jeffrey, 266
Rostenkowski, Dan, 477
rote, 498
R. R. Moton High School, Virginia, *62*,
    63–64
rule of four, 547
Russia, 129, *129*
    aging populations, *19*
    disinformation campaign, for Trump,
        D., 320
    media censorship in, 295
    sanctions against, 619
    Ukraine invasion of, 295, *297*, 460,
        461, *608*, 609, 619
    women in legislature, *197*
Ruzicka, Marla, 10–11, *11*
Rwanda, *197*

safe districts, 335
salary gap, 49
Salerno, Lillian, *521*
salutary neglect, 65
same-sex couples, 142, *142*, 563
same-sex marriage, 91, 213–14, 223,
    224f, 268
sample size, 236f, 237t

sampling error, 235, 236*f*
sampling frame, 233
sanctuary cities, 105–6
Sanders, Bernie, 36, *42*, 263,
    317–19, 366
*Santa Clara Co. v. Southern Pacific
    Railroad*, 558
Saturday Press, 154
Saudi Arabia, *197*, *619*
Savimbi, Jonas, 401
Scalia, Antonin, 144–45, 157–58,
    531, 550
Scalise, Steve, 426
Schedule F, 515–16
Schenck, Charles, 148, 560
Schenck v. United States, 148, 560
Schlafly, Phyllis, 198
Schlesinger, Arthur, Jr., 456, 474*t*
Schlesinger, Arthur, Sr., 473, 474*t*
Scholz, Olaf, *624*
school. *See also* education
    busing, 192
    equal protections in, 205
    prayer in, *100*
science, politicizing, 577
Scott, Dred, 180–81, 529, 541,
    557–58, *558*
the Scottsboro Boys, *163*
search and seizure, 160–61
search warrants, 160*f*
Sears, Winsome Earle, 305–6
Second Amendment, 157–59
Second Continental Congress, 71
Section 504, Rehabilitation Act (1973),
    212
Securities and Exchange
    Commission, 512*f*
security trap, 612
segregation, 185–90, *186*, 202
SEIU (Service Employees International
    Union), 384–85
select committees, 428*t*
selective incorporation, 137
self-driving cars, *110*
self-interest, 230
self-rule, 8, 27, 30, 79
    Constitution on, 31
    in Declaration of Independence, 72*t*
    defining, 31
    democracy, 31–32
    republic, 32–33
Senate, U.S., 38, 81, 325–26. *See also*
    bills; Congress, U.S.
    advice and consent, 415
    bipartisanship in, *371*
    checks and balances on, 83–85, 84*f*
    committees, 427–30, 429*t*
    conference committee, 438–39
    Constitution Article 1 on, 88–89
    diversity of, 416–20, 417*f*
    filibusters, *414*, 414–15, 437–38, 437*f*
    floor action, 435, 435–38, *436*, 437*f*
    Johnson, L. B., in, 604
    on judicial nominees, 415, 535–36
    leaders, 427
    legislative hold in, 413, 415

partisanship in, 369
permanent standing committees of,
    428*t*, 429*t*
in separation of powers, 83–85, 84*f*
unanimous consent of, 436
whips, 427
women in, 195–96
Senate Finance Committee, 435
Seneca Falls Convention, *176*, 195
senior citizens, 14, 585–86
separate but equal, 183, *186*, 561
separation of powers, 83–85, 84*f*
September 11, 2001, 166, 228, *473*,
    507, 636
Serial, 279
Service Employees International Union
    (SEIU), 384–85
Seventeenth Amendment, 79
Seventh-Day Adventists, 145
severe discrimination, 192
sex, between consenting adults, 142, *142*
sexual harassment, 199, 548
sexual orientation, 213–15
Shapiro, Robert, 240
Shays, Daniel, 75, *75*
Shays's Rebellion, *75*, 75–76, *76*
Shelby County v. Holder, 126*t*
Sherbert, Adell, 145–46
Sherbert balancing test, 145–46, *146*
Sherman, Brad, 434
Sherman, Roger, 81, 95–96
Sides, John, 359
signing statements, *464*, 464–65
Silent Generation, 268*f*, 269*f*
Simpson, O. J., 162
Sinema, Kyrsten, *371*
Singapore, *35*, *55*
single-party systems, 350
Sioux Nation, 211
*Sipuel v. Board of Regents of University
    of Oklahoma*, 186*t*
Sirius XM, 281
Sitting Bull, 210
Sixth Amendment, 162–63, *163*
Skocpol, Theda, 265, 402
Skowronek, Stephen, 475
slander, 156
the Slants, *132*, 133–34
slavery, 18
    abolition movement against,
        74, *86*, 180
    Constitutional Convention on, 85–87,
        85*t*, *86*
    Declaration of Independence
        and, 74
    Dred Scott v. Sanford on, 180–81,
        529, 541, 557–58, *558*
    economics of, 180
    Emancipation Proclamation, 181
    enslaved population, in 1790, 85*t*
    Freedmen's Bureau, 183
    fugitive slaves, 86–87
    grandfather clause, 183
    Lincoln on, 87, 354
    Missouri Compromise and, 180,
        181*f*, 541

as national calamity, 87
outlawed, in Northwest Ordinance, 75
politics of, 180
revolt against, 179–84
slave trade, 86, *86*
Washington and, 85
Slovakia, *262*
Slovenia, *262*
Smalls, Robert, 182, *183*
Smith, Howard, 197
Smith, Rogers, 30
Smith v. Allright, 185
Snapchat, 266*f*
Snowden, Edward, 154
social butterflies, 390*t*
social capital, 258–59, *259*
social conflict, 43
social democracy, 40–41
social equality, 48–49
Socialist Party of Philadelphia, 148
social media. *See also specific platforms*
    active use of, 274
    age and choice of, 266*f*
    campaigns using, 299
    censorship of, 295
    concerns with, 283–84
    COVID-19 vaccine disinformation
        on, 273, *274*
    democracy challenged by, 266–67
    democracy improved by, 265–66
    freedom of speech on, 149, 153, 154
    as news source, 279, 279*f*
    in political participation,
        265–68, 266*f*
    regulation of, 291–92, 292*f*
    rise of, 283
    Trump, D.'s, tweets, 266
social mobility, *47*
social movement theory, 7*t*, 8
social policy, 583–89
Social Security, 14, 30, 39, 356, 583, *585*,
    585–86
Social Security Act (1935), 585
Social Security Administration,
    500, 506*t*
social welfare programs, 30
society
    government setting rules for, 14–15
    three sectors of, *12*, 12–13
soft power, 613, *613*
sole executive agreements, 627
solidarity, 41, *42*, 43, *44*
solidarity benefits, 386
Solle, Ashley, 389–90
SOPs (standard operating procedures), 497
Soros, George, 386
Sotomayor, Sonia, 166, 539, *547*,
    552*t*, 554
sound bite, 298
South Africa, *197*
South Carolina, 85, 85*t*, 94*t*,
    145–46, 186*t*
southern strategy, 357
South Korea
    citizen satisfaction in, *35*
    diversity acceptance in, *55*

taxes, 15f
voter turnout, *262*
women in legislature, *197*
Spain, 68f, 75, 129, *129*, 349
    citizen satisfaction in, *35*
    diversity acceptance in, *55*
    social mobility in, *47*
    voter turnout, *262*
Spanberger, Abigail, 337
Speaker of the House, 425–26, *426*
special interests, 378. *See also* interest
        groups; lobbying
specialized courts, 537–38, 538f
speech. *See* freedom of speech
spending, by government, 14, 590, 596
Spikes, Harry, *424*
spilling the tea, 390t
The Spirit of the Laws
        (Montesquieu), 84
split-ticket voters, 360
spoils system, 494
sports, transgender athletes and, 214, *215*
Squid Games, 209
staff, Congressional, 423–25, *424*
Stamp Tax, 69
standard operating procedures
        (SOPs), 497
standing, 547
standing committees, 428–29, 428t, 429t
stare decisis, 553
state and local courts, 534
state authority, in Constitution,
        116–17, 116f
State Department, U.S., 460, 505, 506t,
        520, 629
state government
    choices in, 110, 112
    COVID-19 responses of, 123
    dual versus cooperative federalism,
        117f, 119t
    education on race and, 111, *111*
    in federalism, 79
    full faith and credit between, 116
    income tax rates by, 110f
    legislatures of, 75, *197*
    marijuana policy and, 580f
    national versus, 79
    protection for individual rights in, 109
    reserved powers of, 115–16
    state judge requirements, 534
    trust in, 108f
state-level policy, 109–10
state militias, 157–58
*State of Missouri ex rel. Gaines v.
        Canada*, 186t
State of the Union address, *343*, 437 462
states
    abortion in, 141
    civil liberties in, 137
    speech of, 150
Statue of Liberty, 56
Sterling, Alton, 179
Stevens, John Paul, 145
Stevenson, Bryan, *532*, 533
Stewart, Potter, 165
Stokes, Donald, 239–40

Stonewall Inn riot, 213
STOP ERA movement, 198–99
"Stop the Steal," 3
Story, Joseph, 353
straight-ticket voters, 360
strategic disengagement, 623, 625
straw polls, 238t
street-level bureaucrats, 502, *502*
strict scrutiny, 177–78, 560
strict separation, of church and state,
        144–45
students
    loans to, 584
    speech of, 152–53
    undocumented, 204f
substantive representation, 418, 419
success, 48
suffrage, 49
    women's, 195–96, 196f, *197*
Sumner, Charles, 441, *441*
sunshine laws, 32
supermajority, 74
super PACs, 314, *315*, 368
super-swirl cake, contested federalism
        as, 117f, 119–20, 121f, 130
Super Tuesday, 319
supremacy clause, 115, 542
Supreme, Vermin, *318*
Supreme Court, U.S., 9, 33, *526*, *549*. See
        also judicial branch; *specific cases*
    on ACA, 562, 587–88
    acts of Congress, nullified by, 542f
    Biden, Joe, on rulings by, 527
    Bill of Rights and, 137
    Brown v. Board of Education, 63,
        186–87, 186t, 198, 219, 529,
        545, 561
    budgets of, 545
    on bureaucracy, 518
    Bush v. Gore, 534
    Carson v. Mankin, 528, 529
    case selection, 547–49
    in checks and balances, 83–85, 84f
    *Chevron v. Resources Defense
        Council*, 518
    *Citizens United v. The Federal
        Elections Commission*, 312,
        314, 562
    clerks, 550
    collegiality on, 555–56
    conferences sessions, written deci-
        sions and, 549–50
    confirmation of justices, 550–52,
        551, 552t
    Constitution Article 3 on, 90–91
    Constitution on, 90–91
    on death penalty, 548
    decision making of, 553–56, 554f
    democracy and, 4
    diversity in, 538–40, 539t
    *Dobbs v. Jackson Women's Health
        Organization*, 126t, 141–42,
        148, 200, 527, 549, 563
    Dred Scott v. Sanford, 180–81, 529,
        541, 557–58, *558*
    on federalism, 125–26, 126t

on fighting words, 151
on Fourteenth Amendment,
        558–59, 561, 563
on freedom of speech, 133–34,
        147–52
Gideon v. Wainwright, 138t, 163, 561
Hamilton on, 90
hearing cases, 546–47
ideology in, 554, 555f
incorporating rights, 97–98, 137, 159
as institution, 556
judicial activism, 543
judicial restraint, 543
judicial review, 541
*Kennedy v. Bremerton School
        District*, 528
Korematsu v. U.S., 560–61, *561*
landmark cases, 557–63
legitimate controversy and, 547
Lemon v. Kurtzman, 144
lobbyists and, 395–96, *396*
Mapp v. Ohio, 138t, 161
Marbury v. Madison, 90–91,
        540–41, 544
McCulloch v. Maryland, 125, 557
*McCutcheon v. Federal Elections
        Commission*, 312, 314
Miranda v. Arizona, 138t, 162
Muller v. Oregon, 559–60, *560*
*National Federation of Independent
        Business v. Sebelius*, 126t, 562
Native Americans and, 211
Near v. Minnesota, 138t, 154
*New York State Rifle & Pistol
        Association v. Bruen*, 527–28
nominations, 552t
by the numbers, 530
Obergefell v. Hodges, 126t, 213–14, 563
oral arguments, 546–47
partisanship of, 370–71, 554, 555f
peer pressure and, 555–56
Planned Parenthood v. Casey, 141
Plessy v. Ferguson, 183, 529,
        558–59, *559*, 561
power of, 528–29, 544–45
on privacy rights, 139–40
public opinion on, 532f, *556*
Roe v. Wade, 126, 126t, 140–42, 200,
        527, 548, 561
rule of four, 547
Schenck v. United States, 148, 560
on search and seizure, 161
on separation of church and state,
        144–45, 528
in separation of powers, 83–85, 84f
Sherbert balancing test and, 145–46
standing and, 547
stare decisis, 553
textualism and, 543
Tinker rule, 152
on voting rights, 216–17
West Virginia v. EPA, 528
on women's rights, 199
writ of certiorari, 547
Surowiecki, James, 240–41
survey research, 242

suspect categories, 177–78
Sweat v. Painter, 186t
Sweden, 129, *129*
    citizen satisfaction in, *35*
    diversity acceptance in, *55*
    economic equality in, *49*
    foreign aid spending, *614*
    on government taking care of poor, *41*
    voter turnout in, *262*
swing states, 322–23
Switzerland, *262*
symbolic expression, 149–50
symbols, public policy and, 604
Syria, 296–97

Taft, William, 243, *467*, 474t
Taiwan, *35*, *55*
Tam, Simon, *132*, 133, 150
Taney, Roger, 180–81, *558*
tax, 557
    American Opportunity Tax
        Credit, 584
    burden, U.S., 15–16, 15f
    Continental Congress on, 75
    deductions, for employee healthcare,
        16–17
    gas, 575–76, 576t
    by nation, 15f
    rates by state government, 110f
    in social democracy, 41
    Stamp Tax, 69
tax cuts, 2017, 590
Taylor, Zachary, 474t
Tea Party political movement, 71,
    259, 336
telecommunications, 395f
Telecommunications Act (1996), 286
Telemundo, 300
television
    cable, 282
    FCC on, 291
    first presidential debates, *321*
    government-owned, 294–95
    infotainment, 282–83
    Kennedy, John F., on, 281, *321*
    late night, 282
    as mass media, 281–83
    as news source, 267f279f, 279
    in polarization, 282
    public, 294–95
Ten Commandments, 144
Tenth Amendment, 115–16
term limits, *339*, 565
terrorism, 128, 166–67, *167*, 296–98. *See
    also* September 11, 2001
    war on terror, 636
Tessler, Michael, 359
Texas, 53, 105–6, 123
    death penalty in, 135
    Lawrence v. Texas, 141–42, *142*
    legislature, 329
    Pointer v. Texas, 138t
    Uvalde, *167*, 277–78, 572–73, 602
    Washington v. Texas, 138t
text-to-donate, 336t
textualism, 543

Thailand, *66*, 151
Theiss-Morse, Elizabeth, 445
Third Amendment, 139
Third House, 390t
third parties, 349–51, 350t, *351*, 372–73
Third Way, 365
Thirteenth Amendment, 182
Thomas, Clarence, 142, 547, *547*,
    552t, 554
Thomas, Lia, 214, *215*
Thoreau, Henry David, 252
Thor: Love and Thunder, 599, 601
Three-Fifths Compromise, 85–86
three strikes laws, 126
Thurmond, Strom, 350t
TikTok, 265, 266f, 273–74, 283, 292,
    299, 336
Timbs, Tyson, 163–64
Timbs v. Indiana, 163–64
time, place, and manner clause, 308
timing, of opinion polling, 234, 237t
Tinker, John, 152
Tinker, Mary Beth, 152
Tinker rule, 152
Title IX, 198
Title VI, 198
Tocqueville, Alexis de, 12, 35, 136, 487
    on civil bodies, 402
    Democracy in America by, 45,
        48, 255
    on economic inequality, 49
    on equality, 48
    on lawyers, 531
To Kill a Mockingbird, 532
top-down policy, 579, *579*
torture, 454
Townshend Acts (1767), 69–70
trade
    associations, 384t, 385
    Biden, Joe, and, 618
    deficit, 616
    fair, 617
    free, 617, 618f
traditional political participation,
    248–52, 250t
transgender individuals, 214
Transparency International, *632*
Transportation Security Authority
    (TSA), 498
travel ban, 450
trials, rights at, 161–62
tribal movement, 210
Tribune Company, 286
trolling, 267
Trone, David, 325
Truman, Harry S., 58, 231
    on decisiveness, 473
    on Eisenhower, 515
    executive orders, *467*
    rating, 475t
    vetoes, 463
Trump, Donald, 9, 36, 305, *342*, 369t,
    370, 628t
    agenda of, 457
    on American First foreign policy,
        636–37

anti-immigrant rhetoric, 321
approval ratings of, 472f, 473
Barrett nomination, 532, 550–51
batting average, 463t
Biden, Joe's, election certification
    fought by, 3, 409–10
birtherism and, 316
on bureaucracy, 522
as businessperson, 316, 317t
cabinet of, 507–8, 510t
campaign promises of, 38
as candidate, 346
clean energy policy and, 122, 122f
climate change and, 122, 224
COVID-19 and campaigning
    of, 299
Dreamers policy of, 205
economy under, 590
election, as upset, 263
Electoral College totals of
    (2020), 83f
Electoral College victory of
    (2016), 321
endorsements of, 306
EOP of, 482
executive orders of, 450, *467*
false, misleading statements by,
    276, 289
federalism of, 120
on flavored e-cigarettes, 381
foreign policy of, 461
on gas tax, 576
Gorsuch nomination, 532
on government, 12
on immigrants, 55–56
on immigration, 105–6
impeachments of, 84, 90
judicial nominees of, 415, 535, 536f
on libel laws, 156–57
on lobbyists, 400–402
media attention and, 287–88
midterms, 329t
multistate lawsuits filed under, 121f
nomination of, 319
on North Korea, 625
partisanship under, 120
presidential appointments of, 465
protectionism of, 618
race of voters for, 228
rating, 475t
religion and, 52
Republican Party factions and, 363
Russian disinformation campaign
    for, 320
Schedule F and, 515–16
shy voters for, 236
Supreme Court nominations of,
    550–51
tax cuts, 590
travel ban, 450
tweets by, 231, 266
unfilled posts, 507
vetoes, 439, 464, 464f
White House of, 483, 484
white support for, 259, 323
Trump, Melania, 486

Trumpists, 363
trust. *See also* public opinion
  in government, 13*f*, 108*f*
  in media, 286*f*
trustee representation, 68, 418–20
TSA (Transportation Security
    Authority), 498
tuition, 31
turf war, 498
Turkey, 15*f*, 148, *262*
Twain, Mark, 31, 257, 413
Twitter, 149, 154, 231, 266, 266*f*, 283,
    301, 383
two-party system, 347–50
Two Treatises on Government
    (Locke, J.), 72
Tyler, John, 474*t*

Udall, Morris, 316
UFW. *See* United Farm Workers
Uihlein, Richard, 386
UK. *See* United Kingdom
Ukraine
  international support for, *624*
  Russia's invasion of, 295, *297*, 460,
      461, *608*, 609, 619
unalienable rights, 74
unanimous consent, 436
underdog effect, 239
undocumented individuals, 105–6,
    204–5, 204*f*
unemployment benefits, *586*, 586–87
unfunded mandate, 123
unicameral legislature, 80
unilateralism, 624
unions, 364–65
unitary actors, 626
unitary executive theory, 456
unitary government, 107, 129, *129*
United Farm Workers (UFW),
    202, *203*
United Kingdom (UK). *See also* Great
    Britain
  aging populations, *19*
  citizen satisfaction in, *35*
  diversity acceptance in, *55*
  economy of, 616*f*
  foreign aid spending, *614*
  Parliament, 430
  social mobility in, *47*
  taxes, 15*f*
  women in legislature, *197*
United Nations, 635
United States (U.S.). *See also specific*
    topics
  aging populations, *19*
  American exceptionalism, 27,
      620–21, *621*
  becoming majority-minority, 263
  citizen satisfaction in, *35*
  colonial, 65–71
  as democratic republic, 33
  demographics, *20*
  diversity acceptance in, *55*
  economy of, 616*f*
  executions in, 164*f*

foreign aid spending, *614*
government, compared to other de-
    mocracies, *90*, 129, *129*
on government taking care of
    poor, *41*
incarceration rate, 160
Latinos as rising force in, 201–3
as nation of immigrants, *18*,
    18–19, 203
religiosity, 52
religious composition of, 52*f*
social mobility in, *47*
taxes, 15–16, 15*f*
views of, abroad, 621–22, 622*f*
voter turnout in, *262*
women in legislature, *197*
United States v. Nixon, 561–62
United States v. Sioux Nation of
    Indians, 211
United States v. Texas, 126*t*
United States v. Windsor, 126*t*
universalistic politics, 494
University of California v. Bakke, 193
Univision, 300
urban design, 25
U.S. *See* United States
USAJobs, 513
USA Patriot Act (2001), 166, 636
Uvalde, Texas, *167*, 277–78,
    572–73, 602

Valelly, Richard, 183
Van Buren, Martin, 474*t*
Vance, J. D., 306
Vandenberg, Arthur, 635
Vanuatu, *197*
vaping, 381
Vargas, Jose Antonio, 105, 130
Vavreck, Lynn, 359
Ventura, Jesse, 351, *351*
Verizon Communications, 398*t*
veterans
  benefits, 584
  Department of Veterans Affairs, 506*t*
  GI Bill, 584
veto power, 454*t*
  over legislation, 439
  overrides, 462–64, 464*f*
  pocket, 463
  in separation of powers, 84, 84*f*
vice president, 479–80, *480*
Vietnam, 152, 297, *298*, 388
Virginia, 94*t*, 95, 186*t*, 194, 305–6
  Davis v. School Board of Prince
      Edward County, 63, 186*t*
  death penalty in, 135
  enslaved population in, 85*t*
  House of Burgesses, 65
  R. R. Moton High School, 63–64
  The Virginia Plan, 79–81
Virginia Military Institute, 178
The Virginia Plan, 79–81, 603–4
voice vote, 438
voluntarism, civic, 128, 255
voter turnout, *251*, 255–58, 257*f*, *262*
voting, 239–40. *See also* suffrage

barriers to, 310–12
base voters, 360
cloture, 437–38, 437*f*
expanding access to, 311*f*
high turnout, *251*
in Iowa City, 310*t*
laws, Democrats, Republicans
    on, 264
low turnout, 255–56
paradox of, 261
party identification in, 360
requiring by law, 270
restrictions, on African Americans,
    183, 216–17, 256
rights, in Fifteenth Amendment, 182
roll-call, 438
self-interest in, 230
split-ticket, 360
straight-ticket, 360
as traditional participation, 248–51
voice, 438
Voting Rights Act (1965), 79, 126, 189,
    216–17, 539

Wagner Act (1935), 560
Walker, Herschel, *304*, 306
Walker, Will, 263–64
Wallace, George, 350*t*
Wall Street, 242, *242*
Wall Street Journal, 283
Wal-Mart, 199
Walton, Alice, *50*
Walton, Sam, *50*
war. *See also* military, U.S.; World War II
  bureaucracy in, 494–95
  in congressional elections,
      328–29
  media coverage, 296–98, *297*
  preemptive, 636
  in presidential elections, 321
  in social policy, 584–85
war on terror, 636
War Powers Act (1973), 459, 460, 627
Warren, Earl, 545, 554, 561
Warren, Elizabeth, 292
Washington (state), 138*t*
Washington, DC, *10*, 186*t*
Washington, George, 32, 49, 53, 346,
    353, 620
  cabinet of, 505
  at Constitutional Convention, 76, 83
  farewell address of, 280
  as first president, 449, 455
  foreign policy experience, 628*t*
  Jefferson and, 413
  on national day of prayer, 143
  on national government, 75
  owning slaves, 85
  on political parties, 344, 468
  rating, 474*t*
Washington, Kerry, *251*
Washington Post, 276, 280
Washington v. Texas, 138*t*
Wasserman Schultz, Debbie, 366
Watergate, 288, 561–62
weak presidency, 456–57

wealth, 6, 45–47, 49–50, 257, 312–15
Weaver, James, 350t
*Webb School v. School District
    No 90*, 186t
Weber, Max, 495
Webster, Daniel, 479
welfare, 506t
    entitlement programs, 588–89, 588f
    percent of federal budget, 14f
Westboro Baptist Church, 148–49, *149*
West Coast Hotel Company v. Parrish,
    560
western expansion, 75
West Virginia v. EPA, 528
westward expansion, 209
WhatsApp, 266f
What's the Matter with Kansas?
    (Frank), 230
Whigs, 352t, 353–54
whistleblower, 517
White, Jerry, 154
White House Office, 481t, 483–84
white nationalism, 128, 130
whites, *20*
    identity politics, 359
    incarceration of, 218f
    life expectancy, poverty rates of, 217t
    police using deadly force against,
        179f
    supporting Trump, D., 323
white supremacists, 184, 194
wholesale campaigning, 336t
WIC (Women, Infants, and Children
    program), 502
Wikileaks, 154, 366
William III (king), 34
Williams, Holly, *297*
Williamson, Hugh, *81*
Williamson, Vanessa, 402

Williams v. Mississippi, 183
Wilson, Darren, 179
Wilson, James, 81
Wilson, Woodrow, 184, 195, 349, *467*,
    474t, 577, 620, 633–34
Wilsonians, 625, 626t
Winfrey, Oprah, 260t
winner-take-all, 319
Winthrop, John, 51, 53
Wisconsin, 53
The Wisdom of Crowds (Surowiecki),
    240–41
Witches' Voice, 146
Witt, James Lee, 509
"woke" attitudes, 214
Wolf v. Colorado, 138t
women. *See also* gender
    in cabinet, 510t
    as CEOs, 200t
    in combat, *178*
    in congressional elections, 327, *327*
    elected to legislatures, 195–96, 196f,
        197
    in Revolutionary War, 74, *74*
Women, Infants, and Children program
    (WIC), 502
women's rights, 30
    Civil Rights Act (1964) and, 198–99
    *Dobbs v. Jackson Women's Health
        Organization*, 126t, 141–42,
        148, 200, 527, 549, 563
    Equal Rights Amendment, 198–99
    #MeToo movement, 200
    Muller v. Oregon, 559–60, *560*
    NOW, 198
    Planned Parenthood v. Casey, 141
    Roe v. Wade, 126, 126t, 140–42, 200,
        527, 548, 561
    Schlafly against, 198

Seneca Falls Convention, *176*, 195
    sexual harassment and, 199
    sports and, 198, *198*
    STOP ERA movement, 198–99
    suffrage, 195–96, 196f, *197*
    Title IX in, 198
    Title VI in, 198
Wood, Gordon, 45, 70, 74
World Health Organization, 636
World Trade Organization (WTO), 617
World War I, 356, 560, 633–34
World War II, 119, 136, 495, 634
    economic prosperity after, 46f
    global alliances after, 461
    government spending during, 590
    Japanese Americans during, 208,
        560–61
    military tribunals, 538
Wounded Knee Incident, 211
Wright brothers, 13
writ of certiorari, 547
written decisions, 549–50
WTO (World Trade Organization), 617

xenophobia, 130
Xi Jinping, *47*

Yanukovych, Victor, 401
Yemen, *197*
Yorktown, Battle of, 28
Youngkin, Glen, 305
YouTube, 265, 266f, 274, 279, 283

Zaller, John, 230
Zelensky, Volodymyr, *624*
Zell, Sam, 286
Zoom, 283
Zuckerberg, Mark, 149